Marine Insurance

Butterworths Insurance Library

First edition 1969
Second edition 1974
Third edition 1979
Fourth edition 1985

Marine Insurance

Fourth edition

E R Hardy Ivamy LLB, PhD, LLD
of the Middle Temple, Barrister,
Professor of Law in the University of London

London
Butterworths
1985

Butterworths Insurance Library

United Kingdom	Butterworth & Co (Publishers) Ltd, 88 Kingsway, LONDON WC2B 6AB and 61A North Castle Street, EDINBURGH EH2 3LJ
Australia	Butterworths Pty Ltd, SYDNEY, MELBOURNE, BRISBANE, ADELAIDE, PERTH, CANBERRA and HOBART
Canada	Butterworth & Co (Canada) Ltd, TORONTO and VANCOUVER
New Zealand	Butterworths of New Zealand Ltd, WELLINGTON and AUCKLAND
Singapore	Butterworth & Co (Asia) Pte Ltd, SINGAPORE
South Africa	Butterworth Publishers (Pty) Ltd, DURBAN and PRETORIA
USA	Butterworth Legal Publishers, ST PAUL, Minnesota, SEATTLE, Washington, BOSTON, Massachusetts, AUSTIN, Texas and D & S Publishers, CLEARWATER, Florida

© Butterworth & Co (Publishers) Ltd 1985

All rights reserved. No part of this publication may be reproduced or transmitted in any form or by any means, including photocopying and recording, without the written permission of the copyright holder, application for which should be addressed to the publisher. Such written permission must also be obtained before any part of this publication is stored in a retrieval system of any nature.

This book is sold subject to the Standard Conditions of Sale of Net Books and may not be re-sold in the UK below the net price fixed by Butterworths for the book in our current catalogue.

British Library Cataloguing in Publication Data

Ivamy, E.R. Hardy
    Marine insurance.——4th ed.
    1. Insurance, Marine——Law and legislation——
    Great Britain
    I. Title
    344.106′8622   KD1845
    ISBN 0 406 25313 7

Typeset by Cotswold Typesetting Ltd, Gloucester
Printed in Great Britain by Billing and Son Limited, Worcester

Preface

Since the last edition of this book was published in 1979 and a Supplement in 1982 a fundamental change has occurred in the law of Marine Insurance for the original Lloyd's form, which was first used in about 1779, has been completely replaced by a new one. In addition, the Institute Clauses which were used in connection with the old form have been modernised to take account of the new situation.

Accordingly, some Chapters of this book have been reorganised and substantially rewritten. These Chapters are Chapter 11 (The Form of the Policy), Chapter 13 (Attachment and Duration of the Risk under the Policy), Chapter 14 (Marine Risks), Chapter 15 (War and Strike Risks), Chapter 17 (The Exceptions), Chapter 33 (Partial Loss of Ship) and Chapter 35 (Partial Loss of Goods). Throughout the work emphasis has been laid on the effect of the Institute Clauses on the Marine Insurance Act 1906 and the common law.

A number of new cases have now been added either to the text or to the footnotes. These include *The Yasin* [1979] 2 Lloyd's Rep 45 (subrogation), *Bruns v Colocotronis: The Vasso* [1979] 2 Lloyd's Rep 412 (p p i policy), *Prudent Tankers Ltd SA v Dominion Insurance Co Ltd: The Caribbean Sea* [1980] 1 Lloyd's Rep 338 (latent defect), *Fuerst Day Lawson Ltd v Orion Insurance Co Ltd* [1980] 1 Lloyd's Rep 656 (goods insured 'from anywhere to anywhere') *West of England Shipowners Mutual Protection and Indemnity Association (Luxembourg) v Aifanouros Shipping SA: The Aifanourios* [1980] 2 Lloyd's Rep 403 (payment of call), *Stolos Compania SA v Ajax Insurance Co Ltd: The Admiral C* [1981] 1 Lloyd's Rep 9, CA (claim to be collected through broker), *First National Bank of Chicago v West of England Shipowners Mutual Protection and Indemnity Association (Luxembourg): The Evelpidis Era* [1981] 1 Lloyd's Rep 54 (assignment), *The Bamburi* [1982] 1 Lloyd's Rep 312 (constructive total loss), *Athens Maritime Enterprises Corporation v Hellenic Mutual War Risks Association (Bermuda) Ltd: The Andreos Lemos* [1982] 2 Lloyd's Rep 483 (piracy), *M Almojil Establishment v Malayan Motor and General Underwriters (Private) Ltd: The Al-Jubail IV* [1982] 2 Lloyd's Rep 637, Singapore Court of Appeal (whether time or voyage policy), *Soya GmbH Mainz Kommanditgesellschaft v White* [1983] 1 Lloyd's Rep 122, HL (inherent vice), *Allden v Raven: The Kylie* [1983] 2 Lloyd's Rep 444 (non-disclosure), *Pindos Shipping Corporation v Raven: The Mata Hari* [1983] 2 Lloyd's Rep 449 (rectification of policy), *Integrated Container Service Inc v British Traders Insurance Co Ltd* [1984] 1 Lloyd's Rep 154, CA (sue and labour clause), *Container Transport International Inc and Reliance Group Inc v Oceanus Mutual Underwriting Association (Bermuda) Ltd* [1984] 1 Lloyd's Rep 476, CA (non-disclosure), *N Michalos & Sons Maritime SA v Prudential Assurance Co Ltd: The Zinovia* [1984] 2 Lloyd's Rep 264 (constructive total loss), *Silver Dolphin Products Ltd v Parcels and General Assurance Association Ltd* [1984] 2 Lloyd's Rep 404 (attachment of risk), *Empresa Lineas Maritimas Argentinas v Oceanus Mutual Underwriting Association (Bermuda) Ltd* [1984] 2 Lloyd's Rep 517 (membership of association), *Black King Shipping*

Corporation v Massie: The Litsion Pride [1985] 1 Lloyd's Rep 437 (duty of good faith) and *Rhesa Shipping Co SA v Edmunds: The Popi M* [1985] 2 All ER 712, HL.

A selection of the Institute Clauses has been reproduced in the Appendices by the kind permission of the Institute of London Underwriters, to whom I tender my thanks. Thos R Miller & Son supplied me with the material on the perils insured against by Protection and Indemnity Associations and the rules of entry and membership, and I am particularly grateful for their help. My thanks are also due to the Association of Average Adjusters who have allowed me to set out in an Appendix their Rules of Practice.

I should like to thank the staff of Butterworths for undertaking the arduous job of preparing the Index and the Tables of Cases and Statutes and for seeing the book through the press.

University College London   E. R. HARDY IVAMY
July 1985

Contents

Preface v
Table of statutes xv
Table of cases xix

PART I—THE MAKING OF THE CONTRACT

Chapter 1—Introduction 3

Chapter 2—The nature of marine insurance 4
   A Contract of indemnity 4
   B 'Losses incident to marine adventure' 7
   C Mixed sea and land risks 7
   D The subject-matter insured 8

Chapter 3—The avoidance of wagering or gaming contracts 11
     The position before 1745 11
     The position after 1745 11

Chapter 4—Insurable interest 16
   A Examples of persons having an insurable interest 16
       Owner 17
       Mortgagor and mortgagee 22
       Master and crew 23
       Agent 24
       Carrier 24
       Lien holder and pawnors 25
       Trustees and executors 25
       Captors 26
       Insurer 26
       Persons expecting a profit from a marine adventure 26
       Lender of money on bottomry or respondentia 27
       Marina operator 27
   B Existence of insurable interest at the time of the loss 27

Chapter 5—The duties of a broker in effecting the policy 30
     Duty to obey his principal's instructions 30
     Duty to use proper skill and care 32
     Duty to carry out the transaction 37

Chapter 6—Non-disclosure 39
   A Duty to disclose material facts 39
       Disclosure by the assured himself 39
       Disclosure by agent effecting insurance 41
   B The test of materiality 44
   C Circumstances which need not be disclosed 45
   D Examples of material and immaterial facts 53
   E The duration of the duty of disclosure 66
   F The effect of non-disclosure 68
   G Broker's liability towards the insurer for non-disclosure 69

viii   *Contents*

Chapter 7—Misrepresentation   71
    The duty of the assured   71
    The duration of the duty   71
    The test of materiality   72
    Construction of representation   72
    Materiality is a question of fact   72
    Withdrawal or correction of representation   77
    Representation to the first underwriter   78
    Effect of misrepresentation   78
    Burden of proof   78
    Evidence   78

Chapter 8—The premium   80
  A   The amount of the premium   80
  B   The time for payment of the premium   82
  C   The responsibility for payment of the premium   82
  D   The effect of acknowledgment of receipt of the premium   82
  E   The return of the premium   82

PART II—THE POLICY

Chapter 9—Introduction   89

Chapter 10—The classification of policies   90
  A   Voyage, time and mixed policies   90
  B   Floating policies   91
      Effect of fraud   93
      Where several policies exist   93
  C   Valued and unvalued policies   93
      Valued policies   93
         1   Conclusiveness of valuation   94
         2   Valuation and constructive total loss   96
         3   Valuation and general average sacrifice   97
         4   Valuation and salvage charges   97
      Unvalued policies   97

Chapter 11—The form of the policy   101
  A   The form set out in the Marine Insurance Act 1906   101
  B   The form used up to 1982   102
  C   The new form   104

Chapter 12—Designation of the subject-matter in the policy   106
  A   The need for reasonable certainty   106
  B   Nature and extent of the interest   111
  C   Interest to be covered   111

Chapter 13—Attachment and duration of the risk under the policy   113
  A   Time policies   113
  B   Voyage policies   114
      Attachment of the risk   114
         1   Voyage policies on ship   115
         2   Voyage policies on goods   117
         3   Voyage policies on freight   118
      Duration of the risk   119
         1   The general rule   119
            Risk on ship   119
            Risk on goods   122
         2   Exceptions to the general rule   126
            1   Implied condition as to commencement of adventure   126

  2 Change of voyage 127
  3 Deviation 129
  4 Delay in voyage 135
  5 Termination clauses 138

Chapter 14—Marine risks 140
 A Hull clauses 140
 B Freight clauses 177
 C Cargo clauses 177
 D General average 182
 E Salvage 192
 F Other risks 194

Chapter 15—War and strike risks 197
 A War risks 197
   Generally 197
   The Institute Clauses 209
   Insurance by the State 211
   Mutual insurance associations 213
 B Strike risks 213

Chapter 16—Risks covered by protection and indemnity associations 215
 A Risks of a general nature 215
 B War risks 220
 C Freight and demurrage risks 224
 D Through transit risks 224

Chapter 17—The exceptions 225
 I Exceptions under the Marine Insurance Act 1906 225
 II Exceptions under the Institute Clauses 256
 III Other exceptions expressly stated in the policy 267
 IV Qualified undertakings of the insurer 268

Chapter 18—Termination and cancellation of the policy 273
 A Termination 273
 B Cancellation 273

Chapter 19—Rectification of the policy 274

Chapter 20—Alteration of the policy 278

Chapter 21—Warranties 280
 A Nature of warranties 280
 B The types of warranty 281
 C Express warranties 281
   Construction of an express warranty 281
   Necessity for inclusion in policy 282
   Examples of express warranties 282
    1 Sailing warranties 282
    2 Warranty as to position of ship 285
    3 Warranty as to number of crew 285
    4 Convoy warranties 286
    5 Warranty as to nationality 286
    6 Warranty as to neutrality 287
    7 Warranty as to part uninsured 288
    8 Other instances 291
 D Implied warranties 296
   Seaworthiness 296
    1 Voyage policies on ship 299

x   Contents

        2   Time policies on ship   302
        3   Mixed policies on ship   306
        4   Voyage policies on goods   307
   Legality   308
E   Excuses for breach of warranty   310
F   Result of breach of warranty   310
G   Waiver of breach of warranty   311

Chapter 22—The assignment of the policy   315

A   Assignability of policies   315
B   Right of assignee to sue in own name   315
C   Defences available to the insurer   316
D   Form of the assignment   319
E   Ineffectiveness of assignment by person having no interest   320
F   Rights of assignor and assignee inter se   321

Chapter 23—The construction of the policy   322

A   Construction and the doctrine of precedent   322
B   Some general rules of construction   322
   Intention of the parties   323
   Construction of policy as a whole   323
   Written and printed words   323
   Ordinary meaning   324
   Context of words   327
   Reasonable construction   327
   'Contra proferentem' rule   328
C   Rules set out in the Marine Insurance Act 1906   330

Chapter 24—The duties, authority and rights of the broker after effecting the policy   331

A   The duties and authority of the broker   331
   Where there are express instructions   331
   Where there are no express instructions   331
B   The rights of the broker   333
   Lien   333
      1   Particular lien   333
      2   General lien   334
   Brokerage   337

PART III—LOSS AND ABANDONMENT   341

Chapter 25—Introduction   341

Chapter 26—The types of loss   342

A   Total loss and partial loss   342
B   Actual total loss and constructive total loss   342
C   Particular average loss and general average loss   343

Chapter 27—Actual total loss   346

A   Actual total loss of ship   346
   Examples of actual total loss   346
   Sale of vessel by master   348
   Missing ships   349
B   Actual total loss of goods   349
C   Actual total loss of freight   350
   Loss of goods   350
   Arrival of goods in unmerchantable condition   352
   Sale of perishable cargo   353

Frustration of chartered voyage 353
Loss of ship before sailing 353
Ship unable to proceed 354
Effect of freight being earned 361

Chapter 28—Constructive total loss 362

  A Definition of 'constructive total loss' 362
      Completeness of definition 363
      Relation between s 60(1) and s 60(2) 364
      Notice of abandonment not an essential ingredient 365
  B Reasonable abandonment of subject-matter 365
  C Deprivation of possession of ship or goods 367
  D Damage to ship 372
  E Damage to goods 374
  F Constructive total loss arising from contract 375
  G Effect of constructive total loss 375
  H Effect of restoration on the extent of the loss 376

Chapter 29—Abandonment 378

  A When the right to abandon arises 378
  B Who may abandon 380
  C Notice of abandonment 381
  D In what cases notice must be given 382
  E Form of notice 385
  F To whom the notice must be given 387
  G Time within which notice must be given 387
  H No obligation on insurer to accept abandonment 389
  I What constitutes an acceptance 389
  J Irrevocability of abandonment 390
  K Waiver of notice of abandonment 392
  L The effect of abandonment 392
      1 Right to take over the subject-matter insured 392
      2 Right to freight 392

Chapter 30—Discovery of ship's papers 397

Discretion of the court 397
Persons against whom an order can be made 400

PART IV—THE MEASURE OF INDEMNITY

Chapter 31—Introduction 405

Chapter 32—Total loss 407

Total loss of freight 407
Effect of devaluation 407

Chapter 33—Partial loss of ship 410

  A Ship insured against total loss only 410
  B Particular average warranties 410
  C 'Deductible' clauses 418
  D Calculating the measure of indemnity 418
  E Procedure for ascertaining the amount payable 426

Chapter 34—Partial loss of freight 427

  A Losses not amounting to the specified percentage 427
  B Losses amounting to the specified percentage 427

Chapter 35—Partial loss of goods 429
- A Particular average warranties 429
- B Apportionment of valuation 432
- C Calculating the measure of indemnity 432
- D Liability of insurer for salvage charges and particular charges 436

Chapter 36—General average contribution and salvage charges 437

Chapter 37—Liabilities to third parties 439

Chapter 38—Successive losses 440

Chapter 39—Sue and labour clause 442
- A Generally 442
  - 'Factors, servants and assigns' 442
  - Expenses properly incurred 443
  - Necessity for existence of peril 447
  - Independent contract 447
  - Need for peril to be covered by policy 447
  - Expenses incurred by the insurer not recoverable 449
  - Scope of s 78(4) 449
  - Position where there is no 'sue and labour' clause 450
- B The Institute Clauses 451
  - Cargo clauses 451
  - Hull clauses 451

PART V—THE RIGHTS OF THE INSURER ON PAYMENT

Chapter 40—Subrogation 455
- A The rights in respect of which subrogation arises 456
- B The exercise of the right of subrogation 458
- C The effects of subrogation 458

Chapter 41—The right of contribution 461

PART VI—REINSURANCE

Chapter 42—Reinsurance 465
- A The relation between the original assured and the reinsurer 465
- B The relation between the reassured and the reinsurer 466
  - Payment under original policy 466
  - Expiry of original policy 466
  - Excess clause 467
  - Insurable interest 467
  - Unseaworthiness 468
  - Proximate cause of loss 469
  - 'Total or constructive loss only' 470

PART VII—MUTUAL INSURANCE

Chapter 43—Mutual insurance 475
- Rules of association 475
- Terms of entry and membership 475
- Contribution by members 476
- The period of insurance 477
- Cesser of insurance 478
- The risks covered 478

Contents xiii

Claims 478
Disputes 478
Certificates 479

APPENDICES

Appendix I—Statutes 483

The Sale of Goods Act 1979, ss 16–20 483
The Merchant Shipping Act 1894, s 506 484
The Marine Insurance Act 1906 484
The Marine Insurance (Gambling Policies) Act 1909 503
The Marine and Aviation Insurance (War Risks) Act 1952 504

Appendix II—Marine policy forms 510

1 Lloyd's form 510
2 Insurance Companies' form 513

Appendix III—The Institute Clauses 516

1 Cargo Clauses 516
   Institute Cargo Clauses (A) 516
   Institute Cargo Clauses (B) 519
   Institute Cargo Clauses (C) 523
   Institute War Clauses (Cargo) 526
   Institute Strikes Clauses (Cargo) 530
2 Hull Clauses 533
   Institute Time Clauses (Hulls) 533
   Institute Voyage Clauses (Hulls) 540
   Institute War and Strikes Clauses (Hulls—Time) 547
   Institute War and Strikes Clauses (Hulls—Voyage) 549
3 Freight Clauses 550
   Institute Time Clauses (Freight) 550
   Institute Voyage Clauses (Freight) 555
   Institute War and Strikes Clauses (Freight—Time) 558
   Institute War and Strikes Clauses (Freight—Voyage) 560
4 Institute Warranties 565

Appendix IV—The York-Antwerp Rules 1974 563

Appendix V—Rules of Practice of the Association of Average Adjusters (1981) 568

Appendix VI—Ship's Papers—Rules of the Supreme Court 595

INDEX 597

Table of statutes

Page references printed in bold type indicate where the Act is set out in part or in full.

	PAGE
Admiralty Court Act 1840	
s 6	25
Arbitration Act 1950	479
British Nationality Act 1948	509
Capital Allowances Act 1965	
s 33 (7)	203
Companies Act 1862	500
Companies Act 1985	
s 519(1)	468
Courts Act 1971	
s 56	13
Sch 9	13
Customs Consolidation Act 1853	
s 170–172	308
Emergency Laws (Miscellaneous Provisions) Act 1947	211
Encouragement of Trade (1663)	
s 6	308
Exportation (1793)	308
Finance Act 1901	
s 11	113
(1), (3)	113
Finance Act 1959	
Sch 8	
Pt II	67, 113
Food and Drugs Act 1938	
s 10	255
Gaming Act 1845	12
Harbours, Docks and Piers Act 1847	
s 56	394
Interpretation Act 1978	
s 9	113
23 (3)	113
Limitation Act 1939	184
s 2 (1)	184
Limitation Act 1980	
s 5	184
Marine and Aviation Insurance (War Risks) Act 1952	211, **505–509**
s 1 (1), (2)	212
2 (1)	211, 213
3 (1)	213
4	213
5 (1)–(4)	213

	PAGE
Marine Insurance Act 1745	11, 12, 36
Marine Insurance Act 1906	7, 149, 225, 309, **484–501**, 508
s 1	4, 7, 330
2 (1)	7
(2)	8
3	141
(1), (2)	4
4	12, 14, 15, 16, 36, 468
(2)	12, 468
5 (1)	16, 123
(2)	16
6 (1)	27, 28, 110
(2)	29
7 (1)	16, 26
9 (1)	26
(2)	465
10	27
11	23
12	20
14 (1)	22
(2)	22, 24
(3)	17
15	320
16	7, 98, 99
(2)	10
18	77
(1)	39, 41, 66, 68
(2)	40, 44
(3)	45, 48, 49, 52
(4)	53
(5)	54
19	41
20	62, 75, 76, 310
(1)	71, 75, 78, 280
(2)	72
(4)	72, 280
(5)	72
(6)	77
(7)	72
21	67, 71, 77
23	104
24 (1), (2)	111

xvi Table of statutes

Marine Insurance Act 1906—contd	PAGE
s 25 (1)	90, 91
26 (1)	106
(2)	111
(3)	112
(4)	106
27 (1)	93
(2)	94
(3)	94, 95, 424
(4)	96, 373
28	97
29 (1), (2)	91
(3)	92
(4)	93
30	330
(1)	101, 330
(2)	9, 330
31 (1), (2)	80
32	458
(1)	5, 461
(2)	5, 461
33 (1)	280
(2)	281
(3)	280, 293, 310
34 (1)	310
(2), (3)	311
35 (1)	281
(2)	280, 282
(3)	281
36 (1)	287
(2)	287, 288
37	286
38	285
39	296
(1)	53, 299, 306
(2)	299
(3)	301
(4)	297
(5)	303, 304, 306
40 (1)	307
(2)	296, 307
41	296, 308, 309, 314
42 (1), (2)	126
43, 44	116, 118
45	127, 128
(1), (2)	127
46	117, 129
(2)	326
47	130
48	67, 135
49	129
(1)	130, 133, 134, 136, 138
(2)	138
50	316, 319
(1)	315
(2)	315, 316, 317, 318
(3)	319
51	321
52	82
53 (1)	82, 86

Marine Insurance Act 1906—contd	PAGE
s 53 (2)	334
54	82
55	486
(1)	226, 227
(2)	50, 142, 168, 194, 196, 228, 231, 232, 247, 248, 250, 254, 255, 256, 450
56	363, 364
(1), (2)	342
(3)–(5)	342
57	363
(1)	10, 165, 342, 346, 391
(2)	343
58	349
59	133, 393
60	363, 364, 366, 376
(1)	10, 350, 362, 363, 364, 365, 366
(2)	165, 362, 364, 365, 366, 367, 374
61	343, 364, 365, 375, 376, 378, 394, 440
62	364, 365
(1)	343, 382
(2)	385
(3)	387
(4), (5)	389
(6)	390, 391, 392
(7)	343, 380, 382, 384
(8)	392
(9)	343, 385
63	364, 393
(1)	392, 393
(2)	394
64 (1)	343, 417
(2)	193, 417
65	194
(1)	192, 194
(2)	192, 443
66 (1)	193, 344
(2)	344
(3)	185, 344
(4)	182, 183
(5)	183
66 (6), (7)	184
67 (1)	96, 405
(2)	105, 405
68	407
69	6, 410, 419, 423
(1), (2)	423
(3)	423, 424
70	10, 427
71	429, 432, 433
(3), (4)	434
72 (1), (2)	432
73 (1), (2)	437
74	439
75 (1)	406

Table of statutes xvii

Marine Insurance Act 1906—contd	PAGE
s 76 (1)	430
(2)	417, 436
(3)	416
(4)	417
77 (1)	414, 440
(2)	440
78 (1)	417, 442, 446
(2)	443
(3)	442
(4)	231, 242, 442, 446, 450
79	6, 394
(1)	5, 455, 459
(2)	5, 455
80	5
(1), (2)	461
81	405, 459
82	86
83	83
84	6, 84
(3)	6, 108
85	475
87	330
(1)	325
88	136, 349, 387
90	4, 9, 433
91	117
(2)	330
Sch 1	145, 322, **501**
Form	101
r 1	330
2	115, 330
3	115, 118, 330
4	330
5	330
6	130, 328, 330
7	141, 330
8	155, 330
9	152, 330
10	330
11	162, 165, 246, 330
12	327, 330
13	411, 330
14	330
15	9, 107, 330
16	3, 107, 330
17	9, 107, 154, 326, 330
Marine Insurance (Gambling Policies) Act 1909	12, **503–504**
s 1 (1)	12, 13
(2)–(5), (7)	13
(8)	12
Merchant Shipping Act 1854	23, 193, **484**
Merchant Shipping Act 1876	
s 5	297
Merchant Shipping Act 1894 (31 *Statutes* 57)	23, 194, 455
s 31–46	22
68	287
157 (1)	23

Merchant Shipping Act 1894—contd	PAGE
s 544	193
(1)	193
742	161
Merchant Shipping Act 1979	
s 44	297
Ministers of the Crown (Transfer of Functions) Act 1946	509
Naval Prize Act 1864 (25 *Statutes* 910)	126
Pacific Islanders Protection Act 1872	308
Pacific Islanders Protection Act 1875	164
Policies of Marine Assurance Act 1868	
s 1	316
Port of Boston Act 1842	
s 29	394
Prize (1782)	26
Restriction of Advertisement (War Risks Insurance) Act 1939	
s 1 (1), (2)	509
Revolted Colonies, America (1776)	308
Sale of Goods Act 1979	**483**
s 6	29
16–19	18
39, 46, 48	18
Sale of Goods Act 1979	
s 6	29
16–20	**483–484**
Slave Trade (1791)	
s 7	308
Stamp Act 1891	500, 508
s 93	113
Summer Time Act 1972	
s 3	113
War Risks Insurance Act 1939:	211, 212, 509

AUSTRALIA

Marine Insurance Act 1909	
s 51	128
63	391
68 (1)	391
(6)	391, 392
84	451
(1)–(3)	451

CANADA

BRITISH COLUMBIA

Marine Insurance Act (RSC 1960 C 231)	
s 20, 43	66, 310

INDIA

Marine Insurance Act 1963	458
Transfer of Property Act	
s 135A	458

UNITED STATES OF AMERICA

Tanker Act (46 US Code 391a)	
s 391a	309

Table of cases

A

	PAGE
Acanthus, The [1902] P 17, 71 LJP 14, 85 LT 696, 18 TLR 160, 9 Asp MLC 276	416, 421
Adamson v Newcastle SS Freight Insurance Association (1879) 4 QBD 462, 48 LJQB 670, 41 LT 160, 27 WR 818, 4 Asp MLC 150, DC	353
Adelaide SS Co v R (1923) 129 LT 161, 16 Asp MLC 178, 14 Ll L Rep 341, HL	200
Admiral C, The. See Stolos Compania SA v Ajax Insurance Co Ltd, The Admiral C	
Admiralty Comrs v Brynawel SS Co Ltd (1923) 40 TLR 78, 17 Ll L Rep 89	202
African Merchants Co v British and Foreign Marine Insurance Co (1873) LR 8 Exch 154, 42 LJ Ex 60, 28 LT 233, 21 WR 484, 1 Asp MLC 558, Ex Ch	132
Agenoria SS Co Ltd v Merchants Marine Insurance Co Ltd (1903) 19 TLR 442, 8 Com Cas 212	422
Aifanourios, The. See West of Scotland Ship Owners Mutual Protection and Indemnity Association (Luxembourg) v Aifanourios Shipping SA, The Aifanourios	
Aitchison v Lohre (1879) 4 App Cas 755, 49 LJQB 123, 41 LT 323, 28 WR 1, 4 Asp MLC 168, HL	193, 375, 379, 420, 443
Ajum Goolam Hossen & Co v Union Marine Insurance Co [1901] AC 362, 70 LJPC 34, 84 LT 366, 17 TLR 376, 9 Asp MLC 167, PC	298
Al-Jubail IV, The. See Almojil (M) Establishment v Malayan Motor and General Underwriters (Private) Ltd, The Al-Jubail IV	
Aldridge v Bell (1816) 1 Stark 498	388
Alexander v Campbell (1872) 27 LT 462, 1 Asp MLC 447	72
Allagar Rubber Estates Ltd v National Benefit Assurance Co Ltd (1922) 10 Ll L Rep 564	8, 123
Allden v Raven, The Kylie [1983] 2 Lloyd's Rep 444	53, 60, 66
Allgemeine Versicherungs-Gesellschaft Helvetia v German Property Administrator [1931] 1 KB 672, 100 LJKB 290, 144 LT 705, CA	393
Allison v Bristol Marine Insurance Co (1876) 1 App Cas 209, [1874–80] All ER Rep 781, 34 LT 809, 24 WR 1039, 3 Asp MLC 178, HL	21, 351
Alluvials Mining Machinery Co v Stowe (1922) 10 Ll L Rep 96	65, 81
Almojil (M) Establishment v Malayan Motor and General Underwriters (Private) Ltd, The Al-Jubail IV [1982] 2 Lloyd's Rep 637	91, 138, 295, 306, 313, 322
Alps, The [1893] P 109, 62 LJP 59, 68 LT 624, 41 WR 527, 9 TLR 285, 7 Asp MLC 337, 1 R 587	229, 267, 428
Alston v Campbell (1779) 4 Bro Parl Cas 476, HL	25
American Employers Insurance Co v St Paul Fire and Marine Insurance Co Ltd [1978] 1 Lloyd's Rep 417	277
Amin Rasheed Shipping Corpn v Kuwait Insurance Co [1982] 1 WLR 961, 126 Sol Jo 343, [1982] 1 Lloyd's Rep 638; affd. [1983] 1 All ER 873, [1983] 1 WLR 228, 127 Sol Jo 51, [1983] 1 Lloyd's Rep 235, CA; affd. [1984] AC 50, [1983] 2 All ER 884, [1983] 3 WLR 241, 127 Sol Jo 492, [1983] 2 Lloyd's Rep 365, HL	103
Anderson v Morice (1875) LR 10 CP 609, 44 LJCP 341, 33 LT 355, 24 WR 30, 3 Asp MLC 31, Ex Ch; affd. sub nom. Anderson v Morice, Morice v Anderson (1876) 1 App Cas 713, 46 LJQB 11, 35 LT 566, 25 WR 14, 3 Asp MLC 290, HL	26, 28, 298
Anderson v Ocean SS Co (1884) 10 App Cas 107, 54 LJQB 192, 52 LT 441, 33 WR 433, 5 Asp MLC 401, HL	444
Anderson v Pacific Fire and Marine Insurance Co (1872) LR 7 CP 65, 26 LT 130, 20 WR 280, 1 Asp MLC 220	74

xx *Table of cases*

	PAGE
Anderson v Pitcher (1800) 2 Bos & P 164	72, 286
Anderson v Royal Exchange Assurance Co (1805) 7 East 38, 3 Smith KB 48	332, 350, 379, 413
Anderson v Wallis (1813) 2 M & S 240, 3 Camp 440	375
Andrews v Mellish (1814) 5 Taunt 496, Ex Ch	131
Angel v Merchants Marine Insurance Co [1903] 1 KB 811, [1900–3] All ER Rep 952, 72 LJKB 498, 88 LT 717, 51 WR 530, 19 TLR 395, 9 Asp MLC 406, 8 Com Cas 179, CA	97, 374
Angerstein v Bell (1795) 1 Park's Marine Insce 7th ed 55	120
Anghelatos v Northern Assurance Co Ltd (1924) 40 TLR 813, 68 Sol Jo 812, 30 Com Cas 31, 19 Ll L Rep 255, HL	237, 243
Anghelatos and London Joint City and Midland Bank v Northern Assurance Co (1922) 13 Ll L Rep 291, CA	397, 400
Annen v Woodman (1810) 3 Taunt 299	115, 299
Apollinaris Co v Nord Deutsche Insurance Co [1904] 1 KB 252, 73 LJKB 62, 89 LT 670, 52 WR 174, 20 TLR 79, 9 Asp MLC 526, 9 Com Cas 91	154, 326
Arcangelo v Thompson (1811) 2 Camp 620	287
Aries Tanker Corpn v Total Transport Ltd, The Aries [1977] 1 All ER 398, [1977] 1 WLR 185, 121 Sol Jo 117, [1977] 1 Lloyd's Rep 334, HL	19
Armar, The. *See* Compania Maritima Astra SA v Archdale, The Armar	
Armet v Innes (1820) 4 Moore CP 150	131
Aron (J) & Co v Miall (1928) 98 LJKB 204, [1928] All ER Rep 655, 139 LT 562, 34 Com Cas 18, 17 Asp MLC 529, 31 Ll L Rep 242, CA	319, 320
Aronsen (Oscar L) Inc v Compton, The Megara [1973] 2 Lloyd's Rep 361; affd. [1974] 1 Lloyd's Rep 590	377, 471
Arrow Shipping Co v Tyne Improvement Comrs, The Crystal [1894] AC 508, 63 LJP 146, 71 LT 346, 10 TLR 551, 7 Asp MLC 513, 6 R 258, HL	393
Asfar & Co v Blundell [1895] 2 QB 196, 64 LJQB 573, 1 Com Cas 75, 15 R 481; affd. [1896] 1 QB 123, 65 LJQB 138, 73 LT 648, 44 WR 130, 12 TLR 29, 40 Sol Jo 66, 8 Asp MLC 106, 1 Com Cas 185, CA	19, 20, 50, 51, 52, 95, 262, 350, 352
Assicurazioni Generali and Schenker & Co v SS Bessie Morris Co Ltd and Browne [1892] 2 QB 652, 61 LJQB 754, 67 LT 218, 41 WR 83, 8 TLR 715, 36 Sol Jo 682, 7 Asp MLC 217, 4 R 33, CA	354
Assicurazioni Generali De Trieste v Empress Assurance Corpn Ltd [1907] 2 KB 814, 76 LJKB 980, 97 LT 785, 23 TLR 700, 51 Sol Jo 703, 10 Asp MLC 577, 13 Com Cas 37	460
Associated Oil Carriers Ltd v Union Insurance Society of Canton Ltd [1917] 2 KB 184, 86 LJKB 1068, 116 LT 503, 33 TLR 327, 14 Asp MLC 48, 22 Com Cas 346	44, 59, 384
Astrovlanis Compania Naviera SA v Linard (The Gold Sky) [1972] 2 QB 611, [1972] 2 All ER 647, [1972] 2 WLR 1414, 116 Sol Jo 176, [1972] 1 Lloyd's Rep 331, CA	243
Astrovlanis Compania Naviera SA v Linard, The Gold Sky [1972] 2 Lloyd's Rep 187	231, 242, 247, 449
Athel Line Ltd v Liverpool and London War Risks Insurance Association Ltd [1946] KB 117, [1945] 2 All ER 694, 115 LJKB 141, 174 LT 81, 62 TLR 81, 79 Ll L Rep 18, CA	200
Athens Maritime Enterprises Corpn v Hellenic Mutual War Risks Association (Bermuda) Ltd [1983] QB 647, [1983] 1 All ER 590, [1983] 2 WLR 425, 126 Sol Jo 577, [1982] 2 Lloyd's Rep 483	157
Atlantic Maritime Carriers SA v Hellenic Mutual War Risks Association Ltd [1968] 2 Lloyd's Rep 124; on appeal sub nom. The Mitera (1969) 113 Sol Jo 282, [1969] 1 Lloyd's Rep 359, CA	223
Atlantic Maritime Co Inc v Gibbon [1954] 1 QB 88, [1953] 2 All ER 1086, [1953] 3 WLR 714, 97 Sol Jo 760, [1953] 2 Lloyd's Rep 294, CA	103, 262, 264, 265, 408
Atlantic Transport Co v R, The Maryland (1921) 9 Ll L Rep 370	199
A-G v Ard Coasters Ltd, Liverpool and London War Risks Insurance Association Ltd v SS Richard de Larrinaga Marine Underwriters [1921] 2 AC 141, 91 LJKB 31, 125 LT 548, 37 TLR 692, 15 Asp MLC 353, 26 Com Cas 352, HL	199, 205
A-G v Glen Line Ltd and Liverpool and London War Risks Insurance Association Ltd (1929) 34 Com Cas 309, CA; revsd. sub nom. Glen Line Ltd v A-G (1930) 46 TLR 451, 36 Com Cas 1, 37 Ll L Rep 55, HL	393, 456, 457, 465

Table of cases xxi

	PAGE
Australasian Insurance Co v Jackson (1875) 33 LT 286, 3 Asp MLC 26, PC	164, 308
Australasian Steam Navigation Co v Morse (1872) LR 4 PC 222, 8 Moo PCCNS 482, 27 LT 357, 20 WR 728, 1 Asp MLC 407	349
Australian Agricultural Co v Saunders (1872) cited in 28 LT 844; affd. (1875) LR 10 CP 668, 44 LJCP 391, 33 LT 447, 3 Asp MLC 63, Ex Ch	133
Australian Coastal Shipping Commission v Green [1971] QB 456, [1971] 1 All ER 353, [1971] 2 WLR 243, 115 Sol Jo 57, [1971] 1 Lloyd's Rep 16, CA	187

B

Bah Lias Tobacco and Rubber Estates Ltd v Volga Insurance Co Ltd (1920) 3 Ll L Rep 155, 202	126
Bain v Case (1829) 3 C & P 496, Mood & M 262	136
Baines v Holland (1855) 10 Exch 802, 3 CLR 593, 24 LJ Ex 204	285
Baines v Woodfall (1859) 6 CBNS 657, 28 LJCP 338, 6 Jur NS 19	83
Baker v Adam (1910) 102 LT 248, [1908–10] All ER Rep 632, 15 Com Cas 227, 11 Asp MLC 368	319, 320
Baker v Towry (1816) 1 Stark 436	411
Baker-Whiteley Coal Co v Marten (1910) 26 TLR 314	413
Balmoral SS Co v Marten [1901] 2 KB 896, 70 LJKB 1018, 85 LT 389, 50 WR 35, 17 TLR 765, 9 Asp MLC 254, 6 Com Cas 298, CA; affd. [1902] AC 511, [1900–3] All ER Rep 961, 71 LJKB 819, 87 LT 247, 18 TLR 802, 9 Asp MLC 321, 7 Com Cas 292, HL	7, 97, 437
Bamburi, The [1982] 1 Lloyd's Rep 312	367, 371, 377
Banco de Barcelona v Union Marine Insurance Co Ltd (1925) 134 LT 350, 69 Sol Jo 747, 16 Asp MLC 604, 30 Com Cas 316, 22 Ll L Rep 209, 317; on appeal 23 Ll L Rep 55, 214, CA	238
Bank of Athens v Royal Exchange Assurance, The Eftychia (1937) 57 Ll L Rep 37; affd. 59 Ll L Rep 67, CA	241
Bank of New South Wales v South British Insurance Co Ltd (1920) 4 Ll L Rep 266	317
Banque Monetaca and Carystuiaki v Motor Union Insurance Co Ltd (1923) 14 Ll L Rep 48	156
Barber v Fleming (1869) LR 5 QB 59, 10 B & S 879, 39 LJQB 25, 18 WR 254	21
Barber v Fletcher (1779) 1 Doug KB 305	78
Barclay v Cousins (1802) 2 East 544	26
Barclay v Stirling (1816) 5 M & S 6	131, 395, 396
Baring v Christie (1804) 5 East 398, 1 Smith KB 462	286
Baring v Clagett (1802) 3 Bos & P 201	282, 286, 287
Baring v Henkle (1801) 1 Marshall on Marine Insces 3rd ed 232	411
Baring Bros & Co v Marine Insurance Co (1894) 10 TLR 276, CA	4, 102, 433
Barker v Blakes (1808) 9 East 283	388
Barker v Janson (1868) LR 3 CP 303, 37 LJCP 105, 17 LT 473, 16 WR 399, 3 Mar LC 28	94, 346
Barrow v Bell (1825) 4 B & C 736, 7 Dow & Ry KB 244, 4 LJOSKB 47	412
Bartlett v Pentland (1830) 10 B & C 760, [1824–34] All ER Rep 144, L & Welsb 235, 8 LJOSKB 264	327
Bates v Hewitt (1867) LR 2 QB 595, 36 LJQB 282, 15 WR 1172	46, 50, 56
Beatson v Haworth (1796) 6 Term Rep 531	130
Becker, Gray & Co v London Assurance Corpn [1918] AC 101, [1916–17] All ER Rep 146, 87 LJKB 69, 117 LT 609, 34 TLR 36, 62 Sol Jo 35, 14 Asp MLC 156, 23 Com Cas 205, HL	230, 264
Beckett v West of England Marine Insurance Co Ltd (1871) 25 LT 739, 1 Asp MLC 185	119
Beckwaite v Nalgrove (Unreported) cited in (1910) 3 Taunt 41	54
Beckwith v Sydebotham (1807) 1 Camp 116	52
Bedouin, The [1894] P 1, 63 LJP 30, 69 LT 782, 42 WR 299, 10 TLR 70, 7 Asp MLC 391, 6 R 693, CA	52, 73, 229, 428
Belcher v Capper (1842) 4 Man & G 502, 5 Scott NR 257, 11 LJCP 274	163
Bell v Bell (1810) 2 Camp 475	115, 121
Bell v Bromfield (1812) 15 East 364	287
Bell v Carstairs (1810) 2 Camp 543	78
Bell v Carstairs (1811) 14 East 374	232

Belle of Portugal, The. See Rosa v Insurance Co of the State of Pennsylvania, The Belle of Portugal
Benlarig, The (1888) 14 PD 3, 58 LJP 24, 60 LT 238, 6 Asp MLC 360 443
Bennett SS Co v Hull Mutual SS Protecting Society [1914] 3 KB 57, 83 LJKB 1179, 111 LT 489, 30 TLR 515, 12 Asp MLC 522, 19 Com Cas 353, CA 172
Bensaude v Thames and Mersey Marine Insurance Co [1897] AC 609, [1895–9] All ER Rep 256, 66 LJQB 666, 77 LT 282, 46 WR 78, 13 TLR 501, 8 Asp MLC 315, 2 Com Cas 238, HL 230, 262, 281
Benson v Chapman (1849) 2 HL Cas 696, 8 CB 950, 13 Jur 696, HL . . . 361
Bergens Dampskibs Assurance Forening v Sun Insurance Office Ltd (1930) 143 LT 435, 46 TLR 543, 74 Sol Jo 568, 18 Asp MLC 172, 37 Ll L Rep 175 470
Berger and Light Diffusers Proprietary Ltd v Pollock [1973] 2 Lloyd's Rep 442 . 40, 41, 56, 57, 62, 67, 97, 99, 350
Berk (F W) & Co Ltd v Style [1956] 1 QB 180, [1955] 3 All ER 625, [1955] 3 WLR 935, 99 Sol Jo 889, [1955] 2 Lloyd's Rep 382 . . . . 253, 448
Bernardi v Motteux (1781) 2 Doug KB 575 287
Berthon v Loughman (1817) 2 Stark 258 79
Biccard v Shepherd (1861) 14 Moo PCC 471, sub nom. Commercial Marine Co v Namaqua Mining Co 5 LT 504, 10 WR 136, 1 Mar LC 165, PC 299, 302
Bird v Appleton (1800) 8 Term Rep 562 . . . . 288, 309
Bird v Brown (1850) 4 Exch 786, 19 LJ Ex 154, 14 LTOS 399, 14 Jur 132 . . 381
Bird's Cigarette Manufacturing Co Ltd v Rouse (1924) 19 Ll L Rep 301 . . 62, 251, 291
Birkley v Presgrave (1801) 1 East 220 344
Birrell v Dryer (1884) 9 App Cas 345, 51 LT 130, 5 Asp MLC 267, HL . . . 328
Bishop v Pentland (1827) 7 B & C 219, 1 Man & Ry KB 49, 6 LJOSKB 6 . . 231, 412
Black King Shipping Corpn v Massie, The Litsion Pride (1984) Times, 17 December . . 39
Blackburn v Haslam (1888) 21 QBD 144, 57 LJQB 479, 59 LT 407, 36 WR 855, 4 TLR 577, 6 Asp MLC 326, CA 43
Blackburn v Liverpool, Brazil and River Plate Steam Navigation Co [1902] 1 KB 290, [1900–3] All ER Rep 67, 71 LJKB 177, 85 LT 783, 50 WR 272, 18 TLR 121, 9 Asp MLC 263, 7 Com Cas 10 143
Blackburn, Low & Co v Vigors (1887) 12 App Cas 531, 57 LJQB 114, 57 LT 730, 36 WR 449, 3 TLR 837, 6 Asp MLC 216, HL 41, 43
Blackenhagen v London Assurance Co (1808) 1 Camp 454 230
Blackett v Royal Exchange Assurance (1832) 2 Cr & J 244, [1824–34] All ER Rep 468, 2 Tyr 266, 1 LJ Ex 101 . . . . 326, 328, 414
Blackett, Magalhaes and Colombie v National Benefit Assurance Corpn (1921) 8 Ll L Rep 293, CA 307
Blackhurst v Cockell (1789) 3 Term Rep 360 285
Blairmore Co Ltd (Sailing Ship) v Macredie [1898] AC 593, 79 LT 217, 14 TLR 513, 8 Asp MLC 429, 3 Com Cas 241, sub nom. The Blairmore 67 LJPC 96, HL . . . 376
Blane Steamships Ltd v Minister of Transport [1951] 2 KB 965, [1951] 2 TLR 763, 95 Sol Jo 577, [1951] 2 Lloyd's Rep 155, CA 394
Blower v Great Western Rly Co (1872) LR 7 CP 655, 41 LJCP 268, 26 LT 883, 36 JP 792, 20 WR 776 250
Boag v Standard Marine Insurance Co Ltd [1937] 2 KB 113, [1937] 1 All ER 714, 106 LJKB 450, 156 LT 338, 53 TLR 414, 81 Sol Jo 157, 19 Asp MLC 107, 42 Com Cas 214, 57 Ll L Rep 83, CA 458
Board of Trade v Hain SS Co [1929] AC 534, [1929] All ER Rep 26, 98 LJKB 625, 141 LT 435, 45 TLR 550, 18 Asp MLC 15, 35 Com Cas 29, HL 200
Bolivia Republic v Indemnity Mutual Marine Assce Co Ltd [1909] 1 KB 785, 99 LT 394, 24 TLR 724, 11 Asp MLC 117; affd. [1908–10] All ER Rep 260, 78 LJKB 596, 100 LT 503, 25 TLR 254, 53 Sol Jo 266, 11 Asp MLC 218, 14 Com Cas 156, CA . 41, 42, 46, 154, 156
Bond v Nutt (1777) 2 Cowp 601 280
Bondrett v Hentigg (1816) Holt NP 149 . . . . 144, 156
Boon and Cheah Steel Pipes Sdn Bhd v Asia Insurance Co Ltd [1975] 1 Lloyd's Rep 452 . 227, 350, 363, 374
Booth v Gair (1863) 15 CBNS 291, 3 New Rep 121, 33 LJCP 99, 9 LT 386, 9 Jur NS 1326, 12 WR 105, 1 Mar LC 393 444

Table of cases xxiii

	PAGE
Boston Corpn v Fenwick & Co Ltd (1923) 129 LT 766, [1923] All ER Rep 583, 39 TLR 441, 16 Asp MLC 239, 28 Com Cas 367, 15 Ll L Rep 85	394
Bosworth (No 3), The (1962). See Grand Union (Shipping) Ltd v London SS Owners' Mutual Insurance Association Ltd, The Bosworth (No 3)	
Bottomley v Bovill (1826) 5 B & C 210, 7 Dow & Ry KB 702, 4 LJOSKB 237	131, 132, 166
Bouillon v Lupton (1863) 15 CBNS 113, 2 New Rep 393, 33 LJPC 37, 8 LT 575, 10 Jur NS 422, 11 WR 966, 1 Mar LC 347	283
Boulton v Houlder Bros & Co [1904] 1 KB 784, 73 LJKB 493, 90 LT 621, 52 WR 388, 20 TLR 328, 48 Sol Jo 310, 9 Asp MLC 592, 9 Com Cas 182, CA	397, 401
Bousfield v Barnes (1815) 4 Camp 228	93, 461
Bousfield v Creswell (1810) 2 Camp 545	332
Bowden v Vaughan (1809) 10 East 415	73
Bowring (C T) & Co Ltd v Amsterdam London Insurance Co Ltd (1930) 36 Ll L Rep 309	251
Boyd v Dubois (1811) 3 Camp 133	151, 250
Braconbush, The. See United Scottish Insurance Co Ltd v British Fishing Vessels Mutual War Risks Association Ltd, The Braconbush	
Bradford v Levy (1825) 2 C & P 137, Ry & M 331	166
Bradford v Symondson (1881) 7 QBD 456, 50 LJQB 582, 45 LT 364, 30 WR 27, 4 Asp MLC 455, CA	86
Bragg v Anderson (1812) 4 Taunt 229	131
Brandeis Goldschmidt & Co v Economic Insurance Co Ltd (1922) 38 TLR 609, 11 Ll L Rep 42	183, 186
Brankelow SS Co v Canton Insurance Office [1899] 2 QB 178, CA; affd. sub nom. Williams & Co v Canton Insurance Office Ltd [1901] AC 462, 70 LJKB 962, 85 LT 317, 17 TLR 696, 9 Asp MLC 247, 6 Com Case 256, HL	351
Brede, The. See Henriksens Rederi A/S v T H Z Rolimpex, The Brede (1972) (1974)	
Brentwood, The. See Coast Ferries Ltd v Century Insurance Co of Canada, The Brentwood	
Bridges v Hunter (1813) 1 M & S 15	44, 55, 57, 78
Briggs v Merchant Traders' Association (1849) 13 QB 167, 18 LJQB 178, 13 LTOS 68, 13 Jur 787	25
Brine v Featherstone (1813) 4 Taunt 869	74
Bristol SS Corpn v London Assurance and Linard, The Delfin [1976] 2 Lloyd's Rep 741	270, 324, 325
Britain SS Co Ltd v R [1921] 1 AC 99, 89 LJKB 881, 123 LT 721, 36 TLR 791, 64 Sol Jo 737, 15 Asp MLC 58, 25 Com Cas 301, HL	198, 203, 204
British American Tobacco Co v Poland (1920); on appeal (1921) 7 Ll L Rep 108, CA	136
British and Burmese Steam Navigation Co Ltd v Liverpool and London War Risks Insurance Association Ltd and British and Foreign Marine Insurance Co Ltd (1917) 34 TLR 140	207
British and Foreign Insurance Co Ltd v Wilson Shipping Co Ltd [1921] 1 AC 188, [1920] All ER Rep 560, 89 LJKB 981, 123 LT 756, 36 TLR 890, 65 Sol Jo 25, 15 Asp MLC 114, 26 Com Cas 13, 4 Ll L Rep 197, 371, HL	440
British and Foreign Marine Insurance Co v Gaunt [1921] 2 AC 41, [1921] All ER Rep 447, 65 Sol Jo 551, 15 Asp MLC 305, 26 Com Cas 247, 7 Ll L Rep 62, HL	8, 107, 154, 178, 179, 326, 448, 449
British and Foreign Marine Insurance Co Ltd v Samuel Sanday & Co [1916] 1 AC 650, [1916–17] All ER Rep 134, 85 LJKB 550, 114 LT 521, 32 TLR 266, 60 Sol Jo 253, 13 Asp MLC 289, 21 Com Cas 154, HL	45, 59, 106, 264
British Dominions General Insurance Co Ltd v Duder [1915] 2 KB 394, [1914–15] All ER Rep 176, 84 LJKB 1401, 113 LT 210, 31 TLR 361, 13 Asp MLC 84, 20 Com Cas 270, CA	466
Broderick v Hollingsworth. See Hollingworth v Brodrick	
Brooking v Maudslay, Son and Field (1888) 38 Ch D 636, 57 LJ Ch 1001, 58 LT 852, 36 WR 664, 4 TLR 421, 6 Asp MLC 296	273, 311
Brooks v MacDonnell (1835) 1 Y & C Ex 500, 4 LJ Ex Eq 60	457
Brotherston v Barber (1816) 5 M & S 418	392
Brough v Whitmore (1791) 4 Term Rep 206	102, 325
Brown v Smith (1813) 1 Dow 349, HL	156, 168
Brown v Stapyleton (1827) 4 Bing 119, 12 Moore CP 334, 5 LJOSCP 121	108

xxiv *Table of cases*

PAGE

Brown v Tayleur (1835) 4 Ad & El 241, 1 Har & W 578, 5 Nev & MKB 472, 5 LJKB
 57 . . . . 116, 131
Brown v Tierney (1809) 1 Taunt 517 131
Brown v Vigne (1810) 12 East 283 120
Bruce v Jones (1863) 1 H & C 769, 1 New Rep 333, 32 LJ Ex 132, 7 LT 748, 9 Jur NS 628, 11
 WR 371, 1 Mar LC 280 461
Bruns v Colocotronis, The Vasso [1979] 2 Lloyd's Rep 412 13
Bryant and May Ltd v London Assurance Corpn (1886) 2 TLR 591 . . . 413
Buchanan & Co v Faber (1899) 15 TLR 383, 4 Com Cas 223 . . . 26, 299
Buckley v Gross (1863) 2 B & S 566, [1861–73] All ER Rep Ext 1844, 1 New Rep 357, 32
 LJQB 129, 7 LT 743, 27 JP 182, 9 Jur NS 986, 11 WR 465 436
Bullen v Denning (1826) 5 B & C 842, 8 Dow & Ry KB 657, 4 LJOSKB 314 . . . 322
Burges v Wickham (1863) 3 B & S 669, 33 LJQB 17, 8 LT 47, 10 Jur NS 92, 11 WR 992, 1
 Mar LC 303 297
Burnard v Rodocanachi (1882) 7 App Cas 333, 51 LJQB 548, 47 LT 277, 31 WR 65, 4 Asp
 MLC 576, HL 456
Burnett v Kensington (1797) 7 Term Rep 210 413
Burton v English (1883) 12 QBD 218, 53 LJQB 133, 49 LT 768, 32 WR 655, 5 Asp MLC 187,
 CA 154
Busk v Royal Exchange Assurance Co (1818) 2 B & Ald 73 . . . . 150, 231
Butler v Wildman (1820) 3 B & Ald 398, [1814–23] All ER Rep 748 153

C

CVG Siderurgicia del Orinoco SA v London SS Owners' Mutual Insurance Association Ltd,
 The Vainqueur José [1979] 1 Lloyd's Rep 557 . . . . . 219, 478
Cachapool, The (1881) 7 PD 217, 46 LT 171, 4 Asp MLC 502 284
Caine v Palace Steam Shipping Co [1907] 1 KB 670, 76 LJKB 292, 96 LT 410, 23 TLR 203,
 51 Sol Jo 170, 10 Asp MLC 380, 12 Com Cas 96 CA; affd. sub nom. Palace Shipping Co
 Ltd v Caine [1907] AC 386, 76 LJKB 1079, 97 LT 587, 23 TLR 731, 51 Sol Jo 716, 10
 Asp MLC 529, 13 Com Cas 51, HL 309
Callander (or Callender or Callendar) v Oelrichs (1838) 5 Bing NC 58, 1 Arn 401, 6 Scott
 761, 8 LJCP 25, 4 LT 341, 2 Jur 967 38
Calmar SS Corpn v Scott, The Portmar [1953] 1 Lloyd's Rep 485 104
Cambridge v Anderton (1824) 2 B & C 691, 1 C & P 213, 4 Dow & Ry KB 203, Ry & M 60,
 2 LJOSKB 141 . . . . 346, 382
Camden v Anderson (1798) 1 Bos & P 272 27
Camden v Cowley (1763) 1 Wm Bl 417 116
Camelo v Britten (1820) 4 B & Ald 184 308
Campbell v Christie (1817) 2 Stark 64 278
Campbell v Innes (1821) 4 B & Ald 423 59
Canada Rice Mills Ltd v Union Marine and General Insurance Co Ltd [1941] AC 55, [1940]
 4 All ER 169, 110 LJPC 1, 164 LT 367, 57 TLR 41, 85 Sol Jo 92, 46 Com Cas 74, 19 Asp
 MLC 391, 67 Ll L Rep 549, PC 143, 147
Canning v Maritime Insurance Co Ltd (1936) 56 Ll L Rep 91 240
Cantiere Meccanico Brindisino v Janson [1912] 3 KB 452, 81 LJKB 1043, 107 LT 281, 28
 TLR 564, 57 Sol Jo 62, 12 Asp MLC 246, 17 Com Cas 332, CA . 47, 50, 53, 54, 74, 297,
  302
Cape Borer, The. See Rudolph (M J) Corpn v Lumber Mutual Fire Insurance Co (Luria
 International, Third Parties), The Cape Borer
Capetandiamantis Compania Maritima SA, Eastern Seas Transport Corpn and Orient
 Shipping Corpn v Hellenic Mutual War Risks Association Ltd [1968] 2 Lloyd's Rep
 124; on appeal sub nom. The Mitera (1969) 113 Sol Jo 282, [1969] Lloyd's Rep 359,
 CA 223
Capital Coastal Shipping Corpn and Bulk Towing Corpn v Hartford Fire Insurance Co
 (United States of America, Third Party), The Christie [1975] 2 Lloyd's Rep 100 . 161,
  249, 295, 298, 313, 329
Caribbean Sea, The. See Prudent Tankers Ltd SA v Dominion Insurance Co Ltd, The
 Caribbean Sea

Caroline, The (1921) 37 TLR 617, 7 Ll L Rep 56 199
Carr v Royal Exchange Assurance Corpn (1864) 5 B & S 941, 5 New Rep 216, 34 LJQB 21,
 11 LT 595, 11 Jur NS 265, 13 WR 204, 2 Mar LC 160 328
Carras v London and Scottish Assurance Corpn Ltd [1936] 1 KB 291, [1935] All ER Rep
 246, 105 LJKB 689, 154 LT 69, 52 TLR 123, 41 Com Cas 120, 18 Asp MLC 581,
 CA 354, 361
Carruthers v Sheddon (1815) 6 Taunt 14, 1 Marsh 416 . . . . 24, 111
Carruthers v Sydebotham (1815) 4 M & S 77 411
Carter v Boehm (1766) 3 Burr 1905, 1 Wm Bl 593 . . . . . 46, 50, 79
Carter v Royal Exchange Assurance (prior to 1746) cited in 2 Stra 1249 130
Case v Davidson (1816) 5 M & S 79; affd. sub nom. Davidson v Case (1820) 2 Brod & Bing
 379, 8 Price 542, 5 Moore CP 116, Ex Ch 393, 395
Caspian Sea, The. See Montedison SpA v Icroma SpA, The Caspian Sea
Castle Insurance Co ltd v Hong Kong Islands Shipping Co Ltd, The Potoi Chau [1984] AC
 226, [1984] 3 All ER 706, [1983] 3 WLR 524, 127 Sol Jo 616, [1983] 2 Lloyd's Rep
 376 185
Castrique v Imrie (1870). See Imrie v Castrique (1860)
Cater v Great Western Insurance Co of New York. See Cator v Great Western Insurance Co
 of New York
Cates (Captain J A) Tug and Wharfage Co Ltd v Franklin Insurance Co [1927] AC 698, 96
 LJPC 132, 137 LT 709, 17 Asp MLC 819, 28 Ll L Rep 161, PC . . 347, 376, 390
Cator v Great Western Insurance Co of New York (1873) LR 8 CP 552, 29 LT 136, 21 WR
 850, 2 Asp MLC 90, sub nom. Cater v Great Western Insurance Co of New York 42
 LJCP 266 227
Chandler v Blogg [1898] 1 QB 32, 67 LJQB 336, 77 LT 524, 14 TLR 66, 8 Asp MLC 349, 3
 Com Cas 18 . . . . 172, 173, 414
Chandris v Argo Insurance Co Ltd (1963) 107 Sol Jo 575, [1963] 2 Lloyd's Rep 65 . . 184
Charente SS Co Ltd v Transports Director (1922) 10 Ll L Rep 514, 38 TLR 434, CA . . 200
Charlesworth v Faber (1900) 5 Com Cas 408 . . . . . . 46, 466
Charlotte, The [1908] P 206, 77 LJP 132, 99 LT 380, 24 TLR 416, 11 Asp MLC 87, CA . 458
Chaurand v Angerstein (1791) Peake 43 72
Cheshire (T) & Co v Thompson (1919) 35 TLR 317, 24 Com Cas 198, CA . . . 36
Cheshire (T) & Co v Vaughan Bros & Co [1920] 3 KB 240, 89 LJKB 1168, 123 LT 487, 84
 JP 233, 15 Asp MLC 69, 25 Com Cas 242, 3 Ll L Rep 213, CA . . 13, 14, 36, 468
China (Republic of), China Merchants Steam Navigation Co and United States of America v
 National Union Fire Insurance Co of Pittsburgh, Pennsylvania, The Hai Hsuan [1958]
 1 Lloyd's Rep 351, CA 167, 199
China (Republic of), China Merchants Steam Navigation Co Ltd and United States of
 America v National Union Fire Insurance Co of Pittsburgh, Pennsylvania, The Hai
 Hsuan (No 2) [1958] 2 Lloyd's Rep 578 13
China SS Co v Commercial Assurance Co (1881) 8 QBD 142, 51 LJQB 132, 45 LT 647, 30
 WR 224, CA 401
China Traders' Insurance Co Ltd v Royal Exchange Assurance Corpn [1898] 2 QB 187, 67
 LJQB 736, 78 LT 783, 46 WR 497, 14 TLR 423, 42 Sol Jo 507, 8 Asp MLC 409, 3 Com
 Cas 189, CA 40, 401
Chippendale v Holt (1895) 65 LJQB 104, 73 LT 472, 44 WR 128, 12 TLR 50, 40 Sol Jo 99, 8
 Asp MLC 78, 1 Com Cas 197 465
Christie, The. See Capital Coastal Shipping Corpn and Bulk Towing Corpn v Hartford Fire
 Insurance Co (United States of America, Third Party), The Christie
Clan Line Steamers Ltd v Board of Trade, The Clan Matheson [1929] AC 514, [1929] All
 ER Rep 17, 98 LJKB 408, 141 LT 275, 45 TLR 408, 18 Asp MLC 1, 35 Com Cas 15, 34
 Ll L Rep 1, HL 204
Clan Line Steamers Ltd v Liverpool and London War Risks Insurance Association Ltd [1943]
 KB 209, [1942] 2 All ER 367, 112 LJKB 209, 168 LT 139, 58 TLR 369, 73 Ll L Rep
 165 . . . . 198, 202
Clan Matheson, The. See Clan Line Steamers Ltd v Board of Trade, The Clan Matheson
Clapham v Langton (1864) 5 B & S 729, 4 New Rep 411, 34 LJQB 46, 10 LT 875, 12 WR
 1011, 2 Mar LC 54, Ex Ch
Clason v Simmonds (1741) cited in 6 Term Rep 533 . . . . . 129, 131

	PAGE
Cleary v McAndrew (Cargo ex), The Galam 2 Moo PCCNS 216, 3 New Rep 254, 9 LT 550, 10 Jur NS 477, 12 WR 495, 1 Mar LC 408, PC	351
Coast Ferries Ltd v Century Insurance Co of Canada, The Brentwood [1973] 2 Lloyd's Rep 232; on appeal (1974) 48 DLR (3d) 310	170
Cobb and Jenkins v Volga Insurance Co Ltd of Petrograd (1920) 4 Ll L Rep 130, 178	148
Cockey v Atkinson (1819) 2 B & Ald 460	116, 131
Cohen v Hinckley (1809) 2 Camp 51	349
Cohen, Sons & Co v National Benefit Assurance Co Ltd (1924) 40 TLR 347, 18 Ll L Rep 199	146
Cohen (G) Sons & Co v Standard Marine Insurance Co Ltd (1925) 41 TLR 232, 69 Sol Jo 310, 30 Com Cas 139, 21 Ll L Rep 30	48, 51, 304, 346, 368, 386, 389
Coker v Bolton [1912] 3 KB 315, 82 LJKB 91, 107 LT 54, 56 Sol Jo 751, 12 Asp MLC 231, 17 Com Cas 313	12, 357, 359
Colby v Hunter (1827) 3 C & P 7, Mood & M 81	285
Colledge v Harty (1851) 6 Exch 205, 20 LJ Ex 146, 16 LTOS 372	282, 285
Collett v Morrison (1851) 9 Hare 162, 21 LJ Ch 878	274
Cologan v London Assurance Co (1816) 5 M & S 447	350, 368
Colvin v Newberry and Benson (1828) 8 B & C 166	163
Comber v Anderson (1808) 1 Camp 523	31, 331
Commercial Marine Co v Namaqua Mining Co. See Biccard v Shepherd	
Commercial Trading Co Inc v Hartford Fire Insurance Co [1974] 1 Lloyd's Rep 179	163, 166
Commonwealth, The (1907). See Welsh Girl, The (1906)	
Companhia Geval de Seguros v Lloyd Continental Insurance Co Ltd (1922) 13 Ll L Rep 26	373
Compania Colombiana de Seguros v Pacific Steam Navigation Co [1965] 1 QB 101, [1964] 1 All ER 216, [1964] 2 WLR 484, 108 Sol Jo 75, [1963] 2 Lloyd's Rep 479	458
Compania Maritima Astra SA v Archdale, The Armar [1954] 2 Lloyd's Rep 95	424
Compania Maritima San Basilio SA v Oceanus Mutual Underwriting Association (Bermuda) Ltd, The Eurysthenes [1977] QB 49, [1976] 3 All ER 243, [1976] 3 WLR 265, 120 Sol Jo 486, [1976] 2 Lloyd's Rep 171, CA	91, 219, 303, 477
Compania Maritima of Barcelona v Wishart (1918) 87 LJKB 1027, 118 LT 705, 34 TLR 251, 14 Asp MLC 298, 23 Com Cas 264	208
Compania Martiartu v Royal Exchange Assurance [1923] 1 KB 650, 92 LJKB 546, 129 LT 1, 16 Asp MLC 189, 28 Com Cas 76, CA; affd. [1924] AC 850, HL	246, 349
Compania Naviera Santi SA v Indemnity Marine Assurance Co Ltd, The Tropaioforos [1960] 2 Lloyd's Rep 469	241
Compania Naviera Vascongada v British and Foreign Marine Insurance Co Ltd (1935) 54 Ll L Rep 35, 80 Sol Jo 110	240, 305
Comunidad Naviera Baracaldo v Norwich Union Fire Insurance Society (1923) 16 Ll L Rep 45, 93, 156	236
Constable v Noble (1810) 2 Taunt 403	116, 326
Container Transport International Inc and Reliance Group Inc v Oceanus Mutual Underwriting Association (Bermuda) Ltd [1984] 1 Lloyd's Rep 476	39, 44, 45, 53, 59, 77
Continental Grain Co Inc v Twitchell [1945] 1 All ER 575n, 173 LT 189, 61 TLR 291, 78 Ll L Rep 251, CA	229
Conway v Gray (1809) 10 East 536	24
Copenhagen, The (1799) 1 Ch Rob 289	343
Corcoran v Gurney (1853) 1 E & B 456, 22 LJQB 113, 20 LTOS 221, 17 Jur 1152	412
Corlett v Gordon (1813) 3 Camp 472	37
Cornfoot v Royal Exchange Assurance Corpn [1904] 1 KB 40, 73 LJKB 22, 89 LT 490, 52 WR 49, 20 TLR 34, 48 Sol Jo 32, 9 Asp MLC 489, 9 Com Cas 80, CA	122
Cory v Burr (1883) 8 App Cas 393, 52 LJQB 657, 49 LT 78, 31 WR 894, 5 Asp MLC 109, HL	164, 226
Cory v Patton (1874) LR 9 QB 577, 43 LJQB 181, 30 LT 758, 23 WR 46, 2 Asp MLC 30	67, 79
Cosmopolitan Shipping Co Inc v Hatton and Cookson Ltd (Liverpool) (1929) 143 LT 296, 18 Asp MLC 130, 35 Com Cas 113, CA	298
Costain-Blankevoort (UK) Dredging Co Ltd v Davenport, The Nassau Bay [1979] 1 Lloyd's Rep 395	198, 203
Cotton v Heyl [1930] 1 Ch 510, [1930] All ER Rep 375, 99 LJ Ch 289, 143 LT 16	316
Coulouras v British General Insurance Co Ltd (1922) 12 Ll L Rep 220	234

Table of cases xxvii

	PAGE
Court v Martineau (1702) 3 Doug KB 161	52, 57
Court Line Ltd v R, The Lavington Court [1945] 2 All ER 357, 173 LT 162, 61 TLR 418, 89 Sol Jo 497, 78 Ll L Rep 390, CA	364
Cousins (H) & Co Ltd v D and C Carriers Ltd [1971] 2 QB 230, [1971] 1 All ER 55, [1971] 2 WLR 85, 114 Sol Jo 882, [1970] 2 Lloyd's Rep 397, CA	8
Coxwold, The. See Yorkshire Dale SS Co Ltd v Minister of War Transport, The Coxwold	
Craufurd v Hunter (1798) 8 Term Rep 13	26, 111
Cressington, The [1891] P 152, 60 LJP 25, 64 LT 329, 7 TLR 208, 7 Asp MLC 27, DC	298
Crocker v General Insurance Co Ltd (1897) 14 TLR 112, 3 Com Cas 22, CA	121
Crocker v Sturge [1897] 1 QB 330, 66 LJQB 142, 75 LT 549, 45 WR 271, 13 TLR 96, 41 Sol Jo 158, 8 Asp MLC 208, 2 Com Cas 43	121
Crofts v Marshall (1836) 7 C & P 597	142
Crouan v Stanier [1904] 1 KB 87, 73 LJKB 102, 19 TLR 664, 9 Com Cas 27, 52 WR 75, 47 Sol Jo 728	449
Crowley v Cohen (1832) 3 B & Ad 478, 1 LJKB 158	24, 108
Crozier v Smith (1840) 1 Man & G 407, 1 Scott NR 338, 4 Jur 581	351
Cruickshank v Janson (1810) 2 Taunt 301	116, 120
Crystal, The (1894). See Arrow Shipping Co v Tyne Improvement Comrs, The Crystal	
Cullen v Butler (1816) 5 M & S 461	145, 150
Cunard v Hyde (1859) 2 E & E 1, 29 LJQB 6, 6 Jur NS 14	308
Cunard SS Co v Marten [1902] 2 KB 624, 71 LJKB 968, 87 LT 400, 18 TLR 825, 9 Asp MLC 342; affd. [1903] 2 KB 511, 72 LJKB 754, 89 LT 152, 52 WR 39, 19 TLR 634, 47 Sol Jo 708, 9 Asp MLC 452, 9 Com Cas 9, CA	102, 324, 444
Currie & Co v Bombay Native Insurance Co (1869) LR 3 PC 72, 6 Moo PCCNS 302, 39 LJPC 1, 22 LT 317, 18 WR 296, 3 Mar LC 369	386, 388
Czarnikow (C) Ltd v Java Sea and Fire Insurance Co Ltd [1941] 3 All ER 256, 166 LT 104, 70 Ll L Rep 319	369

D

Da Costa v Edmunds (1815) 4 Camp 142	46, 154, 326
Dakin v Oxley (1864) 15 CBNS 646, 33 LJCP 115, 10 LT 268, 10 Jur NS 655, 12 WR 557, 2 Mar LC 6	19
Daneau v Laurent Gendron Ltée, Union Insurance Society of Canton Ltd (Third Party) [1964] 1 Lloyd's Rep 220	312
Davidson v Case (1820). See Case v Davidson (1816)	
Davidson v Willasey (1813) 1 M & S 313	21, 353
Davies v National Fire and Marine Insurance Co of New Zealand [1891] AC 485, 60 LJPC 73, 65 LT 560, PC	78, 92
Davis v Garrett (1830) 6 Bing 716, L & Welsb 276, [1824–34] All ER Rep 286, 4 Moo & P 540, 8 LJOSCP 253	129
De Costa v Scandret (1723) 2 P Wms 170	40, 55
De Cuadra v Swann (1864) 16 CBNS 772	133
De Hahn v Hartley (1786) 1 Term Rep 343	285
Delany v Stoddart (1785) 1 Term Rep 22	134
Delfin, The. See Bristol SS Corpn v London Assurance and Linard, The Delfin	
De Marco and Gazan v Scottish Metropolitan Assurance Co (1923) 14 Ll L Rep 173, 220	208
De Mattos v Saunders (1872) LR 7 CP 570, 27 LT 120, 20 WR 801, 1 Asp MLC 377	144, 413
Demetriades v Northern Assurance Co, The Spathari (1923) 17 Ll L Rep 327	246
Demetriades & Co v Northern Assurance Co (1926) 21 Ll L Rep 265, HL	60, 75
De Monchy v Phoenix Insurance Co of Hartford (1928) 138 LT 703, CA; affd. sub nom. Phoenix Insurance Co of Hartford v De Monchy (1929) 141 LT 439, [1929] All ER Rep 531, 45 TLR 543, 18 Asp MLC 7, 35 Com Cas 67, 34 Ll L Rep 201, HL	194
Dennistoun v Lillie (1821) 3 Bli 202, HL	71, 73
Dent v Smith (1869) LR 4 QB 414, 10 B & S 249, 38 LJQB 144, 20 LT 868, 17 WR 646, 3 Mar LC 251	144, 286
De Rothschild v Royal Mail Steam Packet Co (1852) 7 Exch 734, 21 LJ Ex 273, 19 LTOS 229	150

xxviii *Table of cases*

PAGE

Devaux v J'Anson (1839) 5 Bing NC 519, 2 Arn 82, 7 Scott 507, 8 LJCP 284, 6 LT 836, 3 Jur 678 22
De Vaux v Salvador (1836) 4 Ad & El 420, 1 Har & W 751, 6 Nev & MKB 713, 5 LJKB 134 . . . . 144, 422
De Wolf v Archangel Insurance Co (1874) LR 9 QB 451, 43 LJQB 147, 30 LT 605, 22 WR 801, 2 Asp MLC 273 126
Diamond, The [1906] P 282, 75 LJP 90, 95 LT 550, 10 Asp MLC 286 297
Dias, The. See Palamisto General Enterprises SA v Ocean Marine Insurance Co Ltd, The Dias
Dickenson v Jardine (1868) LR 3 CP 639, 37 LJCP 321, 18 LT 717, 16 WR 1169, 3 Mar LC 126 . . . . 153, 182, 183
Dickson & Co v Devitt (1916) 86 LJKB 315, 32 TLR 547, 21 Com Cas 291 . . 32
Diederichsen v Farquharson Bros [1898] 1 QB 150, 67 LJQB 103, 77 LT 543, 46 WR 162, 14 TLR 59, 42 Sol Jo 65, 8 Asp MLC 333, 3 Com Cas 87, CA 154
Dixon v Reid (1822) 5 B & Ald 597, 1 Dow & Ry KB 207 . . . . . 156, 168
Dixon v Sadler (1839) 5 M & W 405, 9 LJ Ex 48; affd. sub nom. Sadler v Dixon (1841) 8 M & W 895, 11 LJ Ex 435, Ex Ch 231, 302
Dixon v Whitworth (1880) 4 CPD 371, 48 LJCP 538, 40 LT 718, 28 WR 184, 4 Asp MLC 326; revsd. 49 LJQB 408, 43 LT 365, 4 Asp MLC 327, CA 25, 443, 447
Dobell (G E) & Co v SS Rossmore Co Ltd [1895] 2 QB 408, [1895–9] All ER Rep 885, 64 LJQB 777, 73 LT 74, 44 WR 37, 11 TLR 501, 8 Asp MLC 33, 14 R 558, CA . . 297
Dobson v Bolton (1799) 1 Marshall on Marine Insces 3rd ed 231, 1 Park's Marine Insce 8th ed 239 411
Dodwell & Co Ltd v British Dominions General Insurance Co Ltd [1955] 2 Lloyd's Rep 391n 254
Domingo Mumbru Société Anon v Laurie (1924) 20 Ll L Rep 122, 189 . . . 238
Dora Forster, The [1900] P 241, 69 LJP 85, 49 WR 271, 16 TLR 380 . . . 440
Doriga Y Sanudo v Royal Exchange Assurance Corpn (1922) 13 Ll L Rep 126, 166 . 235
Doyle v Dallas (1831) 1 Mood & R 48 . . . . 348, 413
Driscol v Bovil (1798) 1 Bos & P 313 72
Driscol v Passmore (1798) 1 Bos & P 200 72
Dudgeon v Pembroke (1874) LR 9 QB 581, 43 LJQB 220, 31 LT 31, 22 WR 914, 2 Asp MLC 323; on appeal (1875) 1 QBD 96, Ex Ch; on appeal (1877) 2 App Cas 284, 46 LJQB 409, 36 LT 382, 25 WR 499, 3 Asp MLC 393, HL 141, 302, 323
Duff v Mackenzie (1857) 3 CBNS 16, 26 LJCP 313, 30 LTOS 103, 3 Jur NS 1025 . 107, 431
Duffell v Wilson (1808) 1 Camp 401 84
Dunbeth, The [1897] P 133, 66 LJP 66, 76 LT 658, 8 Asp MLC 284 . . . 130
Dunlop Bros & Co v Townend [1919] 2 KB 127, [1918–19] All ER Rep 575, 88 LJKB 1129, 121 LT 159, 14 Asp MLC 517, 24 Com Cas 201 . . . . . . 92, 112
Duthie v Hilton (1868) LR 4 CP 138, 38 LJCP 93, 19 LT 285, 17 WR 55, 3 Mar LC 166 . 351

E

Eagle Oil Transport Co Ltd v Board of Trade (1925) 42 TLR 201 200
Eagle, Star and British Dominions Insurance Co Ltd v Reiner (1927) 43 TLR 259, 71 Sol Jo 176, 27 Ll L Rep 173 277
Earle v Harris (1780) 1 Doug KB 357 280
Earle v Rowcroft (1806) 8 East 126 . . . . 162, 164, 165, 166, 169
Eastern Prince, The. See Link v General Insurance Co of America, The Eastern Prince
Ebsworth v Alliance Marine Insurance Co (1873) LR 8 CP 596, 42 LJCP 305, 29 LT 479, 2 Asp MLC 125; revsd. (1874) 43 LJCP 394n, Ex Ch 24, 25
Eddystone Marine Insurance Co, Re, ex p Western Insurance Co [1892] 2 Ch 423, 61 LJ Ch 362, 66 LT 370, 40 WR 441, 8 TLR 393, 36 Sol Jo 308, 7 Asp MLC 107 . . 466
Eden v Parkison (1781) 2 Doug KB 732 286
Edie v East India Co (1761) 1 Wm Bl 295, 2 Burr 1216 326
Edwards v Footner (1808) 1 Camp 530 73
Edwards (John) & Co v Motor Union Insurance Co Ltd [1922] 2 KB 249, 91 LJKB 921, 128 LT 276, 38 TLR 690, 16 Asp MLC 89, 27 Com Cas 367, 11 Ll L Rep 122, 170 . 455, 456
Eenrom, The (1799) 2 Ch Rob 1, 1 Eng Pr Cas 118; affd. (1802) 6 Ch Rob ix . . 309

Eftychia, The. See Bank of Athens v Royal Exchange Assurance, The Eftychia
Elkin v Janson (1845) 13 M & W 655, 14 LJ Ex 201, 9 Jur 353 . . . . . 57, 78
Elliot v Wilson (1776) 4 Bro Parl Cas 470, HL 129
Elton v Brogden (1747) 2 Stra 1264 166
Elton v Larkins (1832) 8 Bing 198, 5 C & P 385, 1 Moo & S 323 57
Emanuel & Co v Andrew Weir & Co (1914) 30 TLR 518 274
Emperor Goldmining Co Ltd v Switzerland General Insurance Co Ltd [1964] 1 Lloyd's Rep 348 450
Empire SSC Incorporated v Threadneedle Insurance Co (1925) 22 Ll L Rep 437, 534 . 238
Empresa Lineas Maritimas Argentinas v Ocean Mutual Underwriting Association (Bermuda) Ltd [1984] 2 Lloyd's Rep 517 475
Empress Assurance Corpn Ltd v C T Bowring & Co Ltd (1905) 11 Com Cas 107 . . 69
Engineer, The. See Tatham, Bromage & Co, The Engineer
Entwistle v Ellis (1857) 2 H & N 549, 27 LJ Ex 105, 3 LT 382, 6 WR 76 431
Etherington and Lancashire and Yorkshire Accident Insurance Co, Re [1909] 1 KB 591, [1908–10] All ER Rep 581, 78 LJKB 684, 100 LT 568, 25 TLR 287, 53 Sol Jo 266, CA 328
Eurysthenes, The. See Compania Maritima San Basilio SA v Oceanus Mutual Underwriting Association (Bermuda) Ltd, The Eurysthenes
Euterpe SS Co Ltd v North of England Protecting and Indemnity Association Ltd (1917) 33 TLR 540 . . . . 207, 349
Evelpidis Era, The. See First National Bank of Chicago v West of England Shipowners Mutual Protection and Indemnity Association (Luxembourg), The Evelpidis Era
Everth v Hannam (1815) 6 Taunt 375, 2 Marsh 72 169
Eyre v Glover (1812) 16 East 218, 3 Camp 276 26

F

Fabrique de Produits Chimiques SA, La v Large [1923] 1 KB 203, [1922] All ER Rep 372, 92 LJKB 370, 128 LT 636, 39 TLR 76, 16 Asp MLC 110, 28 Com Cas 248, 13 Ll L Rep 269 . . . . 152, 431
Fairfield Shipbuilding and Engineering Co Ltd v Gardner, Mountain & Co Ltd (1911) 104 LT 288, 27 TLR 281, 11 Asp MLC 594 336
Fairlie v Christie (1817) 7 Taunt 416, 1 Moore CP 114 278
Falkner v Ritchie (1814) 2 M & S 290 168
Farmer v Legg (1797) 7 Term Rep 186 308
Farnworth v Hyde (1865) LR 2 CP 204, 36 LJCP 33, 15 LT 395, 12 Jur NS 997, 15 WR 340, 2 Mar LC 429, Ex Ch 348, 374
Federation Insurance Co of Canada v Coret Accessories Inc and Hirsh (trading as S A Hirsh & Co) [1968] 2 Lloyd's Rep 109 248
Feise v Parkinson (1812) 4 Taunt 640 . . . . 73, 84
Fenwick v Robinson (1828) 3 C & P 323, Dan & Ll 8 419
Field SS Co v Burr [1899] 1 QB 579, 68 LJQB 426, 80 LT 445, 47 WR 341, 15 TLR 193, 43 Sol Jo 258, 8 Asp MLC 529, 4 Com Cas 106, CA 421
Fillis v Brutton (1782) 1 Park's Marine Insurances (8th Edn) 414 . . . . . 57, 73
Firemen's Fund Insurance Co v Western Australian Insurance Co Ltd and Atlantic Insurance Co Ltd (1927) 138 LT 108, [1927] All ER Rep 243, 43 TLR 680, 17 Asp MLC 332, 33 Com Cas 36, 28 Ll L Rep 243 . . . . 465, 466, 468
First National Bank of Chicago v West of England Shipowners Mutual Protection and Indemnity Association (Luxembourg), The Evelpidis Era [1981] 1 Lloyd's Rep 54 . 477
Fisher v Cochran 5 Tyr 496, 4 LJ Ex 328, Ex Ch 284
Fisher v Smith (1878) 4 App Cas 1, 48 LJQB 411, 39 LT 430, 27 WR 113, 4 Asp MLC 60, HL 334, 336
Fisk v Masterman (1841) 8 M & W 165, 10 LJ Ex 306, 7 LT 442 . . . . 85, 461
Fitzgerald v Pole 4 Bro Parl Cas 439, HL 11
Fitzherbert v Mather (1785) 1 Term Rep 12 . . . . . . 41, 44, 55, 71
Fleming v Smith (1848) 1 HL Cas 513, HL 383, 388
Fletcher v Inglis (1819) 2 B & Ald 315 142
Flint v Flemyng (1830) 1 B & Ad 45, L & Welsb 257, 8 LJOSKB 350 . . . 21, 22
Foley v Moline (1814) 5 Taunt 430, 1 Marsh 117 57

xxx Table of cases

	PAGE
Foley v Tabor (1861) 2 F & F 663	53
Foley v United Fire and Marine Insurance Co of Sydney (1870) LR 5 CP 155, 39 LJCP 206, 22 LT 108, 18 WR 437, 3 Mar LC 352, Ex Ch	21, 115, 118
Fomin v Oswell (1813) 3 Camp 357	287
Fooks v Smith [1924] 2 KB 508, 94 LJKB 23, 132 LT 486, 16 Asp MLC 435, 30 Com Cas 97, 19 Ll L Rep 297, 414	379
Forbes v Aspinall (1811) 13 East 323	9, 85, 95, 98
Forestal Land, Timber and Rlys Co Ltd v Rickards [1940] 4 All ER 96; revsd. [1941] KB 225, [1940] 4 All ER 395, 57 TLR 139, 68 Ll L Rep 45, CA; affd. sub nom. Rickards v Forestal Land, Timber and Rlys Co Ltd [1942] AC 50, [1941] 3 All ER 62, 110 LJKB 593, 165 LT 257, 57 TLR 672, 46 Com Cas 335, 70 Ll L Rep 173, HL	5, 127, 134, 156, 163, 167, 265, 329, 362, 364, 367, 370, 376
Forrester v Pigou (1813) 1 M & S 9	78
Forster v Christie (1809) 11 East 205	230
Fort v Lee (1811) 3 Taunt 381	52, 57
Foster v Reeve. See Koster v Reed	
Foster v Wilmer (1746) 2 Stra 1249	130
Fowler v English and Scottish Marine Insurance Co Ltd (1865) 18 CBNS 818, 6 New Rep 66, 34 LJCP 253, 12 LT 381, 11 Jur NS 411, 13 WR 658, 2 Mar LC 202	375
Fracis, Times & Co v Sea Insurance Co Ltd (1898) 79 LT 28, 47 WR 119, 42 Sol Jo 634, 8 Asp MLC 418, 3 Com Cas 229	308
Francis v Boulton (1895) 65 LJQB 153, 73 LT 578, 44 WR 222, 12 TLR 75, 40 Sol Jo 145, 8 Asp MLC 79, 1 Com Cas 217	435, 444
Franco v Natusch (1836) Tyr & Gr 401	298
Frangos v Sun Insurance Office Ltd (1934) 49 Ll L Rep 354	304, 306
Freeland v Glover (1806) 7 East 457, 6 Esp 14, 3 Smith KB 424	44, 52
Friere v Woodhouse (1817) Holt NP 572	57
Fuerst Day Lawson Ltd v Orion Insurance Co Ltd [1980] 1 Lloyd's Rep 656	8, 90, 180
Furness Withy & Co Ltd v Duder [1936] 2 KB 461, [1936] 2 All ER 119, 105 LJKB 473, 154 LT 663, 80 Sol Jo 488, 18 Asp MLC 623, 55 Ll L Rep 52	174

G

Gabay v Lloyd (1825) 3 B & C 793, [1824–34] All ER Rep 422, 5 Dow & Ry KB 641, 3 LJOSKB 116	142, 326
Gagniere & Co Ltd v Eastern Co of Warehouses Insurance and Transport of Goods with Advances Ltd (1921) 8 Ll L Rep 365, CA	275
Gairdner v Senhouse (1810) 3 Taunt 16	131, 328
Gambles v Ocean Marine Insurance Co of Bombay (1876) 1 Ex D 141, 45 LJQB 366, 34 LT 189, 24 WR 384, 3 Asp MLC 120, CA	121
Gandy v Adelaide Insurance Co (1871) LR 6 QB 746, 40 LJQB 239, 25 LT 742, 1 Asp MLC 188	53
Garrels v Kensington (1799) 8 Term Rep 230	288
Garthwaite (Sir William) (Insurance) Ltd v Port of Manchester Insurance Co Ltd (1930) 37 Ll L Rep 194, CA	397
Gedge v Royal Exchange Assurance Corpn [1900] 2 QB 214, [1900–3] All ER Rep 179, 69 LJQB 506, 82 LT 463, 16 TLR 344, 9 Asp MLC 57, 5 Com Cas 229	13, 309, 314
Gee and Garnham Ltd v Whittall [1955] 2 Lloyd's Rep 562	252
Geelong, The. See Peninsular and Oriental Branch Service v Commonwealth Shipping Representative, The Geelong	
General Insurance Co Ltd of Trieste v Royal Exchange Assurance Corpn 2 Com Cas 144	431
General Insurance Co of Trieste (Assicurazioni Generali) v Cory [1897] 1 QB 335, 66 LJQB 313, 13 TLR 130, 2 Com Cas 58	289
General Shipping and Forwarding Co v British General Insurance Co Ltd (1923) 15 Ll L Rep 175	95, 289
General Steam Navigation Co v R (1927) 27 Ll L Rep 366	349
General Steam Navigation Co Ltd v Commercial Union Assurance Co Ltd (1915) 31 TLR 630	349
General Steam Navigation Co Ltd v Janson (1915) 31 TLR 630	207

Table of cases xxxi

	PAGE
Gernon v Royal Exchange Assurance (1815) 6 Taunt 383, Holt NP 53n, 2 Marsh 88	387, 388
Geyer v Aguilar (1798) 7 Term Rep 681	287
Gibson v Mair (1813) 1 Marsh 39	288
Gibson v Small (1853). See Small v Gibson (1849) (1850)	
Gibson v Winter (1833) 5 B & Ad 96, 2 Nev & MKB 737, 2 LJKB 130	316
Gladstone v King (1813) 1 M & S 35	41, 55
Glaser v Cowie (1813) 1 M & S 52	35
Glasgow Assurance Corpn Ltd v William Symondson & Co (1911) 104 LT 254, 27 TLR 245, 11 Asp MLC 583, 16 Com Cas 109	59, 70
Gledstanes v Royal Exchange Assurance (1864) 5 B & S 797, 5 New Rep 40, 34 LJQB 30, 11 LT 305, 11 Jur NS 108, 13 WR 71, 2 Mar LC 142	93, 349
Glen Line Ltd v A-G (1930). See A-G v Glen Line Ltd and Liverpool and London War Risks Insurance Association Ltd (1929)	
Glenlivet, The [1894] P 48, 63 LJP 45, 69 LT 706, 42 WR 97, 10 TLR 97, 38 Sol Jo 78, 7 Asp MLC 395, CA	102, 413
Glennie v London Assurance Co (1814) 2 M & S 371	350
Glover v Black (1763) 3 Burr 1394, 1 Wm Bl 422	27, 108
Glynn v Margetson & Co [1893] AC 351, 62 LJQB 466, 69 LT 1, 9 TLR 437, 1 Asp MLC 366, 1 R 193, HL	131
Godin v London Assurance Co (1758) 1 Burr 489, 2 Keny 254, 1 Wm Bl 103	461
Gold Sky, The. See Astrovlanis Compania Naviera SA v Linard, The Gold Sky [1972] 2 Lloyd's Rep 187	
Gold Sky, The. See Astrovlanis Compania Naviera SA v Linard, The Gold Sky	
Goldschmidt v Whitmore (1811) 3 Taunt 508	164
Gooding v White (1913) 29 TLR 312	57
Goole and Hull Steam Towing Co Ltd v Ocean Marine Insurance Co Ltd [1928] 1 KB 589, [1929] All ER Rep 621, 97 LJKB 175, 138 LT 548, 44 TLR 133, 72 Sol Jo 17, 17 Asp MLC 409, 33 Com Cas 110, 29 Ll L Rep 242	5, 6, 7, 422, 460
Goram v Sweeting (1670) 2 Saund 200	151
Gordon v Rimmington (1807) 1 Camp 123	150
Gorsedd SS Co Ltd v Forbes (1900) 16 TLR 566, 5 Com Cas 413	83
Goulart v Trans-Atlantic Marine Inc and Enos [1970] 2 Lloyd's Rep 389	216
Gould v Oliver (1837) 4 Bing NC 134, 3 Hodg 307, 5 Scott 445, 7 LJCP 68	46, 154, 326
Graham v Barras (1834) 5 B & Ad 1011, 3 Nev & MKB 125	283
Graham Joint Stock Shipping Co v Motor Union Insurance Co [1922] 1 KB 563, [1921] All ER Rep 394, 91 LJKB 370, 126 LT 620, 15 Asp MLC 445, 27 Com Cas 130, CA	400
Graham Joint Stock Shipping Co Ltd v Merchants Marine Insurance Co Ltd [1924] AC 294, 93 LJKB 122, 130 LT 706, 40 TLR 192, 68 Sol Jo 273, 16 Asp MLC 300, 29 Com Cas 107, 17 Ll L Rep 44, 241, HL	318
Grainger v Martin (1863) 4 B & S 9, 2 New Rep 191, sub nom. Martin v Granger 8 LT 796, 11 WR 758, 1 Mar LC 365, Ex Ch	373, 388
Grand Union (Shipping) Ltd v London SS Owners' Mutual Insurance Association Ltd, The Bosworth (No 3) (1962) 106 Sol Jo 689, [1962] 1 Lloyd's Rep 483	194
Grant v Paxton (1809) 1 Taunt 463	46
Grant, Smith & Co and McDonnell Ltd v Seattle Construction and Dry Dock Co [1920] AC 162, [1918–19] All ER Rep 378, 89 LJPC 17, 122 LT 203, PC	145
Gratitudine, The (1801) 3 Ch Rob 240, [1775–1802] All ER Rep 283	153, 345
Grauds v Dearsley (1935) 79 Sol Jo 271, 51 Ll L Rep 203	239
Gravesend Barge Case (1608). See Mouse's Case	
Gray v Lloyd (1812) 4 Taunt 136	308
Grazebrook, Re, ex p Chavasse (1865) 4 De GJ & Sm 655, 6 New Rep 6, 34 LJ Bcy 17, 12 LT 249, 11 Jur NS 400, 13 WR 627, 2 Mar LC 197	309
Great Indian Peninsula Rly Co v Saunders (1862) 2 B & S 266, 31 LJQB 206, 6 LT 297, 9 Jur NS 198, 10 WR 520, 1 Mar LC 211, Ex Ch	444, 447
Great Indian Peninsula Rly Co v Turnbull 53 LT 325, 33 WR 874, 1 TLR 570, 5 Asp MLC 465	21
Green v British India Steam Navigation Co Ltd [1921] 1 AC 99, 89 LJKB 881, 123 LT 721, 36 TLR 791, 64 Sol Jo 737, 15 Asp MLC 58, 25 Com Cas 301, HL	204
Green v Brown (1743) 2 Stra 1199	349

xxxii *Table of cases*

PAGE

Green v Elmslie (1794) Peake 278 226
Green v Royal Exchange Assurance Co (1815) 6 Taunt 68, 1 Marsh 447 . . . 353, 383
Green Lion, The. See Sipowicz v Wimble, The Green Lion
Greenhill v Federal Insurance Co [1927] 1 KB 65, 95 LJKB 717, 135 LT 244, 70 Sol Jo 565,
    17 Asp MLC 62, 31 Com Cas 289, 24 Ll L Rep 383, CA 50, 51, 52, 58
Greenock SS Co v Maritime Insurance Co [1903] 1 KB 367, 72 LJKB 59, 88 LT 207, 51 WR
    447, 19 TLR 107, 8 Com Cas 78; affd. [1903] 2 KB 657, 72 LJKB 868, 89 LT 200, 52
    WR 186, 19 TLR 680, 47 Sol Jo 761, 9 Asp MLC 463, 9 Com Cas 41, CA . . 81, 226, 301
Greer v Poole (1880) 5 QBD 272, 49 LJQB 463, 42 LT 687, 28 WR 582, 4 Asp MLC 300,
    DC 226
Gregory v Christie (1784) 3 Doug KB 419 120
Gregory Maritime Ltd v Thos R Miller & Son, United Kingdom Mutual SS Assurance
    Association Ltd and United Kingdom Freight, Demurrage and Defence Association Ltd
    [1966] 1 Lloyd's Rep 296 477
Gregson v Gilbert (1783) 3 Doug KB 232 . . . . 142, 145
Griffiths v Bramley-Moore (1878) 4 QBD 70, 48 LJQB 201, 40 LT 149, 27 WR 480, 4 Asp
    MLC 66, CA 19
Grill v General Iron Screw Collier Co (1866) LR 1 CP 600, Har & Ruth 654, 35 LJCP 321,
    14 LT 711, 12 Jur NS 727, 14 WR 893, 2 Mar LC 362; affd. (1868) LR 3 CP 476, 37
    LJCP 205, 18 LT 485, 16 WR 796, 3 Mar LC 77, Ex Ch 164
Gulf and Southern SS Co Inc v British Traders Insurance Co Ltd [1930] 1 KB 451, [1929] All
    ER Rep 601, 99 LJKB 208, 142 LT 406, 35 Com Cas 198, 18 Asp MLC 94, 35 Ll L Rep
    203 351
Gulfstream Cargo Ltd v Reliance Insurance Co, The Papoose [1971] 1 Lloyd's Rep 178: 53, 58
Gurney v Grimmer (1923) 38 Com Cas 7, 44 Ll L Rep 189, CA 471
Guthrie v North China Insurance Co Ltd (1902) 18 TLR 412, 7 Com Cas 130, CA . . 353

H

Hadkinson v Robinson (1803) 3 Bos & P 388 . . . . . . 227, 230
Hagedorn v Whitmore (1816) 1 Stark 157 144
Hahn v Corbett (1824) 2 Bing 205, 9 Moore CP 390, 3 LJOSCP 253 . . . 144, 231
Hai Hsuan, The. See China (Republic of), China Merchants Steam Navigation Co and United
    States of America v National Union Fire Insurance Co of Pittsburgh, Pennsylvania, The
    Hai Hsuan
Hai Hsuan (No 2), The. See Repulic of China Merchants Steam Navigation Co Ltd and
    United States of America v National Union Fire Insurance Co of Pittsburgh, Pennsylvania,
    The Hai Hsuan (No 2)
Halhead v Young (1856) 6 E & B 312, 25 LJQB 290, 2 Jur NS 970, 4 WR 530, sub nom.
    Hallhead v Young 27 LTOS 100 . . . . 26, 108
Hall v Hayman [1912] 2 KB 5, 81 LJKB 509, 106 LT 142, 28 TLR 171, 56 Sol Jo 205, 12 Asp
    MLC 158, 17 Com Cas 81 . . . . 97, 372, 374
Hall v Janson (1855) 4 E & B 500, 24 LJQB 97, 24 LTOS 289, 1 Jur NS 571, 3 WR 213, 3
    CLR 737 . . . . 107, 326
Hall Bros SS Co Ltd v Young, The Trident [1939] 1 KB 748, [1939] 1 All ER 809, 108 LJKB
    313, 160 LT 402, 55 TLR 506, 83 Sol Jo 175, 19 Asp MLC 269, 44 Com Cas 146, 63 Ll L
    Rep 143, CA 175
Hallhead v Young. See Halhead v Young
Hamilton v Mendes (1761) 2 Burr 1198, 1 Wm Bl 276 379
Hamilton v Sheddon (1837) 3 M & W 49, Murp & H 334, 7 LJ Ex 1, 6 LT 479 . . 136, 270
Hamilton & Co v Eagle Star and British Dominions Insurance Co Ltd (1924) 19 Ll L Rep
    242 74
Hamilton, Fraser & Co v Pandorf & Co (1887) 12 App Cas 518, 57 LJQB 24, 57 LT 726, 52
    JP 196, 36 WR 369, 3 TLR 768, 6 Asp MLC 212, HL 141, 142, 145, 150
Hammond v Reid (1820) 4 B & Ald 72 132
Harding v Bussell [1905] 2 KB 83, 74 LJKB 500, 92 LT 531, 21 TLR 401, 10 Asp MLC 50,
    10 Com Cas 184, CA 398
Hare v Travis (1827) 7 B & C 14, 9 Dow & Ry KB 748, 5 LJOSKB 348 . . . 117

	PAGE
Harland and Wolff Ltd v J Burstall & Co (1901) 84 LT 324, 17 TLR 338, 9 Asp MLC 184, 6 Com Cas 113	26
Harman v Vaux (1813) 3 Camp 429	411
Harmonides, The [1903] P 1, 72 LJP 9, 87 LT 448, 51 WR 303, 19 TLR 37, 9 Asp MLC 354	373
Harocopus v Mountain (1934) 49 Ll L Rep 267	300
Harper (A C) & Co v Mackechnie & Co [1925] 2 KB 423, 95 LJKB 162, 134 LT 90, 31 Com Cas 21	60
Harrison v Universal Marine Insurance Co (1862) 3 F & F 190	141
Harrisons Ltd v Shipping Controller [1921] 1 KB 122, 90 LJKB 384, 124 LT 540, 36 TLR 880, 15 Asp MLC 270	201
Harrower v Hutchinson (1869) LR 4 QB 523, 17 WR 731; revsd. LR 5 QB 584, 10 B & S 469, 39 LJQB 229, 22 LT 684, 3 Mar LC 44, Ex Ch	56, 116
Hart v Standard Marine Insurance Co Ltd (1889) 22 QBD 499, 58 LJQB 284, 60 LT 649, 37 WR 366, 5 TLR 229, 6 Asp MLC 368, CA	281
Hartley v Buggin (1781) 3 Doug KB 39	136
Haughton v Empire Marine Insurance Co (1866) LR 1 Exch 206, 35 LJ Ex 117, 15 LT 80, 14 WR 645, 2 Mar LC 406, sub nom. Houghton v Empire Marine Insurance Co 4 H & C 44, 12 Jur NS 376	115
Havelock v Hancill (1789) 3 Term Rep 277	164
Haversham Grange, The [1905] P 307, 74 LJP 115, 93 LT 733, 53 WR 675, 21 TLR 628, 10 Asp MLC 156, CA	416, 421
Haywood v Rodgers (1804) 4 East 590, sub nom. Heyward v Rodgers 1 Smith KB 289	53
Hearne v Edmunds (1819) 1 Brod & Bing 388, 4 Moore CP 15	412
Hedburg v Pearson (1816) 7 Taunt 154, 12 Marsh 432	431
Hedley v Pinkey & Sons SS Co [1894] AC 222, 63 LJQB 419, 70 LT 630, 42 WR 497, 10 TLR 347, 7 Asp MLC 483, 6 R 106, HL	297
Helen, The (1865) LR 1 A & E 1, 35 LJ Adm 2, 13 LT 305, 11 Jur NS 1025, 14 WR 136, 2 Mar LC 293	309
Helmville Ltd v Yorkshire Insurance Co Ltd, The Medina Princess [1965] 1 Lloyd's Rep 361	97, 341, 374, 422, 423, 424
Henchman v Offley (1782) 3 Doug KB 135, 2 Hy Bl 345n	93, 461
Henderson Bros v Shankland & Co [1896] 1 QB 525, 65 LJQB 340, 74 LT 238, 44 WR 401, 12 TLR 250, 40 Sol Jo 334, 8 Asp MLC 136, 1 Com Cas 333, CA	372
Henkle v Royal Exchange Assce Co (1749) 1 Ves Sen 317, [1558–71] All ER Rep 450	274
Henriksens Rederi A/S v T H Z Rolimpex, The Brede [1974] QB 233, [1973] 3 All ER 589, [1973] 3 WLR 556, 117 Sol Jo 600, [1973] 2 Lloyd's Rep 333, CA	19
Herring v Janson (1895) 1 Com Cas 177	98
Heselton v Allnutt (1813) 1 M & S 46	130
Hewitt v London General Insurance Co Ltd (1925) 23 Ll L Rep 243	80, 117, 135, 467
Hewitt Bros v Wilson [1915] 2 KB 739, 84 LJKB 1337, 113 LT 304, 31 TLR 333, 13 Asp MLC 111, 20 Com Cas 241, CA	109
Heyman v Parish (1809) 2 Camp 149, 11 RR 688	167
Heyward v Rodgers. See Haywood v Rodgers	
Hibbert v Carter (1787) 1 Term Rep 745, [1775–1802] All ER Rep 222	25, 320
Hibbert v Martin (1808) 1 Camp 538	169
Hibbert v Pigou (1783) 3 Doug KB 224	293
Hickie and Borman v Rodocanachi (1859) 4 H & N 455, 28 LJ Ex 273, 33 LTOS 150, 5 Jur NS 550, 7 WR 545	395
Hicks v Shield (1857) 7 E & B 633, 26 LJQB 205, 29 LTOS 106, 3 Jur NS 715, 5 WR 536	21
Hide v Bruce (1783) 3 Doug KB 213	281
Hill v Patten (1807) 8 East 373, [1803–13] All ER Rep 479, Holt NP 333n	108
Hill v Scott [1895] 2 QB 713, 65 LJQB 87, 73 LT 458, 12 TLR 58, 8 Asp MLC 109, 1 Com Cas 200, CA	24
Hills v London Assurance Corpn (1839) 5 M & W 569, 9 LJ Ex 25, 11 LT 159	431
Hindustan Steam Shipping Co v Admiralty Comrs (1921) 8 Ll L Rep 230	199
Hobbs v Hannam (1811) 3 Camp 93	17, 20, 163
Hodgson v Glover (1805) 6 East 316	26
Hodgson v Malcolm (1806) 2 Bos & PNR 336	145
Hoffman & Co v British General Insurance Co (1922) 10 Ll L Rep 434	299

	PAGE
Holland v Russell (1863) 4 B & S 14, 2 New Rep 188, 32 LJQB 297, 8 LT 468, 11 WR 757, Ex Ch	55
Hollingworth v Brodrick (1837) 7 Ad & El 40, 8 LJQB 80, 1 Jur 430, sub nom. Broderick v Hollingsworth 2 Nev & PKB 608, Will Woll & Dav 689	302
Holman v Johnson (1775) 1 Cowp 341, [1775–1802] All ER Rep 98	309
Holt Hill Sailing Ship Co v United Kingdom Marine Association [1919] 2 KB 789, 88 LJKB 1155, 121 LT 420, 35 TLR 367, 14 Asp MLC 463	375
Honour v Equitable Life Assurance Society of US [1900] 1 Ch 852, 69 LJ Ch 420, 82 LT 144, 48 WR 347, 44 Sol Jo 313	273
Hood v West End Motor Car Packing Co [1917] 2 KB 38, 86 LJKB 831, 116 LT 365, 61 Sol Jo 252, 14 Asp MLC 12, CA	110
Hoop, The (1799) 1 Ch Rob 196, [1775–1802] All ER Rep 129, 1 Eng Pr Cas 107	309
Hopper v Wear Marine Insurance Co (1882) 46 LT 107, 4 Asp MLC 482	119
Hore v Whitmore (1778) 2 Cowp 784	280
Hornal v Neuberger Products Ltd [1957] 1 QB 247, [1956] 3 All ER 970, [1956] 3 WLR 1034, 100 Sol Jo 915, CA	247
Horncastle v Suart (1806) 7 East 400	21
Horneyer v Lushington (1812) 15 East 46, 3 Camp 85	33, 115, 121, 287
Houghton v Empire Marine Insurance Co. See Haughton v Empire Marine Insurance Co	
Houstman v Thornton (1816) Holt NP 242	392, 457
Howard, Houlder and Partners v Union Marine Insurance Co Ltd (1922) 38 TLR 515, 10 Ll L Rep 627, HL	409
Hubbard v Glover (1812) 3 Camp 313	74
Hudson v Bilton (1856) 6 E & B 565, 26 LJQB 27, 27 LTOS 154, 2 Jur NS 784	283
Hudson v British and Foreign Marine Insurance Co. See Leitrim, The	
Hudson v Harrison (1821) 3 Brod & Bing 97, 6 Moore CP 288	388, 390
Hull v Cooper (1811) 14 East 479	126
Humfrey v Dale (1857) 7 E & B 266	327
Hunt v Royal Exchange Assurance (1816) 5 M & S 47	361, 389
Hunter v Northern Marine Insurance Co Ltd (1888) 13 App Cas 717, HL	122, 326
Hunter v Potts (1815) 4 Camp 203	142
Hunter v Wright (1830) 10 B & C 714, L & Welsb 138, 5 Man & Ry KB 611, 8 LJOSKB 259	83
Hunter, The (1815) 1 Dods 480, 2 Eng Pr Cas 208	287
Hutton v Warren (1836) 1 M & W 466, [1835–42] All ER Rep 151, 2 Gale 71, Tyr & Gr 646, 5 LJ Ex 234	325
Hydarnes SS Co v Indemnity Mutual Marine Assurance Co [1895] 1 QB 500, 64 LJQB 353, 72 LT 103, 11 TLR 173, 7 Asp MLC 553, 14 R 216, CA	102, 119, 324
Hyderabad (Deccan) Co v Willoughby [1899] 2 QB 530, 68 LJQB 862, 15 TLR 449, 4 Com Cas 270	8, 136, 178

I

Imperial Marine Insurance Co v Fire Insurance Corpn Ltd (1879) 4 CPD 166, 48 LJQB 424, 27 WR 680, sub nom. Maritime Marine Insurance Co Ltd v Fire Re-insurance Corpn Ltd 40 LT 166, 4 Asp MLC 71	92
Imrie v Castrique (1860) 8 CBNS 405, Ex Ch; affd. sub nom. Castrique v Imrie (1870) LR 4 HL 414, [1861–73] All ER Rep 508, 39 LJCP 350, 23 LT 48, 19 WR 1, 3 Mar LC 454, HL	25
Indian City, The. See Reardon Smith Lines Ltd v Black Sea and Baltic General Insurance Co Ltd, The Indian City	
Inglis v Stock (1885) 10 App Cas 263, 54 LJQB 582, 52 LT 821, 33 WR 877, 5 Asp MLC 422, HL	26, 108
Inman SS Co v Bischoff (1882) 7 App Cas 670, [1881–5] All ER Rep 440, 52 LJQB 169, 47 LT 581, 31 WR 141, 5 Asp MLC 6, HL	52, 228, 267
Integrated Container Service Inc v British Traders Insurance Co Ltd [1981] 2 Lloyd's Rep 460, [1981] Com LR 212	446
Integrated Container Service Inc v British Traders Insurance Co Ltd [1984] 1 Lloyd's Rep 154, CA	446, 447, 450
Ionides v Harford (1859) 29 LJ Ex 36, 33 LTOS 186	321

Ionides v Pacific Insurance Co (1871) LR 6 QB 674, 41 LJQB 33, 25 LT 490, 1 Asp MLC 141; affd. (1872) LR 7 QB 517, 41 LJQB 190, 26 LT 738, 21 WR 22, 1 Asp MLC 330, Ex Ch 67, 73, 91, 93
Ionides v Pender (1872) 27 LT 244, [1861] All ER Rep 898, 1 Asp MLC 432 . . . 26
Ionides v Pender (1874) LR 9 QB 531, 43 LJQB 227, 30 LT 547, 22 WR 884, 2 Asp MLC 266 57
Ireland v Livingston (1872) LR 5 HL 395, [1861–73] All ER Rep 585, 41 LJQB 201, 27 LT 79, 1 Asp MLC 389, HL 30
Irvin v Hine [1950] 1 KB 555, [1949] 2 All ER 1089, 65 TLR 768, 83 Ll L Rep 162 . . 363, 423, 424, 425, 449
Irving v Manning (1847) 1 HL Cas 287, 6 CB 391, 6 LT 108, 10 LT 877, HL . . 94, 97, 375, 378
Irving v Richardson (1831) 2 B & Ad 193, 1 Mood & R 153, 9 LJOSKB 225 . . 22, 111, 461
Irwin v Eagle Star Insurance Co Ltd, The Jonie [1973] 2 Lloyd's Rep 489 . . . 159
Issaias v Marine Insurance Co Ltd (1923) 15 Ll L Rep 186, CA . . 167, 236, 244, 245, 246

J

Jackson v Isaacs (1858) 3 H & N 405, 27 LJ Ex 392 21
Jackson v Mumford (1904) 52 WR 342, 20 TLR 172, 9 Com Cas 114, CA . . . 8, 159
Jackson v Union Marine Insurance Co Ltd (1873) LR 10 CP 125, [1874–80] All ER Rep 317, 44 LJCP 27, 31 LT 789, 23 WR 169, 2 Asp MLC 435, Ex Ch . . . 228, 267, 354
Jacob v Gaviller (1902) 87 LT 26, 50 WR 428, 18 TLR 402, 7 Com Cas 116 . . . 8, 178
James Yachts Ltd v Thames and Mersey Marine Insurance Co Ltd [1977] 1 Lloyd's Rep 206 . . . . 8, 66, 310
Jamieson and Newcastle SS Freight Insurance Association, Re [1895] 2 QB 90, 64 LJQB 560, 72 LT 648, 43 WR 530, 11 TLR 416, 7 Asp MLC 593, 14 R 444, CA . . 268, 354
Janson v Driefontein Consolidated Mines Ltd [1902] AC 484, [1900–3] All ER Rep 426, 71 LJKB 857, 87 LT 372, 51 WR 142, 18 TLR 796, 7 Com Cas 268, HL . . . 8
Janson v Poole (1915) 84 LJKB 1543, 31 TLR 336, 20 Com Cas 232 467
Janson (or Jamson) v Ralli. See Ralli v Janson
Jardine v Leathley (1863) 3 B & S 700, 1 New Rep 394, 32 LJQB 132, 7 LT 783, 9 Jur NS 1035, 11 WR 432, 1 Mar LC 288 381
Jenkins v Power (1817) 6 M & S 282 309
Joel v Law Union and Crown Insurance Co [1908] 2 KB 863, 77 LJKB 1108, 99 LT 712, 24 TLR 898, 52 Sol Jo 740, CA 54
John W Hill, The. See Wells Fargo Bank International Corpn v London Steam-Ship Owners' Mutual Insurance Association Ltd, The John W Hill
John Worthington, The. See Standard Oil Co of New Jersey v United States, The John Worthington
Johnson v Chapman (1865) 19 CBNS 563, 35 LJCP 23, 14 WR 264, sub nom. Shooting Star, The, Johnson v Chapman 15 LT 70, 2 Mar LC 404 154
Johnson v Sheddon (1802) 2 East 581 435
Johnston v Sutton (1779) Doug KB 254 308
Jones v Neptune Marine Insurance Co (1872) LR 7 QB 702, 41 LJQB 370, 27 LT 308, 1 Asp MLC 416 119
Jones v Nicholson (1854) 10 Exch 28, 2 CLR 1236, 23 LJ Ex 330, 23 LTOS 146 . . 164
Jonie, The. See Irwin v Eagle Star Insurance Co Ltd, The Jonie
Joyce v Kennard (1871) LR 7 QB 78, 71 LJQB 17, 25 LT 932, 20 WR 233, 1 Asp MLC 194 24
Joyce v Realm Insurance Co (1872) LR 7 QB 580, 41 LJQB 356, 27 LT 144, 1 Asp MLC 396 . . . . 323, 466
Jupiter (No 3), The [1927] P 122 168

K

Kacianoff v China Traders Insurance Co Ltd [1914] 3 KB 1121, 83 LJKB 1393, 111 LT 404, 12 Asp MLC 524, 19 Com Cas 371, CA 230
Kahn (or Kann) v W H Howard Bros & Co Ltd [1942] AC 50, [1941] 3 All ER 62, 110 LJKB 593, 165 LT 257, 57 TLR 672, 46 Com Cas 335, 70 Ll L Rep 173, HL . . . 371

Table of cases

PAGE

Kaltenbach v Mackenzie (1878) 3 CPD 467, 48 LJQB 9, 39 LT 215, 26 WR 844, 4 Asp MLC 39, CA 348, 388, 389
Keevil and Keevil Ltd v Boag [1940] 3 All ER 346, 163 LT 238, 84 Sol Jo 560, 19 Asp MLC 387, CA 397, 399
Keighley, Maxsted & Co v Durant [1901] AC 240, 70 LJKB 662, 84 LT 777, 17 TLR 527, 45 Sol Jo 536, HL 381
Keith v Burrows (1877) 2 App Cas 636, HL 395
Kelly v Walton (1808) 2 Camp 155 388
Kemp v Halliday (1866) LR 1 QB 520, 6 B & S 723, 35 LJQB 156, 14 LT 762, 12 Jur NS 582, 14 WR 697, 2 Mar LC 370, Ex Ch 373, 413
Kewley v Ryan (1794) 2 Hy Bl 343 . . . . 93, 130
Kidston v Empire Marine Insurance Co (1867) LR 2 CP 357, 36 LJCP 156, 16 LT 119, 15 WR 769, 2 Mar LC 468, Ex Ch 444
King v Glover (1806) 2 Bos & PNR 206 23
King v Victoria Insurance Co Ltd [1896] AC 250, 65 LJPC 38, 74 LT 206, 44 WR 592, 12 TLR 285, PC 8, 458
King v Walker (1864) 3 H & C 209, 33 LJ Ex 325, 11 Jur NS 43, 13 WR 232, Ex Ch . . 385
Kingsford v Marshall (1832) 8 Bing 458, 1 Moo & S 657, 1 LJCP 135 . . . 412
Kingston v Phelps (1795) cited in 7 Term Rep 165 130
Kirby v Smith (1818) 1 B & Ald 672 . . . . 40, 57, 72
Kleinwort v Shepard (1859) 1 E & E 447, 28 LJQB 147, 32 LTOS 313, 5 Jur NS 863, 7 WR 227 156
Knight v Cambridge (1724) 8 Mod Rep 230, 2 Ld Raym 1349, 1 Stra 581 . . 164
Knight v Faith (1850) 15 QB 649, 19 LJQB 509, 15 LTOS 277, 14 Jur 1114 . . 348, 383
Knill v Hooper (1877) 2 H & N 277, 26 LJ Ex 377, 29 LTOS 229, 5 WR 791 . . 302
Knox v Wood (1808) 1 Camp 543 26
Koebel v Saunders (1864) 17 CBNS 71, 4 New Rep 403, 33 LJCP 310, 10 LT 695, 10 Jur NS 920, 12 WR 1106, 2 Mar LC 68 250
Koster v Reed (1826) 6 B & C 19, 9 Dow & Ry KB 2, sub nom. Foster v Reeve 5 LJOSKB 73 349
Kuehne and Nagel Inc v Baiden [1977] 1 Lloyd's Rep 90, USCA 24
Kulukundis v Norwich Union Fire Insurance Society [1937] 1 KB 1, [1936] 2 All ER 242, 1488n, 105 LJKB 703, 155 LT 114, 52 TLR 591, 80 Sol Jo 445, 41 Com Cas 239, 19 Asp MLC 37, 55 Ll L Rep 55, CA 10, 103, 330, 354, 355
Kylie, The. See Allden v Raven, The Kylie
Kynance Sailing Ship Co v Young (1911) 104 LT 397, 27 TLR 306, 11 Asp MLC 596, 16 Com Cas 123 . . . . 116, 120

L

Ladbroke v Lee (1850) 4 De G & Sm 106 22
Laertes, The (Cargo Ex) (1887) 12 PD 187, 56 LJP 108, 57 LT 502, 36 WR 111, 6 Asp MLC 174 302
Laing v Glover (1813) 5 Taunt 49 282
Laing v Union Marine Insurance Co Ltd (1895) 11 TLR 359, 1 Com Cas 11 . . 56, 132
Lakeland, The (1927) 29 Ll L Rep 293, CA 234
Landauer v Asser [1905] 2 KB 184, 74 LJKB 659, 93 LT 20, 53 WR 534, 21 TLR 429, 10 Com Cas 265, DC 321
Lane v Nixon (1866) LR 1 CP 412, Har & Ruth 585, 35 LJCP 243, 12 Jur NS 392, 14 WR 641 307
Lang v Anderdon (1824) 3 B & C 495, 5 Dow & Ry KB 393, 3 LJOSKB 62 . . 284, 285
Langhorn v Allnutt (1812) 4 Taunt 511 132
Langhorn v Cologan (1812) 4 Taunt 330 . . . . 85, 278
La Nippon Marine Insurance Co v London General Insurance Co (1923) 14 Ll L Rep 298 397
Lanyon v Blanchard (1811) 2 Camp 597 336
Lapwing, The [1940] P 112, 109 LJP 66, 165 LT 217, 56 TLR 520, 19 Asp MLC 363, 45 Com Cas 164, 66 Ll L Rep 174 160
Larchgrove (Owners) v R (1919) 36 TLR 108, 1 Ll L Rep 408, 498 . . . 204
Laroche v Oswin (1810) 12 East 131 133
Latvijas Banka (Bank of Latvia) v Adams (1936) 54 Ll L Rep 82 398

Table of cases xxxvii

PAGE

Laurel, The, Stewart v Greenock Marine Insurance Co (1848). See Stewart v Greenock Marine Insurance Co
Laveroni v Drury (1852) 8 Exch 166, 22 LJ Ex 2, 16 Jur 1024, 1 WR 55, sub nom. Leveroni v Drury 20 LTOS 178 142
Lavington Court, The. See Court Line Ltd v R, The Lavington Court
Lawrence v Aberdein (1821) 5 B & Ald 107 . . . . . . 142, 324, 328
Leatham v Terry (1803) 3 Bos & P 479 396
Leathly v Hunter (1831) 7 Bing 517, 1 Cr & J 423, 5 Moo & P 457, 2 Tyr 355, 9 LJOS Ex 118, Ex Ch 131
Lee v Southern Insurance Co (1870) LR 5 CP 397, 39 LJCP 218, 22 LT 443, 18 WR 863, 3 Mar LC 393 444
Lehigh and Wilkes-Barre Coal Co v Globe and Rutgers Fire Insurance Co (1925) 26 Ll L Rep 82 172
Leigh v Adams (1871) 25 LT 566, 1 Asp MLC 147 55
Leitrim, The [1902] P 256, 71 LJP 108, 87 LT 240, 51 WR 158, 18 TLR 819, 9 Asp MLC 317, sub nom. Hudson v British and Foreign Marine Insurance Co 8 Com Cas 6 . . 344, 416
Lemos v British and Foreign Marine Insurance Co Ltd (1931) 39 Ll L Rep 275 . . . 341
Leon v Casey [1932] 2 KB 576, [1932] All ER Rep 484, 101 LJKB 578, 147 LT 165, 48 TLR 452, 37 Com Cas 330, 18 Asp MLC 300, CA 398
Leonard v Leyland & Co (1902) 18 TLR 727 297
Letchford v Oldham (1880) 5 QBD 538, 49 LJQB 458, 28 WR 789, CA . . . 412
Leveroni v Drury. See Laveroni v Drury
Levy v Barnard (1818) 2 Moore CP 34, 8 Taunt 149 337
Lewis v Rucker (1761) 2 Burr 1167 . . . . 434, 435
Leyland Shipping Co v Norwich Union Fire Insurance Society [1918] AC 350, [1918–19] All ER Rep 443, 87 LJKB 395, 118 LT 120, 34 TLR 221, 62 Sol Jo 307, 14 Asp MLC 258, HL 228
Liberian Insurance Agency Inc v Mosse [1977] 2 Lloyd's Rep 560 . . 62, 69, 77, 80, 109, 110, 111
Lidgett v Secretan (1870) LR 5 CP 190, 39 LJCP 196, 22 LT 272, 18 WR 692, 3 Mar LC 365 122
Lind v Mitchell (1928) 98 LJKB 120, [1928] All ER Rep 447, 140 LT 261, 45 TLR 54, 17 Asp MLC 562, 34 Com Cas 81, 32 Ll L Rep 70, CA . . . 145, 160, 232, 365
Lindsay v Janson (1859) 4 H & N 699, 28 LJ Ex 315, 3 LT 341 119
Lindsay v Klein, The Tatjana [1911] AC 194, 80 LJPC 161, 104 LT 261, 11 Asp MLC 562, HL 298
Link v General Insurance Co of America, The Eastern Prince (1944) 77 Ll L Rep 431 . 199
Lishman v Northern Maritime Insurance Co (1875) LR 10 CP 179, 44 LJCP 185, 32 LT 170, 23 WR 733, 2 Asp MLC 504, Ex Ch 67, 289
Litsion Pride, The. See Black King Shipping Corpn v Massie, The Litsion Pride
Liverpool and London War Risks Association Ltd v Ocran SS Co Ltd [1948] AC 243, [1947] 2 All ER 586, [1948] LJR 304, 177 LT 623, 63 TLR 594, 92 Sol Jo 25, 81 Ll L Rep 1, HL 201, 206
Liverpool and London War Risks Insurance Association Ltd v Marine Underwriters of SS Richard de Larrinaga [1921] 2 AC 141, [1921] All ER Rep 72, 91 LJKB 31, 125 LT 548, 37 TLR 692, 15 Asp MLC 353, 26 Com Cas 352, 7 Ll L Rep 151, HL . . . 199
Livie v Janson (1810) 12 East 648 440
Livingstone, The (1904) 130 Fed Rep 746 459
Lloyd v Fleming (1872) LR 7 QB 299, 41 LJQB 93, 20 WR 296, sub nom. Loyd v Fleming, Loyd v Spence 25 LT 824, 1 Asp MLC 192 . . . . 28, 320
Lloyd (J J) Instruments Ltd v Northern Star Insurance Co Ltd, The Miss Jay Jay [1985] 1 Lloyd's Rep 264 150
Lockyer v Offley (1786) 1 Term Rep 252 169
London and North Western Rly Co v Glyn (1859) 1 E & E 652, 28 LJQB 188, 33 LTOS 199, 5 Jur NS 1004, 7 WR 238 25
London County Commercial Reinsurance Office Ltd, Re [1922] 2 Ch 67, 91 LJ Ch 337, 127 LT 20, 38 TLR 399, 15 Asp MLC 553, 10 Ll L Rep 100, 370 . . . . 7, 14, 37

xxxviii *Table of cases*

PAGE

London General Insurance Co v General Marine Underwriters' Association [1921] 1 KB 104, 89 LJKB 1245, 124 LT 67, 36 TLR 887, 15 Asp MLC 94, 26 Com Cas 52, 4 Ll L Rep 38, CA 44, 47, 59, 465
Loraine v Thomlinson (1781) 2 Doug KB 585 83
Lothian v Henderson (1803) 3 Bos & P 499, HL 286, 288
Lower Rhine and Württemberg Insurance Association v Sedgwick [1898] 1 QB 739, 67 LJQB 330, 46 WR 380, 78 LT 496, 14 TLR 226, 8 Asp MLC 380; revsd. [1899] 1 QB 179, 68 LJQB 186, 80 LT 6, 47 WR 261, 15 TLR 65, 8 Asp MLC 466, 4 Com Cas 14, CA . 28, 79
Lower Rhine and Württemberg Insurance Association v Sedgwick [1899] 1 QB 179, 68 LJQB 186, 80 LT 6, 47 WR 261, 15 TLR 65, 8 Asp MLC 466, 4 Com Cas 14, CA . . 467
Lowlands SS Co Ltd v North of England Protecting and Indemnity Association (1921) 6 Ll L Rep 230 274
Loyd v Fleming. See Lloyd v Fleming
Loyd v Spence. See Lloyd v Fleming
Lubbock v Potts (1806) 7 East 449, 3 Smith KB 401 35
Lubbock v Rowcroft (1803) 5 Esp 50 230
Lucena v Craufurd (1806) 2 Bos & PNR 269, HL 16, 26, 111
Luckie v Bushby (1853) 13 B & C 864, 1 CLR 685, 22 LJCP 220, 21 LTOS 186, 17 Jur 625, 1 WR 455 185
Luke v Lyde (or Lloyd) (1759) 2 Burr 882, 1 Wm Bl 190 395
Lynch v Hamilton (1810) 3 Taunt 37; affd. sub nom. Lynch v Dunsford (1811) 14 East 494, Ex Ch 40, 55, 69, 73

M

Maanss v Henderson (1801) 1 East 335 335
M'Andrew v Bell (1795) 1 Esp 373 . . . . 54, 57, 320
Macbeth & Co v King (1916) 86 LJKB 1004, 115 LT 221, 32 TLR 581, 13 Asp MLC 442 . . . . 207, 349
M'Carthy v Abel (1804) 5 East 388, 1 Smith KB 524 . . . . . . 359, 361
M'Connell v Hector (1802) 3 Bos & P 113 286
M'Cowan v Baine and Johnston, The Niobe [1891] AC 401, [1891-4] All ER Rep 343, 65 LT 502, 7 TLR 713, 7 Asp MLC 89, HL 172, 414
McDermott v National Benefit Life Assurance Co (1921) 7 Ll L Rep 97 . . . 314
M'Dougle v Royal Exchange Assurance Co (1815) 4 Camp 283 411
Macdowall v Fraser (1779) 1 Doug KB 260 73
Mackenzie v Whitworth (1875) 1 Ex D 36, 45 LJQB 233, 33 LT 655, 24 WR 287, 3 Asp MLC 81, CA 26, 108, 111
Mackintosh v Marshall (1843) 11 M & W 116, 12 LJ Ex 337, 6 LT 581 . . . 44
M'Swiney v Royal Exchange Assurance (1849) 14 QB 634; revsd. sub nom. Royal Exchange Assurance v M'Swiney (1850) 14 QB 646, 19 LJQB 222, 16 LTOS 22, 14 Jur 998, Ex Ch 26, 27, 108
Magnus v Buttemer (1852) 11 CB 876, 21 LJCP 119, 18 LTOS 276, 16 Jur 480 . . 413
Maignen & Co v National Benefit Assurance Co Ltd (1922) 38 TLR 257, 10 Ll L Rep 30 275
Main, The [1894] P 320, 63 LJP 69, 70 LT 247, 10 TLR 242, 7 Asp MLC 424, 6 R 775 . 85, 94
Mallough v Barber (1815) 4 Camp 150 32
Man v Shiffner (1802) 2 East 523 335
Manchester Liners Ltd v British and Foreign Marine Insurance Co Ltd (1901) 86 LT 148, 18 TLR 183, 9 Asp MLC 266, 7 Com Cas 26 228
Manfield v Maitland (1821) 4 B & Ald 582 21
Mann v Forrester (1814) 4 Camp 60 336
Mann Macneal and Steeves Ltd v Capital and Counties Insurance Co Ltd [1921] 2 KB 300, 90 LJKB 846, 124 LT 778, 37 TLR 247, 15 Asp MLC 225, 26 Com Cas 132, 5 Ll L Rep 203, 424, CA 50, 51, 53
Mansell & Co v Hoade (1903) 20 TLR 150 348
Marazura Navegacion SA v Oceanus Mutual Underwriting Association (Bermuda) Ltd and John Laing (Management) Ltd [1977] 1 Lloyd's Rep 283 479

Table of cases xxxix

	PAGE
Margetts and Ocean Accident and Guarantee Corpn, Re [1901] 2 KB 792, 70 LJKB 762, 85 LT 94, 49 WR 669, 17 TLR 538, 45 Sol Jo 557, 9 Asp MLC 217, DC	172
Marine Insurance Co v China Transpacific SS Co (1886) 11 App Cas 573, 56 LJQB 100, 55 LT 491, 35 WR 169, 2 TLR 857, 6 Asp MLC 68, HL	416, 421
Marine Insurance Co Ltd v Grimmer [1944] 2 All ER 197, 77 Ll L Rep 461, CA	32
Marine Sulphur Queen, The [1970] 2 Lloyd's Rep 285	456
Maris v London Assurance (1935) 52 Ll L Rep 211, CA	240
Maritime Insurance Co v Stearns [1901] 2 KB 912, 71 LJKB 86, 50 WR 238, 17 TLR 613, 6 Com Cas 182	126
Maritime Marine Insurance Co Ltd v Fire Re-Insurance Corpn Ltd. *See* Imperial Marine Insurance Co v Fire Insurance Corpn Ltd	
Marmion v Johnston (1928) 31 Ll L Rep 78	58
Marryat v Wilson (1799). *See* Wilson v Marryat (1798)	
Marsden v Reid (1803) 3 East 572	78, 130
Marstrand Fishing Co Ltd v Beer [1937] 1 All ER 158, 156 LT 196, 53 TLR 287, 81 Sol Jo 36, 19 Asp MLC 100, 56 Ll L Rep 163	165, 347, 366, 369
Marten v Nippon Sea and Land Insurance Co Ltd (1898) 14 TLR 333, 3 Com Cas 164	466
Marten v SS Owners' Underwriting Association (1902) 71 LJKB 718, 87 LT 208, 50 WR 587, 18 TLR 613, 9 Asp MLC 339, 7 Com Cas 195	97, 374, 465
Marten v Vestey Bros Ltd [1920] AC 307, [1920] All ER Rep 603, 89 LJKB 663, 122 LT 785, 36 TLR 228, 14 Asp MLC 600, 25 Com Cas 175, 2 Ll L Rep 113, HL	103, 120
Martin v Crokatt (1811) 14 East 465	382
Martin v Granger. *See* Grainger v Martin	
Martin v Sitwell (1691) 1 Show 156, 1 Holt KB 25	85
Maryland, The. *See* Atlantic Transport Co v R, The Maryland	
Mata Hari, The. *See* Pindos Shipping Corpn v Raven, The Mata Hari	
Mathie v Argonaut Marine Insurance Co Ltd (1925) 21 Ll L Rep 145, HL	63, 64
Matveieff & Co v Crossfield (1903) 51 WR 365, 19 TLR 182, 47 Sol Jo 258, 8 Com Cas 120	326
Mazarakis Bros v Furness, Withy & Co (1924) 18 Ll L Rep 152, CA	200
Medina Princess, The. *See* Helmville Ltd v Yorkshire Insurance Co Ltd, The Medina Princess	
Mees v Importers' and Exporters' Marine Insurance Co Ltd (1923) 15 Ll L Rep 201, CA	397
Megara, The. *See* Aronsen (Oscar L) Inc v Compton, The Megara	
Mellish v Allnutt (1813) 2 M & S 106	33
Mellish v Andrews (1812) 15 East 13	379, 380
Mentz, Decker & Co v Maritime Insurance Co [1910] 1 KB 132, 79 LJKB 104, 101 LT 808, 11 Asp MLC 339, 15 Com Cas 17	9, 81, 135, 165
Mercantile Marine Insurance Co v Titherington (1864) 5 B & S 765, 5 New Rep 82, 34 LJQB 11, 11 LT 340, 11 Jur NS 62, 13 WR 141	122, 323
Mercantile SS Co Ltd v Tyser (1881) 7 QBD 73, 29 WR 790, 5 Asp MLC 6n	52, 228, 267
Merchant Shipping Co v Armitage (1873) LR 9 QB 99, 43 LJQB 24, 29 LT 809, 2 Asp MLC 185, Ex Ch	351
Merchants' Marine Insurance Co v Liverpool Marine and General Insurance Co (1928) 97 LJKB 589, [1928] All ER Rep 452, 139 LT 184, 44 TLR 512, 17 Asp MLC 475, 33 Com Cas 294, 31 Ll L Rep 45, CA	469
Merchants' Marine Insurance Co Ltd v North of England Protecting and Indemnity Association (1926) 43 TLR 107, 71 Sol Jo 82, 32 Com Cas 165, 26 Ll L Rep 201, CA	173
Metcalfe v Britannia Ironworks Co (1877) 2 QBD 423, 46 LJQB 443, 36 LT 451, 25 WR 720, 3 Asp MLC 407, CA	351
Metcalfe v Parry (1814) 4 Camp 123	131
Meyer v Ralli (1876) 1 CPD 358, [1874–80] All ER Rep 1086, 45 LJQB 741, 35 LT 838, 24 WR 963, 3 Asp MLC 324	227, 442
Miceli v Union Marine and General Insurance Co Ltd (1938) 60 Ll L Rep 275, CA	147
Michael v Gillespy (1857) 2 CBNS 627, 26 LJCP 306, 29 LTOS 162, 3 Jur NS 1219	28
Michael, The. *See* Piermay Shipping Co SA and Brandt's Ltd v Chester, The Michael	
Michalos (N) & Sons Maritime SA v Prudential Assurance Co Ltd, The Zinovia [1984] 2 Lloyd's Rep 264	242, 247
Middlewood v Blakes (1797) 7 Term Rep 162	56
Miller v Tetherington (1862) 7 H & N 954, 31 LJ Ex 363, 9 LT 231, 8 Jur NS 1039, 10 WR 356, 1 Mar LC 388, Ex Ch	327

xl *Table of cases*

PAGE

Miller v Warre (1825). See Warre v Miller
Miller v Woodfall (1857) 8 E & B 493, 27 LJQB 120, 30 LTOS 240, 4 Jur NS 302 . . 395
Milles v Fletcher (1779) 1 Doug KB 231 353
Milward v Hibbert (1842) 3 QB 120, 2 Gal & Dav 142, 11 LJQB 137, 7 LT 76, 6 Jur
  706 . . . . 154, 326
Minett v Anderson (1794) Peake 277 121
Miss Jay Jay, The. See Lloyd (J J) Instruments Ltd v Northern Star Insurance Co Ltd, The
  Miss Jay Jay
Mitera, The (1969). See Atlantic Maritime Carriers SA v Hellenic Mutual War Risks
  Association Ltd, Capetandiamantis Compania Maritima SA, Eastern Seas Transport
  Corpn and Orient Shipping Corpn v Hellenic Mutual War Risks Association Ltd (1968)
Mitrovitch Bros & Co v Merchants Marine Insurance Co Ltd (1923) 14 Ll L Rep 25 . . 208
Moir v Royal Exchange Assurance Co (1815) 3 M & S 461 . . . . . 284, 285
Montedison SpA v Icroma SpA, The Caspian Sea [1979] 3 All ER 378, [1980] 1 WLR 48,
  123 Sol Jo 551, [1980] 1 Lloyd's Rep 91 19
Montgomery & Co v Indemnity Mutual Marine Insurance Co [1902] 1 KB 734, 71 LJKB
  467, 86 LT 462, 50 WR 440, 18 TLR 479, 46 Sol Jo 410, 9 Asp MLC 289, 7 Com Cas
  120, CA 184
Montoya v London Assurance Co (1851) 6 Exch 451, 20 LJ Ex 254, 17 LTOS 82 . . 143
Montreal Light, Heat and Power Co v Sedgwick [1910] AC 598, 80 LJPC 11, 103 LT 234, 26
  TLR 657, 11 Asp MLC 437, PC 350
Moor Line v King and United Kingdom Mutual War Risks Association (1920) 36 TLR 799,
  4 Ll L Rep 286 204
Moore v Evans [1918] AC 185, 87 LJKB 207, 117 LT 761, 34 TLR 51, 62 Sol Jo 69, 23 Com
  Cas 124, HL 362
Moore v Mourgue (1776) 2 Cowp 479 30
Moore v Taylor (1834) 1 Ad & El 25, 3 Nev & MKB 406, 3 LJKB 132 120
Moran, Galloway & Co v Uzielli [1905] 2 KB 555, 74 LJKB 494, 54 WR 250, 21 TLR 378,
  10 Com Cas 203 . . . . 9, 19, 25
Morck v Abel (1802) 3 Bos & P 35 84
Mordy v Jones (1825) 4 B & C 394, 6 Dow & Ry KB 479, 3 LJOSKB 250 . . . 227
Morgan v Price (1849) 4 Exch 615, 19 LJ Ex 201, 14 LTOS 257 461
Morice v Anderson (1876). See Anderson v Morice (1875) (1876)
Morrison v Universal Marine Insurance Co (1873) LR 8 Exch 197, 42 LJ Ex 115, 21 WR
  774, Ex Ch 40, 55, 67
Moss v Byrom (1795) 6 Term Rep 379 165
Moss v Smith (1850) 9 CB 94, 19 LJCP 225, 14 LTOS 376, 14 Jur 1003 354
Motteux v Governor & Co of London Assurance (1739) 1 Atk 545 274
Mount v Larkins (1831) 8 Bing 108, 1 Moo & S 165, 1 LJCP 20 . . . . 126, 136
Mountain v Whittle [1921] 1 AC 615, [1921] All ER Rep 626, 90 LJKB 699, 125 LT 193, 65
  Sol Jo 415, 15 Asp MLC 255, 6 Ll L Rep 378, HL 144, 148, 268, 306
Mouse's Case (1608) 12 Co Rep 63, cited in 2 Bulst 280, sub nom. Gravesend Barge Case 1
  Roll Rep 79 153
Moxon v Atkins (1812) 3 Camp 200 . . . . 46, 116, 326
Muirhead v Forth and North Sea Steamboat Mutual Insurance Association [1894] AC 72, 10
  TLR 82, 6 R 59, HL 288
Muller v Thompson (1811) 2 Camp 610 282
Munro, Brice & Co v Marten [1920] 3 KB 94, 89 LJKB 1009, 123 LT 562, 36 TLR 241, 15
  Asp MLC 45, 25 Com Cas 112, 2 Ll L Rep 2, CA 208, 349
Munro, Brice & Co v War Risks Association [1918] 2 KB 78, [1916–17] All ER Rep 981n,
  88 LJKB 509, 118 LT 708, 34 TLR 331, 14 Asp MLC 312 349
Munroe, The [1893] P 248, 70 LT 246, 7 Asp MLC 407, 1 R 642 414

N

Nassau Bay, The. See Costain-Blankevoort (UK) Dredging Co Ltd v Davenport, The Nassau
  Bay
National Benefit Assurance Co Ltd (Application of Sthyr), Re (1933) 45 Ll L Rep 147 . 18,
    178

Table of cases xli

	PAGE
Naviera de Canarias SA v Nacional Hispanica Aseguradora SA [1978] AC 853, [1977] 1 All ER 625, [1977] 2 WLR 442, 121 Sol Jo 186, [1977] 1 Lloyd's Rep 457, HL	230, 263
Navigators and General Insurance Co Ltd v Ringrose [1962] 1 All ER 97, [1962] 1 WLR 173, 106 Sol Jo 135, [1961] 2 Lloyd's Rep 415, CA	269
Navone v Haddon (1850) 9 CB 30, 19 LJCP 161, 14 LTOS 419	350
Naylor v Taylor (1829) 9 B & C 718, Dan & Ll 240, 4 Man & Ry KB 526, 7 LJOS 311	376
Near East Relief v King, Chasseur & Co Ltd [1930] 2 KB 40, 99 LJKB 522, 35 Com Cas 104, 36 Ll L Rep 91	337
Neilson v De Lacour (1797) 2 Esp 618	327
Nelson v Empress Assurance Corpn Ltd [1905] 2 KB 281, 74 LJKB 699, 93 LT 62, 53 WR 648, 21 TLR 555, 10 Asp MLC 68, 10 Com Cas 237, CA	465
Nelson v Salvador (1829) Dan & Ll 219, Mood & M 309	283
Nesbitt v Lushington (1792) 4 Term Rep 783	156
Neter (N E) & Co v Licenses and General Insurance Co Ltd [1944] 1 All ER 341, 170 LT 165, 60 TLR 201, 77 Ll L Rep 202	149
Neue Fischmehl Vertribs-Gesellschaft Haselhorst mbH v Yorkshire Insurance Co Ltd (1934) 50 Ll L Rep 151	76, 300
New Zealand Shipping Co Ltd v Duke [1914] 2 KB 682, 83 LJKB 1300, 111 LT 37, 30 TLR 385, 12 Asp MLC 507, 19 Com Cas 223	9
Nicholson v Power (1869) 20 LT 580, 3 Mar LC 236, Ex Ch	67
Nickels & Co v London and Provincial Marine and General Insurance Co (1900) 70 LJQB 29, 17 TLR 54, 6 Com Cas 15	230
Niger Co Ltd v Guardian Assurance Co Ltd (1922) 13 Ll L Rep 75, HL	67, 137
Niobe, The. See M'Cowan v Baine and Johnston, The Niobe	
Noble v Kennoway (1780) 2 Doug KB 510, [1775–1802] All ER Rep 439	46, 326
Nonnen v Kettlewell (1812) 16 East 176	72
North Atlantic SS Co Ltd v Bure (1904) 20 TLR 266, 9 Com Cas 164	97, 374
North British Fishing Boat Insurance Co Ltd v Starr (1922) 13 Ll L Rep 206	46, 47, 59
North British Rubber Co v Cheetham (1938) 61 Ll L Rep 337, CA	398
North Shipping Co Ltd v Union Marine Insurance Co Ltd (1919) 35 TLR 292, 24 Com Cas 161, CA	83
North of England Iron SS Insurance Association v Armstrong (1870) LR 5 QB 244, 39 LJQB 81, 21 LT 822, 18 WR 520, 3 Mar LC 330	94
North of England Oil-Cake Co v Archangel Insurance Co (1875) LR 10 QB 249, [1874–80] All ER Rep 875, 44 LJQB 121, 32 LT 561, 24 WR 162, 2 Asp MLC 571, DC	28, 321
Northwestern Mutual Life Assurance Co v Linard, The Vainqueur [1973] 2 Lloyd's Rep 275	234, 243
Norwich Union Fire Insurance Society v Colonial Mutual Fire Insurance Co [1922] 2 KB 461, [1922] All ER Rep 513, 91 LJKB 881, 128 LT 121, 38 TLR 822, 66 Sol Jo 720, 16 Asp MLC 98, 28 Com Cas 20	278
Norwich Union Fire Insurance Society Ltd v Price Ltd [1934] AC 455, [1934] All ER Rep 352, 103 LJPC 115, 151 LT 309, 50 TLR 454, 78 Sol Jo 412, 40 Com Cas 132, 49 Ll L Rep 55, PC	348, 390
Nottebohn v Richter (1886) 18 QBD 63, 56 LJQB 33, 35 WR 300, 3 TLR 30, CA	102
Nourse v Liverpool Sailing Ship Owners' Mutual Protection and Indemnity Association [1896] 2 QB 16, 65 LJQB 507, 74 LT 543, 44 WR 500, 12 TLR 406, 8 Asp MLC 144, 1 Com Cas 388, CA	193
Nutt v Bourdieu (1786) 1 Term Rep 323	162, 163

O

Ocean, A/S v Black Sea and Baltic General Insurance Co Ltd (1935) 51 Ll L Rep 305, CA	329, 420
Oceanic SS Co v Faber (1907) 97 LT 466, 23 TLR 673, 10 Asp MLC 515, 13 Com Cas 28, CA	159
Oceanic Steam Navigation Co Ltd v Evans (1934) 51 TLR 67, 78 Sol Jo 838, 40 Com Cas 108, 50 Ll L Rep 1, CA	394
Olive v Smith (1813) 5 Taunt 56, 2 Rose 122	334
Oliverson v Brightman (1846) 8 QB 781, 15 LJQB 274, 7 LTOS 81, 10 Jur 875	133
Oliverson v Loughnan (1815) cited in 2 B & Ald 322	299

xlii Table of cases

PAGE

Oriental Fire and General Insurance Co Ltd v American President Lines Ltd and Cotton
 Trading Corpn of San Francisco [1968] 2 Lloyd's Rep 372 458
Oswell v Vigne (1812) 15 East 70 287
Otago Farmers' Co-op Association of New Zealand v Thompson [1910] 2 KB 145, 79 LJKB
 692, 102 LT 711, 11 Asp MLC 403, 15 Com Cas 28 326
Ougier v Jennings (1800) 1 Camp 505n 46, 130
Overseas Commodities Ltd v Style [1958] 1 Lloyd's Rep 546 . . . 108, 227, 254, 292
Overseas Marine Insurance Co Ltd, Re (1930) 36 Ll L Rep 183, CA . . . 468

P

Pacific Queen Fisheries v L Symes, The Pacific Queen [1963] 2 Lloyd's Rep 201, CA . 49, 52,
66, 169, 306, 309
Padre Island, The. See Socony Mobil Oil Co Inc, Mobil Oil Co Ltd and Mobil Oil AG v West
 of England Ship Owners Mutual Insurance Association (London) Ltd, The Padre Island
Padre Island, The. See Steam Tanker Padre Island Inc and Pullman Bank and Trust Co v
 London Assurance, Guildhall Insurance Co, The Padre Island
Palace Shipping Co Ltd v Caine. See Caine v Palace Steam Shipping Co
Palamisto General Enterprises SA v Ocean Marine Insurance Co Ltd, The Dias [1972] 2 QB
 625, [1972] 2 WLR 1425, 116 Sol Jo 685, [1972] 2 Lloyd's Rep 60, sub nom. Dias, The,
 Palamisto General Enterprises SA v Ocean Marine Insurance Co Ltd [1972] 2 All ER
 1112, CA 243
Palmer v Blackburn (1822) 1 Bing 61, 7 Moore CP 339, 1 LJOSCP 1 427
Palmer v Naylor (1854) 10 Exch 382, 2 CLR 1202, 23 LJ Ex 323, 24 LTOS 83, 18 Jur 961, 2
 WR 621, Ex Ch 156
Palmer v Warren Insurance Co (1840) 1 Story 360 328
Palyart v Leckie (1817) 6 M & S 290 84
Panamanian Oriental SS Corpn v Wright [1970] 2 Lloyd's Rep 365; on appeal [1971] 2 All
 ER 1028, [1971] 1 WLR 882, 115 Sol Jo 345, [1971] 1 Lloyd's Rep 487, CA . 261, 348,
371, 385
Papadimitriou v Henderson [1939] 3 All ER 908, 55 TLR 1035, 45 Com Cas 29, 64 Ll L Rep
 345 . . . . 96, 233, 359
Papoose, The. See Gulfstream Cargo Ltd v Reliance Insurance Co, The Papoose
Parente (Robert A) v Bayville Marine Inc and General Insurance Co of America [1975] 1
 Lloyd's Rep 333 254
Parfitt v Thompson (1844) 13 M & W 392, 14 LJ Ex 73, 4 LTOS 116, 138 . . 302
Park v Hamond (or Hammond) (1816) 2 Marsh 189, 6 Taunt 495, Holt NP 82n, 4 Camp
 344 33
Parker v Potts (1815) 3 Dow 23, HL 298
Parkin v Dick (1809) 11 East 502, 2 Camp 221 308
Parkin v Tunno (1809) 11 East 22, 2 Camp 59 230
Parmeter v Cousins (1809) 2 Camp 235 . . . . 115, 299
Parmeter v Todhunter (1808) 1 Camp 541 353
Pateras v Royal Exchange Assurance (1934) 78 Sol Jo 569, 49 Ll L Rep 400 . 239, 245
Paterson v Harris (1861) 1 B & S 336, 30 LJQB 354, 5 LT 53, 7 Jur NS 1276, 9 WR 743, 1
 Mar LC 124 . . . . 27, 142
Patrick v Eames (1813) 3 Camp 441 . . . . 21, 353
Patterson v Ritchie (1815) 4 M & S 393 376
Pawson v Watson (1778) 1 Doug KB 12n, 2 Cowp 785 . . . . . 78, 281
Payne v Hutchinson (1810) 2 Taunt 405n 116
Pearson v Commercial Union Assurance Co (1876) 1 App Cas 498, 45 LJQB 761, 35 LT 445,
 24 WR 951, 3 Asp MLC 275, HL 270
Pelly v Royal Exchange Assurance Co (1757) 1 Burr 341, [1558–1774] All ER Rep 405 326
Pelton SS Co Ltd v North of England Protecting and Indemnity Association, The Zelo (1925)
 22 Ll L Rep 510 172
Peninsular and Oriental Branch Service v Commonwealth Shipping Representative, The
 Geelong (1922) 13 Ll L Rep 230 200
Pentland, The (1897) 13 TLR 430 297

Table of cases xliii

PAGE

Pesquerias Secaderos de Espana SA v Beer (1946) 175 LT 495, 79 Ll L Rep 417; revsd. (1947) 80 Ll L Rep 318, CA; on appeal [1949] 1 All ER 845n, 93 Sol Jo 371, 82 Ll L Rep 501, HL 392
Petros M Nomikos Ltd v Robertson 64 Ll L Rep 45, HL 329, 357, 358, 363, 364, 365, 375
Petros M Nomikos Ltd v Robertson. See Robertson v Petros M Nomikos Ltd
Phelps v Auldjo (1809) 2 Camp 350 128
Phillips v Irving (1844) 7 Man & G 325, 8 Scott NR 3, 13 LJCP 145, 3 LTOS 55 . . 136
Phillips v Nairne (1847) 4 CB 343, 16 LJCP 194, 9 LTOS 295, 11 Jur 455 . . 302, 372
Philpott v Swann (1861) 11 CBNS 270, 30 LJCP 358, 5 LT 183, 7 Jur NS 1291, 1 Mar LC 151 227
Phoenix Insurance Co of Hartford v De Monchy (1929) 141 LT 439, [1929] All ER Rep 531, 45 TLR 543, 18 Asp MLC 7, 35 Com Cas 67, 34 Ll L Rep 201, HL 142
Phoenix Insurance Co of Hartford v De Monchy (1929). See De Monchy v Phoenix Insurance Co of Hartford (1928)
Phyn v Royal Exchange Assurance Co (1798) 7 Term Rep 505 . . . . 162, 166
Pickersgill (William) & Sons Ltd v London and Provincial Marine and General Insurance Co Ltd [1912] 3 KB 614, [1911–13] All ER Rep 861, 82 LJKB 130, 107 LT 305, 28 TLR 591, 57 Sol Jo 11, 12 Asp MLC 263, 18 Com Cas 1 317
Pickup v Thames and Mersey Marine Insurance Co Ltd (1878) 3 QBD 594, 47 LJQB 749, 39 LT 341, 26 WR 689, 4 Asp MLC 43, CA 298
Piermay Shipping Co SA and Brandt's Ltd v Chester, The Michael [1979] 1 Lloyd's Rep 55 . . . . 167, 245
Pillgrem v Cliff Richardson Boats Ltd and Richardson (Switzerland General Insurance Co, third party) [1977] 1 Lloyd's Rep 297 . . . . 27, 418
Pindos Shipping Corpn v Raven, The Mata Hari [1983] 2 Lloyd's Rep 449 . . 277, 296
Pink v Fleming (1890) 25 QBD 396, 59 LJQB 151, 559, 63 LT 413, 6 TLR 432, 6 Asp MLC 554, CA 228
Piper v Royal Exchange Assurance (1932) 44 Ll L Rep 103 . . . . 17, 48, 61, 239
Pipon v Cope (1808) 1 Camp 434 . . . . 162, 164, 168
Pirie v Steele (1837) 8 C & P 200, 2 Mood & R 49, 3 LT 382 419
Pirie & Co v Middle Dock Co (1881) 44 LT 426, 4 Asp MLC 388 151
Pitman v Universal Marine Insurance Co (1882) 9 QBD 192, 51 LJQB 561, 46 LT 863, 30 WR 906, 4 Asp MLC 544, CA 379, 425
Pittegrew v Pringle (1832) 3 B & Ad 514 283
Planche v Fletcher (1779) 1 Doug KB 251, [1775–1802] All ER Rep 409 . . 46, 308
Poingdestre v Royal Exchange Corpn (1826) Ry & M 378 419
Pollard v Bell (1800) 8 Term Rep 434 288
Polpen Shipping Co Ltd v Commercial Union Assurance Co Ltd [1943] KB 161, [1943] 1 All ER 162, 112 LJKB 198, 168 LT 143, 59 TLR 106, 87 Sol Jo 129, 74 Ll L Rep 157 . 174
Polurrian SS Co Ltd v Young (1913) 84 LJKB 1025, 109 LT 901, 30 TLR 126, 12 Asp MLC 449, 19 Com Cas 143; affd. [1915] 1 KB 922, [1914–15] All ER Rep 116, 84 LJKB 1025, 112 LT 1053, 31 TLR 211, 59 Sol Jo 285, 13 Asp MLC 59, 20 Com Cas 152, CA . . 364, 366, 367, 369, 376, 377
Pomeranian, The [1895] P 349, 65 LJP 39 . . . . 4, 433, 444
Popi M, The. See Rhesa Shipping Co SA v Edmunds, The Popi M
Portmar, The. See Calmar SS Corpn v Scott, The Portmar
Portvale SS Co Ltd v Royal Exchange Assurance Corpn (1932) 147 LT 217, [1932] All ER Rep 810, 48 TLR 441, 76 Sol Jo 415, 18 Asp MLC 309, 43 Ll L Rep 161 . . . 415
Potoi Chau, The. See Castle Insurance Co Ltd v Hong Kong Islands Shipping Co Ltd, The Potoi Chau
Potter v Campbell (1867) 2 LJNC 223, 17 LT 474n, 16 WR 399, 401, 3 Mar LC 29n . . 389
Potter v Rankin (1868) LR 3 CP 562; revsd. (1870) LR 5 CP 341, Ex Ch; affd. sub nom. Rankin v Potter (1873) LR 6 HL 83, 42 LJCP 169, 29 LT 142, 22 WR 1, 2 Asp MLC 65, HL 354
Powell v Gudgeon (1816) 5 M & S 431 226
Powles v Innes (1843) 11 M & W 10, 12 LJ Ex 163 . . . . . . 27, 321
Preston v Greenwood (1784) 4 Doug KB 28 120
Price v Livingstone (1882) 9 QBD 679, 53 LJQB 118, 47 LT 629, 5 Asp MLC 13, CA . 283
Price v Maritime Insurance Co (1900) [1901] 2 KB 412, 70 LJKB 780, 85 LT 101, 49 WR 645, 17 TLR 559, 45 Sol Jo 575, 9 Asp MLC 213, 6 Com Cas 168, CA . . . 9

xliv *Table of cases*

	PAGE
Price v Noble (1811) 4 Taunt 123	153
Price & Co v AI Ships' Small Damage Insurance Association (1889) 22 QBD 580, 58 LJQB 269, 61 LT 278, 37 WR 566, 5 TLR 356, 6 Asp MLC 435, CA	416
Princess Charlotte, The (1863) Brown & Lush 75, 33 LJPM & A 188	287
Probatina Shipping Co Ltd v Sun Insurance Office Ltd [1974] 2 All ER 478, [1973] 2 Lloyd's Rep 520; on appeal [1974] QB 635, [1974] 2 All ER 478, [1974] 2 WLR 666, 118 Sol Jo 331, [1974] 1 Lloyd's Rep 369, CA	398, 399
Property Insurance Co Ltd v National Protector Insurance Co Ltd (1913) 108 LT 104, 57 Sol Jo 284, 12 Asp MLC 287, 18 Com Cas 119	465, 466
Proudfoot v Montefiore (1867) LR 2 QB 511, 8 B & S 510, 36 LJQB 225, 16 LT 585, 15 WR 920, 2 Mar LC 512	41, 44, 55
Provincial Insurance Co of Canada v Leduc (1874) LR 6 PC 244, 43 LJPC 49, 31 LT 142, 22 WR 929, 2 Asp MLC 538, PC	17, 282, 285, 311, 326, 390
Prudent Tankers Ltd SA v Dominion Insurance Co Ltd, The Caribbean Sea [1980] 1 Lloyd's Rep 338	114, 160, 250
Pyman v Marten (1906) 24 TLR 10, 13 Com Cas 64, CA	83

Q

Quebec Marine Insurance Co v Commercial Bank of Canada (1870) LR 3 PC 234, 7 Moo PCCNS 1, 39 LJPC 53, 22 LT 559, 18 WR 769, 3 Mar LC 414, PC	301, 302, 311

R

R v Arnaud (1846) 9 QB 806, 16 LJQB 50, 8 LTOS 212, 10 JP 821, 11 Jur 279	27
Raine v Bell (1808) 9 East 195	133
Ralli v Janson (1856) 6 E & B 422, sub nom. Janson (or Jamson) v Ralli 25 LJQB 300, 27 LTOS 139, 2 Jur NS 566, 4 WR 568, Ex Ch	431
Ralli v Universal Marine Insurance Co (1862) 4 De GF & J 1, 31 LJ Ch 313, 6 LT 34, 37, 8 Jur NS 495, 10 WR 278, 327, 1 Mar LC 194, 197	321
Randal v Cockran (1748) 1 Ves Sen 98	457
Rankin v Potter (1873) LR 6 HL 83, 42 LJCP 169, 29 LT 142, 22 WR 1, 2 Asp MLC 65, HL	348, 353, 356, 381, 383
Rankin v Potter (1873). See Potter v Rankin (1868) (1870)	
Ratcliffe v Shoolbred (1780) 1 Park's Marine Insce 8th ed 413	72
Rayner v Godmond (1821) 5 B & Ald 225	411
Rayner v Preston (1881) 18 Ch D 1, 50 LJ Ch 472, 44 LT 787, 45 JP 829, 29 WR 547, CA	321
Reardon Smith Lines Ltd v Black Sea and Baltic General Insurance Co Ltd, The Indian City [1939] AC 562, [1939] 3 All ER 444, 108 LJKB 692, 161 LT 79, 55 TLR 929, 83 Sol Jo 796, 19 Asp MLC 311, 45 Com Cas 1, HL	326
Red Sea, The [1895] P 293, 64 LJP 89, 73 LT 462, 8 Asp MLC 102, 11 R 801; on appeal [1896] P 20, 65 LJP 9, 73 LT 462, 44 WR 306, 12 TLR 40, 40 Sol Jo 64, 8 Asp MLC 102, CA	21, 395, 396
Redman v Wilson (1845) 14 M & W 476, 14 LJ Ex 333, 9 Jur 714	144, 231
Redmond v Smith (1844) 7 Man & G 457, 2 Dow & L 280, 8 Scott NR 250, 13 LJCP 159, 3 LTOS 162, 8 Jur 711	308
Reed (A E) & Co v Page, Son & East Ltd [1927] 1 KB 743, 96 LJKB 390, 137 LT 77, 43 TLR 272, 17 Asp MLC 231, 32 Com Cas 243, CA	301
Reid v Allan (1849) 4 Exch 326, 19 LJ Ex 39, 7 LT 75, 13 Jur 1082	105
Reid v Darby (1808) 10 East 143	299
Reid v Standard Marine Assurance Co Ltd (1886) 2 TLR 807	349
Reimer v Ringrose (1851) 6 Exch 263, 20 LJ Ex 175, 17 LTOS 18	374
Reischer v Borwick [1894] 2 QB 548, 63 LJQB 753, 71 LT 238, 10 TLR 568, 7 Asp MLC 493, 9 R 558, CA	228
Reliance Marine Insurance Co v Duder [1913] 1 KB 265, 81 LJKB 870, 106 LT 936, 28 TLR 469, 12 Asp MLC 223, 17 Com Cas 227, CA	467
Renpor, The (1883) 8 PD 115, 52 LJP 49, 48 LT 887, 31 WR 640, 5 Asp MLC 98, CA	443

Table of cases xlv

PAGE

Renton (G H) & Co Ltd v Black Sea and Baltic General Insurance Co Ltd [1941] 1 KB 206, [1941] 1 All ER 149, 110 LJKB 329, 164 LT 190, 57 TLR 133, 85 Sol Jo 178, 46 Com Cas 113, 19 Asp MLC 396, 68 Ll L Rep 71 . . . . 8, 125
Renton (G H) & Co Ltd v Cornhill Insurance Co Ltd (1933) 149 LT 280, [1933] All ER Rep 577, 49 TLR 414, 18 Asp MLC 407, 46 Ll L Rep 14 430
Rhesa Shipping Co SA v Edmunds, The Popi M [1983] 2 Lloyd's Rep 235; revsd. (1985) Financial Times 22 May 170, 250
Rhind v Wilkinson (1810) 2 Taunt 237 28
Rich v Parker (1798) 7 Term Rep 705, 2 Esp 615 287
Rickards v Forestal Land, Timber and Rlys Co Ltd. See Forestal Land, Timber and Rlys Co Ltd v Rickards
Rickards v Murdock (1830) 10 B & C 527, L & Welsb 132, 5 Man & Ry KB 418, 8 LJOSKB 210 . . . . 57, 79
Rickman v Carstairs (1833) 5 B & Ad 651, 2 Nev & M KB 562, 3 LJKB 28 . . . 85
Ridsdale v Newnham (1814) 3 M & S 456 283
Rivaz v Gerussi (1880) 6 QBD 222, 50 LJQB 176, 44 LT 79, 4 Asp MLC 377, CA . 65, 69, 93
Robertson v Clarke (1824) 1 Bing 445, 8 Moore CP 622, 2 LJOSCP 71 . . . 116
Robertson v Ewer (1786) 1 Term Rep 127 . . . . 164, 422
Robertson v French (1803) 4 East 130 . . . . 33, 323
Robertson v Marjoribanks (1819) 2 Stark 573 78
Robertson v Money (1824) Ry & M 75 116
Robertson v Petros M Nomikos Ltd [1939] AC 371, [1939] 2 All ER 723, 108 LJKB 433, 160 LT 542, 55 TLR 779, 83 Sol Jo 583, 19 Asp MLC 296, 44 Com Cas 303, sub nom. Petros M Nomikos Ltd v Robertson 64 Ll L Rep 45, HL 263, 364
Robinson v Touray (1811) 3 Camp 158 92
Roddick v Indemnity Mutual Marine Insurance Co [1895] 2 QB 380, 64 LJQB 733, 72 LT 860, 44 WR 27, 11 TLR 480, 39 Sol Jo 620, 8 Asp MLC 24, 14 R 516, CA . 107, 288, 291
Rodocanachi v Milburn (1886) 18 QBD 67, 56 LJQB 202, 56 LT 594, 35 WR 241, 3 TLR 115, 6 Asp MLC 100, CA 21
Rodoconachi v Elliott (1874) LR 9 CP 518, 43 LJCP 255, 31 LT 239, 2 Asp MLC 399, Ex Ch 8, 368
Roelandts v Harrison (1854) 9 Exch 444, 2 CLR 995, 23 LJ Ex 169, 22 LTOS 289 . 282
Rohl v Parr (1796) 1 Esp 445 142
Rosa v Insurance Co of the State of Pennsylvania, The Belle of Portugal [1970] 2 Lloyd's Rep 386 . . . . 113, 151, 161
Roscow v Corson (1819) 8 Taunt 684 165
Rosetto v Gurney (1851) 11 CB 176, 20 LJCP 257, 17 LTOS 242, 15 Jur 1777 . . 354, 374
Ross v Hunter (1790) 4 Term Rep 33 . . . . 162, 167, 169
Roura and Forgas v Townend [1919] 1 KB 189, [1918–19] All ER Rep 341, 88 LJKB 393, 120 LT 116, 35 TLR 88, 14 Asp MLC 397, 24 Com Cas 71 . . . 376, 409
Routh v Thompson (1809) 11 East 428 26
Routh v Thompson (1811) 13 East 274 26
Roux v Salvador (1835) 3 Bing NC 266, 2 Hodg 209, 4 Scott 1, 7 LJ Ex 328 . 348, 350, 382, 388
Rowland and Marwood SS Co Ltd v Maritime Insurance Co Ltd (1901) 17 TLR 516, 6 Com Cas 160 375
Royal Exchange Assurance v M'Swiney (1850). See M'Swiney v Royal Exchange Assurance (1849)
Royal Exchange Assurance Co Ltd v Compania Naviera Santi SA (1962) 106 Sol Jo 312, [1962] 1 Lloyd's Rep 410 241
Royal Exchange Shipping Co v Dixon (1886) 12 App Cas 11, 56 LJQB 266, 56 LT 206, 35 WR 461, 3 TLR 172, 6 Asp MLC 92, HL 154
Ruabon SS Co v London Assurance [1900] AC 6, [1895–9] All ER Rep 677, 69 LJQB 86, 81 LT 585, 48 WR 225, 16 TLR 90, 44 Sol Jo 116, 9 Asp MLC 2, 5 Com Cas 71, HL . 416, 421
Rudolph (M J) Corpn v Lumber Mutual Fire Insurance Co (Luria International, Third Parties), The Cape Borer [1975] 2 Lloyd's Rep 108 218
Russell v Niemann (1864) 17 CBNS 163, 5 New Rep 190, 34 LJCP 10, 10 LT 786, 13 WR 93, 2 Mar LC 72 150
Russell v Provincial Insurance Co Ltd [1959] 2 Lloyd's Rep 275 . . . 270, 272, 300

xlvi *Table of cases*

	PAGE
Russell v Thornton (1859) 4 H & N 788	53
Russell v Thornton (1860) 6 H & N 140, 30 LJ Ex 69, 2 LT 574, 6 Jur NS 1080, 8 WR 615	55
Russian Bank for Foreign Trade v Excess Insurance Co [1918] 2 KB 123, 87 LJKB 872, 118 LT 645, 34 TLR 383, 14 Asp MLC 316, 23 Com Cas 325; affd. [1919] 1 KB 39, 88 LJKB 209, 119 LT 733, 35 TLR 42, 63 Sol Jo 40, 14 Asp MLC 362, CA . .	262, 386
Ruys v Royal Exchange Assurance Corpn [1897] 2 QB 135, 66 LJQB 534, 77 LT 23, 13 TLR 444, 8 Asp MLC 294, 2 Com Cas 201	376

S

Sadler v Dixon (1841). See Dixon v Sadler (1839)
Safadi v Western Assurance Co (1933) 46 Ll L Rep 140 . . . . . 124, 319
St Margaret's Trust Ltd v Navigators and General Insurance Co Ltd (1949) 82 Ll L Rep 752 . . . . 48, 247, 347, 445
Salvador v Hopkins (1765) 3 Burr 1707 . . . . 46, 326
Samuel v Royal Exchange Assurance Co (1828) 8 B & C 119, 6 LJOSKB 315 . 119, 120, 136
Samuel (P) & Co Ltd v Dumas [1923] 1 KB 592, 92 LJKB 465, 128 LT 706, 39 TLR 154, 67 Sol Jo 336, CA; affd. [1924] AC 431, [1924] All ER Rep 66, 93 LJKB 415, 130 LT 771, 40 TLR 375, 68 Sol Jo 439, 16 Asp MLC 305, 29 Com Cas 239, 17 Ll L Rep 47, 67, 217, HL 22, 23, 145, 227, 232, 235, 244, 290, 312, 318
Sanderson v Busher (1814) 4 Camp 54n 280, 286
Sanderson v M'Cullom (1819) 4 Moore CP 5 278
Sanderson v Symonds (1819) 1 Brod & Bing 426, 4 Moore CP 42 278
Sarguy v Hobsun. See Sarquy v Hobson
Sarquy v Hobson (1827) 4 Bing 131, sub nom. Sarguy v Hobsun 1 Y & J 347, 12 Moore CP 474, Ex Ch 226
Sasson (E D) & Co Ltd v Yorkshire Insurance Co Ltd (1923) 14 Ll L Rep 167; affd. 16 Ll L Rep 129, CA 251, 254
Sassoon (E D) & Co v Western Assurance Co [1912] AC 561, [1911–13] All ER Rep 438, 81 LJCP 231, 106 LT 929, 12 Asp MLC 206, 17 Com Cas 274, PC . . . 145, 147
Saunders v Baring (1876) 34 LT 419, 3 Asp MLC 132 350
Sawtell v Loudon (1814) 5 Taunt 359, Marsh 99 54
Schauer v Webster & Co (1929) 35 Ll L Rep 31 455
Schloss v Stevens (1905) 10 Com Cas 224, CA 398
Schloss Bros v Stevens [1906] 2 KB 665, 75 LJKB 927, 96 LT 205, 22 TLR 774, 10 Asp MLC 331, 11 Com Cas 270, CA 8, 46, 178
Schroder v Thompson (1817) 7 Taunt 462, 1 Moore CP 163 136
Scindia Steamships (London) Ltd v London Assurance [1937] 1 KB 639, [1937] 3 All ER 895, 106 LJKB 425, 157 LT 496, 42 Com Cas 121, 19 Asp MLC 86, 56 Ll L Rep 136 158
Scott v Coulson [1903] 2 Ch 249, 72 LJ Ch 600, 88 LT 653, 19 TLR 440, CA . . 274
Scott v Globe Marine Insurance Co Ltd (1896) 1 Com Cas 370 . . . . 25, 92
Scottish Marine Insurance Co v Turner (1853) 4 HL Cas 312n, 21 LTOS 10, 17 Jur 631, 1 WR 537, 1 Macq 334, HL 359, 361
Scottish Metropolitan Assurance Co Ltd v Groom (1924) 41 TLR 35, 20 Ll L Rep 44, CA 445
Scottish Metropolitan Assurance Co Ltd v Stewart (1923) 39 TLR 407 . . 276, 324
Scottish National Insurance Co Ltd v Poole (1912) 107 LT 687, 29 TLR 16, 57 Sol Jo 45, 12 Asp MLC 266, 18 Com Cas 9 467
Scottish Shire Line Ltd v London and Provincial Marine and General Insurance Co Ltd [1912] 3 KB 51, 81 LJKB 1066, 107 LT 46, 56 Sol Jo 551, 12 Asp MLC 253, 17 Com Cas 240 . . . . 21, 57, 230
Sea Insurance Co v Blogg [1898] 2 QB 398, 67 LJQB 757, 78 LT 785, 47 WR 71, 14 TLR 474, 42 Sol Jo 590, 8 Asp MLC 412, 3 Com Cas 218, CA 284
Sea Insurance Co v Hadden (1884) 13 QBD 706, 53 LJQB 252, 50 LT 657, 32 WR 841, 5 Asp MLC 230, CA 395, 456
Sea Insurance Co of Scotland v Gavin (1829) 4 Bli NS 578, 2 Dow & Cl 129, HL . 116
Seagrave v Union Marine Insurance Co (1866) LR 1 CP 305, Har & Ruth 302, 35 LJCP 172, 14 LT 479, 12 Jur NS 358, 14 WR 690, 2 Mar LC 331 24
Seaman v Fonereau (1743) 2 Stra 1183 . . . . . . 40, 41, 69, 73, 79

Table of cases xlvii

	PAGE
Sewell v Royal Exchange Assurance Co (1813) 4 Taunt 856	309
Sharp v Gladstone (1805) 7 East 24, 3 Smith KB 39	396
Shawe v Felton (1801) 2 East 109	98, 121
Shelbourne & Co v Law Investment and Insurance Corpn [1898] 2 QB 626, 67 LJQB 944, 79 LT 278, 8 Asp MLC 445, 3 Com Cas 304	226, 228, 421
Sheriff v Potts (1803) 5 Esp 96	132
Shirley v Wilkinson (1781) 3 Doug KB 41	57
Shoolbred v Nutt (1782) 1 Park's Marine Insce 8th ed 493, 1 Marshall on Marine Insces 3rd ed 474	53
Shooting Star, The, Johnson v Chapman. See Johnson v Chapman	
Sibbald v Hill (1814) 2 Dow 263, 1 Moo PCC 133n, 49 Lords Journals 1106, HL	73
Silver Dolphin Products Ltd v Parcels and General Assurance Association Ltd [1984] 2 Lloyd's Rep 404	117
Simeon v Bazett (1813) 2 M & S 94	44
Simon, Israel & Co v Sedgewick [1893] 1 QB 303, 62 LJQB 163, 67 LT 785, 41 WR 163, 9 TLR 104, 7 Asp MLC 245, 4 R 128, CA	117
Simond v Boydell (1779) 1 Doug KB 268	102
Simonds v Hodgson (1832) 3 B & Ad 50, 1 LJKB 51	108
Simons (trading as Acme Credit Services) v Gale [1958] 2 All ER 504, [1958] 1 WLR 678, 102 Sol Jo 452, [1958] 2 Lloyd's Rep 1, PC	293
Simpson v Thomson (1877) 3 App Cas 279, 38 LT 1, 3 Asp MLC 567, HL	456, 458
Sipowicz v Wimble, The Green Lion [1974] 1 Lloyd's Rep 593	147, 159
Slattery v Mance [1962] 1 QB 676, [1962] 1 All ER 525, [1962] 2 WLR 569, 106 Sol Jo 113, [1962] 1 Lloyd's Rep 60	62, 77
Sleigh v Tyser [1900] 2 QB 333, 69 LJQB 626, 82 LT 804, 16 TLR 404, 9 Asp MLC 97, 5 Com Cas 271	4, 302, 311, 433
Small v Gibson (1849) 16 QB 141, Ex Ch; affd. sub nom. Gibson v Small (1853) 4 HL Cas 353, 21 LTOS 240, 17 Jur 1131, 1 CLR 363, HL	282
Small v United Kingdom Marine Mutual Insurance Association [1897] 2 QB 42, 66 LJQB 412, 76 LT 326, 13 TLR 290, 8 Asp MLC 255, 2 Com Cas 133; affd. [1897] 2 QB 311, 66 LJQB 736, 76 LT 828, 46 WR 24, 13 TLR 514, 8 Asp MLC 293, 2 Com Cas 267, CA	163, 227
Smith v Accident Insurance Co (1870) LR 5 Exch 302, 39 LJ Ex 211, 22 LT 861, 18 WR 1107	328
Smith v Cologan (1788) 2 Term Rep 188n	37
Smith v Lascelles (1788) 2 Term Rep 187	37, 38
Smith v Scott (1811) 4 Taunt 126	144
Smith Hill & Co v Pyman Bell & Co [1891] 1 QB 742, 60 LJQB 621, 64 LT 436, 39 WR 466, 7 TLR 417, 7 Asp MLC 7, CA	21
Snook v Davidson (1809) 2 Camp 218	335
Soares v Thornton (1817) 7 Taunt 627, 1 Moore CP 373	163, 167
Société Belge Des Betons SA v London and Lancashire Insurance Co Ltd [1938] 2 All ER 305, 158 LT 352, 82 Sol Jo 316, 60 Ll L Rep 225	369
Société d'Avances Commerciales (SA Egyptienne) v Merchants' Marine Insurance Co (1924) 20 Ll L Rep 74	237, 238
Socony Mobil Oil Co Inc, Mobil Oil Co Ltd and Mobil Oil AG v West of England Ship Owners Mutual Insurance Association (London) Ltd, The Padre Island [1984] 2 Lloyd's Rep 408	479
Solly v Whitmore (1821) 5 B & Ald 45	131
Soussanis v Liverpool Marine Insurance Co Ltd (1935) 51 Ll L Rep 1, CA	398
South British Fire and Marine Insurance Co of New Zealand v Da Costa [1906] 1 KB 456, 75 LJKB 276, 94 LT 435, 54 WR 420, 22 TLR 305, 50 Sol Jo 292, 10 Asp MLC 227, 11 Com Cas 81	307, 467
Soya GmbH Mainz Kommanditgesellschaft v White [1982] 1 Lloyd's Rep 136, [1982] Com LR 22, CA; on appeal [1983] 1 Lloyd's Rep 122, 133 NLJ 64, [1983] Com LR 46, HL	49, 195, 255
Spalding v Crocker (1897) 13 TLR 396, 2 Com Cas 189	121, 274
Sparkes v Marshall (1836) 2 Bing NC 761, 2 Hodg 44, 3 Scott 172, 5 LJCP 286	28, 320
Spathari, The. See Demetriades v Northern Assurance Co, The Spathari	

xlviii   *Table of cases*

PAGE

Spence v Union Marine Insurance Co Ltd (1868) LR 3 CP 427, 37 LJCP 169, 18 LT 632, 16 WR 1010, 3 Mar LC 82 . . . . 431, 436
Spitta v Woodman (1810) 2 Taunt 416, 16 East 188n 33
Stainback v Fenning (1851) 11 CB 51, 20 LJCP 226, 17 LTOS 255, 15 Jur 1082 . . 27
Stainbank v Shepard (or Shepherd) (1853) 13 CB 418, 1 CLR 609, 22 LJ Ex 341, 22 LTOS 158, 17 Jur 1032, 1 WR 505, Ex Ch 27
Stamma v Brown (1742) 2 Stra 1173 . . . . 162, 166
Standard Oil Co of New Jersey v United States, The John Worthington [1951] 2 Lloyd's Rep 36 199
Stanley v Western Insurance Co (1868) LR 3 Exch 71, 37 LJ Ex 73, 17 LT 513, 16 WR 369 143
Steam Tanker Padre Island Inc and Pullman Bank and Trust Co v London Assurance, Guildhall Insurance Co et al, The Padre Island [1971] 2 Lloyd's Rep 431 . . 162, 244
Stearns v Village Main Reef Gold Mining Co Ltd (1905) 21 TLR 236, 10 Com Cas 89, CA 456
Steel v Lacy (1810) 3 Taunt 285 73
Steel v State Line SS Co (1877) 3 App Cas 72, [1874–80] All ER Rep 145, 37 LT 333, 3 Asp MLC 516, HL 297
Steel Wing Co Ltd, Re [1921] 1 Ch 349, [1920] All ER Rep 292, 90 LJ Ch 116, 124 LT 664, 65 Sol Jo 240, [1920] B & CR 160 316
Steinman & Co v Angier Line [1891] 1 QB 619, 60 LJQB 425, 64 LT 613, 39 WR 392, 7 TLR 398, 7 Asp MLC 46, CA 152
Stephens v Australasian Insurance Co (1872) LR 8 CP 18, 42 LJCP 12, 27 LT 585, 21 WR 228, 1 Asp MLC 458 . . . . 24, 92
Stevenson v Snow (1761) 3 Burr 1237, 1 Wm Bl 318 . . . . . . 85, 323
Stewart v Bell (1821) 5 B & Ald 238 . . . . 46, 326
Stewart v Dunlop (1785) 4 Bro Parl Cas 483, HL 41
Stewart v Greenock Marine Insurance Co (1848) 2 HL Cas 159, sub nom. The Laurel, Stewart v Greenock Marine Insurance Co 2 LT 809, HL 380, 395
Stewart v Merchants' Marine Insurance Co (1885) 16 QBD 619, 55 LJQB 81, 53 LT 892, 34 WR 208, 2 TLR 156, 5 Asp MLC 506, CA 102, 414
Stirling v Vaughan (1809) 11 East 619, 2 Camp 225 . . . . . . 16, 25, 26
Stitt v Wardell (1797) 2 Esp 610 132
Stockdale v Dunlop (1840) 6 M & W 224, 9 LJ Ex 83, 7 LT 804, 4 Jur 681 . . . 27
Stolos Compania SA v Ajax Insurance Co Ltd, The Admiral C [1981] 1 Lloyd's Rep 9, [1980] Com LR 4, CA 325
Stone v Marine Insurance Co Ocean Ltd of Gothenburg (1876) 1 Ex D 81, 45 LJQB 361, 34 LT 490, 24 WR 554, 3 Asp MLC 152 . . . . 85, 119, 120
Strass v Spillers and Bakers Ltd [1911] 2 KB 759, 80 LJKB 1218, 104 LT 284, 11 Asp MLC 590, 16 Com Cas 166 321
Street v Royal Exchange Assurance (1914) 111 LT 235, 30 TLR 495, 12 Asp MLC 496, 19 Com Cas 339, CA 471
Stribley v Imperial Marine Insurance Co (1876) 1 QBD 507, 45 LJQB 396, 34 LT 281, 24 WR 701, 3 Asp MLC 134 . . . . 41, 57
Stringer v English and Scottish Marine Insurance Co (1870) LR 5 QB 599, 10 B & S 770, 39 LJQB 214, 22 LT 802, 18 WR 1201, 3 Mar LC 440, Ex Ch . . . 346, 368, 379
Sunderland SS Co and North of England Iron SS Insurance Association, Re (1894) 11 TLR 106, 14 R 196, CA 375
Sutherland v Pratt (1843) 11 M & W 296, 2 Dowl NS 813, 12 LJ Ex 235, 7 Jur 261 . 25
Swan and Cleland's Graving Dock and Slipway Co v Maritime Insurance Co and Croshaw [1907] 1 KB 116, 76 LJKB 160, 96 LT 839, 23 TLR 101, 12 Com Cas 73, 10 Asp MLC 450 320

T

Tabbs v Benedelack (1801) 3 Bos & P 207n, 4 Esp 108 286
Tannenbaum & Co v Heath [1908] 1 KB 1032, 77 LJKB 634, 99 LT 237, 24 TLR 450, 52 Sol Jo 375, 13 Com Cas 264, CA 398
Tanner v Bennett (1825) Ry & M 182 232
Tasker v Scott (1815) 6 Taunt 234 25
Tate v Hyslop (1885) 15 QBD 368, [1881–5] All ER Rep 875, 54 LJQB 592, 53 LT 581, 1 TLR 532, 5 Asp MLC 487, CA 56

Table of cases xlix

	PAGE
Tatham v Hodgson (1796) 6 Term Rep 656	142, 145
Tatham, Bromage & Co v Burr, The Engineer [1898] AC 382, 67 LJP 61, 78 LT 473, 46 WR 530, 14 TLR 369, 8 Asp MLC 400, HL	323
Tatjana, The. See Lindsay v Klein, The Tatjana	
Taylor v Briggs (1827) 2 C & P 525, Mood & M 28	108
Taylor v Dunbar (1869) LR 4 CP 206, 38 LJCP 178, 17 WR 382	143, 153, 228
Taylor v Liverpool and Great Western Steam Co (1874) LR 9 QB 546, 43 LJQB 205, 30 LT 714, 22 WR 752, 2 Asp MLC 275	152
Teneria Moderna Franco Espanola v NZ Insurance Co [1924] 1 KB 79, 93 LJKB 169, 130 LT 139, 16 Asp MLC 236, CA	397, 401
Tenneco Oil Co v Tug Tony Coastal Towing Corpn [1972] 1 Lloyd's Rep 514	456
Thames and Mersey Marine Insurance Co v British and Chilian SS Co [1916] 1 KB 30, [1914–15] All ER Rep 239, 85 LJKB 384, 114 LT 34, 32 TLR 89, 13 Asp MLC 221, 21 Com Cas 150, CA	460
Thames and Mersey Marine Insurance Co v Gunford Ship Co [1911] AC 529, 80 LJPC 146, 105 LT 312, 27 TLR 518, 55 Sol Jo 631, 12 Asp MLC 49, 16 Com Cas 270, HL	56, 63, 64
Thames and Mersey Marine Insurance Co v Pitts, Son and King [1893] 1 QB 476, 68 LT 524, 41 WR 346, 37 Sol Jo 216, 7 Asp MLC 302, 5 R 168, DC	20, 94, 95
Thames and Mersey Marine Insurance Co Ltd v Hamilton, Fraser & Co (1887) 12 App Cas 484, [1886–90] All ER Rep 241, 56 LJQB 626, 57 LT 695, 36 WR 337, 3 TLR 764, 6 Asp MLC 200, HL	145
Thames and Mersey Marine Insurance Co Ltd v Van Laun & Co (1905) [1917] 2 KB 48n, 86 LJKB 840n, 116 LT 368n, 14 Asp MLC 14n, HL	110, 117
Thelluson v Fletcher (1793) 1 Esp 73	385
Thellusson v Fergusson (1780) 1 Doug KB 360	130
Thellusson v Staples (circa 1780) cited in 1 Doug 366n	284
Theodorou v Chester [1951] 1 Lloyd's Rep 204	179
Thin v Richards & Co [1892] 2 QB 141, 62 LJQB 39, 66 LT 584, 40 WR 617, 8 TLR 571, 36 Sol Jo 501, 7 Asp MLC 165, CA	301
Thomas v Tyne and Wear SS Freight Insurance Association [1917] 1 KB 938, 86 LJKB 1037, 117 LT 55, 14 Asp MLC 87, 22 Com Cas 239	303
Thompson v Gillespy (1855) 5 E & B 209, 3 CLR 1368, 24 LJQB 340, 25 LTOS 174, 1 Jur NS 779, 3 WR 505	283
Thompson v Hopper (1856) 6 E & B 172, 25 LJQB 240, 26 LTOS 308, 2 Jur NS 608, 4 WR 360	145
Thompson v Hopper (1858) EB & E 1038, 27 LJQB 441, 32 LTOS 38, 5 Jur NS 93, 6 WR 857, Ex Ch	129, 232
Thompson v Rowcroft (1803) 4 East 34	396
Thompson v Taylor (1795) 6 Term Rep 478	21
Thompson v Whitmore (1810) 3 Taunt 227, [1843–60] All ER Rep 698	142, 413
Thornley v Hebson (1819) 2 B & Ald 513	379
Thornton v Knight (1849) 16 Sim 509	273
Thrunscoe, The [1897] P 301, 66 LJP 172, 77 LT 407, 46 WR 175, 13 TLR 566, 8 Asp MLC 313, DC	143
Tidswell v Ankerstein (1792) Peake 151	25
Tierney v Etherington (1743) cited in 1 Burr 348	133, 325, 328
Tobin v Harford (1864) 17 CBNS 528, 4 New Rep 373, 34 LJCP 37, 10 LT 817, 10 Jur NS 850, 12 WR 1062, 2 Mar LC 34, Ex Ch	85
Todd v Reid (1821) 4 B & Ald 210	327
Todd v Ritchie (1816) 1 Stark 240	167
Toulmin v Anderson (1808) 1 Taunt 227	167
Towse v Henderson (1850) 4 Exch 890, 19 LJ Ex 163, 14 LTOS 400	298
Traders and General Insurance Association Ltd, Re, ex p Continental and Overseas Trading Co [1924] 2 Ch 187, 93 LJ Ch 464, 131 LT 626, 40 TLR 561, 68 Sol Jo 615, 16 Asp MLC 384, 29 Com Cas 302, 18 Ll L Rep 450	123, 124
Traders and General Insurance Association Ltd v Bankers and General Insurance Co Ltd (1921) 38 TLR 94, 9 Ll L Rep 223	194
Trident, The (1939). See Hall Bros SS Co Ltd v Young, The Trident	

l *Table of cases*

PAGE

Trim Joint District School Board of Management v Kelly [1914] AC 667, 83 LJPC 220, 111 LT 305, 30 TLR 452, 58 Sol Jo 493, 7 BWCC 274, HL 145
Trinder, Anderson & Co v Thames and Mersey Marine Insurance Co [1898] 2 QB 114, 67 LJQB 666, 78 LT 485, 46 WR 561, 14 TLR 386, 8 Asp MLC 373, 3 Com Cas 123, CA
. . . . 232, 383, 450
Tropaioforos, The. See Compania Naviera Santi SA v Indemnity Marine Assurance Co Ltd, The Tropaioforos
Turnbull v Janson (1877) 36 LT 635, 3 Asp MLC 433, CA 297
Turnbull, Martin & Co v Hull Underwriters' Association [1900] 2 QB 402, [1900–3] All ER Rep 85, 69 LJQB 588, 82 LT 818, 16 TLR 359, 9 Asp MLC 93, 5 Com Cas 248 . 230, 262
Twemlow v Oswin (1809) 2 Camp 85 349
Tyson v Gurney (1789) 3 Term Rep 477 286

U

Uhde v Walters (1811) 3 Camp 16 . . . . 116, 326
Undaunted, The (1860) Lush 90, 29 LJPM & A 176, 2 LT 520 443
Union Castle Mail SS Co Ltd v United Kingdom Mutual War Risks Association Ltd [1958] 1 QB 380, [1958] 1 All ER 431, [1958] 2 WLR 274, 102 Sol Jo 125, [1958] 1 Lloyd's Rep 58 220
Union Insurance Society of Canton Ltd v George Wills & Co [1916] AC 281, 85 LJPC 82, 114 LT 245, 32 TLR 196, 13 Asp MLC 233, 21 Com Cas 169, PC . . 93, 282
United Kingdom Mutual SS Assurance Associtaion Ltd v Boulton (1898) 3 Com Cas 330 . . . . 359, 395
United Mills Agencies Ltd v R E Harvey, Bray & Co [1952] 1 All ER 225n, [1952] 1 TLR 149, 96 Sol Jo 121, [1951] 2 Lloyd's Rep 631 332
United Scottish Insurance Co Ltd v British Fishing Vessels Mutual War Risks Association Ltd, The Braconbush (1944) 78 Ll L Rep 70 . . . . . 209, 349
United Shipping Co Ltd v Assicurazioni Generali (1929) 34 Ll L Rep 323, CA . . 291
United States Shipping Co v Empress Assurance Corpn [1907] 1 KB 259, 76 LJKB 225, 23 TLR 137, 12 Com Cas 142; affd. [1908] 1 KB 115, 77 LJKB 120, 24 TLR 45, 13 Com Cas 90, CA 20, 428
Usher v Noble (1810) 12 East 639 . . . . 99, 435
Uzielli v Boston Marine Insurance Co (1884) 15 QBD 11, 54 LJQB 142, 52 LT 787, 33 WR 293, 1 TLR 49, 5 Asp MLC 405, CA 385, 443, 466

V

Vacuum Oil Co v Union Insurance Society of Canton Ltd (1926) 32 Com Cas 53, 25 Ll L Rep 546, CA 368, 381, 384, 386, 387
Vainqueur José, The. See CVG Siderurgicia del Orinoco SA v London SS Owners' Mutual Insurance Association Ltd, The Vainqueur José
Vainqueur, The. See Northwestern Mutual Life Assurance Co v Linard, The Vainqueur
Vallance v Dewar (1808) 1 Camp 503, [1803–13] All ER Rep 619 . . . 46, 130
Vallejo v Wheeler (1774) 1 Cowp 143, Lofft 631 . . . . 161, 163, 165
Vandyck v Hewitt (1800) 1 East 96 84
Vasso, The. See Bruns v Colocotronis, The Vasso
Village Main Reef Gold Mining Co v Stearns (1900) 5 Com Cas 246 . . . 398
Violett v Allnutt (1811) 3 Taunt 419 132
Virginia Carolina Chemical Co v Norfolk and North American Shipping Co (1912) 107 LT 320, 28 TLR 513, 56 Sol Jo 722, 12 Asp MLC 233, 17 Com Cas 277 . . . 297
Visscherij Maatschappij Nieuw Onderneming v Scottish Metropolitan Assurance Co Ltd (1922) 38 TLR 458, 27 Com Cas 198, 10 Ll L Rep 579, CA . . . 62, 234
Volkswagenwerk AG and Wolfsburger Transport Gesellschaft mbH v International Mutual Strike Assurance Co (Bermuda) Ltd [1977] 2 Lloyd's Rep 503, CA . . . 476
Vortigern, The [1899] P 140, [1895–9] All ER Rep 387, 68 LJP 49, 80 LT 382, 47 WR 437, 15 TLR 259, 8 Asp MLC 523, 4 Com Cas 152, CA 301
Vrondissis v Stevens [1940] 2 KB 90, [1940] 3 All ER 74, 109 LJKB 615, 163 LT 1, 56 TLR 713, 84 Sol Jo 515, 45 Com Cas 225, 19 Asp MLC 368, 67 Ll L Rep 55 . . . 360

Table of cases li

W

Case	Page
Wadsworth Lighterage and Coaling Co Ltd v Sea Insurance Co Ltd (1929) 45 TLR 597, 35 Com Cas 1, 34 Ll L Rep 285, CA	248
Wait and James v British and Foreign Marine Insurance Co (1921) 9 Ll L Rep 518, 552	429
Wake v Atty (1812) 4 Taunt 493	33
Walford (Leopold) (London) Ltd v National Benefit Assurance Co Ltd (1921) 7 Ll L Rep 39	271
Walker v Maitland (1821) 5 B & Ald 171	231
Walker (F B) & Sons Inc v Valentine [1970] 2 Lloyd's Rep 429	169, 294
Wallace v Tellfair (1786) 2 Term Rep 188n	38
Waples v Eames (1745) 2 Stra 1243	120
Warre v Miller (1825) 4 B & C 538, 7 Dow & Ry KB 1, sub nom. Miller v Warre 4 LJOSKB 8	21, 116
Warwick v Scott (1814) 4 Camp 62	286
Waters and Steel v Monarch Fire and Life Assurance Co (1856) 5 E & B 870, [1843–60] All ER Rep 654, 25 LJQB 102, 26 LTOS 217, 2 Jur NS 375, 4 WR 245	25
Wavertree Sailing Ship Co v Love [1897] AC 373, 66 LJPC 77, 76 LT 576, 13 TLR 419, 8 Asp MLC 276, PC	185
Way v Modigliani (1787) 2 Term Rep 30	117, 129
Webster v De Tastet (1797) 7 Term Rep 157	34
Webster v Foster (1795) 1 Esp 407	43
Weir v Aberdeen (1819) 2 B & Ald 320	52, 53, 311
Weir & Co v Girvin & Co [1899] 1 QB 193, 68 LJQB 170, 47 WR 365, 79 LT 596, 15 TLR 69, 8 Asp MLC 470, 4 Com Cas 56; affd. [1900] 1 QB 45, 69 LJQB 168, 81 LT 687, 48 WR 179, 16 TLR 31, 9 Asp MLC 7, 5 Com Cas 40, CA	19
Weissberg v Lamb (1950) 84 Ll L Rep 509	447
Wells v Hopwood (1832) 3 B & Ad 20	411, 412
Wells Fargo Bank International Corpn v London Steam-Ship Owners' Mutual Insurance Association Ltd, The John W Hill [1977] 1 Lloyd's Rep 213	479
Welsh Girl, The (1906) 22 TLR 475; affd. sub nom. The Commonwealth [1907] P 216, 76 LJP 106, 97 LT 625, 23 TLR 420, 51 Sol Jo 386, 10 Asp MLC 538, CA	459
West of England Bank v Canton Insurance Co (1877) 2 Ex D 472	400
West of Scotland Ship Owners Mutual Protection and Indemnity Association (Luxembourg) v Aifanourios Shipping SA, The Aifanourios [1980] 2 Lloyd's Rep 403, Ct of Sess	476, 477
Westbury v Aberdein (1837) 2 M & W 267, Murp & H 49, 6 LJ Ex 83, 1 Jur 201	40, 55, 57
Western Assurance Co of Toronto v Poole [1903] 1 KB 376, 72 LJKB 195, 88 LT 362, 9 Asp MLC 390, 8 Com Cas 108	102, 324, 465, 466
Westport Coal Co v McPhail [1898] 2 QB 130, 67 LJQB 674, 78 LT 490, 46 WR 566, 14 TLR 388, 8 Asp MLC 378, 3 Com Cas 140, CA	164, 231
Westwood v Bell (1815) 4 Camp 349, Holt NP 122	335
Wharton (J) (Shipping) Ltd v Mortleman [1941] 2 KB 283, [1941] 2 All ER 261, 111 LJKB 321, 165 LT 342, 57 TLR 514, 46 Com Cas 244, CA	202
Whiting v New Zealand Insurance Co Ltd (1932) 44 Ll L Rep 179	252, 433
Whitwell v Harrison (1848) 2 Exch 127, 18 LJ Ex 465, 7 LT 75	120
Wilkinson v Hyde (1858) 3 CBNS 30, 27 LJCP 116, 7 LT 442, 4 Jur NS 482	108, 431
Williams v Atlantic Assurance Co Ltd [1933] 1 KB 81, [1932] All ER Rep 32, 102 LJKB 241, 148 LT 313, 37 Com Cas 304, 18 Asp MLC 334, 43 Ll L Rep 177, CA	22, 58, 75, 99, 315, 316, 320
Williams v East India Co (1802) 3 East 192	244
Williams v North China Insurance Co (1876) 1 CPD 757, 35 LT 884, 3 Asp MLC 342, CA	95
Williams v Shee (1813) 3 Camp 469	132, 133
Williams & Co v Canton Insurance Office Ltd [1901] AC 462, 70 LJKB 962, 85 LT 317, 17 TLR 696, 9 Asp MLC 247, 6 Com Case 256, HL	228
Williams & Co v Canton Insurance Office Ltd (1901). See Brankelow SS Co v Canton Insurance Office (1899)	
Williamson v Innes (1831) 8 Bing 81n, 1 Mood & R 88	115
Willis & Co v Baddeley [1892] 2 QB 324, 61 LJQB 769, 67 LT 206, 40 WR 577, 36 Sol Jo 592, CA	401

Table of cases

Willis SS Co Ltd v United Kingdom Mutual War Risks Association Ltd (1947) 80 Ll L Rep 398 206
Willmott v General Accident Fire and Life Assurance Corpn Ltd (1935) 53 Ll L Rep 156 . 68, 76, 305
Wilson v Boag [1956] 2 Lloyd's Rep 564 . . . . 91, 128
Wilson v Jones (1867) LR 2 Exch 139, 36 LJ Ex 78, 15 LT 669, 15 WR 435, 2 Mar LC 452, Ex Ch 27
Wilson v Marryat (1798) 8 Term Rep 31; affd. sub nom. Marryat v Wilson (1799) 1 Bos & P 430, Ex Ch 309
Wilson v Rankin (1865) LR 1 QB 162, 6 B & S 208, 35 LJQB 87, 13 LT 564, 14 WR 198, 2 Mar LC 287, Ex Ch 309
Wilson v Salamandra Assurance Co of St Petersburg (1903) 88 LT 96, 19 TLR 229, 9 Asp MLC 370, 8 Com Cas 129 42
Wilson Bros Bobbin Co Ltd v Green [1917] 1 KB 860, 86 LJKB 713, 116 LT 637, 14 Asp MLC 119, 22 Com Cas 185 444
Wilson, Holgate & Co Ltd v Lancashire and Cheshire Insurance Corpn Ltd (1922) 13 Ll L Rep 486 . . . . 64, 250, 276
Wilson, Sons & Co v Xantho (Cargo Owners) (1887) 12 App Cas 503, 56 LJP 116, 57 LT 701, 36 WR 353, 3 TLR 766, 6 Asp MLC 207, HL . . . 143, 144, 145, 150
Wolff v Horncastle (1798) 1 Bos & P 316 . . . . 24, 25
Wood v Smith, The City of Cambridge LR 5 PC 451, 43 LJ Adm 11, 30 LT 439, 22 WR 578, 2 Asp MLC 239, PC 283
Woodley v Michell (1883) 11 QBD 47, 52 LJQB 325, 48 LT 599, 31 WR 651, 5 Asp MLC 71, CA 144
Woodside v Globe Marine Insurance Co [1896] 1 QB 105, 65 LJQB 117, 73 LT 626, 44 WR 187, 12 TLR 97, 40 Sol Jo 115, 8 Asp MLC 118, 1 Com Cas 237 . . . 94
Wooldridge v Boydell (1778) 1 Doug KB 16 116
Woolmer v Muilman (1763) 1 Wm Bl 427, 3 Burr 1419 311
Wright v Marwood (1881) 7 QBD 62, 29 WR 673, 50 LJQB 643, 45 LT 297, 4 Asp MLC 451, CA 154
Wright v Shiffner (1809) 11 East 515, 2 Camp 247 284
Wyllie v Povah (1907) 23 TLR 687, 12 Com Cas 317 9
Wynnstay SS Co v Board of Trade (1925) 23 Ll L Rep 278 202

X

Xenos v Fox (1869) LR 4 CP 665, 38 LJCP 351, 17 WR 893, Ex Ch . . . 443
Xenos v Wickham (1866) LR 2 HL 296, 36 LJCP 313, 16 LT 800, 16 WR 38, 2 Mar LC 537, HL 273, 333

Y

Yasin, The [1979] 2 Lloyd's Rep 45 . . . . 24, 456
Yates v Whyte (1838) 4 Bing NC 272, 1 Arn 85, 5 Scott 640, 7 LJCP 116 . . . 458
Yero Carras (Owners) v London and Scottish Assurance Corpn Ltd (1935) 53 Ll L Rep 131 . . . . 10, 354
Yorkshire Dale SS Co Ltd v Minister of War Transport, The Coxwold [1942] AC 691, [1942] 2 All ER 6, 111 LJKB 512, 167 LT 349, 58 TLR 263, 86 Sol Jo 359, 73 Ll L Rep 1, HL 198, 200, 205
Yorkshire Insurance Co Ltd v Nisbet Shipping Co Ltd [1962] 2 QB 330, [1961] 2 All ER 487, [1961] 2 WLR 1043, 105 Sol Jo 367, [1961] 2 Lloyd's Rep 479 . . . 5, 459

Z

Zachariessen (or Zachariassen) v Importers' and Exporters' Marine Insurance Co (1924) 40 TLR 297, 29 Com Cas 202, 18 Ll L Rep 98, CA 208, 349
Zelo, The. See Pelton SS Co Ltd v North of England Protecting and Indemnity Association, The Zelo
Zinovia, The. See Michalos (N) & Sons Maritime SA v Prudential Assurance Co Ltd, The Zinovia

PART I
The making of the contract

CHAPTER 1

Introduction

This book deals exclusively with Marine Insurance. Although to a certain extent it is complete in itself, it should be read in conjunction with the first volume in this series,[1] especially with regard to such matters as the construction of the policy, the premium, the doctrine of proximate cause, and the rights, duties and authority of insurance agents and brokers.

Marine Insurance is a contract of indemnity.[2] Contracts in the nature of wagering or gaming are void,[3] and, as in other types of insurance, it is essential for the assured to have an insurable interest in the subject-matter insured.[4]

Where a marine insurance broker is employed to effect the policy, he has certain duties to perform.[5]

The assured must disclose to the insurers all material facts,[6] and must not make any misrepresentations during the negotiations for the contract.[7] He must pay the premium, and the insurer must issue the policy when the premium has been paid or tendered.[8]

---

[1] Ivamy, *General Principles of Insurance Law* (4th Edn, 1979, Supplement 1982).
[2] See Chapter 2, post.
[3] See Chapter 3, post.
[4] See Chapter 4, post.
[5] See Chapter 5, post.
[6] See Chapter 6, post.
[7] See Chapter 7, post.
[8] See Chapter 8, post.

CHAPTER 2

The nature of marine insurance

In a contract of marine insurance the insurer undertakes, in consideration of a premium, to indemnify the assured against loss occasioned by perils incident to a marine adventure.

The definition given by Roccus is:[1]

> '*Assecuratio est contractus quo quis alienae rei periculum in se suscepit, obligando se sub certo pretio ad eam compensandam si illa perierit.*'

Section 1 of the Marine Insurance Act 1906[2] states:

> 'A contract of marine insurance is a contract whereby the insurer undertakes to indemnify the assured, in manner and to the extent thereby agreed, against marine losses, that is to say, the losses incident to marine adventure.'

Section 3(1) states:

> 'Subject to the provisions of this Act, every lawful marine adventure may be the subject of a contract of marine insurance.'

Section 3(2) goes on to state that:

> 'In particular there is a marine adventure where:
>
> *a* Any ship, goods or other moveables[3] are exposed to maritime perils. Such property is referred to in this Act as "insurable property";
> *b* The earning or acquisition of any freight, passage money, commission, profit, or other pecuniary benefit, or the security for any advances, loan, or disbursements, is endangered by the exposure of insurable property to maritime perils;
> *c* Any liability to a third party may be incurred by the owner of, or other person interested in or responsible for, insurable property, by reason of maritime perils.
>
> "Maritime perils" means the perils consequent on, or incidental to, the navigation of the sea, that is to say, perils of the seas, fire, war perils, pirates, rovers, thieves, captures, seizures, restraints, and detainments of princes and peoples, jettisons, barratry, and any other perils, either of the like kind, or which may be designated by the policy.'

A   CONTRACT OF INDEMNITY

A contract of marine insurance is a contract of indemnity, i e the amount recoverable is measured by the extent of the assured's pecuniary loss.[4]

---

[1] *De Assec*, not I.
[2] References in whatever terms in this Act to ships, vessels, or boats or activities or places connected therewith are extended to include hovercraft or activities or places connected with hovercraft: Hovercraft (Application of Enactments) Order 1972 (SI 1972/971).
[3] 'Moveables' means 'any moveable tangible property, other than the ship, and includes money, valuable securities, and other documents': Marine Insurance Act 1906, s 90. See, e g *Baring Bros & Co v Marine Insurance Co* (1894) 10 TLR 276 (postal packet containing stock certificates); *The Pomeranian* [1895] P 349 (live cattle); *Sleigh v Tyser* [1900] 2 QB 333 (live cattle).
[4] For other examples of contracts of indemnity, see Ivamy, *General Principles of Insurance Law* (4th edn, 1979) pp 9–10, and Ivamy, *Fire and Motor Insurance* (4th edn, 1984), pp 8–10.

In *Rickards v Forestal Land, Timber and Rlys Co Ltd*[5] Lord Wright said:[6]

> 'The object both of the Legislature and of the Courts has been to give effect to the idea of indemnity, which is the basic principle of insurance, and to apply it in the diverse complications of fact and law in respect of which it has to operate. In this way, the law merchant has solved, or sought to solve, the manifold problems which have been presented by insurances of maritime adventures.'

Accordingly, where the assured has no insurable interest[7] in the subject-matter insured, he can recover nothing under the policy, for he has suffered no loss and the insurer is under no duty to indemnify him.

Again, where he has over-insured the subject-matter by double insurance,[8] he may, unless the policy otherwise provides, claim payment from the insurers in such order as he may think fit, provided that he is not entitled to receive any sum in excess of the indemnity allowed by the Marine Insurance Act 1906.[9] Where the policy under which the assured claims is a valued policy,[10] he must give credit, as against the valuation, for any sum received by him under any other policy without regard to the actual value of the subject-matter insured.[11] Where the policy under which he claims is an unvalued policy,[12] he must give credit, as against the full insurable value, for any sum received by him under any other policy.[13] Where he receives any sum in excess of the indemnity allowed by the Act of 1906, he is deemed to hold such sum in trust for the insurers, according to their right of contribution amongst themselves.[14]

Further, by the doctrine of subrogation[15] the assured cannot recover more than an indemnity, for if the insurer has paid the assured in respect of a total or partial loss, the insurer is subrogated to any rights which the assured may have against a third party.[16] Thus, if the insured vessel is sunk as a result of the negligent navigation of another vessel, and the insurer pays the assured in respect of a total loss, any sum which the assured may recover from the owners of the vessel at fault will belong to the insurer. But under the doctrine of subrogation the insurer is not entitled to any sum in excess of that which he has paid to the assured.[17]

Again, where the assured has recovered part of the cost of repairing his vessel, which has collided with another vessel, from the owners of that vessel, he must give credit for that amount in making any claim against his insurers.

Thus, in *Goole and Hull Steam Towing Co Ltd v Ocean Marine Insurance Co Ltd*[18] a

---

[5] [1941] 3 All ER 62, HL.
[6] Ibid, at 76.
[7] As to 'insurable interest', see pp 16–29, post.
[8] 'Double insurance' is defined by s 32(1) of the Marine Insurance Act 1906 in the following terms: 'Where two or more policies are effected by or on behalf of the assured on the same adventure and interest or any part thereof, and the sums insured exceed the indemnity allowed by this Act, the assured is said to be over-insured by double insurance.' See further, p 461, post.
[9] Marine Insurance Act 1906, s 32(2)(a).
[10] As to 'valued policies', see pp 93–97, post.
[11] Marine Insurance Act 1906, s 32(2)(b).
[12] As to 'unvalued policies', see pp 97–100, post.
[13] Marine Insurance Act 1906, s 32(2)(c).
[14] Ibid, s 32(2)(d). As to the 'right of contribution', see ibid, s 80 and p 461, post.
[15] As to 'subrogation', see pp 455–460, post.
[16] Marine Insurance Act 1906, s 79(1), (2).
[17] *Yorkshire Insurance Co Ltd v Nisbet Shipping Co Ltd* [1962] 2 QB 330, [1961] 2 All ER 487, QBD.
[18] (1927) 29 LlL Rep 242, KBD.

vessel was insured under a valued policy for her full value of £4,000. She collided with another vessel and repairs to her cost £5,000. Both vessels were held to blame, and the owners of the other vessel paid the assured £2,500. The assured claimed on the policy, contending that the damage suffered was the cost of the repairs less the sum paid by the owners of the other vessel, i e a total sum of £2,500, and as this sum was less than the sum insured (viz £4,000) they were entitled to recover the whole of it from the insurers.

MacKinnon J, held that this was the wrong basis of calculation. The amount payable under the policy was £4,000 less the amount received by the assured as damages (viz £2,500) i e the assured could only claim £1,500. Although the insurers were primarily liable to pay up to £4,000, the assured had already been paid a sum in respect of damages, and the insurers were entitled by their right of subrogation to be given credit for that sum. His Lordship observed:[19]

'It is quite true in this case that the payment of £4,000 has not fully indemnified the assured for their expenditure of £5,000 on the repairs; they have not put back into their pocket all that they have paid out; but according to the bargain they have made under the policy I think they have been indemnified according to this Act for the whole of the particular average loss which they have sustained as promised under s 69, and therefore, as they have been, according to this Act, fully indemnified for that particular average loss, the underwriters under s 79 are entitled to all the rights and remedies of the assured in respect of that loss, because they have fully indemnified them for that loss.

When the underwriters, in respect of a particular average loss, have paid the assured the indemnity agreed under this provision, when, in particular, they have paid a sum not exceeding the insured amount, in this case £4,000, I think the underwriters are entitled to say: "We have paid the agreed indemnity for the whole of the particular average loss you have sustained, and not merely for a part of it"; they are, therefore, entitled to be subrogated, or to take credit, for the whole sum which the assured may recover from a third party in respect of that particular average damage.'

Another example of the principle that the contract of marine insurance is a contract of indemnity is to be found in the rules relating to the return of premium.[20] Thus, e g where the insured goods have never been imperilled because they have never been loaded, the premium is returnable.[1]

In *Goole and Hull Steam Towing Co Ltd v Ocean Marine Insurance Co Ltd*[2] MacKinnon J, pointed out that a marine insurance was often said to be a contract of indemnity, yet it must always be remembered that it was not a contract of indemnity ideally, but of an indemnity according to the conventional terms of the bargain. When a loss had happened, the question was hardly ever: 'How much is the assured out of pocket?' That might be the proper question if the object of the contract was to provide an ideal indemnity. The real question in any case was: 'What is the measure of indemnity which by the convention of the parties had been promised to the assured?' That might in some cases be less than an ideal pecuniary indemnity, and in some cases it might be more.

As illustrations of the measure of indemnity being based on the convention of the parties his Lordship observed:[3]

'If the assured has undervalued his ship in the valuation he has agreed upon, he may find that

---

[19] Ibid, at 245.
[20] As to the 'return of premium', see Marine Insurance Act 1906, s 84 and pp 82–86, post.
[1] Marine Insurance Act 1906, s 84(3)(b).
[2] (1927) 29 LlL Rep 242, KBD.
[3] Ibid, at 244.

he has suffered pecuniary loss outside any insurable indemnity. That happened very strikingly in *Balmoral SS Co v Marten*;[4] indeed, theoretically the same result might arise upon an unvalued policy because, by the convention of the policy, the insurable value of the vessel under s 16 is the value at the commencement of the risk, and theoretically you might have some loss happening at the end of a long voyage when the market value of the ship, owing to change of conditions, had considerably increased. Then, as I mentioned just now in argument, by the terms of the bargain, as interpreted in the cases and the Act, the insurable interest in freight allows the gross freight to be insured. That again is laid down in s 16, and obviously if freight is lost at an early stage of a long voyage, the assured recovers a great deal more than he ought to upon any ideal pecuniary estimation of his loss. Similarly, in some other cases of total loss.'

He then went on to examine the case of a partial loss of goods, and said:[5]

'When a partial loss occurs, there are various conventional bases for ascertaining the measure of indemnity that is promised. In the case of goods, you have to find the proportion of the damaged value to the sound value of the goods and apply that to the insured value, or the insurable value. That again may well result in an artificial indemnity differing from the real pecuniary loss to the assured, as for instance, supposing, as may well be, the valuation includes freight payable at the destination and the particular average loss of goods in question is a total loss of part of the insured goods in the course of the voyage; upon them no freight would have to be paid, and to that extent in recovering the insured value of those goods the assured would be making an actual profit; that is to say, there is an artificial measure of indemnity which differs from the real.'

B 'LOSSES INCIDENT TO MARINE ADVENTURE'

For the contract to be one of marine insurance it is essential that the loss which is insured against is one incident to a marine adventure.

In *Re London County Commercial Reinsurance Office Ltd*[6] a policy of insurance was issued by an insurance company, the risk insured being against a total loss in the event of peace not being declared between Great Britain and Germany on or before 31 March 1918. The policy was in the marine form. A question arose as to whether it was, in fact, a marine policy, and, therefore, governed by the Marine Insurance Act 1906. It was held by the Chancery Division that it was not a marine policy, and so the Act did not apply to it. P O Lawrence J, said:[7]

'The first question . . . is as to the validity of the peace policies. In my judgment these policies are not contracts of marine insurance. It is true that they are made out on the printed form which the company generally uses for its marine policies, but that fact alone does not, in my opinion, make them marine policies. None of the printed clauses contained in these policies have any application to the subject-matter of the insurance, and when the substance of these policies is looked at, it is obvious that the losses insured against are not losses incident to any marine adventure. These policies, therefore, do not come within the definition of contracts of marine insurance contained in s 1 of the Marine Insurance Act 1906, and the provisions of that Act do not apply to them.'

C MIXED SEA AND LAND RISKS

Section 2(1) of the Marine Insurance Act 1906 states:

'A contract of marine insurance may, by its express terms, be extended so as to protect the

---

[4] [1902] AC 511.
[5] (1927) 29 LlL Rep 242 at 245.
[6] (1922) 127 LT 20, ChD.
[7] Ibid, at 24.

assured against losses on inland waters or on any land risk which may be incidental to any sea voyage.'

Thus, in *Hyderabad (Deccan) Co v Willoughby*[8] bullion was insured 'at and from Boodini to London, including all risks of every description, from the mines by escort to railway station at Raichur, thence by rail to Bombay, and thence to London'. In *Schloss Bros v Stevens*[9] goods were insured against all risks by land or by water from Cartagena to any place in the interior of Colombia. In *Allagar Rubber Estates v National Benefit Assurance Co Ltd*[10] some cases of rubber were insured under a 'tree to buyer' policy, which stated that the risk was to commence 'from time of entry at receiving house on the estate and until safe delivery taken by the purchaser in London'. Again, in *H Cousins & Co Ltd v D and C Carriers Ltd*[11] a consignment of ladies' clothing and shoes was insured from Hong Kong to the Port of London, and thence by road to Scotland. Further, in *Fuerst Day Lawson Ltd v Orion Insurance Co Ltd*[12] oil was insured in steel or iron drums on steamer and/or steamers and/or conveyances or any other method of transportation from 'anywhere to anywhere'.

Section 2(2) of the Marine Insurance Act 1906 states:

> 'Where a ship in course of building or the launch of a ship, or any adventure analogous to a marine adventure is covered by a policy in the form of a marine policy, the provisions of this Act, in so far as applicable, shall apply thereto.'

Thus, in *Jackson v Mumford*[13] vessels in the course of construction were insured against 'fire in shops and on board on stocks, trials, and all marine risks to completion and acceptance by Admiralty'. Again, in *James Yachts Ltd v Thames and Mersey Marine Insurance Co Ltd*[14] a builders' risk policy in the 'British Columbia Builders' Risk Form (1946)' covered 'Hull, tackle ... boats and other furniture and fixtures and all material belonging to and/or destined for inclusion in all vessels being built at the premises of the assured as specified elsewhere herein'.

D   THE SUBJECT-MATTER INSURED

The principal types of subject-matter which may be insured under a marine insurance policy are:

1   a ship;
2   goods;
3   freight;

---

[8] [1899] 2 QB 530.
[9] [1906] 2 KB 665.
[10] (1922) 10 LlL Rep 564, KBD. As to the interpretation of this clause, see p 123, post. Other cases of mixed sea and land risks include *Rodoconachi v Elliott* (1874) LR 9 CP 518, Ex Ch (goods detained in the Siege of Paris in the Franco-German war of 1870); *King v Victoria Insurance Co* [1896] AC 250, PC (wool); *Janson v Driefontein Consolidation Mines* [1902] AC 484 (bullion); *Jacob v Gaviller* (1902) 87 LT 26 (dog); *British and Foreign Marine Insurance Co v Gaunt* [1921] 2 AC 41, HL (wool); *G H Renton & Co Ltd v Black Sea and Baltic General Insurance Co Ltd* [1941] 1 All ER 149, KBD (timber).
[11] [1971] 2 QB 230, [1971] 1 All ER 55, CA.
[12] [1980] 1 Lloyd's Rep 656, QBD (Com Ct).
[13] (1904) 9 Com Cas 114, CA.
[14] [1977] 1 Lloyd's Rep 206 (British Columbia SC).

4   profits[15] and commission;[16]
5   wages;
6   the liability of a shipowner to the owner of the cargo;
7   loans, advances[17] and disbursements.[18]

The meaning of the first three of these terms must now be considered.

1 'Ship'

Rule 15 of the Rules for Construction of the Policy[19] set out in the First Schedule to the Marine Insurance Act 1906 states:

> 'The term "ship" includes the hull, materials and outfit, stores and provisions for the officers and crew, and, in the case of vessels engaged in a special trade, the ordinary fittings requisite for the trade, and also, in the case of a steamship, the machinery, boilers, and coals and engine stores, if owned by the assured.'

2 'Goods'

Rule 17 of the Rules for Construction of the Policy set out in the First Schedule to the Marine Insurance Act 1906 states:

> 'The term "goods" means goods in the nature of merchandise, and does not include personal effects or provisions and stores for use on board.'

3 'Freight'

Meaning of the term

Section 90 of the Marine Insurance Act 1906 states:

> ' "Freight" includes the profit derivable by a shipowner from the employment of his ship to carry his own goods or moveables, as well as freight payable by a third party, but does not include passage money.'

Hence, the expression 'freight' is employed in three senses:

    i   Ordinary freight.
   ii   Chartered freight.
  iii   Owner's trading freight.

i   Ordinary freight

Ordinary freight means the reward paid to the shipowner for carrying goods in his ship to the port of delivery.

Here the term 'shipowner' includes the charterer who employs a ship which he has chartered from the actual shipowner to carry goods for third parties.

The meaning of 'ordinary freight' was explained by Lord Ellenborough CJ, in *Forbes v Aspinall*[20] in the following words:[1]

---

[15] See, eg *Wyllie v Povah* (1907) 12 Com Cas 317.
[16] See, eg *Mentz Decker & Co v Maritime Insurance Co* [1910] 1 KB 132.
[17] See, eg *Price v Maritime Insurance Co* [1901] 2 KB 412, CA.
[18] See, eg *Moran, Galloway & Co v Uzielli* [1905] 2 KB 555; *New Zealand Shipping Co Ltd v Duke* [1914] 2 KB 682.
[19] These Rules apply subject to the provisions of the Marine Insurance Act 1906, and unless the context of the policy otherwise requires: Marine Insurance Act 1906, s 30(2).
[20] (1811) 13 East 323.
[1] Ibid, at 325.

'Freight is the profit earned by the shipowner in the carriage of goods on board his ship, and an insurance upon freight is an insurance made in order to secure that profit to the shipowner in case he is prevented by any of the perils insured against from actually earning such profit.... In every action upon such a policy, evidence is given, either that the goods were put on board from the carriage of which freight would result, or that there was some contract under which the shipowner, if the voyage were not stopped by the perils insured against, would have been entitled to demand freight.'

ii Chartered freight

Chartered freight means the sum of money paid to the shipowner by the charterer for the use of the entire ship for a voyage or for a period of time, whether the payment be by a lump sum, or at specified rates for the cargo carried, or at specified rates for a period of time.

When insuring chartered freight it is prudent to insure it under that designation, thereby giving the insurer notice of the charter-party.

iii Owner's trading freight

Owner's trading freight means that addition to the cost of his own goods carried in his own ship which the shipowner charges at the port of delivery as the price of carriage. The 'shipowner' here includes the charterer who carries his own goods in the chartered ship.

The shipowner or charterer does not pay himself for the carriage of the goods, and there is consequently no freight in the usual meaning of the term. At the same time, his goods may be augmented in value, by carriage to another port, to an amount which will cover both prime cost and carriage, and this amount may be insured as freight.

References to freight insurance in Marine Insurance Act 1906

The references to freight insurance in the Marine Insurance Act 1906 are particularly sparse. Thus, Lord Wright MR, said in *Yero Carras (Owners) v London and Scottish Assurance Corpn Ltd*:[2]

'It is well known that the Act did not deal expressly with the subject of freight insurance except in s 16(2), where it defined the insurable value of an interest in freight as the gross amount of the freight at the risk of the assured plus the charges of insurance, and in s 70, where it gave the rules for adjusting a partial loss on freight. It may indeed be that part of the definition of actual loss in s 57(1), that is, the words "where the assured is irretrievably deprived" of the subject-matter insured, may apply to an actual loss[3] of freight such as the present; similarly, the relevant words of s 60(1) may apply to a constructive total loss[4] of freight.'

In *Kulukundis v Norwich Union Fire Insurance Society*[5] Scott LJ, said:[6]

'This case raises for decision certain questions of principle left open by Parliament when it passed the Marine Insurance Act 1906. It is said on what seems to be good authority that the distinguished lawyers who settled the drafting of the Bill were unable to agree upon the law as to insurance of freight, and that is why the Act says so little about it.'

---

[2] (1935) 53 LlL Rep 131 at 137, CA.
[3] See Chapter 27, post.
[4] See Chapter 28, post.
[5] [1936] 2 All ER 242, CA.
[6] Ibid, at 269.

CHAPTER 3

The avoidance of wagering or gaming contracts

The position before 1745

The invention of marine insurance was due to the desirability of making good to the merchant and shipowner any loss arising from the destruction of property by tempest or other sea peril.

Grotius says that insurance was a contract *praestandae indemnitatis circa casus fortuitos*.[1]

The cardinal principle of insurance, therefore, is the principle of indemnity, and in early times insurances were always effected on the understanding that the person insuring was possessed of property which was about to be subjected to the dangers of a sea voyage.

At times, however, insurances were procured by persons who had no property at risk, and who had no intention of risking property, and whose only object was to take the chance of obtaining from the insurer a sum of money by staking merely the premium. For reasons which it is difficult to support, such insurances were sometimes upheld,[2] though, as Emerigon points out, an insurance without an object at risk can never be a true insurance.

Insurances were, however, formerly classed with lotteries, on the ground that they approximated more nearly to wagers than to any other form of contract.[3]

The support given to insurances where there was no property to insure, combined with the placing of insurances in the same category as lotteries, led to the recognition of a class of insurances which were simply wagers, i e the assured had no property at stake, but simply speculated with his premium on the event of the voyage.[4]

The position after 1745

Such was the position at common law prior to the passing of a series of statutes from 1745 onwards.

In that year the Marine Insurance Act enacted:

> 'That no assurance or assurances shall be made by any person or persons or bodies corporate or politic, on any ship or ships belonging to His Majesty or any of his subjects, or on any goods, merchandises, or effects laden or to be laden on board of any such ship or ships, interest or no interest, or without further proof or interest than the policy, or by way of gaming or wagering, or without benefit of salvage to the assurer, and that every such assurance shall be null and void to all intents and purposes.'

---

[1] *De Jure Belli*, ii, 12.
[2] Roccus, *De Assecurationibus*, vol X.
[3] Puffendorf, *Law of Nature*, p 25.
[4] See the cases tried on policies 'interest or no interest', circa 1740, cited in *Fitzgerald v Pole* (1754) 4 Bro Parl Cas 439 at 445.

The limited nature of the prohibition of wagering policies by this Act ceased to be of any real importance on the passing of the Gaming Act 1845, which declared all contracts by way of gaming and wagering to be void.

The Marine Insurance Act 1745 was finally repealed by the Marine Insurance Act 1906, s 4 of which provides:

> '(1) Every contract of marine insurance by way of gaming or wagering is void.
> (2) A contract of marine insurance is deemed to be a gaming or wagering contract—
>   a where the assured has not an insurable interest as defined by this Act, and the contract is entered into with no expectation of acquiring such an interest; or
>   b where the policy is made "interest or no interest" or "without further proof of interest than the policy itself" or "without benefit of salvage to the insurer" or subject to any other like term:
>
> Provided that, where there is no possibility of salvage, a policy may be effected without benefit of salvage to the insurer.'

It will be seen from s 4(2)(b) that the Act in its terms is inclusive, and that no mere phraseology is aimed at.

In order to come within the subsection the terms of the policy must be such as to show a clear intention to depart from the principle of indemnity, and where such intention is shown, the policy is void.[5]

It will, therefore, be seen that, although wager policies were at one time enforced in English courts of law, only those policies are now recognised which effect insurances upon property in which the assured has an interest apart from the policy itself. Thus, in the present view of the law, policies of insurance have reverted to the legitimate use for which they were originally devised, i e to protect from loss the merchant who risks his ship or goods in a maritime adventure.

Section 4 of the Marine Insurance Act 1906 has been carried a step further by the Marine Insurance (Gambling Policies) Act 1909.[6]

This Act states that if any person effects a contract of marine insurance without having any bona fide interest, direct or indirect, either in the safe arrival of the ship in relation to which the contract is made or in the safety or preservation of the subject-matter insured, or a bona fide expectation of acquiring such an interest, the contract shall be deemed to be a contract by way of gambling on loss by maritime perils.[7] The contract is also deemed to be a contract by way of gambling on loss by maritime perils where any person in the employment of the owner[8] of a ship, not being a part-owner of a ship, effects a contract of marine insurance in relation to the ship, and the contract is made 'interest or no interest' or 'without further proof of the interest than the policy itself' or 'without benefit of salvage to the insurer' or subject to any other like term.[9]

In each of the above cases, the person effecting the policy is guilty of an offence, and is liable on summary conviction to imprisonment for a term not exceeding six months or to a fine not exceeding £100.[10] If he is found guilty, he

---

[5] *Coker v Bolton* [1912] 3 KB 315 at 318.
[6] See Appendix I, pp 503–504, post.
[7] See s 1(1)(a).
[8] The expression 'owner' includes charterer: Marine Insurance (Gambling Policies) Act 1909, s 1(8).
[9] Ibid, s 1(1)(b).
[10] Ibid, s 1(1).

is liable to forfeit to the Crown any money he may receive under the contract.[11]

Any broker or other person through whom, or any insurer with whom, any such contract is effected, is guilty of an offence and liable on summary conviction to the like penalty if he acted knowing that the contract was by way of gambling on loss by maritime perils within the meaning of the statute.[12]

Proceedings under the Act cannot be instituted without the consent of the Attorney-General.[13] They must not be instituted against a person (other than a person in the employment of the owner of the ship in relation to which the contract was made) alleged to have effected a contract by way of gambling on loss by maritime perils until an opportunity has been afforded him of showing that the contract was not such a contract, and any information given by him for that purpose is not admissible as evidence against him in any prosecution under the Act.[14]

If proceedings are taken against any person (other than a person in the employment of the owner of the ship in relation to which the contract was made) for effecting such a contract, and the contract was made 'interest or no interest', or 'without further proof of interest than the policy itself' or 'without benefit of salvage to the insurer' or subject to any other like term, the contract shall be deemed to be a contract by way of gambling on loss by maritime perils unless the contrary is proved.[15]

Any person aggrieved by an order or decision of the court of summary jurisdiction may appeal to the Crown Court.[16]

Notwithstanding the statutory prohibition, the practice of effecting insurances of this kind still continues, particularly in regard to such interest as disbursements and commissions.

The policies usually contain a clause in the following form:

'In the event of loss the production of this policy to be deemed a sufficient proof of interest.'

The clause is styled a p p i clause (i e 'policy proof of interest'). Such policies are also termed 'honour policies', because the assured has to rely entirely on the honour of the insurer in the event of a loss, the policy not being enforceable at law.[17]

A p p i policy is void even though the assured may in fact have had an insurable interest.[18]

---

[11] Ibid, s 1(1).
[12] Ibid, s 1(2).
[13] Ibid, s 1(3).
[14] Ibid, s 1(4).
[15] Ibid, s 1(5).
[16] Ibid, s 1(7), as amended by the Courts Act 1971, s 56, Sch 9, Part I.
[17] See *Gedge v Royal Exchange Assurance* [1900] 2 QB 214; *T Cheshire & Co v Vaughan Bros & Co* [1920] 3 KB 240 at 251. For the difference between p p i policies in the United States and in England, see *Republic of China, China Merchants Steam Navigation Co Ltd and United States of America v National Union Fire Insurance Co of Pittsburgh, Pennsylvania, The Hai Hsuan* (No 2) [1958] 2 Lloyd's Rep 578 (US Dist Ct). For a case where the plaintiffs were not seeking to enforce a gaming policy or to enforce rights arising under it, but were seeking to enforce an obligation on the part of the defendant to share with them the proceeds of such a policy which he had already received, see *Bruns v Colocotronis, The Vasso* [1979] 2 Lloyd's Rep 412, QBD Com Ct. (See the judgment of Robert Goff J, ibid, at 420.)
[18] *T Cheshire & Co v Vaughan Bros & Co* (1920) 123 LT 487, CA. The facts and decision are set out in more detail at pp 36–37, post.

Thus, in *Thomas Cheshire & Co v Vaughan Bros & Co*[19] exporters of some nitrate from South America instructed their brokers to effect a p p i policy on their prospective profits. The brokers did so, but the policy was unenforceable against the insurers because they failed to disclose a material fact. When the brokers were sued by the exporters for damages for negligence, they pleaded that they were not liable because the policy, being a p p i one, was in any event void under the Marine Insurance Act 1906, s 4. It was held by the Court of Appeal[20] that this defence succeeded even though the exporters had an insurable interest in fact.

Scrutton LJ, said:[1]

> '[Counsel] says, [section] 4 of the Marine Insurance Act 1906 is not really so strict as it appears to be. It says: "(1) Every contract of marine insurance by way of gaming or wagering is void. (2) A contract of marine insurance is deemed to be a gaming or wagering contract: (*a*) where the assured has not an insurable interest as defined by this Act, and the contract is entered into with no expectation of acquiring such an interest; or (*b*) where the policy is made 'interest or no interest', or 'without further proof of interest than the policy itself'." That only means, if I understand [Counsel's] argument, that it is prima facie a gaming and wagering contract and you may defeat it if you can show you either had a real interest or a probability of obtaining it. That is, in effect, to read sub-s (*a*) of sub-s 2 into sub-s (*b*). I see no ground for cutting down the section that way.'

Where at the time of issue a policy has a detachable p p i clause, it is void under the Marine Insurance Act 1906, s 4, even though at the time of a claim under it the clause may have been detached by the assured.[2]

Thus, in *Re London County Commercial Reinsurance Office Ltd*[3] an insurance company issued a number of policies on vessels. Attached to the policies were detachable p p i clauses. When claims were made by the assured under the policies, in some cases the clauses had been detached, but in others the clauses were left attached. The company went into liquidation, and the liquidator refused to pay the claims on the ground that the policies were void. It was held by the Chancery Division that he was entitled to refuse to pay. All the policies were void under the Marine Insurance Act 1906, s 4. It made no difference whether or not the p p i clause had been detached.

P O Lawrence J, said:[4]

> 'The first question which arises on these policies is whether the fact that a detachable p p i clause was gummed on to the policies when they were signed and issued does not render them void under s 4 of the Marine Insurance Act 1906. In my judgment there is no difference between those policies which still have the p p i clause attached to them and those from which the p p i clause has been detached. It is not necessary to consider what course the Court would have adopted if before the policies had been brought to its attention the p p i clause had been detached, and neither of the litigating parties had raised the point that such a clause had ever formed part of the policies, because in the present case evidence has been adduced on behalf of the liquidator which proves clearly that the p p i clause was attached to all the policies when they were signed and handed to the assured. In my judgment the proper time to judge whether these policies are valid or void is at the time when they are issued. The subsequent tearing off of the p p i clause by the assured (even though it was done with the permission of the insurers) cannot in my opinion have the effect of rendering the policies valid if they were null and void

---

[19] (1920) 123 LT 487, CA.
[20] Bankes, Scrutton and Atkin LJJ.
[1] (1920) 123 LT at 493.
[2] *Re London County Commercial Reinsurance Office Ltd* [1922] 2 Ch 67, ChD.
[3] (1922) 127 LT 20, ChD.
[4] Ibid, at 26.

when they were issued. It was contended, however, that the Court ought not to regard any of the policies as p p i policies because of the introductory words preceding the p p i clause on the detachable slip, which stipulated that the p p i clause was no part of the policy but was to be binding in honour on the underwriters, and might be removed by the assured. In my opinion that contention cannot prevail. The stipulation relied upon is a palpable and, in my opinion, wholly futile attempt to evade the provisions of s 4 of the Act of 1906. A stipulation that an important clause affecting the whole tenor of the policy should form no part of the policy, and might be removed by the assured, stands self-condemned, and cannot, in my opinion, have the effect of making the policy what it is not, namely, a policy not containing such a clause.'

CHAPTER 4

Insurable interest[1]

A contract of marine insurance being a contract of indemnity, and policies 'interest or no interest' being void by s 4 of the Marine Insurance Act 1906, it follows that an assured seeking to recover under a policy must show that he has suffered a financial loss by reason of the non-completion of the adventure; that the loss was caused by a peril insured against; and that the subject-matter in respect of which the loss has taken place was covered by the policy.[2]

Such a financial loss can only result from some relation between the assured and the thing insured.[3] The range of such possible relations is very wide, varying from absolute ownership to a mere presumptive interest or expectation of profit at the end of the adventure.

Indefeasibility of property is not the criterion of interest.[4]

Section 5(1) of the Marine Insurance Act 1906 states:

> 'Every person has an insurable interest who is interested in a marine adventure.'

Section 5(2) goes on to state:

> 'In particular, a person is interested in a marine adventure where he stands in any legal or equitable relation to the adventure or to any insurable property at risk therein, in consequence of which he may benefit by the safety or due arrival of insurable property, or may be prejudiced by its loss, or by damage thereto, or by the detention thereof, or may incur liability in respect thereof.'

Section 5 is based on the words of Lawrence J, in *Lucena v Craufurd*:[5]

> 'A man is interested in a thing to whom advantage may arise or prejudice happen from the circumstances which may attend it.... Interest does not necessarily apply to the whole or part of a thing, nor necessarily and exclusively that which may be the subject of privation, but the having some relation to, or concern in, the subject of insurance, which relation or concern, by the happening of the perils insured against may be so affected as to produce a damage, detriment or prejudice to the person insuring.'

A EXAMPLES OF PERSONS HAVING AN INSURABLE INTEREST

Various persons may have an insurable interest in the subject-matter of the insurance. They can be conveniently considered under the following heads:

    1   Owner.
    2   Mortgagor and mortgagee.

---

[1] See further, Ivamy, *General Principles of Insurance Law* (4th edn, 1979), pp 20–31.
[2] See pp 106–112, post.
[3] See pp 16–27, post.
[4] *Stirling v Vaughan* (1809) 11 East 619. See further, Marine Insurance Act 1906, s 7(1).
[5] (1806) 2 Bos & PNR 269 at 302.

3   Master and crew.
4   Agent.
5   Carrier.
6   Lien holders and pawnors.
7   Trustees and executors.
8   Captors.
9   Insurer.
10 Persons expecting a profit from a marine adventure.
11 Lender of money on bottomry or respondentia.
12 Marina operator.

1 Owner

In considering the various modes of insurable interest, the most important is ownership, which is the simplest form of insurable interest.

(a) Ownership of ship

The interest of the owner remains although he may have let out his ship under a charter-party upon terms which would entitle him to recover from the charterer the value of the ship in the event of her loss. He is not bound to trust to the charterer or to the charterer's underwriters, but he may insure the ship with other underwriters on his own account.[6]

Thus, s 14(3) of the Marine Insurance Act 1906 provides:

> 'The owner of insurable property has an insurable interest in respect of the full value thereof, notwithstanding that some third person may have agreed, or be liable, to indemnify him in case of loss.'

The ownership of a vessel is not usually a difficult matter to ascertain.

Thus, in *Piper v Royal Exchange Assurance*[7] a yacht in Norway was bought in 1926 'as she lies' by the plaintiff, and was at the risk of the seller until she arrived in London. The plaintiff effected a policy in respect of her, and claimed against the insurers for damage which she had suffered by stranding in 1928.[8] The insurers counterclaimed for £346 15s 10d (which they had paid him in respect of damage suffered by her on the voyage from Norway to London in 1926) on the ground that he had no insurable interest in her.

Roche J, held that the counterclaim succeeded on this ground, and observed:[9]

> 'Now, in those circumstances the underwriters say: "We insured the plaintiff through the broker on the basis that he had an interest, and we paid him on the basis that he had an interest, and he had not, and in those circumstances we claim the recovery back of the sum which we paid in settlement of this particular average claim."
>
> In my judgment, the underwriters are so entitled.
>
> Suffice it to say that in my judgment the plaintiff had no interest here. It is unnecessary to decide, but it is probable that he had an interest, not in the ship itself, but in its arrival, which might have been insured and constituted an insurable contingent interest, but I think it ought to have been so described, and this is just one of those matters of interest which requires to be

---

[6] *Hobbs v Hannam* (1811) 3 Camp 93; *Provincial Insurance Co of Canada v Leduc* (1874) LR 6 PC 244 at 244.
[7] (1932) 44 LlL Rep 103, KBD.
[8] As to this point, see p 239, post.
[9] (1932) 44 LlL Rep 103 at 116.

defined, because it is necessary still to define the subject-matter insured, although it is not necessary to specify the nature and extent of the injuries to the subject-matter insured.

I am not saying that the plaintiff ought to or could have insured it under the designation of profits; I am only saying that he could not insure it under the title of the ship itself so as to enable him to recover for particular average to that ship upon a voyage in a case when he was not concerned with what happened to the ship by way of damage on that voyage, and where he had nothing to pay by reason of any particular average which was suffered by the ship.'

(b) Ownership of cargo

The ownership of cargo sometimes gives rise to discussion, turning on the rights of seller and buyer. The question of insurable interest in the cargo depends on the terms of the contract of sale, and on the stage at which the property in the goods sold passes from the seller to the buyer.

The passing of the property in the goods is governed by the Sale of Goods Act 1979, ss 16 to 19.[10]

In *Re National Benefit Assurance Co Ltd (Application of H L Sthyr)*,[11] which concerned an 'all risks' policy in respect of thirty bales of woollen goods 'from Tilbury to Novorossisk for Rostoff-on-Don', one of the issues[12] which arose was whether the goods had been sold by the assured to the purchaser, or whether they had only been sold subject to their safe arrival at Rostoff-on-Don. In fact, the goods never reached Rostoff-on-Don. When the assured claimed for a loss under the policy, the insurers contended that he had no insurable interest in them because he had already sold them.

Maugham J, held that the claim succeeded, for the assured had an insurable interest, since the sale was only conditional on the arrival of the goods. He observed:[13]

> 'Then remains the more serious question as to whether there was not an out-and-out sale to Mr Vitouchnovsky and the present claimant is unable to make a valid claim. In that matter there is this difficulty, that all the documents which were in existence at the time, or practically all of them, have been destroyed and the records of the Russo-Scandinavian Bank have been taken over by the People's Bank and there is some difficulty in ascertaining the facts. Mr Harald Sthyr says that no sale was made until the bank had information that the goods had arrived at Rostoff-on-Don and payment made not later than 45 days afterwards. Mr Vitouchnovsky and Mr Harald Sthyr have been called, and the former says he never saw the goods and that the sale was conditional on the goods reaching Rostoff-on-Don. I think that taking into consideration what took place when the State Bank took possession, I should be quite wrong in coming to the conclusion that the property passed before the goods reached Rostoff-on-Don.'

An unpaid seller who has divested himself of the property and the possession of goods which are in the course of transit to the buyer has the right to resume possession of them in the event of the buyer becoming insolvent.[14] This right which is known as the seller's right of stoppage in transit is exercised by the seller physically retaking possession of the goods or by his giving notice to the carrier or other bailee in whose possession the goods are,[15] and its effect is to give the seller a lien on the goods for payment of the price.[16]

---

[10] These sections are set out in Appendix I, pp 483–484, post.
[11] (1933) 45 LlL Rep 147, ChD.
[12] The case also concerned the question of the burden of proof of a loss under an 'all risks' policy. As to this point, see pp 178–179, post.
[13] (1933) 45 LlL Rep 147 at 151.
[14] Sale of Goods Act 1979, s 39 et seq.
[15] Ibid, s 46.
[16] Ibid, s 48.

Once this right of stoppage in transit has been exercised, the seller, although not in law the owner of the goods, has an insurable interest in them by virtue of his lien.

Whether the mere existence of the right and the possibility that the seller may exercise it is in itself sufficient to constitute an insurable interest is more doubtful, although support for the affirmative view is to be found in *Moran v Uzielli*.[17]

(c)   Ownership of freight

I ORDINARY FREIGHT

In the case of ordinary freight[18] the insurable interest is in the shipowner, who will receive the price for the carriage of the goods only on their arrival at the port of destination.

Thus, Lord Russell CJ, said in *Weir & Co v Girvin & Co*:[19]

> 'Freight is a payment to be made to the ship for carriage and delivery, and until there has been carriage and delivery, the shipowner is not under ordinary circumstances entitled to demand freight at all.'

In this definition, 'delivery' does not mean the actual handing over of the goods carried, but merely that the goods have arrived at the port of delivery, and that the shipowner is in a position to deliver them.

As a general rule, if the goods are put ashore at some point short of their destination, freight is not earned, even though this may have been the only alternative to a certain loss of the goods. The freight is, therefore, at risk when the ship starts on her voyage, and it may be totally lost to the owner by any peril which prevents the arrival of the ship and the goods at the port of destination.[20]

On the other hand, as long as the cargo delivered is, commercially speaking, identical with that which was loaded, the full freight is payable even though the goods are delivered in a damaged condition.[1]

It follows that the cargo owner, as well as the shipowner, has an insurable interest in the freight to this extent—i e that if he has to pay full freight for goods which arrive in a damaged condition, he suffers a loss on the elements which go to make up the price of goods at the port of delivery. These elements are:

1   prime cost;
2   freight;
3   port dues;
4   profits.

---

[17] [1905] 2 KB 555.
[18] For the meaning of 'ordinary freight', see pp 9–10, ante.
[19] [1899] 1 QB 193 at 196.
[20] *Dakin v Oxley* (1864) 15 CBNS 646; *Asfar & Co v Blundell* [1896] 1 QB 123; *Henriksens Rederi A/S v T H Z Rolimpex (The 'Brede')* [1974] QB 233, [1973] 3 All ER 589, CA; *Aries Tanker Corporation v Total Transport Ltd* [1977] 1 All ER 398, [1977] 1 WLR 185, HL; *Montedison SpA v Icroma SpA, The Caspian Sea* [1979] 3 All ER 378, [1980] 1 WLR 48, QBD (Com Ct).
[1] Accordingly, in *Griffiths v Bramley-Moore* (1878) 4 QBD 70, where the policy was expressed to cover 'only one-third loss of freight in consequence of sea-damage as per charter-party' and the charter-party provided that in the event of any of the cargo being sea-damaged, freight on such portion was to be reduced by one-third, it was held on the happening of this event that there had been a total loss of one-third of the freight.

If, therefore, the goods arrive in a damaged condition, so that the owner only receives three-fourths of the price of sound goods, the loss embraces one-fourth of each of the elements which make up the price of sound goods, and thus he loses one-fourth of the freight.[2]

This point is, however, purely academic, and it only applies to goods arriving in a damaged condition. Since goods are usually insured under a valued policy, a loss of freight as being part of the value of the goods would be provided for.[3] In many cases the shipper of goods under a bill of lading is required to pay freight in advance either on shipment of the goods or on the signing of the bills of lading or on the sailing of the vessel. Such a person is, of course, entitled to insure the freight which he has paid in advance.

Thus, s 12 of the Marine Insurance Act 1906 states:

> 'In the case of advance freight, the person advancing the freight has an insurable interest, in so far as such freight is not repayable in case of loss.'

II CHARTERED FREIGHT

Chartered freight[4] may give rise to three forms of insurable interest, the existence of which will, however, depend on the terms of the charter-party.

The shipowner is entitled to insure the chartered freight if its payment is contingent on some event which may be frustrated by maritime or other perils, e g by the operation of the 'off-hire clause'.

If, however, the whole or part of the chartered freight is paid in advance, the shipowner cannot insure that which is so paid, since it is not at risk. But the right to insure it is in the charterer, since the risk is his.

Thus, s 12 of the Marine Insurance Act 1906 states:

> 'In the case of advance freight, the person advancing the freight has an insurable interest, in so far as such freight is not repayable in case of loss.'

The charterer may also insure freight to be earned by the ship for him if he has chartered her for use as a general ship.

In such a case, however, if he has paid freight in advance and insured it, he would not be entitled to recover both on the policy insuring his advance freight and on the policy insuring his bills of lading freight, unless that policy showed a loss on the advance freight, in which event the difference would be recoverable as lost advance freight.

In such a case the charterer may insure profit freight;[5] and, of course, if by his contract the charterer incurs any liability in respect of the loss—either total or partial—of the ship, he has an insurable interest in the ship herself, quite apart from freight.[6]

A question often arises whether an advance of money to the ship by the charterer, which is not expressed to be a payment of freight in advance, nor a payment on account of freight, is really advance freight, or whether it comes under some other designation, such as a loan.

---

[2] See Benecke, *Principles of Indemnity*, p 24.
[3] See *Thames and Mersey Marine Insurance Co Ltd v Pitts, Son and King* [1893] 1 QB 476.
[4] For the meaning of 'chartered freight', see p 10, ante.
[5] *Asfar & Co v Blundell* [1895] 2 QB 196; affd [1896] 1 QB 123. See further, *United States Shipping Co v Empress Assurance Corpn* [1907] 1 KB 259.
[6] *Hobbs v Hannam* (1811) 3 Camp 93.

Such payments being made usually at the ship's port of loading, the chief test of the nature of the payment is whether or not it was intended to be insured; if there was an intention to insure such a payment, it is deemed to be advance freight.[7]

The difference between the two forms of advance payments was thus stated by Bayley J, in *Manfield v Maitland*:[8]

> 'If the memorandum of charter-party had clearly expressed that the money advanced should be in part payment of the freight, then it would follow that the loss of the ship would produce a loss of the money advanced to the freighter, and he would have an insurable interest in it. But if that be not so, and it be only a loan by the freighter, he would have no insurable interest, having a remedy against the owner for the debt.'

In *Hicks v Shield*[9] the charter-party provided 'cash for ship's disbursements to be advanced to the extent of £300 free of interest, but subject to insurance and £2 10s per cent commission . . . the freight to be paid on unloading and right delivery of cargo as follows, say, in cash less 2 months' interest at 5 per cent per annum, and if required £300 to be paid in cash on arrival, less 2 months' interest.' It was held that the stipulated advance of £300 was an advance of freight, and that on the loss of the ship the charterer could not recover back that advance on the ground that it was a loan.

Lord Campbell CJ, said:[10]

> 'This mention of insurance seems to me to stamp the transaction indelibly as a payment on account of freight, and not as a mere loan; for if the advance was to be insured, it must be an advance of freight, which is insurable, whereas a loan is not. There is nothing necessarily inconsistent in the other clause that "the freight is to be paid on unloading and right delivery of cargo". This may refer to the payment of the residue of the freight not already advanced.'

The allowance of insurance in such cases imposes no obligation on the shipowner to insure the advance freight.[11]

Indeed, except that the shipowner allows the freighter the amount required to insure the advance, the mention of insurance in no way affects the contract of hire or of carriage.[12]

Where chartered freight is insured, it is essential that there should exist some definite and binding contract under which freight is payable,[13] although it is not necessary that the contract should be in writing.[14]

Moreover, some step must have been taken under the contract towards earning the freight.

Thus, in *Barber v Fleming*[15] Blackburn J, said:[16]

---

[7] *Allison v Bristol Marine Insurance Co* (1876) 1 App Cas 209; *Hicks v Shield* (1857) 7 E&B 633; *The Red Sea* [1895] P 293; on appeal [1896] P 20.
[8] (1821) 4 B&Ald 582 at 585.
[9] (1857) 26 LJQB 205.
[10] Ibid, at 208.
[11] *Jackson v Isaacs* (1858) 3 H&N 405.
[12] *Smith, Hill & Co v Pyman, Bell & Co* [1891] 1 QB 742. See also, *Rodocanachi v Milburn* (1886) 18 QBD 67; *Great Indian Peninsular Rly Co v Turnbull* (1885) 53 LT 325.
[13] *Flint v Flemyng* (1830) 1 B&Ad 45; *Scottish Shire Line Ltd v London and Provincial Marine and General Insurance Co Ltd* [1912] 3 KB 51.
[14] *Warre v Miller* (1825) 4 B&C 538; *Patrick v Eames* (1813) 3 Camp 441.
[15] (1869) LR 5 QB 59.
[16] Ibid, at 67. See also, *Davidson v Willasey* (1813) 1 M&S 313; *Thompson v Taylor* (1795) 6 Term Rep 478; *Horncastle v Suart* (1806) 7 East 400; *Foley v United Fire and Marine Insurance Co of Sydney* (1870) LR 5 CP 155.

'When a shipowner has got a contract with another person under which he will earn freight, and has taken steps and incurred expense upon the voyage towards earning it, then his interest ceases to be a contingent thing, but becomes an inchoate interest, and is an interest which, if afterwards destroyed by one of the perils insured against, is lost, and ought to be paid for by the underwriters.'

III OWNER'S TRADING FREIGHT[17]

When the shipowner carries his own goods in his own ship, he is permitted to insure, as freight, that increase in price which he, as shipowner, will earn on his own goods by carrying them in his own ship. In other words, under an insurance on freight the assured may recover the profits expected to be made by carrying his own goods in his own ship on the voyage insured.[18]

Where a shipowner is carrying his own goods in his own ship, two conditions are required in order to establish an insurable interest in freight:

1   the ship must be ready to carry a cargo; and
2   there must exist a cargo intended to be shipped, for until such a cargo is ready she cannot be in a position to earn freight.[19]

2 Mortgagor and mortgagee

Section 14(1) of the Marine Insurance Act 1906 states:

'Where the subject-matter insured is mortgaged, the mortgagor has an insurable interest in the full value thereof . . .'

The reason for this is that he is the owner, and he is under covenant to repay the mortgage debt.

Where the mortgage instrument contains a covenant by the mortgagor to insure the vessel on behalf of the mortgagee, the mortgagor is deemed to be a trustee for the mortgagee of any proceeds of the policy.[20]

Section 14(1) of the Marine Insurance Act 1906 states:

'Where the subject-matter insured is mortgaged . . . the mortgagee has an insurable interest in respect of any sum due or to become due under the mortgage.'

Further, s 14(2) states:

'A mortgagee . . . may insure on behalf and for the benefit of other persons interested as well as for his own benefit.'

If the mortgagee's advance is not equal to the value of the ship, and he insures the ship to her full value, he will not be able to recover more than the value of his advance unless he can show that at the time when he executed the policy, he intended to insure the interest of the mortgagor.[1]

An unregistered mortgagee of a Greek ship has an insurable interest in the ship notwithstanding that according to Greek law all unregistered mortgages are void.[2]

---

[17] For the meaning of 'owner's trading freight', see p 10, ante.
[18] *De Vaux v J'Anson* (1839) 5 Bing NC 519.
[19] *Flint v Flemyng* (1830) 1 B&Ad 45; *De Vaux v J'Anson*, supra.
[20] *Swan & Cleland's Graving Dock and Slipway Co v Maritime Insurance Co, & Croshaw* [1907] 1 KB 116. As to the legal position of a mortgagee of a ship, see the Merchant Shipping Act 1894, ss 31 to 46.
[1] *Irving v Richardson* (1831) 2 B&Ad 193; *Ladbroke v Lee* (1850) 4 Dé G&Sm 106. See further, *Williams v Atlantic Assurance Co Ltd* [1933] 1 KB 81.
[2] *P Samuel & Co Ltd v Dumas* [1924] AC 431.

In *P Samuel & Co Ltd v Dumas*[3] a shipowner purported to mortgage a Greek vessel to a mortgagee to secure moneys due and to become due under a current account. The mortgage was to be registered in Greece, but, in fact, it never was registered. The vessel was lost and a firm of shipbrokers, who had insured her under a time policy on behalf of the mortgagee, claimed against the insurer under the policy. One of the grounds[4] on which the insurer denied liability was that the mortgagee had no insurable interest.

The House of Lords[5] held that he had an insurable interest under s 5(1) of the Marine Insurance Act 1906, for he had an equitable right to a mortgage, and so was 'interested in a marine adventure'.

Viscount Cave observed:[6]

> 'In the present case the appellant held a British mortgage on the ship and a deed of covenant which recited an agreement by the owner to deliver to the mortgagee a "formal first mortgage of the said steamship duly executed and registered in Greece", and contained a covenant by him to "take such steps as might be necessary to effect the complete registration of the said steamship as a Greek steamship": and he was entitled in equity to enforce these agreements. This being so, I think it impossible to say that he was not interested in the adventure within the meaning of the above section; and, if so, he clearly had an insurable interest to the extent of the sum secured by the mortgage.'

3 Master and crew

Prior to the Merchant Shipping Act 1854 the rule of maritime law was that 'freight is the mother of wages'. It followed that if a vessel were lost in the course of her voyage, nothing was due to the seamen on account of wages.

Moreover, by way of further identifying the interest of the crew with the success of the adventure it was deemed to be contrary to public policy to permit a seaman to insure his wages, although the master was placed at no such disadvantage.[7]

This distinction was done away with by the Merchant Shipping Act 1854 (since repealed) and now by the Merchant Shipping Act 1894 a seaman is entitled in the event of the loss of his ship to his wages up to the date of loss.

Section 157(1) of the Merchant Shipping Act 1894 provides:

> 'The right to wages shall not depend on the earning of freight; and every seaman and apprentice who would be entitled to demand and recover any wages, if the ship in which he has served had earned freight, shall, subject to all other rules of law and conditions applicable to the case, be entitled to demand and recover the same, notwithstanding that freight has not been earned . . .'

Section 11 of the Marine Insurance Act 1906 states:

> 'The master or any member of the crew of a ship has an insurable interest in respect of his wages.'

---

[3] [1924] AC 431, HL.
[4] Other aspects of the case concerned a breach of warranty, waiver of a breach of warranty, connivance of the owner at the scuttling of the vessel, and the meaning of 'perils of the sea'. As to these points, see pp 290–291, post, p 312, post, p 235, post, and p 145, post, respectively.
[5] Viscount Haldane LC, Viscount Cave, Viscount Finlay, Lord Sumner and Lord Parmoor.
[6] [1924] All ER Rep 66 at 74. See also, the speech of Lord Sumner, ibid, at 82, and that of Viscount Finlay, ibid, at 77.
[7] *King v Glover* (1806) 2 Bos&PNR 206.

4 Agent

An agent has no insurable interest if his only relationship to the goods is that of agent for another person.

Thus, in *Seagrave v Union Marine Insurance Co*[8] a broker sold as agent on commission a cargo of goods, and the bill of lading was made out to his order or assigns, and he held the bill of lading until the purchaser had given an acceptance for the amount of the goods. It was held that he could not recover on a policy which he had effected in respect of the goods, as he had no interest in the cargo, and, being a mere agent, incurred no liability and suffered no damage through the loss.

On the other hand, an agent, who has made advances, may insure the goods consigned to him to the extent, at any rate, of the advances he has made upon them.

Thus, in *Ebsworth v Alliance Marine Insurance Co*,[9] where consignees gave acceptances against consignments of cotton and insured the consignments and their advances by open cover on which they declared from time to time, it was held that they had an insurable interest for the amount of an advance on a particular consignment which was lost by perils insured against.

Similarly, an agent may have an insurable interest in profits or commission which he expects to earn on goods consigned to him, eg a shipbroker in the brokerage on a vessel addressed to him. There must, however, be a legal and binding contract under which the profits or commission are payable, and mere expectation is not sufficient.

An agent having himself an insurable interest in respect of advances, profits or commission, as the case may be, is entitled to insure not only on his own behalf but also on behalf of all other persons interested in the same subject-matter.

Thus, s 14(2) of the Marine Insurance Act 1906 states:

'A . . . person having an interest in the subject-matter insured may insure on behalf and for the benefit of other persons interested as well as for his own benefit.'

In the event of his doing so it would seem that in any action brought by the agent upon the policy it is necessary to allege the interests of such other persons.[10]

5 Carrier

A carrier has an insurable interest in the goods committed to him for carriage.[11]
Although he is not the actual owner, he may insure and also sue on the policy

---

[8] (1866) LR 1 CP 305. See further, *Wolff v Horncastle* (1798) 1 Bos&P 316; *Conway v Gray* (1809) 10 East 536 at 547; *Carruthers v Sheddon* (1815) 6 Taunt 14.
[9] (1873) LR 8 CP 596. See further, *Wolff v Horncastle*, supra.
[10] See, however, the opinions of Bovill CJ, and Denman J, to the contrary in *Ebsworth v Alliance Marine Insurance Co* (1873) LR 8 CP 596.
[11] *Crowley v Cohen* (1832) 3 B&Ad 478; *Joyce v Kennard* (1871) 71 LJQB 17; *Stephens v Australasian Insurance Co* (1872) LR 8 CP 18; *Hill v Scott* [1895] 2 QB 713; *The Yasin* [1979] 2 Lloyd's Rep 45 at 53, QBD (Com Ct) (per Lloyd J). For an example of a policy issued to a charterer in respect of loss of or damage to cargo owned by third parties, see *Kuehne and Nagel Inc v Baiden* [1977] 1 Lloyd's Rep 90 (NY Ct App), where it was held that the cargo owner's claim for damage had been reasonably settled by the assignees of the assured. (See the judgment of Gabrielli J, ibid, at 92.)

provided he sues as trustee for the owner; otherwise he may be unable to recover, if under the terms of his contract of carriage he has incurred no risk.[12]

6 Lien holders and pawnors

A person who has a lien on the property has an insurable interest in it to the amount of his lien, and the pawnee of goods which are assigned to him by indorsement of the bill of lading can insure them.[13]

Again, a ship's carpenter having a lien for repairs has an insurable interest.[14]

But no right of lien on a ship is conferred on the lender who advances money for the ship on bills of exchange; and the judgment of the French Court in *Castrique v Imrie*,[15] given against the master 'en sa qualité de capitaine et par privilége sur le navire', purporting to apply English law to a British ship, and expressing a contrary view, was erroneous; although the decision was held not to be examinable in this country, it being a judgment in rem. But where advances had been made for necessaries, thereby conferring a right to enforce the debt by an action in rem under s 6 of the Admiralty Court Act 1840, the creditor had an insurable interest in the ship to the extent of the advances.[16]

Salvors have a lien on the ship salved. Therefore, where an owner paid the salvage claim, he was held to have a lien on the cargo for that share of the claim which was due from the cargo, and consequently to have an insurable interest to that extent in the cargo.[17]

The pawnor has also an insurable interest, if the transaction by which the ship has been hypothecated is, in fact, a pledge and not a sale.[18]

Where a shipowner has incurred liabilities to salvors in respect of services rendered during the voyage, he has an insurable interest in the other interests on board to the extent to which he may be liable to contribute in general average to satisfy the claims of the salvors whether claimed on a salvage bond or otherwise.[19]

7 Trustees and executors

Legal ownership is vested in trustees and executors by virtue of the office which they hold, and they have an insurable interest in the property so vested, such interest enuring for the benefit of the beneficial owners, heirs, or legatees.

Thus, in *Stirling v Vaughan*[20] Lord Ellenborough CJ, said:[1]

> 'What is the case of an executor; probate is necessary to complete his title, yet before probate he has title sufficient to enable him to insure.'

---

[12] *Scott v Globe Marine Insurance Co Ltd* (1896) 1 Com Cas 370.
[13] *Sutherland v Pratt* (1843) 11 M&W 296. See also, *Hibbert v Carter* (1787) 1 Term Rep 745; *Wolff v Horncastle* (1798) 1 Bos&P 316; *Ebsworth v Alliance Marine Insurance Co* (1873) LR 8 CP 596.
[14] *Tasker v Scott* (1815) 6 Taunt 234.
[15] (1860) 8 CBNS 405.
[16] *Moran, Galloway & Co v Uzielli* [1905] 2 KB 555.
[17] *Briggs v Merchant Traders' Association* (1849) 13 QB 167. See also *Dixon v Whitworth* (1880) 4 CPD 371.
[18] *Alston v Campbell* (1779) 4 Bro Parl Cas 476.
[19] *Briggs v Merchant Traders' Association* (1849) 13 QB 167.
[20] (1809) 11 East 619.
[1] Ibid, at 628. See further, *Tidswell v Ankerstein* (1792) Peake 151; *London and North-Western Rly Co v Glyn* (1859) 1 E&E 652; *Waters v Monarch Life Assurance Co* (1856) 5 E&B 870.

8 Captors

Captors have an insurable interest in property captured in time of war, by reason of possession with its attendant liabilities, e g a liability to be ordered to restore the property and pay costs.

Section 7(1) of the Marine Insurance Act 1906 states:

> 'A defeasible interest is insurable, as also is a contingent interest.'

There must, however, be something more than mere expectation in the captor; there should be a vesting of the property by virtue of the Prize Act. Failing a right under the Prize Act, captors should insure on behalf of the Crown, though an insurance made by captors for the benefit of all concerned is held to be made under the implied authority of the Crown. The insurable interest exists notwithstanding the fact that captors are liable to be dispossessed by an order of release made by the Crown before adjudication; for indefeasibility of property is not a criterion of insurable interest.[2]

9 Insurer

An insurer has an insurable interest in the thing insured to the extent of his liability in the event of a loss, and he is entitled to protect himself by reinsuring. Thus, s 9(1) of the Marine Insurance Act 1906 states:

> 'The insurer under a contract of marine insurance has an insurable interest in his risk, and may reinsure in respect of it.'

An insurer is not bound to state that he is reinsuring. If he has insured on goods, he may reinsure by describing the interests as 'on goods'.[3]

In practice, however, it is almost invariable for a reinsurance policy to contain a clause stating:

> 'Being a reinsurance subject to the same clauses and conditions as the original policy and to pay as may be paid thereon.'[4]

10 Persons expecting a profit from a marine adventure

Profits which may naturally be expected to result from the successful termination of the adventure are insurable.[5]

But this form of insurable interest should be specifically described in the policy as 'profits'.[6]

It must, however, be shown that there was a well-founded and reasonable probability of a profit being made[7] since a mere expectation of gain at the close of a voyage is not sufficient to create an insurable interest.[8]

---

[2] *Stirling v Vaughan*, supra; *Routh v Thompson* (1809) 11 East 428; subsequent proceedings (1811) 13 East 274. See further, Marine Insurance Act 1906, s 7(1).

[3] *Mackenzie v Whitworth* (1875) 1 ExD 36. See further, *Craufurd v Hunter* (1798) 8 Term Rep 13; *Lucena v Craufurd* (1806) 2 Bos&PNR 269; *Stirling v Vaughan* (1809) 11 East 619.

[4] As to the effect of this clause, see p 466, post.

[5] *Barclay v Cousins* (1802) 2 East 544; *Anderson v Morice* (1875) LR 10 CP 609; *Harland and Wolff v J Burstall & Co* (1901) 84 LT 324.

[6] *McSwiney v Royal Exchange Assurance Corpn* (1849) 14 QB 634; *Halhead v Young* (1856) 6 E&B 312; *Inglis v Stock* (1885) 10 App Cas 263.

[7] *Hodgson v Glover* (1805) 6 East 316; *Eyre v Glover* (1812) 16 East 218; *Ionides v Pender* (1872) 27 LT 244.

[8] *Knox v Wood* (1808) 1 Camp 543; *Buchanan & Co v Faber* (1899) 4 Com Cas 223.

To give rise to a claim under an insurance on profits, it must be shown that the loss arose by a peril insured against and not merely from a fall in the market. Moreover, the goods on which the profit is expected to be made must be at risk and the assured must have an insurable interest in them.[9]

A shareholder in a limited company has no insurable interest in the property of the company, since that property is vested in the company itself and not in any individual member.[10]

But he can insure profits which may be expected to result from any maritime adventure on which the company embarks, although his right to such profits would only exist by reason of his position as a shareholder.[11]

11 Lender of money on bottomry or respondentia

Section 10 of the Marine Insurance Act 1906 states:

> 'The lender of money on bottomry or respondentia has an insurable interest in respect of the loan.'

The existence of these interests depends on the due arrival of the ship and the goods. Therefore, where the advance is on ship, freight and cargo, and is to be repaid in any event, there is no interest insurable as bottomry.[12]

It is suggested by Emerigon that the lender cannot also be the insurer, since, in such a case the loan would lose its maritime character and become a simple usurious loan.[13]

12 Marina operator

A marina operator may insure against legal liability for loss of or damage to craft belonging to third parties whilst in his care.[14]

B EXISTENCE OF INSURABLE INTEREST AT THE TIME OF THE LOSS[15]

Since the principle of indemnity is the very foundation of marine insurance, it follows that a person who, at the date of the loss, has parted with his interest, or, though in negotiation for, has not yet acquired an interest in the thing insured, cannot successfully prosecute a claim under a policy.

Section 6(1) of the Marine Insurance Act 1906 states:

> 'The assured must be interested in the subject-matter insured at the time of the loss though he need not be interested when the insurance is effected.'

Thus, in *Powles v Innes*[16] in January 1838, the plaintiffs, insurance agents, by

---

[9] *Stockdale v Dunlop* (1840) 6 M&W 224; *McSwiney v Royal Exchange Assurance Corpn* (1849) 14 QB 634. Cf *Wilson v Jones* (1866) LR 1 Exch 193; on appeal (1867) LR 2 Exch 139.
[10] *Paterson v Harris* (1861) 1 B&S 336. See further, *R v Arnaud* (1846) 9 QB 806.
[11] *Wilson v Jones* (1866) LR 1 Exch 193.
[12] *Stainbank v Fenning* (1851) 11 CB 51; *Stainbank v Shepard* (1853) 13 CB 418.
[13] See *Glover v Black* (1763) 3 Burr 1394.
[14] See e g *Pillgrem v Cliff Richardson Boats Ltd and Richardson; (Switzerland General Insurance Co, Third Party)* [1977] 1 Lloyd's Rep 297 (Supreme Court of Ontario), where the question was whether the loss had occurred in the 'alteration, repair or maintenance' of a cabin cruiser.
[15] See also, Ivamy, *General Principles of Insurance Law* (4th edn, 1979), pp 28–31.
[16] (1843) 11 M&W 10. See also, *Camden v Anderson* (1798) 1 Bos&P 272.

directions from, and on account and for the benefit of, Robert Page and Robert Chamberlain, effected a time policy in respect of two-thirds of the ship 'Commerce', which was lost in January 1839, during the currency of the policy. Before the loss Page conveyed his share to Sarah Banks, who already owned one-third. On the day after the sale Sarah Banks effected a policy in respect of her two-thirds, upon which she was paid as for a total loss. The defendant was an underwriter for £150, and paid £75 as being due to Chamberlain in respect of his share. It was held that as Page had parted with his interest before the loss, he was not entitled to recover.

Again, in *North of England Oil Cake Co v Archangel Insurance Co*,[17] the insurance was effected in November 1871, on goods. In February 1872, the owners sold the goods, which were still on the voyage, for cash payable fourteen days after the goods were ready for delivery at the port. On 21 February 1872, the bills of lading were indorsed to the buyers. On 26 February the ship arrived in port, and two days later, while unloading overside into lighters, one lighter sank alongside the buyers' wharf. The loss was within the policy, being occasioned by perils insured against. When afterwards an action was brought by the buyers, to whom the policy had been assigned after the loss, it was held that, inasmuch as on the sale of the goods the policy was not assigned to the buyers, the interest under the policy remained vested in the sellers, and on delivery of the goods the interest of the sellers ceased, and the policy became a nullity, and no subsequent assignment could revive it.[18]

These decisions do not, of course, affect the right of an assignee to recover on a policy, though he had no interest in the subject-matter of the insurance at the time when the policy was executed. It is sufficient that at the date of the loss he was entitled both to the policy and to the goods.[19]

Like any other interest, if it exists at the time of the loss, an insurable interest in freight may be recovered in an action on the policy. This will also be the case under a time policy, even though that policy must have expired before the freight could have been earned.[20]

'*Lost or not lost*'

Insurances are often effected without any information being forthcoming as to the safety of the ship or cargo. If, therefore, either ship or cargo should be lost before the insurance is effected, the interest of the assured will have ceased to exist, and he would be unable to recover on the policy, although it was executed in perfect good faith and in ignorance of the loss.

In order to avoid this result, the words 'lost or not lost' are introduced into the policy, and these words render the insurer liable, although, in fact, at the date of the policy the loss may have taken place and the interest of the assured may have ceased to exist.

Hence s 6(1) of the Marine Insurance Act 1906 provides that:

'. . . where the subject-matter is insured "lost or not lost", the assured may recover although he

---

[17] (1875) LR 10 QB 249. See also, *Anderson v Morice* (1876) 1 App Cas 713.
[18] As to assignment, see generally pp 315–321, post.
[19] *Lower Rhine and Wurtemburg Insurance Association v Sedgewick* [1898] 1 QB 739 at 745; *Rhind v Wilkinson* (1810) 2 Taunt 237; *Sparkes v Marshall* (1836) 2 Bing NC 761; *Lloyd v Fleming* (1872) LR 7 QB 299.
[20] *Michael v Gillespy* (1857) 26 LJCP 306.

may not have acquired his interest until after the loss, unless at the time of effecting the contract of insurance the assured was aware of the loss, and the insurer was not.'

Section 6(2) states:

'Where the assured has no interest at the time of the loss, he cannot acquire interest by any act or election after he is aware of the loss.'

It may be noted that where there is a contract for the sale of specific goods, and the goods without the knowledge of the seller have perished at the time when the contract was made, the contract is void.[1]

---

[1] Sale of Goods Act 1979, s 6.

CHAPTER 5

The duties of a broker in effecting the policy

Where a broker is employed to effect a policy, certain duties must be performed by him.

Thus, he must:

1 obey his principal's instructions;
2 use proper skill and care;
3 carry out the transaction.

1 Duty to obey his principal's instructions

The primary duty of the broker is to obey the assured's instructions and effect a policy accordingly.[1]

In considering the law on the matter it must be pointed out that in many of the reports of the early cases the words 'agent' or 'correspondent' are used with reference to the person effecting the policy. It would appear that these terms often mean 'broker', for at that time the profession of brokers was not fully organised, and those engaged in mercantile transactions might at the same time fulfil the triple functions of brokers, underwriters and agents.

Perhaps the chief rule that the Courts evolved was that the broker was under a duty to act bona fide in all cases, and this was particularly so when no special instructions regarding the policy had been given to him by his principal.[2]

One of the earliest cases is *Moore v Mourgue*[3] decided by Lord Mansfield. The action was brought by the plaintiff, who was a merchant at Alicante, against the defendant, his agent in London, on the ground that he had not insured his goods according to instructions. The goods consisted of fruit, and no evidence was given to show that any particular instructions had been given as to how or with whom he was to effect the policy. The defendant insured with the London Assurance Office which, in policies on fruit, always put in the exception 'free

---

[1] See further, Ivamy, *General Principles of Insurance Law* (4th edn, 1979), pp 550–551.
[2] Similarly, if the agent receives ambiguous instructions and acting bona fide puts on them a reasonable interpretation, he will not be liable for negligence, if it turns out that the instructions were otherwise interpreted by his principal. See e g the judgment of Lord Chelmsford in *Ireland v Livingston* (1872) LR 5 HL 395 at 416: 'Now it appears to me that if a principal gives an order to an agent in such uncertain terms as to be susceptible of two different meanings, and the agent bona fide adopts one of them and acts upon it, it is not competent to the principal to repudiate the act as unauthorised, because he meant the order to be read in the other sense of which it is equally capable. It is a fair answer to such an attempt to disown the agent's authority, to tell the principal that the departure from his intention was occasioned by his own fault and that he should have given his order in clear and unambiguous terms.'
[3] (1776) 2 Cowp 479.

from particular average'.[4] The loss which ensued was not a total loss, for though the goods were at first under water, some were saved.

The jury found a verdict for the defendant, and one of the jurymen said that the ground of the verdict was 'because they thought he had acted bona fide to the best of his judgment'. Lord Mansfield gave judgment accordingly, and on a motion for a new trial his decision was supported by three other Judges. On this motion he himself was present, and explained the reason for his decision and his directions to the jury. He said that the plaintiff, if he pleased, might have given orders to the defendant not to insure at the London Assurance Office, but at some other office where the exception concerning fruit would not have been insisted upon. Since he gave no instructions, he left it to the defendant's discretion, and therefore if the defendant acted bona fide, there was complete freedom to elect between the underwriters. Further, since the premium was the same, there could be no temptation as to his choice between them.

A similar case is *Comber v Anderson*.[5] This was an action against the defendants, as insurance brokers, respecting a cargo of wheat, which the plaintiff had bought at Waterford to be conveyed by the ship 'Fanny' from there to Liverpool. The plaintiff alleged that it was the duty of the defendants to have caused such a policy of insurance to be effected on the wheat as would have indemnified him from any partial loss which should or might arise in the event of the ship being stranded. The defendants effected the policy with the Royal Exchange Assurance Co, whose policy contained a clause that the company was to be 'free from all average upon corn, unless general, or otherwise specially agreed'. No special agreement was entered into by the defendants, and the ship later stranded, and a partial loss was incurred. It appeared that the plaintiff had not given the defendants any special directions concerning the insurance of the cargo, and he did not complain of the policy having been effected with the Royal Exchange Assurance Co, until some time after the loss had happened. Lord Ellenborough CJ, had no hesitation in giving judgment for the defendants. He said that the plaintiff must be taken to have been cognisant of the existence of the Chartered Companies and the tenor of their policies—matters which since the publication of Park's book on Insurance[6] were familiar to all persons in the least degree conversant with these subjects. If he had wished that the policy upon the cargo was not to be effected on the terms offered by the Royal Exchange Assurance Co, he ought to have given special directions to the defendants for this purpose; and at any rate, having been so late in reproaching them for what they had done, he had acquiesced and adopted the policy which they actually effected.

It is doubtful however whether *Moore v Mourgue*[7] would necessarily be followed at the present time. No proof was given that the plaintiff, who was a foreigner, was actually acquainted with the difference in the terms offered by the underwriters and those offered by the London Assurance Co, and further it would seem that the agent had not exercised reasonable skill, since he had not insured under a policy which afforded the more complete protection.

The principal must be able to rely on the broker carrying out his instructions faithfully, and it is no defence to an action for negligence for the broker to claim

---

[4] As to particular average warranties, see pp 429–432, post.
[5] (1808) 1 Camp 523.
[6] Park JA, *A System of the Law of Marine Insurance* (1786).
[7] Supra.

that the principal ought to have examined the policy to see that he had gained full protection. In *Dickson & Co v Devitt*[8] the plaintiffs instructed the defendant, an insurance broker, to insure goods 'per steamship "Suwa Maru" and/or steamers,[9] London to Port Dickson', against marine and war risks. A 'slip' in accordance with the instructions was prepared, but the underwriter to whom it was shown would only insure the marine risk, as he was full up with war risks. The defendant's clerk who was taking the 'slip' round, then struck out the words 'and war', and prepared another 'slip' for the war risk alone, and in doing so he accidentally left out the words 'and/or steamers', so that the insurance of the goods against war risk was only on the 'Suwa Maru'. This 'slip' in that form was in due course underwritten by an underwriter.

Debit notes were prepared and sent by the defendant to Dickson & Co, the debit note in respect of the marine risk purporting to be on the goods per 'Suwa Maru' and/or steamers, while the note in respect of the war risk purported to be on the goods per 'Suwa Maru' only. Policies embodying the same distinction followed later. It was the usual practice in Dickson & Co's office to check the debit notes, when received, with the instructions given to the broker. No one in the office, however, discovered the discrepancy between the instructions and debit note in respect of the war risk insurance. The two debit notes were sent pinned together, and it was suggested that the clerk checked the debit note in respect of the marine risk, which was on the top, and finding that it was all right, made only a cursory examination of the debit note in respect of the war risk.

On being sued for negligence, the broker claimed that the plaintiffs were themselves negligent, and that therefore he was not liable, but Atkin J, gave judgment against him. He thought a client was entitled to rely on the insurance broker carrying out his instructions, especially as the client might quite easily overlook a difference which ought to be perfectly plain to a person who had special knowledge of insurance matters. The principal would not know whether the document did, in fact, carry out his instructions. Business could not be carried on, if, when a person had been employed to use skill and care with regard to a matter, the employer was bound to use his own skill and care to see whether the person employed had done what he was employed to do.

2 Duty to use proper skill and care

It is the duty of the broker to act with proper skill and care.[10]

The Courts soon held that it was the duty of the broker to insert all the clauses which were usual and ordinary in the type of voyage concerned. In *Mallough v Barber*[11] the defendants, who were insurance brokers, were sued for negligence in effecting a policy of insurance for the plaintiff. He had instructed them to effect a policy for £550 on the ship 'Expedition' and her freight 'at and from Tenerife to London at 10 guineas per cent'.

They effected the policy in the words communicated to them. The 'Expedition' took some goods on board at Tenerife, and then proceeded to Lanzarote to complete her cargo. Lanzarote was another island in the Canary

---

[8] (1916) 86 LJKB 315.
[9] For the meaning of this term, see *Marine Insurance Co Ltd v Grimmer* [1944] 2 All ER 197, CA.
[10] See further, Ivamy, *General Principles of Insurance Law* (4th edn, 1979), pp 551–555.
[11] (1815) 4 Camp 150.

Group, but not on the direct route to London. The vessel was later captured, and the underwriters naturally refused to pay on the ground of deviation.

Lord Ellenborough CJ, gave judgment for the plaintiff, because the defendants had not inserted the usual clauses. A great number of insurance brokers gave evidence to show that where instructions were given to effect insurance 'at and from Tenerife', it was the invariable practice, even though no special orders were given, to insert in the policy a clause giving 'liberty to touch and stay at all or any of the Canary Islands', because ships seldom loaded the whole of their cargoes at Tenerife, but generally went to some of the other islands to complete their loading.

It was naturally vital for the broker to ensure that the commencement of the risk was properly described, for otherwise no money would be recoverable on the policy in the event of loss. This was the question to be decided in *Park v Hammond*.[12] The material facts in this case were that the plaintiff, who was a merchant at Malaga, wrote a letter to the defendant, who was an insurance broker in London, instructing him to insure goods from Gibraltar to Dublin, stating that he would himself take the risk on the goods from Malaga to Gibraltar Bay. The insurance was effected and the clause concerning the commencement of the risk was in the common printed form without alteration or addition: 'beginning the adventure upon the said goods and merchandise from the loading thereof aboard the same ship'. The ship sailed from Malaga, and arrived in Gibraltar Bay, but did not touch at Gibraltar itself because of plague, and went to Algeciras to put letters ashore. She then continued her voyage, and was totally lost off the coast of Ireland. The underwriters refused to pay on the policy, because the risk had not been insured against, so the plaintiff sued the defendant for negligence, and judgment was given for the plaintiff.

Gibbs CJ, who decided the case, said that the instructions were abundantly sufficient to show that the goods to be insured from Gibraltar had been loaded at Malaga. It was, therefore, the duty of the defendant to have stated this fact in the policy. It had been settled that a policy on goods 'beginning the adventure from the loading thereof aboard the said ship' without any addition, or 'aboard the said ship as above' only attached to goods loaded at the port which was the terminus a quo of the risk insured.[13] Insurance brokers were bound to know that this was the law, and to act accordingly for the benefit of their employers. They were expected to display competent skill as well as diligence in their business.

One of the earliest cases showing the course of a broker's business at the beginning of the nineteenth century is *Wake v Atty*,[14] and here the Court had to consider whether a broker had to be on permanent full-time duty in his office. An underwriter was sued on a policy of insurance, and one of the questions to be decided was whether a want of diligence on the part of the broker avoided the policy.

It appeared that the insurance broker first effected the policy upon the 'Monarch' on 15 October in consequence of instructions dated 13 October from Sunderland. He had not, however, completed it until 17 October, on which day

---

[12] (1815) 4 Camp 344.
[13] *Robertson v French* (1803) 4 East 130; *Spitta v Woodman* (1810) 2 Taunt 416; *Horneyer v Lushington* (1812) 15 East 46; *Mellish v Allnutt* (1813) 2 M&S 106.
[14] (1812) 4 Taunt 493.

at about 10 o'clock in the morning he left his house in Southampton Buildings, Chancery Lane, with the policy in his pocket, prepared for the execution by the underwriters, and went to the Royal Exchange where he procured the signature of the Lloyd's underwriter at about 11 o'clock, without having previously called at an office which he had in the Coal Exchange, and to which letters addressed to him on business were usually directed. It was his habit to go to the Royal Exchange and transact his business there on the way to his office. On arriving at his office on 17 October, he found there a letter which had come by that morning's post from his principal at Sunderland written on 15 October and stating that he had received on 14 October from the wife of the master of the 'Monarch' a letter, in which her husband stated that the ship had been captured 9 days after leaving Malta on the passage to Gibraltar. In directing the jury Mansfield CJ, left it to them to say whether the broker ought first to have gone to his office and got his letters, and whether the omission was 'gross and palpable negligence' in him. The jury decided that the broker was not negligent, and a new trial was asked for on the ground of misdirection. The underwriter contended that it would open a door to great frauds in the effecting of policies, if a broker might choose whether he would inspect his advices of the day or not before he transacted his business at Lloyd's, for in that case where he had reason to expect intelligence of losses, he would effect his insurances without reading his letters. In London, where persons were in the general habit of receiving letters from the country on subjects relating to their business, they ought to look at their letters before they proceeded to transact their affairs.

On the other hand, it was maintained that the broker had on 17 October no reason to expect any further instructions relative to the effecting of the policy. It was, therefore, no negligence on his part to proceed to its completion without searching his office for further advices. There was no reason to think the 'Monarch' a lost or missing ship. It was unreasonable to say that a merchant or broker must invariably open all his letters of the day, to however remote a part of the town they might be directed, before he could venture to transact any business.

Gibb J, saw no grounds for disturbing the verdict of the jury in finding that the broker was entitled to presume that he had all the information on which he was to effect the policy. Mansfield CJ, was of the same opinion, laying stress on the fact that the policy was begun a day or two before the underwriter signed it, and said that it was just by chance that the master of the ship happened to write to his wife about the loss, and that she had informed the plaintiff.

Effect of illegality of policy

It was early realised that a broker sued for negligence in not effecting a policy could plead the defence of illegality. That this might be so can be seen from *Webster v de Tastet*.[15] In this case the plaintiff had been hired to go as a mate in a ship from the coast of Africa to Havana for which he was to receive wages at the rate of £5 per month and three privilege slaves free of expense on the ship arriving at the port of sale. He directed the defendant, who was his agent in Liverpool, to get an insurance effected on the slaves, but he neglected to do so. The defendant contended that the plaintiff could not recover the value of the slaves, because they were not the legal subject of insurance. Counsel for the

---
[15] (1797) 7 Term Rep 157.

plaintiff admitted that if a policy had been effected, the plaintiff could not have recovered the value of the privilege slaves in an action against the underwriter, but contended that the plaintiff was entitled to damages because in point of fact these kinds of slaves were frequently the subject of insurance by mates at Liverpool, where the loss was always paid by the underwriters without disputing the question, but the Court of King's Bench decided against him.

The question of partial illegality had to be considered in the later case of *Glaser v Cowie*[16] where the principle on which the case was decided would be equally applicable to brokers. The defendants, who were merchants in London, received from the plaintiffs, who resided and carried on business at Stralaund, a letter dated 20 April 1810, and written by their managing clerk, which gave orders to effect an insurance according to the terms of a memorandum enclosed. The memorandum contained directions for an insurance on goods to the amount of £7,000, and particularly described the adventure to be insured, and said that it was to include loss by British as well as foreign capture, and at the conclusion (in a postscript written in German) it contained these words: 'Observe the premium on this value is also to be insured.' At the time of the receipt of this letter and its enclosure, the defendants also received another letter from the plaintiffs, enclosing a duplicate of the above memorandum, dated 23 April, and written by the same person as the former, in which he wrote thus: 'I confirm all what I said belonging to the insurance, and send you to-day the note in English to avoid all misunderstanding. I added *British* capture, though I know it is not lawful, but hope you will take care for an insurer with whom a policy of honour may be trusted as good and lawful.' The defendants upon the receipt of these letters effected an insurance in general terms against loss or capture by any power whatsoever, on the sum of £7,000, but not on the premium. It was objected by the defendants that the order for the insurance was illegal inasmuch as it contained a direction to include loss by British capture, and therefore could not be made a ground of action against the defendants for not complying with it. The jury gave the verdict for the plaintiffs. On appeal the order for a new trial was refused.

The case was heard before Lord Ellenborough CJ, who had presided at the Court of trial at Guildhall. He and the other Judges of the King's Bench were of the opinion that this omission was certainly a slip of the defendants, which probably arose from the direction respecting the insurance of the premium being in a foreign language, and occurring in a few words at the end of a letter of considerable length. But still, as the first letter contained a specific direction which was confirmed by the subsequent letter, the defendants were bound to attend to it. It was true that the plaintiffs said in their second letter that they added British capture, though they knew it was not lawful, but it was not a crime to insure against British capture, so as to make the whole policy illegal and void, as the Court seemed to have thought in *Lubbock v Potts*,[17] though perhaps such insurance would have been void pro tanto. In this respect the defendants conducted themselves with adroitness by effecting an insurance in general terms which would be construed to extend to such captures only as they might lawfully insure against.

---

[16] (1813) 1 M&S 52.
[17] (1806) 7 East 449.

Position where policy is void

The position where the broker has effected a void policy was considered in *T Cheshire & Co v Vaughan Bros & Co*.[18] The plaintiffs were Liverpool warehousemen, who used to receive cargoes of nitrate for warehousing at three ports. The trade at that time was under the control of the Government, so that ships which started for a particular port might be diverted to other ports or other countries. The warehousemen desired to insure the profits which they expected to make from the nitrate coming to their warehouse, by insuring the non-arrival of the ship by reason of her diversion in such an event. They accordingly gave the defendants, a firm of brokers, instructions to effect policies which would cover this loss. In view of the difficulty of proving the actual loss, because, when they knew the ship was not coming, they would naturally endeavour to fill the vacant space in their warehouse with other goods, and a somewhat complicated question might arise as to the amount of the loss, they intended that their policies should have on them a p p i clause whereby the mere production of the policy would be evidence of interest to the full amount mentioned in the policy.

The ship was diverted to Italy for economic reasons, and because full disclosure of the nature of the special risk had not been made to them, the underwriters refused to pay on the policy.[19] The plaintiffs thereupon sued the brokers for negligence. The defence raised was that they were not entitled to recover any damages, because the p p i policy was void under the Marine Insurance Act 1906, s 4,[20] and this contention was upheld by the Court of Appeal.

Scrutton LJ, observed that even if the contract were null and void, the strong probability was that, except for the defendants' negligence in not disclosing the risk, the plaintiffs would have recovered on the policy, as the underwriters would not have taken objection to the p p i clause. Nevertheless, in his view, the principle on which the case should be decided was that a contract, which was declared by the law to be null and void, could not be either directly or indirectly the basis of a legal claim. The Court left open the question whether such a contract might also be void on the ground of public policy. Bankes LJ, observed that it might be that the making of a p p i policy was against public policy in spite of the change that had been introduced by the repeal of the Marine Insurance Act 1745, which made such an assurance illegal, and the substitution of the Marine Insurance Act 1906, s 4, which merely made it void as a gaming and wagering contract, because the main evil which it was intended that the earlier Act should deal with as recited in the preamble was as great when the

---

[18] [1920] 3 KB 240.
[19] *Cheshire v Thompson* (1919) 24 Com Cas 114 at 198.
[20] Section 4 states:
   (1) 'Every contract of marine insurance by way of gaming or wagering is void.
   (2) A contract of marine insurance is deemed to be a gaming or wagering contract—
      (*a*) where the assured has not an insurable interest as defined by this Act, and the contract is entered into with no expectation of acquiring such interest; or
      (*b*) where the policy is made "interest or no interest"; or "without further proof of interest than the policy itself"; or "without benefit of salvage to the insurer" or subject to any other like term:
      Provided that where there is no possibility of salvage, a policy may be effected without benefit of salvage to the insurer.'

Act of 1906 was passed as it was in 1745. It might to some extent have changed its form, but the evil was the same evil, and the mere alteration of the language of the statute could not be readily accepted as indicating an alteration in the view of the legislature in reference to such a contract.[1]

3 Duty to carry out the transaction[2]

It was settled in *Smith v Lascelles*[3] that a broker could not be compelled by the principal to effect an insurance.

But Ashurst J, stated that if directions were given to a person to whom the application would be made in the usual course of business, and he did not give notice of dissent, he would probably be answerable for negligence, because he had deprived the other of any opportunity of applying elsewhere to procure the insurance.

An illustration of this rule is provided by *Corlett v Gordon*.[4] The plaintiff, being at Paramiribo in South America, enclosed a bill of lading in respect of some cotton addressed to the defendants, who were merchants in London, requesting them to effect an insurance to the full amount. The defendants had not done business with the plaintiff before, and had not promised to act as his consignees. For some reason they wished to decline to do so, and on receiving the bill of lading, they endorsed it over to one Major, a friend and creditor of the plaintiff. Major effected the insurance and received the goods, which never came into the possession of the defendants. Major afterwards became insolvent with the proceeds in his hands.

The plaintiff claimed the value of the goods, and judgment was given for him. Lord Ellenborough CJ, remarked that the defendants had no right to endorse the bill of lading. They could not devolve on another person the authority conferred upon them, and turn over the property to a stranger. It was difficult to say what they ought to have done; but he was quite clear that they were not justified in doing what they did. They could elect either to take or reject the bill of lading. If they took it, they were bound to take it according to the terms of the consignment by which they themselves were bound to insure and sell the goods. They appeared to have acted with a good conscience, but they were not correct in point of law.

If the broker cannot get the insurance effected in the usual way, is he bound to take any further steps to carry out his principal's instructions, and will he be liable if a loss results? This question came before the Court in *Smith v Cologan*.[5] Strictly speaking, this case concerns insurance agents, but the principle would be equally applicable to brokers. This was an action on the case for neglecting to effect an insurance on goods. The defendants, who were the correspondents of the plaintiffs, sent their broker, one Anderson, to Lloyd's Coffee House to get their orders effected. Anderson could not get the policy underwritten at the

---

[1] But see *Re London County Commercial Reinsurance Office Ltd* [1922] 2 Ch 67, where it was held that ppi policies were merely void, and that when the liquidator of the insuring company repudiated liability, the premium must be returned to the assured.
[2] See further, Ivamy, *General Principles of Insurance Law* (4th edn, 1979), p 550.
[3] (1788) 2 Term Rep 187.
[4] (1813) 3 Camp 472.
[5] (1788) 2 Term Rep 188n.

premium of 5 to 6 guineas per cent which he offered. This was not because the premium offered was too low for such a risk, but because the underwriters would not engage in the risk at all on account of the ship not being registered at Lloyd's.

Buller J, considered it immaterial to consider whether the defendants ought to have approached the Public Offices, i e the two Chartered Companies, because they went further in their quest for underwriters and their acts were adopted by the plaintiffs. The next step they took was to write to GK & Co, who were the shipowners living at Newcastle, thinking them the most likely persons to get the insurance effected, which they accordingly did. When the loss became known, the defendants endeavoured to get the policy out of the hands of GK & Co, and they applied repeatedly, but could not succeed. GK & Co maintained that they had other sums to recover on the same policy, and, therefore, could not let it go out of their hands. The only way in which the defendants might have recovered the policy was by bringing an action, and the Judge considered that their failure to do so did not constitute negligence. Later the matter was discussed at a meeting between the defendants and one of the plaintiffs who approved of their conduct, and considered Anderson as his agent. In these circumstances judgment was given for the defendants.

The decision appears unsatisfactory for two reasons. First, it leaves open the question whether the defendants would have been guilty of a breach of duty in approaching GK & Co at all in the event of non-ratification, and secondly, there is no evidence to show that the plaintiff who approved of the defendant's actions had the authority of the other plaintiffs to do so.

In some circumstances, a broker would be bound to effect the insurance if required to do so by a person residing abroad. Once more the case relates strictly to insurance agents, but is equally applicable to brokers. In 1786 Buller J, in *Wallace v Tellfair*[6] ruled that where a merchant residing in this country had accepted an order for insurance, and limited a broker to too small a premium in consequence of which no insurance could be procured, he was liable to make good the loss to the foreign merchant. The same Judge enlarged on this principle 2 years later in *Smith v Lascelles*[7] in which he said that there were three instances in which such an order must be obeyed.

First, where a merchant abroad has effects in the hands of his correspondent here, he has a right to expect that he will obey an order to insure, because he is entitled to call his money out of the other's hands when and in what manner he pleases. Secondly where the merchant abroad has no effects in the hands of his correspondent, yet if the course of dealing between them be such that the one has been used to send orders for insurance, and the other to comply with them, the former has a right to expect that his order for insurance will still be obeyed, unless the latter gives him notice to discontinue that course of dealing. Thirdly, if the merchant abroad sends bills of lading to his correspondent here, he may engraft on them an order to insure as the implied condition on which the bills of lading shall be accepted which the other must obey, if he accepts them, for it is one entire transaction.[8]

---

[6] (1786) 2 Term Rep 188n.
[7] (1788) 2 Term Rep 187.
[8] See *Callender v Oelrichs* (1838) 5 Bing NC 58.

CHAPTER 6

Non-disclosure[1]

In his book on 'Marine Insurance' Park said:

> 'Insurance is a contract of speculation. The facts upon which the risk is to be computed, lie, for the most part, within the knowledge of the assured only. The underwriter must therefore rely upon him for all necessary information; and must trust to him that he will conceal nothing, so as to make him form a wrong estimate. If a mistake happens, without any fraudulent intention, still the contract is annulled, because the risk is not the same which the underwriter intended. Good faith forbids either party by concealing what he privately knows to draw the other into a bargain from his ignorance of the fact and his belief to the contrary.'

In the Marine Insurance Act 1906 the duty of good faith is expressed in s 17 in the following terms:

> 'A contract of marine insurance is a contract based upon the utmost good faith, and, if the utmost good faith be not observed by either party, the contract may be avoided by the other party.'

Section 17 of the Act restates the long established duty of the utmost good faith in contracts of marine insurance. It is not necessary, even if it were possible, to go into degrees of good faith or the question what degree of good faith may apply to other contracts. It is enough that much more than an absence of bad faith is required of both parties to all contracts of insurance. The general principle is stated in s 17 because the special sections which follow are not exhaustive. The sections concerned must be read in the light of s 17 and all their references to insurer and assured follow the statutory duty of utmost good faith on each party.[2]

A DUTY TO DISCLOSE MATERIAL FACTS

1 Disclosure by the assured himself

Section 18(1) of the Marine Insurance Act 1906 states:

> 'Subject to the provisions of this section, the assured must disclose to the insurer, before the contract is concluded, every material circumstance which is known to the assured, and the assured is deemed to know every circumstance which, in the ordinary course of business, ought to be known by him. If the assured fails to make such disclosure, the insurer may avoid the contract.'

---

[1] See further, Ivamy, *General Principles of Insurance Law* (4th edn, 1979), pp 132–170.
[2] *Container Transport International Inc and Reliance Group Inc v Oceanus Mutual Underwriting Association (Bermuda) Ltd* [1984] 1 Lloyd's Rep 476 at 525, CA (per Stephenson LJ), where the learned Lord Justice quoted with approval the statement in Chalmers' *Marine Insurance Act 1906* (9th edn, by E R Hardy Ivamy, 1983), p 24. The obligation of utmost good faith continues after the execution of the contract: *Black King Shipping Corpn v Massie, The Litsion Pride* (1984) Times, 17 December, QBD (Com Ct), where the duty of good faith was held to apply to the requirement to give notice to the insurers under the war risk trading warranties and to the making of claims.

Section 18(2) goes on to provide:

> 'Every circumstance is material which would influence the judgment of a prudent insurer in fixing the premium, or determining whether he will take the risk.'

It is to be emphasized that not only must material circumstances known by the assured be disclosed but also material circumstances which he is deemed to know.

Thus, in *Berger and Light Diffusers Pty Ltd v Pollock*[3] the fact that a bill of lading in respect of some steel injection moulds was 'claused' in that it stated that the moulds were 'unprotected', 'secondhand' and 'insufficiently packed' was deemed to be known to the assured, for it was known by their shipping agents.[4]

The non-disclosure may be either fraudulent or innocent, i e the information may be designedly withheld, or the party not making the disclosure may regard it as unimportant and not necessary to be disclosed. But in each case the result is the same. The contract is voidable at the option of the insurer.

The wider the risk the greater the burden on the assured to make full disclosure of material circumstances. A policy 'on ship or ships', or 'on steamer or steamers', or a policy on goods with an indorsement of different lines of steamers on which the goods insured may be carried, requires greater care on the part of the assured than a policy on goods to be shipped on a named ship. His duty in both cases is the same, but the possibility of innocent non-disclosure is much greater in the one case than in the other.

Mere disclosure of part of the information will not avail the assured if that which remains undisclosed is found to be material.[5]

The same principle applies to contracts of reinsurance. Thus, in *China Traders' Insurance Co v Royal Exchange Assurance Corpn*[6] Vaughan Williams LJ, said:[7]

> 'A reinsurer is himself an assured who takes upon himself, not only before but after the contract comes into operation, to act with the greatest good faith.'

All information with regard to material facts which have been received must be disclosed, even if there are good grounds for doubting the correctness of the information. It is no defence to say that the source of the information was unreliable, nor will the assured be protected if the information turns out in the event to be untrue. His duty is to disclose the facts and their source, and to leave the underwriter to form his own opinion as to the correctness of the report, and its effect on the proposed contract.

Thus, in *De Costa v Scandret*[8] Lord Macclesfield LC, said:

> 'The insured has not dealt fairly with the insurers in this case; he ought to have disclosed to them what intelligence he had of the ship's being in danger, and which might induce him at least to fear that it was lost, though he had no certain account of it.'

Similarly, in *Lynch v Hamilton*[9] Sir James Mansfield CJ, said:[10]

---

[3] [1973] 2 Lloyd's Rep 442, QBD, Com Ct.
[4] See the judgment of Kerr J, ibid, at 461.
[5] *Kirby v Smith* (1818) 1 B&Ald 672; *Westbury v Aberdein* (1837) 2 M&W 267.
[6] [1898] 2 QB 187.
[7] Ibid, at 193.
[8] (1723) 2 P Wms 170.
[9] (1810) 3 Taunt 37.
[10] Ibid, at 44. See also, *Lynch v Dunsford* (1811) 14 East 494; *Seaman v Fonereau* (1743) 2 Stra 1183; *Morrison v Universal Marine Insurance Co* (1873) LR 8 Exch 197.

> 'I cannot distinguish this from the case of *Seaman v Fonereau*,[11] where a letter received stated that the vessel insured had been seen in the night leaky, and had disappeared the next day, and though that rumour was false, inasmuch as the ship kept her course and was afterwards captured, it was held that for want of that disclosure the underwriters were not liable.'

The existence of an open cover between the assured's brokers and the insurers does not relieve the assured of his duty under s 18(1) to disclose material circumstances which are known to him.[12]

2 Disclosure by agent effecting insurance

The duty of making a full disclosure of material circumstances lies on the assured, whether the insurance is effected by himself or by an agent.[13]

The agent must be as diligent in disclosure as his principal, and all persons are connecting links—either as owners or agents—between the thing insured and the insurer, and must pass their knowledge from one to another with the utmost assiduity until the information reaches the insurer.

There may only be the owner contracting directly with the insurer; there may be the owner and his broker, or the shipping agent, owner and broker, and the chain may include the master of the ship.

The failure of any of these to do his duty may involve non-disclosure of a material fact caused either by the owner directly, or by an agent for whose acts or omissions he is responsible. Neither fraud nor neglect on the part of any agent will or ought to excuse the principal, who will be held responsible for his representatives in this respect. If the law were otherwise, the door would be open to dishonest practices of the worst kind.[14]

Section 19 of the Marine Insurance Act 1906 states:

> 'Subject to the provisions of the preceding section as to circumstances which need not be disclosed, where an insurance is effected for the assured by an agent, the agent must disclose to the insurer—
>
> *a* every material circumstance which is known to himself, and an agent to insure is deemed to know every circumstance which in the ordinary course of business ought to be known by, or to have been communicated to, him; and
>
> *b* every material circumstance which the assured is bound to disclose, unless it come to his knowledge too late to communicate it to the agent.'

Some agents so far represent the principal that in all respects their acts and intentions and their knowledge may truly be said to be the acts and intentions and the knowledge of the principal. An early Scots case in 1785 indicates that when a clerk of the assured knew that a loss had occurred, his knowledge was deemed to be that of the principal.[15] Again, in 1813 in *Gladstone v King*[16] the master of a ship was considered to be under a duty to communicate information about damage she had sustained. Similarly, in 1867 in *Proudfoot v Montefiore*,[17]

---

[11] (1743) 2 Stra 1183.
[12] *Berger and Light Diffusers Pty Ltd v Pollock* [1973] 2 Lloyd's Rep 442, QBD (Com Ct). (See the judgment of Kerr J, ibid, at 460.)
[13] See further, Ivamy, *General Principles of Insurance Law* (4th edn, 1979), pp 579–583.
[14] *Fitzherbert v Mather* (1785) 1 Term Rep 12; *Proudfoot v Montefiore* (1867) LR 2 QB 511; *Stribley v Imperial Marine Insurance Co* (1876) 1 QBD 507; *Blackburn, Low & Co v Vigors* (1887) 12 App Cas 531.
[15] *Stewart v Dunlop* (1785) 4 Bro Parl Cas 483, HL.
[16] (1813) 1 M&S 35; *Stribley v Imperial Marine Insurance Co* (1876) 1 QBD 507.
[17] (1867) LR 2 QB 511. See also, *Fitzherbert v Mather*, supra; *Bolivia Republic v Indemnity Mutual Marine Assurance Co Ltd* [1909] 1 KB 785.

where the general agent of a shipowner knew that the ship was lost and purposely refrained from communicating with the owner until the latter had effected the insurance, his guilty knowledge was considered to be that of his employer.

In *Bolivia Republic v Indemnity Mutual Marine Assurance Co Ltd*[18] a cargo was insured for a voyage up the Amazon from Para to Puerto Alonzo and/or other places on the River Acre and in that district. It consisted of stores for the Bolivian Government troops, who were in that area for the purpose of resisting an expedition which was seeking to overthrow the Government and establish a republic. The cargo was seized when the vessel was intercepted by the expedition. The agent of the insured knew that the expedition was actually being fitted out for the purpose of intercepting the cargo, but did not disclose this fact to the insurers when effecting the policy. Pickford J, held that the fact was material, and that since it had not been disclosed, the insurers were entitled to avoid liability under the policy.

He observed:[19]

> 'The fact that an expedition was actually at that moment being fitted out for the very purpose of intercepting the goods shipped by the Bolivian Government upon the *Labrea*, it seems to me, must be material to the mind of anybody who was considering whether he would effect an insurance upon these goods. It may be that the insurer ought to be taken to have had knowledge of there being disturbances in the territory of Colonias or El Acre—I do not decide, but I will assume that. But even assuming he had, it seems to me that the additional fact that there was at that moment an expedition fitting out for the purpose of intercepting the goods was an additional fact which he cannot be taken to have had knowledge of, and a very material fact. I have had evidence that it was material; and I agree that it was a most material fact to be disclosed.'

His Lordship also considered the situation which arose under an open cover which could be used for the goods of different owners, and said:[20]

> 'It seems to me if a person opens a cover which may be used for the goods of different owners, and he knows facts which are material to the insurance of the goods of one and not material to the insurance of the goods of another—though possibly when he declares the goods to which the facts are not material, it may not be necessary for him to disclose these facts which are material to the goods of the other—as soon as he uses that cover for the purpose of insuring goods, to which the facts he knows at the time of opening the cover are material, it is his duty to disclose them, and he cannot say that the first declaration he made upon the cover was in respect of goods to which the facts are not material, and as the date of the initialling of the slip has to be looked at as the date at which the concealment must take place to avoid the policy when goods are afterwards declared upon it, to which the facts are material, he is not bound to disclose them, and his policy is not void.'

But to lay down an abstract proposition of law that every agent, no matter how limited the scope of his agency, would bind his principal by his acts is on the face of it absurd. The nature of the agency must be such as to place the agent under a duty to communicate the information to his principal.

Accordingly, in *Wilson v Salamandra Assurance Co of St Petersburg*[1] it was held that members of Lloyd's were not affected by information contained in surveys by Lloyd's agents abroad.

---

[18] (1908) 99 LT 394, KBD.
[19] Ibid, at 398.
[20] Ibid, at 398.
[1] (1903) 88 LT 96.

In *Blackburn Low & Co v Vigors*[2] the plaintiffs instructed a broker to insure an overdue ship. Whilst acting for the plaintiffs, the broker received information material to the risk and did not communicate it to them, but no policy was actually effected by him. Later the plaintiffs gave instructions to another broker, who effected the policy with the defendant. Both the plaintiffs and the second broker acted in good faith, and the question was whether the knowledge of the first broker would affect the policy and enable the defendant to treat it as voidable.

The House of Lords decided that the policy was not vitiated on the ground that the first broker was not one of those agents whose duty it was to give information to the principal. The basis for the decision was that the responsibility of an innocent assured for the non-communication of facts which happened to be within the private knowledge of persons whom he merely employed to obtain an insurance on a particular risk ought not to be carried beyond the person who actually made the contract on his behalf. Lord Watson considered that there was no authority whatever for enlarging his responsibility beyond that limit, unless it were to be found in the decisions relating to captains and ship's agents; and these cases did not appear to him to have any analogy to the case of agents employed to effect a policy. He considered that there was a material difference in the relations of those two classes of agents to their employer. The one class was specially employed for the purpose of communicating to him the very facts which the law required him to divulge to his insurer, the other was employed not to procure or furnish information concerning the ship, but to effect an insurance. There was also an important difference in the position of those two classes with respect to the insurer. He was entitled to contract, and did contract on the basis that all material facts connected with the vessel insured known to the agent employed for that purpose had been communicated by him in due course to his principal. So also when an agent to insure was brought into contact with an insurer, the latter transacted on the footing that the agent had disclosed every material circumstance within his personal knowledge, whether it was known to his principal or not; but it could not be reasonably suggested that the insurer relied to any extent on the private information possessed by persons of whose existence he presumably knew nothing.

But the opposite conclusion was reached on the facts of a case decided in the next year by the Divisional Court,—*Blackburn v Haslam*[3]—and with good reason. In this case a firm of underwriters endeavoured to effect a reinsurance policy on an overdue ship, and gave instructions to some Glasgow brokers to that effect. The Glasgow brokers wired to their London agents to insure at a rate which their principals had named. While the negotiations were going on, the Glasgow brokers received information that the ship, the subject of the insurance, had been lost. But such information was given in confidence, and for that reason was not communicated to their principals. The principals afterwards effected the reinsurance through the London agents of the Glasgow firm. It was held that there had been merely a handing over of the negotiations by the Glasgow brokers to their principals, and, therefore, the non-disclosure by the Glasgow brokers of the loss of the ship was non-disclosure by their

---

[2] (1887) 12 App Cas 531, HL.
[3] (1888) 21 QBD 144. See also, *Webster v Foster* (1795) 1 Esp 407.

principals, and the reinsurance was voidable at the instance of the reinsurers.

Pollock B, declared that if the view which the court had taken of the facts and of the law which arose out of them were the true view, his judgment in no way conflicted with the decision in *Blackburn Low & Co v Vigors*.[4] Although the opinion was expressed in that case that it was not the duty of the agents to communicate to their principals the information which they had received, he considered that opinion as applying to the particular facts before the House which showed that before the negotiations for the policy sued upon had commenced, all connection of the plaintiff with his former brokers had ceased. He could not suppose it would be intended to apply to the facts proved in the present case, which showed that so far from the connections between the principals and their agents ceasing, the brokers used the name of the principals to continue the negotiations, and the principals adopted the act and themselves continued and carried out what their brokers had commenced.

If a material circumstance comes to the knowledge of the assured soon after he has given instructions to effect an insurance, it becomes his duty to communicate at once with his broker in order that the new fact may be laid before the insurer. The assured is under a duty to use the same diligence in relieving the insurer of an increase in the risk as he would employ to procure a lower rate or premium if the new fact would entitle him to stipulate for a reduction.

If news of loss has reached him, he must communicate his news to the insurer with as much alacrity as he would display in countermanding the insurance if he heard of the safe arrival of the vessel and the consequent termination of the risk.[5]

Whether the material circumstance comes to the assured's knowledge too late to communicate it to the agent is, of course, a question of fact.[6]

B THE TEST OF MATERIALITY

The test of materiality is laid down by s 18(2) of the Marine Insurance Act 1906 which states:

> 'Every circumstance is material which would influence the judgment of a prudent insurer in fixing the premium, or determining whether he will take the risk.'

In some cases the premium paid is an index to the nature of the risk which was assumed by the insurer, and may be of assistance in determining whether the fact in question was disclosed or not.[7]

The meaning of the term 'prudent insurer' was considered by Atkin J, in *Associated Oil Carriers Ltd v Union Insurance Society of Canton Ltd*.[8] In this case the

---

[4] Supra.
[5] *Fitzherbert v Mather* (1785) 1 Term Rep 12; *Proudfoot v Montefiore* (1867) LR 2 QB 511; *London General Insurance Co v General Marine Underwriters' Association* [1921] 1 KB 104.
[6] *Container Transport International Inc and Reliance Group Inc v Oceanus Mutual Underwriting Association (Bermuda) Ltd* [1984] 1 Lloyd's Rep 476, CA, where it was held that it was not too late for the assured to have communicated their knowledge of the figures relating to a previous claim. (See the judgment of Parker LJ, ibid, at 518.)
[7] *Bridges v Hunter* (1813) 1 M&S 15; *Simeon v Bazett* (1813) 2 M&S 94; *Freeland v Glover* (1806) 7 East 457; *Mackintosh v Marshall* (1843) 11 M&W 116.
[8] [1917] 2 KB 184.

question was whether it was material on 31 July 1914 to disclose the fact that the charterers of a vessel were of German nationality. This fact had been held material in *British and Foreign Marine Insurance Co Ltd v Samuel Sanday & Co*,[9] which had been decided by the House of Lords in 1916, but his Lordship observed:[10]

> '[Counsel] said that a prudent insurer within the meaning of the section must be taken to know the law as laid down in *Sanday*'s case. Knowing so much, he would clearly have been influenced. I think that this standard of prudence indicates an insurer much too bright and good for human nature's daily food. There seems no reason to impute to the insurer a higher degree of knowledge and foresight than that reasonably possessed by the more experienced and intelligent insurers carrying on business in that market at that time. The evidence satisfies me that if the standard of prudence is the ideal one contended for by [Counsel], there were in July 1914, no prudent insurers in London, or if there were, they were not to be found in the usual places where one would seek for them.'

The word 'influence' in s 18(2) means that the disclosure is one which would have had an impact on the formation of the insurer's opinion and on his decision-making process in relation to the matters covered by that sub-section.[11]

In determining whether there has been a non-disclosure within the meaning of the sub-section the yardstick is the prudent insurer and not the particular insurer.[12] There is no requirement that the particular insurer should have been induced to take the risk or charge a lower premium than he would otherwise have done as a result of the non-disclosure.[13]

The Court cannot choose one prudent insurer rather than another. The very choice of a prudent insurer as the yardstick indicates that the test intended is one which can sensibly be answered in relation to prudent insurers in general. It is possible to say that prudent insurers in general would consider a particular circumstance as bearing on the risk and exercising an influence on their judgment towards declining the risk or loading the premium.[14]

C CIRCUMSTANCES WHICH NEED NOT BE DISCLOSED

Section 18(3) of the Marine Insurance Act 1906 states:

> 'In the absence of inquiry the following circumstances need not be disclosed, namely:
>
> a any circumstance which diminishes the risk;
> b any circumstance which is known or presumed to be known to the insurer. The insurer is presumed to know matters of common notoriety or knowledge, and matters which an insurer in the ordinary course of his business, as such, ought to know;
> c any circumstance as to which information is waived by the insurer;
> d any circumstance which it is superfluous to disclose by reason of any express or implied warranty.'[15]

---

[9] [1916] 1 AC 650, HL.
[10] [1917] 2 KB 184 at 192.
[11] *Container Transport International Inc and Reliance Group Inc v Oceanus Mutual Underwriting Association (Bermuda) Ltd* [1984] 1 Lloyd's Rep 476 at 492, CA (per Kerr LJ).
[12] Ibid, at 510 (per Parker LJ).
[13] Ibid, at 510 (per Parker LJ).
[14] Ibid, at 511 (per Parker LJ).
[15] As to warranties, see pp 280–314, post.

1 Facts tending to diminish the risk

In *Carter v Boehm*[16] Lord Mansfield illustrated this point when he said:[17]

> 'The underwriter need not be told what lessens the risque agreed and understood to be run by the express terms of the policy. . . . If he insures for three years, he need not be told any circumstance to shew it may be over in two; or if he insures a voyage, with liberty of deviation, he need not be told what tends to shew there will be no deviation.'

2 Facts within the actual or presumed knowledge of the insurer

The insurer is presumed to know and to contract with reference to every trade usage which may operate on the subject-matter of the insurance.

Thus, the assured is under no duty to disclose:

i   The mode of loading at the ports mentioned in the policy.[18]
ii The mode of unloading at the port of destination.[19]
iii That stowage on deck may in certain cases be in accordance with the usage of the trade.[20]
iv The general nature and circumstances of the branch of trade to which the policy relates.[1]
v   The course of the old East India Trade, the terms of the charter-party, and the destination of India ships.[2]

Even if the trade is newly established, the usages are presumed to be known to the insurer.[3]

The insurer is also presumed to know that war is imminent,[4] or that a state of war exists in some remote part of the globe.[5]

A reinsurer is presumed to know that the original insurance policy may contain a 'continuation' clause.[6]

It would, however, seem that the facts of which knowledge is presumed must be of recent date, for it has been held that previous knowledge of a matter which was at one time notorious does not relieve the assured from referring to it and recalling it to the mind of the insurer, if it is material.[7]

In *Bolivia Republic v Indemnity Mutual Marine Assurance Co Ltd*,[8] which concerned a cargo insured for a voyage up the Amazon, Pickford J, assumed but did not decide that the insurers ought to have had knowledge of there being disturbances in the territory of Colonias or El Acre, near where the goods were being carried.[9]

---

[16] (1766) 3 Burr 1905.
[17] Ibid, at 1910.
[18] *Moxon v Atkins* (1812) 3 Camp 200.
[19] *Stewart v Bell* (1821) 5 B&Ald 238; *Gould v Oliver* (1837) 4 Bing NC 134.
[20] *Da Costa v Edmunds* (1815) 4 Camp 142.
[1] *Vallance v Dewar* (1808) 1 Camp 503; *North British Fishing Boat Insurance Co Ltd v Starr* (1922) 13 LlL Rep 206.
[2] *Salvador v Hopkins* (1765) 3 Burr 1707; *Grant v Paxton* (1809) 1 Taunt 463.
[3] *Noble v Kennoway* (1780) 2 Doug KB 510 at 512; *Ougier v Jennings* (1800) 1 Camp 505n.
[4] *Planché v Fletcher* (1779) 1 Doug KB 251.
[5] *Schloss Bros v Stevens* [1906] 2 KB 665; *Bolivia Republic v Indemnity Mutual Marine Assurance Co* [1909] 1 KB 785.
[6] *Charlesworth v Faber* (1900) 5 Com Cas 408.
[7] *Bates v Hewitt* (1867) LR 2 QB 595.
[8] (1908) 99 LT 394, KBD.
[9] Ibid, at 398.

In *Cantiere Meccanico Brindisino v Janson*,[10] which concerned the insurance of a floating dock for a voyage from Avonmouth to Brindisi, Buckley LJ, said that the insurers must be presumed to know that a dry dock was not an ocean-going craft, and that unless she had been built with a view to or had been strengthened for a voyage, she was not seaworthy.[11]

An insurer is not deemed to know the contents of a casualty slip relating to a vessel which at the time he receives the information would have had no interest to him at all.[12]

Thus, in *London General Insurance Co Ltd v General Marine Underwriters' Association Ltd*[13] the plaintiffs on 24 September insured 'lost or not lost' the cargo of a vessel which was on a voyage from Italy to the United Kingdom. On the evening of that day she put into port with her cargo on fire. Notice of the fire was posted on the casualty board at Lloyd's on 25 September at 10 a m. At about 4 p m on that day the plaintiffs effected a reinsurance policy on the cargo 'lost or not lost' with the defendants. Neither the plaintiffs nor the defendants knew of the casualty at the date of effecting the reinsurance. The plaintiffs claimed for a loss under the reinsurance policy, but the defendants contended that the occurrence of the fire should have been disclosed to them, and that consequently they were not liable. The plaintiffs, however, maintained that since the defendants ought to have known in the course of their business the contents of casualty slips, this was a circumstance which they were not bound to communicate to them.

The Court of Appeal[14] held that the defendants were not deemed to know the contents of casualty slips about a vessel which, at the time they received the information, would have had no interest to them at all, and that therefore the plaintiffs' contention failed.

Lord Sterndale MR, said:[15]

> 'There remains another point, and that is this: It is said that if that is true of the plaintiffs, it is equally true of the defendants, and, as they ought to have known in the course of their business the contents of the casualty slips, it was a circumstance which the plaintiffs were not bound to communicate to them. The learned Judge has taken the view—again I do not see my way to differ from it—that the defendants were not upon the risk in the *Vigo*. I think that is right, and he has then taken this—that you could not expect the defendants, supposing they had looked at the casualty slips, to have present to their minds always the information about a vessel which at the time they got the information, if they did get it, would have had no interest to them at all.'

In *North British Fishing Boat Insurance Co Ltd v Starr*[16] an insurance company claimed on a reinsurance policy in respect of a motor fishing vessel which was destroyed by fire. The reinsurer refused to pay the claim on the ground that the company had not disclosed a material fact,[17] viz that there had been an exceptional increase in the number and amount of fire losses among motor fishing vessels insured by the company.

---

[10] (1912) 107 LT 281, CA.
[11] Ibid, at 287.
[12] *London General Insurance Co Ltd v General Marine Underwriters' Association Ltd* (1920) 124 LT 67, CA.
[13] (1920) 124 LT 67, CA.
[14] Lord Sterndale MR, Warrington and Younger LJJ.
[15] (1920) 124 LT at 70.
[16] (1922) 13 LlL Rep 206, KBD.
[17] The evidence as to materiality is set out ibid, at 206–209.

Rowlatt J, held that the defence failed because under s 18(3)(b) of the Marine Insurance Act 1906 the assured was under no duty to disclose facts which the insurer knew or ought to know. In the present case the reinsurer ought to know the losses which were taking place in motor fishing vessels.

His Lordship observed:[18]

> 'I must look at the underwriter in this case as a person doing the business of insuring ships and as necessarily conversant with the course of losses affecting particular classes of ships. What he is not bound to know in the ordinary course of his business are particular circumstances specially affecting ships or lines of ships, and specially affecting some limited number of ships.
>
> In my judgment this action must succeed and the defence fails, because I think that whether motor boats fishing round the coast of England as a whole are or are not suffering losses making a particular premium worth while taking is a matter which the underwriter ought to find out, or is supposed to know, because it is his business to know that class of thing, and, therefore, the assured is not bound to go into these matters or disclose these matters when he comes with his business.'

In *George Cohen, Sons & Co v Standard Marine Insurance Co Ltd*[19] an obsolete battleship was insured whilst being towed from Chatham to Brake (in Germany) where she was to be broken up. She went ashore off the Dutch coast. The insurers sought to avoid liability on the ground that the assured had failed to disclose a material fact, i e that the vessel would have no steam power with which to assist her steering gear.

It was held in the King's Bench Division that there was no need for the assured to disclose the fact, for it was a matter of common notoriety that vessels of this type were sent to sea in this condition.

Roche J, said:[20]

> 'Here, having regard to the evidence as to the frequency with which vessels of this character, dismantled warships, are sent to sea without any steam at all, and having regard to the knowledge that the underwriters certainly had that the vessel was not going to have steam for the main purposes of the voyage and for propulsion, I think it was a matter which they must have known, or must be presumed to have known. Whenever one of these vessels goes to sea, and apparently their number has been considerable, casualties have been not unknown, and, apparently also from the evidence before me, underwriters have interested themselves in these matters. I think they must be presumed or taken to have known that a vessel such as this, at any rate, might be going to sea in the condition in which the *Prince George* went to sea. In those circumstances the inference that I draw is that they waived—they asked about a good many of the things—disclosure of any further facts as to what was proposed to be done with regard to the *Prince George* before she went to sea.'

One of the issues[1] in *Piper v Royal Exchange Assurance*[2] was whether the insurers should have known any facts material to the actual value of a yacht, which was excessively overvalued to the knowledge of the assured. When she was damaged by fire, the insurers sought to disclaim liability on the ground that the assured was guilty of non-disclosure of material facts, but the assured contended that he was excused from disclosing them by reason of s 18(3)(b) of the Marine Insurance Act 1906.

---

[18] Ibid, at 210.
[19] (1925) 21 LlL Rep 30, KBD.
[20] Ibid, at 38.
[1] Another issue was whether the assured knew that the yacht was excessively overvalued. As to this aspect of the case, see pp 61–62, post.
[2] (1932) 44 LlL Rep 103, KBD.

Roche J, held that the facts were not deemed to be known to the insurers, and that the assured's contention failed. He observed:[3]

> 'With regard to that, various comments have been made, and perhaps I have made some of them, on the organisation of the defendant's business. The fact is that some things are known to one department which are not known to another, and some things were not known to people who were underwriting the later insurance which might well, under a better business organisation—which, I understand has now been introduced—have been known to them, but they were not the facts which I have found ought to have been the subject-matter of disclosure on this occasion. They knew from the reports which they had received both from the voyage damage and in respect of the stranding damage that there were defects in this ship which would affect her value. Of course, she was not valued at the value of a new ship, which would be many times more than £2,500, and there was little to show that a number, at any rate, of those defects of which they had been made aware were not remedied by subsequent repair, and certainly what they did not know was of the progress of the deterioration on board the ship, evidenced by her manifest unsaleability and evidenced by the resolution of the plaintiff himself to make the best he could of her for himself, whatever that might be, instead of continuing to put her upon the market. I am not saying, and it was never contended on the part of the defendants that those were facts which ought to have been disclosed eo nomine or specifically to the underwriters, but what was said was that this deterioration and these facts with regard to her value were matters which were known to the assured and were not known to the underwriters. I think that is true, and, therefore, I hold that the plaintiff is not saved by the provisions of s 18(3)(b) of the Marine Insurance Act 1906.'

In *St Margaret's Trust Ltd v Navigators and General Marine Insurance Co Ltd*[4] the insurance company knew the age, type, condition and agreed value of a ketch, and the intended manner in which she was going to be laid up. Morris J, held that it was unnecessary for the assured to describe the neglected state of her topsides caulking.

The learned Judge observed:[5]

> 'In the present case, the defendant company had insured this craft when she was owned by the Hardway Company. They had insured her without survey when she was in a mud berth at Fareham Creek, and they had insured her without survey after she was moved to deep water moorings at Gosport. When asked for quotation assuming that the craft was to be used as a houseboat, they said: "Our quotation then is 2 per cent, provided that there is a satisfactory survey on the underwater part of the hull and the moorings." Afterwards the defendants were told that the quotation was not sought for the craft to be used as a houseboat, but it was sought for her when in mud berth and for a time when she would be out of commission, during which time she would be worked on by Mr Griffin, who was an experienced man in connection with yachts. The defendants knew that the *Vishela* was an old craft; that she was 43 years old.'

In *Pacific Queen Fisheries v L Symes: The Pacific Queen*[6] the United States Court of Appeals, Ninth Circuit,[7] held that an altered method of handling gasoline on board vessels of the same type as the vessel insured was not a matter which the insurer was deemed to know, and was therefore a matter which the assured was under a duty to disclose.

In *Soya GmbH Mainz Kommanditgesellschaft v White*[8] cargoes of soya beans were loaded on the vessels 'Welsh City' and 'Corfu Island' at an Indonesian port. They arrived at Antwerp in a heated condition. When the assured claimed under the policy, the insurers repudiated liability on the ground of non-

---

[3] Ibid, at 120.
[4] (1949) 82 LlL Rep 752, KBD.
[5] Ibid, at 762.
[6] [1963] 2 Lloyd's Rep 201, (US 9th Cir).
[7] Circuit Judge Pope, Circuit Judge Barnes and Circuit Judge Hamley.
[8] [1982] 1 Lloyd's Rep 136, CA.

disclosure of a material fact, i e that a similar cargo on the 'Teviotbank' had been shipped earlier and had also arrived heated. The Court of Appeal[9] held that the defence failed and that there would be judgment for the assured for, on the evidence, the insurers had been told of the damage suffered by the cargo on board the 'Teviotbank' and that that damage was insignificant and negligible.[10]

3 Facts as to which information is waived

If the assured satisfies the requirements of the contract by acting honestly in his disclosures, and by showing an endeavour to treat the insurer fairly, he will not be held responsible for not explicitly disclosing a fact which afterwards turns out to be material, if the information which he has given discloses sufficient to warn the insurer that such a fact existed.

If the disclosure was one that should have put a careful man of business upon inquiry, the requirements of the contract will have been fulfilled. The fact that no such inquiry was made by the other party makes no difference, for he is presumed to have waived the need for specific information on the point in question.

In *Carter v Boehm*[11] Lord Mansfield said:[12]

> 'The insured need not mention what the underwriter ought to know, what he takes upon himself the knowledge of, or what he waives being informed of.'

Similarly, in *Asfar & Co v Blundell*[13] Mathew J, briefly stated the rule thus:[14]

> 'It is a well settled principle of insurance law that underwriters are not entitled to be told what they waive all enquiry about. In this particular case they were told that there was a charter, and if they wanted to learn the contents of that charter, they had only to enquire.'

If, however, it appears from the evidence that it has become the established practice to disclose a certain fact when it exists, non-disclosure of that fact cannot be taken to be waived merely by the omission to inquire whether it exists or not.[15]

In *Cantiere Meccanico Brindisino v Janson*[16] a floating dock in tow of two tugs was insured for a voyage from Avonmouth to Brindisi. The policy contained a clause stating 'seaworthiness admitted'. The dock was lost on the voyage and the assured claimed for a total loss. The insurers refused to indemnify the assured on the ground that there had been a failure by them to disclose a material fact, viz that the dock had not been specially strengthened for the voyage.

---

[9] Waller, Donaldson and O'Connor LJJ.
[10] See the judgment of Donaldson LJ: [1982] 1 Lloyd's Rep 136 at 142. The case subsequently went to the House of Lords on another point, i e the prima facie rule in the Marine Insurance Act 1906, s 55(2)(c) that the insurer was not liable for loss by inherent vice had been effectively excluded by the words of the policy. See pp 255–256, post.
[11] (1766) 3 Burr 1905.
[12] Ibid, at 1910.
[13] [1895] 2 QB 196.
[14] Ibid, at 202. Cf *Bates v Hewitt* (1867) LR 2 QB 595.
[15] *Mann, Macneal and Steeves Ltd v Capital and Counties Marine Insurance Co* [1921] 2 KB 300; *Greenhill v Federal Insurance Co* [1927] 1 KB 65.
[16] [1912] 3 KB 452, CA.

The Court of Appeal[17] held that the action succeeded. The insurers, by the use of the clause 'seaworthiness admitted', had waived any duty on the assured's part to disclose the want of special strengthening.

In *Mann, Macneal and Steeves Ltd v General Marine Underwriters*[18] a wooden ship was insured for a voyage from America to France and back again. Part of the cargo which she had contracted to carry from America consisted of petrol, but the assured did not disclose this fact. It was held by the Court of Appeal[19] that in the circumstances of the case the insurers had waived disclosure of the contract by not making inquiry.

Bankes LJ, said:[20]

> 'I do, however, consider that the appellants are entitled to succeed upon either of two grounds with which the learned Judge does not deal. In the first place, I think that the evidence as to the practice in relation to the non-disclosure of the character of cargo when effecting a policy on hull does not only justify, but requires, the court to hold that an underwriter waives any information in relation to what may be fairly described as a parcel of ordinary cargo of lawful merchandise, which this parcel was. In the second place, I think that the plea of waiver can be supported on the ground indicated by Lord Esher MR, in *Asfar v Blundell*,[1] where in dealing with the question of concealment he says: "But it is not necessary to disclose minutely every material fact; assuming that there is a material fact which he"—the assured—"is bound to disclose, the rule is satisfied if he discloses sufficient to call the attention of the underwriters in such a manner that they can see that if they require further information, they ought to ask for it." In my opinion the disclosure in the present case that this vessel was a wooden vessel with auxiliary motor engines was a disclosure of the fact that it was proposed to carry cargo from the United States to France in a vessel specially and dangerously liable to fire damage, and that such a disclosure was, within Lord Esher's language, a sufficient disclosure to put the underwriter on inquiry.'

In *George Cohen, Sons & Co v Standard Marine Insurance Co Ltd*[2] Roche J, held[3] that the insurers had waived the non-disclosure of the fact that the assured intended to send an obsolete battleship, which was being towed from Chatham to Brake (in Germany) to be broken up, to sea without any steam power on board.

The omission to make inquiry is no waiver if the insurers are not put on inquiry. Waiver is not to be easily presumed.[4]

Thus, in *Greenhill v Federal Insurance Co Ltd*[5] celluloid was shipped from Halifax, Nova Scotia, to Nantes, and arrived in a damaged condition. When a claim was made under the policy, the insurance company repudiated liability on the ground that there had been non-disclosure of the fact that the celluloid had been previously carried from New York to Halifax on a very slow steamer, and that the cargo had been exposed to rough weather on deck and had been left on an open quay on arrival at Halifax. It was held by the Court of Appeal[6] that the pre-carriage of goods was a material fact and ought to have been disclosed. Accordingly, the insurance company was entitled to avoid liability.

---

[17] Vaughan Williams, Fletcher Moulton and Buckley LJJ.
[18] (1920) 124 LT 778, CA.
[19] Bankes, Atkin and Younger LJJ.
[20] (1920) 124 LT 778 at 780.
[1] [1896] 1 QB 123.
[2] (1925) 21 LlL Rep 30, KBD.
[3] Ibid, at 38.
[4] *Greenhill v Federal Insurance Co Ltd* (1926) 135 LT 244, CA.
[5] (1926) 135 LT 244, CA.
[6] Lord Hanworth MR, Scrutton and Sargant LJJ.

There had been no waiver of non-disclosure arising from the absence of inquiry by the company as to the manner in which the celluloid had been brought to Halifax.

Sargant LJ, said:[7]

'But it is said that here there was, within s 18, sub-s (3), sub-head (c), a waiver by the insurer of information as to the previous history of the goods so far as pre-carriage was concerned, and this because such goods were known not to have originated in Halifax; that there must have been some pre-carriage, and that it was therefore for the insurers to make inquiries as to the circumstances of such pre-carriage. Had the pre-carriage necessarily or ordinarily involved incidents—vicissitudes—of the same character as those which occurred in the actual pre-carriage here, there would have been much in favour of this argument. But it is clear from the evidence that this is not so, and that the circumstances of the pre-carriage were so exceptional that they would necessarily be material and ought to have been disclosed. Indeed, the argument of the plaintiffs, if pressed to its logical conclusion, would in almost every case negative mere non-disclosure as a defence, since in almost every case appropriate inquiries would have got behind the non-disclosure and have elicited the material circumstances, unless indeed they had resulted in a positive mis-statement by the assured.'

In *Inman SS Co v Bischoff*[8] notice was given to the insurers that the vessel insured was chartered to a third party under a charter-party. The insurers did not ask for particulars of the charter-party. It was held that the assured was under no duty to disclose them for, on the facts, information as to them had been waived.

Again, in *The Bedouin*[9] there was an insurance on chartered freight. The 'slip' stated 'Freight chartered and/or as if chartered on board or not on board one-third diminishing each month'. This showed the insurer that he was insuring 'time chartered freight'. It was held that the insurer had waived information as to the fact that such a charter-party contained the usual 'off-hire' clause.

In *Freeland v Glover*[10] a letter was disclosed which mentioned an earlier letter. The insurer did not ask for the earlier letter to be shown to him. It was held that the information as to this letter had been waived.

In *Weir v Aberdeen*[11] the ship was overloaded, and so strained and laboured in her passage from London to the Downs that the owners asked leave to put some cargo ashore at Ramsgate, which was granted. It was held that there was no necessity to inform the insurers specifically that she had laboured heavily, for they had waived information as to this since the request to discharge the cargo was a sufficient intimation of her condition.

In *Pacific Queen Fisheries v L Syme: The Pacific Queen*[12] the insurers of a wooden-hulled motor vessel were held not to have waived[13] information as to an increase in her gasoline carrying capacity and an altered method of carrying gasoline, and accordingly were held entitled to avoid liability for the loss of the

---

[7] (1926) 135 LT 244 at 253.
[8] (1882) 7 App Cas 670.
[9] [1894] P 1. It is to be noted that in this case it was proved that it was a common usage to insert a cesser clause in a charter-party in regard to time freight; while in the earlier case of *Mercantile SS Co v Tyser* (1881) 7 QBD 73 the non-disclosure of a cancelling clause in a policy on chartered freight was held to be non-disclosure of a material fact.
[10] (1806) 7 East 457. See also, *Court v Maritineau* (1782) 3 Doug KB 161; *Fort v Lee* (1811) 3 Taunt 381; *Asfar & Co v Blundell* [1896] 1 QB 123 at 129.
[11] (1819) 2 B&Ald 320. See also, *Beckwith v Sydebotham* (1807) 1 Camp 116.
[12] [1963] 2 Lloyd's Rep 201 (US Court of Appeals 9th Cir).
[13] The evidence as to the alleged waiver is set out ibid, at 209–210.

vessel on the ground that these facts, which were material, had not been disclosed to them by the assured.

In *Gulfstream Cargo Ltd v Reliance Insurance Co: The Papoose*[14] it was held by the United States, Court of Appeals, Fifth Circuit,[15] that the insurers of a vessel had not waived information of material facts, eg that she had unusual rhythmic vibrations, leaked excessively and was unfit for any use off shore.[16]

In *Allden v Raven: The Kylie*,[17] where a claim was made in respect of the total loss of a yacht Parker J, held that, on the evidence,[18] the insurers had not waived the non-disclosure by the assured that he had been previously convicted of handling a stolen dinghy, and that the yacht had been built from a kit.

In *Container Transport International Inc and Reliance Group Inc v Oceanus Mutual Underwriting Association (Bermuda) Ltd*[19] the Court of Appeal[20] held that the assured had not established waiver of the non-disclosure of an inaccurate and misleading claims record, and of a refusal of a previous insurer to renew a policy.[1]

4 Facts the disclosure of which is unnecessary by reason of a warranty

Section 39(1) of the Marine Insurance Act 1906 states:

> 'In a voyage policy there is an implied warranty that at the commencement of the voyage the ship shall be seaworthy for the purpose of the particular adventure insured.'

Accordingly, information in the possession of the assured which tends to show that the vessel insured under a voyage policy was not seaworthy need therefore not be disclosed.[2] On the other hand, there is no such implied warranty in time policies, and in such cases full disclosure must be made.[3]

Again, where the nature of the cargo would necessarily cause bad stowage, information to this effect must be disclosed to the insurer, though the implied warranty of seaworthiness is broken by bad stowage or overloading.[4]

D EXAMPLES OF MATERIAL AND IMMATERIAL FACTS

Section 18(4) of the Marine Insurance Act 1906 states:

> 'Whether any particular circumstance, which is not disclosed, by material or not is, in each case, a question of fact.'

---

[14] [1970] 1 Lloyd's Rep 178.
[15] Brown ChJ, Tuttle and Godbold CtJJ.
[16] See the judgment of Brown ChJ [1970] 1 Lloyd's Rep 178 at 183.
[17] [1983] 2 Lloyd's Rep 444, QBD (Com Ct).
[18] See ibid, at 445–448.
[19] [1984] 1 Lloyd's Rep 476, CA.
[20] Stephenson, Kerr and Parker, LJJ.
[1] See the judgment of Kerr LJ ([1984] 1 Lloyd's Rep 476 at 500, and 506), and that of Stephenson LJ, ibid, at 529–530.
[2] *Schoolbred v Nutt* (1782) 1 Park's Marine Insurances (8th Edn), p 493; *Haywood v Rodgers* (1804) 4 East 590; *Gandy v Adelaide Insurance Co* (1871) LR 6 QB 746.
[3] *Russell v Thornton* (1859) 4 H&N 788; *Cantiere Meccanico Brindisino v Janson* [1912] 3 KB 452, CA.
[4] *Foley v Tabor* (1861) 2 F&F 663. See further, *Weir v Aberdeen* (1819) 2 B&Ald 320; *Mann, Macneal and Steeves v Capital and Counties Insurance Co Ltd* [1921] 2 KB 300.

Section 18(5) provides:

'The term "circumstance" includes any communication made to, or information received by, the assured.'

In *Cantiere Meccanico Brindisino v Janson*,[5] which concerned a floating dock insured for a voyage from Avonmouth to Brindisi, Buckley LJ, emphasized that the material circumstance referred to in s 18(4) was a material circumstance of fact, and observed:[6]

'But by material circumstance is, I think, meant a material circumstance of fact to the exclusion of a material circumstance of opinion. Whether the dry dock here tendered for insurance required to be strengthened for the voyage or not was, I think, a question of opinion. The assured honestly believed, and had the authority of Watkins' report for believing, that she did not require to be strengthened for the voyage, but might safely be towed to a Mediterranean port provided that suitable arrangements for towing were made. The assured was bound to disclose that report as soon as he had it. He did so. If he had received any other report, say to a contrary effect, the existence of the opinion which it contained was a matter of fact, and its disclosure was necessary as being a material circumstance.'

It does not necessarily follow that because a fact has been held to be immaterial in one case, a similar fact is not material in another.

The question is to be decided, if necessary, by a jury, as representing reasonable men.[7]

A number of cases decided before and after the passing of the Marine Insurance Act 1906 concerning the question of materiality are considered below.

Sailing without convoy

In *Sawtell v Loudon*[8] it was known at Lloyd's that the 'Sophia' was at sea without convoy. The broker insured 'on ship' instead of 'on goods'. The owner wrote to the broker saying that the ' "Sophia" was the same ship, but he supposed that she had been unable to join her convoy'. The letter was not disclosed to the underwriter when the policy was altered from 'ship' to 'goods'. It was held that the letter was material and ought to have been disclosed.

Presence of enemy

In *Beckwaite v Nalgrove*[9] a letter received from the Cape of Good Hope saying that two or three French privateers were in those seas was held to be material.

Readiness to sail

In *McAndrew v Bell*[10] on 24 November a letter dated 8 November, stating that the vessel was ready to sail, was received. Insurance was effected on 2 December. It was held that the letter ought to have been disclosed.

---

[5] (1912) 107 LT 281, CA.
[6] Ibid, at 287.
[7] *Joel v Law Union and Crown Insurance Co* [1908] 2 KB 863, CA (life insurance) per Fletcher Moulton LJ, at 884.
[8] (1814) 5 Taunt 359.
[9] Unreported, cited in (1810) 3 Taunt 41.
[10] (1795) 1 Esp 373.

Missing ship

In *Bridges v Hunter*[11] a letter was received containing bills of lading marked 'with convoy'. If the bills of lading had been disclosed, the underwriters would have seen that the ship was not in Lloyd's convoy list and was missing. The bills of lading were held to be material.

Grounding of vessel

In *Russell v Thornton*[12] the fact that a ship had grounded and had sprung a leak was held to be material.

Capture doubtful

In *De Costa v Scandret*[13] a merchant, on hearing that a vessel similar to his own was captured, effected an insurance without disclosing to the underwriters this information which was uncertain. It was held that he ought to have done so.

Ships parting in storm

In *Westbury v Aberdein*[14] a policy dated 3 November was effected on the 'King George' which sailed from Malaga in company with the 'Fruiter' on 10 October. The 'Fruiter' arrived and reported that she had parted with the 'King George' in a storm off Oporto. This fact was held to be material, and ought to have been disclosed.

Loss of vessel

In *Fitzherbert v Mather*[15] a letter from the shipper's agent dated 16 September stated: 'Goods shipped this day on board the "Joseph", which immediately sailed.' The policy was effected on goods on 21 September. It was held that the fact that the ship had gone ashore, and that the goods had been lost, should have been disclosed by the agent who knew about it.

Vessel on rock

In *Gladstone v King*[16] insurance on a vessel was effected on 25 October. On the preceding 5 July she had been driven on to a rock. She got off, and her master wrote on 5 August without mentioning the matter as he thought her undamaged. She was in fact damaged. It was held that the fact that she had been on the rock was material, and ought to have been disclosed.

Name of vessel

In *Lynch v Hamilton*[17] a ship was posted at Lloyd's on 22 November as seen at sea

---

[11] (1813) 1 M&S 15.
[12] (1860) 6 H&N 140. See also, *Holland v Russell* (1863) 4 B&S 14.
[13] (1723) 2 P Wms 170.
[14] (1837) 2 M&W 267.
[15] (1785) 1 Term Rep 12.
[16] (1813) 1 M&S 35. See also, *Morrison v Universal Marine Insurance Co* (1873) LR 8 Exch 197; and *Proudfoot v Montefiore* (1867) LR 2 QB 511.
[17] (1810) 3 Taunt 37. See also, *Lynch v Dunsford* (1811) 14 East 494 and *Leigh v Adams* (1871) 25 LT 566.

leaky and deeply laden. A policy 'on ship or ships' was effected on 26 November. The name of the vessel was not given, but she had in fact been captured. It was held that this was a material fact, and ought to have been disclosed.

Previous history of vessel

In *Bates v Hewitt*[18] it was held that the assured should have disclosed that the insured vessel, which was a merchant ship, had formerly been a Confederate cruiser.

Liability of lightermen

In *Tate v Hyslop*,[19] when effecting a policy with risks on craft and lighters, not specified to be without recourse against lightermen, the assured did not disclose the fact that he had contracted with the lightermen on terms which excluded their liability for negligence. It was held that this was a material fact, and that the insurer could avoid liability.

Nature of port

In *Harrower v Hutchinson*[20] the assured did not disclose that under a policy 'at and from Buenos Aires to port or ports of call' the ship was going to a place to complete her cargo where there was no natural or artificial port, but only a kind of bay—a place which was then unknown to underwriters as a port of loading. This fact was held to be material.

Previous history of master

The fact that the master of the insured vessel had not been to sea for 20 years and had then lost his ship has been held not to be a material fact.[1]

Previous history of goods

In *Berger and Light Diffusers Pty Ltd v Pollock*[2] the fact that some steel injection moulds which were insured for a voyage from Australia to England had previously been found by various companies interested in using them for large-scale production to be unsuitable in their present state was held to be immaterial.[3]

Sailing orders

If the master sails under special orders which cause him to deviate from the customary route, or which fetter his discretion, they should be disclosed by the assured, otherwise the policy may be avoided both on the ground of non-disclosure and of deviation.[4]

---

[18] (1867) LR 2 QB 595.
[19] (1885) 15 QBD 368.
[20] (1869) LR 4 QB 523. See also, *Laing v Union Marine Insurance Co* (1895) 1 Com Cas 11.
[1] *Thames and Mersey Marine Insurance Co Ltd v Gunford Ship Co Ltd* [1911] AC 529, HL.
[2] [1973] 2 Lloyd's Rep 442, QBD (Com Ct).
[3] See the judgment of Kerr J, ibid, at 465.
[4] *Middlewood v Blakes* (1797) 7 Term Rep 162.

Date of arrival of vessel

In *Scottish Shire Line Ltd v London and Provincial Marine and General Insurance Co Ltd*[5] the assured took out a freight policy in respect of apples to be carried from Tasmania to England. The apple season at Hobart was confined to the months of March and April. The assured had entered into a contract with the shippers of the apples to have the vessel at Hobart on or about 20 March, but this fact was not disclosed to the insurers. Hamilton J, in holding that this fact was material, said:[6]

> 'The risk, if there was no date in this contract, would be that when the vessel arrived at Hobart, there might be no apples, in which case she could not earn freight by carrying them, and that she might be prevented from arriving at Hobart, while there were apples to ship, by perils of the sea. Considering that she was about to leave English waters at the end of the year, and considering that the apple season at Hobart appears to extend for about two months, to which, I suppose, must be added a few days—three or four, whichever it may be—during which apples in case may remain awaiting shipment without deterioration, the underwriter would in that view have a very considerable time range within which the vessel might arrive and save her freight.
>
> I do not say that the risk of her being injured, and so losing that freight, would not be a considerable one, but it would be a risk measured by the extent of the range of time within which she could arrive and save it. If the time was to be about 20 March, not much before and not much after, it seems to me that the risk is intrinsically altered, and the likelihood of the underwriter being called upon to pay in the event of accident is considerably increased.'

Date of sailing

In some early cases the date of sailing was held to be always a material fact.[7] It is, however, now settled that the question whether the date of sailing is a material fact depends entirely upon the circumstances of the particular case, and is not to be assumed against the assured.[8] The same observation applies to ships other than the vessel insured or concerned in the policy, which may have sailed at the same time.[9]

Overvalued cargo

In *Ionides v Pender*[10] the assured did not disclose that the real value of the insured cargo was £970, but he insured it for £2,800. The insurer was held to be entitled to avoid liability because the overvaluation was material.

In *Berger and Light Diffusers Pty Ltd v Pollock*,[11] where the assured had stated that some steel injection moulds were worth £20,000, it was held that the insurers had failed to prove that the alleged overvaluation was material.

---

[5] (1912) 107 LT 46, KBD.
[6] Ibid, at 53.
[7] *Fillis v Brutton* (1782) 1 Park's Marine Insurances (8th Edn), p 414; *Shirley v Wilkinson* (1781) 3 Doug KB 41; *Bridges v Hunter* (1813) 1 M&S 15.
[8] *Fort v Lee* (1811) 3 Taunt 381; *Foley v Moline* (1814) 5 Taunt 430; *Rickards v Murdock* (1830) 10 B&C 527; *Elkin v Janson* (1845) 13 M&W 655; *Stribley v Imperial Marine Insurance Co* (1876) 1 QBD 507; *Scottish Shire Line Ltd v London and Provincial Marine and General Insurance Co* [1912] 3 KB 51.
[9] *Kirby v Smith* (1818) 1 B&Ald 672; *Elton v Larkins* (1832) 8 Bing 198; *Friere v Woodhouse* (1817) Holt NP 572; *Court v Martineau* (1782) 3 Doug KB 161; *McAndrew v Bell* (1795) 1 Esp 373; *Westbury v Aberdein* (1837) 2 M&W 267.
[10] (1874) LR 9 QB 531. See also, *Gooding v White* (1913) 29 TLR 312.
[11] [1973] 2 Lloyd's Rep 442, QBD (Com Ct). (See the judgment of Kerr J, ibid, at 465.)

In *Williams v Atlantic Assurance Co Ltd*[12] the insurers repudiated liability for the loss of a cargo of textile goods shipped from Alexandria to Liverpool, on the ground that they had been grossly overvalued. They contended that they had been told that they were worth £8,000 whereas in fact their value was only £250.

Scrutton LJ, giving judgment in the Court of Appeal, held (obiter) that this plea failed because the underwriters had not given evidence in support of their allegation, and said:[13]

> 'The underwriters have not taken the course, which, in my view, should always be pursued, of going into the box and saying what they knew and what was the material fact which they did not know. In my view an underwriter pleading concealment must come and say what he was or was not told. He may not remember directly, but may be able to say, as he said in *Greenhill v Federal Insurance Co Ltd*,[14] that he cannot have been told this material fact—that if he had known it, he would never have dreamed of writing this policy at the ordinary rate of premium. ... The underwriter ... was not called. ... In my view, in a plea of concealment, the underwriter must be called to say what he was told, unless all communications are in writing. ... If therefore the case had turned only on concealment,[15] I should have refused to decide against the plaintiff on it, as I think the matter of such general importance that calling the underwriter should be strictly required ...'

Unseaworthiness of vessel

In *Marmion v Johnston*[16] a derrick barge over 50 years old was insured under a time policy against perils of the sea. She sank during a gale at her moorings in the North Carriers' Dock, Liverpool. She was raised, but repairs were found to be impracticable, and the assured claimed for a constructive total loss. The insurer repudiated liability on the ground that the barge was unseaworthy, and that the assured had not disclosed her unseaworthy condition.

A special jury found that the barge was seaworthy,[17] and that her sinking was caused by the gale. Charles J, gave judgment for the assured.

In *Gulfstream Cargo Ltd v Reliance Insurance Co: The Papoose*[18] the insurers were held to be entitled to avoid liability under a time policy in respect of the insured vessel because the assured had not disclosed that (i) in June 1961 the master had reported to the assured that the vessel had unusual rhythmic vibrations and leaked excessively; (ii) after a period in a shipyard she again leaked excessively; and (iii) in September 1961 a marine surveyor had reported that she was unfit for any use off shore.[19]

Refusal of risk by another insurer

In marine insurance it is unnecessary for the assured to disclose that the risk has been previously refused by other insurers.[20]

---

[12] [1932] All ER Rep 32, CA.
[13] Ibid, at 36.
[14] [1927] 1 KB 65.
[15] The case turned principally on the question whether the value of the goods insured under an unvalued policy had been proved to the satisfaction of the Court. As to this point, see p 99, post.
[16] (1928) 31 LlL Rep 78 (Liverpool Assizes).
[17] As to the evidence on this point, see ibid, pp 78–79.
[18] [1971] 1 Lloyd's Rep 178 (US Court of Appeals 5th Cir).
[19] See the judgment of Brown ChJ, ibid, at 182.
[20] But in other branches of the law of insurance such a refusal of the risk has been held to be material. See Ivamy, *General Principles of Insurance Law* (4th edn, 1979), p 146.

Thus, in *Glasgow Assurance Corpn Ltd v William Symondson & Co*[1] Scrutton J, said:[2]

> 'The ordinary man in the street would, I am sure, think it material to know that the risk he was offered had been previously refused by six other underwriters; and many life insurance offices expressly ask the question: "Has your life been refused by any other office?" But it is elementary marine insurance law that such refusals need not be disclosed to another underwriter. The ordinary business man would, I am sure, think it material to know that the underwriter wanting to reinsure thought so badly of the risk that he was ready to pay a higher premium than he received to get rid of it; but no one has ever suggested that this need be disclosed.'

Again, in *North British Fishing Boat Insurance Co Ltd v Starr*[3] Rowlatt J, observed:[4]

> 'Now, no one contends that the mere fact that other underwriters have refused a risk ought to be disclosed. The underwriter sits there to receive offers of business and to accept or refuse them as he thinks fit, and what one man thinks good business another man may not care to take. And he sits there to gauge the situation, and to quote for himself.'

Previous claims record

In *Container Transport International Inc and Reliance Group Inc v Oceanus Mutual Underwriting Association (Bermuda) Ltd*[5] the assured was held to have been guilty of non-disclosure of a material circumstance in putting forward an inaccurate or incomplete and misleading claims record.

Reinsured goods already lost

In *London General Insurance Co v General Marine Underwriters' Association*[6] the original insurers of a cargo did not disclose to the reinsurers that the insured cargo had already been damaged by fire on 24 September. News of the casualty was posted at Lloyd's on the morning of 25 September, and should have been seen by the insurers. The policy of reinsurance was effected on the afternoon of 25 September. It was held that the reinsurers could avoid liability on the ground of non-disclosure of a material fact.

Nationality of assured

In *Campbell v Innes*[7] it was held that the non-disclosure of the nationality of the assured was material and a ground on which the insurer could avoid liability.

But in *Associated Oil Carriers Ltd v Union Insurance Society of Canton Ltd*[8] where the insured vessel had been chartered to a German shortly before the outbreak of the First World War, it was held that it was unnecessary for the assured to disclose the charterer's nationality as this was not a material fact.

---

[1] (1911) 104 LT 254.
[2] Ibid, at 257.
[3] (1922) 13 LlL Rep 206, KBD.
[4] Ibid, at 210.
[5] [1984] 1 Lloyd's Rep 476, CA.
[6] [1921] 1 KB 104.
[7] (1821) 4 B&Ald 423.
[8] [1917] 2 KB 184. Cf *British and Foreign Marine Insurance Co Ltd v Samuel Sanday & Co* [1916] 1 AC 650, HL.

In *Demetriades & Co v Northern Assurance Co*[9] a cargo was insured for a voyage from Leith to Piraeus. The vessel carrying it sank off the coast of Portugal. When the assured claimed for a loss under the policy, one of the grounds[10] on which the insurers repudiated liability was that there had been non-disclosure of a material fact, viz that there was a Greek interest in the vessel, and that this was material to the risk in view of the attitude of underwriters with regard to Greek ships.

The House of Lords[11] held that this was a material fact which ought to have been disclosed, and that consequently the insurers were entitled to avoid liability.

Lord Shaw of Dunfermline said:[12]

> 'A material representation which should have been made, and was not made but was concealed, was that this was a Greek ship. In my opinion, as I have said, that was material enough to avoid the contract if the falsehood in regard to that matter was upon the register. But when we come to the actual fact of the nationality of the vessel, how material it is appears from the evidence of Mr Harper, the shipping editor of "Lloyd's List and Shipping Gazette", who gives the official statistics with regard to a long period of time, namely, the period from 1 September 1920 to 30 November 1921. During that period, 14 British vessels of over 500 tons were lost, and during the same period 27 Greek vessels were lost, that is to say, nearly double the number of Greek vessels to British. But, my Lords, that is not really the substantial comparison. The substantial comparison is the relation of Greek losses to Greek tonnage afloat as compared with British losses compared with British tonnage afloat, and the startling fact is that for every 22,000 Greek tons afloat one vessel was lost, whereas in the case of British registered ships one loss only occurred in the case of 1,570,000 tons afloat, a contrast so startling that it requires very little evidence in a law court to convince me that in the insurance and shipping world any representation which would conceal the Greek nationality of the vessel was a material matter for the contracting parties. That misrepresentation or concealment on the subject having occurred, the defence is completely justified.'

Previous conviction of assured

In *Allden v Raven, The Kylie*,[13] where the assured claimed for a total loss of a yacht, he admitted that the non-disclosure of a previous conviction[14] for handling a stolen dinghy was material,[15] but sought to prove that the insurers had waived such non-disclosure. Parker J, dismissed the claim on the ground that, on the evidence,[16] no waiver had been established.

Vessel already sailed

In *A C Harper & Co Ltd v R D Mackechnie & Co*[17] the sellers had sold some glacial acetic acid to the buyers c i f Singapore. The buyers contended that the sellers

---

[9] (1926) 21 LlL Rep 265, HL.
[10] Another ground was that there had been a misrepresentation of a material fact. As to this aspect of the case, see p 75, post.
[11] Viscount Cave LC, Lord Dunedin, Lord Shaw of Dunfermline, Lord Sumner and Lord Buckmaster.
[12] (1925) 21 LlL Rep at 269. See also the speech of Lord Sumner, ibid, at 269.
[13] [1983] 2 Lloyd's Rep 444, QBD (Com Ct).
[14] For previous convictions, see further Ivamy, *General Principles of Insurance Law* (4th edn, 1979), pp 156, 159–160.
[15] The assured also admitted that the fact that the yacht had been built from a kit was also a material one. See p 66, post.
[16] See [1983] 2 Lloyd's Rep 444 at 445–448.
[17] (1925) 22 LlL Rep 514.

had not tendered to them a valid policy of insurance because the insurance company had refused to pay in respect of a loss covered by it, on the ground that there had been a non-disclosure of a material fact, viz that the vessel carrying the goods had sailed at the time when the insurance was effected.

Roche J, held that the insurance company was entitled to do so, and that the policy was invalid. Accordingly, the buyers were awarded damages against the sellers for breach of the terms of the c i f contract. He observed:[18]

> 'So far as I can judge, the objection by the insurance company is a good one. It is not denied on behalf of the defendants that under ordinary circumstances it is material that the underwriter should be told, if he is insuring, not that the goods are to proceed on a voyage, but whether they have proceeded on a voyage. There are reasons as to the season and the weather which makes it desirable to be known. What is argued and supported by evidence for the defendants is the proposition that under the broad circumstances of the case the underwriter either was told all that was material or waived disclosure of further facts. I have heard all the witnesses; and I am satisfied that no more was made plain to the underwriters than this, that the business which the brokers had done with the other insurance companies was to be transferred to them; and I find there was no disclosure of the fact that the sailing in question was a past sailing and that there was no waiver by the underwriters of any information material to be given.'

Overvaluation of vessel

In *Piper v Royal Exchange Assurance*[19] a vessel was insured for £2,500. She stranded on the Buxey Sands while on a voyage to Burnham-on-Crouch. The assured claimed under the policy, but was met with the defence that she was overvalued and that therefore there had been non-disclosure of a material fact, and that the insurers accordingly were entitled to avoid liability.

Roche J, held that the claim succeeded. At the time of the stranding the assured was endeavouring to sell her at a price rather less than the insured value, and it could not be said that he was aware of her actual value, which was little more than the value of her lead keel. His Lordship observed:[20]

> 'In my judgment the vessel never was worth £2,500; but it does not follow that the overvaluation was one which avoided the policy.... I think [the assured] was hoping against hope that he might sell this vessel, and might sell her at somewhere about £2,000, or perhaps rather less. It may not have been very honest, from some points of view, to sell a vessel with those defects, but still, it is not a matter quite unknown in business and I am not prepared to find that he so knew at that date of her deficiency in value and that he ought to have told his underwriters in 1928. In other words, that was his asking price at that time, and I am not prepared to find that he ought to have declared her at a lower figure.'

Another issue in *Piper v Royal Exchange Assurance*[1] concerned a later policy in respect of the same yacht, and this issue also was whether she was overvalued. The insurers repudiated liability in respect of damage to her by fire on the ground that she had been overvalued to the assured's knowledge. It was proved that she was only worth half the sum for which he insured her, and there was little chance of selling her, and repairs which had been carried out on her had not been effective to get rid of the real trouble that affected her saleable value.

---

[18] Ibid, at 515.
[19] (1932) 44 LlL Rep 103, KBD. The case also concerned insurable interest and the question whether the stranding was accidental. As to these matters, see pp 17–18, ante, and p 239, post, respectively.
[20] (1932) 44 LlL Rep 103 at 119.
[1] Ibid.

Roche J, held that the vessel was overvalued to the knowledge of the assured, and that the insurers were not liable. He observed:[2]

> 'I am satisfied that at that time the vessel was worth little more than, if as much as, half the value at which she was insured; that £1,000 or £1,200 would have represented the whole value of the ship—her mast, her sails, and everything. That, in my judgment, is a material circumstance which the assured knew, and which would have made a difference to the underwriters so that they would not have insured the risk at all. I accept the evidence given on that matter by the underwriters. The matter had been progressive ever since the beginning. The inherent defects in this ship, and her want of saleability, had been becoming progressively known to the assured, and at that date, at any rate, if not before, he ought to have disclosed the decrease in value to the underwriters if he wanted them to insure her at that value.'

In *Slattery v Mance*[3] a yacht was insured for £4,450. The assured failed to disclose that a month before the policy was effected, he would have been willing to accept an offer of £2,250 for her from a prospective buyer. This fact was held to be material and a ground on which the insurer could avoid liability, because the overvaluation had not been disclosed.

Customer's complaints as to state of goods

In *Bird's Cigarette Manufacturing Co Ltd v Rouse*[4] the assured effected a policy in respect of some cigarettes in a warehouse in Cologne, but did not disclose the fact that complaints had been made by customers that some of them were mildewed. Bailhache J, held that this was a material fact which ought to have been disclosed to the insurers, and since it had not been disclosed, they were entitled to avoid liability for a loss arising under the policy.[5]

Condition of goods on shipment

In *Berger and Light Diffusers Pty Ltd v Pollock*[6] the fact that the bills of lading relating to some steel injection moulds which were insured for a voyage from Australia to England were 'claused' in that they described the goods as 'unprotected', 'secondhand' and 'insufficiently packed' was held not to be material.[7]

In *Liberian Insurance Agency Inc v Mosse*[8] a cargo described as 'enamelware (cups and plates) in wooden cases' was insured for a voyage from Hong Kong to Monrovia and arrived in a damaged condition. Donaldson J, held that the insurers could avoid liability on the ground of non-disclosure of material facts viz (i) the cargo included 823 cartons as contrasted with wooden cases; (ii) a significant proportion of the enamelware had been touched up by overpainting; and (iii) the cargo was an end of stock or job lot purchase and had been bought at a cheap rate.

---

[2] Ibid, at 120.
[3] [1962] 1 QB 676. See further, *Visscherij Maatschappij Nieuw Onderneming v Scottish Metropolitan Assurance Co Ltd* (1922) 27 Com Case 198, CA (overvalued trawler).
[4] (1924) 19 LlL Rep 301, KBD.
[5] His Lordship also held that the insurers were entitled to avoid liability on the ground that there had been a breach of a warranty. As to this point, see p 291, post.
[6] [1973] 2 Lloyd's Rep 442, QBD (Com Ct).
[7] See the judgment of Kerr J, ibid, at 465.
[8] [1977] 2 Lloyd's Rep 560, QBD. (See the judgment of Donaldson J, ibid, at 565.) The learned Judge also held that the insurers could avoid liability under the Marine Insurance Act 1906, s 20 for there had been material misrepresentations as to the state of the cargo in the respects mentioned above. See p 77, post.

Other insurance policies effected by assured

The fact that the assured, in addition to effecting a hull policy, had also taken out a policy on freight and disbursements has been held to be a material one which he must disclose to the insurers.[9]

Thus, in *Thames and Mersey Marine Insurance Co Ltd v Gunford Ship Co Ltd*[10] the assured effected a valued policy in respect of a vessel for a voyage from Hamburg to Santa Rosalia, the sum insured being £18,500, whilst her real value was only £9,000. But the insurance company was not told that the assured had also taken out policies to a large amount on freight and disbursements. She was wrecked off the Brazilian coast. It was held by the House of Lords[11] that the insurance company could avoid liability on the ground of non-disclosure of a material fact.

Lord Shaw of Dunfermline said:[12]

> 'I do not find myself able to agree with the judgment of either House of the Court of Session. It follows upon the nature of the argument there presented that no duty rests upon the owners, or agent, to disclose to the insurers of the hull facts of the character found in this case. I cannot assent or give any countenance to such a view. The learned Lord Ordinary says: "I cannot see that there is any duty whatever on the part of the assured to disclose to the underwriter on hull, who accepts the vessel at a declared value, that he is also effecting insurances upon freight and disbursements." The opinion of all your Lordships is to an opposite effect, and I humbly agree with that opinion. So far as the effecting of insurances upon freight is concerned that is sound business, because it is grounded upon a stipulation for true indemnity; but so far as disbursements, wherever they are duplications of freight, are concerned, these, when freight has already been insured, form no part of a contract of indemnity, but the insurance upon them is merely a gamble, discountenanced by sound principle and not enforceable by law.'

In *Mathie v Argonaut Marine Insurance Ltd*[13] the plaintiff sent his vessel in ballast from a port in the United Kingdom to Delagoa Bay to load a cargo there for Mauritius. He took out a freight policy for £6,000 in the form 'Freight and anticipated freight and/or chartered freight on board or not'. On the arrival of the vessel at Delagoa Bay a cargo for Mauritius was not available, so the plaintiff supplied a cargo of coal for Bombay and insured it for £6,000. The cargo was lost in the course of the voyage to Bombay. The plaintiff claimed against the insurers, but they repudiated liability on the ground that he had not disclosed the fact that there was already in existence a policy for £6,000 on freight. They contended that the actual freight upon the coal from Delagoa Bay to Bombay might have been something from £1,800 to £2,000, and that, if the insurance of the cargo and the freight were added together, there was no doubt that it was considerably in excess of the total value of the cargo and the freight which, calculated on the price at which the plaintiff thought that he could sell the cargo at Bombay, was £7,200.

The House of Lords[14] held that the action succeeded, for there had been no

---

[9] *Thames and Mersey Insurance Co Ltd v Gunford Ship Co Ltd* [1911] AC 529, HL.
[10] [1911] AC 529, HL.
[11] Lord Loreburn LC, Lord Macnaghten, Lord Alverstone, Lord Shaw of Dunfermline and Lord Robson.
[12] (1911) 105 LT 312 at 317.
[13] (1925) 21 LlL Rep 145, HL.
[14] Lord Buckmaster, Lord Dunedin, Lord Atkinson, Lord Sumner and Lord Wrenbury.

non-disclosure of a material fact. Lord Buckmaster adopted[15] the test used by Bailhache J, who had said in the trial court:[16]

> 'As I understand it, in order to find out whether existing insurances ought to be disclosed when a fresh insurance is taken out one has to consider this: of course, one must take the figures, but one has to consider whether the discrepancy between the insured value and the actual insurable value is of such a nature as to change the character of the risk from a business risk to a speculative risk.'

He himself saw no reason to differ from the conclusion of fact reached by Bailhache J, to the effect that in the circumstances of the case there had been no change in the character of the risk.

Lord Dunedin said that there was a vital difference between the present case and *Thames and Mersey Insurance Co Ltd v Gunford Ship Co Ltd*,[17] where it had been held that the risk was entirely speculative. His Lordship observed:[18]

> 'But here if these underwriters had been told about the Liverpool policy and had then asked the question "How came you to insure freight for £6,000?", they would have been told: "I insured it for £6,000 because that was the limit, seeing the value of the hull, to which I was entitled to go." In other words, they would have been told that the transaction was a perfectly ordinary one. It does not seem to me that anything happened to change what was a perfectly usual and legitimate business transaction into a purely speculative one.'

In *Wilson, Holgate & Co Ltd v Lancashire and Cheshire Insurance Corpn Ltd*[19] 657 barrels of palm oil were insured for a voyage from Singapore to Liverpool. The policy contained the following clause:

> 'Average payable on each package separately or as customary including risks of leakage, and breakage from any cause whatsoever irrespective of percentage.'

One hundred and seven of the barrels were found to be damaged on arrival at Liverpool. The assured claimed for a loss under the policy, but the insurers denied liability on the ground that the assured had failed to disclose that they had effected another insurance against marine risks 'f p a and warranted free from all claims for leakage and breakage however caused'. The insurers also contended that the assured had not disclosed the fact that the bills of lading, under which the goods were shipped, contained a marginal note which stated 'Not responsible for leakage, old casks'.

Bailhache J, held that the defence of non-disclosure failed, and that the insurers were liable.[20]

As to the failure to disclose that another insurance policy had been effected in respect of the goods, he observed:[1]

> 'Then it is said that there has been non-disclosure of material facts. The first material fact non-disclosed is that there was an insurance effected with the Marine Insurance Society of Canton. That was an insurance against marine risks f p a, and warranted free from all claims from leakage and breakage, however caused. It did not cover the particular risk intended to be

---

[15] (1925) 21 LlL Rep 145 at 146.
[16] (1924) 18 LlL Rep 118 at 121.
[17] [1911] AC 529, HL.
[18] (1925) 21 LlL Rep 145 at 146.
[19] (1922) 13 LlL Rep 486, KBD.
[20] Other defences were that the loss of the goods was due to inherent vice, and that the goods had not been properly described in the policy. As to these matters, see pp 250–251, post, and p 276, post, respectively.
[1] (1922) 12 LlL Rep 486 at 488.

covered by this policy, and, in my opinion, there was no reason why the fact of that insurance should be disclosed to the underwriters in this case.'

As to the failure to disclose the condition of the casks, his Lordship said:[2]

'Then it is said that the ... bill of lading contained the following marginal clause: "Not responsible for leakage, old casks". No point is made about the words "not responsible for leakage", but it is said that the fact that the bill of lading contained the marginal clause "old casks" ought to have been communicated to the underwriters. Now, it has to be borne in mind that the casks contained oil. It is better to use second-hand casks than new casks, and once you get as far as that I do not see how a man is to distinguish between second-hand casks and old casks. Two of the underwriters have said that if they knew these marginal words were on the bill of lading, they would not have insured. That is all very well. But the first witness said, and the second one agreed with him, that in the whole of his experience of 30 years as an underwriter he has never been told what sort of casks oil was contained in.

He made that statement in answer to a question by me, because my impression was that the class of casks in which oil is contained never is stated on the "slip" which is submitted to an underwriter, and he has no information about it. In my opinion, if the underwriter had asked about it, he would have been entitled to be told. He was not entitled to be told inasmuch as he asked no question about it.

Evidently it is not the practice to tell underwriters what sort of casks the oil is contained in.'

Undervaluation in floating policy

In *Rivaz v Gerussi*[3] the undervaluation of interests in floating policies for named sums to cover shipments 'to be declared and valued as interest might appear' was held to be a material fact.

Carriage of insured cargo on deck

In *Alluvials Mining Machinery Co v Stowe*[4] 68 barrels of kerosene were insured from a port in the United Kingdom to some mines in Nigeria. The assured had arranged for the goods to be carried as deck cargo at shipper's risk, but this fact was not disclosed to the insurer. The barrels contained 2,135 gallons of oil, but only 200 gallons arrived at the mines. When sued under the policy, the insurer repudiated liability on the ground that there had been non-disclosure of a material fact.

Greer J, held that this defence succeeded, and that the action failed.[5] He observed:[6]

'Even if the carriage of the goods on deck amounted to a variation of the risk by reason of the exercise of the liberty granted to the shipowner, the risk to carry goods on deck is a very grave risk—so grave that, though I do not accept the view that it is absolutely impossible at any premium to get anyone at Lloyd's to insure such a risk, it is almost impossible and very difficult, and not in the ordinary course of business for any such risk to be taken up. And in these circumstances this is a most material fact.

Even assuming the shipowner might carry the goods on deck, still it seems to me it would be a most material fact to be disclosed if in fact an agreement has been made that they should be carried on deck, because there is a great difference between the state of affairs which arises when a contract is made that the goods shall run a particular risk, and when it is a mere possibility that this risk may arise.'

---

[2] Ibid, at 488.
[3] (1880) 6 QBD 222.
[4] (1922) 10 LlL Rep 96, KBD.
[5] His Lordship also held that the loss was not covered by the policy because there had been no variation of risk within the meaning of clause 5 of the Institute Clauses. As to this point, see pp 81–82, post.
[6] (1924) 10 LlL Rep at 98.

Vessel's gasoline carrying capacity

In *Pacific Queen Fisheries v L Symes: The 'Pacific Queen'*[7] one of the issues was whether the insurers of a wooden-hulled motor vessel were entitled to repudiate liability for her loss on the ground that the assured had failed to disclose increases in risk caused by an increase in the gasoline carrying capacity of the vessel from 3,000 to 8,000 gallons and the extra-hazardous methods of carriage.[8]

The United States Court of Appeals Ninth Circuit[9] held[10] that these facts were material, and that this defence of the insurers succeeded.

Use of premises

In *James Yachts Ltd v Thames and Mersey Marine Insurance Co Ltd*,[11] the insurers were held[12] to be entitled under the Marine Insurance Act of British Columbia (RSC 1960 c 231), s 20[13] to avoid liability under a builders' risk policy on the ground that the assured had failed to disclose the fact that (i) the local authority had refused to give him permission to use the premises consisting of a boat yard for any industrial use because they were a high hazard risk, and (ii) the assured was in financial difficulties and would be less able to maintain the equipment used and thereby would increase the hazard.[14]

Yacht built from kit

In *Allden v Raven, The Kylie*[15] the insurers sought to repudiate liability in respect of the loss of a yacht on the ground that the assured had not disclosed the fact that he had built it from a kit.[16] The assured admitted that this fact was material but alleged that non-disclosure of it had been waived by the insurers. Parker J, however, held that, on the evidence,[17] the claim for the loss of the vessel failed because no such waiver on the part of the insurers had been established.

E THE DURATION OF THE DUTY OF DISCLOSURE

The assured is under a duty to disclose to the insurer all material facts 'before the contract is concluded'.[18]

---

[7] [1963] 2 Lloyd's Rep 201 (US Court of Appeals 9th Cir).
[8] The evidence is set out at [1963] 2 Lloyd's Rep at 203–5.
[9] Circuit Judge Pope, Circuit Judge Barnes and Circuit Judge Hamley.
[10] [1963] 2 Lloyd's Rep 201 at 210.
[11] [1977] 1 Lloyd's Rep 206 (Supreme Court, British Columbia).
[12] See the judgment of Ruttan J, ibid, at 212. It was also held that the assured was in breach of the implied warranty of legality set out in the Marine Insurance Act of British Columbia (RSC 1960, c 231), s 43. As to this point, see p 310, post.
[13] Which corresponds to the (English) Marine Insurance Act 1906, s 18.
[14] For the evidence, see [1977] 1 Lloyd's Rep at 208–211.
[15] [1983] 2 Lloyd's Rep 444, QBD (Com Ct).
[16] He also admitted that a previous conviction for handling a stolen dinghy was material and ought to have been disclosed. See p 60, ante.
[17] [1983] 2 Lloyd's Rep 444 at 445–448.
[18] Marine Insurance Act 1906, s 18(1).

Section 21 of the Marine Insurance Act 1906 states:

> 'A contract of marine insurance is deemed to be concluded when the proposal of the assured is accepted by the insurer, whether the policy be then issued or not; and for the purpose of showing when the proposal was accepted, reference may be made to the slip or covering note or other customary memorandum of the contract . . .'[19]

Similarly, in a case decided before the Act, it was said:[20]

> 'The "slip" is in practice, and according to the understanding of those engaged in marine insurance, the complete and final contract between parties fixing the terms of the contract and the premium so that neither party without the assent of the other can deviate from the terms thus agreed upon without a breach of faith.'

Hence, if everything material be communicated up to the time of the initialling of the 'slip' by the underwriter, but something material arising between that time and the time of executing the policy is not communicated, there is no non-disclosure so as to vitiate the policy.[1]

Where, however, the underwriter issues the policy under protest, after he has received information that a material circumstance has not been disclosed, he is not estopped from disputing his liability on the ground of such non-disclosure, merely because he has issued the policy.[2]

In *Niger Co Ltd v Guardian Assurance Co Ltd*,[3] which concerned a loss of goods stored in a warehouse at Burutu whilst in transit from the United Kingdom to Africa and from Africa to the United Kingdom, an excessive accumulation of goods occurred there due to the difficulty of getting shipping space. The policy was effected in January 1916, and the accumulation occurred after that date. When they were sued under the policy, one of the defences[4] pleaded by the insurers was that the assured should have disclosed the accumulation, and since no disclosure had been made, they could avoid liability under the policy.

It was held by the House of Lords[5] that this defence failed, and that the claim under the policy succeeded, because there had been no non-disclosure, since non-disclosure was a matter which went only to the formation of the contract, and once the contract had been concluded no further disclosure was necessary.

Lord Sumner observed:[6]

> 'There remains the question of non-disclosure. The object of disclosure being to inform the underwriter's mind on matters immediately under his consideration, with reference to the taking or refusing of a risk then offered to him, I think it would be going beyond the principle to say that each and every change in an insurance contract creates an occasion on which a

---

[19] This section is printed in the text as amended by the Finance Act 1959, Eighth Schedule, Part II.

[20] *Ionides v Pacific Fire and Marine Insurance Co* (1871) LR 6 QB 674 at 684.

[1] *Cory v Patton* (1874) LR 9 QB 577; *Lishman v Northern Maritime Insurance Co* (1875) LR 10 CP 179; *Ionides v Pacific Fire and Marine Insurance Co*, supra; *Berger and Light Diffusers Pty Ltd v Pollock* [1973] 2 Lloyd's Rep 442, QBD (Com Ct), where it was held that there was a continuing duty of disclosure between the date of the 'cross-slip' and the 'signing slip'. (See the judgment of Kerr J, ibid, at 461.)

[2] *Nicholson v Power* (1869) 20 LT 580; *Morrison v Universal Marine Insurance Co* (1873) LR 8 Exch 197.

[3] (1922) 13 LlL Rep 75, HL.

[4] Another defence was that the adventure had not been prosecuted with reasonable despatch as required by s 48 of the Marine Insurance Act 1906. As to this point, see p 137, post.

[5] Lord Buckmaster, Lord Atkinson, Lord Sumner and Lord Wrenbury.

[6] (1922) 13 LlL Rep 75 at 82. See also the speech of Lord Buckmaster, ibid, at 76–77, and that of Lord Atkinson, ibid, at 78–79.

general disclosure becomes obligatory, merely because the altered contract is not the unaltered contract, and therefore the alteration is a transaction as the result of which a new contract of insurance comes into existence. This would turn what is an indispensable shield for the underwriter into an engine of oppression against the assured.'

In *Willmott v General Accident Fire and Life Assurance Corpn*[7] a motor boat, which was insured under a time policy, sank during a gale while lying at moorings off Anchor Head near Weston-super-Mare. When a claim in respect of a total loss was made by the assured, the insurers denied liability on the ground that he had not disclosed the fact that the vessel would be habitually moored off Anchor Head.[8] When the policy was entered into, he had no intention that she should ever be moored anywhere except in Knightstone Harbour, and, in fact, she was not moved to Anchor Head until 2 months later.

Branson J, held that this defence failed, and that the action succeeded. The change of plan as to mooring was made subsequent to the date of the policy, and such a change was not prohibited by the policy. Consequently the question of non-disclosure of that material fact did not arise.

He observed:[9]

'The position with regard to that is this, that until some time after Whitsuntide, which happened in June, this policy having been entered into in April, there seems to have been no intention on the part of the plaintiff that the ship should ever be moored anywhere but in Knightstone Harbour. No doubt in June, when it was discovered that sometimes it shortened the period during which the vessel would be available for running passenger trips, moorings were put down in this Gut and afterwards the ship was very frequently moored there, but the fact that that state of things arose in June is nothing to do with the allegation that there was a failure to disclose the material fact in April. It was not a fact in April that she was going to be moored off Anchor Head; that was simply something which came about at a subsequent time altogether. As I said in the course of the argument, had the defendants desired to make it a contractual obligation on the part of the plaintiff to keep his boat in Knightstone Harbour and nowhere else, they could have made a condition to that effect, but they did not, and the result is that though they may have complained if he had intended, when he gave his answers to the questionnaire, to keep this boat at Anchor Head and not at Knightstone Harbour—of course, they could have complained then—they cannot complain, if the answer was true at the time it was given, because a subsequent change of plans, which is not prohibited by the contract into which he has entered, has not prevented him from keeping her not infrequently, or indeed very often, at another and less safe mooring.'

F THE EFFECT OF NON-DISCLOSURE

The effect of non-disclosure is set out in s 18(1) of the Marine Insurance Act 1906 which states:

'If the assured fails to make such disclosure, the insurer may avoid the contract.'

The insurer is entitled in such a case to elect which course he will adopt. He may either return the premium and declare the contract at an end, or he may retain the premium and allow the contract to stand.

The right to avoid the contract exists from the time when it is made and continues until the insurer, with full knowledge of the non-disclosure, affirms or is deemed to affirm the contract. Full knowledge of the facts is essential before

---

[7] (1935) 53 LlL Rep 156, KBD.
[8] Other defences were that the vessel was unseaworthy, and that the assured had made a material misrepresentation as to her value. As to these defences, see p 305, post, and pp 76–77, post.
[9] (1935) 53 LlL Rep 156 at 158.

there can be any question of affirmation; being put on inquiry is insufficient. Even when the insurer has full knowledge of the facts, he is still entitled to a reasonable time in which to decide whether to affirm the contract. In a situation in which the insurer has taken no action to affirm or repudiate the contract and a reasonable time for making up his mind has elapsed, he will be deemed to have affirmed the contract if either so much time has elapsed that the necessary inference is one of affirmation or the assured has been prejudiced by the delay in making an election or rights of third parties have intervened.[10]

It is not necessary to the exercise of the right of election that the fact which is not disclosed should be in any way connected with, or have any influence upon, the loss. The right to avoid the policy exists because the material facts have not been within the knowledge of both parties at the time of effecting the insurance.

When the fact in question comes to the knowledge of the insurer, he is in a position to affirm the contract if he so desires. The influence of the fact which is not disclosed upon the loss has no bearing on the question as to whether there is a valid contract or not, and therefore the right of the insurer to avoid the contract is not affected thereby.[11]

Thus, in *Rivaz v Gerussi*[12] an assured effected a number of insurances by taking out floating policies for certain named sums to cover shipments to be declared and valued 'as interest might appear'. The policies were to succeed each other in order of date, but the value of the shipments was systematically and fraudulently understated by the assured. The fact that they had been so undervalued was not disclosed to the insurer. This was held to be a ground on which the insurer could avoid the contract, although there could be no possible connection between the value of a shipment and the cause of its loss.

G BROKER'S LIABILITY TOWARDS THE INSURER FOR NON-DISCLOSURE

Cases in the early part of this century established the principle that an insurer could not hold a broker liable for innocent non-disclosure of a material fact.[13]

In *Empress Assurance Corpn Ltd v C T Bowring & Co Ltd*[14] a firm of insurance brokers effected with an insurance company a number of open covers for the purpose of reinsuring risks taken by their principals. The premiums under the open covers were to be the same as those received by the original insurers less a brokerage to the firm. The brokers in declaring risks under the open covers stated definite amounts of premiums, without explaining what deductions had been made by the original insurers, their principals, in order to determine the rates received by them. In each case policies were drawn up by the company containing the premiums stated by the brokers. The insurance company, afterwards learning the facts, disputed the correctness of these deductions, and

---

[10] *Liberian Insurance Agency Inc v Mosse* [1977] 2 Lloyd's Rep 560 at 565, QBD (per Donaldson J). See further, Ivamy, *General Principles of Insurance Law* (4th edn, 1979), pp 169–170. In *Liberian Insurance Agency Inc v Mosse* (supra) it was held that a reasonable time had not expired. (See the judgment of Donaldson J, [1977] 2 Lloyd's Rep 560 at 565–566).
[11] *Lynch v Hamilton* (1810) 3 Taunt 37; *Seaman v Fonereau* (1743) 2 Stra 1183.
[12] (1880) 6 QBD 222.
[13] See further on this subject, Ivamy, *General Principles of Insurance Law* (4th edn, 1979), p 594.
[14] (1905) 11 Com Cas 107.

sued the brokers for breach of duty to the company in not securing correct amounts of premium. The brokers had throughout acted in good faith.

The Court held that the brokers owed no duty to the insurance company and could not be held liable on such a claim, even if negligence on their part were proved. Kennedy J, said that the defendants never became responsible to the plaintiffs as their agents or brokers. He knew of no case or legal authority which could be cited to show that the broker who was instructed to effect a marine insurance policy, either directly by the person intending to insure, or indirectly through another broker, became for any part of the business of effecting the insurance the agent also of the underwriter. If such were the case, the curious inference, he supposed, would follow that the knowledge of the broker would be the knowledge also of the underwriter. He could see no reason why there should be any difference where the insurance was effected by a system of open cover, as in the present case. Stress was laid by the plaintiffs on the fact that in the conduct of this business the defendants ought naturally to expect that the plaintiffs would rely on the accuracy of their declarations in regard to the attachment of risks and in regard to premiums. But the mere fact of the reliance of one person on the accuracy of the statements of another made to him in regard to a matter of business in which such reliance was natural enough, although not obligatory, was not of itself sufficient to make negligence on the part of that other person in regard to some statement made honestly but inaccurately an actionable wrong.

In *Glasgow Assurance Corpn Ltd v William Symondson & Co*[15] it was held that if a broker disclosed the name of the ship and the perils affecting her, he could not be sued for negligence or for concealment of a material fact, if he did not state the name of the person interested in her who was desiring to insure or reinsure his interest. Scrutton J, said that it was never done in practice. The underwriter, when he entered into a policy insuring the broker as well in his own name as for and in the name of any other person, must expect to find the broker declaring his own interest or the interest of any other principal. If the underwriter wanted to know who was the assured, he must ask. It was true that the underwriter must have confidence in the broker to make such an agreement as was found in this case, but so he must have in every open cover where he reinsured part of risks of which he knew nothing except that they were to be written by someone else. No one had ever suggested in the latter case that the assured owed any duty of agency or selection to the underwriter, though without confidence such a contract would not be renewed.

The plaintiffs alleged that the defendants concealed from them that three of the four partners constituting the defendants' firm were underwriting members of Lloyd's who underwrote policies on their behalf, and that they intended to place with the plaintiffs reinsurances of risks underwritten by such partners in their capacity as underwriters at a premium greater than that payable to the plaintiffs, and thereby to make profits greatly in excess of their agreed commission. Scrutton J, said that it was common knowledge in marine insurance that many brokerage firms in London had partners who were also underwriters at Lloyd's, and that when an underwriter contracted with the brokers he might find them putting forward their own risks or those of the underwriting members as principals or other people's risks as agents.

---

[15] (1911) 16 Com Cas 109.

CHAPTER 7

Misrepresentation

1 The duty of the assured

Section 20(1) of the Marine Insurance Act 1906 states:

> 'Every material representation made by the assured or his agent to the insurer during the negotiations for the contract, and before the contract is concluded, must be true. If it be untrue the insurer may avoid the contract.'

A representation is either made spontaneously by the assured or in answer to questions put to him by the insurers.

It is often found that the assured has made a representation with the object of inducing the insurer to accept the liability at a smaller premium than he would otherwise require, by impressing him with a more favourable view of the risk, or with the object of securing from him an insurance which would otherwise be refused.

Between misrepresentation and non-disclosure there is this difference: that whereas in non-disclosure the undisclosed fact would tend to show the risk to be greater than it would otherwise seem to be, in cases of misrepresentation the fact so stated would make the risk appear smaller than it was in reality.

It should be observed that s 20(1) of the Marine Insurance Act 1906 applies to any representation whether made by the assured or his agent.

Thus, the assured is responsible for the representations made by his broker, and also for the truth of the information communicated to the broker by his agents, or communicated to himself by his agents and by him communicated to the broker, when such information is laid before the insurer as a statement of fact.

If the assured desires to avoid the responsibility for the falsity of such information, he should take care that the insurer is told that the assured will not vouch for its truth.[1]

2 The duration of the duty

It should be noticed that the representation must be made 'during the negotiations for the contract, and before the contract is concluded'.

As to the time when the contract is concluded, s 21 of the Marine Insurance Act 1906 states:

> 'A contract of marine insurance is deemed to be concluded when the proposal of the assured is accepted by the insurer, whether the policy be then issued or not; and for the purpose of showing when the proposal was accepted, reference may be made to the slip or covering note or other customary memorandum of the contract.'

---

[1] *Fitzherbert v Mather* (1785) 1 Term Rep 12; *Dennistoun v Lillie* (1821) 3 Bli 202.

3 The test of materiality

Section 20(2) of the Marine Insurance Act 1906 states:

> 'A representation is material which would influence the judgment of a prudent insurer in fixing the premium, or determining whether he will take the risk.'

4 Construction of representation

A representation must be construed according to its plain and accepted meaning, and need not necessarily receive a literal construction. Accordingly, when the ordinary commercial meaning is wider than the literal intepretation, neither the assured nor the insurer will be permitted to narrow the meaning of the words.[2]

In construing a representation, regard must be had to any trade usage or to any special meaning which the words would convey to a person engaged in the class of business covered by the policy.[3]

Section 20(4) of the Marine Insurance Act 1906 states:

> 'A representation as to a matter of fact is true, if it be substantially correct, that is to say; if the difference between what is represented and what is actually correct would not be considered material by a prudent insurer.'

Section 20(5) provides:

> 'A representation as to a matter of expectation or belief is true if it be made in good faith.'

The question whether the representation is substantially correct is a question of fact for the jury, and will depend on the nature of the representation considered in reference to the risk and all the surrounding circumstances.

Thus, in *Pawson v Watson*[4] the assured represented the ship carried 12 guns and 20 men. In fact, she carried 9 guns, 6 swivels, 16 men, and 9 boys. It was held that the representation was substantially correct.

5 Materiality is a question of fact

The question whether the representation had a material bearing on the risk is a question of fact for the jury to determine.

Thus, s 20(7) of the Marine Insurance Act 1906 states:

> 'Whether a particular representation be material or not, is, in each case, a question of fact.'

One class of representation is nearly always material. This is the class which consists of answers to the questions put by the insurer. From the question itself the insurer is presumed to regard the fact as material, and since he is entitled to all the information which he requires before making a contract, the assured must answer it to the best of his ability, clearly stating whether the information is certain or uncertain, whether reliable or of doubtful authenticity.

It is not necessary that such a fact should per se be material to or affect the

---

[2] *Ratcliffe v Shoolbred* (1780) 1 Park's Marine Insurances (8th edn), p 413; *Kirby v Smith* (1818) 1 B&Ald 672.
[3] *Chaurand v Angerstein* (1791) Peake 43; *Anderson v Pitcher* (1800) 2 Bos&P 164.
[4] (1778) 2 Cowp 785. See also, *Alexander v Campbell* (1872) 27 LT 462; *Driscol v Passmore* (1798) 1 Bos&P 200; *Driscol v Bovil* (1798) 1 Bos&P 313; *Nonnen v Kettlewell* (1812) 16 East 176.

risk. Accordingly, it will not avail an assured to show that a loss which has occurred is wholly unconnected with the fact misrepresented.[5]

Where the representation is made fraudulently, it would seem that the question of materiality does not arise, and that it is sufficient to show that the insurer relied on the representation and was thereby induced to accept the risk.[6]

Examples of material and immaterial misrepresentations

In *Fillis v Brutton*[7] a broker was informed by the assured that the vessel was ready to sail on 24 December, and he represented to the insurer that she was in port. In fact, she had sailed on 23 December. It was held that the insurer was entitled to avoid the contract on the ground that the representation was a material one. Lord Mansfield CJ, said:

> 'In all insurances it is essential to the contract that the assured should represent the true state of the ship to the best of his knowledge. On that information the underwriters engage.'

In *Macdowall v Fraser*[8] a broker represented to the underwriter that the vessel 'was seen safe in the Delaware on 11 December by a ship which arrived at New York'. In fact, the vessel was lost on 9 December by running against *chevaux de frise*[9] placed across the river. The representation was held to be material, and the underwriter was held to be entitled to avoid liability.

Lord Mansfield CJ, said:[10]

> 'The difference between the fact as it turns out and as represented must be material. The case of the *Julius Caesar* was very different from this.... It was only said what was meant to be done, and was done, though different, was as advantageous, or more so, than what had been represented.'

Other cases in which the representation made by the assured was held to be material concern statements that:

  i   The vessel was American.[11]
  ii Goods were on board the 'Socrates', which was a new vessel, when, in fact, they were on board the 'Socrate', which was an old ship.[12]
  iii The ship had a French licence to trade.[13]
  iv The vessel would sail with convoy.[14]

In *Bowden v Vaughan*[15] the assured in an action on a policy on goods 'at and from Lisbon to London' had received a letter from Lisbon dated 27 October in which it was stated that the vessel would sail in a few days. The letter was not shown to the underwriters, but the broker made a statement to them to the

---

[5] *Seaman v Fonereau* (1743) 2 Stra 1183; *Lynch v Hamilton* (1810) 3 Taunt 37.
[6] *Sibbald v Hill* (1814) 2 Dow 263; *The Bedouin* [1894] P 1.
[7] (1782) 1 Park's Marine Insurances (8th edn), 414.
[8] (1779) 1 Doug KB 260.
[9] Iron spikes set in timber to guard a wall.
[10] (1779) 1 Doug KB 260 at 261. See also, *Dennistoun v Lillie* (1821) 3 Bli 202; *Bowden v Vaughan* (1809) 10 East 415.
[11] *Steel v Lacy* (1810) 3 Taunt 285.
[12] *Ionides v Pacific Fire and Marine Insurance Co* (1872) LR 7 QB 517.
[13] *Feise v Parkinson* (1812) 4 Taunt 640.
[14] *Edwards v Footner* (1808) 1 Camp 530.
[15] (1809) 10 East 415.

same effect. If it had been stated that the vessel was not to sail in less than a month, the insurance could not have been effected, as the French army was daily expected at Lisbon. The representation was held material since the vessel did not sail until 29 November, and was stopped by the enemy on 30 November before she left the Tagus. The jury were of the opinion that the representation had been made bona fide and on probable expectation. On a motion for a new trial the Court took the same view, especially as the assured had no control over the event.

In *Hubbard v Glover*[16] the policy was on ship 'at and from St Petersburg or Cronstadt to London'. The underwriters wanted a warranty to be included in the policy to the effect that the vessel was to sail before 1 August. The broker stated: 'There is no occasion for that; the ship has sailed some time, and must now be off Gothenburg. There is a cargo ready for her, and she is sure to be an early ship.' The policy was signed on 13 June 1811. The ship had reached Gothenburg some days before the conversation, and she performed the voyage to Cronstadt without any accident or delay; but the cargo was not ready, the first part of it being sent alongside on 8 September. On 30 September she sailed homewards, and was wrecked on 11 November. Before she sailed from Cronstadt the winter risk had begun. Lord Ellenborough CJ, said that if the desired warranty had been introduced, the underwriters would have been discharged. But the representation was only a matter of conjecture and the subject of expectation and belief, and the underwriters were liable, although the delay quite changed the nature of the risk.

In *Brine v Featherstone*[17] Gibbs J, said that there was a wide distinction between stating a fact and an opinion. What the broker had stated in that case was only an inference which he drew from the facts. If the underwriter did not inquire what the facts were on which the broker founded his conclusion, the fallacy of the conclusion did not avoid the policy.

In *Cantiere Meccanico Brindisino v Janson*,[18] which concerned a floating dock insured for a voyage from Avonmouth to Brindisi, the insurers refused to indemnify the assured in respect of her loss, alleging that there had been a misrepresentation during the negotiations of the policy, viz that she had been specially strengthened for the voyage. The Court of Appeal[19] held that the misrepresentation had not been proved, and gave judgment for the assured.[20]

In *Hamilton & Co v Eagle Star and British Dominions Insurance Co Ltd*[1] the assured were a firm of produce merchants and importers, who had insured under an open cover in respect of consignments of apples for 12 months from 1 July 1922, to 30 June 1923. During the negotiations for the insurance the assured's broker stated that the clauses of the cover note, which the insurer was asked to quote for and which contained a 'prolongation of voyage clause',[2] were clauses which

---

[16] (1812) 3 Camp 313.
[17] (1813) 4 Taunt 869 at 870. See also, *Dennistoun v Lillie* (1821) 3 Bli 202; *Anderson v Pacific Fire and Marine Insurance Co* (1872) LR 7 CP 65.
[18] (1912) 107 LT 281, CA.
[19] Vaughan Williams, Fletcher Moulton and Buckley LJJ.
[20] See the judgment of Vaughan Williams LJ (1912) 107 LT at 283, that of Fletcher Moulton LJ, ibid, at 284, and that of Buckley LJ, ibid, at 286.
[1] (1924) 19 LlL Rep 242, KBD.
[2] This clause stated: 'In case of prolongation of the voyage over . . . days . . . to pay any damage to or deterioration of the apples.'

were in force in the existing policies of the assured. This was incorrect because such a clause had been deleted as from 20 April 1922, in the existing policies. The representation was an honest one, and had been made in good faith. A loss occurred, and the insurer sought to repudiate liability under s 20 of the Marine Insurance Act 1906 on the ground that there had been a misrepresentation of a material fact.

Bailhache J, held that the defendant was entitled to do so, and said:[3]

> 'I decide this case upon the ground that there was an innocent misrepresentation; that the omission to state that the prolongation of the voyage clause had been deleted was an omission which made the statement that was made materially untrue, and made it untrue in a matter which was material to the consideration of the risk. If nothing has been said, nothing need be said: but if anything was to be said in this case, having regard to what was omitted, the fact ought to have been stated that the New Zealand Insurance Co had had this trouble about the prolongation of the voyage clause, and that that clause had been deleted.'

In *Demetriades v Northern Assurance Co*[4] a cargo had been insured for a voyage from Leith to Piraeus. The vessel on which it was loaded was a total loss off the Portuguese coast. When the assured claimed under the policy, one of the grounds[5] on which the insurers repudiated liability was that he was guilty of misrepresentation of a material fact, and that consequently the policy was voidable under s 20(1) of the Marine Insurance Act 1906. The vessel was, in fact, Greek owned but she was falsely certified as British and was falsely entered on the British register, and had been represented to the insurers as sailing under the British flag.

The House of Lords[6] held that the insurers were entitled to avoid liability. The representation that the vessel was sailing under the British flag implied that she was entitled to be registered as a British ship, and this was untrue.

Lord Sumner observed:[7]

> 'The representation that the *Spathari* was a British ship was in a sense true. She had been placed on the British Register ad hoc, but it was really an untruth, told, in my opinion so far as Mr Borthwick and Mr Demetriades are concerned, with intent to deceive. Under the Merchant Shipping Act the interest which Mr Demetriades had in her was such that the *Spathari* was not qualified to be placed on the British Register, and, when the facts became known, was liable to be seized and in due course forfeited to the Crown, with serious consequences to such persons as made or were privy to the making of the misleading declarations by which registration was obtained. To represent her to the underwriters as a British ship, when she never should have had the appearance of a British ship and was liable to be removed at any time from the register, is in my opinion a misrepresentation of fact which was false to the knowledge of these two persons.'

In *Williams v Atlantic Assurance Co Ltd*[8] the assured stated that a cargo of textile goods was worth £8,000, but, in fact, it was worth only £250. Giving judgment in the Court of Appeal Slesser LJ, held obiter that the insurers were

---

[3] (1924) 19 LlL Rep 242 at 246.
[4] (1926) 21 LlL Rep 265, HL.
[5] Another ground was that there had been non-disclosure of a material fact, viz a Greek interest in the vessel. As to this aspect of the case, see p 60, ante.
[6] Viscount Cave LC, Lord Dunedin, Lord Shaw of Dunfermline, Lord Sumner and Lord Buckmaster.
[7] (1925) 21 LlL Rep 265 at 269. See also, the speech of Viscount Cave LC, ibid, at 267, and that of Lord Shaw of Dunfermline, ibid, at 268.
[8] [1933] 1 KB 81, CA.

entitled to avoid liability on the ground that there had been a misrepresentation, and observed:[9]

> 'The misrepresentation that the goods were worth £8,000 when, in fact, they were worth, as I find, at any rate not more than £250, is an overvaluation so gross that it is calculated to influence and must, in fact, have influenced the underwriters in taking the risk. The misrepresentation ... is apparent on the face of the documents, and, if I am wrong on the technical question of assignment,[10] I hold that under s 20 of the 1906 Act, the underwriters were entitled to avoid the contract for an untrue material misrepresentation. That is to say, I find the value which was declared at £8,000 to have been, in fact, £250 and no more.'

In *Neue Fischmehl Vertriebs-Gesellschaft Haselhorst mbH v Yorkshire Insurance Co Ltd*[11] the assured insured an old steamer, which was used as a shrimp drying factory, for a voyage in the tow of a tug from Friedrichskoog to Cuxhaven and while there for a period of 10 days. She started on her voyage, and after getting not more than 100 yards from Friedrichskoog, the tug anchored her and went back to Cuxhaven intending to return when the weather was more favourable. The steamer was then towed by some fishermen who anchored her. When the tide fell, she grounded and broke her back. The assured claimed for a constructive total loss. The insurers refused to indemnify the assured on the ground that there had been a material misrepresentation in that the assured had stated that the vessel was of extraordinary stable construction 'and had been fully overhauled in 1926 and rebuilt most solidly and strengthened by iron beams', whereas those statements were not true.[12]

MacKinnon J, held that this defence succeeded, and that the action failed.[13] The misrepresentations which had been made were material. The iron beams had been put in to support a factory which was put on deck. The work had not been done for the purpose of strengthening the hull as a floating and water-resisting structure. Further, she had not been fully overhauled, nor was it true to say that she was rebuilt.[14]

In *Wilmott v General Accident Fire and Life Assurance Corpn Ltd*[15] a motor boat, which was insured under a time policy, sank during a gale while lying at moorings off Anchor Head near Weston-super-Mare. The assured claimed for a total loss. One of the defences[16] pleaded by the insurers was that he had made a material misrepresentation as to the boat's value.

Branson J, held that this defence failed, and that the action succeeded. The incorrect answer made by the assured as to the value of the vessel was probably due to the fact that he was incorrectly questioned by the insurers' agent, who himself completed the proposal form.

His Lordship observed:[17]

---

[9] Ibid, at 42.
[10] As to this point, see pp 315–316, post.
[11] (1934) 50 LlL Rep 151, KBD.
[12] The insurers also maintained that the vessel was unseaworthy. As to this aspect of the case, see p 300, post.
[13] (1934) 50 LlL Rep 151 at 153.
[14] As to the evidence, see ibid, at 153.
[15] (1935) 53 LlL Rep 156, KBD.
[16] Other defences pleaded by the insurers were that the vessel was unseaworthy, and that the assured had not disclosed a material fact. As to these defences, see p 305, post and p 68, ante respectively.
[17] (1935) 53 LlL Rep 156 at 159.

'Neither Mr Willmott nor Mr Gibbons in giving their evidence were really clear in the distinction between the questions, "What price did you pay?" or, "What did the motor boat cost you?" or, "What was the value of the motor boat?". Mr Gibbons when he was in the box said first of all: "I asked him the value," and then, "I asked him the price." I said to him, "What did you do; did you ask the value or the price?", and he said "I read out the questions." Now, that shows that in his mind to ask the value is equivalent to reading out the questions, and, if that is so, how can I be sure when he put the words in front of Mr Willmott "price paid by you", he did not look up from the questionnaire and say: "How much did it cost?" and that is what Mr Willmott said he did say. Mr Willmott said: "He asked me what is the cost," and, further, Mr Willmott said, "There would have been no excuse for saying the price I paid was £200, because I had not paid £200, but when the question was: "what did it cost you?", I thought it right and fair to add up what I had paid for the hull, the shafting, the engine, the re-panelling and the re-decking, etc, of this craft, and that plus an addition for wages and a profit on the wages for any men who were used out of my own business for this purpose, was not unfairly stated." It would have been obviously a most fraudulent thing for him, if the question put to him had been: "What was the price paid by you?" to have responded "£200", but one can see how an honest man in the circumstances might have answered the question: "What did they cost you?" by the sum of £200, and I find that that was the answer Mr Willmott gave. The result is that upon that ground also I think the defence fails and the plaintiff is entitled to recover.'

In *Slattery v Mance*[18] the assured stated that the value of the insured yacht was £4,500. The jury found that this representation was material and false, for a month before it had been made he had said that he would be willing to accept an offer of £2,250 for her from a prospective buyer. Salmon J, accordingly held that the insurer could avoid liability.

In *Liberian Insurance Agency Inc v Mosse*[19] a cargo described as 'enamelware (cups and plates) in wooden cases' was insured for a voyage from Hong Kong to Monrovia, and arrived in a damaged condition. Donaldson J, held that the insurers could avoid liability on the ground that the assured had made material misrepresentations as to the state of the cargo in that (i) the cargo included 823 cartons as contrasted with wooden cases; (ii) a significant proportion of the enamelware had been touched up by overpainting; and (iii) the cargo was an end of stock or job lot purchase and had been bought at a cheap rate.

In *Container Transport International Inc and Reliance Group Inc v Oceanus Mutual Underwriting Association (Bermuda) Ltd*[20] a statement concerning the claims record of the assured was held by the Court of Appeal[1] to be material, and since the statement was untrue, the insurers were entitled to repudiate liability.[2]

6 Withdrawal or correction of representation

Section 20(6) of the Marine Insurance Act 1906 states:

'A representation may be withdrawn or corrected before the contract is concluded.'[3]

---

[18] [1962] 1 QB 676. The evidence as to the overvaluation is set out ibid, at 67–70. The jury found that the representation by the assured had not been made fraudulently.
[19] [1977] 2 Lloyd's Rep 560, QBD. (See the judgment of Donaldson J, ibid, at 565.) The learned Judge also held that the insurers could avoid liability under the Marine Insurance Act 1906, s 18 for there had been non-disclosure of material facts as to the state of the cargo in the respects mentioned above. See p 62, ante.
[20] [1984] 1 Lloyd's Rep 476, CA.
[1] Stephenson, Kerr and Parker LJJ.
[2] See the judgment of Kerr LJ: [1984] 1 Lloyd's Rep 476 at 500.
[3] As to the time when the contract is deemed to be concluded, see Marine Insurance Act 1906, s 21, and p 71, ante.

7 Representation to the first underwriter

Whether a representation made to the first underwriter, should it prove to be untrue and material, is available to enable subsequent underwriters to avoid the contract is not clear.

In *Barber v Fletcher*[4] Lord Mansfield CJ, said:[5]

> 'It has certainly been determined in a number of cases that a representation made to the first underwriter extends to the others.'

In *Forrester v Pigou*[6] Lord Ellenborough CJ, expressed some doubt on the point, while in *Robertson v Marjoribanks*[7] Abbott CJ, ruled that evidence of a communication to the first underwriter was only admissible when it was for the benefit of all the underwriters, by showing the risks to appear less than they would otherwise seem to be. He rejected the evidence of such a communication when it showed the risks to be greater. In other words, the evidence might be given when it minimised the risks, but not when it burdened the underwriter by increasing them.

There is no modern reported case in which the rule that a representation made to the first underwriter is available to subsequent underwriters, and no reference is made to any such rule in the Marine Insurance Act 1906.

8 Effect of misrepresentation

Where the representation turns out to be untrue, the insurer will be entitled to avoid the contract.[8]

His right to avoid the contract, however, must be exercised with the same promptitude as in cases of non-disclosure, for the reasons already pointed out in that connection.[9]

9 Burden of proof

Misrepresentation is usually set up by the insurer as a defence to an action on the policy, and on him therefore will rest the burden of proof, and the misrepresentation relied on must be established very clearly.[10]

10 Evidence

The rate of premium affords some guidance as to the risk assumed by the underwriter.[11]

---

[4] (1779) 1 Doug KB 305. See also, *Pawson v Watson* (1778) 2 Cowp 785; *Bell v Carstairs* (1810) 2 Camp 543; *Marsden v Reid* (1803) 3 East 572.
[5] (1779) 1 Doug KB at 306.
[6] (1813) 1 M&S 9 at 13.
[7] (1819) 2 Stark 573.
[8] Marine Insurance Act 1906, s 20(1).
[9] See p 69, ante.
[10] *Davies v National Fire and Marine Insurance Co of New Zealand* [1891] AC 485. See also *Elkin v Janson* (1845) 13 M&W 655. See further, Ivamy, *General Principles of Insurance Law* (4th Edn, 1979), pp 193–196.
[11] *Bridges v Hunter* (1813) 1 M&S 15. See also, Ivamy, op cit, p 195.

The 'slip' may be looked at in order to show whether the representation was a material one.[12] Evidence as to whether a fact is material or not may be given by experts in insurance business accustomed to fixing premiums in accordance with the risks.[13]

---

[12] *Cory v Patton* (1874) LR 9 QB 577; *Lower Rhine and Wurtemburg Insurance Association v Sedgwick* [1898] 1 QB 739 at 747.
[13] *Seaman v Fonereau* (1743) 2 Stra 1183 at 1185; *Berthon v Loughman* (1817) 2 Stark 258 at 259; *Carter v Boehm* (1766) 3 Burr 1905; *Rickards v Murdock* (1830) 10 B&C 527.

CHAPTER 8

The premium[1]

The premium is the consideration which the insurers receive from the assured in exchange for their undertaking to pay the sum insured in the event insured against.[2]

A THE AMOUNT OF THE PREMIUM

The amount of the premium may be fixed when the contract is made. But sometimes the amount of the premium is to be arranged later.[3] Again, the parties may arrange to pay an additional premium in certain events, e g if there has been a change of voyage.[4] Thus, clause 10 of the Institute Cargo Clauses (A)[5] states:

> '*Change of Voyage Clause*. Where after attachment of this insurance, the destination is changed by the Assured, held covered at a premium and on conditions to be arranged[6] subject to prompt notice being given to the Underwriters.'

In cases where no arrangement has been made as to the amount of the original premium, s 31(1) of the Marine Insurance Act 1906 states:

> 'Where an insurance is effected at a premium to be arranged, and no arrangement is made, a reasonable premium is payable.'

Where the parties have not agreed on the amount of an additional premium, s 31(2) of the Act provides:

> 'Where an insurance is effected on the terms that an additional premium is to be arranged in a given event, and that event happens but no arrangement is made, then a reasonable additional premium is payable.'

In *Hewitt v London General Insurance Co Ltd*[7] a cargo of nitrate was insured for a voyage from Tocopilla to La Pallice, France, via the Panama Canal. The policy contained a clause which stated:

> 'In the event of the voyage being changed or of any deviation from the terms of this policy, the same to be held covered at premium to be arranged hereafter.'

---

[1] See further, Ivamy, *General Principles of Insurance Law* (4th edn, 1979), pp 197–222.
[2] Ibid, p 197.
[3] Ibid, p 198.
[4] See pp 127–129, post.
[5] These clauses are set out in Appendix III, pp 516–519, post.
[6] The word 'arranged' means 'agreed or, in default of agreement fixed by an arbitrator or by the court.': *Liberian Insurance Agency Inc v Mosse* [1977] 2 Lloyd's Rep 560 at 568 (per Donaldson J). An assured can rely on such a clause only if the premium to be arranged would be such as could properly be described as a reasonable commercial rate: ibid, at 568. See p 109, post.
[7] (1925) 23 LlL Rep 243, KBD.

The insurers of the cargo reinsured their risk under a reinsurance policy, which was expressed to be subject to the same terms, clauses and conditions contained in the original policy.

The vessel sailed on her voyage and called at Colon, which was on the contractual route, but there she was ordered to go to New Orleans. She deviated to get to that port, and after sailing from there some weeks later was lost with all her cargo. One of the issues[8] which arose for decision in the action brought against the reinsurers by the insurers, who had paid the original assured for a total loss, was whether the reinsurers were entitled to the payment of an additional premium.

Branson J, held that they were not entitled to such payment. He said that the rule for the ascertainment of an extra premium in such a case was laid down in *Greenock SS Co v Maritime Insurance Co Ltd*.[9] This test was that the parties must assume that the breach was known to them at the time when it happened, and ascertain what it would then have been reasonable to charge. Applying this test to the present case, he observed:[10]

> 'The evidence as to the usual course of a voyage to France from Colon was very slight. It depends on the bunkering capacity of the vessel in question and the price of coal at various ports which might be used to provide coal. A steamer might go to a coaling port on the Atlantic seaboard of the US or to the French West Indies. So in view of all the evidence and although the putting in to New Orleans was clearly a deviation, it was not in my opinion at all a serious one. It is said to have lengthened the voyage by some 500 miles. The voyage was 5,000 miles so the lengthening was in my opinion not more than 10 per cent of the total. The policy subscribed by [the insurers] permits of much greater variations in the voyage than this without any change of premium. It was stated and not denied that upon the original policy no extra premium was asked in respect of the deviation, because it was considered that the deviation did not cause any material addition to the risk.'

In *Alluvials Mining Machinery Co v Stowe*[11] 68 barrels of kerosene were insured from a port in the United Kingdom to some mines in Nigeria. The policy contained a clause stating:

> 'Held covered on premium to be arranged in case of deviation or change or other variation of risk by reason of the exercise of any liberty granted to the shipowner or charterer, etc.'

The assured had arranged for the cargo to be carried as deck cargo. The barrels contained 2,135 gallons of oil, but only 200 gallons arrived at the mines. The assured contended that the loss fell within the clause set out above on the payment of an additional premium. But the insurer repudiated liability on the ground that there had been no 'variation of risk' within the meaning of the clause.

Greer J, held that this defence succeeded, and gave judgment for the insurer.[12] He observed:[13]

---

[8] Other issues were whether the risk had attached, and whether the original assured had an insurable interest at the time of the loss. As to these aspects of the case, see pp 467–468, post, and pp 117–118, post, respectively.
[9] [1903] 1 KB 367 at 375 (per Bigham J). See also, *Mentz, Decker & Co v Maritime Insurance Co Ltd* (1909) 15 Com Cas 17 at 26 (per Hamilton J).
[10] (1925) 23 LlL Rep 243 at 246.
[11] (1922) 10 LlL Rep 96, KBD.
[12] His Lordship also held that the action failed on the ground that there had been non-disclosure of a material fact, i e that the goods were carried on deck. As to this point, see p 65, ante.
[13] (1922) 10 LlL Rep 96 at 97.

'In order to come within this clause it is necessary to decide if the risk which arises from the peril of being loaded on deck and carried on deck was a variation of the risk by reason of the exercise of any liberty granted to the shipowner. It seems to me there was no variation of risk on this voyage at all, because the risk from the start to the end of the contract of carriage was a risk of goods to be loaded on deck.

The facts are not in dispute. On 12 July the goods were handed to the shipowner for carriage upon the terms of a shipping note which says:"Please receive from Messrs Holt & Co, and ship per steamship *Gambia* the following goods," and here the goods are described: "being barrels of paraffin on deck at shippers' risk". Thus from the very commencement of the contractual relations between the plaintiffs, and the shipowners there was a consent on the part of the [assured] and an agreement between the parties that the goods were to be carried on deck, and there never was any variation of that risk from the beginning of the transaction to the end. . . . There was not, in my judgment, a variation in the risk at all; or, rather, there was no variation of the risk by reason of the exercise of any liberty granted to the shipowner. There was no liberty granted to the shipowner in the contract of affreightment to carry these goods on deck, in the sense of the words that he was free to carry them on deck, because it was part of the contract to carry on deck.

I think those words mean the contract of carriage is for ordinary carriage of goods in the usual place and way, but there are liberties reserved to the shipowner to vary that from time to time in certain ways, and the facts in this case do not show any exercise of liberty to vary that risk within the meaning of the words.'

B THE TIME FOR PAYMENT OF THE PREMIUM

Section 52 of the Marine Insurance Act 1906 states:

'Unless otherwise agreed, the duty of the assured or his agent to pay the premium and the duty of the insurer to issue the policy to the assured or his agent, are concurrent conditions, and the insurer is not bound to issue the policy until payment or tender of the premium.'

C THE RESPONSIBILITY FOR PAYMENT OF THE PREMIUM

Section 53(1) of the Marine Insurance Act 1906 states:

'Unless otherwise agreed, where a marine policy is effected on behalf of the assured by a broker, the broker is directly responsible to the insurer for the premium . . . .'

D THE EFFECT OF ACKNOWLEDGMENT OF RECEIPT OF THE PREMIUM[14]

Section 54 of the Marine Insurance Act 1906 states:

'Where a marine policy effected on behalf of the assured by a broker acknowledges the receipt of the premium, such acknowledgment is, in the absence of fraud, conclusive as between the insurer and the assured but not as between the insurer and the broker.'

E THE RETURN OF THE PREMIUM[15]

In some cases the right of the assured to a return of the premium is expressly set

---

[14] See further, Ivamy, *General Principles of Insurance Law* (4th edn, 1979), pp 203–204.
[15] See further, Ivamy, op cit, pp 212–222.

out in the terms of the policy. He can also claim that the premium be returned to him by the insurer where there has been a failure of consideration.

The enforcement of the right to a return will vary according to whether the premium has been paid or not. The insurer remains directly liable to the assured for its return.

1 Return of premium by agreement

Section 83 of the Marine Insurance Act 1906 states:

> 'Where the policy contains a stipulation for the return of the premium, or a proportionate part thereof, on the happening of a certain event, and that event happens, the premium, or, as the case may be, the proportionate part thereof, is thereupon returnable to the assured.'

Policies contain various provisions for the return of premium.

Thus, clause 22 of the Institute Time Clauses (Hulls) sets out a very detailed provision as to the return of the premium where the vessel is laid up in port or is under repair.[16] Similar provisions are to be found in clause 16 of the Institute Time Clauses (Freight).[17]

The meaning of the expression 'laid up in port' was considered in *North Shipping Co v Union Marine Insurance Co*,[18] where it was held that the evidence established a custom that the words were extended to cover various operations in port, which might occur in the normal course of discharging. But they did not cover the case of a vessel remaining in port for a considerable time with steam up and being moved from time to time for the purpose of supplying coal to various ships in the port.

In *Hunter v Wright*[19] a clause in the policy stated that the premium was returnable if the vessel was 'sold or laid up'. After being laid up for several months she was again employed during the currency of the policy. It was held that no premium was returnable on the ground that the clause did not cover a temporary laying up.

In *Pyman v Marten*,[20] where the premium was returnable if the vessel was sold or transferred to new management, it was held that her capture did not satisfy this condition, and that the premium could not be claimed by the assured.

Clauses providing for the return of premium on condition that the vessel is not employed in certain trades or areas are also found.[1]

If in a time policy there is a provision for a return of premium in respect of the time unexpired, and that premium is returned, the effect is to cancel the policy for that unexpired period and to prevent the assured from recovering any loss which takes place during the time in respect of which the premium has been returned.[2]

Where the vessel is in safety in port during a portion of the time insured, there is no right to a return of premium for that portion of time, in the absence of an express provision in the policy.[3]

---

[16] See pp 539–540, post.
[17] See pp 553–554, post.
[18] (1919) 24 Com Cas 161, CA.
[19] (1830) 10 B&C 714.
[20] (1906) 13 Com Cas 64.
[1] E g *Gorsedd SS Co Ltd v Forbes* (1900) 5 Com Cas 413.
[2] *Baines v Woodfall* (1859) 6 CBNS 657.
[3] *Loraine v Thomlinson* (1781) 2 Doug KB 585.

84 *The premium*

2 Return of premium for failure of consideration

The circumstances in which, apart from an express provision in the policy, a return of premium may be claimed, are set out in s 84 of the Marine Insurance Act 1906:

> '(1) Where the consideration for the payment of the premium totally fails and there has been no fraud or illegality on the part of the assured or his agents, the premium is thereupon returnable to the assured.
>
> (2) Where the consideration for the payment of the premium is apportionable and there is a total failure of any apportionable part of the consideration, a proportionate part of the premium is, under like conditions, thereupon returnable to the assured.
>
> (3) In particular—
>
> > *a* Where the policy is void, or is avoided by the insurer as from the commencement of the risk, the premium is returnable, provided that there has been no fraud or illegality on the part of the assured; but if the risk is not apportionable, and has once attached, the premium is not returnable;
> >
> > *b* Where the subject-matter insured, or part thereof, has never been imperilled, the premium, or, as the case may be, a proportionate part thereof, is returnable:
> > Provided that where the subject-matter has been insured "lost or not lost", and has arrived in safety at the time when the contract is concluded, the premium is not returnable unless, at such time, the insurer knew of the safe arrival;
> >
> > *c* Where the assured has no insurable interest throughout the currency of the risk the premium is returnable, provided that this rule does not apply to a policy effected by way of gaming or wagering;
> >
> > *d* Where the assured has a defeasible interest which is terminated during the currency of the risk, the premium is not returnable;
> >
> > *e* Where the assured has over-insured under an unvalued policy, a proportionate part of the premium is returnable;
> >
> > *f* Subject to the foregoing provisions, where the assured has over-insured by double insurance, a proportionate part of the several premiums is returnable:
> > Provided that, if the policies are effected at different times, and any earlier policy has at any time borne the entire risk, or if a claim has been paid on the policy in respect of the full sum insured thereby, no premium is returnable in respect of that policy, and when the double insurance is effected knowingly by the assured no premium is returnable.'

Fraud

Where the assured is guilty of fraud in procuring the policy, although the contract will on that account be voidable, the premium is not returnable.[4]

The assured may, on the other hand, recover the premium if the insurer is guilty of fraud.[5]

Illegality

Where the contract is illegal and by reason of such illegality the policy is void, the Courts will not assist either of the parties where both of them are in pari delicto, and will neither enforce the contract to pay nor compel the return of the premium if it has been paid and the risk has commenced.[6]

Indeed, it would seem that the premium cannot be recovered back even if the risk has never commenced, unless perhaps the assured clearly and at an earlier date repudiates the illegal contract.[7]

---

[4] *Feise v Parkinson* (1812) 4 Taunt 640.
[5] *Duffell v Wilson* (1808) 1 Camp 401.
[6] *Vandyck v Hewitt* (1800) 1 East 96; *Morck v Able* (1802) 3 Bos&P 35.
[7] *Palyart v Leckie* (1817) 6 M&S 290.

Again, the premium will not be returned when the assured materially alters the policy without the consent of the insurer, although such an alteration will render the policy void.[8]

Short interest

When the interest is short, e g where a full cargo is insured and only half of it is shipped, the assured is entitled to a return of the premium proportionate to the shortage.[9]

Thus, in *The Main*[10] a proportionate part of the premium was ordered to be returned where a payment on the valuation in the policy was ordered to be reduced in an equal ratio to the actual amount at risk.

Double insurance

In the same way premiums on the amount of double insurance have been ordered to be returned.

Thus, in *Fisk v Masterman*[11] an insurance was effected on 12 April by five policies at 50 gns per cent on a cargo of cotton then at sea. On 13 April, news having arrived that the ship was safe, a further insurance was bona fide effected by six different policies at 10 gns and 5 gns per cent. The first set of policies alone did not exceed the value of the interest, but both sets together did exceed it. It was held that the assured were entitled to a return of premium on the double insurance from the insurer on the second set in proportion to the sums insured by them on 13 April, but no return of premium was to be made by the insurers in respect of the first set. The reason was that the first group of insurers might have been liable on their policies, the vessel having sailed on 8 February and being overdue. If all the policies had been effected on 12 April there would have been a proportionate return by all the insurers.

Effect of risk never attaching

Where, as may happen, some error or misunderstanding results in no risk being run, the insurer must return the premium.

Thus, in *Stevenson v Snow*[12] Lord Mansfield CJ, said:[13]

> 'Equity implies a condition that the insurer shall not receive the price of running a risk if he runs none.'

Accordingly, the premium will be returnable if the assured insures goods on the wrong ship by mistake.[14]

Effect of attachment of risk

In *Stone v Marine Insurance Co Ocean Ltd of Gothenburg*[15] a ship was bound for

---

[8] *Langhorn v Cologan* (1812) 4 Taunt 330.
[9] *Forbes v Aspinall* (1811) 13 East 323; *Rickman v Carstairs* (1833) 5 B&Ad 651; *Tobin v Harford* (1864) 17 CBNS 528.
[10] [1894] P 320.
[11] (1841) 8 M&W 165.
[12] (1761) 3 Burr 1237.
[13] Ibid, at 1240.
[14] *Martin v Sitwell* (1691) 1 Show 156.
[15] (1876) 1 ExD 81.

Antwerp with a cargo of wheat, and the parties, not knowing her destination and believing her to be at sea, endorsed on the policy leave to change the destination and to allow the ship to go to Antwerp on payment of an additional premium. On that day the ship was in the outer dock at Antwerp, but had not finished her voyage, having yet to go into the inner dock to discharge her cargo. It was held that the insurers were entitled to retain the additional premium since the risk had attached.

Again, in *Bradford v Symondson*[16] where a vessel was overdue, the insurers on cargo reinsured it 'lost or not lost' at a heavy premium. The vessel had, in fact, arrived safely. It was held that the reinsurer was entitled to the agreed premium as the risk had attached.

3 Enforcement of return

Section 82 of the Marine Insurance Act 1906 states:

> 'Where the premium, or a proportionate part thereof, is, by this Act, declared to be returnable—
> *a* If already paid, it may be recovered by the assured from the insurer; and
> *b* If unpaid, it may be retained by the assured or his agent.'

4 Direct responsibility of the insurer to the assured

Section 53(1) of the Act states:

> 'Unless otherwise agreed, where a marine policy is effected on behalf of the assured by a broker, . . . the insurer is directly responsible to the assured for the amount which may be payable in respect of . . . returnable premium.'

---

[16] (1881) 7 QBD 456.

PART II
The policy

CHAPTER 9

Introduction

There are various ways in which policies may be classified, eg (i) voyage policies and time policies; (ii) valued policies and unvalued policies.[1]

The form and contents of the Lloyd's policy are substantially the same as those of a policy issued by a marine insurance company.[2]

The subject-matter insured must be designated in the policy with reasonable certainty.[3]

The policy specifies the attachment and duration of the risk,[4] and lists the perils insured against.[5] A policy may provide cover in respect of war and strikes risks.[6] Certain risks are covered by Protection and Indemnity Associations.[7]

A number of risks which the insurer is not willing to bear are excluded from the cover provided by the policy.[8]

The policy may be determined by the parties, or cancelled by the insurer, eg where he has been induced by fraud on the part of the assured to issue it.[9] If the policy contains terms which have not been agreed upon by both parties, it may be rectified.[10] If a material alteration of the terms of the policy is made by the assured without the consent of the insurer, the insurer is entitled to avoid liability under it.[11]

The policy often contains a promissory warranty, eg a warranty by which the assured undertakes that some particular thing shall or shall not be done, eg that the insured vessel will sail by a specified date.[12]

Policies of marine insurance can be assigned where there is no provision in them to the contrary.[13]

There are various rules relating to the construction of a policy.[14]

After the policy has been effected by him, a broker has certain duties, authority and rights.[15]

---

[1] See Chapter 10, post.
[2] See Chapter 11, post.
[3] See Chapter 12, post.
[4] See Chapter 13, post.
[5] See Chapter 14, post.
[6] See Chapter 15, post.
[7] See Chapter 16, post.
[8] See Chapter 17, post.
[9] See Chapter 19, post.
[10] See Chapter 20, post.
[11] See Chapter 21, post.
[12] See Chapter 18, post.
[13] See Chapter 22, post.
[14] See Chapter 23, post.
[15] See Chapter 24, post.

CHAPTER 10

The classification of policies

Policies are sometimes classified according to the subject-matter insured, e g a hull policy, a goods policy, a freight policy.

Another classification is into lawful policies and 'honour policies',[1] i e those not legally enforceable but binding in honour only.

A major division, however, is that of 'voyage' policies,[2] 'time' policies[3] and 'mixed' policies.[4]

Where the insurance is described in general terms and leaves the name of the ship and other particulars to be defined by subsequent declaration, the policy is known as a 'floating' policy.[5]

Another method of classification is that of 'valued' and 'unvalued' policies.[6]

A VOYAGE, TIME AND MIXED POLICIES

Voyage policy

Section 25(1) of the Marine Insurance Act 1906 states:

> 'Where the contract is to insure the subject-matter "at and from", or from one place to another or others, the policy is called a "voyage policy".'

Thus, a vessel may be insured 'at and from London to New York', or 'from Liverpool to Calcutta'.

Again, goods may even be insured from 'anywhere to anywhere'.[7]

Time policy

Section 25(1) of the Marine Insurance Act 1906 states:

> 'Where the contract is to insure the subject-matter for a definite period of time the policy is called a "time policy".'

Thus, a vessel may be insured 'for twelve months commencing 1 January 1985'.

The word 'definite' means that the period must be specified. It is sufficiently specified if it specifies a stated period even though that period is determinable

---

[1] See infra.
[2] See infra.
[3] See infra.
[4] See p 91, post.
[5] See pp 91–93, post.
[6] See pp 93–100, post.
[7] *Fuerst Day Lawson Ltd v Orion Insurance Co Ltd* [1980] 1 Lloyd's Rep 656, QBD (Com Ct).

on notice, and even though the insurance will be renewed or continued automatically at the end of the period unless determined.[8]

Mixed policy

Section 25(1) of the Marine Insurance Act 1906 states:

> 'A contract for both voyage and time may be included in the same policy.'

Such a policy is known as a 'mixed' policy, e g a vessel may be insured from London to Hong Kong and whilst there for 6 months.[9]

B FLOATING POLICIES

'Floating' policies are those in which the class of the subject-matter insured is named, and also the maximum limit of value fixed. But the specific things insured and their value individually have to be subsequently declared by the assured.

Sometimes the vessel by which the goods are to be carried is not stated otherwise than 'by ship or ships', or by some suitable variation of this form, such as 'by ship or ships' of the Universal SS Co Ltd.

This method of insuring is not modern. It was discussed by Magens in 1755.[10]

Section 29(1) of the Marine Insurance Act 1906 states:

> 'A floating policy is a policy which describes the insurance in general terms, and leaves the name of the ship or ships and other particulars to be defined by subsequent declaration.'

Section 29(2) goes on to state:

> 'The subsequent declaration or declarations may be made by endorsement on the policy, or in other customary manner.'

The advantages afforded to a merchant by 'floating' policies are obvious. Goods may be dispatched to him at his risk; and until he is notified by his consignor, he may be ignorant of the fact that the consignment has been

---

[8] *Compania Maritima San Basilio SA v Oceanus Mutual Underwriting Association (Bermuda) Ltd: The 'Eurysthenes'* [1976] 2 Lloyd's Rep 171 at 177, CA (per Lord Denning MR). In that case the certificate of entry of a vessel in a mutual insurance association stated that the risk was to commence on 17 February 1972. By the rules of the association it attached until noon on 20 February 1972, when the policy year began, and continued thereafter from year to year until determined. It was still in existence in April 1974 when the vessel stranded. The Court of Appeal rejected the shipowners' contention that the insurance was not for a 'definite period of time' because it continued indefinitely until determined by one side or the other. The association's argument that the insurance was for a 'definite period of time' i e until 20 February 1972, and the fact that it continued after that date did not make it any the less a time policy was upheld. As to mutual insurance associations, see pp 475–479, post.

[9] See *Wilson v Boag* [1956] 2 Lloyd's Rep 564 (NSW), where a motor launch was insured for $4\frac{1}{2}$ months while used within a limited radius, and a loss was sustained while on a voyage to a port outside the limits, and the policy was held to be a 'time' policy and not a 'mixed' policy; *M Almojil Establishment v Malayan Motor and General Underwriters (Private) Ltd, The Al-Jubail IV* [1982] 2 Lloyd's Rep 637 (Sing CA), where a vessel was insured for 12 months from and on the voyage from Singapore to the Persian Gulf and whilst trading within the Gulf and it was held that the policy was a 'mixed' policy. (See the judgment of Lai Kew Chai J, ibid, at 640.)

[10] For the general nature of this class of policy as described, see Blackburn J, in *Ionides v Pacific Insurance Co* (1871) LR 6 QB 674 at 682.

forwarded, and have no knowledge of its value or of the ship by which the carriage is effected. Nevertheless he is able to protect himself from the consequences of loss by effecting an insurance in the form of a 'floating' policy.

Similarly, where a seller of goods has contracted to sell them c i f over a period, he may decide to take out a 'floating' policy in respect of the various consignments which he may ship during the period of shipment allowed under the contract.

Where a policy is effected on goods by ship or ships to be thereafter declared, the policy attaches to the goods as soon as, and in the order in which, they are shipped. Every shipment must be declared, for the assured is not entitled to be his own insurer as to some or any of the shipments.[11]

Section 29(3) of the Marine Insurance Act 1906 states:

> 'Unless the policy otherwise provides, the declarations must be made in the order of dispatch for shipment. They must, in the case of goods, comprise all consignments within the terms of the policy, and the value of the goods or other property must be honestly stated, but an omission or an erroneous declaration may be rectified even after loss or arrival, provided the omission or declaration was made in good faith.'

The assured may correct any mistake in the declaration if there is no fraud, and the insurer is not prejudiced thereby.[12]

This right to correct the order of declarations in accordance with the order of shipment is binding on a company whose business is fire insurance, if as reinsurers they insure, against fire at sea, ships to be thereafter declared, for such a risk is a marine risk, and the principles of the law of marine insurance apply.[13]

Declarations must be made as early as possible, and the obligation to do so is not dispensed with by a term in the policy requiring declarations to be made within a certain time of shipment from an intermediate port.

Thus, in *Davies v National Fire and Marine Insurance Co of New Zealand*,[14] in a

---

[11] See *Stephens v Australasian Insurance Co* (1872) LR 8 CP 18; *Dunlop Bros & Co v Townend* [1919] 2 KB 127.

[12] See *Robinson v Touray* (1811) 3 Camp 158; *Scott v Globe Marine Insurance Co Ltd* (1896) 1 Com Cas 370.

[13] *Imperial Marine Insurance Co v Fire Insurance Corpn Ltd* (1879) 4 CPD 166, where Lopes J, observed (at 171): 'The defendants contended that they, the defendants, not being a marine insurance company, the usage stated in *Stephens v Australasian Insurance Co* (1872) LR 8 CP 18 did not attach. As the case depends mainly on whether this custom applies or not, it is convenient first to consider that question. I think it does. The argument is that the usage does not attach because the plaintiffs are insurers against marine risks, and the defendants are insurers against fire. It is conceded, however, that it is within the powers of the defendant company to reinsure against loss by fire in case of ships at sea. The plaintiffs here insure against perils by sea generally, and in order to ease their liability, they reinsure their risks in respect of coal-laden vessels for a limited amount in each case and in respect of fire only, and between specified ports, with the defendants. The contract with the defendants is a contract of fire insurance no doubt, but a contract of fire insurance in respect of a marine risk. The defendants when they entered into that contract were doing the trade or business of marine insurance. The plaintiffs in the course of their business undertook certain marine risks, the defendants for their own benefit take upon themselves to indemnify the plaintiffs against one of those marine risks (being a risk against fire). It was a marine risk in the hands of the plaintiffs, and did not become less so when undertaken by the defendants. When the defendants contracted with the plaintiffs, they contracted with them according to the usage of the particular trade or business to which the contract related. It related to the trade or business of marine insurance. I think, therefore, the usage in *Stephens v Australasian Insurance Co*, supra, applies.'

[14] [1891] AC 485.

floating policy on goods from Melbourne to Sydney per steamers of a named line, and from Sydney to London per steamers of another specified line, it was stipulated that declarations should be made within 48 hours after the departure of steamers from Sydney. It was held that this stipulation did not dispense with the necessity of declaring the risks from Melbourne to Sydney.

Section 29(4) of the Marine Insurance Act 1906 states:

> 'Unless the policy otherwise provides, where a declaration of value is not made until after notice of loss or arrival, the policy must be treated as an unvalued policy as regards the subject-matter of that declaration.'[15]

Although the declaration may ordinarily be made at any time, where the policy expressly provides a time for the making of a declaration, this amounts to a warranty, and non-compliance is unaffected by s 29(4) of the Marine Insurance Act 1906.[16]

Effect of fraud

Fraud in regard to the declaration will render the policy voidable.

Thus, in *Rivaz v Gerussi*[17] an assured effected a series of floating policies for certain named sums to cover shipments to be declared and valued as interest might appear. The policies were to succeed each other in order of date, but the value of the shipments was systematically and fraudulently under-stated by the assured. The fact that they had been so under-stated was concealed from the insurer. It was held that the policy was voidable.

Where several policies exist

Where the assured has effected two or more floating policies, one is usually expressed to be in succession to the other, and where this is the case, the shipments must be declared accordingly.

But where there is no such provision, so that the interest may be covered by either policy, the assured may declare on either policy in respect of such interest.[18]

C VALUED AND UNVALUED POLICIES

Section 27(1) of the Marine Insurance Act 1906 states:

> 'A policy may be either valued or unvalued.'

Unvalued policies are, in fact, very rarely found.

1 Valued policies

Valued policies are those in which the value of the thing insured is agreed on by the parties and the amount set out in the policies.[19]

---

[15] See *Gledstanes v Royal Exchange Assurance* (1864) 5 B&S 797; *Ionides v Pacific Fire and Marine Insurance Co* (1871) LR 6 QB 674; *Union Insurance Society of Canton Ltd v George Wills & Co* [1916] 1 AC 281.
[16] *Union Insurance Society of Canton Ltd v George Wills & Co* [1916] AC 281.
[17] (1880) 6 QBD 222.
[18] *Kewley v Ryan* (1794) 2 Hy Bl 343; *Henchman v Offley* (1782) 2 Hy Bl 345n.
[19] *Bousfield v Barnes* (1815) 4 Camp 228.

Thus, s 27(2) of the Marine Insurance Act 1906 provides:

'A valued policy is a policy which specifies the agreed value of the subject-matter insured.'

Conclusiveness of valuation

The value fixed by the policy is generally conclusive, but it is only binding on the parties and their assignees,[20] for s 27(3) of the Marine Insurance Act 1906 states:

'Subject to the provisions of this Act, and in the absence of fraud, the value fixed by the policy is, as between the insurer and assured, conclusive of the insurable value of the subject intended to be insured, whether the loss be total or partial.'

Thus, in *The Main*[1] a policy was effected on freight valued at £5,500, the valuation having been made in accordance with the rates of freight then current. The ship, however, met with an accident, and in consequence of her detention in port for repairs some engagements for cargo had to be cancelled. Meanwhile freight rates declined considerably, and when the ship sailed, she carried a freight of only £3,250. On a claim for a total loss it was contended by the insurers that, having regard to the fall in freight rates, the valuation could be opened, or at all events payment should be made only on the freight actually risked, which was £3,250 less £952 paid in advance. It was held that the parties were bound by the valuation.

Again, in *Barker v Janson*[2] a ship suffered damage which made her a constructive total loss, but neither party knew it, and a time policy was effected on her for £8,000, during the currency of which she was totally lost. It was held that the value was conclusive, there being no fraud.

In *Woodside v Globe Marine Insurance Co*[3] the valuation in a marine policy against 'fire' was held to be binding where the vessel, having been damaged by stranding to such an extent as to become a constructive total loss, was afterwards totally destroyed by fire, although the insurers were not liable on the policy for a loss by stranding.

In *Thames and Mersey Marine Insurance Co v Pitts, Son and King*,[4] where goods were valued at £7,940, including £1,360 for advance on freight, it was held that £7,940 was the true value of the goods and that, although it included a sum for advance on freight, those words only helped to show the way in which the parties had arrived at the valuation. Further, the inclusion of freight in the value of the goods did not affect the principle that calculations for payment in the event of loss must be based on the valuation contained in the policy. For the purpose of estimating particular average losses it was not permissible to deduct the advance freight from the value of the goods and to treat such advance freight as a separate insurance.

---

[20] The valuation has no other effect, notwithstanding the judgment of Lord Campbell CJ, in *Irving v Manning* (1847) 1 HL Cas 287, where he said that the valuation was 'for *all* purposes', and that of Mellor J, in *North of England Iron SS Insurance Association v Armstrong* (1870) LR 5 QB 244, where he said that 'all questions as to the mutual rights of the assurer and the assured must be governed by the value stated in the policy'.

[1] [1894] P 320.
[2] (1868) LR 3 CP 303.
[3] [1896] 1 QB 105.
[4] [1893] 1 QB 476.

The valuation of freight in a valued policy may be opened if the ship does not carry the whole of the goods, but only a part.[5]

Where the insurance was on charterer's profit-freight valued at £2,000, the assured was only allowed to recover the difference between the chartered freight and the bills of lading freight, which difference amounted to £790.[6]

In *General Shipping and Forwarding Co v British General Insurance Co Ltd*[7] a vessel was insured for £2,000 in December 1921 under a policy in which she was valued at £5,000. In fact, her market value was about £1,500. She became a total loss on 23 September 1923 near the Skerries during the currency of the policy. The assured claimed £2,000 under the policy, but the insurers repudiated liability on the ground that she was grossly overvalued.[8]

It was held that the claim succeeded. Although the vessel was considerably over-insured, probably to the extent of twice her value,[9] the insurers were just as able to estimate her market value as her owners were. There was no fraud, and under s 27(3) of the Marine Insurance Act 1906 the value fixed by the policy was conclusive.

Bailhache J, observed:[10]

> 'Now it is sought to reopen the valuation upon the ground of excessive insurance. In considering that one must bear in mind that this was an insurance of hull and machinery and not an insurance of goods. One must bear in mind that the underwriter had at his hand in Lloyd's Register of ships all the information about the *Borre* that the owners had, except, of course, the price at which she had changed hands, and the circumstances under which she became the property of the Janet SS Co. The defendants had been on the risk twice before; and on this third occasion they increased their risk to £2,000. The underwriters were just as well able in my judgment to estimate what the market value of the *Borre* was as were the people who owned her; and with all the information before them and the same possibilities of estimating her value they chose to accept this valuation and to make a contract on these terms and to take premiums on this valuation of £5,000. Now they seek to upset it on the ground that it is an over-valuation so excessive as to entitle them to be off the risk. Now, where the subject-matter of the case is goods, the matter is on a different footing. There the underwriter has no means of knowing the value of the goods except the statement of the assured. He has not, as in this case, all the information to his hand when he comes to insure goods; and it is much more easy to infer fraud from over-insurance of goods than from over-insurance of ships when both parties are in approximately the same position to know what the market value of the ship proposed to be insured is.
>
> Moreover, it must be borne in mind that underwriters who know their business very well and make large sums of money out of it for the most part favour over-valuation of hull and machinery. They particularly favour it not only when they cover total loss and constructive total loss but particular average loss as well, because the 3 per cent franchise is harder to get over when the value is high than when the value is small. But there are good reasons why they should accept over-valuation in the case of total and constructive total loss, particularly where, as is always the case now, the insured value and the repaired value are to be taken at the same figure. But it is no business of mine to tell underwriters how to conduct business which they do very successfully. It suffices that they prefer over-valuation of hull and machinery.'

---

[5] *Forbes v Aspinall* (1811) 13 East 323; *Williams v North China Insurance Co* (1876) 1 CPD 757. On the effect of including advance freight in the value of the goods as set out in the valuation, see *Thames and Mersey Marine Insurance Co v Pitts* [1893] 1 QB 476.
[6] *Asfar & Co v Blundell* [1895] 2 QB 196; on appeal [1896] 1 QB 123.
[7] (1923) 15 LlL Rep 175, KBD.
[8] Another defence was that there had been a breach of a warranty. As to this aspect of the case, see pp 289–290, post.
[9] For the evidence as to her value, see (1923) 15 LlL Rep 175 at 176.
[10] Ibid, at 176.

In *Papadimitriou v Henderson*[11] a policy in respect of freight and/or chartered freight and/or anticipated freight was effected for a period of 3 months as employment might offer. The sum insured was £3,500. Clause 5 of the Institute Time Clauses (Freight)[12] was incorporated into the policy and stated:

> 'In the event of the total loss, whether absolute or constructive, the amount underwritten by this policy shall be paid in full.'

The vessel was chartered for a voyage from Odessa to Marseilles for the carriage of lorries and spare parts consigned to agents for the Spanish Republican Government. She was captured by an insurgent warship 160 miles east of Malta and taken to Palma, Majorca, and condemned as prize, and so was a constructive total loss.[13] The assured claimed for a loss of freight under the terms of the policy set out above.

Goddard J, held that the action succeeded, and that the full amount insured could be recovered even though there was evidence that the freight which would be earned under a later charter-party which had been fixed was a lesser sum. He observed:[14]

> 'The parties are saying, I think, by the policy, "I, the shipper, have a profit-earning ship, a ship with which I can earn profit, and I want to insure that if this ship is seized during the time the policy is current and effective, I shall recover a certain sum which is anticipated"—"anticipated freight" I think it means—"because it is anticipated that I shall be able to earn at least that sum, if not more, during the period." As I say, it is certain that she could have earned £2,842 upon one voyage, not a very great distance from Marseilles round to Hamburg, and there would have been time, of course, after that voyage—I have not had any evidence as to the exact time that it would take or might be anticipated to take for a voyage from the South of France round to Hamburg, but it would not be very long, and thereafter the ship would have an opportunity of earning further freight.
>
> It seems to me to be well settled by the cases to which [Counsel] has referred me, that there can be no doubt as to the right to recover where a contract has been fixed and where the ship has started on a voyage in anticipation of a future voyage.'

His Lordship then went on to say that his attention had been called to s 67(1) of the Marine Insurance Act 1906 in relation to the measure of indemnity, and said:[15]

> 'Now, the measure of indemnity here it seems to me is fixed in the same way as when you are insuring goods you fix them by valuation. It is fixed at £3,500. I think, therefore, that I am justified in holding that the plaintiff is entitled here to recover £3,500 of freight.'

Valuation and constructive total loss

Section 27(4) of the Marine Insurance Act 1906 states:

> 'Unless the policy otherwise provides, the value fixed by the policy is not conclusive for the purpose of determining whether there has been a constructive total loss.'[16]

Thus, the valuation in the policy is not, apart from a term in the contract,

---

[11] (1939) 64 LlL Rep 345, KBD.
[12] For the modern version of this clause, see clause 15 of the Institute Time Clauses (Freight) set out in Appendix III, p 553, post.
[13] As to this aspect of the case, see pp 359–360, post.
[14] (1939) 64 LlL Rep 345 at 350.
[15] Ibid, at 351.
[16] As to constructive total loss, see pp 362–377, post.

conclusive for the purpose of determining whether a vessel is a constructive total loss, since for *that* purpose the repaired value must be considered.[17]

But the valuation will be conclusive where there is a term to that effect.[18] Thus, clause 17 of the Institute Time Clauses (Hulls) states:

'In ascertaining whether the Vessel is a constructive total loss the insured value shall be taken as the repaired value. . . .'

Again, clause 15 of the Institute Time Clauses (Freight) states:

'. . . In ascertaining whether the Vessel is a constructive total loss, the insured value in the insurances on hull and machinery shall be taken as the repaired value. . . .'

Valuation and general average sacrifice

Where there is a general average sacrifice,[19] although the contributing value of the interests and the amount of the contribution are ascertained for the purposes of adjustment quite independently of the valuation in the policy, the insurer is only bound by the valuation in the policy.

Where therefore the ship is valued in the policy at less than her value in the general average statement, the insurer is only liable to pay to her owner an amount which bears the same ratio to the ship's contribution as the valuation in the policy bears to the valuation in the general average statement.[20]

Valuation and salvage charges

The same rule[1] applies to the insurer's liability for salvage charges in like circumstances.[2]

2 Unvalued policies

Unvalued policies are those in which the value of the thing would have to be ascertained in the event of a loss.

Thus s 28 of the Marine Insurance Act 1906 states:

'An unvalued policy is a policy which does not specify the value of the subject-matter insured, but, subject to the limit of the sum insured, leaves the insurable value to be subsequently ascertained in the manner hereinbefore specified.'

Unvalued policies are found only rarely.[3]

Manner of ascertaining value

The manner of ascertaining the insurable value is set out in s 16 of the Marine

---

[17] *Irving v Manning* (1847) 1 HL Cas 287.
[18] See e g *Helmville Ltd v Yorkshire Insurance Co Ltd, The Medina Princess* [1965] 1 Lloyd's Rep 361, QBD (Com Ct); *Marten v SS Owners' Underwriting Association Ltd* (1902) 71 LJKB 718; *Angel v Merchants' Marine Insurance Co* [1903] 1 KB 811, CA; *North Atlantic SS Co v Burr* (1904) 9 Com Cas 164; *Hall v Hayman* [1912] 2 KB 5.
[19] As to general average sacrifice, see p 183, post.
[20] *SS Balmoral v Marten* [1902] AC 511.
[1] Ibid.
[2] As to salvage charges, see pp 192–193, post.
[3] For an example of an unvalued policy, see *Berger and Light Diffusers Pty Ltd v Pollock* [1973] 2 Lloyd's Rep 442, QBD (Com Ct), which concerned some steel injection moulds. (See the judgment of Kerr J, ibid, at 459.)

Insurance Act 1906. This manner varies according as to whether the subject-matter insured is:

 i a ship;
 ii freight;
 iii goods;
 iv any other subject-matter.

i Insurable value of ship

Section 16 of the Marine Insurance Act 1906 states:

> 'In insurance on ship the insurable value is the value at the commencement of the risk, of the ship, including her outfit, provisions and stores for the officers and crew, money advanced for seamen's wages, and other disbursements (if any) incurred to make the ship fit for the voyage or adventure contemplated by the policy, plus the charges of insurance upon the whole:
>
> The insurable value, in the case of a steamship, includes also the machinery, boilers, and coals and engine stores if owned by the assured, and in the case of a ship engaged in a special trade, the ordinary fittings requisite for that trade.'

Thus, the value of a ship insured under a voyage policy is that which she is worth at the port where the voyage commences, including all her stores and money advanced for seamen's wages, the whole being covered by the premium and commission for effecting the insurance. This is the present method of valuation,[4] and was the view expressed by Stevens.[5] It was adopted by Lawrence J, in *Shawe v Felton*[6] and by Lord Ellenborough CJ, in *Forbes v Aspinall*.[7]

The value, however, on departure or arrival of the vessel will be, in fact, approximate to the true value at the date of the loss according as the loss takes place soon after departure or just before arrival. But to take the value at the port where the voyage commences as the true estimate seems to place the assured in rather a favoured position, especially when he is entitled to insure his freight as well. Still, it has the advantage that the insurer, if he so desires, is able to ascertain with some certainty the actual value at the time, while the difficulties of ascertaining the value at any other time would be very great, if not insurmountable.[8]

It is to be noticed that the more modern practice is to insure disbursements separately and not as part of the ship's valuation.

ii Insurable value of freight

Section 16 of the Marine Insurance Act 1906 states:

> 'In insurance on freight, whether paid in advance or otherwise, the insurable value is the gross amount of freight at the risk of the assured, plus the charges of insurance.'

iii Insurable value of goods

Section 16 of the Marine Insurance Act 1906 states:

---

[4] Cf Benecke, *Principles of Indemnity*, pp 40, 64.
[5] *Stevens on Average*, p 172.
[6] (1801) 2 East 109 at 116.
[7] (1811) 13 East 323 at 329.
[8] See *Herring v Janson* (1895) 1 Com Cas 177.

> 'In insurance on goods or merchandise, the insurable value is the prime cost of the property insured, plus the expenses of and incidental to shipping and the charges of insurance upon the whole.'

Thus, the value of goods will be their value on board at the place of loading plus the insurance premium and commission.[9]

The words 'prime cost' mean the prime cost to the assured at or about the time of shipment or at any rate when the prime cost could be reasonably deemed to represent their value to the owner at the date of shipment.

Thus, in *Williams v Atlantic Assurance Co*[10] Greer LJ, said:[11]

> 'In my opinion, s 16 of the Marine Insurance Act 1906 is to be construed in the light of the consideration that the object of all insurance is indemnity: see especially per Lord Esher MR (then Brett LJ) and Bowen LJ, in *Castellain v Preston*.[12] I think the words "prime cost" in that section mean the prime cost to the assured at or about the time of shipment, or at any rate at some time when the prime cost can be reasonably deemed to represent their value to their owner at the date of shipment. To hold that the prime cost at a period of boom long past must by statute be taken to be the value at a time when values had become diminished by 50 per cent would have the effect of enabling the assured to recover under his right to indemnity for loss during the voyage a sum which would represent a loss incurred long before the voyage started.'

Where the policy is unvalued, the assured is not entitled to claim for the estimated profit he would realise from the sale of the insured goods.[13]

iv Insurable value of any other subject-matter

Section 16 of the Marine Insurance Act 1906 states:

> 'In insurance on any other subject-matter the insurable value is the amount at the risk of the assured when the policy attaches plus the charges of insurance.'

Necessity for proof of value

In *Williams v Atlantic Assurance Co Ltd*[14] an unvalued policy to the extent of £8,000 was effected in respect of 20 cases of textile goods for a voyage from Alexandria to Liverpool. The goods were lost on the voyage. The assignee of the policy claimed under it in respect of the loss, but the Court of Appeal[15] held that the action failed because it was essential that the value of the lost goods should be proved and that this had not been done.

Scrutton LJ, observed:[16]

> 'I am unable to make any finding in view of the innumerable frauds and contradictions which the plaintiff, himself innocent, put forward to support his assignor's claim. If Constantinou

---

[9] *Berger and Light Diffusers Pty Ltd v Pollock* [1973] 2 Lloyd's Rep 442, QBD (Com Ct), where the insurable value of some steel injection moulds was found to be £5,316.20. (See the judgment of Kerr J, ibid, at 456.)
[10] [1932] All ER Rep 32.
[11] Ibid, at 40.
[12] [1881–5] All ER Rep 493 at 495, 499.
[13] *Usher v Noble* (1810) 12 East 639, where Lord Ellenborough CJ, said (at 646): 'The invoice price at the loading port, including premiums of insurance and commission, is for all purposes of either total or average loss the usual standard of calculation resorted to for the purpose of ascertaining the value in the case of an open policy.'
[14] (1932) 43 LlL Rep 177, CA.
[15] Scrutton, Greer and Slesser LJJ.
[16] (1932) 43 LlL Rep 177 at 183. See also, the judgment of Slesser LJ, ibid, at 189.

and Valsamis were plaintiffs, I should unhesitatingly say they had not satisfied me of any amount of value. As it is, the first £1,000 recovered by Mr Williams, if he should recover anything, will go to Messrs Constantinou, Valsamis & Co. I have very carefully considered the evidence, and the plaintiff has not satisfied me of any value that I can reasonably place on whatever goods were contained in the 20 cases described in the manifest as "20 caisses manufacture", which I am satisfied were shipped in the *Parthian* by Messrs Constantinou, Valsamis & Co.'

CHAPTER 11

The form of the policy

A form of policy is set out in the Marine Insurance Act 1906. For nearly 200 years a form was adopted by Lloyd's and the insurance companies and continued in use despite considerable criticism. In 1982 a new form came into use.

A THE FORM SET OUT IN THE MARINE INSURANCE ACT 1906

There are no restrictions as to the form which a marine insurance policy may take. All that s 30(1) of the Marine Insurance Act 1906 states is:

'A policy may be in the form in the First Schedule to this Act.'

The form set out in the First Schedule is as follows:

FORM OF POLICY.

BE IT KNOWN THAT   as well in own name as for and in the name and names of all and every other person or persons to whom the same doth, may, or shall appertain, in part or in all doth make assurance and cause

and them, and every of them, to be insured lost or not lost, at and from

Upon any kind of goods and merchandises, and also upon the body, tackle, apparel, ordnance, munition, artillery, boat, and other furniture, of and in the good ship or vessel called the

whereof is master under God, for this present voyage,
or whosoever else shall go for master in the said ship, or by whatsoever other name or names the said ship, or the master thereof, is or shall be named or called; beginning the adventure upon the said goods and merchandises from the loading thereof aboard the said ship,

upon the said ship, etc

and so shall continue and endure, during her abode there, upon the said ship, etc. And further, until the said ship, with all her ordnance, tackle, apparel, etc, and goods and merchandises whatsoever shall be arrived at

upon the said ship, etc, until she hath moored at anchor twenty-four hours in good safety; and upon the goods and merchandises, until the same be there discharged and safely landed. And it shall be lawful for the said ship, etc, in this voyage, to proceed and sail to and touch and stay at any ports or places whatsoever

without prejudice to this insurance. The said ship, etc, goods and merchandises, etc, for so much as concerns the assured by agreement between the assured and assurers in this policy, are and shall be valued at

Touching the adventures and perils which we the assurers are contented to bear and do take upon us in this voyage: they are of the seas, men of war, fire, enemies, pirates, rovers, thieves, jettisons, letters of mart and countermart, surprisals, takings at sea, arrests, restraints, and detainments of all kings, princes, and people, of what nation, condition, or quality soever, barratry of the master and mariners, and of all other perils, losses, and misfortunes, that have or shall come to the hurt, detriment, or damage of the said goods and merchandises, and ship, etc, or any part thereof. And in case of any loss or misfortune it shall be lawful to the assured, their factors, servants and assigns, to sue, labour, and travel for, in and about the defence, safeguards, and recovery of the said goods and merchandises, and ship, etc, or any part thereof, without prejudice to this insurance; to the charges whereof we, the assurers, will contribute each one according to the rate and quantity of his sum herein assured. And it is especially declared and agreed that no acts of the insurer or insured in recovering, saving, or preserving the property insured shall be considered as a waiver, or acceptance of abandonment. And it is agreed by us, the insurers, that this writing or policy of assurance shall be of as much force and effect as the surest writing or policy of assurance heretofore made in Lombard Street, or in the Royal Exchange, or elsewhere in London. And so we, the assurers, are contented, and do hereby promise and bind ourselves, each one for his own part, our heirs, executors, and goods to the assured, their executors, administrators, and assigns, for the true performance of the premises, confessing ourselves paid the consideration due unto us for this assurance by the assured, at and after the rate of

IN WITNESS whereof we, the assurers, have subscribed our names and sums assured in London.

NB—Corn, fish, salt, fruit, flour, and seed are warranted free from average, unless general, or the ship be stranded—sugar, tobacco, hemp, flax, hides and skins are warranted free from average, under five pounds per cent, and all other goods, also the ship and freight, are warranted free from average, under three pounds per cent unless general, or the ship be stranded.

B THE FORM USED UP TO 1982

Lloyd's developed their own form of policy, but the wording of a marine insurance company's policy was substantially the same.

The form of the Lloyd's policy, which had been in use for about 200 years, was still employed to cover all kinds of marine risks, any variations which the newer developments of commerce necessitated being made by means of clauses which were incorporated with the policy in various ways.

Sometimes clauses were printed on slips and gummed to the policy, or they were written, printed, or stamped on the margin of the policy.

In other cases, variations were incorporated by reference to some other document, e g when it was intended that the policy should embody the rules of an association or protection club, or any other rules recognised in the shipping world, such as the York–Antwerp Rules 1974.[1]

The result was that, instead of having a policy expressly drawn to meet the special risks, the old form was packed with clauses and exceptions, and became a document of some complexity, the construction of which was often a matter of great difficulty.

The contract thus formed was often the subject of adverse judicial comment. Indeed, the judicial view of marine policies would seem to be well summarised in the words of Buller J, which form a criticism as applicable today as when they were uttered in *Brough v Whitmore*[2] in 1791:

'Without commenting on the words of the policy, it is sufficient to say that a policy of assurance has at all times been considered in courts of law as an absurd and incoherent instrument.'

---

[1] The York–Antwerp Rules 1974 are set out in Appendix IV, pp 563–567, post.
[2] [1791] 4 Term Rep 206 at 210. See also, *Simond v Boydell* (1779) 1 Doug KB 268 at 270 (per Lord Mansfield CJ); *Stewart v Merchants' Marine Insurance Co* (1885) 16 QBD 619 at 621 (per Lord Esher MR); *Hydarnes SS Co v Indemnity Mutual Marine Assurance Co* [1895] 1 QB 500; *The Glenlivet* [1894] P 48 at 53 (per Lindley LJ); *Cunard SS Co v Marten* [1902] 2 KB 624 at 626 (per Walton J); *Western Assurance Co of Toronto v Poole* [1903] 1 KB 376 at 388 (per Bigham J); *Baring Bros & Co v Marine Insurance Co* (1894) 10 TLR 276; *Nottebohn v Richter* (1886) 18 QBD 63.

In *Marten v Vestey Bros Ltd*[3] Lord Dunedin referred to the Lloyd's policy in the following words:[4]

> 'The form known as "Lloyd's Policy" is a very ancient document. It undoubtedly owed its original form to the time, now long past, when the ordinary state of affairs was that the shipowner and the merchant were one and the same person. Like Antonio in "The Merchant of Venice", he sent out his argosy laden with his own goods to be disposed of in foreign lands and to bring back foreign goods in exchange.
>
> The oldest policy known in England is of date 1613, a copy of it being preserved in the Bodleian Library at Oxford, and differs little from the policy of the present day; but the actual printed form of policy which we now have was arranged in 1779 at a general meeting of members of Lloyd's, who undertook to establish a particular form of marine insurance policy and not to allow any alterations in that policy. With the exception of the introduction in 1874 of what is known as the "Waiver Clause", and the alteration in 1850 of the phrase at the commencement of the policy, "In the name of God, Amen", to "Be it known that", the printed policy at present is the policy of 1779.'

He then went on to consider the practice of making additions to the form, and said:[5]

> 'Now, undoubtedly it might have been better—it would have saved this and, perhaps, other controversies—if, when modern times had come, the underwriters had reformed this document and adopted a separate form for insurance on ship, goods and freight respectively when the insurance was only to cover one of these three things. But they have not done so. Nay, more, they have not in practice even taken the trouble, when a policy is effected on one, to delete the phrases obviously only applying to the other two things which may be insured. But they leave blanks in the policy, and these blanks are filled up so as to fix what is the subject insured, and additional and special clauses are often written on the margin or affixed to the policy by gum. This may be a bad practice, but it is a universal practice.'

In *Kulukundis v Norwich Union Fire Insurance Society*[6] Scott LJ, said:[7]

> 'The archaic words of our ancient form of marine policy, set out in the schedule to the Act and embodied in the policy sued upon, afford little guidance in the way of description or explanation as to the circumstances which the insurer agrees shall constitute a loss for which he has to pay. Indeed the statutory form is inapt to cover freight at all, although it is habitually used by Lloyd's for insurance of freight by adding written or typed words to the printed form, regardless of grammar, so as to bring in that subject-matter.'

In *Atlantic Maritime Co Incorporated v Gibbon*[8] Sir Raymond Evershed MR, said:[9]

> 'The policy is in a form which, I gather, is common in cases of this kind; that is to say, it is based upon the standard form of Lloyd's policy to which numerous slips, ten in all, have been added,

---

[3] [1920] All ER Rep 603, HL.
[4] Ibid, at 606.
[5] Ibid, at 606.
[6] [1937] 1 KB 1, [1936] 2 All ER 242, CA.
[7] Ibid, at 270.
[8] [1953] 2 Lloyd's Rep 294, CA.
[9] Ibid, at 299. See also, the judgment of Sellers J, in the court below: [1953] 1 Lloyd's Rep 278 at 285, where he said that freight insurance entered into on the old form of policy with deletions and additions to adapt it to the intended contract had almost invariably given rise to difficulties of interpretation, and he did not regard the present case as one of the exceptions. See further, *Amin Rasheed Shipping Corpn v Kuwait Insurance Co, The Al Wahab* [1983] 2 Lloyd's Rep 365 at 370, HL, where Lord Diplock said that the adoption of the obsolete language of the Lloyd's policy made it impossible to discover what were the legal incidents of the mutual rights and obligations accepted by the insurers and the assured as having been brought into existence by the contract, unless recourse was had not only to the Rules for Construction of the Policy contained in the Schedule to the Marine Insurance Act 1906 but also to the substantive provisions of the Act. For the Rules for Construction of the Policy, see p 330, post.

so that little indeed is left of the original foundation. . . . I have no doubt that those engaged in this class of business find it convenient that their policies should take this form. But it cannot, I think, be denied that the effect produced is in some degree one of taking away with one hand what has been given with the other, and the task of the courts in construing the resultant document or documents is certainly rendered more difficult. The very numerous cases to which we have been referred make it not, indeed, easy to contend that those entering into this class of business well understand the conventional accumulation of clauses which constitute the policy.'

An echo of this sentiment is to be found in the American case of *Calmar SS Corpn v Scott, The Portmar*,[10] where Frankfurter J, said that the policy had been assembled by imposing on the age-old Lloyd's form layer upon layer of warranties and riders. Warranties freed the underwriters from obligation imposed by riders, and subsequently riders then reimposed obligations thus avoided. Construing such conglomerate provisions required a skill not unlike that called for in the decipherment of obscure palimpsest texts.

C THE NEW FORM

In January 1982 Lloyd's and the marine insurance companies issued new forms of policies.[11]

The forms contain a statement that in consideration of the payment of the premium the insurers agree to insure the subject-matter against loss, damage, liability or expense in the proportions and manner provided. Then follows a schedule stating (i) the policy number; (ii) the name of the assured;[12] (iii) the name of the vessel; (iv) the voyage or period of insurance; (v) the subject-matter insured; (vi) the agreed value (if any); (vii) the amount insured; (viii) the premium; and (ix) clauses, endorsements, special clauses and warranties.[13]

As from 1 January 1982 new Institute[14] Clauses for use with the new forms have been issued. In general, these set out (a) the risks covered; (b) the exceptions; (c) the duration of the policy; (d) the circumstances in which a claim can be made; (e) the assured's duty to minimize losses; and (f) the fact that English law and practice are to apply.

The more important of these clauses are:

1. The Institute Cargo Clauses (A).[15]
2. The Institute Cargo Clauses (B).[16]
3. The Institute Cargo Clauses (C).[17]
4. The Institute War Clauses (Cargo).[18]
5. The Institute Strikes Clauses (Cargo).[19]

---

[10] [1953] 1 Lloyd's Rep 485 at 488.
[11] See Appendix II, pp 510–515, post.
[12] The Marine Insurance Act 1906, s 23 states: 'A marine policy must specify (1) the name of the assured, or of some person who effects the insurance on his behalf . . .'
[13] As to warranties, see pp 280–314, post.
[14] I e the Institute of London Underwriters. The clauses are revised from time to time to meet the changing needs of the marine insurance world.
[15] See Appendix III, pp 516–519, post.
[16] See Appendix III, pp 519–522, post.
[17] See Appendix III, pp 523–526, post.
[18] See Appendix III, pp 526–529, post.
[19] See Appendix III, pp 530–532, post.

6   The Institute Time Clauses (Hulls).[20]
7   The Institute Voyage Clauses (Hulls).[1]
8   The Institute War and Strikes Clauses (Hulls–Time).[2]
9   The Institute War and Strikes Clauses (Hulls–Voyage).[3]
10 The Institute Time Clauses (Freight).[4]
11 The Institute Voyage Clauses (Freight).[5]
12 The Institute War and Strikes Clauses (Freight–Time).[6]
13 The Institute War and Strikes Clauses (Voyage–Freight).[7]

Section 24 of the Marine Insurance Act 1906 states:

> 'A marine policy must be signed by or on behalf of the insurer, provided that in the case of a corporation the corporate seal may be sufficient, but nothing in this section shall be construed as requiring the subscription of a corporation to be under seal.'[8]

At one time the assured's broker obtained the underwriters' signatures to a Lloyd's policy, but now they are affixed by Lloyd's Policy Signing Office.

Strictly speaking each underwriter should sign for himself but where as is usually the case, the underwriters work in syndicates, one person signs as their agent.[9]

Section 67(2) of the Marine Insurance Act 1906 states:

> 'Where there is a loss recoverable under the policy, the insurer, or each insurer if there be more than one, is liable for such proportion of the measure of indemnity as the amount of his subscription bears to the value fixed by the policy, in the case of a valued policy,[10] or to the insurable value in the case of an unvalued policy.'[11]

---

[20] See Appendix III, pp 533–540, post.
[1] See Appendix III, pp 540–547, post.
[2] See Appendix III, pp 547–548, post.
[3] See Appendix III, pp 549–550, post.
[4] See Appendix III, pp 550–554, post.
[5] See Appendix III, pp 555–558, post.
[6] See Appendix III, pp 558–559, post.
[7] See Appendix III, pp 560–561, post.
[8] Where the insurer is a partnership, the name of the firm is sufficient: *Reid v Allan* (1849) 4 Exch 326. But nowadays partnerships between underwriters are forbidden by usage.
[9] As to syndicates, see Ivamy, *General Principles of Insurance Law* (4th edn, 1979), p 597.
[10] As to valued policies, see pp 93–97, ante.
[11] As to unvalued policies, see pp 97–100, ante.

CHAPTER 12
Designation of the subject-matter in the policy

The subject-matter insured must be stated in the policy with reasonable certainty, but the nature and extent of the assured's interest in the subject-matter need not be specified. If the subject-matter insured is designated in general terms, the policy is construed to apply to the interest intended by the assured to be covered.

A THE NEED FOR REASONABLE CERTAINTY

Section 26(1) of the Marine Insurance Act 1906 states:

> 'The subject-matter insured must be designated in a marine policy with reasonable certainty.'

Section 26(4) provides:

> 'In the application of this section regard shall be had to any usage regulating the designation of the subject-matter insured.'

1 Usage

By usage it is understood that when the 'subject-matter insured' consists of goods, not only are the goods themselves insured but so is the adventure.[1]

Thus, Earl Loreburn said:[2]

> 'There are many things that may be at risk, and in respect of which insurance may be effected—ship, goods, freight, profits, and so on. There are also familiar even antique, expressions constantly used from long ago in marine policies, and continued because they are well understood in the business, or have been interpreted by Judges. This section says that regard is to be had to any usage regulating the designation of the subject-matter assured. The words of this policy have for generations been understood and held by Judges to designate not merely the goods but also the adventure. So far from abrogating this designation of subject-matter I should have thought the Act took pains to preserve it and others like it. I will merely in a sentence refer to s 91(2) of the Act which preserves the rules of the Common Law, including the law merchant, save in so far as they are inconsistent with the express provisions of this Act.
> It seems to me that Parliament has triply guarded against the danger that the Act should be construed in the sense urged upon us by Counsel for the [insurers]. It has refrained from saying that the old rule shall be altered, which of itself would suffice. It has twice warned us that we are to regard and preserve rules and usages in terms that are applicable to this rule. Accordingly, I take with me the conclusion that the adventure was a subject-matter insured.'

---

[1] *British and Foreign Marine Insurance Co Ltd v Samuel Sanday & Co* [1916–17] All ER Rep 134, HL.
[2] Ibid, at 137.

2 Describing subject-matter briefly

The subject-matter insured is often merely referred to briefly, e g 'freight', 'ship', 'goods'.

i 'Freight'

Rule 16 of the Rules for Construction of Policy set out in the First Schedule to the Marine Insurance Act 1906 states:

> 'The term "freight" includes the profit derivable by a shipowner from the employment of his ship to carry his own goods or moveables,[3] as well as freight payable by a third party, but does not include passage money.'[4]

Advance freight may be insured under the simple designation of 'freight', and need not be described as 'advance'.[5]

ii 'Ship'

Rule 15 of the Rules for Construction of Policy set out in the First Schedule to the Marine Insurance Act 1906 states:

> 'The term "ship" includes the hull, materials and outfit, stores and provisions for the officers and crew, and, in the case of vessels engaged in a special trade, the ordinary fittings requisite for the trade, and also, in the case of a steamship, the machinery, boilers, and coals and engine stores, if owned by the assured.'

The word 'hull' in a policy on 'hull and machinery' does not cover coal, engine room and deck stores, provisions and cabin stores, port expenses and advances or premiums.[6]

iii 'Goods'

Rule 17 of the Rules for Construction of Policy set out in the First Schedule to the Marine Insurance Act 1906 states:

> 'The term "goods' means goods in the nature of merchandise, and does not include personal effects[7] or provisions and stores for use on board.
> In the absence of any usage to the contrary, deck cargo and living animals must be insured specifically, and not under the general denomination of goods.'

The words 'in the absence of any usage to the contrary' mean a usage in the trade and not a usage of the business of insurance.[8]

Thus, in *British and Foreign Marine Insurance Co v Gaunt*,[9] where part of a cargo of wool, which had been insured from South America to England, had been carried on deck on a local steamer to the port of shipment for loading on to an

---

[3] 'Moveables' means 'any moveable tangible property other than the ship and includes money, valuable securities, and other documents': Marine Insurance Act 1906, s 90.
[4] The term 'freight' is also defined in similar terms in the Marine Insurance Act 1906, s 90.
[5] *Hall v Janson* (1855) 4 E&B 500, in which case, however, the interest was described as 'money advanced on account of freight'.
[6] *Roddick v Indemnity Mutual Marine Insurance Co* [1895] 2 QB 380, CA.
[7] Personal belongings may be insured as 'effects': *Duff v Mackenzie* (1857) 3 CBNS 16.
[8] *British and Foreign Marine Insurance Co Ltd v Gaunt* [1921] 2 AC 41, HL.
[9] [1921] All ER Rep 447, HL. The case also concerned the burden of proving a loss under an 'all risks' policy. As to this point, see p 178, post.

ocean steamer, the insurers repudiated in respect of this part on the ground that it ought to have been insured specifically.

The House of Lords[10] rejected this contention, and held that there was a usage in the trade to carry deck cargo, and that the insurance company was liable even if it did not know of the usage.

Lord Birkenhead LC, said:[11]

> 'It was contended for the [insurers] that the "usage" contemplated by the rule was a usage in the insurance business as to the description for the purposes of insurance. This cannot be so. In the first place this construction would involve such a departure from the principles of law existing when the Act was passed that we ought not so to construe the words unless such an alteration was most plainly intended; secondly, inasmuch as an insurer is bound to know the usages of trade, if a usage exists in the trade to carry goods of a particular kind on deck, he knows that such goods are likely to be so carried, and there is little reason for requiring a specific statement that such a method of carriage will or may be employed. The "usage", therefore, must be a trade usage, and it was abundantly established in the case which your Lordships are considering. There was, therefore, no need to insure the wool specifically as deck cargo, and the omission to do so does not afford any defence to the [insurers].'

The term 'goods' will cover substituted cargoes where the policy is 'out and home', or when it insured voyages to successive ports, or is a time policy.[12]

It will also cover the produce of a fishing expedition,[13] the interest of a carrier,[14] and the outfit of an emigrant.[15]

But it will not cover jewellery worn on the person[16] nor profits.[17] Accordingly, if profits are to be insured, they should be specifically described as such in the policy.[18]

Bottomry and respondentia are not covered by the term 'goods', and should be specifically described in the policy, unless a usage can be proved in any particular trade under which it is usual to insure such interests under general words.[19]

'Cotton in bales' will cover 'pressed bales', if that is the meaning of the term in the particular trade.[20]

In *Overseas Commodities Ltd v Style*[1] some cases of tinned pork were insured under an 'all risks' policy under which each case had to be marked 'L 26 NMS'. Some of the cases were not so marked, and it was held that the policy attached only to such of the cases that complied with this requirement, and the insurer was under no liability in respect of the loss of any cases not so marked.

---

[10] Lord Birkenhead LC, Viscount Finlay, Viscount Cave, Lord Atkinson and Lord Sumner.
[11] [1921] All ER Rep 447 at 450. See also the speech of Viscount Finlay, ibid, at 453–454, and that of Lord Sumner, ibid, at 455–458.
[12] *Hill v Patten* (1807) 8 East 373.
[13] Ibid.
[14] *Crowley v Cohen* (1832) 3 B&Ad 478.
[15] *Wilkinson v Hyde* (1858) 3 CBNS 30.
[16] *Brown v Stapyleton* (1827) 4 Bing 119.
[17] *Inglis v Stock* (1885) 10 App Cas 263.
[18] *Royal Exchange Assurance Corpn v M'Swiney* (1850) 14 QB 646; *Inglis v Stock* supra; *Halhead v Young* (1856) 6 E&B 312; *Crowley v Cohen*, supra; *Mackenzie v Whitworth* (1875) 1 ExD 36.
[19] *Glover v Black* (1763) 3 Burr 1394; *Simonds v Hodgson* (1832) 3 B&Ad 50.
[20] *Taylor v Briggs* (1827) 2 C&P 525.
[1] [1958] 1 Lloyd's Rep 546, QBD (Com Ct).

3 Error in description

A clause[2] may state:

> 'Held covered at a premium to be arranged in case of . . . any omission or error in the description of the interest, vessel or voyage.'

The clause may refer to a 'note' in the policy stating:

> 'It is necessary for the Assured when they become aware of an event which is held covered under this insurance to give prompt notice to Underwriters and the right to such cover is dependent upon compliance with this obligation.'

Premium to be arranged

The word 'arranged' means 'agreed or, in default of agreement, fixed by an arbitrator or by the court.'[3]

The clause does not contemplate any alteration in the terms of the insurance other than in respect of premium.[4]

The clause applies only if the assured on the basis of an accurate declaration of all the facts affecting the risk but excluding knowledge of what was to happen in the event, could have obtained a quotation in the market at a premium which could properly be described as a 'reasonable commercial rate'.[5]

Thus, in *Liberian Insurance Agency Inc v Mosse*[6] evidence was given to the effect that no insurer, knowing that the insured consignment of enamelware was an end of production consignment containing a variety of qualities including a high proportion of seconds and that a significant proportion of the cargo was packed in export cartons, would have quoted a reasonable commercial rate of premium on all risks terms, unless he was protected by a fpa warranty.[7]

Good faith

The 'held covered' clause has no application when the omission or error in the description was intended to deceive.[8]

Interest

The word 'interest' in the 'held covered' clause means 'subject-matter insured' as was held in *Hewitt Bros v Wilson*,[9] where four cases of printing machinery were insured for a voyage from London to Malta. A portion of the machinery was damaged by breakage during the voyage, and the assured claimed an indemnity in respect of it. The policy contained a clause stating:

---

[2] As in clause 4 of the Institute Cargo Clauses (FPA) which are now replaced by the Institute Cargo Clauses (A) set out in Appendix III, pp 516–519, post. The new Clauses, however, do not contain a 'held covered' clause in case of any omission or error in the description of the interest.
[3] *Liberian Insurance Agency Inc v Mosse* [1977] 2 Lloyd's Rep 560, QBD (Com Ct), at 568 (per Donaldson J).
[4] Ibid, at 568 (per Donaldson J).
[5] Ibid, at 567 (per Donaldson J).
[6] [1977] 2 Lloyd's Rep 560, QBD (Com Ct).
[7] As to the fpa warranty, see pp 429–432, post.
[8] *Liberian Insurance Agency Inc v Mosse* [1977] 2 Lloyd's Rep 560 at 567 (per Donaldson J); *Hewitt Bros v Wilson* [1915] 2 KB 739, CA.
[9] (1915) 113 LT 304, CA.

'In the event of . . . any incorrect definition of the interest insured, it is agreed to hold the assured covered at a premium (if any) to be arranged.'

The insurers contended that the words 'interest insured' meant 'insurable interest'. But the Court of Appeal[10] held that this was not their true meaning. Lord Reading LCJ, said:[11]

'I have looked through the statute and have asked if Counsel could point to anything in it which shows that the use of the phrase "interest insured" is applicable to the insurable interest. The words "interest insured" can, to my mind, be explained as a useful phrase to indicate that it is the subject-matter insured in which the person insuring has an interest in the goods themselves.

I have no hesitation in coming to the conclusion that that is the true meaning of the words used.'

Swinfen Eady LJ, observed:[12]

'I can see no reason for upholding the contention that the words "interest insured" in the "held covered clause" relate to the insurable interest which the assured had in the goods insured under the policy. It is not necessary more particularly to describe or deal with the insurable interest under the policy. It is not necessary that the assured should have an insurable interest in the subject-matter of the insurance at the time when the insurance is effected. (See Marine Insurance Act 1906, s 6(1)). In my opinion the words "interest insured" do not refer to insurable interest, but only to the subject-matter of the insurance, so that the words "any incorrect definition of the interest insured" mean, therefore, "any incorrect definition of the subject-matter of the insurance".'

Bray J, said:[13]

'It is said that the words "interest insured" mean "insurable interest" in the subject-matter of the insurance, and not the subject-matter itself. I agree that we ought to apply the ordinary principles of construction to the words. Under the Marine Insurance Act 1906, and under the ordinary law merchant, it is not necessary to define the interest of the assured at all. Therefore the words "definition of interest" (if "interest" is to be taken as meaning insurable interest) do not describe anything that is usually to be found in policies of insurance. But I can see no reason for giving to these words any such meaning. The term is a good one to use in order to describe the subject-matter of the insurance, and I can see no reason why any artificial meaning should be attributed to it, more especially when it is remembered that in this same policy there is another clause in which the word "interest" is clearly used to mean the subject-matter of the insurance.'

Effect of the 'note'

In *Liberian Insurance Agency Inc v Mosse*[14] Donaldson J, said[15] that, as he had indicated in argument, he entertained some doubt as to whether the 'note', which was not a numbered clause, was to be construed as having contractual effect. But he was satisfied that the 'note' accurately stated the law, whether or not it was contractual.

---

[10] Lord Reading LCJ, Swinfen Eady LJ and Bray J.
[11] (1915) 113 LT 304 at 306.
[12] Ibid, at 307.
[13] Ibid, at 307.
[14] [1977] 2 Lloyd's Rep 560, QBD (Com Ct).
[15] Ibid, at 566. See also *Hood v West End Motor Car Packing Co Ltd* [1917] 2 KB 38, CA; *Thames and Mersey Marine Insurance Co Ltd v H T Van Laun & Co* [1917] 2 KB 48, HL.

'Prompt notice'

In *Liberian Insurance Agency Inc v Mosse*[16] his Lordship said[17] that if the assured was to take advantage of the 'held covered' clause, he must give notice[18] to the insurers expressly or impliedly seeking a cover in accordance with the clause within a reasonable time of learning of the change of voyage or of the omission or error in the description. What time was reasonable would depend on all the circumstances. Thus, if the assured learnt the true facts while the risk was still current, a reasonable time would usually be a shorter period than when that occurred when the adventure had already ended. If the assured learnt the true facts when it was in the grip of a peril, a reasonable time would be very short indeed.

His Lordship went on to say[19] that it might be objected that it was unfortunate to use the words 'prompt notice' when what was meant was notice within a reasonable time. But in the context of a clause which might impose on insurers, and indirectly on reinsurers, risks which they had never specifically accepted, he did not think that notice which was other than prompt could ever be said to be given within a reasonable time. The use of the word 'prompt' was not only justifiable but also desirable in explanation of the obligation which was implicit in the clause itself.

B NATURE AND EXTENT OF THE INTEREST

Section 26(2) of the Marine Insurance Act 1906 states:

> 'The nature and extent of the interest of the assured in the subject-matter insured need not be specified in the policy.'

Thus, it is not necessary for the policy to state the particular way in which the assured is interested in the subject-matter insured, e g as owner, trustee, mortgagor or mortgagee. It is sufficient if that thing is insured out of which his particular interest springs.[20]

Similarly, the policy need not specify that the insurer is reinsuring. Thus, if he has insured on goods, it is sufficient if the reinsurance policy merely states that it is 'on goods'.[1] But it is the usual practice for a reinsurance policy to contain a clause stating: 'Being a reinsurance subject to the same clauses and conditions as the original policy and to pay as may be paid thereon.'

C INTEREST INTENDED TO BE COVERED

Section 26(3) of the Marine Insurance Act 1906 states:

---

[16] [1977] 2 Lloyd's Rep 560, QBD (Com Ct).
[17] Ibid, at 566.
[18] In *Liberian Insurance Agency Inc v Mosse*, supra, the assured did not put the full facts before the insurers and did not seek the protection of the clause. All that happened was that the fact that part of the consignment was in cartons instead of in wooden cases was revealed incidentally in the course of a survey report. (See the judgment of Donaldson J, ibid, at 568.)
[19] Ibid, at 566.
[20] *Irving v Richardson* (1831) 2 B&Ad 193: *Carruthers v Sheddon* (1815) 6 Taunt 14.
[1] *Mackenzie v Whitworth* (1875) 1 ExD 36; *Craufurd v Hunter* (1798) 8 Term Rep 13; *Lucena v Craufurd* (1806) 2 Bos&PNR 269.

'Where the policy designates the subject-matter insured in general terms, it shall be construed to apply to the interest intended by the assured to be covered.'

The word 'interest' in the Marine Insurance Act 1906, s 26(3), means the interest which the assured has in the subject-matter of the insurance.[2]

Thus, Bailhache J, said:[3]

'Subsection (3) has been the subject of a good deal of judicial criticism on the ground that it is difficult to understand. I think the chief difficulty about it is due to the fact that the word "interest" is very often used in marine insurance in two senses. It is very often used to mean the nature of the interest which the assured has in the subject-matter of the insurance, and it is also often used in the looser sense to indicate the subject-matter of the insurance itself. When, however, the same section of an Act of Parliament contains the word "subject-matter" and the word "interest" used together, it seems to me quite clear that the word "interest" must be construed in its stricter and proper sense. I think that sub-s (3) means that where the policy designates the subject-matter insured in general terms, as, for instance, in this case, merchandise, it shall be construed to apply to the interest—that is to say, the pecuniary or insurable interest which the assured intended should be covered, whether that interest be that of the owner or whether it be that of a person who has made advances, or of a person who is interested in the safe arrival of the goods by reason of the commission which he shall get on the sale, and, of course, the policy applies to a case where a person takes out a floating policy not to cover any pecuniary interest of his own, but to cover the liabilities and interest of persons on whose behalf he is instructed to insure.'

---

[2] *Dunlop Bros & Co v Townend* [1918–19] All ER Rep 575.
[3] Ibid, at 578.

CHAPTER 13

Attachment and duration of the risk under the policy

The attachment and duration of the risk, ie the period during which the insurer is liable for any loss or damage which may be suffered by the subject-matter insured will depend on whether the policy is a time policy or a voyage policy.

A TIME POLICIES

The attachment and duration of the risk under the policy will depend on its terms. Thus, for example, a vessel may be insured 'From 12 noon 1 January 1986 to 12 noon on 1 January 1987.

Under a policy in this form the risk will normally terminate on 1 January 1987 at 12 noon, but policies often contain a 'continuation clause'. An example is provided by clause 2 of the Institute Time Clauses (Hulls)[1] which states:

> 'Should the Vessel at the expiration of this Policy be at sea or in distress or at a port of refuge or of call, she shall, provided previous notice be given to the Underwriters, be held covered at a pro rata monthly premium to her port of destination.'

At one time no policy could be made for a period exceeding 12 months,[2] but now there are no such restrictions.[3]

The hour of the day on which the risk is to commence and terminate is almost invariably expressed in all English time policies, and, subject to the Summer Time Act 1972, s 3, the time referred to, unless it is otherwise specifically stated, is Greenwich mean time.[4]

Sometimes the policy attaches on the happening of a specified event. Thus, in *Rosa v Insurance Co of the State of Pennsylvania: The Belle of Portugal*,[5] cargo was insured under a policy which stated:

> 'Insurance to attach when vessel advise Carl and Carl Insurance, Inc of the amount of fish on board. Vessel is permitted to report at various times throughout the voyage. No insurance to

---

[1] These clauses are set out in Appendix III, pp 533–540, post.
[2] Stamp Act 1891, s 93. But s 11(1) of the Finance Act 1901 rendered valid a policy containing a continuation clause as defined by s 11(3) of that Act. Viz 'The expression "continuation clause" means an agreement to the following or the like effect, namely, that in the event of the ship being at sea or the voyage not otherwise completed on the expiration of the policy, the subject-matter of the insurance shall be held covered until the arrival of the ship or for a reasonable time thereafter not exceeding thirty days.'
[3] Finance Act 1959, Eighth Schedule, Part II which repealed, inter alia, s 93 of the Stamp Act 1891, and s 11 of the Finance Act 1901.
[4] Interpretation Act 1978, ss 9, 23(3).
[5] [1970] 2 Lloyd's Rep 386, US Ct of Appeals, Ninth Circuit, where it was held that the failure to report the amount of fish on board was caused by heavy rain which curtailed the sending capacity of the vessel's radio, and was therefore excused by the clause set out above.

attach hereunder unless message is received and confirmed in San Diego that the vessel had taken on a load of not less than one-fourth of her loading carrying capacity.

This policy shall not be prejudiced by any unintentional delay or omission in the reporting hereunder.'

The policy may contain a 'termination clause', as in clause 4 of the Institute Time Clauses (Hulls)[6] providing for its automatic termination, e g in the case of

    i   change of the classification society of the vessel;
    ii change of the vessel's class;[7]
    iii change in the ownership of the vessel;
    iv change in the flag of the vessel;
    v   transfer of the vessel to new management;
    vi charter on a bareboat basis;
    vii requisition for title or use of the vessel.[8]

Clause 5 of the Institute Time Clauses (Freight) is similar to effect.[8]

Further, clause 5 of the Institute War and Strikes (Hulls–Time)[9] and clause 5 of the Institute War and Strikes (Hulls–Voyage)[10] state that the insurance may be cancelled by either party on giving 7 days' notice, and that whether or not such notice has been given, the insurance terminates automatically:

    i   on the occurrence of any hostile detonation of any nuclear weapon of war;
    ii on the outbreak of war (whether there is a declaration of war or not) between any of the following countries: United Kingdom, United States of America, France, the Union of Soviet Socialist Republics, the People's Republic of China;
    iii in the event of the vessel being requisitioned for title or use.

B VOYAGE POLICIES

A *Attachment of the risk*

For purposes of convenience voyage policies may be considered under the following heads:

    1 Voyage policies on ship.
    2 Voyage policies on goods.
    3 Voyage policies on freight.

---

[6] These clauses are set out in Appendix III, pp 533–540, post.
[7] For a case where a vessel's class was held not to have been altered, see *Prudent Tankers Ltd SA v Dominion Insurance Co Ltd, The Caribbean Sea* [1980] 1 Lloyd's Rep 338. QBD (Com Ct). (See the judgment of Robert Goff J, ibid, at 349.)
[8] These clauses are set out in Appendix III, pp 550–554, post.
[9] These clauses are set out in Appendix III, pp 547–548, post.
[10] These clauses are set out in Appendix III, pp 549–550, post.

1 Voyage policies on ship

The attachment of the risk will depend on whether the voyage is described as 'from' a port or 'at and from' a port.

Further, the risk will never attach at all if the vessel does not sail from the port of departure stated in the policy or sails for a different destination.

'From'

Where the voyage is described in the policy as, e g 'from London to Montreal', the word 'from' only covers the risk after the vessel sails from London.

Rule 2 of the Rules for Construction of Policy set out in the First Schedule to the Marine Insurance Act 1906 states:

> 'Where the subject-matter is insured from a particular place, the risk does not attach until the ship starts on the voyage insured.'

'At and from'

The words 'at and from' will protect the ship in the named port if she is there in good safety:[11] but she must have been at the port in good safety, otherwise the risk will not attach[12] except where the insurance is effected 'lost or not lost'.

Rule 3(a) of the Rules for Construction of Policy set out in the First Schedule to the Marine Insurance Act 1906 states:

> 'Where a ship is insured at and from a particular place, and she is at that place in good safety when the contract is concluded, the risk attaches immediately.'

It is not, however, necessary that a ship so insured should be at the place where the adventure commences when the contract is concluded.

Thus, Rule 3(b) of the Rules for Construction of Policy set out in the First Schedule to the Marine Insurance Act 1906 states:

> 'If she be not at that place when the contract is concluded, the risk attaches as soon as she arrives there in good safety, and, unless the policy otherwise provides, it is immaterial that she is covered by another policy from a specified time after arrival.'

If in an insurance 'at and from' a vessel arrives at the port named as that at which the risk is to commence in such a condition as to be incapable of lying there in safety until she can be repaired for her voyage, the risk will not attach.[13]

But 'good safety' means 'good physical safety' only. Accordingly, in *Bell v Bell*,[14] where a ship was insured 'at and from Riga' to her port of discharge in the United Kingdom, and upon arrival at Riga was seized and condemned, it was held that, the vessel once having been in Riga in good physical safety, the risk had attached.

Where the risk is to commence at a named port, the word 'port' is to be understood in the sense in which it is commonly understood by seamen and merchants, and may be defined as a place resorted to by shipping for the

---

[11] *Williamson v Innes* (1831) 8 Bing 81n; *Foley v United Fire and Marine Insurance Co of Sydney* (1870) LR 5 CP 155.
[12] *Parmeter v Cousins* (1809) 2 Camp 235.
[13] *Parmeter v Cousins*, supra; *Annen v Woodman* (1810) 3 Taunt 299; *Haughton v Empire Marine Insurance Co* (1866) LR 1 Exch 206.
[14] (1810) 2 Camp 475. See further, *Horneyer v Lushington* (1812) 15 East 46.

discharge and loading of cargo, including even an open roadstead where so used.[15]

Thus, where the policy was 'at and from Carmarthen to London', it was held that goods loaded at Llanelly were not covered,[16] and a loading at Bridport was held not to be covered by an insurance 'at and from Lyme to London'.[17]

Similarly, where an insurance is expressed to be 'at and from' an island or other geographical term comprising a number of ports, the term is to be understood in its customary sense, and includes all the ports or places within the named district.[18]

It will be appreciated that one effect of the attachment of an insurance 'at and from' in respect of a homeward voyage may be to cause the vessel to be doubly insured.[19] This is usually provided against by a clause 'risk to commence on expiration of previous policy'.

Thus, in *Kynance Sailing Ship Co v Young*,[1] where a ship was insured from Australia to port or ports on the west coast of America, and by a later policy 'at and from Valparaiso and/or port or ports on the west coast of South America to European ports', the risk to commence on expiration of previous policy, and the vessel discharged part of her Australian cargo at Valparaiso and was lost whilst proceeding thence to Tocopilla with the remainder, it was held that the loss fell within the earlier policy.

Alteration of port of departure

It is provided by s 43 of the Marine Insurance Act 1906 that:

'Where the place of departure is specified by the policy, and the ship, instead of sailing from that place, sails from any other place, the risk does not attach.'

Thus, if the vessel were insured for a voyage from London to Sydney, and instead sailed from Liverpool, the policy would not attach.

In modern policies the insured vessel is not bound to sail from a particular port, for there is often a term in the policy that the voyage is to be from, e g 'any port in the United Kingdom'.

Sailing for different destination

Section 44 of the Marine Insurance Act 1906 states:

'Where the destination is specified in the policy, and the ship instead of sailing for that destination, sails for any other destination, the risk does not attach.'

Thus, in *Woolridge v Boydell*[2] a vessel was insured from Maryland to Cadiz.

---

[15] *Cockey v Atkinson* (1819) 2 B&Ald 460; *Sea Insurance Co of Scotland v Gavin* (1829) 4 Bli NS 578; *Harrower v Hutchinson* (1869) LR 4 QB 523.
[16] *Payne v Hutchinson* (1810) 2 Taunt 405n.
[17] *Constable v Noble* (1810) 2 Taunt 403. See *Moxon v Atkins* (1812) 3 Camp 200; *Brown v Tayleur* (1835) 4 Ad&El 241.
[18] As to what is meant by 'The Baltic', see *Uhde v Walters* (1811) 3 Camp 16; 'The East India Islands', see *Robertson v Money* (1824) Ry&M 75; and *Robertson v Clarke* (1824) 1 Bing 445; 'Jamaica', see *Camden v Cowley* (1763) 1 Wm Bl 417; 'The West India Islands', see *Cruickshank v Janson* (1810) 2 Taunt 301; and *Warre v Miller* (1825) 4 B&C 538.
[19] As to 'double insurance', see p 461, post.
[1] (1911) 104 LT 397.
[2] (1778) 1 Doug KB 16.

She cleared from Maryland to Falmouth, and was captured in Chesapeake Bay. It was held by the Court of King's Bench that the policy never attached because the voyage which then had been commenced was not the one insured, so the insurer was not liable.

2 Voyage policies on goods

The general rule is that the risk attaches in accordance with the 'transit' ('warehouse to warehouse') clause.[3]

As in the case of policies on ship, the risk will not attach if the vessel on which the goods are loaded sails from a port not specified in the policy,[4] or sails for a different destination.[5]

Provided that the terminus a quo and the terminus ad quem remain unaltered, the policy attaches notwithstanding an intention to deviate existing before the inception of the voyage.[6]

In *Hewitt v London General Insurance Co Ltd*[7] the plaintiffs were the insurers of a cargo of nitrate belonging to the assured to be carried from Tocopilla to La Pallice, France, via the Panama Canal. They reinsured their risk with the defendants, the reinsurance policy being subject to the same terms as the original policy. The vessel sailed from Tocopilla with orders to proceed to Beaumont, Texas, unless otherwise instructed at Colon. At Colon the ship received orders to go to New Orleans. She arrived there and took in further cargo. She sailed from there, and was a total loss with all her cargo in a collision. The plaintiffs paid the assured and claimed under the reinsurance policy. One of the grounds on which the defendants denied liability was that the original policy had not attached because the vessel had sailed from Tocopilla with the intention to deviate.

Branson J, held that this defence failed, and observed:[8]

> 'Firstly, it is said that the policy never attached at all. It is said that at common law a voyage policy does not attach where the ship sails with an intention to deviate, if the deviation is sufficiently material; that there is no express provision on the point in the Marine Insurance Act 1906; and that consequently the common law rule is preserved by s 91. In my opinion that proposition is untenable. Neither of the two cases[9] cited by Mr Dickinson supports his contention as to the common law.
>
> The cases cited[10] by Mr Davies, on the other hand, show conclusively to my mind that at common law the policy will attach, notwithstanding an intention to deviate existing before the inception of the voyage, provided that the terminus a quo and the terminus ad quem remain unaltered.... Were the common law otherwise, the statute in my opinion would have altered it, for it expressly provides in s 46 that an intention to deviate is immaterial. There must be a material deviation in fact to discharge liability under the contract. It is of the essence of Mr Dickinson's argument that the existence of an intention to deviate before the voyage

---

[3] See pp 122–126, post. For an unusual case where it was held that the policy was a voyage policy but that the risk commenced only from a specified date, see *Silver Dolphin Products Ltd v Parcels and General Assurance Association Ltd* [1984] 2 Lloyd's Rep 404, QBD (Com Ct). (See the judgment of Neill J, ibid, at 407.)
[4] See supra.
[5] See supra.
[6] *Hewitt v London General Insurance Co Ltd* (1925) 23 LlL Rep 243, KBD.
[7] (1925) 23 LlL Rep 243, KBD.
[8] Ibid, at 245.
[9] Ie *Way v Modigliani* (1787) 2 Term Rep 30; *Thames and Mersey Marine Insurance Co Ltd v H T Van Laun & Co* (1905) [1917] 2 KB 48n, HL.
[10] Ie *Hare v Travis* (1827) 7 B&C 14; *Simon, Israel & Co v Sedgewick* [1893] 1 QB 303, CA.

commences, if the intended deviation is sufficiently material, makes the voyage a different voyage. That is expressly negatived, it seems to me, by the statute to which I have referred. One may add that it would be strange indeed to find the statute providing expressly two cases in which the policy is not to attach, as it does in ss 43 and 44, and making no mention of the third one if the third one in fact existed. The argument founded on suggested hardship to the insurer, if the law is as thus expressed, fails to impress me.'

'*Transit*' clause

The Institute Cargo Clauses (A),[11] (B)[12] and (C)[13] each contain a 'transit clause'[14] which specifies the time when the risk attaches, stating:

> 'This insurance attaches from the time the goods leave the warehouse or place of storage at the place named in the policy for the commencement of the transit, continues during the ordinary course of transit . . .'

A similar clause is to be found in the Institute War Clauses (Cargo)[15] and the Institute Strikes Clauses (Cargo).[16]

3 Voyage policies on freight

It has already been noticed that the term 'freight' includes not only freight due under a bill of lading, but charter-party freight and the profit to be derived by the shipowner from the carriage of his own goods.[17]

As far as chartered freight is concerned, Rule 3(c) of the Rules for Construction of Policy set out in the First Schedule to the Marine Insurance Act 1906 states:

> 'Where chartered freight is insured at and from a particular place and the ship is at that place in good safety when the contract is concluded, the risk attaches immediately. If she be not there when the contract is concluded, the risk attaches as soon as she arrives there in good safety.'

In the case of chartered freight the risk commences as soon as there is an inception of performance by the ship of the terms of the charter-party.

Thus, in *Foley v United Fire and Marine Insurance Co of Sydney*,[18] where a vessel was chartered to proceed from Calcutta to Mauritius, there to discharge her cargo and to proceed thence with a return cargo to the United Kingdom, chartered freight was insured 'at and from Mauritius to the Rice Ports and thence to the United Kingdom'. It was held that, the vessel having been wrecked at Mauritius before her outward cargo had been discharged, there was nevertheless a loss of the homeward freight within the meaning of the policy.

With regard to freight other than chartered freight, Rule 3(d) of the Rules for Construction of Policy set out in the First Schedule to the Marine Insurance Act 1906 states:

> 'Where freight other than chartered freight is payable without special conditions and is insured at and from a particular place, the risk attaches pro rata as the goods or merchandise

---

[11] Clause 8. These clauses are set out in Appendix III, pp 516–519, post.
[12] Clause 8. These clauses are set out in Appendix III, pp 519–522, post.
[13] Clause 8. These clauses are set out in Appendix III, pp 523–526, post.
[14] The clause was formerly known as the 'warehouse to warehouse' clause.
[15] Clause 5. These clauses are set out in Appendix III, pp 526–529, post.
[16] Clause 5. These clauses are set out in Appendix III, pp 530–532, post.
[17] See p 9, ante.
[18] (1870) LR 5 CP 155.

are shipped; provided that if there be cargo in readiness which belongs to the shipowner, or which some other person contracted with him to ship, the risk attaches as soon as the ship is ready to receive such cargo.'

The time when the risk under a freight policy attaches may be varied by express terms.

Thus, in *Beckett v West of England Marine Insurance Co*,[19] where a vessel was chartered to carry a cargo from Liverpool to the West Coast of Africa, there to discharge and take on board a return cargo, her homeward freight was insured at and from Lagos under a policy, which contained a clause stating:

> 'The insurance aforesaid shall commence upon the freight and goods or merchandise aforesaid from the loading of the said goods or merchandise on board the said ship or vessel at as above.'

The vessel arrived on the West coast of Africa, delivered part of her cargo, and in attempting to cross Lagos Bar to discharge the remainder, ran aground. It was held that the risk had not attached.

B Duration of the risk

The duration of the risk will depend on whether the policy is on ship or on goods.

But the risk may terminate even before the time when it usually expires where the adventure has not been commenced within a reasonable time, or there has been a change of voyage, or a deviation of the vessel from the contractual route, or where the adventure is not prosecuted throughout its course with reasonable dispatch, or where the insurance is terminated under a 'termination' clause.

(1) The general rule

1 Risk on ship

The risk on ship ceases on her arrival at the port named in the policy.

Whether the ship has arrived or not is a question of fact, but the rule is that a ship has arrived when she has reached the place at which ships of that tonnage and kind usually cast anchor, and until then she has not arrived.[20]

Thus, in *Stone v Marine Insurance Co Ocean Ltd of Gothenburg*[1] leave was endorsed on a policy on 2 January enabling a vessel on payment of an extra premium to take her cargo to Antwerp. At Antwerp it was usual for vessels to discharge in the inner dock. On that date, unknown to the parties, the vessel had arrived in the outer dock at Antwerp, and was waiting to go into the inner dock. It was held that the insurer was entitled to retain the additional premium, because at the time the leave was given the risk had not ceased, and would not cease until the ship was berthed in the inner dock.

Again, in *Samuel v Royal Exchange Assurance*[2] the vessel on arriving in London was ordered to go to the King's Dock at Deptford, but the master moored near

---

[19] (1871) 1 Asp MLC 185. See further, *Jones v Neptune Marine Insurance Co* (1872) LR 7 QB 702; *Hopper v Wear Marine Insurance Co* (1882) 46 LT 107; *Hydarnes SS Co v Indemnity Mutual Marine Assurance Co* [1895] 1 QB 500.
[20] *Lindsay v Janson* (1859) 4 H&N 699.
[1] (1876) 1 Ex D 81.
[2] (1828) 8 B&C 119.

the dock gates, it being impossible to enter the dock on account of the ice in the river. She remained there some days, and afterwards, when being warped to the docks, she went aground on account of the breaking of the rope. It was held that the vessel had not been moored in good safety, as she had not entered the dock which was her proper place of discharge, and therefore at the time of the loss the risk had not ceased.

The ship must be moored in the usual place and manner, so as to be able, if she so desires, to begin to discharge cargo.

Thus, in *Waples v Eames*[3] a vessel, which was ordered out to the quarantine ground as soon as she dropped anchor, was protected by the policy whilst in quarantine because she was not 'moored' within the meaning of the term.

But if the vessel is lying where vessels usually cast anchor at the port, and is only waiting to come up to the quay, she is 'moored' within the meaning of the clause;[4] and a ship too large to get inside to her named berth, but moored outside as near as she could be, was held to be 'moored'.[5]

Where the destination is general—e g the Baltic, or Jamaica, or to 'ports of discharge'—the risk ceases when the ship has been at the first port of discharge at which she called to discharge the bulk of her cargo.[6]

Express terms

Of course, the protection of the policy may be extended by express terms to the 'final' or 'last' port of discharge, not necessarily the last port originally intended, but the last available;[7] or it may be extended by usage,[8] or by a new agreement endorsed on the policy.[9]

In *Marten v Vestey Bros Ltd*[10] a vessel was insured 'from any port or ports place or places on the River Plate . . . to any port or ports place or places in France and/or United Kingdom (final port)'. She sailed from Buenos Aires to Dakar, and was there ordered to discharge part of her cargo at St Nazaire and the rest at Le Havre. She did so, and then sailed for Barry for bunkers, and was lost on her voyage there. The assured claimed under the policy, but the insurer refused to indemnify him because the words 'final port' meant the final port of discharge either in the United Kingdom or in France, and in fact the cargo had been discharged at Le Havre, and accordingly the vessel was not on the insured voyage at the time of the loss.

The House of Lords[11] held that this defence succeeded, and that the claim failed. Viscount Haldane observed:[12]

'I find it difficult to construe the meaning as being that the ship is to continue insured after she has discharged her cargo, and during an unlimited further period in which she may cruise

---

[3] (1745) 2 Stra 1243; cf *Samuel v Royal Exchange Assurance* (1828) 8 B&C 119.
[4] *Angerstein v Bell* (1795) 1 Park's Marine Insurance (7th Edn), p 55.
[5] *Whitwell v Harrison* (1848) 2 Exch 127.
[6] *Cruickshank v Janson* (1810) 2 Taunt 301; *Moore v Taylor* (1834) 1 Ad&El 25.
[7] *Brown v Vigne* (1810) 12 East 283; *Moore v Taylor*, supra. See further, *Kynance Sailing Ship Co v Young* (1911) 16 Com Cas 123, where the policy was 'to port or ports of call and/or discharge'.
[8] *Gregory v Christie* (1784) 3 Doug KB 419; *Preston v Greenwood* (1784) 4 Doug KB 28.
[9] *Stone v Marine Insurance Co Ocean Ltd of Gothenburg* (1876) 1 Ex D 81.
[10] [1920] All ER Rep 603, HL.
[11] Viscount Haldane, Lord Dunedin, Lord Atkinson and Lord Buckmaster.
[12] [1920] All ER Rep 603 at 604. See also the speech of Lord Dunedin, ibid, at 607–608, that of Lord Atkinson, ibid, at 609–610, and that of Lord Buckmaster, ibid, at 610.

from port to port, for instance along the coast of Ireland and in the Hebrides, picking up new freight. I cannot read it as meaning that the ship may turn herself into a tramp going about from port to port indefinitely round the United Kingdom, and still remaining insured although running heavy risks from submarines and otherwise, and yet with no increase of the single premium of 27s 6d per cent, which is all that is to be paid. It is difficult to see how terms so vague could define an agreement. I think that, however oddly drawn the document may be, there is one duty from which only an Act of Parliament can absolve Judges who have to construe it, and that is to try to attach some significance to every expression that is at once appropriate and is yet not nullified by other and governing words within the four corners of the instrument. If the practice of Lloyd's really militated against this principle, serious questions might arise. But I cannot think that it really does so. Applying the test, it appears to me that the words to which I have referred do indicate an intention, not excluded by any other expression the policy, to make the voyage terminate with the discharge of the cargo. That took place in France, and there seems to me to be no reason for supposing that the voyage insured was to extend to an indefinite period following on this discharge. That is surely an interpretation which is as reasonable as it is natural. I may add that I agree with Scrutton LJ, in his impression that the words "final port" are not limited to the United Kingdom. They seem to me as they stand in their context to apply to France as well. But, for the reason I have already given, I find it very difficult to take the expression "final port" so read as satisfied by "the last port in fact in the United Kingdom at which the vessel is".'

Again, in *Crocker v Sturge*,[13] where the clause was varied so as to read 'at and from A to B and to any port or ports, place or places; in any order on the west coast of C, and for 30 days after arrival in a final port, however employed', the words 'port or ports, place or places', coupled with the phrase 'however employed', were held not to be limited to ports of discharge, but included ports of loading for the homeward voyage in the district named.

In good safety

Further, the ship must be moored in physical safety. Thus, a ship which arrived in a sinking condition, and in a short time sank, was never moored 'in good safety'.[14]

So also, a vessel which entered a port where there was an embargo on vessels of her nationality was not 'in good safety';[15] but in the absence of an embargo she was held to be 'in good safety', although, in fact, she was seized in the port.[16]

In *Gambles v Ocean Marine Insurance Co of Bombay*[17] a policy was expressed to be 'at and from Pomaron to Newcastle-on-Tyne and for fifteen days whilst there after arrival'. The ship arrived, and, being chartered for coals outwards, took in some coals as stiffening and moved to a berth to complete her cargo, and whilst there was lost in a storm. The court held that the policy when applied to the period of 15 days must be construed on the same principles as a time policy, and not on the principles applicable to a voyage policy. On this construction the insurers were held to be liable, though, if the policy had remained a voyage policy throughout, they would have been under no liability, as the ship was engaged in something quite unconnected with the voyage insured.

---

[13] [1897] 1 QB 330. See also, *Spalding v Crocker* (1897) 2 Com Cas 189 and *Crocker v General Insurance Company of Trieste* (1897) 3 Com Cas 22.
[14] *Shawe v Felton* (1801) 2 East 109.
[15] *Minett v Anderson* (1794) Peake 277; *Horneyer v Lushington* (1812) 15 East 46.
[16] *Bell v Bell* (1810) 2 Camp 475.
[17] (1876) 1 Ex D 141.

But in *Hunter v Northern Marine Insurance Co*,[18] where the clause ran 'whilst in port during thirty days after arrival', the insurers were held not liable for a loss within the 30 days while the vessel was proceeding in tow down the Clyde outside Greenock, at which port she had discharged her cargo and been repaired.

The days are reckoned as consecutive periods of 24 hours each, commencing from the time when the ship is moored at anchor in good safety.[19]

In *Lidgett v Secretan*[20] the risk was 'at and from London to Calcutta and for thirty days after arrival', with the usual 24 hours' mooring clause. The ship sustained sea damage, and was kept afloat by pumping until her arrival at Calcutta, where she was safely moored till her cargo was discharged, a process which occupied nearly a fortnight. She was then removed to dry dock for repairs, and after the period of 30 days had expired was accidentally destroyed by fire. It was held that there was no liability on the insurers in respect of either period, and the loss took place after the 30 days. The construction given to the clause was that after the expiration of 30 days from the arrival and mooring of the vessel, the ship having remained as a vessel and in the possession and control of her owners—though not sound—the insurers were not responsible.

2 Risk on goods

'Transit' clause

The risk on goods will continue until the happening of one of the events specified in the 'transit' clause, which is one of the clauses in the Institute Cargo Clauses (A),[1] (B)[2] or (C).[3]

Thus, clause 8 of the Institute Cargo Clauses (A) states:

'8.1   This insurance attaches from the time the goods leave the warehouse or place of storage at the place named herein for the commencement of the transit, continues during the ordinary course of transit and terminates either

8.1.1   on delivery to the Consignees' or other final warehouse or place of storage at the destination named herein,

8.1.2   on delivery to any other warehouse or place of storage, whether prior to or at the destination named herein, which the Assured elect to use either

8.1.2.1   for storage other than in the ordinary course of transit or

8.1.2.2   for allocation or distribution,

or

8.1.3   on the expiry of 60 days after completion of discharge overside of the goods hereby insured from the oversea vessel at the final port of discharge,

whichever shall first occur.

8.2   If, after discharge overside from the oversea vessel at the final port of discharge, but prior to termination of this insurance, the goods are to be forwarded to a destination other than that to which they are insured hereunder, this insurance, whilst remaining subject to termination as provided for above, shall not extend beyond the commencement of transit to such other destination.

8.3   This insurance shall remain in force (subject to termination as provided for above and to the provisions of Clause 9 below) during delay beyond the control of the Assured, any

---

[18] (1888) 13 App Cas 717.
[19] *Cornfoot v Royal Exchange Assurance* [1904] 1 KB 40; *Mercantile Marine Insurance Co v Titherington* (1864) 5 B&S 765.
[20] (1870) LR 5 CP 190.
[1] These clauses are set out in Appendix III, pp 516–519, post.
[2] These clauses are set out in Appendix III, pp 519–522, post.
[3] These clauses are set out in Appendix III, pp 523–526, post.

deviation, forced discharge, reshipment or transhipment and during any variation of the adventure arising from the exercise of a liberty granted to shipowners or charterers under the contract of affreightment.'

The wording of the clause has varied from time to time. A number of the cases which have interpreted the meaning of the words used in it are considered below.

In *Allagar Rubber Estates Ltd v National Benefit Assurance Co Ltd*[4] some cases of rubber were insured under a 'tree to buyer' policy. The policy contained a clause stating:

'The risk to commence from time of entry at receiving house on the estate and until safe delivery taken by the purchaser.'

The cases arrived in this country, and some of them were warehoused in a warehouse at Lower Oliver's Wharf, Stepney, where they were destroyed by fire after they had been there for 8 months. The assured claimed for a loss under the policy, but the insurers contended that the rubber was covered only for a reasonable period, and that in the present case the delay was unreasonable. It appeared that before the First World War 30 days was the usual period for which an assured was covered by this type of policy.

It was held by Bailhache J, that the action succeeded. In the absence of a special provision to the contrary, the rubber was covered until delivery to the purchaser. There was no implication that the period was limited except possibly to a reasonable time, but the delay, in fact, had not been unreasonable. He observed:[5]

'The clause says the risk to commence from the time of entry at receiving house or shed on the estate, and continue until safe delivery is taken by the purchaser. Reading in purely literal terms it might continue for an indefinite time, but it is conceded, and I think must indeed be conceded, that notwithstanding the wide words of the clause the risk must come to an end after reasonable delay on the part of the assured in disposing of the goods.

On the whole, I have come to the conclusion, having regard to the state of the rubber trade in that year, that the time taken by the plaintiffs was not unusually long under the circumstances, but longer than would be anticipated in an ordinary year. I am confirmed in that opinion by the fact that of the 715 cases plaintiffs disposed of all but 82. On the whole, therefore, I come to the conclusion that the claim succeeds.'

In *Re Traders and General Insurance Association Ltd, ex p Continental and Overseas Trading Co*[6] a policy of insurance had been effected in respect of 10 bales of blankets from Antwerp to Calcutta and Karachi. The policy contained a 'warehouse to warehouse' clause[7] which stated:

'The insured goods are covered subject to the terms of this policy from the time of leaving the shippers' or manufacturers' warehouse during the ordinary course of transit until on board the vessel, during transhipment, if any, and from the vessel whilst on quays, wharves or in sheds during the ordinary course of transit until safely deposited in consignees' or other warehouse at destination named in policy.'

In March and April 1920 the assured purchased 10 bales of blankets from a firm in Termonde (in Belgium) which forwarded them on 7 October 1920 from Termonde to Antwerp for shipment on a steamer, which was due to sail from

---

[4] (1922) 10 LlL Rep 564, KBD.
[5] Ibid, at 565.
[6] (1924) 18 LlL Rep 450, ChD.
[7] Now known as the 'transit' clause. See pp 121–122, ante.

Antwerp on 12 October. The goods were placed in a warehouse at Antwerp, and were damaged by a fire there on 11 October. The assured claimed for a loss under the policy on the ground that the goods were covered from the time they left Termonde, or alternatively from the time they were placed in the warehouse at Antwerp. The insurers contended that they could not be considered to have insured the goods against a risk, which might involve undisclosed and lengthy land transit, and which ought specifically to have been mentioned in the specification in those cases in which it was to be included. Further, they maintained that the discharge or delivery at Antwerp was not a delivery from a warehouse but from a barge, and consequently the 'warehouse to warehouse' clause did not apply.

Eve J, held that the claim failed, and accepted both the above defences pleaded by the insurers. He observed:[8]

> 'The clause undoubtedly extends the liability of the insurers to risk incurred prior to shipment, but the nature and area of that extension must, in my opinion, be ascertained in each case by reference to the terms of the specification relating to the particular goods. Where goods are specified as consigned from Paris, Lyons and other centres necessarily involving land transit, the additional risks of that transit would, in my opinion, be covered, but where, as in the case with the two parcels out of which this claim arises, the terminus a quo mentioned in the specification is the port of shipment and the transit is in terms "by steamer", I cannot accept the view that the clause ought to be construed as imposing liability from the commencement of the transit from the factory or, indeed, at any points outside an area which, having regard to the local conditions might fairly be held to be within what [Counsel] has aptly spoken of as the ambit of the terminus a quo. Nor, in my opinion, ought I to treat the discharge ex barge on 8 October as equivalent to the leaving of the warehouse referred to in the clause.'

In *Safadi v Western Assurance Co*[9] cotton goods were insured from Manchester to Damascus under a policy containing a 'warehouse to warehouse' clause[10] which provided (inter alia):

> 'When the destination to which the goods are insured is without the limits of the port of discharge of the overseas vessel the risks covered by this policy continue until the goods are safely deposited in the consignee's or other warehouse at the destination named in the policy or until the expiry of 30 days from midnight of the day in which the discharge of the goods hereby insured from the overseas vessel is completed, whichever may first occur. Transhipment, if any, other than as above, and/or delay, arising from circumstances beyond the control of the assured, held covered at a premium to be arranged.'

The goods were discharged at Beirut, and were placed in a Customs warehouse. After being there for about 10 weeks they were destroyed by fire. The plaintiff as assignee[11] of the policy claimed for a loss under the policy, but the insurers repudiated liability on the ground that the goods were not covered because they had been in the warehouse at Beirut for more than 30 days. The plaintiff, however, maintained that the policy covered delay arising from circumstances beyond his control, and that the delay was due to the unsettled state[12] of the territory between Beirut and Damascus.

Roche J, held that the claim failed because the goods had been left in the

---

[8] (1924) 18 LlL Rep 450 at 451.
[9] (1933) 46 LlL Rep 140, KBD.
[10] Now known as the 'transit' clause. See pp 121–122, ante.
[11] His Lordship held (obiter) that in any event he was not an assignee of the policy: (1933) 46 LlL Rep 140 at 144. As to this point, see pp 319–320, post.
[12] For the evidence on this point, see (1933) 46 LlL Rep 140 at 142.

warehouse for business reasons, and not because of probable danger to them. He observed:[13]

> 'I am satisfied that although there may have been some danger of the rebels trying to get goods such as these cotton goods, that was not a real danger and it was not one which was influencing Messrs Sabeh and Kahaleh. The truth is that they left the goods in the Customs House at Beirut because they did not want to pay for them. They had got credit and they chose to extend the credit.
>
> I am satisfied that it was for supposed business reasons such as those that Sabeh and Kahaleh left the goods in the Customs House at Beirut and not because they were in fact afraid of anything happening to them in transit. It is significant that they did, in fact, give orders to certain forwarding agents to take delivery of the goods on 20 May or thereabouts a few days before they were destroyed. The facts were no different then as regards the security or insecurity of the railway from the condition of affairs which had prevailed in the weeks before. So I am confirmed in my view that there was no real danger, neither was there apprehension of danger, as the governing cause moving Messrs Sabeh and Kahaleh to keep the goods in the Customs House at Beirut.'

He further held that the assured could not rely on the clause concerning 'circumstances beyond the control of the assured' because the circumstances as to the state of insurrection in the area were known to the assured when the policy was effected, and said:[14]

> 'There is this further matter to be borne in mind. There is a good deal of doctrine and authority to the effect that you cannot apply language such as "cause or circumstances and matters beyond the control of the assured" to excuse performance when those causes and circumstances and matters are represented by causes and circumstances and matters in existence and known to be in existence by the person relying upon them at the time he makes the contract from the performance of which he seeks to be excused. These circumstances as to the state of the war and the operations of the Druses were known to everybody at the time these policies were taken out and at the time these goods were sent forward and the documents representing them were sent forward.'

In *G H Renton & Co Ltd v Black Sea and Baltic General Insurance Co Ltd*[15] timber was insured for a voyage from Igarka to London. The policy contained the Timber Trade Federation Insurance Clauses, clause 2 of which stated:

> 'Including risks of... non-delivery... from the time of leaving mill, warehouse, factory, yard or premises at the place from which the goods are loaded... whilst on board the ocean-going vessel until discharged at the port of destination; and whilst in transit by land and/or water to final destination there or in the interior.'

In accordance with the usage of the Port of London, the cargo was discharged from the ship on to the quay alongside, and stacked regardless of marks, size or description. It was subsequently sorted by the Port of London Authority and piled in a shed. The discharge of the goods began on 23 September. It was completed on 12 October. Meanwhile the piling began on 26 September and finished on 7 November. Counting started on that date, and continued until a day or two before 30 November when the landing returns were made out. A part of the cargo was then found to be missing. The assured claimed for a loss under the policy, but the insurers contended that the risk had ended when the goods were discharged on to the quayside.

Lord Caldecote LCJ, accepted this contention, and held that the claim failed. The final destination could not be determined by reference to the right which

---

[13] Ibid, at 142.
[14] Ibid, at 143.
[15] [1941] 1 All ER 149, KBD.

the assured had from the Port of London Authority to take possession of the cargo after it had been sorted and landing returns made out. The final destination was the shed or space to which the cargo was delivered on the quayside.

His Lordship observed:[16]

> 'The question which arises in this case, on the facts of the case, is whether the final destination was the place at which the goods arrived when they were bulked or stacked, or whether the final destination had not then been reached. In the view which I have formed, the facts do not justify a conclusion that the goods were still in transit for the purposes of this clause after they had reached the quayside or the shed in which they were placed in bulk. If the [assured's] contention is right, the final destination of the cargo, which might be taken in exceptional circumstances from the pile, but before the piling is completed and before the counting is completed, would be different from the final destination in the case of goods which had to wait until the final piling and counting had been finished.
>
> I think that the final destination for the purposes of this case and this particular parcel of goods was the shed or the space to which the goods were delivered, and the mere fact that they had been moved to another part of that shed and piled according to their marks seems to me to make no difference at all. It is quite conceivable that the goods might have been put under their marks and sizes as they were delivered from the ship, but, according to the usage of the port, the goods are bulked without regard to their marks and sizes, and the fact that they were moved to another part of the shed does not, in my view, prevent the shed from being their final destination.'

(2) Exceptions to the general rule

1 Implied condition as to commencement of adventure

Section 42(1) of the Marine Insurance Act 1906 states:

> 'Where the subject-matter is insured by a voyage policy "at and from" or "from" a particular place, it is not necessary that the ship should be at that place when the contract is concluded, but there is an implied condition that the adventure shall be commenced within a reasonable time, and that if the adventure be not so commenced the insurer may avoid the contract.'

The effect of delay in the commencement of an adventure may be to vary the risk from that which was within the contemplation of the parties to the contract of insurance. A summer risk may become a winter one or may, for other reasons, become more hazardous.

Thus, in *De Wolf v Archangel Marine Insurance Co*,[17] where a policy 'at and from Montreal to Monte Video' was made on 13 July, and the ship did not arrive at Montreal until 30 August this was held to be an unreasonable delay as it caused the voyage to become a winter instead of a summer risk. Accordingly, the insurer was held entitled to avoid liability under the policy.

The implied condition, however, may not apply in every case, for s 42(2) of the Marine Insurance Act 1906 states:

> 'The implied condition may be negatived by showing that the delay was caused by circumstances known to the insurer before the contract was concluded, or by showing that he waived the condition.'

In *Bah Lias Tobacco and Rubber Estates v Volga Insurance Co Ltd*[18] the insured effected a policy in June 1917 in respect of the 1916–17 tobacco crop 'at and

---

[16] Ibid, at 151.
[17] (1874) LR 9 QB 451. See *Hull v Cooper* (1811) 14 East 479; *Mount v Larkins* (1831) 8 Bing 108; *Maritime Insurance Co v Stearns* [1901] 2 KB 912.
[18] (1920) 3 LlL Rep 155 at 202, KBD (Com Ct).

from Sumatra to London and/or ports in Holland'. The policy included the risk of fire antecedent to shipment. On 18 July part of the crop was destroyed by fire whilst it was in store in Sumatra. A claim was made under the policy, but the insurers refused to indemnify the assured on the ground that there had been unreasonable delay in the commencement of the adventure.

Shearman J, held that the defence failed, and that the claim succeeded. Since the insurers had accepted an additional premium to cover a period during which the loss occurred, they were precluded from raising the defence of unreasonable delay.

2 Change of voyage

It is provided by s 45 of the Marine Insurance Act 1906 that:

> '(1) Where after, the commencement of the risk, the destination of the ship is voluntarily changed from the destination contemplated by the policy, there is said to be a change of voyage.
> (2) Unless the policy otherwise provides, where there is a change of voyage, the insurer is discharged from liability as from the time of change, that is to say, as from the time when the determination to change it is manifested; and it is immaterial that the ship may not in fact have left the course of voyage contemplated by the policy when the loss occurs.'

Whether the determination to change the destination contemplated by the policy is a matter of fact in each case.

The insurer is only entitled to avoid liability if the voyage has been changed voluntarily.

In *Rickards v Forestal Land, Timber and Rlys Co Ltd*[19] a cargo was insured for carriage on a German vessel from South American ports to Hong Kong or Shanghai. The vessel arrived at Rio on 25 August 1939. War was declared on 3 September 1939. Her master sailed from Rio on 6 September 1939 in compliance with an order from the German Government that all German vessels should seek refuge in neutral ports or to return to Germany, or as a last resort to scuttle themselves. Subsequently she was scuttled off the Faroe Islands to avoid capture by a British warship. One of the issues which arose was whether there had been a 'change of voyage' within s 45(1) of the Marine Insurance Act 1906.

The House of Lords[20] held that there had been no such change because the destination of the vessel had not been *voluntarily* changed as required by that subsection.

Lord Wright said:[1]

> 'There was a change of voyage when the vessel sailed from Rio on the voyage or adventure to run the blockade on the orders of the German Government. That change of voyage was certainly not voluntary. On that ground, therefore, it could not be said that the insurer was discharged from liability under s 45(2) of the Act, because the change of voyage which discharges the underwriter is defined in s 45(1), and the definition includes the element that the voyage is voluntarily changed.'

Lord Porter observed:[2]

> 'It is said, however, that, in addition to, or instead of, deviating, the master at some stage changed his voyage. I do not think that he did in the sense in which those words are used in the

---
[19] [1941] 3 All ER 62, HL.
[20] Viscount Simon LC, Viscount Maugham, Lord Thankerton, Lord Wright and Lord Porter.
[1] [1941] 3 All ER 62 at 78.
[2] Ibid, at 96.

Marine Insurance Act 1906. Change of voyage is now defined in s 45 of the Act as occurring when, after the commencement of the risk, the destination of the ship is voluntarily changed from the destination contemplated by the policy. There was no voluntary change in the case of the *Minden*. The master was acting, not on his own initiative, but on the orders which, to use the words of Lord Ellenborough in *Phelps v Auldjo*,[3] morally as a good subject he ought not to have resisted.'

Even where there has been a change of voyage, the insurer will still be liable if the assured can bring himself within the terms of a 'held covered' clause in the policy, e g clause 10 of the Institute Cargo Clauses (A)[4] states:

'Change of Voyage Clause. Where after attachment of this insurance the destination is changed by the Assured, held covered at a premium and on conditions to be arranged subject to prompt notice being given to the underwriters.'

Again, clause 2 of the Institute Voyage Clauses (Hulls)[5] states:

'Change of voyage. Held covered in case of . . . change of voyage . . . provided notice be given to the Underwriters immediately after receipt of advices and any amended terms of cover and any additional premium[6] required by them be agreed.'

In *Wilson v Boag*[7] a motor launch was insured under a time policy from 12 February 1953 to 30 June 1953, and a clause stated that she was covered

'whilst the same is used for private and pleasure purposes only on the waters of Port Stephens and within a radius of 50 miles thereof against all loss or damage caused by stress of weather, stranding, any latent defect in the machinery or hull or by negligence of paid hands, and against salvage charges.'

During the period of the policy she left Port Stephens on a voyage undertaken for private and pleasure purposes to Sydney which was 90 miles away. While she was still within the 50-mile perimeter, she became disabled, drifted for several days, and salvage charges were incurred.

The plaintiff (suing as the executrix of the assured) claimed an indemnity in respect of the salvage charges, but the insurer disclaimed liability on the ground that there had been a 'change of voyage' within the meaning of s 51 of the (Australian) Marine Insurance Act 1909,[8] for at the time of the loss she was proceeding to Sydney which was a port outside the 50-mile radius, and not a port of destination contemplated by the policy.

The Supreme Court of New South Wales[9] held that the policy should be regarded as a time policy under which the insurer was liable for losses occurring within the defined geographical area irrespective of the voyage on which the vessel was engaged, and observed:[10]

'On the whole we are of opinion that the policy here in question should not be construed as a voyage policy attaching only to voyages intended to begin and end within the perimeter and to remain wholly within it. It is to be regarded rather as a time policy in which is contained a limitation of the liability of the insurer to loss sustained while the launch is within a defined geographical area. We think that the policy covers loss occurring within the perimeter even

---

[3] (1809) 2 Camp 350.
[4] These clauses are set out in Appendix III, pp 516–519, post.
[5] These clauses are set out in Appendix III, pp 533–540, post.
[6] For the payment of an additional premium, see p 80, ante.
[7] [1956] 2 Lloyd's Rep 564 (NSW).
[8] Which corresponds to s 45 of the (English) Marine Insurance Act 1906.
[9] Street CJ, and Owen and Walsh JJ.
[10] [1956] 2 Lloyd's Rep at 565.

though the launch was then in the course of proceeding to a point outside it. That seems to us to be the natural meaning to be given to the relevant words.

There appear to be no reported cases precisely in point, and to apply the rules of law relating to commercial voyage policies to this case seems to us to be somewhat unreal, and not to be warranted by anything to be found in the terms of the contract.'

3 Deviation

Section 46 of the Marine Insurance Act 1906 states:

'(1) Where a ship, without lawful excuse,[11] deviates from the voyage contemplated by the policy, the insurer is discharged from liability as from the time of deviation, and it is immaterial that the ship may have regained her route before any loss occurs.

(2) There is a deviation from voyage contemplated by the policy—
  a Where the course of the voyage is specifically designated by the policy, and that course is departed from; or
  b Where the course of the voyage is not specifically designated by the policy, but the usual and customary course is departed from.

(3) The intention to deviate is immaterial; there must be a deviation in fact to discharge the insurer from his liability under the contract.'

The extent of the deviation has no bearing on its effect. It is immaterial whether the deviation is trivial or extensive.[12] The deviation will not be cured even if the ship returned to her proper course before any loss occurred.[13]

Nor need the insurer prove a connection between the deviation and the loss. It is enough that the policy has been avoided by the variation of the risk which the deviation introduced.[14]

Where the course is specifically designated

Where the voyage is described or defined in the policy with any detail, the vessel must follow the route specified, even though it may be one not customarily taken by shipping.

Thus, in *Elliot v Wilson*:[15]

Goods were insured from Carron to Hull with liberty to touch at Leith. A loss occurred after the vessel had proceeded to Morrison's Haven, which was a place at which all vessels sailing down the Firth of Forth habitually touched.

Held, the insurers were not liable.

Where the course of the voyage is not specifically designated

The voyage set out in the policy must be performed in the way in which voyages of that class are usually performed. Any departure from the course usually taken by vessels pursuing voyages of that class will be a deviation.

Thus, in *Clason v Simmonds*:[16]

A policy described the voyage as 'at and from London to her ports of discharge in the Straits as high as Messina with power to stop or stay at any ports in places whatsoever'. The ship called at Falmouth, at which port it was unusual for ships on that voyage to call.

Held, that this was a deviation.

---

[11] For the circumstances in which deviation is excused, see s 49, and pp 133–134, post.
[12] *Elliot v Wilson* (1776) 4 Bro Parl Cas 470.
[13] *Way v Modigliani* (1787) 2 Term Rep 30.
[14] *Elliot v Wilson*, supra; *Davis v Garrett* (1830) 6 Bing 716; *Thompson v Hopper* (1858) EB&E 1038.
[15] (1776) 4 Bro Parl Cas 470.
[16] (1741) cited in 6 Term Rep 533.

Further, where it is customary for vessels engaged in certain classes of trade to perform intermediate voyages not specified in the policy, a ship engaging in such an intermediate voyage is not guilty of a deviation.[17]

Mere intention not a deviation

A mere intention or design to deviate has per se no effect on the contract, and, unless it is carried into effect, will not vary or in any way affect the risk.[18]

Thus, in *Kingston v Phelps*:[19]

> The master sailed with an intention of deviating to call at an unauthorised port. Before reaching the point at which the deviation was to take place he was forced by stress of weather into that very port.
>
> *Held,* that there was no deviation, for the intention was never carried into effect, and the actual deviation arose from necessity and was therefore excused.[20]

Several ports of discharge

The Marine Insurance Act 1906, s 47 states:

> '(1) Where several ports of discharge are specified by the policy, the ship may proceed to all or any of them, but, in the absence of any usage or sufficient cause to the contrary, she must proceed to them, or such of them as she goes to, in the order designated by the policy. If she does not there is a deviation.
>
> (2) Where the policy is to "ports of discharge", within a given area, which are not named, the ship must, in the absence of any usage or sufficient cause to the contrary, proceed to them, or such of them as she goes to, in their geographical order. If she does not there is a deviation.'

Moreover, to revisit is to deviate.[1]

There is, however, no obligation on the ship to call at *all* the ports named, and where several ports of discharge are specified by the policy and she clears for only one of them, this is not a deviation.[2]

If the ports are not particularly specified, they must be visited in the order in which they lie on the ship's course, i e in their geographical order.

Thus, in *The Dunbeth*[3] a ship proceeding from Gibraltar was held to be guilty of a deviation when she called at King's Lynn and then went to Cardiff, instead of taking those ports in the reverse order.

Liberty to touch and stay

The policy may contain a clause stating that a vessel has 'liberty to touch and stay at any port whatsoever.'[4]

Rule 6 of the Rules for Construction of Policy set out in the First Schedule to the Marine Insurance Act 1906 states:

> 'In the absence of any further license or usage, the liberty to touch and stay "at any port or

---

[17] *Vallance v Dewar* (1808) 1 Camp 503; *Ougier v Jennings* (1800) 1 Camp 505n.
[18] *Foster v Wilmer* (1746) 2 Stra 1249; *Heselton v Allnutt* (1813) 1 M&S 46.
[19] (1795) cited in 7 Term Rep 165; *Carter v Royal Exchange Assurance* (prior to 1746), cited in 2 Stra 1249; *Thellusson v Fergusson* (1780) 1 Doug KB 360; *Kewley v Ryan* (1794) 2 Hy Bl 343.
[20] See now Marine Insurance Act 1906, s 49(1)(d).
[1] *Beatson v Haworth* (1796) 6 Term Rep 531; *Marsden v Reid* (1803) 3 East 572.
[2] *Marsden v Reid,* supra.
[3] [1897] P 133.
[4] But it should be noted that there is no such clause in the Institute Voyage Clauses (Hulls), which are set out in Appendix III, pp 540–547, post.

place whatsoever" does not authorize the ship to depart from the course of her voyage from the port of departure to the port of destination.'

The liberty to touch and stay will be construed and limited with reference to the general purposes of the voyage.[5] Thus, in *Gairdner v Senhouse*[6] Sir James Mansfield said:[7]

> 'And the larger the words are, the more necessary is this construction, else the ship might trade and barter without any termination.'

Accordingly, a 'liberty to stop and stay at any port or places whatsoever'[8] gives no liberty to call at a port quite unconnected with the purposes of the voyage.[9]

So also, however wide the wording of the policy may be, the liberty to stay must be construed with regard to the main object of the adventure, and a liberty to stay 'for any purpose whatsoever' will only cover purposes connected with the objects of the voyage.

In *Bragg v Anderson*[10] a vessel was insured 'at and from Martinique and all or any of the West Indian Islands to London, with liberty in that voyage to proceed and sail to and touch at any ports or places whatsoever'. She sailed from Martinique for St Domingo, where she loaded a cargo for London. In holding that there had been no deviation, Mansfield CJ, said:[11]

> 'There is not getting over these words; instead of "all", you must substitute the words "some of the West Indian Islands, such as lie between Martinique and London", and you would make quite a new engagement.'

In *Leathly v Hunter*[12] goods were insured by the ships 'Albion, Bolivar, Java Packet, and Blora', 'all or any as interest might appear and with leave to declare the same thereafter at and from Singapore, Penang, Malacca, and Batavia, all or any, to the ship's port or ports of discharge in Great Britain or to any port or ports in the United Netherlands or to Altona or Hamburg, or all or any, with leave to touch, stay, and trade at all or any ports or places whatsoever and wheresoever in the East Indies, Persia, or elsewhere or in any direction and for any purpose necessary or otherwise, particularly Singapore, Penang, Malacca, Batavia, the Cape of Good Hope, and St Helens'. A quantity of coffee was loaded on the 'Java Packet' at Batavia, whence the vessel sailed for Sombaya, which lies some 400 miles to the east of Batavia and out of the course from Batavia or any of the other three named ports to Europe. It was held that there had been no deviation.

In *Solly v Whitmore*[13] a policy described the risk as 'at and from Hull to her

---

[5] *Barclay v Stirling* (1816) 5 M&S 6; *Leathly v Hunter* (1831) 7 Bing 517; *Brown v Tayleur* (1835) 4 Ad&El 241.
[6] (1810) 3 Taunt 16.
[7] Ibid, at 22. See also, *Glynn v Margetson & Co* [1893] AC 351.
[8] The words 'any port or ports whatsoever' will include 'places', if the purpose of the voyage so requires: *Cockey v Atkinson* (1819) 2 B&Ald 460. See also *Brown v Tierney* (1809) 1 Taunt 517, cited in 4 Taunt 394.
[9] *Clason v Simmonds* (1741) cited in 6 Term Rep 533.
[10] (1812) 4 Taunt 229.
[11] Ibid, at 230.
[12] (1831) 7 Bing 517. See also, *Bottomley v Bovill* (1826) 5 B&C 210; *Andrews v Mellish* (1814) 5 Taunt 496; *Metcalfe v Parry* (1814) 4 Camp 123; *Armet v Innes* (1820) 4 Moore CP 150.
[13] (1821) 5 B&Ald 45.

port or ports of loading in the Baltic Sea and Gulf of Finland, with liberty for the ship in the said voyage to proceed and sail to and touch and stay at any ports or places whatsoever and wheresoever for *all* purposes, particularly at Elsinore, without it being deemed a deviation'. The ship delivered goods at Elsinore and Danzig. It was held that there had been a deviation. Abbott CJ, said:[14]

> 'The liberty given by this policy to "touch at any ports for all purposes" must be construed to mean purposes connected with the voyage. Here the voyage was from Hull to a loading port in the Baltic, and if the ship had gone to Elsinore or Danzig to see if she could get a cargo, that would have been a purpose connected with the voyage, and consequently would not have been a deviation. But the vessel in fact went to those ports for the purpose of delivering goods, which was wholly unconnected with the voyage insured. I am therefore of opinion that this was a deviation.'

In *Hammond v Reid*[15] a vessel was insured 'at and from Para to New York, during her stay there and at and from thence to Para, with leave to call at all or any of the Windward or Leeward Islands and colonies on her passage to New York, with leave to discharge, exchange and take on board the whole or any part of any cargo or cargoes at any port or places she might call at or proceed to, particularly at all or any of the Windward or Leeward Islands'. She sailed from Para for New York, but with orders to proceed first to Barbados, where the master was directed to load an exchange cargo. This was done, and the vessel left Barbados for New York, intending to call on her way at St Bartholomew's and St Thomas's Islands in order to ascertain the state of the markets there for the purpose of another cargo, which her owner proposed to ship by another vessel. It was held that there was a deviation in putting into St Bartholomew's and St Thomas's Islands.

Intermediate voyages

In the case of 'intermediate voyages' the same principle applies, and the ship is 'protected by the policy so long only as she is sailing on an intermediate voyage undertaken with a view to the accomplishment of one or other of the voyages pointed out by the policy as the principal object in the contemplation of the parties'.[16]

Trading at port of call

So strictly was the rule applied that it was formerly held that 'liberty to touch and stay' did not permit of trading at the port of call, and where a ship took in a fresh cargo at a port of call, it was held to be a deviation, although it produced no delay, the ship being delayed through waiting for a convoy or by an adverse wind.[17]

Nowadays, however, trading at a port of call will not be a deviation if there is no additional delay or change of risk caused by it.

---

[14] Ibid, at 46.
[15] (1820) 4 B&Ald 72. See also, *Violett v Allnutt* (1811) 3 Taunt 419; *Langhorn v Allnutt* (1812) 4 Taunt 511; *Williams v Shee* (1813) 3 Camp 469; *Bottomley v Bovill* (1826) 5 B&C 210; *Company of African Merchants v British and Foreign Marine Insurance Co* (1873) LR 8 Exch 154; *Laing v Union Marine Insurance Co* (1895) 1 Com Cas 11.
[16] *Bottomley v Bovill* (1826) 5 B&C 210 at 218 (per Abbott CJ).
[17] *Sheriff v Potts* (1803) 5 Esp 96. See also, *Stitt v Wardell* (1797) 2 Esp 610.

Thus, in *Raine v Bell*[18] Lawrence J, said:[19]

> 'If the doing of a thing do not alter the risk of the underwriter and be not expressly prohibited to be done, I cannot say that it vitiates the policy.'

The rule that the principles of law relating to deviation apply whether the policy is on goods or on ship, extends to this phase of it also so that, if the policy is on goods, the ship may trade at ports of call if she can do so without alteration of the risk.[20]

But if such trading at the port of call, where there is only a liberty to touch and stay, causes additional delay, or otherwise varies the risk, it will be a deviation.[1]

Transhipment

Where it is clearly necessary for the preservation of the goods to tranship them, they are protected on board the new ship until they are landed at the port of destination named in the policy or intended by the parties.[2]

But if there is no liberty to tranship the cargo, the necessity for doing so must be very clear, otherwise the transhipment may amount to a deviation.[3]

Where transhipment does not put an end to the risk, the insurer is liable for any loss which may occur in the course of transhipment, landing, and re-shipment, including risk of lighterage where customary.[4]

Section 59 of the Marine Insurance Act 1906 states:

> 'Where, by a peril insured against, the voyage is interrupted at an intermediate port or place, under such circumstances as, apart from any special stipulation in the contract of affreightment, to justify the master in landing and re-shipping the goods or other moveables, or in transhipping them, and sending them on to their destination, the liability of the insurer continues, notwithstanding the landing or transhipment.'

Where the policy contains a 'transit' clause, the risk continues during transhipment.

Thus the Institute Cargo Clauses (A),[5] (B)[6] and (C)[7] state:

> 'This insurance shall remain in force ... during transhipment ...'

Excuses for deviation

Section 49(1) of the Marine Insurance Act 1906 states:

> 'Deviation or delay in prosecuting the voyage contemplated by the policy is excused—
> a Where authorised by any special term in the policy; or
> b Where caused by circumstances beyond the control of the master and his employer; or
> c Where reasonably necessary in order to comply with an express or implied warranty; or
> d Where reasonably necessary for the safety of the ship or subject-matter insured; or

---

[18] (1808) 9 East 195.
[19] Ibid, at 201.
[20] *Laroche v Oswin* (1810) 12 East 131.
[1] *Williams v Shee* (1813) 3 Camp 469.
[2] *De Cuadra v Swann* (1864) 16 CBNS 772; *Oliverson v Brightman* (1846) 8 QB 781.
[3] *Oliverson v Brightman*, supra.
[4] *Tierney v Etherington* (1743) cited in 1 Burr at 348; *Oliverson v Brightman*, supra; *Australian Agricultural Co v Saunders* (1875) LR 10 CP 668.
[5] These clauses are set out in Appendix III, pp 516–519, post.
[6] These clauses are set out in Appendix III, pp 519–523, post.
[7] These clauses are set out in Appendix III, pp 523–526, post.

e For the purpose of saving human life, or aiding a ship in distress where human life may be in danger; or

f Where reasonably necessary for the purposes of obtaining medical or surgical aid for any person on board the ship; or

g Where caused by the barratrous conduct of the master or crew, if barratry[8] be one of the perils insured against.'

In *Forestal Land, Timber and Rlys Co Ltd v Rickards*,[9] where a German vessel carrying the insured goods was ordered by the German Government to seek refuge at a neutral port on the outbreak of the Second World War, and her master did so, the House of Lords[10] held that the deviation was excused under s 49(1)(b).[11] Lord Wright said:[12]

'The deviation thus comes within the protection of s 49(1)(b) of the Act, which enacts that deviation is excused (inter alia) where it is caused by circumstances beyond the control of the master and his employer. Here the deviation was caused by circumstances beyond the control of the master, who was, as already stated, bound to obey the orders of his Government equally with his employer, the German shipowner. The deviation was certainly beyond the control of the assured, if that is material.'

Effect of the 'transit' clause

It should be noted that where there is a 'transit' clause[13] in the policy, the goods are still covered even though there has been a deviation for the clause states:

'This insurance shall remain in force ... during any deviation ...'

Duty to resume course

Section 49(2) of the Marine Insurance Act 1906 states:

'When the cause excusing the deviation ... ceases to operate, the ship must resume her course, and prosecute her voyage, with reasonable dispatch.'

But it is not necessary for her to return to the point of deviation and pursue her original route.[14]

'Held covered' clause

Although the general rule is that the insurer is entitled to avoid liability under the policy where there has been a deviation, he cannot do so where the assured brings himself within the terms of a 'held covered' clause e g clause 2 of the Institute Voyage Clauses (Hulls)[15] which states:

---

[8] See pp 122–126, ante.
[9] (1941) 70 LlL Rep 173, HL.
[10] Viscount Simon LC, Viscount Maugham, Lord Thankerton, Lord Wright and Lord Porter.
[11] Their Lordships reached a similar conclusion in *Middows Ltd v Robertson* and *W W Howard Bros & Co Ltd v Kann* (which were heard and reported with *Forestal Land, Timber and Rlys Co Ltd v Rickards*, supra, where the same point arose).
[12] (1941) 70 LlL Rep at 189. See also the speech of Lord Porter, ibid, at 201, where his Lordship also said: 'The master's act was both necessitated by moral force and reasonably necessary for the safety of the ship which unless such steps were taken, might well fall into the hands of the British Navy.'
[13] For the 'transit' clause, see pp 122–126, ante.
[14] *Delany v Stoddart* (1785) 1 Term Rep 22.
[15] These clauses are set out in Appendix III, pp 540–547, post. Clause 3 of the Institute Voyage Clauses (Freight), which are set out in Appendix III, pp 555–558, post) is in the same terms.

'Held covered in case of deviation . . . provided notice be given to Underwriters immediately after receipt of advices and any amended terms of cover and any additional premium[16] required by them be agreed.'

Whether the notice has been given promptly will, of course, depend on the circumstances.

Usually such a clause requires the assured to give prompt notice of the deviation to the insurers. If he does not do so, the insurers will not be liable for any loss of or damage to the subject-matter insured.

In *Hewitt v London General Insurance Co Ltd*[17] a cargo of nitrate was insured for a voyage from Tocopilla to La Pallice, France. The policy contained a clause which stated:

'In the event of the voyage being changed or of any deviation from the terms of this policy the same to be held covered at premium to be arranged hereafter.'

The insurers reinsured their risk under a reinsurance policy which was expressed to be 'subject to the same terms, clauses and conditions' as the original policy. The vessel deviated to New Orleans, and was subsequently lost with all her cargo. The insurers paid the sum insured to the original assured, and claimed an indemnity from the reinsurers. The reinsurers, however, repudiated liability on the ground[18] that the insurers had failed to give notice of deviation within a reasonable time, and that therefore they could not rely on the 'held covered' clause.

Branson J, held that this defence failed. The insurers did not know of the deviation until the loss had happened, and then they found it out only because the loss was posted at Lloyd's and advertised in the ordinary way. Once the loss had occurred no practical benefit would have accrued to the reinsurers from being told any sooner than they, in fact, were told of the deviation or subsequent loss. They knew it as soon as the knowledge was of any good to them at all. His Lordship added:[19]

'That being so the case of *Mentz, Decker & Co v Maritime Insurance Co*[20] shows that a delay in giving notice is no bar to the [assured] recovering. Hamilton J, says[1] regarding the deviation clause: "The clause must be read as it stands, and I think it is a mutual agreement to hold covered subject to a proviso which is satisfied by the giving of such notice which the assured can give after the receipt of advice, and as there was nothing practicable to be done on the receipt of the advice, the notice was given sufficiently early for the purposes of the present case at the time it was given."

I asked here if it could be suggested that anything practicable could have been done by [the insurers] had they received notice any earlier than they did, and I was told that nothing could be suggested.'

4 Delay in voyage

The Marine Insurance Act 1906, s 48 states:

---

[16] For the payment of an additional premium, see p 80, ante.
[17] (1925) 23 LlL Rep 243, KBD.
[18] Other grounds on which they repudiated liability were that the assured under the original policy had no interest at the time of the loss, and that the risk under the original policy had not attached. As to these aspects of the case, see pp 467–468, post, and pp 117–118, ante, respectively.
[19] (1925) 23 LlL Rep at 246.
[20] (1909) 15 Com Cas 17.
[1] Ibid, at 27.

'In the case of a voyage policy, the adventure insured must be prosecuted throughout its course with reasonable despatch, and, if without lawful excuse[2] it is not so prosecuted, the insurer is discharged from liability as from the time when the delay became unreasonable.'

Not only must the voyage be commenced within a reasonable time and be carried out without deviation from the vessel's proper course, but it must be prosecuted with reasonable despatch. Thus, any unreasonable delay in the course of the voyage is equivalent to a deviation and has the same effect in avoiding the policy.[3] The question as to what is a reasonable delay depends upon the circumstances of each case.[4]

Thus, in *Mount v Larkins*:[5]

> A master of a vessel stayed so long at a port of call that he was able to build a house and also to fit out a schooner on a sealing voyage, manning her with sailors from the insured ship.
> *Held*, the insurer could avoid liability.

Tindal CJ, said:[6]

> 'The voyage, commenced after an unreasonable interval of time, would have become a voyage at a different period of the year, at a more advanced age of the ship, and, in short, a different voyage than if it had been prosecuted with proper and ordinary diligence.'

But where a ship was detained in a river by ice, and was thereby prevented from getting into dock, it was held that there was no unreasonable delay.[7]

Similarly, where the delay was caused by the ship waiting to get a crew, Lord Ellenborough said:

> 'To discharge the policy there must be a clear imputation of waste of time. Mere length of time elapsing between the sailing of the vessel and the underwriting of the policy is not of itself sufficient to avoid the policy; it is capable of explanation.'

Delay in order to obtain cargo has been held to be justifiable.[8]

Further, delay while awaiting permission to land a cargo has also been excused.[9]

Again, where a ship with liberty 'to touch, stay and trade' remained in one of the ports from 3 June to 10 January following, it was said that the delay was not unreasonable since it had arisen from necessary repairs and the state of the freight market.[10]

But where a ship sailed to Benin and remained there for 13 months on purposes unconnected with the insured voyage, the delay was held to be unreasonable.[11]

Again, where goods en route were kept for a month at a railway station, the delay was held to be too long, and consequently the insurer was discharged.[12]

In *British American Tobacco Co v Poland*[13] the assured insured a quantity of

---

[2] See Marine Insurance Act 1906, s 49(1).
[3] *Hartley v Buggin* (1781) 2 Park 652.
[4] Marine Insurance Act 1906, s 88.
[5] (1831) 8 Bing 108.
[6] Ibid, at 122.
[7] *Samuel v Royal Exchange Assurance* (1828) 8 B&C 119.
[8] *Schroder v Thompson* (1817) 7 Taunt 462.
[9] *Bain v Case* (1829) 3 C&P 496.
[10] *Phillips v Irving* (1844) 7 Man&G 325.
[11] *Hamilton v Sheddon* (1837) 3 M&W 49.
[12] *Hyderabad (Deccan) Co v Willoughby* [1899] 2 QB 530.
[13] (1921) 7 LlL Rep 108, CA.

twine under a Lloyd's policy against a number of risks including fire for a voyage from London to Kavella, a port in Greece, on the 'Bosphoru' or other steamer. Under normal conditions the goods would have been shipped by a through bill of lading and have been transhipped at Piraeus to a coasting steamer for carriage to Kavella. Owing to war conditions the only means of forwarding the goods was to consign them to the British Consul at Piraeus, and request him to forward them. They were delayed at Piraeus for 3 months whilst awaiting a permit from the British Government.[14] On arrival off Kavella a coasting steamer to which the goods had been transferred was refused permission to land them, so her master decided to take them back to Piraeus for further instructions. On the return voyage the goods were destroyed by fire. The assured claimed for a loss under the policy, but the insurer refused to pay on the ground that there had been an unreasonable delay at Piraeus.

The Court of Appeal[15] rejected this contention and held that the action succeeded, for there had been no unreasonable delay.[16] Bankes LJ, said[17] that he agreed with the judgment of Bailhache J, in the court below[18] on that point. Bailhache J, had said[19] that there had been undoubtedly a considerable loss of time at Piraeus, but the goods had been shipped on board the coasting steamer at the very earliest opportunity.

In *Niger Co Ltd v Guardian Assurance Co and Yorkshire Insurance Co*[20] the plaintiffs were West African merchants. They insured some goods against all risks from West and South West Africa. The policy covered them in the interior of Africa and during the period when they were awaiting re-shipment at Burutu. The plaintiffs' course of business was to collect native produce in the interior and transport it down the Niger at stated periods to Burutu, where it was stored awaiting shipment overseas. A fire took place at Burutu in January 1916 and the goods were destroyed. Owing to war conditions they had been lying at Burutu for varying periods up to 8 months. The plaintiffs claimed under the policy, but the insurers repudiated liability[1] on the ground that the delay in shipment which had taken place at Burutu constituted a failure to prosecute the adventure with reasonable dispatch within the meaning of s 48 of the Marine Insurance Act 1906.

It was held by the House of Lords[2] that this defence failed, and that the action succeeded. The policy showed that the parties contemplated a reasonable delay at Burutu awaiting re-shipment and, in the circumstances prevailing in January 1916, the delay was not unreasonable.

---

[14] A permit was necessary because Kavella was being blockaded as there were considerable doubts as to the position taken up by the Greek army, and as to whether they would be likely to be loyal to the Allies or go over to Germany. See on this point the judgment of Bailhache J, in the court below: (1920) 5 LlL Rep 347 at 348, KBD.
[15] Bankes, Warrington and Scrutton LJJ.
[16] (1921) 7 LlL Rep at 109.
[17] Ibid, at 109.
[18] (1920) 5 LlL Rep 347, KBD.
[19] Ibid, at 349.
[20] (1922) 13 LlL Rep 75, HL.
[1] Another defence was that there had been non-disclosure of a material fact, viz that there was a large accumulation of goods at Burutu. As to this point, see pp 67–68, ante.
[2] Lord Buckmaster, Lord Atkinson, Lord Sumner and Lord Wrenbury.

Lord Buckmaster observed:[3]

> 'It was then urged that there had been unreasonable delay in forwarding the goods, evidenced by the amount of the goods in the warehouse at the time of the fire. This is largely a question of fact, and has been found adversely to the appellants in both the courts. I agree with the decisions so reached; the facts that the high river season was just passed, that the river had been good, so that abundant produce had been shipped, and the scarcity of shipping are sufficient to explain the quantity of produce, which was stated to be equivalent to a collection of eight months. The figures as to the previous annual shipments support this view.'

In *M Almojil Establishment v Malayan Motor and General Underwriters (Private) Ltd, The Al-Jubail IV*,[4] where a vessel was insured for 12 months from and on a voyage from Singapore to the Persian Gulf and whilst trading within the Gulf, and was delayed at Colombo for 79 days whilst repairs were effected to her, the Singapore Court of Appeal[5] held that the delay was reasonable.[6]

Excuses for delay

Delay in prosecuting the voyage contemplated by the policy is excused by the same reasons which justify a deviation.[7]

Effect of 'transit' clause

It should be noted that the risk continues where the policy includes a transit clause even though there has been a delay.

Thus, e g the 'transit' clause set out in the Institute Cargo Clauses (A)[8] states:

> 'This insurance shall remain in force . . . during delay beyond the control of the Assured . . .'

Duty to resume course

Section 49(2) of the Marine Insurance Act 1906 states:

> 'When the cause excusing the . . . delay ceases to operate, the ship must resume her course and prosecute her voyage, with reasonable despatch.'

5 Termination clauses

The risk may terminate earlier than in the general rule where in the case of goods there is a 'termination of contract of carriage' clause in the policy.

Thus, clause 9 of the Institute Cargo Clauses (A)[9] states that if owing to circumstances beyond the control of the assured either the contract of carriage is terminated either at a port or place other than the destination named in it or the transit is terminated before delivery of the goods as provided in the 'transit' clause, the insurance is to cease, but may remain in force if prompt notice is given to the underwriters and the payment of an additional premium, if so required by them, is made.

---

[3] (1922) 13 LlL Rep 75 at 76. See also the speech of Lord Atkinson, ibid, at 81 and that of Lord Sumner, ibid, at 82.
[4] [1982] 2 Lloyd's Rep 637, Sing CA.
[5] Wee Chong Jin CJ, Lai Kew Chai and Chua JJ.
[6] See the judgment of Lai Kew Chai J: [1982] 2 Lloyd's Rep at 641.
[7] Marine Insurance Act 1906, s 49(1). See pp 133–134, ante.
[8] These clauses are set out in Appendix III, pp 516–519, post.
[9] These clauses are set out in Appendix III, pp 516–519, post.

Further in the Institute War and Strikes Clauses (Hulls–Voyage)[10] the insurance terminates under a 'termination clause' on the happening of any events specified in the Institute Time Clauses (Hulls–Time)[11] e g

   i   the occurrence of any hostile detonation of any nuclear weapon of war;
  ii   the outbreak of war between certain named countries.

---

[10] These clauses are set out in Appendix III, pp 549–550, post.
[11] See p 114, ante.

CHAPTER 14

Marine risks

The set of Institute Clauses to be attached to the policy will depend on whether the subject-matter in respect of which cover for marine risks is needed is the hull,[1] the freight[2] or the cargo.[3]

All the clauses refer to the insurers' liability for general average[4] and salvage.[5]

Other risks may also be insured against.[6]

A HULL CLAUSES

The Institute Time Clauses (Hulls)[7] and the Institute Voyage Clauses (Hulls)[8] contain provisions setting out the extent of the cover in respect of:

1   the loss of or damage to the insured vessel;[9]
2   damage caused to another vessel;[10] and
3   general average and salvage.[11]

1 LOSS OF OR DAMAGE TO INSURED VESSEL

The Institute Time Clauses (Hulls)[12] and the Institute Voyage Clauses (Hulls)[13] each cover loss of or damage to the vessel caused by

a   a number of perils irrespective of want of due diligence by the assured;
b   a number of perils where the assured is not guilty of want of due diligence; and
c   steps to mitigate a pollution hazard.

---

[1] See pp 140–177, ante.
[2] See p 177, post.
[3] See pp 177–182, post.
[4] See pp 182–192, post.
[5] See pp 192–194, post.
[6] See pp 194–196, post.
[7] These clauses are set out in Appendix III, pp 533–540, post.
[8] These clauses are set out in Appendix III, pp 540–547, post.
[9] See pp 140–170, post.
[10] See pp 170–176, post.
[11] See pp 176–194, post.
[12] These clauses are set out in Appendix III, pp 533–540, post.
[13] These clauses are set out in Appendix III, pp 540–547, post.

(a) Perils irrespective of want of due diligence

The insurance[14] covers loss of or damage to the vessel caused by

1. perils of the seas, rivers, lakes or other navigable waters;
2. fire and explosion;
3. violent theft by persons from outside the vessel;
4. jettison;
5. piracy;
6. breakdown of or accident to nuclear installations or reactors; and
7. contact with aircraft or similar objects, or objects falling therefrom, land conveyance, dock or harbour equipment or installation.

Of the above perils some require special mention. Some of the reported cases, however, concern loss of or damage to cargo, yet the principles established by them apply equally to the loss of or damage to a ship.

Perils of the sea

A peril of the sea is a danger arising from the action of the sea which cannot be expressly guarded against, such as storms, or leakage of the ship, whether caused by agencies working from without or from within.[15]

To come within the meaning of the expression 'perils of the seas' the occurrences must not be such as can be foretold as, e g the gradual decay of a ship's timbers by the action of the water. Something fortuitous and unexpected is involved in the word 'peril' or 'accident'.[16]

Similarly, Rule 7 of the Rules for Construction of Policy set out in the First Schedule to the Marine Insurance Act 1906 states:

> 'The term "perils of the seas" refers only to fortuitous accidents or casualties of the sea. It does not include the ordinary action of the winds and waves.'[17]

Hence, insurers are answerable for casualties arising from the violent action of the elements, as distinguished from the silent, natural, and the gradual action of the elements upon the vessel itself, which properly relate to wear and tear.

They insure against casualties which might happen, and not consequences which must happen. In *The Golden Fleece*[18] Lush J, directed the jury that in the case before them the question was this: Was the leak on which the vessel foundered attributable to injury or violence from without or to weakness from within? For if it was not attributable to perils of the seas—i e to the violent action of the elements from without, or any other casualty involved in perils of the seas—the jury would come to no other conclusion than that it was due to an inherent infirmity in the ship herself.

The dividing line has therefore to be drawn between that which is accidental, fortuitous, and unexpected, and that which is natural, ordinary, and usual in its nature, having regard to the particular circumstances.[19]

---

[14] See the Institute Time Clauses (Hulls), cl 6 (p 534, post), and the Institute Voyage Clauses (Hulls), cl 4 (p 541, post).
[15] *Hamilton Fraser & Co v Pandorf & Co* (1887) 12 App Cas 518.
[16] Ibid.
[17] See further, Marine Insurance Act 1906, s 3.
[18] Cited by Blackburn J, in *Dudgeon v Pembroke* (1874) LR 9 QB 581.
[19] *Harrison v Universal Marine Insurance Co* (1862) 3 F&F 190.

Section 55(2)(c) of the Marine Insurance Act 1906 states:

> 'Unless the policy otherwise provides, the insurer is not liable for ordinary wear and tear, ordinary leakage and breakage, inherent vice or nature of the subject-matter insured, or for any loss proximately caused by rats or vermin, or for any injury to machinery not proximately caused by maritime perils.'

A loss occasioned by the natural chemical action of salt water, as distinguished from a loss by the violence of the waves, is not recoverable as a loss by perils of the seas;[20] and leakage from casks is not a loss from sea perils unless the cargo has shifted in a gale,[1] in the absence of special terms in the policy.[2]

Further, where, in the ordinary course of navigation, the ship takes the ground at low water, a straining of the ship is not a loss by sea perils, in the absence of any unusual circumstance.[3]

Nor was it a loss by sea perils where a transport had been laid down on Gosport Beach to be cleansed and caulked in the ordinary way, and the tide rose and knocked away the shoring, thereby causing her to fall over.[4]

Where, however, a ship took ground at low water in harbour in the ordinary way, and the rising of the tide was accompanied by a heavy swell, which set into the harbour, causing the ship to strike the ground and damage herself, the damage was held to result from sea perils.[5]

But, on the other hand, where the ship was destroyed by the action of worms on the timbers, this, being a thing which could not be said to be unexpected or accidental, was not a loss by sea perils.[6] A similar decision was reached where a vessel was detained at Antigua for a considerable time, and rats made holes in the bottom of the ship, so that she was condemned.[7]

Moreover the loss must be a peril of the *sea* in the sense that the sea or salt water must be the destroying agent.

Thus, where cattle were injured by the rolling and pitching of the ship, the loss was one by sea perils;[8] and also where horses were injured in like manner in a storm.[9]

But where the master took a wrong course, and so lengthened his voyage that fodder ran short and cattle were lost for lack of food, the loss was not one by sea perils;[10] nor even where unfavourable winds lengthened the voyage and caused a loss of cattle for lack of food.[11]

Where a cargo of cheese was damaged by rats, it was held not to be a peril of the seas;[12] but damage to a cargo of rice, caused by the incursion of water through holes made by rats, is a loss by perils of the seas.[13]

Where a cargo of hides was rendered putrid by the shipping of large

---

[20] *Paterson v Harris* (1861) 1 B&S 336.
[1] *Crofts v Marshall* (1836) 7 C&P 597.
[2] See eg *Phoenix Insurance Co of Hartford v De Monchy* (1928) 35 Com Cas 67.
[3] *Magnus v Buttemer* (1852) 11 CB 876.
[4] *Thompson v Whitmore* (1810) 3 Taunt 227.
[5] *Fletcher v Inglis* (1819) 2 B&Ald 315.
[6] *Rohl v Parr* (1796) 1 Esp 445.
[7] *Hunter v Potts* (1815) 4 Camp 203.
[8] *Lawrence v Aberdein* (1821) 5 B&Ald 107.
[9] *Gabay v Lloyd* (1825) 3 B&C 793.
[10] *Gregson v Gilbert* (1783) 3 Doug KB 232.
[11] *Tatham v Hodgson* (1796) 6 Term Rep 656.
[12] *Laveroni v Drury* (1852) 8 Exch 166.
[13] *Hamilton Fraser & Co v Pandorf & Co* (1887) 12 App Cas 518.

quantities of sea water, thereby imparting to a consignment of tobacco a nauseous flavour, it was held that the damage to the tobacco was caused by perils of the seas.[14]

Again, where ventilators had to be closed in bad weather and the accumulated hot air injured the cargo, the damage was held to be caused by an 'accident of the sea'.[15]

In *Canada Rice Mills Ltd v Union Marine and General Insurance Co Ltd*[16] a floating policy in respect of shipments of rice as from time to time declared had been effected by the assured. The policy covered loss occasioned by (inter alia) perils of the sea 'and all other perils losses and misfortunes that have or shall come to the hurt detriment or damage of the subject-matter of the insurance'. Rice was shipped on a vessel at Rangoon bound for the Fraser River. On arrival there it was found that the rice was overheated due to the closing of the ventilators and hatches in heavy seas to prevent the incursion of sea water. The assured claimed for a loss under the policy.

The Judicial Committee of the Privy Council[17] held that the action succeeded because the damage, which was not caused by the incursion of sea water but by action to prevent incursion, was recoverable as a loss by perils of the sea.

Lord Wright observed:[18]

> 'There remains the second question—namely, whether the damage which was caused, not by the incursion of sea water, but by action taken to prevent the incursion, is recoverable as a loss by perils of the seas. It is curious that, so far as their Lordships know, there is no express decision on this point under a policy of marine insurance, but, in their Lordship's judgment, the question should be answered in the affirmative, as they think the jury did. The answer may be based on the view that, where the weather conditions so require, the closing of the ventilators is to be regarded, not as a separate or independent cause, interposed between the peril of the sea and the damage, but as being such a mere matter of routine seamanship necessitated by the peril that the damage can be regarded as the direct cause of the peril.... In cases of fire insurance, it has been said that loss caused from an apparently necessary and bona fide attempt to put out a fire by spoiling goods by water, and in other ways, is within the policy: per Kelly CB, in *Stanley v Western Insurance Co.*[19] Their Lordships agree with this expression of opinion, and accordingly are prepared to hold that the damage to the rice, which the jury have found to be due to action necessarily and reasonably taken to prevent the peril of the sea affecting the goods, is a loss due to a peril of the sea, and is recoverable as such.'

Where cargo was damaged by sea water negligently let in by the engineer through a tank valve, it was held to be a loss by perils of the sea.[20]

On the other hand, where a very long delay caused a cargo of meat to become putrid, the loss was said not to be a loss by sea perils, though the delay was caused by tempest.[1]

A loss by foundering, the result of a collision, is a loss by perils of the sea, for, as was pointed out by Lord Bramwell in *Wilson, Sons & Co v Xantho (Cargo*

---

[14] *Montoya v London Assurance* (1851) 6 Exch 451.
[15] *The Thrunscoe* [1897] P 301; *Canada Rice Mills Ltd v Union Marine and General Insurance Co Ltd* [1941] AC 55, [1940] 4 All ER 169, PC.
[16] [1940] 4 All ER 169, PC.
[17] Viscount Maugham, Lord Russell of Killowen, Lord Wright and Lord Porter.
[18] [1940] 4 All ER 169 at 177.
[19] (1868) LR 3 Exch 71 at 74. See further, Ivamy, *Fire and Motor Insurance* (4th edn, 1984), p 152.
[20] *Blackburn v Liverpool, Brazil and River Plate Steam Navigation Co* [1902] 1 KB 290.
[1] *Taylor v Dunbar* (1869) LR 4 CP 206.

Owners), *The Xantho*,[2] there can be no difference as to the cause of a loss which results from a hole in the ship, whether that hole be small or large, whether in the one case the hole be made by a plank starting, or whether the hole be caused by another ship. In each case it would be occasioned by a peril of the sea, and it can make no difference that one of the causes which led up to the loss was the negligence of some of the parties concerned.

So the loss of, or damage to, a ship occasioned by the negligence of another ship colliding with her, is a loss by perils of the sea,[3] and so is the loss of a vessel owing to her being negligently towed into harbour.[4]

On the other hand, where a shipowner is made liable by legal proceedings to pay damages for injuries done to another ship by the insured ship in a collision, such damages will not, as regards the insured ship, be a loss under her policy by perils of the sea.[5]

Where goods were sold under a decree of the Admiralty Court in a salvage suit, and the proceeds were entirely swallowed up by the costs, it was held that this was not a loss by perils of the sea.[6]

Again, it would seem that where a collision is brought about without waves or winds or difficulties of navigation contributing to the accident, the loss is not one by perils of the sea.[7]

The following are further examples of loss by perils of the sea:

i   A ship was taken in tow by a man-of-war, and, in order to keep up with her, had to carry an excess of canvas in a gale, and consequently she shipped a large quantity of water, which damaged her cargo.[8]

ii   A cargo had been negligently stowed, and the ship, becoming leaky, was beached to save her from sinking.[9]

iii   The capture of a cargo in a stranded ship.[10]

iv   A loss occasioned by wreckers plundering the cargo.[11]

v   Where a ship had come into the control of a foreign power by sea perils, the charges levied on the cargo were recovered as a loss by perils of the sea.[12]

vi   Where two members of a crew went ashore to cast off a rope, and were seized by the press gang before they had accomplished their duty, and

---

[2] (1887) 12 App Cas 503.
[3] *Smith v Scott* (1811) 4 Taunt 126.
[4] *Mountain v Whittle* [1921] 1 AC 615.
[5] *De Vaux v Salvador* (1836) 4 Ad&El 420. See the 'Collision Clause', which is considered at pp 170–176, post.
[6] *De Mattos v Saunders* (1872) LR 7 CP 570.
[7] *Woodley v Michell* (1883) 11 QBD 47. But as to this, see *Wilson, Sons & Co v Xantho (Cargo Owners), The Xantho* (1887) 12 App Cas 503, where it was laid down that the meaning of the term 'perils of the sea' in bills of lading and in policies of insurance was the same; but that whereas in a policy the causa proxima alone was to be regarded, in a bill of lading the Court would consider not merely the causa proxima, but also the causa sine qua non, in order to determine whether the shipowner had, by his conduct in relation to the causes as a whole, merited the benefit of the exception.
[8] *Hagedorn v Whitmore* (1816) 1 Stark 157.
[9] *Redman v Wilson* (1845) 14 M&W 476.
[10] *Hahn v Corbett* (1824) 2 Bing 205.
[11] *Bondrett v Hentigg* (1816) Holt NP 149.
[12] *Dent v Smith* (1869) LR 4 QB 414.

in consequence the ship was driven ashore, the loss was held to be one by perils of the sea.[13]

Where a friendly ship was fired upon in mistake for an enemy's ship, Lord Ellenborough CJ, intimated that the loss in such a case was not by perils of the seas, although, being ejusdem generis, it came under the general words at the end of the perils clause. 'Perils of the seas' did not mean 'perils *on* the seas'.[14]

But a loss arising from ignorance and want of skill is not a loss by a peril of the sea.[15] Nor is a ship which is intentionally scuttled.[16]

In *P Samuel & Co Ltd v Dumas*[17] the House of Lords[18] held by a majority[19] that a loss of a vessel by scuttling was not a 'peril of the sea', for the term 'peril of the sea' referred only to fortuitous accidents and casualties. Consequently even an innocent mortgagee of a vessel, which was scuttled with the connivance of her owner, could not recover under a policy of insurance in respect of her.

Viscount Cave observed:[20]

> 'Then, was the loss a loss by perils of the sea? Surely not. The term "perils of the seas" is defined in Sch 1 to the Act as referring only to "fortuitous accidents or casualties of the seas". The word "accident" may be ambiguous, and has even been held in another connection to include a wilful murder: *Trim Joint District School Board of Management v Kelly*.[1] But the word "fortuitous", which is at least as old as *Thompson v Hopper*,[2] involves an element of chance or ill luck which is absent where those in charge of a vessel deliberately throw her away. In *Wilson, Sons & Co v Xantho (Cargo Owners)*,[3] Lord Herschell said that in order that there might be a peril of the seas
>
> "there must be some casualty, something which could not be foreseen as one of the necessary incidents of the adventure. The purpose of the policy is to secure an indemnity against accidents which may happen, not against events which must happen".
>
> In *Hamilton, Fraser & Co v Pandorf & Co*,[4] Lord Bramwell approved the definition of Lopes LJ, "it is a sea damage occurring at sea and nobody's fault". In *E D Sassoon & Co v Western Assurance Co*,[5] Lord Mersey, in delivering the judgment of the Judicial Committee of the Privy Council, adopted a similar view, which is also to be found in the judgment of the Judicial Committee in *Grant, Smith & Co and McDonnell Ltd v Seattle Construction and Dry Dock Co.*[6] On this view the expression "perils of the sea", while it may well include a loss by accidental collision or negligent navigation, cannot extend to a wilful and deliberate throwing away of a ship by those in charge of her.'

In *Lind v Mitchell*[7] a schooner was damaged by ice and started leaking. Her master caused her to be prematurely abandoned, and set her on fire to prevent her from being a danger to navigation. She was later sighted by another vessel

---

[13] *Hodgson v Malcolm* (1806) 2 Bos&PNR 336.
[14] *Cullen v Butler* (1816) 5 M&S 461; *Thames and Mersey Marine Insurance Co Ltd v Hamilton Fraser & Co* (1887) 12 App Cas 484.
[15] *Tatham v Hodgson* (1796) 6 Term Rep 656 at 659 (per Lawrence J). See *Gregson v Gilbert* (1783) 3 Doug KB 232.
[16] *P Samuel & Co Ltd v Dumas* [1924] AC 431, HL.
[17] [1924] AC 431, HL.
[18] Viscount Haldane LC, Viscount Cave, Viscount Finlay, Lord Sumner and Lord Parmoor.
[19] Viscount Cave, Viscount Finlay and Lord Parmoor: Lord Sumner dissenting.
[20] [1924] All ER Rep 66 at 76. See also the speech of Viscount Finlay, ibid, at 79.
[1] [1914] AC 667, HL.
[2] (1856) 6 E&B 172.
[3] (1887) 12 App Cas 503, HL.
[4] (1887) 12 App Cas 518, HL.
[5] [1912] AC 561, PC.
[6] [1920] AC 162, PC.
[7] [1928] 32 LlL Rep 70, CA.

which approached her and found her on fire, but floating high in the water. She was never seen again. One of the issues which arose in the case was whether she had been wilfully cast away by the master. The Court of Appeal[8] held that there was no evidence pointing to this, and that she had been lost by a peril of the seas.

Scrutton LJ, observed:[9]

> 'Having read the evidence carefully, I can find no evidence on which a jury would be entitled to convict the master in this case of wilfully and deliberately abandoning the ship not from any consideration of the existing danger from her leaks but simply because he wanted to get rid of her.
> One of the matters which influences me in that decision is the complete absence of motive of the master. In all the scuttling cases one has been able to prove a distinct advantage to the assured from the vessel being cast away, heavy over-insurance, impecuniosity of the assured, and matters like that. In this case it is not alleged that the assured or the managing owner are guilty of misconduct or have given any instructions for misconduct. The master is not insured; the master will get nothing by the vessel going to the bottom, except that he will lose his employment. I entirely fail to see any evidence on which you can find that the abandonment of the ship was wilful casting away by the master.'

In *Cohen, Sons & Co v National Benefit Assurance Co Ltd*[10] a policy in the usual Lloyd's form[11] was taken out in respect of the German submarine U124 'from Southampton to Swansea and for four months while breaking up covering all and every risk'. She was taken from Southampton to Swansea. While the work of breaking up was going on, she sank in a dock.[12] The assured were called upon by the insurers to raise her and commenced operations. After spending £2,000 they refused to continue them, and claimed an indemnity from the insurers in respect of this sum. But the insurers repudiated liability on the ground that her sinking was not due to a peril insured against, but was due to want of care by those who were dismantling her.

Bailhache J, held that the claim succeeded, for the loss was due to a peril of the sea, and observed:[13]

> 'In my view, the unintentional admission of sea water into a ship, whereby the ship sinks, is a peril of the sea. There is no warranty in this policy against negligence; there is no exception of negligence; and the fact that the unintentional admission of water into the ship is due to negligence is, in my opinion, totally and absolutely immaterial. There is a peril of the sea whenever a ship is afloat in the sea, and water from the sea is unintentionally admitted into her which causes a loss, either to the cargo or to the ship.'

He also considered that the words of the policy 'all and every risk' were sufficiently wide to cover the negligence of the workmen, and said:[14]

> 'Suppose I turn away from the construction of this as a marine peril and construe the words "covering all and every risk" as being words to be construed in their full signification without being qualified at all by the printed words of the policy. One of the ordinary risks of dismantling a ship is that somebody or other on board may be negligent; and in my opinion that is exactly what the [insurers] have proved in this case. There was negligence by somebody which caused this water to come into the ship and caused the damage. I have no doubt at all that if the words are not to be qualified by the printed words of the policy, "Southampton to

---

[8] Scrutton, Lawrence and Sankey LJJ.
[9] (1928) 32 LlL Rep at 74.
[10] (1924) 18 LlL Rep 199, KBD.
[11] It was not a Lloyd's but an insurance company's policy.
[12] The circumstances of the sinking are set out (1924) 18 LlL Rep 199 at 201.
[13] Ibid, at 202.
[14] Ibid, at 202.

Swansea, and for four months while breaking up, covering all and every risk" undoubtedly covers the negligence of the workmen. [Counsel] has pointed to the fact—which he seems to think is in his favour—that these people had broken up a great many submarines without anything of this sort having happened at all; that being urged as something to support his case as showing, as I understand it, that this was one of the almost inevitable risks of breaking up a ship. To my mind it shows exactly the opposite thing. The fact that they had broken up 18 or 19 ships without risk shows that this was not an accident which must inevitably have happened, but a risk which does not happen unless somebody is negligent. I find that is a fact, because [the insurers'] witnesses conclusively proved that fact.'

In *Miceli v Union Marine and General Insurance Co Ltd*[15] a cargo of wet salted and dried codfish[16] was insured for a voyage from the Faroe Islands to Naples. Heavy weather was experienced in the Bay and in the Gulf of Lions. The cargo arrived in a damaged condition. The assured claimed for a loss by perils of the sea, but the Court of Appeal[17] held that the action failed because he had not discharged the burden of showing that the damage had been caused by sea water.[18]

In the course of his speech in *Canada Rice Mills Ltd v Union Marine and General Insurance Co Ltd*[19] Lord Wright alluded to the meaning to be given to the words, and said that the incursion of sea water through the ventilators and hatches of a vessel fell within their ambit. He observed:[20]

> 'The jury may have pictured the tramp motor vessel, heavily laden with 5,000 tons of rice, driving into the heavy head seas, pitching and rolling tremendously and swept by seas or spray. Their Lordships do not think that it can properly be said that there was no evidence to justify their finding. On any voyage, a ship may, though she need not necessarily, encounter a storm, and a storm is a normal incident on such a passage as the *Segundo* was making, but, if, in consequence of the storm, cargo is damaged by the incursion of the sea, it would be for the jury to say whether or not the damage was due to a peril of the sea. They are entitled to take a broad commonsense view of the whole position.... Storms at sea may be frequent, in some cases seasonal, like typhoons in the China seas. A ship may escape them, and they are outside the ordinary accidents of wind and sea. They may happen on the voyage, but it cannot be said that they must happen. In their Lordships' judgment, it cannot be predicated that, where damage is caused by a storm, even though its incidence or force is not exceptional a finding of loss by perils may not be justified.'

The term 'perils of the sea' does not cover damage by seawater entering a vessel through holes in her caused by natural decay.[1] A cargo of opium was stored in a wooden hulk moored in the River Huang-Pu at Shanghai, and was insured against 'perils of the sea'. The hulk became leaky due to the natural decay of her hull. Water from the river found its way into her and damaged the opium. The assured claimed that the damage was caused by a 'peril of the seas'. The Judicial Committee of the Privy Council[2] held that the loss was not caused by a 'peril of the seas', and that the action failed.

---

[15] (1938) 60 LlL Rep 275, CA.
[16] The meaning of these terms is explained ibid, at 275.
[17] Sir Wilfred Greene MR, Scott and Mackinnon LJJ.
[18] The evidence is set out at (1938) 60 LlL Rep 275 at 276–278.
[19] [1940] 4 All ER 169, PC.
[20] Ibid, at 177.
[1] *E D Sassoon & Co v Western Assurance Co* [1912] AC 561, PC. See also, *Sipowicz v Wimble, The Green Lion* [1974] 1 Lloyd's Rep 593 (District Court of Southern District of New York), where the loss of the vessel was held not to be caused by a 'peril of the seas' but was due to the water entering her because of the bad condition of the metal fastenings securing the keel to the rest of the hull. (See the judgment of Cannella DJ, ibid, at 598.)
[2] Lord Macnaghten, Lord Atkinson, Lord Shaw and Lord Mersey.

Lord Mersey observed:[3]

'The learned judge held that the damage was not due to a sea peril at all, but was solely due to the weakness of the hulk, and he thereupon dismissed the action. Their Lordships are of opinion that the learned Judge was right. There was no weather, nor any other fortuitous circumstance, contributing to the incursion of the water; the water merely gravitated by its own weight through the opening in the decayed wood and so damaged the opium. It would be an abuse of language to describe this as a loss due to perils of the sea. Although sea water damaged the goods, no peril of the sea contributed either proximately or remotely to the loss.'

In *Cobb and Jenkins v Volga Insurance Co Ltd of Petrograd*[4] a policy had been effected in respect of some woollen goods during transit from London to Hull and then to Petrograd. Perils of the sea were included in the risks insured against. On arrival at Petrograd it was found that some of the goods had been damaged by water, but the Lloyd's surveyor, who inspected them, did not state whether the damage had been caused by salt water or fresh water. The goods had been shipped at Hull and had reached Trondhjem undamaged. They had been sent by rail from Trondhjem to Lulea. There they were put on board a vessel and carried across the Gulf of Bothnia to Uleaborg. They were sent on from there by rail to Tornea, where they remained for 4 months. They were then taken in sledges across a frozen river and carried by rail to Petrograd. The assured claimed for a loss under the policy on the ground that the damage had been caused by perils of the sea, i e sea water, because from the time that the goods arrived at Uleaborg until they reached Petrograd, the temperature was below freezing point so that no moisture could have reached them.

Greer J, held that the claim failed because the assured had not shown that the loss had been caused by perils of the sea.[5] He concluded his judgment by saying:[6]

'Apparently they managed to get accommodation on the railway before the thaw. If so, they must have been taken across the river in sledges or carried across. If so, they were never waterborne and had no chance of falling into the water. In these circumstances, it is impossible for me to hold that they did, and I am satisfied that they did not, suffer from any sea perils while at Tornea. Mr Guisberg's evidence is not confirmed by an expert opinion in Petrograd, and it may be that there are no experts left in Petrograd. I am not satisfied that Mr Guisberg is right when he says that he could determine definitely by looking at the goods that they were damaged by salt water. I think it is quite possible and just as likely as not that the damage he saw was damage by fresh water, for which the insurers would not be responsible.

On the whole, I am not satisfied that the damage happened from a peril insured against. It is an unfortunate mystery, and it will remain a mystery for the rest of time how the damage happened.'

In *Mountain v Whittle*[7] a houseboat was insured under a time policy against, inter alia, perils of the sea. The assured wished to have her cleaned, so he arranged for her to be towed to a convenient yard 7 miles away. The tug which was employed was larger than was usual for this type of operation, and caused an unusually high breast wave, which entered the vessel and caused her to sink. The House of Lords[8] held that the loss was caused by a peril of the seas, and that the assured was entitled to recover under the policy.

---

[3] [1911–13] All ER Rep 430 at 439.
[4] (1920) 4 LlL Rep 130 at 178, KBD.
[5] The evidence is set out ibid, at 178.
[6] Ibid, at 178.
[7] [1921] 1 AC 615, HL. Other aspects of the case related to the construction of 'liberty to shift clause' and a 'docking clause'. See pp 268–269, post.
[8] Lord Birkenhead LC, Viscount Haldane, Viscount Finlay, Viscount Cave, and Lord Sumner.

Lord Birkenhead LC, said:[9]

> 'In my opinion, the nature of this wave constituted a 'sea peril'. The elements which are necessary to form a sea peril have frequently been collected and explained in this House. But it is no longer necessary, unless for the purposes of illustration, to go further than the statutory provisions of the Marine Insurance Act 1906, that the term "perils of the seas" refers only to fortuitous accidents or casualties of the seas, and does not include the ordinary action of winds or waves. In my opinion, the incidence and dimensions of the wave in question amounted to a fortuitous casualty of the seas and were not accounted for merely by the ordinary action of winds or waves.'

Viscount Finlay observed:[10]

> 'If the water was in a normal condition and got into the houseboat simply owing to the defective character of the seams, there would be no loss by peril of the seas—the loss would have been by the defective condition of the vessel. A loss caused by the entrance of sea water is not necessarily a loss by perils of the seas. There must be some special circumstance, such as heavy waves causing the entrance of the sea water, to make it a peril of the seas. Was there such a peril here? Both Bailhache J, and the Court of Appeal find that there was, and upon the evidence I cannot doubt that they were right. It seems to be quite clear that the *Dorothy* was exposed to a wash of an extraordinary character from the great size and power of the *Dorrington*, the tug to which she was lashed. The breast wave so occasioned amounted to a peril of the seas just as much as if it had been occasioned by a high wind. No attempt was made on behalf of the underwriters to show that the water would have made its way into the houseboat to the same extent if the wash and breast wave had been normal. The wash occasioned by passing vessels at sea may constitute a peril of the seas if of an extraordinary character, and if the wash here was occasioned by something abnormal in the strength and size of the tug or the mode of towage, it was equally a peril of the sea.'

Damage caused by rough weather may be a 'peril of the sea' if the cargo has been properly stowed, even if such weather is expected.[11]

In *N E Neter & Co v Licenses and General Insurance Co Ltd*[12] a cargo of china clay was insured for a voyage from Fowey to Bombay. The assured alleged that a large part of the clay was found on arrival at Bombay to have been stained due to rough weather in the Bay of Biscay causing some casks of dye-stuff stowed with the clay to be stoved in. The King's Bench Division held that the assured had not discharged the burden of proving that the proximate cause of the damage to the cargo was the rough weather, but that the damage caused by rough weather would have been a peril of the sea, even though such weather was expected, provided that the cargo had been properly stowed.

Tucker J, said:[13]

> 'I think it is clearly erroneous to say that, because the weather was such as might reasonably be anticipated, there can be no peril of the seas. There must, of course, be some element of the fortuitous or unexpected to be found somewhere in the facts and circumstances causing the loss, and I think such an element exists when you find that properly stowed casks, in good condition when loaded, have become stoved in as a result of the straining and labouring of a ship in heavy weather. It is not the weather by itself that is fortuitous; it is the stoving in due to the weather, which is something beyond the ordinary wear and tear of the voyage. This appears to me to be "something which could not be foreseen as one of the necessary incidents of the adventure". It was "an accident which might happen, not an event which must happen".'

---

[9] [1921] All ER Rep 626 at 629.
[10] Ibid, at 632. See also the speech of Lord Sumner, ibid, at 634.
[11] *N E Neter & Co v Licenses and General Insurance Co Ltd* [1944] 1 All ER 341, KBD.
[12] [1944] 1 All ER 341, KBD.
[13] Ibid, at 343.

Although the phrase 'perils of the seas' has the same meaning in a bill of lading, charter-party, or policy of insurance,[14] it would seem that the risk of pirates would not now be included under the words 'perils of the sea'—at all events, not in a policy of insurance, it being rather a peril *on* the sea.[15]

Where a yacht was insured under a time policy in respect of loss and damage 'directly caused by external accidental means', and she was damaged in the course of a voyage from Deauville to Hamble in a confused sea with the wind of about Force 4 and waves 3 metres high, it was held that the insurers were liable, for there was no material distinction between 'external accidental means' and 'perils of the sea', and the assured had proved that she was damaged in that way.[16]

Fire

The term 'fire' needs no definition; but the extent of its application to policies of marine insurance is not so clear. Amongst the earliest references to fire as a cause of danger to the ship is that of Malynes:

> 'It hath oftentimes happened that by a candle unadvisably used by the boys or otherwise before the ships were unladen they have been set on fire and burnt to the very keel with all the goods in them, and the assurers have paid the sums of money by them assured.'

The earliest reported case on the subject is *Gordon v Rimmington*.[17] In this case the 'Reliance' was burnt off the coast of Africa in 1804 by her captain and crew to prevent her falling into the hands of an enemy privateer. Lord Ellenborough CJ, in his judgment gave some examples of the various grounds upon which the assured might be entitled to recover under this head:[18]

> 'Fire is expressly mentioned in the policy as one of the perils against which the underwriters undertake to indemnify the assured, and if the ship is destroyed by fire, it is of no consequence whether this is occasioned by a common accident or by lightning or by an act done in duty to the State. Nor can it make any difference whether the ship is thus destroyed by third persons, subjects of the King, or by the captain and crew acting with loyalty and good faith; fire is still the causa causans and the loss is covered by the policy.'

In *Busk v Royal Exchange Assurance*[19] the 'Carolina' was frozen up for the winter in a Russian port and, according to the custom of the country, the crew were paid off. The ship was left in charge of the mate who lit a fire in his cabin, but negligently omitted to see that it was extinguished before he went to bed. The ship was set on fire and burnt to the water's edge. It was held that the mere negligence of the mate was not a ground for relieving the insurers, for, although the fire was due to negligence, the loss was caused by fire.

Again, in *Rosa v Insurance Co of the State of Pennsylvania: The Belle of Portugal*,[20] where a vessel was lost by fire, which was one of the perils insured against, and

---

[14] *Hamilton Fraser & Co v Pandorf & Co* (1887) 12 App Cas 518.
[15] Cf the judgment of Byles J, in *Russell v Niemann* (1864) 34 LJCP 10 at 14 and that of Lord Ellenborough CJ, in *Cullen v Butler* (1816) 5 M&S 461. See further, *Hamilton Fraser & Co v Pandorf & Co*, supra, where Lord Esher (at 475) defined perils of the sea as 'perils to which people who carry on their business on that dangerous element are liable because they carry on their business on the sea. They are perils of the sea, not the perils of journeying.' See also *De Rothschild v Royal Mail Steam Packet Co* (1852) 21 LJ Ex 273; *Wilson, Sons & Co v Xantho (Cargo Owners), The Xantho* (1887) 12 App Cas 503; *Samuel v Dumas*, supra.
[16] *J J Lloyd Instruments Ltd v Northern Star Insurance Co Ltd, The Miss Jay Jay* [1985] 1 Lloyd's Rep 264, QBD (Com Ct). See the judgment of Mustill J, ibid, at p 272.
[17] (1807) 1 Camp 123.
[18] Ibid, at 123.
[19] (1818) 2 B&Ald 73.

the fire was caused by the negligence of a shore-side electrician, the United States Court of Appeals, Ninth Circuit,[21] held that the assured was entitled to recover under the policy.[1]

But although negligence will not excuse the insurer, yet if the fire is caused by an inherent vice in the thing insured, he will succeed upon the ground that the assured has himself occasioned the loss by having the goods in that condition, e g if spontaneous combustion took place in a cargo of hemp owing to its having been put on board in a damaged condition, the insurer would escape liability.[2] Similarly, he would not be liable where coals were lost by spontaneous combustion.[3]

Theft

The term 'pirates' presents no difficulty in regard to its use in marine policies, but the same observation is not applicable to the term 'thieves'. In the Florentine policy of 1523 the words employed are 'Robberies of Friends and Foes'. In the policy in *Goram v Sweeting*[4] the terms employed are 'Pirates, Rovers, Thieves', while in some American policies the words used are 'Pirates, Robbers or Rovers, and Thieves'.[5] In each of the above policies the insurer was liable for a loss by barratry.

There is an historical connection between barratry and simple theft, arising from the fact that neither was regarded as being a casus fortuitus, and therefore, apart from express words, the insurer would not be liable for a loss under either head. Accordingly, where the insurer was liable for barratry, he might reasonably be expected to be liable for a loss by theft. So Magens, in the marginal note to the section of his essay which treats of barratry,[6] says that the insurers must pay for the faults and thefts of the master and crew.

On the other hand, Malynes dealing with losses by 'Pirates, Rovers, Thieves' says:

'The losses which ordinarily according to the season of the year happen upon the seas are unknown; the like is more or less, with men of war, Enemies, Pirats, Rovers, Theevs, especially with men of war in times of hostility, as it is in time of peace by Pirats, Rovers, and Theevs which are assailing theevs; for otherwise if there be theevs on shipboard within themselves, the master of the ship is to answer for that, and to make it good, so that the assurers are not charged with any such loss; which sometimes is not observed.'

Malynes thus limits the loss by theft to the case of 'assailing theevs', but Park[7] says that a loss by thieves from without is undoubtedly recoverable, and he questions the soundness of the limitation by Malynes to a loss from 'assailing theevs', pointing out that there is a non sequitur in Malynes's reasoning that because the shipowner is liable for a loss by simple theft, therefore the policy does not cover it.

Park says:

'To be sure, it is not a necessary consequence, that because the owner is liable in such a case, therefore, the insurer, if an insurance has been made, must be discharged.'[8]

---

[20] [1970] 2 Lloyd's Rep 386.
[21] Merrill and Ely Ct JJ, and Crocker DJ.
[1] See the judgment of Merrill Ct J: [1970] 2 Lloyd's Rep 386 at 387.
[2] *Boyd v Dubois* (1811) 3 Camp 133.
[3] *Pirie & Co v Middle Dock Co* (1881) 44 LT 426.
[4] (1670) 2 Saund 200.
[5] Phillips s 1106.
[6] Section 63.
[7] Park on *Insurance*, p 28.
[8] Ibid, p 27.

Indeed, Malynes himself says that the rule is not always observed.

Phillips[9] is of opinion that a loss by simple larceny is covered by the word 'thieves', and says:

> 'Where the policy is against "thieves" simply, the provision is too explicit and definite to admit of the exclusion of all simple larceny, since it would cancel this provision, since larceny by violence is insured against as robbery.'

Roccus,[10] however, in dealing with the liability under Neapolitan law for losses of this kind, says that it depends upon the kind of theft, and he enumerates three kinds:

1. Theft by Pirates and Robbers—'*Furtum committatur in mari per pyratas et latrones*'; such a loss was recoverable in Naples because it was a casus fortuitus.
2. The second incidence is of theft committed on board the ship, and he proceeds to say that the underwriter is not liable for theft on board, because either the master of the ship or the owner of the goods is responsible for the safe custody of the thing stolen, and it is a loss from negligence and not a casus fortuitus and for the same reason the underwriter was not liable in Naples for a loss by barratry.
3. The third instance is that of theft committed by land thieves while the ship is in port, and for this form of loss the underwriter is not liable, since an insurance against shipwreck, enemies, and pirates will not cover such a loss, and he will not be responsible for such a loss unless he has specially made himself liable for it.

Thus far the authorities cited, with the possible exception of Malynes, would seem to be at least logical in their view of the subject, Roccus, on the one hand, classing a loss by theft with a loss by barratry, and pronouncing against the insurer's liability, while Magens, Park, and Phillips, discussing a system of insurance in which barratry is a loss insured against and in which mere negligence does not affect the liability of the insurers, declare that a loss by thieves covers a loss by theft.

English writers, purporting to follow Malynes, have, however, assigned to the term 'thieves' a meaning which renders the employment of that word in the policy useless and unnecessary. It is said that the word denotes persons, not members of the crew, who commit *robbery with violence*; that it does not cover a loss by simple theft, but only refers to *latrocinium*, as distinguished from *furtum*.

This view is adopted by Rule 9 of the Rules for Construction of Policy in the First Schedule to the Marine Insurance Act 1906:

> 'The term "thieves" does not cover clandestine theft or a theft committed by any one of the ship's company whether crew or passengers.'

In *La Fabrique de Produits Chimiques SA v F N Large*[11] two cases of vanillin and one case of caffeine were insured 'at and from London to Brugg (in Switzerland)'. The policy contained a 'warehouse to warehouse' clause.[12] The

---

[9] Phillips, *Insurance*, p 650.
[10] *De Assec*, not 41–43.
[11] (1922) 13 LlL Rep 269, KBD. The case also concerned the point whether there had been a partial loss of the goods or a total loss of part of them. As to this, see pp 431–432, post. See further, *Taylor v Liverpool and Great Western Steam Co* (1874) LR 9 QB 546; and *Steinman & Co v Angier Line* [1891] 1 QB 619.
[12] Now known as the 'transit' clause. See pp 122–126, ante.

two cases of vanillin were stolen from the warehouse of the forwarding agents, who had arranged for them to be put on board a vessel bound for Bordeaux, at night whilst she was unattended. One of the defences to the claim made by the insured was that this did not constitute 'theft' in marine insurance as no violence had been used.

Bailhache J, held that, without deciding whether in a 'warehouse to warehouse' policy the word 'theft' ought to be limited to theft by violence in the same way as it was in a purely marine policy, there had clearly been a theft by violence. Two sets of doors had been smashed by crowbars.[13] Further, theft by violence did not necessarily involve an assault on some person or other.

His Lordship observed:[14]

> 'I am reminded that the risk of thieves in a policy of marine insurance does not cover the ordinary clandestine theft, but only theft accompanied by violence, and that certainly is so when the policy is a policy of marine insurance pure and simple; and it is said that the same rule must apply when it is a "warehouse to warehouse" policy as when it is a marine policy, because of clause 5 of the Institute Cargo Clauses annexed to the policy; and it is said that the risk of thieves in a 'warehouse to warehouse' policy must have the same construction as in a marine insurance policy, as there was no violence in a case like this, where the goods were left unattended by night.
>
> I am not sure that in a "warehouse to warehouse" policy the word "theft" ought to be limited to theft by violence in the same way as it is in a purely marine policy. However that may be, this was clearly a theft by violence. There was a smashing of two sets of doors by crowbars, and it seems to me that clearly was a theft by violence. I do not think by violence there must be an assault on some person or other.
>
> It seems to me that when a person comes along and by crowbars smashes in doors, he breaks in and steals by violence, and the facts of this case answer the description of a theft by violence.'

Jettison

Jettison is the voluntary sacrifice in time of peril of something in or upon the ship, by throwing it overboard, with the intention of preserving the ship and cargo.[15]

So, where the captain threw overboard a quantity of dollars to prevent them falling into the hands of the enemy, who was pressing him and subsequently captured his ship, the loss was held to be by jettison.[16]

Where the jettison is rendered necessary by an inherent vice, and not by the perils insured against, the insurer is not liable.[17]

It would seem that if the jettison be in fact justifiable, it is not necessary that it should have been made by the order of the master, for any person performing the act would be deemed to be the agent of the owner for that purpose.[18]

The insurance against jettison is independent of any right to general average contribution, though the insurer, after payment of the loss, would be entitled to such rights as the assured possessed.[19]

Goods carried on deck are not protected against loss by jettison unless it is the custom so to carry them or unless specifically insured as such.

---

[13] As to the evidence, see (1922) 13 LlL Rep 269.
[14] Ibid, at 269.
[15] *The Gratitudine* (1801) 3 Ch Rob 240.
[16] *Butler v Wildman* (1820) 3 B&Ald 398.
[17] *Taylor v Dunbar* (1869) LR 4 CP 206.
[18] *Mouse's Case* (1608) 12 Co Rep 63. Cf *Price v Noble* (1811) 4 Taunt 123.
[19] *Dickenson v Jardine* (1868) LR 3 CP 639.

The reason for this is that Rule 17 of the Rules for Construction of Policy set out in the First Schedule to the Marine Insurance Act 1906 states:

'In the absence of any usage to the contrary deck cargo . . . must be insured specifically, and not under the general denomination of goods.'

If, however, the cargo is usually loaded on deck, then the insurer assumes liability for the loss of it when occasioned by any of the perils insured against;[20] and it seems that the rule against deck cargoes does not extend to inland river voyages at all.[1]

Where cotton was carried on deck according to the custom of the trade, the witnesses who proved the custom also proved that the shipowner so shipped it at his own risk and not at cargo-owner's risk. In order therefore to recover under the policy, such a risk would have to be specially insured, and would not be recoverable under the general term 'jettison'.[2]

Where a deck cargo was carried at merchant's risk, and a stipulation so to carry it was contained in a charter-party, and part of the deck cargo was properly jettisoned, it was held that, although the cargo so carried on deck was at merchant's risk, yet that did not relieve the shipowners, who by a charter-party permitted it to be so carried, from a claim for contribution in respect of the jettisoned cargo. The cargo being timber from the Baltic, it was proved to be customary for such ships to carry a deck-load of timber.[3]

In a case arising out of the carriage of a cargo of cattle, there was no evidence given of any custom allowing cattle to be carried on deck. But the contract for carriage stipulated that part of the upper deck was to be used for the purpose of carrying cattle, 'Vessel not to be responsible for mortality or accident of any kind'. The bill of lading provided that the cattle should be delivered in good order and condition, danger of the seas only excepted, and there was also a marginal note, 'Not accountable for mortality or any accident or injury of any kind or nature whatsoever'. The whole of the cattle were rightly jettisoned, but it was held that there was no liability on any other interest to contribute to the loss: first, because the cargo owners were not consenting parties to the loading on deck, and, there being no custom to bind them, the deck-load would not be a lawful deck-cargo; and, secondly, the ship being a general ship, there was no *express* liability on the shipowner in respect of the cargo, nor could any liability be implied, because that would import the principle of general average restricted in its application to the shipowner only.[4]

Piracy

Pirates are persons who without legal commission for the purpose plunder other vessels indiscriminately on the high seas for their own ends.

Thus, in *Bolivia Republic v Indemnity Mutual Marine Assurance Co Ltd*[5] a cargo being carried on a vessel up the Amazon was insured under a policy by which the insurance company agreed to indemnify the assured against loss arising

---

[20] *Da Costa v Edmunds* (1815) 4 Camp 142; *Gould v Oliver* (1837) 4 Bing NC 134; *Milward v Hibbert* (1842) 3 QB 120; *British and Foreign Marine Insurance Co v Gaunt* [1921] 2 AC 41.
[1] *Apollinaris Co v Nord Deutsche Insurance Co* [1904] 1 KB 252.
[2] *Royal Exchange Shipping Co v Dixon* (1886) 12 App Cas 11.
[3] *Burton v English* (1883) 12 QBD 218; *Johnson v Chapman* (1865) 19 CBNS 563.
[4] *Wright v Marwood* (1881) 7 QBD 62. Cf *Diederichsen v Farquharson Bros* [1898] 1 QB 150.
[5] [1909] 1 KB 785.

from various perils including piracy. The cargo consisted of stores and provisions, which were being sent up river by the Bolivian Government to their troops in the neighbourhood of El Acre, who were there for the purpose of resisting an organised expedition seeking to overthrow the Government. The vessel was intercepted by the expedition, and the cargo was seized. The assured claimed an indemnity under the policy on the ground that the loss had been caused by 'piracy'. The Court of Appeal[6] held that the action failed. 'Pirates' were persons who plundered indiscriminately for their own ends. The expedition consisted of persons who were simply operating against the property of the Government for a public end.

Vaughan Williams LJ, said:[7]

> 'The first one cited, which is from *Molloy* (book 1, chap 4, s 1) is "a sea thief, a hostis humani generis, who, to enrich himself either by surprise or open force, sets upon merchants or other traders by sea". A writer with whom I confess I am not acquainted, *Riquelme*, is cited in the same note, and he says that a pirate is a person who is preying by force contra los buques de todos los pueblos. And *Ortolan*, cited in the same note, says he is a man who is pillaging by arms les navires de toutes les nations. Those two definitions (I have not read the whole of them) seem to be either taken from the same source, or the one copied from the other, and there are other definitions which embody the same idea. No doubt there are definitions which do not embody that idea, but that, I think, is the common and ordinary meaning—to adopt the words of Pickford J:
>
>> "... a man who is plundering indiscriminately for his own ends and not a man who is simply operating against the property of a particular State for a public end, the end of establishing a government, although that act may be illegal, although that act may be criminal, and although he may not be acting on behalf of a society which is, to use the expression in *Hall on International Law*, politically organised. It may be piracy within the meaning of the doctrines of international law, but, in my opinion, it is not piracy within the meaning of a policy of insurance, because, as I have already said, I think you have to attach to 'piracy' a popular or business meaning, and I do not think, therefore, that this was a loss by piracy. There is another passage in *Hall on International Law* (5th edn), at p 262, which throws some light upon the matter; that is speaking of
>>
>>> 'Depredations committed at sea upon the public or private vessels of a State, or descents upon its territory from the sea by persons not acting under the authority of any politically organised community, notwithstanding that the objects of the persons so acting may be professedly political,'
>>
>> and he says such acts as those are, within the meaning of international law, piratical. But he goes on to say this:
>>
>>> 'Sometimes they are wholly political in their objects, and are directed solely against a particular State, with careful avoidance of depredation or attack upon the persons or property of the subjects of other States. In such cases, though the acts done are piratical with reference to the State attacked, they are for practical purposes not piratical with reference to other States, because they neither interfere with nor menace the safety of those States nor the general good order of the seas. It will be seen presently that the difference between piracy of this kind and piracy in its coarser forms has a bearing upon usage with respect to the exercise of jurisdiction.'
>>
>> I think the meaning of 'piracy' in a policy of insurance is what is called in this book piracy in its coarser sense, and, therefore, I do not think this is a loss by piracy within the meaning of this policy."
>
> I adopt the statement of Pickford J's, as the basis of my judgment.'

Rule 8 of the Rules for Construction of Policy set out in the First Schedule to the Marine Insurance Act 1906 states:

> 'The term "pirates" includes passengers who mutiny and rioters who attack the ship from the shore.'

---

[6] Vaughan Williams, Farwell and Kennedy LJJ.
[7] [1908–10] All ER Rep 260 at 264.

The crew of a ship who mutiny, and seize her and then carry her off, are pirates,[8] though in such a case the loss might also be ascribed to barratry.[9]

So the seizure of a ship by a body of emigrants is piratical, and the insurers would be liable under the word 'pirates' if the policy contained no f c and s clause.[10]

The carrying away of a ship by coolie emigrants, who had mutinied and murdered the master and some of the crew, is an act of piracy, and the loss is covered by the word 'pirates'.[11]

In *Nesbitt v Lushington*[12] Lord Kenyon CJ, held that a mob, who boarded the ship and plundered her, were pirates within the meaning of the policy. But in *Bondrett v Hentigg*[13] plundering by wreckers was said to be a loss by perils of the seas.

In *Banque Monetaca and Carystuiaki v Motor Union Insurance Co Ltd*[14] a Greek motor schooner was insured under a policy against war risks, i e capture, seizure or arrest and the consequences thereof whether before or after a declaration of war. The policy, however, excluded loss by piracy. The insured vessel called at Kerasounde (a port in the Black Sea on the coast of Turkey) in June 1920, when a state of war existed between Greece and Turkey. She was seized by Osman Agha, a brigand, who controlled the town, and was never heard of again. No prize court proceedings had been taken. The assured claimed for a total loss by the perils insured against, but the insurers refused to indemnify them on the ground that the vessel had been lost as a result of 'piracy'.

Roche J, held that the loss was due to capture and seizure by an enemy,[15] and not due to a raid by brigands, and observed:[16]

> 'I am satisfied, so far as I have the evidence, that in this case there was a loss from seizure and not from piracy. My reasons are as follows: There is no doubt that the person mentioned in the allegations, Osman Agha, was, by common consent, a person of low character, and that he was and had been a brigand. At the time, however, it is established upon evidence, upon which I ought to act, that he had arrived—as even a brigand might do—at a position of considerable authority, and that he was virtually controlling, as dictator, the region in which this seizure took place. . . . Of course, capture or seizure among civilised people is always identified with the form of taking the ship seized before the Prize Court. Osman Agha or the Kemalists did not indulge in that form, but the absence of the legal form does not seem to me to alter the substance of the matter, which is that this purported to be a seizure and capture of an enemy vessel rather than a raid by brigands upon such vessel.'

In *Rickards v Forestal Land, Timber and Rlys Co Ltd*[17] shortly before the outbreak of the Second World War a master of a German vessel was ordered to seek a neutral port or to return to Germany or as a last resort to scuttle her. War broke out and the vessel sailed from Rio for Germany and scuttled herself off the Faroe Islands to avoid capture by a British warship, and the insured cargo was

---

[8] *Brown v Smith* (1813) 1 Dow 349.
[9] *Dixon v Reid* (1822) 5 B&Ald 597.
[10] *Kleinwort v Shepard* (1859) 1 E&E 447.
[11] *Palmer v Naylor* (1854) 10 Exch 282.
[12] (1792) 4 Term Rep 783.
[13] (1816) Holt NP 149.
[14] (1923) 14 LlL Rep 48, KBD.
[15] As to the evidence, see ibid, pp 48–51.
[16] Ibid, at 50. His Lordship adopted (ibid, at 49) the definition of 'piracy' given by Pickford J, in *Bolivia Republic v Indemnity Mutual Marine Assurance Co Ltd* [1909] 1 KB 785 at 791. The decision in that case was later affirmed by the Court of Appeal: [1909] 1 KB 785 at 796.
[17] [1941] 3 All ER 62, HL.

lost. The House of Lords[18] held that the loss of the cargo could not be regarded as caused by piracy, because the master's act in sailing from Rio was done on the express orders of the German Government.[19]

There is no reason to limit piracy to acts outside territorial waters.[20] If a vessel is in the ordinary meaning of the phrase 'at sea' or if the attack on her can be described as a 'maritime offence', then she is in a place where piracy can be committed.[1]

Theft without force or threat of force is not piracy.[2]

Thus, in *Athens Maritime Enterprises Corpn v Hellenic Mutual War Risks Association (Bermuda) Ltd, The Andreas Lemos*[3] armed men came on board a vessel intending and expecting to steal without violence but anticipated the possibility of some resistance or interference. They intended to use force or the threat of force if that possibility materialised. Staughton J, held that there was no loss by piracy in regard to the ship's equipment which they threw into the sea. The loss was due to clandestine theft.[4]

Clandestine thieves who use or threaten violence in order to escape after the theft has been committed, do not give rise to a loss by piracy.[5]

(b) Perils where the assured is not guilty of want of due diligence

Clause 6 of the Institute Time Clauses (Hulls)[6] and clause 4 of the Institute Voyage Clauses (Hulls)[7] each state that provided the loss has not resulted from want of due diligence by the assured, the owners or the managers, the insurance covers loss of or damage to the vessel caused by

1. accidents in loading, discharging or shifting cargo or fuel;
2. bursting of boilers, breakage of shafts or any latent defect in the machinery or hull;
3. negligence of master, officers, crew or pilots;[8]
4. negligence of repairers or charterers provided such repairers or charterers are not an assured under the policy;
5. barratry of master, officers or crew.

---

[18] Viscount Simon LC, Viscount Maugham, Lord Thankerton, Lord Wright and Lord Porter.
[19] See the speech of Lord Wright: [1941] 3 All ER 62 at 76.
[20] *Athens Maritime Enterprises Corpn v Hellenic Mutual War Risks Association (Bermuda) Ltd, The Andreas Lemos* [1982] 2 Lloyd's Rep 483, QBD (Com Ct) at 490 (per Staughton J).
[1] Ibid, at 490 (per Staughton J).
[2] Ibid, at 491 (per Staughton J).
[3] [1982] 2 Lloyd's Rep 483, QBD (Com Ct).
[4] Ibid, at 491. His Lordship also observed (ibid, at 491): 'The very notion of piracy is inconsistent with clandestine theft... It is not necessary that the thieves raise the pirate flag and fire a shot across the victims's bows before they can be called pirates. But piracy is not committed by stealth.'
[5] Ibid, at 491 (per Staughton J).
[6] These clauses are set out in Appendix III, pp 537–540, post.
[7] These clauses are set out in Appendix III, pp 540–547, post.
[8] The master, officers, crew or pilots are not to be considered 'owners' within the meaning of the clause should they hold shares in the vessel: Institute Time Clauses (Hulls), cl 6; Institute Voyage Clauses (Hulls), cl 4.

Breakage of shafts

In *Scindia SS (London) Ltd v London Assurance*[9] a vessel was insured under a time policy which contained a clause stating:

> 'This insurance also specially to cover (subject to free of average warranty) loss of or damage to hull or machinery directly caused by accidents in loading, discharging or handling cargo, or in bunkering or in taking in fuel, or caused through the negligence of master, mariners, engineers or pilots, or through explosions, bursting of boilers, breakage of shafts, or through any latent defect in the machinery or hull.'

The vessel went into dry dock for the purpose of renewing the lower half of the wood lining of the stern bush. It was necessary to remove the propeller and withdraw the tailshaft. The shaft broke, and it fell into the dock with the propeller attached to it. One blade of the propeller was broken.

The assured claimed in respect of the damage to the propeller, and the insurers admitted liability for it. But there was also a claim for the cost of replacing the tailshaft, which had fractured owing to a latent defect.

It was held by Branson J, that the cost was not recoverable. He said that even apart from the words of the clause, the breakage of the shaft was not covered and observed:[10]

> 'Now, what is said on the part of the [insurers] is, that that is a latent defect, and, except under those words of this clause which deal with latent defects, damage caused by latent defects are excluded from this clause by virtue of s 55(2)(c), of the Marine Insurance Act. That seems to me to be a sound proposition. Where you have in the policy express words dealing with latent defects, and you try to isolate from that portion of the policy certain other words, and say that they insure against a particular peril simpliciter, I think to these words so isolated the general provisions of marine insurance law, as indicated by the section to which I have referred, must be applied and words so isolated must be read subject to those conditions of the law.'

His Lordship said that it had been argued that the clause could be read as expressly covering breakage of shafts. But this was not the true construction because the clause referred to *damage caused by breakage of shafts*, which was a different matter entirely. He remarked:[11]

> 'It seems to me that to try to isolate these words, "bursting of boilers, breakage of shafts", from their context and to read them as if they were taken out from their position and written in immediately after the clause in brackets "subject to free of average warranty" so that the clause should read, "This insurance also specially to cover (subject to free of average warranty) bursting of boilers, breakage of shafts", you are doing such violence to the language of the clause that it is not possible to put such a construction upon it. It seems to me that the words must be read in the position in which they are found and in the context in which they are found, and, so reading them, one finds that they appear following one set of circumstances introduced by the words "directly caused by", another set of circumstances introduced by the words "or caused through", and themselves introduced by the words "or through". When one looks at them from that point of view, it becomes quite obvious that they cannot be isolated in the way contended for by the plaintiffs.'

It had also been argued that 'shafts' were a portion of hull or machinery, and that 'loss or damage to machinery caused by the breakage of shafts' included the actual breaking of the shaft itself. But he considered that this argument also should be rejected, and said:[12]

---

[9] (1936) 56 LlL Rep 136, KBD.
[10] Ibid, at 138.
[11] Ibid, at 138.
[12] Ibid, at 138.

'It is said "shafts" are a portion of hull or machinery; they are a portion of machinery, and "loss of or damage to machinery caused by the breakage of shafts" includes the actual breaking of the shaft itself. That, it seems to me, is a forced construction of the language and not the ordinary meaning which, reading the clause as a bit of English prose, one would be inclined to put upon it. It comes following other clauses in which obviously the loss or damage happens to something different from the thing by which the damage is said to be caused. The first clause is 'caused by accidents in loading", and so forth; "caused through the negligence of master, mariners", and so forth. Both of those clauses obviously envisage, as it seems to me, a state of affairs in which the main cause produces damage which has an effect upon something else; and I see no reason why, when one comes down after those two clauses to the one with which I have particularly to deal, one should read it in any other way.'

His Lordship then went on to express his own view of what the clause meant, and said:[13]

'It seems to me, therefore, that the proper reading is that the breakage of the shaft itself is not covered, nor can you properly say that the breakage of the shaft is a loss of or damage to machinery caused by the breakage of the shaft. The breakage of the shaft is the breakage of the shaft, and if, by reason of the breakage of the shaft, the machine is torn to pieces, then one would get damage caused by the breakage of the shaft. But in this case the only damage beyond the damage to the propeller, which has been paid for, is the actual damage which happened to the shaft itself, to wit, the breakage of the shaft, and the breakage of the shaft is not caused by the breakage of the shaft, and if that is damage to the machinery which the breakage of the shaft has caused, it seems to me you get a confusion both of thought and language which I think should not be introduced into the construction of a clause of this kind.'

Latent defect

In *Jackson v Mumford*[14] it was held that weakness of design was not a 'latent defect' within the clause, nor was the breakage of an engine connecting rod.

Moreover, a pre-existing latent defect itself is not damage in respect of which an indemnity is recoverable, even though by wear and tear it becomes visible during the policy.

Thus, in *Oceanic SS Co v Faber*[15] a crack was discovered in the tail shaft of a vessel insured under a port policy, which contained the 'Inchmaree' clause, and a new shaft had to be fitted. It was held that the insurers were not liable for its cost because the crack in the old shaft had been gradually developing from a latent flaw for 10 years, and there was no damage other than the latent defect itself.

In *Irwin v Eagle Star Insurance Co Ltd: The Jonie*[16] a yacht was insured under a policy containing an 'Inchmaree' clause covering her in respect of loss through 'any latent defect in the machinery or hull'. An air conditioning firm joined together a steel pipe and a brass pipe which was usually submerged in bilge water. The joint should not have been made, for when it was exposed to the presence of air and salt water, electrolysis resulted. It was painted over and the assured was not aware of the condition of the piping. Six months after the installation the yacht sank due to a nipple in the pipe breaking. The United

---

[13] Ibid, at 139.
[14] (1904) 9 Com Cas 114.
[15] (1907) 13 Com Cas 28.
[16] [1973] 2 Lloyd's Rep 489. See also *Sipowicz v Wimble, The Green Lion* [1974] 1 Lloyd's Rep 593, District Court of Southern District of New York, where it was held that the defect was not a 'latent' one because the assured knew of the condition of the metal fastenings and had performed certain work in order to restore them. (See the judgment of Cannella DJ, ibid, at 599.)

States Court of Appeals, Fifth Circuit,[17] held that the assured was not entitled to an indemnity under the policy for there was no defect in the metal, but only a mistake by the air conditioning firm in joining steel and brass together. Accordingly, there was no 'latent defect in the machinery or hull' within the meaning of the policy.[18]

In *Prudent Tankers Ltd SA v Dominion Insurance Co Ltd, The Caribbean Sea*[19] a defect consisting of fatigue cracks in a wedge-shaped nozzle which was joined to a vessel's plate was held to be a 'latent' one,[20] and her loss was directly due to that defect.

Robert Goff J, was of the opinion that a 'latent' defect was one which could not be discovered on such an examination as a reasonably careful skilled man would make.[1]

Negligence

In *Lind v Mitchell*[2] the mortgagees of a wooden schooner insured her under a time policy against perils of the sea. The policy incorporated a clause which stated:

> 'This insurance specially to cover loss of vessel directly caused by accidents in loading, discharging or handling caused through the negligence of master, mariners, engineers or pilots.'

The schooner was returning to Burgeo, Newfoundland, after being holed by ice. She was intentionally set on fire by her master and prematurely abandoned. She was subsequently found by another vessel still on fire but floating high in the water. That was the last seen of her. The assured claimed for a total loss, but the insurers repudiated liability on the ground that the assured had failed to prove a loss by perils of the sea, and that she had in fact been lost by the wilful act of the master and crew in abandoning her and setting fire to her.

The Court of Appeal[3] held that the insurers were liable to indemnify the assured because the master had been negligent, and clause 8 covered the assured against loss of the vessel through the master's negligence.

In *Baxendale v Fane: The Lapwing*[4] a yacht was insured under a time policy. Clause 5 provided:

> 'This insurance also specially to cover ... loss of or damage to hull or machinery directly caused by ... negligence of master, mariners, engineers or pilots.'

She was negligently docked by the manager of a ship-repairing company whilst being placed in a tidal dock to have her bottom cleaned, and suffered damage. The assured claimed for a loss under the policy, and one of the defences raised by the insurer was that the manager was not the 'master' for the purpose of the clause set out above, and therefore the assured could not rely on it.

---

[17] Wisdom, Coleman and Simpson CtJJ.
[18] See the judgment of Coleman CtJ, in [1973] 2 Lloyd's Rep 489 at 491.
[19] [1980] 1 Lloyd's Rep 338, QBD (Com Ct).
[20] For the evidence, see ibid, at 345–346.
[1] Ibid, at 347.
[2] (1928) 98 LJKB 120, CA.
[3] Scrutton, Lawrence and Sankey LJJ.
[4] (1940) 66 LlL Rep 174, PDA.

Hodson J, held that the claim succeeded, for the manager was the 'master' within the meaning of s 742 of the Merchant Shipping Act 1894, and that the loss was therefore covered by the policy. He observed:[5]

> '"Master" has been defined in many statutes. In the Merchant Shipping Act 1894, s 742,
> '"Master" includes every person (except a pilot) having command or charge of any ship.'
> I have no doubt that O'Connor was the master of the vessel at the time of the first docking. He was still in charge of her. The fact that he was at the same time manager of the yacht works and was the servant of the yacht works, not of the plaintiff, seems to me to make no difference. Indeed, his dual position enables his negligence to be the more clearly established, because he was in a position to know what was the nature of the bottom of the dock in which he was placing the vessel.'

In *Rosa v Insurance Co of the State of Pennsylvania, The Belle of Portugal*[6] the fishing vessel 'Belle of Portugal' and her skiff were insured under a policy which covered (inter alia) 'loss or damage to hull directly caused by negligence of master, charterers, mariners, engineers or pilots'. The vessel was lost due to an electrical fire, and her crew took to the boats. They were picked up by the motor vessel 'Port Adelaide'. The crew of the 'Port Adelaide' tried to hoist the skiff on board, and it was lost. The assured claimed an indemnity from the insurers, but they repudiated liability on the ground that the skiff was not covered because it was lost through the negligence of the crew of the 'Port Adelaide'. The United States Court of Appeals, Ninth Circuit,[7] held that the action succeeded, for there was no proof that the crew of the Port Adelaide had been negligent, and even if they had been, the clause covered losses due to the negligence of 'mariners'.[8]

In *Capital Coastal Shipping Corpn and Bulk Towing Corpn v Hartford Fire Insurance Co (United States of America, Third Party), The Christie*,[9] where a tug was insured under a policy containing such a clause, the District Court for the Eastern District of Virginia, Norfolk Division, held[10] that even if the person operating her had been negligent and his negligence was the cause of the loss, the assured could not recover under the policy because there had been a breach of warranty.[11]

Barratry

This peril appeared in Florentine policies as early as 1523 where the underwriters assumed the risk 'di Barratteria di Padrone' and Magens, citing Stracca, says that it appeared in policies in London and Antwerp about the same time. The term 'barratry' comprehends all wrong done by the master or mariners against the interests of the owner of the ship, but it does not include errors of judgment or cases of ordinary negligence.

The difficulty of definition was discussed in the early case of *Vallejo v Wheeler*,[12] where the headnote states that 'barratry is every species of fraud or knavery in the Master or mariners of the ship by which the owners or freighters

---

[5] (1940) 66 LlL Rep 174 at 181.
[6] [1970] 2 Lloyd's Rep 386.
[7] Merrill and Ely CtJJ, and Crocker DJ.
[8] See the judgment of Merrill CtJ: [1970] 2 Lloyd's Rep 386 at 387.
[9] [1975] 2 Lloyd's Rep 100.
[10] See the judgment of Hoffman DJ, ibid, at 107.
[11] As to the warranty in this case, see p 295, post.
[12] (1774) 1 Cowp 143.

are injured', a definition which was cited with approval by Willes J, in *Lockyer v Offley*.[13]

In *Vallejo v Wheeler*[14] many definitions were cited, and Lord Mansfield said:[15]

> 'I take the word—i e barratry—to have been originally introduced by the Italians, who were the first great traders of the modern world. In the Italian dictionary, the word barratrare means "to cheat" and whatsoever is by the master a cheat, a fraud, a cozening, or a trick, is barratry in him: nothing can be so general.'

Lord Ellenborough CJ, in the later case of *Earle v Rowcroft*[16] said:[17]

> 'A breach of duty by the Master in respect to his owners with a criminal intent or ex maleficio is barratry.'

Lord Mansfield in *Nutt v Bourdieu*[18] and Lord Ellenborough CJ, in *Earle v Rowcroft*[19] both expressed surprise that liability for loss to the owner resulting from the misconduct of the master should by the policy be thrown on the insurer when the master is selected and appointed by the owner himself. Such an objection, however, would not apply to a policy on goods; and in regard to policies on ships, in early times the insurer probably knew as much about the master as the owner did, and in any case received due notice of the name of the master who was to sail in command of the ship, by its insertion in the policy.

The definition given in Rule 11 of the Rules for Construction of Policy in the First Schedule of the Marine Insurance Act 1906 is:

> 'The term "barratry" includes every wrongful act wilfully committed by the master or crew to the prejudice of the owner, or, as the case may be, the charterer.'[20]

The act of barratry must be performed without the owner's consent, for against a willing and consenting owner barratry cannot be committed, since it is obviously impossible to cheat or defraud one who orders or consents to the act of cheating or of fraud.

Not only is barratry—in its original sense—impossible against a willing and consenting owner, but a barratrous act, to which the owner consented, could not be a ground for recovering under the policy any loss caused by that act, for no one can take advantage of his own wrong.[1] Therefore where the master is himself the owner, the loss occasioned by his barratrous conduct could not be recovered under the policy as a loss by barratry,[2] and Emerigon says that where the assured himself commands the ship, the insurers will in no case be

---

[13] (1786) 1 Term Rep 252.
[14] Supra.
[15] (1774) 1 Cowp 43 at 154.
[16] (1806) 8 East 126.
[17] Ibid, at 134. See also *Phyn v Royal Exchange Assurance* (1798) 7 Term Rep 505.
[18] (1786) 1 Term Rep 323.
[19] Supra.
[20] For the definition of barratry given in a US case, see *Steam Tanker Padre Island Inc and Pullman Bank and Trust Co v London Assurance, Guildhall Insurance Co et al, The Padre Island* [1971] 2 Lloyd's Rep 431 (District Court for the Southern District of Texas) at 432 (per Garza DJ). In this case a vessel ran aground on the Hen and Chickens Rocks in the Bahamas, and it was held that she had been deliberately stranded by the master at the command of the owners, and that consequently a loss by barratry had not been shown. For the evidence on this point, see ibid, pp 437–438.
[1] *Stamma v Brown* (1742) 2 Stra 1173; *Pipon v Cope* (1808) 1 Camp 434.
[2] *Ross v Hunter* (1790) 4 Term Rep 33.

responsible for his barratry, although this could not be extended to the barratry of the mariners in which the master took no part.[3]

It has been said that the owner of a ship under charter cannot recover for a loss occasioned by an illegal and barratrous act committed by the charterers' agent.[4]

On the other hand, if the master with the sanction of the real owner commits an act of barratry towards the charterer who is pro tempore the owner, the assured on goods may recover,[5] the general rule being that the owner of goods is bound by the conduct of the person who is for the time being the owner of the ship,[6] and cannot recover for a loss occasioned by any barratrous act sanctioned by him.[7] If the real owner, acting as master, intentionally runs the ship ashore, this will be barratry against the charterer.[8]

One of the points which was argued in *Rickards v Forestal Land, Timber and Rlys Co Ltd* in the King's Bench Division[9] (though not when the case went to the Court of Appeal[10] and the House of Lords[11]) was whether barratry could be committed against a cargo owner.

In this case a cargo was insured from South American ports to Hong Kong or Shanghai. The vessel on which the goods were loaded was a German one. She sailed from Buenos Aires on 16 August 1939. War was declared between Great Britain and Germany on 3 September. On 29 September the master, acting under the orders of the German Government, scuttled her off the Faroe Islands to avoid capture by a British warship. The cargo owners in their claim against the underwriters maintained that the cause of the loss was the barratry of the master and crew. Hilbery J, gave judgment for the underwriters, citing with approval[12] the words of Lord Mansfield CJ, in *Nutt v Bourdieu*:[13]

> 'The point to be considered is whether barratry, in the sense in which it is used in our policies of insurance, can be committed against any but the owners of the ship. It is clear beyond contradiction that it cannot. For barratry is something contrary to the duty of the master and the mariners, the very terms of which imply that it must be in the relation in which they stand with the owners of the ship.'

Again, in *Commercial Trading Co Inc v Hartford Fire Insurance Co*[14] the United States Court of Appeals, Fifth Circuit,[15] held that where a master delivered the insured goods to a person who did not produce all the bills of lading in respect of them, the assured's claim for a loss by 'criminal barratry of the master' would be dismissed, since criminal barratry could be committed only against the shipowners.[16]

---

[3] Emerigon, xii, 3.
[4] *Hobbs v Hannam* (1811) 3 Camp 93. But see *Small v United Kingdom Marine Mutual Insurance Association* [1897] 2 QB 311.
[5] *Vallejo v Wheeler* (1774) 1 Cowp 143; *Soares v Thornton* (1828) 7 Taunt 627.
[6] On the question as to when the freighter becomes *pro tempore* the owner of the vessel, see *Belcher v Capper* (1842) 4 Man&G 502 and *Colvin v Newberry and Benson* (1828) 8 B&C 166.
[7] *Nutt v Bourdieu*, supra.
[8] *Soares v Thornton*, supra.
[9] [1940] 4 All ER 96.
[10] [1940] 4 All ER 395, CA.
[11] [1941] 3 All ER 62, HL.
[12] [1940] 4 All ER 96 at 112.
[13] (1786) 1 Term Rep 323 at 330.
[14] [1974] 1 Lloyd's Rep 179.
[15] Brown ChJ, Ingraham and Roney CtJJ.
[16] See the judgment of Brown ChJ: [1974] 1 Lloyd's Rep at 180.

It has been held that a part-owner may commit barratry against his co-owners,[17] e g where the master being part-owner fraudulently sold the ship and cargo, and applied the proceeds to his own use.[18]

The most common instances of barratry are those which spring from smuggling, some breach of international or municipal regulations, or which arise from deviation or scuttling.

Smuggling

Cases of smuggling are the most frequent; and if the master commits barratry by smuggling, the insurer is liable, although the terms of the policy are confined to 'any lawful trade'.[19]

Where, however, the revenue authorities had seized the ship in consequence of smuggling by the master, the insurer escaped liability because of the f c and s warranty, although the dominant cause of the loss was barratry.[20]

In another case, where the ship had been seized and forfeited, the insurer escaped liability because of the negligence of the assured, who should have prevented the repeated acts of smuggling.[1]

Breach of international or municipal regulations

Besides smuggling, any other breach of either municipal or international law which results in a loss to the assured will be barratrous. The earliest reported case on barratry is an action on a policy of insurance, which was tried in 1724, where the fraudulent neglect of the captain to pay port dues resulted in the forfeiture of the ship, and was held to be barratry.[2]

Breach of an embargo is also barratry;[3] and the conduct of the captain came under the same designation where a breach of blockade was intentionally committed, which resulted in the seizure and condemnation of the ship.[4]

Trading with the enemy is barratry,[5] and so is the shipping of Kanaka labourers in violation of the Pacific Islanders Protection Act 1875.[6]

The non-observance of the rule of the road at sea by starboarding instead of porting the helm is not barratry, although it is a violation of the rules made under the authority of an Act of Parliament;[7] so in cases of this class regard must be had to the special circumstances in each instance, and to the presence or absence of fraudulent intent in performance of the act complained of.

Deviation

Deviation by the master for his own purposes is barratry. Thus, where the master sailed out of the course of the voyage to trade on his own account, and in

---

[17] See also *Westport Coal Co v McPhail* [1898] 2 QB 130, where in regard to negligence the Court drew a distinction between negligence of the master as master, and as co-owner.
[18] *Jones v Nicholson* (1854) 10 Exch 28.
[19] *Havelock v Hancill* (1789) 3 Term Rep 277.
[20] *Cory & Sons v Burr* (1883) 8 App Cas 393.
[1] *Pipon v Cope* (1808) 1 Camp 434.
[2] *Knight v Cambridge* (1724) 2 Ld Raym 1349.
[3] *Robertson v Ewer* (1786) 1 Term Rep 127.
[4] *Goldschmidt v Whitmore* (1811) 3 Taunt 508.
[5] *Earle v Rowcroft* (1806) 8 East 126.
[6] *Australasian Insurance Co v Jackson* (1875) 33 LT 286.
[7] *Grill v General Iron Screw Collier Co* (1868) LR 1 CP 600.

the deviation the ship was lost, such deviation, being fraudulent, was held to be barratrous.[8]

In *Mentz, Decker & Co v Maritime Insurance Co Ltd*[9] a policy was effected on commissions expected to be earned in respect of a vessel due to sail from San Juan del Sur, and thence to a port of loading in Costa Rica and thence to a port of discharge in the United Kingdom or on the Continent. She sailed from San Juan del Sur to Punta Arenas for orders. There her master received orders to go to load a cargo at Cocos Bay in Costa Rica. But instead of going there the master went on a voyage to the Cocos Islands, which were 250 miles away, merely to land an explorer, who was anxious to get there quickly. Hamilton J, held that this conduct amounted to barratry, and observed:[10]

> 'The question, therefore, which arises first of all is: In deviating did the captain commit a barratrous act? The Marine Insurance Act in the schedule in rule 11 states that, "The term 'barratry' includes every wrongful act wilfully committed by the master or crew to the prejudice of the owner, or, as the case may be, to the charterer." The authorities prior to the Act show that where a captain is engaged in doing that which he must, as an ordinary man of common sense, know to be a serious breach of his duty to his owners, and is engaged in doing it for his own benefit, then he is acting barratrously. He may act quite barratrously in many other ways, but I think it is quite clear that if he is disregarding his duty to his owners and breaking his duty to them for the sake of private purposes and ends, his conduct is barratrous.'

A similar instance is provided by *Marstrand Fishing Co Ltd v Beer*.[11] In this case the master of a fishing vessel named the 'Girl Pat' was instructed by his owners to fish in the North Sea. Instead he ran off with her with the intention of trading with her and ultimately selling her.[12] Porter J, held that an act of barratry had been committed, but that the taking of a vessel by barrators was not in itself sufficient evidence of irretrievable loss to constitute an 'actual total loss'[13] within the meaning of s 57(1) of the Marine Insurance Act 1906, nor had it been proved that the vessel was a 'constructive total loss'[14] under s 60(2)(i)(a).

The same view obtained where the master, in violation of the instructions of his owners, cruised for prizes, in consequence of which the vessel was afterwards lost, the fraud in this case being shown by the omission of the cruising from the log-book.[15]

There was also a loss by barratry where the master of a British ship trading at a British settlement proceeded to a Dutch settlement, and traded with the enemy without the consent of the owners, in consequence of which his ship was seized and condemned as a prize for trading with the enemy.[16]

'Detention, if done in the prosecution of a barratrous act, is part of the barratry for which the underwriters are liable, and not a deviation by which they are excused.'[17]

A deviation caused by the crew taking the ship on a different voyage is barratry.

---

[8] *Vallejo v Wheeler* (1774) 1 Cowp 143.
[9] (1909) 101 LT 808, KBD.
[10] Ibid, at 810.
[11] [1937] 1 All ER 158, KBD.
[12] For the evidence on this point, see ibid, pp 159–161.
[13] As to 'actual total loss', see pp 346–361, post.
[14] As to 'constructive total loss', see pp 362–377, post.
[15] *Moss v Byrom* (1795) 6 Term Rep 379.
[16] *Earle v Rowcroft* (1806) 8 East 126.
[17] Per Richardson J, in *Roscow v Corson* (1819) 8 Taunt 684.

On the other hand, where the master, sailing with a letter of mart[18] had taken a prize, and was compelled by the mariners to put back to Bristol, although his orders were to send the prize back with a prize crew and to proceed himself to Newfoundland, it was held that this was not barratry, as there was no attempt to defraud the owners. In this case the prize got in safely, but the ship was captured.[19]

Nor was it barratry where the master, instead of sailing to Marseilles, sailed for Genoa with the intention of returning to Marseilles, the ship on the way back being blown up in an engagement with a Spanish ship, for the Court found that the master acted for the benefit of the owners, and not in his own interest.[20]

Where the deviation proceeds from ignorance or want of skill and not from fraud, it is not barratry, although it may be against the interest of the owners;[1] for unless accompanied by fraud or criminal intent, no case of deviation will fall within the true definition of barratry.[2]

So, in the case of a loss by detention, the cause of the detention must have been wilful, since mere mistake is not enough. 'In order to establish barratry you must give positive proof of fraud',[3] for barratry means an act of the master in fraud of his duty to his owners.

Similarly, Abbott LCJ, said in *Bottomley v Bovill*:[4]

'A mere mistake by the captain as to the meaning of the instructions, or a misapprehension of the best mode of acting under the instructions and carrying them into effect, would not amount to barratry. The jury were to find for the assured if they were of opinion that the captain acted in fraud of his duty to his owner when he went to A instead of to B; but if they thought, on the other hand, that he merely mistook the meaning of the instructions or the best mode of acting for the purpose of carrying them into effect, then to find for the underwriter.'

Thus, where the master took his ship into a port of refuge because she had sprung a leak, and before survey he broke up her ceiling and end bows with crowbars, it was suggested that this was done in order to secure the condemnation of the vessel. Lord Ellenborough CJ, thereupon said:

'In order to constitute barratry, which is a crime, the captain must be proved to have acted

---

[18] Letters of Mart and Countermart were letters granted by the Crown to subjects whose ships or other effects had been captured or arrested, independently of war, by the subjects of other States, and such letters conferred on the recipients the liberty of indemnifying themselves for what had been unjustly taken from them. They had no other object than that of repairing the wrong that had been done, and were in the form of reprisals limited to that extent. Any person fitting out a ship for purposes of war unprovided with some such royal commission would be deemed a pirate. There was no authority to grant such a commission except in the Crown. Privateering having been ended by the Declaration of Paris 1856, the subject has lost all its former importance.
[19] *Elton v Brogden* (1747) 2 Stra 1264.
[20] *Stammar v Brown* (1742) 2 Stra 1173.
[1] *Phyn v Royal Exchange Assurance* (1798) 7 Term Rep 505.
[2] *Earle v Rowcroft* (1806) 8 East 126. See also, *Commercial Trading Co Inc v Hartford Fire Insurance Co* [1974] 1 Lloyd's Rep 179, (US Court of Appeals, 5th Cir) at 182 (per John R Brown ChJ). In this case where a master had misdelivered the insured cargo to a third party who did not produce all the outstanding bills of lading, the Court held that barratry could not be committed against a cargo owner, and in any event, the master's acts did not show any criminal intent to defraud or in any way harm the owners.
[3] Per Abbott LCJ, in *Bradford v Levy* (1825) Ry&M 331.
[4] (1826) 5 B&C 210 at 212.

against his better judgment; as the case stands, there is a whole ocean between you and barratry.'[5]

Scuttling

Barratry often takes the form of intentional scuttling by the master or members of the crew. Thus, in *Elfie A Issaias v Marine Insurance Co Ltd*[6] the vessel was sunk by the intentional admission of sea water into her by the acts of the master and engineer in removing a pipe in the condenser and removing the sea connections.[7] The Court of Appeal[8] held that this was an act of barratry for which the insurance company must indemnify the assured.[9]

In *Rickards v Forestal Land, Timber and Rlys Co Ltd*[10] a cargo was insured for carriage on a German vessel from South American ports to Hong Kong or Shanghai. The vessel arrived at Rio on 25 August 1939. War was declared on 3 September 1939. After 16 August 1939 all German owned shipping had been taken control of by the German Government, and all vessels and their masters had been ordered to take refuge in neutral ports or to return to Germany, or as a last resort to scuttle themselves. The vessel sailed from Rio on 6 September 1939 and was subsequently scuttled off the Faroe Islands to avoid capture by a British warship and the insured cargo was lost as well. The House of Lords[11] held that the loss of the cargo could not be regarded as caused by barratry 'because it must be assumed that [the master's] owners were equally with himself sympathetic with, or subject to the orders of the German Government'.[12]

In *Piermay Shipping Co SA and Brandt's Ltd v Chester, The Michael*[13] a vessel sank and became a total loss, and the assured claimed for a loss by barratry.[14] It was common ground that she had been deliberately sunk by the second engineer. The insurers denied liability contending that he had acted with the assured's knowledge and consent. Kerr J, held that the action succeeded for, on the evidence,[15] the thought of sinking the vessel never crossed the assured's mind. The decision was subsequently affirmed[16] by the Court of Appeal.[17]

Changing sides in a civil war

In *Republic of China Merchants Steam Navigation Co Ltd and United States of America v National Union Fire Insurance Co of Pittsburgh, Pennsylvania, The Hai Hsuan*[18] six

---

[5] *Todd v Ritchie* (1816) 1 Stark 240. Examples of barratry in this sense are to be found in *Ross v Hunter* (1790) 4 Term Rep 33; *Toulmin v Anderson* (1808) 1 Taunt 227; *Heyman v Parish* (1809) 2 Camp 149; and *Soares v Thornton* (1817) 7 Taunt 627.
[6] (1923) 15 LlL Rep 186, CA.
[7] The evidence on this point is set out ibid, at 187–188, 190.
[8] Lord Sterndale MR, Warrington and Atkin LJJ.
[9] The Court also considered the question of the burden of proof in the case of a claim for loss by barratry. This aspect of the case is to be found at pp 245–247, post.
[10] [1942] AC 50, [1941] 3 All ER 62, HL.
[11] Viscount Simon LC, Viscount Maugham, Lord Thankerton, Lord Wright and Lord Porter.
[12] [1941] 3 All ER at 76 (per Lord Wright).
[13] [1979] 1 Lloyd's Rep 55, QBD (Com Ct).
[14] The insured risk sued upon was not perils of the sea but barratry alone, which appeared to be unprecedented: ibid, at 56 (per Kerr J.)
[15] The evidence is set out ibid, at 60–62, 64–66, 72–88.
[16] [1979] 2 Lloyd's Rep 1.
[17] Roskill and Brandon LJJ, and Sir David Cairns.
[18] [1958] 1 Lloyd's Rep 351 (US Court of Appeals, 4th Cir).

vessels at Hong Kong belonging to the Chinese Nationalist Government were ordered to sail to Formosa or to Japan. Instead of going there the masters of the vessels concerned ran up the Red Flag, and held them for the benefit of the Chinese Communist Government. The United States Court of Appeals[19] held that this constituted 'barratry'. Circuit Judge Soper said that the insurance company had contended that masters and mariners who changed sides during a civil war could not be considered to have committed barratry, and observed:[20]

> 'The answer to this is simply that the characterization of an act as barratrous is independent of the motives which provoked the act. In *The Jupiter (No 3)*[1] the master, who had been placed in command of a vessel by the administrator for White Russian interests, allowed the USSR to gain possession of his ship. The Court decided that the master "may have acted as a loyal subject of the USSR, but he betrayed his trust to his employers".'

Another Chinese Nationalist vessel in the case was under a charter-party from Spain to Japan. She was directed to proceed to Formosa, but the crew refused to carry out the orders of her master, who intended to comply with his owners' instructions. When she was about 30 miles west of Singapore, the engine-room staff stopped the engine and turned off the telemotor. The master ordered the anchor to be dropped to avoid a possible danger to her. He had had no food for several days and was sick with fear. On the master's refusal to take her to Singapore, the chief officer sailed her there himself, and on the same day, the master was admitted to Singapore General Hospital. Two days later the vessel flew the Communist flag. The Court held that these acts constituted 'barratry'.

Effect of owner's negligence

The insurer will not be liable when the assured is guilty of gross negligence, and might have prevented the acts of barratry.

Thus, where a ship was seized for smuggling at Weymouth, and after being liberated was again seized at Jersey for another act of smuggling, and after being again liberated was seized at Weymouth for a third offence, Lord Ellenborough CJ, said:

> 'This is a clear case of *crassa negligentia* on the part of assured. It was his duty to have prevented these repeated acts of smuggling by the crew. By his neglecting to do so, and allowing the risk to be so monstrously enhanced, the underwriters are discharged.'[2]

Date of liability

The liability of the insurer commences from the time when the barratrous act which results in the loss is committed, e g from the commencement of a barratrous deviation.[3]

But Lord Ellenborough CJ, held that where the conduct of the master resulted in the condemnation and sale of the ship, the cause of action did not accrue to the assured until delivery of the ship to the purchaser, and

---

[19] Chief Judge Parker, Circuit Judge Soper and Circuit Judge Haynsworth.
[20] [1958] 1 Lloyd's Rep at 361.
[1] [1927] P 122.
[2] *Pipon v Cope* (1808) 1 Camp 434; and see Marine Insurance Act 1906, s 55(2)(a).
[3] *Brown v Smith* (1813) 1 Dow 349; *Falkner v Ritchie* (1814) 2 M&S 290; *Dixon v Reid* (1822) 5 B&Ald 597.

consequently that was the date from which the Statute of Limitations began to run.[4]

The insurer is not liable unless the actual loss takes place while the policy attaches, and the fact that the act of barratry was committed during the life of the policy makes no difference.

Thus, where the ship was insured for a voyage, and during the voyage the master committed an act of smuggling which resulted in the seizure of the ship after she had been moored 24 hours in good safety, the insurer was held not liable for the loss.[5]

Evidence

A condemnation proceeding upon an attempt to commit a breach of a blockade is by no means conclusive evidence of a loss by barratry.[6]

It is never necessary for the assured to prove that the master was not the owner.[7]

Where the acts and the evidence relied on as constituting barratry are consistent with ignorance on the part of the master and with obedience to the orders of the owners, such acts would be deemed innocent and not barratrous,[8] unless, of course, they are accompanied by fraud or crime.[9]

Want of due diligence

In *Pacific Queen Fisheries v L Symes, The Pacific Queen*[10] a wooden-hulled motor vessel was insured under a policy containing such a clause, and was lost as a result of an explosion and a fire. The United States Court of Appeals, Ninth Circuit,[11] held that the insurers were not liable to indemnify the assured because the loss fell within the proviso to the clause, viz 'provided such loss or damage has not resulted from want of due diligence by the Owners of the Vessel, or any of them, or by the Managers', and had resulted from want of due diligence on the part of the assured to prevent the explosion.[12]

In *F B Walker & Sons Inc v Valentine*[13] a tug was insured under a policy which contained a clause stating that it covered 'loss of or damage to the vessel insured directly caused by the negligence of the master. . . .; Provided such loss has not resulted from want of due diligence by the assured'. The vessel sank at a wharf due to excessive leakage of water through the rudder post and main engine stuffing boxes. The United States Court of Appeals, Fifth Circuit,[14] held that the insurers were liable on the policy, for, on the evidence, although it was good

---

[4] *Hibbert v Martin* (1808) 1 Camp 538.
[5] *Lockyer v Offley* (1786) 1 Term Rep 252.
[6] *Everth v Hannam* (1815) 6 Taunt 375.
[7] *Ross v Hunter* (1790) 4 Term Rep 33.
[8] *Everth v Hannam*, supra.
[9] *Earle v Rowcroft* (1806) 8 East 126 at 139.
[10] [1963] 2 Lloyd's Rep 201 (US Court of Appeals, 9th Cir).
[11] Circuit Judge Pope, Circuit Judge Barnes and Circuit Judge Hamley.
[12] [1963] 2 Lloyd's Rep at 212-3.
[13] [1970] 2 Lloyd's Rep 429. The case also concerned a breach of warranty. As to this point, see pp 294-295, post.
[14] Brown ChJ, Jones and Carswell CtJJ.

seamanship to tighten up the main engine stuffing boxes and this had not been done, it was not due to any 'want of due diligence' by the assured.[15]

In *Coast Ferries Ltd v Century Insurance Co of Canada, The Brentwood*[16] the assured had insured a vessel under a time policy, which stated (inter alia) that they were covered in respect of loss or damage to her directly caused by the negligence of the master 'provided such loss or damage has not resulted from want of due diligence by the assured'. The vessel sailed with a freeboard of only 18 inches at the stem. A bow wave entered the ventilators. She lost stability, rolled over, and had to be beached. The proximate cause of the loss was unseaworthiness caused by negligent loading by the master. The Court of Appeal of British Columbia[17] held that the assured were not entitled to an indemnity under the policy, for they had failed to furnish the master with sufficient information about minimum freeboard and trim for the vessel to enable him to exercise sound judgment in loading in the light of his skill and experience. Accordingly, the loss had resulted from 'want of due diligence' on their part.[18]

In *Rhesa Shipping Co SA v Edmunds, The Popi M*,[19] where a vessel was thought to have collided with a submerged submarine,[20] Bingham J, at first instance held that in all probability she would have been lost without the negligence of the crew because her aftermost compartments would not have been flooded. But the insurers' defence that there was a want of due diligence on the part of the assured failed for no matter how assiduous and careful owners or managers might be, they could not be expected to instruct sea-going officers to take steps and precautions so elementary and obvious to those which were neglected in the present case.[1]

(c) Pollution hazard

Clause 6 of the Institute Time Clauses (Hulls)[2] and clause 4 of the Institute Time Clauses (Voyage)[3] state that the policy covers loss of or damage to the vessel caused by any governmental authority acting under the powers vested in it to prevent or mitigate a pollution hazard, or threat of it, resulting directly from damage to the vessel for which the insurers are liable under the policy.

But the insurers are under no liability where the act of the governmental authority has resulted from any want of due diligence by the assured, the owners or the managers of the vessel.[4]

2 DAMAGE CAUSED TO ANOTHER VESSEL

Clause 8 of the Institute Times Clauses (Hulls)[5] and clause 6 of the Institute

---

[15] See the judgment of Brown ChJ: [1970] 2 Lloyd's Rep at 430.
[16] [1973] 2 Lloyd's Rep 232.
[17] Nemetz, Taggart and Davey JJ.
[18] See [1973] 2 Lloyd's Rep at 234.
[19] [1983] 2 Lloyd's Rep 235, QBD (Com Ct).
[20] As to this aspect of the case, see p 250, post.
[1] See [1983] 2 Lloyd's Rep 235 at 250. The House of Lords, however, subsequently held that the assured had failed to prove that the vessel was lost by a peril insured against, and the claim therefore failed: (1985) Financial Times, 22 May. See p 250, post.
[2] These clauses are set out in Appendix III, pp 533–540, post.
[3] These clauses are set out in Appendix III, pp 540–547, post.
[4] Masters, officers, crew or pilots are not to be considered 'owners' within the meaning of the clause should they hold shares in the vessel: Institute Time Clauses (Hulls), cl 6; Institute Voyage Clauses (Hulls), cl 4.
[5] These clauses are set out in Appendix III, pp 533–540, post.

Voyage Clauses (Hulls)[6] each contain a '3/4ths Collision Liability' Clause, which states that

  i the insurers agree to indemnify the assured for 3/4 of any sum or sums paid by the assured to any other person or persons by reason of the assured becoming legally liable by way of damages for
   a loss of or damage to any other vessel or property on any other vessel;
   b delay or loss of use of any such other vessel or property on her; and
   c general average of, salvage of, or salvage under contract of, any such other vessel or property on her,
   where such payment by the assured is in consequence of the insured vessel coming into collision with any other vessel.
  ii where the insured vessel is in collision with another vessel and both vessels are to blame, then, unless the liability of one or both vessels becomes limited by law, the indemnity must be calculated on the basis of cross-liabilities as if the respective owners had been compelled to pay to each other such proportion of each other's damage as may have been properly allowed in ascertaining the balance or sum payable by or to the assured in consequence of the collision;
  iii in no case will the insurers' liability exceed their proportionate part of 3/4 of the insured value of the insured vessel in consequence of the collision;
  iv the insurers will pay 3/4 of the legal costs incurred by the assured or which the assured may be compelled to pay in contesting liability or taking proceedings to limit liability, with the prior consent of the insurers; and
  v the indemnity in no case extends to any sum which the assured pays for or in respect of
   a removal or disposal of obstructions, wrecks, cargoes or any other thing whatever;
   b any real or personal property or thing whatsoever except other vessels or property on other vessels;
   c the cargo, or other property on, or the engagements of, the insured vessel;
   d loss of life, personal injury or illness; or
   e pollution of or contamination of any real or personal property or thing whatsoever (except other vessels with which the insured vessel is in collision or property on such other vessels).

Clause 9 of the Institute Time Clauses (Hulls) and clause 7 of the Institute Voyage Clauses (Hulls) also contain a 'sister ship' clause which states

  a if the insured vessel comes into collision with or receives salvage services from another vessel belonging wholly or partly to the same owners or the same management, the assured has the same rights under the policy as they would have if the other vessel were entirely the property of owners not interested in the insured vessel; and
  b in such cases the liability for the collision or the amount payable for the

---

[6] These clauses are set out in Appendix III, pp 540–547, post.

services rendered must be referred to a sole arbitrator to be agreed on between the insurers and the assured.

'Vessel'

The word 'vessel' in the 'collision clause' has received a very extended meaning.[7]

In *Chandler v Blogg*[8] the word 'ship' was held to cover a collision with a sunken barge, which was subsequently raised and sailed home. She was therefore in a position analogous to that of a vessel at anchor. It would seem, however, that the governing factor in the case of a sunken vessel is whether she still retains character as a ship or has become merely a wreck. Where she is a wreck, a collision with her would not be within the meaning of the words 'collision with any other ship or vessel'.

An anchor is part of a vessel, and therefore a tug striking a ship's anchor comes into collision with a 'vessel'.[9]

But where a ship fouled the nets of a fishing vessel, it was held not to be a 'collision' within the meaning of the clause.[10]

In *Pelton SS Co Ltd v North of England Protecting and Indemnity Association, The Zelo*[11] the owners of a steamship claimed against a mutual indemnity association in respect of a collision between her and the wreck of another vessel. Soon after the other vessel had sunk, salvage operations were begun in order to raise her from 30 feet of water, but these were unsuccessful. When the insured vessel struck her, part of the other vessel's forecastle and a considerable part of the stem were further damaged, and any salvage operation became hopeless. The assured claimed against the insurers under the 'collision clause', but they refused to pay on the ground that the wreck was no longer a 'vessel', so the assured brought an action against the mutual indemnity association for the whole of the loss. The association paid one-quarter of the loss, but contended that they were not liable for the remaining three-quarters because she was a 'vessel' at the time of the collision.

Greer J, accepted this contention and held that the claim in respect of the remaining three-quarters failed. The question whether the other vessel was a 'vessel' at the time of the collision depended on whether or not any reasonably minded owner would have continued salvage operations on her in the hope of completely recovering her and by subsequent repair. In his opinion, they did have such a reasonable expectation, and he observed:[12]

> 'In my judgment the salvors at the time of the loss had a reasonable expectation that they would be able to salve the vessel. It is not necessary for the purpose of my judgment to decide whether in fact that reasonable expectation would have been converted into fact by their further operations. If they had reasonable expectation of being able to salve this vessel so that

---

[7] *McCowan v Baine and Johnston, The Niobe* [1891] AC 401.
[8] [1898] 1 QB 32.
[9] *Re Margetts and Ocean Accident and Guarantee Corpn* [1901] 2 KB 792.
[10] *Bennett SS Co v Hull Mutual SS Protecting Society* [1914] 3 KB 57. See also *Lehigh and Wilkes-Barre Coal Co v Globe and Rutgers Fire Insurance Co* (1925) 26 LlL Rep 82 (US Court of Appeals, 2nd Cir), where it was held that a barge, which had been damaged when it came into contact with the bank of a canal, had not been involved in a 'collision' within the meaning of the 'collision clause', nor had another barge which had struck some steep rocks along the shore.
[11] (1925) 22 LlL Rep 510, KBD.
[12] Ibid, at 512.

she could be repaired and again navigated, she remained a vessel within the meaning of the clause in the principal policy and within the meaning of the rules to which I have referred.'

His Lordship said that he did not agree with the test of 'navigability' suggested in *Chandler v Blogg*,[13] and remarked:[14]

'The only case which is at all near this to which my attention has been called is the case of *Chandler v Blogg*,[15] where it was held that a barge which was lying at the bottom and was damaged by collision by another ship was still a ship or vessel although at the moment of collision it could not be navigated, if it was capable of being easily raised, and it became navigable as soon as it was raised; and the judgment of Bigham J, rather suggests that he accepted in some sense the test of navigability as a test of whether the thing in question was or was not a ship or vessel, not as an absolute test, because it is clear in that case that at the moment of collision the vessel was not navigable, but he seemed to base his judgment upon the fact that the vessel had become navigable the moment she was brought to the surface.

It seems to me, with great respect, that navigability cannot be the test as to whether the thing is or is not a ship or vessel. I mean navigability at the time of collision, because in this case, *Chandler v Blogg*,[16] the vessel was not navigable at the time of collision. It does not seem to me you can test whether a vessel at the bottom is or is not a ship or vessel by saying she will be navigable immediately she comes to the surface. You must apply some other test; and I cannot find any better test than the question whether or not any reasonably minded owner would continue salvage operations in the hope of completely recovering the vessel by those operations and subsequent repair.'

In *Merchants' Marine Insurance Co Ltd v North of England Protecting and Indemnity Association*[17] the plaintiffs were the insurers of a vessel against maritime risks, and claimed from the defendants, who were an indemnity association of which the owner of the vessel was a member, an indemnity against liability incurred for damage arising out of a collision between her and a pontoon crane in the River Charente.

Under the rules of the indemnity association a member was protected against damages to the extent of one-fourth which he might become liable to pay in respect of collision between his vessel and 'any other ship or vessel'. Under another rule he was protected against the *whole* damage,

'which the member or owner may become liable to pay . . . in respect of damage done by the steamship to any harbour, dock, or pier, or quays, or works connected therewith or to jetties, erections or any fixed or moveable things, other than ships or vessels.'

The Court of Appeal[18] held that the plaintiffs were entitled to an indemnity in respect of the *whole* of the damage because the pontoon crane was not a 'ship or vessel' within the rules of the indemnity association. The primary purpose for which it was designed and adapted was to float and to lift, and not to navigate, and that adaptability for navigation was an essential element of a 'ship or vessel'.

Bankes LJ, said:[19]

'Now what do we find with regard to the structure? It is, in fact, a structure upon which a crane is fixed, and permanently fixed. It has no motive power of its own. I do not attach much

---

[13] [1898] 1 QB 32.
[14] (1925) 22 LlL Rep at 512.
[15] Supra.
[16] Supra.
[17] (1926) 26 LlL Rep 201, CA.
[18] Bankes, Scrutton and Sargant LJJ.
[19] (1926) 26 LlL Rep at 202. See also the judgment of Scrutton LJ, ibid, at 203, and that of Sargant LJ, ibid, at 203.

importance to that, but it is an incident. It is not capable of being steered: it has no rudder. I think that again is only an incident, but I think it is rather an important incident. It is undoubtedly capable of being moved, but it is obviously so unseaworthy that it can only be moved short distances, or comparatively short distances, and only when the weather is exactly favourable. It is a most unwieldy structure. Its arm, or jib, is 70 ft long: it is fixed athwart the platform with two fixed struts, and obviously, upon looking at it, it is a most unseaworthy structure. We have also its life history, to this extent, that it was built very many years ago—in 1868, I think the date is. Everyone agrees that the fact that it had to be towed a considerable distance to the place where the crane was fitted is immaterial for the present purposes. One has to consider what it is and what it has been since it became a floating crane, and, so far as the information goes, it has only been moved very occasionally during all these years. I think there are about five or six times when it has been moved since 1914, and therefore, although it is obviously movable and it obviously must be moved, in order to make it an effective crane, from time to time, the conclusion I come to is that, for this purpose and for the purpose of the construction of this rule, it is more accurately described as a floating platform for this crane than as a ship or vessel. I desire to say, speaking for myself, that I do not think it is possible to frame an exhaustive definition which will be of assistance in other cases, or to attempt an exhaustive test to apply for the purpose of deciding whether any particular object is a ship or vessel.'

In *Polpen Shipping Co Ltd v Commercial Union Assurance Co Ltd*[20] a ship was insured under a policy containing a 'collision clause', which provided that the insurer would indemnify the assured 'if the ship hereby insured shall come into collision with any other ship or vessel and the assured shall in consequence thereof become liable to pay and shall pay by way of damages to any other person . . . any sum'. The insured ship negligently collided with a flying boat causing damage which the assured paid. The assured claimed an indemnity from the insurer. It was held by the King's Bench Division that the action failed. The words 'ship or vessel' did not include a flying boat.

Atkinson J, said:[1]

'The conclusion at which I have arrived is that in this policy it is impossible to hold that the words "ship or vessel" include this flying boat. I do not want to attempt a definition, but I think a ship or vessel does involve two ideas. If I had to define them, I should say a vessel was any hollow structure intended to be used in navigation, that is, intended to do its real work upon the seas or other waters, and which is capable of free and ordered movement from one place to another. Its ability to navigate is not merely incidental to the work for which it is really intended. A seaplane's real work is to fly. That is its real work and what it is built for, and its ability to float and navigate short distances is merely incidental to its real work, and to my mind that is where the real difference lies. A ship or vessel must be something which is intended to do its real work upon the waters, and it has got to be capable of free and ordered movement.'

'Damages'

The clause covers only collision damages payable in respect of a tort. It does not cover liability arising in contract.[2]

Thus, in *Furness Withy & Co Ltd v Duder*[3] a marine insurance policy included the 'collision clause' by which the insurer agreed to indemnify the assured 'if the ship hereby insured shall come into collision with any other ship or vessel and the assured shall in consequence thereof become liable to pay by way of damages to any other person any sum . . .' An Admiralty tug was engaged by the assured to tow the insured ship. The towage contract contained a clause

---

[20] [1943] KB 161, [1943] 1 All ER 162, KBD.
[1] Ibid, at 165.
[2] *Furness Withy & Co Ltd v Duder* [1936] 2 KB 461, [1936] 2 All ER 119, KBD.
[3] [1936] 2 All ER 119, KBD.

under which the assured agreed 'to make good to the Admiralty all damage suffered by the Admiralty through injury to Admiralty property . . . by reason of or arising out of . . . the service [of the tug]'. The insured ship collided with the tug owing to the negligent navigation of the tug. The assured paid the amount of the damage to the Admiralty, and claimed an indemnity from the insurer under the 'collision clause'.

It was held by the King's Bench Division that the action failed. The clause only applied to liability arising in tort, and not to liability arising out of a towage contract.

Branson J, said:[4]

> 'The question here is whether the £119 12s 8d, which the plaintiffs have paid to the Admiralty is a sum which they became liable to pay in consequence of the ship having come into collision with another ship, and became liable to pay by way of damages. Mr Miller urges that the collision was the proximate cause of the liability on the part of the plaintiffs to pay, and therefore that it can correctly be described as the cause in consequence of which the plaintiffs became liable to pay. But my view is that the [collision] clause must be read as one sentence. It does not help to divide it into two and to ask oneself whether payment arose in consequence of the collision, and was it, if it did so arise, a payment in consequence of damage. It leads to a clearer view of the meaning of the clause to read it as it was written in one sentence and to ask oneself, "What did the parties mean? What are the circumstances that the parties contemplated?" It may be that this is no more than a case of first impression. Looking at it from that point of view, I think that the sentence means that where, as a result of the collision, there arises a legal liability upon the shipowners to pay something which may be described as damages, then the underwriters will indemnify. The expression "become liable to pay and shall pay by way of damages" indicates a method of liability arising by way of tort and not by way of contract. There is no such liability here.'

In *Hall Bros SS Co Ltd v Young, The Trident*[5] a vessel was insured under a policy which contained a 'collision clause' in the usual form, viz:

> 'And it is further agreed that if the ship hereby insured shall come into collision with any other ship or vessel and shall in consequence thereof become liable to pay and shall pay by way of damages to any other person or persons any sum or sums in respect of such collision the undersigned will pay the assured such proportion of three-fourths of such sum or sums so paid as their respective subscriptions hereto bear to the value of the ship hereby insured . . .'

After the insured vessel arrived off Dunkirk a pilot boat approached her. The pilot boat's steering gear broke down, and a collision occurred. The insured vessel was in no way to blame.

Under article 7 of the French Law dated 28 March 1928 it was provided that:

> 'Except in cases of gross negligence of the pilot, the "*avaries*" sustained by the pilot vessel in the course of pilotage operations and in the course of embarking or disembarking the pilot is chargeable to the ship.'

Under this law the assured paid £432 7s 6d to the Pilotage Administration, and claimed to recover from the insurers three-fourths of that sum.

It was held by the Court of Appeal[6] that the insurers were not liable. The 'collision clause' only extended to liabilities which arose by way of damages.

Sir Wilfred Greene MR, considered that the very special liability imposed by

---

[4] Ibid, at 120.
[5] (1939) 63 LlL Rep 143, CA.
[6] Sir Wilfred Greene MR, MacKinnon and Finlay LJJ.

French law was not one which fell under the head of damages, and observed:[7]

> 'The result in my opinion is, in a sentence, that the very special liability imposed by art 7 of the French law of 28 March 1928, is not one which, upon the true construction of the "[collision] clause", falls under the head of a sum which the assured became liable to pay by way of damages in respect of the collision. Whatever else it may be, it is in its nature outside the word "damages" as used in the clause.'

MacKinnon LJ, held further that the liability was not one 'in consequence of the collision but in consequence of French law', and said:[8]

> 'This liability, in my view, was not proximately caused by the collision, and it was not caused by the collision at all. This liability was caused by the French law, which created a liability on the ship to pay for any damage caused to the pilot boat by any cause, and, of course, "any cause" included collision. I think the liability for this expense was not a liability in consequence of the collision but in consequence of the French law, even though by the operation of that law the damage to the pilot boat did arise by reason of this collision.'

Finlay J, was also of the same opinion, for he said:[9]

> 'This was not a payment by way of damages in any possible sense in which that word could be used in an English clause of this character, and in the second place it appears to me to result, as my brother MacKinnon has pointed out, that the payment, whatever it was, was not made in consequence of the collision but was made because the French law has imposed a liability—nothing to do with collision, though collision is one of the matters which may arise—to make a payment in case of damage suffered by the pilot vessel during the pilotage, during the manoeuvres necessary for embarking and disembarking the pilot.'

3 GENERAL AVERAGE AND SALVAGE

Clause 11 of the Institute Time Clauses (Hulls)[10] and clause 9 of the Institute Voyage Clauses (Hulls)[11] each state that

    a the policy covers the vessel's proportion of salvage,[12] salvage charges[13] and/or general average,[14] reduced in respect of any under-insurance, but in case of general average sacrifice of the vessel the assured may recover in respect of the whole loss without first enforcing their right of contribution from other parties;

    b adjustment is to be according to the law and practice obtaining at the place where the adventure ends, as if the contract of affreightment contained no special terms on the subject, but where the contract so provides the adjustment is to be according to the York–Antwerp Rules 1974;[15]

    c where the vessel sails in ballast, the provisions of the York–Antwerp Rules 1974 apply;[16] and

---

[7] (1939) 63 LlL Rep at 147. See also the judgments of MacKinnon LJ, ibid at 148, and of Finlay LJ, ibid, at 148.
[8] (1939) 63 LlL Rep at 148.
[9] Ibid, at 148.
[10] These clauses are set out in Appendix III, pp 533–540, post.
[11] These clauses are set out in Appendix III, pp 540–547, post.
[12] See pp 192–194, post.
[13] See pp 192–193, post.
[14] See pp 182–192, post.
[15] See pp 187–192, post.
[16] Except Rules XX and XXI. The voyage for this purpose is deemed to continue from the port or place of departure until the arrival of the vessel at the first port or place thereafter other than a

d no claim lies where the loss was not incurred to avoid or in connection with the avoidance of a peril insured against.

B FREIGHT CLAUSES

The Institute Time Clauses (Freight)[17] and the Institute Voyage Clauses (Freight)[18] contain clauses similar to those in the Institute Time Clauses (Hulls)[19] and the Institute Voyage Clauses (Hulls)[20] in that they set out

1. the extent of the cover in respect of the loss of the freight;[1]
2. the insurers' liability should the vessel come into collision with another vessel;[2]
3. provisions relating to general average and salvage.[3]

C CARGO CLAUSES

The Institute Cargo Clauses are of three types, the risks insured against being different in each case:

1. The Institute Cargo Clauses (A);
2. The Institute Cargo Clauses (B); and
3. The Institute Cargo Clauses (C).

1 THE INSTITUTE CARGO CLAUSES (A)

The Institute Cargo Clauses (A)[4] contain

i a risks clause;
ii a general average clause; and
iii a 'both to blame collision' clause.

(i) Risks clause

Clause 1 of this set of clauses states that with certain specified exceptions,[5] the policy covers all risks of loss or damage to the cargo.

---

port or place of refuge or place of call for bunkering only: Institute Time Clauses (Hulls), cl 11; Institute Voyage Clauses (Hulls), cl 9. If at any such intermediate port or place there is an abandonment of the adventure originally contemplated, the voyage is thereupon deemed to be terminated: ibid.

[17] These clauses are set out in Appendix III, pp 550–554, post.
[18] These clauses are set out in Appendix III, pp 555–558, post.
[19] See pp 535–542, post.
[20] See pp 544–551, post.
[1] See the Institute Time Clauses (Freight), cll 7 and 8, and the Institute Voyage Clauses (Freight) cll 5 and 6.
[2] See cll 9 and 10, and cll 7 and 8 respectively.
[3] See cl 11 and cl 9 respectively.
[4] These clauses are set out in Appendix III, pp 516–522, post.
[5] For the exceptions, see pp 256–257, post.

Examples from the reported decisions

The precise wording of 'all risks' clauses varies as can be seen from the reported cases on the subject.[6]

In *British and Foreign Marine Insurance Co v Gaunt*[7] a cargo of wool had been insured from Patagonia to England under a policy which stated:

> 'Including all risk of craft, fire, coasters, hulks, transhipment and inland carriage by land and/or water, and all risk from the sheep's back and/or station, while awaiting shipment and/or forwarding and until safely delivered ... with liberties as per bill of lading.'

On delivery the wool was found to have been damaged by wet.

In an action on the policy by the buyers of the wool to whom the policy had been assigned, it was proved that the wool was sometimes stored in the open, that it was frequently carried on deck on the local steamers to the port of shipment where it was loaded on to ocean steamers, and that they had experienced bad weather while the wool was in transit. The damage sustained was exceptional. The insurers contended that the buyers had failed to establish affirmatively a loss by an insured peril.

The House of Lords[8] held that the claim succeeded. Since the policy was against 'all risks', it was sufficient to show that the loss was caused by a casualty or something accidental without proving the exact nature of the casualty or accident which caused the loss. There was evidence in the present case of an abnormal incident.

Lord Birkenhead LC, observed:[9]

> 'The damage proved was such as did not occur, and could not be expected to occur, in the course of a normal transit. The inference remains that it was due to some abnormal circumstance, some accident or casualty. We are, of course, to give effect to the rule that the plaintiff must establish his case, that he must show that the loss comes within the terms of his policies; but where all risks are covered by the policy and not merely risks of a specified class or classes, the plaintiff discharges his special onus when he has proved that the loss was caused by some event covered by the general expression, and he is not bound to go further and prove the exact nature of the accident or casualty which, in fact, occasioned his loss. In this case the respondent established that the loss must have been due to some casualty.'

In *Re National Benefit Assurance Co Ltd (Application of H L Sthyr)*[10] 30 bales of woollen goods were insured under an 'all risks' policy from Tilbury to Novorossisk for Rostoff-on-Don. The policy contained a clause stating:

> 'This insurance also covers the risks excluded by the following clause in marine policies on English conditions: "Warranted free of capture, seizure, arrest, restraint, or detainment, and the consequences of hostilities or warlike operations whether before or after declaration of war".'

---

[6] E g *Hyderabad (Deccan) Co v Willoughby* [1899] 2 QB 530 (bullion insured 'at and from Boodini to London, including all risks of every description, from the mines by escort to railway station at Raichur, thence by rail to Bombay, and thence to London'); *Jacob v Gaviller* (1902) 7 Com Cas 116 (fox terrier insured 'against all risks from London to Bombay, and thence by rail to Lahore'); *Schloss Bros v Stevens* [1906] 2 KB 665 (goods insured 'against all risks by land or by water' from Cartagena to any place in the interior of Colombia).

[7] [1921] All ER Rep 447, HL. The case also concerned a trade usage to carry cargo on deck. As to this point, see pp 107–108, ante.

[8] Lord Birkenhead LC, Viscount Finlay, Viscount Cave, Lord Atkinson and Lord Sumner.

[9] [1921] All ER Rep at 450. See also the speech of Viscount Finlay, ibid, at 452, and that of Lord Sumner, ibid, at 455.

[10] (1933) 45 LlL Rep 147, ChD. Another aspect of this case i e whether the assured had an insurable interest is considered at p 18, ante.

The goods, which were for sale on arrival at Rostoff-on-Don, arrived at Novorossisk on 4 September 1919. They were ordered to be forwarded to Rostoff-on-Don, where they were to be delivered to a person who had agreed to buy them provided that they arrived there. The goods were never heard of after leaving Novorossisk. They had not reached Rostoff-on-Don by April 1920. Fighting was going on between the Bolshevist and Czarist forces in the district. The assured claimed for a loss under the policy.[11]

It was held by Maugham J, that the action succeeded. The prima facie inference to be drawn from the facts was that the goods had been lost by a risk within the policy. The burden of proving that the loss was due to an excepted peril lay on the insurers, and this burden had not been discharged.

His Lordship observed:[12]

> 'I am fully justified therefore in saying that the inference to be drawn was that the goods had not arrived even in the month of April, some time after the Bolshevists had got possession of Rostoff-on-Don and when there would not have been any serious difficulty in getting the goods there. I conclude therefore that there is sufficient evidence that the goods never reached Rostoff-on-Don at all, they having arrived at Novorossisk in August; and having the evidence I have of the terrible state of the country at the time, I think the proper inference to be drawn is that the goods never did reach Rostoff-on-Don and that there has been a total loss.
>
> Supposing that is the whole of the case, that the goods were lost and that there is no evidence to show how they were lost—whether they were seized by the Whites or the Reds or by bandits taking advantage of the unsettled state of things to loot or whether they were destroyed by accident I cannot tell. There is here, on my view of the facts, a loss of the goods under an all risks policy with an exception, and it would be for the underwriters to show that the events did happen within the exception.'

In *Theodorou v Chester*[13] some bleached sponges were insured from London to New York for sale there, but since no sale took place, they were insured from New York to London under a policy covering them 'against all risks of loss and/or damage however arising, irrespective of percentage'. The sponges were tightly packed in wooden cases or in bales wrapped in hessian. The assured found that they were damaged, and claimed against the insurers. He alleged that the goods were stained by water, dirt, paint and other substances penetrating the hessian and the cases. The insurers, on the other hand, maintained that the damage was due to normal transit risks of dust and dirt combined with the atmospheric pressure.

It was held that the action succeeded. Croom-Johnson J, held that the assured under an 'all risks' policy was required to prove that the loss was due to an abnormal peril. He was also required to disprove any counter-theory put forward by the insurers which was designed to show that the loss was due to normal transit risks. On the balance of proof the assured had shown that the damage to the sponges was due to an extraneous and accidental cause.

His Lordship adopted[14] the principles relating to the burden of proof set out by the House of Lords in *British and Foreign Marine Insurance Co v Gaunt*,[15] and then observed:[16]

---

[11] As to the evidence, see (1933) 45 LlL Rep 147 at 150.
[12] Ibid, at 150.
[13] [1951] 1 Lloyd's Rep 204, KBD.
[14] Ibid at 218–219.
[15] [1921] All ER Rep 447, HL. See p 178, ante.
[16] [1951] 1 Lloyd's Rep at 238.

'The onus of proof is, of course, upon the plaintiff to establish those things which I indicated earlier in this judgment. There is no onus on the defendants either to account for or to explain or to satisfy me in any way about the matters which have been raised on behalf of the plaintiff. The defendants, as they are entitled to do, have put everything in issue and have in effect said to the plaintiff "Prove your case"; but they have done something else, which, within my one-time considerable experience of underwriting cases, they are also fully entitled to do. They are entitled to present to the court all sorts of theories, suggestions and all the rest of it, not with a view to accepting any onus, but simply with a view to saying: "Now, then, here are all these possibilities. You, the plaintiff, must see to it that these reasonable other explanations are negatived by your evidence, so that you do not leave anything unproved or unsustained by the case which you make to the court."

Now, approaching the matter on that basis, it is not for the defendants to satisfy me that their theories are right. It is, I think, for the plaintiff to satisfy me that these theories, if I come to the conclusion that they are reasonably possible theories, are not right.'

In *Fuerst Day Lawson Ltd v Orion Insurance Co Ltd*[17] a cargo of oil drums was insured against all risks. On arrival the drums were found to contain water with slight traces of oil. Mocatta J, gave judgment for the insurers because the assured had failed to discharge the burden of proof that the oil had ever started on its transit. He considered that there was a possibility, to put it no higher, that the drums from the outset contained water with a thin film of essential oils for deception purposes.

(ii) General average clause

Clause 2 of this set of clauses states that the policy covers general average and salvage charges, adjusted or determined according to the contract of affreightment and/or the governing law and practice, incurred to avoid or in connection with the avoidance of loss from any cause except those causes which are excluded.

(iii) 'Both to blame collision' clause

Clause 3 states that the policy is extended to indemnify the assured against such proportion of liability under the contract of affreightment 'Both to Blame Collision' clause as is recoverable in respect of a loss under the policy. Clause 3 further provides that in the event of a claim by the shipowners under the 'Both to Blame Collision' clause the assured agree to notify the insurers who are to have the right, at their own cost and expense, to defend the assured against such a claim.

2 THE INSTITUTE CARGO CLAUSES (B)

The Institute Cargo Clauses (B)[18] contain

    i   a risks clause;
    ii a general average clause; and
    iii a 'both to blame collision' clause.

---

[17] [1980] 1 Lloyd's Rep 656, QBD (Com Ct).
[18] These clauses are set out in Appendix III, pp 519–522, post.

(i) Risks clause

Clause 1 of this set of clauses states that with certain specified exceptions,[19] the policy covers

- a loss of or damage to the cargo reasonably attributable to
  1. fire or explosion;
  2. the vessel or craft being stranded, grounded, sunk or capsized;
  3. the overturning or derailment of a land conveyance;
  4. the collision or contact of the vessel, craft or conveyance with any external object other than water;
  5. the discharge of the cargo at a port of distress; and
  6. earthquake, volcanic eruption or lightning.
- b the loss of or damage to the cargo caused by
  1. general average sacrifice;
  2. jettison or washing overboard, and
  3. the entry of sea, lake or river water into the vessel, craft, hold, conveyance, container, liftvan, or place of storage.
- c the total loss of any package lost overboard or dropped whilst loading on to or unloading from the vessel or craft.

(ii) General average clause

This clause is in the same form as clause 2 of the Institute Cargo Clauses (A).[1]

(iii) 'Both to blame collision' clause

This clause is in the same form as clause 3 of the Institute Cargo Clauses (A).[2]

3 THE INSTITUTE CARGO CLAUSES (C)

The Institute Cargo Clauses (C)[3] also contain

  i   a risks clause;
  ii   a general average clause; and
  iii a 'both to blame collision' clause.

(i) Risks clause

Clause 1 of this set of clauses states that with certain exceptions, the policy covers

- a loss of or damage to the cargo reasonably attributable to
  1. fire or explosion;
  2. the vessel or craft being stranded, grounded, sunk or capsized;
  3. the overturning or derailment of a land conveyance;
  4. the collision or contact of the vessel, craft or conveyance with any external object other than water; and

---

[19] For the exceptions, see pp 257–258, post.
[1] See p 180, ante.
[2] See p 180, ante.
[3] These clauses are set out in Appendix III, pp 523–526, post.

    5   the discharge of the cargo at a port of distress.
  b the loss of or damage to the cargo caused by
    1   general average sacrifice;
    2   jettison.

(ii) General average clause

This clause is in the same form as clause 2 of the Institute Cargo Clauses (A).[4]

(iii) 'Both to blame collision' clause

This clause is in the same form as clause 3 of the Institute Cargo Clauses (A).[5]

D GENERAL AVERAGE[6]

General average is an incident of a marine adventure and is related to marine insurance by reason of the fact that through the operation of the principle of subrogation the insurer who has to pay the loss on the interest sacrificed is, on payment of the loss, entitled to the contribution due from the owners of the interests saved.[7] On the other hand, the insurer on interests saved has to make good the loss incurred by his assured in having to contribute to general average if the loss is due to a peril insured against.

The contract of indemnity given by the policy is an independent contract, and has to be satisfied irrespective of the right to a general average contribution.

Thus, where the assured receives a general average contribution from the other interests saved before payment by the insurer on the policy, the insurer is only liable to pay the balance of the loss.

If the insurer pays the loss before payment or adjustment of general average, he becomes entitled to the rights of the assured in respect of a general average contribution.

The assured cannot keep both the sum paid to him by the insurer and also the general average contribution from the other interests involved in the adventure.[8]

1 INSURER'S LIABILITY IN RESPECT OF GENERAL AVERAGE EXPENDITURE

Section 66(4) of the Marine Insurance Act 1906 states:

---

[4] See p 180, ante.

[5] See p 180, ante.

[6] A detailed discussion of the law relating to general average would appear to be out of place in a book such as the present on marine insurance, for this is a matter which relates to the carriage of goods by sea rather than to marine insurance. In this book, therefore, it is only the insurer's liability in respect of general average which is considered. For a detailed survey of the law of general average, see R Lowndes and G R Rudolf, *The Law of General Average* (10th edn by Sir John Donaldson, C S Staughton and D J Wilson), 1975 (published as *British Shipping Laws*, Volume 7).

[7] As to subrogation, see pp 455–460, post.

[8] *Dickenson v Jardine* (1868) LR 3 CP 639.

> 'Subject to any express provision in the policy, where the assured has incurred a general average expenditure, he may recover from the insurer in respect of the proportion of the loss which falls upon him ...'

Thus, the insurer is only liable for the proper proportion of the expenditure which the person making the expenditure is himself liable for.[9] It is obvious in that case the liability cannot be ascertained until there has been some adjustment of the various contributory values and something in the nature of an average statement, not necessarily an average statement made out by an average adjuster, but an average statement made out by someone, by the owner or the master of the vessel.[10]

2 INSURER'S LIABILITY IN RESPECT OF GENERAL AVERAGE SACRIFICE

Section 66(4) of the Marine Insurance Act 1906 states:

> 'Subject to any express provision in the policy ... in the case of a general average sacrifice, he may recover from the insurer in respect of the whole loss without having enforced his right of contribution from the other parties liable to contribute.'

Thus, the insurer is immediately liable for a general average sacrifice independently of any average statement being prepared, and quite independently of the working out of any proportion or contribution.[11]

Where the insurer has indemnified the assured, he is entitled to be subrogated to the rights of the assured against the owners of other interests which are liable to contribute.[12]

3 INSURER'S LIABILITY IN RESPECT OF GENERAL AVERAGE CONTRIBUTION

Section 66(5) of the Marine Insurance Act 1906 states:

> 'Subject to any express provision in the policy,[13] where the assured has paid or is liable to pay a general average contribution in respect of the subject insured, he may recover therefor from the insurer.'

Commenting on this subsection Bailhache J, observed:[14]

> 'Where he makes a contribution, he may recover the whole amount of the contribution, just as when he makes a sacrifice as distinct from expenditure, he recovers the whole amount. Both those things differ from expenditure because in the case of expenditure he only recovers the proportion of the expenditure which the person making the expenditure is liable to pay himself.'

---

[9] *Brandeis, Goldschmidt & Co Ltd v Economic Insurance Co Ltd* (1922) 11 LlL Rep 42 at 44, KBD (per Bailhache J).
[10] Ibid.
[11] *Brandeis, Goldschmidt & Co Ltd v Economic Insurance Co Ltd* (1922) 11 LlL Rep 42 at 44, KBD (per Bailhache J).
[12] *Dickenson v Jardine* (1868) LR 3 CP 639. As to subrogation, see generally pp 455–460, post.
[13] For an express provision in the policy whereby there had to be an adjustment before the insurer would be liable, see *Brandeis, Goldschmidt & Co v Economic Insurance Co Ltd* (1922) 11 LlL Rep 42 at 44, KBD.
[14] *Brandeis, Goldschmidt & Co Ltd v Economic Insurance Co Ltd* (1922) 11 LlL Rep 42 at 44, KBD.

4 WHERE LOSS INCURRED NOT FOR PURPOSE OF AVOIDING PERIL INSURED AGAINST

Section 66(6) of the Marine Insurance Act 1906 states:

> 'In the absence of express stipulation, the insurer is not liable for any general average loss or contribution where the loss was not incurred for the purpose of avoiding, or in connection with the avoidance of, a peril insured against.'

5 DIFFERENT INTERESTS OWNED BY SAME ASSURED

General average contribution is a charge upon the interests concerned in the general average act and falls upon the insurer of each interest, and whether the interests are in one hand or several hands makes no difference to the liability of the insurer.[15]

Section 66(7) of the Marine Insurance Act 1906 states:

> 'Where ship, freight, and cargo, or any two of those interests, are owned by the same assured, the liability of the insurer in respect of general average losses or contributions is to be determined as if those subjects were owned by different persons.'

6 PERIOD OF LIMITATION

In *Chandris v Argo Insurance Co Ltd*[16] a general average loss in respect of an insured vessel had been incurred more than 6 years before the issue of the writ, although a general average statement had been completed and issued within 6 years before this date. When sued by the assured, the insurance company pleaded that the action was statute-barred under the Limitation Act 1939, s 2(1),[17] contending that it was not liable since the period of limitation began to run from the date of the loss, or alternatively from the date of the termination of the adventure in the course of which the loss was incurred.

The assured, on the other hand, claimed that there was an implied term in the contract of insurance that time should not run at all. Megaw J, held[18] that, although the evidence[19] which had been adduced showed that the Limitation Act 1939 had never been pleaded by insurers on the London market in answer to claims on marine policies on hulls, it did not lead to the conclusion that there ought to be implied in all such contracts that insurers agreed not to invoke their rights under the statute.

In the alternative the assured contended that the period of limitation did not begin to run until a general average statement had been completed and issued. In support of this argument they cited clause 8 of the Institute Time Clauses (Hulls), which were incorporated into the policy.

Clause 8 provided:

---

[15] *Montgomery & Co v Indemnity Mutual Insurance Co* [1902] 1 KB 734, CA.
[16] [1963] 2 Lloyd's Rep 65, QBD (Com Ct).
[17] Which provides that: 'The following actions shall not be brought after the expiration of six years from the date on which the cause of action accrued, that is to say, (a) actions founded on simple contract . . .' See now Limitation Act 1980, s 5.
[18] [1963] 2 Lloyd's Rep at 75.
[19] As to the evidence, see ibid, at 75.

'General average . . . to be adjusted according to the law and practice obtaining at the place where the adventure ends, as if the contract of affreightment contained no special terms upon the subject; but where the contract of affreightment so provides the adjustment shall be according to York–Antwerp Rules 1890 . . . or York–Antwerp Rules 1924.'[20]

That showed, they said, that the preparation and the issue of a general average adjustment was a condition precedent to the accrual of liability on the part of the insurer.

The contention was also rejected by the learned Judge who observed;[1]

'As a preliminary observation on this question, I would say that *Luckie v Bushby*[2] and *The Wavertree*[3] case, both of which I have previously cited, show that, in the absence of express contractual provision, an average adjustment when prepared is in no way conclusive. The insurer, or another party to the adventure is free to say that the adjustment is wrong, on the facts or the manner of computation, or both. If so, the shipowner must prove his case in the Courts, and he does not prove it by merely producing an average adjustment, even one prepared by an independent professional adjuster. It is difficult, in my view, to suggest that the production of an adjustment, which, when produced is in no way binding or conclusive, would as a matter of business efficacy be regarded by the parties as a condition precedent to a cause of action; that is, as an event which causes time to start to run.

Further, it must be observed that if the plaintiffs are right, it means that the assured has it in his power to postpone indefinitely the accrual of the cause of action and the commencement of the running of time under the statute, unless, indeed, some further term is to be implied into the contract of insurance, requiring reasonable expedition in the preparation of the adjustment and its issue when prepared.'

His Lordship also said[4] that s 66(3) of the Marine Insurance Act 1906 showed that the right to receive and the liability to pay the contribution arose on the occurrence of the general average loss.

Again, in his opinion,[5] clause 8 of the Institute Time Clauses (Hulls) did not mean that an adjustment under the York–Antwerp Rules was a condition precedent to the accrual of the insurer's liability.

In the words of his Lordship:[6]

'In my judgment, that clause, looking at it for the moment without reference to the Rules themselves, does not say, or mean, that an adjustment under the York–Antwerp Rules 1924 is a condition precedent to the accrual of the insurer's liability. It pre-supposes that liability. It shows that an average adjustment is contemplated by the parties and that the code to be used in ascertaining the amount of the insurer's liability shall be the code prescribed in the 1924 Rules. It prescribes the method of computing the amount of liability. It does not say, or imply, that there shall be no liability on the insurer, or that time shall not run, until the amount has been thus computed. As I have mentioned, the computation in the adjustment is in no way binding. It does not operate to fix or settle the amount so that it cannot be disputed.'

But where the parties sign a general average bond, the period of limitation runs from the time when the general average statement has been completed by the average adjuster.[7]

---

[20] The contract of affreightment, in fact, provided for adjustment according to the York–Antwerp Rules, 1924. See ibid, at 77.
[1] [1963] 2 Lloyd's Rep at 76.
[2] [1853] 13 B&C 864.
[3] Ie *Wavertree Sailing Ship Co Ltd v Love* [1897] AC 373.
[4] [1963] 2 Lloyd's Rep at 76–77.
[5] Ibid, at 77.
[6] Ibid, at 77.
[7] *Castle Insurance Co Ltd v Hong Kong Islands Shipping Co Ltd, The Potoi Chau* [1983] 2 Lloyd's Rep 376, PC. (See the judgment of Lord Diplock, ibid, at 382–383.)

7 APPLICATION OF FOREIGN LAW OR YORK–ANTWERP RULES 1974

The policy almost invariably provides that either a foreign law or the York–Antwerp Rules 1974 shall apply.

Thus, clause 11 of the Institute Time Clauses (Hulls)[8] states:

> 'General average . . . to be adjusted according to the law and practice obtaining at the place where the adventure ends, as if the contract of affreightment contained no special terms upon the subject; but where the contract of affreightment so provides the adjustment shall be according to York–Antwerp Rules.
>
> When the Vessel sails in ballast, not under charter, the provisions of the York–Antwerp Rules 1974 (excluding Rules XX and XXI) shall be applicable, and the voyage for this purpose shall be deemed to continue from the port or place of departure until the arrival of the Vessel at the first port or place thereafter other than a port or place of refuge or a port or place of call for bunkering only. If at any such intermediate port or place there is an abandonment of the adventure originally contemplated the voyage shall thereupon be deemed to be terminated.'

a Foreign adjustment clause

At one time before this clause was adopted, insurers in this country took exception to foreign average statements. Thus, Bailhache J, remarked:[9]

> 'Foreign average statements often included matters as being the proper subject of general average which by Common Law in this country were not included; and underwriters used to say: "We carry on business in this country. Our contract is English, and we are liable for general average by English Common Law; and the only general average we are obliged to pay is such a general average as is recovered under English law"; and they used to object to foreign statements; and very often there was trouble between them and the assured, the assured having to pay a foreign statement and the underwriter questioned the foreign statement because it was not in accordance with English law. Therefore this clause making a general average payable according to foreign statement was put in; and it was put in in aid of the assured and to prevent these disputes with the underwriters.'

Under such a clause the insurer is not liable until an adjustment has actually been made.

Thus, in *Brandeis, Goldschmidt & Co Ltd v Economic Insurance Co Ltd*[10] a parcel of zinc ore was insured by its owners from Australia to Antwerp or Rotterdam. It was loaded on a German vessel. On the outbreak of the First World War the vessel sought refuge at Syracuse, which was a neutral port. A fire broke out. This constituted a general average loss, and the assured became liable to contribute. The master took from them the ordinary general average bond. The vessel was seized by the Italian Government when Italy came into the war in April 1915. The assured sold the zinc ore and wanted to take delivery of it, but the Italian Government said that they must pay a deposit of 40 per cent of its value by way of security against any contribution to which they might be found liable in general average. The assured paid the deposit, and claimed to recover it from the insurers. The policy contained a clause which stated:

> 'General average . . . payable according to foreign statement or per York–Antwerp Rules if in accordance with the contract of affreightment.'

---

[8] Clause 11 is set out in full in Appendix III, pp 533–540, post.
[9] *Brandeis, Goldschmidt & Co Ltd v Economic Insurance Co Ltd* (1922) 11 LlL Rep 42 at 44, KBD.
[10] (1922) 11 LlL Rep 42, KBD.

The insurers contended that no foreign statement or statement according to the York–Antwerp Rules had been prepared, and that their liability to repay the deposit did not arise until this had been done.

Bailhache J, accepted this contention, and held that the claim failed. His Lordship observed:[11]

> 'It is quite clear that the amount of a contribution which persons have to pay towards a general average loss can only be ascertained by adjustment; and inasmuch as an adjustment is necessary to this ascertainment—general average being payable according to foreign statement—it seems to me that I must hold that there is an express provision in the policy which prevents the code applying in its simplicity and prevents the assured from recovering unless and until someone or other has made an adjustment either according to foreign law or according to York–Antwerp Rules, an adjustment which would show precisely what is the sum payable by these underwriters.'

b The York–Antwerp Rules 1974

The York–Antwerp Rules 1974 are divided into 'lettered' and 'numbered' rules. These apply to the exclusion of any law and practice inconsistent therewith. Except as provided by the numbered rules, general average must be adjusted according to the lettered rules.

i *The lettered rules*

The lettered rules provide a definition of a general average act, what losses are allowed, the effect of the fault of one of the parties, the onus of proof, substituted expenses, and the basis of adjustment.

DEFINITION OF GENERAL AVERAGE ACT

There is a general average act when, and only when, any extraordinary sacrifice or expenditure is intentionally and reasonably made or incurred for the common safety for the purpose of preserving from peril the property involved in a common maritime adventure.[12]

In *Australian Coastal Shipping Commission v Green*[13] the plaintiffs insured the m v 'Bulwarra' and the m v 'Wangara' with the defendant underwriter under a marine insurance policy which incorporated the York–Antwerp Rules 1950. The moorings of the 'Bulwarra' were carried away on 13 July 1960, in heavy weather. The plaintiffs employed the tug 'Hero' on the United Kingdom Standard Towage Conditions to assist her. The tow-rope parted and fouled the 'Hero's' propeller and she became a total loss. Her owners sued the plaintiffs under Condition 1(3), which stated:

---

[11] Ibid, at 44. The learned Judge said (ibid, at 45) that he did not approve of the action of the insurers in insisting that there must be a general average statement in a case where the money had been undoubtedly paid and would never be recovered, and there was no doubt that the matter never would be adjusted at all. Counsel, however, indicated (ibid, at 45) that the action had been fought by the insurers on a question of principle as to whether they could be made legally liable to repay the deposit. But he said that he was now instructed to say that they would approach the other underwriters, and were in fact doing so, and no doubt some settlement would be made which would satisfy the assured. His Lordship then said (ibid, at 45) that he was very glad to hear it because it was obviously a loss which ought to fall, with every consideration of fairness on the underwriters.
[12] Rule A.
[13] [1971] 1 Lloyd's Rep 16, CA.

'The Tugowner shall not, whilst towing, be liable for damage . . . done to the tug . . . or for loss of the tug . . . and the hirer shall pay for all loss or damage . . . and shall also indemnify the Tugowner against all consequences thereof. . . . Provided that any such liability for loss or damage as above set out is not caused by want of reasonable care on the part of the Tugowner to make his tugs seaworthy.'

but the claim was dismissed by the Supreme Court of New South Wales because it had been caused by the tug's unseaworthiness. The 'Wangara' went aground on 18 November 1961 and the plaintiffs hired the tug 'Walumba' on the United Kingdom Standard Towage Conditions. The tow-rope parted and fouled the 'Walumba's' propeller. The 'Walumba' accepted salvage services from salvors. She was also damaged. The salvors sued the tugowners, who joined the plaintiffs as third parties on the ground that they were liable to indemnify the tugowners. The plaintiffs claimed from the defendant (i) an indemnity in respect of the costs incurred in defending the action brought by the owners of the 'Hero'; and (ii) an indemnity in respect of over £20,000 made up of (a) the claim by the owners of the 'Walumba' for damage to her; (b) the salvage award made in favour of the salvors; and (c) costs.

The Court of Appeal[14] held that the action succeeded for the employment of the 'Hero' and the 'Walumba' was a general average act under Rule A of the York–Antwerp Rules. Lord Denning MR, observed:[15]

'The "general average act" was I think the contract made by the shipowners with the tug. In each case the vessel was in dire peril and the shipowners called upon the tug for help. If the tug had rendered salvage services on the usual terms of "no cure—no pay", the contract would undoubtedly have been a "general average act". If the services had been successful, the owners would have been liable to pay a very high reward: which would count as "general average expenditure". If the services had been unsuccessful, they would have had to pay nothing. . . . Instead of entering into such a contract, the shipowners made a towage contract on the United Kingdom Standard Towage Conditions. That was a very reasonable contract to make for both sides. It is well known that there is a substantial risk in towage operations that the tow-rope may break and foul the propeller of the tug: and that, if that happens, the tug may run aground or be damaged and have to be rescued. In a salvage agreement, the tugowners take that risk on themselves in return for the chance of a very high salvage reward. In a hiring agreement, at a fixed rate of hire, they cannot be expected to take the risk on themselves. It is only right and fair that they should ask for and receive an indemnity. The benefit to the shipowners is that, if the service is successful, he pays much less than he would under a salvage award: but, in return, he has to give an indemnity to the tugowner. In these circumstances, I have no doubt that the towage contract is a "general average act". It was intentionally and reasonably made for the common safety.'

He then went on to state[16] that the costs in defending the action brought by the owners of the 'Hero' and the expenditure incurred in relation to the 'Walumba' were the direct consequence of the general average act, and could therefore be recovered from the defendant under Rule C.[17]

ALLOWABLE LOSSES

Only such losses, damages or expenses which are the direct consequence of the general average act shall be allowed as general average. Loss or damage

---

[14] Lord Denning MR, Phillimore and Cairns LJJ.
[15] [1971] 1 Lloyd's Rep 16 at 20. See also the judgment of Phillimore LJ, ibid, at 23, and that of Cairns LJ, ibid, at 25.
[16] Ibid, at 22. See also the judgment of Phillimore LJ, ibid, at 23–24, and that of Cairns LJ, ibid, at 25.
[17] Supra.

sustained by the ship or cargo through delay, whether on the voyage or subsequently, such as demurrage, and any indirect loss whatsoever, such as loss of market, shall not be admitted as general average.[18]

EFFECT OF FAULT

Rights to contribution in general average shall not be affected, though the event which gave rise to the sacrifice or expenditure may have been due to the fault of one of the parties to the adventure, but this shall not prejudice any remedies which may be open against that party for such fault.[19]

ONUS OF PROOF

The onus of proof is upon the party claiming in general average to show that the loss or expense claimed is properly allowable as general average.[20]

SUBSTITUTED EXPENSES

Any extra expense incurred in place of another expense which would have been allowable as general average shall be deemed to be general average and so allowed without regard to the saving, if any, to other interests, but only up to the amount of the general average expense avoided.[1]

BASIS OF ADJUSTMENT

General average shall be adjusted as regards both loss and contribution upon the basis of values at the time and place when and where the adventure ends. This rule shall not affect the determination of the place at which the average statement is to be made up.[2]

ii The numbered rules

The principal numbered rules concern jettison of cargo, damage by jettison and sacrifice for the common safety, extinguishing fire on shipboard, cutting away wreck, voluntary stranding, salvage remuneration, damage to machinery and boilers, expenses of lightening a ship, ship's materials and stores burnt for fuel, expenses at a port of refuge, wages and maintenance of the crew in a port of refuge, damage to cargo in discharging, deductions from cost of repairs, loss of freight, amount to be made good for cargo lost or damaged by sacrifice, contributory values, undeclared or wrongfully declared cargo.

JETTISON OF CARGO

No jettison of cargo is to be made good as general average, unless such cargo is carried in accordance with the recognised custom of the trade.[3]

---

[18] Rule C.
[19] Rule D.
[20] Rule E.
[1] Rule F.
[2] Rule G.
[3] Rule I.

DAMAGE BY JETTISON AND SACRIFICE FOR THE COMMON SAFETY

Damage done to a ship and cargo or either of them, by or in consequence of a sacrifice made for the common safety, and by water which goes down a ship's hatches opened or other opening made for the purpose of making a jettison for the common safety, must be made good as general average.[4]

EXTINGUISHING FIRE ON SHIPBOARD

Damage done to a ship and cargo, or either of them, by water or otherwise, including damage by beaching or scuttling a burning ship, in extinguishing a fire on board the ship, shall be made good as general average. But no compensation is made for damage by smoke or heat however caused.[5]

CUTTING AWAY WRECK

Loss or damage caused by cutting away wreck or parts of the ship which have previously been carried away or are effectively lost by accident, are not made good as general average.[6]

VOLUNTARY STRANDING

When a ship is intentionally run on shore for the common safety, whether or not she might have been driven on shore, the consequent loss shall be allowed in general average.[7]

SALVAGE REMUNERATION

Expenditure incurred by parties to the adventure on account of salvage,[8] whether under contract or otherwise, is allowed in general average to the extent that the salvage operations were undertaken for the purpose of preserving from peril the property involved in the common maritime adventure.[9]

DAMAGE TO MACHINERY AND BOILERS

Damage caused to machinery and boilers of a ship which is ashore and in a position of peril, in endeavouring to refloat, are allowed in general average when shown to have arisen from an actual intention to float the ship for the common safety at the risk of such damage.[10]

But where a ship is afloat, no loss or damage caused by working the propelling machinery and boilers is in any circumstances to be made good as general average.[11]

EXPENSES OF LIGHTENING

When a ship is ashore and cargo and ship's fuel and stores or any of them are

---

[4] Rule II.
[5] Rule III.
[6] Rule IV.
[7] Rule V.
[8] As to salvage, see pp 192–194, post.
[9] Rule VI.
[10] Rule VII.
[11] Ibid.

discharged as a general average act, the extra cost of lightening, lighter hire and reshipping (if incurred), and the loss or damage sustained thereby, are allowable as general average.[12]

SHIP'S MATERIALS AND STORES BURNT FOR FUEL

Ship's materials and stores, or any of them, necessarily burnt for fuel for the common safety at a time of peril are allowed as general average, when and only when an ample supply of fuel had been provided.[13]

But the estimated quantity of fuel that would have been consumed, calculated at the price current at the ship's last port of departure at the date of her leaving, must be credited to the general average.[14]

EXPENSES AT PORT OF REFUGE

When a ship has entered a port or place of refuge, the expenses of entering it are admitted as general average.[15] When she sails from there with her original cargo, or part of it, the expenses of leaving the port are also admitted as general average.[16]

The cost of handling on board or discharging cargo, fuel or stores whether at a port or place of loading, call or refuge are admitted as general average when the handling or discharge was necessary for the common safety or to enable damage to the ship caused by sacrifice or accident to be repaired, if the repairs were necessary for the safe prosecution of the voyage.[17]

WAGES AND MAINTENANCE OF CREW IN PORT OF REFUGE

Wages and maintenance of master, officers and crew reasonably incurred and fuel and stores consumed during the prolongation of the voyage occasioned by a ship entering a port or place of refuge or returning to her port or place of loading are admitted as general average when the expenses of entering the port or place are allowable in general average in accordance with Rule X.[18]

DAMAGE TO CARGO IN DISCHARGING

Damage to or loss of cargo, fuel or stores caused in the act of handling, discharging, storing, reloading and stowing must be made good as general average, when and only when the cost of those measures respectively is admitted as general average.[19]

DEDUCTIONS FROM COST OF REPAIRS

In adjusting claims for general average, repairs to be allowed in general average are not subject to deductions in respect of 'new for old' where old

---

[12] Rule VIII.
[13] Rule IX.
[14] Ibid.
[15] Rule X.
[16] Ibid.
[17] Ibid.
[18] Rule XI.
[19] Rule XII.

material or parts are replaced by new unless the ship is over 15 years old in which case there is a deduction of one-third.[20]

LOSS OF FREIGHT

Loss of freight arising from damage to or loss of cargo are to be made good as general average, either when caused by general average, or when the damage to or loss of cargo is so made good.[1]

AMOUNT TO BE MADE GOOD FOR CARGO LOST OR DAMAGED BY SACRIFICE

The amount to be made good as general average for damage to or loss of cargo sacrificed is the loss sustained thereby, based on the value at the time of discharge ascertained from the commercial invoice rendered to the receiver or if there is no such invoice, from the shipped value.[2]

CONTRIBUTORY VALUES

The contribution to a general average must be made upon the actual net value of the property at the termination of the adventure. To these values must be added the amount made good as general average for property sacrificed, if not already included, deduction being made from the shipowner's freight and passage money at risk of such charges and crew's wages as would not have been incurred in earning the freight had the ship and cargo been totally lost at the date of the general average act, and have not been allowed as general average.[3]

UNDECLARED OR WRONGFULLY DECLARED CARGO

Damage or loss caused to goods loaded without the knowledge of the shipowner or his agent or goods wilfully misdescribed at time of shipment are not allowed as general average, but such goods remain liable to contribute, if saved.[4]

E SALVAGE

The insurers are usually liable under the policy for the payment of salvage and for salvage charges.[5]

1   SALVAGE CHARGES

The Marine Insurance Act 1906, s 65(1) states:

> 'Subject to any express provision in the policy, salvage charges incurred in preventing a loss by perils insured against may be recovered as a loss by those perils.'

The expression 'salvage charges' is defined in s 65(2) in the following terms;

---

[20] Rule XIII.
[1] Rule XV.
[2] Rule XVI.
[3] Rule XVII.
[4] Rule XIX.
[5] Eg as in the Institute Time Clauses (Hulls), cl 11. See p 176, ante.

'"Salvage charges" means the charges recoverable under maritime law by a salvor independently of contract. They do not include the expenses of services rendered by the assured or his agents, or any person employed for hire by them, for the purpose of averting a peril insured against. Such expenses where properly incurred, may be recovered as particular charges[6] or as a general average loss[7] according to the circumstances under which they were incurred.'

Accordingly, where a ship is salved by salvors who intervene voluntarily and not under contract, the insurer is under no liability to pay any sum in excess of the sum insured.

Thus, in *Aitchison v Lohre*[8] a vessel was insured for £1,200 and was salved by salvors with whom no contract was made. They obtained a salvage award for £800. The assured elected to repair the vessel and the cost of the repairs came to £1,200. He claimed an indemnity in respect of this amount and also of the salvage award. It was held by the House of Lords that the insurer was only liable to pay the £1,200 as this was the full sum insured.

But if the salvage services are rendered under a contract, any sum which the assured is liable to pay for them may be recovered under the 'sue and labour' clause[9] in addition to the sum insured, for the salvors are in that case the 'factors, servants and assigns' of the assured within the meaning of that clause.

2 LIFE SALVAGE

Until 1854 a salvor who had saved lives alone and had not rendered a salvage service to a vessel or her cargo, was not entitled to a salvage award. But in 1854 the Merchant Shipping Act of that year enabled him to claim one. The relevant provision of that statute is now re-enacted in the Merchant Shipping Act 1894, s 544.[10]

Where a salvor rendered services to the vessel and her cargo and also to lives, it was always the practice of the Admiralty Court to give him an enhanced award, the enhancement being a reflection of the value of the services rendered in the saving of life.

In *Nourse v Liverpool Sailing Ship Owners' Mutual Protection and Indemnity Association*[11] the question arose as to whether an assured, who was liable to pay a salvage award to a salvor in respect of life salvage only, could claim an indemnity from the insurer under a Lloyd's policy. Mathew J, held that he

---

[6] This term is defined by s 64(2) of the Marine Insurance Act 1906 in the following way: 'Expenses incurred by or on behalf of the assured for the safety or preservation of the subject-matter insured other than general average and salvage charges are called "particular charges".' See generally p 417, post.

[7] This term is defined by s 66(1) of the Marine Insurance Act 1906 in the following way: 'A general average loss is a loss caused by or directly consequential on a general average act. It includes a general average expenditure as well as a general average sacrifice.' See pp 344–345, post.

[8] (1879) 4 App Cas 755, HL.

[9] As to the 'sue and labour' clause, see pp 442–452, post.

[10] Section 544(1) states: 'Where services are rendered wholly or in part within British waters in saving life from any British or foreign vessel, or elsewhere in saving life from any British vessel, there shall be payable to the salvor by the owner of the vessel, cargo, or apparel saved, a reasonable amount of salvage, to be determined in case of dispute in manner hereinafter mentioned.'

[11] [1896] 2 QB 16.

could not, and, after referring to the position before the Merchant Shipping Act 1894 had been enacted, observed:[12]

> 'There is nothing to show that the statutes were intended to impart any new meaning to the policy of marine insurance, which existed long before the legislation in favour of salvors of life . . .'

This decision was subsequently affirmed[13] by the Court of Appeal.[14]

In *Grand Union (Shipping) Ltd v London SS Owners' Mutual Insurance Association Ltd, The Bosworth (No 3)*[15] the material facts were different because the salvors had rendered salvage services to a ship and her cargo in distress in the North Sea, and saved the lives of all her crew. McNair J, held that the salvage award in respect of both lives and property which the salved vessel had to pay was recoverable from the insurers under a Lloyd's policy. In the words of his Lordship:[16]

> 'The plaintiffs are not entitled to recover any part of the *Wolverhampton Wanderers*' award from the club for the simple reason that it is recoverable under the terms of Lloyd's policy. It is true, of course, that the construction may involve a slight forcing of the language of s 65 of the Marine Insurance Act 1906, because salvage, of course, is covered under a Lloyd's policy not by reason of any express provision in the policy but by reason of the Common Law now embodied in the Marine Insurance Act 1906. Section 65(1) of the Marine Insurance Act says this:
> "Subject to any express provision in the policy, salvage charges incurred in preventing a loss by perils insured against may be recovered as a loss by those perils."
> It needs possibly a little stretching of the language to say that a salvage award in so far as it reflects an element of life salvage gives rise to a charge incurred in preventing a loss by perils insured against. I think the answer to that is that by the practice of the Admiralty Court an award made in these circumstances is treated as being, and is in fact, an award for services rendered to the ship and cargo.'

F OTHER RISKS

Other risks which may be insured against include (i) leakage; and (ii) heat, sweat and spontaneous combustion.

LEAKAGE

As is stated later, the liability of the insurer for leakage is excluded by the Marine Insurance Act 1906, s 55(2)(c).[17] But the risk of leakage can be specially insured against.

Thus, in *De Monchy v Phoenix Insurance Co of Hartford*[18] some barrels of turpentine were insured from Jacksonville, Florida, to Rotterdam. The certificate of insurance stated: 'To pay leakage from any cause in excess of 1 per

---

[12] Ibid, at 19.
[13] [1896] 2 QB at 21, CA.
[14] Lord Esher MR, Smith and Rigby LJJ.
[15] [1962] 1 Lloyd's Rep 483, QBD (Com Ct).
[16] Ibid, at 490.
[17] See p 256, post.
[18] (1929) 34 LlL Rep 201, HL. See also *Traders and General Insurance Association v Bankers and General Insurance Co* (1921) 9 LlL Rep 223, where a reinsurance policy in respect of a consignment of soya bean oil contained a clause stating 'including leakage in excess of 2 per cent over trade ullage'.

cent'. A claim was made against the insurers for loss due to leakage. The insurers denied liability on the ground that 'leakage' meant such leakage as was visible on the barrels on discharge.

The House of Lords[19] rejected this contention, and held that the claim succeeded. 'Leakage' meant any escape of turpentine whether through a hole in the barrel which might or might not be discernible, or through the pores of the material of which the barrel was made.

Viscount Dunedin observed:[20]

> 'The answer of the underwriters was simple. They said that no leakage could be held as proved which did not leave signs of it on the cask. That at once raises the question of "What is the meaning of leakage?" Leakage I take to mean any stealthy escape either through a small hole which might be discernible, or through the pores of the material of which the cask is composed. Turpentine has a very great power of penetration. It even penetrates through metal containers, but it evaporates rapidly, and having penetrated it leaves no sign or external mark. It is clear, therefore, that if the underwriters' view were right, there would be no leakage except when an actual hole was shown in the cask. The provision as to an average leakage and the elaborate provision as to comparing the contents of the casks on arrival with what they had been at starting, all point clearly to the inadmissibility of such a construction.[1] It is not, therefore, surprising that when the case came into Court little or nothing was heard of this defence.'

HEAT, SWEAT AND SPONTANEOUS COMBUSTION

In *Soya GmbH Mainz Kommanditgesellschaft v White*[2] a cargo of soya beans was insured against the risk of heat, sweat and spontaneous combustion on a voyage from an Indonesian port to Antwerp and arrived in a heated condition. The House of Lords[3] held that the assured were entitled to an indemnity. Lord Diplock said[4] that the words 'heat, sweat and spontaneous combustion' were words which were descriptive of the perils insured against, not of the loss occasioned by those perils nor of what caused the heat, sweat or spontaneous combustion to occur. 'Heat', if it stood alone as descriptive of a peril, would be equally apt to describe both the heating of the insured cargo from an external source and its becoming hot as a result of some internal chemical, biological or bacterial process taking place in the cargo itself. But 'heat' did not stand alone. It appeared in conjunction with two other perils insured against, 'sweat' and 'spontaneous combustion'. 'Sweat' meant the exudation of moisture from within the goods to their exterior as a result of something which happened inside them. 'Spontaneous combustion' could refer only to a chemical reaction which took place inside the goods, and resulted in their becoming incandescent

---

[19] Lord Hailsham LC, Viscount Dunedin, Viscount Sumner, Lord Buckmaster and Lord Atkin.
[20] (1929) 34 LlL Rep 201 at 204.
[1] The clause referred to stated: 'Where barrels with contents are weighed at a port of shipment and destination, loss, if any, due to leakage shall be ascertained by a comparison of the gross shipped and gross landed weights. Where barrels with contents are weighed at port of shipment and contents of barrels only weighed at destination, loss, if any, due to leakage shall be ascertained by a comparison of the gross shipped weight, after deducting 80 lb tare for each barrel, and the net landed weight.'
[2] [1983] 1 Lloyd's Rep 122, HL. The case in the lower courts also concerned an alleged non-disclosure of a material fact. See pp 49–50, ante.
[3] Lord Diplock, Lord Keith of Kinkel, Lord Scarman, Lord Roskill and Lord Templeman.
[4] [1983] 1 Lloyd's Rep at 126.

or bursting into flames. The two expressions were clearly intended to be descriptive of particular kinds of inherent vice. 'Heat' appearing in immediate conjunction with them was apt to include heating of the cargo as a result of some internal action inside the cargo itself. The words used displaced the prima facie rule of construction laid down in the Marine Insurance Act 1906, s 55(2)(c)[5] that the insurer was not liable for 'inherent vice or nature of the subject-matter insured'. It did so to the extent that such inherent vice consisted of a tendency to become hot, to sweat or to combust spontaneously. To hold otherwise would be contrary to commercial common sense.

---

[5] See pp 250–256, post.

CHAPTER 15

War and strikes risks

It may be desirable to insure against the risks of war and/or strikes, liability for which is excluded by a 'war exclusion clause'[1] or a 'strikes exclusion clause'[2] in most sets of the Institute Clauses.

A WAR RISKS

The subject of war risks insurance may be considered.

1   generally;[3]
2   under the Institute Clauses;[4]
3   in relation to insurance by the State;[5] and
4   in relation to insurance by mutual insurance associations.[6]

1 GENERALLY

The principal risks which are covered by war risks insurance are, of course, war and hostile acts by belligerents.

The reported cases, however, deal mainly with the meaning of 'hostilities' and 'warlike operations' which were the terms used in earlier times.

The cases have not principally been concerned with policies incorporating the Institute War Clauses, but are cases dating back to the First World War when merchant vessels were requisitioned by the Government and chartered under a form of charter-party known as 'T.99' under which the marine risks were left with the marine underwriters, and the Government undertook the risk of damage from 'all consequences of hostile or warlike operations'. A number of cases decided in the Second World War also interpreted these words where vessels had been similarly requisitioned.

The cases concerned the interpretation of war clauses which covered the risks excluded by the 'free of capture and seizure' clause which at that time stated:

'Warranted free of capture and seizure ... and also from all consequences of hostilities or warlike operations, whether before or after declaration of war.'

Thus, any loss which was the result of hostilities or warlike operations was a

---

[1] See pp 257, 258, 260, post.
[2] See pp 257, 258, 260, post.
[3] See pp 197–209, post.
[4] See pp 209–211, post.
[5] See p 211–213, post.
[6] See pp 213–214, post.

war risk and not a marine risk, even though it had not been directly caused by a hostile act by or against a belligerent power, so that if a vessel were lost as a result of coming into collision with a warship, the war risk insurers were liable even if no enemy vessel was involved at all.

But the 'free of capture and seizure' clause was altered as a result of *Yorkshire Dale SS Co Ltd v Minister of War Transport, The Coxwold*,[7] so that the clause did not exclude

> 'contact with any fixed or floating object[8] . . . stranding, heavy weather or fire unless caused directly (and independently of the nature of the voyage or service which the vessel concerned or, in the case of a collision, any other vessel involved therein, is performing) by a hostile act by or against a belligerent power . . .'

The position therefore was that, a loss which was not directly caused by a hostile act was a marine risk and not a war risk.

Consequently a number of the cases considered in the pages which follow have lost their importance, but are still of interest in showing the meaning of the terms 'hostilities' and 'warlike operations'.

'Hostilities'

The meaning of the term 'hostilities' was stated by Lord Wrenbury in *Britain SS Co Ltd v R*[9] in the following terms:[10]

> 'All the decisions have I think proceeded, and in my judgment have rightly proceeded, upon the footing that the word "hostilities" does not mean "the existence of a state of war" but means "acts of hostility" or (to use the noun substantive which follows) "operations of hostility". The sentence may be read "all consequences of operations of hostility (or war) or operations warlike (similar to operations of war) whether before or after declaration of war". To attribute to the word the longer meaning—namely, "all consequences of the existence of a state of war"—would give the expression a scope far beyond anything which one can conceive as intended. To define the meaning of "operation" in this connection is, no doubt, a matter of great difficulty, and for the purpose of these cases is not, I think, necessary.'

'Warlike operations'

i Meaning

The meaning of the term 'warlike operations' was reviewed by Atkinson J, in *Clan Line Steamers Ltd v Liverpool and London War Risks Insurance Association Ltd*,[11] where he said:[12]

> 'The conclusion at which I have arrived from a careful examination of the authorities to which I have referred is that a warlike operation is one which forms part of an actual or intended belligerent act or series of acts by combatant forces; that part may be performed preparatory to the actual act or acts of belligerency, or it may be performed after the actual act or acts of belligerency, but there must be a connection sufficiently close between the act in question and the belligerent act or acts to enable a tribunal to say with at least some modicum of common

---

[7] [1942] AC 691, HL. See p 201, post.
[8] For a case on whether 20 mm shells sucked up by a dredger were 'fixed or floating objects', see *Costain-Blankevoort (UK) Dredging Co Ltd v Davenport, The Nassau Bay* [1979] 1 Lloyd's Rep 395. See the judgment of Walton J, ibid, at 405–406, where the meaning of 'contact' was also considered.
[9] [1921] 1 AC 99, HL.
[10] Ibid, at 133.
[11] [1942] 2 All ER 367, KBD.
[12] Ibid, at 374.

sense, as Lord Dunedin suggests, that it formed part of acts of belligerency. If military equipment is being taken in a ship to a place behind the fighting front from which the forces engaged, or about to be engaged on that front, may be supplied, that ship may beyond question be said to be taking part in a warlike operation. If a ship is bringing home such equipment after it has been employed on a fighting front, or had been lying available for and at the service of a fighting front, again beyond question, in view of the decisions, she is taking part in a military operation.'

ii Examples of 'warlike operations'[13]

In *A-G v Ard Coasters*[14] the House of Lords[15] held that a vessel, which was run down by a warship patrolling in the North Sea, was lost as a consequence of a 'warlike operation'.

In *Caroline (Owners) v War Risk Underwriters*[16] an armed trawler was leading a convoy at night. She blew up as a result of the explosion of a mine or torpedo. In the confusion two other vessels in the convoy came into collision. Shearman J, held that the armed trawler was engaged in a warlike operation, and the collision was a direct result of it.

In *Liverpool and London War Risks Insurance Association v Marine Underwriters of SS Richard de Larrinaga*[17] a vessel was proceeding in convoy, and came into collision with a warship, which was on her way to pick up a convoy. The House of Lords held that at the time of the collision, the warship was engaged in a 'warlike operation', and the collision was a consequence of that operation. No distinction could be drawn between proceeding under orders to a spot to carry out a 'warlike operation' and the actual carrying out of the 'warlike operation'. Both formed part of the 'warlike operation'.

In *Atlantic Transport Co v R: The Maryland*[18] a vessel, which had been to Salonika with a cargo of horses and stores for the use of the forces there, was proceeding from Salonika to Algiers for bunkers and thence to Gibraltar for orders. She collided with another vessel, which was on a voyage to Salonika with a cargo of frozen meat for the forces. Both vessels were steaming without lights in accordance with Admiralty instructions. It was held that, although sailing without lights was not in itself a 'warlike operation', both vessels were engaged in a 'warlike operation'.

In *Hindustan Steam Shipping Co v Admiralty Comrs*[19] a vessel was loaded with a cargo of steam coal, and was sent to Malta and then to Tenedos. She was employed there as a supply ship for submarines. Her master drew the attention of the naval authorities to the danger of leaving a cargo of steam coal in the hold for an indefinite time. Fire broke out in the hold, and she suffered damage. It was held that although spontaneous combustion of coal was a marine risk, a

---

[13] Cases concerning war risk clauses decided in the United States courts include: *Link v General Insurance Co of America, The Eastern Prince* (1944) 77 LlL Rep 431, District Court for the Western District of Washington (Northern Division); *Standard Oil Co of New Jersey v United States, The John Worthington* [1951] 2 Lloyd's Rep 36, United States Supreme Court; *Republic of China, China Merchants Steam Navigation Co Ltd and United States of America v National Union Fire Insurance Co of Pittsburgh, Pennsylvania, The Hai Hsuan* [1958] 1 Lloyd's Rep 351 (US Court of Appeals).
[14] [1921] 2 AC 141, HL.
[15] Viscount Finlay, Lord Dunedin, Lord Sumner, Lord Parmoor and Lord Wrenbury.
[16] (1921) 7 LlL Rep 56, KBD.
[17] (1921) 7 LlL Rep 151, HL.
[18] (1921) 9 LlL Rep 370, KBD.
[19] (1921) 8 LlL Rep 230, KBD.

new risk had come into existence when the vessel became a combatant ship. The fire was the proximate and direct result of the new risk, and was a consequence of 'hostilities or warlike operations'.

In *Charente SS Co v Director of Transports*[20] a collision occurred between a merchant vessel and a vessel being used as a troopship to carry American forces from the United States to Europe. Both vessels were sailing without lights in accordance with Admiralty instructions. No negligence on the part of either master was established. The Court of Appeal[1] held that the loss was a consequence of 'hostilities or warlike operations'.

In *Peninsular and Oriental Branch Service v Commonwealth Shipping Representative: The Geelong*[2] a vessel was carrying ambulance wagons and other Government stores from Mudros to Alexandria when she was involved in a collision. The House of Lords[3] held that she was engaged in a 'warlike operation'.

In *Adelaide SS Co v R*[4] a hospital ship carrying wounded men was involved in collision. The House of Lords[5] held that she was engaged in a 'warlike operation'.

In *Mazarakis Bros v Furness, Withy & Co*[6] a vessel while proceeding on a voyage from Huelva to Nantes collided with a warship. The Court of Appeal[7] held that the warship was engaged in a 'warlike operation' at the time of the collision.

In *Eagle Oil Transport Co v Board of Trade*[8] a vessel was employed by the British Government in carrying oil fuel for the British fleet. While manoeuvring inside the boom defences of Invergordon Harbour, she collided with a Government oil tanker. Rowlatt J, held that she was engaged in a 'warlike operation'.

In *Board of Trade v Hain SS Co*[9] a vessel was employed as a mine-layer in the United States Navy. Whilst returning from a European port to the United States with 720 mines on board, she collided with another vessel on 25 December 1918 (shortly after the Armistice). The House of Lords[10] held that she was engaged in a 'warlike operation'.

In *Athel Line Ltd v Liverpool and London War Risks Insurance Association Ltd*[11] a vessel was carrying a full cargo of oil from Trinidad to naval bases at Loch Alsh and Scapa Flow. She was instructed to anchor at Loch Alsh to await orders to discharge. She was holed by sitting on a rock while swinging to her anchor. The Court of Appeal[12] held that she was engaged in a 'warlike operation', and that the damage arose as a consequence of that operation. The anchoring of the vessel at the time and place in question was an essential part of the operation, and the fact that she had anchored in the course of her voyage did not of itself suspend the 'warlike operation'.

---

[20] (1922) 10 LlL Rep 514, CA.
[1] Bankes, Warrington and Scrutton LJJ.
[2] (1922) 13 LlL Rep 230 at 455, HL.
[3] Viscount Cave LC, Lord Finlay, Lord Dunedin, Lord Atkinson and Lord Sumner.
[4] (1923) 14 LlL Rep 341 at 549, HL.
[5] Viscount Cave LC, Lord Shaw, Lord Sumner, Lord Parmoor and Lord Wrenbury.
[6] (1924) 18 LlL Rep 152, CA.
[7] Bankes, Scrutton and Sargant LJJ.
[8] (1925) 23 LlL Rep 301, KBD.
[9] [1929] AC 534, HL.
[10] Lord Buckmaster, Viscount Dunedin, Lord Sumner, Lord Warrington of Clyffe and Lord Atkin.
[11] [1946] KB 117, [1945] 2 All ER 694, CA.
[12] Lord Greene MR, MacKinnon and Tucker LJJ.

In *Yorkshire Dale SS Co Ltd v Minister of War Transport, The Coxwold*[13] it was admitted that a vessel, which was carrying petrol for the use of HM forces, was engaged in a 'warlike operation' at the time of her stranding near the Damsel Rocks near the Isle of Skye.

Lord Wright in giving judgment in the House of Lords said:[14]

> 'Under certain circumstances, a trading or merchant vessel has been held to be for purposes of the war risk clause engaged in a warlike operation. As illustrative of these circumstances, I may take those of a merchant ship carrying troops, ammunition, guns, tanks, or other military machines or equipment to a theatre of war, or away from a theatre of war, as in the evacuation of the British forces from Norway, Greece or Crete or elsewhere. Such a vessel may be regarded pro hac vice as serving the belligerent purposes of the country and as taking her share in hostilities against the enemy. She is therefore, it is said, to be deemed to be engaged on a warlike operation within the meaning of the war risk cover; so it has been laid down by this House under T 773 or T 99, the charter-party used in the last war. If that vessel is lost or damaged or damages other vessels by reason of the acts which she does in executing the warlike operation, the loss or damage is held to be by a consequence of the warlike operation.'

Lord Porter said:[15]

> 'If the *Coxwold* had been on an ordinary mercantile voyage, no doubt, as a result of the decisions in your Lordships' House, the risk would be a marine one, whether its cause was absence of lights or sailing in convoy or obeying the orders of the commodore vessel or inability to see the Neist Light because it was dimmed. But in the circumstances the cause of the *Coxwold* being at that place at that time in those conditions was her warlike operation and the loss was in my view not only in the course of but caused by that operation.'

In *Liverpool and London War Risks Insurance Association Ltd v Ocean SS Co Ltd*[16] a vessel sailed from Liverpool for Alexandria on 2 December 1942, with a cargo of war stores. The urgency of the voyage necessitated the carriage of a heavy deck cargo. Very heavy weather was experienced resulting in the deck cargo breaking adrift and causing damage.

The House of Lords[17] held that the vessel was engaged in a 'warlike operation', which had resulted in the damage done by the deck cargo.

iii Examples of operations held not to be 'warlike'

In *Harrison's Ltd v Shipping Controller*[18] a vessel was loaded with hospital stores for the British Government, and had on board a few British troops and officers. She sailed from Salonika to Taranto, and whilst in the vicinity of Taranto was ordered to follow a pilot escort into Taranto harbour. Her master lost sight of the pilot escort's lights, and, seeing a red light on his port bow, put the helm to port and she was stranded. McCardie J, held that she was not engaged in a 'warlike operation' because the dominant features of the ship and the dominant object of her voyage must be looked at. It could not be said that the presence of a few soldiers on board, whether wounded or unwounded, turned a merchant ship into a transport, or changed an otherwise peaceful voyage into a 'warlike operation'.

---

[13] [1942] AC 691, HL.
[14] Ibid, at 11.
[15] Ibid, at 16.
[16] [1948] AC 243, [1947] 2 All ER 586, HL.
[17] Lord Thankerton, Lord Wright, Lord Porter, Lord Uthwatt and Lord Normand.
[18] [1920] 1 KB 122, KBD.

In *Admiralty Comrs v Brynawel SS Co*[19] a collier was damaged by bumping up against a minesweeper which she was coaling. The minesweeper was taking in coal preparatory to resuming minesweeping operations. Rowlatt J, held that she was not engaged in 'warlike operations'.

In *Wynnstay SS Co v Board of Trade*[20] a vessel was at anchor off Staten Island, and was in ballast inward bound to load a cargo of grain for carriage to France. She collided with another vessel also at anchor, which was also in ballast inward bound after supplying a cargo of fuel oil to units of the US Fleet in European waters. At the time of the collision she had been requisitioned by the US Government, and was commanded by US Naval officers.

Rowlatt J, held that the collision had not resulted from a 'warlike operation', and said:[1]

> 'The cases have gone a long way in giving a wide meaning to the words "warlike operation", but I cannot conceive anyone saying that this injury was in consequence of a warlike operation. If you can say that when once a vessel becomes a unit of a belligerent navy, either as a fighting ship or as a ship supporting the fighting ships by way of supply, that from that time her whole life is one continuous warlike operation, then I think the award in this case would be wrong. But I think you would have to go as far as that in order to quarrel with this award, because here she had carried oil, was prepared to carry it again, and might carry it either for a warship or for anybody else. But she was not carrying it, and she was not going anywhere to fetch it. She had come back, and was lying at anchor awaiting orders.
>
> As pointed out by the Attorney-General, if she had been told, instead of dropping her anchor, to go into dock, and it had happened on the way to dock, it is contrary to the meaning of the words to say that she was engaged in a warlike operation. She was waiting there to see what was to be done with her next. I cannot see that she was engaged in any warlike operation.'

In *J Wharton (Shipping) Ltd v Mortleman*[2] a requisitioned vessel was bound for Southampton for orders. It was the Government's intention to employ her for the transport of Army equipment to a war base. Her master was unaware of the purpose for which she would be used. She collided with another vessel. The Court of Appeal[3] held that she was not engaged in a 'warlike operation' MacKinnon LJ, said:[4]

> 'There are dicta to the effect that, when a warship is proceeding to the scene of warlike operations, although at the moment she is not actually engaged in them, none the less during that preliminary passage to the scene of warlike operations she is herself exercising a warlike operation. No doubt that is perfectly correct, but it seems to me to have no bearing upon this totally different question as regards this purely commercial vessel, which was engaged at the time of the disaster in question in a purely commercial and unwarlike operation, and I am quite satisfied that, if the authors of those dicta to which I have referred had had this particular problem brought to their attention, and if they had been asked whether they would come to the same conclusion in such a case, they would readily, and with some asperity perhaps, have said that that was a totally illegitimate extension of anything which they intended to say, and a quite improper inference.'

In *Clan Line Steamers Ltd v Liverpool and London War Risks Insurance Association Ltd*[5] the insured vessel was on a voyage from Liverpool to Rouen and Dunkirk,

---

[19] (1923) 17 LlL Rep 89, KBD.
[20] (1925) 23 LlL Rep 278, KBD.
[1] Ibid, at 279.
[2] [1941] 2 KB 283, [1941] 2 All ER 261, CA.
[3] MacKinnon and Luxmoore LJJ, and Stable J.
[4] [1941] 2 All ER 261 at 263.
[5] [1943] KB 209, [1942] 2 All ER 367, KBD.

and was carrying steel rounds for the making of shells intended for the French Ministry of Munitions. She came into collision with another vessel in the English Channel. Atkinson J, held that she was not engaged in a 'warlike operation', and said:[6]

> 'To hold that to carry steel rounds on behalf of the French Armament Mission from Manchester to a port mainly used for commercial purposes (albeit also at times used for receiving supplies of munitions of war) for the purpose of carriage to some factory or factories doubtless to be chosen because of their distance from the fighting front is a warlike operation would be to hold something which, in my judgment, would be completely out of harmony with the substance of everything said since *Britain SS Co Ltd v R*.[7] The cargo was not yet military equipment. I do not say that that is in itself conclusive. It is unnecessary so to decide. Army workshops may for all I know have to handle much material not yet in its final usable form, but it was not destined for a force in the field, only for a factory; it was not being carried to a place where it would be available for an army in the field; that is, an army engaged in or about to engage in acts of belligerency; it was not connected with any belligerent act or acts of any army in being; and, in my judgment, it is outside everything indicated in the cases to which I have referred.'

In *Costain-Blankevoort (UK) Dredging Co Ltd v Davenport: The Nassau Bay*[8] a dredger was engaged in a dredging operation off the coast of Mauritius when she sucked up a number of 20 mm Oerlikon shells, which had been dumped in the sea by the British armed forces at the end of World War II. An explosion in the dredger's discharge pump occurred and she sank. Her owners collected the insurance money in respect of her. The Special Commissioners held that a balancing charge of £607,433 under the Capital Allowances Act in respect of that sum would be imposed in an assessment to corporation tax. The owners appealed on the ground that they were entitled to rely on the exemption given by s 33(7) of the Act, which stated:

> 'Where the loss of a ship is due to a war risk connected with any war in which His Majesty was engaged on 15 June 1945, then, notwithstanding that the loss occurs after the conclusion of. . . that war, no balancing charge shall be made by reason of the loss in respect of expenditure on the ship.'

That subsection said that 'war risk' meant any risk falling within the definition of 'war risk' contained in the form of policy set out in Sch 1 to an agreement for reinsurance of British ships made by the Minister of War Transport on 16 September 1943. That form stated that 'war risk' meant

> 'The risks of war which would be excluded from an ordinary English policy of marine insurance by the following, or similar, but not more extensive clause: "Warranted free of the consequences of hostilities or warlike operations . . .".'

Walton J, held that the appeal would be dismissed. The dumping of the ammunition was the very reverse of a warlike operation. It involved the very opposite for it was the destruction of war stores which was surely an act of pacification.[9]

---

[6] Ibid, at 374.
[7] [1921] 1 AC 99, HL.
[8] [1979] 1 Lloyd's Rep 395.
[9] Ibid, at 405. His Lordship, however, said ibid, at 405 that the dumping might have been a 'warlike operation' if eg Mauritius had been about to be overrun by enemy forces and ammunition and all kinds of other warlike stores had been dumped in the sea so as to deny their use to the enemy, but there was not the slightest evidence of anything so dramatic in the present case.

'Consequences of hostilities or warlike operations'

In order to recover under a war risks policy the assured must show that the loss has occurred as a *consequence* of 'hostilities or warlike operations'.

In *Moor Line v King and United Kingdom Mutual War Risks Association*[10] a vessel was lost by stranding. The marine risk underwriters denied liability, and contended that this was due to her altering course to avoid a floating mine, and was therefore the consequence of a warlike operation. It was held that the loss was due to negligent navigation, so the war risk insurers were not liable and the loss fell upon the marine risk underwriters.

In *Larchgrove (Owners) v R*[11] a vessel collided with an American cargo ship, which had been chartered to the US Navy and manned by naval ratings, and was carrying munitions from the United States to France. Roche J, held that the loss was a marine risk. The collision had been caused solely by the American vessel. The negligence on the part of those navigating her was a lapse by them as ordinary seamen, and not in their capacity of members of the US armed forces. She was not engaged as a warship at the moment of the collision, but was only a cargo ship.

In *Britain SS Co v R*[12] two vessels were proceeding without lights in accordance with instructions issued by the Admiralty and came into collision. No evidence was given at the trial of the presence in the neighbourhood of any enemy or friendly warship. The House of Lords[13] held that in the circumstances sailing without lights was neither a warlike operation nor was the collision the consequence of one.

In *Green v British Indian Steam Navigation Co*[14] a vessel was sailing on convoy. She zigzagged in accordance with the orders of the officer in charge of the escorting warships. She stranded and became a total loss. The loss took place in the Mediterranean in an area known to be infested with enemy submarines. But there was no evidence of the presence of a submarine at the time of the loss. It was held by the House of Lords[15] that the loss was not the consequence of a 'warlike operation'.

In *Clan Line Steamers Ltd v Board of Trade*[16] an insured vessel proceeding in convoy, and carrying stores for the civil commissariat and stores for the military authorities from New York to Nantes, collided with another vessel, which was carrying a cargo entirely made up of war stores. It was admitted that the other vessel was engaged on a warlike operation. The collision was found to be due to the breakdown of the steering gear of the insured vessel. The House of Lords[17] held that the loss was therefore not a consequence of a 'warlike operation'.

Lord Hailsham LC, observed:[18]

---

[10] (1920) 4 LlL Rep 286, KBD (Com Ct).
[11] (1919) 36 TLR 108, KBD.
[12] [1921] 1 AC 99, HL.
[13] Viscount Cave, Lord Atkinson, Lord Shaw, Lord Sumner and Lord Wrenbury.
[14] [1921] 1 AC 99, HL. The case was tried together with *Britain SS Co v R*, supra.
[15] Viscount Cave, Lord Atkinson, Lord Shaw, Lord Sumner and Lord Wrenbury.
[16] (1929) 34 LlL Rep 1, HL.
[17] Lord Hailsham LC, Viscount Sumner, Lord Buckmaster, Lord Blanesburgh and Lord Warrington of Clyffe.
[18] (1929) 34 LlL Rep 1 at 5.

'In the present case the facts found by the arbitrator show that the collision was due, and was due solely, to the breakdown of the steering-gear of the *Clan Matheson*. From the moment that that breakdown occurred nothing which could be done by those in charge of either vessel could prevent the collision, and in my opinion in law as well as in ordinary parlance the collision was the consequence of that breakdown.

The conclusion which I have reached is supported by the high authority of Lord Sumner in *The Warilda*, to which I have already referred. Lord Sumner says, [1923] AC at 305; 14 LlL Rep at 552:

"When damage is done by two ships coming into collision, one being engaged in a warlike operation, and the other on an ordinary commercial voyage, the collision is a risk falling on the marine policy, unless it is taken out of it by being proved to be caused by warlike operations, and this proof fails, when it is shown to be caused by the action of the officer in charge of the commercial operation, all the more so if his action is negligent and blameworthy; but I think the result would be the same, if his action was only an error of judgment or wrong but excusable in what is called the agony of the moment, so long as it is his action that causes the collision effectively and proximately, for the ship engaged in the warlike operation may play a minor part, since it takes two to make a collision." '

In *Yorkshire Dale SS Co Ltd v Minister of War Transport: The Coxwold*[19] a vessel carrying petrol for HM forces stranded near the Damsel Rocks on the Isle of Skye. She was in convoy and was following a zigzag course, but lost touch with the rest of the convoy. There was an unexpected and unexplained tidal set, which carried her some miles off course and she took the ground. The House of Lords[20] held that the effective and predominant cause of the stranding was the warlike operation[1] on which the vessel was engaged.

Viscount Simon LC, said:[2]

'It is not correct to say that, because a vessel is engaged in a warlike operation, therefore everything that happens to her during her voyage is proximately caused by a warlike operation or is a proximate consequence of a warlike operation. Neither is it correct to say that because the accident is of a kind which arises from a marine risk (e g stranding or collision), therefore the particular accident can in no circumstances be regarded as the consequence of a warlike operation. The truth lies between these two extremes. It seems to me that there is no abstract proposition, the application of which will provide the answer in every case, except this: one has to ask oneself what was the effective and predominant cause of the accident that happened, whatever the nature of that accident may be. It is well settled that a marine risk does not become a war risk merely because the conditions of war may make it more probable that the marine risk will operate and a loss will be caused. It is for this reason that sailing without lights, or sailing in convoy, are regarded as circumstances which do not in themselves convert marine risks into war risks. But where the facts as found by the Judge establish that the operation of a war peril is the 'proximate' cause of the loss in the above sense, then the conclusion that the loss is due to war risk follows.'

Lord Atkin observed:[3]

'If in the course of a warlike operation the direction of the ship's course against another ship is a consequence of a warlike operation (*A-G v Ard Coasters* [1921] 2 AC 141), it is surely impossible to distinguish the case where the course of the ship is directed against a rock, and this whether negligently or without negligence, and whether the ship is deflected by tide or current or wind.'

Lord Macmillan stated:[4]

---

[19] (1942) 73 LlL Rep 1.
[20] Viscount Simon LC, Lord Atkin, Lord Macmillan, Lord Wright and Lord Porter.
[1] The fact that she was engaged in a 'warlike operation' was admitted.
[2] (1942) 73 LlL Rep 1 at 6.
[3] Ibid, at 7.
[4] Ibid, at 8. See also the speeches of Lord Wright, ibid, at 11, and of Lord Porter, ibid, at 14–16, especially at 14, where he summarises the effect of a number of the relevant decisions.

'The learned arbitrator has found that the casualty suffered by the "Coxwold" was "the direct consequence of the warlike operation" in which she was engaged. Your Lordships have therefore only to decide whether that conclusion is justified on the facts which the arbitrator has found and set out in the case which he has stated. These facts have been narrated by the Lord Chancellor, and, in my opinion, they justify the arbitrator's conclusion. I think that the ordinary man if asked what caused the casualty would reply that it was by the vessel, in obedience to orders from the commodore of the convoy, deviating from a safe course in order to avoid a suspected enemy submarine. It is true that there was an unexpected tidal set which contributed to carry the vessel to the eastward, but there is no finding that this tidal set would have caused the stranding apart from the change of course. Certainly the vessel would not have gone ashore where she did but for the order which she received and obeyed to change her course to the eastward to avoid apprehended enemy action.'

In *Liverpool and London War Risks Insurance Association Ltd v Ocean SS Co Ltd*,[5] where a vessel was carrying war stores from Liverpool to Alexandria, the House of Lords[6] held that damage due to the maintenance of high speed and zigzagging in heavy weather to avoid enemy submarines was not a consequence of a 'warlike operation', for the damage was not shown to be due to anything more than bad weather aggravated by war conditions.

Lord Porter observed:[7]

'As Lord Wright pointed out in *The 'Coxwold'*,[8] the basis of the decisions seems to be that the casualty can be traced to definite action on the part of those on board the quasi-warship in directing the course of the vessel to carry out the warlike operation. That direction may take her into collision with another vessel or on to a rock, but incidents may occur in the course of the voyage without being caused by such definite action on the part of those directing it. In the case of stranding or collision the progress of the ship brings her on to the rock or into the other vessel. The rock does not move; it is static. If the other vessel runs into her and it is that vessel's action which causes the injury, it is the progress of that ship and not that of the damaged vessel which causes the injury, and whether that injury is a war or marine loss depends on whether the other ship, not the damaged vessel, is engaged on a warlike operation or on an ordinary mercantile adventure. Where the ship is struck and injured by the sea, in substance it is not the movement of the vessel, but the motion of the sea which causes the damage. The doctrine has never been extended to cover mere sea damage without more. Possibly, it may cover a case where the ship is pressed into the sea for war purposes, but that is a deliberate extension of the risk in order to assist in the war effort. No such act was done in the present case, and damage caused by the force of wind or sea is not, in my view, war damage even though it would not have occurred if the vessel had not zigzagged or kept her speed, provided, of course, that her action in doing so did not differ from that which a ship carrying an ordinary mercantile cargo would undertake in the conditions of war.'

In *Willis SS Co Ltd v United Kingdom Mutual War Risks Association Ltd*[9] the insured vessel was carrying Army stores from Barry to the Middle East via the Cape of Good Hope. She arrived at Durban on her outward voyage with damage in the vicinity of her tailshaft. The shaft was found to be misaligned, and the rivets were renewed. Further repairs were effected at Durban on her homeward voyage. The lignum vitae lining in the tailshaft was found to be excessively worn down, and the assured contended that this was due to the maintenance of high speed during heavy weather causing excessive vibration and consequent misalignment of the propeller shaft.

Lewis J, held that the vessel was engaged on a warlike operation, but that

---

[5] [1947] 2 All ER 586, HL.
[6] Lord Thankerton, Lord Wright, Lord Porter, Lord Uthwatt and Lord Normand.
[7] [1947] 2 All ER 586 at 598.
[8] (1942) 73 LlL Rep 1, HL.
[9] (1947) 80 LlL Rep 398, KBD.

the damage was not a consequence of that operation. It was due solely to the faulty lignum vitae lining in the tailshaft. He observed:[10]

> 'In the view that I have formed, and on the evidence before me, I am unable to find that any undue or excessive vibration was set up as a consequence of a warlike operation which aggravated the already existing damage. If I were satisfied that the manoeuvring of the ship as one of the essential parts of the warlike operation had been responsible, though even only responsible by contributing in causing excessive vibration, and that the true cause of the damage was not solely the defective lignum vitae, I should on the authorities have been bound to find in favour of the plaintiffs; but on the facts I have found I am of the opinion that this action fails.'

Proof of loss or damage by war risks[11]

Whether a vessel has been lost by a war risk or by a marine risk is a matter of fact, and the burden of proof of loss lies on the assured.

In *General Steam Navigation Co Ltd v Janson*[12] the 'Oriole' left London for Havre in a seaworthy condition on 29 January 1915. She was last seen off Dungeness on 30 January. On that day two other vessels had been torpedoed off Le Havre by an enemy submarine. Bailhache J, held that on the evidence[13] she had been lost by a war risk. Three of her lifebuoys were picked up on 6 February at Rye, Dymchurch and Hastings. A bottle containing a General Steam Navigation Co Ltd's envelope with the words 'Oriole torpedoed—sinking' written in pencil was picked up on 20 March off the Channel Islands.

In *Macbeth & Co v King*[14] a vessel sailed from Hull for the Tyne on 15 February 1915. She reached the Spurn lightship where her Humber pilot left her. She was never seen again. Bailhache J, held that she was lost by a war risk in view of the fact that the seas in which she was sailing were rendered dangerous owing to the possibility of mines from an English minefield having got adrift. Further, there were German mines and submarines in the area.[15]

In *Euterpe SS Co Ltd v North Of England Protecting and Indemnity Association Ltd*[16] a vessel was passing up the East Coast of England on 7 January 1917. She passed Great Yarmouth. Nothing more was heard of her. Rowlatt J, held that the vessel had been lost by a war risk.[17] She had probably struck a mine or had been torpedoed. She had evidently perished from a sudden disaster, for no pieces of wreckage or bodies were found, and no distress signals were heard.

In *British and Burmese Steam Navigation Co Ltd v Liverpool and London War Risks Insurance Association Ltd, and British and Foreign Marine Insurance Co Ltd*[18] a vessel left Liverpool for Rangoon via the Cape of Good Hope on 26 January 1917. She was in a seaworthy condition on sailing, but was never heard of again. She was believed to have passed through an area in which an enemy submarine had been operating. Other vessels had been lost by war risks about the same time near the course that she had probably taken. The disaster to her was sudden.

---

[10] Ibid, at 410.
[11] As to the burden of proof, see generally Ivamy, *General Principles of Insurance Law* (4th edn, 1979), pp 439–449.
[12] (1915) 31 TLR 630, KBD.
[13] For the evidence set out in detail, see ibid, at 630–631.
[14] (1916) 86 LJKB 1004, KBD (Com Ct).
[15] For the evidence, see ibid, at 1005.
[16] (1917) 33 TLR 540, KBD.
[17] For the evidence see ibid, at 540–541.
[18] (1917) 34 TLR 140, KBD.

She had wireless, but no message was received. There was evidence that an explosion sometimes threw wireless apparatus out of gear. Bailhache J, held that she had been lost by a war risk. There was sufficient evidence that she had been sunk by an enemy submarine.[19]

In *Compania Maritima of Barcelona v Wishart*[20] a vessel left the Tyne for a Spanish port on 17 November 1916, and was never heard of again. Evidence[1] was given that she was seaworthy. But the weather in the North Sea was bad at the time and other vessels had been lost in the vicinity of where she was. Roche J, held[2] that she had been lost by a marine risk, and that she had not been torpedoed nor mined. The weather was far too bad to admit of effective submarine operations.

In *Munro Brice & Co v F W Marten*[3] a sailing vessel left Gulfport for Fleetwood on 21 March 1917. In the ordinary way she would have arrived in 40 to 60 days. But nothing was ever heard of her. She had to pass through an area rendered dangerous by enemy submarines. The Court of Appeal[4] held that her loss was due to a war risk for, since she had not arrived, the necessary conclusion was that if she was shown to have entered that area, she must have been torpedoed. It was improbable that she had foundered owing to bad weather.

In *Mitrovitch Bros & Co v Merchants Marine Insurance Co Ltd*[5] a sailing vessel disappeared whilst on a voyage from Mejillones (Chile) to Brest in 1917. In August 1917, when she was considerably overdue, a coat belonging to a member of her crew and a barrel marked with her name were picked up off Penmarch in an area in which enemy submarines were operating.[6] Rowlatt J, held that the proper conclusion was that she had been torpedoed, and that her cargo had been lost by war perils.

In *De Marco and Gazan v Scottish Metropolitan Assurance Co*[7] a vessel was insured against war risks. Whilst she was about 22 miles north of Cape Dukato, a thud was felt all over her. The hatches of one of the holds were blown off and she sank in half an hour. The assured claimed for a loss under the policy on the ground that she had been lost by a mine.[8] The insurer refused to pay, and alleged that she had been wilfully cast away by means of a bomb placed in her cargo.[9] Roche J, held that the action failed because the assured had failed to prove that she had been lost by a war peril.

In *Zachariassen v Importers' and Exporters' Marine Insurance Co Ltd*[10] a four-master barque was insured in November 1920 against 'mine risks only as per Norwegian conditions including missing'. She left Newport News for

---

[19] For the evidence see ibid, at 140–141.
[20] (1918) 23 Com Cas 264.
[1] For the evidence see ibid, at 267–270.
[2] See ibid, at 268. The vessel was a Spanish one and her loss caused intense interest and hot debates in Spain. See ibid, at 269–270.
[3] (1920) 2 LlL Rep 2, CA.
[4] Bankes, Scrutton and Atkin LJJ.
[5] (1923) 14 LlL Rep 25.
[6] For the evidence in detail, see ibid, at 27–28.
[7] (1923) 14 LlL Rep 173 at 220.
[8] Evidence was given at the trial as to the presence of mines in the neighbourhood and the effect of mine explosions, etc. See ibid, at 226–227.
[9] Evidence was given as to her cost, value and earning power at the time of the loss, and as to the over-insurance of the ship and cargo. See ibid, at 227–228.
[10] (1923) 18 LlL Rep 98, CA.

Gothenburg on 1 October 1920, and was not heard of again. She was posted as missing in March 1921. Evidence was given that, at about the time of the voyage, vessels had been lost through mines in the North Sea. The Court of Appeal[11] held that the assured had failed to prove that the vessel had been lost by a mine, but that upon its true construction the policy covered a case where the vessel was engaged on a voyage which involved mine risks and was not heard of again. Consequently the assured could recover on the policy.

Bankes LJ, said:[12]

> 'It seems to me, taking this evidence and these reports as a whole, that it leaves the Court entirely unable to say that this vessel did not come within the mine area and therefore was not exposed to a mine risk. If she was exposed or may have been exposed to a mine risk, it seems to me that her case comes within the words of this policy in which the parties deliberately included words which were intended to cover a case where, if the vessel might have been exposed to a mine risk, and was missing in the sense that nobody could say exactly how she came to her end, then it is a case covered by the insurance.'

In *General Steam Navigation Co v R*[13] a vessel sailed from Bordeaux to London in March 1918. On arrival in London her bottom was found to be damaged. The assured contended that she had collided with an enemy submarine on the night of 13–14 March. MacKinnon J, held that on the evidence[14] they had failed to discharge the burden of proof. The damage had probably been caused when she had run over a submerged wreck in the previous August.[15]

In *United Scottish Insurance Co Ltd v British Fishing Vessels Mutual War Risks Association Ltd: The Braconbush*[16] a steam trawler sailed from Aberdeen for the West Coast fishing grounds on 28 January 1942. An underwater explosion occurred when she was off Duncansby Head. She vibrated heavily, and later water was found to be coming in. Her pumps were unable to cope and she sank. Atkinson J, held that the assured had discharged the burden of showing that she had been holed as the result of contact with an explosive float, and that she had therefore been lost by a war risk. The suggestion that she had been holed by submerged wreckage was not borne out by the evidence.[17]

2 THE INSTITUTE CLAUSES

The Institute War Clauses provide cover in respect of war risks, the extent of it depending on whether the subject-matter insured is cargo, hull or freight.

(a) Cargo clauses

Clause 1 of the Institute War Clauses (Cargo)[18] states that the insurance covers (subject to specified exceptions[19]) loss of or damage to the cargo caused by

---

[11] Bankes, Scrutton and Sargant LJJ.
[12] (1924) 18 LlL Rep at 100.
[13] (1927) 27 LlL Rep 366, KBD.
[14] For the evidence, see ibid, at 368–371.
[15] See ibid, at 371.
[16] (1944) 78 LlL Rep 70, KBD.
[17] For the evidence, see ibid, at 76–82.
[18] These clauses are set out in Appendix III, pp 526–529, post.
[19] For the exceptions, see p 258, post.

1 war, civil war, revolution, rebellion, insurrection or civil strife arising therefrom, or any hostile act by or against a belligerent power;
2 capture, seizure, arrest, restraint or detainment, arising from the above risks, and the consequences thereof or any attempt thereat; and
3 derelict mines, torpedoes, bombs or other derelict weapons of war.

Clause 2 states that the insurance also covers general average[20] and salvage charges,[1] adjusted or determined according to the contract of affreightment and/or the governing law and practice, incurred to avoid or in connection with the avoidance of loss from a risk mentioned above.

(b) Hull clauses

Clause 1 of the Institute War and Strikes Clauses (Hulls–Time)[2] states that subject to certain specified exceptions[3] the insurance covers loss of or damage to the vessel caused by

i war, civil war, revolution, rebellion, insurrection, or civil strife arising therefrom, or any hostile act by or against a belligerent power;
ii capture, seizure, arrest, restrain or detainment, and the consequences thereof or any attempt thereat;
iii derelict mines, torpedoes, bombs or other derelict weapons of war;
iv any terrorist or any person acting maliciously or from a political motive; and
v confiscation or expropriation.[4]

Clause 1 of the Institute War and Strikes Clauses (Hulls–Voyage)[5] is to similar effect.

(c) Freight clauses

Clause 1 of the Institute War and Strikes Clauses (Freight–Time)[6] and of the Institute War and Strikes Clauses (Freight–Voyage)[7] each state that subject to specified exceptions[8] the insurance covers

i loss (total or partial) of the freight caused by
   a war, civil war, revolution, rebellion or insurrection, or civil strife arising therefrom, or any hostile act by or against a belligerent power;
   b capture, seizure, arrest, restraint or detainment, and the consequences thereof or any attempt thereat; and
   c derelict mines, torpedoes, bombs or other derelict weapons of war; and

---

[20] As to 'general average', see pp 176–192, ante.
[1] As to salvage charges, see pp 192–193, ante.
[2] These clauses are set out in Appendix III, pp 547–549, post.
[3] For the exceptions, see p 261, post.
[4] Clause 2 of this set of clauses also incorporates some of the Institute Time Clauses (Hulls) including e g the 'Pollution Hazard' clause. As to this clause see p 170, ante.
[5] These clauses are set out in Appendix III, pp 549–550, post.
[6] These clauses are set out in Appendix III, pp 558–559, post.
[7] These clauses are set out in Appendix III, pp 560–561, post.
[8] For the exceptions, see pp 264–267, post.

ii loss (total or partial) of the freight arising from loss of or damage to the vessel caused by
   a any terrorist or person acting maliciously or from a political motive;
   b confiscation or expropriation.

3 INSURANCE BY THE STATE

The effect of war or the imminence of war on the marine insurance rate can be seen by a reference to the state of the market in 1914 and in 1938 at the time of the Munich crisis.

On 1 August 1914 the rates went up by 150 per cent. On 14 September 1938 the rates rose from one shilling to five shillings per cent, on 15 September to thirty-five shillings and on 16 September to as much as £5 per cent for continental marine insurance.

i The War Risks Insurance Act 1939

It was as a result of the chaos that ensued that the War Risks Insurance Act 1939 was passed. Part I of the Act secured that on the outbreak of hostilities ships would not be laid up and commerce interrupted by any lack of insurance facilities. Powers were confirmed by the Government enabling them to insure ships and cargoes in wartime, and also to cover them against 'King's enemy risks' in advance of an outbreak of war, if reasonable and adequate facilities for such insurance were not otherwise available.

The powers given by the Act of 1939 were extended by the Defence Regulations which had to be re-enacted annually under the Emergency Laws (Miscellaneous Provisions) Act 1947.

ii The Marine and Aviation Insurance (War Risks) Act 1952

The principal purpose of the Act of 1952 was to repeal Part I of the Act of 1939, and those provisions of Part III which relate to the insurance of ships and cargoes. Additional powers which are provided by the Act of 1952 are:

  i The power to insure or reinsure aircraft;
  ii To enter into agreements in peace time to reinsure foreign ships against war risks when this country is at war or involved in other hostilities; and
  iii To insure goods moving between ship or aircraft and warehouse, or vice versa, at overseas ports.[9]

It is desirable that the Government should have the power to insure or re-insure aircraft because British civil aircraft may continue to operate commercially during a future war, and there is a possibility that certain foreign aircraft may be taken on charter during war for commercial purposes, or that owing to the circumstances of the war, foreign aircraft may be based on this country. As regards the insurance of goods moving between ship or aircraft and warehouse or vice versa, the Act of 1939 applied only in the United Kingdom,

---

[9] Marine and Aviation Insurance (War Risks) Act 1952, s 2(1).

the Isle of Man and the Channel Islands, and it is felt that owing to the wider range of modern warfare this cover should be given also to overseas countries.

The Act of 1939 authorised the insurance of foreign ships in wartime, but it became necessary during the last war to undertake the reinsurance of foreign ships, and the Act was amended in 1940 by Defence Regulation to make this possible. But there was no power to conclude in peace time any agreements with foreign countries for the reinsurance of their ships, and it is important that this new power should be given by the Act of 1952 so that they can know in advance that their ships can be adequately protected by insurance.

The Act of 1939, as amended, authorised insurance or reinsurance by the Government only against King's enemy risks. The Act of 1952 concerns 'war risks'. This expression means:

> 'Risks arising from any of the following events, that is to say, hostilities, rebellion, revolution and civil war, from civil strife consequent on the happening of any of those events, or from action taken (whether before or after the outbreak of any hostilities, rebellion, revolution or civil war, for repelling an imagined attack or preventing or hindering the carrying out of any attack, and includes piracy.'[10]

Similarly, in many parts of the Act reference is made to 'war or other hostilities in which Her Majesty is engaged'.

The arrangement of the Act of 1939 has been followed in the Act of 1952. The Secretary of State may, after the approval of the Treasury has been granted, enter into agreements with any authorities or persons—

> *a* whereby he undertakes the liability of reinsuring any war risks against which a ship or aircraft is for the time being insured; and
>
> *b* whereby he undertakes the liability of reinsuring any war risks against which the cargo carried in a ship or aircraft is for the time being insured.

But the Secretary of State is not allowed to enter into an agreement whereby he undertakes the liability of reinsuring any war risks against which a foreign ship or aircraft is for the time being insured, except insofar as they arise during the continuance of any war or other hostilities in which Her Majesty is engaged, or arise after any such war or hostilities in consequence of things done or omitted during the continuance thereof.[11]

When an agreement has been made, it must be laid as soon as possible before each House of Parliament.[12]

If either House within 14 days resolves that the agreement be annulled, it becomes void, except in so far as it confers rights or imposes obligations in respect of things previously done or omitted to be done, without prejudice, however, to the making of a new agreement.[13]

With the approval of the Treasury the Secretary of State has power to carry on business:

> *a* at any time when it appears to him that reasonable and adequate facilities for the insurance of British ships or British aircraft against war risks or any description of such risks, are not available, for the insurance by him of such ships, or as the case may be, such aircraft, against such risks or, as the case may be, that description thereof;

---

[10] Ibid, s 1.
[11] Ibid, s 1(1).
[12] Ibid, s 1(2).
[13] Ibid, s 1(2).

b during the continuance of any war or other hostilities in which Her Majesty is engaged, for the insurance by him of ships and aircraft (whether British or not);

c at any time when it appears to him that reasonable and adequate facilities for the insurance of cargoes carried in ships or aircraft against war risks, or any description of such risks are not available, for the insurance by him of such cargoes against such risks or, as the case may be, that description thereof;

d during the continuance of any war or other hostilities in which Her Majesty is engaged, for the insurance by him of cargoes carried in ships or aircraft;

e during the continuance of any such war or hostilities, for the insurance by him of goods consigned for carriage by sea or by air, while the goods are in transit between the premises from which they are consigned and the ship or aircraft or between the ship and aircraft and their destination.[14]

The cover may be against war risks and no other, unless he is satisfied that in the interests of the defence of the realm or the efficient prosecution of any such war or hostilities it is necessary or expedient to extend the cover.

The Act contains transitional provisions for compensation in respect of goods lost or damaged in transit after discharge or before shipment within the first 7 days of the opening of a Government Office to undertake war risks insurance.[15]

The right of the assured to be paid direct by the Secretary of State as reinsurer in the event of an insurer becoming insolvent is preserved.[16]

A Fund under the control of the Minister is to be established and is to be called 'The Marine and Aviation Insurance (War Risks) Fund'.[17] Into it are to be paid the premiums received by the Secretary of State under the Act.[18] Any deficit in the Fund after payment of claims is to be charged on the Consolidated Fund,[19] and any excess paid into the Exchequer.[20]

Accounts must be laid before Parliament in each financial year, except where the Treasury certifies that in the interests of the defence of the realm or the efficient prosecution of any war or other hostilities in which Her Majesty is engaged, it is inexpedient to do so.[1]

4 MUTUAL INSURANCE ASSOCIATIONS

War risk insurance is also undertaken by mutual insurance associations in respect of vessels entered with them.[2]

B STRIKES RISKS

The risks of a strike may be insured against under the Institute Clauses, the particular set of clauses to be used depending on whether the subject-matter is cargo, hull or freight.

---

[14] Ibid, s 2(1).
[15] Ibid, s 3(1).
[16] Ibid, s 4.
[17] Ibid, s 5(1).
[18] Ibid, s 5(1).
[19] Ibid, s 5(2).
[20] Ibid, s 5(3).
[1] Ibid, s 5(4).
[2] See pp 220–224, post.

(a) Cargo clauses

Clause 1 of the Institute Strikes Clauses (Cargo)[3] states that the insurance covers with specified exceptions,[4] loss of or damage to the cargo caused by

1. strikers, locked-out workmen or persons taking part in labour disturbances;
2. any terrorist or any person acting from a political motive.

Clause 2 states that the insurance covers general average[5] and salvage charges,[6] adjusted or determined according to the contract of affreightment and/or governing law and practice, incurred to avoid or in connection with the avoidance of a risk mentioned above.

(b) Hull clauses

Clause 1 of the Institute War and Strikes Clauses (Hulls–Time)[7] and the Institute War and Strikes Clauses (Hulls–Voyage)[8] each include cover with certain specified exceptions in respect of loss of or damage to the vessel caused (inter alia) by

> 'strikers locked-out workmen or persons taking part in labour disturbances, riots or civil commotions'.

(c) Freight clauses

Clause 1 of the Institute War and Strikes Clauses (Freight–Time)[9] and the Institute War and Strikes Clauses (Freight–Voyage)[10] each state that insurance cover includes, with certain exceptions, loss (total or partial) of the freight arising from loss of or damage to the vessel caused by

1. strikers, locked-out workmen or persons taking part in labour disturbances, riots or civil commotions;
2. any terrorist or any person acting maliciously or from a political motive; and
3. confiscation or appropriation.

---

[3] These clauses are set out in Appendix III, pp 530–532, post.
[4] For the exceptions, see pp 258–259, post.
[5] As to 'general average', see pp 176–192, ante.
[6] As to 'salvage charges', see pp 192–193, ante.
[7] These clauses are set out in Appendix III, pp 547–548, post.
[8] These clauses are set out in Appendix III, pp 549–550, post.
[9] These clauses are set out in Appendix III, pp 558–559, post.
[10] These clauses are set out in Appendix III, pp 560–561, post.

CHAPTER 16

Risks covered by protection and indemnity associations[1]

Various risks are covered by the Protection and Indemnity Associations. These will depend on the particular type of Association concerned, e g whether the Association gives protection in the case of risks of a general nature, war risks, freight and demurrage risks, and through transit risks.

A RISKS OF A GENERAL NATURE

The cover afforded by the United Kingdom Mutual Steamship Assurance Association (Bermuda) Ltd is typical of that provided by similar Associations.

The principal risks insured against by this Association are:

1. Damages or compensation for the loss of life or personal injury or illness.
2. Expenses incurred under statute or collective or special agreements in respect of loss of life, personal injury or illness.
3. Repatriation.
4. Crew substitute expenses.
5. Loss of effects.
6. Distressed seamen's expenses.
7. Port and deviation expenses.
8. Life salvage.
9. Collision liability.
10. Fixed and floating objects.
11. Damage to vessels or property other than by collisions.
12. Liability under towage contracts.
13. Liability arising under indemnities and contracts.
14. Removal of wrecks.
15. Quarantine expenses.
16. Liability for loss or shortage of cargo or other property.
17. Liability for damage to or responsibility in respect of cargo or other property.
18. General average.
19. Fines.
20. Legal expenses.

---

[1] For the history and development of Protection and Indemnity Clubs, see 'Report of Advanced Study Group No 109 of the Insurance Institute of London', which was presented at a special meeting of members held on 8 January 1957, and reprinted by permission of the Institute.

1 Damages or compensation for loss of life or personal injury

The shipowner is entitled to damages or compensation for loss of life of or personal injury to or illness of any person in or on board[2] or near the vessel, including hospital, medical or funeral expenses, for which the owner may in consequence be liable, arising out of the negligent navigation or management of the ship or other negligent act or omission on board of or in relation to the ship.

2 Expenses incurred under statute or special agreement in respect of loss of life or personal injury

The Association will indemnify the owner in respect of hospital, medical and funeral expenses incurred under statutory obligation or in accordance with any collective or special agreement approved by the Directors of the Association in consequence of loss of life of or personal injury to or illness of any master or seaman on board the vessel, or any member of the crew of the ship who is proceeding to or from such ship, including expenses incurred in consequence of any master or seaman being by reason of injury or illness temporarily removed from the ship.

Such expenses, including the expense of repatriation in consequence of illness, incurred in respect of the master of the ship without statutory obligation or collective or special agreement, is recoverable if the Directors determine that such expenses should not, having regard to all the circumstances of the case, be borne by or charged against the master.

3 Repatriation

The owner can recover repatriation expenses incurred under statutory obligation in respect of any member of the crew of the ship, or any master or seaman who is proceeding to or from such ship.

But no expenses are recoverable if they arise out of or ensue upon the termination of any agreement either in accordance with the terms thereof or by mutual consent, or the sale of the ship, or any other act of the shipowner in respect of the ship.

4 Crew substitute expenses

The owner can recover expenses necessarily incurred in sending abroad substitutes, or in securing, engaging, repatriating or deporting a substitute engaged abroad, to replace any master or seaman on board ship who has died, or who has been left ashore or in consequence of injury, illness, desertion or in any other case in which the Directors of the Association shall determine that such expenses were reasonably incurred.

No such expenses are recoverable if they arise out of or ensue on the termination of any agreement either in accordance with the terms thereof or by mutual consent, or the breach by the owner of any of the statutory or

---

[2] For a case where a protection and indemnity association excluded a particular fisherman from the coverage of the policy, and he unsuccessfully sued them and the shipowners for damages for preventing him from obtaining employment, see *Goulart v Trans-Atlantic Marine Inc and Enos* [1970] 2 Lloyd's Rep 389, Mass SC.

contractual obligations, or of the terms or conditions of any collective agreement.

5 Loss of effects

The owner is entitled to recover payments made to masters and seamen in respect of the loss of their effects by marine perils under the National Maritime Board Agreements or similar Agreements approved by the Directors of the Association or under statutory obligation.

6 Distressed seamen's expenses

The owner is entitled to recover expenses incurred by or chargeable to him under statutory obligations for the relief of distressed seamen.

7 Port and deviation expenses

The owner can recover port and other charges solely incurred for the purpose of landing or disposing of stowaways or landing or securing the necessary treatment for an injured or sick person being carried in the ship including the net loss to the owner in respect of fuel, insurance, wages, stores, and provisions incurred for such purpose or while awaiting a substitute for such person.

8 Life salvage

Life salvage is recoverable to the extent only that it is not recoverable from hull underwriters on the ship or from cargo owners or underwriters.

9 Collision liability

One-fourth of an owner's liability, with costs incidental thereto, for damage done by collision with any other ship or vessel including the one-fourth liability which is not covered under the usual Lloyd's policy on hull with the Institute Time Clauses (Hulls)[3] attached, and which may not be covered under other forms of hull policy approved by the Managers of the Association, is recoverable.

10 Fixed and floating objects

The owner is entitled to an indemnity in respect of loss of or damage to any harbour, dock, pier, jetty or any other fixed or moveable thing whatsoever.

He is also entitled to an indemnity for any loss or damage for which he is liable as a party to any agreement which relates to the cost of cleaning up pollution caused by oil which escapes from his ship.

11 Damage to vessels or property other than by collision

The owner can recover for loss of or damage to any other ship or any property therein occasioned otherwise than by collision with the ship arising out of the negligent navigation or management of the ship or other negligent act or omission on board of or in relation to the ship.

---

[3] See pp 170–176, ante. The Institute Time Clauses (Hulls) are set out in Appendix III, pp 533–540, post.

12 Liability under towage contracts

The owner is entitled to an indemnity in respect of loss or damage arising out of or during the course of customary towage of the ship in the ordinary course of trading for which he may become liable under the terms of the towage contract but only to the extent to which such liability is not recoverable under the hull policies.

The Directors of the Association can reject or reduce a claim if they decide that it was unreasonable, having regard to all the circumstances of the case, to perform the particular towage or to enter into the particular contract of towage, or if in their opinion the particular contract of towage should reasonably have provided that the relevant risks and liabilities did not fall upon the owner of the tow.

13 Liability arising under indemnities and contracts

The owner is entitled to claim from the Association in respect of loss, damage or injury to persons (including loss of life and illness) or to any property whatsoever (including ships other than his own and any cargo intended to be or being or having been carried in his ship) for which he may be liable under the terms of an indemnity or contract given or made by him, or by the Association at his request, in consideration of the provision of any facilities afforded to or to be afforded to or in connection with his ship.

14 Removal of wreck

The owner is entitled to an indemnity in respect of the costs and expenses of or incidental to the raising, removal, destruction, lighting or marking of the wreck of the ship, when such raising, removal, destruction, lighting or marking is compulsory by law or the costs thereof are legally recoverable from him.[4]

The value of all stores and materials saved as well as of the wreck itself, must first be deducted from such costs, charges, and expenses, and only the balance thereof, if any, is recoverable from the Association.

15 Quarantine expenses

The owner is entitled to recover in respect of quarantine expenses and extraordinary expenses incident to the outbreak of infectious disease upon the ship incurred for or by way of the disinfection of her or of persons on board her under quarantine or public health enactments, regulations or orders, including the cost of taking in fuel in quarantine, and of loading and discharging cargo and of the victualling of the crew and passengers after deducting the ordinary expenses of loading, discharging and victualling.

He can also recover in respect of the fuel consumed for towage in proceeding to and from and lying at a special station or place in accordance with such enactments, regulations or orders.

Expenses directly consequent upon bearing up for, or putting into, a port or place of refuge and resuming the voyage thereafter by reason solely of the outbreak of infectious or contagious disease upon the ship are also recoverable.

---

[4] See e g *M J Rudolph Corpn v Lumber Mutual Fire Insurance Co* (*Luria International, Third Parties*): *The Cape Borer* [1975] 2 Lloyd's Rep 108 (District Court, Eastern District of New York).

16 Liability for loss or shortage of cargo or other property

The owner is entitled to recover in respect of loss of cargo or other property intended to be or being or having been carried in the ship arising out of any breach of him or by any person for whose acts, neglect or default he may be legally liable of his obligation or duty as a carrier by sea properly to load, handle, stow, carry, keep, care for, discharge and deliver such cargo or property, or out of unseaworthiness or unfitness of the ship.[5]

17 Liability for damage to or responsibility in respect of cargo or other property

The owner can recover an indemnity in respect of damage to or responsibility in respect of cargo or other property intended to be or being or having been carried in the ship arising out of any breach by him or by any person for whose acts, neglect or default he may be legally liable of his obligation or duty as a carrier by sea properly to load, handle, stow, carry, keep, care for, discharge and deliver the cargo or property, or arising out of unseaworthiness or unfitness of the ship.

He is also entitled to recover the extra cost (in excess of the cost which would normally have been incurred by him under the contract of carriage) of discharging or disposing of damaged or worthless cargo, provided that he is liable for such cost and has no recourse to recover it from any other party.

18 General average

The owner can recover an indemnity in respect of the ship's proportion of general average, special charges or salvage not recoverable under the hull policies by reason of the value of the ship being assessed for contribution to general average or salvage at a sound value in excess of the insured value under the hull policies.

The Directors of the Association may for the purpose of assessing any sum recoverable determine the proper value at which the ship should have been insured under the hull policies, and the Association will pay only the amount, if any, of the ship's proportion of general average which would not have been recoverable under the hull policies, even if she had been insured thereunder at such value.

19 Fines

The owner is entitled to recover an indemnity in respect of fines imposed upon him in respect of a ship by any court, tribunal or authority of competent jurisdiction for failure to maintain safe working conditions in respect of the ship. An indemnity may also be recovered in respect of a fine imposed on him for oil pollution, or on any seaman whom he may be liable to reimburse.

---

[5] See e g *Compania Maritima San Basilio SA v Oceanus Mutual Underwriting Association (Bermuda) Ltd: The Eurysthenes* [1977] QB 49, [1976] 3 All ER 243, [1976] 2 Lloyd's Rep 171, CA; *C V G Siderurgicia del Orinoco SA v London SS Owners' Mutual Insurance Association Ltd: The Vainqueur José* [1979] 1 Lloyd's Rep 557, QBD (Com Ct).

20 Legal expenses

The owner is entitled to recover in respect of costs and expenses, including legal costs and charges, which he may incur in respect of or in avoiding or attempting to avoid any liability or expenditure against which he is wholly or partly insured by the Association.

But no such costs or expenses are recoverable unless they have been incurred with the prior consent in writing of the Managers, or the Directors determine that they were reasonably incurred.

B WAR RISKS

Various Associations are concerned with war risks,[6] e g the United Kingdom Mutual War Risks Association Ltd.

a Detention of vessel and prolongation of voyage

The Rules of an Association sometimes provide cover in respect of

'Expenses incurred by the assured by reason of:
(1) the detention of the insured ship in pursuance of the orders or directions or with the approval of the Committee of [the mutual insurance Association] or of any British Government Department or official or British military authority given in order to avoid loss of or damage to the insured ship by any peril hereby insured;
(2) prolongation of the voyage arising out of compliance with such orders or directions, or with such approval as aforesaid.... Nothing shall be payable in respect of the first 7 days of each such period of detention or prolongation and the amount recoverable shall be assessed by the Committee whose decision shall in all respects be final.'

i *'Directions'*

In *Union-Castle Mail SS Co Ltd v United Kingdom Mutual War Risks Association Ltd*[7] a warning had been issued by the Admiralty on 30 October 1956 stating that

'In view of the situation between Israel and Egypt, merchant shipping is advised, for the time being and until further notice, to keep clear of the Suez Canal and Egyptian and Israeli waters.'

Diplock J, held that this warning did not constitute 'directions' for the purpose of the clause set out above because this term did not include a warning, the ignoring of which would give rise to no legal sanctions.

His Lordship observed:[8]

'Was the Admiralty warning a "direction" of a British Government Department? In terms, it purports to be no more than "advice"; and indeed, neither the Admiralty nor any other British Government Department had power to do any more than to advise as to action to be taken to avoid loss of or damage to a British merchant vessel. Such advice has no legal sanction behind it.
But the words "orders or directions" "of any British Government Department or official or British military authority" have a familiar and indeed an ominous ring. During the last war

---

[6] A number of cases concerning War Risk Associations are considered in chapter 15, for it appeared to be convenient to treat them there rather than in the present chapter.
[7] [1958] 1 Lloyd's Rep 58, QBD (Com Ct).
[8] Ibid, at 67. The learned Judge said that little assistance in interpreting the word was given by other clauses in the policy: ibid, at 67–68.

very wide powers to make orders by statutory instrument, and to give directions by less formal documents, enforceable by sanctions, were granted to Government Departments and officials, and, bearing in mind that this is a war risks policy, which contemplates the possibility of a state of war, I should have little hesitation in holding that the words "orders or directions . . . of any British Government Department or official or British military authority" applied only to instructions, the ignoring of which would give rise to legal sanctions and did not include advice, warnings or exhortations which the shipowner was at liberty to accept or disregard, as he pleased.'

ii 'Approval'

In *Union-Castle Mail SS Co Ltd v United Kingdom Mutual War Risks Association Ltd*[9] Diplock J, said[10] that whether a particular step had been taken with the 'approval' of the Government authority within the meaning of the clause set out above was a question of fact. The approval need not be given in any particular form. It might be given in advance. It might be given retrospectively. It might be given generally to all ships or specifically to individual ships. If advice given by the Admiralty to ships generally was taken, steps taken in accordance with that advice were taken with the 'approval' of the Admiralty within the meaning of the clause.

In this case the 'Dunnottar Castle' and the 'Rhodesia Castle' were insured under a war risks policy containing a clause in the form set out above.

The 'Dunnottar Castle' was on a voyage round Africa in a clockwise direction, and arrived at Port Said on 30 October 1956. She was ordered by the assured to turn and proceed to Mombasa via the Cape of Good Hope, and return to London via the Cape of Good Hope. Diplock J, held[11] that in turning her back from Port Said out of the area covered by the Admiralty warning they were acting with the approval of the Admiralty. The fact that they were influenced by the probability that the Suez Canal was blocked was irrelevant.

The 'Rhodesia Castle' was on a voyage round Africa in an anti-clockwise direction. On 2 November 1956 the assured ordered her to turn at Mombasa and return to London via the Cape of Good Hope and Mediterranean ports. The learned Judge held[12] that in turning round at Mombasa and failing to proceed to Aden and Port Sudan, which were scheduled ports of call, she was not acting with Admiralty approval.

iii 'Prolongation'

In *Union-Castle Mail SS Co Ltd v United Kingdom Mutual War Risks Association Ltd*[13] Diplock J, held (obiter) that the word 'prolongation' was used not in a geographical sense but in a temporal one and observed:[14]

---

[9] Supra.
[10] [1958] 1 Lloyd's Rep 58 at 68.
[11] Ibid, at 69.
[12] Ibid, at 70. His Lordship also held (ibid, at 68–69) that there was no approval express or implied by the Committee of the defendant Association of any of the steps taken by the assured. The Committee's failure to raise objections to those steps could not give rise to an estoppel because there was no duty upon the Committee to speak. Further, the Committee's admission that they would have given approval, if asked, did not include an admission that the approval of the re-routing instructions would have been given 'in order to avoid loss of or damage to the insured ship by any peril hereby insured'. But, in any event, there could not be an implied approval when none was in fact sought.
[13] Supra.
[14] [1958] 1 Lloyd's Rep at 71.

'What he is entitled to recover is: "Expenses incurred by reason of the prolongation of the voyage." If those words stood by themselves, "prolongation" might conceivably be construed in a geographical sense, although this is not the primary sense in which I would read it. Alternatively, it might be construed as meaning that the assured could recover the difference between the expenses actually incurred by him during the whole of the prolonged voyage and those which would have been incurred if the voyage had been carried out as originally contemplated.

But these words do not stand alone. That "prolongation" is used in a purely temporal sense appears from the reference to "period of prolongation" in the last part of the clause; there may be deviation without "prolongation". The provision that nothing shall be payable in respect of the first seven days of such period of "prolongation" seems to me to make two things plain: First, that "prolongation" does not start until the date on which the voyage normally would have ended; and secondly, that it is the actual expenses incurred during the voyage, after the expiry of such seven days, which are recoverable, although no doubt this is a figure which may in practice have to be estimated.'

iv *'Voyage'*

Diplock J, said[15] that the peril insured against was the prolongation of the voyage, and that this meant

'the voyage upon which the vessel is engaged at the moment at which the steps are taken with the Admiralty approval in order to avoid loss of, or damage to, the insured ship by a peril insured. At that stage it is open to the owner to continue the voyage with a deviation, in which case he may have a claim under the policy, or to abandon the voyage, or to change the voyage, in which case he has no claim under the policy. Which of these courses he has in fact adopted is in each case a question of fact, and, indeed, may be one of degree.'

He considered that in each of the present cases the voyage, on which the vessel was engaged at the moment at which steps were taken to avoid the area referred to in the Admiralty warning, was changed. Consequently the assured had no claim under the policy in respect of either vessel.

As far as the 'Dunnottar Castle' was concerned he observed:[16]

'It does not seem to me that the movements which she, in fact, undertook after turning back from the Suez area can be considered as a continuation of the same voyage on which she was engaged when she turned back. A call at Las Palmas for bunkers would no doubt not affect the identity of the voyage; nor would an omission to call at ports within the area to which the Admiralty warning applied; nor should I be understood as saying that some minor variation in the order of calling at scheduled ports must necessarily amount to a change of voyage. But, calls at four South African ports and one Portuguese East African port to carry new passengers in the reverse direction from the original voyage, the omission to call at Aden and two other ports (I exclude Suez which was in the warning area), however sensible it may be as a matter of commercial common sense, seems to me to amount to a new or changed voyage, and not to a prolongation of the voyage within the meaning of the policy.'

He said that similar considerations applied to the 'Rhodesia Castle', for five ports on the original route had not been called at, and four ports had been called at a second time on the return voyage.[17]

v *Savings and benefits*

His Lordship also held[18] (obiter) that neither any savings in dues before

---

[15] Ibid, at 70.
[16] Ibid, at 70.
[17] Ibid, at 71.
[18] Ibid, at 70.

prolongation, nor benefits which accrued as a result of prolongation, should be taken into consideration in assessing the claim under the policy, and observed:

> 'It does not seem to me that any savings made in consequence of the deviation which resulted in the prolongation of the voyage have any relevance to this calculation, any more than any additional expenses which may have been incurred before the expiry of the seven days after the date upon which the voyage would normally have ended.
>
> The same considerations apply to benefits. The clause relates to expenses only; but the kind of benefit which has been discussed in the present cases seems to me to be unlikely to accrue except in cases where there has been a change of voyage, in which case, as I have held, there is no claim under the policy.
>
> It is, I suppose, possible that by reason of late arrival at intermediate ports consequent upon deviation, a shipowner might obtain additional passengers or freight for onward carriage, but it does not seem to me that the policy or the clause is concerned with such matters, any more than it is concerned with loss of booked passengers or freight for onward carriage which results from such delay.'

vi Deviation

His Lordship said that the view that the Admiralty approval did not operate on anything outside the area of the warning put the matter too high, and observed:[19]

> 'If the result of keeping away from the defined area is necessarily to cause a deviation which prolongs the length of the voyage upon which an insured vessel is engaged, the expenses incurred as a result of that prolongation would, in my view, be recoverable, subject to the franchise[20] under the policy. I gave, in the course of the argument, the example of a vessel on a voyage to Bombay which, as a result of the Admiralty warning, went round the Cape instead of through the Canal. The expenses incurred by the prolongation of the voyage to Bombay would, in my view, be recoverable, subject to the franchise.'

b Diversion of vessel

In *Atlantic Maritime Carriers SA v Hellenic Mutual War Risks Association Ltd; Capetandiamantis Compania Maritima SA; Eastern Seas Transport Corpn and Orient Shipping Corpn v Hellenic Mutual War Risks Association Ltd*[1] the plaintiffs had insured three[2] vessels which they owned—the 'Mitera', the 'Kyriakoula D Lemos' and the 'Corsair'—with the defendants, who were a P & I Club. The policies covered inter alia:

> 'The net extra expenses reasonably incurred by the Assured in consequence of... diversion of the insured ship on a voyage already commenced, arising from compliance with orders, directions or recommendations by the Committee given in order to avoid loss or damage to the insured ship by any peril hereby insured.'

On 6 June 1967 the Suez Canal was closed as a result of hostilities between Israel and the United Arab Republic. On 8 June the defendants issued a circular letter stating that no ships insured by them should proceed through the Canal.

The 'Mitera' was chartered on 27 April for a voyage from Sunderland to China. She arrived in ballast at Sunderland on 28 May, commenced loading on 29 May and sailed on 21 June. She arrived off Gibraltar on 30 June and because of the defendants' circular letter went round the Cape of Good Hope to China.

---

[19] Ibid, at 71.
[20] Viz the first 7 days of the period of prolongation.
[1] [1968] 2 Lloyd's Rep 124, QBD (Com Ct).
[2] The fourth plaintiffs' claim in respect of another vessel was not pursued. See ibid, at 125.

The 'Kyriakoula D Lemos' was chartered on 12 April to carry a cargo from Casablanca to China. She sailed in ballast from Japan on 22 May for Casablanca. She arrived there on 28 June, and after loading went round the Cape of Good Hope to China.

The 'Corsair' was chartered on 2 May for a voyage from Gdansk to Japan. She arrived in ballast at Gdansk on 9 June, and sailed for Japan on 12 June via the Panama Canal in compliance with the defendants' letter.

The plaintiffs contended that extra expenses were incurred in consequence of the diversion of the insured ships 'on a voyage already commenced', and that the defendants were liable to indemnify them.

Roskill J, held that the action failed, for none of the cases fell within the coverage of the policies. The commencement of the loaded voyages which was after 8 June 1967 could not be related back to the point of time at which the respective ballast 'legs' began.

His Lordship observed:[3]

> 'I have difficulty in seeing why, with all respect to Mr MacCrindle's argument, it is legitimate to consider the whole of the antecedent contractual arrangements pursuant to which the ship is doing that which she is doing at the moment of diversion and pursuant to which she is at the particular geographical point at a particular moment of time. I think the introduction of those words "on a voyage already commenced" does introduce something, as Mr Kerr put it, in the nature of a geographical concept. You have to ask yourself, "What was she doing? Was she on a voyage already commenced when she was diverted?" It seems to me that it cannot be argued that any of them were at the material time on a voyage which had already commenced unless the commencement of that voyage can in each case be, as it were, related back temporally to the point of time at which the respective ballast legs began. In the first case the ship sailed on the loaded voyage during which she went round the Cape of Good Hope well after 8 June 1967. The same is true in relation to the material part of the second case. It is also true of the third case.'

The Court of Appeal[4] affirmed the decision.[5] Lord Denning MR, said that in the case of all three vessels the voyage did not begin until after the circular letter had been issued, so the expenses which had been incurred were not recoverable.

C FREIGHT AND DEMURRAGE RISKS

Some Associations have been formed to cover expenses incurred in enforcing the rights of a vessel in respect of freight and demurrage, and in defending her in respect of claims made against her, e g the United Kingdom Freight, Demurrage and Defence Association Ltd.

D THROUGH TRANSIT RISKS

Through transit risks incurred by combined transport operators in the carriage of containers are insured by some Associations e g the Through Transit Mutual Assurance (Bermuda) Ltd.

---

[3] [1968] 2 Lloyd's Rep 124 at 133.
[4] Lord Denning MR, Winn and Fenton Atkinson LJJ.
[5] [1969] 1 Lloyd's Rep 359, CA.

CHAPTER 17

The exceptions

The Marine Insurance Act 1906 sets out a number of exceptions which apply to all policies unless there is a term in them to the contrary.[1]

The Institute Clauses which are generally attached to the policy contain a number of clauses exempting the insurer from liability where the loss of or damage to the subject-matter insured arises from certain causes.[2]

Other exceptions are sometimes found expressly stated in a policy.[3]

Further, the undertaking of the insurer may be qualified so that he is not liable, e g if the subject-matter insured is outside an area defined in the policy or is not being used in a specified manner at the time of the loss or damage.[4]

I EXCEPTIONS UNDER THE MARINE INSURANCE ACT 1906

There are various losses referred to in the Marine Insurance Act 1906 for which the insurers are not liable. These are:

1. losses not proximately caused by perils insured against;
2. losses caused by the wilful misconduct of the assured;
3. losses caused by delay;
4. losses caused by ordinary wear and tear;
5. losses caused by inherent vice; and
6. other losses e g those caused by vermin.

1 LOSSES NOT PROXIMATELY CAUSED BY PERILS INSURED AGAINST[5]

A rule which is applicable rather to the consideration of the facts of the loss than to the terms of the policy is that which decides to which of several contributing causes a loss must be assigned.

The principle which prevails is that the loss must be attributed to the actual and direct cause, so that where there are a number of events successive in order of time, each producing the one which follows it, the last event preceding and producing the loss is held to be the cause of such a loss.

No question can arise when one cause only has come into operation. Discussion only ensues when there are two or more possible causes. Often it may

---

[1] See pp 225–256, post.
[2] See pp 256–267, post.
[3] See pp 267–268, post.
[4] See pp 268–272, post.
[5] For the doctrine of proximate cause, see further, Ivamy, *General Principles of Insurance Law* (4th edn, 1979), pp 404–419, and Ivamy, *Fire and Motor Insurance* (4th edn, 1984) pp 147–154.

appear that one of the earlier events is the dominant cause in producing the damage. It may be the causa sine qua non, while the actual causa causans may seem to be comparatively insignificant. Nevertheless, the law does not regard the relative importance of causes in the production of loss, since such an inquiry, if pursued, would open up a wide field of speculation and lead to considerable uncertainty.

In order therefore that the liability of the parties, in relation to the question whether the loss has been caused by any one of the perils insured against, may be ascertained and settled with some degree of certainty, the rule applied is causa proxima non remota spectatur.

Thus, Bacon said:[6]

> 'It were infinite for the law to judge of the causes of causes and their impulsions one of another; therefore it contenteth itself with the immediate cause, and judgeth of acts by that, without looking to any further degree.'

Hence s 55(1) of the Marine Insurance Act 1906 states:

> 'Subject to the provisions of this Act, and unless the policy otherwise provides, the insurer is liable for any loss proximately caused by a peril insured against, but, subject as aforesaid, he is not liable for any loss which is not proximately caused by a peril insured against.'

Thus, the assured can only recover on the policy when the loss is a direct and immediate consequence of any peril insured against and not a remote consequence of that peril.[7]

So, in *Cory v Burr*,[8] where the master was guilty of smuggling, which led to the seizure of the ship by the revenue authorities, it was held that the actual loss was occasioned by the capture or seizure on the part of the authorities, and not by the barratrous act of smuggling.

Lord Fitzgerald put the matter in this way:[9]

> 'If in place of the Spanish cruiser having seized this vessel she had failed to seize her, but in the attempt to seize her and in the pursuit had sunk the ship, I should put the same question, "What caused the loss?", and the proper answer would have been not the barratrous act of the captain, but the sinking of the vessel by the Spanish cruiser.'

Again, in *Greenock SS Co v Maritime Insurance Co*,[10] where the master was negligent in not procuring a sufficient supply of coal, and burnt the ship's fittings, it was held that the proximate cause of the loss was the short supply of coal, and not the negligence of the master.

Where a ship, disabled by perils of the sea, put into port for repairs, and in order to raise money for the repairs the master sold part of the cargo, it was held that the goods so sold were lost by the sale, and not by perils of the sea.[11]

Further, where a ship was blown by a gale into enemy waters and there captured, it was held that the loss was a loss by capture.[12]

In *Greer v Poole*[13] a ship was detained by an action on a bottomry bond, and after the sale of the ship, the balance due to the bondholder had to be paid by

---

[6] *Max*, reg 1.
[7] *Shelbourne & Co v Law Investment and Insurance Corpn Ltd* [1898] 2 QB 626.
[8] (1883) 8 App Cas 393.
[9] Ibid, at 406.
[10] [1903] 1 KB 367.
[11] *Powell v Gudgeon* (1816) 5 M&S 431; *Sarquy v Hobson* (1827) 4 Bing 131.
[12] *Green v Elmslie* (1794) Peake 278.
[13] (1880) 5 QBD 272.

the assured on cargo out of his own pocket. The payment by the cargo owner was held not to be a loss by a peril insured against, but the proximate cause of the loss was the inability of the shipper's agent to pay off the charge which had been created.

In *Cator v Great Western Insurance Co of New York*[14] part of a cargo was damaged by sea-water, and as a result suspicion attached to the remainder, which produced a diminution of the price on sale. Such diminution was a loss caused by suspicion, and not by sea perils.

In *Mordy v Jones*,[15] where the master prudently sold damaged goods, and paid the proceeds to the parties concerned, it was held that the freight was lost by the action of the master in selling, and not by a peril insured against.

In *Meyer v Ralli*,[16] where a sale of cargo was ordered by the court in order to pay advances incurred at a port of refuge, the loss was held to have been caused by the sale and not by perils of the sea.

In *P Samuel & Co Ltd v Dumas*,[17] where the proximate cause of the loss of a vessel was scuttling, the House of Lords[18] held that the insurers were not liable, for by s 55(1) of the Marine Insurance Act 1906 they were only liable for any loss proximately caused by a peril insured against, and scuttling was not a peril insured against.[19]

Viscount Finlay observed:[20]

'The scuttling of this vessel occurred on the seas, but it was not due to any peril of the seas; it was due entirely to the fraudulent act of the owner. The scuttling was not fortuitous, but deliberate, and had nothing of the element of accident or casualty about it. Storms are "fortuitous", the ordinary action of the waves is not, and fraudulent scuttling is even more decisively out of the region of accident. The entrance of the sea water cannot for this purpose be separated from the act which caused it.'

But in a dissenting speech Lord Sumner indicated that a scuttled ship was proximately lost by perils of the sea, and said:[1]

'I find it impossible not to be influenced by the consideration that if a scuttled ship is not proximately lost by perils of the sea, then every cargo-owner who loses his goods with her is as uninsured as the scuttling shipowner. Curious results may follow. An owner-skipper of a craft of small value laden with, say, bullion, finds his anchor dragging as he lies in shelter and in shallow water, and to save his cargo from total loss if his vessel faces the gale outside and sinks in deep water, blows a hole in her stern and drops her on the mud in four fathoms, where the bullion is easily raised. I take it this, if reasonably done, is a general average sacrifice of the vessel and, subject to the ship's contribution, is directly recoverable from cargo-owners and freighters. Can the captain not recover anything on his hull policy, nor the cargo-owners

---

[14] (1873) LR 8 CP 552. See further *Overseas Commodities Ltd v Style* [1958] 1 Lloyd's Rep 546, QBD (Com Ct) at 562 (per McNair J); *Boon and Cheah Steel Pipes Sdn Bhd v Asia Insurance Co Ltd* [1975] 1 Lloyd's Rep 452, Malaysia High Court, at 455 (per Raja Azlan Shah J).
[15] (1825) 4 B&C 394. See also, *Hadkinson v Robinson* (1803) 3 Bos&P 388; *Philpott v Swann* (1861) 11 CBNS 270.
[16] (1876) 1 CPD 358.
[17] [1924] AC 431, HL.
[18] Viscount Haldane LC, Viscount Cave, Viscount Finlay and Lord Parmoor; Lord Sumner dissenting on this point.
[19] Their Lordships overruled a dictum in *Small v United Kingdom Marine Mutual Insurance Association* [1897] 2 QB 42, where it had been held obiter that where a vessel was scuttled, the mortgagee would have been entitled to recover for a loss by perils of the sea if he had not taken part in appointing the master. See the speech of Viscount Cave [1924] All ER Rep 66 at 77, and that of Viscount Finlay, ibid, at 79–80.
[20] [1924] All ER Rep 66 at 79.
[1] Ibid, at 89.

anything on theirs, a loss by general average sacrifice being a loss by perils of the seas? That result follows from the respondent's argument, but I think it is not a result which underwriters desire or intend.'

In *Pink v Fleming*[2] two ships came into collision, and one of them had to put into port for repairs. To effect the repairs her cargo of fruit had to be discharged and subsequently reloaded, in consequence of which, and also by reason of the delay, the fruit was damaged. It was held that the loss of the fruit did not arise from the collision.

With regard to loss by delay s 55(2)(b) of the Marine Insurance Act 1906 states:

> 'Unless the policy otherwise provides, the insurer on ship or goods is not liable for any loss proximately caused by delay, although the delay be caused by a peril insured against.'

The doctrine of proximate cause is not always easy to apply. An example of the difficulty occurred in *Reischer v Borwick*,[3] where a ship proceeding up a river collided with a snag,[4] and the collision caused a leak. The ship was anchored, the pumps were worked, and the leak plugged. But while the vessel was being towed to the nearest dock for repairs, the plug fell out. The captain ordered the tug to run the ship ashore. This was done, and the ship was abandoned. In an action against the underwriters Lindley LJ, said:[5]

> 'It appears to me that an injury to a ship may fairly be said to cause its loss if, before that injury is or can be repaired, the ship is lost by reason of the existence of that injury—i e under circumstances which but for that injury would not have affected her safety.'

The court, therefore, arrived at the conclusion that the collision was the proximate cause of the loss, although the towing of the ship through the water might have been a concurrent cause.

Application to chartered freight

In *Inman SS Co v Bischoff*[6] the charterers had the option of putting the ship off-hire if she was disabled, and they did so on that ground, the ship having struck on a rock and requiring repairs. It was held that the insurers on freight were not liable for the unpaid hire, because the loss was not caused by a peril insured against, but by the act of the charterers in putting the vessel off-hire.

On the other hand, in *Jackson v Union Marine Insurance Co*[7] a charter-party provided that the ship should proceed with all convenient speed from Liverpool to Newport, and there load a cargo for San Francisco, the freight to be paid on right delivery of the cargo. On the passage from Liverpool to Newport the

---

[2] (1890) 25 QBD 396. See also *Taylor v Dunbar* (1869) LR 4 CP 206; *Shelbourne & Co v Law Investment and Insurance Corpn Ltd* [1898] 2 QB 626.

[3] [1894] 2 QB 548. See further, *Leyland Shipping Co v Norwich Union Fire Insurance Society Ltd* [1918] AC 350, where a vessel, which was insured under a policy containing a f c and s clause, was torpedoed by a German submarine and brought into harbour, she took the ground on each side and finally broke her bulkheads and became a total loss. It was held that the loss was a loss from an act of hostilities.

[4] I e the trunk of a tree fixed at one end in the bottom of a river.

[5] [1894] 2 QB 548 at 551.

[6] (1882) 7 App Cas 670. See also *Mercantile SS Co v Tyser* (1881) 7 QBD 73; *Williams & Co and Brankelow SS Co v Canton Insurance Office* [1901] AC 462; *Manchester Liners Ltd v British and Foreign Marine Insurance Co Ltd* (1901) 7 Com Cas 26.

[7] (1874) LR 10 CP 125.

vessel ran on to some rocks and sustained damage, the repairs of which would have taken so long as to frustrate the contract. It was held that the underwriters of a policy on the chartered freight were liable for the loss of freight consequent on the charterers cancelling the charter-party.

Similarly, in *The Alps*[8] the charter-party provided for the payment of hire at so much per month, and stated that in the event of loss of time from want of repairs preventing the working of the vessel for more than 24 working hours, the payment should cease from the hour when the detention began. The vessel was damaged by fire. It was held that the insurers on a policy on chartered freight were liable in respect of the hire lost.

The distinction between *Inman SS Co v Bischoff*[9] and *Jackson v Union Marine Insurance Co*[10] and *The Alps*[11] is that in the last two cases the loss of hire was the immediate result of the perils insured against, whereas in the first case the loss was a result of the exercise of an option.

In *Continental Grain Co Inc v Twitchell*[12] a floating policy for 12 months from 1 June 1937 had been effected by the plaintiffs, who declared monthly the different ships, the profits which they wanted to insure and the anticipated profits in respect of each ship. In September 1937 they declared the m v 'Oakre', which was chartered to them under a time charter-party, and a policy was issued to them. This policy insured them in respect of:

> 'Anticipated earnings and/or interest, warranted free of all average. Only against total and/or constructive total loss of vessel as per clause attached hereto.'

In September 1937 the plaintiffs sub-chartered her to Lamport & Holt Line Ltd for a voyage from St Johns, Newfoundland, to the River Plate. In October she stranded on Grand Manan Island in the Bay of Fundy, and sustained serious damage. She was repaired in $2\frac{1}{2}$ months, but the repairs cost so much that she was a constructive total loss. But she was not treated as such, and was put back into service by the plaintiffs. Lamport & Holt Line Ltd paid $5,000 to be relieved of the sub-charter-party, and she was engaged on other voyages until July 1938, when the plaintiffs paid $35,000 to be relieved of the head charter-party because the freight market had gone heavily against them.

The plaintiffs claimed under the policy in respect of the loss of anticipated earnings on the ship, or, alternatively, the loss of gross freight between the date of the stranding and the completion of her repairs.

The Court of Appeal[13] held that the claim failed. The proximate cause of the loss experienced subsequent to repairs being effected was the fall in the market, and not the constructive total loss of the vessel. Accordingly, there was no total loss of earnings due to the constructive total loss of the vessel.

Lord Goddard said:[14]

> 'I think I cannot do better than read two paragraphs of Atkinson J's[15] judgment, with which I entirely agree and which seem to me to be conclusive of this case. "A total loss of earnings", he

---

[8] [1893] P 109. See further, *The Bedouin* [1894] P 1.
[9] Supra.
[10] Supra.
[11] Supra.
[12] (1945) 78 LlL Rep 251, CA.
[13] Lord Goddard, Du Parco LJ and Uthwatt J.
[14] (1945) 78 LlL Rep 251 at 255.
[15] In the court below: (1945) 78 LlL Rep 107.

says,[16] "necessarily results from a total loss of the ship, but there is not necessarily a total loss of earnings after a constructive total loss of a ship. If the ship is repaired before the expiration of the charter and is again in service, there has been only a partial loss of earnings due to the constructive total loss. If the repairs are not completed until after the termination of the charter, then there is a total loss of earnings due to the constructive total loss of the ship."

Later on he said: "To succeed on the policy the plaintiffs must prove that there has been a total loss of such earnings, that is, of the valued earnings, of which the proximate cause was the constructive total loss of the ship. The only earnings lost by reason of the constructive total loss of the ship were those that would have been made between 31 October and 15 February. That which was lost as the result of the stranding was only part of that which had been valued. Any loss after 15 February was not attributable in any way to the constructive total loss. The policy did not insure against a loss of profits while the ship was in service, but against a total loss through being out of service."'

Sometimes the underwriter is protected by a special clause. Thus, clause 14 of the Institute Time Clauses (Freight)[17] states:

'This insurance does not cover any claim consequent on loss of time whether arising from a peril of the sea or otherwise.'[18]

Loss by apprehension of peril

In accordance with the rule, if a loss be occasioned through conduct arising out of or caused by an expectation of loss by a peril, such a loss is not recoverable by a claim for loss by that peril, for the peril did not cause the loss.

Thus, Lord Alvanley CJ, said in *Hadkinson v Robinson*:[19]

'Where underwriters have insured against capture and restraint of princes, and the captain, learning that if he entered the port of his destination, the vessel will be lost by confiscation, avoids that port, whereby the object of the voyage is defeated, such circumstances do not amount to a peril operating to the total destruction of the thing insured. . . . A peril insured against . . . must be a peril acting upon the subject insured immediately and not circuitously.'

In *Lubbock v Rowcroft*[20] a ship was bound from London to Messina, and at an intermediate port it was ascertained that, Messina being in the hands of the enemy, the ship could not go there without danger of capture. It was held that the assured on goods was not entitled to abandon and claim for a total loss, since the abandonment arose from an apprehension of capture by the enemy, and not from a loss within the terms of the policy.

Similarly, in *Forster v Christie*,[1] due to fear of an embargo at the port of destination the voyage was not pursued. It was held that the loss was not attributable to 'arrest or detainments of kings, princes, and people'.

---

[16] Ibid, at 113.
[17] See Appendix III, pp 550–554, post.
[18] *Bensaude v Thames and Mersey Marine Insurance Co* [1897] AC 609; *Turnbull, Martin & Co v Hull Underwriters' Association* [1900] 2 QB 402; *Scottish Shire Line Ltd v London and Provincial Marine and General Insurance Co* [1912] 3 KB 51; *Naviera de Canarias SA v Nacional Hispanica Asseguradora SA: The Playa de Las Nieves* [1978] AC 853, [1977] 1 All ER 625, HL. As to this clause, see pp 262–264, post.
[19] (1803) 3 Bos&P 388 at 392.
[20] (1803) 5 Esp 50.
[1] (1809) 11 East 205; *Blackenhagen v London Assurance Co* (1808) 1 Camp 454; *Parkin v Tunno* (1809) 11 East 22; *Nickels & Co v London and Provincial Marine and General Insurance Co* (1900) 6 Com Cas 15; *Kacianoff v China Traders Insurance Co Ltd* [1914] 3 KB 1121; *Becker, Gray & Co v London Assurance Corpn* [1918] AC 101.

Negligence as the dominant cause

There are some cases in which the dominant cause of the loss—i e the causa sine qua non—is the negligence of the master or crew, such negligence having produced the cause which in its turn had brought about the loss. In all such cases, if the cause from which the loss has resulted is one of the perils insured against, the insurer will be liable, notwithstanding the fact that the loss might not have occurred but for the negligence of the assured or his servants or agents. Thus, s 55(2)(a) of the Marine Insurance Act 1906 states:

> 'The insurer is not liable for any loss attributable to the wilful misconduct of the assured, but, unless the policy otherwise provides, he is liable for any loss proximately caused by a peril insured against, even though the loss would not have happened but for the misconduct or negligence of the master or crew.'[2]

Accordingly, underwriters have been held liable in the following cases:

i   Fire caused by the negligence of the mate.[3]
ii Sloop running ashore through the negligence of the crew in going to sleep and keeping no watch.[4]
iii Negligence of the crew in lashing the ship to pier posts with a rope of insufficient strength, thus causing a loss by stranding.[5]
iv Negligence of the master in throwing too much ballast overboard, thereby making the ship top-heavy, thus causing a loss by perils of the sea.[6]
v   Negligent stowage causing a loss by sea perils.[7]
vi Where for want of a pilot a ship stranded and became a wreck, the perils of the sea formed the causa proxima and not the seizure and confiscation of the wreck by the Spanish Government.[8]

It is sometimes said that if the negligence of the assured or his agents is the immediate cause of the loss, the insurer will not be liable. It would, however, seem that this proposition must be very limited in its application, for it would not include cases of barratry, and would appear to be confined in practice to those cases where the assured had neglected to make the ship fit for the purpose for which it was intended—i e where there has been a breach of the implied warranty of seaworthiness in the extended meaning which this warranty has acquired, in which case the insurer would escape liability whether the breach of warranty was intentional or due to negligence. It is difficult to conceive of negligence per se as the cause of loss, although in a few cases the loss has been ascribed to it.[9]

---

[2] For the relation between this subsection and s 78(4) of the Marine Insurance Act 1906, which states that it is the duty of the assured and his agents in all cases to take such measures as may be reasonable for the purpose of averting or minimising the loss, see *Astrovlanis Compania Naviera SA v Linard: The Gold Sky* [1972] 2 Lloyd's Rep 187, QBD (Com Ct) at 221 (per Mocatta J). See further, pp 449–450, post.
[3] *Busk v Royal Exchange Assurance* (1818) 2 B&Ald 73.
[4] *Walker v Maitland* (1821) 5 B&Ald 171.
[5] *Bishop v Pentland* (1827) 7 B&C 219.
[6] *Dixon v Sadler* (1839) 5 M&W 405.
[7] *Redman v Wilson* (1845) 14 M&W 476.
[8] *Hahn v Corbett* (1824) 2 Bing 205.
[9] See *Westport Coal Co v McPhail* [1898] 2 QB 130.

In *Bell v Carstairs*[10] a ship was condemned through the negligence of the owners in not supplying her with proper documents, and the condemnation expressly proceeded on the ground of want of documents. Lord Ellenborough CJ, held that the assured could not recover for a loss thus occasioned by their own neglect.

Similarly, in *Tanner v Bennett*[11] the insurer was held to be under no liability where a ship was allowed to be broken up by the agents of the assured after being surveyed in a negligent manner.

2 WILFUL MISCONDUCT OF THE ASSURED

Section 55(2)(a) of the Marine Insurance Act 1906 states:

'The insurer is not liable for any loss attributable to the wilful misconduct of the assured, but, unless the policy otherwise provides, he is liable for any loss proximately caused by a peril insured against, even though the loss would not have happened but for the misconduct or negligence of the master or crew.'

Wilful misconduct is equivalent to the wilful performance of the act which causes the loss. In such a case the insurers are not liable,[12] as the law will permit no man to take advantage of his own wrong.[13]

In *P Samuel & Co Ltd v Dumas*,[14] where a vessel insured under a time policy was scuttled with the connivance of her owner, one of the defences pleaded by the insurer when a claim was made under the policy was that, assuming that the insurance was for the joint benefit of the mortgagee of the vessel and her owner, the policy was avoided by the misconduct of the owner.

In giving judgment in the House of Lords, Viscount Cave held that the interest of the mortgagee was separate from that of the owner, so the question of a joint interest did not arise. He observed:[15]

'In support of this contention, a well-known American authority (*Duer on Marine Insurance*, Lecture III, s 15) was cited; and it was pointed out that the proposition contended for is not inconsistent with the English case of *Trinder, Anderson & Co v Thames and Mersey Marine Insurance Co*,[16] which was a case of negligent navigation and not of wilful misconduct. There is a force in this argument, but I am not prepared to say that in the present case it should prevail. It may well be that, when two persons are jointly insured and their interests are inseparably connected so that a loss or gain necessarily affects them both, the misconduct of one is sufficient to contaminate the whole insurance: *Phillips on Insurance* (5th edn), vol I, s 235. But in this case there is no difficulty in separating the interest of the mortgagee from that of the owner; and if the mortgagee should recover on the policy, the owner will not be advantaged, as the insurers will be subrogated as against him to the rights of the mortgagee. In such a case the "assured" referred to in s 55(2) is the particular assured to whom it is sought to make the insurer liable. In my opinion, therefore, this contention also fails.'

In *Lind v Mitchell*,[17] where a schooner was damaged by ice and started leaking, one of the issues was whether she had been lost by the 'wilful

---

[10] (1811) 14 East 374.
[11] (1825) Ry&M 182.
[12] *Thompson v Hopper* (1858) EB&E 1038.
[13] This principle is applied in all branches of insurance. See Ivamy, *General Principles of Insurance Law* (4th edn, 1979), pp 283–286.
[14] [1924] All ER Rep 66, HL.
[15] Ibid, at 75.
[16] [1898] 2 QB 114, CA.
[17] (1928) 32 LlL Rep 70, CA.

misconduct of the assured'. The Court of Appeal[18] held that, since such a contention had not been made in the court below,[19] it could not be raised on the appeal. So it was held that the loss was not attributable to his 'wilful misconduct'.[20]

In *Papadimitriou v Henderson*[1] a policy had been effected in respect of freight and/or chartered freight and/or anticipated freight for a period of three months. The vessel was chartered for a voyage from Odessa to Marseilles for the carriage of lorries and spare parts consigned to agents for the Spanish Republican Government. She was captured by an insurgent warship and taken to Palma, Majorca, and condemned as prize. When the assured claimed for a loss of freight, the insurers repudiated liability on the ground that the loss had been caused by his wilful misconduct in continuing the voyage after the master had received warnings of possible interference by insurgent warships off Cap Bon.

Goddard J, held that this defence failed, and that the assured was entitled to claim the whole of the sum insured under the policy.[2] He observed:[3]

'The owner was under no obligation that I know of to divert his vessel from that voyage unless, of course, she was obviously running into danger. He would not want to lose his ship, and no doubt he would give instructions to his captain if he could. The only definite warning that the owner had, or that anybody had, was that some trouble, that is to say, some search or stoppage for the purpose of search, might be expected off Cap Bon; and when the owner was asked to order the ship to proceed to Malta for orders, as soon as terms were arranged under which she should proceed to Malta where he was not bound to allow her to go, he gave those orders. As soon as he was requested, and the terms were arranged under which she should put about and go back to Piraeus, she did, and there is no evidence before me to show that anybody was expecting that one of the Spanish warships belonging to the insurgent forces was lurking, to use a familiar expression, east of Malta. Even if there had been, I think it would be a very dangerous doctrine to lay down in the Courts of this country that the captain of a neutral ship or the owner of a neutral ship or the owner of a ship belonging to a country not at war, is guilty of wilful misconduct if he tries to proceed with his contract voyage, simply because there is a risk of capture, as there must always be a risk of capture during a war, which is the very reason why shipowners and merchants insure against war risks.'

But his Lordship went on to say that in certain circumstances the position might be different and remarked:[4]

'Of course, if it was a case in which the shipowner got warning that a blockade had been established at a particular port or that a ship was lying waiting at a particular point, and the shipowner deliberately sent his ship forward to that point to run the blockade, it may be that there would be, in certain cases, an inference to be drawn that he was not endeavouring to carry out the voyage, but what he was endeavouring to do was to get his ship captured, and that, of course, would be wilful misconduct.'

Evidence of assured's connivance at scuttling

A general guide as to the circumstances to be taken into account when considering whether a vessel has been intentionally cast away is to be found in

---

[18] Scrutton, Lawrence and Sankey LJJ.
[19] (1928) 31 LlL Rep 262.
[20] (1928) 32 LlL Rep 70 at 73.
[1] (1939) 64 LlL Rep 345, KBD.
[2] As to this aspect of the case, see p 96, ante.
[3] (1939) 64 LlL Rep 345 at 348.
[4] Ibid, at 349.

the judgment of MacKinnon J, in *Lemos v British and Foreign Marine Insurance Co Ltd*,[5] where he said:[6]

> 'I think that three aspects have been considered, and have been properly considered; first of all, the circumstances of the actual loss of the ship, the nature of the casualty. In many of the cases to which I allude the ship was lost by being sunk at sea, and it was alleged that she struck sunken wreckage, or had been blown up by a mine, a very different thing from a case of a steamer which runs upon a rock. The second circumstance, or set of circumstances, to be considered, I think, is the nature and extent of the opportunity for communications between the master, the crew, and the owner, and the nature of the communications which are, in fact, alleged to have passed between them. The third set of circumstances that has always been considered, and which, obviously, is very material to consider, is the motives which operated to induce either the master or the owner, or both, to get rid of the ship by a pretended loss; for instance, the extent to which the owner would profit by the loss of his ship, having regard to the over-insurance of the ship, and the nature of his pecuniary position, his need for money, and various things of that sort. In some cases, if I remember aright, the same sort of considerations applied to the master; whether the master had himself effected insurances on which he might stand to gain if the ship was lost. Those, I think, are the three types of facts which one has to consider in such a case as this.'

In *Visscherij Maatschappij Nieuwe Onderneming v Scottish Metropolitan Assurance Co*[7] a trawler sank 10 miles off shore in broad daylight. She was travelling at the rate of 1 knot. During the First World War she had been very profitable to her owners, but after the War she had been working at a loss. When she sank, her value was very substantially less than her insured value. The insurers contended that she had been cast away by the assured.

The Court of Appeal[8] held that this defence succeeded. Having regard to the financial position of the assured, to the untrue explanation put forward by the crew and to the absence of motive in the crew apart from the owners' interest, she must be presumed to have been cast away with the owners' consent.

In *Coulouras v British General Insurance Co Ltd*[9] the insured vessel sank in calm weather close to the West Hinder Lightvessel whilst on a voyage from Ghent to Southampton. She was insured for four times her actual market value.[10] It was doubtful whether she was making any real profit.[11] Shortly before she sank the master ordered the cook to prepare a meal for the crew as he (the master) was going to sink her.[12] The insurers contended that she had been wilfully cast away with the connivance of the assured. Rowlatt J, held that this contention succeeded, and that the claim failed. He observed:[13]

> 'Serious as the issue is, I must honestly say I have no doubt on the point that this ship was sunk by the captain, and that it was sunk with the connivance of the owner.
>
> There was no sort of reason for thinking the captain would sink her without the connivance of the owner, and without finding that any undue sums were given to the crew—as to which the evidence is obscure—certainly one would have thought that the owner, confronted with a

---

[5] (1931) 39 LlL Rep 275, KBD.
[6] Ibid, at 283. For American cases in which scuttling was alleged, see *The Lakeland* (1927) 29 LlL Rep 293 (US Court of Appeals 6th Cir); *Northwestern Mutual Life Insurance Co v Linard The Vainqueur* [1973] 2 Lloyd's Rep 275 (SDNY). This decision was subsequently affirmed by the (US Court of Appeals 2nd Cir) [1974] 2 Lloyd's Rep 398.
[7] (1922) 10 LlL Rep 579, CA.
[8] Lord Sterndale MR, Warrington and Scrutton LJJ.
[9] (1922) 12 LlL Rep 220 at 266, KBD.
[10] Ibid, at 277.
[11] Ibid, at 277–278.
[12] Ibid, at 280.
[13] Ibid, at 280.

story of this kind, and honest in the matter, would most certainly have conducted some sort of investigation as between himself and the captain. There is no trace of that at all from first to last.'

In *Doriga Y Sanudo v Royal Exchange Assurance Corpn*[14] the insured vessel left Newport (Mon) for Pasajes. Early morning next day she sank off Bull Point in a calm sea. The insurers repudiated liability for her loss on the ground that she had been wilfully cast away with the privity of the assured. She was worth not much below her insured value. The freight market was bad.

Bailhache J, held that scuttling had not been proved, and that the claim succeeded. He observed:[15]

> 'My view is that the handling of the *Marianela* after water was found in her was entirely discreditable. The crew left her much sooner than they should have done. With any decent seamanship she would have been safely beached, or, as I think, kept afloat. I attribute her handling to panic, and not to a desire to sink her. Had there been such a desire, I do not see why she should have been anchored within five to seven miles of Bull Point, lighted as brilliantly as oil lamps could.'

In *Ansoleaga Y Cia v Indemnity Mutual Marine Insurance Co*[16] the insured vessel sank in the Gulf of Cadiz. She was insured for £245,000 under a policy which expired within a month. Her actual value at the time of the loss was £55,000.[17] The assured owed four-fifths of her purchase price, and the vessel had ceased to make any profit. Water was found to be entering the vessel. Without sounding or taking steps to investigate, the master gave orders to abandon her. It was a calm night. The vessel sank in the direct line of shipping passing from the north of Europe to Gibraltar. The insurers contended that she had been cast away with the connivance of the assured. The Court of Appeal[18] held that this defence succeeded, and that the action failed.

In *P Samuel & Co Ltd v Dumas*[19] a Greek vessel was insured under a time policy for 12 months by persons to whom she had been mortgaged. While on a voyage from Philippeville to the Tyne, she foundered in calm weather off the coast of Spain. When a claim was made by the mortgagee, one of the defences put forward by the insurers was that the loss was due to the wilful misconduct of the owner in procuring or conniving at the sinking of the vessel.

Bailhache J, held that if the owners had claimed under the policy, the claim would have failed because connivance at the scuttling had been proved,[20] but that the innocent mortgagee was entitled to an indemnity under the policy. The House of Lords,[1] however, held that the learned Judge was wrong on this point[2] because scuttling was not a peril of the sea and so was a peril not covered by the policy.[3] Consequently the action by the mortgagee failed.

---

[14] (1922) 13 LlL Rep 126 at 166, KBD.
[15] Ibid, at 192.
[16] (1922) 13 LlL Rep 231, CA.
[17] Scrutton LJ, said (ibid, at 245) that it was common knowledge that at the time of a great slump in shipping values a number of losses of ships happened under peculiar circumstances. This was the first case in which the Court of Appeal came to give judgment. It had already heard three other cases, and there were a large number of others waiting.
[18] Bankes and Scrutton LJJ, and Eve J.
[19] (1922) 11 LlL Rep 241, KBD; (1922) 12 LlL Rep 73.
[20] The evidence is set out at (1922) 12 LlL Rep at 87–90.
[1] Viscount Haldane LC, Viscount Cave, Viscount Finlay, Lord Sumner and Lord Parmoor.
[2] [1924] All ER Rep 66, HL.
[3] As to this aspect of the case, see p 145, ante.

In *Elfie A Issaias v Marine Insurance Co Ltd*[4] a new wooden vessel sustained damage in August 1920 in the Atlantic on her first voyage from Baltimore to Piraeus. The damage disabled the engines and caused a small amount of water to enter her. She was taken in tow by another vessel, but after some hours her master signalled that she was sinking and that he wished to be taken off. The master and chief engineer of the other vessel went on board her, and found that water was entering her rapidly owing to a pipe in the engine room having been intentionally disconnected. Efforts were made to salve her, but she sank. Her value at the time of the loss was about £40,000 less than her insured value. The insurers refused to indemnify the assured, and alleged that she had been intentionally cast away with his connivance.

The Court of Appeal[5] held the insurers had failed to prove this,[6] and that the loss was due to an act of barratry.[7]

In *Comunidad Naviera Baracaldo v Norwich Union Fire Insurance Society*[8] a vessel was insured under a time policy for £150,000. Whilst on a voyage from Vivero to Rotterdam, she was alleged to have struck a submerged object. Water entered her in six places. She sank shortly afterwards. The weather was calm. The assured claimed for a total loss, but the insurers contended that she had been wilfully cast away with the assured's knowledge and consent.

At the trial it was proved that her value was substantially less than £150,000.[9] The assured owed their bankers £100,000 in respect of her purchase price.[10] They were, however, in a sound financial position at the time of the loss.[11] Before the loss they had attempted to lower her insured value.[12] Further, they had attempted to fix her for other voyages after the voyage on which she had been lost.[13]

Greer J, held that the vessel had been lost by a peril of the sea. The defence had not been made out and the claim succeeded.

In *Compania Naviera Martiartu v Royal Exchange Assurance Corpn*[14] a vessel was insured for £174,000 under time policies which expired in less than a month after she sank on a voyage from Vivero to Rotterdam south of Ushant. The insurers contended that she had been wilfully cast away by those on board her with the knowledge and consent of the assured, and repudiated liability under the policies.

It was proved that her real value was only £14,000. She was on a course which would have taken her ashore inside Armen Rock instead of on a course which would have enabled her to pass clear of the dangers of Ushant. The sea was smooth and there was little or no wind. The vessel did not founder until 5 hours after the crew had taken to their boats. No attempt was made to attract attention or secure assistance by means of rockets. The logs and papers were lost.

---

[4] (1923) 15 LlL Rep 186, CA.
[5] Lord Sterndale, Warrington and Atkin LJJ.
[6] The evidence is set out at (1921) 15 LlL Rep at 187–188, 190.
[7] As to barratry, see pp 161–169, ante.
[8] (1923) 16 LlL Rep 45 at 93, 156, KBD.
[9] Ibid, at 45.
[10] Ibid, at 157.
[11] Ibid, at 157.
[12] Ibid, at 159.
[13] Ibid, at 158.
[14] (1924) 18 LlL Rep 247, 19 LlL Rep 95, HL.

The House of Lords[15] held that the claim failed, for she had been scuttled with the connivance of the assured.

The Earl of Birkenhead said:[16]

> 'The owners, on the other hand, had a gigantic interest in the scuttling. The loss of the vessel at that particular moment meant indeed the difference to the company between solvency and insolvency. When once the fact of deliberate scuttling is established, the probability which remains to be balanced is as to whether such scuttling took place with or without the privity of the owners. Their Counsel pressed upon us the terms in which the minutes of the meetings were couched in the period immediately preceding the loss. I find this argument particularly unconvincing. If a man, who has an immense pecuniary interest in casting away his ship, has decided to commit this fraud, I should not expect any hint of it to be contained in his papers. On the contrary, unless besides being a rogue he was also a fool, I should expect his papers carefully to convey the impression that he was engaged in arranging for the further employment of his vessel.
>
> Applying the general test which I have already indicated, I am satisfied that the [insurers] have discharged the task which this case imposed upon them. In other words, they have proved facts from which there springs an irresistible inference that the owners were accomplices in the fraudulent destruction of the vessel.'

In *Anghelatos v Northern Assurance Co Ltd*[17] the insured vessel was on a voyage from Newport News to Haifa when she ran ashore on the Formigas Rocks near the Azores. She became a total loss. The insurers contended that she had been deliberately cast away by the instructions and with the privity of the assured. There was inconsistency of evidence with regard to her position.[18] There were no ship's papers.[19] Money had been distributed to her crew.[20] There were telegrams sent by the master to the chief officer as to the evidence to be given.[1] The assured's financial position was desperate.[2]

The House of Lords[3] held that the claim failed. The vessel had been wilfully cast away by the master with the connivance of the assured. Lord Shaw said:[4]

> 'I am of opinion that the vessel did not perish by accident, but was deliberately run on the rocks. Her value was between £15,000 and £16,000, and she was insured for the sum of £150,000 on ship alone. The enormous financial advantage of a loss or wreck to the owner is admitted, but the evidence as regards the owner is not relevant to this case, for it says that he was not superior to this class of temptation. This class of nefarious adventure was not unknown to him. After full inquiry by a court of law, he had been adjudged guilty of these malpractices on at least one former occasion. He is, in short, a convicted scuttler, and he was at the period of this occurrence in desperate straits for money. This was not the first ship he had dishonestly sent to the bottom of the sea. There are further details, but they do not abate, but add to the grossness of this scheme. This, in my opinion, is a case to be judged upon the whole evidence. I only express this separate opinion in order to say that I decline to accept this case as ruled or even assisted by any presumption in favour of accidental loss.'

In *Société d'Avances Commerciales (SA Egyptienne) v Merchants' Marine Insurance*

---

[15] Earl of Birkenhead, Viscount Finlay, Lord Dunedin, Lord Sumner and Lord Carson.
[16] (1924) 19 LlL Rep at 97. See also the speech of Viscount Finlay, ibid, at 98, and that of Lord Sumner, ibid, at 99.
[17] (1924) 19 LlL Rep 255, HL.
[18] Ibid, at 256.
[19] Ibid, at 258.
[20] Ibid, at 259.
[1] Ibid, at 260.
[2] Ibid, at 257.
[3] Earl of Birkenhead, Lord Atkinson, Lord Shaw, Lord Sumner and Lord Wrenbury.
[4] (1924) 19 LlL Rep at 261. See also the speech of the Earl of Birkenhead, ibid, at 260, and that of Lord Sumner, ibid, at 262.

Co^5 the insured vessel was carrying a cargo of onions from Alexandria to New York, and sank in calm weather 50 miles off the North African coast when 3 days out on her voyage. The insurers refused to pay for the loss, contending that she was scuttled at the instance of one Schemeil, who was part owner of her to the extent of 75 per cent, and was also the owner of the onions. The Court of Appeal[6] held that the irresistible evidence was that she had been wifully cast away, and that the claim failed.

In *Domingo Mumbru Société Anon v Laurie*[7] a vessel was steering a course unusually close to the shore. An explosion was said to have occurred in a bunker. Her master turned her towards the shore, and she stranded shortly afterwards. She got off without assistance and sank while being towed into Cavalaire Bay. The weather was fine and calm. She was insured for £180,000. Her market value did not exceed £30,000. The insurers contended that she had been wilfully cast away with the connivance of her owners. At the trial divers gave evidence that they had found tank tops off and valves open. Rowlatt J, held that the defence succeeded, and that the claim failed.

In *Banco de Barcelona v Union Marine Insurance Co Ltd*[8] the plaintiffs had insured their cargo of bales of cloth on the steamer 'Cruz' for a voyage from Barcelona to Galatz. The vessel was abandoned by her crew except for her master off Sardinia. She later sank, the master going down with her. A diver found the tank injection valves to the tanks over two of the holds open, and both main injection Kingston valves and the port bilge injection valve open. The plaintiffs had taken over the cloth as purchasers, and had credited the price to the original owners. When a claim was made under the policy, the insurers contended that the loss was brought about by the wilful misconduct of the plaintiffs in procuring or conniving at the casting away of the vessel.

Greer J, held that the claim failed. The vessel had been scuttled with the connivance of the owners[9] and some of those responsible for the management of the plaintiffs.[10]

In *Empire SS Co Inc v Threadneedle Insurance Co*[11] a special jury returned a verdict[12] that a vessel, which had been lost by fire whilst in port at Claremont on the James River in the United States, had been intentionally set on fire by the assured, and that she had been fraudulently over-insured. Branson J, accordingly entered judgment for the insurers.

In *Lemos v British and Foreign Marine Insurance Co Ltd*[13] the insured vessel was in the course of entering Axim Bay in the Gold Coast, and stranded on the Hoever Rock, and became a hopeless wreck. The insurers repudiated liability on the ground that the loss was due to the wilful misconduct of the assured in procuring or conniving at the casting away of the vessel.

---

[5] (1924) 20 LlL Rep 74 at 140, CA.
[6] Bankes, Atkin and Sargant LJJ.
[7] (1924) 20 LlL Rep 122 at 189, KBD.
[8] (1925) 22 LlL Rep 209 at 317, KBD.
[9] His Lordship said that it was quite impossible in the present case to make out a case of barratry: ibid, at 329.
[10] For further proceedings concerning security of costs pending on appeal, see (1925) 23 LlL Rep 55, 214, CA.
[11] (1925) 22 LlL Rep 437, 534.
[12] Ibid, at 537.
[13] (1931) 39 LlL Rep 275, KBD.

MacKinnon J, held that the claim succeeded. The stranding, although the result of negligence, was accidental.[14] There was an absence of evidence of connivance.[15] Further, the vessel was not over-insured,[16] and there was no proof that the assured was financially unsound.[17]

In *Piper v Royal Exchange Assurance*[18] a yacht stranded on the Buxey Sands whilst on a voyage to Burnham-on-Crouch. When the assured claimed under the policy which he had effected in respect of her, the insurers refused to indemnify him on the ground that the stranding was not accidental. Roche J, held[19] that the claim succeeded. Her topmast had broken by accident, and there was no reason to suppose that she had got on to the sands otherwise than by accident.

In *Pateras v Royal Exchange Assurance*[20] a vessel was found to have been wilfully cast away[1] on a rock near the Burling Light off the Portuguese coast. Roche J, held that this had been done with the connivance of the owner. Amongst the evidence leading him to that conclusion was the fact that she was being employed very unprofitably round about the period of the loss, and that the chief officer, who had been her master, had been succeeded for the particular voyage by the owner's son.

In the words of the learned Judge:[2]

> 'The interests of the owners point to the desirability of such an end to the ship and that includes, if it were done, that it was not done otherwise than with their consent. The fact was that the vessel was over-insured; she was worth about £5,000 and she was insured against total loss, ship and freight, for about £15,000. This is a matter of which the owners were themselves fully cognisant, but it is not a matter which influences me at all in arriving at my conclusion that the ship was cast away. But when that fact co-exists with a conclusion that the ship was cast away by her navigators, and when it is also clear that the ship was, as most ships were, navigated very unprofitably about this period, and when I think it is also plain that by an arrangement to which the late Mr Pateras was a party, this master, his son, whom I have found guilty of the conduct which I have described, and who became master for this voyage and arranged, rather unusually, the particular employment which she should go upon, I think the conclusion is inevitable that the late Mr Pateras was a party to what was done.'

In *Grauds v Dearsley*[3] a vessel foundered in the Bay of Biscay. Talbot J, held that her loss was not due to an explosion, as her owner alleged, but was due to scuttling with his connivance. He reached this decision after consideration of a number of matters[4] including the fact that the evidence of the chief engineer was different at different times, the master's conclusion, in a few minutes after receiving the engineer's report, that the ship was sinking and must be abandoned as soon as possible, the absence of any real attempt to investigate

---

[14] Ibid, at 287.
[15] Ibid, at 287–288.
[16] Ibid, at 288.
[17] Ibid, at 288.
[18] (1932) 44 LlL Rep 103, KBD. The case also concerned insurable interest and the defence of non-disclosure of a material fact. As to these matters, see pp 17–18, ante, and pp 61–62, ante, respectively.
[19] (1932) 44 LlL Rep 103 at 118.
[20] (1934) 49 LlL Rep 400, KBD.
[1] For the evidence on this point, see ibid, at 407–409.
[2] Ibid, at 409.
[3] (1935) 51 LlL Rep 203, KBD. The learned Judge sat with Mr John McLaren as an assessor.
[4] See ibid, at 231.

further or to save the ship, and the false evidence which had been given as to the weather and sea conditions while she slowly sank.

In *Maris v London Assurance*[5] the insured vessel sank at night after striking a submerged rock off the island of Brusnik in the Adriatic. The insurers repudiated liability on the ground that she had been wilfully cast away with the connivance of the assured. Evidence was given that the weather was fine and that the sea was smooth. The vessel was abandoned soon after striking the rock. The chart and official log were brought away. There was no evidence of previous preparation or that the master and crew had brought away more than the barest belongings.

The Court of Appeal[6] held that the assured's claim succeeded, for it had been shown that the casualty was fortuitous.

In *Compania Naviera Vascongada v British and Foreign Marine Insurance Co Ltd*[7] a vessel was insured under a time policy. While on a voyage in ballast from Larne to Port Talbot, she sprang a leak through striking the quayside when manoeuvring to leave Larne Harbour, and through heavy weather sank in the Irish Sea. The assured claimed for a total loss, but the insurers contended that she had not been lost by the perils insured against, and had been intentionally lost by those in charge of her at the instigation or with the connivance of the assured.[8]

Branson J, held that the action succeeded. The assured had discharged the burden of proof of showing that the loss was fortuitous,[9] the master honestly believing that the vessel was so nearly in a sinking condition that it was time to abandon her and useless to try to tow her to port.

In *Canning v Maritime Insurance Co Ltd*[10] a vessel was lost off the Isle of Wight. It was found that she had been scuttled by her owner, though the master was not a party to his act.[11] Branson J, held that the claim under the policy failed. It was true that the share in the insurance money which the assured would have received was not large. But the ship was his living, and an accident had happened to the stuffing box, and there was no money available to repair it. His Lordship observed:[12]

> 'It is said that the plaintiff had so little to gain by the loss of the ship that it is inconceivable that he took such a risk for so small an advantage. But was that so? True, the share he would get in the insurance money was not large, but as he himself said, the ship was his living, an accident had happened to the stuffing box and there was no money available to repair it. He showed himself, in the witness box, to be a man of agile mind, and I have no doubt that he came to the conclusion that the best way to meet the difficulty was to sink the ship. His own story of his going to the captain when he himself did not believe that the ship would sink and suggesting that she should be beached and evidently persuading the captain that beaching was the only way to save the ship points in the same direction. Furthermore, it is very significant that the well in the hold was never sounded. I cannot conceive why it was not, except on the basis that the plaintiff knew that water was going in there.'

---

[5] (1935) 52 LlL Rep 211, CA.
[6] Greer, Slesser and Roche LJJ.
[7] (1935) 54 LlL Rep 35, KBD.
[8] Another aspect of the case, viz whether she had been sent to sea in an unseaworthy condition with the privity of the assured is considered at pp 305–306, post.
[9] As to the evidence, see (1935) 54 LlL Rep at 50–57.
[10] (1936) 56 LlL Rep 91, KBD.
[11] See ibid, at 104.
[12] Ibid, at 104.

In *Bank of Athens v Royal Exchange Assurance*[13] the insured vessel had been stranded near the Cape Saint Vito lighthouse owing to a wilful act of the master.[14] Branson J, held that a claim by the assured to recover for a constructive total loss failed on the ground that the stranding had been done at his instigation. In giving judgment he observed:[15]

> 'But once one is convinced, as I am, that the master wilfully cast the ship away, the inference that he did so with the connivance of the owner becomes irresistible when the owner has given false evidence in the box, when he had every inducement to throw his ship away, and when he neither asks for nor receives any explanation from the master of how the loss came about for at least three weeks after the event.'

This decision was subsequently affirmed[16] by the Court of Appeal.[17]

The vessel in *Compania Naviera Santi SA v Indemnity Marine Assurance Co Ltd: The Tropaioforos*[18] was registered in Panama and was insured for £160,000. At the time of her loss in good weather in the Bay of Bengal it was clear that she could not have much of a future as a trading vessel because freight rates had slumped alarmingly and she was nearly 40 years old. The assured claimed under their policy for a loss by perils of the sea.

Pearson J, held that on a balance of probabilities they had failed to prove their case, and that the vessel had been scuttled.[19] The evidence which led his Lordship to this conclusion was composed of a great many facts pointing the same way. Instead of an SOS message being sent out, the master had sent a private telegram to the ship's London agents stating that water had entered the engine and boiler room, and that he had ordered the crew to abandon her. The

---

[13] (1937) 57 LlL Rep 37, KBD.
[14] For the evidence on this point, see ibid, at 57–58.
[15] Ibid, at 62.
[16] (1937) 59 LlL Rep 67, CA.
[17] Greer, Slesser and Scott LJJ.
[18] [1960] 2 Lloyd's Rep 469, QBD (Com Ct). The case lasted 42 days, and the costs were reported to have amounted to £90,000.
[19] The subsequent history of the case is noteworthy. Judgment was given in December 1960. The assured lodged an appeal against the decision, but in October 1961 applied to the Court of Appeal for it to be withdrawn, and this application was granted. The vessel had been insured with 53 other insurance companies besides the Indemnity Marine Assurance Co Ltd, and also with 2,093 Lloyd's underwriters, and the assured company, when it commenced the action, agreed to be bound by the result. Nevertheless in June 1961 it started proceedings in the Greek Courts against two of the companies in respect of the loss of the vessel, and in the following October instituted further proceedings against some of the other insurance companies and the underwriters concerned. In December 1961 all the insurance companies and underwriters issued a writ against the assured claiming an injunction to restrain all proceedings against them in any country whatsoever. The assured did not enter an appearance or deliver a defence. The injunction was granted by McNair J, in January 1962. The case again came before the court sub nom *Royal Exchange Assurance v Compania Naviera Santi SA: The Tropaioforos (No. 2)* [1962] 1 Lloyd's Rep 410, QBD (Com Ct) on an application by the assured for the injunction to be set aside. Megaw J, declined to do so. He said (ibid, at 418) that the assured had litigated in this country deliberately and voluntarily in respect of the very matters concerning which it now sought to obtain a reversal of the decision of the courts of this country, and had done so when it was still exercising its right of appeal in this country. Further, the litigation here had been conducted on the basis of an agreement that it would not litigate elsewhere. But the assured had broken the agreement, and had commenced proceedings in the Greek courts in respect of the same matters. Although the assured was not resident within the jurisdiction and had no assets here, his Lordship considered that he was entitled to order the stay of all further proceedings because its conduct amounted to 'an abuse of the process of the court'. It was at any rate vexatious and oppressive.

telegram was false, for it gave her position wrongly. It had been sent deliberately to prevent early discovery of the vessel. When an SOS message was sent out 30 minutes later, once again the wrong position was given. Two and three-quarter hours later the ship went down, and the correct position was then sent out. When her crew were picked up by another ship, they were found to have brought their luggage with them, and the master was perfectly dressed and clean shaven. But, when he was asked for the logs, he said that they had gone down with the ship.

In *Astrovlanis Compania Naviera SA v Linard (The Gold Sky)*[20] a vessel sank off Gibraltar and the assured claimed an indemnity from the insurer in respect of a total loss by perils of the sea. They contended that a large vertical crack in the shell plating on the port side low down in the engine room had developed and the resulting jet of seawater which came in had proved impossible to control. The insurer put the assured to strict proof that the vessel had been lost by perils of the sea, and, in the alternative, alleged that she had been scuttled with the assured's connivance.[1] Evidence was adduced to show that the vessel had sunk with a salvage tug standing by, and that she had refused offers of assistance by the tug.

Mocatta J, held that the insurer had not proved beyond reasonable doubt that the vessel had been scuttled,[2] but that the assured had not proved, on a balance of probabilities, that her loss was fortuitous.[3] Accordingly, the claim failed.

In *N Michalos & Sons Maritime SA v Prudential Assurance Co Ltd, The Zinovia*[4] a vessel ran aground in the Gulf of Suez and became a constructive total loss. The assured claimed an indemnity under the policy on the ground that she had been lost by a peril of the sea. The insurers repudiated liability alleging that the assured had recruited a person as chief officer to join the vessel at Port Said with a view to running her aground. Bingham J, gave judgment for the assured for, on the evidence,[5] the insurers had not satisfied the court that the vessel had been deliberately cast away, and the owners had succeeded in showing that the loss was caused by a peril of the sea, i e grounding due to negligent navigation and her subsequent pounding on the bottom.

Particulars of scuttling

Where the insurers allege that a vessel has been scuttled, RSC Ord 18, r 12(1)[6]

---

[20] [1972] 2 Lloyd's Rep 187, QBD (Com Ct).
[1] The insurer also contended that the assured was in breach of the duty imposed by the Marine Insurance Act 1906, s 78(4). As to this point, see pp 449–450, post.
[2] [1972] 2 Lloyd's Rep at 217.
[3] Ibid, at 216.
[4] [1984] 2 Lloyd's Rep 264, QBD (Com Ct).
[5] The evidence is set out ibid, at 273–303.
[6] Which states:
'Subject to paragraph (2), every pleading must contain the necessary particulars of any claim, defence or other matter pleaded including, without prejudice to the generality of the foregoing words—
   a   particulars of any misrepresentation, fraud, breach of trust, wilful default or undue influence on which the party pleading relies; and
   b   where a party pleading alleges any condition of the mind of any person, whether any disorder or disability of mind or any malice, fraudulent intention or other condition of mind except knowledge, particulars of the facts on which the party relies.'

and Ord 72, r 7(2),[7] and fair treatment require that so far as practicable the matter should be pleaded with particularity so that the assured may know what case he has to meet.[8] This does not mean that the assured is entitled to know what evidence will be adduced against him, nor is he entitled to particulars of circumstantial matters from which inferences will be sought to be drawn.[9] But he is entitled to have the best particulars available of those circumstances which the insurers will, whether by direct evidence or by inference, attempt to establish as constituting scuttling.[10]

Burden of proving connivance by assured

The question as to whether the burden of proving[11] that a vessel has been wilfully cast away with the privity of the assured lies on the insurer was alluded to in *Anghelatos v Northern Assurance Co*,[12] but the House of Lords left it open. The Earl of Birkenhead observed:[13]

> 'It has, for instance, been much discussed whether, when a plaintiff produces an insurance policy and gives evidence of the stranding of the ship, he thereby shifts on to the insurance company the onus of showing that the stranding was not accidental, but was the result of fraudulent contrivance. Some difference of judicial opinion has appeared in the courts below. It is said, on the one hand, that if the plaintiff adduces evidence that the ship has been sunk, it is then for the underwriters to discharge effectively the onus of showing that the ship was not accidentally, but dishonestly, sunk. It is said by some judges, on the other hand, that it is for the plaintiff in such cases to show not only that the ship perished, but that the ship perished by the risk insured against. My Lords, it is almost certain that this matter will one day require careful consideration by your Lordships when it arises as an issue which actually requires decision in this House, but, having regard to the view which I have formed, and as I understand your Lordships have all found, this is not such a case. It is not, in other words, for us, differing from our usual practice, to lay down a rule in abstracto when the conclusion we have reached absolves us from the necessity of a general pronouncement.'

Further, Lord Sumner said:[14]

> 'It is unnecessary on this occasion to deal with the onus of proof. In view of what was said by Scrutton LJ, I think it is desirable to say this explicitly: That the question whether *Samuel v*

---

[7] Which states:
'Without prejudice to Ord 18, r 12(1), no particulars shall be applied for or ordered in an action in the Commercial List except such particulars as are necessary to enable the party applying to be informed of the case he has to meet or as are for some other reason necessary to secure the just, expeditious and economical disposal of any question at issue in the action.'
[8] *Palamisto General Enterprises SA v Ocean Marine Insurance Co Ltd, The Dias* [1972] 2 Lloyd's Rep 60 at 73, CA (per Buckley LJ).
[9] Ibid, at 73 (per Buckley LJ).
[10] Ibid, at 73 (per Buckley LJ). See further, *Astrovlanis Compania Naviera SA v Linard (The Gold Sky)* [1972] 1 Lloyd's Rep 331, CA, where an order for particulars of scuttling would have been made, but was not made, in fact, because the application had been made too late, for it should have been made as soon as the defence was delivered. (See the judgment of Lord Denning MR, ibid, at 333, that of Edmund Davies LJ, ibid, at 338, and that of Stephenson LJ, ibid, at 339.)
[11] For an American case concerning the question of the burden of proof in a case of alleged scuttling, see *Northwestern Mutual Life Insurance Co v Linard (The Vainqueuer)* [1973] 2 Lloyd's Rep 275 (SDNY). (See the judgment of Ward DJ, ibid, at 280–282.) In this case it was held that although the proof was insufficient for the court to find that the vessel had been scuttled, the assured had failed to discharge the burden of proving that the loss fell within the policy. This decision was subsequently affirmed by the United States Court of Appeals, Second Circuit: [1974] 2 Lloyd's Rep 398.
[12] (1924) 19 LlL Rep 255, HL. For the facts of the case, see p 237, ante.
[13] (1924) 19 LlL Rep at 256.
[14] Ibid, at 262.

Dumas,[15] a decision of your Lordships' House this year, has not now in any way affected the burden of proof is a question that will have to be seriously considered at some time. If it is the case that loss by wilful misconduct by the assured is a mere exception out of a prima facie general liability from loss by stranding or by foundering, then I can well understand why the law says those who allege that exception must prove it, namely, the underwriters, but if it be that the law as I understand it lays down finally that an assured is insured against accidental stranding, but not against designed stranding, then it may well be that the assured only brings himself within the proposition that he has proved a loss by perils insured against, if he proves the circumstances of the loss were circumstances of accidental stranding. I, therefore, think that point should explicitly be kept open for future decision.'

The important question of the burden of proof in the case of a claim for a loss by barratry was considered by the Court of Appeal[16] in *Elfie A Issaias v Marine Insurance Co Ltd*[17] in which it had to be decided whether the scuttling[18] of the vessel had been carried out by the orders or with the concurrence of the owner. Warrington LJ, observed:[19]

'In the present case the cause of the loss has been ascertained and is no longer in dispute. Prima facie it was an act of barratry and would be one of the perils insured against; and it is for the underwriters to show that the wrongful act of the master was not committed "to the prejudice" of the owner inasmuch as it was connived at by him. I apprehend that to cast away a man's ship without his consent is "to his prejudice" although the pecuniary effect may be to his advantage.'

To similar effect is a passage in the judgment of Atkin LJ:[20]

'The charge of privity against the owner makes against him an allegation of what would be a crime if committed in respect of an English ship, and what, in the absence of evidence to the contrary, I am entitled to assume is a crime by Greek law if committed in respect of a Greek ship; and is in any case a charge of very serious dishonesty. The plaintiff is entitled to invoke in his favour a principle of English law so well established that it is somewhat surprising to find little reference to it in some recent cases, the principle of presumption of innocence. I will cite from Stephen on Evidence, Art 94: "The burden of proving that any person has been guilty of a crime or wrongful act is on the person who asserts it, whether the commission of such act is or is not directly in issue in the action."

It is hardly necessary to cite authority, but I will refer to *Williams v East India Co* (1802) 3 East 192, per Lord Ellenborough at 199, an interesting case, for it threw on the plaintiff the burden of proving a negative:

"The rule of law is that where any act is required to be done on the one part, so that the party neglecting it would be guilty of a criminal neglect of duty in not having done it, the law presumes the affirmative and throws the burthen of proving the contrary, that is, in such case of proving a negative, on the other side."

One might refer to numerous works of authority in support, for example, Taylor on Evidence, 11th edn, s 112, and passages there cited. The same article in Stephen begins with a proposition which I also think is well established: "If the commission of a crime is directly in issue in any proceeding, criminal or civil, it must be proved beyond reasonable doubt."

These propositions are the very cornerstone of British justice, and have contributed more

---

[15] [1924] All ER Rep 66, HL.
[16] Lord Sterndale MR, Warrington and Atkin LJJ.
[17] (1923) 15 LlL Rep 186, CA. In *Steam Tanker Padre Island Inc and Pullman Bank and Trust Co v London Assurance, Guildhall Insurance Co, The Padre Island* [1971] 2 Lloyd's Rep 431 (SDNY), where the assured contended that the loss of the vessel resulted from barratry, Garza DJ, said (ibid, at 432) that there had been much discussion about which party had the burden of proof on the particular issues, and that it was sufficient to say that regardless of which party had the various burdens, the evidence produced by the insurers carried the burden as to all relevant issues.
[18] As to this aspect of the case, see p 236, ante.
[19] (1923) 15 LlL Rep at 189.
[20] Ibid, at 191. See also the judgment of Lord Sterndale MR, ibid, at 189.

than any other to establishing its fame: and I venture to think, despite the uneasiness felt at the suggestion by Counsel for the defendants, that they apply even to actions brought against underwriters. The question, therefore, is whether the defendants have succeeded in proving beyond reasonable doubt that the owner was privy to the act of the captain in scuttling the ship—not necessarily by knowing or directing the particular act but by procuring, either by direct order or by hint or suggestion, or by even omitting to prevent a known or suspected intention in some way wilfully to lose the ship.'

In *Pateras v Royal Exchange Assurance: The Sappho*[1] Roche J, said:[2]

'But substantially in my view the rule as to onus of proof is quite correctly stated by Lord Justice Bankes when the case of the *Compania Martiartu* was in the Court of Appeal. It is there reported in [1923] 1 KB 650, and the gist of the matter is that although there is, of course, and must be, a strong presumption against the commission of an act so criminal as the wilful throwing away of a ship, yet if the matter be really uncertain as between that explanation of the loss and a fortuitous explanation of the loss, the onus of proof is on the plaintiffs. Here, I have come to a conclusion definitely adverse to the plaintiff; but at all events I should, as Lord Justice Bankes did in that case, be of opinion that I should find it impossible to say that the plaintiffs had established to my satisfaction that the loss of the vessel was due to a peril covered by the policy, that is to say, that it was fortuitous.'

He then went on to say that in his opinion the question of the burden of proof was seldom of importance, and observed:[3]

'It is a matter not only of reluctance but of mixed opinion on my part, that one must be very slow to assume against anybody that they would be guilty of the act of throwing away a ship, and, accordingly, the prima facie explanation of accidental loss is easily established and is easily founded, and it takes a good deal to persuade me at any rate that there is a rival explanation of sufficient plausibility to displace the presumption that there was an accident. But such things are done, and in this case I have, after giving the matter the most anxious consideration, arrived at the conclusion that the explanation of this case is not accident but design.'

In *Piermay Shipping Co SA and Brandt's Ltd v Chester: The 'Michael'*,[4] however, Kerr J, said[5] that the assured must establish a loss by barratry, which involved establishing both a deliberate sinking and the absence of the assured's consent. If at the end of the day the court was left in doubt whether the assured consented or not, then the claim would fail.

He said that in *Elfie A Issaias v Marine Insurance Co Ltd*[6] the assured claimed in the court of first instance that the loss was due to perils of the sea as against scuttling, and Bailhache J, held that the vessel had been scuttled. The assured failed to persuade the Court of Appeal that the sinking was accidental and not deliberate. But they then also contended in the alternative that they could rely on a loss by barratry and attacked the Judge's findings on the question of privity, although barratry had not been pleaded and had never been raised before. The Court of Appeal allowed the appeal to proceed on that basis, and disagreed with the inference of privity drawn by the Judge. It was suggested as one of the arguments for the insurers that, once the court was satisfied that the vessel had been sunk deliberately by a member of the crew, a presumption of privity at once arose. That was unanimously negatived by the court and it was

---

[1] (1934) 49 LlL Rep 400, KBD.
[2] Ibid, at 407.
[3] Ibid, at 407.
[4] [1979] 1 Lloyd's Rep 55, QBD (Com Ct).
[5] Ibid, at 66.
[6] (1923) 15 LlL Rep 186, CA. See p 236, ante.

held that the presumption was the other way because the assured could rely on the presumption of innocence. But perhaps because the issue arose in that way the judgments contained passages which lent themselves to the interpretation that even in a claim for barratry alone, an assured need prove no more than that the vessel was sunk deliberately, and the burden of establishing privity then shifted to the insurers.

Kerr J, said[7] that he could not think that that was correct in principle. In the ultimate analysis one must distinguish between what the assured had to establish in order to raise a prima facie case of a loss by an insured peril i e barratry and what the insurers must establish by way of defence if (but only if) the assured first made out a prima facie case. The insurers had two strings to their bow. They could say that there was no case to answer because the assured had failed to make out a prima facie case; and they could go further and seek to establish a positive defence of scuttling. He thought that the relevant passages in the *Elfie A Issaias v Marine Insurance Co Ltd*[8] were directed to the latter aspect where the burden of establishing privity would clearly be on the insurers. When the case went[9] to the Court of Appeal,[10] Roskill LJ, said:[11]

'But we wish to repeat what we said in giving a brief judgment formally dismissing the appeal, that the fact that we are agreeing with the conclusion reached by the learned Judge must not be taken as approval by this court of his views upon the question of burden of proof. It may assist if and when this question arises for decision if we indicate how the argument might perhaps be advanced the other way, an argument seemingly not fully advanced below since its logical result, if correct, must have been, we would have thought, that underwriters should have opened the case on the basis that once deliberate sinking was admitted the entire burden of proving privity rested on them. The learned Judge appears to have reached his view because of the definition of barratry in r 11 of the Rules of Construction annexed to the Marine Insurance Act 1906. But with respect, he does not appear to have paid much regard to the decision of this Court in *Elfie A Issaias v Marine Insurance Co Ltd*.[12] The Court of Appeal hearing that appeal included both Lord Sterndale MR, and Atkin LJ (as he then was). The reports of their judgments contain statements clearly inconsistent with the learned Judge's view. We have not overlooked that in *Demetriades v Northern Assurance Co (The Spathari)*,[13] a majority of the Second Division of the Inner House appear to have treated the *Issaias* case as irreconcilable with *Compania Martiartu v Royal Exchange Assurance*.[14] When *The Spathari* reached the House of Lords,[15] the appeal failed without the question of scuttling or of privity or onus being further considered. We draw attention to the fact that in the *Issaias* case this court regarded the *Martiartu* case as irrelevant. In *Martiartu* the plaintiffs asserted but failed to prove a fortuitous loss. The burden was on them to do so. Underwriters sought to prove scuttling with privity. The burden was on them to do so. They succeeded. But in the *Issaias* case, as the facts were determined in the Court of Appeal, the sinking was held to be, as in the present case it was agreed to be, not fortuitous but deliberate. The only remaining issue, there as here, was privity. Atkin LJ, and the other members of the court clearly thought and said that in such a situation the burden of proof was on underwriters and that the assured was entitled to the benefit of the presumption of innocence. We ask but do not answer, for it is not necessary so to do, whether in these circumstances it was open to the learned Judge, or would, indeed, be open to us in this court, not to follow the decision in the *Issaias* case in the present case in which deliberate sinking was admitted and the only issue was privity. Finally we think it right to

---

[7] [1979] 1 Lloyd's Rep 55 at 67.
[8] Supra.
[9] [1979] 2 Lloyd's Rep 7.
[10] Roskill and Brandon LJJ, and Sir David Cairns.
[11] [1979] 2 Lloyd's Rep 7 at 12.
[12] (1923) 15 LlL Rep 186. See p 236, ante.
[13] (1923) 17 LlL Rep 327.
[14] [1923] 1 KB 650, CA; affd [1924] AC 850, HL.
[15] (1925) 21 LlL Rep 265.

record, with reference to a passage in the judgment of Mocatta J, in *Astrovlanis Compania Naviera SA v Linard, The Gold Sky*[16] on onus of proof, that Mr Evans frankly accepted that in that case as counsel for underwriters he had failed to remind the learned Judge of the decision of this court in *Hornal v Neuberger Products*,[17] to which Kerr J refers.'[18]

In *N Michalos & Sons Maritime SA v Prudential Assurance Co Ltd, The Zinovia*[19] Bingham J, said that in the case of barratry it was necessary to prove the loss and its causation by that peril. This would involve the assured in proving a deliberate casting away and the absence of consent on his part. In the absence of suspicious circumstances, lack of consent might readily be inferred, and very little in the way of proof might be necessary. But it would still seem wrong in principle that the burden of disproving an essential ingredient of the assured's claim should be laid on the insurers.

Accordingly, he was of the opinion that once the assured had proved a casting away by the deliberate act of the master or crew it was for the insurers to prove that the owners consented to or connived at the casting away.[20]

Standard of proof

The issue of barratry is effectively concerned with the presence or absence of fraud on the part of the assured. The issue arises in a civil case and the standard of proof required is therefore less than in a criminal case. Generally, issues of fact in civil cases are decided on a balance of probability, but the more serious the issue, the higher will be the standard of proof required. This consideration has to be borne in mind in relation to the contentions on both sides, which are really obverse sides of the same coin. It clearly applies to the insurers' positive allegation of scuttling and to some extent in the converse way to the assured because it may well be that they start with some measure of a presumption of innocence in their favour. At the end of the case the issue is then whether, on the balance of probability, they can still rely on the presumption.[1]

3 LOSS CAUSED BY DELAY

Section 55(2)(b) of the Marine Insurance Act 1906 states:

> 'Unless the policy otherwise provides, the insurer on ship or goods is not liable for any loss proximately caused by delay, although the delay be caused by a peril insured against.'

In *St Margaret's Trust Ltd v Navigators & General Insurance Co Ltd*[2] a ketch insured under a time policy was put on a mud berth at Lymington. She slipped over and filled with water, and was later raised and towed to Pylewell Creek. No further steps were taken, and she gradually deteriorated and had no more than her break up value. Morris J, held that the assured was not entitled to an

---

[16] [1972] 2 Lloyd's Rep 187 at 216–217.
[17] [1957] 1 QB 247, [1956] 3 All ER 970.
[18] [1979] 1 Lloyd's Rep 55 at 67.
[19] [1984] 2 Lloyd's Rep 264, QBD (Com Ct).
[20] Ibid, at 272.
[1] [1979] 1 Lloyd's Rep at 67. See further *N Michalos & Sons Maritime SA v Prudential Assurance Co Ltd, The Zinovia* (supra), where Bingham J, at 272, alluded to the high standard required for proof of fraud in a civil case.
[2] (1949) 82 LlL Rep 752, KBD.

indemnity for a total loss under the policy because her eventual deterioration resulted from delay. All that he could recover, on the evidence adduced, was the expenses in raising her, which had been incurred under a 'sue and labour' clause[3] in the policy, and the estimated damage to her fittings caused by the submersion.

In *Federation Insurance Co of Canada v Coret Accessories Inc and Hirsh (trading as S A Hirsh & Co)*[4] a case of handbag parts were insured for a voyage from Barcelona to Montreal under a policy which contained a clause stating:

> 'Warranted free of claim for loss or damage arising from loss of market, or for loss, damage or deterioration arising from delay, whether such delay be caused by a peril of the sea or otherwise, unless the risk of delay be expressly assumed in writing hereon.'

The case was not delivered at Montreal, so the insurers paid the sum insured to the assured in exchange for a receipt signed by the assured's agent.[5] The receipt provided that:

> 'If at any time non-delivered goods be found in whole or in part, the undersigned undertakes to accept such goods and to reimburse the [insurers] to the extent of the insured value of the goods.'

The case was subsequently found and was delivered to the assured, who refused to accept delivery on the ground that the goods were seasonal, and as they had arrived late, could not be used. The insurers claimed repayment of the sum insured.

Collins J, giving judgment in the Quebec Superior Court, held that the action succeeded. He said that the loss had been caused by delay. The policy did not cover the event which gave rise to the loss, so the assured had no claim under it, and he must return the money paid by the insurers on the presumed loss. The learned Judge observed:[6]

> 'The fact that the [assured] was unable to use them when they were delivered because of their seasonal nature does not affect the legal situation. While the failure to deliver on time resulted in a monetary loss to the [assured] such a loss was not insured against. The [assured] was unable to satisfy the court that the loss covered by such a delay was covered by any term of the policy. Loss or damage arising from loss of market as well as loss, damage or deterioration arising from delay are specifically excluded. It was delay which caused the loss or damage. There was no obligation to deliver within a specified time. Consequently as the policy did not cover the event which gave rise to the loss, the [assured] has no claim under the policy and the money paid in good faith on a presumed loss must be returned by the [assured].'

4 ORDINARY WEAR AND TEAR

Section 55(2)(c) of the Marine Insurance Act 1906 states:

> 'Unless the policy otherwise provides, the insurer is not liable for ordinary wear and tear...'

In *Wadsworth Lighterage and Coaling Co Ltd v Sea Insurance Co Ltd*[7] a steam barge over 50 years old was insured under a time policy which provided:

---

[3] As to this aspect of the case, see pp 445–446, post.
[4] [1968] 2 Lloyd's Rep 109, Quebec Superior Court, District of Montreal.
[5] The court found that the agent was authorised by the assured to sign the receipt. As to this point, see ibid, at 110–111.
[6] Ibid, at 111.
[7] (1929) 34 LlL Rep 285, CA.

'This insurance is against the risks of total and/or constructive and/or arranged loss, including general average and salvage and damage to such vessel by collision with any other vessel, or with any fixed, floating or other object, or by fire, lightning, stranding or sinking.'

One night the vessel sank in the Coburg Dock, Liverpool. No one was on board at the time. There was no evidence of any accident which caused her to sink. The assured claimed for a total loss.

The Court of Appeal[8] held that the claim failed since the loss of the vessel was due to ordinary wear and tear.[9]

In the course of his judgment Greer LJ, observed:[10]

'A barge at some time or other comes to the end of its working life; it has had so much wear and tear that it is no longer able to withstand the wear and tear that is the ordinary incident of its every-day work. I think that the learned Judge has found that that was the reason why this vessel sank in dock on a quiet night when there was no wind and, so far as anybody could ascertain or imagine, no effective cause for making a barge which was in good condition sink. I not only see no reason for differing from the learned Judge but I see very strong reasons for agreeing with those findings. I think the explanation that was suggested by Mr Little in his evidence is one which cannot be accepted having regard to the other facts proved in this case. If there had been on the way to the dock or in passing into the dock an unusual bump, one would have expected that those on board would have known about it, and if they suffered the next morning the loss of their vessel, they would have had no difficulty in recollecting that there was an extraordinary bump the night before. In addition to that, I find it difficult to suppose that if there had been an unusual bump, it would not have been ascertained when the pumps were put on at four o'clock, $1\frac{1}{2}$ hours after the barge got into the dock, possibly two or three hours after the bump, certainly at least $1\frac{1}{2}$ hours after the bump; I feel a difficulty in supposing that it would not have been discovered that there was more than the normal amount of leakage with this particular barge.'

It was further held that, on the true construction of the policy, the clause set out above did not cover a loss due to wear and tear. On this point Scrutton LJ, said:[11]

'The Act says: "Unless the policy otherwise provides, the insurer is not liable for ordinary wear and tear"; and giving the best consideration I can to the matter, the policy does not seem to provide otherwise; it does not seem to me to provide that the insurer is liable for ordinary wear and tear. It would be very unusual that he should be, and I can find no words which do make him liable for ordinary wear and tear. The result will be, of course, that if the assured on this policy says: "I claim for total loss", the answer is that in the first part of the clause the total loss is only a total loss caused by the perils in the policy, which do not include wear and tear. If, as [Counsel] concluded in his argument, he says: "Very well, if I cannot get total loss, then I want the loss as partial under the latter part of the clause, by sinking," the answer seems to me again to be the same, that it is only sinking by perils insured against, and ordinary wear and tear is not one of the perils insured against in the body of the policy.'

Again, in *Capital Coastal Shipping Corpn and Bulk Towing Corpn v Hartford Fire Insurance Co (United States of America, Third Party): The Christie*,[12] where a tug sank and the assured claimed under the policy for a loss by perils of the sea, the District Court for the Eastern District of Virginia, Norfolk Division, gave judgment[13] for the insurers for, on the evidence, she had sunk through ordinary wear and tear.[14]

[8] Scrutton, Greer and Slesser LJJ.
[9] (1918) Lloyd's List and Shipping Gazette, 10 April 1918: [1955] 2 Lloyd's Rep at 391n.
[10] [1958] 1 Lloyd's Rep 546, QBD (Com Ct).
[11] Ibid, at 289. See also the judgment of Greer LJ, ibid, at 289–290, and that of Slesser LJ, ibid, at 290–291.
[12] [1975] 2 Lloyd's Rep 100.
[13] See the judgment of Hoffman DJ, ibid, at 104.
[14] The evidence is set out ibid, at 101–104.

In *Prudent Tankers Ltd SA v Dominion Insurance Co Ltd, The Caribbean Sea*[15] in the course of a voyage in the Pacific Ocean off the coast of Nicaragua, the vessel sank although the wind was Force 4 the weather fine and the sea and swell moderate. When the assured claimed for a loss under the policy, the insurers repudiated liability on the ground that it was caused by ordinary wear and tear. Robert Goff J, held that the claim succeeded for, on the evidence,[16] the loss was not due to that cause but to a 'latent defect in the machinery or hull', consisting of a defect in a wedge-shaped nozzle joined to the vessel's plate, and that loss was covered by the policy.[17]

In *Rhesa Shipping Co SA v Edmunds, The Popi M*[18] the insurers contended that a vessel which sank in the Eastern Mediterranean in calm seas and fair weather was lost due to her defective deteriorated and decayed condition. Bingham J, rejected this submission and held that, on the evidence,[19] the loss of the vessel was due to perils of the sea for the cause of water entering her was contact with a submerged submarine.[20] The House of Lords,[21] however, reversed the decision on the ground that the burden of proving that the loss was caused in this way lay on the assured, and they had failed to discharge it.[22]

5 INHERENT VICE

The doctrine of proximate cause involves the further proposition that the insurer is not liable for the loss occasioned by any inherent vice in the thing itself, e g spontaneous combustion, disease, decay or fermentation. Thus, s 55(2)(c) of the Marine Insurance Act 1906 states:

> 'Unless the policy otherwise provides, the insurer is not liable for . . . inherent vice or nature of the subject-matter insured . . .'

Willes J, said in *Blower v Great Western Rly Co*:[1]

> 'By the expression "vice" is meant only that sort of vice which by its internal development tends to the destruction or the injury of the animal or thing to be carried.'

Thus, in *Boyd v Dubois*[2] the insurer was held not liable for the spontaneous combustion of flax put on board in a damp condition.

In *Wilson, Holgate & Co Ltd v Lancashire and Cheshire Insurance Corpn Ltd*[3] 657 barrels of palm oil were insured for a voyage from Singapore to Liverpool. On arrival at Liverpool 107 of the casks were found to be in a very damaged condition, and there had been a leakage of about 4 per cent of the oil. When

---

[15] [1980] 1 Lloyd's Rep 338, QBD (Com Ct).
[16] The evidence is set out ibid, at 347–348.
[17] As to this aspect of the case, see p 160, ante.
[18] [1983] 2 Lloyd's Rep 235, QBD (Com Ct).
[19] For the evidence, see ibid, at 248.
[20] The insurers also contended that the vessel was lost through the negligence of the crew and that there had been a 'want of due diligence' on the part of the assured. As to this aspect of the case, see p 170, ante.
[21] Lord Fraser of Tullybelton, Lord Diplock, Lord Roskill, Lord Brandon of Oakbrook and Lord Templeman.
[22] (1985) Financial Times, 22 May.
[1] (1872) LR 7 CP 655 at 662.
[2] (1811) 3 Camp 133. See also *Koebel v Saunders* (1864) 17 CBNS 71.
[3] (1922) 13 LlL Rep 486, KBD.

the assured claimed for a loss under the policy, the insurers denied liability[4] on the ground that the loss was due to the insufficiency of the casks, i e inherent vice.

Bailhache J, held that the damage was due to bad stowage and not to inherent vice, and observed:[5]

> 'The first thing I have to determine is what was the cause of this leakage and the state of the casks when they arrived at Liverpool. I have come to the conclusion that the cause of it was the way in which and the hold in which these goods were stowed. Palm oil is a substance which has the consistency of thick grease. It is the sort of stuff you see put into the axle-boxes of railway carriages, and if stowed in a suitable hold with suitable ventilation and away from heat, when coming from a hot sea into a cold sea, has a tendency not to get more liquid but to get more solid. Palm kernel oil is a liquid oil which will penetrate almost anything. On the facts I have come to the conclusion that the barrels were in sufficiently good order when the consignment left Singapore, and the state in which they arrived was not due to the fact that the oil was originally packed in inefficient barrels.'

In *E D Sassoon & Co Ltd v Yorkshire Insurance Co*[6] 70 tin-lined cases of cigarettes were insured from Glasgow to Baghdad. The policy covered the ordinary marine risks and also damage by fresh water, mould or mildew. When the cases arrived at Baghdad, the cigarettes were mildewed and the tin linings of the cases were rusty on the inside and on the outside as well. When the assured claimed under the policy, they were met with the defence that the damage by mildew was due to an inherent vice in the goods.

The Court of Appeal[7] held that the claim succeeded because the loss was not due to inherent vice, but was due to a fortuitous risk covered by the policy. Bankes LJ, observed:[8]

> 'The [assured] by their evidence did negative the suggestion that the mischief arose as the result of inherent vice. The learned Judge did not find definitely what the cause of the mischief was, but he appears to have been strongly influenced by the evidence of one of the witnesses who suggested the cause of the mischief was condensation on the outside of the tin case which rusted through the tin as I understand it, and caused the rusty appearance both on the inside and outside of the tin lining and, as the result of that, moisture was admitted to the interior of the tin which caused the growth of the spores. The learned Judge did not definitely find that as the cause but he did find in favour of the assured that the two causes which were said to have operated necessarily to produce the mould or mildew complained of had no existence in fact.
>
> Under those circumstances, have the [assured] established their case? Have they established that the damage complained of was the result of some fortuitous circumstance and not the result of inherent vice? In my opinion they have.'

In *Bird's Cigarette Manufacturing Co Ltd v Rouse*[9] cigarettes were insured for a voyage from London to Cologne, and were found to be mildewed. The insurers refused to indemnify the assured on the ground that the loss had been caused by inherent vice. Bailhache J, held that this defence only partly succeeded, for while it was true that some of the cigarettes contained more moisture than they should have done for safe keeping and were foredoomed to mildew, others had been damaged by salt water,[10] and for such damage the insurers were liable.

---

[4] Other defences were that the goods were not properly described in the policy, and that there was non-disclosure of a material fact, viz the existence of another policy in respect of the goods, and the condition of the casks as stated in the bill of lading. As to these defences, see p 276, post, and pp 64–65, ante, respectively.
[5] (1922) 13 LlL Rep 486 at 487.
[6] (1923) 16 LlL Rep 129, CA.
[7] Bankes, Scrutton and Atkin LJJ.
[8] (1923) 16 LlL Rep 129 at 130. See also the judgment of Scrutton LJ, ibid, at 132–133, and that of Atkin LJ, ibid, at 133.
[9] (1924) 19 LlL Rep 301, KBD.
[10] As to the evidence, see ibid, at 302–303.

In *C T Bowring & Co Ltd v Amsterdam London Insurance Co Ltd*[11] some consignments of Chinese groundnuts were insured from Tsingtao to European ports. The policies covered the goods against the usual marine risks, and contained the following clause:

> 'To pay average and/or damage from sweating and/or heating when resulting from external cause if amounting to three per cent on each bag or on the whole.'

On arrival at various European ports the groundnuts were found to be damaged to a considerable extent by heating due to moisture. On a claim being made by the assured in respect of the loss, Wright J, held that the action failed because the heating was due to internal moisture, i e inherent vice,[12] and that the clause set out above protected the insurers from liability, and observed:[13]

> 'It seems to me, therefore, that the only explanation of the damage observed at the ports of discharge, the only explanation which fits in with all the theories and conditions to be considered, is the explanation which meets with the approval of the practical men; and the explanation is that the damage was solely and entirely due to the condition in which the goods where shipped.'

In *Whiting v New Zealand Insurance Co Ltd*[14] a cargo of paper hats shipped in wooden cases was insured under a policy containing a 'warehouse to warehouse' clause for a voyage from Kobe (in Japan) to London. On arrival some of the contents of the cases were found to be mouldy. When sued under the policy, the insurers denied liability on the ground that the damage had been caused by inherent vice. Evidence was given that other consignments had arrived in sound condition.

Roche J, held that the action succeeded. The mould was the result of fresh water damage sustained by the wooden cases on the quay before shipment.[15] His Lordship observed:[16]

> 'That which happened must have happened when they were on the quay before they were carried into the ship or in the lighter. I think there was wet on the quay which affected these cases, and from the cases went into the goods themselves in the form of moisture. I do not mean in the form of running water. The wet which affected the cases would set up that moist atmosphere which is shown to encourage the growth of this fungus, mould. Moisture of that sort originated in most of the cases through fresh water. Standing in pools on the quay is a peril which is insured against. Accordingly, I hold that the [insurers] are liable for damage occasioned by that cause.'

In *Gee and Garnham Ltd v Whittall*[17] 17 consignments of 112,000 aluminium kettles were insured under an 'all risks' policy from Hamburg to the United Kingdom. The Institute Cargo Clauses (Wartime Extension) were incorporated into the policy. Clause 6 of those clauses stated:

> 'This insurance shall in no case be deemed to extend to cover loss damage or expense proximately caused by delay or inherent vice or nature of the subject-matter insured.'

---

[11] (1930) 36 LlL Rep 309, KBD.
[12] The evidence is set out ibid, at 320–324.
[13] Ibid, at 324.
[14] (1932) 44 LlL Rep 179, KBD. The case also concerned the measure of indemnity. As to this aspect, see pp 433–434, post.
[15] (1932) 44 LlL Rep 179 at 180.
[16] Ibid, at 180.
[17] [1955] 2 Lloyd's Rep 562, QBD.

On arrival some of the kettles were found to be dented and others water-stained. Sellers J, considered that they were made of very thin metal, and that it was quite possible that some of the damage had been caused by uneven distribution or inadequate provision of wood wool resulting in pressure of one metal part against another during the handling of the goods.[18] Inadequate packing constituted 'inherent vice', and accordingly he gave judgment for the insurer, who had been sued for a loss under the policy.

His Lordship observed:[19]

> 'In those circumstances, I have come to the conclusion that the claim here of the underwriters that the damage in the bulk of the cases was due to the inadequate packing or even before transit started at all has been made out; and, inadequate packing, of course, brings the case under the plea of inherent vice in the goods.'

The learned Judge found that the stains on the kettles had been caused by the use of wood wool which was too wet because it had not been properly seasoned.[20] This too constituted 'inherent vice' for which the insurer was not liable.[1]

In *F W Berk & Co Ltd v Style*[2] the assured claimed to recover from the insurers the expenses of re-bagging and landing a cargo of kieselguhr[3] packed in paper bags, which burst whilst being transferred from the ship's hold to a lighter. The goods were insured on a voyage from Mostaganem to London against all risks of loss and/or damage from whatsoever cause arising. The policy incorporated the Institute Cargo Clauses (Wartime Extension), clause 6 of which stated:

> 'This insurance shall in no case be deemed to extend to cover loss damage or expense proximately caused by delay or inherent vice or nature of the subject-matter insured.'

The insurers denied liability on the ground that the kieselguhr was packed in paper bags, which were defective and inadequate to withstand the ordinary incidents of the transit in that the seams opened, because there was no adhesive or inadequate adhesive matter to keep them firmly closed and the contents secure during ordinary and necessary handling and carriage.

Sellers J, gave judgment for the insurers. He said that the subject-matter insured was kieselguhr packed in paper bags, and that the bags were defective on shipment,[4] and observed:[5]

> 'Notwithstanding the affidavit evidence about the bags used, and the samples recently sent to the plaintiffs and produced in court, I find that the [assured's] consignment of kieselguhr was packed in faulty and inadequate bags which leaked because they were insufficient to endure the ordinary contemplated handling and carriage. The faults in the manufacture of the bags could be accounted for by a failure in the machine or in the processes or by the inexperience or negligence of an operative or operatives concerned with making them; but whatever the cause, I find that the evidence establishes that the bags must have been inadequate from the outset.'

---

[18] As to the evidence of this point, see ibid, at 567–568.
[19] As to the evidence of this point, see ibid, at 569.
[20] For the evidence on this point, see ibid, at 569–570.
[1] The learned Judge, however, held that as regards a small proportion of the consignment which was wet-stained, there was evidence that it might have been wetted by rain while on the quay in London, and that such damage was recoverable. See ibid, at 570–571.
[2] [1955] 2 Lloyd's Rep 382, QBD.
[3] I e a diatomaceous earth, used as an absorbent of nitro-glycerine in the manufacture of dynamite: *Shorter Oxford English Dictionary* (3rd edn, revised 1964), Vol I, p 1084.
[4] As to the evidence on this point, see [1955] 2 Lloyd's Rep at 386–387.
[5] Ibid, at 387.

Contracting out of the protection of the Act

Section 55(2)(c) of the Marine Insurance Act 1906 contemplates that the parties may contract out of the statutory protection with regard to a loss due to the inherent vice of the goods.[6]

Thus, in *E D Sasson & Co Ltd v Yorkshire Insurance Co*,[7] Atkin LJ, said (obiter):[8]

> 'I think it is quite plain from the words of the Marine Insurance Act, s 55, sub-s 2(c) that a policy may provide, if it is done in express words, for the insurer being liable for losses which are excepted, the ordinary wear and tear, ordinary leakage and breakage and inherent vice from the nature of the subject-matter insured. The particular kind of loss, the amount of the loss, is one which, within the words of Lord Sterndale, is a loss that may or may not happen and not one which certainly must happen; if it was a loss which certainly must happen within the voyage, I doubt whether it could ever be made properly the subject-matter of a policy of insurance. It seems to me conceivable if apt words are used, that an assured might cover a loss occasioned by mould which he does not know enough about to know whether it will or will not happen during the voyage, and which, in fact, may happen during the voyage but which may not happen during the voyage.'

In *Dodwell & Co Ltd v British Dominions General Insurance Co Ltd*,[9] the assured were importers of two shipments of barrels of oil carried from Hankow, including transhipment at Shanghai to the United Kingdom. In the course of the transit there was a very serious and abnormal leakage of oil from the barrels. Heat on the voyage caused the staves of the barrels to shrink, and loosened the hoops. This was accentuated by the prolonged voyage and perhaps bad stowage. The two policies sued on covered all risks, i e war risks, general marine risks and particularly leakage. Bailhache J, gave judgment for the assured for the loss occasioned by the leakage, in so far as it was in excess of the ordinary leakage, under one policy. But in the case of the other policy the insurers had used the words 'including risk of leakage from any cause whatsoever'. His Lordship held them bound by their own expression, and said that the words 'clearly included all leakage to which these barrels of oil were subjected'. Accordingly, under the second policy the insurers had to pay for the whole of the leakage proved.

In *Overseas Commodities Ltd v Style*[10] a consignment of tins of pork had been insured from France to England. The principal question was whether the assured had complied with a warranty that all the tins were marked by the manufacturers with a code for verification of the date of manufacture.[11] But another matter which arose in the case was the interpretation of a clause[12] in the policy which stated that the perils insured against were:

---

[6] For an American case where a boat was insured under a policy covering 'latent defects', see *Robert A Parente v Bayville Marine Inc and General Insurance Co of America* [1975] 1 Lloyd's Rep 333, State of New York Supreme Court (Appellate Division), where it was held that a latent defect was one which could not be discovered by any ordinary test. (See the judgment of Judge Hopkins, ibid, at 333.)

[7] (1923) 16 LlL Rep 129, CA.

[8] Ibid, at 133.

[9] (1918) *Lloyd's List and Shipping Gazette*, 10 April 1918: [1955] 2 Lloyd's Rep 391n.

[10] [1958] 1 Lloyd's Rep 546, QBD (Com Ct).

[11] As to this point, see pp 292–293, post.

[12] Counsel for the assured said that this was the first case in which a policy, which specifically insured against inherent vice, had fallen to be decided. It was shown in the course of the trial that at the time in question it was the established practice in the United Kingdom, as between

'All risks of whatsoever nature and/or kind. Average irrespective of percentage. Including blowing of tins. Including inherent vice and hidden defect. Condemnation by authorities to take place within three months of the date of arrival in final warehouse in the United Kingdom but not exceeding five months in all from the date of manufacture.'

McNair J, said[13] that the policy, though it retained in the printed Institute Cargo Clauses (Extended Cover) a clause expressly excluding inherent vice, did in terms specially devised by the typed words defining the scope of the policy, contract out of the statutory protection, as s 55(2)(c) of the Act of 1906 contemplated might be done. But, in view of this departure from the normal form of cover, it was not unreasonable to suppose that the insurers would seek to limit the extension within certain bounds. The critical question was whether by the words used they had done so, or whether they had added a further peril in addition to inherent vice.

His Lordship held (obiter)[14] that it was clear that 'condemnation by authorities' meant condemnation on the grounds of unfitness for human consumption. Further, the words plainly imported a condition or qualification upon that which had gone before (i e 'Including blowing of tins. Including inherent vice and hidden defect'), and, as a matter of construction, they were the equivalent of 'Provided that condemnation takes place'.[15]

On this part of the case he concluded:[16]

'Furthermore, having regard to the peculiar nature of the subject-matter—namely, a pasteurized and not wholly sterilized pig product—it seems inconceivable that the underwriters should, with their eyes open, have accepted liability for loss by inherent vice developing at any time in the future, since such a product must inevitably, if not consumed within a limited period, suffer loss from inherent vice, for, being perishable, it necessarily contains the seeds of its own ultimate destruction.'

His Lordship also added[17] that if the solving of this question had been material for his judgment, he would have accepted the argument of Counsel for the insurer that if the assured claimed for a loss by inherent vice or hidden defect, he must show condemnation within the specified limits.

He said (obiter)[18] that for the purpose of the policy there was a 'condemnation by authorities' when the local inspecting officer certified that the goods in question were unfit for human consumption. The words were not to be construed strictly, and there was no need for the full procedure laid down by s 10 of the Food and Drugs Act 1938 to be carried out, viz the bringing of the food before the Justices of the Peace by the authorised officer of the local authority so that it could be condemned.

In *Soya GmbH Mainz Kommanditgesellschaft v White*[19] where a cargo of soya beans was insured against 'heat, sweat and spontaneous combustion', the House

---

the importer and the first wholesaler, for the importer to agree to indemnify him in respect of any tins condemned by the local authority as unfit for human consumption within ninety days from the date of the invoice. It was to protect themselves against this risk that the assured as importers had taken out the policy of insurance.
[13] [1958] 1 Lloyd's Rep 546 at 560.
[14] Ibid, at 560.
[15] Ibid, at 560.
[16] Ibid, at 560.
[17] Ibid, at 560.
[18] Ibid, at 560–561.
[19] [1983] 1 Lloyd's Rep 122, HL.

of Lords[20] held that by those words the policy 'otherwise provided' so as to displace the prima facie rule laid down in s 55(2)(c) of the Act that the insurer was not liable for loss through inherent vice.[21]

6 OTHER PERILS EXCEPTED BY THE MARINE INSURANCE ACT 1906

Section 55(2)(c) of the Marine Insurance Act 1906 states:

> 'Unless the policy otherwise provides, the insurer is not liable for . . . ordinary leakage and breakage . . . of the subject-matter insured, or for any loss proximately caused by rats or vermin, or for any injury to machinery not proximately caused by maritime perils.'

II EXCEPTIONS UNDER THE INSTITUTE CLAUSES

Various exceptions are to be found in the Institute Clauses and their extent depends on whether the particular set of clauses is concerned with the insurance of cargo, or hulls or freight.

1 CARGO CLAUSES

a The Institute Cargo Clauses (A)

The Institute Cargo Clauses (A),[22] contain:

  i a general exclusions clause;
  ii an unseaworthiness and unfitness exclusion clause;
  iii a war exclusion clause; and
  iv a strikes exclusion clause.

It will be observed that many of the exceptions under these clauses are substantially the same as those to be found in the Marine Insurance Act 1906.[23]

i General exclusions clause

By this clause the insurers exclude liability for

  a loss, damage or expense attributable to the wilful misconduct of the assured;
  b ordinary leakage, ordinary loss in weight or volume, or ordinary wear and tear of the subject-matter insured;
  c loss, damage or expense caused by insufficiency or unsuitability of packing[1] or preparation of the subject-matter insured;
  d loss, damage or expense caused by inherent vice or nature of the subject-matter insured;

---

[20] Lord Diplock, Lord Keith of Kinkel, Lord Scarman, Lord Roskill and Lord Templeman.
[21] At p 126.
[22] See Appendix III, pp 516–519, post.
[23] See pp 225–256, ante.
[1] 'Packing' is deemed to include stowage in a container or liftvan but only when such stowage is carried out prior to the attachment of the insurance or by the assured or their servants.

e loss, damage or expense proximately caused by delay, even though the delay caused by a risk insured against except expenses payable as a result of general average and salvage charges;
f loss, damage or expense arising from insolvency or financial default of the owners, managers, charterers or operators of the vessel; and
g loss, damage or expense arising from the use of any weapon of war employing atomic or nuclear fission and/or fusion or other like reaction or radioactive force or matter.

ii Unseaworthiness and unfitness clause

By this clause the insurers exempt themselves from liability for loss, damage or expense arising from:

a unseaworthiness of vessel or craft; or
b unfitness of vessel, craft, conveyance, container or liftvan for the safe carriage of the subject-matter insured,

where the assured or their servants are privy to such unseaworthiness or unfitness at the time the subject-matter insured is loaded in it.

But the insurers waive any breach of the implied warranties of the seaworthiness of the ship and fitness of the ship to carry the subject-matter insured to the destination unless the assured or their servants are privy to such unseaworthiness or unfitness.

iii War exclusion clause

This clause states that in no case does the insurance cover loss, damage or expense caused by

a war, civil war, revolution, rebellion, insurrection[2] or civil strife arising therefrom, or any hostile act by or against a belligerent power;
b capture, seizure, arrest or detainment (piracy excepted) and the consequences thereof or any attempt thereat; and
c derelict mines, torpedoes, bombs or other derelict weapons of war.

iv Strikes exclusion clause

This clause exempts the insurers from liability for loss, damage or expense

a caused by strikers, locked-out workmen or persons taking part in labour disturbances, riots or civil commotions; or
b resulting from strikes, lock-outs, labour disturbances, riots or civil commotions; or
c caused by any terrorist or any person acting from a political motive.

b The Institute Cargo Clauses (B) and (C)

The Institute Cargo Clauses (B)[3] and (C)[4] contain the same four clauses as in the Institute Cargo Clauses (A) except that

---

[2] For the meaning of this term, see Ivamy, *General Principles of Insurance Law* (4th edn, 1979) p 280.
[3] See Appendix III, pp 519–523.
[4] See Appendix III, pp 525–528.

i *to the 'General exclusions clause'* is added a further exception which states that the insurers will not be liable for

> 'deliberate damage to or deliberate destruction of the subject-matter insured or any part thereof by the wrongful act of any person or persons.'

ii *in the 'War exclusion clause'* the exception of detainment also excludes liability for detainment caused by piracy.

c The Institute War Clauses (Cargo)

i   The Institute War Clauses (Cargo)[5] contain

   a   a *'general exclusions' clause* which sets out the same exceptions as those set out in the Institute Cargo Clauses (B)[6] and (C),[7] but does not cover any claim based on loss or frustration of the voyage or adventure;
   b   an *unseaworthiness and unfitness exclusion clause* in the same form as in the Institute Cargo Clauses (A),[8] (B)[9] and (C)[10] thereof or any attempt thereat;
   c   derelict mines, torpedoes, bombs or other derelict weapons of war.

ii A *'strikes exclusion' clause* exempts the insurers from loss, damage, liability or expense caused by

   a   strikers, locked-out workmen, or persons taking part in labour disturbances, riots or civil commotions; and
   b   any terrorist or any person acting from a political motive.

iii A *'malicious acts' exclusion clause* states that the policy does not cover loss, damage or liability or expense arising from

   a   the detonation of an explosive.
   b   any weapon of war.

   and caused by any person acting maliciously or from a political motive.

iv A *'nuclear exclusion' clause* states that in no case does the policy cover loss.

d The Institute Strikes Clauses (Cargo)

These clauses[11] contain a 'general exclusions clause' and an 'unseaworthiness and unfitness exclusion clause'.

(1) General exclusions clause

This clause[12] exempts the insurers from liability for

---

[5] See Appendix III, pp 528–531, post.
[6] See pp 257–258, ante.
[7] See pp 257–258, ante.
[8] See pp 256–257, ante.
[9] See pp 257–258, ante.
[10] See pp 257–258, ante.
[11] See Appendix III, pp 528–532, post.
[12] See Institute Strike Clauses (Cargo), cl 3.

i loss damage or expense attributable to wilful misconduct of the assured;
ii ordinary leakage, ordinary loss in weight or volume or ordinary wear and tear of the subject-matter insured;
iii loss, damage or expense caused by insufficiency or unsuitability of packing[13] or preparation of the subject-matter insured;
iv loss, damage or expense caused by inherent vice or nature of the subject-matter insured;
v loss, damage or expense proximately caused by delay, even though the delay is caused by a risk insured against (except expenses payable as a result of general average and salvage charges);
vi loss, damage or expense arising from insolvency or financial default of the owners, managers, charterers or operators of the vessel;
vii loss, damage or expense arising from the absence, shortage or withholding of labour of any description whatsoever resulting from any strike, lock-out, labour disturbance, riot or civil commotion;
viii any claim based on loss of or frustration of the voyage or adventure;
ix loss, damage or expense arising from the use of any weapon of war employing atomic or nuclear fission and/or fusion or other like reaction or radioactive force or matter; and
x loss, damage or expense caused by war, civil war, revolution, rebellion, insurrection or civil strife arising therefrom, or any hostile act by or against a belligerent power.

(2) Unseaworthiness and unfitness clause

This clause[14] is in the same form as the Institute Cargo Clauses (A),[15] (B)[16] and (C),[17] and the Institute War Clauses (Cargo).[18]

2 HULL CLAUSES

The Institute Time Clauses (Hulls)[19] and the Institute Voyage Clauses (Hulls)[20] each contain the same clauses excepting liability:

i War exclusion clause;
ii Strikes exclusion clause;
iii Malicious acts exclusion clause;
iv Nuclear exclusion clause;
v Navigation clause; and
vi Three-fourths collision liability clause.

---

[13] 'Packing' is deemed to include stowage in a container or liftvan but only when such stowage is carried out prior to attachment of the insurance or by the assured or their servants.
[14] See Institute Strike Clauses (Cargo), cl 4.
[15] See pp 516–519, post.
[16] See pp 519–523, post.
[17] See pp 523–526, post.
[18] See pp 526–529, post.
[19] See Appendix III, pp 533–540, post.
[20] See Appendix III, pp 540–547, post.

i War exclusion clause

This clause[1] states:

> 'In no case shall this insurance cover loss, damage, liability or expense caused by
>
>> war, civil war, revolution, rebellion, insurrection or civil strife arising therefrom, or any hostile act by or against a belligerent power.
>>
>> capture, seizure, arrest, restraint or detainment (barratry and piracy excepted) and the consequences thereof or any attempt thereat.
>>
>> derelict mines, torpedoes, bombs or other derelict weapons of war.'

ii Strikes exclusion clause

This clause[2] states:

> 'In no case shall this insurance cover loss, damage, liability or expense caused by
>
>> strikers, locked-out workmen, or persons taking part in labour disturbances, riots or civil commotions.
>>
>> any terrorist or any person acting from a political motive.'

iii Malicious acts exclusion clause

This clause[3] states:

> 'In no case shall this insurance cover loss, damage, liability or expense arising from
>
>> the detonation of an explosive
>>
>> any weapon of war
>
> and caused by any person acting maliciously or from a political motive.'

iv Nuclear exclusion clause

This clause[4] states:

> 'In no case shall this insurance cover loss, damage, liability or expense arising from any weapon of war employing atomic or nuclear fission and/or fusion or other like reaction or radioactive force or matter.'

v Navigation clause

This clause[5] states:

> 'In the event of the vessel being employed in trading operations which entail cargo loading or discharging at sea from or into another vessel (not being a harbour or inshore craft no claim shall be recoverable under this insurance for loss or damage to the Vessel or liability to any other vessel arising from such loading or discharging operations, including whilst approaching, lying alongside and leaving, unless previous notice that the Vessel is to be employed in such operations has been given to the Underwriters and any amended terms of cover and any additional premium required by them have been agreed.'

---

[1] See Institute Time Clauses (Hulls), cl 23, and Institute Voyage Clauses (Hulls), cl 20.
[2] See Institute Time Clauses (Hulls), cl 24, and Institute Voyage Clauses (Hulls), cl 21.
[3] See Institute Time Clauses (Hulls), cl 25, and Institute Voyage Clauses (Hulls), cl 22.
[4] See Institute Time Clauses (Hulls), cl 26, and Institute Voyage Clauses (Hulls), cl 23.
[5] Institute Time Clauses (Hulls), cl 1, and Institute Voyage Clauses (Hulls), cl 1.

vi   The three-fourths collision liability clause

This clause[6] states that in no case does it extend to

   a removal or disposal of obstructions, wrecks, cargoes or any other thing whatsoever;

   b any real or personal thing whatsoever except other vessels or property on other vessels.

   c the cargo or other property on or the engagements of the insured vessel.

   d loss of life, personal injury or illness.

   e pollution or contamination of any real or personal property or thing whatsoever (except other vessels with which the insured vessel is in collision or property on such other vessels).

Institute War and Strikes Clauses (Hulls) (Time) and Institute War and Strikes Clauses (Hulls) (Voyage)

These clauses[7] include exceptions stating that (inter alia) the insurers are not responsible for loss, damage, liability or expense arising from

1. any detonation of any weapon of war employing atomic or nuclear fission and/or fusion or other like reaction or radioactive force or matter.
2. the outbreak of war (whether there be a declaration of war or not) between any of the following countries:

   United Kingdom, United States of America, France, the Union of Soviet Socialist Republics, the People's Republic of China.
3. requisition or pre-emption;
4. capture, seizure arrest, restraint detainment, confiscation or expropriation by or under the order of the government of any public or local authority of the country in which the Vessel is owned or registered;
5. arrest, restraint, detainment, confiscation or expropriation under quarantine regulations or by reason of infringement of any customs or trading regulations;
6. the operation of ordinary judicial process, failure to provide security or to pay any fine or penalty or any financial cause;
7. piracy.

In *Panamanian Oriental SS Corpn v Wright*[8] a vessel was insured under a policy which excluded liability for loss arising from (inter alia)

'arrest, restraint or detainment under quarantine regulations or by reason of infringement of any customs regulations.'

The vessel was boarded by Vietnamese customs officials. Unmanifested goods were found on board. A special military court acquitted the master of smuggling offences, but convicted some of the crew. The vessel was ordered to be confiscated. When the assured claimed for a loss under the policy, the

---

[6] Institute Time Clauses (Hulls), cl 8, and Institute Voyage Clauses (Hulls), cl 6.
[7] See Appendix III, pp 547–548, 549–554, post.
[8] [1971] 1 Lloyd's Rep 487, CA.

insurers repudiated liability on the ground that the exception was set out above applied. The Court of Appeal[9] held that they were entitled to do so, for they had proved the breach of customs regulations, and that the confiscation was the result of it. It was unnecessary for them to show that the special military court acted in good faith within its jurisdiction and free from political interference.[10]

3 FREIGHT CLAUSES

a Institute Time Clauses (Freight) and Institute Voyage Clauses (Freight)

The Institute Time Clauses (Freight)[11] and the Institute Voyage Clauses (Freight)[12] each contain the same exceptions as those in the Institute Time Clauses (Hulls)[13] but in addition state

> 'This insurance does not cover any claim consequent on loss of time whether arising from a peril of the sea or otherwise.'

In *Bensaude & Co v Thames and Mersey Marine Insurance Co*[14] a freight policy was effected in respect of a vessel under a charter-party. The policy contained a clause stating 'free from any claim consequent on loss of time, whether arising from a peril of the sea or otherwise'. The vessel broke down after being at sea for a day. On putting back to a port for repairs it was seen that the time that they would take would destroy the adventure. Consequently the charter-party was cancelled by the charterers. The owners sued on the policy for a total loss of freight. It was admitted that the vessel had been disabled consequent on a peril of the sea. It was held that the claim arose by reason of a loss of time, and that the loss of time was occasioned by a peril of the sea, and that the insurers were not liable.

Again, in *Turnbull, Martin & Co v Hull Underwriters' Association*[15] the policy was upon 'freight of frozen meat, chartered or as if chartered'. The refrigerating apparatus of the vessel was destroyed by fire before arrival at the port of loading, thereby rendering it impossible to carry the frozen meat. It was held that the claim made under the policy was 'consequent on loss of time' within the meaning of the clause, and the fact that the freight was not chartered freight made no difference, having regard to the words 'chartered or as if chartered'.

In *Atlantic Maritime Co Inc v Gibbon*,[16] where a vessel was prevented from entering the port of Taku Bar by the presence of a Chinese Nationalist warship during the civil war and it was held that this constituted a restraint of princes, the Court of Appeal[17] also held that the assured's claim for a loss under a freight

---

[9] Lord Denning MR, Fenton Atkinson LJ, and Sir Gordon Willmer.
[10] See the judgment of Lord Denning MR, [1971] 1 Lloyd's Rep at 493, that of Fenton Atkinson LJ, ibid, at 495, and that of Sir Gordon Willmer, ibid, at 495.
[11] See Appendix III, pp 550–554, post.
[12] See Appendix III, pp 555–558, post.
[13] See Appendix III, pp 533–540, post.
[14] [1897] AC 609.
[15] [1900] 2 QB 402. See also *Russian Bank of Foreign Trade v Excess Insurance Co* [1918] 2 KB 123. Cf *Asfar & Co v Blundell* [1896] 1 QB 123.
[16] [1953] 2 Lloyd's Rep 294, CA.
[17] Sir Raymond Evershed MR, Jenkins and Morris LJJ.

policy was barred by a 'frustration' clause.[18] The policy also contained a clause stating:

> 'Warranted free from any claim consequent on loss of time whether arising from a peril of the sea or otherwise.'

Sir Raymond Evershed MR, said obiter[19] that it was unnecessary for him to express a final view on the matter, but said that he considered that the clause did not apply to a case like the present one. Here the time element was relevant,[1] not as a consequence of the mishap, but in order to ascertain correctly the nature and quality of the accident. He then continued:[2]

> 'If, because of the length of time which is likely to subsist during which the peril lasts, it is justifiable to say "This finally disposes of the bargain", then the freight is lost then and there immediately upon the happening of the insured peril, and is attributable solely to that peril. The time element has only been essential in order to estimate correctly the extent of the peril; and if in point of fact the peril ceased a week or two weeks afterwards, that fact would be quite immaterial provided that the original decision was held, in the circumstances, to have been reasonably justified.'

Morris LJ, also said[3] that he considered it unnecessary to express any concluded opinion. If he might treat the matter as an open one as directed by Lord Atkin in *Robertson v Petros M Nomikos Ltd*[4] in the sense that the decided cases could merely be regarded as questions of fact which were not to trammel a fresh determination of the facts of a new case, then he expressed the doubt whether on the facts of the present case it could be said that the claim made was one consequent on loss of time.[5]

In *Naviera de Canarias SA v Nacional Hispanica Aseguradora SA: The Playa de las Nieves*[6] a vessel was let out under a time-charter-party containing an 'off hire' clause by which hire would cease to be payable in the event of a breakdown of machinery. Her owners took out a freight policy containing a clause stating:

> 'Warranted free from any claim consequent on loss of time whether arising from a peril of the sea or otherwise.'

The vessel sustained damage by breakdown of machinery and had to be repaired. She was 'off hire' during this period, and the owners claimed from the insurers the amount of hire which they had lost.

The House of Lords[7] held that the claim failed for the ensuing loss of hire could not be more appropriately described than as 'consequent on loss of time'.[8] Lord Diplock said[9] that it was a matter of common knowledge that

---

[18] As to the 'frustration' clause, see pp 264–267, post.
[19] [1953] 2 Lloyd's Rep at 312.
[1] Ibid, at 311.
[2] Ibid, at 311.
[3] Ibid, at 318.
[4] [1939] AC 371 at 377, HL.
[5] Jenkins LJ, said [1953] 2 Lloyd's Rep at 316 that he wished to add nothing to what Sir Raymond Evershed MR, had said.
[6] [1977] 1 Lloyd's Rep 457, HL.
[7] Lord Diplock, Viscount Dilhorne, Lord Simon of Glaisdale, Lord Salmon and Lord Fraser of Tullybelton.
[8] See the judgment of Lord Diplock: [1977] 1 Lloyd's Rep at 459.
[9] Ibid, at 459. Lord Diplock, however, considered that while it was not easy to envisage a case where **partial loss of hire** under a time charter-party would not be excluded by the clause, general average contribution and salvage charges on chartered freight would be covered by the policy.

there were available in the market policies which expressly covered loss by delay arising from perils insured against. It was exceptional however, for them to be taken out by shipowners because periods when a vessel came 'off hire' during the currency of a time charter-party were by no means uncommon and the uncertainty in the amount of the liability to which the insurer was exposed made the premium required for that type of insurance much higher than for a policy which contained a clause in the same form as in the present case. The premium for the cover on freight in the present case was 1·16 per cent, and represented about one-third of the amount of hire payable for a single day. It was difficult to believe that either shipowners or insurers ever supposed that for the premium cover was being given for 1 year against loss of hire withheld under the 'off hire' clause.

b Institute War and Strikes (Freight) Clauses

The Institute War and Strikes (Freight) Clauses[10] contain the same exceptions as those in the Institute War and Strikes Clauses (Hulls–Time)[11] but in addition state that the policy excludes liability for

> 'any loss based upon loss or frustration of the adventure.'

This clause is known as the 'Frustration Clause'.[12]

In *Atlantic Maritime Co Inc v Gibbon*[13] the Court of Appeal[14] decided by a majority that the loss of freight was caused by a restraint of princes, but held that the liability of the insurers was excluded by the 'frustration' clause.

Sir Raymond Evershed MR, stated:[15]

> 'If the adventure was lost, whether strictly the contract of affreightment was frustrated, by which I mean "frustrated" according to our law of contract—if the view taken by the master and the owners was justified, then the circumstances were such as had the equivalent effect and the adventure was lost—then the freight it would earn would have been lost also. But in my judgment, as I have earlier indicated, if the adventure was so lost, and was lost by reason of this interference by the warships, then I have come to the conclusion that the underwriters are absolved from liability by the frustration clause in the policy which I have already read. I repeat its terms here: "Nevertheless this policy is warranted free of any claim based upon loss of, or frustration of, any voyage or adventure caused by . . . restraints . . . of . . . princes", etc. I think, according to the plain sense of the language and the plain sense of the facts, it was on this hypothesis so lost, and the case falls within, and exactly within, the ordinary meaning of that paragraph.'

Morris LJ, was of the same opinion, and said:[16]

> 'The underwriters are, however, in my view relieved from liability by the terms of the clause

---

[10] See Appendix III, pp 558–561, post.
[11] See Appendix III, pp 547–549, post.
[12] This clause was introduced in policies as a result of the decision of the House of Lords in *British and Foreign Marine Insurance Co Ltd v Sanday & Co* [1916] 1 AC 650, where it was held that even though the insured goods were safe, a claim could be based upon loss of the adventure by reason of a peril insured against, viz a restraint of princes. See further, *Becker, Gray & Co v London Assurance Corpn* [1918] AC 101, HL. The history of the clause is summarised in Lord McNair and A D Watts, *Legal Effects of War* (4th edn, 1966), pp 270–275.
[13] [1953] 2 Lloyd's Rep 294, CA. The facts of this case are set out at pp 262–263, ante.
[14] Sir Raymond Evershed, and Morris LJ: Jenkins LJ, dissenting on this point.
[15] [1953] 2 Lloyd's Rep 294 at 306.
[16] Ibid, at 317. See also the judgment of Jenkins LJ, ibid, at 315, though his remarks were obiter on this point because he said that the loss was not caused by a restraint of princes.

which has been called the "frustration clause". Here the claim of the plaintiffs is that they have suffered the loss of the voyage or adventure, the subject of the charter-party of 16 July, and that such loss was caused by the restraint of "Kings Princes Peoples Usurpers or persons attempting to usurp power". That is in reality the claim made by the plaintiffs, even though they choose merely to say that the loss was caused by civil war. The purpose of the words in the frustration clause is to exclude a liability otherwise arising. The word "Nevertheless" by which the clause is introduced demonstrates that. It seems to me that the only question here is whether these words apply. In my view they do, and the claim made by the plaintiffs is covered by this exception clause which relieves the underwriters from liability.'

Restraint of princes imposed in civil war

In *Atlantic Maritime Co Inc v Gibbon*[17] the assured also contended that, although the prohibition was a restraint of princes, the intervention of the destroyers was also an incident or the consequence of a civil war and a warlike operation, and, as such, sufficed to support a claim based on one or other of those insured perils irrespective of its character as a restraint of princes.

Jenkins LJ, refused to accept this contention, and said that if the peril giving rise to the loss was a restraint of princes, and the warranty clearly operated as a bar to the claim, it made no difference that the restraint was imposed in the course of or in consequence of civil war. The only action taken by the destroyers relevant to the claim was the prohibition or restraint of loading at Taku Bar. Apart from such prohibition or restraint, there was nothing in their activity (whether regarded as civil war or warlike operations) which could be said to have brought about the loss of freight to which the claim related. The claim could not be effectively formulated otherwise than by alleging the prohibition or restraint. Clearly, the mere fact of civil war or warlike operations did not make performance of the voyage impossible. The vessel had made at least one voyage to and from Taku Bar while the civil war was in progress. The learned Lord Justice then observed:[18]

> 'Moreover, considering the matter purely as one of construction, I see no ground for construing the reference to restraints as meaning restraints imposed otherwise than in the course of or in consequence of civil war or warlike operations. That mode of construction, carried to its logical conclusion, would for practical purposes nullify the exception, for restraint of princes would seldom if ever occur otherwise than in association with another or others of the various perils insured against.'

Inapplicability to claim for loss of goods themselves

In *Forestal Land, Timber and Rlys Co Ltd v Rickards*[19] the policy in respect of a cargo to be carried from Buenos Aires for Hong Kong/Shanghai contained a clause stating:

> 'Warranted free of any claim based upon loss of, or frustration of the insured voyage or adventure caused by arrests restraints or detainments of Kings Princes Peoples Usurpers or Persons attempting to usurp power.'

The vessel carrying the goods deviated, and sought refuge in neutral ports on the orders of the German Government. She attempted to get back to Germany, but was scuttled by her crew to avoid being captured in the Allied blockade.[20]

---

[17] [1953] 2 Lloyd's Rep 294, CA.
[18] Ibid, at 315. See also the judgment of Sir Raymond Evershed MR, ibid, at 307.
[19] (1941) 70 LlL Rep 173, HL.
[20] The facts of the case are more fully stated at pp 127–128, ante.

When a claim was made under the policy, the insurers contended that it was barred by the 'frustration' clause.

The House of Lords[1] held that this contention failed. The policies covered both the goods themselves against their destruction, damage or deprivation, and also the expected benefit from their arrival. The 'frustration' clause did not operate to exclude a claim for loss of or damage to the goods themselves, which was notionally severable from a claim for loss of the adventure.

Lord Wright[2] said that the 'frustration' clause could not be applied to a case where the assured was claiming for loss of or damage to the actual physical things or chattels. He was entitled to resist the application of the clause on the ground that the primary subject-matter was the goods, and that the adventure was merely ancillary or accessory. A claim in respect of the loss of the adventure was an added benefit granted to the assured over and above his interest in the goods themselves. The exception was expressly by its language limited to the loss of, or frustration of, the insured voyage or adventure. Its language could not be twisted to make it cover a claim for actual loss or damage to the goods themselves.

Viscount Simon LC, said[3] that the proper interpretation of the frustration clause was not 'free of any claim which on the facts might be based on loss of the insured voyage'. Its proper meaning must be 'free of any claim which is in fact based and can only be based, upon loss of the insured voyage'.

Viscount Maugham said[4] that he could not see why the assured should not be able to claim an indemnity simply on the basis of loss of goods, and as if the doctrine of loss of adventure had never been accepted as part of our maritime law. The contract was an insurance against loss of two different kinds in relation to the goods. The first involved loss or damage to the goods themselves. The second involved merely that they had not reached their destination, though they might be perfectly safe. The 'frustration' clause was free from ambiguity. It relieved the insurers from liability in the cases under the second head, but it left their liability unaffected in cases under the first head, provided, of course, that the risk had not come to an end. Some importance must be attributed to the fact that the clause was limited to claims 'based upon' the loss of or frustration of the insured voyage.[5] The words, in their natural meaning, pointed to the way in which the claims were framed, and could not easily be read as extending to claims which might truly be said to be occasioned by the loss of or frustration of the adventure, but were really based upon the loss of or damage to the goods themselves.

Lord Porter said[6] that once the master sailed for a German port the goods were a constructive total loss at a moment when they were still being carried in the vessel and on the voyage insured in the policy. It was true that the adventure was put an end to by that loss, but the adventure was lost through the loss of the goods. The goods were not lost by reason of the loss of the adventure. The 'frustration' clause therefore had no application to the circumstances of the case. It was meant to deal, and its wording appropriately dealt, with a case where

---

[1] Viscount Simon LC, Viscount Maugham, Lord Thankerton, Lord Wright and Lord Porter.
[2] (1941) 70 LlL Rep at 193.
[3] Ibid, at 181.
[4] Ibid, at 183.
[5] Ibid, at 184.
[6] Ibid, at 203.

the assured, if he was to recover at all, must rely upon the loss of the adventure and could not rely upon the loss of the goods. His Lordship said that he would take this view even if the wording of the clause had been 'frustration of the adventure by restraint of princes always excepted'. But his view was strengthened when he found that the phrase used was 'warranted free of any claim based upon loss of the adventure'. No doubt it could be said that 'based upon' bore the same meaning as 'founded upon'. But whichever word was used, it was the claim which must be based or founded upon frustration in order to exonerate the insurers. 'Claim' suggested the form of claim adopted by the assured, not a possible claim which he might have made had he so desired.

III OTHER EXCEPTIONS EXPRESSLY STATED IN THE POLICY

CANCELLATION CLAUSE

Policies on freight often contain a clause stating:

> 'No claim arising from the cancelling of any charter shall be allowed.'

Such a clause is intended to apply to the case of charter-parties with cancelling clauses under which the charterer may cancel the charter-party for named causes, the most common of which is the non-arrival of the vessel at the port of loading by a specified time.

In time charter-parties, the right to freight may continue until cancellation, notwithstanding detention or delay on the part of the vessel caused, e g by perils insured against in the policy. In such cases the loss of freight would not arise until cancellation, and would be consequent on the cancellation and not on the peril causing the delay.[7]

Further, even in a voyage policy the loss of freight will be attributed to the exercise of the option to cancel, although the delay might be due to a peril insured against.[8]

But in a voyage charter-party with no such option the chartered freight may be lost by a peril insured against which detains the ship so long that it would not be reasonable to hold the charterer to his contract to provide a cargo. In such a case the insurer would be liable to pay the assured the freight so lost.[9]

In *The Alps*[10] it was held that where a cesser clause was put into operation through the direct action of perils insured against, the insurer was liable for the loss of freight.

Meaning of 'cancelling'

The cancellation must arise from some agreement between the parties, made either by a term in the charter-party enabling the charterer to cancel it on the happening of some named event, or by a special agreement arrived at during the existence of the charter-party.

But if no such agreement is made, the charter-party is not 'cancelled' and the

---

[7] *Inman SS Co v Bischoff* (1882) 7 App Cas 670.
[8] *Mercantile SS Co v Tyser* (1881) 7 QBD 73.
[9] *Jackson v Union Marine Insurance Co* (1874) LR 10 CP 125.
[10] [1893] P 109.

happening which prevents the vessel earning her freight is not a cancellation within the meaning of the clause in the policy, although the event may be such as to relieve the charterer from finding a cargo and from paying the chartered freight.

Thus, if a vessel under a charter-party on her way to the port of loading goes to the bottom, or is so delayed that the charterer is released from the obligation of finding a cargo and there is thus a loss of chartered freight, this does not operate as a cancellation of the charter-party under this clause so as to relieve the insurer.

If it had that effect, a policy on chartered freight with such a clause would be almost valueless to the assured.[11]

IV QUALIFIED UNDERTAKINGS OF THE INSURER

Sometimes the undertaking of the insurer is qualified by the terms of the policy. If a loss occurs which is outside the scope of the limit of the undertaking, there is no liability.

Thus, the undertaking of the insurer may be qualified by:

1. The Institute Trading Warranties.
2. Other clauses referring to the area of operation of the insured vessel.
3. Clauses concerning the towing of the vessel.
4. Clauses relating to deck cargo.
5. Clauses relating to the experience of the crew.

1 THE INSTITUTE TRADING WARRANTIES[12]

These state that the vessel is not covered by the terms of the policy if she is, e g in the Great Lakes between certain dates or St Lawrence Seaway west of Montreal between certain dates, the Behring Sea.

Nor will she be covered if she sails from any port or place in Siberia except Nakhodka and/or Vladivostock.

There are certain periods of time in which she will not be covered if she sails with a cargo of Indian coal.

2 OTHER CLAUSES AS TO AREA OF OPERATION

In *Mountain v Whittle*[13] a houseboat was insured under a time policy against, inter alia, perils of the sea 'whilst anchored in a creek off Netley, however employed, with liberty to shift . . . including all risk of docking, undocking, changing docks, and going on gridiron or graving docks as may be required'. The vessel needed cleaning, so the assured arranged for her to be towed to a yard at Northam, which was the nearest place where she could be docked. A tug

---

[11] *Re Jamieson and Newcastle SS Freight Insurance Association* [1895] 2 QB 90.
[12] These warranties are set out in Appendix III, pp 561–562, post.
[13] [1921] 1 AC 615, HL.

was employed for the purpose, but she was too powerful, and an unusually high breast wave from her caused the houseboat to sink. When a claim for a loss by perils of the sea[14] was made under the policy, the insurer contended that the loss was not covered because the 'liberty to shift' clause and the 'docking' clause were not apt to cover a voyage of 7 miles to a different part of the coast.

The House of Lords[15] held that the claim succeeded. The 'liberty to shift' clause was not apt to cover the 7 mile voyage, but the 'docking' clause was, for it must be construed as extending the policy to cover a voyage to such a dock or gridiron as a reasonable assured would in all the circumstances be justified in employing. In the present case the assured was justified in employing the dock at Northam.

Lord Birkenhead LC, observed:[16]

> 'I think that the words "with liberty to shift" are to be construed as an extension of the scope of the policy, which would otherwise only protect the vessel while it was actually anchored in the creek. In other words, if the freedom to shift had not been stipulated for, the vessel would have been unprotected during the innumerable small movements which circumstances may from time to time have required. I do not think that the words were intended to cover a voyage of seven or eight miles to a different part of the coast. But the "docking" clause must be determined with reference to quite other considerations.
>
> No reasonable meaning can be given to the "docking" clause, unless it is construed as extending the protection to the course of a voyage to a dock or gridiron such as a reasonable owner might in all the circumstances of the case be expected to employ and be justified in employing. I am not impressed by the arguments used in order to illustrate the supposed extravagant consequences of this construction. If an insurer extends the protection of the vessel insured to a voyage for the purpose of docking the vessel, he may be expected to acquaint himself with the measure of his liability by ascertaining where docks are reasonably to be found and how far the "changing docks and going on gridiron" to which he has assented will increase his liability, and ought to be reflected in the rate to be charged.'

In *Navigators and General Insurance Co Ltd v Ringrose*[17] a catamaran had been insured under a dinghy insurance policy 'whilst within the United Kingdom ashore or afloat'. The assured sailed on a voyage from Teignmouth to the Channel Islands. When the craft was between 25 and 30 miles to the south of Portland Bill, she was dismasted and taken in tow by an Italian tramp steamer, which later claimed a salvage award. This was paid by the insurance company without any admission of liability on the promise of the assured to repay it, if the company were found to be under no liability.

The Court of Appeal[18] held that the company was not liable under the policy, and consequently could recover from the assured the sum which had been paid, because the place where the casualty happened must determine whether or not the loss fell within its terms. The place where it did happen, being substantially mid-way between England and France, fell outside them for it could not by any test be held to be within the United Kingdom. The court said that it was unnecessary to give a meaning to the words 'United Kingdom'.

Holroyd Pearce LJ, observed[19] that it had been suggested in argument that they covered an area within sight of land, a wide area which differed greatly

---

[14] As to this aspect of the case, see pp 148–149, ante.
[15] Lord Birkenhead LC, Viscount Haldane, Viscount Finlay, Viscount Cave and Lord Sumner.
[16] [1921] All ER Rep 626 at 629. See also the speech of Viscount Finlay, ibid, at 631, and that of Lord Sumner, ibid, at 633–634.
[17] [1962] 1 All ER 97, CA.
[18] Holroyd Pearce, Willmer and Davies LJJ.
[19] [1962] 1 All ER 97 at 99.

according to the type of land, the size of the ship and various physical conditions. In the context of the policy that was a possible contention. It was also suggested that it covered the waters over which Her Majesty claimed jurisdiction. That seemed to him to provide the most clear and ascertainable limitation of the area included in the policy.

Willmer LJ, thought[20] that there was much to be said for this last view.

Davies LJ, felt[1] that whatever test one chose would give rise to anomalies. If the test of 'waters over which Her Majesty claims jurisdiction' were applied, it would do so. On a straight line of coast, presumably, those waters would mean the 3 mile limit. If, in the course of a voyage intended to be within that limit or in the course of a race intended to be within that area, a vessel were carried, say, a quarter of a mile beyond the limit owing to conditions of wind and tide, to say that, in those circumstances, she would cease to be insured when she sailed more than 3 miles from the shore, would seem to him to be an affront to common sense.

In *Pearson v Commercial Union Assurance*[2] in a 3 months' policy against fire the words were 'on the hull of the SS "Indian Empire" with her tackle furniture and stores on board belonging, lying in the Victoria Dock London with liberty to go into dry dock'. The vessel was so large that she could only go into a dry dock 2 miles up the river, and then it was necessary to remove the lower halves of her paddle-wheels. After repairs she was towed down the river and moored for the purpose of replacing the lower halves of the paddle-wheels. While so moored, she was totally destroyed by fire. It was held that, though the ship would be covered by the policy while in either dock and during transit, yet her mooring was effected for quite another purpose, i e to have her paddle-wheels replaced, and her loss therefore was not covered by the policy.

In *Bristol SS Corpn v London Assurance and Linard: The Delfini*[3] a vessel was insured under a time policy

> 'Whilst at Hirohata within breakwaters . . . With leave to shift, in tow or otherwise and including docking, undocking, overhauling, fitting out and whilst on trial trips within port limits . . .'

During the currency of the policy she was moved to Osaka, where she collided with another vessel and was damaged. When the assured claimed an indemnity under the policy, the insurers contended that they were not liable because they were no longer at risk from the time the vessel left Hirohata. Bonsal DJ, giving judgment in the District Court for the Southern District of New York, accepted this argument and held that the claim failed.[4]

3 TOWING

In *Russell v Provincial Insurance Co Ltd*[5] a motor boat was insured under a time policy which provided:[6]

---

[20] Ibid, at 100.
[1] Ibid, at 100.
[2] (1876) 1 App Cas 498. See also *Hamilton v Sheddon* (1837) 3 M&W 49.
[3] [1976] 2 Lloyd's Rep 741.
[4] See the judgment ibid, at 743.
[5] [1959] 2 Lloyd's Rep 275, QBD (Com Ct).
[6] The policy was not in common marine form, but was in the company's own form. See ibid, at 277.

'No claim shall attach to this policy while the vessel is being towed (except as is customary or when in need of assistance), or while undertaking towing or salvage services under a pre-arranged contract.'

The insured vessel was used for 'white weeding'.[7] She and another motor boat named the 'Lynn Vivian' were breasted together, and both used their engines at reduced power, whilst proceeding from Burnham-on-Crouch to Southend. The steering was done from the 'Lynn Vivian'. The insured vessel bumped on the bottom when the two boats cut across a sandbank. The assured claimed for a total loss, but the insurers denied liability[8] on the ground that she was 'being towed' at the time of the loss.

McNair J, held that the claim succeeded. He said that it was customary for vessels to proceed breasted together,[9] that that operation did not constitute towing, and that it was an operation which was not excluded from the policy. He observed:[10]

'It was submitted on behalf of the [insurers], with some force, that, even on those findings of fact—that the steering was being done from the other vessel and part of the motive power was being provided by the other vessel—the insured vessel was under tow. But, having regard to the evidence, which I accept, that it is quite common and customary in this trade for these vessels, even though both are perfectly navigable and fit, to proceed in company abreast, economising on fuel by using the two engines and economising in labour by having one man only at the wheel, I think that it is quite wrong on this policy to hold that the operation constitutes towing. If the [insurers] wish to exclude that form of operation from this policy, they have got to do it, so far as I am concerned, in very much clearer language than they have done.'

As far as towage is concerned, clause 1 of the Institute Time Clauses (Hulls)[11] states:

'The vessel is covered . . . at all times and has leave to . . . assist and tow vessels or craft in distress but it is warranted that the Vessel shall not be towed, except as is customary or to the first safe port or place when in need of assistance, or undertake towage or salvage services under a contract previously arranged by the Assured and/or Owners and/or Managers and/or Charterers. This clause shall not exclude customary towage in connection with loading and discharging.'

4 DECK CARGO

In *Leopold Walford (London) Ltd v National Benefit Assurance Co Ltd*[12] the assured claimed on a declaration under a floating policy for damage to goods carried on deck in a vessel from Liverpool to Bremen. The declaration contained the following words:

---

[7] I e a process of obtaining seaweed or weed from the river and estuary of the Crouch and submitting it to some kind of process when it is eventually sold. See ibid, at 278.
[8] Other defences were that she was unseaworthy, and that the loss had been caused by 'the inexperience of the person in control'. As to these aspects of the case, see pp 300–301, post, and p 272, post, respectively.
[9] As to the evidence, see [1959] 2 Lloyd's Rep 275 at 279.
[10] [1959] 2 Lloyd's Rep 275 at 280.
[11] These clauses are set out in Appendix III, pp 533–540, post. The relevant clause in the Institute Voyage Clauses (Hulls), the Institute Time Clauses (Freight) and the Institute Voyage Clauses (Freight) is to similar effect.
[12] (1921) 7 LlL Rep 39, KBD.

'539 bales of cotton. . . . This policy to pay in full up to the amount insured any loss or liability of shipowners in respect of cargo carried on deck for which bills of lading have been given as under-deck.'

It was held by Greer J, that the action failed because the assured had failed to show that the goods carried on deck were carried on the terms of an under-deck bill of lading.

His Lordship observed:[13]

'The [assured] suing upon a document can only sue successfully if they establish a state of facts which entitle them upon the terms of the document to succeed; and in my judgment what the [assured] were insured against was loss on a cargo carried on deck for which bills of lading had been given as under-deck; and unless the [assured] can show that they had a cargo on a vessel in respect of which bills of lading had been given as under-deck, but, notwithstanding the fact that bills of lading had been given as under-deck, they had been carried by the carrier on deck and then lost—unless they can make that out, they cannot recover on this contract. They cannot recover merely because if they had stated the true facts, they could probably have insured at the same rate as they did insure upon the statement of facts in this case. They have got to bring themselves within the terms of the contract upon which they sue, and in my judgment they have failed to do so.'

5 EXPERIENCE OF CREW

One of the defences[14] pleaded by the insurers in *Russell v Provincial Insurance Co Ltd*[15] to a claim in respect of the total loss of a motor boat after bumping on a sandbank, whilst on a voyage from Burnham-on-Crouch to Southend, was that the loss was excluded by a condition of the policy[16] which stated:

'No claim shall attach to this policy for any . . . loss . . . caused by the inexperience of the person in control.'

McNair J, rejected this defence, and held[17] that the claim succeeded, for, on the evidence, the persons in control of her were men of first rate and long experience. They were of good standing in their particular line and perfectly capable and experienced in handling craft like the insured vessel.

---

[13] Ibid, at 40.
[14] Other defences were that the vessel was unseaworthy, and that she was not covered by the policy at the time of the loss because she was 'being towed'. As to these aspects of the case, see pp 300–301, post, and pp 270–271, ante, respectively.
[15] [1959] 2 Lloyd's Rep 275, QBD (Com Ct).
[16] The policy was not in common marine form, but was in the company's own form. See ibid, at 277.
[17] Ibid, at 281.

CHAPTER 18

Termination and cancellation of the policy

A TERMINATION

The parties may terminate the policy by mutual consent.[1]

When a broker terminates a policy, he must have clear authority for that purpose. When the seal of the insurance company is affixed to the policy, the contract is complete, the company then becoming merely the custodian of the policy for the assured. Where a broker, subsequent to the sealing of the policy without authority procured its cancellation, such termination was held to be ineffective and the assured was entitled to recover.[2]

B CANCELLATION

The mere fact that there is a good defence to an action on a policy, quite apart from fraud, e g a defence of unseaworthiness or deviation, will not entitle the court to cancel the policy. The court is not concerned with defences to an action on a contract which is, in fact, found to exist.[3]

But where it is shown that the policy was obtained by fraud or a fraudulent misrepresentation, the court will order it to be delivered up to be cancelled.[4]

---

[1] See Ivamy, *General Principles of Insurance Law* (4th edn, 1979), pp 248–249.
[2] *Xenos v Wickham* (1866) LR 2 HL 296.
[3] *Thornton v Knight* (1849) 16 Sim 509; *Brooking v Maudslay, Son and Field* (1888) 38 ChD 636. See further, Ivamy, op cit, p 252.
[4] *Honour v Equitable Life Assurance Society of United States* [1900] 1 Ch 852. See further, Ivamy, op cit, pp 252–253.

CHAPTER 19

Rectification of the policy

The general power of the court to rectify mistakes in a document has often been exercised in relation to policies of marine insurance.[1]

The earliest reported case is *Motteux v London Assurance*,[2] where the policy was expressed to be on the ship 'Eyles' 'from Fort St George in the East Indies to London'. Before the execution of the policy, a label of the agreement had been entered in the insurance company's book, signed by the assured's agent and by two directors on behalf of the company. In the book the risk was described to be 'at and from' Fort St George. The loss was not recoverable on the policy as it stood, but if the policy were made to agree with the entry in the book, the claim could be sustained. Lord Hardwicke LC, held that the intention of the parties was made clear by the label, and the variance in the policy, being a clerical error, ought to be rectified.

The mistake must not, however, be merely that of one party to the contract, but must be a mutual, or, as it is sometimes called, a common mistake,[3] and the party desirous of correcting it should commence the necessary proceedings immediately the error is discovered.

He must not delay the expectation of events which may make the mistake operate in his favour, since in that case he would be held to have adopted the policy as executed.[4]

In *Lowlands SS Co v North of England Protecting and Indemnity Association*[5] a vessel was insured with a mutual insurance association against war risks. She was taken over by the Admiralty and manned by naval ratings for the purpose, as her owners believed, of proceeding to block a port in enemy occupation. This operation would have inevitably led to her destruction. Her owners thereupon informed the association of the proposed voyage, and it was agreed that the policy should be cancelled as from the date of her sailing. Two days later she was lost on a voyage under an ordinary Admiralty charter, and had not sailed on any expedition to the enemy port. Her owners maintained that they were entitled to recover for a total loss on the ground that the agreement to cancel had been entered into under a mutual mistake.

The arbitrator to whom the dispute was referred found that there was no mutual mistake, and that the agreement had not been made on a condition

---

[1] For the power of the court to rectify, see further, Ivamy, *General Principles of Insurance Law* (4th edn, 1979), chapter 24.
[2] (1739) 1 Atk 545. See further, *Collett v Morrison* (1851) 9 Hare 162; *Henkle v Royal Exchange Assurance* (1749) 1 Ves Sen 317.
[3] *Spalding v Crocker* (1897) 2 Com Cas 189; *Scott v Coulson* [1903] 2 Ch 249; *Emanuel & Co v Andrew Weir & Co* (1914) 30 TLR 518. See further, Ivamy, op cit, p 257.
[4] See Ivamy, op cit, pp 258–259.
[5] (1921) 6 LlL Rep 230, KBD.

which had not been fulfilled, i e the vessel's taking part in the expedition. His decision that the owners' claim failed was affirmed by Sankey J, who observed:[6]

> '[Counsel] said, with regard to the question of mutual mistake, that this being an agreement founded on mutual mistake, the agreement to cancel cannot stand. Mutual mistake was a question of fact, and the arbitrator has found there was no mutual mistake, and that it was all on one side, viz a mistake by someone in the applicants' service or firm as to the destination of the vessel. There was no mutual mistake, but that was a question of fact for the arbitrator and not for me.
>
> The last point was that it was an agreement to cancel only if the vessel went on a particular voyage—that she did not go on that particular voyage, and therefore the condition on which alone the agreement to cancel was made had never been fulfilled. The arbitrator found that the vessel went on some expedition, but that there was no evidence to show what expedition. I read the arbitrator's finding as being that the applicants had not discharged the onus of proving that the agreement to cancel was made on a condition which had not been fulfilled, and that therefore he came to the conclusion that the applicants were not entitled to recover £5,000. On the facts as they were before the arbitrator he was entitled to come to the conclusion he did, and there is nothing wrong in law with the award.'

In *Gagniere & Co Ltd v Eastern Co of Warehouses Insurance and Transport of Goods with Advances Ltd*[7] the Court of Appeal[8] refused to rectify a policy relating to a number of cases of woollen goods being sent from England to Russia because the terms of the contract had not been clearly proved.

Bankes LJ, observed:[9]

> 'There is really no sufficient evidence to establish what the contract between the parties really was, and, in the absence of clear evidence as to what the contract really was, it seems to me to be very difficult to persuade a court that the policy should be rectified.'

In *Maignen & Co v National Benefit Assurance Co*[10] the assured had effected a policy in respect of 138 hogsheads of burgundy from Beaune to Boulogne and London. The policy contained the words: 'Including leakage or breakage, however caused, irrespective of percentage.' On the arrival of the goods in London, it was found that a large quantity of wine had been lost by leakage. When a claim was made under the policy, the insurers contended that the policy was not in accordance with the 'slip'[11] under which leakage was not a peril insured against, and that the policy should be rectified accordingly.

Greer J, held that the 'slip' did cover leakage, and that the claim succeeded. The question of rectification did not arise. He observed:[12]

> 'Under these circumstances, I need not give consideration to the other question that was discussed as to whether or not—assuming that upon the interpretation of the "slip" the contract was different from that ultimately entered into by means of the actual policy—the policy could be rectified to make it correct. I am inclined to think that where a closing "slip" is sent forward for the purpose of preparing a policy, it is an intimation "these are our terms", the terms which the insurer is willing to have in the final document that is to be binding between the parties; and if these are exceeded in the writing out of the contract and the document is executed and the contract signed, I am inclined to think the insurer is bound by what he has done, notwithstanding the fact that if it had been done in time, it might have been said :"What

---

[6] Ibid, at 231.
[7] (1921) 8 LlL Rep 365, CA.
[8] Bankes, Warrington and Scrutton LJJ.
[9] (1921) 8 LlL Rep 365 at 367.
[10] (1922) 10 LlL Rep 30, KBD.
[11] As to the 'slip', see p 67, ante.
[12] (1922) 10 LlL Rep at 31.

you are representing is not in accordance with the arrangement we made when the slip was initialled; and therefore I will not sign the policy." It is, however, unnecessary for me to decide the point here because I think the "slip" covers the insurance of leakage, etc., during the whole of the voyage, Beaune to London, carriage upon the railway, while being handled and put on board ship, leakage on the ship and leakage on the railway subsequently.'

In *Wilson, Holgate & Co Ltd v Lancashire and Cheshire Insurance Corpn Ltd*[13] the insurers contended that they were entitled to repudiate liability in respect of damage to 107 out of 657 barrels of palm oil which were insured for a voyage from Singapore to Liverpool, on the ground that the goods were not properly described under the policy, for in the policy they were stated to be 'palm oil kernels'.[14]

Bailhache J, held that the goods had been properly described in the 'slip',[15] and that the assured were entitled to rectification of the policy. He observed:[16]

'The [insurers] have raised since then two or three other defences. In the first place, they say that "the said goods which were in fact palm oil, were not properly described under the policy". That stands in this way. The original "slip" submitted to the underwriters described these goods as palm oil, but for some reason or another, and by a mistake, the covering instructions and the policies themselves called the stuff palm kernel oil. But I must have regard to the original contract, which, as one of the underwriters said, is the real contract he made, and in the original contract the goods are described as palm oil, and I disregard the mistake made afterwards. If necessary I should rectify the policy. I should be the more ready to rectify it because it is clear that palm oil is a better subject from an underwriters' point of view than palm kernel oil.'

In *Scottish Metropolitan Assurance Co v Stewart*[17] the 'slip' stated that a vessel was reinsured 'from 20 September 1922 until noon on 20 February 1923' whereas the reinsurance policy expressly included 20 September. The vessel was a total loss on 20 September. The reinsurer contended that the risk did not attach until midnight on 20 September, and denied that the policy was in operation at the time of the loss. He claimed rectification of the policy to agree with the 'slip'. Rowlatt J, held that there were no grounds for rectification, and that 20 September was included in the period of the risk. He observed:[18]

'The word "from" is not to be treated as a technical word, but it is to be construed with reference to the circumstances of the case and the intention of the parties to be inferred from those circumstances. This is not a case where the period of time is named and then the day from which it is to run is also named. There you have to say whether you exclude a day at the beginning or exclude a day at the end in order to get the proper length of time. Here we have a case where merely the day indicating the commencement is mentioned and a particular point of time at the other end and the length of time depends upon those facts and not upon an independent declaration of its length. . . . I act upon what I think is the meaning of this language as ordinarily used, without pretending to find elaborate reasons for it. When you say from one day to another and say nothing more, you mention the days which prima facie you include—you mention days with which you are concerned. You do not mention those with which you are not concerned.'

---

[13] (1922) 13 LlL Rep 486, KBD.
[14] Other 'defences' were that the loss of the goods was due to inherent vice, and that there had been non-disclosure of a material fact, viz the existence of another policy in respect of the goods, and the condition of the goods as stated in the bill of lading. As to these defences, see pp 250–251, ante, and pp 64–65, ante, respectively.
[15] As to the 'slip', see p 67, ante.
[16] (1922) 13 LlL Rep at 487.
[17] (1923) 15 LlL Rep 55, KBD.
[18] Ibid, at 58.

In *Eagle Star and British Dominions Insurance Co Ltd v A V Reiner*[19] a reinsurer was held to be entitled to rectification of a reinsurance policy so that it correctly set out the terms of the 'slip'. Salter J, said[20] that the policy was not in accordance with the contract which the parties made, and that there was a mistake[1] common to them both. The contract, which they had made in fact, appeared on the 'slip' and was one under which the risk attached, and was meant by both of them to attach 'at and from and off' Gibraltar, and not from Spain as stated in the reinsurance policy.

In *American Employers Insurance Co v St Paul Fire and Marine Insurance Co Ltd*[2] some barges were insured under a policy giving coverage on a 'per vessel' basis. The barges were destroyed in an accident whilst being towed. When the assured claimed under the policy, the insurers denied liability on the ground that the parties intended coverage to be on a 'per occurrence' basis, and claimed rectification of the policy. Maxwell DJ, giving judgment in the District Court for the Northern District of West Virginia, refused to grant the application because the insurers had not shown that there had been a mutual mistake.[3]

In *Pindos Shipping Corpn v Raven, The Mata Hari*[4] a policy in respect of a yacht contained a warranty[5] which stated 'warranted class maintained'. She became a constructive total loss after sinking in a storm. At the time of the loss she was not in class. When a claim was made on the policy, the insurers repudiated liability on the ground that the warranty had been broken. The assured applied for rectification of the policy on the ground that at the time of the initialling of the 'slip'[6] they and the insurers intended that there should be no such warranty in the policy. Bingham J, refused to rectify the policy for even if the assured had intended that there should be no such warranty, it was not an intention common to both parties and that was fatal to the assured's claim.[7]

---

[19] (1927) 27 LlL Rep 173, KBD.
[20] Ibid, at 177.
[1] As to the evidence of a mistake having been made, see ibid, at 175.
[2] [1978] 1 Lloyd's Rep 417.
[3] See the judgment ibid, at 422.
[4] [1983] 2 Lloyd's Rep 449, QBD (Com Ct).
[5] As to warranties, see chapter 21, post.
[6] As to the 'slip', see p 67, ante.
[7] See the judgment at [1983] 2 Lloyd's Rep at 453.

CHAPTER 20

Alteration of the policy

Policies may be altered with the consent of those concerned.[1] Alterations are usually made by endorsement on the policy, signed or initialled by the parties. Only those who consent to the alteration will be bound by it, and if the policy is varied in any material respect by the assured alone, it becomes void. But such a result can only arise when the alteration is material.[2]

Therefore, in *Sanderson v Symonds*,[3] where the policy allowed the ship 'to sell, barter, and exchange goods at any of the ports to which under the terms of the policy she might proceed during her stay', and the assured inserted the words 'and trade' after the words 'her stay', the court held that the alteration was not material. Accordingly, the insurer was liable although he had not signed the alteration.

But alterations in the nature of the voyage, by changing the port of destination, the route, or the day of sailing, have been held to be material alterations by which the policy was avoided, except in regard to those insurers who had signed or initialled the alterations.[4]

In *Norwich Union Fire Insurance Co v Colonial Mutual Fire Insurance Co Ltd*[5] a vessel was insured for £15,000 by her owners under a policy issued by the plaintiffs. The policy stated that her hull and machinery were valued at £313,050. The plaintiffs reinsured £2,500 of their risk with the defendants. The reinsurance policy stated:

'The said ship and goods and merchandise . . . are and shall be valued at £2,500 on hull and machinery, etc, valued at £313,050. . . . Being against the risks of total and/or constructive and/or arranged total loss of steamer only. . . . Subject to the same clauses and conditions as the original policy . . . and to pay as may be paid thereon.'

During the currency of the original policy the plaintiffs and the owners of the vessel agreed to an alteration as to the terms concerning the hull and machinery, and the original policy was altered to read:

'Agree to reduce policies on hull and machinery valued at £313,050. To pay only £225,000 in event of total loss, constructive total loss and return premium 10 per cent gross on £313,050 . . .'

The defendants did not assent, and were not aware of the alteration in the original policy. Shortly afterwards the vessel sank and became a total loss. The owners claimed from the plaintiffs the original value of the vessel, viz £313,050,

---

[1] See further, Ivamy, *General Principles of Insurance Law* (4th edn, 1979), p 254.
[2] See further, Ivamy, op cit, p 255.
[3] (1819) 1 Brod&Bing 426. See further, *Sanderson v McCullom* (1819) 4 Moore CP 5.
[4] *Langhorn v Cologan* (1812) 4 Taunt 330; *Campbell v Christie* (1817) 2 Stark 64; *Fairlie v Christie* (1817) 7 Taunt 416.
[5] (1922) 12 LlL Rep 94, 215, KBD.

but ultimately compromised for £225,000. The plaintiffs paid them £12,200, which was their proportion of the compromised value. The defendants paid to the plaintiffs £2,036 8s 4d, which was the compromised proportion of the £2,500 which was the sum insured under the reinsurance policy. The plaintiffs, however, claimed the balance of the £2,500.

McCardie J, held that the action failed because the alteration was a material one, and had been made without the assent or knowledge of the defendants, who were accordingly discharged from further liability under it. He observed:[6]

> 'The parties first embodied their new bargain in a "slip" and then endorsed the effect of the "slip" on the reinsurance policy. If this was not a variation, and a variation moreover of a material character, I know not what a material variation can be. The original rights and obligation under the head policy were altered in substantial fashion. Premiums were varied and returned and the amount payable on total loss, constructive total loss, and/or arranged total loss was deliberately altered to a striking extent, viz from £313,050 to £225,000. It cannot, I think, possibly be said that the policy as altered was the same as the original policy. The very object of the parties was to effect a "thing", ie the physical subject-matter of the reinsurance policy remained the same, but the foundation of the reinsurance policy, to wit, the head policy, was changed in substantial manner. In other words, the original foundation of the reinsurance policy had, in my view, ceased to exist. The original policy had, in substance, become a fresh policy with different terms.
>
> The alteration had been effected without the assent or even the knowledge of the defendants.
>
> The only sound rule seems to be that the head policy cannot be altered save with the consent of the reinsurer. It is not without interest to refer to a branch of the law, which although different in some ways, yet presents many features in common with insurance. I refer to suretyship. It is well settled that if a creditor, without the consent of the surety, varies the terms of his bargain with the debtor, the surety is prima facie discharged.'

---

[6] Ibid, at 218.

CHAPTER 21
Warranties

Warranties are often included in policies. These are undertakings by the assured, and are of a promissory nature. There are two types of warranty: (i) an express warranty; and (ii) an implied warranty. If there has been a breach of warranty, the insurer is entitled to avoid liability on the policy as from the time when the breach takes place. There are various excuses available to the assured who is guilty of a breach of warranty. In certain circumstances the insurer will be held to have waived the breach of warranty.

A NATURE OF WARRANTIES

Section 33(1) of the Marine Insurance Act 1906 states:

> 'A warranty . . . means a promissory warranty, that is to say, a warranty by which the assured undertakes that some particular thing shall or shall not be done, or that some condition shall be fulfilled, or whereby he affirms or negatives the existence of a particular state of facts.'

A warranty must be exactly complied with, for s 33(3) of the Marine Insurance Act 1906 states:

> 'A warranty, as above defined, is a condition which must be exactly complied with, whether it be material to the risk or not.'

Thus, in *Bond v Nutt*,[1] where a ship was warranted 'to have sailed on or before 1 August', Lord Mansfield said:[2]

> 'Had she or had she not sailed on or before that day? No matter what cause prevented her, if the fact is that she had not sailed, though she stayed behind for the best reasons, the policy was void.'[3]

In this connection a warranty differs from a representation, for s 20(4) of the Marine Insurance Act 1906 provides that:

> 'A representation as to a matter of fact is true, if it be substantially correct, that is to say, if the difference between what is represented and what is actually correct would not be considered material by a prudent insurer.'

Again, a representation is not embodied in the policy, for it is 'made by the assured or his agent to the insurer during the negotiations for the contract'.[4]

On the other hand, s 35(2) states:

---

[1] (1777) 2 Cowp 601. See further, *Hore v Whitmore* (1778) 2 Cowp 784; *Earle v Harris* (1780) 1 Doug KB 357; *Sanderson v Busher* (1814) 4 Camp 54n.
[2] (1777) 2 Cowp at 606.
[3] The word 'void' means, of course, 'voidable'.
[4] Marine Insurance Act 1906, s 20(1).

'An express warranty must be included in, or written upon, the policy, or must be contained in some document incorporated by reference into the policy.'

In order to ensure the exact compliance with any representation made by the assured, the insurer should take care that the representation is inserted in the policy, and thus be converted into a warranty.

It has been held that a representation does not become a warranty by folding the paper containing it inside the policy.[5]

It was formerly said that if the representation was only wafered to the policy, it was not a warranty.[6] If, however, it is, in fact, a written term of the contract, the mode of attachment will not now constitute an objection to its status as a warranty.[7]

While exact compliance is required, it is all that is required, and the obligation of the assured is limited to such compliance and extends to nothing else.[8]

B THE TYPES OF WARRANTY

Section 33(2) of the Marine Insurance Act 1906 states:

'A warranty may be express or implied.'

Section 35(3) states:

'An express warranty does not exclude an implied warranty, unless it be inconsistent therewith.'

C EXPRESS WARRANTIES

A *Construction of an express warranty*

The word 'warranted' is not essential to constitute a warranty.

Thus, s 35(1) of the Marine Insurance Act 1906 states:

'An express warranty may be in any form of words from which the intention to warrant is to be inferred.'

The words will be interpreted in a business sense.

Thus, in *Hart v Standard Marine Insurance Co Ltd*,[9] where there was a warranty stating 'Warranted no iron or ore exceeding the net registered tonnage', it was said that an ordinary businessman would consider that steel was comprised in the common meaning of the word 'iron'.

But in the absence of some necessity for a special construction, the warranty will only mean what it says, and it will not be extended to put a further liability or disability on the assured in relation to the contract.

Consequently, in *Hide v Bruce*[10] a warranty that a ship 'will carry 20 guns'

---

[5] *Pawson v Watson* (1778) 1 Doug KB 12n.
[6] Ibid.
[7] *Bensaude v Thames and Mersey Marine Insurance Co* [1897] AC 609 at 612 (per Lord Halsbury LC).
[8] *Hide v Bruce* (1783) 3 Doug KB 213.
[9] (1889) 22 QBD 499, CA.
[10] (1783) 3 Doug KB 213.

was held not to mean that she would have the necessary men to work them.

Similarly, in *Laing v Glover*,[11] where a vessel was warranted 'to sail with convoy', and sailed with the convoy, but was driven back by bad weather, and the convoy went on without her, it was held that the warranty did not mean that she was bound to wait for a fresh convoy.

Again, in *Muller v Thompson*[12] an insurance 'on cargo being 1,031 hogsheads of wine' did not involve a warranty that no other cargo would be shipped.

The court will not allow a warranty to be constituted by putting a strained construction on the words used, but will interpret them by the same rules of construction applied to the interpretation of all commercial documents in order to determine the real intention of the parties, and to see whether they intended the words to constitute a warranty.[13]

Where the words are plain and bear an unmistakable meaning, no evidence will be admitted for the purpose of putting a different construction on them.[14]

B Necessity for inclusion in policy

As has been stated above, a warranty must be included in the policy or incorporated into it by reference, for s 35(2) provides:

> 'An express warranty must be included in, or written upon, the policy, or must be contained in some document incorporated by reference into the policy.'

C Examples of express warranties

A large number of instances of express warranties are to be found in the reported cases. These may be classified under the following heads:

1 Sailing warranties.
2 Warranty as to position of ship.
3 Warranty as to number of crew.
4 Convoy warranties.
5 Warranty as to nationality.
6 Warranty as to neutrality.
7 Warranty as to part uninsured.
8 Other instances.

1 Sailing warranties

Sometimes there is included in the policy a sailing warranty, e g 'warranted to sail on or before 10 May 1985'.

In this kind of warranty the important question to be decided is whether the ship has 'sailed' within the meaning of the warranty.

Parke B, in *Roelandts v Harrison*[15] defined a 'sailing' in the following words:

> 'That period of time when the vessel breaks ground, being at that time fully fit for sea, having the cargo on board which he intends to carry, with a constant crew, and having permission to leave by having the Custom House clearances on board.'

---

[11] (1813) 5 Taunt 49.
[12] (1811) 2 Camp 610.
[13] *Baring v Clagett* (1802) 3 Bos&P 201; *Small v Gibson* (1849) 16 QB 141; *Colledge v Harty* (1851) 6 Exch 205; *Union Insurance Society of Canton Ltd v George Wills & Co* [1916] AC 281.
[14] *Provincial Insurance Co of Canada v Leduc* (1874) LR 6 PC 244.
[15] (1854) 9 Exch 444 at 456.

Thus, to constitute a sailing, three conditions must be complied with:

1 The ship must be ready and equipped for the first stage of her voyage if the voyage is necessarily divisible into stages, or for the whole of the voyage if it is not divisible.
2 She must unmoor and proceed on her course.
3 When she leaves her moorings, the master must have the intention of then actually proceeding on the voyage.

a Readiness of vessel

The ship must be ready and equipped with her crew, papers, and all requisites.

In *Ridsdale v Newnham*[16] a vessel was insured 'at and from Portneuf to London'. The policy contained a warranty 'to sail on or before 28 October'. The vessel sailed from Portneuf on 26 October with a crew sufficient to take her to Quebec, where she got her clearances, and took on board the rest of her crew. She left Quebec on 30 October. Lord Ellenborough CJ, said:[17]

> 'The warranty could only be satisfied by a commencement of the voyage with a crew competent to carry the ship to her port of destination. When the ship was lying at Quebec obtaining her clearances and taking in her crew, how can she be considered as having sailed on her voyage?'

On the other hand, in *Bouillon v Lupton*[18] a vessel was insured 'from Lyons to Galatz, ship warranted to have sailed before 15 August'. She left Lyons for the voyage down the river Rhone before the day named in the warranty, but with only her river crew and without her full tackle for the sea voyage. She could not have made her river voyage rigged for sea, and it was usual to take her masts and heavy tackle on board at Marseilles. She took them on board at Marseilles without delay, and sailed from there on 23 August. It was held that the warranty had been complied with.

b Unmooring and proceeding on the voyage

The vessel must unmoor and proceed on her voyage.

In *Nelson v Salvador*[19] a vessel was warranted 'to sail on or before 10 August'. She cleared outwards on 9 August, her passengers and cargo being on board. On the morning of 10 August one of the two anchors was weighed, some sails were set, and she was moved about 30 fathoms by hauling on the cable of the remaining anchor. Before she heaved anchor, a heavy swell was observed setting into the bay, and the ship remained as she was until the morning of 11 August, when she actually left the port. It was held that the warranty had not been complied with.

But in *Wood v Smith, The City of Cambridge*[20] a vessel left dock with a pilot on

---

[16] (1815) 3 M&S 456. See also *Graham v Barras* (1834) 5 B&Ad 1011, where the crew was not shipped in time; *Pittegrew v Pringle* (1832) 3 B&Ad 514, where the ballast was not shipped; *Hudson v Bilton* (1856) 2 Jur NS 784; *Price v Livingstone* (1882) 9 QBD 679; *Thompson v Gillespy* (1855) 5 E&B 209.
[17] (1814) 4 Camp 111. The Court of King's Bench later refused to grant a new trial: (1815) 3 M&S 456.
[18] (1863) 15 CBNS 113.
[19] (1829) Mood & M 309.
[20] (1874) LR 5 PC 451.

board, and anchored some distance down the river with the object of crossing the bar earlier next day than she could have done if she remained in dock until the next morning. It was held that this operation was a 'proceeding to sea' within the meaning of a local Harbour Act.

On the other hand, in *The Cachapool*,[1] where a vessel in leaving dock on her voyage sustained damage and anchored in the river for repairs, it was held that when so anchored, she was not 'proceeding to sea'.

c Intention to proceed to sea

The third element of a 'sailing' is the intention of the master to proceed on his voyage in the usual and customary way.

The question therefore is 'What was the object and intention of the master when he weighed anchor?'

The element of a 'sailing' was put in the form of the following proposition by Counsel for the insurer in *Thellusson v Staples*:[2]

> 'To constitute a "sailing" within the meaning of the warranty the vessel, at the time of her sailing from the port of loading, must be in the contemplation of the captain at absolute and entire liberty to proceed to her port of delivery in a mathematical line if it were possible.'

Thus, in *Sea Insurance Co v Blogg*[3] in a reinsurance policy on goods 'per steamers as attached sailing on or after 1 March 1896', the assured declared on the 'Massacoit'. The vessel completed her loading about 10 pm on 29 February, and, having cleared the Custom House, was ready for sea. The master moved her from the wharf about 500 yards into the stream and there anchored until the morning, his object being to prevent the crew going ashore and getting drunk. On the following morning, 1 March, at about 8 am the ship weighed anchor and proceeded to sea. It was held that the warranty had been complied with, and that the movement of the vessel on 29 February was not a 'sailing' because there was no intention on the part of the master of then proceeding to sea.

Further, in *Wright v Shiffner*,[4] sailing from the port of departure to a place of rendezvous outside the direct and usual course of the voyage to await a convoy, was held to be a compliance with the warranty if the intention of the master was to sail with the convoy in the usual way.

WARRANTY 'TO DEPART'

The warranty 'to depart' from a port means to leave the port, not merely to sail towards the mouth or entrance of the port.

In *Moir v Royal Exchange Assurance Co*[5] a vessel was insured 'at and from Memel'. She was warranted 'to depart on or before 15 September'. She cleared on 9 September and sailed on her voyage, but before she got out of the harbour, the wind changed and she came to anchor within the harbour's mouth, and was detained until after 15 September. Lord Ellenborough CJ, said:[6]

---

[1] (1881) 7 PD 217.
[2] Cited in 1 Doug 366n.
[3] [1898] 2 QB 398. See also *Fisher v Cochran* (1835) 5 Tyr 496; *Lang v Anderdon* (1824) 3 B&C 495.
[4] (1809) 2 Camp 247.
[5] (1815) 3 M&S 461.
[6] Ibid, at 462.

'If this had been a warranty "to sail", there was a sailing abundantly proved. But "to depart" raises a question of grammatical construction. A warranty to depart on a particular day is, I think, a warranty to be out of port on or before that day.'

WARRANTY 'TO SAIL FROM'

The words 'to sail *from*' have received the same judicial interpretation as the words 'to depart'.[7]

WARRANTY 'TO SAIL TO'

The warranty 'to sail to' means '*to sail towards*', and does not mean 'to arrive at'.[8]

2 Warranty as to position of ship

Warranties are sometimes inserted declaring the whereabouts or condition of the vessel on a date named, the object being to give the insurer a better idea of the risk.

Section 38 of the Marine Insurance Act 1906 states:

'Where the subject-matter insured is warranted "well" or "in good safety" on a particular day, it is sufficient if it be safe at any time during that day.'

In *Blackhurst v Cockell*[9] a policy on a ship contained a warranty stating 'Lost or not lost. Warranted well on 9 December'. The policy was subscribed between 1 pm and 3 pm on 9 December. The vessel was, in fact, lost at about 8 am on that day. It was held that the warranty was complied with by the fact that the vessel was safe at some time on the day when the underwriters subscribed the policy, although she was not safe at the particular hour when they subscribed it. The warranty protected them against all losses before that day, but not against losses on that day.

A warranty that a ship was in port on a day named is not equivalent to a warranty that the ship was 'safe' on the day named. The vessel must be in the named port, and not elsewhere.

Thus, in *Colby v Hunter*[10] a policy on a ship stated 'at and from Hamburg to Vigo. Warranted in port on 19 October'. On that date the ship was in the port of Cuxhaven, which was 90 miles outside the limits of the port of Hamburg. It was held that the warranty had not been complied with.

3 Warranty as to number of crew

Sometimes the policy contains a warranty as to the number of crew to be carried.

Thus, in *De Hahn v Hartley*[11] a policy on a ship contained a warranty stating that she was 'to sail from Liverpool with 50 hands or upwards'. She left Liverpool with only 46 hands, but at Beaumaris took six more hands on board.

---

[7] *Moir v Royal Exchange Assurance* (1815) 3 M&S 461; *Lang v Anderdon* (1824) 3 B&C 495; *Baines v Holland* (1855) 10 Exch 802.
[8] *Colledge v Harty* (1851) 6 Exch 205; *Provincial Insurance Co of Canada v Leduc* (1874) LR 6 PC 244.
[9] (1789) 3 Term Rep 360.
[10] (1827) Mood & M 81.
[11] (1786) 1 Term Rep 343.

It was held that the warranty had not been complied with, even though the full number had been made up at Beaumaris.

4 Convoy warranties

In time of war, policies have often contained warranties that vessels shall sail under the protection of an armed convoy.

In warranties of this class the rule requiring an exact compliance with the warranty has always been regarded as one of special importance, and the excuse that a ship was prevented by stress of weather from sailing with the convoy would not avail the assured.[12]

A warranty 'to sail with convoy for the voyage, with leave to go to the place of rendezvous and join the convoy' means that a ship must receive her sailing instructions at the place of rendezvous, or the warranty will not be complied with.

Thus, in *Anderson v Pitcher*[13] a vessel received her sailing instructions after the convoy had been under way for 2 days. It was held that at the time of sailing she was not part of the convoyed fleet, since she had no sailing instructions at the place of rendezvous.

But where the warranty is that the ship shall sail with convoy, she may sail without convoy from the port of loading to the place of rendezvous, there to join her convoy for the voyage even though there may be a convoy for ships bound for other destinations between the loading port and the place of rendezvous.[14]

5 Warranty as to nationality

Section 37 of the Marine Insurance Act 1906 states:

> 'There is no implied warranty as to the nationality of a ship, or that her nationality shall not be changed during the risk.'

The mere possession of a characteristic national name is not a warranty that the ship is of any particular nationality. Still less is it a warranty that the nationality of the ship shall remain unchanged either during the continuance of the voyage or during the currency of the policy. If a ship is warranted to be of a certain nationality, the warranty is complied with if she is of the specified nationality at the time when the warranty attaches, and if the insurer requires the nationality of the ship to remain unchanged during the risk, he must expressly state that in the policy.[15]

As to what establishes nationality, Lord Kenyon LCJ, held in *Tabbs v Benedelack*[16] that persons residing in a country carrying on a trade, by which both they and the country were benefited, were to be considered as the subjects of that country, and were so considered by the law of nations, at least, so far as to subject their property to capture by a country at war with the country in which they lived.

---

[12] *Sanderson v Busher* (1814) 4 Camp 54n.
[13] (1800) 2 Bos&P 164.
[14] *Warwick v Scott* (1814) 4 Camp 62, NP.
[15] *Eden v Parkison* (1781) 2 Doug KB 732; *Tyson v Gurney* (1789) 3 Term Rep 477; *Dent v Smith* (1869) LR 4 QB 414.
[16] (1802) 4 Esp 108. See also *M'Connell v Hector* (1802) 3 Bos&P 113; *Baring v Clagett* (1802) 3 Bos&P 201; *Lothian v Henderson* (1803) 3 Bos& P 499; *Baring v Christie* (1804) 5 East 398.

In that case a ship 'warranted to be American property' was captured by the French, and on a claim being made by the assured the insurer alleged a breach of the warranty. The assured was an American living in England married to an English woman. The vessel had been built in America, bought in America from an American, brought to England, and properly documented as an English ship, but the assured was not domiciled in England. The insurer, however, succeeded in establishing the breach of warranty on the ground stated by the Lord Chief Justice.

To comply with a warranty of nationality, a ship must not only be of the nationality specified, but she must carry the usual documents and other things which are necessary to prove it. These are the flag, the certificate of registry, log-book, bill of health, invoices, bills of lading, certificates of origin etc.[17] She is, however, only bound to carry those documents which are prescribed either by international usage or by treaty.

By the Merchant Shipping Act 1894, s 68, the national character of a ship has to be declared before she clears, and the customs officer inscribes that name on the clearance; and, moreover, the ship may be detained until such declaration is made.[18]

The flag which the ship flies when there is no danger, and the nationality of the consul on whom the master calls when he is in port, are two elements which will form strong evidence of the national character of the ship.[19]

6 Warranty as to neutrality

Section 36(1) of the Marine Insurance Act 1906 states:

> 'Where insurable property, whether ship or goods, is expressly warranted neutral, there is an implied condition that the property shall have a neutral character at the commencement of the risk, and that so far as the assured can control the matter, its neutral character shall be preserved during the risk.'

Section 36(2) goes on to state:

> 'Where a ship is expressly warranted "neutral" there is also an implied condition that, so far as the assured can control the matter, she shall be properly documented, that is to say, that she shall carry the necessary papers to establish her neutrality, and that she shall not falsify or suppress her papers, or use simulated papers. If any loss occurs through breach of this condition the insurer may avoid the contract.'

The employment of simulated papers is a breach of the warranty, for it renders the ship liable to capture and condemnation. The fact that the ship cannot trade without them makes no difference,[20] although it is open to the insurer to agree to the use of such papers.[1]

Moreover, the destruction of the ship's papers may be a breach of the warranty, for, like mutilation, erasure, or alteration of documents, it is a circumstance of great suspicion, which will always justify arrest, and may lead to condemnation.[2]

---

[17] *Geyer v Aguilar* (1798) 7 Term Rep 681. See also *Kindersley v Chase* (1801) 2 Park's Marine Insce 8th Edn 743; *Rich v Parker* (1798) 2 Esp 615; *Baring v Clagett* (1802) 3 Bos&P 201.
[18] See *The Princess Charlotte* (1863) Brown & Lush 75.
[19] *Arcangelo v Thompson* (1811) 2 Camp 620, NP.
[20] *Horneyer v Lushington* (1812) 15 East 46; *Oswell v Vigne* (1812) 15 East 70; *Fomin v Oswell* (1813) 3 Camp 357.
[1] *Bell v Bromfield* (1812) 15 East 364.
[2] *The Hunter* (1815) 1 Dods 480; *Bernardi v Motteux* (1781) 2 Doug KB 575.

Where the ship is condemned by a foreign court for a breach of neutrality, the sentence of the court is admissible in evidence to show the grounds upon which it proceeded.[3] So also is the sentence of a British Vice-Admiralty Court.[4]

But if it should appear that the condemnation proceeded on the basis of a breach of a local or domestic law, as distinguished from international law or the obligations of a treaty between the country of the ship and that of the court passing sentence, the warranty will not have been broken, e g where condemnation proceeds on the basis of a violation of certain laws relating to navigation.[5]

It has been said that the warranty is broken if the forfeiture of the protection which neutrality affords is brought about by the wilful act of the master,[6] but the effect of such conduct will depend on the circumstances of each particular case, as it may amount to barratry.[7]

Effect of breach of warranty of neutrality

The effect of a breach of warranty of neutrality is ordinarily to render the policy voidable at the instance of the insurer, even although the breach may have had no connection with any loss that may have occurred.

Hence, where the assured is responsible for a breach of neutrality in relation to a policy on goods, the insurer may avoid liability as from the date of the breach.

This is, however, not the case where a ship warranted neutral is nevertheless not properly documented, since in that event s 36(2) of the Marine Insurance Act 1906 expressly provides that the insurer can avoid liability only where this is the cause of the loss.

7 Warranty as to part uninsured

Sometimes the policy contains a warranty stating that the assured is to keep a certain part of the value of the subject-matter uninsured.

Clauses of this kind had their origin in the old custom of requiring the assured to be his own insurer for a part of the value. The Ordinance of Louis XIV of 1681 required the assured to run the risk of one-tenth, unless the policy specially provided that the whole was to be insured. The intention was doubtless to ensure greater care on the part of the assured, and probably it had some practical value when the connection of the assured with the ship was closer than it is in modern times.

In *Muirhead v Forth and North Sea Mutual Insurance Association*[8] a warranty that 'the assured shall keep one-fifth uninsured' was held to mean that the assured should be his own insurer for one-fifth, and that if he effected an insurance or insurances for more than four-fifths, the underwriters on the policy containing the warranty were not liable.

In *Roddick v Indemnity Mutual Marine Insurance Co*[9] it was held that the

---

[3] *Lothian v Henderson* (1803) 3 Bos&P 499.
[4] *Gibson v Mair* (1813) 1 Marsh 39.
[5] *Pollard v Bell* (1800) 8 Term Rep 434; *Bird v Appleton* (1800) 8 Term Rep 562.
[6] *Garrels v Kensington* (1799) 8 Term Rep 230.
[7] As to barratry, see pp 161–169, ante.
[8] [1894] AC 72.
[9] [1895] 2 QB 380

warranty was broken if part of the amount warranted uninsured had been insured under a p p i policy, even though such a policy would be unenforceable at law.

But if an insurer stops payment, and the assured in good faith insures again for the estimated deficiency, the mere existence of a policy of such doubtful value is not a breach of warranty, for there can be no breach of warranty unless the insurance alleged to constitute a breach of the warranty is effective and really available to the assured.

Thus, in *General Insurance Co of Trieste v Cory*[10] a policy relating to a vessel valued at £12,000 contained a warranty stating 'warranted £2,400 uninsured'. Of the remaining £9,600, £5,000 was insured with a syndicate, who stopped payment and advised their assured to effect new insurances. Thereupon, the assured, estimating that £2,000 out of the £5,000 was still effective, procured a fresh policy elsewhere for £3,000, and consequently held policies for £12,600. It was held that, in the circumstances, there was no breach of warranty.

The warranty sometimes takes the form of a stipulation that the subject-matter of the insurance shall not be insured for more than a named sum.

Thus, in *Lishman v Northern Marine Insurance Co*[11] a warranty of this kind stipulated that the hull should not be insured for more than £2,700 after 20 March. A further insurance for £500, which would expire on 20 March, but would be renewed unless the assured gave notice not to renew, was not discontinued by express notice. The vessel was lost on 16 March, and the loss was known on the next day. It was held that the warranty was complied with, for the loss of the vessel before 20 March relieved the assured from the obligation of giving express notice of non-renewal, there being no vessel in existence to form the subject-matter of a renewed insurance.

In *General Shipping and Forwarding Co v British General Insurance Co Ltd*[12] a vessel was insured under a time policy containing the Institute Time Clauses (Hulls) warranty, which stated:

> 'Warranted that, except as hereinafter mentioned, the amount insured for account of assured ... on premiums, freight, hire, profit, disbursements, commissions, or other interests, policy proof of interest or full interest admitted, or on excess or increased value of hull or machinery, however described, shall not exceed 15 per cent of the value of the hull and machinery as stated herein, but this warranty shall not restrict the assured's right to cover:—PREMIUMS: Any amount not in excess of actual premiums on all interests of whatsoever nature insured including estimated premium on any Club Insurances, but in all cases reducing monthly by a proportionate amount of the whole.'[13]

The vessel became a total loss, and the assured claimed under the policy. One of the defences[14] pleaded by the insurers was that the assured had insured the premiums on a premium-reducing policy for £581, and to that policy was pinned a p p i slip, and that this amounted to a breach of the warranty set out above.

---

[10] [1897] 1 QB 335.
[11] (1875) LR 10 CP 179.
[12] (1923) 15 LlL Rep 175, KBD.
[13] For the modern version of this clause see the Institute Time Clauses (Hulls), cl 21, set out in Appendix III, pp 540–541, post.
[14] Another defence pleaded by the insurers was that the vessel had been overvalued. As to this point, see p 95, ante.

It was held that there had been no breach of warranty, and that the action succeeded.

Bailhache J, said:[15]

> 'The policy is undoubtedly a policy for the actual amount of premium; and it is for 12 months; and it is a monthly reducing policy. So far, it is quite clear it is within the terms of the warranty and the insurance is justified. But for some reason someone or other has pinned on this policy a p p i slip. There is no sort of reason why premiums should be insured on p p i terms at all. It is the actual sum which the owner is out of pocket and which he is perfectly entitled to insure; and there can be no question of any proof of interest. His interest in the matter is obvious. I do not know how the slip came to be pinned on to the policy and I do not know whether the proposal was to insure on p p i terms. I have not seen the slip submitted to the underwriter and initialled by him. But assuming that it was, in my opinion it was no breach of this warranty, which says "This warranty shall not restrict the assured's right to cover", and to cover premiums in precisely the same way as these were covered, except that the policy has attached to it the p p i slip. I cannot think that this was any breach of the warranty. The warranty is not quite easy to construe: but in my judgment there is nothing in the warranty to prevent such an insurance upon premiums as in this case.'

Again, in *P Samuel & Co Ltd v Dumas*[16] a vessel was insured under a time policy which included clause 22 of the Institute Time Clauses (Hulls),[17] which stated:

> 'Warranted that (except as hereinafter mentioned) the amount insured for account of assured and/or their managers on . . . freight . . . shall not exceed 15 per cent of the values of the hull and machinery as stated herein but this warranty shall not restrict the assured's right to cover . . . freight and/or chartered freight on board or not on board, insured for twelve months or other time. Any amount not exceeding 25 per cent of the value of the hull and machinery as stated herein, but if the insurance be for less than twelve months, the 25 per cent to be proportionately reduced . . .'

The value of the vessel's hull and machinery was stated in the policy as £110,000, so the maximum amount for which the assured was entitled to insure freight under the above warranty by p p i or f i a policies for 6 months was £13,750. In fact, the assured insured the freight by f i a policy against war risks for 6 months for £27,500. The vessel was lost, and a claim was made under the policy. The insurers repudiated liability on the ground that there had been a breach of warranty.

The House of Lords[18] held that there had been a breach of warranty by reason of the over-insurance of the freight against war risks, since the word 'insured' in clause 22 must be construed in its natural and ordinary sense, and therefore covered all kinds of marine insurance.

Viscount Cave observed:[19]

> 'That clause contained a warranty or condition that the amount insured on freight, etc (p p i or f i a), should not exceed (in the event which happened) 12½ per cent of the stated value of the hull and machinery, or £13,750, and, as the f i a insurance of the freight against war risks was for £27,500, there was a clear breach of the warranty unless the word "insured" in the warranty is to be confined to insurances against the perils insured against by the policy in question, that is to say, to insurances against marine perils only to the exclusion of war perils. I see no sufficient ground for so restricting the meaning of the word. The word "insured" in a policy of marine

---

[15] (1923) 15 LlL Rep at 177.
[16] [1924] All ER Rep 66, HL.
[17] For the modern version of this clause see clause 21 of the Institute Time Clauses (Hulls), set out in Appendix III, pp 538–539, post.
[18] Viscount Haldane LC, Viscount Cave, Viscount Finlay, Lord Sumner and Lord Parmoor.
[19] [1924] All ER Rep at 73.

insurance prima facie covers all insurances against sea risks, including war risks; and there is in the policy in question in this case no context sufficient to cut down the natural meaning of the word. It is true that the insurer of a ship against ordinary marine risks is not directly interested in the amount of the insurance of the freight against war risks. But it is said that an over-insurance of freights by honour policies against war risks may tempt the owner to throw away his ship with a view to claiming under the war risk policies, and, alternatively, under the ordinary marine policies, and so may involve the marine underwriters in litigation and loss; and certainly the course of events in the present case supports that view. Upon the whole I think that the word "insured" must be construed in its natural and ordinary sense, and as including all kinds of marine insurance.'

But their Lordships held that the breach of warranty had been waived by the insurers.[20]

The operation of the clause will be confined to the subject-matter of the policy.

Thus, in *Roddick v Indemnity Mutual Marine Insurance Co*[1] a policy for £1,000 on hull and machinery valued at £10,000 contained a clause '£5,000 warranted uninsured'. The assured had effected policies on hull and machinery for a total £5,000, and had also effected insurances of £2,600 on disbursements. It was held that there was no breach of warranty as the two sets of policies did not cover the same subject-matter.

8 Other instances

In *Bird's Cigarette Manufacturing Co Ltd v Rouse*[2] cigarettes in a warehouse in Cologne were insured under a policy containing the words 'Warranted no complaints'. In fact, before the policy was effected, complaints that some of the cigarettes, which had been in the warehouse and had been sold to customers, were mildewed had been received by the assured. When a claim was made in respect of a loss under the policy, the insurers refused to indemnify the assured on the ground that there had been a breach of warranty. Bailhache J, held that this defence succeeded.[3]

In *United Shipping Co Ltd v Assicurazioni Generali*[4] the plaintiffs sold a steamer to an Italian. He paid part of the purchase price, the remainder being left on mortgage, the plaintiffs receiving a statutory mortgage and insurance policies effected by him and approved by them. One-third of the sum insured was insured by the defendants and the other two-thirds by Sicilian companies. The defendants gave the plaintiffs a guarantee of the proper fulfilment by the Sicilian companies under the policy. A clause in the policy stated:

> 'The assured [i e the purchaser of the vessel] is obliged under penalty of forfeiture of the benefits accrued from the present insurances to maintain the steamer during the year of insurance in the first class of the Registro Italiano or other equivalent register recognised by the underwriters. If this condition is not complied with, the said steamer is covered solely against total loss and this of course until the restoration of the above-mentioned first class.'

The vessel was classified BS*. This meant that she was in the BS class of the British Corporation, which was a well-known classification society. The star

---

[20] As to this point, see p 312, post.
[1] [1895] 2 QB 380.
[2] (1924) 19 LlL Rep 301, KBD.
[3] His Lordship also held that the defence of non-disclosure of a material fact, viz that there had been complaints, also succeeded. As to this point, see p 62, ante.
[4] (1929) 34 LlL Rep 323, CA.

indicated that she was built under the Corporation's survey. The BS* class was the only class in the Corporation's books. The Corporation's register was equivalent to the first class of the Registro Italiano. Under the Corporation's rules the vessel was subject to periodical surveys at periods of 4 years. The Corporation had power to extend the periods for a further year. Her second special survey No 2 was due in June 1925, and the facultative extension of 1 year brought the normal permissible period down to June 1926. Some work in connection with the survey was done in April 1925, but before the survey was completed she proceeded to India, and arrived back at Dunkirk in October 1926. At Dunkirk the British Corporation's surveyor refused to grant a further 6 months' extension, but in November 1926 gave an interim certificate enabling 'the vessel to go to any port of the Continent or of the United Kingdom where complete repairs are to be made under the survey of the British Corporation'. In January 1927 the Italian purchaser of the vessel obtained a further certificate from the surveyor at Dunkirk, and this enabled her to proceed to a port in the United Kingdom to load coal and thence to proceed to Ancona, Italy, for discharging and to Trieste for repairs.

She went to Cardiff to load coal, proceeded on her voyage to Ancona, but suffered particular average damage, and had to be towed to Brest. The plaintiffs claimed for a particular average loss under the policies. The two Sicilian companies repudiated liability on the ground that the vessel had lost her class, and that the warranty as to classification had been broken, so the plaintiffs sued the defendants on the guarantee.

The Court of Appeal[5] held by a majority that the defendants were liable. The vessel had maintained her class during the voyage from Dunkirk to Cardiff and thence to Trieste, and there had been no breach of the warranty to maintain her classification. The British Corporation had a discretion in granting extensions of the time for completing the classification survey.

Scrutton LJ, said:[6]

> 'I read the clause as being: "I undertake that my vessel shall be maintained by the British Corporation in the first class, that is to say, in their class," Was she? There seems to be only one answer to that. She was. She was in the register book during the whole of the period. It is not a case where there was a mistake, as if there had been an omission in the register book to cancel her class. It was not a case of any collusion between the British Corporation and the shipowner to defeat the Sicilian underwriters. The British Corporation intended to maintain her in her class. They intentionally left her there because they had not withdrawn her class. They intended it.'

He then went on to say[7] that the matter was one entirely for the judgment of the British Corporation. If they chose to maintain the class, no third party could come and say: 'You ought not to have done it under your rules.' It was no business of third parties. The only question was whether the Corporation had maintained the vessel in the first class.

In *Overseas Commodities Ltd v Style*[8] the assured had effected an 'all risks' policy in respect of some tins of canned pork. The policy contained a warranty stating 'warranted all tins marked by manufacturers with a code for verification of date of manufacture'. Many of the tins were not marked in the stipulated

---

[5] Scrutton and Greer LJJ; Slesser LJ, dissenting.
[6] (1929) 34 LlL Rep at 324. See also the judgment of Greer LJ, ibid, at 327–328.
[7] Ibid, at 325.
[8] [1958] 1 Lloyd's Rep 546, QBD (Com Ct).

manner. The assured discovered that some of the tins were blown, and claimed under the policy. McNair J, held that the action failed because the breach of warranty excused the insurers.

His Lordship observed:[9]

'In my judgment, the use of the words "for verification" point clearly and definitely to the conclusion that tins must be marked in a manner which will identify the actual date of manufacture. Verification, in its ordinary sense, means the establishment of the truth or correctness of a particular fact. There was no evidence before me that the term has any meaning according to the understanding of merchants other than this ordinary meaning. In my judgment, this warranty quite plainly means that the tins must be marked in the stipulated manner; that is, by a manufacturers' code so that the true or correct date of manufacture may be established. This seems to me to be the natural meaning of the words, and I am reinforced in my belief that it is the true meaning in these policies by the fact that, so read, it fits in with, and is consistent with, the earlier clause which provides that condemnation by authorities is to take place "not exceeding 5 months in all from date of manufacture". In that clause, "date of manufacture" clearly means "true or correct date of manufacture", and not merely the date stated by the code marks to be the date of manufacture.'

He then concluded:[10]

'It has long been well-established law that an express warranty requires a strict and literal performance: see now the Marine Insurance Act 1906, s 33(3). As is stated in Arnould on Marine Insurance, 14 edn, s 632,

"Every policy, in fact, in which an express warranty is inserted is a conditional contract, to be binding if the warranty be literally complied with, but not otherwise."

In the language of Lord Mansfield in *Hibbert v Pigou* (1783), as reported in "A Treatise on the Law of Insurance", by Samuel Marshall (1823), Vol 1, at 375; and "A Treatise of the Law of Marine Insurance, Bottomry, and Respondentia" (1861), also by Samuel Marshall, at 280.

"... the contract depends on an event taking place. There is no latitude, no equity; the only question is, has that event happened?"'

Counsel for the assured had contended that the warranty should be read distributively so as to excuse the insurer only in respect of the particular tins not marked as required by the warranty. His Lordship, however, considered[11] that it was wholly artificial and illegitimate to sever the policies in this way. The premium was a single premium calculated at the rate of 22s per £100 of the amount insured, and not at a rate per tin. Even if it were true that this view was unduly legalistic, the assured was still left with an insuperable difficulty that the suggested construction involved, at least, reading in words which were not in the warranty or re-writing the warranty in a different form, such as 'Underwriters are freed from liability in respect of any tins not marked...' The argument based on the hardship or unreasonableness in this construction was met by the very nature of the express warranty in marine insurance law, i e that such a warranty required a strict and literal performance.

In *Simons (Trading as Acme Credit Services) v Gale: The Cap Tarifa*[12] the assured advanced £A29,000 for a firm which proposed buying a vessel lying at Noumea, New Caledonia for the purpose of transporting cattle from Townsville, Queensland, to Manila. To enable him to finance the adventure he got in touch with insurance brokers, and on 13 December 1955, they issued him with a certificate stating that he was insured with Lloyd's underwriters, who

---

[9] Ibid, at 557.
[10] Ibid, at 558.
[11] Ibid, at 558.
[12] [1958] 2 Lloyd's Rep 1, PC.

agreed 'to pay a total loss of £A29,000 in the event of the vessel not completing loading Townsville within 90 days from sailing from Noumea from any cause whatsoever'. Also included in the certificate was the following condition:

'Warranted animals available for loading and all arrangements for conversion of vessel made at inception of this insurance.'

It was anticipated that the vessel would leave Noumea about 20 December 1955, arrive in Brisbane about 27 December for conversion so that she could carry cattle, sail from Brisbane about 11 January 1956, arrive at Townsville about 14 January, and, after loading, sail for Manila about 18 January.

In fact, she did not sail from Noumea until 10 January 1956. She arrived at Brisbane on 16 January, but she was never converted and never proceeded to Townsville. The assured claimed for a total loss under the policy, but the underwriters repudiated liability on the ground that there had been a breach of warranty, for 'all arrangements for conversion had not been made at the inception of this insurance'. The Judicial Committee of the Privy Council[13] accepted this contention, and held that the action failed.

The assured's argument was that the words 'inception of this insurance' meant the date when the vessel sailed. But their Lordships considered that it meant the moment of time when insurance cover was obtained.[14] The language was quite inappropriate to describe 'the date of sailing', which could, and no doubt would, have been used if that had been the date intended. The facts showed that by 13 December no arrangements had been made for the conversion of the ship, but on 14 December some ship repairers, in answer to a telephone inquiry made on behalf of the assured, said that they could convert the ship, if she arrived about the first week in January, but would give no firm quotation. There the matter rested until 23 December.

Their Lordships considered that, if the decisive date were 13 December, the warranty had not been complied with. Even if the time were extended to 14 December, no contractual obligation had then been incurred either by the assured or by the ship repairers. If something less than a contractual arrangement would suffice, something more definite and precise than the tentative undertaking given by the ship repairers would be required.

Lord Tucker observed:[15]

'The word "all" is important and precludes a construction which would be satisfied by "some arrangement".'

In *F B Walker & Sons Inc v Valentine*[16] a tug was insured under a policy which stated (inter alia):

---

[13] Viscount Kilmuir LC, Viscount Simonds, Lord Morton of Henryton, Lord Tucker and Lord Clyde.
[14] Counsel submitted that there was an obvious commercial reason for relating the warranty to the time of the making of the contract rather than to the time of the sailing from Noumea. Obviously the length of time required for the conversion of the vessel into a cattle-carrying ship was a most important and material fact for the underwriters. The vessel was suspect as to the boilers, a risk the underwriters were prepared to take. Adding to that danger the possibility of a lengthy period for the work necessary for the conversion, it was material for the underwriters to have some reasonable assurance that the conversion could be done within a space of time which would make the voyage likely to be performed within 90 days. See [1958] 2 Lloyd's Rep at 4.
[15] Ibid, at 7.
[16] [1970] 2 Lloyd's Rep 429. The case also concerned the interpretation of a clause relating to the perils insured against. As to this point, see pp 169–170, ante.

'It is agreed that when this Vessel is tied up and moored it shall be at all times in charge of a watchman in the employ of the Assured whose duty it shall be to make careful examination of the Vessel throughout at reasonable intervals, including inspection of the bilges.'

The vessel sank at a wharf due to excessive leakage of water through the rudder post and main engine stuffing boxes. The United States Court of Appeals, Fifth Circuit,[17] held[18] that the assured's claim for a loss under the policy failed, for they had not complied with the clause set out above. The watchman had not been instructed to make a careful examination of the tug throughout including inspection of the bilges, nor was instruction given as to what would or would not be 'reasonable intervals' at which the examination should be carried out.[19]

In *Capital Coastal Shipping Corpn and Bulk Towing Corpn v Hartford Fire Insurance Co (United States of America, Third Party): The Christie*[20] a warranty in a time policy relating to a tug stated:

'Warranted the master of the insured vessel shall be Captain C T Chism and except in the event of emergency or distress, this policy does not provide coverage [when] operated by any other master.'

The vessel sank and when the assured claimed under the policy, the insurers repudiated liability on the ground that there had been a breach of warranty in that at the time of the sinking, Captain Chism was not her master. The District Court for the Eastern District of Virginia, Norfolk Division, upheld[1] this contention and gave judgment for the insurers for there was no such emergency as to allow the warranty to be breached.

In *M Almojil Establishment v Malayan Motor and General Underwriters (Private) Ltd, The Al-Jubail IV*[2] a vessel was insured under a 'mixed policy'[3] for 12 months as from and on a voyage from Singapore to the Persian Gulf and whilst trading within the Gulf. The policy contained a warranty which stated:

'Warranted . . . (c) subject to satisfactory condition survey by approved surveyors.'

The vessel was lost off the coast of Iran while on her 'delivery voyage' over the Indian Ocean. The assured claimed for a total loss but the insurers repudiated liability on the ground that the warranty had been broken. Evidence was given that a survey report had been issued by a Mr Vesuna, a naval architect in practice as a marine engineer and ship surveyor. The report only touched on the hull and condition for classification purposes and did not deal with the question whether the vessel could withstand the 'delivery voyage' over the Indian Ocean. The Singapore Court of Appeal[4] held that there had been a breach of warranty and that the assured's claim failed for (i) the survey carried out by Mr Vesuna was not a 'satisfactory condition survey' within the contemplation of the warranty; and (ii) Mr Vesuna was not an 'approved surveyor' for that term meant a 'surveyor approved by underwriters in Singapore'.[5]

---

[17] Brown ChJ, Jones and Carswell CtJJ.
[18] The court found it unnecessary to determine whether or not the clause was a warranty. (See the judgment of Brown ChJ: [1970] 2 Lloyd's Rep at 432.)
[19] See the judgment of Brown ChJ: ibid, at 433.
[20] [1975] 2 Lloyds' Rep 100.
[1] See the judgment of Hoffman DJ, ibid, at 107.
[2] [1982] 2 Lloyd's Rep 637, Singapore Court of Appeal.
[3] For 'mixed policies', see p 91, ante.
[4] Wee Chong Jin CJ, Lai Kew Chai and Chua JJ.
[5] See the judgment of Chua J, ibid, at 641–642.

In *Pindos Shipping Corpn v Raven, The Mata Hari*[6] a yacht was insured under a policy containing a warranty which stated 'warranted class maintained'. She became a constructive total loss after sinking in a storm. At the time of the loss she was not in class. Bingham J, held that the insurers were entitled to repudiate liability on the policy on the ground that there had been a breach of warranty.[7]

Another instance of a warranty is provided by clause 1(1) of the Institute Time Clauses (Hulls),[8] which states:

> 'The Vessel is covered subject to the provisions of this insurance at all times and has leave to sail or navigate with or without pilots, to go on trial trips and to assist and tow vessels or craft in distress, but it is warranted that the Vessel shall not be towed, except as is customary or to the first safe port or place when in need of assistance, or undertake towage or salvage services under a contract previously arranged by the Assured Owners and/or Managers and/or Charterers. This clause 1(1) shall not exclude customary towage in connection with loading and discharging.'

D IMPLIED WARRANTIES

There are three implied warranties set out in the Marine Insurance Act 1906:

1. A warranty of seaworthiness of the ship (s 39).[9]
2. In a voyage policy on goods an implied warranty that at the commencement of the voyage the ship is not only seaworthy as a ship, but also that she is reasonably fit to carry the goods to the destination contemplated by the policy (s 40(2)).[10]
3. An implied warranty that the adventure insured is a lawful one, and that, so far as the assured can control the matter, the adventure shall be carried out in a lawful manner (s 41).[11]

The above warranties may conveniently be considered under the following heads:

   A Seaworthiness.
      1 Voyage policies on ship.
      2 Time policies on ship.
      3 Mixed policies on ship.
      4 Voyage policies on goods.
   B Legality.

A *Seaworthiness*

There is no absolute condition of a vessel recognised by law as satisfying the warranty of seaworthiness. The term is a relative one, and seaworthiness is that condition in which a ship should be to enable her to counter whatever perils of

---

[6] [1983] 2 Lloyd's Rep 449, QBD (Com Ct).
[7] See the judgment ibid, at 453. The assured unsuccessfully applied for rectification of the policy on the ground that the parties had not intended that the warranty should be included in the policy. See p 277, ante.
[8] These clauses are set out in Appendix III, pp 533–540, post.
[9] See pp 296–308, post.
[10] See pp 307–308, post.
[11] See pp 308–310, post.

the sea a ship of her kind, and laden as she is, may fairly be expected to encounter in performing the voyage concerned.[12]

Thus, s 39(4) of the Marine Insurance Act 1906 states:

'A ship is deemed to be seaworthy when she is reasonably fit in all respects to encounter the ordinary perils of the seas of the adventure insured.'

Thus, in *Burges v Wickham*[13] a small vessel of light draught constructed for river navigation was insured 'from the Clyde to Calcutta'. Although she could not be made as fit for ocean navigation as an ordinary sea-going vessel, she was made as seaworthy as such a vessel could be. It was held that the insurers were liable on the policy for her loss at sea.

Again, in *Clapham v Langton*[14] a river-going iron vessel of only 3 ft draught was insured under a voyage policy 'from the Tyne to Odessa'. Since she had been made as fit for sea navigation as it was possible to make her, she was held to be seaworthy.

Not merely must the vessel be sound in hull and tackle, but she must be well found in everything necessary for the voyage insured.

Her master must be competent and her crew sufficient.

If in any part of the voyage a pilot is required, she must obtain one.

The stores must be adequate, and, if the voyage is of such a character as to require the services of a doctor, he should be provided with the requisite drugs and instruments.

The vessel should be properly supplied with fuel and her machinery should be sound.

A ship is not unseaworthy if she is properly found in all requisite appliances, although, through the negligence of the persons responsible, such appliances are not used.

Thus, in *Hedley v Pinkney & Sons SS Co*[15] the omission to fix stanchions and rails, which were on board, although it constituted negligence in the master, was held not to be unseaworthiness in the vessel within the meaning of s 5 of the Merchant Shipping Act 1876.[16]

In *Steel v State Line SS Co*,[17] where a vessel sailed on her voyage with a porthole insecurely fastened, through which the sea entered and damaged the cargo, Lord Blackburn took the view that if the porthole was in a place where it would in practice be left open from time to time, but yet was capable of being speedily shut when occasion required, the vessel could not be said to be unfit to encounter the perils of the voyage; and if, when weather threatened, it was not shut, that would be negligence of the crew, and not unseaworthiness.

But a distinction was drawn in *G E Dobell & Co v SS Rossmore & Co Ltd*[18]

---

[12] *Steel v State Line SS Co* (1877) 3 App Cas 72.
[13] (1863) 3 B&S 669.
[14] (1864) 10 LT 875. See further, *Turnbull v Janson* (1877) 36 LT 635; *Cantiere Meccanico Brindisino v Janson* [1912] 3 KB 452.
[15] [1894] AC 222.
[16] See now, Merchant Shipping Act 1979, s 44.
[17] (1877) 3 App Cas 72. See further, *Hedley v Pinkney & Sons SS Co* [1894] AC 222 at 225 (per Lord Herschell); *Leonard v Leyland* (1902) 18 TLR 727; *The Diamond* [1906] P 282; *Virginia Carolina Chemical Co v Norfolk and North American Shipping SS Co* (1912) 17 Com Cas 277; *The Pentland* (1897) 13 TLR 430, where it was held that the vessel was not unseaworthy when one of her two boilers required minor repairs, and was out of commission.
[18] [1895] 2 QB 408.

where an insufficiently fastened porthole could not be closed without removing the cargo, which was then impracticable. It was said that, although the ship was well found with appliances to close the porthole, yet the neglect of the ship's carpenter to close it properly before loading and sailing rendered the vessel unseaworthy.

The mode in which cargo is stowed may sometimes be important, for if, by reason of the adoption of an improper mode of stowage, the ship starts in an unseaworthy condition, the policy may be avoided.

Improper or unsuitable dunnage may render the ship unseaworthy for the specific cargo.[19]

The warranty does not imply that the owner of the vessel undertakes that she shall be free from suspicion of unseaworthiness. It is enough if she is seaworthy in fact.[20]

The suitability of the term 'seaworthiness' as describing the warranty in modern times is open to question, for though in common use, yet, except as applied to the material condition of the hull or vessel in regard to her fitness for prosecuting the voyage, the term in its wider application seems hardly appropriate to the purposes of the warranty—e g when used in reference to the competency of the master or the number of the crew.

Burden of proof

The burden of proving a breach of the implied warranty of seaworthiness lies on the insurer where he alleges it.[1]

The fact that a ship springs a leak soon after commencing her voyage, although no doubt a matter for the jury to consider when deciding whether she was seaworthy at the time of sailing, does not per se affect the general principle that the party alleging unseaworthiness must prove it, nor does it by itself shift the burden of proof on to the assured.[2]

Thus, in *Pickup v Thames and Mersey Marine Insurance Co*[3] Brett LJ, said:[4]

> 'But when facts are given in evidence, it is often said certain presumptions, which are really inferences of fact, arise, and cause the burden of proof to shift; and so they do as a matter of reasoning, and, as a matter of fact, for instance, where a ship sails from a port, and soon after she has sailed sinks to the bottom of the sea, and there is nothing in the weather to account for such a disaster, it is a reasonable presumption to be made that she was unseaworthy when she started; and a jury may be properly told that, upon such uncontradicted evidence, they may presume as a matter of reasoning and inference from the facts, the vessel must have been in an unseaworthy condition when she started.'

In *Capital Coastal Shipping Corpn and Bulk Towing Corpn v Hartford Fire Insurance Co (United States of America, Third Party): The Cristie*,[5] where a tug was insured under a time policy and sank in port in calm water, the District Court for the

---

[19] *The Cressington* [1891] P 152.
[20] *Towse v Henderson* (1850) 4 Exch 890.
[1] *Parker v Potts* (1815) 3 Dow 23; *Franco v Natusch* (1836) Tyr & Gr 401; *Pickup v Thames and Mersey Marine Insurance Co* (1878) 3 QBD 594, CA.
[2] *Pickup v Thames and Mersey Marine Insurance Co*, supra.
[3] Supra. See further, *Anderson v Morice* (1876) 1 App Cas 713; *Ajum Goolam Hossen & Co v Union Marine Insurance Co* [1901] AC 362; *Lindsay v Klein* [1911] AC 194; *Cosmopolitan Shipping Co (Inc) v Hatton and Cookson Ltd* (1929) 143 LT 296.
[4] (1878) 3 QBD at 600.
[5] [1975] 2 Lloyd's Rep 100.

Eastern District of Virginia, Norfolk Division, held[6] that the presumption that she was unseaworthy had not been satisfactorily rebutted by the assured.[7]

In *Reid v Darby*[8] it was held that the sentence of a Vice-Admiralty Court, ordering a sale of a vessel on account of unseaworthiness, was not of itself evidence of the facts on which the finding was based.

1 Voyage policies on ship

Time from which the warranty applies

Section 39(1) of the Marine Insurance Act 1906 states:

> 'In a voyage policy there is an implied warranty that at the commencement of the voyage the ship shall be seaworthy for the purpose of the particular adventure insured.'

Thus, where a vessel is insured 'from London', she need only be seaworthy when she sails on her voyage. It is immaterial whether she was seaworthy when she was lying in the port.

Section 39(2) of the Marine Insurance Act 1906 states:

> 'Where the policy attaches while the ship is in port, there is also an implied warranty that she shall, at the commencement of the risk, be reasonably fit to encounter the ordinary perils of the port.'

Thus, in *Parmeter v Cousins*[9] where the policy was 'at and from Surinam to London', the vessel was sound enough to float in port, but she was unseaworthy for the voyage. She was lost after starting on her voyage. It was held that the assured was unable to recover on the policy. But if she had been lost in port, eg by fire, the insurers would have been liable under the word 'at', since she was seaworthy for that portion of the contract.

Where a vessel is insured 'at and from' a certain port, it is not necessary for her to be seaworthy for the voyage at the time when she is lying in port.[10]

In *Hoffman & Co v British General Insurance Co*[11] a wooden schooner was insured for a voyage from Uleaborg to Gweek. She met with contrary winds and put into Elsinore. She left there, but was caught in a heavy summer gale and had to return there, floating on the strength of the buoyancy of her cargo of timber. The assured claimed for a constructive total loss, but the insurer denied liability on the ground that she was unseaworthy at the commencement of the voyage.

Bailhache J, accepted this contention, and held that the claim failed. The schooner was built in 1894, and had undergone her last survey in 1911. In 1914 after a voyage in warm weather she arrived at Uleaborg and loaded a cargo of timber there. War broke out, and she could not leave. In 1920 certain repairs including caulking were carried out.[12] His Lordship said that her planks were worm-eaten, and that the caulking had been badly done. He observed:[13]

---

[6] See the judgment of Hoffman DJ, ibid, at 105.
[7] For the evidence, see ibid, at 101–103.
[8] (1808) 10 East 143.
[9] (1809) 2 Camp 235. See also *Biccard v Shepherd* (1861) 14 Moo PCC 471.
[10] *Annen v Woodman* (1810) 3 Taunt 299; *Oliverson v Loughnan* (1815) cited in 2 B&Ald at 322; *Buchanan & Co v Faber* (1899) 15 TLR 383.
[11] (1922) 10 LlL Rep 434, KBD.
[12] As to the evidence, see ibid, at 436–437.
[13] Ibid, at 437.

'I have come to the conclusion also that she was badly worm-eaten. Nobody who gave a seaworthy certificate knew that. I do not mean that the worms had eaten through the planks, but that they were so far worm-eaten that they were weakened. I have come to the conclusion that the caulking which was done was inefficiently and badly done through no fault of the surveyors or the master, but owing to the difficulties there were about getting the services of experienced workmen; and I have come to the conclusion that she needed caulking well and efficiently, not only between the light draught line and the loading line, but right down to the keel. I am very much influenced, but I hope not unduly, by the fact that immediately these repairs were done and the vessel had been reloaded, she made more water—7 in against 1 in— in twenty four hours. I am also impressed by the fact that, without heavy weather to account for it, when she had been at sea for six or seven days, she made so much more water that it was necessary to pump her every watch instead of only morning and evening; and I have come to the conclusion that she was altogether too weak to encounter the weather that she did encounter, and that the weather she did encounter was not so abnormal on a voyage of this description at this time of the year as she ought not to have been able to withstand with safety.'

In *Harocopus v Mountain*[14] two dumb barges carrying petroleum[15] in bulk were separately insured for a voyage from Batum to Istanbul. One was lost in the Black Sea in August 1922 and the other was also lost there in October 1922 while performing the voyage. The assured contended that the losses were due to bad weather, but the insurer denied liability on the ground that the barges were unseaworthy at the commencement of the voyage.

Roche J, held that this defence succeeded, and that the action failed. Both barges were unseaworthy by reason of their steering badly, having too little freeboard and insufficient bulkheads.[16] Further, in the case of the barge lost on the second occasion, the tug towing her was insufficiently coaled for the voyage, and on this ground also the implied warranty of seaworthiness had been broken.[17]

In *Neue Fischmehl Vertriebs-Gesellschaft Haselhorst mbH v Yorkshire Insurance Co Ltd*[18] an old steamer was used as a shrimp drying factory, and was insured for a voyage in the tow of a tug. She broke her back, and the assured claimed for a constructive total loss. The insurers refused to indemnify the assured on the ground that there had been a material misrepresentation by the assured, and also on the ground that the vessel was unseaworthy.

MacKinnon J, held that the action failed on the ground that the representation was material and was false,[19] and held (obiter) that the vessel was unseaworthy. The caulking was in such a condition that it could be pushed out by running one's finger over it.[20]

In *Russell v Provincial Insurance Co Ltd*[1] the insured's motor boat was insured under a time policy[2] against inter alia 'stress of weather, stranding, sinking'. She

---

[14] (1934) 49 LlL Rep 267, KBD.
[15] At the time in question the Allies were in possession and occupation of Istanbul. There were a considerable number of troops and other persons in the city, and there was a large demand for petroleum. A number of vessels were pressed into service which had never had the same experience before. These river barges were not uncommonly used for the purpose. See the judgment of Roche J, ibid, at 270.
[16] Ibid, at 270–271.
[17] Ibid, at 271–272.
[18] (1934) 50 LlL Rep 151, KBD.
[19] This aspect of the case is considered at p 76, ante.
[20] As to the evidence, see (1934) 50 LlL Rep at 154.
[1] [1959] 2 Lloyd's Rep 275, QBD (Com Ct).
[2] The policy was not in common marine form but was in the company's own form. See ibid, at 277.

sank on a voyage from Burnham-on-Crouch to Southend whilst cutting across a sandbank. When the assured claimed for a total loss, one of the defences[3] raised by the insurers was that she was unseaworthy, and that the assured had not kept her in a proper state of repair and seaworthiness as required by the policy.

McNair J, held that this defence failed, for she was seaworthy, and that she sank as a result of a genuine casualty.

He observed:[4]

> 'I think it is quite clear from the evidence of Mr Carlin and Mr Polkinghorn which I accept, that something in the way of a casualty—not a serious blow, but something in the way of a casualty—did occur to this craft as she was passing over the Whitaker Spit. It may well be that she struck something harder than the sand, because there was evidence that on these sandbanks, as one might expect, there are hard objects—possibly the remains from the war: pieces of wreckage and matters of that kind—which might damage a wooden vessel quite severely. Although she had drawn a little water while she was at her moorings, she had apparently come down the Crouch to this particular spot without any difficulty, and although whatever it was that caused the water to come in was nothing very serious in the way of a casualty, I think, in view of the fact that she had been recently repaired, that it would be quite wrong for me to hold that, when she left the Crouch, she was in any way unseaworthy. I also find that there was a genuine casualty resulting in the craft sinking substantially, in a way to surprise these two men.'

Voyage in stages

Where a voyage is divisible into stages, and the stages of the voyage require either the same or a different class of equipment, the absence of that equipment at the commencement of any stage will render the ship unseaworthy for that stage.[5]

Section 39(3) of the Marine Insurance Act 1906 states:

> 'Where the policy relates to a voyage which is performed in different stages during which the ship requires different kinds of or further preparation or equipment, there is an implied warranty that at the commencement of each stage the ship is seaworthy in respect of such preparation or equipment for the purposes of that stage.'

Thus, in *Quebec Marine Insurance Co v Commercial Bank of Canada*[6] the steamship 'West' was insured under a voyage policy 'at and from Montreal to Halifax in Nova Scotia'. She sailed from Montreal to Quebec in safety. But after leaving Quebec, on getting into salt water, her boiler leaked, and she was taken to Hookee Cove and repaired. She again proceeded on her voyage, but when near her destination she was driven ashore in a storm, and became a total loss. She was held to be unseaworthy by reason of the defect in her boiler, which rendered her unfit to encounter the seas when she entered the salt water. Lord Penzance pointed out that the vessel must be seaworthy for each stage of the voyage, though each stage might require a different type of equipment.

Again, in *The Vortigern*[7] a vessel, which was not adequately provided with coal for each stage of the voyage, was held to be unseaworthy.

---

[3] Other defences were that she was not covered by the policy at the time of the loss because she was 'being towed', and that the loss had been caused by 'the inexperience of the person in control'. As to these aspects of the case, see pp 270–271, ante, and p 272, ante, respectively.
[4] [1959] 2 Lloyd's Rep at 280.
[5] *The Vortigern* [1899] P 140; *Thin v Richards & Co* [1892] 2 QB 141; *Greenock SS Co v Maritime Insurance Co* [1903] 2 KB 657; *A E Reed & Co v Page, Son and East Ltd* [1927] 1 KB 743.
[6] (1870) LR 3 PC 234. See further, *Bouillon v Lupton* (1863) 15 CBNS 113.
[7] Supra.

Whether a voyage is one which is capable of being regarded as divided into stages depends upon necessity, and once the insurer has shown that the vessel was unseaworthy for the voyage from its outset, it lies upon the assured to prove the necessity for dividing the voyage into stages.[8]

Salved ship

Even in the case of a salved ship, which, having been abandoned by her original crew, is taken into a foreign port and sails from there to the United Kingdom, there is an implied warranty of seaworthiness in the policy on the voyage home.[9]

No warranty of continued seaworthiness

Although the ship must be seaworthy at the commencement of the risk, or at the commencement of each stage of the voyage if it is divisible into stages, yet there is no implied warranty that the ship shall continue seaworthy, for the possibility of the ship being rendered unseaworthy by certain perils, and of loss accruing thereby, forms the very risk which the insurer takes on himself when he enters into the contract.[10]

Dispensing with the warranty

The insurers may dispense with the implied warranty of seaworthiness, but in such a case the assured should see that this is done in terms which are plain and unmistakable.[11]

In *Parfitt v Thompson*[12] in a policy on a vessel from 'Bristol to Sierra Leone, and thence to her port of discharge in the United Kingdom', it was stated that she should be considered to be seaworthy in her hull. On her arrival at The Gambia she was found to be unseaworthy, and, since there was no place in which to repair her, she was sold. Pollock CB, said:[13]

> 'It appeared to me that if the vessel had foundered in a perfectly calm sea from a leak occasioned by rottenness on the day after the policy was effected, the underwriters would have been liable.'

2 Time policies on ship

A general application of the implied warranty of seaworthiness to time policies would be attended with great difficulty, for a time policy often attaches when a ship is at sea, or in a position where her owners would be quite unable to refit her in order to comply with the warranty when the policy attached.

Moreover, the purpose for which she is to be employed under a time policy

---

[8] *The Vortigern*, supra.
[9] *Knill v Hooper* (1877) 2 H&N 277.
[10] *Hollingworth v Brodrick* (1837) 7 Ad&El 40; *Dixon v Sadler* (1841) 8 M&W 895; *Biccard v Shepherd* (1861) 14 Moo PCC 471; *Dudgeon v Pembroke* (1877) 2 App Cas 284.
[11] *Parfitt v Thompson* (1844) 13 M&W 392. See also *Quebec Marine Insurance Co v Bank of Canada* (1870) LR 3 PC 234; *Sleigh v Tyser* [1900] 2 QB 333; *Cantiere Meccanico Brindisino v Janson* [1912] 3 KB 452.
[12] Supra. See also *Phillips v Nairne* (1847) 4 CB 343; *The Cargo ex Laertes* (1887) 12 PD 187, where the bill of lading stated 'warranted seaworthy only so far as ordinary care can provide'.
[13] (1844) 13 M&W at 395.

cannot often be set out with the same definite exactness as to voyage, cargo, and other incidents as it can in a voyage policy.

Section 39(5) of the Marine Insurance Act 1906 states:

> 'In a time policy there is no implied warranty that the ship shall be seaworthy at any stage of the adventure, but where, with the privity of the assured, the ship is sent to sea in an unseaworthy state, the insurer is not liable for any loss attributable to unseaworthiness.'

Meaning of 'privity of the assured'

In *Compania Maritima San Basilio SA v Oceanus Mutual Underwriting Association (Bermuda) Ltd: The Eurysthenes*,[14] where the parties applied to the court to determine the meaning of the words 'privity of the assured' in s 39(5), the Court of Appeal[15] held that they meant 'with his knowledge and consent'. In the course of his judgment Lord Denning MR, said:[16]

> 'When the old common lawyers spoke of a man being "privy" to something being done, or of an act being done "with his privity", they meant that he knew of it beforehand and concurred in it being done. If it was a wrongful act done by his servant, then he was liable for it if it was done "by his command or privity", that is, with his express authority or with his knowledge and concurrence. "Privity" did not mean that there was any wilful misconduct by him, but only that he knew of the act beforehand and concurred in it being done. Moreover, "privity" did not mean that he himself personally did the act, but only that someone else did it and that he knowingly concurred in it. Hence, in the later Merchant Shipping Acts, the owner was entitled to limit his liability if the act was done without his "actual fault or privity". Without his "actual fault" meant without any actual fault by the owner personally. Without his "privity" meant without his knowledge or concurrence.
>
> Such is, I think, the meaning we should attach to the word "privity" in s 39(5). If the ship is sent to sea in an unseaworthy state, with the knowledge and concurrence of the assured personally, the insurer is not liable for any loss attributable to unseaworthiness, that is, to unseaworthiness of which he knew and in which he concurred.
>
> To disentitle the shipowner, he must, I think, have knowledge not only of the facts constituting the unseaworthiness but also knowledge that those facts rendered the ship unseaworthy, that is, not reasonably fit to encounter the ordinary perils of the sea: And, when I speak of knowledge, I mean not only positive knowledge but also the sort of knowledge expressed in the phrase "turning a blind eye". If a man, suspicious of the truth, turns a blind eye to it, and refrains from inquiry—so that he should not know it for certain—then he is to be regarded as knowing the truth. This "turning a blind eye" is far more blameworthy than mere negligence. Negligence in not knowing the truth is not equivalent to knowledge of it.'

He then went on to say:[17]—

> 'The knowledge must also be the knowledge of the shipowner personally, or his alter ego, or, in the case of a company, its head men or whoever may be considered their alter ego. It may be inferred from evidence that a reasonably prudent owner in his place would have known the facts and have realised that the ship was not reasonably fit to be sent to sea. But, if the shipowner satisfies the court that he did not know the facts or did not realise that they rendered the ship unseaworthy, then he ought not to be held privy to it, even though he was negligent in not knowing.'

Examples

In *Thomas v Tyne and Wear Steamship Freight Insurance Association*[18] a vessel

---

[14] [1976] 2 Lloyd's Rep 171, CA.
[15] Lord Denning MR, Roskill and Geoffrey Lane LJJ.
[16] [1976] 2 Lloyd's Rep at 179.
[17] Ibid, at 179. See also the judgment of Roskill LJ, ibid, at 184, and that of Geoffrey Lane, LJ, ibid, at 188.
[18] (1917) 117 LT 55, KBD.

insured under a time policy was totally lost on a voyage from Appledore to Birkenhead. When she left Appledore, she was unseaworthy in two respects: (a) she was unfit for the voyage in consequence of damage which she had sustained in consequence of having twice taken the ground during voyages in the previous month; and (b) her crew was insufficient. The assured was not privy to the unseaworthiness with regard to the hull, but was privy to the insufficiency of the crew. The vessel was lost solely as a result of the previous damage to the hull. The assured claimed for a total loss under the policy.

Atkin J, held that the action succeeded. He considered that s 39(5) of the Marine Insurance Act 1906 meant that the insurer was not to be liable for a loss attributable to unseaworthiness to which the assured was privy, and observed:[19]

> 'In the case of insurance under a time policy the intention of the Legislature was that the assured should be unable to recover in respect of a loss occasioned by his own fault. That was the rule previous to the Act. In order to prevent the assured recovering under a time policy it was always necessary to show that the loss was the result of some misconduct on the part of the assured. The statute has now defined the degree of misconduct necessary to prevent the assured recovering as being the sending of the ship to sea in an unseaworthy state with the privity of the assured. When a ship is sent to sea in a state of unseaworthiness in two particulars, and the assured is privy to the one and not to the other, the insurer is not protected unless the loss is caused by the particular unseaworthiness to which the insured was privy. The contrary construction of the section is unreasonable. For example, if a ship were sent on a voyage with a defective equipment and subsequently during the course of the voyage became unseaworthy in some wholly different aspect which caused her loss, according to the [insurers'] contention the assured could not recover.'

In *George Cohen, Sons & Co v Standard Marine Insurance Co*,[20] which concerned an obsolete battleship insured under a time policy, Roche J, held that even if she was unseaworthy, this matter was quite unknown to the assured, who could therefore recover for a loss under the policy.

In *Frangos v Sun Life Insurance Office Ltd*[1] a Greek steamer was insured under a time policy by the assured, who were Greek citizens. Whilst on a voyage from Cardiff to Istanbul, she sank. She was about 30 years old, and had been in the ownership of the assured for 3 years. When the assured claimed for a total loss, the insurers contended that they were not liable because she had been sent in an unseaworthy state with the privity of the assured.

Roche J, held that the action succeeded, because, although possibly the vessel was in an unseaworthy state at the inception of the voyage,[2] that state was not known to the owners. The loss was due to the springing of a leak owing to the labouring of the vessel in a heavy sea, which was a loss by perils of the sea.[3]

His Lordship observed:[4]

> 'I am satisfied that there must have been a straining in the shell plating of this vessel in the neighbourhood of the afterpeak tank and of No 4 hold, probably a seam which extended over both those compartments in the vessel, and that that straining was due to the weather. I do not know what the condition of that seam or part of the vessel was when she started. It may be that the vessel was not in that respect seaworthy when she started; it may be that there was an old

---

[19] Ibid, at 56.
[20] (1925) 20 LlL Rep 133, 168; 21 LlL Rep 30, KBD.
[1] (1934) 49 LlL Rep 354, KBD.
[2] As to the evidence on this point, see ibid, at 358.
[3] Ibid, at 359.
[4] Ibid, at 358.

hurt which dated back some time, but which had not yet resulted in particular mischief, or it may not be so. I am disposed to think by the readiness with which the afterpeak bulkhead gave way, that it was in a dubious and shaky condition, whether by corrosion or otherwise I do not know.'

He also said that it was unnecessary to consider a very interesting point which was raised in the course of the case, viz what would be the effect if one part owner knew of the unseaworthiness which contributed to the loss, and the other part owner did not, and stated:[5]

'I reserve that point for consideration in any case in which it really arises. In this case it does not arise, and it would be as improper as it is unnecessary to express an opinion upon that interesting point.'

In *Willmott v General Accident Fire and Life Assurance Corpn Ltd*[6] a motor boat was insured under a time policy. She sank during a gale while lying at moorings off Anchor Head near Weston-super-Mare. When the assured claimed for a total loss, the insurers repudiated liability on the ground that she had been sent to sea in an unseaworthy condition to which he was privy.[7]

Branson J, held that this defence failed, and that the action succeeded. He observed:[8]

'Then it is said that the vessel was, to the knowledge of the [assured], unseaworthy and was sent to sea, to wit, these moorings, in an unseaworthy state and so the loss was occasioned. Now, I have this evidence: that this motor boat, as with the others that ply for passenger hire off Weston-super-Mare, is periodically examined by an inspector appointed by the Urban District Council, and I have had the advantage of Mr Shearmur's evidence in the witness-box. It amounts to this: that before this boat went out to sea or was commissioned after the winter of 1933–34, that is to say, in April 1934, she was examined by him and certain defects were pointed out and orders were given that those defects should be remedied, and when those defects had been remedied, she was again inspected before she was commissioned. It must have been done properly, of course, because the Urban District Council have to see to the safety of the passengers who come down and go for sea trips in these motor boats, and I cannot believe that when she was allowed by Mr Shearmur to go to sea and to carry passengers, she could have been in any proper sense of the word unseaworthy. Mr Shearmur would have been grossly negligent in his duty if he had allowed her to go to sea if she was unseaworthy, and I have not any doubt that she was not.'

In *Compania Naviera Vascongada v British and Foreign Marine Insurance Co Ltd*[9] a vessel was insured under a time policy. While on a passage in ballast from Larne to Port Talbot, she sprung a leak through striking the quayside when manoeuvring to leave Larne Harbour, and through heavy weather foundered in the Irish Sea. The assured claimed for a loss by perils of the sea, but the insurers denied liability on the ground[10] that she had been sent to sea in an unseaworthy state with the privity of the assured, thereby causing the loss. It was proved that the vessel was classed under the highest class of the Bureau Veritas, although her annual survey was 5 months overdue.

---

[5] Ibid, at 358.
[6] (1935) 53 LlL Rep 156, KBD.
[7] Other defences pleaded by the insurers were that the assured had not disclosed a material fact, and had made a material misrepresentation as to the boat's value. As to these defences, see p 68, ante, and pp 76–77, ante, respectively.
[8] (1935) 53 LlL Rep at 157.
[9] (1935) 54 LlL Rep 35, KBD.
[10] Another defence was that the vessel had been intentionally sunk at the instigation or with the connivance of the assured. As to this aspect of the case, see p 240, ante.

Branson J, held that the claim succeeded, and observed:[11]

'The Marine Insurance Act 1906 contains no definition of the expression "with the privity of the assured", which is used in s 39(5), the sub-section upon which the defendants must rely. Nor has its exact meaning been argued or defined in any decided case. It is contended by Mr Willink for the plaintiffs, that actual knowledge of the unseaworthiness to which the loss is attributable, must be proved. For this he relies upon the *dictum* of Lord Birkenhead in *Mountain v Whittle* [1921] 1 AC 615 at 618, and of Roche J, as he then was, in *Frangos v Sun Insurance Office* (1934) 49 LlL Rep 354 at 357, and upon the definition of "privy" in the Oxford Dictionary: "participating in knowledge—accessory". Mr Willink also referred to *Dudgeon v Pembroke* (1877) 2 App Cas 284 at 297, but that was a case decided before the Act which I have to construe, and so I prefer to leave it out of consideration.

Mr Miller, on the other hand, contends that when there has been a deliberate omission to have the ship surveyed when according to the rules of her Society a survey is due, where the age of the ship is such that her owners must have realised that only regular surveys could obviate the risk of her going to sea in an unseaworthy condition, the owners are privy to any unseaworthiness which the survey, if held, would presumably have discovered. In my opinion, this contention places a heavier burden upon the owner than that imposed by the Act. I think that if it were shown that an owner had reason to believe that his ship was, in fact, unseaworthy, and deliberately refrained from an examination which would have turned his belief into knowledge, he might properly be held privy to the unseaworthiness of his ship. But the mere omission to take precautions against the possibility of the ship being unseaworthy cannot, I think, make the owner privy to any unseaworthiness which such precaution might have disclosed.'

In *Pacific Queen Fisheries v L Symes: The Pacific Queen*[12] a wooden-hulled vessel was sent to sea in an unseaworthy state by reason of the hazardous condition caused by an increase in her gasoline carrying capacity from 3,000 to 8,000 gallons and by reason of an alteration in the method of discharging the gasoline. The vessel was lost as a result of an explosion and a fire, but the insurers refused to indemnify the assured on the ground that they were privy to her being sent to sea in such a condition. The United States Court of Appeals, Ninth Circuit,[13] held[14] that this defence succeeded, and that the claim of the assured must be dismissed.

3 Mixed policies on ship

Although neither s 39(1) nor s 39(5) of the Marine Insurance Act 1906 expressly mentions a mixed policy,[15] nevertheless a warranty of seaworthiness is implied in that type of policy.[16]

Thus, in *M Almojil Establishment v Malayan Motor and General Underwriters (Private) Ltd, The Al-Jubail IV*,[17] where a vessel was insured for 12 months as from and on a voyage from Singapore to the Persian Gulf and whilst trading in the Gulf, the Singapore Court of Appeal[18] held that there was an implied warranty of seaworthiness. Lai Kew Chai J, said[19] that the assured was in

---

[11] (1935) 54 LlL Rep at 57.
[12] [1963] 2 Lloyd's Rep 201, US Ct of Appeals, Ninth Circuit.
[13] Circuit Judge Pope, Circuit Judge Barnes and Circuit Judge Hamley.
[14] [1963] 2 Lloyd's Rep at 210–212.
[15] For 'mixed policies', see p 91, ante.
[16] *M Almojil Establishment v Malayan Motor and General Underwriters (Private) Ltd, The Al-Jubail IV* [1982] 2 Lloyd's Rep 637, Singapore Court of Appeal.
[17] [1982] 2 Lloyd's Rep 637, Singapore Court of Appeal.
[18] Wee Chong Jin CJ, Lai Kew Chai and Chua JJ.
[19] See the judgment at [1982] 2 Lloyd's Rep 640.

possession and control of the vessel before she left Singapore and began what would clearly be the most turbulent part of her life in the 12 months' period. That part of the cover was between two termini and the policy, so far as the 'delivery voyage' over the Indian Ocean was concerned, had all the attributes of a voyage policy. On the evidence, she was suitable for coastal and local trade and not for an ocean voyage.[20]

4 Voyage policies on goods

The implied warranty of seaworthiness does not extend to goods, for the underwriter is not responsible for their condition, apart from the action of the perils insured against.

Section 40(1) of the Marine Insurance Act 1906 states:

> 'In a policy on goods or other movables there is no implied warranty that the goods or moveables are seaworthy.'

Section 40(2) provides:

> 'In a voyage policy on goods or other movables there is an implied warranty that at the commencement of the voyage the ship is not only seaworthy as a ship, but also that she is reasonably fit to carry the goods or other movables to the destination contemplated by the policy.'

In *Blackett, Magalhaes and Colombie v National Benefit Assurance Co*[1] a deck cargo of cotton was insured 'at and from Liverpool to Oporto'. Some of the cargo was lost overboard by perils insured against. The assured claimed under the policy, but the insurers repudiated liability on the ground that the vessel had sailed in an unseaworthy condition in that she was improperly stowed, with all the light cargo in the hold and the heavy cargo on deck, thus tending to make her top-heavy and unable to resist the action of the winds and waves whereby she took a heavy list resulting in the loss alleged. Moreover they contended that the deck cargo was insufficiently secured.

Swift J, found that the evidence did not satisfy him that the vessel was unseaworthy, and held that the claim succeeded. The Court of Appeal[2] affirmed his decision.

The implied warranty of seaworthiness is limited to the vessel herself, and does not extend to a lighter or other craft used to convey the goods to the ship.

The insurer in a policy on goods 'until the same be safely landed in the port of discharge, including all risks to and from the ship', insures the risk of landing by lighters in the manner customary at the port, but the implied warranty of seaworthiness does not attach to the lighters so used.[3]

But the insurer will be liable for the loss or damage to the goods if the assured is not privy to the unseaworthiness of the vessel where the policy contains a clause in the form of clause 5 of the Institute Cargo Clauses (A), (B) or (C),[4] which states:

---

[20] For the evidence, see ibid, at 640–641.
[1] (1921) 8 LlL Rep 293, CA.
[2] Bankes, Warrington and Scrutton LJJ.
[3] *Lane v Nixon* (1866) LR 1 CP 412; *South British Fire and Marine Insurance Co of New Zealand v Da Costa* [1906] 1 KB 456.
[4] These clauses are set out in Appendix III, pp 516–526, post.

'*Unseaworthiness and Unfitness Exclusion Clause*
(1) In no case shall this insurance cover loss damage or expense arising from
unseaworthiness of vessel or craft,
unfitness of vessel craft conveyance container or liftvan for the safe carriage of the subject-matter insured,
where the Assured or their servants are privy to such unseaworthiness or unfitness at the time the subject-matter insured is loaded therein.
(2) The Underwriters waive any breach of the implied warranties of seaworthiness of the ship and fitness of the ship to carry the subject-matter insured to destination unless the Assured or their servants are privy to such unseaworthiness or unfitness.'

B Legality

Section 41 of the Marine Insurance Act 1906 states:

'There is an implied warranty that the adventure insured is a lawful one, and that so far as the assured can control the matter, the adventure shall be carried out in a lawful manner.'

Thus, in *Redmond v Smith*[5] Tindal CJ, said:

'A policy on an illegal voyage cannot be enforced, for it would be singular if the original contract being invalid and, therefore, incapable to be enforced, a collateral contract founded upon it could be enforced.'

An adventure may be illegal either by the common law or by statute or because it may be contrary to the war policy of this country.

The illegality must, however, be one arising under the law of England.[6] Whether a statute is such as to render any adventure in violation of its terms illegal or whether its scope is limited to the mere infliction of a penalty is often a difficult question to determine, and depends on a proper construction of the statute concerned in order to determine what was the intention of the Legislature.

As examples of cases in which statutes have been held to render the particular adventure illegal the following may be quoted:

i Loading cargo on deck in violation of the Customs Consolidation Act 1853, ss 170, 171, 172.[7]
ii Violating the repealed Act of 31 Geo III, c 54, s 7 as to the competence of the master.[8]
iii Exporting gunpowder contrary to 33 Geo III, c 2.[9]
iv Exporting naval stores in violation of the same Act.[10]
v Exporting provisions without a licence, contrary to 16 Geo III, c 5.[11]
vi Violating the Pacific Islanders Protection Act 1872.[12]
vii Exporting manufactures contrary to 15 Chas II, c 7, s 6.[13]

---

[5] (1844) 7 Man&G 457 at 474.
[6] *Planche v Fletcher* (1779) 1 Doug KB 251; *Fracis, Times & Co v Sea Insurance Co* (1898) 3 Com Cas 229.
[7] *Cunard v Hyde* (1859) 2 E&E 1.
[8] *Farmer v Legg* (1797) 7 Term Rep 186.
[9] *Camelo v Britten* (1820) 4 B&Ald 184.
[10] *Parkin v Dick* (1809) 11 East 502.
[11] *Johnston v Sutton* (1779) Doug KB 254.
[12] *Australasian Insurance Co v Jackson* (1875) 33 LT 286.
[13] *Gray v Lloyd* (1812) 4 Taunt 136.

In the same way a policy covering an adventure in violation of a treaty will be void, for a treaty is part of the law of the contracting States.[14]

In time of war, so long as this country remains neutral, it is not illegal to carry contraband to one of the belligerents or to run his blockade, even though to do so would constitute a breach of neutrality and so subject the property insured to the risk of capture.[15]

Once, however, this country becomes a belligerent not only is it illegal for any of its subjects to trade to an enemy country or with an enemy subject,[16] but any adventure on the part of a neutral which constitutes a breach of neutrality becomes, from the point of view of this country, an illegal adventure. In short, it may be said that whenever any property becomes liable to British capture, according to the principles of the Law of Prize, its insurance is illegal.

Prior to the Marine Insurance Act 1906 it was held that where the act complained of as being illegal was the act of the master, there must be circumstances from which the knowledge of the owners might be presumed in order that they might be affected by such act.[17]

The principle of this decision, however, seems to have been somewhat extended by the Marine Insurance Act 1906, s 41. It is submitted that an assured will not be excused from the consequences of some illegality on the part of the master unless it is clear that not only was the act done without his knowledge and consent, but that nothing in his own conduct conduced to the illegality being committed.

If an entire voyage is insured, any illegality committed or to be committed at any stage of it will vitiate the insurance.[18]

Where an insurance is effected in order to cover a part of the voyage only, it would seem necessary that the illegality must exist in that part, and that the insurance is not affected by illegality at some previous or succeeding part of the voyage.[19]

In all cases the question of illegality affects the insurer as well as the assured, so that where the illegality is established, the insurer will be able to recover his premium,[20] and if the risk is illegal, the insurer will be discharged from all liability, although he was aware of the illegality and although he may not desire to defend the action on that ground. The court will itself refuse to give an effect to an insurance which is seen to be illegal.[1]

In *Pacific Queen Fisheries v L Symes, The Pacific Queen*[2] the United States Court of Appeals, Ninth Circuit,[3] declined to express a view as to whether the fact that a wooden-hulled motor vessel was in breach of the Tanker Act[4] because she carried bulk gasoline without a certificate, rendered the voyage illegal.

---

[14] *The Eenrom* (1799) 2 Ch Rob 1; *Wilson v Marryat* (1798) 8 Term Rep 31; *Bird v Appleton* (1800) 8 Term Rep 562.
[15] *Re Grazebrook, ex p Chavasse* (1865) 4 De GJ&Sm 655; *The Helen* (1865) LR 1 A&E 1; *Caine v Palace SS Co* [1907] 1 KB 670.
[16] *The Hoop* (1799) 1 Ch Rob 196.
[17] *Wilson v Rankin* (1865) LR 1 QB 162.
[18] *Bird v Appleton*, supra; *Wilson v Marryat*, supra.
[19] *Sewell v Royal Exchange* (1813) 4 Taunt 856.
[20] *Jenkins v Power* (1817) 6 M&S 282.
[1] *Holman v Johnson* (1775) 1 Cowp 341; *Gedge v Royal Exchange Assurance Corpn* [1900] 2 QB 214.
[2] [1963] 2 Lloyd's Rep 201, US Ct of Appeals, Ninth Circuit.
[3] Circuit Judge Pope, Circuit Judge Barnes and Circuit Judge Hamley.
[4] 46 US Code Sect 391a.

Circuit Judge Barnes observed:[5]

> 'We feel there exists a question, under the circumstances here presented, whether or not the bulk gasoline carried by the *Pacific Queen* could come within the term "fuel or stores". More importantly, other fishing vessels, performing a similar role as that played by the *Pacific Queen*, are (or very shortly will be) engaged in fishing adventures. Some carry bulk gasoline for the same purposes as those of the *Pacific Queen*. Many are insured, either by [the defendants] or other underwriters. If a loss occurred, this case would be an important and perhaps controlling precedent. The Commandant of the Coast Guard said:
>
> > "3. Since full compliance with either the regulations under the Tanker Act or the Dangerous Cargo Act, neither of which regulations were designed to cover this type of vessel and operation, which is presumably fishing, is impossible, or impracticable of accomplishment and further, since it is possible that the legal responsibilities of the owners of this type of vessel are not sufficiently clear, the file in this case will be referred to the Merchant Marine Council for study and action towards issuing such clarifying regulations as may be indicated."
>
> Therefore, we prefer not to make an unnecessary decision on a non-controlling issue until the Merchant Marine Council (an expert body which can hold hearings and consider all ramifications of the question) has determined by regulation whether vessels of the *Pacific Queen's* type and operation should or should not be within the purview of the Tanker and Dangerous Cargo Acts.'

In *James Yachts Ltd v Thames and Mersey Marine Insurance Co Ltd*[6] the Supreme Court of British Columbia held[7] that the insurers were entitled to avoid liability under a builders' risk policy on the ground that the assured was in breach of the implied warranty in the Marine Insurance Act of British Columbia (RSC 1960, c 231) s 43[8] in that he was operating an unlawful business in carrying on boat building at his yard when forbidden to do so pursuant to the byelaws and regulations of the local authority.

E EXCUSES FOR BREACH OF WARRANTY

Section 34(1) of the Marine Insurance Act 1906 states:

> 'Non-compliance with a warranty is excused when, by reason of a change of circumstances, the warranty ceases to be applicable to the circumstances of the contract, or when compliance with the warranty is rendered unlawful by any subsequent law.'

F RESULT OF BREACH OF WARRANTY

The result of a breach of warranty is stated in s 33(3) of the Marine Insurance Act 1906 which provides:

> '... If [the warranty] be not so complied with, then, subject to any express provision in the policy, the insurer is discharged from liability as from the date of the breach of warranty, but without prejudice to liability incurred by him before that date.'

The warranty so becomes part of the thing insured as to render it different from what it would be if there were no such warranty, and therefore if the thing

---

[5] [1963] 2 Lloyd's Rep at 214.
[6] [1977] 1 Lloyd's Rep 206.
[7] See the judgment of Ruttan J, ibid, at 212. It was also held that the assured was guilty of non-disclosure of material facts under the Marine Insurance Act of British Columbia (RSC 1960, c 231), s 20. As to this point, see p 66, ante.
[8] Which corresponds to the (English) Marine Insurance Act 1906, s 20.

without the performed warranty is lost from whatever cause, the thing so lost is a different thing from that in reference to which the contract was made.

Thus, in *Woolmer v Muilman*,[9] where a ship 'warranted neutral ship and property' was lost by perils of the sea, and it was shown that the ship was not neutral property, Lord Mansfield CJ, said:[10]

> 'This was no contract, for the man insured neutral property: and this was not neutral property.'

From this point of view, therefore, it cannot matter from what cause the breach of warranty arises, nor from what cause the loss takes place.

Nor is a breach of warranty affected by the fact that it may have had no bearing upon any loss which may have occurred.

Further, s 34(2) of the Marine Insurance Act 1906 states:

> 'Where a warranty is broken, the assured cannot avail himself of the defence that the breach has been remedied, and the warranty complied with, before loss.'

Thus, in *Quebec Marine Insurance Co v Commercial Bank of Canada*[11] a vessel insured 'at and from Montreal to Halifax' sailed from Montreal with a defective boiler which was only discovered when she reached salt water. She had to return to Montreal for repairs which were effected. She then sailed again from Montreal. It was held that the insurers were not liable in respect of her subsequent loss at the mouth of the St Lawrence.

G WAIVER OF BREACH OF WARRANTY

Section 34(3) of the Marine Insurance Act 1906 states:

> 'A breach of warranty may be waived by the insurer.'

Thus, in *Weir v Aberdeen*[12] a vessel was insured 'at and from London to Bahia'. She sailed from London in an unseaworthy condition by reason of her being overloaded. She was forced to put in at Ramsgate to unload part of her cargo, and then, with the consent of the insurers, proceeded on her voyage and was lost. It was held that the breach of the implied warranty of seaworthiness had been waived, and that the insurers were liable for the loss.

In *Sleigh v Tyser*[13] the implied warranty of seaworthiness was held not to be waived in a cattle policy by a clause which provided for 'fittings and condition of cattle to be approved by Lloyd's agent's surveyor', for, although this condition had been complied with, it was merely an extra precaution for the insurer.

Nor is the legal effect of a breach of warranty destroyed by a custom which prevails amongst insurers to pay innocent shippers of goods the amount of the loss where there is a good defence of unseaworthiness. Such a custom is a matter of honour only, and cannot be supported as a legal right.[14]

---

[9] (1763) 3 Burr 1419.
[10] Ibid, at 1420.
[11] (1870) LR 3 PC 234.
[12] (1819) 2 B&Ald 320; *Provincial Insurance Co of Canada v Leduc* (1874) LR 6 PC 244.
[13] [1900] 2 QB 333.
[14] *Brooking v Maudslay, Son and Field* (1888) 38 ChD 636.

In *P Samuel & Co Ltd v Dumas*[15] a vessel was insured under a time policy, and a warranty contained in it stated that the assured was entitled to insure freight for a period of 6 months for $12\frac{1}{2}$ per cent of the value of the hull and machinery. The value of the hull and machinery was stated in the policy as £110,000, so the maximum for which the assured was entitled to insure the freight under warranty by p p i or f i a policies for 6 months was £13,750. In fact, the assured insured the freight by f i a policy against war risks for 6 months for £27,500. The vessel was lost, and, when a claim was made under the policy, the insurer repudiated liability on the ground that there had been a breach of warranty.

The House of Lords[16] held that there had been a breach of warranty,[17] but also held[18] that the breach had been waived by the insurer.

Viscount Cave LC,[19] considered that the insurer was prevented from taking advantage of the breach of warranty by the circumstance that he was a party to the excessive insurance on freight which constituted the breach, and said:[20]

> 'Now a right may be waived either by express words or by conduct inconsistent with the continuance of the right; and even where there is no actual waiver, the person having the right may so conduct himself that it becomes inequitable for him to enforce it. Here the [insurer], who must be assumed to have been aware that the assured was prevented by the terms of the policy of insurance on the vessel from taking out honour policies on the freight for six months for any sum in excess of £13,750, joined in the issue of such policies for double that amount and took his share of the premiums on those policies; and I can conceive no conduct more inconsistent with an intention on his part to enforce the restriction. It is argued that at the moment when the representative of the [insurer] initialled the war risk "slip" the amount underwritten if apportioned between the ship, freight, and disbursements was not in excess of the amount allowed; but the answer is that the "slip" then already contained the words: "Hull and machinery, £110,000; freight, f i a, £27,500; disbursements, f i a, £10,500", and specified the period as six months, so that it was obvious on the face of the document that the underwriters were taking a share in an insurance of that character and amount and expected and intended it to be carried through. Further, when the policy was issued in October, it was known that the full amount specified in the "slip" had been underwritten; and Mr Dumas through his representatives, who must be taken (in the absence of any evidence to the contrary) to have acted with his authority, was a party to the issue of the policy. In my opinion, the [insurer] and the other underwriters who took that course are prevented by waiver or acquiescence from treating the marine policy on the vessel as void for breach of the warranty.'

In *Daneau v Laurent Gendron Ltée: Union Insurance Society of Canton Ltd (Third Party)*[1] a scow was leased to the defendant by its owner. One of the conditions under which she was leased was that the defendant would insure her. He effected a policy with the Union Insurance Society of Canton Ltd. The policy contained a warranty which stated:

> 'Period of Lay-up—Warranted that the vessel is to be laid up and out of commission between 16 November and 30 April, both inclusive, unless otherwise specifically agreed.'

The scow became a total loss, and the plaintiff sued the defendant for breach

---

[15] [1924] AC 431, HL.
[16] Viscount Haldane LC, Viscount Cave, Viscount Finlay, Lord Sumner and Lord Parmoor.
[17] As to this point, see pp 290–291, ante.
[18] Viscount Cave and Lord Parmoor; Viscount Finlay and Lord Sumner dissenting. Viscount Haldane LC, expressed no opinion on the matter.
[19] Lord Parmoor agreed on all points with the speech of Viscount Cave LC.
[20] [1924] All ER Rep at 94. For the dissenting speech of Lord Sumner, see ibid, at 91–94, and that of Viscount Finlay, ibid, at 78.
[1] [1964] 1 Lloyd's Rep 220, Exchequer Court, Quebec Admiralty District.

of contract in that the defendant had failed to return her. The defendant brought in the insurance company as a third party, but the insurance company denied liability on the ground that there had been a breach of the warranty set out above in that the defendant had failed to lay up the scow within the period stipulated or in the proper manner.

Arthur I Smith J, giving judgment in the Exchequer Court of the Quebec Admiralty District, held that there had been no breach of warranty, and that the insurance company must indemnify the defendant. He said that the vessel had been laid up in accordance with the policy requirements,[2] and that the company had participated in the arrangements for the repair of the vessel. The company did not cancel the policy or indicate that it considered that the defendant had forfeited the right to claim under the policy. Accordingly, the company must be deemed to have waived compliance with the warranty.

The learned Judge observed:[3]

> 'It was argued moreover, that in any event the third-party defendant is precluded from complaining in respect of the time, place and manner of lay-up, it having waived such right of complaint, if any, as it may have had.
>
> The proof shows that the third-party defendant was advised of the location at which the scow was laid up, and of the damage sustained by her, in the spring of 1962. Upon receipt of this advice the third-party defendant instructed its agents, Hayes, Stewart & Co to take charge of the matter and henceforth there was close co-operation between the defendant, the owner and Hayes, Stewart & Co in arranging for the repair of the vessel and in the course of action followed subsequent to her repair.
>
> It is the defendant's submission that in such circumstances the third-party defendant must be deemed to have waived such right, if any, as it may have had to complain that the terms of the policy had been violated in respect of the time, place or manner of lay-up.
>
> It is noteworthy that the policy contains no non-waiver clause and that the third-party defendant's representatives, generally without reservation, actively participated in, and in some respects actually directed and approved the arrangements made for the attempted repairs of the scow.
>
> At no time did the third-party defendant act to cancel the policy or in any way indicate that it considered that the insured had forfeited its right to claim thereunder. It was only by its statement of defence filed in October 1963, that it for the first time offered to tender back to the defendant the insurance premium paid by him.
>
> In the court's opinion the proof justifies the conclusion that the third-party defendant, with full knowledge of the circumstances which it now complains of as constituting a violation of the conditions of the policy, nevertheless so acted and dealt with the defendant that it must be deemed to have waived compliance with these conditions, if violation there was.'

In *Capital Coastal Shipping Corpn and Bulk Towing Corpn v Hartford Fire Insurance Co (United States of America, Third Party), The Cristie*,[4] where a warranty stated that a particular person should be the master of the insured tug, the District Court for the Eastern District of Virginia, Norfolk Division, held[5] that the evidence did not establish that a breach of that warranty had been waived by the insurers.[6]

In *M Almojil Establishment v Malayan Motor and General Underwriters (Private) Ltd, The Al-Jubail IV*[7] where a vessel was insured under a mixed policy[8] for

---

[2] As to the evidence on this point, see ibid, at 223.
[3] Ibid, at 223.
[4] [1975] 2 Lloyd's Rep 100.
[5] See the judgment of Hoffman DJ, ibid, at 107.
[6] The evidence is set out ibid, at 107.
[7] [1982] 2 Lloyd's Rep 637, Singapore Court of Appeal.
[8] For 'mixed policies', see p 91, ante.

12 months as from and on a voyage from Singapore to the Persian Gulf and whilst trading in the Gulf, the assured was in breach of the implied warranty that she should be seaworthy on leaving Singapore on her 'delivery voyage' over the Indian Ocean. She sank off the coast of Iran and when the assured claimed for a total loss, one of the issues which arose was whether the insurers had waived the breach of warranty. The Singapore Court of Appeal[9] held that, on the evidence, no proof of waiver had been established.[10]

In *McDermott v National Benefit Life Assurance Co*[11] a vessel was insured under a voyage policy which was on a cargo form and contained inter alia the Institute Cargo Clauses, one of which stated that as between the insurers and the assured it was admitted that the vessel was seaworthy.[12] In fact, the vessel was unseaworthy and had stranded at the time when the policy was effected. She was later wrecked on her voyage from Holyhead to Birkenhead. The assured claimed for a total loss, and contended that the implied warranty of seaworthiness had been waived by the insertion of the clause mentioned above. The insurers maintained that it was merely by an oversight that the clause had not been struck out of the form.

It was held by the Court of Appeal (Ireland)[13] that this contention failed because the Institute Cargo Clauses were solely referable to cargo, and were inapplicable in the present case.

Often the policy contains a clause concerning the waiver of a breach of warranty by the insurer as long as the assured is willing to pay an additional premium.

Thus, clause 3 of the Institute Time Clauses (Hulls) states:

> 'Held covered in case of any breach of warranty as to cargo, trade, locality, towage, salvage services or date of sailing, provided notice be given to the Underwriters immediately after receipt of advices and any amended terms of cover and any additional premium required by them be agreed.'[14]

Clause 4 of the Institute Time Clauses (Freight) is to similar effect.[15]

The implied warranty set out in s 41 of the Marine Insurance Act 1906 that the adventure insured is a lawful one, and that, so far as the assured can control the matter, the adventure shall be carried out in a lawful manner, is a warranty which an insurer cannot waive.[16]

---

[9] Wee Chong Jin CJ, Lai Kew Chai and Chua JJ.
[10] See the judgment of Lai Kew Chai J [1982] 2 Lloyd's Rep 637 at 642.
[11] (1921) 7 LlL Rep 97.
[12] The 'Seaworthiness admitted clause', which is referred to in this case, has now been replaced by the 'Unseaworthiness and Unfitness Exclusion Clause'. See pp 307–308, ante.
[13] Sir James Campbell LC, Ronan and O'Connor LJJ.
[14] See Appendix III, pp 533–540, post.
[15] See Appendix III, pp 550–554, post.
[16] *Gedge v Royal Exchange Assurance Corpn* [1900] 2 QB 214.

CHAPTER 22

The assignment of the policy

Generally a marine insurance policy is assignable.[1] The assignee has a right to sue in his own name, but may be met by any defence available to the insurer against the assignor. The policy can be assigned by indorsement. An assured who has no interest cannot assign. The rights of the assignor and assignee inter se depend on the terms of the assignment.

A   ASSIGNABILITY OF POLICIES

Section 50(1) of the Marine Insurance Act 1906 states that:

> 'A marine policy is assignable unless it contains terms expressly prohibiting assignment. It may be assigned either before or after loss.'

In the case of a policy on goods there is generally no prohibition against assignment of the policy. This is not so in the case of an assignment of a policy on ship, or a policy on freight.

Thus, clause 5 of the Institute Time Clauses (Hulls)[2] states:

> 'No assignment of or interest in this insurance or in any moneys which may be or become payable thereunder is to be binding on or recognised by the Underwriters unless a dated notice of such assignment or interest signed by the Assured, and by the assignor in the case of subsequent assignment, is endorsed on the Policy and the Policy with such endorsement is produced before payment of any claim or return premium thereunder.'

Clause 3 of the Institute Time Clauses (Freight)[3] is in identical language.

B   RIGHT OF ASSIGNEE TO SUE IN OWN NAME

Section 50(2) of the Marine Insurance Act 1906 states:

> 'Where a marine policy has been assigned so as to pass the beneficial interest in such policy, the assignee of the policy is entitled to sue thereon in his own name . . .'

In *Williams v Atlantic Assurance Co Ltd*[4] an unvalued policy to the extent of £8,000 was effected by the firm of Constantinou, Valsamis & Co to cover 20 cases of textile goods on a voyage from Alexandria. The goods were lost at sea. The plaintiff had established a claim against the firm for £7,000. The claim was settled on the terms that the policy was assigned to him, the firm retaining

---

[1] See further as to assignment of policies, Ivamy, *General Principles of Insurance Law* (4th edn, 1979), chapter 34.
[2] These clauses are set out in Appendix III, pp 533–540, post.
[3] These clauses are set out in Appendix III, pp 550–554, post.
[4] [1933] 1 KB 81, CA.

the right to receive the first £1,000 of any sum recovered. The plaintiff sued the insurance company in his own name, but the Court of Appeal[5] held that the action failed because he had not proved the value of the goods which had been lost.[6]

Greer and Slesser LJJ, also held that the assignment to the plaintiff did not pass to him the whole beneficial interest, and that, since he was a mere equitable assignee, he could not sue on the policy without joining the firm as co-plaintiff.

Greer LJ, said:[7]

> 'But the [insurers] also contended that, inasmuch as in assigning the policy to [the plaintiff] Williams, Constantinou, representing the firm, stipulated as part of the arrangement that the first £1,000 received under the policy should be paid to him, the beneficial interest in the policy was partly in Constantinou as representing the firm and partly in Williams, and that, even if the interest of Constantinou in the first £1,000 had been created by a separate transaction, it would have amounted to an equitable assignment of an interest in the policy. It seems to me this is established by the decision of Lawrence LJ, then P O Lawrence J, in *Re Steel Wing Co*[8] and the decision of Luxmoore J, in *Cotton v Heyl*.[9] I think that these decisions correctly lay down the law, and that it is impossible to say that the plaintiff Williams obtained the beneficial interest in the policy which would be necessary to enable him to sue in his own name under s 50 of the Marine Insurance Act. It is not material whether the beneficial interest in part of the policy moneys arose after an assignment by the beneficial owner of the whole interest, or, as in the present case, by a retention of part of the beneficial interest by the assignor at the time of the assignment.'

Slesser LJ, observed:[10]

> 'At common law the assignee could not sue in his own name on the policy, but an action could be brought by the assignor as trustee for the assignee: *Gibson v Winter*.[11] The power of the assignee to sue in his own name was conferred by the Policies of Marine Assurance Act 1868, s 1, and amended by the Act of 1906, and it is incumbent upon an assignee who wishes so to sue and does not join the assignor to satisfy the section. For the reasons I have stated Mr Williams has failed to bring himself within the Act, for he is not, in my view, possessed of more than part of the beneficial interest in the policy, part of which is either still in the legal ownership of the liquidator on behalf of the assignors or at least is impressed with an equitable interest in their favour: see per P O Lawrence J, in *Re Steel Wing Co*,[12] and Luxmoore J, in *Cotton v Heyl*.[13] In neither view has the beneficial interest passed within the meaning of the 1906 statute.'

C DEFENCES AVAILABLE TO THE INSURER

The assignee is liable to be met by any defence arising out of the policy which the insurer could have raised against the original assured, for s 50(2) of the Marine Insurance Act 1906 states:

> '... the defendant [i e the insurer] is entitled to make any defence arising out of the contract

---

[5] Scrutton, Greer and Slesser, LJJ.
[6] As to this point, see pp 99–100, ante.
[7] [1932] All ER Rep 32 at 39. But a contrary view was expressed by Scrutton LJ, ibid, at 38.
[8] [1921] 1 Ch 349.
[9] [1930] 1 Ch 510.
[10] [1932] All ER Rep 32 at 41. Greer and Slesser LJJ, also held that an equitable assignee could not sue in his own name at common law without joining the assignors as co-plaintiffs. See ibid, at 39, 41.
[11] (1833) 5 B&Ad 96.
[12] Supra.
[13] Supra.

which he would have been entitled to make if the action had been brought in the name of the person by or on behalf of whom the policy was effected.'

Thus, in an action by the assignee of the policy, the insurers are not entitled to set up a counter-claim which they may have against the original assured.[14]

On the other hand, the assignee may be defeated by the insurers showing that the policy was voidable owing to non-disclosure of a material fact by the assured.[15]

Thus, in *William Pickersgill & Sons Ltd v London and Marine Provincial Insurance Co Ltd*[16] the assignors of a marine insurance policy failed to disclose a material fact to the insurance company. The insured vessel was lost, and the assignees of the policy, who did not know of the non-disclosure, claimed against the insurance company. It was held by the King's Bench Division (Commercial Court) that the insurance company was entitled to rely on s 50(2), and avoid liability under the policy on the ground of non-disclosure even against an innocent assignee.

Hamilton J, said:[17]

'Attention has been drawn properly enough to the hardship which the plaintiffs have sustained by reason of the fact that, having trusted the British Standard Company to make the proper disclosures, the policy is disputed because the proper disclosures were not made. I am quite satisfied, however, that that is a risk which is certainly not of a character that ought to affect my judgment in deciding whether the defence of concealment is available against the plaintiffs or not. Whatever hardship may be inflicted on the plaintiffs in this case, the case is exceptional; whereas to hold the contrary, and in favour of the plaintiffs to exclude the defendants from raising this defence, would, in my judgment, revolutionise the position of underwriters, and entirely shake the basis upon which their business is done, which is that they are entitled to rely as against all persons interested now or hereafter in the policy upon proper disclosure and true representations having been made when the policy was first negotiated.'

In *Bank of New South Wales v South British Insurance Co Ltd*[18] the defendant insurance company had insured the Electrolytic Refining & Smelting Co of Australia Ltd 'as well in their own name as in that of those to whosoever the same may appertain' in respect of some copper ingots 'at and from Port Kemble to Hamburg'. The policy was against the usual perils, and included capture, seizure, detention and all the consequences of hostilities or warlike operations. The plaintiffs advanced to a German firm, Messrs Aron Hirsch & Sohn, who had bought the copper, the invoice price of copper on receiving the bill of lading and the insurance policy as security. The vessel carrying the copper arrived in London shortly after the outbreak of the First World War, and the copper was seized and condemned as enemy property and lawful prize.

The plaintiffs claimed under the policy in respect of a constructive total loss of the amount which they had advanced, on the ground that they were interested as pledgees.

It was held by the Court of Appeal[19] that they were in the position of assignees of the policy from Aron Hirsch & Sohn, and consequently under s 50(2) of the Marine Insurance Act 1906 had no greater rights than Aron

---

[14] *Pellas & Co v Neptune Marine Insurance Co* (1879) 5 CPD 34; *Baker v Adam* (1910) 15 Com Cas 227.
[15] *W Pickersgill & Sons Ltd v London and Provincial Marine and General Insurance Co Ltd* [1912] 3 KB 614.
[16] (1912) 107 LT 305, KBD (Com Ct).
[17] Ibid, at 307.
[18] (1920) 4 LlL Rep 266, 384, CA.
[19] Bankes and Scrutton LJJ, and Eve J.

Hirsch & Sohn, as regards whom the policy was null and void as they were enemy aliens.

Bankes LJ, observed:[20]

> 'If the title was that of assignees of the policy so as to pass a beneficial interest in it, then under s 50(2) of the Marine Insurance Act 1906 the defendants are entitled to make any defence arising out of the contract which they would have been entitled to make if the action had been brought in the name of the person by or on behalf of whom the policy was effected. The case has been argued on the assumption that if the policy was not effected wholly or partly on behalf of the plaintiffs, it was effected on behalf of Messrs Aron Hirsch & Sohn. No question has been raised in reference to the Electrolytic Company's interest in the policy. If, therefore, the title of the plaintiffs was that of assignee of the policy, the defendants were entitled to rely on the fact that Messrs Aron Hirsch & Sohn were at all material times alien enemies, and the goods enemy property. It is not clear that the plaintiffs were assignees of the policy, but, whatever the exact nature of their title, so long as it was derivative only, they could not be in a better position than as assignees.'

In *Graham Joint Stock Shipping Co Ltd v Merchants' Marine Insurance Co Ltd*[1] the insured vessel was a total loss off the south coast of Spain. She was found to have been wilfully cast away by the assured, who had made an equitable assignment[2] of the policy to mortgagees. The mortgagees claimed an indemnity from the insurers in respect of the loss.

It was held by the House of Lords[3] that the claim failed, for the wrongful act of the assured debarred him and consequently the mortgagees from recovering on the policy.

In *P Samuel & Co Ltd v Dumas*,[4] where a vessel insured under a time policy had been scuttled with the connivance of her owner, one of the issues which arose was as to whether the insurer could rely on s 50(2) as against a mortgagee of the vessel, since it was alleged that the mortgagee was entitled to sue on the policy only by reason of the fact that he was an assignee of it.

The House of Lords[5] held that this defence failed, and that the mortgagee was separately insured under the policy, and was not an assignee of it. Viscount Cave observed:[6]

> 'Secondly, it is said that the mortgagee was not originally insured by the policy sued upon, but was a mere assignee of the policy from the owner, and, accordingly, that as the owner, having scuttled his ship, could not sue upon the policy, this defence is available under s 50(2) of the Act against the mortgagee. In my opinion, the evidence shows clearly that Mr Samuel, the mortgagee, was an original party to the insurance, which was effected on his personal instructions, and that the brokers, when they took out the policy
> "as well in their own name as for and in the name and names of all and every other person or persons to whom the same doth, may, or shall appertain in part or in all",
> intended to and did enter into the contract of insurance on behalf of the mortgagee as well as on behalf of the owner. This was sworn to by three witnesses, who were neither cross-examined nor contradicted on this point; and I think that the learned Judge was fully entitled to find (as he did) that the policy was to be taken out on behalf of the mortgagee to secure the joint

---

[20] (1920) 4 LlL Rep at 385.
[1] (1923) 17 LlL Rep 44, 241, HL.
[2] There was no evidence to show that the policy had been effected on behalf of the owner and the mortgagees so that the mortgagees would have been directly insured: ibid, at 242 (per Viscount Cave LC).
[3] Viscount Cave LC, Viscount Haldane, Viscount Finlay, Lord Sumner and Lord Parmoor.
[4] [1924] AC 431, HL.
[5] Viscount Cave LC, Viscount Haldane, Viscount Finlay, Lord Sumner and Lord Parmoor.
[6] [1924] All ER Rep 66 at 75. See also the speech of Viscount Finlay, ibid, at 77, and that of Lord Sumner, ibid, at 82.

interest of himself and the mortgagor, and that there was no question of an assignment. If so, that disposes of this point.'

D FORM OF THE ASSIGNMENT

Section 50(3) of the Marine Insurance Act 1906 states:

'A marine policy may be assigned by indorsement thereon or in other customary manner.'

It was held in *Baker v Adam*[7] that delivery did not constitute a sufficient assignment. In that case Hamilton J, said:[8]

'I do not entertain any doubt that Messrs Chandler, Hargreaves, and Co handed over the policy with the assent and concurrence of the assured, Messrs Green, who had been their principals, and I think it is clear also that they handed it over with the intention, whether it was an effectual intention or not, to assign such interest in the policy as could be assigned. Section 50 of the Marine Insurance Act 1906 provides that "a marine policy may be assigned by indorsement thereon, or in other customary manner", and it is suggested that what Messrs Chandler, Hargreaves and Co did amounted to an assignment in a customary manner—namely, by delivery. In any case I think it is clear that the delivery to satisfy those words, must be one with the intention of assigning, and, in fact, I think there is sufficient evidence to show that there was such an intention to assign, but I do not think that, so far as the Marine Insurance Act is concerned, that mode of dealing with the policy constituted any sufficient assignment. What is the customary manner of assigning a marine policy appears to me to be essentially a question of evidence.'

In *J Aron & Co v Miall*[9] the method of indorsing the policy in blank in order to constitute an assignment was referred to by Scrutton LJ, in the following words:[10]

'One finds on the policy an assignment of the policy in the ordinary form in which policies are assigned in England, that is to say, the brokers who effected the policy have signed their name, and the agent of the first seller has signed his name. That indorsement in blank, according to my experience and according to the custom of marine insurance in England, assigns all claims on the policy to the holder of the policy, and it is made more precise in this case by Messrs Aron, the holders of the policy, indorsing on it a request that the claim shall be paid to them. In my view, the effect of effecting the assignment of the policy in that way in the ordinary manner in which policies are assigned in England assigns to the person holding the policy the right to sue on any claim which the assignor has on the policy, irrespective of the fact that the assignee was not at the time of loss interested in the subject-matter lost or damaged.'

One of the issues raised[11] in *Safadi v Western Assurance Co*[12] was whether there had been an assignment of the policy 'by indorsement or in other customary manner'. Roche J, held that no assignment of the policy had been proved, and observed:[13]

'It is said first of all against the plaintiff that there is not an assignment; that an assignment should be by indorsement and that there is none here that is material to this case. On that point s 50(3) of the Marine Insurance Act says that "a marine policy may be assigned by

---

[7] (1910) 102 LT 248.
[8] Ibid, at 249.
[9] (1928) 31 LlL Rep 242, CA.
[10] (1928) 31 LlL Rep 242 at 244, CA. See also the judgments of Greer LJ, and Sankey LJ, ibid, at 246 and 247 respectively.
[11] Another aspect of the case concerned the duration of the risk. As to this point, see pp 124–125, ante.
[12] (1933) 46 LlL Rep 140, KBD.
[13] Ibid, at 144.

indorsement thereon or in other customary manner". I think that makes it plain that, upon proof, assignment in some customary manner other than by written assignment or indorsement thereon can be a good assignment, and I am of that opinion. The case of *Baker v Adam* (1910) 15 Com Cas 227, I think amounted to this, that Hamilton J, as he then was, was not satisfied that the policy had been assigned in the customary manner. If that were the only point in the case, I think I should be satisfied here that the policy was assigned in the customary manner. I have no doubt myself that policies often are assigned otherwise than by indorsement. In the case of c i f contracts they are so often handed over without any indorsement being made upon them that I should be surprised if it could not be proved that that is a customary manner of assigning policies. But here I am not in the least satisfied that there was any intention to assign at all. I am unable to accept the evidence of Mr Safadi or the evidence of his partners on this point. It is entirely unsatisfactory. I think the strong probability is that those on the other side did not want to mix themselves up in this case, either because they did not want to be troubled about discovery of documents or about security of costs or both, and the true fact is that Mr Safadi was merely given the policies in order that he might sue for everybody concerned.'

E INEFFECTIVENESS OF ASSIGNMENT BY PERSON HAVING NO INTEREST

Although it is not necessary that the assured should be named in the policy, the protection which it affords is confined in the first instance to those on whose behalf it was effected, and is only available to a person to whom the assured has transferred his interest in the subject-matter if the assured has either expressly or impliedly agreed to assign the policy to him or to hold it for his benefit.

Thus, s 15 of the Marine Insurance Act 1906 states that:

'Where the assured assigns or otherwise parts with his interest in the subject-matter insured, he does not thereby transfer to the assignee his rights under the contract of insurance, unless there be an express or implied agreement with the assignee to that effect . . .'

Hence the assignee of the policy must be the assignee of the thing insured, if its exists. But if the thing insured is lost, it becomes incapable of assignment, though the right of action on the policy remains in the assured, and will pass to the assignee on an assignment of the policy; i e after loss, an assignment of the goods and the policy are valid, and the assignee may sue upon the policy in his own name.

The property, which is then covered by the assigned policy, is the interest in the damage or the chose in action.[14]

Therefore, on the sale of a cargo at sea, the purchaser should stipulate that the interest under the policy insuring the goods should pass to him, otherwise the interest of the seller would cease on sale, and the goods would be uninsured, for a sale of the goods destroys the interest of the seller in the property, and his policy becomes ineffective.

Although the assignment by indorsement of a bill of lading prima facie transfers the property in the goods, this depends entirely on the intention of the parties. If it is an absolute assignment, the full interest passes to the assignee; but the circumstances must be considered in order to see what was in fact intended to be transferred.[15]

---

[14] *Lloyd v Fleming* (1872) LR 7 QB 299; *Sparkes v Marshall* (1836) 2 Bing NC 761; *Swan and Cleland's Graving Dock and Slipway Co v Maritime Insurance Co and Croshaw* [1907] 1 KB 116; *Baker v Adam* (1910) 15 Com Cas 227; *J Aron & Co v Miall* (1928) 34 Com Cas 18.
[15] *Hibbert v Carter* (1787) 1 Term Rep 745; *M'Andrew v Bell* (1795) 1 Esp 373; *Williams v Atlantic Assurance Co Ltd* [1933] 1 KB 81, CA.

Further, the purchaser under a subsequent assignment of the policy cannot revive the policy in his own interest.[16]

Thus, s 51 of the Marine Insurance Act 1906 states that:

> 'Where the assured has parted with or lost his interest in the subject-matter insured, and has not, before or at the time of so doing, expressly or impliedly agreed to assign the policy, any subsequent assignment of the policy is inoperative.
>
> Provided that nothing in this section affects the assignment of a policy after loss.'

F RIGHTS OF ASSIGNOR AND ASSIGNEE INTER SE

As between assignor and assignee the rights of the parties to the proceeds of the policy assigned depend on the terms of the assignment. If by the terms of the assignment the assignee was to be entitled to the whole of the proceeds, he will not be accountable to the assignor notwithstanding that the policy may have afforded a measure of protection fuller than that upon which he was entitled to insist.

Thus, in *Landauer v Asser*[17] goods were sold afloat on c i f terms, insurance for 5 per cent over invoice amount to be effected by the sellers for the account of the buyers. The sellers insured in excess of 5 per cent, and handed the policy to the buyers against payment. It was held that the buyers were entitled to the full proceeds, and were not trustees for the sellers in respect of the excess over 5 per cent.

---

[16] *North of England Oil Cake Co v Archangel Insurance Co* (1875) LR 10 QB 249; *Rayner v Preston* (1881) 18 ChD 1; *Powles v Innes* (1843) 11 M&W 10.

[17] [1905] 2 KB 184. See also, *Ralli v Universal Marine Insurance Co* (1862) 4 De GF&J 1; *Strass v Spillers and Bakers Ltd* [1911] 2 KB 759; *Ionides v Harford* (1859) 29 LJ Ex 36.

CHAPTER 23

The construction of the policy

The construction of policies is affected by the doctrine of precedent. Various rules exist for the guidance of the court in construing the words contained in them. In addition, there are some rules for construction of policies set out in the First Schedule to the Marine Insurance Act 1906.

A CONSTRUCTION AND THE DOCTRINE OF PRECEDENT

Where words have been the subject of discussion in courts of law, the meaning which has been assigned to them will be taken to be the meaning intended in subsequent cases, unless the parties stipulate that some other meaning shall be adopted.[1]

B SOME GENERAL RULES OF CONSTRUCTION

The history of the Lloyd's policy, its creation and existence in commerce long before it came within the cognisance of the law, together with the conservative habits of businessmen, who hesitate to make any change which may bring into question the rights relating to valuable interests, all render it difficult to lay down any rigid rules of construction.

The rules for the construction of a policy are the same in all branches of insurance.[2] Among those which are of special importance in marine insurance are the following:

1 The intention of the parties must prevail.
2 The whole of the policy must be looked at.
3 The written words must be given more effect than the printed words.
4 The ordinary meaning of the words will be adopted.
5 The meaning of a particular word may be limited by the context.
6 In case of ambiguity the reasonable construction is to be preferred.
7 In case of ambiguity the 'contra proferentem' rule may be applied.

Thus, in *M Almojil Establishment v Malayan Motor and General Underwriters (Private) Ltd, The Al-Jubail IV*[3] Lai J, said:[4]

---

[1] *Bullen v Denning* (1826) 5 B&C 842. See further, Ivamy, *General Principles of Insurance Law* (4th edn, 1979), pp 353–355.
[2] See Ivamy, op cit, p 355.
[3] [1982] 2 Lloyd's Rep 637, Singapore Court of Appeal.
[4] Ibid, at 640.

'In construing this policy and ascertaining the intention of the parties, we look at the whole policy and the terms used in it for their plain, ordinary and popular sense. We also look at all the surrounding circumstances known to the parties at the time the contract of insurance was made.'

1 Intention of the parties

The cardinal principle is that the intention of the parties should be looked at.[5] Thus, Lord Mansfield CJ, said in *Stevenson v Snow*:[6]

'These contracts are to be taken with great latitude; the strict letter of the contract is not to be so much regarded as the object and intention of it.'

2 Construction of policy as a whole

The policy must be construed as a whole.[7]
Thus, Lord Halsbury LC, said in *Tatham, Bromage & Co v Burr*:[8]

'In looking at a document between businessmen, I do not think it is wise to look at technical rules of construction. I think it is well to look at the whole document, to look at the subject-matter with which the parties are dealing, and then to take the words in their natural and ordinary meaning and construe the document in that way.'

3 Written and printed words

Where terms have been added to the printed policy, they will, should they in any way conflict with the words of the printed policy, be treated as overriding the printed words, and be deemed to be the final expression of the intention of the parties.[9]

Thus, in *Robertson v French*[10] Lord Ellenborough CJ, said:[11]

'The words superadded in writing (subject always to be governed in point of construction by the language and terms with which they are accompanied) are entitled nevertheless, if there should be any reasonable doubt upon the sense and meaning of the whole, to have greater effect attributed to them than to the printed words, inasmuch as the written words are the immediate language and terms selected by the parties themselves for the expression of their meaning, and the printed words are a general formula adapted equally to their case and that of all other contracting parties, upon similar occasions and subjects.'

Thus, in *Mercantile Marine Insurance Co v Titherington*,[12] where in the old form[13] of the Lloyd's printed policy there was the usual 24 hours' safety clause,[14] covering the ship for 24 hours after her arrival and also a written clause protecting the ship for 30 days in port, the insurers were held liable for a loss within the 30 days.

Where the parties have added a clause to a printed form of policy, and words have been allowed to remain which may either render the document

---

[5] See Ivamy, op cit, pp 355–356.
[6] (1761) 3 Burr 1237 at 1240.
[7] See Ivamy, op cit, pp 356–359.
[8] [1898] AC 382 at 386.
[9] *Robertson v French* (1803) 4 East 130. See Ivamy, op cit, pp 359–361.
[10] (1803) 4 East 130.
[11] Ibid, at 136. See also *Joyce v Realm Marine Insurance Co* (1872) LR 7 QB 580; *Dudgeon v Pembroke* (1877) 2 App Cas 284.
[12] (1864) 5 B&S 765.
[13] For the old form of the Lloyd's policy, see pp 102–103, post.
[14] There is no such clause in the new form of the Lloyd's policy. For the new form, see pp 104–105, ante.

meaningless or frustrate the intention of the parties, the court in construing such a document may strike out the inconsistent words.

Thus, in *Cunard SS Co v Marten*[15] Walton J, said:[16]

> 'It is obviously necessary in every case to consider carefully the description of the risk or special kind of indemnity expressed in the written words of the policy in order to ascertain whether any particular clause of the printed form applies to the insurance effected by the policy. It is most unusual to find that the superfluous or inapplicable words have been struck out of the printed form.'

In *Hydarnes SS Co v Indemnity Mutual Marine Assurance Co*[17] there was a policy on freight in respect of meat, covering all loss caused by breakdown of the machinery until the final sailing of the vessel. The insurance was stated to be 'at and from Montevideo to any ports or places . . . in the River Plate . . . and then to . . . the United Kingdom . . . The insurance shall commence upon the freight . . . from the loading of the said goods on board the said ship or vessel at Montevideo'. Meat was not intended to be loaded at Montevideo, nor was it in the course of trade ever loaded there. The refrigerating machinery broke down after the vessel left Montevideo, at one of the ports of loading, and so no meat was, in fact, loaded. The purpose of the policy was to protect the assured from loss of freight by breakdown of machinery, so it was held that the printed words 'from the loading of the said goods on board the said ship or vessel' should be struck out, and that the assured was entitled to recover the loss of freight.

4 Ordinary meaning

Unless it can be shown that some special meaning is attached to the words either by judicial decisions, by usage, or by the special circumstances or terms of the contract, the words of the policy are to be construed in their ordinary and popular sense.[18]

Thus, in *Lawrence v Aberdein*[19] Abbott CJ, said:[20]

> 'If there be any one case in which effect can be given to the words, understanding them in their ordinary and popular sense, they ought not to be extended beyond that sense.'

Similarly, in *Bristol SS Corpn v London Assurance and Linard, The Delfini*[1] Bonsal DJ, said:[2]

> 'An insurance contract must be interpreted in context, giving effect to the plain meaning of the terms and to each of the provisions included.'

In *Scottish Metropolitan Assurance Co Ltd v Stewart*[3] a vessel was reinsured 'from 20 September 1922, until noon on 20 February 1923'. The reinsurer contended that the risk did not attach until midnight on 20 September. Rowlatt J, rejected

---

[15] [1902] 2 KB 624.
[16] Ibid, at 627. See also *Western Assurance Co of Toronto v Poole* [1903] 1 KB 376.
[17] [1895] 1 QB 500.
[18] See Ivamy, op cit, pp 362–374.
[19] (1821) 5 B&Ald 107.
[20] Ibid, at 110.
[1] [1976] 2 Lloyd's Rep 741, District Court for the Southern District of New York.
[2] Ibid, at 743.
[3] (1923) 15 LlL Rep 55. The case also concerned the question of whether the policy should be rectified to agree with the 'slip'. As to this point, see p 276, ante.

this argument and held that the ordinary meaning of the words used was that 20 September was included in the period of the risk.[4]

In *Bristol SS Corpn v London Assurance and Linard, The Delfini*[5] the words 'port risk' were held to mean 'a risk upon a vessel while lying in port and before she has taken her departure on another voyage'.[6]

In *Stolos Compania SA v Ajax Insurance Co Ltd, The Admiral C*[7] a term in the policy that claims were to be 'collected' through certain brokers was held to mean 'collected in cash' and not 'brought into account between brokers and insurers in the manner customary in the market'.[8]

The end and aim of interpretation is to ascertain its meaning from the document. But it has to be remembered that the policy is a form used by businessmen for business purposes. It must, therefore, be read from the point of view of men of the class who employ it, and if its terms or phrases have in the world of commerce a special meaning, apart from their ordinary signification, they must be so interpreted.

In this way the usage of trade is of importance, for if the contract relates to any special branch of commerce, e g the timber trade or the tea trade, whatever usages in that trade would by a businessman be regarded as affecting the meaning of the document must have due effect given to them in determining its true interpretation. The aim should be to see what was the intention of businessmen, who had a business end in view, when the contract was made which resulted in the execution of the policy.

Thus, in *Hutton v Warren*[9] Parke B, said:[10]

'It has long been settled that in commercial transactions extrinsic evidence of custom and usage is admissible to annex incidents to written contracts in matters with respect to which they are silent. The same rule has also been applied to contracts in other transactions of life in which known usages have been established and prevailed; and this has been done upon the principle of presumption that in such transactions the parties did not mean to express in writing the whole of the contract by which they intended to be bound, but to contract with reference to those known usages.'

Again, in *Brough v Whitmore*[11] Buller J, said:[12]

'The policy is founded on usage, and must be governed and construed by usage.'

Similarly, s 87(1) of the Marine Insurance Act 1906 states:

'Where any right, duty, or liability would arise under a contract of marine insurance by implication of law, it may be negatived or varied . . . by usage, if the usage be such as to bind both parties to the contract.'

The policy will, therefore, be construed with reference to the usage of the specific branch of trade with which it is concerned. 'Policies ought to be construed according to the course of trade and the methods usual at the place'.[13]

---

[4] The relevant passage in the judgment of Rowlatt J, is set out at p 276, ante.
[5] [1976] 2 Lloyd's Rep 741, District Court for the Southern District of New York.
[6] See the judgment of Bonsal DJ, ibid, at 743.
[7] [1981] 1 Lloyd's Rep 9, CA.
[8] See the judgment of Sir David Cairns: ibid, at 10.
[9] (1836) 1 M&W 466 (tenancy of land).
[10] Ibid, at 475.
[11] (1791) 4 Term Rep 206.
[12] Ibid, at 210.
[13] Per Lee CJ, in *Tierney v Etherington* (1743) cited in 1 Burr 343 at 346.

Thus, in *Stewart v Bell*[14] goods were insured from London to Jamaica and were destined for a particular port on that island. The custom was in such cases for the vessel to tranship the cargo into shallops[15] at an adjoining port. It was held that the insurers were liable in respect of loss of the goods whilst they were on the shallops.

Although, as a general principle, the insurer is not liable for damage to goods carried on deck, yet if he insures cargo which is usually loaded in that way, he assumes liability for any loss of it.[16]

Rule 17 of the Rules for Construction of Policy set out in the First Schedule to the Marine Insurance Act 1906 states:

> 'In the absence of any usage to the contrary, deck cargo ... must be insured specifically, and not under the general denomination of goods.'

It is an implied term of the contract that the vessel shall take the customary route for the voyage, and the insurer is only liable for loss incurred while the ship is pursuing that course,[17] or whilst doing things which are customary on that voyage, or at a port or place properly visited on the voyage.

Thus, s 46(2) of the Marine Insurance Act 1906 states:

> 'There is a deviation from the voyage contemplated by the policy ... (b) where the course is not specifically designated by the policy, but the usual and customary is departed from.'

The customary route may be proved by extrinsic evidence.

Usage must be notorious

In order that the usage may control the policy it must be 'an usage so established and settled amongst merchants and traders as to be clear and plain and beyond doubt'.[18]

But even if the usage is not general, yet if it can be shown or implied that the parties contracted with reference to it, they will be bound by it, though not otherwise.[19]

Usage must not contradict the policy

The evidence of usage is only admissible to explain or control the meaning of the policy. It will not be allowed to be given for the purpose of contradicting the plain terms of the policy.

Thus, in *Blackett v Royal Exchange Assurance Co*[20] in an action on a policy on

---

[14] (1821) 5 B&Ald 238. For other instances, see *Pelly v Royal Exchange Assurance Co* (1757) 1 Burr 341; *Brough v Whitmore* (1791) 4 Term Rep 206; *Moxon v Atkins* (1812) 3 Camp 200; *Otago Farmers' Co-Operative Association of New Zealand v Thompson* [1910] 2 KB 145.
[15] Light open boats for use in shallow water.
[16] *Da Costa v Edmunds* (1815) 4 Camp 142; *Gould v Oliver* (1837) 4 Bing NC 134; *Milward v Hibbert* (1842) 3 QB 120; *Apollinaris Co v Nord Deutsche Insurance Co* [1904] 1 KB 252; *British and Foreign Marine Insurance Co Ltd v Gaunt* [1921] 2 AC 41.
[17] *Salvador v Hopkins* (1765) 3 Burr 1707; *Reardon Smith Lines Ltd v Black Sea and Baltic General Insurance Co Ltd: The Indian City* [1939] AC 562, [1939] 3 All ER 444, HL; *Pelly v Royal Exchange Assurance Co*, supra; *Noble v Kennoway* (1780) 2 Doug KB 510; *Constable v Noble* (1810) 2 Taunt 403; *Uhde v Walters* (1811) 3 Camp 16; *Hunter v Northern Marine Insurance Co* (1888) 13 App Cas 717.
[18] *Edie v East India Co* (1761) 2 Burr 1216 at 1221; *Salvador v Hopkins*, supra.
[19] *Gabay v Lloyd* (1825) 3 B&C 793; *Matveieff & Co v Crossfield* (1903) 8 Com Cas 120.
[20] (1832) 2 Cr&J 244. See also *Hall v Janson* (1855) 4 E&B 500; *Provincial Insurance Co of Canada v Leduc* (1874) LR 6 PC 224.

'the ship "Thames", her tackle, apparel, ordnance, munitions, boat and other furniture' it was contended that there was a usage at Lloyd's not to pay for boats slung on the outside of the ship on the quarter. Evidence to that effect was rejected by Vaughan B, at the trial. On appeal, Lord Lyndhurst CB, said:[1]

> 'Usage may be admissible to explain what is doubtful; it is never admissible to contradict what is plain.'

Accordingly, after discussing the admissibility of evidence of usage in regard to deck loading, he held that the evidence was rightly rejected. On the other hand, in *Miller v Tetherington*[2] it was held that a usage at the port of Liverpool not to pay general average in respect of the jettison of deck cargo did not contradict the terms of a Lloyd's policy, and was, therefore, admissible in evidence.

For a custom to be inconsistent with the contract it 'must be such as if expressed in the written contract would make it insensible and inconsistent'.[3]

Usage must not be contrary to law

The usage must not be contrary to law. Therefore, where an insurer sets off a general balance due to him from the broker against a loss payable to the assured, such a practice, though founded on usage, cannot prevail, because it is illegal.[4]

5 Context of words

Sometimes the words have a special meaning owing to the very nature of the circumstances in which they are employed. In such a case the words will be construed with that special meaning.[5]

Thus, in *Neilson v De Lacour*[6] the words 'islands in the West Indies not in the possession of the British' were held not to be regarded as coming within the expression 'Windward or Leeward Islands'.

Further, the 'ejusdem generis' rule will be applied in the construction of marine insurance policies.[7] A particular instance occurs in the case of the perils insured against.

Thus, rule 12 of the Rules for Construction of Policy set out in the First Schedule to the Marine Insurance Act 1906 states:

> 'The term "all other perils" includes only perils similar in kind to the perils specifically mentioned in the policy.'

6 Reasonable construction

The construction must not lead to an unreasonable result, so as to put a burden on either of the parties which would be unusual and inequitable, having regard to the premium paid by the assured.[8]

---

[1] (1832) 2 Cr&J at 249.
[2] (1862) 7 H&N 954.
[3] *Humfrey v Dale* (1857) 7 E&B 266 at 275 (per Lord Campbell CJ).
[4] *Todd v Reid* (1821) 4 B&Ald 210; *Bartlett v Pentland* (1830) 10 B&C 760.
[5] See Ivamy, op cit, pp 374–379.
[6] (1797) 2 Esp 619.
[7] See Ivamy, op cit, pp 376–379.
[8] See Ivamy, op cit, pp 384–386.

Thus, in *Gairdner v Senhouse*[9] a policy covered a risk which was worded 'from London to Trinidad or the Spanish Main, with leave to call at all or any of the West India Islands or settlements, with liberty to touch and stay at any port or places whatsoever and wheresoever'. On the construction of this risk Sir James Mansfield CJ, said:[10]

> 'It must be confined to the voyage insured—that is to some port in the course of the voyage to Trinidad and the Spanish Main—otherwise I do not see where the voyage is to end. . . . The larger the words are, the more necessary is this construction, else the ship might trade and barter without any termination.'

7 'Contra proferentem' rule

If, however, any doubt arises as to the meaning and effect of the words, they may be construed in the sense most favourable to the assured, and any narrow or refined meaning may be discarded.[11]

> 'In the construction of policies the strictum jus or apex juris is not to be laid hold on; but they are to be construed largely, for the benefit of trade, and for the insured.'[12]

This rule is invariably applied in the case of exceptions, for the policy is mainly the insurer's document. He alone signs it, and any exception which it contains is usually for his benefit. Therefore, if the words have more than one meaning, and there is any doubt as to which meaning the parties intended the words to bear, that construction is adopted which is most favourable to the assured.

Thus, in *Blackett v Royal Exchange Assurance Co*:[13]

> 'The rule of construction as to exceptions is that they are to be taken most strongly against the party for whose benefit they are introduced. The words in which they are expressed are considered as his words; and if he do not use words clearly to express his meaning, he is the person who ought to be the sufferer.'

Accordingly, in *Lawrence v Aberdein*[14] a policy in respect of horses contained a clause stating 'warranted free of jettison and mortality'. The horses were killed and injured by the rolling of the ship. The words were construed against the insurer, who was held liable to indemnify the assured against the loss.

Similarly, in *Palmer v Warren Insurance Co*[15] a claim was made in respect of a time policy for a loss which had occurred on a voyage. The policy contained a clause excluding, during the term, 'all ports and places in Mexico and Texas and also the West Indies from 15 July to 15 October'. The insurers were held liable though the loss took place on a *voyage* from the West Indies to New York.

---

[9] (1810) 3 Taunt 16.
[10] Ibid, at 22. See further, Rule 6 of the Rules for Construction of Policy set out in the First Schedule to the Marine Insurance Act 1906 which states: 'In the absence of any further license or usage, the liberty to touch and stay "at any port or place whatsoever" does not authorise the ship to depart from the course of her voyage from the port of departure to the port of destination'.
[11] See Ivamy, op cit, pp 386, 392.
[12] *Tierney v Etherington* (1743) cited in 1 Burr 348 at 349. See further, *Carr v Royal Exchange Assurance Corpn* (1864) 5 B&S 941.
[13] (1832) 2 Cr&J 244. See also *Birrell v Dryer* (1884) 9 App Cas 345; *Smith v Accident Insurance Co* (1870) LR 5 Exch 302; *Re Etherington and Lancashire and Yorkshire Accident Insurance Co* [1909] 1 KB 591 at 596.
[14] (1821) 5 B&Ald 107.
[15] (1840) 1 Story 360.

The clause was construed as being confined to risks in port. It was to be read as if it had been written: 'Excepting all risks *in* all ports and places in Mexico and Texas and also in the West Indies from, etc.'

In *A/S Ocean v Black Sea and Baltic General Insurance Co Ltd* [16] Maugham LJ, said[17] that, having regard to the fact that the clause, which was alleged to be ambiguous, was contained not in the printed form of policy but in an addition in typescript added to the policy, he saw no reason for coming to the conclusion that the insurers were the proferentes, and accordingly there was no room for the application of the 'contra proferentem' rule.

In *Petros M Nomikos Ltd v Robertson*[18] the clauses in a freight policy stated:

> '5. In the event of the total loss whether absolute or constructive of the steamer the amount underwritten by this policy shall be paid in full, whether the steamer be fully or only partly loaded, or in ballast, chartered or unchartered.
> 8. Warranted free from any claim consequent on loss of time whether arising from a peril of the sea or otherwise.'

In considering the true construction of these two clauses Lord Porter said:[19]

> 'Read together it is possible to construe them in either of two ways. They may mean either (1) "If loss of freight be caused by loss of time, the underwriters shall not be liable, provided that if the vessel is a constructive total loss, then the underwriters will pay in full whether the cause of the loss of freight be loss of time or not", or they may mean (2) "In no case will the underwriters be liable for loss caused by loss of time, whether the vessel be a constructive total loss or not". For myself I prefer the former of the two constructions, but it is enough to say that the meaning is doubtful, that the proviso as to loss of time is an exception to the general liability of underwriters, and if they leave their exemption of liability doubtful, they cannot rely upon the exception but must pay the loss.'

In *Forestal Land, Timber and Rlys Co Ltd v Rickards*[20] Lord Wright in holding that the 'frustration' clause[1] in a policy was not applicable to a claim for actual loss or damage to the goods themselves, said:[2]

> 'Even if I felt any doubt about this, which I do not, I should still say that it is for an underwriter who has undertaken a particular insurance if he desires to make exceptions from it, to do so in clear terms. However, I do not think the exception is even ambiguous.'

Viscount Maugham said in the same case:[3]

> 'The first thing that occurs to one is that it would have been exceedingly easy to draft the clause as undoubtedly to have this wider effect [i e against the risk of claims for loss of goods as well as for claims based upon loss of the insured voyage] if that had been the intention. Next, if the matter is left in doubt, the clause must be construed contra proferentes, plainly in this case the underwriters. It might be sufficient, in the circumstances, to leave the problem here; but further examination of the clause seems to me to show that it is deliberately framed so as to have the narrow construction.'

In *Capital Coastal Shipping Corpn and Bulk Towing Corpn v Hartford Fire Insurance Co (United States of America, Third Party), The Cristie*,[4] where a warranty provided that a particular person should be master of a vessel, and a different person was

---

[16] (1935) 51 LlL Rep 305, CA.
[17] Ibid, at 310. See also the judgment of Greer LJ, ibid, at 307.
[18] (1939) 64 LlL Rep 45, HL.
[19] Ibid, at 55.
[20] (1941) 70 LlL Rep 173, HL.
[1] As to the 'frustration' clause, see pp 264–267, ante.
[2] (1941) 70 LlL Rep at 193.
[3] Ibid, at 185.
[4] [1975] 2 Lloyd's Rep 100.

her master at the time of her sinking, the District Court for the Eastern District of Virginia, Norfolk Division, refused[5] to construe the warranty contra proferentem because the evidence indicated that the assured had a clear understanding of the importance and operation of the warranty and could not contend that it was too vague.[6]

C RULES SET OUT IN THE MARINE INSURANCE ACT 1906

Section 30(1) of the Marine Insurance Act 1906 states:

'A policy may be in the form in the First Schedule to this Act.'

Section 30(2) goes on to provide:

'Subject to the provisions of this Act, and unless the context of the policy otherwise requires,[7] the terms and expressions mentioned in the First Schedule to this Act shall be construed as having the scope and meaning in that Schedule assigned to them.'

There are seventeen rules set out in the First Schedule,[8] and these concern the meaning of the following terms:

1. 'Lost or not lost'.
2. 'From'.
3. 'At and from'.
4. 'From the loading thereof'.
5. 'Safely landed'.
6. 'Touch and stay'.
7. 'Perils of the seas'.
8. 'Pirates'.
9. 'Thieves'.
10. 'Restraint of princes'.
11. 'Barratry'.
12. 'All other perils'.
13. 'Average unless general'.
14. 'Stranded'.
15. 'Ship'.
16. 'Freight'.
17. 'Goods'.

---

[5] See the judgment of Hoffman DJ, ibid, at 106.
[6] The evidence is set out ibid, at 106.
[7] Thus, in *Kulukundis v Norwich Union Fire Insurance Society* [1936] 2 All ER 242, CA, Scott LJ, drew attention to the fact that the special terms of the policy might vary the interpretation to be placed on it when he said (ibid, at 269): 'In the analysis of marine insurance cases it is often difficult to keep interpretation and application wholly separate, and the present is no exception; but so far as practicable it is helpful to clear thinking to endeavour to do so. It is also important not to forget that most of the law of marine insurance is in essence pure interpretation of the contract contained in the common form of marine policy. We have all got into the mental habit of thinking of it as substantive law, particularly since its codification in statutory shape; but the Act has made no difference to the essence of the legal problem—as is made plain by ss 1, 30, 87 and 91(2) and the "Rules for Construction of Policy" contained in the Schedule. It is as it always was, primarily a problem of interpretation; the Act merely fixed the interpretation which it requires the court to put on the old form of policy unless the special terms of the particular contract vary it. I emphasise the point, because on a difficult question such as that in debate in the present case, it seems to me helpful to keep the interpretation aspect prominently in mind and to remember that we are trying to determine what was the intention of the parties in respect of loss of freight as disclosed by their written contract, and especially in respect of the events and conditions in which the right to payment for a loss of freight should become operative.'
[8] See Appendix I, pp 502–503, post.

CHAPTER 24

The duties, authority and rights of the broker after effecting the policy

A THE DUTIES AND AUTHORITY OF THE BROKER

The duties of the broker after the policy has been effected will depend in the first instance on whether he has received express instructions from the assured. If there are no such instructions, he must carry out such duties as are implied by law as imposed on brokers.

Where there are express instructions

Sometimes the assured prefers to transact all business on his own behalf after the policy has been effected. At other times he may prefer to leave the policy in the hands of the broker with instructions, e g to cancel the policy, to give notice of abandonment to the insurer, to collect the sum insured in a case of loss.

In these circumstances the broker must carry out his instructions with proper skill and care. If he does not do so, he can be sued for damages for breach of duty.[1]

Where there are no express instructions

In the absence of express instructions the duties of a broker are such as are usually established by decided cases as being impliedly imposed on him, and his authority depends on the 'usual authority' given to persons in his position.[2]

1 Duty to give notice of abandonment[3]

It was held as early as 1803 in *Comber v Anderson*[4] that a broker, who had the policy in his hands, was responsible for giving due notice of abandonment. In this case an action was brought against the defendants, who were insurance brokers, for not giving notice to the underwriters, so that the plaintiff was unable to recover for a total loss. On 28 January, as the ship was proceeding down the river from Waterford on a voyage to Liverpool, she struck a rock and immediately filled with water. The greater part of the plaintiff's wheat was saved, but was so much damaged by salt water that it only produced £95 13s 4d. The abandonment was not made till 18 February.

On 2 February the plaintiff, who resided at Liverpool, wrote a letter to the defendants, which they received in London on 4 February, and in which, after

---

[1] See further Ivamy, *General Principles of Insurance Law* (4th edn, 1979), pp 551–555.
[2] See further Ivamy, ibid, pp 561–566.
[3] As to notice of abandonment, see p 381, post.
[4] (1808) 1 Camp 523.

mentioning the stranding of the ship, he said: 'In the meantime, if any steps can be taken for my interest with your underwriters, I trust to your usual goodness to do the needful. I should wish to abandon if it be admitted of.' The defendants by return of post wrote back that it would be imprudent to say anything to the underwriters without learning some further particulars. The plaintiff did not write to them again till 9 February, when he neither complained of the abandonment not being made, nor directed them to abandon. However, they sent in a notice of abandonment on 18 February, which in *Anderson v Royal Exchange Assurance Co*[5] was held by the Court of King's Bench to be too late.

Lord Ellenborough, in giving judgment, said that no negligence could be imputed to the defendants for not abandoning before 18 February. The plaintiff's letter of 2 February left it to the defendants' discretion to act as they should think most expedient; and if he was dissatisfied with their conduct, he ought immediately to have said so. Instead of that he did nothing until 9 February; and even then did not complain, or give them any fresh orders upon this subject. Had he positively requested them to abandon, they would have been answerable for not complying with his request as soon as possible. But he had referred them to their own judgment, and it seemed as if he himself at the time had thought that they acted judiciously. So the plaintiff was non-suited.

2 Duty to collect sum insured

In 1810 the court had to consider whether the broker by keeping the policy in his own hands was under a duty to collect the sum insured. In *Bousfield v Cresswell, Executor of Whitfield*[6] the defendant's testator was an insurance broker, and had effected a policy for the plaintiff and a total loss had occurred. This was an action for his not having duly called upon certain of the underwriters, who had since become insolvent, to settle the loss and pay the sums insured by them. It appeared that Whitfield had been employed as a broker to get the policy underwritten; but there was no evidence to show that he ought to have called on the underwriters to settle and pay, except that the policy remained in his hands after the loss had occurred.

In giving judgment for the plaintiff on the merits of the case Lord Ellenborough CJ, observed that if an insurance broker kept the policy in his hands, he should be presumed to promise that he would collect the sums due from the underwriters on a loss happening, in consideration of the commission he received for effecting the insurance. Here the testator, if he chose to part with his lien, might have handed over the policy to the assured as soon as it was effected, and his responsibility would then have been at an end. But as he retained it, he was bound to use all reasonable diligence to bring the underwriters to a settlement of the loss according to the usage of trade in this respect.

3 No duty to state terms of cover note

In *United Mills Agencies Ltd v R E Harvey Bray & Co*[7] McNair J, held that there was no duty in law requiring insurance brokers to notify clients of the terms of a

---

[5] (1805) 7 East 38.
[6] (1810) 2 Camp 545.
[7] [1952] 1 TLR 149, KBD.

cover note as soon as possible, though in practice it was usual to do so. His Lordship observed:[8]

> 'That seems to be good business and prudent office management, but on the evidence I am completely unable to hold that it is part of the duty owed by the broker to the client so to notify him, in the sense that a failure so to notify him would involve him in legal liability. No case was cited in which any broker had ever been held liable, or had ever paid any client money in respect of such a failure. It seems to me to put a quite intolerable and unreasonable burden on a broker to say that as a matter of law, apart from prudent practice, he is bound to forward the cover note as soon as possible. It is no doubt prudent to do so, both to allay the client's anxiety and possibly to enable the client to check the terms of insurance. That is a very different thing from saying it is part of his duty.'

4 No authority to cancel policy

In *Xenos v Wickham*[9] the plaintiffs' broker agreed with the defendants, a marine insurance company, to effect an insurance of the plaintiffs' ship on certain terms. A policy of insurance under seal was duly executed in the absence of the broker. According to the usual practice the deed was retained in the company's office to await the broker's application for it, and the broker debited with the premium. When the premium became payable and was demanded, the broker who had been paid the amount by the plaintiffs, declared that the insurance was a mistake, and without the plaintiffs' authority had the deed cancelled. The ship was lost, and the plaintiffs brought an action on the deed.

It was held that, although retained in the defendants' office under the above circumstances, the deed was fully perfected and constituted a complete contract of insurance between the parties, and, as the broker had no authority to cancel it, the action was maintainable.

Lord Cranworth LC, observed that the insurers had a right to consider the broker as having authority to do all which the broker could do in discharge of his duty in effecting a policy, and they might safely settle with him in a case of loss if that were the ordinary mercantile usage, but there was no suggestion that it was the part of the ordinary duty or power of a broker to cancel agreements once validly and completely entered into.

B THE RIGHTS OF THE BROKER

After the policy has been effected the broker is entitled to

    A   a lien
    B   brokerage.

A *Lien*

The broker is entitled to a particular lien on the policy and in certain circumstances a general lien as well.[10]

1 Particular lien

The broker is entitled to retain the policy until the premium and the charges

---

[8] Ibid, at 154.
[9] (1866) LR 2 HL 296.
[10] See further, Ivamy, *General Principles of Insurance Law* (4th edn, 1979), p 548.

due to him have been paid by the assured. Thus, s 53(2) of the Marine Insurance Act 1906 states:

> 'Unless otherwise agreed, the broker has, as against the assured, a lien upon the policy for the amount of the premium and his charges in respect of the policy.'

In *Fisher v Smith*,[11] Fisher was a shipowner in Barrow-in-Furness, and instructed Skinner & Co to insure one of his vessels for him. He knew that Skinner & Co usually employed Smith, an insurance broker in Liverpool to effect policies for their principals as there were no brokers in Barrow-in-Furness. Smith knew that Fisher was the principal in this case. A loss occurred, and Smith claimed that he was entitled to retain the policy until Fisher himself paid him the premiums which had not been paid over to Smith by Skinner & Co.

The House of Lords[12] held that the claim succeeded. Lord Penzance observed:[13]

> 'Under these circumstances it appears to me that the ordinary rule of law that a lien would arise in favour of the broker could not but be applicable to this case. It is precisely the same as if there had been no intermediate agent at all, and as if Mr Fisher had written direct to Mr Smith to ask him to open a policy for him.'

Even though the principal's agent has no authority to delegate his duty to a sub-agent to effect a policy, the broker will still have a lien if the principal exercises his power to ratify[14] the sub-agent's acts.

2 General lien

The broker may also claim a general lien in respect of any balance on an insurance account provided that he can bring himself within the terms of s 53(2) of the Marine Insurance Act 1906 which provides:

> 'Unless otherwise agreed ... where [the broker] has dealt with the person who employs him as a principal, he has also a lien on the policy in respect of any balance on any insurance account which may be due to him from such person, unless when the debt was incurred he had reason to believe that such person was only an agent.'

When lien arises

This subsection is based on a long established Lloyd's custom to the same effect. Thus, in *Olive v Smith*[15] Gibbs J, said that he came to London in 1775, and was 'pretty early conversant with marine insurance business', and never remembered any doubt existing as to whether a broker had a general lien on the balance of an insurance account.

As can be seen from the terms of the subsection, whether the broker has a general lien depends on whether he has dealt with his employer as a principal or had reason to believe that he was only an agent.

---

[11] (1878) 4 App Cas 1, HL.
[12] Earl Cairns LC, Lord Penzance, Lord O'Hagan and Lord Selborne.
[13] (1878) 4 App Cas at 8.
[14] As to ratification, see generally *Bowstead on Agency*, 14th edn (1976), pp 37–63; R Powell, *The Law of Agency*, 2nd edn (1961), pp 120–147; and Ivamy, *General Principles of Insurance Law* (4th edn, 1979), pp 569–577.
[15] (1813) 5 Taunt 56 at 65.

I DEALING WITH EMPLOYER AS A PRINCIPAL

In 1815 in *Westwood v Bell*[16] it was held that, if the broker reasonably believed that his immediate employer was himself the principal, his general lien would be upheld. Here the plaintiff, through a number of intermediate agents, had authorised one Clarkson to effect a policy of insurance for him with the defendants, who were insurance brokers. Clarkson represented that the policy was for himself, and the defendants accordingly effected the policy for him.

On finding out that the plaintiff was the real principal, they successfully claimed against him for a general balance of their account with Clarkson. In the course of his judgment Gibbs CJ, observed:[17]

> 'I hold that if a policy of insurance is effected by a broker in ignorance that it does not belong to the persons by whom he is employed, he has a lien upon it for the amount of the balance which they owe him. In this case Clarkson has misconducted himself and is liable for not disclosing that he was a mere agent in the transaction; but the defendants, who had every reason to believe that he was the principal, are entitled to hold the policy. If goods are sold by a factor in his own name, the purchaser has a right to set-off a debt due from him in an action by the principal for the price of the goods. The factor may be liable to his employer for holding himself out as the principal, but that is not to prejudice the purchaser who bona fide dealt with him as the owner of the goods, and gave him credit in that capacity. The lien of the policy broker rests on the same foundation. The only question is whether he knew or had reason to believe that the person by whom he was employed was only an agent; and the party who seeks to deprive him of his lien must make out the affirmative. The employer is to be taken to be the principal till the contrary is proved.'

II BELIEVING EMPLOYER WAS ON AN AGENT

In *Maanss v Henderson*[18] the plaintiff was a Prussian residing at Stettin, and consigned a vessel to Jennings with orders to effect an insurance on her. Jennings effected the policy in the usual way in his own name with the defendants, who were brokers. He had been in the habit of effecting insurances with them on account of others as well as for himself. Nothing was said by Jennings as to whether the policy was opened on his own account, except that he said it was 'neutral'. The ship sailed on the voyage and a partial loss was incurred. Jennings later told the defendants that he had acted only as an agent, and, on being sued by the plaintiff, they claimed a general lien and a set-off of some premiums on other insurances that Jennings had effected with them, but this was refused.

Lord Kenyon said:[19]

> 'If the agent disclose his principal at the time, it is clear that he cannot pledge the property of such principal to another with whom he is dealing for his own private debt. It is true that he did not name him at the time, but he did in effect the same thing by saying it was for a "neutral". Supposing the agent had said to the defendant, "It is true that I am an agent for a foreigner, but nevertheless you may retain the money due to him for my debt". Could such a transaction be sustained? But that which is now contended for is in effect the same thing.'

This case was followed in 1802 in *Man v Shiffner*.[20] In *Snook v Davidson*[1] in 1809 the person who employed the defendants to effect a policy said it was 'for a

---

[16] (1815) 4 Camp 349.
[17] Ibid, at 352.
[18] (1801) 1 East 335.
[19] Ibid, at 337.
[20] (1802) 2 East 523.
[1] (1809) 2 Camp 218.

correspondent in the country', and it was there held that the defendants had no general lien. Similar notice to the defendant prevented him from having a general lien in *Lanyon v Blanchard*[2] in 1811.

Again, in *Mann v Forrester*[3] in 1814 the plaintiff, who was a merchant in Rostock, ordered White and Lubbern, who were merchants in London, to send him a cargo of colonial produce on his separate account. They did so, and employed the defendants to effect a policy on the cargo, without mentioning to whom it belonged. The defendants effected the policy, and debited them with the premiums. A loss occurred. The policy was allowed to remain in the defendants' hands, and before they had notice of the plaintiff's interest, they received £650 from the underwriter, and £200 afterwards. When they had the notice, they were creditors of White and Lubbern to the extent of £167. This sum they deducted from the £200 subsequently received, and paid over £33 to the assignees of White and Lubbern, who had become bankrupt.

The plaintiff admitted that he had no right to the £650, but claimed the whole of the £200. But judgment was given for him to the extent of £33 only. Lord Ellenborough observed:[4]

> 'The defendants having had no notice that this policy was not for White and Lubbern, they had a lien upon it for their general balance. They must be supposed to have made advances on the credit of the policy, which was allowed to remain in their hands. Therefore they had a right to satisfy their general balance from the money received under the policy whether before or after the notice communicated to them of the plaintiffs' interest. But after that notice, I think the excess beyond the satisfaction of their balance was money had and received by them to the plaintiff's use.'

In *Fisher v Smith*[5] the facts of which are mentioned above,[6] there could be no question of Smith having a general lien because he knew that Skinner & Co were only agents, and that Fisher was the real principal.

'*Unless otherwise agreed*'

The significance of the words 'unless otherwise agreed' was shown by *Fairfield Shipbuilding and Engineering Co Ltd v Gardner, Mountain & Co Ltd*.[7] There the plaintiffs chartered the 'Volturno' to RS & Co, under a time charter which provided that the charterers were to insure the hull in the owners' name for £40,000 all risks, and £20,000 total loss only. RS & Co instructed the defendants, who were insurance brokers, to effect those policies and also policies on disbursements and freight of the 'Volturno'. The defendants, at the request of RS & Co, wrote to the plaintiffs informing them of the insurances for £40,000 and £20,000 and added: 'We have received instructions from RS & Co to hold the above policies to your order, which we undertake to do, subject to our lien on same for unpaid premiums if any.'

Scrutton J, held that the defendants were estopped from setting up against the plaintiffs a general lien for premiums due from RS & Co in respect of policies on the 'Volturno', other than those for £40,000 and £20,000. He said that the 'undertaking' did not seem to him to be a contract, for there was no

---

[2] (1811) 2 Camp 597.
[3] (1814) 4 Camp 60.
[4] Ibid, at 61.
[5] (1878) 4 App Cas 1.
[6] See p 334, ante.
[7] (1911) 27 TLR 281.

consideration for it. But he thought it was a statement of the defendants' position, which they were estopped from contradicting. If it had been unqualified, the defendants would not have been estopped from asserting against the plaintiffs that they held the policies subject to any lien, whether general or particular. But it was qualified, 'subject to our lien on same for unpaid premiums, if any'. He thought this reservation must be read against the defendants, and it was not clear enough to reserve their general lien.

Non-revival of general lien

In *Near East Relief v King Chasseur & Co Ltd*[8] it was held that the general lien did not revive if the broker, having parted with the possession of the policy, knew or had reason to believe, when it came into his hands again, that his employer was only an agent. Wright J, observed:[9]

> 'Generally, a lien which is lost on parting with possession revives when possession is resumed, but there is authority[10] for the proposition that the rule does not apply to a general lien if, after possession is parted with, and before possession is resumed, the person claiming the general lien becomes aware that his immediate employer is only an agent and not a principal.'

His Lordship said that general liens which involved charging one person's property for another person's debt were not to be encouraged. In the present case when possession of the policy was resumed, the position was subject to the then state of knowledge of the broker, who received the policy back into his possession in accordance with the position then existing.

B Brokerage

Brokerage is paid to the broker not by the assured, but by the insurer by means of a deduction from the premium.

---

[8] [1930] 2 KB 40.
[9] Ibid, at 44.
[10] *Levy v Barnard* (1818) 2 Moore CP 34.

PART III

Loss and abandonment

CHAPTER 25

Introduction

Losses may be divided into various types, viz total loss, partial loss, actual total loss, constructive total loss, particular average loss and general average loss.[1]

Any loss which is not a total loss is a partial loss.[2]

An actual total loss occurs where the subject-matter is destroyed or so damaged as to cease to be a thing of the kind insured, or the assured is irretrievably deprived of it.[3]

A constructive total loss occurs where the subject-matter is reasonably abandoned on account of its actual total loss appearing to be unavoidable, or because it could not be preserved from actual total loss without an expenditure which would exceed its value when the expenditure had been incurred.[4]

A particular average loss means a loss which is not a total loss, and towards which there is no liability upon the other interests involved in the adventure to contribute.[5]

A general average loss is a loss caused by or directly consequential on a general average act. It includes a general average expenditure as well as a general average sacrifice.[6]

Where there is a constructive total loss, the assured is entitled to abandon the subject-matter to the insurer and claim for a total loss.[7]

The assured must bring the action within 6 years from the date of the loss.[8] Sometimes, however, the policy provides that he is only allowed a shorter period in which to sue.[9]

When a loss occurs, the court may, on the application of the insurer, make an order for 'discovery of ship's papers' whereby all relevant documents in the possession of the assured and other persons are to be produced to the insurer.[10]

---

[1] See chapter 26, post.
[2] See p 342, post.
[3] See chapter 27, post.
[4] See chapter 28, post.
[5] See pp 343–344, post.
[6] See pp 344–345, post.
[7] See chapter 29, post.
[8] Limitation Act 1980, s 5.
[9] See e g *Magna Mercantile Co Inc v Great American Insurance Co* [1970] 1 Lloyd's Rep 350, New York County Supreme Ct, where the policy required the action to be commenced within 1 year after the date of the loss.
[10] See chapter 30, post.

CHAPTER 26

The types of loss

Losses may be classified in a variety of ways, viz:
- A Total loss and partial loss.
- B Actual total loss and constructive total loss.
- C Particular average loss and general average loss.

A TOTAL LOSS AND PARTIAL LOSS

Section 56(1) of the Marine Insurance Act 1906 states:

> 'A loss may be either total or partial. Any loss other than a total loss, as hereinafter defined, is a partial loss.'

Section 56(4) provides that:

> 'Where the assured brings an action for a total loss and the evidence proves only a partial loss, he may, unless the policy otherwise provides, recover for a partial loss.'[1]

Further, s 56(5) of the Act states:

> 'Where goods reach their destination in specie, but by reason of obliteration of marks, or otherwise, they are incapable of identification, the loss, if any, is partial and not total.'

B ACTUAL TOTAL LOSS AND CONSTRUCTIVE TOTAL LOSS

Section 56(2) of the Marine Insurance Act 1906 states:

> 'A total loss may be either an actual total loss or a constructive total loss.'

Section 56(3) provides that:

> 'Unless a different intention appears from the terms of the policy, an insurance against total loss includes a constructive as well as an actual total loss.'

The term 'actual total loss' is defined in s 57(1) which states:

> 'Where the subject-matter insured is destroyed, or so damaged as to cease to be a thing of the kind insured, or where the assured is irretrievably deprived thereof, there is an actual total loss.'

'Constructive total loss', on the other hand, is defined by s 60(1) in the following terms:

---

[1] See, eg *Helmville Ltd v Yorkshire Insurance Co Ltd: The Medina Princess* [1965] 1 Lloyd's Rep 361, QBD (Com Ct), where the assured failed to prove that the vessel was a constructive loss, and was held to be entitled to claim for a partial loss.

'Subject to any express provision in the policy, there is a constructive total loss where the subject-matter insured is reasonably abandoned on account of its actual total loss appearing to be unavoidable, or because it could not be preserved from actual total loss without an expenditure which would exceed its value when the expenditure had been incurred.'

There is no exact dividing line between actual and constructive total loss. The two classes merge into each other. But it may be said, in general, that where the thing insured, after suffering damage caused by a peril insured against, is of measurable value, and available to the parties in the place where it lies, the loss comes under the head of constructive total loss.

Hence it is that, the contract of marine insurance being a contract of indemnity, the insurer is entitled in almost all[2] cases of constructive total loss to receive from the assured if he wishes to claim for this type of loss[3] a notice of abandonment[4] in respect of the subject-matter insured in order that the insurer may be given the opportunity of taking such steps as he may desire, with a view to its salvage. This constitutes the great practical distinction between the two kinds of total loss, for s 57(2) of the Marine Insurance Act 1906 provides that:

'In the case of an actual total loss no notice of abandonment need be given.'

C PARTICULAR AVERAGE LOSS AND GENERAL AVERAGE LOSS

Particular average loss

'Particular average' is the term employed to describe a loss on any one interest which is not a total loss, and towards which there is no liability upon other interests to contribute.

Particular average is thus distinguished from general average for, while in the case of particular average the loss remains where it falls, in general average the loss is borne proportionately by all the interests concerned.

Section 64(1) of the Marine Insurance Act 1906 states:

'A particular average loss is a partial loss of the subject-matter insured, caused by a peril insured against, and which is not a general average loss.'

Damage to the ship by storm, injury to the cargo by fire, the loss of freight consequent on the destruction of some part of the cargo, are examples of particular average loss—the damage to the ship falling on the shipowner, the damage to the cargo falling on the cargo owner, while loss of freight is borne by the shipowner or the charterer, as the case may be.

Thus, Sir William Scott observed:[5]

---

[2] Notice of abandonment is unnecessary 'where at the time when the assured receives information of the loss there would be no probability of benefit to the insurer if notice were given to him': Marine Insurance Act 1906, s 62(7). Further, by s 62(9), 'where an insurer has reinsured his risk, no notice of abandonment need be given by him'. As to these exceptional cases, see pp 382–385, post.

[3] The assured is not bound to claim for a constructive total loss, for s 61 of the Marine Insurance Act 1906 states that: 'Where there is a constructive total loss the assured may either treat the loss as a partial loss, or abandon the subject-matter insured to the insurer and treat the loss as if it were an actual total loss.' As to this point, see pp 375–376, post.

[4] Marine Insurance Act 1906, s 62(1). As to the notice of abandonment, see p 381, post.

[5] In *The Copenhagen* (1799) 1 Ch Rob 289 at 293.

> 'Simple or particular average is not a very accurate expression, for it means damage incurred by or for one part of the concern, which part must bear alone, so that in fact it is no average at all; but still the expression is sufficiently understood, and received into familiar use. The loss of an anchor or cable, the starting of a plank, are matters of simple or particular average for which the ship alone is liable. Should a cargo of wine turn sour on the voyage, it would be a matter of simple average which the goods alone must bear, and there might be a simple average for which each would be severally liable under a misfortune happening to both ship and cargo at the same time, and from a common cause, as if a water-spout should fall on a cargo of sugar, and a plank from the same violence should start at the same time.'

The term is in general use and is well understood. 'It is more expressive than the term "partial loss", which may also convey the idea of a total loss of a part, in which sense it is sometimes used.'

To ascertain the measure of particular average damage is in many cases a matter of considerable difficulty requiring the exercise of great skill and special knowledge.

It involves alike in the case of a ship and her appliances, and also in the case of the various kinds of cargo, the necessity of drawing a distinction between damage caused by ordinary wear and tear or by the operation of natural causes on the one hand, and damage caused by the perils insured against on the other.

The work of drawing the distinction between these two forms of depreciation is performed by average adjusters, and the Rules of Practice of the Association of Average Adjusters,[6] based on long experience, contain directions as to the manner in which particular average is to be ascertained in a considerable number of cases relating to a ship and her appliances, as well as to various kinds of cargo.

General average loss

Section 66(1) of the Marine Insurance Act 1906 states:

> 'A general average loss is a loss caused by or directly consequential on a general average act. It includes a general average expenditure as well as a general average sacrifice.'

Section 66(2) of the Act provides that:

> 'There is a general average act where any extraordinary sacrifice or expenditure is voluntarily and reasonably made or incurred in time of peril for the purpose of preserving the property imperilled in the common adventure.'

'General average' is the term used to express the liability of all the owners of the interests concerned to make good the losses of interests which are sacrificed in whole or in part for the safety of the adventure.

In *Birkley v Presgrave*,[7] Lawrence J, thus defined it:[8]

> 'All loss which arises in consequence of extraordinary sacrifices made or expenses incurred for the preservation of the ship and cargo come within general average, and must be borne proportionately by all who are interested.'[9]

---

[6] The Rules are set out in Appendix V, pp 568–594, post.
[7] (1801) 1 East 220.
[8] Ibid, at 228.
[9] This expression does not include loss arising from loss of time caused by the general average act, as the loss is common to all interests and is not included in the computation; and a fortiori, where the delay results in a loss caused by the operation of a cesser clause in a charter-party, the cargo owners are not liable to contribute as they are not parties to this contract: *The Leitrim* [1902] P 256.

This doctrine is part of the maritime law of all nations, and is of ancient origin being derived from the Rhodian, through the Roman, law:

> '*Lege Rhodia cavetur, ut si levandae navis gratia jactus mercium factus est, omnium contributione sarciatur quod pro omnibus datum est.*'[10]

The loss must be incurred in a time of danger to the adventure, when the ship is in imminent peril and it becomes necessary to sacrifice something for the common safety. The most common examples of 'general average sacrifice' are jettison of cargo to lighten the ship, damage to cargo by water used to extinguish fire, and damage done to the ship in case of necessity, e g cutting away the masts to right the ship. The extent of the sacrifice is limited only by the necessities of the case.[11]

When a monetary liability is incurred or money is spent to save the adventure from imminent peril, the general average loss sustained is called a 'general average expenditure'.

All the interests contribute to make good the loss in proportion to their value, and the amount which such interest pays is termed a 'general average contribution'.

Thus, s 66(3) of the Marine Insurance Act 1906 states:

> 'Where there is a general average loss, the party on whom it falls is entitled, subject to the conditions imposed by maritime law, to a rateable contribution from the other parties interested, and such contribution is called a general average contribution.'

---

[10] Digest XIV.2.
[11] *The Gratitudine* (1801) 3 Ch Rob 240.

CHAPTER 27

Actual total loss

Section 57(1) of the Marine Insurance Act 1906 states:

> 'Where the subject-matter insured is destroyed, or so damaged as to cease to be a thing of the kind insured, or where the assured is irretrievably deprived thereof, there is an actual total loss.'

Thus, there may be an actual total loss of:

A Ship.
B Goods.
C Freight.

A ACTUAL TOTAL LOSS OF SHIP

1 Examples of actual total loss

When a ship founders or is entirely destroyed by fire, that is an actual total loss brought about by its physical destruction.

If a vessel is reduced to a mere congeries of planks, it is clear that as a ship she has ceased to exist; or if captured by the enemy in time of war or seized by pirates, although she continues to exist, the vessel is no longer available to the parties interested.[1]

Further, if a ship is so injured that she cannot sail without repairs and cannot be taken to a port at which the necessary repairs can be executed, there is an actual total loss.[2]

In *George Cohen, Sons & Co v Standard Marine Insurance Co Ltd*[3] an obsolete battleship was insured whilst being towed from Chatham to Brake (in Germany) where she was to be broken up. She went ashore on the Dutch coast. Evidence was given that she could be got off, but that the operation would be expensive. The Dutch authorities would not allow her to be moved in case the sea defences in the area were damaged thereby, but their decision was subject to appeal to a higher tribunal. It was held by the King's Bench Division that the vessel was not an actual total loss within the meaning of s 57(1), for the assured had not been irretrievably deprived of her.

Roche J, said:[4]

> 'Having regard to the whole of the evidence, not merely the evidence for the defendants but the evidence given for the plaintiffs by several witnesses, and in particular by Captain

---

[1] See *Cambridge v Anderton* (1824) 2 B&C 691; *Stringer v English and Scottish Marine Insurance Co* (1870) LR 5 QB 599.
[2] *Barker v Janson* (1868) LR 3 CP 303 at 305 (per Willes J).
[3] (1925) 21 LlL Rep 30, KBD.
[4] Ibid, at 33.

Richards, to whose evidence I attach great importance, I am of opinion that this vessel physically could be got off. It would be a matter of great elaboration and difficulty, but at all events, putting the matter at the highest, I am not satisfied that she could not. On the whole I think that she could. It would be an engineering feat requiring considerable preparation and, as I shall subsequently decide, very high expenditure, but it could be done so far as the physical feat was concerned. Though I think Captain Richards regards it as doubtful, he is not prepared to say that it cannot be done. In these circumstances, there has been no irretrievable deprivation which a court can find by reason of physical impossibility.'

In *Captain J A Cates Tug and Wharfage Co Ltd v Franklin Insurance Co*,[5] where a tug sank in shallow water after a collision and was quickly raised, the Judicial Committee of the Privy Council[6] held that she was not an actual total loss.

In *Marstrand Fishing Co Ltd v Beer*[7] the master of the insured fishing vessel was instructed to fish in the North Sea and return to Grimsby. Instead of doing so he called at Dover, where he took on board provisions for 5 weeks. The engineer was purposely left behind at Dover. The vessel sailed from there, and nothing was heard of her for 6 weeks, when it was learnt that she had called at Corcubion, a port in Spain, and had later sailed. The master had incurred by fraud a bill for necessaries, corroborating the suspicion that he and the crew had feloniously taken possession of her. The assured, who were the owners of the vessel, claimed an indemnity from the insurers on the ground that she was an actual total loss.[8]

Porter J, held that the action failed, and said:[9]

'In my view, no one could say here that the vessel was irretrievably lost to her owners. Under the Marine Insurance Act loss by barratry is not necessarily an actual total loss, and in this case I find there was no actual total loss.'

In *St Margaret's Trust Ltd v Navigators and General Insurance Co Ltd*[10] a ketch was insured under a time policy and was put on a mud berth at Lymington. She was subsequently moved across the river to another mud berth where she slipped over at low tide, and filled with water owing to the neglected state of her topside caulking. She was raised and towed to Pylewell Creek, where she was left until another mud berth became available. No further steps were taken, and she gradually deteriorated and had no more than her break-up value. The assured claimed for an actual total loss.

Morris J, held that the action failed on this ground.[11] There was no proof that the ketch was a total loss, as the only evidence adduced was to the effect that, when she had been raised, she could have been put approximately into the condition in which she was when first submerged, and her eventual deterioration resulted from delay.

His Lordship said:[12]

---

[5] (1927) 137 LT 709, PC.
[6] Lord Haldane, Lord Sumner, Lord Shaw, Lord Merrivale and Lord Warrington.
[7] (1936) 56 LlL Rep 163, KBD.
[8] The assured also claimed that she was a 'constructive total loss'. But the action failed on this ground too. As to this aspect of the case, see p 369, post.
[9] (1936) 56 LlL Rep at 173.
[10] (1949) 82 LlL Rep 752, KBD.
[11] But the assured was held entitled to recover, as a partial loss, the amount paid by them in connection with the refloating of the ketch and the estimated damage to her fittings caused by the submersion.
[12] (1949) 82 LlL Rep at 766.

'In my judgment, it would be quite wrong to hold that the *Vishela* became an actual total loss. When she was raised, she was towed across to Pylewell Creek, and thereafter she was examined by a surveyor on behalf of the plaintiffs. Mr Griffin was not really able to say much as to her condition after she went to Pylewell Creek; he saw her on one day and noticed that a lot of the equipment had been taken from the craft. I have not, however, had the evidence of the surveyor who saw her; I have not had the evidence of anyone from Messrs Smith & Marshall; and it does not seem to me that it would be right for me to infer that this craft was on 15 October 1947, in such a state that she could not be repaired so as to be in the state that she was in on 17 September.'

In *Panamanian Oriental Steamship Corpn v Wright*[13] a vessel was boarded by Vietnamese customs officials. Unmanifested goods were found on board her, and she was escorted into port. A special military court acquitted the master of smuggling offences, but convicted some of the crew. The vessel was ordered to be confiscated. Mocatta J, held that there had been no actual total loss, for, on the evidence, it had not been shown that the assured had been irretrievably deprived of her.[14]

2 Sale of vessel by master

Another class of actual total loss is illustrated by cases in which a vessel, having sustained damage amounting to a constructive total loss, has been sold by the master acting in the interests of those concerned without consulting his owners in the matter.

Thus, in *Roux v Salvador*[15] a vessel laden with timber ran aground near St André on the River Saint Lawrence and surveyors reported, advising that, having regard to the extent of her damage and to her position, she should be sold as she lay, together with her cargo. The jury found that the master was justified in acting on this advice. It was held that the assured was entitled to recover as for an actual total loss, notwithstanding that notice of abandonment had not been given.

Such action on the part of a master can, however, be justified only in cases of extreme necessity, e g cases in which, owing to lack of funds or the absence of other facilities, he is unable to repair the damage done and where in the absence of repair, actual total loss appears inevitable.

Hence, in *Kaltenbach v Mackenzie*[16] a vessel ran aground and was taken into Saigon, and was there surveyed and reported to be a constructive total loss because her repairs would cost more than her repaired value. Whilst anchored there in smooth water and in no imminent danger, she was sold. It was held that the assured was not entitled to recover for a total loss, no notice of abandonment having been given.

It should be noticed that in these cases it is not the mere fact of sale which entitles the assured to treat the loss as an actual total loss.

Thus, Bayley B, said in summing up to the jury in *Doyle v Dallas*:[17]

---

[13] [1970] 2 Lloyd's Rep 365, QBD (Com Ct). The decision in the case was later reversed on another ground: [1971] 1 Lloyd's Rep 487, CA. See pp 261–262, ante.

[14] See the judgment of Mocatta J: [1970] 2 Lloyd's Rep at 383.

[15] (1836) 3 Bing NC 266; *Farnworth v Hyde* (1866) LR 2 CP 204; *Rankin v Potter* (1873) LR 6 HL 83.

[16] (1878) 3 CPD 467. See also, *Knight v Faith* (1850) 15 QB 649; *Rankin v Potter*, supra; *Mansell & Co v Hoade* (1903) 20 TLR 150; *Norwich Union Fire Insurance Society Ltd v Price Ltd* [1934] AC 455, PC.

[17] (1831) 1 Mood & R 48 at 54.

'The question in this case is, whether you are satisfied there has been a total loss by perils of the sea. I know of no such head of insurance law as loss by sale. If the situation of the ship be such that by no means within the master's reach it can be treated so as to retain the character of a ship, it is a total loss. If the captain, by means within his reach, can make an experiment to save it with a fair hope of restoring it to the character of a ship, he cannot by selling it turn it into a total loss.'

Moreover, if a master can communicate with the owners of the vessel insured, he is not justified in selling her without doing so,[18] and for this reason it is thought that cases of actual total loss of this type will now be seldom met.

3 Missing ships

When a ship does not arrive at her port of destination, and no news is received of her after a reasonable period has elapsed, she is presumed to have foundered at sea, and the insurers become liable as for a loss by perils of the sea.

Thus, s 58 of the Marine Insurance Act 1906 states:

'Where the ship concerned in the adventure is missing, and after the lapse of a reasonable time no news of her is received, an actual total loss may be presumed.'

What is a reasonable time is in each case a question of fact,[19] and depends on the class of ship, her cargo, and the nature and length of her voyage.[20]

But it is necessary to establish that the vessel sailed on the voyage insured;[1] and the presumption of loss by perils insured against will be rebutted by the insurers offering some reasonable explanation of another reason for the loss.[2]

Thus, in *Koster v Reed*[3] a prima facie case was made out where the plaintiff proved that the ship sailed on the voyage insured, and never arrived at the port of destination, but that 3 or 4 days after she had sailed a witness heard that she had foundered at sea, but that the crew had been saved. The plaintiff was not bound to call any of the crew, or to show that he was unable to procure their attendance.[4]

In some Continental countries there are fixed periods for presuming the loss of a missing ship, the general period being 1 year from the sailing of the vessel.

B ACTUAL TOTAL LOSS OF GOODS

Although a total loss of a ship often involves a total loss of cargo, this is not

---

[18] *Australasian Steam Navigation Co v Morse* (1872) LR 4 PC 222.
[19] Marine Insurance Act 1906, s 88.
[20] *Green v Brown* (1743) 2 Stra 1199.
[1] *Koster v Reed* (1826) 6 B&C 9; *Cohen v Hinckley* (1809) 2 Camp 51.
[2] *Compania Martiartu v Royal Exchange Assurance* [1923] 1 KB 650. See further, the following cases as to the burden of proof in claims against war risk underwriters in respect of missing ships: *General Steam Navigation Co v Commercial Union Assurance Co* (1915) 31 TLR 630; *Euterpe SS Co Ltd v North of England Protecting Association Ltd* (1917) 33 TLR 540; *Macbeth & Co v King* (1916) 32 TLR 581; *Munro Brice & Co v War Risks Association* [1918] 2 KB 78; *Munro Brice & Co v Marten* [1920] 3 KB 94; *Zachariessen v Importers and Exporters Marine Insurance Co* (1924) 29 Com Cas 202; *United Scottish Insurance Co Ltd v British Fishing Vessels Mutual War Risks Association Ltd* (1944) 78 LlL Rep 70 (ship holed by contact with an explosive float).
[3] (1826) 6 B&C 19.
[4] See further, *Twemlow v Oswin* (1809) 2 Camp 85. As to the necessity in similar circumstances of showing that the ship foundered within the currency of a time policy, see *Gledstanes v Royal Exchange Assurance* (1864) 5 B&S 797, and *Reid v Standard Marine Assurance Co Ltd* (1886) 2 TLR 807.

necessarily the case. The cargo may be transhipped before the vessel sinks, and cases are not infrequent where goods are destroyed although the ship remains intact, e g in the case of jettison, perishable cargoes, etc.

Actual total loss of goods takes place whenever they cease to be available to their owner for any purpose whatever, except, perhaps, as waste or refuse.

Thus, in *Berger and Light Diffusers Pty Ltd v Pollock*,[5] where some steel injection moulds were insured for a voyage from Australia to England, and on arrival were found to be damaged by rust due to being immersed in water after the fracture of a pipe in her hold, it was held that there was an actual total loss.[6]

Where the goods insured are perishable in their nature, and arrive damaged by a peril insured against, the test applied in order to determine whether the insurer is to pay for a total or a partial loss[7] is whether the goods, though arriving in specie, are of merchantable quality—i e whether they have ceased to be things of the kind insured.

Thus, Lord Ellenborough CJ, said in *Cologan v London Assurance*:[8]

'Considering the contract of insurance as a contract of indemnity, it surely cannot be less a total loss because the commodity subsists in specie, if it subsist only in the form of a nuisance. There is a total loss of the thing if by any of the perils insured against it is rendered of no use whatever, although it may not be entirely annihilated.'

Thus, in *Roux v Salvador*,[9] where hides become rotten by the admission of water from leakage occasioned by a peril insured against, and the jury found that they could not have arrived as hides at their destination, Lord Abinger held that this was an actual total loss.

But where the goods arrive, although damaged, without loss of species, there is no actual total loss.[10]

In *Boon and Cheah Steel Pipes Sdn Bhd v Asia Insurance Co Ltd*[11] all except 12 steel pipes out of a total consignment of 668 insured under a policy were lost, and the 12 arrived in a damaged condition. The Malaysia High Court held that there was not an actual total loss, and that the *de minimis* rule did not apply for the 12 pipes contituted a proportion too high to bring the rule into operation.[12]

C ACTUAL TOTAL LOSS OF FREIGHT[13]

1 Loss of goods

Where freight is payable on delivery of the goods at the port of destination, if

---

[5] [1973] 2 Lloyd's Rep 442, QBD (Com Ct).
[6] See the judgment of Kerr J, ibid, at 456.
[7] As to partial loss, see pp 429–436, post.
[8] (1816) 5 M&S 447 at 455.
[9] (1836) 3 Bing NC 266 at 279. See also, *Saunders v Baring* (1876) 34 LT 419; *Asfar & Co v Blundell* [1896] 1 QB 123, CA; *Montreal Light Heat and Power Co v Sedgewick* [1910] AC 598.
[10] *Glennie v London Assurance* (1814) 2 M&S 371; *Anderson v Royal Exchange Assurance Co* (1805) 7 East 38; *Navone v Haddon* (1850) 9 CB 30.
[11] [1975] 1 Lloyd's Rep 452.
[12] See the judgment of Raja Azlan Shah J, ibid, at 460, where he said that it might well be that in the case of a single pipe or two out of the whole consignment the rule would apply, but he failed to see how it was possible to hold that 12 pipes could be ignored or treated as trifling and to be brushed aside.
[13] Constructive total loss of freight is not mentioned in the Marine Insurance Act 1906, and presumably is governed by the general provisions contained in s 60(1). The reported cases,

there is a total loss of them before arrival there, there is a total loss of freight. A total loss of freight ensues when the shipowner *from any cause whatever* has been unable to carry the goods to their port of destination.[14]

The same principle applies in cases where lump sum freight is payable on delivery of the cargo.[15]

Indeed, the rule is the same in all cases of freight payable on delivery, except where the inability to deliver the cargo is the result of acts of the cargo owner.[16]

Where the consignee is allowed a specified time in which to take delivery of the goods on arrival, a total loss of the goods before the time has expired will involve a total loss of freight.

Thus, in *Duthie v Hilton*,[17] where freight was to be paid within 3 days after the arrival of the ship and before delivery of the goods, and the night after the ship berthed, she was scuttled to extinguish a fire which had broken out, in consequence of which some casks of cement were destroyed, it was held that the freight could not be recovered.

In the case of freight paid in advance there can be no loss to the shipowner, for it is not at risk, but where cargo is carried for a lump sum freight and half the freight is paid in advance, while only half of the cargo is delivered, no further freight is payable to the carrier. The half freight paid in advance was never at risk, but there is a total loss of the freight which was at risk, and for this the insurer on freight will be liable.[18]

In *Gulf and Southern SS Co Inc v British Traders' Insurance Co Ltd*[19] the assured were shipowners, who effected an insurance policy in respect of risks to cargo carried by them for third parties. The policy stated:

> 'It is agreed that the term "cargo" as used in this policy includes goods, wares, merchandise, livestock, express matter (except in the custody of an express company) and baggage of every description, and where used in this form it includes also advances made by and payment of back charges made by or due from said assured and/or charges of said assured upon said cargo or any portion thereof . . . and the said assurers agree and undertake to indemnify and hold harmless the said assured against hurt, detriment, damage to or loss of such cargo from any and all such risks, perils, acts or misfortunes, to the extent which the assured may be held by the owners thereof, under any liability the assured shall have assumed as common carriers, insurers or otherwise, and for any and all claims which said cargo may be called upon to contribute in general average, and/or salvage, landing, warehousing and/or special charges, and to cover in like manner any cargo owned by the assured, and also any advances made by or due from said assured and/or charges of said assured upon said cargo or any portion thereof.'

The vessel carrying goods belonging to third parties was sunk in a collision whilst on a voyage from New Orleans to Miami and Key West, and was a total loss with all her cargo. The assured claimed (inter alia) an indemnity from the insurers in respect of the freight, which was in the process of being earned by them at the time of the casualty, and became payable only on delivery of the

---

however, make no clear distinction between constructive total loss of freight and actual total loss of freight. It seems preferable to consider both types of loss of freight in this chapter rather than in chapter 28 which concerns 'Constructive Total Loss'.

[14] *Metcalfe v Britannia Iron Works Co* (1877) 2 QBD 423.
[15] *Crozier v Smith* (1840) 1 Man&G 407. A loss of lump sum freight, however, does not take place unless the whole of the cargo is lost: *Merchant Shipping Co v Armitage* (1873) LR 9 QB 99; *Brankelow SS Co v Canton Insurance Office* [1899] 2 QB 178.
[16] *Cleary v McAndrew, The Galam (Cargo ex)* (1863) 2 Moo PCCNS 216.
[17] (1868) LR 4 CP 138.
[18] *Allison v Bristol Marine Insurance Co* (1876) 1 App Cas 209.
[19] (1929) 35 LlL Rep 203, KBD.

goods. The insurers refused to pay on the ground that the terms of the policy could not cover unearned freight.

It was held by the King's Bench Division that the claim succeeded. The words 'charges upon cargo' used in the policy were intended to cover freight which was in the process of being earned. Roche J, said:[20]

> '[Counsel] seeks to make a point that the phrase is not "charges in respect of cargo" but "charges upon cargo"? I think myself that distinction is too fine and is an unreal one to be applied in consideration of this document. But even if the word "upon" is to be pressed, I think it would be an unreal distinction to say that freight is not at the time of loss a charge upon cargo because the freight itself was not earned at the time of the loss. The truth is that back charges also in all these matters as between the assured and the owners of the cargo are only charged upon or earned when the voyage is accomplished, but the insurance is one directed to reimburse the assured against the contingency of the voyage not being accomplished.
>
> I think that in using the words "charges upon cargo" the parties have made it plain to my mind that they intended to cover that which is the principal charge upon and in respect of cargo, namely, freight that was in process of being earned by the shipowners.'

2 Arrival of goods in unmerchantable condition

Further, where goods of a perishable nature arrive, but in such a condition as to be unmerchantable, there is a total loss of goods and also a total loss of freight, assuming that the consignee refuses to accept delivery when tendered.[1]

In *Asfar & Co v Blundell*[2] a vessel carrying a cargo of dates was sunk in the Thames. The owners of the vessel had insured the freight payable in respect of the dates on delivery to the consignees. The dates were recovered from the river, but were in a state which rendered them unfit for human food. They were, however, sold for distilling purposes. The assured claimed against the insurer for a total loss of freight. It was held by the Court of Appeal[3] that the claim succeeded. No freight was payable by the consignees because the goods delivered were, for business purposes, something different from those shipped, and were not in merchantable condition. Consequently there had been a total loss of freight.

Lord Esher MR, said:[4]

> 'The first point taken by the [insurers] was, that there was not a total loss of the dates. The subject-matter is a quantity of dates, in a commercial sense, and these dates were under water for two days, and were then examined by a businessman, who said that they were then in a filthy mess and not dates at all. It is said that there was no change in their nature, and that they were still dates. The well-known test under such circumstances is whether, as a matter of business and of mercantile dealing, the subject-matter has been altered in its nature. If, as a matter of business, it has become something else, and the question is whether there has been a total loss, then, if by the perils of the sea its nature has been so altered, in a commercial and business view, that it has become unmerchantable, there has been a total loss. That is the test; and that test has been fulfilled in this case. Mathew J,[5] came to the conclusion that, as a matter of business, the dates had become so deteriorated as not to be dates at all, and to be unmerchantable as dates. That is a total loss. If there was a total loss, then no freight was due from the consignees of the dates to the charterers.'

---

[20] Ibid, at 206.
[1] *Asfar & Co v Blundell* (1896) 73 LT 648, CA.
[2] (1896) 73 LT 648, CA.
[3] Lord Esher MR, Lopes and Kay LJJ.
[4] (1896) 73 LT at 649.
[5] In the court below: (1895) 64 LJQB 573.

3 Sale of perishable cargo

The same result follows on the sale of a perishable cargo.

Thus, in *Milles v Fletcher*[6] a ship was captured and recaptured, and the master on recapture, acting fairly for the benefit for all concerned, sold the ship and her cargo. It was held that the insurers on freight were liable. Lord Mansfield CJ, said that it was unreasonable for the cargo to be kept in a perishable state in a leaky ship.

But in *Mordy v Jones*[7] a vessel, damaged by a peril insured against, put back to port, where part of the cargo was found to be wet and damaged, and would of necessity have to be dried. This operation would take about 6 weeks. The master sold the goods with the approval of the shipper of the goods. His conduct was found to be that of a prudent uninsured owner, but the court held that the insurer on freight was not liable, presumably on the ground that the loss was not inevitable, for though the circumstances might have caused delay, the liability for mere delay could not fall on the insurer on freight.

It seems that where the ship and goods are improperly sold, there is not a total loss of freight.[8]

But where the circumstances justify a sale, e g where the cargo is salved at sea by salvors, there is a total loss of freight, though the place of the sale is the port of destination.[9]

4 Frustration of chartered voyage

In *Adamson v Newcastle SS Freight Insurance Association*[10] a time policy for a year on freight contained the usual clause 'restraints of princes', etc. The charterparty provided that 'in the event of war, blockade, or prohibition of export preventing loading, this charter to be cancelled'. War having broken out and the ports specified in the charter-party being closed, the ship went to Constantinople and sailed to England with a freight less than the chartered freight. It was held that the chartered voyage was never begun, and there was no loss on that, the charter-party having become void before the ship had the chance of loading or had started on the voyage to the loading port. The voyage performed was a separate venture, which was completed without loss of freight.

5 Loss of ship before sailing

There is a total loss of freight in a valued policy where a ship is lost while taking in her cargo, if she has a full cargo ready for shipment, or even if there is only a contract for one.[11]

Thus, in *Rankin v Potter*,[12] where a vessel was so damaged that she was abandoned to the insurer before the cargo was shipped, and the assured on freight could not in consequence earn his freight, there was a total loss of freight.

---

[6] (1779) 1 Doug KB 231.
[7] (1825) 4 B&C 394.
[8] *Parmeter v Todhunter* (1808) 1 Camp 541; *Green v Royal Exchange Assurance Co* (1815) 6 Taunt 68.
[9] *Guthrie v North China Insurance Co Ltd* (1902) 7 Com Cas 130, CA.
[10] (1879) 4 QBD 462.
[11] Marine Insurance Act 1906, First Schedule, rule 3(d). See further, *Patrick v Eames* (1813) 3 Camp 441; *Davidson v Willasey* (1813) 1 M&S 313.
[12] (1873) LR 6 HL 83.

6 Ship unable to proceed

Where the goods are not destroyed, but the ship cannot proceed, the master has to consider whether the cost of transhipping the goods and conveying them by another ship or in some other way to their destination will exceed their value on arrival. If it appears that there will probably be a loss on the transaction, and therefore the master does not tranship, there will be a total loss of freight.[13]

But a cargo is capable of being sent on when the cost of the various necessary operations (e g unshipping, drying, warehousing, reshipping, salvage, if any, and if into a new bottom, the increase of freight) will not exceed the value of the salved cargo on the arrival at the port of destination.[14] Hence loss of ship does not necessarily involve loss of freight.

Freight may also be lost and the shipowner be relieved of his obligation to carry the cargo if the vessel is so damaged and disabled as to be incapable of being repaired except at an expense exceeding her value when repaired.[15]

But a shipowner is not entitled to claim against the insurer on freight for a total loss of freight unless the vessel suffers such sea damage as will free the shipowner from his obligation under the contract of affreightment to carry the cargo to its destination.[16]

In *Jackson v Union Marine Insurance Co*[17] a ship under charter, with no cancelling clause, left Liverpool on 2 January in tow, and the next day got on the rocks in Caernarvon Bay, where she remained until 18 February, and was ultimately taken back to Liverpool and sold by auction in June. In these circumstances it was held that the charterers were released from their contract by reason of the delay, and that the insurers were liable for the total loss of the chartered freight.

In *Yero Carras (Owners) v London and Scottish Assurance Corpn Ltd*[18] the owners of a vessel had insured 'freight and/or anticipated freight' under a policy which covered the usual marine risks and included the Institute Voyage Clauses (Freight). Clause 4 of these stated:

> 'In the event of the total loss, whether absolute or constructive of the vessel, the amount underwritten by this policy shall be paid in full whether the vessel be fully or only partly loaded or in ballast, chartered or unchartered.'

Clause 5 stated:

> 'In ascertaining whether the vessel is a constructive total loss the insured value in the policies on ship shall be taken as the repaired value and nothing in respect of the damaged or break-up value of the vessel or wreck shall be taken into account.'

The vessel was chartered to proceed to Valparaiso to load a cargo for Europe. The charter-party contained the usual exceptions including perils of the seas. She stranded in the Straits of Magellan on the voyage to Valparaiso. Notice of

---

[13] *Assicurazioni Generali and Schenker & Co v Bessie Morris SS Co Ltd and Browne* [1892] 2 QB 652 at 657.
[14] *Rosetto v Gurney* (1851) 11 CB 176; *Moss v Smith* (1850) 9 CB 94.
[15] *Assicurazioni Generali and Schenker & Co v Bessie Morris SS Co Ltd and Browne* [1892] 2 QB 652. See also, *Rankin v Potter* (1873) LR 6 HL 83; *Kulukundis v Norwich Union Fire Insurance Society* [1937] 1 KB 1, [1936] 2 All ER 242.
[16] *Carras v London and Scottish Assurance Corpn* [1936] 1 KB 291.
[17] (1874) LR 10 CP 125. See also, *Re Jamieson and Newcastle SS Freight Insurance Association* [1895] 2 QB 90.
[18] (1935) 53 LlL Rep 131, CA.

abandonment[19] was given to the hull underwriters, who compromised the claim by paying 100 per cent of the sum insured and a proportion of the 'sue and labour' charges.[20] The owners then claimed the sum insured under the freight policy. She was later refloated and brought into port by salvors. The insurers allowed the owners to retain the vessel. The owners remained liable to the salvors, and surrendered her to them in discharge of their claim. The insurers denied liability, and contended that the vessel had not become a constructive total loss, and therefore the sum insured was not payable.

The Court of Appeal[1] held that the action succeeded. It was clear that the charter-party had been discharged by perils of the sea, which had damaged the vessel to such an extent that she could not be repaired except at an expense exceeding her actual value, and thus for the purposes of the adventure she had been lost to her owners because it was impossible in a commercial sense to repair her. Accordingly, there was an actual total loss of freight under the policy.

Lord Wright MR, said that the freight policy did not expressly or by implication provide that a total loss of freight should be recoverable only in the event of an actual or constructive total loss of the ship under the hull policies, and therefore it was unnecessary to invoke clause 5 to determine whether there was a constructive total loss within the meaning of that clause.

He observed:[2]

> 'I do not think that apart from express terms the right to claim a total or constructive total loss under this policy can depend upon whether there is a constructive total loss under the hull policies. Certainly clause 5 contains no such condition. Clause 5 by its terms can only apply when it is the constructive total loss of the ship that is an essential condition of recovery under the freight policy. The first part of clause 4 deals with the case referred to above where the shipowner, but for the clause, would lose his freight on the ground that it has been earned by the ship after it had been abandoned to underwriters, and the clause in such an event gives an added right of recovery of the full freight. But there is no other condition of the freight policy which postulates or refers to a constructive total loss of the ship; the term is nowhere else used than in clauses 4 and 5 of the policy. Clause 5 gives no added right and imposes no new condition save when it is necessary to establish a constructive total loss of the ship. The clause if more correctly expressed would read: "Whenever it is necessary to prove the total loss, actual or constructive, of the ship", etc. But that can only apply where the contract of insurance requires the ascertainment of that fact as a condition of recovering. Clause 5 does not import any such condition.'

In *Kulukundis v Norwich Union Fire Insurance Society*[3] a vessel was chartered for a voyage from ports in South America via the Straits of Magellan to ports in England. The owners effected a freight policy in respect of 'freight and/or chartered freight'. The charter-party provided for a lump sum freight of £8,000 payable in London upon discharge. The vessel stranded in the Straits of Magellan. She was successfully salved and was brought to Magellanes under her own steam. The hull underwriters agreed with the owners that she should be abandoned, paid them £7,500 and took over all the vessel's liabilities. The cargo owners were notified that the adventure was at an end, and were paid on

---

[19] As to notice of abandonment, see p 381, post.
[20] As to 'sue and labour' charges, see pp 442–452, post.
[1] Lord Wright MR, Slesser and Greene LJJ.
[2] (1935) 53 LlL Rep at 138. See also, the judgment of Slesser LJ, ibid, at 140, and that of Greene LJ, ibid, at 143.
[3] [1937] 1 KB 1, [1936] 2 All ER 242, CA.

a total loss. Temporary repairs were carried out by the salvors. She then sailed for and arrived at Rotterdam with part of the original cargo. The cost of temporary repairs including salvage charges exceeded the value of the ship when repaired.

The owners claimed for a total loss of freight under the freight policy. They alleged that the damage sustained was such that a prudent uninsured owner would not have proceeded with the voyage, that to repair the damage so as to enable the vessel to complete the voyage would have cost more than her value when repaired, and that the repairs would have cost more than the benefit to be derived from the freight to be earned.

The Court of Appeal[4] held that the action succeeded, but the decision was based on differing grounds.

Greene LJ, said[5] that the substantial question in issue was whether the owners were entitled to recover as for a total loss of chartered freight on proof that the cost of temporary repairs to the vessel sufficient to enable her to carry her cargo to its destination would have exceeded her repaired value or whether they must prove that the cost of permanent and complete repairs would have exceeded the repaired value. In many cases the distinction was in practice an academic one. If a vessel, when temporarily repaired, was worth less than the cost of the temporary repairs, it was likely that her value, if she were permanently and completely repaired, would be less than the cost of so repairing her, particularly if to that cost was added the cost of the temporary repairs necessary to enable her to reach a port where she could be permanently and completely repaired. But in the present case the distinction was of vital importance.

The learned Lord Justice said[6] that the rule that a shipowner was to be freed from his obligations to the freighter if the vessel was lost in a commercial sense was now well established, and it could not be treated as the same rule, or branch of the same rule, as that which applied between owner and hull underwriter. In all cases where repair was possible, the prima facie duty of the shipowner under his contract of affreightment was to carry out such repairs to the ship (whether temporary or permanent and complete, as the case might be), to enable her to carry the cargo to its destination. He was excused from the duty to carry out the appropriate repairs if he could prove that the cost of doing so would exceed the repaired value of the vessel. A consideration of the cost of repairs which were not the appropriate repairs in the particular case was irrelevant. In the present case the temporary repairs would have exceeded the value of the ship so repaired. Completion of the voyage was not therefore commercially possible.

Slesser LJ, was of the same opinion, and said[7] that what had to be decided was whether the cost of repairs sufficient to complete the voyage were to be the subject of consideration, or the cost of repairs sufficient permanently to restore the ship, regardless of the specific obligation of carriage. He considered that the question had already been decided by authority, for Lord Chelmsford had said in *Rankin v Potter*,[8] where it had been stated that the cost of repairs were those

---

[4] Slesser, Greene and Scott LJJ.
[5] [1936] 2 All ER 242 at 255.
[6] Ibid, at 257 et seq.
[7] Ibid, at 253.
[8] (1873) LR 6 HL 83.

necessary to make the ship seaworthy and enable her to bring home the cargo:[9]

> 'A plain and clear view upon the facts and circumstances of the case can only be obtained by removing the policy on the ship out of the way, and looking at the case as if there were no other policy in existence but that on freight . . . the only question is whether, by the perils of the sea, the ship was so damaged . . . during the term of the policy, as to be rendered incapable, unless sufficiently repaired, of performing the voyage . . . for which she was chartered.'

Scott LJ, agreed that the owners were entitled to recover, but said[10] that the cost of temporary repairs by itself did not constitute any test. The basic condition under the charter-party was the continued existence and availability of the vessel throughout the voyage. If she should at any time during the voyage be rendered by sea perils incapable of completing the voyage within a reasonable time to earn the freight, then, whether the incapability was physical or commercial, the basic condition of the contract would be broken and the charter-party discharged. It was clear that, if the ship were so damaged that it would not be worth the owner's while to incur the cost of repairs, the ship would be commercially lost. The vessel in the present case was a commercial loss, for she was incapable of completing the contract voyage within a reasonable time.

In *Petros M Nomikos Ltd v Robertson*[11] the owners of a vessel chartered her to carry a cargo of oil from Venezuela to the United Kingdom. The vessel herself was insured by them for £28,000 under a time policy, which stated that her insured value was deemed to be her repaired value. The owners also effected a policy for £4,110 in respect of her freight. The clauses in this policy stated:

> '5. In the event of the total loss, whether absolute or constructive of the steamer the amount underwritten by this policy shall be paid in full, whether the steamer be fully or only partly loaded, or in ballast, chartered or unchartered.[12]
> 6. In ascertaining whether the vessel is a constructive total loss the insured value in the policies on ship shall be taken as the repaired value . . .
> 8. Warranted free from any claim consequent on loss of time whether arising from a peril of the sea or otherwise.'

---

[9] Ibid, at 155.
[10] [1936] 2 All ER at 274.
[11] (1939) 64 LlL Rep 45, HL.
[12] In *Petros M Nomikos Ltd v Robertson* (1939) 64 LlL Rep 45 Lord Wright said (at 51) that the final words of the clause 'whether the steamer be fully or only partly loaded or in ballast, chartered or unchartered' were not words of limitation, but were words inserted to provide as far as possible for every circumstance in reference to insurable interest in freight which was likely to arise. The loss of the ship to the owners must involve in fact the loss of the vessel's freight-earning capacity. The final part of the clause 'whether the steamer be fully or partly loaded' might have been introduced as Hamilton J, said in *Coker v Bolton* [1912] 3 KB 315 at 320; 'for the purpose of meeting the hardship that has long been felt to exist that a shipowner, who has given notice of abandonment and has consequently lost his right to the freight subsequently earned, is precluded from suing on the policy on freight'. This hardship might be excluded in practice as it was done in the instant case and in *Coker v Bolton*, supra, by a clause in the hull policy. But the words of the clause might have a wider application if required by the facts of any particular case. The remaining words of the clause 'or in ballast, chartered or unchartered' seemed to be intended to exclude in the most unqualified manner any other question of an assured's insurable interest in freight. The policy was a time policy and the intention might be to secure that, even if the vessel at the time of the casualty had no cargo on board (i e was in ballast) and had no charter-party, there should be no question of insurable interest though it was not likely that any underwriter would think of raising such a question in a case of this type. The intention might be to provide that the owner's interest in the profit-earning capacity of his ship, which was certainly a good interest in a business sense, should be deemed a sufficient insurable interest for the purposes of the policy.

The vessel was at Rotterdam being repaired before proceeding in ballast to Venezuela. A fire broke out and this was followed by an explosion. The cost of the repairs was £37,000, and her value when repaired was £45,000. The assured did not abandon her and claim for a constructive total loss as they were entitled to do, but elected to have her repaired and claimed for a partial loss up to £27,000,[13] and were paid that sum by the hull underwriters. The charterparty was never performed, and no freight was paid by the charterers. The assured now claimed £4,110 from the underwriters under the freight policy.

The House of Lords[14] held that the action succeeded, for there had been a constructive total loss of the vessel. In considering the right of the assured to recover under the policy, the test as to whether there was a constructive total loss of the vessel was external, and did not depend on whether the assured had elected to give notice of abandonment to the hull underwriters.[15] Further, it was held by a majority of their Lordships[16] that the loss of freight was not consequent on loss of time within the meaning of clause 8, the loss being complete at the date of the fire, none the less so because the assured retained and repaired the vessel.

Lord Wright observed:[17]

> 'I do not think that on the facts of this case the claim was consequent on loss of time within clause 8. Clause 8 must be read with clause 5. Under clause 5 the underwriter's liability to pay depends on the loss, actual or constructive, of the vessel. That liability accrues at once when the casualty happens even if the exact position is not ascertained till later. If the assured has rightly given notice of abandonment of the ship, the loss dates back retrospectively to the date of the casualty. The property in the vessel then passes to the hull underwriters and the shipowner is not interested whether there is a loss of time or not. He can claim on his freight policy under clauses 5 and 6 in a proper case. Equally, here, the loss is complete at the date of the fire. The question of loss of time after the casualty does not enter into the question of liability. The claim under clause 5 does not depend on loss of time in the prosecution of the voyage within the language used by Lord Herschell. The fact that the vessel could not be repaired in time to make her cancelling date is immaterial under clause 5. In one sense every case of a constructive total loss based on the cost of repairs or on deprivation of possession implies that it will take some time to make the repairs or recover possession, and if a claim under clause 5 were treated as a claim consequent on loss of time, the operation of clause 5 would be defeated in the vast majority of cases by clause 8, except in the case of actual total loss. But in my opinion that is not the true construction of either clause 5 of clause 8. The loss under clause 5 occurs eo instanti and does so none the less because the shipowner has retained and repaired the vessel. The sole condition under clause 5 is that the vessel should be an actual or constructive total loss. Clauses 5 and 8 must be read together.'

In *Petros M Nomikos Ltd v Robertson*[18] it was contended that the above clause involved some extension of the list of perils insured against which were enumerated in the policy. Lord Wright said that he wished to reserve his opinion on this matter, and observed:[19]

> 'I do not think it necessary to express any final view on an argument which was strenuously urged on behalf of the [assured]. This argument was to the effect that clause 5 involved some

---

[13] This sum represented the total amount of the insured value less a deductible franchise of £1,000.
[14] Lord Atkin, Lord Thankerton, Lord Russell of Killowen, Lord Wright and Lord Porter.
[15] As to this point, see p 397, post.
[16] Lord Russell of Killowen, Lord Wright and Lord Porter. Lord Atkin and Lord Thankerton reserved their opinion as to whether there the claim was, in any view, consequent on loss of time. See (1939) 64 LlL Rep at 48.
[17] (1939) 64 LlL Rep at 52. See also, the speech of Lord Porter, ibid, at 55.
[18] (1939) 64 LlL Rep 45.
[19] Ibid, at 51.

extension of the list of perils insured against, which were enumerated in the policy. It was contended that all that it was necessary to prove under the clause was that the loss of the vessel was due to perils insured against. Thereupon, it was said, the underwriters were liable to pay for any loss of freight, even though due to some extraneous cause, such as the bankruptcy or default of the consignee. In other words, that the condition on which payment became due was the loss, actual or constructive, of the vessel by perils insured against, as the stipulated event in which the sum due under the freight policy became payable, though it had no actual effect in causing the loss of freight.'

But he went on to say that he would not be prepared to accept that construction, and expressed himself in the following words:[20]

'I shall, however, out of respect to the argument advanced, add that as at present advised, I should not be prepared to accept that construction. It would mean that the policy, pro tanto, was not a policy of indemnity, which appears to me to be inconsistent with the view of Hamilton J, in *Coker v Bolton*.[1] It would also mean that in this particular respect it was not a policy of marine insurance. But Hamilton J, regarded it as a contract of marine insurance, because he held that the underwriters' title to salvage and the provisions of the Marine Insurance Act applied. The contention construes the policy as a policy pro tanto covering other than marine risks, for instance, insolvency or default of the consignee. But clauses 5 and 6 are only parts of a contract of marine insurance which is limited to the perils set out in the body of the policy. There are no express words adding these outside risks. The loss, actual or constructive, of the ship is not an added peril but a loss or casualty operating on the freight through the ship.'

Lord Porter also said:[2]

'In *Scottish Marine Insurance Co v Turner*,[3] where there were no provisions such as those to be found in clause 5 and the ship was abandoned, but freight was earned, it was held that the assured on freight were unable to recover because freight was, in fact, earned and in *M'Carthy v Abel*[4] it was pointed out by Lord Ellenborough that the loss was not due to a peril of the seas but to the abandonment which was the act of the assured themselves. In *Coker v Bolton*,[5] however, and *United Kingdom Mutual Steamship Assurance Association Ltd v Boulton*[6] the assured recovered owing to the presence of a clause identical with or similar to clause 5 in the present policy. In the latter case Bigham J, held a promise to pay a loss of freight "in the event of the total or constructive total loss of the vessel" to mean that the underwriters would pay a loss of freight in circumstances similar to those existing in the *Scottish Marine* case. Such a loss was in his view recoverable not because it was a loss by perils of the seas but because the terms of the policy covered a loss by abandonment.

The learned Judge's view, if right, involves an addition to the perils insured against so as to include amongst them the peril of abandonment, but even such an extension does not go so far as to determine that the mere coincidence of a constructive total loss of the ship with a loss of freight, however caused, is sufficient to enable the assured to recover under the terms of clause 5 of the policy. It is not, however, necessary to come to any final decision upon this point in the present case.'

In *Papadimitriou v Henderson*[7] a policy had been effected in respect of freight and/or chartered freight and/or anticipated freight and the sum insured was to be payable in full in the event of the constructive total loss of the vessel. She was chartered for a voyage from Odessa to Marseilles for the carriage of lorries and spare parts consigned to agents for the Spanish Republican Government. She was captured by an insurgent warship and taken to Palma, Majorca, and

---

[20] Ibid, at 51.
[1] [1912] 3 KB 315.
[2] Ibid, at 56. See also, the speech of Lord Thankerton, ibid, at 48.
[3] (1853) 1 Macq 334, HL.
[4] (1804) 5 East 388.
[5] [1912] 3 KB 315.
[6] (1898) 3 Com Cas 330.
[7] (1939) 64 LlL Rep 345, KBD.

condemned as prize. Goddard J, held that she was a constructive total loss, and that the sum insured under the policy was payable in full.[8]

He observed:[9]

> 'Whether there was a regularly constituted Prize Court or not sitting at Palma, I have no evidence, nor have I any evidence upon which I can find the ground upon which she was condemned. One may speculate on it as much as one likes; the fact was, of course, that the bills of lading clearly showed that the goods which were on board were destined for the Spanish Government. It was the buying organisation of the then Spanish Government who were the consignees of the goods, and the goods were certainly of the class which, when consigned to the Government of a country then at war, would be regarded as contraband; they were in a class of what is commonly called conditional contraband, goods which might be of assistance to the Army Forces and which, if consigned to the Government of the country, a Prize Court would probably have no difficulty in considering to be contraband. But in the policy they were goods which were expressly allowed to be carried on the ship. The policy excluded the vessel from going to any Spanish port or Spanish possession in the Mediterranean. It warranted that no arms or ammunition or instruments of war or materials of a similar nature should be carried, but the warranty was not to exclude the carriage of cars or trucks, benzine, coal, coke or similar things. So the policy expressly allowed this cargo to be carried, albeit it was a cargo, as I have said, which was in the nature of conditional contraband; and, it being consigned to a port so near to Spain as Oran, I have no doubt, if it was considered by a Prize Court, that no Court would have any difficulty in applying the doctrine of continuous voyage. So it is at least likely—I do not say more than that—that if this ship was brought into a Prize Court, she was condemned because she was carrying a cargo of contraband. However that may be, the ship was condemned. The seizure was made on the high seas and it took place on 19 May, and she became a constructive total loss to her owners.'

In *Vrondissis v Stevens*[10] the assured claimed under a freight policy in respect of the freight of a vessel, which went aground near the Kem Reef in Northern Russia while on a voyage from Kem to Hull with a cargo of timber. She was unable to continue her voyage.

The policy provided that:

> 'In the event of total loss and/or constructive and/or arranged and/or compromised total loss of vessel, total loss and/or constructive total loss of freight arising therefrom is not recoverable hereunder.'

The policy was subject to the Institute Time Clauses (Freight), clause 5 of which stated:

> 'In the event of the total loss, whether absolute or constructive of the steamer the amount underwritten by this policy shall be paid in full.'

Clause 6 of the Time Clauses stated:

> 'In ascertaining whether the vessel is a constructive total loss the insured value in the policies on ship shall be taken as the repaired value and nothing in respect of the damaged or break-up value of the vessel or wreck shall be taken into account.'

A preliminary point of law was taken as to whether on the true construction of the policy, the assured was entitled to recover, the parties admitting that there had been a constructive total loss of the vessel, the total or, alternatively, constructive total loss of freight.

Atkinson J, held that if, at the trial of the action, the facts showed that the freight was lost because, although the ship could have been repaired and enabled to complete her voyage, yet the cost of temporary repairs, allowing for

---

[8] As to this aspect of the case, see p 96, ante.
[9] (1939) 64 LlL Rep at 348.
[10] (1940) 67 LlL Rep 55, KBD.

general average contribution, would have exceeded her repaired value, then the assured would be entitled to recover under his freight policy, and the fact that the vessel was a constructive total loss under the hull policy was irrelevant. If, on the other hand, the ship could not have been rendered fit to have completed the voyage, the loss of freight would be said to have arisen therefrom, and the assured could not recover.

He observed:[11]

> 'In my judgment, if it be the fact that the freight was lost in this case because, although the ship could have been repaired and enabled to complete the voyage, yet it would have cost more to effect such temporary repairs, allowing for general average contribution, than the repaired value of the ship, such loss did not arise from the fact, if it be the fact, that the cost of permanent repairs, allowing nothing for general average contribution, would have exceeded the sum of £11,000. On the other hand, if it was not a matter of expense, if the ship could not have been rendered fit to complete the voyage with her cargo of timber, I think it may fairly be said that the loss of freight did, within the meaning of this clause, arise from the fact (if it be the fact) that there was a constructive total loss of the ship in the sense that total loss appeared to be unavoidable and there was a physical impossibility of repair.'

His Lordship said[12] that he considered that the test of commercial loss for the purpose of establishing constructive total loss of vessel and the test of commercial loss for the purpose of establishing loss of freight were different. In the case of a constructive total loss of the vessel, it was the cost of permanent repairs, allowing nothing for general average contribution, compared with a *repaired value which might be artificial*. But in the case of establishing a loss of freight it was the cost of temporary repairs, allowing for general average contribution as compared with the *actual repaired value*.

7 Effect of freight being earned

Where, however, the freight is earned, there is no liability on the insurer in respect of it, and it does not matter that some person other than the assured is entitled to receive the freight, because it can only be so receivable by reason of a right derived from the assured. If the freight is lost to the assured, it is lost by his own act.

Thus, in *Benson v Chapman*[13] a vessel was damaged by perils insured against, and the repairs executed were paid for by borrowing on a bottomry bond, which charged the ship, freight and cargo. The ship duly arrived, and the freight was paid to the obligees of the bottomry bond. The insurers on freight were held not to be liable, for, although the freight was not received by the owner of the vessel, it was received under his authority.

In *Scottish Marine Insurance Co v Turner*[14] the vessel arrived in a bad state, but brought her cargo safely to the port of destination. The assured claimed in respect of a total loss of the vessel from the insurer on ship, and judgment was given for him. Thereupon the insurer on ship was subrogated to the rights of the assured on ship and received the freight. The owner of the ship, being also the assured on freight, claimed for a total loss of freight from the insurers on freight. But the House of Lords held that, freight having been actually earned, there was no liability on those insurers.

---

[11] Ibid, at 60.
[12] Ibid, at 60.
[13] (1849) 2 HL Cas 696.
[14] (1853) 1 Macq 334. See also, *M'Carthy v Abel* (1804) 5 East 388; *Benson v Chapman* (1849) 2 HL Cas 696; *Hunt v Royal Exchange Assurance* (1816) 5 M&S 47; *Carras v London and Scottish Assurance Corpn* [1936] 1 KB 291.

CHAPTER 28

Constructive total loss

The doctrine of constructive total loss is confined to marine insurance.[1]

A constructive total loss is a device intended to subserve the purpose of indemnity by enabling the assured, when by insured perils the postulated danger of loss or deprivation is caused, to disentangle himself, subject to definite limits and conditions, from the danger and throw the burden on the insurers.[2]

Suppose a vessel has stranded. In order to save her it may be necessary to take out her cargo, pump out the water, and raise her. When raised, she may require extensive repairs, and the cost of these operations may be so great that a prudent uninsured owner might well come to the conclusion that it is not worth while to save her at such cost. These operations would involve a financial loss, unless the value of the vessel so recovered and repaired exceeded the cost of the operations; and the assured is entitled to decline to incur such a loss, and may call on the insurers to pay him for a constructive total loss.

A DEFINITION OF 'CONSTRUCTIVE TOTAL LOSS'

'Constructive total loss' is defined in s 60(1) of the Marine Insurance Act 1906 in the following terms:

> 'Subject to any express provision in the policy,[3] there is a constructive total loss where the subject-matter insured is reasonably abandoned on account of its actual total loss appearing to be unavoidable, or because it could not be preserved from actual total loss without an expenditure which would exceed its value when the expenditure had been incurred.'

Section 60(2) goes on to state:

> 'In particular, there is a constructive total loss—
> i   Where the assured is deprived of the possession of his ship or goods by a peril insured against, and (a) it is unlikely that he can recover the ship or goods as the case may be, or (b) the cost of recovering the ship or goods, as the case may be, would exceed their value when recovered; or
> ii In the case of damage to a ship, where she is so damaged by a peril insured against, that the cost of repairing the damage would exceed the value of the ship when repaired.
>
> In estimating the cost of repairs, no deduction is to be made in respect of general average contributions to those repairs payable by other interests, but account is to be taken of the expense of future salvage operations and of any future general average contributions to which the ship would be liable if repaired; or

---

[1] *Moore v Evans* [1918] AC 185 at 194, HL.
[2] *Rickards v Forestal Land, Timber and Rlys Co Ltd* [1941] 3 All ER 62 at 79, HL (per Lord Wright).
[3] The effect of these words is considered under the heading 'Constructive total loss arising from contract', at p 375, post.

iii In the case of damage to goods,[4] where the cost of repairing the damage and forwarding the goods to their destination would exceed their value on arrival.[5]

Completeness of definition

In *Petros M Nomikos Ltd v Robertson*[6] Lord Porter pointed out that the definition of 'constructive total loss' given in s 60 was a complete one, for he said:[7]

> 'That s 60 is intended to be a complete and not a partial definition appears to follow from the wording of s 56 when it says, "Any loss other than a total loss, *as hereinafter defined*, is a partial loss". But it does not follow that the first sub-section lays down the general rule, whereas the second gives certain particular instances already covered by the general rule. Indeed, whatever may be the case with regard to sub-s 2(i), sub-ss (2)(ii) and (iii) do not appear to be covered in terms by the definition in sub-s (1).
>
> But in any case unless there is some reason to the contrary, a definition must be held to include the whole of its wording, and if particular instances are given which include matters which are outside the more general definition, that is no reason for supposing that their application is limited by the more general words. They do no merely illustrate—they add to the terms of the definition. Section 60 does not confine constructive total loss to cases where the subject-matter of insurance has been abandoned, though in some instances there may be no constructive total loss unless abandonment has taken place.'

In *Irvin v Hine*[8] during the Second World War a trawler was being towed to a dry dock. She stranded, and was severely damaged. At all material times the assured would have been unlikely to obtain a licence to repair her or to place her in a dry-dock within a reasonable time. The assured claimed that she was a constructive total loss. It was held by the King's Bench Division that, since the type of loss did not fall within any of the heads of loss stated in s 60, there was no constructive total loss. The assured, therefore, was entitled to claim for a partial loss only.

Devlin J, said:[9]

> 'If any loss outside s 57 (which defines actual total loss) and s 60 were to be held to be a total loss, it could not be a partial loss, as that would be inconsistent with the express provision of s 56. I see no answer to this argument except possibly that it puts too literal a construction on the words of s 56. That makes it material to consider whether such a construction is out of harmony with the object of s 60, as shown in its marginal note, and with the general purpose of the Act. The marginal note is "Constructive total loss defined". This is in keeping with the words of s 56 "total loss, as hereinafter defined" and shows that s 60 is intended to contain a definition. I have used the words "complete definition", as Lord Porter did,[10] as a convenient and expressive term. I dare say it is not meticulously accurate, for, strictly speaking, a definition must be complete, else it is not a definition at all. The question really is whether s 60 is a definition section, defining constructive total loss as a whole, and not merely categories of it, or whether, as Counsel for the [assured] in terms argued, all it does is to lay down the main

---

[4] See e g *Boon and Cheah Steel Pipes Sdn Bhd v Asia Insurance Co Ltd* [1975] 1 Lloyd's Rep 452, Malaysia High Court, where it was held that the amount of the damage suffered must be strictly proved. See p 374, post.

[5] It will be noticed that s 60 does not expressly deal with the constructive total loss of freight. Presumably, it is governed by the general provision of s 60(1). The cases, however, concerning freight have related to an actual total loss of freight, and it seems preferable to consider them in chapter 27, ante.

[6] (1939) 64 LlL Rep 45, HL.

[7] Ibid, at 54.

[8] [1950] 1 KB 555, [1949] 2 All ER 1089, KBD.

[9] Ibid, at 1091. But his Lordship said that he had arrived at his conclusion without relying on the authority of Lord Porter's dictum, but that his conclusion was greatly strengthened by the high persuasive authority of such a dictum.

[10] In *Petros M Nomikos Ltd v Robertson* (1939) 64 LlL Rep 45 at 54, HL.

characteristics of a constructive total loss. This argument gives no weight to the word "defined", both in s 56 and in the marginal note to s 60. I think that the word shows conclusively that s 60 is intended to *define* a constructive total loss, which is the same as saying that s 60 circumscribes completely the conception of constructive total loss. As to the general purpose of the Act, it is described in its title as a codifying Act, and it would, I think, be surprising if its framers had not included in it a comprehensive definition of constructive total loss, or that, if they had intended only to define categories, they would not have made their intention clear.'

He said that Counsel for the assured claimed that in 1913 Pickford J, in *Polurrian SS Co Ltd v Young*[11] had, in effect, treated s 60 as incomplete by adding the qualification 'within a reasonable time' to the provision about recovery of the ship or goods in s 60(2)(i). But it seemed to be clear from the passage referred to that Pickford J, was doing no more than to give the provision what he thought was the right construction. Devlin J, then said:[12]

'The subsection is silent as to whether the deprivation of possession has to be perpetual or not, and so is open to either construction. Even if the right construction of the language, taken by itself, is that the deprivation of possession is to be perpetual, it is clear that the Act does not textually cover the point, and accordingly there would be a lacuna which the common law could fill without inconsistency with any express provision.'

Relation between s 60(1) and s 60(2)

In *Petros M Nomikos Ltd v Robertson*[13] Lord Wright referred to the two definitions given in s 60, and observed:[14]

'The objective definition of a constructive total loss is found in ... section [60] of the Act. Some difficulty has been found in interpreting that section because it consists of two parts. Sub-section (2) of s 60 is purely objective; it gives the two cases of constructive total loss of ship, the first being deprivation of possession, the second the cost of repairs. This is completely consistent with s 61. But sub-s (1) is said to be inconsistent because it makes the constructive total loss depend on the condition that the subject-matter is reasonably abandoned for either of the reasons stated. This, I think, does not qualify the definition in sub-s (2). The two subsections contain two separate definitions, applicable to different conditions of circumstances. But I do not find any inconsistency between s 60(1) and s 61. Section 60(1) deals with actual abandonment, which is also an objective fact, not notice of abandonment, which may be necessary for a claim for a constructive total loss even after actual abandonment of the subject-matter insured. But if there is any inconsistency between s 61 and s 60(1) there is, in my opinion, no inconsistency at all between s 61 and s 60(2), which latter is the definition material in the present case.'

His Lordship also pointed out in *Rickards v Forestal Land, Timber and Rlys Co Ltd*[15] that s 60(2) was additional to s 60(1) and was not merely illustrative, and said:[16]

'It has been observed that this section raises great difficulties of construction. That is perhaps inevitable, and is certainly excusable when it is sought in a brief section, supplemented though it is by ss 61 to 63, to embody the complicated problems of law and fact which experience has shown to arise in the case of a constructive total loss. Some aspects of the section have been recently discussed in this House in *Robertson v Petros M Nomikos Ltd.*[17] In particular, the

---

[11] (1913) 109 LT 901 at 903.
[12] [1949] 2 All ER 1089 at 1092.
[13] (1939) 64 LlL Rep 45, HL.
[14] Ibid, at 50.
[15] [1941] 3 All ER 62, HL.
[16] Ibid, at 79. See also, *Court Line Ltd v R: The Lavington Court* [1945] 2 All ER 357 at 368, CA (per Stable J).
[17] [1939] AC 371, sub nom *Petros M Nomikos Ltd v Robertson* (1939) 64 LlL Rep 45, HL.

difficulty of fitting together the two sub-sections of s 60 and reading them together with s 61 was there considered. I think the view which this House arrived at was that the two sub-sections contain two separate definitions, which may be applied to different conditions of fact. Thus, an assured can base his claim on the terms of sub-s (2), which give an objective criterion in each case, ship, goods or freight, not only more precise than, but substantially different from, that in sub-s (1). Sub-section (2), as compared with sub-s (1), is thus additional, and not merely illustrative.'

Notice of abandonment not an essential ingredient

Notice of abandonment is not an essential ingredient of a constructive total loss. Thus, Lord Wright observed in *Petros M Nomikos Ltd v Robertson*:[18]

'The appellant's argument confuses two different concepts, because it confuses constructive total loss with the right to claim for a constructive total loss. The right to claim except in certain cases depends on due notice of abandonment under s 62 of the Act. The distinction is explicitly stated in s 61 of the Marine Insurance Act, which is as follows:

"Where there is a constructive total loss the assured may either treat the loss as a partial loss, or abandon the subject-matter insured to the insurer and treat the loss as if it were an actual total loss."

The section makes it clear that the right to abandon only arises when there is a constructive total loss in fact. That is the necessary precondition to a right to abandon. The frame of the section makes it impossible to treat the right to abandon as identical with the constructive total loss. It is a superimposed right of election where there is a constructive total loss. Nor is it even a necessary ingredient of a constructive total loss, because though there is a constructive total loss the assured may still treat it as a partial loss.'

To similar effect are the words of Lord Porter:[19]

'Section 61 no doubt gives the assured an election whether to treat the loss as total or partial, and s 62 makes it a condition precedent to a claim for a total loss, that notice of abandonment should be given. But, in terms, s 61 contemplates the existence of a constructive total loss even where the loss is treated as partial. It was not contended before us that there could not be a constructive total loss where no notice of abandonment was given; it was admitted that notice of abandonment was merely a condition precedent to recovery in a case where a constructive total loss had already occurred.

Having regard to the wording of s 61, abandonment may be a condition or consequence of recovery and not a condition precedent to the existence of a total loss whether actual or constructive. A constructive total loss may exist, but if the assured wishes to take advantage of it, he must give notice of abandonment, at any rate in a case where there would be any possibility of benefit to the insurer. If he does give notice and the underwriters accept the abandonment, or if the assured recover as for a total loss, the property insured thereby becomes the property of the underwriters.'

B   REASONABLE ABANDONMENT OF SUBJECT-MATTER

In *Lind v Mitchell*,[20] where a schooner was damaged by ice and started leaking, one of the issues which arose was whether she was a constructive total loss within the meaning of s 60(1) of the Marine Insurance Act 1906, for it was alleged that she had been 'reasonably abandoned on account of her actual total loss appearing to be unavoidable'. Before leaving her the master set fire to her. Later she was sighted by a steamer, which approached her and found her on fire but floating high in the water.

---

[18] (1939) 64 LlL Rep 45 at 50, HL.
[19] Ibid, at 55.
[20] (1928) 32 LlL Rep 70, CA.

The Court of Appeal[1] held that she had been prematurely abandoned, and was not a constructive total loss. Scrutton LJ, observed:[2]

> 'Was this, in the language of s 60 of the Act, which deals with constructive total loss, a reasonable abandonment "on account of its actual total loss appearing to be unavoidable"; that is to say, total loss probable from the leak appearing, judged to be unavoidable, and therefore a reasonable abandonment of the vessel which it is reasonably thought will anyhow be lost by perils of the sea?
> Now I am satisfied that the abandonment was unreasonable. The vessel was within 15 miles of her home port. The lifeboat into which the crew got, according to the evidence, was able to sail and row in with a north-east wind. If the lifeboat could sail, the schooner could equally have sailed with the north-east wind. The schooner was still floating high in the water seven or eight hours after she was abandoned. I assumed in my judgment that the abandonment by the master was unreasonable.'

The words 'appearing to be' unavoidable in s 60(1) of the Marine Insurance Act 1906 mean 'appearing on the true facts as known'. They do not mean 'appearing on the facts as known to the assured'.[3]

In *Marstrand Fishing Co Ltd v Beer*[4] Porter J, said:[5]

> 'The second question, namely, on what must the person making the claim be taken to have acted, depends upon s 60(1), (2) of the Act. If the decision depended upon s 60(2), then the question is: Was the recovery on the proper date unlikely or not? Prima facie, that means: Was the recovery unlikely on the true facts as then existing and not upon the facts as known to the assured? But it may be said that s 60(2) is a particular instance of which s 60(1) is the general expression, and, if so, the meaning of the general must govern that of the particular which is an instance or example of it. Even if this be so, the phrase in s 60(1)—that is, that there is a constructive total loss when the subject-matter insured is reasonably abandoned on account of its actual total loss appearing to be unavoidable—may mean because, on the facts as known, the vessel's loss appears unavoidable, or because, on the true facts, the loss appears unavoidable. I prefer the latter of those two constructions, (a) because the particular instance in s 60(2) would seem to point to the true facts being the criterion, and (b) because that was, I think, the view accepted in the *Polurrian* case.[6] If that be an accurate view, the word "appears" is used because the future of the vessel is still unknown, and her loss must still be described as appearing unavoidable, since certainty can never be predicted of the future. It would be curious if that were not so, since the result of the other would at least be an odd one. One example may suffice. If the decision were to depend on the apparent facts, an owner, whose credible information was that the ship had been driven ashore in such circumstances that her loss appeared to be unavoidable, could give notice of abandonment, issue his writ, and recover, though it was found the next day that the vessel was safe and sound in harbour.'

The wording of s 60(1) is substantially repeated in clause 13 of the Institute Cargo Clauses (A),[7] which are often incorporated into the policy. This clause states:

> 'No claim for Constructive Total Loss shall be recoverable hereunder unless the subject-matter insured is reasonably abandoned either on account of their actual total loss appearing to be unavoidable or because the cost of recovering, reconditioning and forwarding the subject-matter to the destination to which it is insured would exceed its value on arrival.'

---

[1] Scrutton, Lawrence and Sankey LJJ.
[2] (1928) 32 LlL Rep 70 at 74.
[3] *Marstrand Fishing Co Ltd v Beer* [1937] 1 All ER 158.
[4] [1937] 1 All ER 158.
[5] Ibid, at 164.
[6] *Polurrian SS Co Ltd v Young* [1915] 1 KB 922.
[7] These clauses are set out in Appendix III, pp 516–519, post.

C DEPRIVATION OF POSSESSION OF SHIP OR GOODS

There is a constructive total loss of a vessel if it is 'unlikely' that the assured can recover her. It is not enough for it to be merely 'uncertain' whether he will be able to recover her.

Thus, in *Polurrian SS Co Ltd v Young*[8] the insured vessel was on a voyage from Newport to Constantinople. During it war broke out between Greece and Turkey. She was stopped by a Greek warship, and escorted into a Greek port because she was carrying contraband. The authorities kept her there, so the assured gave notice of abandonment, and claimed for a constructive total loss. Six weeks later the vessel was released. It was held by the Court of Appeal[9] that the assured could not recover for a constructive total loss because, at the date of the commencement of the action,[10] the assured had not shown that it was 'unlikely' that he would recover the vessel. To show that it was 'uncertain' was insufficient.

Warrington J, said:[11]

> 'To enable the [assured] to succeed they must establish fully, (i) that at the date of the commencement of this action they had been deprived of the possession of the *Polurrian*; and (ii) that it was not merely quite uncertain whether they would recover her within a reasonable time, but that the balance of probability was that they could not do so. They have, as my brother Pickford has held, and I quite agree with him, made the first point good—the Greek captors did deprive the [assured] of the possession of their ship. Have they also shown that there was more likelihood that the [assured] would not, than that they would, recover her? The test, in my humble judgment, is one the application of which in this case is, and generally in similar cases of capture would be, very difficult to apply with any sense of satisfaction, because it necessarily involves conjecture and speculation as to what is likely to be the outcome of a number of possible contingencies. Addressing myself, however, to the best of my ability to the question which this s 60 directs me to consider, my conclusion is that, while I hold that on 26 October—the crucial date, because the date of the commencement of the [assured's] action—the recovery of the *Polurrian* by her owners was quite uncertain, I do not feel myself justified in holding that the balance of probabilities has been proved so clearly against her recovery that I can say that such recovery was "unlikely". This being so, the [assured] must be held to have failed to make out their case.'

Commenting in *Rickards v Forestal Land, Timber and Rlys Co Ltd*[12] on this decision, Lord Wright agreed that the Marine Insurance Act 1906, s 60(2)(i) had altered the previous law by substituting the test of 'unlikelihood' for 'uncertainty' of recovery of the subject-matter insured, and said:[13]

> 'There is a real difference in logic between saying that a future happening is uncertain and saying that it is unlikely. In the former, the balance is even. No one can say one way or the other. In the latter, there is some balance against the event. It is true that there is nothing in the Act to show what degree of unlikelihood is required. If, on the test of uncertainty, the scales

---

[8] [1915] 1 KB 922, CA.
[9] Lord Cozens-Hardy MR, Kennedy LJ and Warrington J.
[10] The insurers had agreed to treat the date of the notice of abandonment as the date of the commencement of the action, and to put the assured in the same position as if a writ had then been issued. See also *The Bamburi* [1982] 1 Lloyd's Rep 312 where Staughton J, sitting as sole arbitrator, said (ibid, at 321): 'If abandonment is declined, it is the usual practice of underwriters, so far as my knowledge goes, to agree to place the assured in the same position as if a writ had been issued'.
[11] [1914–15] All ER Rep 116 at 123.
[12] [1941] 3 All ER 62, HL.
[13] Ibid, at 81.

are level, any degree of unlikelihood would seem to shift the balance, however slightly. It is not required that the scale should spring up and kick the beam.'

Where goods are detained en route in a city which is either besieged or so circumstanced that the goods cannot be forwarded to their destination, this may result in a constructive total loss;[14] for if, by reason of forcible detention, there is such a long delay as to constitute a change in the circumstances affecting the risk and affecting the position of the assured in relation thereto, he may be entitled to abandon the goods to the insurers and treat the case as one of constructive total loss.[15]

In *George Cohen Sons & Co v Standard Marine Insurance Co Ltd*[16] the 'Prince George', an obsolete battleship, was insured whilst being towed from Chatham to Brake (in Germany), where she was to go to be scrapped. She went ashore on the Dutch coast. The Dutch authorities would not allow her to be moved in case the sea defences in the area were damaged thereby. Their decision, however, was subject to appeal to a higher tribunal. Roche J, held that she was a constructive total loss, and said:[17]

> 'In my judgment there was a distinct unlikelihood, although recourse could be had to the Courts, that under any circumstances, or on any terms which the shipowners as commercial men were likely to be able to offer, the Courts would ever have allowed the operation to have been attempted. For those reasons I decide that the vessel, the *Prince George*, was a constructive total loss.'

In *Vacuum Oil Co v Union Insurance Society of Canton*[18] 10,000 tins of petroleum were insured for a voyage from Alexandria to Cyprus. The vessel carrying them stranded and became a total loss. The tins floated ashore, and were salved by the local agent of the assured. About 8,000 tins were recovered, and a large number of them were leaking. The leaking tins were repaired and filled up from other tins with the result that there were 5,570 full tins and about 2,000 empty tins. One of the issues[19] which arose was whether there was a constructive total loss.

The Court of Appeal[20] held that there had been a constructive total loss having regard to the unlikelihood of obtaining a shipowner to carry damaged tins of petroleum and the probable cost of transhipment.

Atkin LJ, said:[1]

> 'I am quite satisfied that it would have been perfectly impossible to get anybody, however optimistic the owner of a sailing vessel trading in the Mediterranean in these ports might be, to carry a cargo of leaking petroleum tins. The estimate made by the underwriters themselves was that about 900 tins might have leaked in the time it would have taken to do the voyage, and 900 tins represent between 3,500 and 4,000 gallons of petroleum, which during this time would have flowed and leaked into the hold of the unfortunate vessel which was supposed to be carrying them.'

---

[14] *Rodoconachi v Elliott* (1874) LR 9 CP 518. See also, *Cologan v London Assurance* (1816) 5 M&S 447.
[15] *Stringer v English and Scottish Marine Insurance Co* (1870) LR 5 QB 599 at 601 (per Kelly CB).
[16] (1925) 21 LlL Rep 30, KBD.
[17] Ibid, at 34.
[18] (1926) 25 LlL Rep 546, CA.
[19] Other issues which arose in the case were whether there was any possibility of benefit to the insurers, and also whether a Lloyd's agent had authority to receive a notice of abandonment. As to these aspects of the case, see pp 384–385, post, and p 387, post, respectively.
[20] Bankes, Atkin and Sargant LJJ.
[1] (1926) 25 LlL Rep at 552. See also the judgment of Bankes LJ, ibid, at 549, and that of Sargant LJ, ibid, at 555.

In *Marstrand Fishing Co Ltd v Beer: The Girl Pat*[2] the master and crew barratrously took possession of a vessel, which had left Grimsby with orders to fish in the North Sea. There was no competent engineer on board. The engine had broken down twice and the log had been falsified. There was no proper chart on board. She had arrived at and sailed from Corcubion, a port in Spain. She had altered her rig by the addition of a bowsprit. Her fishing numbers had been blacked out. The assured claimed for a constructive total loss.[3]

Porter J, held that the action failed, for it could be said that on a balance of probabilities her recovery was 'uncertain', but not 'unlikely'. His Lordship observed:[4]

> 'She was not lost by a peril of the seas, but a clear act of barratry had been committed, and any loss following that barratry would, I think, be a loss by barratry. (See Arnould, s 858.) In those circumstances, she might have escaped and been sold, or gone ashore, or perhaps been seized by necessaries men, or come into collision with another ship. All these things were possible, and, indeed, not unlikely, but I cannot say that, in my view, on a balance of probabilities, she was more likely to be lost than recovered.
>
> To my mind, it is a case exactly on all fours with the *Polurrian* case,[5] her recovery being uncertain, but not unlikely. If I had been asked to say: "Is she more likely to be lost or recovered?"—I should have felt obliged to reply: "I do not know".'

In *Société Belge des Betons, SA v London and Lancashire Insurance Co Ltd*[6] some vessels and appurtenances, which were used in connection with the construction of some harbour works at Valencia, were insured under a policy against risk of loss by 'restraints of peoples'. The Spanish Civil War broke out in July 1936, and on 2 September 1936 the insured property was seized by the assured's workmen. The workmen were supported by the Popular Executive Committee, which was the de facto and de jure Government of Valencia at that time. On 6 November 1936 the Popular Executive Committee issued a decree of incautacion.[7] Porter J, held (obiter) that there had been a constructive total loss of the property,[8] for its recovery was 'unlikely', and observed:[9]

> 'It is clear from *Polurrian SS Co Ltd v Young*,[10] that to constitute a constructive total loss it must be proved that the assured was unlikely to recover within a reasonable time. If the seizure was a seizure by peoples, in my opinion, in any view of the facts, by 10 November the recovery of the vessels insured was unlikely and certainly unlikely within any reasonable time.'

In *C Czarnikow Ltd and Leslie and Anderson Ltd v Java Sea and Fire Insurance Co Ltd*[11] cargoes were insured for voyages on German vessels for voyages from Singapore and Bombay to Hamburg. On 26 and 28 August 1939 the masters of the vessels acting in compliance with the orders of the German Government put

---

[2] (1936) 56 LlL Rep 163, KBD.
[3] The assured also claimed that there had been an actual total loss of the vessel. But the action on this ground failed also. As to this aspect of the case, see p 347, ante.
[4] (1936) 56 LlL Rep at 174.
[5] [1915] 1 KB 922, CA.
[6] (1938) 60 LlL Rep 225, KBD.
[7] Porter J, in considering the meaning of this word, said (ibid, at 232): 'It was originally used legislatively of the expropriation of the property of the late King of Spain, without compensation, and has since been commonly used. It means the taking possession by a competent tribunal or authority; it is final, has some suggestion of punishment and none of return'.
[8] His Lordship held that, in any event, there had been a total loss by 'restraints of peoples'.
[9] (1938) 60 LlL Rep 225 at 234.
[10] [1914–15] All ER Rep 116, CA.
[11] (1941) 70 LlL Rep 319, KBD.

into Massowah (in Eritrea) and remained there. War broke out on 3 September 1939, and the port authorities refused to permit transhipment or delivery of any cargo except where the ports of shipment and destination were neutral. Abortive attempts were made by the cargo owners to obtain release of the cargoes, and on 16 and 20 October 1939 they gave notice of abandonment to the insurers. But the insurers refused to accept the notice. The assured claimed that there had been a constructive total loss of the goods.

Lord Caldecote LCJ, held that the action succeeded. The assured had been deprived of their goods by restraints of princes or people, and it was more unlikely than likely that they could recover them.

In considering the evidence on this point his Lordship concluded:[12]

'On 30 October the ship with her cargo on board had been at Massowah in a very hot climate for over two months. Mr Worters, the plaintiffs' general manager, said that two months of the hot season would make the copra almost useless for human consumption and in his opinion also for industrial use. Next, though Massowah was nominally a neutral port, in fact, Italy, who did not come into the war till June 1940, was, to use a phrase which with a new meaning has now become familiar, a "non-belligerent"—that is to say, one of the Axis Powers and hand in glove with Germany and not the least likely to do anything which the German Government did not wish. She was more likely than not to do all that was within her power, short of actual war at that stage, to hamper and cripple British cargo owners as well as to support German activities. The reports made by Mr Miles never held out any hopes that either the German captain or the Italian port authorities were likely to be amenable to his efforts. On 11 October the captains of German ships were taking up a position which however fantastic was at any rate significant. They maintained a right to hold all merchandise on board their ships as prize cargo. By this time the attitude of the port commandant was in Mr Miles's words "another difficulty to be overcome", and, in addition, the possibility of any acquiescence on the part of the shipowners was reported to be "extremely remote". As against these facts, I was pressed particularly to say that even assuming the German Government ever seized the cargo, the seizure ended, and the goods were well on their way to release, on 16 October. At that date the German Consul issued instructions that came from the German Foreign Office to the effect that the interests of the cargo were to be protected and that the cargo owners could not be refused delivery nor the right to tranship. Mr Miles, writing on 16 November from Massowah, though this entirely changed the position, and the port commandant who had no instructions from his Government at Addis Ababa, showed a disposition to permit transhipment subject to the fulfilment of certain conditions. There is also the fact that the Board of Trade was taking an interest in the release of the cargoes at Massowah and on 9 October gave the licence to cargo owners to make payments to that end which would otherwise have been illegal as trading with the enemy. Moreover, the London Chamber of Commerce was active, and on 25 October held meetings of cargo owners to discuss the general question of British cargoes detained on board German vessels taking refuge in neutral ports. At that time anyone attending that meeting might perhaps have had his hopes raised by talk of the way in which the Chamber proposed to handle the release and reshipment of goods. It was evident, however, that this at best was going to be a long process, and anyone who was aware of the state of things at Massowah would, I think, have been over-optimistic if he had thought the chances that the cargo would be recovered were then more than very slight. On the whole of the true facts as existing on 30 October I find that on that date it was unlikely, that is to say, more unlikely than likely, that a cargo owner could recover his goods.'

In *Rickards v Forestal Land, Timber and Rlys Co Ltd*[13] a cargo was insured for carriage on the 'Minden', which was a German vessel, from South American ports to Hong Kong or Shanghai. The vessel arrived at Rio on 25 August 1939. War was declared on 3 September 1939. After 16 August 1939 all German owned shipping had been taken control of by the German Government, and all vessels and their masters had been ordered to take refuge in neutral ports or to

---
[12] Ibid, at 328.
[13] [1942] AC 50, [1941] 3 All ER 62, HL.

return to Germany, or as a last resort to scuttle themselves. The vessel sailed from Rio on 6 September 1939. The assured claimed for a constructive total loss of the goods on the ground that their recovery was 'unlikely'.

The House of Lords[14] accepted this contention, and held that the action succeeded.

Lord Wright observed:[15]

> 'In the present case, in my opinion, it was unlikely that the goods would be recovered. The odds were all against it. When the *Minden* sailed from Rio under the orders of the German government, it was, I think, not merely uncertain that she would evade the British blockade. It was, in my opinion, unlikely. If she had been captured, it was no doubt likely that the assured would have regained possession of his goods, but the orders of the German Government had provided against that contingency by requiring the master to scuttle the ship, as he in fact did.'

In *W W Howard Bros & Co Ltd v Kann*[16] a cargo was insured for carriage on the 'Halle', which was a German vessel, from Bunbury, Australia for London via the Cape of Good Hope. She passed the Cape of Good Hope on 18 August 1939 and on a normal voyage she would have reached London on 16 September. In compliance with the orders of the German Government she put into Bissao, Portuguese Guinea, on 6 September, and remained there until 13 October when she sailed and attempted to get back to Germany. The assured claimed for a constructive total loss of the goods on the ground that it was 'unlikely' that they would be recovered.

The House of Lords[17] held that the action succeeded. The goods were constructively lost when the master determined to return to Germany and acted on the German Government's orders.

Lord Porter said:[18]

> 'Let me therefore assume that the question is, was the owner unlikely to recover them once the German Government's orders were acted upon? At that moment I think it was much more likely that they would be lost than that they would survive, and I regard the escape of the *Wagoni* as exceedingly fortunate. In my judgment they were more likely to go to the bottom of the sea than to reach Germany, and even if they reached Germany the assured was unlikely to recover them. If this be the true inference, then once the master sailed for a German port the goods were a constructive total loss at a moment when they were still being carried in the ship mentioned and on the voyage insured in the policy.'

In *Panamanian Oriental Steamship Corpn v Wright*[19] the insured vessel was boarded by Vietnamese customs officials and unmanifested goods were found on board. A special military court ordered her to be confiscated. Mocatta J, held that the assured's claim for a constructive total loss succeeded, for it was unlikely that they could recover possession of her.[20]

In *The Bamburi*[1] a vessel was detained in the Shatt-al-Arab Roads by the Iraqi authorities during a war between Iran and Iraq, and was forbidden to

---

[14] Viscount Simon LC, Viscount Maugham, Lord Thankerton, Lord Wright and Lord Porter.
[15] [1941] 3 All ER at 81. See also, the speech of Viscount Maugham (ibid, at 72), and that of Lord Porter, ibid, at 98.
[16] (1941) 70 LlL Rep 173, HL. This case was heard at the same time and reported together with *Forestal Land, Timber & Rlys Co|Ltd v Rickards*, supra.
[17] Viscount Simon LC, Viscount Maugham, Lord Thankerton, Lord Wright and Lord Porter.
[18] (1941) 70 LlL Rep at 203. See also the speech of Viscount Maugham, ibid, at 185, and that of Lord Wright, ibid, at 197.
[19] [1970] 2 Lloyd's Rep 365, QBD (Com Ct). The decision in this case was later reversed on another ground: [1971] 1 Lloyd's Rep 487, CA. See pp 261–262, ante.
[20] See the judgment of Mocatta J: [1970] 2 Lloyd's Rep at 383.
[1] [1982] 1 Lloyd's Rep 312.

leave. Notice of abandonment[2] was given on 30 September and 14 October 1981. Staughton J, sitting as sole arbitrator, held that the claim for a total constructive loss succeeded because it was unlikely that the assured owners would recover possession of her within 12 months of either of those dates.[3] The loss of 'free use and disposal' of the vessel amounted to 'loss of possession' within the meaning of the policy.[4]

Detainment clause

Special provisions relating to the constructive total loss of a vessel due to her detention are to be found in the Institute Clauses.

Clause 3 of the Institute War and Strikes Clauses (Hulls–Time).[5]

> 'In the event that the Vessel shall have been the subject of capture, seizure, arrest, detainment, confiscation or expropriation, and the Assured shall thereby have lost the free use and disposal of the vessel for a continuous period of 12 months, then for the purpose of ascertaining whether the Vessel is a constructive total loss the Assured shall be deemed to have been deprived of the possession without any likelihood of recovery.'

Clause 3 of the Institute War and Strikes Clauses (Hulls–Voyage)[6] is in the same words.

D DAMAGE TO SHIP

In estimating whether the cost of repairs to the ship will exceed her value when repaired, the assured need not allow a deduction of one-third new for old on repairs, that deduction only being made where repairs are actually executed and not in any other case.[7]

Further, no allowance need be made in the case of the constructive total loss of an old and decrepit vessel for repairs which, had she been in perfect condition, would not have been necessary.[8]

The value of the wreck cannot be added to the cost of repairs for the purpose of determining whether there is a constructive total loss.[9]

Thus, in *Hall v Hayman*[10] the cost of repairing a vessel would have amounted to $30,500. Her value when repaired would have been $34,000. The assured sought to add to the cost of repairs the value of the wreck, viz $14,000, in order to claim that the vessel was a constructive total loss. It was held by the King's Bench Division that he was not entitled to do so.

Bray J, said:[11]

> 'I have also got, undoubtedly, to look at the words in sub-s 2 in the second branch of it: "In the case of damage to a ship, where she is so damaged by a peril insured against that the cost of repairing the damage would exceed the value of the ship when repaired." I cannot come to the

---

[2] See p 381, post.
[3] [1982] 1 Lloyd's Rep 312 at 322.
[4] Ibid at 321.
[5] These clauses are set out in Appendix III, pp 547–548, post.
[6] These clauses are set out in Appendix III, pp 549–550, post.
[7] *Henderson Bros v Shankland* [1896] 1 QB 525.
[8] *Phillips v Nairne* (1847) 4 CB 343.
[9] *Hall v Hayman* (1912) 106 LT 142.
[10] (1912) 106 LT 142.
[11] Ibid, at 147.

conclusion that there is any ambiguity about these words at all—the cost of repairing the damage. Then: "In estimating the cost of repairs, no deduction is to be made in respect of general average contributions to those repairs payable by other interests, but account is to be taken of the expense of future salvage operations, and of any future general average contributions to which the ship would be liable if repaired." It seems to me that this section is plain. It is inconsistent with what is now admitted to have been the common law or the law merchant before, because it has now been decided by the House of Lords since the passing of this Act that, with reference to a wreck that had occurred before it came into operation, according to the common law the value of the wreck should be included in the calculation that I am making; but, as I have said, I have come to the conclusion that the words of the statute are inconsistent with that, and, therefore, I have no right to import the common law.'

Similarly, clause 17 of the Institute Time Clauses (Hulls),[12] which are frequently incorporated into the policy, states:

'In ascertaining whether the Vessel is a constructive total loss . . . nothing in respect of the damaged or break-up value of the Vessel or wreck shall be taken into account.'

In deciding whether there is a constructive total loss, while the assured may take into account all the costs he will have to incur to recover her—including the cost of repairs at the particular time and place, the cost of refloating her, and any general average contribution to which she may be liable if repaired—yet he must give credit for such portion of the cost of saving her as he may be entitled to recover in general average from the owners of other interests concerned if the operation is successfully carried out.[13]

In the absence of a market value the test is what the vessel was fairly worth to her owners from a business point of view.[14]

In *Companhia Geval de Seguros v Lloyd Continental Insurance Co Ltd*[15] an insurance company claimed from the defendants under a reinsurance policy in respect of a Portuguese sailing lugger lost off the Portuguese coast whilst on a voyage from the Newfoundland Banks to Aveiro (a port in Portugal). The vessel experienced bad weather off the Tagus, and had to be beached.[16] The amount of damage to her hull was 84.9 per cent. Sankey J, held that the assured were entitled to claim for a constructive total loss,[17] and said:[18]

'It is suggested that the vessel was not a total loss by the perils insured against, and that the plaintiffs have not proved their case. I come to the conclusion clearly with regard to the hull that there was constructive or actual total loss. The vessel was in a very bad condition. She was in the sand and those on the spot, I should think, acted prudently in dismantling the vessel with a view of salving what could be saved, and it must be recollected what the loss was, 84 per cent. Therefore, I think that with regard to the hull the plaintiffs are entitled to succeed. They were under a liability to pay their assured, and defendants were liable to pay them.'

The general rule is that in estimating the value for the purpose of determining whether or not there is a constructive total loss, any agreed value in the policy is to be ignored.

Section 27(4) of the Marine Insurance Act 1906 states:

---

[12] These clauses are set out in Appendix III, pp 533–540, post.
[13] *Kemp v Halliday* (1866) LR 1 QB 520.
[14] *The Harmonides* [1903] P 1; *Grainger v Martin* (1863) 4 B&S 9.
[15] (1922) 13 LlL Rep 26, KBD.
[16] As to the evidence, see ibid, at 27–28.
[17] His Lordship also held that there was a constructive total loss of the cargo, which had been reinsured under another policy. See ibid, at 28–29.
[18] Ibid, at 28.

'Unless the policy otherwise provides, the value fixed by the policy is not conclusive for the purpose of determining whether there has been a constructive total loss.'

Usually, however, there is a clause in the policy relating to this matter.[19] Thus, clause 17 of the Institute Time Clauses (Hulls)[20] states:

'In ascertaining whether the Vessel is a constructive total loss the insured value shall be taken as the repaired value . . .'

Similarly, clause 15 of the Institute Time Clauses (Freight)[1] states:

'. . . In ascertaining whether the Vessel is a constructive total loss, the insured value in the insurances on hull and machinery shall be taken as the repaired value. . . .'

E DAMAGE TO GOODS

Where goods are saved in a damaged state at a place other than that of their destination, the mode of computation to be adopted, in order to decide whether or not there is a constructive total loss, is to take the whole cost of getting them to their destination, which will have to be incurred by reason of their position and condition. This will include such charges as landing, drying, or warehousing, reshipping, and carriage to their port of destination.

It is essential for the amount of damage to be calculated.

Thus, in *Boon and Cheah Steel Pipes Sdn Bhd v Asia Insurance Co Ltd*,[2] where there was a claim for the constructive total loss of some steel pipes, the Malaysia High Court held that the action failed because the assured had not notified the insurers and had not obtained a survey report from them, and without a detailed examination one could not know for certain the actual damage suffered.[3]

In *Farnworth v Hyde*[4] it was held that credit must be given for the freight payable on delivery under the original bill of lading. A similar decision was given in *Rosetto v Gurney*.[5]

But it would appear from the wording of s 60(2)(iii) of the Marine Insurance Act 1906 that no such deduction should be made, for the words of that subsection clearly state that the whole cost of forwarding, and not merely the excess cost is to be considered.

The debt and costs paid to holders of a bottomry bond must not be included in calculating whether there has been a constructive total loss of the goods.[6]

If, when unshipped at an intermediate port, the damaged cargo could have been sold for an amount exceeding the expense of drying it and bringing it home, there will not be a constructive total loss of cargo.[7] Further, where the

---

[19] See, e g *Marten v SS Owners' Underwriting Association Ltd* (1902) 7 Com Cas 195; *Angel v Merchants' Marine Insurance Co* [1903] 1 KB 811, CA; *North Atlantic SS Co v Bure* (1904) 9 Com Cas 164; *Hall v Hayman* [1912] 2 KB 5; *Helmville Ltd v Yorkshire Insurance Co Ltd*; *The Medina Princess* [1965] 1 Lloyd's Rep 361, QBD (Com Ct).
[20] These clauses are set out in Appendix III, pp 533–540, post.
[1] These clauses are set out in Appendix III, pp 550–554, post.
[2] [1975] 1 Lloyd's Rep 452.
[3] See the judgment of Raja Azlan Shah J, ibid, at 458.
[4] (1866) LR 2 CP 204.
[5] (1851) 11 CB 176. See also, *Moss v Smith* (1850) 9 CB 94.
[6] *Rosetto v Gurney* (1851) 11 CB 176.
[7] *Reimer v Ringrose* (1851) 6 Exch 263.

adventure failed because of the loss of the voyage, it was held that if the goods existed in specie, although in a damaged state, the fact that they would be subject to a claim for general average was not enough to constitute a constructive total loss.[8]

In regard to the relations of freight and cargo, there is not a constructive total loss of cargo when the goods on arrival are of less value than the freight, for any such doctrine would put on the insurer on goods a liability arising out of a contract made by the assured to pay certain, perhaps heavy, rates of freight.

As in the case of a constructive total loss of ship, the valuation agreed on in the policy does not determine the question whether there has been a constructive total loss of goods.

The valuation is only inserted for the purpose of ascertaining the amount to be paid to the assured in the event of loss and for no other purpose.[9]

F CONSTRUCTIVE TOTAL LOSS ARISING FROM CONTRACT

Constructive total loss may also arise from contract.

Thus, in *Rowland and Marwood's SS Co v Maritime Insurance Co*[10] it was agreed that a ship should be deemed to be a constructive total loss if she was stranded for 6 months, and it was impracticable in that period to save her. The ship stranded for that period, and it was held that she was a constructive total loss, though it was quite possible that she would be saved in the near future.

G EFFECT OF CONSTRUCTIVE TOTAL LOSS

Section 61 of the Marine Insurance Act 1906 states:

> 'Where there is a constructive total loss the assured may either treat the loss as a partial loss, or abandon the subject-matter insured to the insurer and treat the loss as if it were an actual total loss.'[11]

Even if the ship is a constructive total loss, the assured may elect to repair her, and he may recover the cost of repairs up to 100 per cent of the valuation, and retain the ship.[12]

Thus, in *Petros M Nomikos Ltd v Robertson*[13] a vessel was insured for £28,000, the policy containing a warranty that 50 per cent was uninsured for a total or constructive loss. She was damaged by an explosion on board. The estimated cost of the repairs was £37,000, and by a term in the policy the insured value was deemed to be the repaired value. The assured elected not to abandon the

---

[8] *Anderson v Wallis* (1813) 2 M&S 240.
[9] *Irving v Manning* (1847) 6 CB 391 at 421 (per Patterson J).
[10] (1901) 6 Com Cas 160. See also, *Re Sunderland SS Co and North of England Iron SS Insurance Association* (1894) 11 TLR 106; *Sailing Ship Holt Hill v United Kingdom Marine Association* [1919] 2 KB 789; *Fowler v English and Scottish Marine Insurance Co* (1865) 18 CBNS 818, where the policy provided that the insurers would pay for a total loss 30 days after official news of capture or embargo.
[11] As to abandonment, see chapter 29, post.
[12] *Aitchison v Lohre* (1879) 4 App Cas 755.
[13] (1939) 64 LlL Rep 45, HL.

vessel and claim for a constructive total loss, but had her repaired and claimed for a partial loss up to £27,000,[14] and were paid that sum by the insurers.

H EFFECT OF RESTORATION ON THE EXTENT OF THE LOSS

Before the Marine Insurance Act 1906 the principle of law in England[15] was that if, in the interval between the date of the loss and the date fixing the legal rights of the parties in relation to the loss, there was a change of circumstances reducing the loss from a total to a partial one, the assured could only recover for a partial loss.[16]

The Marine Insurance Act 1906, however, is entirely silent as to this principle of 'ademption of loss', and it may therefore be that the rule of law which obtained before the Act was passed is now abrogated.[17]

But Lord Wright said in one case:[18]

> 'By the English common law, the date of giving notice of abandonment was not treated as the decisive date, which was taken to be the date of issuing the writ in the action. This was fully established by a number of authorities dating back at least to the time of Lord Mansfield. These authorities were collected by Collins J, in *Ruys v Royal Exchange Assurance Corpn*.[19] The Marine Insurance Act 1906 is silent on the point, and this has led to some question, which Viscount Sumner in *Captain J A Cates Tug and Wharfage Co v Franklin Insurance Co*,[20] found it unnecessary to consider. However, in *Polurrian SS Co Ltd v Young*[1] where, in the changing circumstances, it was material to determine what was the material date at which the justification for giving notice of abandonment was to be judged, the Court of Appeal accepted the date of the commencement of the action. They thus held that the Act had not changed the old rule. In my opinion, this was the sound conclusion. Section 91(2) requires that the express provisions of the Act should be inconsistent with the old rule if the old rule is to be abrogated. I cannot find any such inconsistency in s 60 or s 61, or elsewhere in the Act. The law of Scotland is different on the point, and weight has been attached in some quarters to the fact that the draft of the Act was changed by omitting a section which expressly provided that the date of the writ should be the material date. However, I do not appreciate how this can properly affect the construction of the actual words of the Act. The old rule is, I think, still the law.'

Much of the practical importance of the rule has been lost owing to the practice of asking insurers, when they refuse to accept notice of abandonment, to put the assured in the same position as if a writ had been issued. In most cases the insurers agree to do so.

---

[14] This sum represented the total amount of the insured value less a deductible franchise of £1,000.

[15] The principle was different in Scotland where the question whether there was a constructive total loss was determined once and for all by the position obtaining at the time when notice of abandonment was given without regard to subsequent events. See *Sailing Ship Blairmore Co v Macredie* [1898] AC 593 at 606, 609. In this case a vessel sank in San Francisco Bay on 9 April. On 15 April the assured gave notice of abandonment, and on 16 July the insurers raised the vessel and tendered her to the assured. It was held that the assured were entitled to recover for a total loss, since the insurers were not entitled even at considerable cost to alter the rights of the assured. Those rights were fixed by Scots law at the date of the abandonment, and if the abandonment when made was justifiable, no person except the assured could bring about a waiver or cancellation of the abandonment.

[16] See *Patterson v Ritchie* (1815) 4 M&S 393; *Naylor v Taylor* (1829) 9 B&C 718.

[17] See, however, *Polurrian SS Co Ltd v Young* (1915) 20 Com Cas 152 at 153; *Roura and Forgas v Townend* (1918) 24 Com Cas 71 at 81; *Captain J A Cates Tug and Wharfage Co Ltd v Franklin Insurance Co* [1927] AC 698, PC.

[18] *Rickards v Forestal Land, Timber and Rlys Co Ltd* [1941] 3 All ER 62 at 80, HL.

[19] [1897] 2 QB 135.

[20] [1927] AC 698 at 703, PC.

[1] [1915] 1 KB 922, CA.

Thus, Pickford J, observed:[2]

'The underwriters are asked in case they refuse to accept the abandonment to put the assured' in the same position as if a writ had been issued. In nine cases out of ten, and probably a much larger proportion, the underwriters agree to do so, and, if they do not, the consequence is that the assured issues his writ immediately, and therefore the two dates in ordinary English insurance practice correspond.'

---

[2] In *Polurrian SS Co Ltd v Young* (1913) 19 Com Cas 143 at 153; *The Bamburi* [1982] 1 Lloyd's Rep 312 at 321 (per Staughton J, sitting as sole arbitrator). See also *Oscar L Aronsen Inc v Compton (The Megara)* [1973] 2 Lloyd's Rep 361 at 363, District Court for the Southern District of New York. The decision in this case was subsequently affirmed by the United States Court of Appeals, Second Circuit: [1974] 1 Lloyd's Rep 590.

CHAPTER 29

Abandonment

Where there has been a constructive total loss, the assured is entitled to abandon the subject-matter to the insurer and claim for a total loss.[1] It is only the assured or his authorised agent who is entitled to abandon.[2] The assured intimates to the insurer that he abandons by giving him 'notice of abandonment'.[3] Notice of abandonment is generally needed, though in some cases it is not necessary.[4] The notice need not be in any special form,[5] but it is to the insurers or their agents that it must be given.[6] The time within which it must be given will depend on the circumstances.[7] There is no obligation on the insurers to accept notice of abandonment.[8] Acceptance may be express or implied.[9] Once the notice has been accepted, the abandonment is irrevocable.[10] The notice of abandonment may be waived by the insurers.[11] Various rights are given to the insurers where the property has been validly abandoned.[12]

A WHEN THE RIGHT TO ABANDON ARISES

Section 61 of the Marine Insurance Act 1906 states:

> 'Where there is a constructive total loss the assured may either treat the loss as a partial loss, or abandon the subject-matter insured to the insurer and treat the loss as if it were an actual total loss.'

Mere expectation or apprehension of total loss does not give a right to abandon. For instance, if a ship strands, there is no right to abandon if she can be got off in any way, but, if she cannot be got off, or begins to break up, then the assured may abandon.[13]

When the assured abandons, he does so at his own risk, and if it turns out that the abandonment was not made in a proper case, e g if by a reasonable outlay

---

[1] See pp 378–380, post.
[2] See pp 380–381, post.
[3] See p 381, post.
[4] See pp 382–385, post.
[5] See pp 385–387, post.
[6] See p 387, post.
[7] See pp 387–389, post.
[8] See p 389, post.
[9] See pp 389–390, post.
[10] See pp 390–392, post.
[11] See p 392, post.
[12] See pp 392–396, post.
[13] *Irving v Manning* (1847) 1 HL Cas 287.

the subject-matter might have been restored, and he has failed to procure the restoration, then the loss, if any, will fall on him.[14]

Therefore, although the assured in the matter of abandonment has an option, its exercise is subject to restrictions. Thus, Lord Mansfield CJ, said:[15]

> 'The insured is not obliged to abandon in any case. He has an election. He cannot elect before advice is received of the loss, and if that advice shows the peril to be over, and the thing in safety, he cannot elect at all, because he has no right to abandon when the thing is safe.'

The assured is not obliged to abandon. He may, if he so chooses, repair the damage and claim on his policy for a partial loss.[16]

But where, by a peril insured against, there is a constructive total loss, and no notice of abandonment is given, then if in the ordinary course of an unbroken sequence of events following upon the peril insured against, the constructive total loss becomes an actual total loss, the insurer is liable in respect of the total loss. The insurer, however, is not liable if the loss is the result of some supervening cause.[17]

Thus, in *Fooks v Smith*[18] a cargo of hides was insured from Calcutta to Bourgas and loaded on an Austrian ship. In view of the imminent outbreak of the First World War Austrian shipowners were instructed to get their vessels to a place of safety. The vessel, on which the goods were loaded, sailed for Trieste, where they were landed and sent up country. The insured gave no notice of abandonment. A year later the goods were requisitioned by the Austrian Government and sold. The insured claim for an actual total loss. It was held by the King's Bench Division that the claim failed, for the actual total loss had been caused by the requisitioning, which was not an event that in the ordinary sequence of events followed the constructive total loss by restraint of princes in the previous year.

Bailhache J, observed:[19]

> 'As I understand the law, it stands in this way: Where, by a peril insured against, there is a constructive total loss and no notice of abandonment is given, then if in the ordinary course of an unbroken sequence of events following upon the peril insured against, the constructive total loss becomes an actual total loss—as, for instance, if there is a capture followed by confiscation—the underwriter is liable in respect of the total loss. If, however, the ultimate total loss is not the result of a sequence of events following in the ordinary course upon the peril insured against, but is the result of supervening cause, the underwriter is not liable. That is an illustration of the doctrine Proxima causa non remota spectatur.
>
> Now, was the total loss in the present case a necessary or natural or direct consequence of the peril insured against? Of course, it is true to say that the restraint of princes which brought these hides into Austria and kept them at Trieste is a sine qua non of the ultimate loss; if they had not been there, the Government could not have seized them. But they came there at a time when this country was not at war with Austria, war being declared on 13 August 1914, and they came there because the Austrian Government did not desire Austrian ships to be in danger on the high seas. But the fact that they came there did not as a necessary, natural, or direct consequence lead to their ultimate seizure and requisitioning and sale by the Austrian Government.
>
> It seems to me that that seizure and sale was a nova causa superveniens, and was not the necessary and direct result of the restraint of princes.'

---

[14] *Thornely v Hebson* (1819) 2 B&Ald 513.
[15] *Hamilton v Mendes* (1761) 2 Burr 1198 at 1211.
[16] *Aitchison v Lohre* (1879) 4 App Cas 755; *Pitman v Universal Marine Insurance Co* (1882) 9 QBD 192.
[17] *Fooks v Smith* (1924) 132 LT 486.
[18] (1924) 132 LT 486.
[19] Ibid, at 488. See also, *Anderson v Royal Exchange Assurance* (1805) 7 East 38; *Mellish v Andrews* (1812) 15 East 13; *Stringer v English and Scottish Marine Insurance Co* (1870) LR 5 QB 599.

When the assured claims to be paid as for a constructive total loss, he has to relinquish to the insurer all his rights over and arising from the thing insured.

If he were permitted to retain such rights, he would have, over and above the value of the thing lost paid for as a total loss, its damaged value, which might in some cases be considerable. Thus, instead of merely recovering an indemnity, he would derive more or less advantage from the damage done to the property.

Theoretically, the result of the settlement of the loss between the insurer and the assured should be the same whether the right of abandonment is exercised or not. For where the thing which is the subject-matter of the insurance is totally lost, there is nothing for the insurer to take as a set-off against the insurance, nor does the assured receive more than his indemnity according to the policy.

In such a case, there being nothing in existence to abandon, there is no necessity to give notice of abandonment. This is provided for by s 62(7) of the Marine Insurance Act 1906, which lays down that:

> 'Notice of abandonment is unnecessary where, at the time when assured receives information of the loss, there would be no possibility of benefit to the insurer if notice were given to him.'[20]

On the other hand, where there is a partial loss, the assured is claiming no more than an indemnity. He is only claiming for the loss occasioned by damage which diminishes the value of the thing insured. In this case the assured only recovers what he has lost.

Where the thing still exists, though in so damaged a condition that the expenditure required to restore it would be considered an extravagant or useless expenditure, the assured is still entitled to be paid what he has lost, and it does not appear on principle how the notice of abandonment can in any way affect the measure of his damage. If the thing so damaged is worthless, his loss is total. If it is of value, the loss is only partial. Consequently the right to an indemnity is precisely the same, whether he does or does not abandon.

This view was stated by Lord Ellenborough CJ, in *Mellish v Andrews*[1] in the following terms:

> 'The general convenience of making an abandonment has led to an opinion that it is more necessary than it really is. A party is not in any case obliged to abandon, neither will the want of abandonment oust him of his claim for that which is, in fact, either an average or a total loss, as the case may be.'

The real advantage of abandonment when it is rightly exercised is to throw on the insurer the responsibility of caring for and realising the value of the property abandoned.[2]

B WHO MAY ABANDON

Notice of abandonment can only be given by or upon the authority of the owner of the interest, and the test of ownership in such a case and for the purpose is whether the person who abandons is in such a position in reference to the interest abandoned that he can effectually assign it.[3]

---

[20] See p 382, post.
[1] (1812) 15 East 13 at 15.
[2] See p 382, post.
[3] *Stewart v Greenock Marine Insurance Co* (1848) 2 HL Cas 159.

Therefore, where there was a mere deposit of the policy of insurance with a bank by way of security for a loan, which in itself conveyed no interest in the ship insured, the deposit gave no implied authority to the pledgee to give notice of abandonment.[4]

Further, the assured is not entitled subsequently to ratify such a notice of abandonment in order to obtain the benefit of it, unless the notice has been given by an agent purporting to act as such.[5]

If there are separate interests in a venture which are separately insured by separate policies in different hands, it is clear that one or all of the assured may abandon each of their respective interests without notice to, or the concurrence of, the assured on other interests.

Further, if the interests are in one hand, but are separately insured under different policies, any one interest may be abandoned by the assured without the necessity of abandoning the interests insured under the remaining policies, and it seems to follow that where the various interests are insured in one policy, but are separately valued in that policy, any one of such interests may be abandoned without abandoning the rest.

On the other hand, if the policy covers various interests under one valuation, it would seem that there can be no abandonment of part, without at all events losing the benefit of the valuation in the policy.

C NOTICE OF ABANDONMENT

Notice of abandonment is the intimation given by the assured to the insurer that he abandons the property and places it at the disposal of insurer.

The notice, however, though useful to both parties, imposes no obligation on the insurer.[6]

It will not avail the assured to enable him to turn a partial loss into a constructive total loss, if the thing insured has been abandoned in circumstances which cannot be justified.

The purpose of giving notice of abandonment was alluded to by Atkin LJ, in *Vacuum Oil Co v Union Insurance Society of Canton*[7] in the following words:[8]

> 'Nevertheless it is a requisite to give notice of abandonment, and in many cases it is a very necessary part of the contract, because the principle of it is that the assured is, as soon as he is aware of the circumstances that make it a constructive total loss, to give notice to the underwriters that the property is to be theirs and that he abandons the property to them, and that from thenceforward, whatever dealings take place with the property, take place for the benefit of and for account of the underwriters. The object of that is twofold. First of all, to enable the underwriters to exercise as soon as they can the care over the goods which otherwise are under the control of the assured; secondly, to prevent the assured from continuing to have an option over the underwriters, so that he may say that the goods are or are not their property in accordance with the eventual state of the goods, and sometimes in accordance with the rise or fall of the market for such goods.'

---

[4] *Jardine v Leathley* (1863) 32 LJQB 132.
[5] Ibid. As to ratification, see generally Bowstead on Agency (14th edn, 1976), pp 37–63; *Bird v Brown* (1850) 4 Exch 786; *Keighley, Maxsted & Co v Durant* [1901] AC 240, HL.
[6] *Rankin v Potter* (1873) LR 6 HL 83.
[7] (1926) 25 LlL Rep 546, CA.
[8] Ibid, at 553.

D IN WHAT CASES NOTICE MUST BE GIVEN

Section 62(1) of the Marine Insurance Act 1906 states:

> 'Subject to the provisions of this section, where the assured elects to abandon the subject-matter insured to the insurer, he must give notice of abandonment. If he fails to do so the loss can only be treated as a partial loss.'

Section 62(7) provides:

> 'Notice of abandonment is unnecessary where, at the time when the assured receives information of the loss, there would be no possibility of benefit to the insurer if notice were given to him.'

Thus, wherever there exists, in regard to the thing insured in respect of which the assured intends to claim for a constructive total loss, anything which may be recovered by the insurer at a profit on the cost of recovery, the insurer ought to be given notice of abandonment.

On the other hand, the loss may take place under such conditions that notice would be useless to him.

The assured should in fairness give the insurer notice in every case where the thing insured still exists. But the question in what cases the law requires notice of abandonment to be given has been much debated. Although a distinction has been drawn between the cases of policies on ship and policies on freight, which are, of course, distinct contracts, it would appear that no valid distinction can exist between these policies in reference to the principles which determine whether notice of abandonment ought or not to be given.

In *Martin v Crokatt*[9] a ship was damaged by perils insured against, and put into a small fishing port on the coast of Sweden. She was surveyed, and reported to be incapable of proceeding on her voyage without undergoing very expensive repairs. The assured gave no notice of abandonment, but wrote to the insurers for directions, and they refused to interfere. The ship and her cargo were sold for £20. The assured claimed for a total loss, but the action failed because he had given no notice of abandonment.

In *Cambridge v Anderton*[10] a ship stranded on some rocks in the River St Lawrence, and the surveyors reported that the expense of getting her off and repairing her would far exceed her value when repaired. Thereupon her master sold her, and the purchaser got her off and repaired her. No notice of abandonment was given, and it was held that no notice was necessary.

Abbott LCJ, said:[11]

> 'If the subject-matter of the insurance remained a ship it was not a total loss, but if it were reduced to a mere congeries of planks, the vessel was a mere wreck; the name which you may think fit to apply to it cannot alter the nature of the thing.'

In *Roux v Salvador*[12] a policy on goods had been effected in respect of a voyage from Valparaiso to Bordeaux. The vessel carrying them met with bad weather and sprung a leak, which so damaged part of the cargo of hides that, on putting into Rio de Janeiro for repairs, the master sold the damaged goods, which were valued in the policy at £1,117, for £273, since they were in a state of incipient

---

[9] (1811) 14 East 465.
[10] (1824) 2 B&C 691.
[11] Ibid, at 692.
[12] (1836) 3 Bing NC 266.

putrefaction. The ship duly arrived at Bordeaux, and the remainder of the cargo was delivered undamaged. The damaged goods were a separate parcel and were separately insured. No notice of abandonment had been given. Lord Abinger CJ, held that notice of abandonment was unnecessary, for it was a case of total loss of the goods since they could never arrive.

In *Knight v Faith*[13] a vessel was valued in a policy at £1,000. She was sold for £72 10s after a survey had been made in a place where she could not be repaired. It was held that notice of abandonment was necessary. Lord Campbell CJ, said:

> 'If the subject-matter insured remains in specie, though in a damaged state, a notice of abandonment is necessary to entitle the assured to make a claim as if it had been actually destroyed. With respect to an insurance on a ship this condition is imposed by the law to give the insurers the means of inquiry and of guarding against fraud, to enable them to repair the ship if they should deem such a proceeding for their advantage, and to secure to them all the advantages to which, if liable for a total loss, they would be entitled as owners of the ship from the time when the damage was sustained to which the loss is ascribed.'

In *Green v Royal Exchange Assurance*[14] Gibbs CJ, expressed the opinion that notice of abandonment to insurers on freight was unnecessary, since he could not understand what was to be abandoned.

The doctrine stated by Lord Campbell CJ, in *Knight v Faith*[15] was considerably modified when the question was considered by the House of Lords in *Rankin v Potter*[16] in an action on a policy on freight. The freight was to be earned under a charter-party by which the ship was to go to New Zealand with her cargo for the owner's benefit, and, after having discharged it, to proceed to Calcutta and load a cargo for the charterers for Liverpool or London. The policy was 'lost or not lost at and from Clyde to Southland, while there, and thence to Otago and for 30 days in port thereafter arrival'. The subject-matter of the insurance was £4,000 on homeward chartered freight. At Southland the ship was damaged, and for lack of funds to repair her she remained in port at New Zealand for nearly 12 months. After undergoing certain repairs she went in ballast to Calcutta where, however, the charterers' agent refused to carry out the charter-party on the ground that the charterers had stopped payment. On the ship being put into dry dock, it was found that the cost of repairing her would exceed her value after being repaired. Notices of abandonment were given to the insurers on freight and to the insurers on ship, but none of the insurers accepted them. It was held by the House of Lords that it was not necessary to give notice of abandonment where no benefit or advantage could accrue to the insurer from such notice.

This principle was followed in *Trinder, Anderson & Co v Thames and Mersey Marine Insurance Co*,[17] which concerned a policy on freight 'from Sydney to Newcastle, NSW, while there and from thence to any port or ports in New Zealand, while there and from thence to San Francisco'. On her voyage from New Zealand to San Francisco with coals the ship put into Honolulu for water, and stranded on a reef owing to negligent navigation. A consultation between the master, a Lloyd's agent, and the harbour master resulted in a sale of the

---

[13] (1850) 15 QB 649.
[14] (1815) 6 Taunt 68.
[15] Supra. See further, *Fleming v Smith* (1848) 1 HL Cas 513.
[16] (1873) LR 6 HL 83.
[17] [1898] 2 QB 114.

vessel and her cargo for £374. In little more than a month the purchaser got the ship off and sold her cargo for £1,000. There was no telegraphic communication between Honolulu and any other place. There was no chance of the cargo being forwarded in a substituted vessel. It was held that the insurers on freight could have done nothing if notice of abandonment had been given to them, and therefore notice was unnecessary.

In *Associated Oil Carriers Ltd v Union Insurance Society of Canton Ltd*[18] the assured had effected a freight policy including a war risk clause in respect of a vessel, which was chartered to a German charterer for consecutive voyages for 3 years from January 1913. War broke out in August 1914. The assured instructed the master of the vessel to abandon the voyage, and proceed to a port in the United States for orders. On the outbreak of war performance of the charter-party became illegal, and the freight was lost to the assured. It was held by the King's Bench Division that there was an actual total loss of freight, and that no notice of abandonment was necessary.

Atkin J, said:[19]

> 'Apart from the charter, as I have already said, on 6 August no reasonable person would have thought of making the insured voyage. Under these circumstances it appears to me that the freight was lost to the owners by restraint of princes.
>
> It was further contended that in any case the loss was a constructive total loss, so that notice of abandonment was necessary. Now, it appears to me that if a vessel insured on freight generally loses, entirely from perils insured against, the only freight in respect of which it has a contractual interest, and no other freight can be obtained on the insured voyage, the loss is an actual and not a constructive loss. If other freight can be obtained on the insured voyage, the question might arise whether it could be earned without an expenditure which would exceed its value when earned, and the loss might then be a constructive total loss or no loss at all. Here, as I have said, no freight could be obtained, and I think the loss an actual loss.
>
> But even were there a constructive total loss in this particular case, I think that notice of abandonment would be unnecessary, for the Marine Insurance Act 1906, by s 62, sub-s 7, declares it to be "unnecessary where, at the time when the assured receives information of the loss, there would be no possibility of benefit to the insurer if notice were given to him".
>
> I am satisfied that the underwriters here could have derived no benefit if notice had been given to them at once.'

In *Vacuum Oil Co v Union Insurance Society of Canton*,[20] where there had been a constructive total loss[1] of some tins of petroleum, one of the issues[2] which arose was whether notice of abandonment should have been given to the insurers. Some of the tins were reconditioned and had been sold by a Lloyd's agent with the assent of the assured's representative. The assured contended that no notice of abandonment was necessary because there was no possibility of benefit to the insurers if notice had been given to them.

The Court of Appeal[3] held that notice of abandonment was necessary, for the goods were in specie after the loss. In construing s 62(7) of the Marine Insurance Act 1906 Bankes LJ, said:[4]

---

[18] (1917) 116 LT 503, KBD.
[19] Ibid, at 505.
[20] (1926) 25 LlL Rep 546, CA.
[1] As to this aspect of the case, see p 368, ante.
[2] Another issue was whether a Lloyd's Agent had authority to receive a notice of abandonment. As to this aspect of the case, see p 387, post.
[3] Bankes, Atkin and Sargant LJJ.
[4] (1926) 25 LlL Rep 546 at 549. See also, the judgment of Atkin LJ, ibid, at 553–554, and that of Sargant LJ, ibid, at 555.

'Now in construing that section it must be borne in mind what the state of the law was at the time of the passing of the statute; and when the statute speaks of no possibility of benefit, it does not mean, as Mr Schiller suggests, that in the events which have happened the underwriter would have been no better off. What it means, as I understand it, and as I understand the law existing at the time when the statute was passed, is that when the circumstances are such that the underwriter, if the goods had been abandoned and he had had the absolute control over them, could have exercised that control and done what he thought best under the circumstances. Of course, if the goods were in such a condition that they were on the point of disappearing, or on the point of dissipation, or whatever the appropriate word is—the word must be varied according to the nature of the subject-matter of the insurance—but in the case of a ship, if a ship was in the act or almost in the act of breaking up, you may say that if notice had been given to the underwriter when the vessel was in that stage, there would have been no possibility of benefit to him, because the ship would have broken up before he could do anything. That is what I understand is aimed at by the words "possibility of benefit". But here, on the facts, it is perfectly obvious that the position of things was this, that if notice of abandonment had been given within a reasonable time, the underwriter had the fullest opportunity of dealing with these goods: they were in existence in specie, they were being reconditioned for the purpose of sale for the benefit of whom it might concern, and they were in a condition in which, if notice of abandonment had been given within a reasonable time, there was every possibility of benefit to the insurer within the meaning of this sub-section, because there were the goods, and he could do what he liked with them.

I think, therefore, that taking that statute merely on the facts as proved, this case does not fall within the exception.'

Although the rule is established that, where no benefit can accrue to the insurer from a notice of abandonment, such notice need not be given, it is still desirable, and indeed safer, for an assured to give notice in all cases where he can possibly do so, whether the policy is on freight, goods, or ship. For if there is a possibility of the insurer deriving an advantage from the notice of abandonment, it will be dangerous for the assured to fail to give it.

Section 62(9) of the Marine Insurance Act 1906 states:

'Where an insurer has reinsured his risk, no notice of abandonment need be given by him.'[5]

This presumably means 'need be given by him to the reinsurer'.

E FORM OF NOTICE

There is no special form in which notice of abandonment must be given, but the notice should be unmistakable in its terms.[6] It should also be absolute and unconditional.[7]

Section 62(2) of the Marine Insurance Act 1906 states:

'Notice of abandonment may be given in writing, or by word of mouth, or partly in writing and partly by word of mouth, and may be given in any terms which indicate the intention of the assured to abandon his insured interest in the subject-matter insured unconditionally to the insurer.'

In *King v Walker*[8] it was held that sufficient notice of abandonment was given by showing the insurers a letter from the master in which he stated that he had

---

[5] See *Uzielli v Boston Marine Insurance Co* (1884) 15 QBD 11.
[6] *Thelluson v Fletcher* (1793) 1 Esp 73; *Panamanian Oriental SS Corpn v Wright* [1970] 2 Lloyd's Rep 365, QBD (Com Ct), where four notices of abandonment were given. The decision in this case was later reversed on another ground: [1971] 1 Lloyd's Rep 487, CA. See pp 261–262, ante.
[7] *M'Masters v Shoolbred* (1794) 1 Esp 236.
[8] (1864) 3 H&C 209.

been advised by Counsel to abandon, and asked his owners to give notice to the insurers.

A mere request to the insurers to give directions for the disposition of the property will not suffice.

Lord Ellenborough CJ, once said that the word 'abandon' should be expressly employed to remove all doubts as to the intention of the assured.[9]

The use of the word 'abandon' is not, however, absolutely necessary, although it is clearly desirable. It will be sufficient if the intimation in the notice is perfectly clear.

Accordingly, in *Currie & Co v Bombay Native Insurance Co*,[10] where the notice of abandonment was couched in the following terms: 'With regard to the "Northland", we regret to say that she is a total wreck, and we have hereby to give you notice that we shall claim payment of the policies we hold against her cargo and disbursements', it was held that this amounted to a notice of abandonment.

That it is essential for the notice to indicate that it is the intention of the assured to abandon his interest unconditionally to the insurer is shown by *Russian Bank for Foreign Trade v Excess Insurance Co*.[11] In this case the owners of cargo insured it from Novorossisk (in the Black Sea) to Falmouth. After the closing of the Dardanelles they telegraphed to their brokers saying 'Agreeable release underwriters from all risks if underwriters will pay difference between present value in Novorossisk and insured value'. This telegram was shown to the underwriter. It was held that there had been no effective notice of abandonment, for the notice had not indicated the intention of the assured to abandon their interest unconditionally.

In *George Cohen, Sons & Co v Standard Marine Insurance Co*[12] the assured claimed against the insurers in respect of a total loss of an obsolete battleship which was stranded on the Dutch coast in the course of a voyage from Chatham to Germany. Roche J, held that the claim constituted a valid notice of abandonment, and said:[13]

'On the whole, if necessary, I think I should decide that where a person claims a total loss and asks to be paid the full sum insured, he does sufficiently make it plain to an intelligent underwriter that he is abandoning his interest in the thing in respect of which he claims to be paid as for a total loss.'

In *Vacuum Oil Co v Union Insurance Society of Canton*,[14] where there had been a constructive total loss[15] of some tins of petroleum, the Court of Appeal[16] held that, even if a notice of abandonment had been properly given, it was not an unconditional one. The evidence merely showed that there had been a conversation between the assured's representative and a Lloyd's Agent[17] in which the representative had said: 'Well, this cargo, the petroleum, is in such a state that I am not prepared to deal with it, and you, Lloyd's Agents, the people

---

[9] *Parmeter v Todhunter* (1808) 1 Camp 541.
[10] (1869) LR 3 PC 72.
[11] [1919] 1 KB 39, CA.
[12] (1925) 20 LlL Rep 133, 168, 21 LlL Rep 30, KBD.
[13] (1925) 21 LlL Rep at 36.
[14] (1926) 25 LlL Rep 546, CA.
[15] As to this aspect of the case, see p 368, ante.
[16] Bankes and Sargant LJJ; Atkin LJ, dissenting on this point.
[17] As to the authority of a Lloyd's Agent to accept notice of abandonment, see p 387, post.

who habitually act in the interests of all concerned, had better take it in hand and deal with it as best you can in the interests of all concerned.'[18]

F TO WHOM THE NOTICE MUST BE GIVEN

Notice must be given to the insurers themselves or to their authorised agent.

In *Vacuum Oil Co v Union Insurance Society of Canton*[19] some tins of petroleum were a constructive total loss, and one of the issues[20] which arose in a claim by the assured was whether, even if it were assumed that notice of abandonment had been given either verbally or in correspondence by the representative of the assured to a Lloyd's Agent, such an agent was authorised to receive it on behalf of the insurers.

The Court of Appeal[1] held that a Lloyd's Agent had no such authority. Atkin LJ, observed:[2]

> 'Now it seems to me plain that inasmuch as notice has to be given to the underwriter, any person who is relying upon notice being given to some person other than the underwriter or an official of the underwriting company, has got to prove the authority, and I am bound to say that I am not satisfied that there was any authority in Mr Fakher to receive notice of abandonment. It seems to me quite outside the usual authority of Lloyd's Agents, and outside the usual course of business, because I am satisfied that the usual course of business is for the assured (when they remember to give notice of abandonment, which they constantly do not) to communicate with the underwriter in London, or wherever he may be, through the insurance broker, and it is the duty of the broker to pass on the notice at once to the underwriter; and inasmuch as rapid means of communication now exist I am satisfied that in the ordinary course of business the assured ought to communicate direct in the way I have mentioned, and give notice in that way directly to the underwriter, and I do not think that Lloyd's Agents in different parts of the world are persons who, in ordinary circumstances, have authority to receive notice of abandonment.'

G TIME WITHIN WHICH NOTICE MUST BE GIVEN

Section 62(3) of the Marine Insurance Act 1906 states:

> 'Notice of abandonment must be given with reasonable diligence after the receipt of reliable information of the loss, but where the information is of a doubtful character the assured is entitled to a reasonable time to make inquiry.'

Section 88 states:

> 'Where by this Act any reference is made to reasonable time . . . or reasonable diligence, the question what is reasonable is a question of fact.'

The assured is entitled to wait a reasonable time in order to acquire a full knowledge of the damage before he elects to abandon or not.[3]

---

[18] See the judgment of Bankes LJ (1926) 25 LlL Rep at 550–551, and that of Sargant LJ, ibid, at 555. Cf the dissenting judgment of Atkin LJ, ibid, at 554.
[19] (1926) 25 LlL Rep 546, CA.
[20] Other issues were whether there was a constructive total loss, and also whether there was any 'possibility of benefit' to the insurers. As to these aspects of the case, see pp 368, 384–385, ante, and supra, respectively.
[1] Bankes, Atkin and Sargant LJJ.
[2] (1926) 25 LlL Rep at 554. See also, the judgment of Bankes LJ, ibid, at 550–551, and that of Sargant LJ, ibid, at 555.
[3] *Gernon v Royal Exchange Assurance* (1815) 6 Taunt 383.

On the other hand, he is not allowed to wait and watch the turn of events before making up his mind.[4]

Thus, in *Hudson v Harrison*[5] Dallas CJ, said:[6]

> 'The law is that the assured shall abandon in reasonable time—that he may not lie by to see whether it be more to his interest not to abandon; he must, therefore, in reasonable time, give notice of abandonment.'

In *Fleming v Smith*[7] a vessel bound for Bombay was forced by stress of weather to put into Mauritius in a much damaged condition. The master wrote to the assured saying that he could only borrow money on bottomry to repair her provided that she sailed direct to England. Lloyd's Agents also wrote saying that to return would be better than going to Bombay on account of the low freights ruling in India. The correspondence lasted from September to December, and, heavy expense having been incurred on repairs with the assured's consent, the ship sailed from Mauritius. She arrived in London on 27 March, and possession of her was taken on behalf of the assured. Three days later they gave notice of abandonment. It was held by the House of Lords that they were too late because the correspondence pointed to an intention to regard the loss as a partial rather than a total loss, and they could not, after awaiting events, turn a partial loss into a total loss by giving notice of abandonment.

The failure to give notice of abandonment within what may in the circumstances be regarded as a reasonable time will prevent the assured from recovering for more than a partial loss.[8]

In *Currie & Co v Bombay Native Insurance Co*,[9] Lord Chelmsford said:[10]

> 'What is a reasonable time must depend on the particular circumstances of each case. On the one hand, the assured is not to delay his notice, when a total loss occurs, in order to keep his chance of doing better for himself by keeping the subject insured, and then, when he finds it more to his advantage to do so, throwing the burden upon the underwriters; while, on the other, the underwriters cannot complain of a suspense of judgment fairly exercised on the part of the assured, to enable him to determine whether the circumstances are such as to entitle him to abandon.'

Thus, in *Kelly v Walton*[11] a vessel with a cargo of flax seed was detained by an embargo in a foreign port. News of this reached the assured on cargo on 11 February. The seed would have been of value if sown before 10 May, but not after. It was held that notice of abandonment should have been given on or before 10 May, and that notice given on 11 June was too late.

Again, in *Aldridge v Bell*[12] the fact of constructive total loss was ascertained by survey on 14 December. Notice of abandonment was not given until 6 January, when it might have been given by post in 4 days. It was held that the notice had been given too late.

---

[4] *Roux v Salvador* (1836) 3 Bing NC 266 at 286 (per Lord Abinger). See also, *Kaltenbach v Mackenzie* (1878) 3 CPD 467.
[5] (1821) 3 Brod&Bing 97.
[6] Ibid, at 106.
[7] (1848) 1 HL Cas 513.
[8] *Barker v Blakes* (1808) 9 East 283.
[9] (1869) LR 3 PC 72. See *Gernon v Royal Exchange Assurance* (1815) 6 Taunt 383; *Grainger v Martin* (1863) 4 B&S 9.
[10] (1869) LR 3 PC at 79.
[11] (1808) 2 Camp 155.
[12] (1816) 1 Stark 498.

Further, in *Hunt v Royal Exchange Assurance*[13] a ship was surveyed and condemned on 11 December. Notice of abandonment was given on 22 December, although it might have been given on 17 December. It was held that it had been given too late.

In *Kaltenbach v Mackenzie*[14] the assured knew of the condition of the insured vessel on 7 February. Notice of abandonment was not given until 11 March. It was held that it had been given too late, for they should have telegraphed or written by the next post.

In *Potter v Campbell*[15] a vessel sustained damage by grounding in Bluff Harbour, New Zealand. After temporary repairs had been effected she proceeded to Port Chalmers to discharge her cargo and, after staying 9 months there, she sailed in ballast for Calcutta, where she was dry-docked and found to be a constructive total loss. On learning the result of this survey, her owners gave notice of abandonment. It was held that the notice had been given too late, and that they were entitled to recover only for a partial loss.

In *George Cohen, Sons & Co v Standard Marine Insurance Co*[16] an obsolete battleship left Chatham in December 1922 for Germany to be broken up. After 2 or 3 days she stranded on the Dutch coast, and became a constructive total loss.[17] In February 1923 the assured claimed for a total loss, and in April 1923 gave formal notice of abandonment. Roche J, held that the claim made in February was a valid notice of abandonment,[18] and had been made within a reasonable time.

H NO OBLIGATION ON INSURER TO ACCEPT ABANDONMENT

Section 62(4) of the Marine Insurance Act 1906 states:

> 'Where notice of abandonment is properly given, the rights of the assured are not prejudiced by the fact that the insurer refuses to accept the abandonment.'

The duty imposed on the assured to decide promptly on the question of abandonment imposes no corresponding obligation on the insurer. The assured abandons at his own risk, and there is no duty on the insurer to accept or reject the abandonment, and being without the information necessary to enable him to form an opinion, he may wait to ascertain what the circumstances really are before he decides either to pay a total loss or to reject the abandonment.

I WHAT CONSTITUTES AN ACCEPTANCE

Section 62(5) of the Marine Insurance Act 1906 states:

> 'The acceptance of an abandonment may be either express or implied from the conduct of the insurer. The mere silence of the insurer after notice is not an acceptance.'

---

[13] (1816) 5 M&S 47.
[14] (1878) 3 CPD 467.
[15] (1867) 2 LJNC 223.
[16] (1925) 30 Com Cas 139, KBD.
[17] As to this point, see p 368, ante.
[18] As to this point, see p 386, ante.

In *Hudson v Harrison*[19] the assured received news that the vessel on which his cargo was being carried had been wrecked on 23 December. He gave notice of abandonment, and on 27 December called a meeting of the underwriters, three of whom attended and gave orders to the assured to do the best for all parties. On 28 February the underwriters interfered, and forbade a sale of the damaged cargo. It was held that in the circumstances the underwriters had impliedly accepted the notice of abandonment.

In *Captain J A Cates Tug and Wharfage Co Ltd v Franklin Insurance Co*[20] a tug was sunk in a collision, and notice of abandonment was given to the insurers. As a result of salvage operations which they instituted, the vessel was raised and towed inshore, and the abandonment was not accepted. Without the knowledge of the assured the salvors verbally made an offer to the insurers to purchase the vessel. The offer was later put into writing, but was withdrawn 3 weeks later. The assured contended that the negotiations between the insurers and the salvors constituted an acceptance of the abandonment. The Judicial Committee of the Privy Council[1] held that no acceptance of abandonment could be implied from the conduct of the insurers.

Lord Sumner said:[2]

> 'It was on this incident that the judgment turned, which the trial Judge gave in favour of the [assured] for a total loss. He held that, by reason of these communications between the underwriters and a third party, there had been a binding acceptance of the abandonment, which had been tendered by the assured, in spite of their formal refusal of it. He held that they had done an act which could only be justified under a right derived from abandonment, "for", said he, "does not the solicitation and receipt of a bona fide bid to purchase necessarily imply power to make title should the bid be accepted"? Their Lordships can only say, as the Court of Appeal said, that it does not. The underwriters in this tentative negotiation did not act as owners of the tug or exercise dominion over it, and they did not purport to sell and convey or to make a title for that purpose. An agreement to sell, had it been concluded, would only have been an executory contract, which they would be able to perform if and when they chose to accept the abandonment, but in itself it could not be an act of ownership. As a matter of fact, this everyday proceeding was nothing more than a precaution, equally available in connection with proving a defence in case they should resist the claim or with preparing to make the best of the loss if they should give up the contest and elect to pay.'

J IRREVOCABILITY OF ABANDONMENT

Section 62(6) of the Marine Insurance Act 1906 states:

> 'Where notice of abandonment is accepted the abandonment is irrevocable. The acceptance of the notice conclusively admits liability for the loss and the sufficiency of the notice.'

Indeed, so changed is the relative position of the parties to the contract that after acceptance the insurer will be debarred from setting up a breach of warranty for the purpose of avoiding the policy;[3] although money paid under a mistake of fact can be recovered.[4]

In *Norwich Union Fire Insurance Society Ltd v Wm Price Ltd*[5] a cargo of lemons

---

[19] (1821) 3 Brod&Bing 97.
[20] (1927) 137 LT 709, PC.
[1] Lord Haldane, Lord Sumner, Lord Shaw, Lord Merrivale and Lord Warrington.
[2] (1927) 137 LT at 711.
[3] *Provincial Insurance Co of Canada v Leduc* (1874) LR 6 PC 224.
[4] *Norwich Union Fire Insurance Society Ltd v Wm H Price Ltd* [1934] AC 455, PC.
[5] (1934) 49 LlL Rep 55, PC.

was insured from Messina to Sydney, NSW. The vessel carrying them was in a collision at Smyrna, but they were undamaged. She proceeded to Gibraltar, where she was ordered by her surveyors to go to Holland for repairs. The lemons were reported to be ripening, and on 5 February 1929 they were sold by the shipowners in Gibraltar at the best price obtainable. They were not damaged by any peril insured against, and the sale was solely because of their condition. The true facts, however, were not known to the assured, who had been informed that the vessel had been in a collision, and that the lemons had been sold consequent on damage due to perils insured against. The assured gave notice of abandonment to the insurer, who paid them the sum insured. When the true facts were discovered, the insurers claimed that they were entitled to be repaid since the money had been paid under a mistake of fact.

The Judicial Committee of the Privy Council[6] (on appeal from the Supreme Court of New South Wales) held that the insurers were entitled to recover. The agreement was one for immediate settlement on the basis of an actual loss, the insurers being subrogated to the proceeds of sale. The need for notice of abandonment did not arise, nor could it be given as the lemons had been sold.

Lord Wright observed:[7]

> 'The information on which they acted was that the lemons had been actually sold. The lemons had thus passed from the actual control and possession of the [assured], who had lost them irretrievably. There was thus an actual total loss within the definition of s 63[8] of the Act. No notice of abandonment need in such a case be given. Indeed, there could not be a notice of abandonment within s 68(1)[9] because that section only applies to an election to abandon the subject-matter insured to the insurer, whereas, the lemons having been sold, there was nothing that the [assured] could abandon. All their right of property in the lemons had gone; it is not even clear that the lemons existed at all, since in all human probability they had been already consumed. The lemons had been sold, it seems, by the shipmaster or his agents, acting as agents of necessity; the sale was not the result of any sea damage or peril insured against affecting the lemons, but of their inherent vice or of delay. The sale, unless, justifiable in consequence of perils insured against, gave no claim against the [insurers]. It could not on any view constitute a constructive total loss.'

It was also held (obiter) that a notice or acceptance of abandonment based on a mistake was a nullity. On this point his Lordship said:[10]

> 'It therefore becomes unnecessary to consider the question so fully discussed in the judgments below as to the construction and effect of s 68(6) of the Act. Their Lordships will only briefly point out with all respect that there may be other matters to be considered than the bare words of the sub-section. No doubt it is not generally permissible in construing the words of the Act to read in conditions and qualifications which are not expressed; and s 4 only permits the application of the rules of the common law and the law merchant so far as is not inconsistent with the express provisions of the Act. But the operative effect of mistake or fraud or duress, in cases where it operates, is not inconsistent with the express words (to take the relevant instance) of s 68(6), because mistake, if established, raises a preliminary or prior question, namely, whether there is in law a notice of abandonment at all, or an acceptance of such notice. Indeed, s 68(6) presupposes something which is not only in form but in reality a notice of abandonment or an acceptance thereof. Thus, if what appears to be the notice or acceptance is void and a nullity, the express words of s 68(6) do not apply at all.'

---

[6] Lord Sankey LC, Lord Blanesburgh, Lord Wright, Sir Lancelot Sanderson, and Sir Sidney Rowlatt.
[7] (1934) 49 LlL Rep at 60.
[8] I e of the (Australian) Marine Insurance Act 1909, which corresponds to s 57(1) of the (English) Marine Insurance Act 1906.
[9] I e of the (Australian) Marine Insurance Act 1909, which corresponds to s 62(6) of the (English) Marine Insurance Act 1906.
[10] (1934) 49 LlL Rep at 60.

It would seem that a notice of abandonment which is itself a nullity cannot become the basis of rights simply because abandonment has been accepted by the underwriters. It further seems that on general principles mutual mistake will have the same effect in regard to the offer and acceptance of abandonment as in regard to any other contract.

It is unnecessary to repeat what has been said ealier in this judgment as to the effect of mistake, but it seems to follow that just as mistake may render a notice of abandonment a nullity, so in the same way it may render an acceptance of the notice a nullity. In other words, though the goods were, in fact, lost to the [assured], such a mistake as is here assumed throughout would prevent not only the notice of abandonment, but also the acceptance of abandonment from being other than a nullity. No case would then exist for the application of the words of s 68(6).'

If the notice of abandonment is not accepted by the insurer, the assured is entitled to withdraw it. Thus, in *Pesquerias y Secaderos de Bacalao de Espana SA v Beer*[11] Atkinson J, said:[12]

'But by a notice of abandonment the assured merely makes an offer, which remains executory unless and until it is accepted. Until it is accepted the assured has the right to look to intervening events which may restore in whole or in part his former situation, and may limit his claim accordingly if it suits him better to claim as for a partial loss. (See *Brotherston v Barber* (1816) 5 M&S 418.) Indeed, if it were not so, s 62(6) of the Marine Insurance Act 1906 would be otherwise expressed. That says:

"Where notice of abandonment is accepted the abandonment is irrevocable. The acceptance of the notice conclusively admits liability for the loss and the sufficiency of the notice."

It would be strange to have that section in those words if a notice of abandonment were irrevocable even if it has not been accepted.'

K WAIVER OF NOTICE OF ABANDONMENT

Section 62(8) of the Marine Insurance Act 1906 states:

'Notice of abandonment may be waived by the insurer.'

The insurer may always waive his right to a notice of abandonment, and such a waiver may be either express or implied. Waiver will be implied where a demand made by the assured is followed by a payment of a total loss by the insurer.[13]

L THE EFFECT OF ABANDONMENT

Where the subject-matter insured has been validly abandoned, the insurer can take over whatever remains of it and all proprietary rights attached to it. He is also entitled to the freight which is in the course of being earned by an insured vessel.

1 Right to take over the subject-matter insured

Section 63(1) of the Marine Insurance Act 1906 states:

---

[11] (1946) 79 LlL Rep 417, KBD. The actual decision given by Atkinson J, in this case was reversed on the facts by the House of Lords: [1949] 1 All ER 845. But the statement of principle made by the learned Judge remains unaffected.
[12] (1946) 79 LlL Rep at 433.
[13] *Houstman v Thornton* (1816) Holt NP 242.

'Where there is a valid abandonment, the insurer is entitled to take over the interest of the assured in whatever may remain of the subject-matter insured, and all proprietary rights incidental thereto.'

In *Allgemeine Versicherungs-Gesellschaft Helvetia v Administrator of German Property*[14] Scrutton LJ, said:[15]

'When the total loss of a thing insured is not actual, but constructive, that is, where the thing insured is in specie, but the cost of preserving and repairing it would be more than its value when preserved or repaired (see Marine Insurance Act 1906, s 60), the assured must give a notice of abandonment. This, in itself does not pass any property or rights in the thing insured to the underwriter. If the underwriter then pays the assured a total loss, it used to be thought that the payment passed the property and rights incidental to it to the underwriter, as benefit of salvage.

But before the Marine Insurance Act was passed in 1906, circumstances arose which rendered it necessary to consider whether an underwriter, merely by paying, necessarily became the "owner" of the thing insured. For it might be a damnosa hereditas, whose ownership only imposed liabilities which the underwriter did not want. The owner of a ship wrecked in a harbour might be liable to the harbour authority for the costs of buoying and removing the wreck . . . And in 1894, in *Arrow SS Co v Tyne Improvement Comrs: The Crystal*[16] the question was raised whether underwriters who had paid a total loss were not "owners" liable for the expense of raising the wreck, and Lord Herschell declined to decide the question. Probably, in consequence of this question having arisen when the Marine Insurance Act 1906 was passed, s 63 was worded thus: "Where there is a valid abandonment, the insurer is entitled to take over the interest of the assured in whatever may remain of the subject-matter insured, and all proprietary rights incidental thereto," thus apparently leaving it open to the underwriter not to "take over" the interest of the assured, though "entitled to take it over".'

In surveying the position of an insurer under s 63(1) where there was a valid abandonment, Lord Atkin said:[17]

'On a valid abandonment the insurer becomes no doubt entitled to proprietary rights incidental to the subject-matter insured as from the time of the loss. He is put in the same position as though the subject-matter insured was assigned to him by way of sale immediately after the event which constitutes the loss. He has no rights until the loss, and he takes over "whatever may remain" of the subject-matter insured. Thus, on abandonment of ship he is entitled to the property in the ship, and if it is used after he has acquired the property, he is entitled to the profits of such use. Therefore, if the ship so abandoned proceeds to earn freight in respect of the voyage on which she was abandoned, the insurer as owner of the vessel becomes entitled to the freight, which had only become payable on the hypothesis by his vessel completing the voyage and delivering the cargo at the port of discharge. (*Case v Davidson* (1816) 5 M&S 79.)'

But his Lordship said that a right to sue a wrongdoer for a wrongful act which gave rise to an abandonment appeared to be something quite different from the proprietary rights incidental to the ship which passed on abandonment. If one treated the insurer by analogy as a purchaser after the marine peril had taken effect, it was plain that the sale by itself would not pass the right to sue, which would remain in the vendor.

He considered that confusion was often caused by not distinguishing the legal rights given by abandonment from the rights of subrogation, and said:[18]

---

[14] (1931) 144 LT 705.
[15] Ibid, at 711.
[16] [1894] AC 508.
[17] *AG v Glen Line Ltd and the Liverpool and London War Risks Insurance Association Ltd* (1930) 37 LlL Rep 55 at 61, HL.
[18] *AG v Glen Line Ltd and the Liverpool and London War Risks Insurance Association Ltd* (1930) 37 LlL Rep 55 at 61, HL.

'No one doubts that the underwriter on hull damaged by collision and abandoned as a constructive total loss is entitled to the benefit of the right of the assured to sue the wrongdoer for the damage to hull. But he derives his right from the provisions of s 79, whereby he is subrogated to "all rights and remedies of the assured in and in respect of the subject-matter", very different words from "all proprietary rights incidental thereto". And it is to be noted that in respect of abandonment the rights exist on a valid abandonment, whereas in respect of subrogation they only arise on payment; and that subrogation will only give the insurer rights up to 20s in the £ on what he has paid.'

Different views have been expressed as to whether insured property, which has been validly abandoned, but has not been taken over by the insurers, becomes res nullius.

In *Boston Corpn v France Fenwick & Co Ltd*[19] a vessel was a constructive total loss, and the assured gave notice of abandonment to the insurers. The vessel blocked the fairway to Boston Harbour. The harbour authority brought an action under s 29 of the Port of Boston Act 1842 and s 56 of the Harbours, Docks and Piers Act 1847 against the assured to recover the expenses of removing her.

Bailhache J, held that the action failed because the expenses could only be recovered under these Acts from the 'owners', and, since the assured had given notice of abandonment, they had ceased to be the owners.

His Lordship added:[20]

'I have refrained from expressing any opinion as to whether a valid notice of abandonment unaccepted by underwriters, while it divests the owner of his property in the wreck, at the same time automatically transfers the property to the underwriters. I will only say that there is a good deal to be said against this view in favour of the wreck in such circumstances becoming a res nullius. The point does not call for direction, and I will leave it.'

But a different view was expressed by Greer LJ, in *Oceanic Steam Navigation Co Ltd v Evans*,[1] where he said (obiter):[2]

'It does not follow that, because notice of abandonment is given to an insurer, therefore the vessel, which may have some value, is abandoned to all the world, so that it has no owner at all, and becomes what lawyers prefer to describe, using the Latin language, as res nullius.'

Commenting on this case *Blane Steamships Ltd v Minister of Transport*,[3] which concerned the frustration of a time charter-party, Cohen LJ, expressed a preference for the view of Greer LJ, mentioned above, and said:[4]

'The view expressed by Bailhache J, seems to me difficult to reconcile (a) with the option given to the assured by s 61 of the Marine Insurance Act 1906 to treat the loss as a partial loss, and (b) with the doctrine of ademption of loss explained in *Chalmers' Marine Insurance Act 1906*, 4th edn, p 89.[5] My inclination therefore is to prefer the opinion expressed by Greer LJ, to that of Bailhache J.'

2 Right to freight

Section 63(2) of the Marine Insurance Act 1906 states:

---

[19] (1923) 15 LlL Rep 85, KBD.
[20] Ibid, at 91.
[1] (1934) 50 LlL Rep 1, CA.
[2] Ibid, at 3.
[3] [1951] 2 Lloyd's Rep 155, CA.
[4] Ibid, at 163.
[5] See now 9th edn (1983) p 98.

'Upon the abandonment of a ship the insurer thereof is entitled to any freight in course of being earned, and which is earned by her subsequent to the casualty causing the loss, less the expenses of earning it incurred after the casualty; and where the ship is carrying the owner's goods, the insurer is entitled to a reasonable remuneration for the carriage of them subsequent to the casualty causing the loss.'

This right of the insurer on ship to the benefit of all freight, which has been earned by her subsequent to the casualty causing the loss, prevails over the right of the insurer on the freight itself.[6]

The provisions of s 63(2) may be modified by agreement, e g clause 20 of the Institute Time Clauses (Hulls) states:

'In the event of total or constructive total loss no claim to be made by the Underwriters for freight whether notice of abandonment has been given or not.'[7]

The insurer on ship is, however, strictly confined to the rights of the assured, and cannot, by reason of the abandonment, acquire rights which the assured never possessed in respect of the thing insured.

Thus, the insurer on ship is not entitled to recover from the assured freight which has been earned by re-shipping the goods and forwarding them to their destination, since the ship did not earn the freight.[8]

Further, in the case of constructive total loss, his rights are limited to benefits accruing after the abandonment. Therefore, he is not entitled to freight earned before the abandonment while the ship is still the property of the assured.[9]

But if the ship had earned the freight after abandonment, the insurer on ship would have been entitled to receive it as being the earnings of a ship which had become his property.[10]

In *Sea Insurance Co v Hadden*[11] a vessel was engaged under a charter-party, and her owner effected separate insurances on ship and on chartered freight with different underwriters. The vessel was lost in collision before the chartered freight had been earned, and the owner abandoned to the insurers on ship. In subsequent litigation the assured recovered damages from the owners of the other ship for the loss of chartered freight, and the insurers on ship claimed to receive this from the assured. It was held that they were not entitled to do so.

In *Miller v Woodfall*[12] a shipowner carried his own goods in his own ship, and insured the ship and the freight under separate policies. On her voyage to Liverpool the ship stranded at Southport, and her owner conveyed part of the goods to Liverpool in lighters at his own expense, and then at his own cost caused the ship, with the remainder of the goods, to be brought to Liverpool. He had abandoned the ship at Southport to the insurers. They accepted the abandonment, but claimed credit for the freight of all the goods conveyed to Southport. It was held that they were not entitled to this credit, but that as regards the goods that were on board the ship from Southport to Liverpool,

---

[6] *Case v Davidson* (1816) 5 M&S 79.
[7] As to the interpretation of this clause, see *United Kingdom Mutual SS Assurance v Boulton* (1898) 3 Com Cas 330.
[8] *Hickie and Borman v Rodocanachi* (1859) 4 H&N 455.
[9] *Stewart v Greenock Marine Insurance Co* (1848) 2 HL Cas 159. See further, *Luke v Lyde* (1759) 2 Burr 882; *Barclay v Stirling* (1816) 5 M&S 6; *Keith v Burrows* (1877) 2 App Cas 636; *The Red Sea* [1896] P 20.
[10] *Case v Davidson* (1816) 5 M&S 79.
[11] (1884) 13 QBD 706.
[12] (1857) 8 E&B 493.

they were entitled to credit at the current rates of freight for that distance only.

When freight does pass to the insurers on ship by abandonment, all expenses incurred subsequent to abandonment may be deducted by the assured from the freight where such expenses are incurred in order to earn the freight.[13]

In *The Red Sea*[14] a vessel, having stranded at the entrance to the port of delivery, was abandoned by her owners, and the abandonment was accepted by the insurers. Her cargo of timber was got out and delivered, and consequently freight became payable. The insurers claimed that the gross bill of lading freight, i e £4,279, was payable, less the expenses of delivery incurred subsequent to the casualty. The assured, however, contended that the deductions to be made were not only those incurred subsequent to the casualty, but also two sums of £1,677 advanced by the charterers to the master at the port of loading for disbursements, and £339, necessarily disbursed for coals at an intermediate port to enable the vessel to complete her voyage and so earn her freight. It was held that the sum of £1,677 was to be deducted, since it was really advance freight, being exposed to maritime perils and insurable, and that the balance was all the freight that the shipowner was entitled to earn at the date of the abandonment, and was therefore all that the insurer acquired by subrogation.[15] The other sum for coals was not allowed to be deducted, since there was no evidence to show that those disbursements were incurred for freight alone, and they could not therefore be regarded as expenses on account of freight.

---

[13] *The Red Sea* [1896] P 20. See also, *Thompson v Rowcroft* (1803) 4 East 34, where there was a specific agreement made when the insurers on freight paid for a total loss that, if the ship should be restored and freight earned, such freight should be paid to the insurers on freight, and it was held that on the restoration the agreement bound the assured, and that it was quite independent of the right to the freight which the insurers on ship possessed: *Sharp v Gladstone* (1805) 7 East 24; *Barclay v Stirling* (1816) 5 M&S 6; *Leatham v Terry* (1803) 3 Bos&P 479.

[14] [1896] P 20.

[15] As to subrogation, see generally pp 455–460, post.

CHAPTER 30

Discovery of ship's papers

Arising out of the characteristic of the contract of marine insurance as a contract of good faith is a rule of practice which is peculiar to actions on marine policies.

When a loss occurs, the insurer knows nothing of the circumstances and the assured or other persons interested may know a great deal. Consequently, as soon as a writ is issued against the insurers in respect of a loss, the court may order the assured to file an affidavit disclosing every material document in his possession, and showing what efforts he has made to obtain any relevant documents which may be in the possession of other persons. In the meanwhile the further progress of the action is stayed.[1]

Discretion of the court

Until 1936 a party was entitled as of right to an order for ship's papers.[2]

An action was often stayed under the practice which had grown up since the end of the eighteenth century, and often involved very great hardship to the assured. The order was of a most comprehensive description, and very often great difficulty was found in making proper compliance with the order, which used to lead to many applications and to constant delay in reaching a hearing of the case.[3]

But in 1936 the rules relating to the matter were altered, and by RSC Order 31, Rule 12A, a discretion was given to the Judge as to whether he would order an order for the production of ship's papers.[4]

---

[1] See RSC Ord 72; *Boulton v Houlder Bros & Co* [1904] 1 KB 784; *Teneria Moderna Franco Española v New Zealand Insurance Co* [1924] 1 KB 79; *Sir William Garthwaite (Insurance) Ltd v Port of Manchester Insurance Co Ltd* (1930) 37 LlL Rep 194, CA.

[2] See *Sir William Garthwaite (Insurance) Ltd v Port of Manchester Insurance Co Ltd* (1930) 37 LlL Rep 194 at 195, CA (per Scrutton LJ); *Anghelatos and London Joint City and Midland Bank v Northern Assurance Co* (1922) 13 LlL Rep 291, CA where Scrutton LJ, said (ibid, at 292): 'The affidavit of ship's papers is peculiar to policies of marine insurance and affords discovery which goes far beyond discovery ordered in ordinary common law actions. An underwriter of a policy of marine insurance is in the nature of things entirely ignorant of the loss, and, as the contract of insurance is one of the utmost good faith, it has for centuries been the practice, the moment a claim is made on the policy of marine insurance, to make an order against the person claiming that he file affidavits by all persons interested. It is not enough for him to say the documents named do so-and-so and do nothing more. He must make all enquiries and file affidavits by all persons interested in the proceedings and in the insurances. He must go to the mortgagees; if he is a shipper of goods, he must go to the shipowner; he must procure discovery and affidavits by all persons who have any interest in the subject-matter of the insurance and in the policy.'

[3] *Keevil and Keevil Ltd v Boag* (1940) 67 LlL Rep 263 at 264, CA (per Goddard LJ).

[4] For cases under the old procedure, see *La Nippon Marine Insurance Co v London General Insurance Co* (1923) 14 LlL Rep 298, CA, where an application was made for variation of an order for ship's papers; *Mees v Importers' and Exporters' Marine Insurance Co Ltd* (1923) 15 LlL Rep 201, CA, where

The rule at present in force is RSC Order 72.[5]
RSC Order 72, Rule 10 states:

'(1) Where in an action in the commercial list relating to a marine insurance policy an application for an order under Order 24, Rule 3, is made by the insurer, then, without prejudice to its powers under that rule, the court,[6] if satisfied that the circumstances of the case are such that it is necessary or expedient to do so, may make an order[7] . . . for the production of such documents as are therein specified or described.

(2) An order under this rule may be made on such terms, if any, as to staying proceedings in the action or otherwise, as the court thinks fit.'

An order of this sort will not be granted where the insurance covers land transit only.[8]

But the fact that part of the transit may be by land does not affect the right.[9]

Thus, in *Leon v Casey*[10] goods were insured from Cairo to Jaffa under a policy which contained the 'warehouse to warehouse' clause.[11] They were destroyed by fire whilst being carried on a lorry from Cairo to Alexandria. It was held by the Court of Appeal[12] that an order for discovery of ship's papers would be made because the policy was substantially a marine one.

Scrutton LJ, said:[13]

'The policy itself is in a marine form, but being drawn up in this form before the declarations were made it is for voyages as specified; and they are specified in the schedule in the policy: "Steamers as specified and (or) steamers and (or) conveyances as specified subject to classification clause as attached for steamers unnamed"—"Interest as specified." It is, therefore, obviously in form a marine policy with land risks before and after the marine risk of the same nature as the "warehouse to warehouse" clause which is also included.

In my view, such a policy comes clearly within the decision of the Court of Appeal in *Harding v Bussell*,[14] and the order for ship's papers should, therefore, be made.'

In *North British Rubber Co v Cheetham*[15] a policy had been taken out by the plaintiffs with the defendant insurer upon rubber 'from Interior French Congo to Leith, via Zenio and/or Bangui . . . Including any method of transit in the interior of Africa—this may include porterage and/or by lorries or canoes or

---

an application for an affidavit of ship's papers was made by the insurers before the defence was put in; *Soussanis v Liverpool Marine Insurance Co Ltd* (1935) 51 LlL Rep 1, CA, where the action was dismissed for want of prosecution because the assured had taken no further steps to prepare for trial after an order for ship's papers had been made and the defence delivered; *Latvijas Banka (Bank of Latvia) v Adams* (1936) 54 LlL Rep 82, CA, where the action was dismissed for want of prosecution because an incomplete affidavit of ship's papers had been filed; *Anghelatos and London Joint City and Midland Bank v Northern Assurance Co*, supra.

[5] See Appendix VI, p 595, post.
[6] In this Rule 'the court' means the Judge, the district registrar of Liverpool or the district registrar of Manchester, as the case may be: RSC Order 72, Rule 10(3). For criticisms of the wording of Form No 94, see *Probatina Shipping Co Ltd v Sun Insurance Office Ltd, The Sageorge* [1974] 2 All ER 478 at 496, CA (per Buckley LJ), and at 502 (per Roskill LJ).
[7] Either in Form No 94 in Appendix K or in such other form as it thinks fit: ibid, Rule 10(2). For Form No. 94, see p 595, post.
[8] *Schloss Bros v Stevens* (1905) 10 Com Cas 224.
[9] *Harding v Bussell* [1905] 2 KB 83; *Tannenbaum & Co v Heath* [1908] 1 KB 1032. Cf *Village Main Reef Gold Mining Co v Stearns* (1900) 5 Com Cas 246.
[10] (1932) 147 LT 165, CA.
[11] This clause is now known as the 'transit' clause. See pp 118, 122–126, ante.
[12] Scrutton, Greer and Slesser LJJ.
[13] (1932) 147 LT at 168.
[14] Supra.
[15] (1938) 61 LlL Rep 337, CA.

river boats'. The rubber was dispatched by lorry from Zenio to Mobaye, and suffered damage due to delay there. The plaintiffs claimed under the policy, and were ordered by Lewis J, to file ship's papers.

The Court of Appeal[16] held that they would not interfere with his discretion to make the order, for it had been based on the view that it was necessary or expedient. Greer LJ, said:[17]

> 'In this particular case I cannot conceive that the learned Judge made the order for ship's papers except upon the view that he took either that it was necessary in this case, or at least that it was expedient to make an order for ship's papers. It may very well be that a rubber trader, who is engaged in buying rubber and getting it down from the place where he buys it to the port from which the ship is to sail, has a far better opportunity than any insurers can possibly have of getting the documents which are relevant to the case. I cannot see any reason for supposing that the learned Judge in any way exercised his discretion for any wrong reason, and he had the full facts of the case before him. He had before him the various matters that have been quite properly urged upon us by [Counsel], and that being so we have not, in my judgment, any power to interfere with his discretion.'

In *Keevil and Keevil Ltd v Boag*[18] a claim was made by the assured under a policy in respect of shipments of eggs from Argentina to the United Kingdom. They were found to be defective on arrival. The insurer applied for an order for ship's papers. Singleton J, in Chambers refused to make the order. On appeal to the Court of Appeal[19] his decision was upheld, for there was no evidence that the discretion had been wrongly exercised.

Goddard LJ, observed:[20]

> 'In this case I will say for myself (and I think I may say for my Lord, too) that if we had been dealing with this case in the first instance, we should have exercised our discretion in exactly the same way. We cannot see any real ground for making the very stringent order for an affidavit of ship's papers in a case of the comparative simplicity of this case. Either these eggs were bad when they were put into the warehouse, or they went bad in the warehouse, or they went bad during transit. Further, we are told in this court something which was not mentioned to the learned Judge. It is a matter which has a great bearing on the case; and I am sure that it would have had a great effect on Singleton J, if it had been mentioned to him. It appears that there is a certificate of quality provided from the proper department of the Government of the Argentine Republic, saying that these goods were in a fit condition to be shipped. If that is so—as the document, as [Counsel] says, is admissible in evidence under the Evidence Act—though it is not conclusive, it affords strong prima facie evidence, at any rate, that the eggs had deteriorated while on the ship.'

In *Probatina Shipping Co Ltd v Sun Insurance Office Ltd, The Sageorge*[1] the owners of the vessel insured her for £75,000. On 29 April 1972, she was stranded on a rocky island off Crete and became a total loss. In August 1972 the assured disclosed to the insurers all immediately available and apparently relevant documents including the chart referred to in the master's statement. In October and November 1972 further documents including the crew list were disclosed. On 5 April 1973, the assured issued a writ claiming an indemnity under the policy. On 5 July 1973, the insurers applied for (i) an order for ship's papers under RSC Order 72, r 10(1); and (ii) a stay of the action under RSC

---

[16] Greer and MacKinnon LJJ.
[17] (1938) 61 LlL Rep at 338.
[18] (1940) 67 LlL Rep 263, CA.
[19] Luxmoore and Goddard LJJ.
[20] (1940) 67 LlL Rep 263 at 265.
[1] [1974] 2 All ER 478.

Order 72, r 10(2) pending compliance with the order for ship's papers. At the same time they stated that a plea of scuttling was going to be made.

The Court of Appeal[2] held that an order for ship's papers should not be made automatically, and no order would be made in the present case. Further, it was in the discretion of the court whether to order a stay pending compliance with an order for ship's papers.

Lord Denning MR, in giving judgment said:[3]

> 'The singular feature about an order for ship's papers is that it is an order on the plaintiff to give discovery of documents before the defendant delivers his defence. This feature should be retained. In scuttling cases it may still serve a useful purpose. When a shipowner claims on a policy for loss by perils of the sea, he will be anxious that the underwriters should admit his claim as soon as may be. He will, therefore, or at any rate should, produce all papers that are relevant to his claim; and, in addition, all other papers that the underwriters reasonably ask to see. If he does not do so, but instead goes ahead with his action, it will be open to the defendants to apply for an order for ship's papers before defence. But the order should not be made automatically. The Judge should see whether or not it is a proper case for it. For this purpose Counsel should put before the Judge the reasons for it. Counsel will not, of course, disclose any material which would be privileged or which it would be inadvisable to mention. But he should give such reasons as he can properly disclose without embarrassment or giving away too much of his client's case.'

Buckley LJ, observed:[4]

> 'In my judgment it is the duty of a Judge, who is asked to make an order for ship's papers, to weigh the advantages which may result in the search for truth against the disadvantages of delay and expense involved in discovery of this kind. That delay and expense may be very substantial. If the Judge considers that the advantages outweigh the disadvantages, he will make an order for ship's papers; but otherwise, in my opinion, he should not, notwithstanding that the defendants indicate that they intend to plead scuttling. It goes without saying that the Judge should not make such an order if he has reason to suppose that it is being sought as a means of extorting a settlement.
>
> Whether on an application for ship's papers Counsel should disclose to the court the grounds on which a plea of scuttling is proposed to be put forward must, in my opinion, be a question for Counsel to decide. The circumstances of the case may be such that the Judge is unlikely to make an order for ship's papers without some indication of the kind of suspicions entertained by the defendants. In such a case Counsel may consider it desirable to tell the court the nature of his client's suspicions. If he chooses to disclose any evidence that may be known to his clients, that is a matter for him. . . . It cannot, I think, be right to require Counsel to disclose his client's case at an interlocutory stage in the action and more particularly before pleadings are closed, but Counsel may very possibly feel able to indicate the nature of the defendants' belief or suspicions without making any undesirable disclosure and he may think that to do so will assist him in his application for an order for ship's papers. The court should not, I think, readily suppose than an experienced and responsible Counsel would associate himself with an allegation of scuttling—a grave charge of fraud—without sufficient reason; but some indication of the basis of the allegation may well be necessary for deciding what kind of discovery of documents would fit the case.'

Persons against whom an order can be made

The order can be obtained against:

    i   The owner of a ship.
    ii A mortgagee who may never have been in possession.[5]

---

[2] Lord Denning MR, Buckley and Roskill LJJ.
[3] [1974] 2 All ER 493 at 494.
[4] Ibid, at 495. See also the judgment of Roskill LJ, ibid, at 500.
[5] *West of England Bank v Canton Insurance Co* (1877) 2 Ex D 472; *Graham Joint Stock Shipping Co v Motor Union Insurance Co* [1922] 1 KB 563; *Anghelatos and London Joint City and Midland Bank v Northern Assurance Co* (1922) 13 LlL Rep 291, CA.

    iii An assured under a policy on goods.[6]
    iv Underwriters suing their reinsurers.[7]
    v An agent suing on behalf of a principal.[8]
    vi An assured in an action by an underwriter for the return of money alleged to have been obtained by a fraud.[9]
    vii An assignee of the proceeds of the insurance policy.[10]
    viii Other persons interested.

In *China SS Co Ltd v Commercial Union Assurance Co*[11] an insurance company applied for an order for discovery of ship's papers against the assured and 'all persons interested in these proceedings, and in the insurance and subject-matter of this action'. It was held by the Court of Appeal[12] that the order applied for would be granted.

Brett LJ, said:[13]

> 'Long before the Judicature Acts in consequence of the peculiarity of insurance actions, a much larger right to discovery was given to underwriters than was given to other plaintiffs or defendants by the ordinary practice either in Chancery or at common law. And it was done for this reason, that underwriters had no means of knowing what was going on with regard to the insured property. The vessel was continually out of the jurisdiction of the law courts, and might be chartered and dealt with and what not at places where the underwriters had no agents, and they could have no means of knowing what was going forward unless such information were supplied them by the owners or by those interested in the vessel and in a position to inform them. Because these underwriters are so much in the dark as to what is going forward, it has always been held that they are entitled to the largest possible discovery, and the way a policy of marine insurance begins gives the key to the way in which this order is made, and it has always been the practice to make these orders not only upon the plaintiffs on the record, but upon all persons interested without any affidavit on behalf of the defendants.... After the Judicature Acts the question was raised whether those Acts altered the old practice.'

---

[6] *Teneria Moderna Franco Española v New Zealand Insurance Co* [1924] 1 KB 79.
[7] *China Traders' Insurance Co v Royal Exchange Assurance Corpn* [1898] 2 QB 187.
[8] *Willis & Co v Baddeley* [1892] 2 QB 324.
[9] *Boulton v Houlder Bros & Co* [1904] 1 KB 784.
[10] *Anghelatos and London Joint City and Midland Bank v Northern Assurance Co*, supra.
[11] (1881) 8 QBD 142, CA.
[12] Jessel MR, Brett and Cotton LJJ.
[13] (1881) 45 LT at 647.

PART IV
The measure of indemnity

CHAPTER 31

Introduction

When a loss takes place, the sum which the assured can recover is called the 'measure of indemnity'.

Section 67(1) of the Marine Insurance Act 1906 states:

> 'The sum which the assured can recover in respect of a loss on a policy by which he is insured, in the case of an unvalued policy[1] to the full extent of the insurable value,[2] or, in the case of a valued policy,[3] to the full extent of the value fixed by the policy, is called the measure of indemnity.'

If the subject-matter is not insured for its full value, then the assured is entitled to recover only a proportion of the sum which he would otherwise recover.

Thus, s 67(2) of the Act provides that:

> 'Where there is a loss recoverable under the policy, the insurer, or each insurer if there be more than one, is liable for such proportion of the measure of indemnity as the amount of his subscription bears to the value fixed by the policy, in the case of a valued policy, or to the insurable value, in the case of an unvalued policy.'

The reason for this rule is that the assured is his own insurer in respect of the uninsured balance.

Thus, in the words of s 81 of the Act:

> 'Where the assured is insured for an amount less than the insurable value, or in the case of a valued policy, for an amount less than the policy valuation, he is deemed to be his own insurer in respect of the uninsured balance.'

Thus, if a vessel which is valued at £1,000,000 is insured for £750,000, and is damaged to the extent of £480,000, the assured will have to bear one-quarter of the loss, i e £120,000.

The measure of indemnity will vary according to the nature of the loss, and the chapters which follow deal with them in the order set out below:

1. Total loss.[4]
2. Partial loss of ship.[5]
3. Partial loss of freight.[6]
4. Partial loss of goods.[7]
5. General average contribution and salvage charges.[8]

---

[1] As to unvalued policies, see pp 97–100, ante.
[2] As to insurable value, see pp 97–100, ante.
[3] As to valued policies, see pp 93–97, ante.
[4] Chapter 32, post.
[5] Chapter 33, post.
[6] Chapter 34, post.
[7] Chapter 35, post.
[8] Chapter 36, post.

Introduction

6   Liabilities to third parties.[9]
7   Successive losses.[10]
8   Expenses incurred under the 'sue and labour' clause.[11]

The above matters are considered in detail in the sections of the Act, but there is also a general provision in s 75(1) as to the measure of indemnity. This section states:

> 'Where there has been a loss in respect of any subject-matter not expressly provided for in the foregoing provisions[12] of this Act, the measure of indemnity shall be ascertained, as nearly as may be in accordance with those provisions, in so far as applicable to the particular case.'

---

[9] Chapter 37, post.
[10] Chapter 38, post.
[11] Chapter 39, post.
[12] Viz ss 67–74.

CHAPTER 32

Total loss

The measure of indemnity for a total loss is set out in s 68 of the Marine Insurance Act 1906. This section states:

'Subject to the provisions of this Act, and to any express provision in the policy, where there is a total loss of the subject-matter insured—
(1) If the policy be a valued policy,[1] the measure of indemnity is the sum fixed by the policy:
(2) If the policy be an unvalued policy,[2] the measure of indemnity is the insurable[3] value of the subject-matter insured.'

Total loss of ship

The measure of indemnity set out in s 68 is modified by clause 1 of the Institute Time Clauses (Hulls)[4] and clause 1 of the Institute Voyage Clauses (Hulls)[5] in the case of a vessel about to be scrapped. Both of these clauses state:

'*Navigation*

In the event of the Vessel sailing (with or without cargo) with an intention of being (a) broken up or (b) sold for breaking up, any claim for loss of or damage to the Vessel occurring subsequent to such sailing shall be limited to the market value of the Vessel as scrap at the time when the loss or damage is sustained unless notice has been given to the Underwriters and any amendments to the terms of cover, insured value and premium required by them have been agreed.'

Total loss of freight

Clause 15 of the Institute Time Clauses (Freight)[6] states that:

i in the event of the actual[7] or constructive total loss[8] of the vessel the amount insured in respect of freight will be paid in full, whether the vessel is fully or partly loaded or in ballast, chartered or unchartered;

ii in ascertaining whether the vessel is a constructive total loss, the insured value in the policies on hull and machinery are to be taken as the repaired value and nothing in respect of the damaged or break-up value of the vessel or wreck is to be taken into account; and

iii if the vessel is a constructive total loss but the claim on the policies on hull and machinery are settled as a claim for partial loss, no payment is due under this clause in respect of freight.

---

[1] As to valued policies, see pp 93–97, ante.
[2] As to unvalued policies, see pp 97–100, ante.
[3] As to insurable value, see pp 97–100, ante.
[4] These clauses are set out in Appendix III, pp 533–540, post.
[5] These clauses are set out in Appendix III, pp 540–547, post.
[6] These clauses are set out in Appendix III pp 550–554, post.
[7] As to actual total loss, see pp 346–361, ante.
[8] As to constructive total loss, see pp 362–376, ante.

Clause 13 of the Institute Voyage Clauses (Freight)[9] is to the same effect. Further, clause 3 of the Institute War and Strikes Clauses (Freight–Time)[10] states:

> '*Detainment*
> In the event that a claim for a constructive total loss of the Vessel is paid on the war risks insurance of the Vessel[11] as a result of the loss of the free use and disposal of the Vessel for a continuous period of 12 months due to capture, seizure, arrest, restraint, detainment, confiscation or expropriation whilst this insurance is in force, the amount insured hereunder shall be paid in full less any claims otherwise arising during the said period of 12 months which have been paid or are recoverable hereunder . . .'

Clause 3 of the Institute War and Strikes Clauses (Freight–Voyage)[12] is in the same terms.

In *Atlantic Maritime Co Incorporated v Gibbon*[13] a vessel was chartered to load a cargo at Taku Bar, and was prevented from loading there by a restraint of princes. So her owners, who had effected a policy in respect of the freight to be earned by her, fixed a new charter-party under which she was to carry a cargo from British Columbia to ports in South America and the east coast of the United States. The assured claimed against the insurers for a loss of freight.

The Court of Appeal[14] held that the claim failed because it was barred by a 'frustration' clause[15] in the policy. The court also held obiter that in any case no freight would be recoverable because the assured had sustained no loss.

Sir Raymond Evershed MR, said[16] that if the second charter-party was made in substitution for the first in the sense that it would not have been made and could not have been made if the first had not been lost, then prima facie it would appear that the assured had suffered no loss. If, on the other hand, the second charter-party could have been made and reasonably might have been expected to have been made notwithstanding performance of the first charter-party, the assured would be entitled to claim the freight which had been lost, and could say that it was immaterial that, after the time for performance of the first charter-party had elapsed, they might or could have anticipated some other freight. He considered that the evidence as to the circumstances of the making of the second charter-party was insufficient, but observed (obiter):[17]

> 'On the facts as they emerge from the agreed facts, there seem at least strong grounds for supposing that in truth the British Columbia charter—the making of which caused the decision of the owners communicated to the master on 9 August—was in substitution for the first charter and would not have been made (so that its freight would not have been earned) had it not been for the loss or abandonment of the first charter. Subject, as I say, to any question of figures, but since the British Columbia charter appears to have produced more for the owners than the first charter, the result would appear prima facie to be that there was, in any case, no loss.
> In the absence of that evidence it is additionally fortunate, to my mind, that I do not find it necessary to express any concluded view.'

---

[9] These clauses are set out in Appendix III, pp 555–558, post.
[10] These clauses are set out in Appendix III, pp 558–559, post.
[11] Under clause 3 of the Institute War and Strikes Clauses (Hulls–Time) (see p 372, ante) or clause 3 of the Institute War and Strikes Clauses (Hulls–Voyage) (see p 372, ante).
[12] These clauses are set out in Appendix III, pp 560–561, post.
[13] [1953] 2 Lloyd's Rep 294, CA.
[14] Sir Raymond Evershed MR, Jenkins and Morris LJJ.
[15] As to the 'frustration' clause, see pp 264–267, ante.
[16] [1953] 2 Lloyd's Rep at 312.
[17] Ibid, at 313.

Morris LJ, also said (obiter):[18]

> 'There is, finally, the question as to what would have been the amount recoverable had recovery been possible. Again I do not find it necessary to express any concluded opinion. The policy covers loss of freight or anticipated freight or chartered freight during a three-month period, and as it is a policy of insurance I think that the reminder given by Roche J, in the case of *Roura and Forgas v Townend*[19] in a passage cited to us by [Counsel] in his argument, is worthy to be borne in mind. Roche J, referred to the principle that an assured cannot, under a contract of indemnity, although he may at one time have suffered a loss, recover in respect of such loss if before action it has already been made good to him. The insurance in this case covered a loss of money to be earned in the employment of the ship. Though I express no final opinion, it would seem to me to be contrary to good sense if, in a case where the ship remained intact as a freight-earning vehicle, no account need be taken or allowance made in respect of earnings resulting from the employment of the ship under a new and substituted contract referable to a period of time covered by a contract which could not be performed.'

Effect of devaluation

In *Howard Houlder & Partners Ltd v Union Marine Insurance Co Ltd*[20] the brokers for the assured effected a policy in respect of a cargo of molasses, which was to be conveyed from the West Indies to ports in Canada. One of the clauses of the policy stated:

> 'Claims, if any, to pay at the rate of $4.15 to £1 sterling.'

The cargo was valued at $108,000 and insured for £26,025 with English insurers. At the time when the policy was issued the exchange rate was $4.15 to the £1. The vessel carrying the cargo was a total loss, and so was the cargo. The insurers paid £26,025, but the assured claimed that another £2,886 was due because in the meanwhile the exchange rate had fallen to $3.94 to the £1 sterling, and another £2,886 was required to purchase $108,000.

The House of Lords[1] held that the policy was a sterling policy, and that only £26,025 was due under it. Consequently the claim failed. The clause set out above did not apply to a total loss, but only to claims which from their nature might require to be met in dollars, e g general average.

In the words of Lord Sumner:[2]

> 'Looking at the policy as a whole, as one has to do, and endeavouring to construe all the operative parts of it so as to give them due effect, I think it is fairly clear that, instead of treating this clause as radically altering the whole character of the policy, the only meaning of the words is to say that it applies to those cases and only those cases in which the transaction as a whole necessitates the conversion of one currency into another. It is a clause to pay at a rate—that is to say, it is a clause providing for a rate of exchange, and has, I should have thought, no application at all where the transaction requires no rate of exchange whatever, and, if that is true, to the payment of a total loss on this policy.'

---

[18] Ibid, at 318. Jenkins LJ, said (ibid, at 316) that he wished to express no opinion about the quantification of the loss if it had been recoverable.
[19] [1919] 1 KB 189.
[20] (1922) 10 LlL Rep 627, HL.
[1] Lord Buckmaster, Lord Dunedin, Lord Atkinson, Lord Sumner and Lord Parmoor.
[2] (1922) 10 LlL Rep at 629. See also, the speech of Lord Buckmaster, ibid, at 628, that of Lord Dunedin, ibid, at 628, that of Lord Atkinson, ibid, at 628, and that of Lord Parmoor, ibid, at 629.

CHAPTER 33

Partial loss of ship

When a vessel is damaged, the insurers will not be liable at all if she is insured against total loss only.[1]

The policy may contain a particular average warranty stating that a loss under a specified percentage is not covered.[2]

Usually the policy contains a 'deductible clause', the effect of which is that even if the claim is successful, the assured has to bear the proportion of the loss specified in the clause e g 10 per cent.[3]

In general, the liability of the insurers is governed by the provisions of the Marine Insurance Act 1906, s 69.[4]

The procedure for ascertaining the amount payable is usually stated in the policy.[5]

A SHIP INSURED AGAINST TOTAL LOSS ONLY

Sometimes a vessel is insured against total loss only. In this case no claim will lie in respect of a partial loss.

An instance is provided by *Gurney v Grimmer*,[6] where a reinsurance policy stated:

> 'Warranted free of all average and to pay only in the event of the total constructive compromised and/or arranged total loss of the vessel.'

B PARTICULAR AVERAGE WARRANTIES

Sometimes the policy contains a clause stating 'warranted free from average' under a specified percentage. This means that the insurers are not liable at all unless the damage to the vessel reaches the specified percentage.

If the damage does reach the percentage, the insurer is liable in full i e the clause is a franchise and is not an 'excess' clause and in this respect is very different from a 'deductible' clause.

Sometimes the words 'unless general, or the ship is stranded, sunk or burnt or the damage is caused by collision' are added to the clause.

---

[1] See infra.
[2] See pp 410–417, post.
[3] See p 418, post.
[4] See pp 418–426, post.
[5] See p 426, post.
[6] (1932) 44 LlL Rep 189, CA.

'Average unless general'

Rule 13 of the Rules for Construction of Policy set out in the First Schedule to the Marine Insurance Act 1906 states:

> 'The term "average unless general" means a partial loss of the subject-matter insured other than a general average loss, and does not include "particular charges".'

'Stranding'

i What constitutes a stranding

The question as to what constitutes a 'stranding' has been much discussed, and the conclusion to be drawn from an examination of the decided cases would seem to be that a stranding takes place when a ship takes the ground and remains quiescent for an appreciable space of time, owing to the operation of some extraneous and accidental cause and not in the ordinary course of navigation.

Thus, in *M'Dougle v Royal Exchange Assurance Co*[7] a vessel struck a rock about a cable's length from the shore as she was going into harbour, and remained there for a minute and a half. Lord Ellenborough CJ, said:[8]

> 'This was not a stranding; ex vi termini stranding means lying on the shore or something analogous to that. To use a vulgar phrase—if it is touch and go with the ship, there is no stranding. . . . If by the force of the elements she is run aground and becomes stationary, it is immaterial whether this be on piles, on the muddy bank of the river, or on rocks on the seashore; but a mere striking will not do, wheresoever that may happen.'

But in *Baker v Towry*[9] the same learned Judge directed a jury that if a ship struck upon a rock and remained on it for from 15 to 20 minutes, it was sufficient to constitute a stranding.

A ship was held to be stranded where, having been improperly fastened by the pilot to the pier of the dock basin, she took the ground when the tide went out, fell over, and filled with water when the tide rose.[10] Further, where a vessel was in a lock from which the water was being drawn in order to enable the lock to be repaired, and she grounded upon some piles not known to be there, it was held to be a stranding.[11]

Where a ship was forced ashore by the wind and remained there for 2 hours until the tide flowed when she got off, it was held to be a stranding.[12]

It was held to be a stranding when a vessel ran on piles and remained there until they were cut away.[13]

But there was no stranding where the ship was driven ashore by fouling two other vessels, although she remained fast for an hour.[14]

Nor was it held to be a stranding where a vessel properly and in the ordinary course of navigation while in charge of a pilot took the ground on account of the

---

[7] (1815) 4 Camp 283.
[8] Ibid, at 284. An application for a new trial was later refused; (1816) 4 M&S 530.
[9] (1816) 1 Stark 436.
[10] *Carruthers v Sydebotham* (1815) 4 M&S 77.
[11] *Rayner v Godmond* (1821) 5 B&Ald 225.
[12] *Harman v Vaux* (1813) 3 Camp 429.
[13] *Dobson v Bolton* (1799) 1 Park's Marine Insurances (8th edn) 239.
[14] *Baring v Henkle* (1801) 1 Marshall on Marine Insurances (3rd edn), 232; *Corcoran v Gurney* (1853) 20 LTOS 221. But see *Wells v Hopwood* (1832) 3 B&Ad 20 at 27 (per Taunton J).

shallowness of the water until the tide rose, for this happened to all vessels going into that particular port.[15]

But where a ship in entering a port of refuge struck an anchor and started leaking, and was then hauled up the harbour into shallow water, where she took ground and remained for half an hour, this was held to be a stranding since she was placed there to avoid the consequences of the leak.[16]

It was held to be no stranding where the ship in a tidal harbour took the ground upon a falling tide, although she struck against some hard substance, which damaged her bottom.[17]

On the other hand, where a vessel in a similar harbour was moored alongside the quay, and the tackle mooring her to the shore proved insufficient so that she fell over on her side, this was held to be a stranding.[18]

Where a ship discharging her cargo alongside a quay grounded on mud at low water, but on a subsequent tide, by reason of a gale and the straining of a rope, was so shifted that she grounded on a bank of stones, this grounding was held to be a stranding.[19]

In *Corcoran v Gurney*[20] where a ship anchored in a bay in bad weather, and, the increasing gale causing her to drag her anchor, she was compelled to slip her anchor and enter a tidal harbour under sail where, it being then low water, she took ground and remained aground for some days, it was held to be a stranding.

Lord Campbell CJ, said:[1]

> 'We have excellent guides in the authorities as to what shall be, and what shall not be, considered a stranding. Lord Tenterden in *Wells v Hopwood* (1832) 3 B&Ad 20 says, "Where a vessel takes the ground in the ordinary and usual course of navigation and management, in a tidal river or harbour, upon the ebbing of the tide or from natural deficiency of water, so that she may float again upon the flow of tide or increase of water, such an event shall not be considered a stranding within the meaning of the Memorandum. But where the ground is taken under any extraordinary circumstances of time or place, by reason of some unusual or accidental occurrence, such an event shall be considered a stranding." And Tindal CJ, in *Kingsford v Marshall* (1832) 8 Bing 458, says that it is a stranding "where the taking of the ground does not happen solely from those natural causes which are necessarily incident to the ordinary course of navigation in which the ship is engaged, either wholly or in part, but from some accidental or extraneous cause . . .". What took place was not in the ordinary course of navigation, though certainly from natural causes, as all perils of the sea may be said to be. But it was because of an extraordinary peril and by reason of that peril that the ship grounded in the harbour, and there lay for some time before she was ever in safety. It seems to me the event was caused by extraordinary circumstances and by perils of the sea; and I see no difference to be made between the event of the ship coming upon the ground outside the harbour, and her being forced to enter the harbour for safety and grounding on account of the tide ebbing at the time.'

In *Letchford v Oldham*[2] a ship entered a tidal harbour, and before reaching the quay grounded on a small bank, by the side of which was a hollow, into which hollow the head of the vessel settled as the tide receded. Both bank and hollow had been caused by the paddles of steamers working at low tide. The existence

---

[15] *Hearne v Edmunds* (1819) 1 Brod&Bing 388.
[16] *Barrow v Bell* (1825) 4 B&C 736.
[17] *Kingsford v Marshall* (1832) 8 Bing 458.
[18] *Bishop v Pentland* (1827) 7 B&C 219.
[19] *Wells v Hopwood* (1832) 3 B&Ad 20.
[20] (1853) 20 LTOS 221.
[1] Ibid, at 221.
[2] (1880) 5 QBD 538.

of the bank and hollow had not been previously known, no vessel having met with a similar accident. It was held that there had been a stranding.

Again, a ship was said to be stranded where, being in distress, she was taken in tow and purposely run on a bank.[3]

The fact that the ship was beached by the master does not prevent it being a stranding.[4]

But the mere fact of taking ground in a tidal harbour in a spot where the vessel was placed for unloading was held not to constitute a stranding, although she sustained damage by the hardness of the ground.[5]

Sinking in deep water is not a stranding.[6]

ii Whole loss recoverable on stranding

On a stranding of a ship the whole damage incurred is claimable, whether traceable to the stranding or not, even when the damage takes place first and the stranding follows, or where the stranding takes place but the ship gets off, and the damage follows later in the course of the voyage.

Thus, in *Burnett v Kensington*[7] Ashurst J, said:[8]

> 'As it is difficult to determine, when the ship has been stranded, whether or not the damage to the cargo arose from the stranding or how much of the damage was owing to that cause, . . . and that when the ship has been stranded, the underwriters consent to ascribe the loss to that cause.'

'Sunk'

In *Bryant and May Ltd v London Assurance*[9] the vessel, laden with matchsplints from Quebec to London, arrived at Gravesend, having sprung a leak, with part of her deck just under water. The jury found that the ship had not sunk; and, of course, being laden with timber, could not sink in the ordinary sense of the word.

It would seem that the vessel must be submerged and must touch bottom to constitute a sinking; though probably the state of things in *Anderson v Royal Exchange Assurance Co*[10] and *Doyle v Dallas*,[11] where the vessels were covered at certain states of wind and tide, would also be embraced by the term.

'Or burnt'

The words 'or burnt' began to be used in the early days of steam-power, in consequence of the damage caused by bunker fires.

The word 'burnt' came under consideration in *The Glenlivet*,[12] which was an action on a time policy, during the continuance of which on three separate voyages fires had occurred in the vessel, in each case in the bunkers. On each

---

[3] *De Mattos v Saunders* (1872) LR 7 CP 570.
[4] *Burnett v Kensington* (1797) 7 Term Rep 210. But see *Thompson v Whitmore* (1810) 3 Taunt 227.
[5] *Magnus v Buttemer* (1852) 11 CB 876.
[6] *Baker-Whiteley Coal Co v Marten* (1910) 26 TLR 314.
[7] (1797) 7 Term Rep 210.
[8] Ibid, at 223.
[9] (1886) 2 TLR 591.
[10] (1805) 7 East 38.
[11] (1831) 1 Mood&R 48. See also, *Kemp v Halliday* (1866) LR 1 QB 520.
[12] [1894] P 48.

occasion the damage to the ship was under the percentage mentioned in the policy, and for that damage it was sought to make the insurer liable. The ship was not by reason of the fire prevented from continuing her voyage, and Gorell Barnes J, held that the test was that the fire must be sufficient to cause some interruption of the voyage, so that the vessel was pro tempore incapable of being properly used for the purpose of the voyage, i e the vessel must be 'temporarily innavigable'.

In the Court of Appeal this test was not adopted. Lindley LJ, said that the ship *as a whole* must be stranded, sunk or burnt, and that any fire doing a little structural damage to the ship would not be a burning of the ship in ordinary language.

'Collision'

'Collision with any other ship or vessel' includes collision by a tug towing the insured ship, or the boats or launch of that ship,[13] collision with a sunken barge,[14] or with a wreck projecting above the sand.[15]

Computation of the percentage

i Voyage policies

In the case of a voyage policy the insurance is for the whole voyage, and therefore for the purpose of estimating the percentage of damage regard must be had to the condition of the thing insured on its arrival. For that purpose it is immaterial that the damage was caused at different periods of the voyage or to different parts of the thing insured. In other words, the liability of the insurer is fixed by the amount of the loss which exists on the arrival of the ship.[16]

Where each separate loss has been made good by repairs or otherwise during the voyage, the total cost of all the repairs, etc (less the usual deductions), will give the measure of the partial loss for the purpose of ascertaining whether the percentage has been reached.[17]

ii Time policies

In a time policy the same principle is applied in estimating the loss in each separate voyage under the policy. But where the vessel has performed two or more distinct voyages during the currency of the time policy, the losses on the separate voyages cannot be added together for the purpose of making the insurer liable where in the aggregate they amount to the named percentage.[18]

Where a voyage extends beyond the expiry date of a time policy, the losses up to that date only may be added together to ascertain the percentage. Further, in the case of a time policy although, as stated above, the amounts of losses

---

[13] *M'Cowan v Baine and Johnston, The Niobe* [1891] AC 401.
[14] *Chandler v Blogg* [1898] 1 QB 32.
[15] *The Munroe* [1893] P 248. See also, the cases cited on pp 172–174, ante.
[16] *Blackett v Royal Exchange Assurance Corpn* (1832) 2 Cr&J 244; *Stewart v Merchants Marine Insurance Co* (1885) 16 QBD 619.
[17] See Marine Insurance Act 1906, s 77(1) which states: 'Unless the policy otherwise provides, and subject to the provisions of this Act, the insurer is liable for successive losses, even though the total amount of such losses may exceed the sum insured.' See pp 440–441, post.
[18] *Stewart v Merchants' Marine Insurance Co*, supra.

incurred in separate and distinct voyages cannot be added together, they can be added together where there is one long voyage performed in separate stages.[19]

In *Portvale SS Co Ltd v Royal Exchange Assurance Corpn*[20] a vessel was insured under a time policy clause which stated:

'Warranted free from particular average under 3 per cent.'

Also included was a clause which provided:

'The warranty and conditions as to average under 3 per cent to be applicable to each voyage as if separately insured and a voyage shall be deemed to commence at one of the following periods to be selected by the assured when making up the claim viz, at any time at which the vessel (1) begins to load cargo or (2) sails in ballast to a loading port. Such voyage shall be deemed to continue during the ensuing period until either she has made one outward and one homeward passage (including an intermediate ballast passage if made) or has carried and discharged two cargoes whichever may first happen, and further, in either case, until she begins to load a subsequent cargo or sails in ballast for a loading port.'

The vessel left Pernambuco in ballast under charter to load in the River Plate for Antwerp. On 17 January 1931 she suffered damage by heavy weather on the way there, and put into Montevideo for repairs. She proceeded to Santa Fe to load, and on 7 February in entering the port, she damaged her bows by striking the quay. She loaded and proceeded to St Vincent for bunkers. While bunkering on 18 March she was damaged in a collision. She proceeded to Antwerp, where she was damaged in a collision on 24 June, and, on coming out of dry dock after repairs had been effected, was further damaged on 9 July. The amount of damage suffered on 17 January, 7 February and 18 March was together over 3 per cent. The damage suffered on 24 June and 9 July was under 3 per cent.

The assured claimed an indemnity in respect of the amount of the damage suffered on each occasion, but the insurers refused to pay in respect of the damage suffered on 24 June and 9 July on the ground that it was not suffered during the same voyage as the other sets of damage.

MacKinnon J, held that they were liable to indemnify the assured in respect of all the damage suffered because the definition of 'voyage' in the clause set out above clearly included the vessel's stay at Antwerp.

His Lordship observed:[1]

'Clearly the assured are correct in saying that under that provision this voyage had not finished by 9 July when the fifth of the series of damages and the second of those when laid up at Antwerp occurred, because he can say that, the voyage having commenced at Pernambuco, it is to be deemed to continue until the vessel has carried and discharged two cargoes and further until she begins to load the subsequent cargo or sails in ballast for the loading port. On the actual words of the clause I think there can be no doubt that the assured is right in saying that the voyage which has been deemed to commence at Pernambuco under this provision must be deemed to be still continuing.'

He then concluded:[2]

'The real truth is that the underwriters, not unnaturally, feel that it is hard that so long a period as this, which amounts to five months, should be included in this voyage which started at

---

[19] Ibid.
[20] (1932) 43 LlL Rep 161, KBD.
[1] Ibid, at 164.
[2] Ibid, at 165.

Pernambuco. But, in my view, upon the clear wording of the clause, though it results in this case in what appears to be a somewhat strange and possibly a hard result—yet upon the clear reading of this clause I do not see my way to say that at the time when these last two pieces of damage were sustained this ship had ceased to be on the voyage which commenced at Pernambuco, under the artificial definition of a voyage provided by this clause.'

Dock dues

In ascertaining the percentage of damage to a ship the test is the cost of repairing the damage.

Therefore in the cost of repairs there must be included the dock dues necessitated by those repairs. Generally speaking, the whole of the dock dues will form part of the cost of the repairs if the ship must be docked for that purpose, even though the owner takes advantage of the fact that the ship is docked to have her surveyed or to effect improvements, provided that he does not thereby lengthen her stay in dock.[3]

But if a ship goes into dry dock for a purpose unconnected with damage insured against—e g for scraping and painting—and then such damage is discovered, to the cost of repairing such damage must be added a proportion of the dock dues necessitated by the repairs.

Thus, in *Marine Insurance Co v China Transpacific SS Co*[4] the insured vessel went into dock to be scraped and painted, but when docked her sternpost was found to be fractured and had to be repaired. The repairing and painting proceeded simultaneously. The repairing lasted from 4 January to 11 January inclusive, whilst the scraping and painting lasted from 4 January to 6 January inclusive. It was held that the dock dues from 4 January to 6 January were to be apportioned equally between scraping and painting on the one hand and repairing on the other, but that the repairing alone was to be charged with the dues from 7 January to 11 January inclusive.

The wages and provisions of the crew during the period occupied by the repair of the ship are not included.[5]

Exclusion of general average loss

The assured is not entitled to add the general average loss to the particular average loss in order to bring the loss up to the required percentage.

Thus, s 76(3) of the Marine Insurance Act 1906 states:

> 'Unless the policy otherwise provides, where the subject-matter insured is warranted free from particular average under a specified percentage, a general average loss cannot be added to a particular average loss to make up the specified percentage.'

In *Price v A1 Ships' Small Damage Insurance Association*[6] a vessel had been compelled to make certain general average sacrifices in the course of her voyage, and had also suffered particular average damage. But she had neither been stranded, sunk, nor burnt. By the addition of the particular average, which was less than 3 per cent, to the amount contributed in general average, the total exceeded 3 per cent. The defendants were insurers of all losses 'not

---

[3] *Ruabon SS Co v London Assurance* [1900] AC 6; *The Acanthus* [1902] P 17.
[4] (1886) 11 App Cas 573. See also, *The Haversham Grange* [1905] P 307.
[5] *The Leitrim* [1902] P 256.
[6] (1889) 22 QBD 580, CA.

covered by other policies of insurance'. These other policies contained the usual free of particular average under 3 per cent clause. On being sued for the particular average loss, the insurers contended that they were not liable on the ground that the total damage was over 3 per cent, and that the plaintiffs ought and could have recovered that from the other insurers, because it was covered by the ordinary Lloyd's policy. The Court of Appeal held that this could not be done, for the particular average loss and the general average loss could not be added together to arrive at the percentage referred to in the policy.

Inclusion of actual loss only

Section 76(4) of the Marine Insurance Act 1906 states:

> 'For the purpose of ascertaining whether the specified percentage has been reached, regard shall be had only to the actual loss suffered by the subject-matter insured. Particular charges and the expenses of and incidental to ascertaining and proving the loss must be excluded.'

Section 64(2) defines 'particular charges' in the following way:

> 'Expenses incurred by or on behalf of the assured for the safety or preservation of the subject-matter insured, other than general average and salvage charges, are called particular charges. Particular charges are not included in particular average.'

'Particular charges' are those expenses which are incurred in preserving the cargo, e g warehousing, drying, packing, etc. They are termed 'charges' to distinguish them from a particular average loss which is caused directly by perils insured against.[7]

'Particular charges' may, however, be recovered, irrespective of the percentage laid down by the policy, under the 'sue and labour' clause.

Thus, s 78(1) of the Marine Insurance Act 1906 states:

> 'Where the policy contains a suing and labouring clause, the engagement thereby entered into is deemed to be supplementary to the contract of insurance, and the assured may recover from the insurer any expenses properly incurred pursuant to the clause, notwithstanding . . . that the subject-matter may have been warranted free from particular average, either wholly or under a certain percentage.'

The cost of ascertaining the percentage must be paid by the party on whom the loss, when ascertained, will fall. Thus, if the loss amounts to the percentage, it must be borne by the insurer. If the cost is below the percentage, the assured will be liable to pay for it.

Liability of insurer for salvage charges and particular charges

Section 76(2) of the Marine Insurance Act 1906 states:

> 'Where the subject-matter is warranted free from particular average . . . under a certain percentage, the insurer is nevertheless liable for salvage charges, and for particular charges and other expenses properly incurred pursuant to the provisions of the suing and labouring clause in order to avert a peril insured against.'

---

[7] See Marine Insurance Act 1906, s 64(1) which states: 'A particular average loss is a partial loss of the subject-matter insured, caused by a peril insured against, and which is not a general average loss.'

C 'DEDUCTIBLE' CLAUSES

Clause 12 of the Institute Time Clauses (Hulls)[8] states that

    i no claim arising from a peril insured against is payable unless the aggregate of all such claims arising out of each separate accident or occurrence (including claims in respect of a collision,[9] general average and salvage,[10] and 'sue and labour' expenses[11]) exceeds a specified percentage;

    ii in the event of the aggregate reaching the specified percentage, the amount concerned must be deducted from the sum which would have been payable under the claim;

    iii claims for damage by heavy weather occurring during a single sea passage between two successive ports are treated as being due to one accident;

    iv in the case of heavy weather extending over a period and wholly covered by the policy the deductible to be applied to the claim is to be the proportion of the deductible that the number of days of such heavy weather falling within the period of the insurance bears to the number of days of heavy weather during the single sea passage;

    v the expression 'heavy weather" is deemed to include contact with floating ice; and

    vi the expense of sighting the bottom after stranding, if reasonably incurred specially for that purpose, will be paid even if no damage is found.

Clause 10 of the Institute Voyage Clauses (Hulls)[12] is to similar effect.

A 'deductible' clause in a Canadian case is instanced by *Pillgrem v Cliff Richardson Boats Ltd and Richardson (Switzerland General Insurance Co, Third Party)*[13] where a marina operator's legal liability policy stated:

> 'DEDUCTIBLE
>
> No claim shall be payable under this policy unless the aggregate liability of the insured arising out of the same accident or occurrence and insured against hereunder exceeds the sum of $1,250 ... and this sum shall be deducted from the amount payable hereunder on account of liability arising from each such accident or occurrence.'

D CALCULATING THE MEASURE OF INDEMNITY

The measure of indemnity depends on whether:

1 the ship has been repaired.
2 the ship has been only partially repaired.
3 the ship has not been repaired and has not been sold in her damaged state during the risk.[14]

---

[8] These clauses are set out in Appendix III, pp 533–540, post.
[9] See pp 170–176, ante.
[10] See pp 176–194, ante.
[11] See pp 442–452, post.
[12] These clauses are set out in Appendix III, pp 540–547, post.
[13] [1977] 1 Lloyd's Rep 297, Supreme Court of Ontario.
[14] As to the duration of the risk see pp 113–139, ante.

4 the ship has not been repaired and *is* sold in her damaged state during the risk.

The first three sets of circumstances are considered in s 69 of the Marine Insurance Act 1906, but the fourth is not.

It should be noted that in all cases the 'deductible' clause is an 'excess' clause and the insurer is liable only for the amount by which the loss or damage exceed the amount stated in the clause i e the assured will have to pay the amount specified in the clause himself.

1 Where the ship has been repaired

Section 69 of the Act states:

> 'Where a ship is damaged, but is not totally lost, the measure of indemnity, subject to any express provision in the policy, is as follows:
> (1) Where the ship has been repaired, the assured is entitled to the reasonable cost of the repairs, less the customary deductions, but not exceeding the sum insured in respect of any one casualty.'

The customary deductions

In the case of wooden ships where repairs have been executed, the insurer is liable for the cost of two-thirds of such repairs.

Apart from special contract the deduction is not made in the case of iron ships, nor in the case of a wooden ship on her first voyage, and a voyage out and home may in the circumstances be one voyage.[15]

Rule D7 of the Rules of Practice of the Association of Average Adjusters[16] states:

> 'The deduction for new work in place of old is fixed by custom at one-third, with the following exceptions:
> Anchors are allowed in full. Chain cables are subject to one-sixth only.
> Metal sheathing is dealt with, by allowing in full the cost of a weight equal to the gross weight of metal sheathing stripped off minus the proceeds of the old metal. Nails, felt, and labour metalling are subject to one-third.
> The rule applies to iron as well as to wooden ships, and to labour as well as material. It does not apply to the expense of straightening bent ironwork, and to the labour of taking out and replacing it.
> It does not apply to graving dock expenses and removals, cartages, use of shears, stages, and graving dock materials.
> It does not apply to a ship's first voyage.'

It is obvious that the rule as to the customary deductions may at times work hardship either on the assured or on the insurer, according to the circumstances of the particular case, for it involves the assumption that the ship has been benefited to the extent of one-third of the repairs beyond the actual damage, and of one-third only.

This would not be the case with a ship which had been put into a thorough state of repair before she sailed on the voyage in which the loss claimed took place, for in such a case the allowance of one-third 'new for old' would be a loss to the assured.[17]

---

[15] See *Fenwick v Robinson* (1828) 3 C&P 323; *Pirie v Steele* (1837) 8 C&P 200.
[16] These Rules are set out in Appendix V, pp 568–584, post.
[17] See *Poingdestre v Royal Exchange Assurance* (1826) Ry&M 378.

On the other hand, the ship may have been in such a bad state of repair before the damage took place that the allowance of one-third is much less than the gain accruing to the ship by the repairs, and therefore the insurer loses by the restriction of the allowances of 'new for old' to one-third only.

Thus, in *Aitchison v Lohre*[18] a ship was valued at £2,600 in the policy, and worth only £3,000 before the damage. She was worth £7,000 after the repairs had been executed, although after the damage and before the repairs had been effected she was only worth £998. The insurers contended that the extreme measure of their liability was the amount which they would have had to pay if the assured had elected to claim for a total loss, and had abandoned the damaged ship, as otherwise the assured would recover far more than an indemnity. But it was held by the House of Lords that where the assured elected to repair, the insurers were liable to pay the cost of the repairs less one-third 'new for old', even though the insurers would be liable for an amount exceeding the total loss minus the value of the abandoned ship, for this unusual result of allowing one-third 'new for old' could not invalidate the general rule.

There is usually a special clause in the policy as to whether any deductions will be made.

Thus, clause 14 of the Institute Time Clauses (Hulls)[19] provides:

> 'Claims payable without deduction new for old.'

In *A/S Ocean v Black Sea & Baltic General Insurance Co*[20] a vessel was insured for a voyage from the United Kingdom or the Continent to the Kara Sea and back. The policy stated that it was 'on Norwegian conditions according to the Norwegian Insurance Plan of 1930'.

Paragraph 76(6) of the Plan stated:

> 'FRANCHISES: In the case of particular average damage to the ship, the insurance is effected without liability for the first . . . Kroner per ton gross. The amount of the franchise shall be deducted from the computed compensation.'

Paragraph 77 provided:

> 'If the damage has been occasioned by striking against, or contact with ice . . . one half[1] is deducted from the amount which the underwriter has to compensate in accordance with the rules of this paragraph, or paragraph 76.'

The policy also contained a term which stated:

> 'It is specially agreed that this policy covers ice damage irrespective of percentage.'

The vessel was damaged by ice, and the assured incurred the cost of repairs to machinery. The insurers claimed that they were entitled to make the deduction of one-half, and that their right to do so was not excluded by the phrase 'irrespective of percentage' mentioned above.

The Court of Appeal[2] held that they were entitled to do so. Maugham LJ, said:[3]

---

[18] (1879) 4 App Cas 755.
[19] These clauses are set out in Appendix III, pp 533–540, post. Clause 12 of the Institute Voyage Clauses (Hulls) is to the same effect. These clauses are set out in Appendix III, pp 540–547, post.
[20] (1935) 51 LlL Rep 305, CA.
[1] This deduction was to be made because the vessel was over 10 years old.
[2] Greer and Maugham LJJ, and Talbot J.
[3] (1935) 51 LlL Rep at 310. See also, the judgment of Greer LJ, ibid, at 307, and that of Talbot J, ibid, at 310.

'Much the same consideration applies to the provision with regard to damage to machinery contained in sub-para (II)(B) of para 77, only here it is more apparent even than it is in sub-para (d) to which I have just referred as regards additional deductions due to contact with ice, that the only object of the clause is to prevent the shipowner getting an altogether excessive compensation for ancient machinery; in other words, it is of the nature of a provision precluding the shipowner from getting for machinery over ten years old entirely new machinery. The result is that one-half of the damage to machinery attributable, among other things, to contact with ice is to be deducted as a general rule for ascertaining or computing the compensation for that special injury. I cannot see any reason for thinking that that is a percentage within the meaning of the phrase which is under consideration, and I am quite convinced that it does not literally fall within the words of "irrespective of percentage".'

Expenses of docking

Where the ship goes into dock for the purpose of repairing damage for which the insurers are liable, the whole of the pilotage, towage, and dock dues will fall upon the insurers. If she is docked for the owner's purposes only, the expenses must be paid by the owner.

The mere fact that either the owner or the insurers obtain a benefit from the docking will not entitle the person, who is liable for the dock expenses, to claim a share of those expenses from the other person, for there is no rule of law requiring a person to contribute to an expense merely because he has derived a benefit from it.

Thus, in *Ruabon SS Co v London Assurance*[4] a vessel was docked for repairs which fell upon the insurers. It was held that the assured were not bound to contribute to the expenses of docking her merely because they took advantage of her position in dock and had her surveyed.

But in *Marine Insurance Co v China Transpacific SS Co*[5] a vessel was docked for the owner's purposes, and damage was discovered for which the insurers were liable. This damage was repaired while the ship was in dock. It was held that the dock expenses were to be apportioned.

Consequential damage

The insurer is not liable for any other consequences of the damage. Thus, an insurer on hull and machinery has been held not liable to pay the cost of removing a putrid cargo;[6] and in another case he was held not liable for damages for loss in consequence of the detention of the vessel during repairs.[7]

Bottom treatment

Clause 15 of the Institute Time Clauses (Hulls)[8] and clause 13 of the Institute Voyage Clauses (Hulls)[9] each state that in no case shall a claim be allowed in respect of scraping, gritblasting and/or other surface preparation or painting of the vessel's bottom except that:

  i gritblasting and/or other surface preparation of new bottom plates ashore and supplying and applying any 'shop' primer to them;

---

[4] [1900] AC 6. See also, *The Acanthus* [1902] P 17; *The Haversham Grange* [1905] P 307.
[5] (1886) 11 App Cas 573.
[6] *Field SS Co v Burr* [1899] 1 QB 579.
[7] *Shelbourne & Co v Law Investment and Insurance Corpn* [1898] 2 QB 626.
[8] These clauses are set out in Appendix III, pp 533–540, post.
[9] These clauses are set out in Appendix III, pp 540–547, post.

ii gritblasting and/or other surface preparation of
  a the butts or area of plating immediately adjacent to any renewed or refitted plating damaged during the course of welding and/or repairs,
  b areas of plating damaged during the course of fairing, either in place or ashore; and
iii supplying and applying the first coat of primer/anti-corrosive to the particular areas mentioned above.

are allowed as part of the reasonable cost of repairs in respect of bottom plating damaged by an insured peril.

Wages and maintenance

The crew's wages cannot be recovered as part of the cost of the repairs.[10]

Clause 16 of the Institute Time Clauses (Hulls)[11] and clause 14 of the Institute Voyage Clauses (Hulls)[12] each state:

> '*Wages and maintenance*
> No claim shall be allowed, other than in general average, for wages and maintenance of the Master, Officers and Crew, or any member thereof, except when incurred solely for the necessary removal of the Vessel from one port to another for the repair of damage covered by the Underwriters, or for trial trips for such repairs, and then only for such wages and maintenance as are incurred whilst the Vessel is under way.'

Surveyor's fees

Reasonable fees for classification and other surveyors are allowable as part of the cost of the repairs.[13]

Maximum amount of indemnity

When a vessel has been repaired, the indemnity given to the assured cannot exceed the sum insured.

Thus, in *Goole and Hull Steam Towing Co Ltd v Ocean Marine Insurance Co Ltd*[14] a vessel was insured for £4,000. She was involved in a collision and the cost of repairing her amounted to £5,000. MacKinnon J, held that any expenditure over £4,000 could not be recovered from the insurers, and observed:[15]

> 'Now the insured vessel suffered a partial loss by way of particular average damage; therefore, in respect of that partial loss the underwriters in proportion to their subscriptions under s 69(1) were liable for the reasonable cost of repairing the damage less the customary deductions which in this case are excluded, because there are clauses saying that there shall be no deduction of thirds, but not exceeding the sum insured in respect of any one casualty. If the insured in fact spends as a reasonable cost of repairs more than the insured amount of £4,000, then that excess he has to bear himself, it is to be noted, not as a sum in respect of which he is his own insurer under s 81, but as an expenditure by him outside any insurance calculation at all.'

---

[10] *Robertson v Ewer* (1786) 1 Term Rep 127; *De Vaux v Salvador* (1836) 4 Ad&El 420; *Helmville Ltd v Yorkshire Insurance Co Ltd, The Medina Princess* [1965] 1 Lloyd's Rep 361, QBD (Com Ct) at 523 (per Roskill J).
[11] These clauses are set out in Appendix III, pp 533–540, post.
[12] These clauses are set out in Appendix III, pp 540–547, post.
[13] *Agenoria SS Co Ltd v Merchants Marine Insurance Co Ltd* (1903) 8 Com Cas 212; *Helmville Ltd v Yorkshire Insurance Co Ltd, The Medina Princess*, supra at 523 (per Roskill J).
[14] (1927) 29 LlL Rep 242, KBD.
[15] Ibid, at 244.

2 Where the ship has been only partially repaired

Section 69 of the Marine Insurance Act 1906 states:

> 'Where a ship is damaged, but is not totally lost, the measure of indemnity, subject to any express provision in the policy, is as follows:
> (2) Where the ship has been only partially repaired, the assured is entitled to the reasonable cost of such repairs, computed as above, and also to be indemnified for the reasonable depreciation, if any, arising from the unrepaired damage, provided that the aggregate amount shall not exceed the cost of repairing the whole damage, computed as above.'

3 Where the ship has not been repaired and has not been sold

Section 69 of the Act states:

> 'Where a ship is damaged, but is not totally lost, the measure of indemnity, subject to any express provision in the policy, is as follows:
> (3) Where the ship has not been repaired and has not been sold in her damaged state during the risk, the assured is entitled to be indemnified for the reasonable depreciation arising from the unrepaired damage, but not exceeding the reasonable cost of repairing such damage computed as above.'

In the case of a voyage policy Devlin J, in *Irvin v Hine*[16] expressed the view that the risk terminated when the insured vessel was abandoned by the assured in circumstances and in language which made it clear that he did not intend to pursue the voyage to its destination. His Lordship added:[17]

> 'Neither side expressly accepted this view, but likewise neither actively dissented from it, and both sides addressed me on the assumption that the case fell within s 69(3). I think that assumption is correct: see *Arnould on Marine Insurance*, 12th edn, Vol 1, p 703, s 504.'

In the case of a time policy the time at which the measure of indemnity under s 69(3) of the Marine Insurance Act 1906 falls to be determined is the time when the policy expires.[18]

Thus, in *Helmville Ltd v Yorkshire Insurance Co, The Medina Princess*,[19] Roskill J, said:[20]

> 'Sub-section (3) is silent as to the point of time at which the measure of indemnity is to be ascertained and quantified. But I think that help is to be derived from the opening words of the sub-section namely,
> "Where the ship has not been repaired, and has not been sold in her damaged state during the risk . . ."
> The ship may be repaired at any time after the casualty and during the risk. If she is then wholly repaired, sub-s (1) operates. If she is then partly repaired, sub-s (2) operates. But if "during the risk" which I construe as meaning "during the period between the casualty and the expiry of the policy whether by effluxion of time or otherwise" she is neither repaired nor sold, then sub-s (3) comes into operation. Until the moment when the risk expires, the ship might be repaired or indeed might be sold. The section is silent as to the position if the ship is sold unrepaired and I need not trouble with that contingency. But it is only when the risk is ended that it can be predicted for certain that neither repair nor sale will take place during the risk. That, in my judgment, is the moment at which sub-s (3) operates and requires that the measure of indemnity shall be ascertained and quantified.'

---

[16] [1949] 2 All ER 1089, KBD.
[17] Ibid, at 1092.
[18] *Helmville Ltd v Yorkshire Insurance Co Ltd, The Medina Princess* [1965] 1 Lloyd's Rep 361, QBD (Com Ct).
[19] [1965] 1 Lloyd's Rep 361, QBD (Com Ct).
[20] Ibid, at 516.

In *Irvin v Hine*,[1] a vessel was damaged and the repairs to her, if they had been carried out, would have amounted to £4,620. The agreed value of her in the policy was £9,000, but her true undamaged value was only £2,000. Her damaged value was £685. The assured contended that, in order to calculate 'the reasonable depreciation arising from the unrepaired damage', the true damaged value must be subtracted from the agreed undamaged value. The insurer, on the other hand, maintained that (i) the true damaged value must be subtracted from her true undamaged value, i e the assured's claim would be limited to £1,315, or (ii) the extent to which the ship had depreciated in value should be ascertained by a comparison between her true undamaged value and her true damaged value, i e approximately two-thirds, and then this proportion should be applied to her agreed value, thus arriving at a figure of about £6,000.

Devlin J, did not accept the first submission of the insurer, but did not express an opinion as to whether the argument of the assured should be preferred to the alternative submission of the insurer, and said:[2]

> 'I do not accept the first of these contentions. Section 27(3) provides that the value fixed by the policy is conclusive of the insurable value of the subject intended to be insured, whether the loss be total or partial. Consequently, I think that, unless the defendant's alternative contention is right, the effect of s 69(3) is that the true damaged value must be subtracted from the conventional undamaged value. This is, indeed, what was contended on behalf of the plaintiff. It produces a figure of over £8,000. It is unnecessary for me to decide whether this contention of the plaintiff is to be preferred to the alternative contention of the defendant, for both methods produce a figure higher than that which I have taken as the cost of repairs, and there is no doubt that the latter figure is overriding.'

Section 69(3) of the Marine Insurance Act 1906 requires the measure of indemnity to be quantified on the basis of what it would have cost to repair the vessel if the repairs had been carried out.[3]

Thus, in *Helmville Ltd v Yorkshire Insurance Co Ltd, The Medina Princess*[4] a vessel grounded at Djibouti and became a partial loss. The cost of towing her from there to Karachi, where repairs could have been carried out, would have been £14,560. It was held that this sum was recoverable as part of the partial loss claim, even though the cost of towing was not, in fact, incurred, since the vessel was never repaired.

Roskill J, said:[5]

> 'It follows that on my findings of fact, towage from Djibouti to Karachi would have been necessary in order to repair the ship. I accordingly hold that the sum of £14,560 which I have found to be the cost of towage is recoverable under the policy as part of the plaintiffs' partial loss claim. That the plaintiffs have not incurred that expenditure is irrelevant. Section 69(3)

---

[1] [1949] 2 All ER 1089, KBD.
[2] Ibid, at 1093. His Lordship said that it was also unnecessary for him to find any figure for the true undamaged value of the vessel, but said that he considered that it was best approached by endeavouring to put a figure on the market value of the vessel in 1942, if she had been in good condition, and then by deducting from it the probable cost of her refitting. He thought that her market value was £9,000 or £10,000, and assessed the cost of refitment at about £3,000. For the method of calculating the measure of indemnity in an American case where a vessel had not been repaired, see *Compania Maritima Astra SA v Archdale, The Armar* [1954] 2 Lloyd's Rep 95 (New York Supreme Court).
[3] *Helmville Ltd v Yorkshire Insurance Co Ltd, The Medina Princess* [1965] 1 Lloyd's Rep 361, QBD (Com Ct).
[4] [1965] 1 Lloyd's Rep 361, QBD (Com Ct).
[5] Ibid, at 521.

requires the measure of indemnity to be quantified on the basis of what it would have cost to repair if the repairs had been carried out.'

In *Irvin v Hine*,[6] where a vessel damaged in 1942 could not have been repaired until 1947, Devlin J, stressed the need for an accurate estimate for repairing the damage and said:[7]

> 'The plaintiff's figures were taken as the cost of repairs in 1946, and I was invited by the defendant to deduct the appropriate percentage so as to reduce them to a 1942 basis. I think this contention is unsound. In estimating the cost of repair for the purpose of a partial loss, I think that the court has to get as near as possible to the actual figure which would have been expended had she been repaired, and, if it be proved to my satisfaction, as it is, that she could not have been repaired earlier than the early part of 1947, I think I ought to take the figures appropriate to that time.'

Clause 18 of the Institute Time Clauses (Hulls)[8] states:

i the measure of indemnity in respect of claims for unrepaired damage is the reasonable depreciation in the market value of the vessel at the time that the insurance terminates arising from such unrepaired damage, but not exceeding the reasonable cost of repairs;
ii in no case are the insurers liable for unrepaired damage in the event of a subsequent total loss (whether or not covered by the policy) sustained during the period covered by the policy or any extension of it; and
iii the insurers are not liable in respect of unrepaired damage for more than the insured value at the time the policy terminates.

Clause 16 of the Institute Voyage Clauses (Hulls) is to the same effect.[9]

4 Where the ship has not been repaired and is sold

In *Pitman v Universal Marine Insurance Co*[10] a vessel was insured under a time policy, and was valued at £3,700. During the currency of the risk she grounded while passing up the river to the port of Moulmein. She remained aground for 4 days, and was then towed into port. The assured decided not to repair her, sold her and her stores for £3,897, and claimed for a partial loss.

The Court of Appeal[11] held by a majority that the measure of indemnity was the estimated cost of repairs less the usual deduction in value of the vessel as ascertained by the sale.

Cotton LJ, observed:[12]

> 'I am of opinion that the estimated cost of repairs, less the usual allowance of one-third new for old, is not, under all circumstances, the sum which the insured is to recover. Where, as in the present case, there is not a constructive total loss, he is not, as against the insurers, entitled to sell so as to bind them by the loss resulting therefrom; but, when he elects to take this course, as in the present case, he, as against himself, fixes his loss; that is, he cannot, as against the underwriters, say that the depreciation of the vessel exceeds that which is ascertained by the result of the sale. Probably the most accurate way of stating the measure of what, under such circumstances, he is to recover, is that it will be the estimated cost of repairs, less the usual deduction, not exceeding the depreciation in value of the vessel as ascertained by the sale. It was urged that the Judge in the court below had no sufficient evidence of what was the value of the vessel at Moulmein in its undamaged state. But this objection cannot, I think, be

---

[6] [1949] 2 All ER 1089, KBD.
[7] Ibid, at 1092.
[8] These clauses are set out in Appendix III, pp 533–540, post.
[9] These clauses are set out in Appendix III, pp 540–547, post.
[10] (1882) 46 LT 863, CA.
[11] Jessel MR, and Cotton LJ; Brett LJ, dissenting.
[12] (1882) 46 LT at 865.

sustained; and, as he found that this value was the same as that of the vessel at the commencement of the risk, the question as to the proper mode of estimating from the sale the depreciation of the vessel does not, I think, arise.'

Jessel MR, delivered a concurring judgment.[13]

Brett LJ, however, in a dissenting judgment said that the measure of indemnity should be the estimated cost of repairs less the usual deductions, and observed:[14]

'A ship damaged in some distant port, though she can there be repaired, cannot be replaced by the purchase of another ship at home; the business inconvenience to the shipowner, i e the loss in his business, can only be met by repairing the ship so as to make her as good a carrying machine as she was before. That is the object he desires to attain by the insurance. The loss he desires to cover, and which the underwriter knows he desires to cover, is therefore the cost of repairs, not the diminution in value of the ship to sell. The cost of repairs is, therefore, the matter to be indemnified. The loss in value to sell is not the loss against which the shipowner insured. The injury to or loss by a sale is no more within the purview of the contract of insurance on ship than is the loss of market in the case of an insurance on goods. Loss or gain by a sale of the ship is therefore not a matter to be considered between the assured and the underwriter in adjusting either a total or a partial loss on ship. This seems to me the reasoning by which all writers on insurance, and all Judges who have dealt with insurance, have laid down the one and sole rule which they have laid down for the adjustment for a partial or average loss on ship.'

E PROCEDURE FOR ASCERTAINING AMOUNT PAYABLE

The procedure for ascertaining the amount payable in the case of a partial loss of a ship is usually set out in the policy. Thus, there are special provisions relating to the necessity of notice[15] of damage being given to the insurers, and the right of the insurers to choose the port of repair, and to take tenders for the repair of the vessel.

Clause 10 of the Institute Time Clauses (Hulls)[16] and clause 8 of the Institute Voyage Clauses (Hulls)[17] each refer to 'Notice of Claim and Tenders' and state that:

    i in the event of accident whereby loss or damage may result in a claim under the policy notice must be given to the insurers prior to survey, and also if the vessel is abroad, to the nearest Lloyd's Agent so that a surveyor may be appointed to represent the insurers should they so desire;

    ii the insurers are entitled to decide the port to which the vessel is to proceed for docking or repair and have a right of veto concerning a place of repair or a repairing firm;

    iii the insurers may also take tenders or may require further tenders to be taken for the repair of the vessel; and

    iv in the event of failure to comply with the conditions mentioned above a deduction of 15 per cent must be made from the amount of the ascertained claim.

---

[13] (1822) 46 LT at 865.
[14] Ibid, at 868.
[15] As to notice of loss, see further, Ivamy, *General Principles of Insurance Law* (4th edn, 1979), pp 420–426.
[16] These clauses are set out in Appendix III, pp 533–540, post.
[17] These clauses are set out in Appendix III, pp 540–547, post.

CHAPTER 34

Partial loss of freight

Freight is lost to the carrier by reason of non-delivery of the goods at the port of destination. The liability to pay freight depends on the terms of the bill of lading or charter-party, as the case may be.

But, speaking generally, it may be said that non-delivery of part of the goods, where freight is to be payable on delivery, involves a particular average loss of freight.

The measure of indemnity will depend upon whether:

    A The loss does not amount to the percentage specified in the policy.
    B The loss amounts to the specified percentage.

A LOSSES NOT AMOUNTING TO THE SPECIFIED PERCENTAGE

If the loss falls within the percentage specified in the policy, the assured cannot make any claim at all in the case of a partial loss of freight.

Thus, clause 12 of the Institute Time Clauses (Freight)[1] states:

> '*Franchise*
>
> This insurance does not cover partial loss, other than general average loss, under 3 per cent, unless caused by fire, sinking, stranding[2] or collision with another vessel. Each craft and/or lighter to be deemed a separate insurance if required by the Assured.'

Clause 10 of the Institute Voyage Clauses (Freight)[3] is to similar effect.

B LOSSES AMOUNTING TO THE SPECIFIED PERCENTAGE

Section 70 of the Marine Insurance Act 1906 states:

> 'Subject to any express provision in the policy, where there is a partial loss of freight, the measure of indemnity is such proportion of the sum fixed by the policy, in the case of a valued policy, or of the insurable value, in the case of an unvalued policy, as the proportion of freight lost by the assured bears to the whole freight at the risk of the assured under the policy.'

The standard of comparison in an unvalued policy is the gross freight.

Thus, in *Palmer v Blackburn*[4] freight was insured under an unvalued policy. The ship was lost just before the termination of the voyage. If she had arrived safely, the freight would have been diminished by £699 for wages, pilotage dues, etc, the liability for which ceased on the loss of the ship. It was established

---

[1] These clauses are set out in Appendix III, pp 550–554, post.
[2] For the meaning of stranding, see pp 411–413, ante.
[3] These clauses are set out in Appendix III, pp 555–558, post.
[4] (1822) 1 Bing 61.

that it was customary to settle such losses by paying the gross freight. The court held that the usage must prevail, notwithstanding that the loss gave the assured more than an indemnity.

Again, in *United States Shipping Co v Empress Assurance Corpn*[5] a policy had been effected in respect of freight and/or chartered freight. While discharging cargo during the currency of the policy, the ship stranded and became a constructive total loss. Part of the cargo undischarged became a total loss, and freight was lost in respect of it. It was held that the loss must be adjusted on the gross and not on the net freight, and that the insurer was not entitled to deduct the hire saved by the operation of a cesser clause in the charter-party exempting the charterer from being liable to pay hire during the stranding.[6]

The Institute Clauses

The Institute Time Clauses (Freight)[7] and the Institute Voyage Clauses (Freight)[8] each provide that:

    i the amount recoverable for any claim for loss of freight shall not exceed the gross freight actually lost; and

    ii Where other insurances on freight are current at the time of the loss, all such insurances must be taken into consideration in calculating the liability under the policy, and the amount recoverable under it shall not exceed the rateable proportion of the gross freight lost, notwithstanding any valuation under this or any other insurance.

---

[5] [1907] 1 KB 259.
[6] See also, *The Alps* [1893] P 109, where it was held that, when a loss of time occasioned by any of the perils insured against resulted in a cesser clause coming into operation, and thereby causing a loss of hire, such a loss was recoverable under a policy on chartered freight as a particular average loss; *The Bedouin* [1894] P 1.
[7] Clause 13, The Institute Time Clauses (Freight) are set out in Appendix III, pp 550–554, post.
[8] Clause 11. The Institute Voyage Clauses (Freight) are set out in Appendix III, pp 555–558, post.

CHAPTER 35

Partial loss of goods

Where there is a partial loss of the goods, the insurers are not liable where the policy contains a particular average warranty e g where it exempts them from liability for partial loss unless the vessel carrying the goods is stranded, sunk or burnt.[1]

Where different species of property are insured under one valuation, the valuation may be apportioned.[2]

In general, the measure of indemnity for a partial loss of goods is that set out in the Marine Insurance Act 1906, s 71.[3]

The insurer is always liable for 'salvage charges' and expenses incurred under the 'sue and labour' clause.[4]

A PARTICULAR AVERAGE WARRANTIES

The policy may contain a particular average warranty, which exempts the insurer from liability in the case of a partial loss unless the vessel be stranded, sunk or burnt.

Grounding

In *Wait and James v British and Foreign Marine Insurance Co*[5] a cargo of middlings was insured for a voyage from Buenos Aires to Avonmouth. The policy covered perils of the seas, and was expressed to be 'free from particular average unless the ship stranded'. It also contained a clause which stated:

> 'Grounding in the River Plate . . . not to be deemed a stranding unless it can reasonably be supposed to have caused or led up to the damage claimed for.'

The vessel grounded in the River Plate, and had to be repaired at Rio. Later she experienced heavy weather, and her ventilators had to be closed. On arrival at Avonmouth it was discovered that her cargo had been damaged by moisture.[6] The assured claimed for a partial loss under the policy.

Roche J, held that the claim failed, for, on the evidence, the plaintiffs had failed to show that the grounding could 'reasonably be supposed to have caused or led up to the damage claimed for'. He observed:[7]

---

[1] See pp 429–432, post.
[2] See p 432, post.
[3] See pp 432–436, post.
[4] See p 436, post.
[5] (1921) 9 LlL Rep 518 at 552, KBD.
[6] As to the evidence, see ibid, at 553–554.
[7] Ibid, at 554.

'I do not think I can, as I said to [Counsel], for philosophical or logical reasons treat "leading or led up to" as meaning the same as "caused" and therefore I think I must take this view. There is something short of proof positive, a something which one cannot take as established against the defendants, yet which may be said to be ground for an opinion at any rate which you may think as probable from the evidence, although you cannot be sufficiently sure of it to say it is proved. I think, although it is very difficult to express the idea, that what was meant by the people who framed these words was that they were anxious to start clear of having a technical effect given to the word "stranding"; that if this stranding was to be considered in connection with the damage, it was to be where there was a real probability that it was the cause of such damage: something of that kind—though it was not practically put in those words—and then if that were so, the claim was to be allowed. I think I may suggest something of that kind. I do not like going upon principles so confused, but I must try and do so. Giving effect to them I am unable to say that the stranding is reasonably supposed to have caused or led up to the damage here, even in the remote cause that there was delay causing the ship to run into a storm, that things cropped up that led in a sense to the ship's stranding, and something happened that reasonably and proximately was the cause of damage.'

Deckload

In *G H Renton & Co Ltd v Cornhill Insurance Co Ltd*[8] a quantity of timber was insured under a policy which stated that the risk attached from the time the goods left the shippers' warehouse. It covered loss by perils of the sea, and incorporated the Timber Trade Federation Insurance Clauses. Clause 1 of these stated:

> 'Each craft or raft or deckload or bill of lading or deckload of each bill of lading to be deemed a separate insurance if required by assured.'

Clause 12 stated:

> 'Deckload warranted free from particular average unless the vessel or craft be stranded, sunk or burnt.'

The practice of loading timber as Mesane was carried on by means of lighters. After the timber insured was in lighters and about to be loaded on to the vessel, part of it was damaged by perils of the sea. The insurers refused to pay for the damage on the ground that it was a loss which fell within clause 12.

Roche J, held that the insurers were liable. The combined effect of clauses 1 and 12 was to make the particular average warranty apply only in case of damage sustained by cargo as a deckload. Although the damaged cargo subsequently formed part of a deckload, the assured were entitled to recover.

His Lordship observed:[9]

> 'I think ... that the whole scope of the insurance, including exceptions is to free the underwriters from liability in the case of damage sustained while the goods are deckload and yet to make them liable for damage sustained while goods are not deckload although they may become deckload at some subsequent period of the voyage.'

Total loss of part

Whether a loss will be treated as a total loss of part or a partial loss of the whole will depend upon the terms of the policy. Generally speaking, unless the part is separately insured and capable of being separately identified by being separately packed, the loss will not be treated as a total loss of part. Thus, s 76(1) of the Marine Insurance Act 1906 states:

[8] (1933) 46 LlL Rep 14, KBD.
[9] Ibid, at 16.

'Where the subject-matter insured is warranted free from particular average, the assured cannot recover for a loss of part, other than a loss incurred by a general average sacrifice, unless the contract contained in the policy be apportionable; but, if the contract be apportionable, the assured may recover for a total loss of any apportionable part.'

In *Hills v London Assurance Corpn*[10] wheat valued at £1,600 was loaded in bulk, and, while water which had been shipped in bad weather was being pumped out, wheat to the value of £75 was pumped out with the water. It was held that the loss could not be claimed as a total loss of a part, and that, since the policy stated that the wheat was 'warranted free from particular average', the insurer was not liable.

A similar decision was reached in *Hedburg v Pearson*[11] in the case of a cargo of sugar where part of each hogshead was saved.

Where, however, the insurance is upon distinct hogsheads or packages which are separately valued, the loss of one hogshead or package will be a total loss of such hogshead or package.[12]

In *Duff v Mackenzie*[13] it was held that, where the master had insured his 'effects' free from all average, this meant free from particular average as to any one or more of the effects, and did not prevent him from claiming for a total loss on any one article, since the word 'effects' was employed to save the necessity of separately naming each article.[14]

But the mere fact that the articles are separately packed is not by itself sufficient to make the loss of one package a total loss of part, if the valuation is in bulk and the goods are all of the same species.[15]

Further, in *Entwisle v Ellis*[16] in the case of a floating policy 'free from particular average' it was held that a declaration in the form '500 bags of rice per Laidmans at 8s 3d per bag, £206 5s', would not effect this purpose, because it was made after the policy was issued.

But in *General Insurance Co Ltd of Trieste v Royal Exchange Assurance*,[17] where there was a reinsurance policy 'free of all average' subject to the terms, etc, of the original policy, which made each craft a separate risk, it was held that there was a total loss of part when the ship and cargo were destroyed by fire, although a part of the cargo in lighters was saved.

In *La Fabrique de Produits Chimiques SA v F N Large*[18] two cases of vanillin and one case of caffeine were insured 'at and from London to Brugg (in Switzerland)'. The policy contained a 'warehouse to warehouse' clause.[19] The two cases of vanillin were stolen[20] from the warehouse of the forwarding agents, who had arranged for them to be put on board a vessel bound for Bordeaux, at night whilst it was unattended. The policy was 'free from particular average',

---

[10] (1839) 5 M&W 569.
[11] (1816) 7 Taunt 154.
[12] *Hills v London Assurance Corpn* (1839) 5 M&W 569.
[13] (1857) 3 CBNS 16.
[14] See also, *Wilkinson v Hyde* (1858) 3 CBNS 30, where a similar decision was reached in the case of a policy on an emigrant's equipment insured against total loss only.
[15] *Ralli v Janson* (1856) 6 E&B 422.
[16] (1857) 2 H&N 549.
[17] (1897) 2 Com Cas 144. See also, *Spence v Union Marine Insurance Co* (1868) LR 3 CP 427.
[18] (1922) 13 LlL Rep 269, KBD.
[19] Now known as the 'transit' clause. See pp 122–126.
[20] As to whether this constituted a 'theft' for the purpose of a policy containing a 'warehouse to warehouse' clause, see pp 152–153.

and when a claim was made under it, the insurer repudiated liability on the ground that the loss was a particular average one.

Bailhache J, held that this defence failed. The loss was not a particular average loss of the whole of the goods, but was a total loss of the goods which were stolen, i e the two cases of vanillin. Not only were the goods of a different species but they were separately valued.

His Lordship observed:[1]

'It has been held, even though the species are the same, yet if contained in cases or packages which are themselves separately valued, that the loss of one of these packages is a total loss of that package, and not a particular average loss of the whole. In this case not only are the goods of different species—the two cases lost being vanillin and the one left being caffeine—but, as a matter of fact, each case has a separate value attributed to it. It is true that the insurance is for a whole sum of £1,100, but that £1,100 is merely an addition of three separate items.

It seems to me in this case not only are the goods of different species, which of itself would be sufficient, but they are separately valued. That is a double reason for saying that the loss was not a particular average loss of the whole of the goods, but was a total loss of the particular goods which were stolen, viz, the two cases of vanillin.'

B APPORTIONMENT OF VALUATION

Sometimes different species of property are insured under one valuation, and the valuation must be apportioned over the different species.

Section 72(1) of the Marine Insurance Act 1906 states:

'Where different species of property are insured under a single valuation, the valuation must be apportioned over the different species in proportion to their respective insurable values,[2] as in the case of an unvalued policy.[3] The insured value of any part of a species is such proportion of the total insured value of the same as the insurable value of the part bears to the insurable value of the whole ascertained in both cases as provided by this Act.'

Section 72(2) states:

'Where a valuation has to be apportioned, and particulars of the prime cost of each separate species, quality, or description of goods cannot be ascertained, the division of the valuation may be made over the net arrived sound values of the different species, qualities, or descriptions of goods.'

In this connection Rule E3 of the Rules of Practice of the Association of Average Adjusters states:

'That where different qualities or descriptions of cargo are valued in the policy at a lump sum, such sum shall, for the purpose of adjusting claims, be apportioned on the invoice values where the invoice distinguishes the separate values of the said different qualities or descriptions; and over the net arrived sound values in all other cases.'

C CALCULATING THE MEASURE OF INDEMNITY

In general, the measure of indemnity is calculated in accordance with s 71 of the Marine Insurance Act 1906.

---

[1] (1922) 13 LlL Rep 269 at 270.
[2] As to insurable value, see pp 97–100, ante.
[3] As to unvalued policies, see pp 97–100, ante.

This section concerns

1 the total loss of a part of the goods.
2 damage to the whole or part of the goods.

1 Total loss of part of goods

The measure of indemnity will depend on whether the goods are insured under a valued policy[4] or an unvalued policy.[5]

a Valued policy

Section 71 states:

> 'Where there is a partial loss of goods, merchandise, or other movables,[6] the measure of indemnity, subject to any express provision in the policy is as follows:
> (1) Where part of the goods, merchandise, or other movables insured by a valued policy is totally lost, the measure of indemnity is such proportion of the sum fixed by the policy as the insurable value of the part lost bears to the insurable value of the whole, ascertained as in the case of an unvalued policy.'

b Unvalued policy

Section 71 states:

> 'Where there is a partial loss of goods, merchandise, or other movables, the measure of indemnity, subject to any express provision in the policy, is as follows:
> (2) Where part of the goods, merchandise, or other moveables insured by an unvalued policy is totally lost, the measure of indemnity is the insurable value of the part loss, ascertained as in the case of total loss.'

2 Damage to whole or part of the goods

Section 71 states:

> 'Where there is a partial loss of goods, merchandise, or other movables, the measure of indemnity, subject to any express provision in the policy, is as follows:
> (3) Where the whole or any part of the goods or merchandise insured has been delivered damaged at its destination, the measure of indemnity is such proportion of the sum fixed by the policy, in the case of a valued policy, or of the insurable value in the case of an unvalued policy, as the difference between the gross sound and damaged values at the place of arrival bears to the gross sound value.'

In *Whiting v New Zealand Insurance Co*[7] a consignment of paper hats was found to be damaged on arrival at the port of discharge. Roche J, held that the assured was entitled to recover under his policy the difference between the estimated sound arrival value (which, since the market price had fallen, was less than the assured's selling price) and the damaged value.

---

[4] As to valued policies, see pp 93–97, ante.
[5] As to unvalued policies, see pp 97–100, ante.
[6] 'Movables' means 'any movable tangible property, other than the ship, and includes money, valuable securities, and other documents': Marine Insurance Act 1906, s 90. See, e g *Baring Bros & Co v Marine Insurance Co* (1894) 10 TLR 276 (postal packet containing stock certificates); *The Pomeranian* [1895] P 349 (live cattle); *Sleigh v Tyser* [1900] 2 QB 333 (live cattle).
[7] (1932) 44 LlL Rep 179, KBD. The case also concerned 'inherent vice' in the goods, but Roche J, held that this had not been established by the insurers, but that the goods had been damaged by an external cause. As to this aspect of the case, see p 252, ante.

The learned Judge observed:[8]

> 'There is really no dispute about the proper measure which governs the case. It is under s 71(3) of the Marine Insurance Act 1906, the difference between the gross sound and the damaged values of the goods in question. I think that means at the place and time of arrival. Of course, the price at the time of arrival may not be able to be gauged by any immediate testing of the market, but I think it means market or other value of the goods at that place and time. The question is what that value was. It is really not contended that the fact that [the assured] had sold these goods at 25s 6d a dozen if they had been sound fixes the sound arrived value. Indeed, it is obvious that it cannot, because that is a matter of which the underwriter cannot have knowledge and with which he had nothing to do. If [the assured] could have replaced these goods with sound goods at a lower price, that would be evidence of sound arrived value. I am satisfied that [the assured] did during discussions of the matter indicate quite truly that the market had fallen considerably, and that 25s 6d was not the sound arrived value at the time. On the other hand, the difference between the sound arrived value and the damaged value, which was 12s, was somewhere between 9s and 9s 6d. If my arithmetic is correct, that will result in a sum of £400, representing the difference between sound arrived value and damaged value.'

Meaning of 'gross value'

Section 71(4) of the Marine Insurance Act 1906 states:

> ' "Gross value" means the wholesale price, or, if there be no such price, the estimated value, with, in either case, freight, landing charges, and duty paid beforehand; provided that in the case of goods or merchandise customarily sold in bond, the bonded price is deemed to be the gross value. "Gross proceeds" means the actual price obtained at a sale where all charges on sale are paid by the sellers.'

The comparison must be of gross values without deductions—i e the values must be inclusive of freight, duty, sale, or other charges falling on the buyers before delivery.

The reason for this is that if a is the gross value of damaged goods, and b is the gross value of sound goods, and n represents deductions for freight, charges, and duty upon goods, then these charges must be deducted from both the sound and damaged values, and there will be no true comparison, for the ratio between the net values is different from that between the gross values.

For $\frac{a}{b}$ is greater than $\frac{a-n}{b-n}$ by $\frac{n(b-a)}{b(b-n)}$, and this difference will rise or fall with the value of n, so that the liability of the insurer will depend upon the greater or less value of the freight, charges, and duty, which are not matters connected with the damage to goods and may not even be payable in respect of the goods at the date of the damage.

Immateriality of rise and fall of the market

The loss must be estimated quite irrespective of the rise or fall in the market at the port of destination. 'If speculative destinations of the merchant, and the success of such speculations, were to be regarded, it would introduce the greatest injustice and inconvenience. The underwriter knows nothing of them.'[9]

---

[8] (1932) 44 LlL Rep 179 at 180.
[9] *Lewis v Rucker* (1761) 2 Burr 1167 at 1173 (per Lord Mansfield CJ).

The rule laid down in *Lewis v Rucker*[10] is stated in the words of Lord Mansfield CJ:[11]

> 'The defendant [underwriter] takes the proportion of the difference between sound and damaged at the port of delivery, and pays that proportion upon the value of the goods specified in the policy, and has no regard to the price in money which either the sound or the damaged goods bore in the port of delivery. He says the proportion of the difference is equally the rule, whether the goods come to a rising or a falling market. For instance, suppose the value in the policy £30; they are damaged but sell for £40; if they had been sound, they would have sold for £50—the difference is a fifth; the insurer, then, must pay a fifth of the prime cost, or value in the policy—that is, £6. E converso, if they come to a losing market and sell for £10 being damaged, but would have sold for £20[12] if sound, the difference is one-half; the insurer must pay half the prime cost, or value in the policy—that is, £15.'

The rule was again considered in *Johnson v Sheddon*,[13] and Lawrence J, in giving the judgment of the court, said that the rule was that laid down by Lord Mansfield, and that in addition to non-liability for fluctuations in the market, the insurer was not responsible for any loss which might be the consequence of port duties or charges after the arrival of the goods at the port of destination. The calculation must therefore be based on gross, and not upon net, proceeds.

The subject was again discussed in *Usher v Noble*[14] before Lord Ellenborough CJ, where the question to be determined was how to ascertain the measure of damage done to goods insured under an unvalued policy. Lord Ellenborough applied the rule laid down in *Lewis v Rucker*[15] which was a case on a valued policy, to goods covered by an unvalued policy, and held that the proportion of loss was to be ascertained by comparing the selling values of sound and damaged goods at the port of destination, and applying the proportion so ascertained to the insurable value of the goods.

Cost of reconditioning goods

The cost of making the goods suitable for sale must not be taken into account in considering the question of indemnity. But the assured may recover the cost of reconditioning them from the insurer under the 'sue and labour' clause.[16]

Liability for loss on freight or profits

The insurer on goods is not liable for loss on freight or profits, however occasioned.

One result of the rule of basing the computation of a loss under an unvalued policy on the insurable value of the goods is to throw on the assured on goods the full liability for freight and port charges in respect of those which arrive in a damaged state.

But as Benecke points out:[17]

> 'The only means to obtain a full indemnity in every case is to insure the sum to be paid for

---

[10] (1761) 2 Burr 1167.
[11] Ibid, at 1169.
[12] The report says £30, but this is obviously a printer's error, for £30 would not be the price in a losing market.
[13] (1802) 2 East 581.
[14] (1810) 12 East 639.
[15] Supra.
[16] *Francis v Boulton* (1895) 1 Com Cas 217. As to the 'sue and labour' clause see pp 442–452, post.
[17] *Principles of Indemnity*, p 22.

freight and charges at the port of delivery independently of the goods, and if the proprietor of these should wish for an indemnity also upon the eventual frustration of his profit, to insure the expected profit also separately.'

Goods accidentally mixed

In *Spence v Union Marine Insurance Co*[18] a vessel carried a cargo of cotton in bales consigned to different owners under different bills of lading, all the bales being properly marked for the purposes of identification. The ship was wrecked, and of her cargo—

- (a) 617 bales arrived, some sound, some damaged, but with the marks intact;
- (b) 1,645 arrived damaged, with the marks and means of identification gone;
- (c) 231 were totally lost.

No question arose with reference to class (a); each owner would receive his goods and claim for the damaged bales. With regard to the owners of the cargo contained in classes (b) and (c), the court held that there had been no total loss of class (b), since the goods had arrived in a saleable though damaged state. The owners who had not received all their goods under class (a) were jointly interested in classes (b) and (c) as tenants in common, and their rights were determined by dividing their losses in the two classes in the same proportion as class (b) bore to class (c).

Thus, if x represented the total undelivered to any one merchant, then,

$$\text{The number of bales apportioned as damaged} = \frac{1645x}{1876};$$

$$\text{The number of bales apportioned as lost} = \frac{231x}{1876}.$$

D LIABILITY OF INSURER FOR SALVAGE CHARGES AND PARTICULAR CHARGES

Even where the policy contains a particular average warranty, the insurer still remains liable in respect of 'salvage charges'[19] and 'particular charges'[20] and expenses incurred under the 'sue and labour'[1] clause, for s 76(2) of the Marine Insurance Act 1906 states:

> 'Where the subject-matter is warranted free from particular average, either wholly or under a certain percentage, the insurer is nevertheless liable for salvage charges, and for particular charges and other expenses properly incurred pursuant to the provisions of the suing and labouring clause in order to avert a loss insured against.'

---

[18] (1868) LR 3 CP 427. See also *Buckley v Gross* (1863) 2 B&S 566.
[19] As to 'salvage charges', see pp 192–193, ante.
[20] As to 'particular charges', see p 417, ante.
[1] As to the 'sue and labour' clause, see pp 442–452, post.

CHAPTER 36

General average contribution and salvage charges

Where the subject-matter liable to contribution is insured for its full contributory value, the measure of indemnity is the full amount of the general average contribution which has been paid or is payable.

Thus, s 73(1) of the Marine Insurance Act 1906 states:

> 'Subject to any express provision in the policy, where the assured has paid, or is liable for, any general average contribution, the measure of indemnity is the full amount of such contribution if the subject-matter liable to contribution is insured for its full contributory value.'

When the contributory interest is under-valued in the policy, or only part of it has been insured, the payment by the insurer will be reduced in proportion to the under-insurance.[1] A further reduction will be made when the interest insured has suffered a particular average loss prior to the general average act, i e the amount of such loss must be deducted from the insured value to fix the high limit liability of the insurer in respect of the general average contribution.

On this point s 73(1) of the Marine Insurance Act 1906 states:

> '... but if such subject-matter be not insured for its full contributory value, or if only part of it be insured, the indemnity payable by the insurer must be reduced in proportion to the under-insurance, and where there has been a particular average loss which constitutes a reduction from the contributory value, and for which the insurer is liable, that amount must be deducted from the insured value in order to ascertain what the insurer is liable to contribute.'

The measure of indemnity in respect of salvage charges[2] is set out in s 73(2) which states:

> 'Where the insurer is liable for salvage charges the extent of his liability must be determined on the like principle.'

Clause 11 of the Institute Time Clauses (Hulls)[3] states that:

   i   the clause covers the vessel's proportion of salvage, salvage charges and/or general average, reduced in respect of any under-insurance, but in case of general average sacrifice of the vessel the assured may recover in respect of the whole loss without first enforcing their right of contribution from other parties; and

   ii no claim under this clause will in any case be allowed where the loss

---

[1] *SS Balmoral Co v Marten* [1901] 2 KB 896.
[2] As to the meaning of 'salvage charges', see pp 192–193, ante.
[3] These clauses are set out in Appendix III, pp 533–540, post.

437

was not incurred to avoid or in connection with the avoidance of a peril insured against.

Clause 9 of the Institute Voyage Clauses (Hulls),[4] clause 11 of the Institute Time Clauses (Freight)[5] and clause 9 of the Institute Voyage Clauses (Freight)[6] are to similar effect.

---

[4] These clauses are set out in Appendix III, pp 540–547, post.
[5] These clauses are set out in Appendix III, pp 550–554, post.
[6] These clauses are set out in Appendix III, pp 555–558, post.

CHAPTER 37

Liabilities to third parties

Section 74 of the Marine Insurance Act 1906 states:

'Where the assured has effected an insurance in express terms against any liability to a third party, the measure of indemnity, subject to any express provision in the policy, is the amount paid or payable by him to such third party in respect of such liability.'

CHAPTER 38

Successive losses

The general rule is that the insurer is liable for successive losses, for s 77(1) of the Marine Insurance Act 1906 states:

> 'Unless the policy otherwise provides, and subject to the provisions of this Act, the insurer is liable for successive losses, even though the total amount of such losses may exceed the sum insured.'

But the insurer is liable for a total loss only where this follows on damage incurred previously but not repaired. On this point s 77(2) of the Act states:

> 'Where under the same policy, a partial loss, which has not been repaired or otherwise made good, is followed by a total loss, the assured can only recover in respect of the total loss:
> Provided that nothing in this section shall affect the liability of the insurer under the suing and labouring clause.'[1]

Thus, if the prior damage has been repaired, the assured is entitled to recover in respect of it even over and above the total loss, unless the repairs were executed on the terms that he should not become personally liable for their cost.[2]

Where there are successive losses not followed by an actual total loss,[3] although producing a constructive total loss,[4] the insurer will be liable to pay for them if the assured elects to repair and not claim for a constructive total loss as he is entitled to do under s 61[5] of the Act, which states:

> 'Where there is a constructive total loss the assured may either treat the loss as a partial loss, or abandon[6] the subject-matter to the insurer and treat the loss as if it were an actual total loss.'

If a total loss is occasioned by a peril which is not one of those insured against, the assured has no claim at all either in respect of the total loss or of a partial loss which has not been repaired.[7]

The legal position as to the liability of the insurer in respect of unrepaired damage followed by a total loss is often expressly stated in the policy.

Thus clause 18 of the Institute Time Clauses (Hulls)[8] states:

---

[1] As to the suing and labouring clause, see pp 442–452, post.
[2] *The Dora Forster* [1900] P 241, where the charterers of the insured vessel paid for the repairs at no cost at all to the assured.
[3] As to actual total loss, see pp 346–361, ante.
[4] As to constructive total loss, see pp 362–377, ante.
[5] As to the effect of a constructive total loss, see pp 375–376, ante.
[6] As to abandonment, see pp 378–396, ante.
[7] *Livie v Janson* (1810) 12 East 648; *British and Foreign Insurance Co v Wilson Shipping Co Ltd* [1921] 1 AC 188, HL.
[8] These clauses are set out in Appendix III, pp 533–540, post.

'*Unrepaired damage*

... In no case shall the Underwriters be liable for unrepaired damage in the event of a subsequent total loss (whether or not covered under this insurance sustained during the period covered by this insurance or any extension[9] thereof.'

Clause 16 of the Institute Voyage Clauses (Hulls)[10] is in the same terms.

---

[9] I e an extension under a 'continuation' clause in the policy. As to 'continuation' clauses, see p 113, ante.
[10] These clauses are set out in Appendix III, pp 540–547, post.

CHAPTER 39

Sue and labour clause

The 'sue and labour' clause takes its name from the clause in the old form of Lloyd's policy,[1] which stated:

> 'And in case of any loss or misfortune it shall be lawful to the assured, their factors, servants and assigns, to sue, labour, and travel for, in and about their defence, safeguards, and recovery of the said goods and merchandises, and ship, etc, or any part thereof, without prejudice to this insurance; to the charges whereof we, the assurers, will contribute each one according to the rate and quantity of his sum herein assured. And it is especially declared and agreed that no acts of the insurer or insured in recovering, saving, or preserving the property insured shall be considered as a waiver or acceptance of abandonment.'

The clause has now been modernised and forms part of the Institute Clauses.[2] It may be conveniently considered

    A generally; and
    B in relation to the Institute Clauses.

A GENERALLY

Section 78(1) of the Marine Insurance Act 1906 provides:

> 'Where the policy contains a suing and labouring clause, the engagement thereby entered into is deemed to be supplementary to the contract of insurance, and the assured may recover from the insurer any expenses properly incurred pursuant to the clause, notwithstanding that the insurer may have paid for a total loss, or that the subject-matter may have been warranted free from particular average, either wholly or under a certain percentage.'

The clause is confined strictly to the cost of efforts made to save the thing insured from damage by the perils insured against in the policy.[3]

Thus, s 78(3) of the Marine Insurance Act 1906 provides:

> 'Expenses incurred for the purpose of averting or diminishing any loss not covered by the policy are not recoverable under the suing and labouring clause.'

Section 78(4) states:

> 'It is the duty of the assured and his agents, in all cases, to take such measures as may be reasonable for the purpose of averting or minimising a loss.'

1 'Factors, servants, and assigns'

The clause only creates the liability when 'the assured, their factors, servants, and assigns' sue and labour. Therefore, unless the persons who sue and labour

---

[1] See pp 101–104, ante.
[2] See pp 104–105, ante.
[3] *Meyer v Ralli* (1876) 1 CPD 358.

come under one or other of these designations, the insurer will not be liable under the clause.

Thus, in *Uzielli v Boston Marine Insurance Co*[4] the insurers on ship reinsured with a French company, which, in turn, reinsured with another company. The last mentioned insurance was in respect of a total loss only, 'to pay as may be paid on the original policy', and incorporated a 'sue and labour' clause. The ship went ashore, and the insurers on ship, after abandonment by her owners, expended large sums in refloating her, and after she had been sold recovered from their reinsurers, who in turn sued the third company. It was held that the latter were not liable to pay under the 'sue and labour' clause since the insurers under the original policy were not the 'factors, servants, or assigns' of the French company.

A salvor rendering services is not regarded as coming within the expression 'factors or servants'.[5]

But this does not exclude the right to claim under the clause salvage expenses which are due for services rendered under a contract in which the rate of payment is fixed.

Thus, s 78(2) of the Marine Insurance Act 1906 states:

> '... salvage charges, as defined by this Act are not recoverable under the suing and labouring clause.'

In this connection s 65(2) states:

> ' "Salvage charges" means the charges recoverable under maritime law by a salvor independently of contract. They do not include the expenses of services in the nature of salvage rendered by the assured or his agents, or any person employed for hire by them, for the purpose of averting a peril insured against. Such expenses, where properly incurred, may be recovered as particular charges or as a general average, according to the circumstances under which they were incurred.'

Accordingly, although ordinary salvage expenses are not recoverable under a 'sue and labour' clause, they may be recovered in most cases as a loss by perils of the sea.[6]

2 Expenses properly incurred

In *Xenos v Fox*[7] it was held that the costs incurred in defending—even successfully—a collision suit were not recoverable under the 'sue and labour' clause, even where the policy contained a 'collision' clause,[8] by which the insurer became liable to indemnify the assured against the payment of damages in case of a collision.

Similarly, in *Dixon v Whitworth*[9] it was held that the costs of a salvage suit were not recoverable under the clause.

Where the policy is not on goods, merchandises, or ships, the 'sue and labour' clause does not necessarily apply.

---

[4] (1884) 15 QBD 11.
[5] *Aitchison v Lohre* (1879) 4 App Cas 755. As to the liability of shipowners to pay in the event of salvage services rendered upon terms agreed upon ending abortively, see *The Renpor* (1883) 8 PD 115. Cf *The Undaunted* (1860) 29 LJPM&A 176; *The Benlarig* (1888) 14 PD 3.
[6] *Aitchison v Lohre* (1879) 4 App Cas 755.
[7] (1869) LR 4 CP 665.
[8] As to the 'collision' clause, see pp 170–176, ante.
[9] (1880) 49 LJQB 408.

Thus, in *Cunard SS Co v Marten*[10] a policy was issued to cover the liability of a shipowner in the case of an omission of a negligence clause in the contract of carriage. It was held that a 'sue and labour' clause had no application.

The cost of refitting a ship is not a charge under the 'sue and labour' clause, although the ship is specially constructed to carry the specific cargo, and any other ship would have been useless for that purpose.[11]

Nor in a policy on goods is the cost, which is incurred in forwarding the goods by other ships owing to the original having become a constructive total loss, recoverable under a 'sue and labour' clause where the goods themselves were in no danger at the time at which the expense was incurred.[12]

Where the policy was on freight insured 'free of particular average', and the subject-matter of the insurance was in danger of being lost by a peril insured against, the cost of averting that danger, by forwarding the goods, was held to be recoverable under a 'sue and labour' clause.[13] Moreover, particular charges, i e the expenses of drying, warehousing and packing, are recoverable under the 'sue and labour' clause in the case of policies on goods, since they are incurred to save the thing insured.[14]

At the same time, the assured must not incur unwarrantable expense, since only the necessary and reasonable expenses will be recoverable. Thus, in *Lee v Southern Insurance Co*[15] a ship was stranded and there was a fair prospect of getting her off and of forwarding the goods in her. It was held that the assured was not allowed the full cost of saving the subject-matter of the insurance, i e freight by sending the goods by railway which was more expensive, but only the estimated cost of forwarding the goods in the same or a similar ship.

It would seem that in all cases the insurer would only be bound to pay reasonable salvage expenses, for owners of interests at stake are themselves only bound to pay such salvage expenses as are in all the circumstances fair and reasonable.[16]

There is no restriction on the form which the expenditure may take as long as it is directed to saving interests in peril at the time the expense is incurred.

Thus, in *The Pomeranian*[17] a policy had been effected on live cattle 'including all risk of shipping, and arising from any cause whatsoever . . . Each animal to be deemed a separate insurance'. The ship's machinery broke down in straining and working in heavy weather, and she had to put into a port of refuge for repairs. It was held that the cost of extra fodder supplied to the cattle during the detention, being an expense incurred to keep them alive and so avert a loss, was recoverable under a 'sue and labour' clause.

In *Wilson Bros Bobbin Co Ltd v Green*[18] a cargo of birch wood was insured for a voyage from Raumo to Garston. The goods were loaded on a Norwegian vessel. The policy was against war risks only and contained a 'sue and labour' clause.

---

[10] [1903] 2 KB 511.
[11] *Dixon v Whitworth*, supra.
[12] *Great Indian Peninsular Rly Co v Saunders* (1862) 2 B&S 266; *Booth v Gair* (1863) 15 CBNS 291.
[13] *Kidston v Empire Marine Insurance Co* (1867) LR 2 CP 357.
[14] *Francis v Boulton* (1895) 1 Com Cas 217.
[15] (1870) LR 5 CP 397.
[16] *Anderson v Ocean SS Co* (1884) 10 App Cas 107; *The Pomeranian* [1895] P 349; *Wilson Bros Bobbin Co Ltd v Green* [1917] 1 KB 860.
[17] [1895] P 349.
[18] (1917) 116 LT 637, KBD.

The vessel sailed in November 1914, and owing to the interference of German warships her master put into Grimstadt, a Norwegian port. The cargo was unloaded and stored there, and was afterwards reshipped to Garston. The assured claimed under the 'sue and labour' clause the expenses incurred. It was held by the King's Bench Division that they were entitled to the cost of the storage until they could with reasonable diligence have secured facilities for reshipment to Garston, and also to the proper cost of reshipping and forwarding the cargo at that date.

Bray J, said:[19]

> 'The goods were at Grimstadt, the port of destination was Garston, and the goods could not be safely got to Garston without incurring the expense of storage at Grimstadt and the cost of reloading and forwarding, and therefore, in my opinion, these were expenses—I will leave out the word "proper" for the moment—incurred in endeavouring to avert that loss. The next question raised by [Counsel] was that the [assured] did not act reasonably; that if they had acted with reasonable diligence, the goods could have been reshipped long before, at a much lower freight, and that they did not take reasonable steps to obtain tonnage as soon as they might have done. Now, I have carefully considered the case, and I am bound to say that I think [Counsel] is right on that point. On the evidence, I think that if the [assured] had acted with reasonable diligence, they could have had a ship ready to load the cargo at Grimstadt by about the middle of April 1915, at a lower rate of freight than they in fact paid.'

In *Scottish Metropolitan Assurance Co Ltd v Groom*[20] the plaintiffs had insured the owners of a vessel against total loss, and reinsured part of their risk with the defendant. The vessel sank in suspicious circumstances, and on a claim made by her owners was found to have wilfully been cast away. The plaintiffs were unable to recover the costs of the action because the owners were insolvent, so they sought to recover them from the defendant on the ground that they were recoverable under the 'sue and labour' clause.

The Court of Appeal[1] held that they were not recoverable under this clause. Bankes LJ, said:[2]

> '[Counsel's] point is that the [assured's] claim is covered by the "sue and labour" clause, which does not contain any provision for payment: but it seems to me that the words of the clause are quite inapt to cover such a claim. I agree that very often in construing documents such as policies of insurance the words are treated as somewhat elastic in order to cover claims which obviously come within the intentions of the parties to such documents; but no one has suggested successfully that such a claim as the present comes within the ordinary language of the "sue and labour" clause; and I certainly am not going to set a precedent by holding that it does. I think, as I have already said, that the words are quite inapt.'

In *St Margaret's Trust Ltd v Navigators and General Insurance Co Ltd*[3] a ketch was insured under a time policy containing a 'sue and labour' clause, which stated:

> 'In the case of misfortune to the insured vessel it shall be lawful to the assured . . . to sue, labour and travel for, in and about the protection, safeguard or repair of the insured vessel, without prejudice to this insurance and all charges thereof including salvage charges, the cost of towing or removing the vessel to a place of safety so necessarily incurred, shall form part of the claim . . .'

---

[19] Ibid, at 639.
[20] (1924) 20 LlL Rep 44, CA.
[1] Bankes, Atkin and Sargant LJJ.
[2] (1924) 20 LlL Rep at 45. The court also held that the plaintiffs had failed to prove either an express or an implied contract that the defendant would bear any share of this particular class of expenditure: ibid, at 45.
[3] (1949) 82 LlL Rep 752, KBD.

The vessel was put on a mud berth at Lymington, and slipped over at low tide. She filled with water on the flood tide. She was left there for a month, and the assured was required by the local harbour authority to raise her and tow her to Pylewell Creek. He did so, and thereby incurred expenses of £87 17s 0d. Morris J, held[4] that this amount could be recovered under the 'sue and labour' clause set out above.

In *Integrated Container Service Inc v British Traders Insurance Co Ltd*[5] intermodal freight containers were insured under a policy containing a 'sue and labour' clause and were leased to a third party. The assured were held to be entitled to an indemnity in respect of the costs incurred in recovering them from the third party who had been adjudged bankrupt.[6]

Standard of proof of reasonableness

In subsequent proceedings[7] in *Integrated Container Service Inc v British Traders Insurance Co Ltd*[8] Eveleigh LJ, had occasion to consider the standard of proof required under the Marine Insurance Act 1906, s 78(1) as to the reasonableness of the expenses.

He said[9] that if the insurers were to have the right under s 78(4)[10] to call on the assured to take all reasonable measures for the purpose of averting or minimising a loss, it could not be right that the insurers should be able to exact from the assured a higher degree of proof than that he acted reasonably for that purpose. There was nothing in the 'sue and labour' clause or the Marine Insurance Act 1906 which required the assured to show that a loss would 'very probably' have occurred. To demand such a high degree of proof would place an assured in a dilemma. He would have to make up his mind whether he could satisfy that burden or do nothing and take the risk that the insurers would be able to show that he should have acted in defence of the goods.

The learned Lord Justice went on to say that s 78(4) seemed to impose a duty to act in circumstances where a reasonable man intent on preserving his property, as opposed to claiming on the insurers, would act. Whether or not the assured could recover should depend on the reasonableness of his assessment of the situation and the action taken by him. It should not be possible for insurers to be able to contend that, on an ultimate investigation and analysis of the facts, a loss, while possible or even probable, was not 'very probable'. As the right to recover expenses was a corollary to the duty to act, the assured should be entitled to recover all extraordinary expenses reasonably incurred. It would be wholly unreasonable to penalise an assured on the basis that, while he had shown that a reasonable man would have done as he did, yet in the light of all that had transpired, the loss would not have been probable. In the vast majority of cases at least the assured would not incur extraordinary expenditure unless he felt it incumbent on him to do so.

---

[4] Ibid, at 766–7.
[5] [1981] 2 Lloyd's Rep 460, QBD (Com Ct).
[6] For subsequent proceedings, see *Integrated Container Service Inc v British Traders Insurance Co Ltd* [1984] 1 Lloyd's Rep 154, CA, where it was held that the expenses which were claimed were reasonable. (See the judgment of Eveleigh LJ, ibid, at 161, and that of Dillon LJ, ibid, at 163.)
[7] [1984] 1 Lloyd's Rep 154, CA.
[8] Supra.
[9] [1984] 1 Lloyd's Rep 154 at 158–159.
[10] See p 442, ante.

3 Necessity for existence of peril

Expenses payable under the 'sue and labour' clause must have been incurred to prevent an impending loss when the subject-matter of the insurance is actually in peril. But if the goods are in safety and undamaged when the expense is incurred, the cost will not be a 'sue and labour' expenditure.[11]

Thus, in *Great Indian Peninsular Rly Co v Saunders*[12] iron rails were shipped at London for Bombay, but the ship met with such heavy weather that she was unable to continue her voyage, and had to put into Plymouth. There the rails were discharged and reshipped in another vessel by her owners at an increased rate of freight to Bombay. But inasmuch as the rails were in safety in the owners' hands when the increased rate of freight was incurred, the extra cost was not a 'sue and labour' expenditure chargeable against the insurers on the rails.

On the other hand, in *Integrated Container Service Inc v British Traders Insurance Co Ltd*[13] the expenses of recovering the intermodal freight containers could be claimed by the assured for, on the evidence,[14] they were not yet free from all the calamities engendered by the event which gave rise to their partial loss.

4 Independent contract

Subject, however, to the condition that the expenses incurred were, in the circumstances, reasonable or inevitable, the 'sue and labour' clause will enable the assured to cover the whole of the charges incurred. He recovers not merely a portion of such expenses proportionate to his interest, but the whole. The reason is that the 'sue and labour' clause is a distinct and independent contract by which the assured may recover even more than the amount underwritten. Of course, on payment, the insurer stands in the place of the assured, and if the assured is entitled to recover a proportion of the 'sue and labour' charges from a third party, the insurer will be subrogated to such rights.[15]

5 Need for peril to be covered by policy

Expenses incurred under the 'sue and labour' clause are only recoverable if they have been incurred for the purpose of averting or diminishing a loss covered by the policy.

In *Weissberg v Lamb*[16] the assured effected an 'all risks' marine insurance policy in respect of the removal of his furniture from Holland to the United Kingdom. Some of the furniture was damaged. The carriers refused to deliver the furniture to him unless they were paid in cash, and the only way he could safeguard and obtain possession of the furniture was by doing so. He paid the

---

[11] *Integrated Container Service Inc v British Traders Insurance Co Ltd* [1984] 1 Lloyd's Rep 154, CA where Eveleigh LJ, said (ibid, at 160): 'In order that the "suing and labouring" clause should cease to apply it is necessary in my opinion for the goods to be restored to the custody and control of the assured to the extent that it could now be said that they were no longer threatened by perils . . . or to put it another way, where it could be said that they were now free from all the calamities engendered by the event which gave rise to their partial loss'.
[12] (1862) 2 B&S 266.
[13] [1984] 1 Lloyd's Rep 154, CA.
[14] See ibid, at 160–161, 163.
[15] *Dixon v Whitworth* (1880) 49 LJQB 408. As to subrogation, see pp 455–460, post.
[16] (1950) 84 LlL Rep 509 (Mayor's and City of London Court).

charges under protest, and sought to recover them under the 'sue and labour' clause in the policy.

Judge A Ralph Thomas held that they were not recoverable, since they were not incurred to prevent a loss for which the insurer would be responsible. There was no evidence of a possible loss for which the insurer would have been liable if the assured had refused to pay the sum demanded. There might have been delay in delivery, but s 55 of the Marine Insurance Act 1906 stated that the insurer was not liable for a loss caused by delay, although the delay was caused by a peril insured against.[17]

In *F W Berk & Co Ltd v Style*[18] kieselguhr[19] packed in bags was insured under a policy covering 'all risks of loss and/or damage from whatsoever cause arising irrespective of percentage'. The bags were defective and burst whilst being transferred from the ship's hold to a lighter. The assured incurred expenditure in rebagging and claimed under the policy.

Sellers J, held that the action failed because the bags were defective on shipment, and that the cost of rebagging was caused by the inherent vice of the goods.[20]

The learned Judge also held that the words 'all risk of loss and/or damage from whatsoever cause arising', restricted as they were by clause 6[1] of the Institute Cargo Clauses (Wartime Extension), did not extend to include the expense of rebagging and were not recoverable as 'sue and labour' charges. Further, the expense incurred was not recoverable under the 'sue and labour' clause because an insurance policy covered a risk, not a certainty, and in this case it was certain that the bags in the condition in which they were on shipment could not safely have contained their contents.

On this point he said:[2]

> 'Clause 6 remains part of the policy, and it is in emphatic terms:
> "This insurance shall in no case be deemed to extend to cover loss damage or expense proximately caused by . . . inherent vice . . ."
> This clause restricts the scope of the clause covering all risks of damage "from whatsoever cause arising", but it is not wholly repugnant to it. Having regard to the established law in the matter, if the [assured] had wished to insure against inherent vice—if indeed they could have done so at any reasonable premium—they should have used specific words to that effect, and at least have had clause 6 or the relevant part of it struck out.
> *British and Foreign Marine Insurance Co Ltd v Gaunt*[3] establishes that the plaintiff in such a case as this must prove that the loss or expense, or the "suing and labouring", was due to an accident or casualty, although not necessarily prove the exact nature of the accident or casualty. I cannot find that there was any accident or casualty. As Lord Sumner pointed out, the policy covers a risk, not a certainty. With the bags in the condition in which these bags must have been, it could be said to be certain that they would not hold their contents in the course of necessary handling and transport, and that if at the end of the sea voyage it was desired to have the kieselguhr in bags, it would be necessary to rebag it. If the underwriters were to be held liable, they would be paying for the cost at the time and place of discharge of putting the goods into bags in the condition in which they ought to have been, but were not, on

---

[17] See generally, pp 247–248, ante.
[18] [1955] 2 Lloyd's Rep 382, QBD.
[19] I e a diatomaceous earth used as an absorbent of nitro-glycerine in the manufacture of dynamite: *Shorter Oxford English Dictionary* (3rd edn, revised 1964), Vol I, p 1084.
[20] As to this point, see p 253, ante.
[1] Clause 6 stated: 'This insurance shall in no case be deemed to extend to cover loss damage or expense proximately caused by delay or inherent vice or nature of the subject-matter insured.'
[2] [1955] 2 Lloyd's Rep 382 at 388.
[3] [1921] 2 AC 41, HL.

shipment. Such cost clearly does not fall within the terms of these two policies of marine insurance.'

Accordingly, the special expenditure incurred in rebagging while in the lighter was due to the inherent vice of the goods.[4]

6 Expenses incurred by the insurers not recoverable

Where the insurer incurs expenses in preserving the property, he cannot recover them from the assured under the 'sue and labour' clause since they were incurred in the interest of the insurer alone.[5]

7 Scope of s 78(4)

What constitutes a breach of duty

The scope of s 78(4) was considered by Lord Sumner in *British and Foreign Marine Insurance Co v Gaunt*,[6] where he observed:[7]

> 'There remains an argument based on the reading of s 78(4) of the Act which is very novel. It is one of the disadvantages of codification that new terms used or even unfamiliar sequences of propositions suggest that the law has been changed where those familiar with the old decisions would not have suspected it. The argument affords a striking instance of this. The section obviously refers to suing and labouring. It cannot possibly be read as meaning that, if the agents of the assured are not reasonably careful throughout the transit, he cannot recover for anything to which their want of care contributes. The point, therefore, fails.'

In *Irvin v Hine*[8] any accurate estimate of the damage to the insured vessel could not be obtained without a survey of her in dry dock, but this was never done. The insurers contended that it was the assured's duty under s 78(4) to cause such a survey to be carried out, and that, because he was in breach of this duty, the claim could not be sustained. In rejecting this argument, Devlin J, said:[9]

> 'Section 78(4) requires an assured to take such measures as may be reasonable for the purpose of averting or minimising a loss. A survey in dry dock in the circumstances of this case would not avert or minimise the loss, but would merely ascertain its extent. Its cost would, I think, be part of the cost incurred by the plaintiff in proving his claim. In so far as the burden of proof lies on him, it may be foolish of him to dispense with the survey, but that is another matter. I do not think he is in breach of any duty under s 78(4).'

In *Astrovlanis Compania Naviera SA v Linard, The Gold Sky*,[10] where a vessel sank off Gibraltar and the assured claimed an indemnity from the insurer in respect of a total loss by perils of the sea, one of the defences[11] pleaded by the insurers was that the assured were in breach of the duty imposed on them by s 78(4), since the master had refused offers of help by a salvage tug which was standing by.

---

[4] [1955] 2 Lloyd's Rep at 388.
[5] *Crouan v Stanier* [1904] 1 KB 87.
[6] [1921] All ER Rep 447, HL.
[7] Ibid, at 458.
[8] [1950] 1 KB 555, [1949] 2 All ER 1089, KBD.
[9] Ibid, at 1092.
[10] [1972] 2 Lloyd's Rep 187, QBD (Com Ct).
[11] The insurers put the assured to strict proof that the vessel had been lost by perils of the sea, and, in the alternative, alleged that she had been scuttled. See p 242, ante.

Mocatta J, held (obiter)[12] that it did not necessarily follow that in the absence of instructions from the owners, the master of a vessel must not be taken to be included within the words 'the assured and his agents' in s 78(4) so that a failure by the master to take such measures as were reasonable would militate against his owners' claim against insurers. The words 'his agents' should in the context and to avoid an acute conflict between s 78(4) and s 55(2)(a) be read as inapplicable to the master or crew, unless expressly instructed by the assured in relation to what to do or not to do in respect of suing and labouring. Many persons other than the masters and members of the crew might be agents of the assured with the duty to act on his behalf in relation to suing and labouring.

His Lordship went on to say that this construction was a rational one which reconciled the operation of the two sub-sections in most cases in which the problem was likely to arise. It also catered for the case of barratry. A possible exception not covered was the case of a master/owner. Negligent navigation by such an assured would not bar his claim under s 55(2)(a),[13] whereas s 78(4) would seem clearly to impose the statutory duty upon him. On the evidence in the present case the master had not been instructed to refuse salvage assistance.[14]

Effect of a breach of duty

While it is not possible to state with certainty all the adverse consequences which will be suffered by an assured who fails to perform his duty under the 'sue and labour' clause, there is no doubt that he incurs a risk of his claim for loss or damage being rejected it if can be shown that he failed to act when he should have done.[15]

8 Position where there is no 'sue and labour' clause

In *Emperor Goldmining Co Ltd v Switzerland General Insurance Co Ltd*[16] a cargo of explosives was insured from the time they left a warehouse at Sydney until they were delivered at Fiji. The policy was an 'all risks' policy, but it did not include a 'sue and labour' clause. The vessel sailed from Sydney, but sprang a leak and had to put back for repairs. The cargo had to be unloaded, and the assured incurred expenses in so doing, and also in storing and reloading it on another vessel. The assured claimed that they were entitled to be indemnified by the insurers, even though there was no 'sue and labour' clause in the policy, for s 84(4) of the (Australian) Marine Insurance Act 1909[17] stated that 'It is the duty of the assured and his agents in all cases to take such measures as may be reasonable for the purpose of averting or minimising a loss', and this was what they had done.

---

[12] [1972] 2 Lloyd's Rep at 221.
[13] *Trinder, Anderson & Co v Thames and Mersey Marine Insurance Co* [1898] 2 QB 114. Section 55(2)(a) states: 'The insurer is not liable for any loss attributable to the wilful misconduct of the assured, but, unless the policy otherwise provides, he is liable for any loss proximately caused by a peril insured against, even though the loss would not have happened but for the misconduct or negligence of the master or crew.' As to this subsection, see pp 232–247, ante.
[14] [1972] 2 Lloyd's Rep at 221.
[15] *Integrated Container Service Inc v British Traders Insurance Co Ltd* [1984] 1 Lloyd's Rep 154 at 157, CA (per Eveleigh LJ).
[16] [1964] 1 Lloyd's Rep 348, Supreme Court of New South Wales (Commercial Causes).
[17] Which corresponds to s 78(4) of the (English) Marine Insurance Act 1906.

Counsel for the insurers contended that the absence of such a standard and well recognised provision as the 'sue and labour' clause pointed to the conclusion that they were not liable. Manning J, giving judgment in the Supreme Court of New South Wales, held that the claim succeeded. He said[18] that the common law was enacted in the Act of 1909. Section 84 dealt with the result which flowed from the inclusion of a 'sue and labour' clause in so far as the extension of the liability of the insurer was concerned. Costs described in the clause were to be recoverable notwithstanding that the insurer had paid for a total loss or that there had been a total or partial warranty of freedom from particular average. His Lordship said that he was unable to read this provision as a duty to be carried out by the assured at his own expense, in the absence of a 'sue and labour' clause in the policy.

By way of comment, it may be suggested that, if the decision is correct, there will no longer be any necessity for a 'sue and labour' clause ever to be included in any policy, for the assured's expenses will always be recoverable provided that they are 'properly' incurred. Again, it is submitted that since sub-ss (1), (2) and (3) of s 84 all expressly mention the presence of the 'sue and labour' clause in the policy, it would be reasonable to suppose that sub-s (4), being part of the same section, is also intended to relate to policies containing such a clause, for if it had not been so meant, the sub-section would have expressly said so, or else there would have been a provision to this effect in a separate section so that the matter would be put beyond doubt.

B THE INSTITUTE CLAUSES

The extent of the duty of the assured and his right to an indemnity under the Sue and Labour clause which is now known as the 'Duty of Assured' clause depends on whether the policy is one on cargo or on hull.

1 Cargo clauses

Clause 16 of the Institute Cargo Clauses (A),[19] (B)[20] and (C)[1] states that:

    i it is the duty of the assured and their servants and agents in respect of any loss recoverable under the policy
        a to take such measures as may be reasonable for the purpose of averting or minimising such loss; and
        b to ensure that all rights against carriers, bailees or other third persons are properly preserved and exercised; and
    ii the insurers will, in addition to any loss recoverable under the policy, reimburse the assured for any charges properly and reasonably incurred in pursuance of those duties.

2 Hull clauses

Clause 13 of the Institute Time Clauses (Hulls)[2] states, in general, that:

---

[18] [1964] 1 Lloyd's Rep at 354.
[19] These clauses are set out in Appendix III, pp 516–519, post.
[20] These clauses are set out in Appendix III, pp 519–522, post.
[1] These clauses are set out in Appendix III, pp 523–526, post.
[2] These clauses are set out in Appendix III, pp 533–540, post.

i in case of any loss or misfortune it is the duty of the assured, their servants and agents to take such measures as are reasonable for the purpose of averting or minimising a loss which would be recoverable under the policy.
ii the insurers will contribute to charges properly and reasonably incurred by the assured, their servants or agents for such measures.
iii General average,[3] salvage charges[4] and collision defence or attack costs are not recoverable under this clause;
iv measures taken by the assured or by the insurers with the object of saving, protecting or recovering the subject-matter insured are not to be considered as a waiver or acceptance of abandonment or otherwise prejudice the rights of either party;
v when expenses are incurred pursuant to this clause, the liability under the policy shall not exceed the proportion of such expenses that the amount insured under it bears to the value of the vessel as stated in the policy or to the sound value of the vessel at the time of the occurrence giving rise to the expenditure if the sound value exceeds that value;
vi when a claim for total loss of the vessel is admitted and expenses have been reasonably incurred in saving or attempting to save the vessel and other property and there are no proceeds or the expenses exceed the proceeds, then the policy bears its pro rata share of such proportion of the expenses or of the expenses in excess of the proceeds, as the case may be, as may reasonably be regarded as having been incurred in respect of the vessel; but if the vessel is insured for less than its sound value at the time of the occurrence giving rise to the expenditure, the amount recoverable under the clause is to be reduced in proportion to the under-insurance;[5] and
vii the sum recoverable under the clause is in addition to the loss otherwise recoverable under the insurance but shall in no circumstances exceed the amount insured under the policy in respect of the vessel.

Clause 11 of the Institute Voyage Clauses (Hulls)[6] is in the same form.

---

[3] As to general average, see pp 182–192, ante.
[4] As to salvage charges, see pp 192–193, ante.
[5] As to under-insurance, see p 405, ante.
[6] These clauses are set out in Appendix III, pp 540–547, post.

PART V

The rights of the insurer on payment

CHAPTER 40

Subrogation[1]

With regard to a total loss, s 79(1) of the Marine Insurance Act 1906 provides:

> 'Where the insurer pays for a total loss, either of the whole, or in the case of goods of any apportionable part, of the subject-matter insured, he thereupon becomes entitled to take over the interest of the assured in whatever may remain of the subject-matter so paid for, and he is thereby subrogated to all the rights and remedies of the assured in and in respect of that subject-matter as from the time of the casualty causing the loss.'

The principle of subrogation also applies in the case of a partial loss. Section 79(2) states:

> 'Subject to the foregoing provisions, where the insurer pays for a partial loss, he acquires no title to the subject-matter insured, or such part of it as may remain, but he is thereupon subrogated to all the rights and remedies of the assured in and in respect of the subject-matter insured as from the time of the casualty causing the loss, in so far as the assured has been indemnified, according to this Act, by such payment for the loss.'

There is no right to subrogation on payment under a p p i policy.

Thus, in *John Edwards & Co v Motor Union Insurance Co Ltd*[2] the insurer issued a p p i time policy on freight to be earned by a chartered vessel. Whilst proceeding to the port of loading, she collided with another vessel, which was found solely to blame. The owners of that vessel limited their liability under the Merchant Shipping Act 1894, and were found liable to pay £416 as damages for loss of hire. The insurers paid the assured the sum insured under the freight policy, viz £5,610, but claimed that under the doctrine of subrogation they were entitled to the £416 due from the owners of the vessel at fault. It was held by the King's Bench Division that they were not so entitled because the freight policy was a p p i policy, and therefore the doctrine of subrogation did not apply.

McCardie J, said:[3]

> 'In my view the essence of the matter is that subrogation springs not from payment only, but from actual payment conjointly with the fact that it is made pursuant to the basic and original contract of indemnity. If then, the right of subrogation rests upon payment under a contract of indemnity, how does the matter stand when the policy of insurance is an honour policy only? In my opinion such a policy is not a contract of indemnity at all. It is the negation of such a contract. I respectfully agree with the statement in Arnould, s 311, that "a wager (or honour) policy may be defined to be one in which the parties, by express terms, disclaim, on the face of it, the intention of making a contract of indemnity". This statement, I think, puts the point forcibly and well.'

---

[1] See further, Ivamy, *General Principles of Insurance Law* (4th edn, 1979), pp 496–513. For a case in which it was held that the French law of subrogation was similar to the English law, see *Schauer v Webster & Co* (1929) 35 LlL Rep 31, KBD.
[2] (1923) 128 LT 276.
[3] Ibid, at 278.

The insurer may, of course, waive the right of subrogation.[4]

Further, the policy may contain an implied term that the insurer will not exercise the right of subrogation.[5]

A THE RIGHTS IN RESPECT OF WHICH SUBROGATION ARISES[6]

The insurer, however, is strictly confined to the rights of the assured, and cannot, by virtue of the doctrine of subrogation, acquire rights which the assured never possessed, e g a right to sue himself when two of his own vessels collide with each other.[7]

He is also restricted to the rights incident to and arising out of the thing insured.

Thus, in *Sea Insurance Co v Hadden*[8] the insured vessel was lost in collision with another ship before the chartered freight was earned. Her owners gave notice of abandonment, and were paid by the insurers for her total loss. It was held that the insurers were not entitled to the benefit of the compensation, which had been received from the owners of the vessel at fault in respect of the loss of freight.

Moreover, the insurer is not entitled to the benefit of a voluntary gift received by the assured unless the gift was made with the intention of reducing the loss insured against.

Thus, in *Burnard v Rodocanachi*[9] a valued policy had been effected on cargo which was destroyed by a warship. The policy included war risks. The United States Government, under an Act of Congress, paid to the assured the difference between the insured value which they had received from the insurers, and the real value of the cargo. The Act under which payment was so made provided that no payment should be made to any party who should then have been paid by an insurer, unless the insurance value should be insufficient

---

[4] See e g *The Marine Sulphur Queen* [1970] 2 Lloyd's Rep 285, District Court, Southern District of New York, where it was alleged that the insurers had waived all rights of subrogation under a clause stating, 'The Assurers hereby agree to waive all rights of subrogation against the steamer and/or the Assured and/or affiliated and/or associated and/or allied companies and/or corporations in the event that the carrying steamer is owned and/or chartered and/or operated by the Assured and/or affiliated and/or associated and/or allied companies and/or corporations', and it was held that the cargo insurers were subrogated to the rights of the assured against the time charterers of the carrying vessel, for the word 'chartered' in the clause set out above meant 'chartered under a demise charter-party'. (See the judgment of Canella DJ, ibid, at 299.) (For subsequent proceedings in the same case, but on a different point, see [1973] 1 Lloyd's Rep 88, US Ct of Appeals, Second Circuit); and *Tenneco Oil Co v Tug Tony and Coastal Towing Corpn* [1972] 1 Lloyd's Rep 514, District Court, Southern District of Texas (Houston Division), where it was held that a clause stating, 'Privilege is granted the assured hereunder to waive subrogation prior to a loss against parties with whom the assured has a working agreement' was not void as being contrary to public policy, and that, on the evidence, the right of subrogation had been waived. (See the judgment of Carl O Bue Jr DJ, ibid, at 516–517.)

[5] *The Yasin* [1979] 2 Lloyd's Rep 45, QBD (Com Ct), where, however, it was held that the policy did not contain such an implied term. (See the judgment of Lloyd J, ibid, at 56.)

[6] See further, Ivamy, op cit, pp 501-515.

[7] *Simpson v Thomson* (1877) 3 App Cas 279; *John Edwards & Co v Motor Union Insurance Co* [1922] 2 KB 249. But see the 'sister ship' clause, pp 171–172, ante.

[8] (1884) 13 QBD 706. See also, *Glen Line Ltd v A-G* (1930) 36 Com Cas 1.

[9] (1882) 7 App Cas 333. See also, *Stearns v Village Main Reef Gold Mining Co* (1905) 10 Com Cas 89.

compensation for the loss. It was held that, having regard to the Act under which payment was made, the insurers were not entitled to recover the compensation so paid.

In *Glen Line Ltd v A-G*[10] Glen Line Ltd insured a vessel, but not her freight, against war risks with the Liverpool & London War Risks Association. On 4 August 1914 the British Government agreed to reinsure the Association against war risks in respect of 80 per cent on vessels insured by the Association. The vessel was at Hamburg on 1 August 1914, and was seized by the German authorities shortly after the outbreak of the First World War. Glen Line Ltd gave notice of constructive total loss to the Association, which accepted the notice of abandonment and paid them £61,753 2s 11d in full settlement of the loss. The vessel was returned to the Association at the end of the war. By the treaty of Versailles it was provided by Art 297(e) that nationals of Allied Powers should be entitled to receive from Germany compensation for damage inflicted on their property in German territory on 1 August 1914, by the application of exceptional war measures. The compensation was to be determined by a Mixed Arbitral Tribunal. The Tribunal awarded Glen Line Ltd £136,699 3s 10d. The British Government claimed that they were entitled to 80 per cent of this sum.

The House of Lords[11] held that the claim failed. The sum awarded by the Tribunal was paid to satisfy a claim which arose once and for all at the time of the loss, and did not enure for the benefit of the Government.

Lord Warrington of Clyffe said:[12]

> 'If I am right in the conclusion at which I have arrived as to the nature of the claim, it is clear that it arose once for all at the time of the loss, and cannot be treated as a series of claims for detention from day to day and therefore enuring for the benefit of the person who was owner at the time of each successive detention—in this case the insurers. It is true that the formal claim before the Tribunal was framed in an unfortunate manner, inasmuch as it alleged that "the claimant, the Glen Line Ltd, is and was prior to the outbreak of war and at all times material to this claim the owner of the steamship 'Glenearn', and claimed for moneys which it would have earned during the period of detention". But I do not think this ought to affect the actual rights of the appellants. If the matter had been fought out, the misstatement of fact might have been corrected.'

The insurers are also entitled to take over what remains of the subject-matter.[13]

Therefore, where the insurer paid the total loss of a ship and she was afterwards recovered, he was held to be entitled to her.[14] So also, where owners whose vessels were captured were granted letters of reprisal, the insurers were entitled to a share in the prizes.[15]

None of these rights will, however, pass to the insurers unless they accept the abandonment and pay the total loss; for instance, if they refuse to accept the abandonment and pay only for a partial loss, they cannot lay claim to the salvage.[16]

---

[10] (1930) 37 LlL Rep 55, HL.
[11] Viscount Dunedin, Lord Warrington of Clyffe, Lord Atkin, Lord Tomlin and Lord Macmillan.
[12] (1930) 37 LlL Rep at 59. See also the judgment of Viscount Dunedin, ibid, at 57, that of Lord Atkin, ibid, at 61, and that of Lord Tomlin, ibid, at 62.
[13] See further, p 455, ante.
[14] *Houstman v Thornton* (1816) Holt NP 242.
[15] *Randal v Cockran* (1748) 1 Ves Sen 98.
[16] *Brooks v MacDonnell* (1835) 1 Y&C Ex 500.

B THE EXERCISE OF THE RIGHT OF SUBROGATION

It is in accordance with the doctrine of subrogation that on indemnifying against costs the insurer may sue in the assured's name any person through whose default or wrongdoing the loss may have occurred.[17]

This rule will apply whether the loss be a total or a partial one. Accordingly, where damage is done by a third party to the thing insured, he may be sued by the insurer in the name of the assured.

But the insurer is entitled to sue in his own name where the assured has assigned to the insurer his right of action in respect of the subject-matter.[18]

C THE EFFECT OF SUBROGATION

The settlement of the loss is a matter which alone concerns the assured and the insurer. A third party against whom the insurer takes proceedings in virtue of rights acquired by subrogation from the assured is not entitled to escape liability by showing that, as between the assured and the insurer, there was not a good claim for a total loss, since subrogation is in the nature of an assignment of a cause of action.[19]

Nor, on the same principle, can the amount paid to the assured by the insurer in respect of collision damage be taken into account or deducted from the damages payable by the wrong-doing vessel to the assured. The assured is a trustee for the insurer in the action brought to recover such damages.[20]

In *Boag v Standard Marine Insurance Co Ltd*[1] a cargo of wheat was insured by its owners for £685 with the Standard Marine Insurance Co Ltd. While the ship was on her voyage, the price of wheat rose and the owner took out an increased value policy for £215 with Lloyd's underwriters. The ship grounded, and the insured cargo was jettisoned. A general average adjustment was made and the owners received £532 4s 8d. Both the Standard Marine Insurance Co Ltd and Lloyd's underwriters paid the amount of the policies in full, and the owners gave them letters of subrogation.

The Standard Marine Insurance Co Ltd claimed to be entitled to the whole of the sum paid to the owners, but the Lloyd's underwriters contended that they were entitled to a proportion of this sum.

The Court of Appeal[2] held that the Standard Marine Insurance Co Ltd was entitled to the whole sum.[3] The subrogation rights, which were vested in them

---

[17] See generally Ivamy, op cit, pp 506–507; *Simpson v Thomson* (1877) 3 App Cas 279 at 293 (per Lord Blackburn); *The Charlotte* [1908] P 206, CA; *Oriental Fire and General Insurance Co Ltd v American President Lines Ltd and Cotton Trading Corpn of San Francisco* [1968] 2 Lloyd's Rep 372, High Court of Bombay, where it was held that the insurers were not entitled to sue a third party in their own names under the (Indian) Transfer of Property Act, s 135A (repealed and re-enacted in the (Indian) Marine Insurance Act XI of 1963).
[18] *Compania Colombiana de Seguros v Pacific Steam Navigation Co* [1965] 1 QB 101, [1964] 1 All ER 216. See Ivamy, op cit, p 507, as to the facts of this case.
[19] *King v Victoria Insurance Co Ltd* [1896] AC 250.
[20] *Yates v Whyte* (1838) 4 Bing NC 272.
[1] (1937) 57 LlL Rep 83, CA.
[2] Lord Wright MR, Romer and Scott LJJ.
[3] There was no question of there being a 'double insurance' under s 32 of the Marine Insurance Act 1906, for the case concerned a subsequent and subsidiary insurance. As to this point, see the judgment of Lord Wright: (1937) 57 LlL Rep at 86.

'as from the time of the casualty causing the loss' as set out in s 79(1) of the Marine Insurance Act 1906, could not be prejudiced by the policy subsequently taken out with the Lloyd's underwriters, which, so far as concerned the insurance company, was res inter alios acta. The contingent right, which had vested in the insurance company at the moment the policy was effected, had become a vested right.

Lord Wright said:[4]

> 'The result is that it is an integral condition of this policy that the Standard Marine Company has a contingent right of subrogation which attaches and which vests in them at the moment when the policy is effected. It is contingent in the sense that the state of affairs postulated may never arise, but the contingent right is there, and here the contingency has arisen, and the right vested as a contingency has become an effective right. In the facts of this case, I can see no answer to that conclusion. . . . It seems to me that there is no foundation at all for any argument that the position under the Standard Marine policies has been in any way affected by the Lloyd's policy, which is for these purposes simply res inter alios acta, and that policy does not affect the position between the Standard Marine Company and the goods owners for any purposes in the facts of this case, and it does not prejudice the rights of subrogation of the Standard Marine Company, nor does any dealing subsequently, such as the letters of subrogation, have any such effect.'

In *Yorkshire Insurance Co Ltd v Nisbet Shipping Co Ltd*[5] a vessel was insured for £72,000. She became a total loss in 1945 as a result of a collision with a Canadian Government vessel. The insurers paid the £72,000 to the assured, who claimed damages from the Canadian Government. The action was successful, but meanwhile the pound sterling had been devalued in 1949, and the loss when quantified and converted into English currency came to nearly £127,000. The assured then repaid the £72,000 to the insurers, but retained the balance of £55,000. The insurers brought an action to recover this sum.

Diplock J, held that the claim failed, for the insurers were not entitled to recover under the doctrine of subrogation any more than they had paid. In the words of his Lordship:[6]

> 'It follows that in my view the insurer's rights in this case were limited to recovering from the assured the amount overpaid, that is to say, £72,000. He is entitled to no more. The principle, I think, is a simple one. It renders irrelevant any consideration of the particular concatenation of circumstances which enable the assured to recover from the Canadian Government a sum in sterling in excess of the value of the ship at the time of the casualty. The fact that the policy was a valued policy, with, as it transpired, a policy value somewhat less than the real value is also irrelevant. The simple principle which I apply is that the insurer cannot recover under the doctrine of subrogation now embodied in s 79 of the Marine Insurance Act 1906 anything more than he has paid.'

Moreover, the doctrine of subrogation is applied to all the insurers, including the assured himself if he is his own insurer for part of the loss.

Thus, *The Welsh Girl*[7] a vessel was insured for £1,000, being valued at

---

[4] (1937) 57 LlL Rep at 86.
[5] [1962] 2 QB 330, [1961] 2 All ER 487, QBD.
[6] Ibid, at 494. Diplock J, said that he was fortified in his view by the fact that the law was the same in the United States, for in *The St Johns* (1900) 101 Fed Rep 469, Brown J, observed (at 474): 'If the amount recoverable from the wrongdoer, after payment of the damage-claims of third parties, were in excess of the amount paid by the underwriters to the assured, no doubt that excess would belong to the latter; since the underwriter's right of subrogation in equity could not extend beyond recoupment or indemnity for the actual payments to the assured.' See further, *The Livingstone* (1904) 130 Fed Rep 746.
[7] (1906) 22 TLR 475. See also, *The Commonwealth* [1907] P 216; *The Charlotte* [1908] P 206. As to under-insurance, see generally s 81 of the Marine Insurance Act 1906, p 405, ante.

£1,350 in the policy. She was sunk in a collision and became a total loss. The insurers paid the assured the £1,000, and on suing the vessel at fault recovered £1,000. It was held that the assured was entitled to recover from the insurers $\frac{350}{1,350}$ of £1,000, since he was his own insurer for £350.

On the other hand, in *Thames and Mersey Marine Insurance Co v British and Chilian SS Co*,[8] after she had collided with another vessel, the insurers paid a total loss on a vessel insured for £45,000 on an agreed value of that amount. Proceedings were taken against the other vessel, and the assured was awarded $\frac{3}{5}$ths of the actual value of his vessel which was £65,000. It was held that the insurers were entitled to the whole of the amount recovered in the collision action.

The doctrine of subrogation also operates in favour of a reinsurer.

Thus, in *Assicurazioni Generali de Trieste v Empress Assurance Corpn Ltd*[9] A reinsured B in respect of certain risks on which B had insured C. B paid C, and A paid B in respect of losses on the policy. It was held that when B recovered C the amount so paid on the ground that he had been induced to pay as a result of a fraudulent misrepresentation, the losses paid not being in fact risks under the policy, the principle of subrogation operated to entitle A to recover from B the amount so recovered. But it was also held that B was entitled to deduct the costs properly incurred in recovering the money from C.

---

[8] [1916] 1 KB 30. See also, *Goole and Hull Steam Towing Co v Ocean Marine Insurance Co* [1928] 1 KB 589.
[9] [1907] 2 KB 814.

CHAPTER 41

The right of contribution[1]

Section 80(1) of the Marine Insurance Act 1906 states that:

> 'Where the assured is over-insured by double insurance, each insurer is bound, as between himself and the other insurers, to contribute rateably to the loss in proportion to the amount for which he is liable under the contract.'

'Double insurance' is defined in s 32(1) of the Act in the following manner:

> 'Where two or more policies are effected by or on behalf of the assured on the same adventure and interest or any part thereof, and the sums exceed the indemnity allowed by this Act, the assured is said to be over-insured by double insurance.'

Where, however, in the same subject-matter there are distinct interests and each is separately insured, there is no double insurance even though the sum insured exceeds the value of the subject-matter.[2]

Nor would there be a double insurance where the risks covered by the policies were different, though the subject-matter in each case was the same.[3]

The principle of marine insurance being that it is a contract of indemnity,[4] double insurances are void to the extent of the over-insurance. Accordingly, if the insurers on one policy are compelled[5] to pay the whole of the sum insured under it, they are entitled to contribution from the insurers under the other policy or policies.[6]

Thus, s 80(2) of the Marine Insurance Act 1906 states:

> 'If any insurer pays more than his proportion of the loss, he is entitled to maintain an action for contribution against the other insurers, and is entitled to the like remedies as a surety who has paid more than his proportion of the debt.'

Where the assured receives more than an indemnity, the position is governed by s 32(2)(d) of the Marine Insurance Act 1906, which states:

> 'Where the assured receives any sum in excess of the indemnity allowed by this Act, he is deemed to hold such sum in trust for the insurers according to their right of contribution among themselves.'

---

[1] See further, Ivamy, *General Principles of Insurance Law* (4th edn, 1979), pp 521–542.
[2] *Godin v London Assurance Co* (1758) 1 Burr 489. See further, Ivamy, op cit, pp 523–526.
[3] See Ivamy, op cit, p 523.
[4] See pp 4–7, ante.
[5] Under s 32(2)(a) of the Marine Insurance Act 1906, which states that: 'The assured, unless the policy otherwise provides, may claim payment from the insurers in such order as he may think fit, provided that he is not entitled to receive any sum in excess of the indemnity allowed by this Act.'
[6] See, e g *Henchmann v Offley* (1782) 3 Doug KB 135; *Godin v London Assurance Co* (1758) 1 Burr 489; *Bousfield v Barnes* (1815) 4 Camp 228; *Irving v Richardson* (1831) 2 B&Ad 193; *Fisk v Masterman* (1841) 8 M&W 165; *Morgan v Price* (1849) 4 Exch 615; *Bruce v Jones* (1863) 1 H&C 769.

PART VI
Reinsurance

CHAPTER 42

Reinsurance

The usual form of reinsurance policy[1] states:

> 'Being a reinsurance subject to the same clauses and conditions as the original policy or policies, and to pay as may be paid thereon.'

A THE RELATION BETWEEN THE ORIGINAL ASSURED AND THE REINSURER

The contracts of insurance and of reinsurance are separate and distinct so that the original assured has no rights in the policy of reinsurance.

Thus, s 9(2) of the Marine Insurance Act 1906 states:

> 'Unless the policy otherwise provides, the original assured has no right or interest in respect of such reinsurance.'

Hence, if an action is brought by the original assured against his insurer, the latter cannot bring his reinsurer in as a third party in the same action;[2] and for the same reason the reinsurer is entitled, when sued, to insist on strict proof of the loss and of the reassured's liability.[3]

Moreover, there may be a defence which is open to the reinsurer but which was not open to the reassured, either on account of some special limitation in the reinsurance policy or arising from the non-disclosure of a material fact by the reassured.[4]

Whether the reinsurer is entitled to claim from the original assured on an abandonment of the subject-matter of the insurance any sum received from a third party by way of indemnity has been left open by the House of Lords[5] which decided the case, in which this issue arose, on other grounds.[6]

---

[1] This chapter concerns marine reinsurance only. The subject of reinsurance generally is dealt with in Ivamy, *Personal Accident, Life and Other Insurances* (2nd ed, 1980), pp 325–338.
[2] *Nelson v Empress Assurance Corpn* [1905] 2 KB 281.
[3] *Chippendale v Holt* (1895) 1 Com Cas 197; *Marten v SS Owners' Underwriters Association* (1902) 7 Com Cas 195; *Western Assurance Co of Toronto v Poole* [1903] 1 KB 376; *Firemen's Fund Insurance Co v Western Australian Insurance Co* (1927) 33 Com Cas 36.
[4] See e g *Property Insurance Co v National Protector Insurance Co* (1913) 18 Com Cas 119; *London General Insurance Co v General Marine Underwriters Association* [1921] 1 KB 104.
[5] Viscount Dunedin, Lord Warrington of Clyffe, Lord Atkin, Lord Macmillan and Lord Tomlin.
[6] *A-G v Glen Line Ltd and the Liverpool War Risks Insurance Association Ltd* (1930) 37 LlL Rep 55, HL. See the speeches of Viscount Dunedin, ibid, at 60, that of Lord Atkin, ibid, at 62, and that of Lord Tomlin, ibid, at 63.

B THE RELATION BETWEEN THE REASSURED AND THE REINSURER

The position as between the reassured and the reinsurer is that when called upon to perform his promise, the reinsurer is 'entitled to require the reassured first to show that a loss of the kind reinsured has, in fact, happened; and, secondly, that the reassured has taken all proper and businesslike steps to have the amount of it fairly and carefully ascertained. That is all. He must then pay'.[7]

1 Payment under original policy

The clause incorporates all the usual terms of the original policy which are not inconsistent with those of the reinsurance policy.[8]

But the words 'to pay as may be paid thereon' do not entitle the reassured to recover from their reinsurers payments which they make under the 'sue and labour' clause in the usual form.

Thus, in *Uzielli v Boston Marine Insurance Co*[9] the reassured sought to recover from the reinsurers a sum which they had paid on a loss which, including 'sue and labour' charges, amounted to 112 per cent. It was held that there was no liability on the reinsurers under the reinsurance policy to pay the charges under the 'sue and labour' clause because the work done under the original policy to preserve the vessel was not done by persons who could be properly described as the 'factors, servants, and assigns' of the reassured.

The effect of the words 'subject to the same clauses and conditions as the original policy or policies and to pay as may be paid thereon' was considered in *Re Eddystone Marine Insurance Co, ex p Western Insurance Co*.[10] In this case a vessel had sustained damage by perils insured against, and the Western Insurance Company had become liable to pay the assured on ship, while the Eddystone Marine Insurance Company would have been liable to pay the Western Insurance Company on the reinsurance policy. Stirling J, held that the payment to be made on the reinsurance policy was regulated by that to be made on the original policy of insurance, and that it was not a condition precedent that payment should *actually* have been made on the original policy to entitle the reassured to recover on the reinsurance policy. The obligation of the reinsurers were unaffected by the reassured going into liquidation.

2 Expiry of original policy

The reinsurance policy is strictly confined to the original policy of which it is expressed to be a reinsurance; or if the policies are not designated, then it is

---

[7] *Western Assurance Co of Toronto v Poole* [1903] 1 KB 376 at 386 (per Bigham J). But see doubts expressed by Scrutton LJ, in *Gurney v Grimmer* (1932) 38 Com Cas 7 at 12; and cf *Firemen's Fund Insurance Co v Western Australian Insurance Co* (1927) 33 Com Cas 36.

[8] *Joyce v Realm Marine Insurance Co* (1872) LR 7 QB 580 ('outward cargo to be considered homeward interest 24 hours after her arrival at her first port of discharge'); *Charlesworth v Faber* (1900) 5 Com Cas 408; *Marten v Nippon Sea and Land Insurance Co* (1898) 3 Com Cas 164 ('warehouse to warehouse' clause); *Property Insurance Co v National Protector Insurance Co* (1913) 18 Com Cas 119 (option to navigate the Canadian Lakes).

[9] (1884) 15 QBD 11. But see *Western Assurance Co of Toronto v Poole* [1903] 1 KB 376 at 386 (per Bigham J); *British Dominions General Insurance Co Ltd v Duder* [1915] 2 KB 394, CA.

[10] [1892] 2 Ch 423.

confined to policies actually in existence at the time when the reinsurance policy was effected.

Thus, in *Lower Rhine and Wurtemburg Insurance Association v Sedgwick*[11] a reinsurance policy was issued with a clause stating 'subject to the same clauses and conditions as the original policy'. Two time policies so reinsured expired during the currency of the reinsurance policy. Then a new time policy was underwritten on the same subject-matter, but with some variation of the details especially as regards the valuation. It was held that the reassured could not recover from the reinsurers in respect of losses paid under the new policy.

3 Excess clause

A reinsurance of '£1,000 in excess of £500' means that the liability of the reinsurer does not arise until the risk of the reassured exceeds £500.

Thus, in *South British Fire and Marine Insurance Co of New Zealand v Da Costa*[12] it was held that a 'craft' clause making each craft a separate insurance 'warranted fpa under 3 per cent' did not exempt the reinsurer for '£1,000 in excess of £500' where a lighter sank and the loss payable by the reassured was £298 on a risk of £400. The reinsurance was for '£1,000 in excess of £500' of the whole shipped cargo on which the risk of the reassured was £1,914. Therefore since there was a risk of more than £500, the reassured recovered although the risk on the lighter which sank was only £400.

4 Insurable interest[13]

In *Hewitt v London General Insurance Co Ltd*[14] a cargo of nitrate was insured for a voyage from Tocopilla to La Pallice, France. It belonged to Anthony Gibbs & Sons. The insurers reinsured their risk under a reinsurance policy. The vessel and the cargo were totally lost. The insurers paid the sum insured to Anthony Gibbs & Sons, and when the insurers claimed an indemnity from the reinsurers, the reinsurers contended that they were under no liability[15] because Anthony Gibbs & Sons had no interest at the time of the loss since at that time the cargo had been requisitioned by the French Government.

Branson J, held that the reinsurers were liable because the risk of loss of the cargo against marine perils was on Anthony Gibbs & Sons at the time of the loss, and they were the real assured, although the war risk was borne by the French Government. His Lordship observed:[16]

> 'The question as to whether the French Government or Anthony Gibbs & Sons were the real assured depends on the contract. The contract is a peculiar one. Mr Dickinson contended that it was, in fact, an ordinary free-alongside contract, and that the risk both as regards marine perils and against war perils passed when the goods were put alongside the steamer from Anthony Gibbs & Sons to the French Government. I do not think it is necessary for me to read the clauses upon which Mr Dickinson on the one side and Mr Davies on the other founded their contentions. The material clauses were 1, 2, 3 and 6. I think it sufficient if I state the

---

[11] [1899] 1 QB 179. See also, *Scottish National Insurance Co v Poole* (1912) 18 Com Cas 9; *Reliance Marine Insurance Co v Duder* [1913] 1 KB 265; *Janson v Poole* (1915) 20 Com Cas 232.
[12] [1906] 1 KB 456.
[13] As to insurable interest, see pp 16–29, ante.
[14] (1925) 23 LlL Rep 243, KBD.
[15] Another ground on which they repudiated liability was that the risk under the original policy had not attached. As to this aspect of the case, see pp 117–118, ante.
[16] (1925) 23 LlL Rep at 246.

conclusions to which I have come, and that is that upon the true construction of the contract the risk of loss by perils of the sea remained upon Anthony Gibbs & Sons throughout the voyage and that they were the real assured.'

In *Re Overseas Marine Insurance Co Ltd*[17] the Insurance Office of Australia Ltd insured a vessel under a policy which had pinned to it a slip containing the words:

> 'Full interest admitted; the policy being deemed sufficient proof of interest. This insurance is without benefit of salvage.'

The insurers reinsured part of the risk with the Overseas Marine Insurance Co Ltd. This company went into liquidation. The assured claimed against the insurers under the original policy, and the insurers sought to prove in the liquidation of the Overseas Marine Insurance Co Ltd for the amount of their contingent liability[18] under the original policy. But the liquidator rejected the claim on the ground that the assured had no legal claim against the insurers under the original policy.

It was held by the Court of Appeal[19] that he was entitled to do so, as the original policy was void under s 4 of the Marine Insurance Act 1906.

Scrutton LJ, said:[20]

> 'The underwriters apparently desire to argue (1) that if you pin a slip to a policy, it is not part of the policy; and (2) whether it is part of the policy or not, if there was, in fact, some interest s 4(2)(b) of the Marine Insurance Act does not apply. Those two points have been clearly raised and decided against the contention of the underwriters in the case of *T Cheshire & Co v Vaughan Bros & Co*.[1] This court is bound by that decision.'

5 Unseaworthiness

In *Firemen's Fund Insurance Co Ltd v Western Australian Insurance Co Ltd and Atlantic Assurance Co Ltd*[2] the plaintiffs had issued to the owners of a cargo of gunpowder a policy of insurance against loss by perils of the sea and jettison in respect of a voyage from New York to La Plata. In this policy there was no 'seaworthiness admitted' clause.[3] The plaintiffs reinsured the risk with the defendants under a policy containing a 'seaworthiness admitted' clause. In addition to the consignment of gunpowder the vessel contained a quantity of other explosives and nearly 3,000 drums of sulphuric acid. In a heavy although not exceptional sea some of the drums shifted, and some were broken and leaked. The acid found its way to the vessel's pumps and disabled them, and also destroyed the oakum in the seams and caused the vessel to leak. She went to a port of refuge, but before she was allowed to enter it the harbourmaster directed the explosives

---

[17] (1930) 36 LlL Rep 183, CA.
[18] Under s 519(1) of the Companies Act 1985 any creditor (including any contingent or prospective creditor) is entitled to present a petition for the winding up of a company.
[19] Scrutton, Greer and Slesser LJJ.
[20] (1930) 36 LlL Rep at 184.
[1] [1920] 3 KB 240, CA.
[2] (1927) 28 LlL Rep 243, KBD.
[3] The 'seaworthiness admitted' clause, which was then in use, stated 'The seaworthiness of the vessel as between the Assured and Underwriters is hereby admitted. In the event of loss the Assured's right of recovery hereunder shall not be prejudiced by the fact that the loss may have been attributable to the wrongful act or misconduct of the shipowners or their servants, committed without the privity of the Assured.' It has now been replaced by the 'Unseaworthiness and Unfitness Exclusion' Clause. See pp 307–308, ante.

to be jettisoned. This was done, and the plaintiffs paid the owners for a total loss, and claimed to be reimbursed by the defendants.

It was held that the claim failed. Bateson J, said that the vessel was unfit to perform the voyage when the gunpowder was put on board[4] her, and that she was unseaworthy. Since the plaintiffs were under no liability on the original policy, they were not entitled to recover from the defendants under the reinsurance policy.

He observed:[5]

> 'Clause 8, "seaworthiness admitted", does not prevent the reinsurer saying that the original underwriter suffered no loss for which he could be made responsible; he had a complete defence against the assured, the defence of unseaworthiness, and there was no necessity to plead unseaworthiness in this case. The original underwriter was not liable at all, and if he was not liable, there is nothing for which he can claim over. The contract for reinsurance is on goods limited to the liability of the original underwriter. The reinsurer's liability is limited to the original insurer's liability under the original policy. It is only a different way of saying the same thing. Another way of putting it is to say that the contract of reinsurance properly understood is a contract to indemnify against losses which the original underwriter has suffered, but not against gifts. This was a voluntary payment so far as the original underwriter is concerned, and he did not insure himself for gifts that he might choose to make to his assured. The contract is expressed to be a reinsurance on the same terms as the original policy to indemnify against liability for goods lost, not an insurance of the goods. The reinsurer says to the original underwriter: "You have no liability, you have no loss, you have no interest". The Institute Clause as to unseaworthiness only applies if and when the original policy contains it, and if and when the original underwriter is liable for unseaworthiness. That is put in ex majore cautela, in case there is such a clause in the original policy.'

6 Proximate cause of loss[6]

In *Merchants' Marine Insurance Co Ltd v Liverpool Marine and General Insurance Co Ltd*[7] the plaintiffs were reinsurers of marine risks including perils of the sea on a Norwegian vessel. They reinsured their risk with the defendants. The original policy and the reinsurance policies were time policies from 1 January 1925 to 31 December 1925. Each of them contained a 'continuation clause' which stated:

> 'In the event of the vessel not being at the place of destination at the date of the expiration of the policy the insurance shall be prolonged until the end of the day when the vessel arrives at the first place of destination.'

Both policies incorporated s 27 of the Norwegian Plan[8] which stated:

> 'If the insured object is in a damaged condition at the time the insurance expires, and the damage comes within the underwriters' responsibility, the risk shall continue for the immediate consequences of such damage until the object, without unreasonable delay, has been repaired or sold.'

The policy expired while the vessel was on a voyage to various ports on the coast of South Africa, beginning with Luderitz Bay and ending with Beira. On 9 January 1926 on entering Luderitz Bay she stranded on the Angra Rocks. Her bottom was holed. She reached Luderitz Bay and anchored there. There were

---

[4] As to the evidence on this point, see (1927) 28 LlL Rep at 250.
[5] Ibid, at 251.
[6] As to the application of the 'proximate cause' rule, see pp 225–232, ante.
[7] (1928) 31 LlL Rep 45, CA.
[8] Which is something like the Institute Clauses in English insurance policies: ibid, at 46 (per Scrutton LJ).

no facilities there for repairing her bottom damage. A diver was sent from Cape Town and he patched the holes from the outside. She sailed to Cape Town and made water very fast, so she was beached on Possession Island, and became a constructive total loss.

The plaintiffs paid for a loss, and claimed an indemnity from the defendants, who repudiated liability on the ground that their liability ceased when the vessel reached her first place of destination, and that her loss was not an immediate consequence of the damage she had sustained on the Angra Rocks.

The Court of Appeal[9] held that the claim succeeded, for the loss of the vessel was an immediate consequence of the still existing damage caused by the stranding.

Scrutton LJ, observed:[10]

> 'When the insurance expired, the ship was in a damaged condition. That damage came within the underwriters' responsibility because it was occasioned by perils of the sea. The risk is therefore to continue until the object without unnecessary delay has been repaired. She has not been repaired and there has been no unnecessary delay. What is the risk which is to continue? The risk which is to continue is for the immediate consequences of such a voyage. Was it an immediate consequence of the damage done by the stranding which was continuing and which had not been repaired that she was unable to stand weather which any ordinary seaworthy ship undamaged would have stood, and that she had to be grounded? In my opinion it was.
>
> Now, the learned Judge has come to an opposite conclusion for this reason, that he has imported into the clause a provision which is not there. He has said the clause shall read "till the object is in a place of safety". But that is just what the clause does not say. The clause says that it continues for immediate consequences until the object without unnecessary delay has been repaired; and it assumes there that, after the damage has been caused and before the ship has been repaired, further damage may be caused by the original damage. That seems to me just to be intended to meet the case where a ship, having been damaged, has to be brought to another port to be repaired. That provision does not cease to apply because, on the way to be repaired efficiently, the vessel is in a place where she can lie in safety so long as she is not repaired, and at a place where there are no facilities for repairing her.'

7 'Total or constructive loss only'

Clauses are often found in reinsurance policies against total or constructive total loss only which are designed to prevent the reinsurer from reopening a settlement made between the original assured and the reassured.

In *Bergens Dampskibs-Assurance Forening v Sun Insurance Office Ltd*[11] the plaintiffs, a Norwegian insurance club and other underwriters, had insured the owners of a vessel against perils of the sea, and effected a reinsurance policy with the defendants 'against total loss and/or constructive total loss and/or arranged total loss'. The vessel stranded, and there was a risk that she would become a total loss. The plaintiffs entered into an agreement with her owners that she should be regarded as a total loss, and that the plaintiffs would pay them a sum which, although it was less than the agreed value in the policy in the case of a total loss, was more than the vessel's repaired value at the time. The plaintiffs brought an action against the defendants on the reinsurance policy to recover the sum which they had paid to the owners.

---

[9] Scrutton, Greer, and Sankey LJJ.
[10] (1928) 31 LlL Rep at 47. See also, the judgment of Greer LJ, ibid, at 48–49, and that of Sankey LJ, ibid, at 49.
[11] (1930) 37 LlL Rep 175, KBD.

It was held by Branson J, that the action failed. The owners had never put forward a definite claim for a constructive total loss. The compromise was not a compromise of such a claim, and a conventional loss could not be created by mere arrangement. His Lordship observed:[12]

> 'But, now, does it go further, and does it mean that if you arrange that a vessel shall be treated as a constructive total loss by way of settling the claim, although it could not be arguably put forward that she was—if you transfer it by mere agreement into the category of total loss, does the policy cover that? [Counsel] has said that this is a policy which is against a total loss—a total loss of a ship which is valued, and the value governing it in this case is 800,000 kr, and it cannot mean that by the agreement of the parties it can be treated otherwise than as a partial loss, that it can be transferred by agreement to the category of a total loss and brought within this policy by virtue of the word "arranged". I think that is the right argument. I think that is the dominant consideration. This is a policy against total loss; and what, if I may use the expression, comes under "total loss"? I do not think it can include a case where by the agreement of the parties a different case is put upon the basis of a total loss by mere arrangement, just as it might have been put upon any other basis. I think there must be either a constructive total loss or a claim for a constructive total loss, which claim is arranged. Although the wording in *Street's* case[13] was different, I think that it bears upon the matter. It shows that the word "arranged" really only means "compromised". It does not mean an artificial total loss created by the will of the parties.'

In *Gurney v Grimmer*[14] the plaintiff was one of a number of underwriters who had insured a vessel against marine risks including total and constructive loss. He reinsured part of the risk with the defendant under a reinsurance policy which stated:

> 'It is agreed that this policy ... is subject to the same terms, clauses and conditions as the original policy ... and to pay as may be paid thereon but warranted free of all average and to pay only in the event of the total constructive compromised and/or arranged total loss of the vessel.'

The vessel stranded in the Straits of Magellan. Notice of abandonment was given by the assured, but was not accepted by the insurers. But after negotiations between the assured and the plaintiff (among other insurers) the assured's claim was settled on the basis of a payment as for a constructive total loss.

The plaintiff claimed against the defendant on a 100 per cent basis, but the defendant contended that the words 'compromised and/or arranged' did not cover a payment in full, and that the vessel was not, in fact, a constructive total loss.[15]

The Court of Appeal[16] held that the claim succeeded, for the words 'compromised and/or arranged' were wider than 'compromised', and covered the nature of the transaction between the assured and the insurers.

Lawrence LJ, observed:[17]

---

[12] Ibid, at 177.
[13] I e *Street v Royal Exchange Assurance* (1914) 111 LT 235, CA.
[14] (1923) 44 LlL Rep 189, CA.
[15] As to constructive total loss, see generally pp 362–377, ante.
[16] Scrutton, Lawrence and Greer LJJ.
[17] (1932) 44 LlL Rep at 196. See also the judgment of Scrutton LJ, ibid, at 194–195, and that of Greer LJ, ibid, at 198–199. As to the meaning of 'compromised total loss', see further, *Oscar L Aronsen Inc v Compton (The Megara)* [1973] 2 Lloyd's Rep 361, District Court for the Southern District of New York, where Lumbard CtJ, said (ibid, at 364): 'Surely it cannot be that whenever a shipowner whose vessel has been partially damaged submits inflated repair estimates and a claim for a constructive total loss along with his claim for a partial loss, a

'The word "arranged" is added to "compromised" either in conjunction with "compromised" or as an alternative to "compromised". I do not intend to give an exhaustive definition of the word "arranged". "Compromised", it is admitted on all hands, assumes that a mutual concession has been made by both parties and that each party has got something less than he claimed. The word "arranged" to my mind is a wider word altogether. In certain cases, and in my judgment in this case, I think it is equivalent to "agreed".

In my judgment, in those circumstances, the payment for the constructive total loss was "arranged" at the full amount. By coming to this conclusion I do not wish it to be understood that I consider that the term "arranged" would include a mere payment in full without any kind of investigation or discussion as to the amount.

As I have said before, I have not attempted to give an exhaustive definition of the word "arranged" as used in this policy. All I do say is that in the circumstances of this case the 100 per cent payment was a payment which was "arranged" between the original insurers and the owner of the vessel.'

The assured had been paid in full for the constructive loss of the vessel, but his claim in respect of 'sue and labour' charges and salvage charges was reduced by agreement between him and the insurers. Scrutton LJ, held further that even though one item of the claim was paid in full and another reduced, the transaction was none the less a compromise of the whole claim, and observed:[18]

'It is possible to say that a term of the compromise was that one item was to be paid in full and that another item was to be very much reduced. In my opinion that does not make any difference; the whole transaction is still a compromise. In consideration of his getting all his claim on one head, the shipowner is ready to reduce his claim very substantially on another head, and the result appears to me to be a compromised loss arrived at by a compromise of all the claims in the action.'

---

compromised constructive total loss occurs upon settlement of the claim. Such a result would be absurd, when, as seems to have been the case here, the submission of the constructive total loss claim by the shipowner was merely a device to bolster his bargaining position with the hull underwriters and inflate his recovery for the damage to his vessel.' This decision was subsequently affirmed by the United States Court of Appeals, Second Circuit: [1974] 1 Lloyd's Rep 590.

[18] (1932) 44 LlL Rep at 195. The other learned Lord Justices did not deal in their judgments with this matter.

PART VII
Mutual insurance

CHAPTER 43

Mutual insurance

With reference to the system of insuring property in mutual insurance associations or protection clubs, s 85 of the Marine Insurance Act 1906 states:

'(1) Where two or more persons mutually agree to insure each other against marine losses there is said to be a mutual insurance.

(2) The provisions of this Act relating to the premium do not apply to mutual insurance, but a guarantee, or such other arrangement as may be agreed upon, may be substituted for the premium.

(3) The provisions of this Act in so far as they may be modified by the agreement of the parties, may in the case of mutual insurance be modified by the terms of the policies issued by the association, or by the rules and regulations of the association.

(4) Subject to the exceptions mentioned in this section, the provisions of this Act apply to a mutual insurance.'

There is nothing in relation to insurances effected by such associations which differs in principle from other insurances, whether effected with Lloyd's underwriters or with a marine insurance company. It is necessary, however, to refer briefly to a few of the leading features of such insurances. These relate to:

1. The Rules of the Association.
2. The terms of entry and membership.
3. Contributions by members.
4. The period of insurance.
5. Cesser of insurance.
6. The risks covered.
7. Claims.
8. Disputes.
9. Certificate of entry.

1 Rules of Association

Each Association has it own set of Rules. The Rules are subject to the Memorandum and the Articles, and contain the terms upon which the Association conducts the insurance business.

2 Terms of entry and membership

The terms of entry and membership[1] will vary according to the Association concerned.

---

[1] For a case where the shipowners sought a declaration that they were not members of the Association concerned, and were not liable to pay calls, see *Empresa Lineas Maritimas Argentinas v Oceanus Mutual Underwriting Association (Bermuda) Ltd* [1984] 2 Lloyd's Rep 517, QBD (Com Ct). For 'calls', see infra.

The Rules of the United Kingdom Mutual Steamship Assurance Association Ltd state that:

> 'Any applicant owner who desires to enter a ship for insurance in the Association shall make application for such entry in such form as may from time to time be required by the Managers and, except as otherwise permitted by these Rules, any application by an applicant owner who is not already a Member of the Association shall be accompanied by an application by him for membership of the Association.'

The particulars given by an applicant owner in the application form will, if the entry of the relevant ship be accepted, be deemed to form the basis of the contract of insurance between the owner and the Association, and it is a condition precedent of the insurance that all such particulars and information were true so far as the owner knew or could with reasonable diligence have ascertained.

The Managers are entitled in their absolute discretion and without assigning any reason, to refuse any application for the entry of a ship for insurance in the Association whether or not the applicant of a ship is a Member of the Association.

As soon as reasonably practicable after accepting any application for the entry of a ship for insurance in the Association the Managers must issue to the owner a Certificate of Entry.[2]

If at any time or from time to time the Managers and the owner of any ship entered for insurance in the Association agree to vary the risks against which the ship is insured, the Managers as soon as reasonably practical must issue to the owner an Endorsement Slip stating the terms of such variation and the date and time from which such variation is to be effective.

3 Contribution by members

The Members who have entered ships for insurance in the Association must provide by way of contributions to be levied from such Members all funds which in the opinion of the Directors are required to meet such of the general expenses of the Association as the Directors may from time to time think fit to charge against the Protection and Indemnity insurance business of the Association, to meet the claims, expenses and outgoings, and for such transfers to reserves or provisions, as the Directors may deem it expedient to make out of the contributions which have been paid.

At the beginning of each policy year the Directors must decide the rate per ton of the contributing tonnage of the entered ships which is to be levied from the Members upon their ship and is to be paid by way of an 'advance call'.[3]

At such subsequent time or times during each policy year as the Directors think fit they may decide to levy from the owners of the entered ship a 'supplementary call' which may be either at such rate per ton of the contributory tonnage of the entered ship or at such a percentage of the 'advance call' as the Directors may think fit.[4]

---

[2] See infra.
[3] See eg *Volkswagenwerk AG and Wolfsburger Transport Gesellschaft mbH v International Mutual Strike Assurance Co (Bermuda) Ltd* [1977] 2 Lloyd's Rep 503, CA.
[4] See *Volkswagenwerk AG and Wolfsburger Transport Gesellschaft mbH v International Mutual Strike Assurance Co (Bermuda) Ltd*, supra. For a case where an Association brought an action to enforce payment of a call, see *West of Scotland Ship Owners Mutual Protection and Indemnity Association*

Every 'advance' or 'supplementary call' is payable in such instalments and on such dates as the Directors may specify.[5]

If an entered ship remains in any safe port for a period of 30 or more consecutive days after finally mooring there, the Member is allowed a return of calls at a specified rate.

The Managers have the right to accept any application for the entry of a ship in the Association on the special terms that a fixed premium shall be payable in respect of the ship and that no liability shall arise to pay contributions or calls in respect thereof. An entry accepted in this way is known as a 'special entry'. The Managers' right to accept ships as 'special entries' can only be exercised in certain cases, e g where the ship concerned operates exclusively on the Great Lakes in Canada and the United States and on the River St Lawrence, and where the applicant owner of the ship concerned is a Government or Governmental or State-owned concern or body.

4 The period of insurance

The insurance by the Association of each entered ship otherwise than for a fixed period continues until the end of the policy year which is current at the date on which such insurance commenced.

The policy year may start e g from noon on 20 February.[6]

If at the end of a current policy year a ship entered for insurance otherwise than for a fixed period is still so entered, the insurance continues for the next following policy year on the same terms as those already in force unless the Managers give notice in writing to the owner that the insurance is to cease or the terms upon which he is to be insured for the next following policy year are to be changed.

In *Gregory Maritime Ltd v Thos R Miller & Son, United Kingdom Mutual Steamship Assurance Association Ltd and United Kingdom Freight, Demurrage and Defence Association Ltd*,[7] the plaintiffs were the owners of the m v 'Eirini', and were members of the Mutual Assurance Association. The managers of the Association stated that they intended to ask its directors to terminate the plaintiffs' membership. The plaintiffs sought an injunction restraining the Association from bringing their membership to an end. Cross J, held that the injunction would not be granted. If it had been granted, the directors would be forced to continue the insurance of the vessel indefinitely and the power to terminate membership of the Association would be transferred from the directors to the court. Further, it was not clear who would decide the terms on

---

(Luxembourg) v Aifanourios Shipping SA, The Aifanourios [1980] 2 Lloyd's Rep 403, Court of Session. For a case where the question was whether an Association could set off an amount due in respect of calls against an amount due from the Association, see *First National Bank of Chicago v West of England Shipowners Mutual Protection and Indemnity Association (Luxembourg), The Evelpidis Era* [1981] 1 Lloyd's Rep 54, QBD (Com Ct).

[5] In *Volkswagenwerk AG and Wolfsburger Transport Gesellschaft mbH v International Mutual Strike Assurance Co (Bermuda) Ltd*, supra, it was held that the association was not bound to administer as a separate fund the calls and claims of members insuring against shore risks only to the exclusion of calls and claims of members insuring against other or additional risks. (See the judgment of Megaw LJ, ibid, at 520.)

[6] See e g *Compania Maritima San Basilio SA v Oceanus Mutual Underwriting Association (Bermuda) Ltd, The Eurysthenes* [1977] QB 49, [1976] 3 All ER 243, CA.

[7] [1966] 1 Lloyd's Rep 296, ChD.

which the vessel would be insured. Again, there was no ground for suspecting that the directors would be influenced by the managers. His Lordship observed:[8]

> 'For myself, I do not believe for one moment that these directors, if satisfied in their minds that [the Managers] took a wrong view of what the Club require, will hesitate for a moment from taking that view simply from a fear of hurting [the Managers'] feelings.'

5 Cesser of insurance

An owner ceases to be insured if he dies or a receiving order is made against him. Similarly, a company which is a Member will cease to be a Member upon the passing of any resolution for voluntary winding up or on an order being made for the compulsory winding up or on dissolution or on a receiver or manager of the company's business or undertaking being appointed.

6 The risks covered

The risks which are covered will vary from Association to Association, and will depend on the nature of the particular Association concerned.[9]

7 Claims

Notice in writing of every casualty or other event likely to lead to a claim on the Association must be given to the Managers or to any representative of the Association expressly authorised by them to accept such notice on its behalf.

An owner must at all times disclose to the Association and produce to the Managers as soon as reasonably possible whenever so required any document or information in his or his agents' power or possession which may be relevant to any loss, damage, expense or liability in respect whereof the owner is insured.

On the occurrence of any event which may give rise to a claim, an owner must not unreasonably refrain from taking such steps as at that present time shall appear proper for the purpose of averting or minimising any loss, damage, expense or liability in respect whereof he may be insured.[10]

No claim must be settled nor any liability be admitted by or on behalf of an owner without the prior consent in writing of the Managers.

Every claim must be notified to the Managers as soon as possible, but in no case later than 12 months after the owner has received notice that the claim is or may be made against him.

8 Disputes

If any difference or dispute arises between an owner and the Association out of or in connection with the Rules or any contract between them or as to the rights or obligations of the Association or the owner thereunder or in connection

---

[8] Ibid, at 305.
[9] See pp 215–224, ante.
[10] See eg *C V G Siderurgicia del Orinoco SA v London SS Owners' Mutual Insurance Association Ltd, The Vainqueur José* [1979] 1 Lloyd's Rep 557, QBD (Com Ct).

therewith, such difference or dispute must in the first instance be referred to and adjudicated upon by the Directors.[11]

If the owner concerned in such difference or dispute does not accept the decision of the Directors, it is referred to arbitration, and the arbitration is subject to the provisions of the Arbitration Act 1950.

9 Certificates of entry

The Certificate of Entry states that the owner has been entered in the Register of Members of the Association, and sets out the risks against which the ship has been entered for insurance in the Association. It states the date and the time from which the entry of the ship for insurance in the Association is to commence, and if such entry has been accepted for a fixed period, states the date and time at which the insurance of such ship by the Association is to cease.

Every Certificate of Entry is conclusive evidence and binding for all purposes as to the risks against which the ship is insured by the Association and as to the date and time from which such insurance is to commence.

If any Certificate of Entry specifies more than one person as the owner of an entered ship or if a ship shall be entered for the names of or on behalf of more persons than one, they shall be jointly and severally liable to pay all contributions or other sums due to the Association in respect of such entry.

---

[11] See e g *Wells Fargo Bank International Corpn v London SS Owners' Mutual Insurance Association Ltd, The John W Hill* [1977] 1 Lloyd's Rep 213, District Court, Southern District of New York; *Marazura Navigation SA v Oceanus Mutual Underwriting Association (Bermuda) Ltd and John Laing (Management) Ltd* [1977] 1 Lloyd's Rep 283, QBD (Com Ct); *Socony Mobil Oil Co Inc v West of England Ship Owners Mutual Insurance Association (London) Ltd, The Padre Island* [1984] 2 Lloyd's Rep 408, QBD (Com Ct).

Appendices

APPENDIX I

Statutes

SALE OF GOODS ACT 1979
(Chapter 54)

Part III

Effects of the Contract

Transfer of Property as between Seller and Buyer

16. Goods must be ascertained.—Where there is a contract for the sale of unascertained goods no property in the goods is transferred to the buyer unless and until the goods are ascertained.

17. Property passes when intended to pass.—(1) Where there is a contract for the sale of specific or ascertained goods the property in them is transferred to the buyer at such time as the parties to the contract intend it to be transferred.

(2) For the purpose of ascertaining the intention of the parties regard shall be had to the terms of the contract, the conduct of the parties and the circumstances of the case.

18. Rules for ascertaining intention.—Unless a different intention appears, the following are rules for ascertaining the intention of the parties as to the time at which the property in the goods is to pass to the buyer.

Rule 1.— Where there is an unconditional contract for the sale of specific goods in a deliverable state the property in the goods passes to the buyer when the contract is made, and it is immaterial whether the time of payment or the time of delivery, or both, be postponed.

Rule 2.—Where there is a contract for the sale of specific goods and the seller is bound to do something to the goods for the purpose of putting them into a deliverable state, the property does not pass until the thing is done and the buyer has notice that it has been done.

Rule 3.—Where there is a contract for the sale of specific goods in a deliverable state but the seller is bound to weigh, measure, test, or do some other act or thing with reference to the goods for the purpose of ascertaining the price, the property does not pass until the act or thing is done and the buyer has notice that it has been done.

Rule 4.—When goods are delivered to the buyer on approval or on sale or return or other similar terms the property in the goods passes to the buyer:—
  (a) when he signifies his approval or acceptance to the seller or does any other act adopting the transaction;
  (b) if he does not signify his approval or acceptance to the seller but retains the goods without giving notice of rejection, then, if a time has been fixed for the return of the goods, on the expiration of that time, and, if no time has been fixed, on the expiration of a reasonable time.

Rule 5.—(1) Where there is a contract for the sale of unascertained or future goods by description, and goods of that description and in a deliverable state are unconditionally appropriated to the contract, either by the seller with the assent of the buyer or by the buyer with the assent of the seller, the property in the goods then passes to the buyer; and the assent may be express or implied, and may be given either before or after the appropriation is made.

(2) Where, in pursuance of the contract, the seller delivers the goods to the buyer or to a carrier or other bailee or custodier (whether named by the buyer or not) for the purpose of transmission to the buyer, and does not reserve the right of disposal, he is to be taken to have unconditionally appropriated the goods to the contract.

19. Reservation of right of disposal.—(1) Where there is a contract for the sale of specific goods or where goods are subsequently appropriated to the contract, the seller may, by the terms of the contract or appropriation, reserve the right of disposal of the goods until certain conditions are fulfilled; and in such a case, notwithstanding the delivery of the goods to the buyer, or to a carrier or other bailee or custodier for the purpose of transmission to the buyer, the property in the goods does not pass to the buyer until the conditions imposed by the seller are fulfilled.

(2) Where goods are shipped, and by the bill of lading the goods are deliverable to the order of the seller or his agent, the seller is prima facie to be taken to reserve the right of disposal.

(3) Where the seller of goods draws on the buyer for the price, and transmits the bill of exchange and bill of lading to the buyer together to secure acceptance or payment of the bill of exchange, the buyer is bound to return the bill of lading if he does not honour the bill of exchange, and if he wrongfully retains the bill of lading the property in the goods does not pass to him.

20. Risk prima facie passes with property.—(1) Unless otherwise agreed, the goods remain at the seller's risk until the property in them is transferred to the buyer, but when the property in them is transferred to the buyer the goods are at the buyer's risk whether delivery has been made or not.

(2) But where delivery has been delayed through the fault of either buyer or seller the goods are at the risk of the party at fault as regards any loss which might not have occurred but for such fault.

(3) Nothing in this section affects the duties or liabilities of either seller or buyer as a bailee or custodier of the goods of the other party.

MERCHANT SHIPPING ACT 1894
(57 & 58 Vict c 60)

506. Insurance of certain risks not invalid.—An insurance effected against the happening, without the owner's actual fault or privity, of any or all of the events in respect of which the liability of owners is limited under this Part of this Act shall not be invalid by reason of the nature of the risk.

THE MARINE INSURANCE ACT 1906
(6 Edw 7 c 41)

An Act to codify the Law relating to Marine Insurance [21st December 1906]

MARINE INSURANCE

1. Marine insurance defined.—A contract of marine insurance is a contract whereby the insurer undertakes to indemnify the assured in manner and to the extent thereby agreed, against marine losses, that is to say, the losses incident to marine adventure.

2. Mixed sea and land risks.—(1) A contract of marine insurance may, by its express terms, or by usage of trade, be extended so as to protect the assured against losses on inland waters or on any land risk which may be incidental to any sea voyage.

(2) Where a ship in course of building, or the launch of a ship, or any adventure analogous to a marine adventure, is covered by a policy in the form of a marine policy, the provisions of this Act, in so far as applicable, shall apply thereto; but, except as by this section provided, nothing in this Act shall alter or affect any rule of law applicable to any contract of insurance other than a contract of marine insurance as by this Act defined.

3. Marine adventure and maritime perils defined.—(1) Subject to the provisions of this Act, every lawful marine adventure may be the subject of a contract of marine insurance.

(2) In particular there is a marine adventure where—
  (a) any ship goods or other movables are exposed to maritime perils. Such property is in this Act referred to as "insurable property";
  (b) the earning or acquisition of any freight, passage money, commission, profit, or other pecuniary benefit, or the security for any advances, loan, or disbursements, is endangered by the exposure of insurable property to maritime perils;
  (c) any liability to a third party may be incurred by the owner of, or other person interested in or responsible for, insurable property, by reason of maritime perils.

"Maritime perils" means the perils consequent on, or incidental to, the navigation of the sea, that is to say, perils of the seas, fire, war perils, pirates, rovers, thieves, captures, seizures, restraints, and detainments of princes and peoples, jettisons, barratry, and any other perils, either of the like kind or which may be designated by the policy.

INSURABLE INTEREST

4. Avoidance of wagering or gaming contracts.—(1) Every contract of marine insurance by way of gaming or wagering is void.

(2) A contract of marine insurance is deemed to be a gaming or wagering contract—
  (a) where the assured has not an insurable interest as defined by this Act, and the contract is entered into with no expectation of acquiring such an interest; or
  (b) where the policy is made "interest or no interest", or "without further proof of interest than the policy itself", or "without benefit of salvage to the insurer", or subject to any other like term:

Provided that, where there is no possibility of salvage, a policy may be effected without benefit of salvage to the insurer.

5. Insurable interest defined.—(1) Subject to the provisions of this Act, every person has an insurable interest who is interested in a marine adventure.

(2) In particular a person is interested in a marine adventure where he stands in any legal or equitable relation to the adventure or to any insurable property at risk therein, in consequence of which he may benefit by the safety or due arrival of insurable property, or may be prejudiced by its loss, or by damage thereto, or by the detention thereof, or may incur liability in respect thereof.

6. When interest must attach.—(1) The assured must be interested in the subject-matter insured at the time of the loss though he need not be interested when the insurance is effected:

Provided that where the subject-matter is insured "lost or not lost", the assured may recover although he may not have acquired his interest until after the loss, unless at the time of effecting the contract of insurance the assured was aware of the loss, and the insurer was not.

(2) Where the assured has no interest at the time of the loss, he cannot acquire interest by any act or election after he is aware of the loss.

7. Defeasible or contingent interest.—(1) A defeasible interest is insurable, as also is a contingent interest.

(2) In particular, where the buyer of goods has insured them, he has an insurable interest, notwithstanding that he might, at his election, have rejected the goods, or have treated them as at the seller's risk, by reason of the latter's delay in making delivery or otherwise.

8. Partial interest.—A partial interest of any nature is insurable.

9. Re-insurance.—(1) The insurer under a contract of marine insurance has an insurable interest in his risk, and may re-insure in respect of it.

(2) Unless the policy otherwise provides, the original assured has no right or interest in respect of such re-insurance.

10. Bottomry.—The lender of money on bottomry or respondentia has an insurable interest in respect of the loan.

11. Master's and seamen's wages.—The master or any member of the crew of a ship has an insurable interest in respect of his wages.

12. Advance freight.—In the case of advance freight, the person advancing the freight has an insurable interest, in so far as such freight is not repayable in case of loss.

13. Charges of insurance.—The assured has an insurable interest in the charges of any insurance which he may effect.

14. Quantum of interest.—(1) Where the subject-matter insured is mortgaged, the mortgagor has an insurable interest in the full value thereof, and the mortgagee has an insurable interest in respect of any sum due or to become due under the mortgage.

(2) A mortgagee, consignee, or other person having an interest in the subject-matter insured may insure on behalf and for the benefit of other persons interested as well as for his own benefit.

(3) The owner of insurable property has an insurable interest in respect of the full value thereof, notwithstanding that some third person may have agreed, or be liable, to indemnify him in case of loss.

15. Assignment of interest.—Where the assured assigns or otherwise parts with his interest in the subject-matter insured, he does not thereby transfer to the assignee his rights under the contract of insurance, unless there be an express or implied agreement with the assignee to that effect.

But the provisions of this section do not affect a transmission of interest by operation of law.

INSURABLE VALUE

16. Measure of insurable value.—Subject to any express provision or valuation in the policy, the insurable value of the subject-matter insured must be ascertained as follows:

(1) in insurance on ship, the insurable value is the value, at the commencement of the risk, of the ship, including her outfit, provisions and stores for the officers and crew, money advanced for seamen's wages, and other disbursements (if any) incurred to make the ship fit for the voyage or adventure contemplated by the policy, plus the charges of insurance upon the whole.

The insurable value, in the case of a steamship, includes also the machinery, boilers, and coals and engine stores if owned by the assured, and, in the case of a ship engaged in a special trade, the ordinary fittings requisite for that trade:

(2) in insurance on freight, whether paid in advance or otherwise, the insurable value is the gross amount of the freight at the risk of the assured, plus the charges of insurance:

(3) in insurance on goods or merchandise, the insurable value is the prime cost of the property insured, plus the expenses of and incidental to shipping and the charges of insurance upon the whole:

(4) in insurance on any other subject-matter, the insurable value is the amount at the risk of the assured when the policy attaches, plus the charges of insurance.

DISCLOSURE AND REPRESENTATIONS

17. Insurance is uberrimae fidei.—A contract of marine insurance is a contract based upon the utmost good faith, and, if the utmost good faith be not observed by either party, the contract may be avoided by the other party.

18. Disclosure by assured.—(1) Subject to the provisions of this section, the assured must disclose to the insurer, before the contract is concluded, every material circumstance which is known to the assured, and the assured is deemed to know every circumstance which, in the ordinary course of business, ought to be known by him. If the assured fails to make such disclosure, the insurer may avoid the contract.

(2) Every circumstance is material which would influence the judgment of a prudent insurer in fixing the premium, or determining whether he will take the risk.

(3) In the absence of inquiry the following circumstances need not be disclosed, namely:

(a) any circumstance which diminishes the risk;
(b) any circumstance which is known or presumed to be known to the insurer. The insurer is presumed to know matters of common notoriety or knowledge, and matters which an insurer in the ordinary course of his business, as such, ought to know;
(c) any circumstance as to which information is waived by the insurer;
(d) any circumstance which it is superfluous to disclose by reason of any express or implied warranty.

(4) Whether any particular circumstance, which is not disclosed, be material or not is, in each case, a question of fact.

(5) The term 'circumstance' includes any communication made to, or information received by, the assured.

19. Disclosure by agent effecting insurance.—Subject to the provisions of the preceding section as to circumstances which need not be disclosed, where an insurance is effected for the assured by an agent, the agent must disclose to the insurer—

(a) every material circumstance which is known to himself, and an agent to insure is deemed to know every circumstance which in the ordinary course of business ought to be known by, or to have been communicated to, him; and
(b) every material circumstance which the assured is bound to disclose, unless it come to his knowledge too late to communicate it to the agent.

20. Representations pending negotiation of contract.—(1) Every material representation made by the assured or his agent to the insurer during the negotiations for the contract, and before the contract is concluded, must be true. If it be untrue the insurer may avoid the contract.

(2) A representation is material which would influence the judgment of a prudent insurer in fixing the premium, or determining whether he will take the risk.

(3) A representation may be either a representation as to a matter of fact, or as to a matter of expectation or belief.

(4) A representation as to a matter of fact is true, if it be substantially correct, that is to say, if the difference between what is represented and what is actually correct would not be considered material by a prudent insurer.

(5) A representation as to a matter of expectation or belief is true if it be made in good faith.

(6) A representation may be withdrawn or corrected before the contract is concluded.

(7) Whether a particular representation be material or not is, in each case, a question of fact.

21. When contract is deemed to be concluded.—A contract of marine insurance is deemed to be concluded when the proposal of the assured is accepted by the insurer, whether the policy be then issued or not; and, for the purpose of showing when the proposal was accepted, reference may be made to the slip or covering note or other customary memorandum of the contract . . .

THE POLICY

22. Contract must be embodied in policy.—Subject to the provisions of any statute, a contract of marine insurance is inadmissible in evidence unless it is embodied in a marine policy in accordance with this Act. The policy may be executed and issued either at the time when the contract is concluded, or afterwards.

23. What policy must specify.—A marine policy must specify—
   (1) The name of the assured, or of some person who effects the insurance on his behalf . . .

24. Signature of insurer.—(1) A marine policy must be signed by or on behalf of the insurer, provided that in the case of a corporation the corporate seal may be sufficient, but nothing in this section shall be construed as requiring the subscription of a corporation to be under seal.

(2) Where a policy is subscribed by or on behalf of two or more insurers, each subscription, unless the contrary be expressed, constitutes a distinct contract with the assured.

25. Voyage and time policies.—(1) Where the contract is to insure the subject-matter "at and from", or from one place to another or others, the policy is called a "voyage policy", and where the contract is to insure the subject-matter for a definite period of time the policy is called a "time policy". A contract for both voyage and time may be included in the same policy.

26. Designation of subject-matter.—(1) The subject-matter insured must be designated in a marine policy with reasonable certainty.

(2) The nature and extent of the interest of the assured in the subject-matter insured need not be specified in the policy.

(3) Where the policy designates the subject-matter insured in general terms, it shall be construed to apply to the interest intended by the assured to be covered.

(4) In the application of this section regard shall be had to any usage regulating the designation of the subject-matter insured.

27. Valued policy.—(1) A policy may be either valued or unvalued.

(2) A valued policy is a policy which specifies the agreed value of the subject-matter insured.

(3) Subject to the provisions of this Act, and in the absence of fraud, the value fixed by the policy is, as between the insurer and assured, conclusive of the insurable value of the subject intended to be insured, whether the loss be total or partial.

(4) Unless the policy otherwise provides, the value fixed by the policy is not conclusive for the purpose of determining whether there has been a constructive total loss.

28. Unvalued policy.—An unvalued policy is a policy which does not specify the value of the subject-matter insured, but, subject to the limit of the sum insured, leaves the insurable value to be subsequently ascertained, in the manner hereinbefore specified.

29. Floating policy by ship or ships.—(1) A floating policy is a policy which describes the insurance in general terms, and leaves the name of the ship or ships and other particulars to be defined by subsequent declaration.

(2) The subsequent declaration or declarations may be made by indorsement on the policy, or in other customary manner.

(3) Unless the policy otherwise provides, the declarations must be made in the order of dispatch or shipment. They must, in the case of goods, comprise all consignments within the terms of the policy, and the value of the goods or other property must be honestly stated, but an omission or erroneous declaration may be rectified even after loss or arrival, provided the omission or declaration was made in good faith.

(4) Unless the policy otherwise provides, where a declaration of value is not made until after notice of loss or arrival, the policy must be treated as an unvalued policy as regards the subject-matter of that declaration.

30. Construction of terms in policy.—(1) A policy may be in the form in the First Schedule to this Act.

(2) Subject to the provisions of this Act, and unless the context of the policy otherwise requires, the terms and expressions mentioned in the First Schedule to this Act shall be construed as having the scope and meaning in that schedule assigned to them.

31. Premium to be arranged.—(1) Where an insurance is effected at a premium to be arranged, and no arrangement is made, a reasonable premium is payable.

(2) Where an insurance is effected on the terms that an additional premium is to be arranged in a given event, and that event happens but no arrangement is made, then a reasonable additional premium is payable.

DOUBLE INSURANCE

32. Double insurance.—(1) Where two or more policies are effected by or on behalf of the assured on the same adventure and interest or any part thereof, and the sums insured exceed the indemnity allowed by this Act, the assured is said to be over-insured by double insurance.

(2) Where the assured is over-insured by double insurance—
  (a) the assured, unless the policy otherwise provides, may claim payment from the insurers in such order as he may think fit, provided that he is not entitled to receive any sum in excess of the indemnity allowed by this Act;
  (b) where the policy under which the assured claims is a valued policy, the assured must give credit as against the valuation for any sum received by him under any other policy without regard to the actual value of the subject-matter insured;
  (c) where the policy under which the assured claims is an unvalued policy he

must give credit, as against the full insurable value, for any sum received by him under any other policy;

(d) where the assured receives any sum in excess of the indemnity allowed by this Act, he is deemed to hold such sum in trust for the insurers, according to their right of contribution among themselves.

WARRANTIES, ETC

33. Nature of warranty.—(1) A warranty, in the following sections relating to warranties, means a promissory warranty, that is to say, a warranty by which the assured undertakes that some particular thing shall or shall not be done, or that some condition shall be fulfilled, or whereby he affirms or negatives the existence of a particular state of facts.

(2) A warranty may be express or implied.

(3) A warranty, as above defined, is a condition which must be exactly complied with, whether it be material to the risk or not. If it be not so complied with, then, subject to any express provision in the policy, the insurer is discharged from liability as from the date of the breach of warranty, but without prejudice to any liability incurred by him before that date.

34. When breach of warranty excused.—(1) Non-compliance with a warranty is excused when, by reason of a change of circumstances, the warranty ceases to be applicable to the circumstances of the contract, or when compliance with the warranty is rendered unlawful by any subsequent law.

(2) Where a warranty is broken, the assured cannot avail himself of the defence that the breach has been remedied, and the warranty complied with, before loss.

(3) A breach of warranty may be waived by the insurer.

35. Express warranties.—(1) An express warranty may be in any form of words from which the intention to warrant is to be inferred.

(2) An express warranty must be included in, or written upon, the policy, or must be contained in some document incorporated by reference into the policy.

(3) An express warranty does not exclude an implied warranty, unless it be inconsistent therewith.

36. Warranty of neutrality.—(1) Where insurable property, whether ship or goods, is expressly warranted neutral, there is an implied condition that the property shall have a neutral character at the commencement of the risk, and that, so far as the assured can control the matter, its neutral character shall be preserved during the risk.

(2) Where a ship is expressly warranted "neutral" there is also an implied condition that, so far as the assured can control the matter, she shall be properly documented, that is to say, that she shall carry the necessary papers to establish her neutrality, and that she shall not falsify or suppress her papers, or use simulated papers. If any loss occurs through breach of this condition, the insurer may avoid the contract.

37. No implied warranty of nationality.—There is no implied warranty as to the nationality of a ship, or that her nationality shall not be changed during the risk.

38. Warranty of good safety.—Where the subject-matter insured is warranted "well" or "in good safety" on a particular day, it is sufficient if it be safe at any time during that day.

39. Warranty of seaworthiness of ship.—(1) In a voyage policy there is an implied warranty that at the commencement of the voyage the ship shall be seaworthy for the purpose of the particular adventure insured.

(2) Where the policy attaches while the ship is in port, there is also an implied warranty that she shall, at the commencement of the risk, be reasonably fit to encounter the ordinary perils of the port.

(3) Where the policy relates to a voyage which is performed in different stages, during which the ship requires different kinds of or further preparation or equipment, there is an implied warranty that at the commencement of each stage the ship is seaworthy in respect of such preparation or equipment for the purposes of that stage.

(4) A ship is deemed to be seaworthy when she is reasonably fit in all respects to encounter the ordinary perils of the seas of the adventure insured.

(5) In a time policy there is no implied warranty that the ship shall be seaworthy at any stage of the adventure, but where, with the privity of the assured, the ship is sent to sea in an unseaworthy state, the insurer is not liable for any loss attributable to unseaworthiness.

40. No implied warranty that goods are seaworthy.—(1) In a policy on goods or other moveables there is no implied warranty that the goods or moveables are seaworthy.

(2) In a voyage policy on goods or other moveables there is an implied warranty that at the commencement of the voyage the ship is not only seaworthy as a ship, but also that she is reasonably fit to carry the goods or other moveables to the destination contemplated by the policy.

41. Warranty of legality.—There is an implied warranty that the adventure insured is a lawful one, and that, so far as the assured can control the matter, the adventure shall be carried out in a lawful manner.

THE VOYAGE

42. Implied condition as to commencement of risk.—(1) Where the subject-matter is insured by a voyage policy "at and from" or "from" a particular place, it is not necessary that the ship should be at that place when the contract is concluded, but there is an implied condition that the adventure shall be commenced within a reasonable time, and that if the adventure be not so commenced the insurer may avoid the contract.

(2) The implied condition may be negatived by showing that the delay was caused by circumstances known to the insurer before the contract was concluded, or by showing that he waived the condition.

43. Alteration of port of departure.—Where the place of departure is specified by the policy, and the ship instead of sailing from that place sails from any other place, the risk does not attach.

44. Sailing for different destination.—Where the destination is specified in the policy, and the ship, instead of sailing for that destination, sails for any other destination, the risk does not attach.

45. Change of voyage.—(1) Where, after the commencement of the risk, the destination of the ship is voluntarily changed from the destination contemplated by the policy, there is said to be a change of voyage.

(2) Unless the policy otherwise provides, where there is a change of voyage, the insurer is discharged from liability as from the time of change, that is to say, as from the time when the determination to change it is manifested; and it is immaterial that the ship may not in fact have left the course of voyage contemplated by the policy when the loss occurs.

46. Deviation.—(1) Where a ship, without lawful excuse, deviates from the voyage contemplated by the policy, the insurer is discharged from liability as from the time of deviation, and it is immaterial that the ship may have regained her route before any loss occurs.

(2) There is a deviation from the voyage contemplated by the policy—
   (a) where the course of the voyage is specifically designated by the policy, and that course is departed from; or
   (b) where the course of the voyage is not specifically designated by the policy, but the usual and customary course is departed from.

(3) The intention to deviate is immaterial; there must be a deviation in fact to discharge the insurer from his liability under the contract.

47. Several ports of discharge.—(1) Where several ports of discharge are specified by the policy, the ship may proceed to all or any of them, but, in the absence of any usage or sufficient cause to the contrary, she must proceed to them, or such of them as she goes to, in the order designated by the policy. If she does not there is a deviation.

(2) Where the policy is to "ports of discharge", within a given area, which are not named, the ship must, in the absence of any usage or sufficient cause to the contrary, proceed to them, or such of them as she goes to, in their geographical order. If she does not there is a deviation.

48. Delay in voyage.—In the case of a voyage policy, the adventure insured must be prosecuted throughout its course with reasonable dispatch, and, if without lawful excuse it is not so prosecuted, the insurer is discharged from liability as from the time when the delay became unreasonable.

49. Excuses for deviation or delay.—(1) Deviation or delay in prosecuting the voyage contemplated by the policy is excused—
   (a) where authorised by any special term in the policy; or
   (b) where caused by circumstances beyond the control of the master and his employer; or
   (c) where reasonably necessary in order to comply with an express or implied warranty; or
   (d) where reasonably necessary for the safety of the ship or subject-matter insured; or
   (e) for the purpose of saving human life, or aiding a ship in distress where human life may be in danger; or
   (f) where reasonably necessary for the purpose of obtaining medical or surgical aid for any person on board the ship; or
   (g) where caused by the barratrous conduct of the master or crew, if barratry be one of the perils insured against.

(2) When the cause excusing the deviation or delay ceases to operate, the ship must resume her course, and prosecute her voyage, with reasonable dispatch.

ASSIGNMENT OF POLICY

50. When and how policy is assignable.—(1) A marine policy is assignable unless it contains terms expressly prohibiting assignment. It may be assigned either before or after loss.

(2) Where a marine policy has been assigned so as to pass the beneficial interest in such policy, the assignee of the policy is entitled to sue thereon in his own name; and the defendant is entitled to make any defence arising out of the contract which he would have been entitled to make if the action had been brought in the name of the person by or on behalf of whom the policy was effected.

(3) A marine policy may be assigned by indorsement thereon or in other customary manner.

51. Assured who has no interest cannot assign.—Where the assured has parted with or lost his interest in the subject-matter insured, and has not, before or at the time of so doing, expressly or implied agreed to assign the policy, any subsequent assignment of the policy is inoperative:

Provided that nothing in this section affects the assignment of a policy after loss.

THE PREMIUM

52. When premium payable.—Unless otherwise agreed, the duty of the assured or his agent to pay the premium, and the duty of the insurer to issue the policy to the assured or his agent, are concurrent conditions, and the insurer is not bound to issue the policy until payment or tender of the premium.

53. Policy effected through broker.—(1) Unless otherwise agreed, where a marine policy is effected on behalf of the assured by a broker, the broker is directly responsible to the insurer for the premium, and the insurer is directly responsible to the assured for the amount which may be payable in respect of losses, or in respect of returnable premium.

(2) Unless otherwise agreed, the broker has, as against the assured, a lien upon the policy for the amount of the premium and his charges in respect of effecting the policy; and, where he has dealt with the person who employs him as a principal, he has also a lien on the policy in respect of any balance on any insurance account which may be due to him from such person, unless when the debt was incurred he had reason to believe that such person was only an agent.

54. Effect of receipt on policy.—Where a marine policy effected on behalf of the assured by a broker acknowledges the receipt of the premium, such acknowledgment is, in the absence of fraud, conclusive as between the insurer and the assured, but not as between the insurer and broker.

LOSS AND ABANDONMENT

55. Included and excluded losses.—(1) Subject to the provisions of this Act, and unless the policy otherwise provides, the insurer is liable for any loss proximately caused by a peril insured against, but, subject as aforesaid, he is not liable for any loss which is not proximately caused by a peril insured against.

(2) In particular,—
   (a) the insurer is not liable for any loss attributable to the wilful misconduct of the assured, but, unless the policy otherwise provides, he is liable for any loss proximately caused by a peril insured against, even though the loss would not have happened but for the misconduct or negligence of the master or crew;
   (b) unless the policy otherwise provides, the insurer on ship or goods is not liable for any loss proximately caused by delay, although the delay be caused by a peril insured against;
   (c) unless the policy otherwise provides, the insurer is not liable for ordinary wear and tear, ordinary leakage and breakage, inherent vice, or nature of the subject-matter insured, or for any loss proximately caused by rats or vermin, or for any injury to machinery not proximately caused by maritime perils.

56. Partial and total loss.—(1) A loss may be either total or partial. Any loss other than a total loss, as hereinafter defined, is a partial loss.

(2) A total loss may be either an actual total loss, or a constructive total loss.

(3) Unless a different intention appears from the terms of the policy, an insurance against total loss includes a constructive, as well as an actual, total loss.

(4) Where the assured brings an action for a total loss and the evidence proves only a partial loss, he may, unless the policy otherwise provides, recover for a partial loss.

(5) Where goods reach their destination in specie, but by reason of obliteration of marks, or otherwise, they are incapable of identification, the loss, if any, is partial, and not total.

57. Actual total loss.—(1) Where the subject-matter insured is destroyed, or so damaged as to cease to be a thing of the kind insured, or where the assured is irretrievably deprived thereof, there is an actual total loss.

(2) In the case of an actual loss no notice of abandonment need be given.

58. Missing ship.—Where the ship concerned in the adventure is missing, and after the lapse of a reasonable time no news of her has been received, an actual total loss may be presumed.

59. Effect of transhipment etc.—Where, by a peril insured against, the voyage is interrupted at an intermediate port or place, under such circumstances as, apart from any special stipulation in the contract of affreightment, to justify the master in landing and re-shipping the goods or other moveables, or in transhipping them, and sending them on to their destination, the liability of the insurer continues, notwithstanding the landing or transhipment.

60. Constructive total loss defined.—(1) Subject to any express provision in the policy, there is a constructive total loss where the subject-matter insured is reasonably abandoned on account of its actual total loss appearing to be unavoidable, or because it could not be preserved from actual total loss without an expenditure which would exceed its value when the expenditure had been incurred.

(2) In particular, there is a constructive total loss—
    (i) where the assured is deprived of the possession of his ship or goods by a peril insured against, and (*a*) it is unlikely that he can recover the ship or goods, as the case may be, or (*b*) the cost of recovering the ship or goods, as the case may be, would exceed their value when recovered; or
    (ii) in the case of damage to a ship, where she is so damaged by a peril insured against that the cost of repairing the damage would exceed the value of the ship when repaired.
        In estimating the cost of repairs, no deduction is to be made in respect of general average contributions to those repairs payable by other interests, but account is to be taken of the expense of future salvage operations and of any future general average contributions to which the ship would be liable if repaired; or
    (iii) in the case of damage to goods, where the cost of repairing the damage and forwarding the goods to their destination would exceed their value on arrival.

61. Effect of constructive total loss.—Where there is a constructive total loss the assured may either treat the loss as a partial loss, or abandon the subject-matter insured to the insurer and treat the loss as if it were an actual total loss.

62. Notice of abandonment.—(1) Subject to the provisions of this section, where the assured elects to abandon the subject-matter insured to the insurer, he must give notice of abandonment. If he fails to do so the loss can only be treated as a partial loss.

(2) Notice of abandonment may be given in writing, or by word of mouth, or partly in writing and partly by word of mouth, and may be given in any terms which indicate the intention of the assured to abandon his insured interest in the subject-matter insured unconditionally to the insurer.

(3) Notice of abandonment must be given with reasonable diligence after the receipt

of reliable information of the loss, but where the information is of a doubtful character the assured is entitled to a reasonable time to make inquiry.

(4) Where notice of abandonment is properly given, the rights of the assured are not prejudiced by the fact that the insurer refuses to accept the abandonment.

(5) The acceptance of an abandonment may be either express or implied from the conduct of the insurer. The mere silence of the insurer after notice is not an acceptance.

(6) Where notice of abandonment is accepted the abandonment is irrevocable. The acceptance of the notice conclusively admits liability for the loss and the sufficiency of the notice.

(7) Notice of abandonment is unnecessary where, at the time when the assured receives information of the loss, there would be no possibility of benefit to the insurer if notice were given to him.

(8) Notice of abandonment may be waived by the insurer.

(9) Where an insurer has re-insured his risk, no notice of abandonment need be given by him.

63. Effect of abandonment.—(1) Where there is a valid abandonment the insurer is entitled to take over the interest of the assured in whatever may remain of the subject-matter insured, and all proprietary rights incidental thereto.

(2) Upon the abandonment of a ship, the insurer thereof is entitled to any freight in course of being earned, and which is earned by her subsequent to the casualty causing the loss, less the expenses of earning it incurred after the casualty; and, where the ship is carrying the owner's goods, the insurer is entitled to a reasonable remuneration for the carriage of them subsequent to the casualty causing the loss.

PARTIAL LOSSES (INCLUDING SALVAGE AND GENERAL AVERAGE AND PARTICULAR CHARGES)

64. Particular average loss.—(1) A particular average loss is a partial loss of the subject-matter insured, caused by a peril insured against, and which is not a general average loss.

(2) Expenses incurred by or on behalf of the assured for the safety or preservation of the subject-matter insured, other than general average and salvage charges, are called particular charges. Particular charges are not included in particular average.

65. Salvage charges.—(1) Subject to any express provision in the policy, salvage charges incurred in preventing a loss by perils insured against may be recovered as a loss by those perils.

(2) "Salvage charges" means the charges recoverable under maritime law by a salvor independently of contract. They do not include the expenses of services in the nature of salvage rendered by the assured or his agents, or any person employed for hire by them, for the purpose of averting a peril insured against. Such expenses, where properly incurred, may be recovered as particular charges or as a general average loss, according to the circumstances under which they were incurred.

66. General average loss.—(1) A general average loss is a loss caused by or directly consequential on a general average act. It includes a general average expenditure as well as a general average sacrifice.

(2) There is a general average act where any extraordinary sacrifice or expenditure is voluntarily and reasonably made or incurred in time of peril for the purpose of preserving the property imperilled in the common adventure.

(3) Where there is a general average loss, the party on whom it falls is entitled, subject to the conditions imposed by maritime law, to a rateable contribution from the other parties interested, and such contribution is called a general average contribution.

(4) Subject to any express provision in the policy, where the assured has incurred a

general average expenditure, he may recover from the insurer in respect of the proportion of the loss which falls upon him; and, in the case of a general average sacrifice, he may recover from the insurer in respect of the whole loss without having enforced his right of contribution from the other parties liable to contribute.

(5) Subject to any express provision in the policy, where the assured has paid, or is liable to pay, a general average contribution in respect of the subject insured, he may recover therefor from the insurer.

(6) In the absence of express stipulation, the insurer is not liable for any general average loss or contribution where the loss was not incurred for the purpose of avoiding, or in connection with the avoidance of, a peril insured against.

(7) Where ship, freight, and cargo, or any two of those interests, are owned by the same assured, the liability of the insurer in respect of general average losses or contributions is to be determined as if those subjects were owned by different persons.

MEASURE OF INDEMNITY

67. Extent of liability of insurer for loss.—(1) The sum which the assured can recover in respect of a loss on a policy by which he is insured, in the case of an unvalued policy to the full extent of the insurable value, or, in the case of a valued policy to the full extent of the value fixed by the policy, is called the measure of indemnity.

(2) Where there is a loss recoverable under the policy, the insurer, or each insurer if there be more than one, is liable for such proportion of the measure of indemnity as the amount of his subscription bears to the value fixed by the policy in the case of a valued policy, or to the insurable value in the case of an unvalued policy.

68. Total loss.—Subject to the provisions of this Act and to any express provision in the policy, where there is a total loss of the subject-matter insured,—
   (1) if the policy be a valued policy, the measure of indemnity is the sum fixed by the policy:
   (2) if the policy be an unvalued policy, the measure of indemnity is the insurable value of the subject-matter insured.

69. Partial loss of ship.—Where a ship is damaged, but is not totally lost, the measure of indemnity, subject to any express provision in the policy, is as follows:
   (1) where the ship has been repaired, the assured is entitled to the reasonable cost of the repairs, less the customary deductions, but not exceeding the sum insured in respect of any one casualty:
   (2) where the ship has been only partially repaired, the assured is entitled to the reasonable cost of such repairs, computed as above, and also to be indemnified for the reasonable depreciation, if any, arising from the unrepaired damage, provided that the aggregate amount shall not exceed the cost of repairing the whole damage, computed as above:
   (3) where the ship has not been repaired, and has not been sold in her damaged state during the risk, the assured is entitled to be indemnified for the reasonable depreciation arising from the unrepaired damage, but not exceeding the reasonable cost of repairing such damage, computed as above.

70. Partial loss of freight.—Subject to any express provision in the policy, where there is a partial loss of freight, the measure of indemnity is such proportion of the sum fixed by the policy in the case of a valued policy, or of the insurable value in the case of an unvalued policy, as the proportion of freight lost by the assured bears to the whole freight at the risk of the assured under the policy.

71. Partial loss of goods, merchandise, etc.—Where there is a partial loss of

goods, merchandise, or other moveables, the measure of indemnity, subject to any express provision in the policy, is as follows:
  (1) where part of the goods, merchandise or other movables insured by a valued policy is totally lost, the measure of indemnity is such proportion of the sum fixed by the policy as the insurable value of the part lost bears to the insurable value of the whole, ascertained as in the case of an unvalued policy:
  (2) where part of the goods, merchandise, or other movables insured by an unvalued policy is totally lost, the measure of indemnity is the insurable value of the part lost, ascertained as in case of total loss:
  (3) where the whole or any part of the goods or merchandise insured has been delivered damaged at its destination, the measure of indemnity is such proportion of the sum fixed by the policy in the case of a valued policy, or of the insurable value in the case of an unvalued policy, as the difference between the gross sound and damaged values at the place of arrival bears to the gross sound value:
  (4) "gross value" means the wholesale price or, if there be no such price, the estimated value, with, in either case, freight, landing charges, and duty paid beforehand; provided that, in the case of goods or merchandise customarily sold in bond, the bonded price is deemed to be the gross value. "Gross proceeds" means the actual price obtained at a sale where all charges on sale are paid by the sellers.

72. Apportionment of valuation.—(1) Where different species of property are insured under a single valuation, the valuation must be apportioned over the different species in proportion to their respective insurable values, as in the case of an unvalued policy. The insured value of any part of a species is such proportion of the total insured value of the same as the insurable value of the part bears to the insurable value of the whole, ascertained in both cases as provided by this Act.

(2) Where a valuation has to be apportioned, and particulars of the prime cost of each separate species, quality, or description of goods cannot be ascertained, the division of the valuation may be made over the net arrived sound values of the different species, qualities, or descriptions of goods.

73. General average contributions and salvage charges.—(1) Subject to any express provision in the policy, where the assured has paid, or is liable for, any general average contribution, the measure of indemnity is the full amount of such contribution, if the subject-matter liable to contribution is insured for its full contributory value; but, if such subject-matter be not insured for its full contributory value, or if only part of it be insured, the indemnity payable by the insurer must be reduced in proportion to the under insurance, and where there has been a particular average loss which constitutes a deduction from the contributory value, and for which the insurer is liable, that amount must be deducted from the insured value in order to ascertain what the insurer is liable to contribute.

(2) Where the insurer is liable for salvage charges the extent of his liability must be determined on the like principle.

74. Liabilities to third parties.—Where the assured has effected an insurance in express terms against any liability to a third party, the measure of indemnity, subject to any express provision in the policy, is the amount paid or payable by him to such third party in respect of such liability.

75. General provisions as to measure of indemnity.—(1) Where there has been a loss in respect of any subject-matter not expressly provided for in the foregoing provisions of this Act, the measure of indemnity shall be ascertained, as nearly as may be, in accordance with those provisions, in so far as applicable to the particular case.

(2) Nothing in the provisions of this Act relating to the measure of indemnity shall affect the rules relating to double insurance, or prohibit the insurer from disproving interest wholly or in part, or from showing that at the time of the loss the whole or any part of the subject-matter insured was not at risk under the policy.

76. Particular average warranties.—(1) Where the subject-matter insured is warranted free from particular average, the assured cannot recover for a loss of part, other than a loss incurred by a general average sacrifice, unless the contract contained in the policy be apportionable; but, if the contract be apportionable, the assured may recover for a total loss of any apportionable part.

(2) Where the subject-matter insured is warranted free from particular average, either wholly or under a certain percentage, the insurer is nevertheless liable for salvage charges, and for particular charges and other expenses properly incurred pursuant to the provisions of the suing and labouring clause in order to avert a loss insured against.

(3) Unless the policy otherwise provides, where the subject-matter is warranted free from particular average under a specified percentage, a general average loss cannot be added to a particular average loss to make up the specified percentage.

(4) For the purpose of ascertaining whether the specified percentage has been reached, regard shall be had only to the actual loss suffered by the subject-matter insured. Particular charges and the expenses of and incidental to ascertaining and proving the loss must be excluded.

77. Successive losses.—(1) Unless the policy otherwise provides, and subject to the provisions of this Act, the insurer is liable for successive losses, even though the total amount of such losses may exceed the sum insured.

(2) Where, under the same policy, a partial loss, which has not been repaired or otherwise made good, is followed by a total loss, the assured can only recover in respect of the total loss:

Provided that nothing in this section shall affect the liability of the insurer under the suing and labouring clause.

78. Suing and labouring clause.—(1) Where the policy contains a suing and labouring clause, the engagement thereby entered into is deemed to be supplementary to the contract of insurance, and the assured may recover from the insurer any expenses properly incurred pursuant to the clause, notwithstanding that the insurer may have paid for a total loss, or that the subject-matter may have been warranted free from particular average, either wholly or under a certain percentage.

(2) General average losses and contributions and salvage charges, as defined by this Act, are not recoverable under the suing and labouring clause.

(3) Expenses incurred for the purpose of averting or diminishing any loss not covered by the policy are not recoverable under the suing and labouring clause.

(4) It is the duty of the assured and his agents, in all cases, to take such measures as may be reasonable for the purpose of averting or minimising a loss.

RIGHTS OF INSURER ON PAYMENT

79. Right of subrogation.—(1) Where the insurer pays for a total loss, either of the whole, or in the case of goods of any apportionable part, of the subject-matter insured, he thereupon becomes entitled to take over the interest of the assured in whatever may remain of the subject-matter so paid for, and he is thereby subrogated to all the rights and remedies of the assured in and in respect of that subject-matter as from the time of the casualty causing the loss.

(2) Subject to the foregoing provisions, where the insurer pays for a partial loss, he acquires no title to the subject-matter insured, or such part of it as may remain, but he is thereupon subrogated to all rights and remedies of the assured in and in respect of the

subject-matter insured as from the time of the casualty causing the loss, in so far as the assured has been indemnified, according to this Act, by such payment for the loss.

80. Right of contribution.—(1) Where the assured is over-insured by double insurance, each insurer is bound, as between himself and the other insurers, to contribute rateably to the loss in proportion to the amount for which he is liable under his contract.

(2) If any insurer pays more than his proportion of the loss, he is entitled to maintain an action for contribution against the other insurers, and is entitled to the like remedies as a surety who has paid more than his proportion of the debt.

81. Effect of under insurance.—Where the assured is insured for an amount less than the insurable value or, in the case of a valued policy, for an amount less than the policy valuation, he is deemed to be his own insurer in respect of the uninsured balance.

RETURN OF PREMIUM

82. Enforcement of return.—Where the premium or a proportionate part thereof is, by this Act, declared to be returnable,—
(a) if already paid, it may be recovered by the assured from the insurer; and
(b) if unpaid, it may be retained by the assured or his agent.

83. Return by agreement.—Where the policy contains a stipulation for the return of the premium, or a proportionate part thereof, on the happening of a certain event, and that event happens, the premium, or, as the case may be, the proportionate part thereof, is thereupon returnable to the assured.

84. Return for failure of consideration.—(1) Where the consideration for the payment of the premium totally fails, and there has been no fraud or illegality on the part of the assured or his agents, the premium is thereupon returnable to the assured.

(2) Where the consideration for the payment of the premium is apportionable and there is a total failure of any apportionable part of the consideration, a proportionate part of the premium is, under the like conditions, thereupon returnable to the assured.

(3) In particular—
   (a) where the policy is void, or is avoided by the insurer as from the commencement of the risk, the premium is returnable, provided that there has been no fraud or illegality on the part of the assured; but if the risk is not apportionable, and has once attached, the premium is not returnable:
   (b) where the subject-matter insured, or part thereof, has never been imperilled, the premium, or, as the case may be, a proportionate part thereof, is returnable:
      Provided that where the subject-matter has been insured "lost or not lost" and has arrived in safety at the time when the contract is concluded, the premium is not returnable unless, at such time, the insurer knew of the safe arrival.
   (c) where the assured has no insurable interest throughout the currency of the risk, the premium is returnable, provided that this rule does not apply to a policy effected by way of gaming or wagering;
   (d) where the assured has a defeasible interest which is terminated during the currency of the risk, the premium is not returnable;
   (e) where the assured has over-insured under an unvalued policy, a proportionate part of the premium is returnable;
   (f) subject to the foregoing provisions, where the assured has over-insured by double insurance, a proportionate part of the several premiums is returnable:
      Provided that, if the policies are effected at different times, and any

earlier policy has at any time borne the entire risk, or if a claim has been paid on the policy in respect of the full sum insured thereby, no premium is returnable in respect of that policy, and when the double insurance is effected knowingly by the assured no premium is returnable.

MUTUAL INSURANCE

85. Modification of Act in case of mutual insurance.—(1) Where two or more persons mutually agree to insure each other against marine losses there is said to be a mutual insurance.

(2) The provisions of this Act relating to the premium do not apply to mutual insurance, but a guarantee, or such other arrangement as may be agreed upon, may be substituted for the premium.

(3) The provisions of this Act, in so far as they may be modified by the agreement of the parties, may in the case of mutual insurance be modified by the terms of the policies issued by the association, or by the rules and regulations of the association.

(4) Subject to the exceptions mentioned in this section, the provisions of this Act apply to a mutual insurance.

SUPPLEMENTAL

86. Ratification by assured.—Where a contract of marine insurance is in good faith effected by one person on behalf of another, the person on whose behalf it is effected may ratify the contract even after he is aware of a loss.

87. Implied obligations varied by agreement or usage.—(1) Where any right, duty, or liability would arise under a contract of marine insurance by implication of law, it may be negatived or varied by express agreement, or by usage, if the usage be such as to bind both parties to the contract.

(2) The provisions of this section extend to any right, duty, or liability declared by this Act which may be lawfully modified by agreement.

88. Reasonable time, etc. a question of fact.—Where by this Act any reference is made to reasonable time, reasonable premium, or reasonable diligence, the question what is reasonable is a question of fact.

89. Slip as evidence.—Where there is a duly stamped policy, reference may be made, as heretofore, to the slip or covering note, in any legal proceeding.

90. Interpretation of terms.—In this Act, unless the context or subject-matter otherwise requires,—
"Action" includes counter-claim and set off:
"Freight" includes the profit derivable by a shipowner from the employment of his ship to carry his own goods or movables, as well as freight payable by a third party, but does not include passage money:
"Movables" means any movable tangible property, other than the ship, and includes money, valuable securities, and other documents:
"Policy" means a marine policy.

91. Savings.—(1) Nothing in this Act, or in any repeal effected thereby, shall affect—
  (a) the provisions of the Stamp Act 1891, or any enactment for the time being in force relating to the revenue;
  (b) the provisions of the Companies Act 1862, or any enactment amending or substituted for the same;
  (c) the provisions of any statute not expressly repealed by this Act.

(2) The rules of the common law including the law merchant, save in so far as they are inconsistent with the express provisions of this Act, shall continue to apply to contracts of marine insurance.

92. *This section was repealed by the Statute Law Revision Act 1927; 24 Halsbury's Statutes (2nd edn) 426.*

93. *This section was repealed by the Statute Law Revision Act 1927; 24 Halsbury's Statutes (2nd edn) 426.*

94. Short title.—This Act may be cited as the Marine Insurance Act 1906.

SCHEDULES

Section 30

FIRST SCHEDULE

FORM OF POLICY

BE IT KNOWN THAT   as well in
own name as for and in the name and names of all and every other person or persons to whom the same doth, may, or shall appertain, in part or in all doth make assurance and cause
and them, and every of them, to be insured lost or not lost, at and from

Upon any kind of goods and merchandises, and also upon the body, tackle, apparel, ordnance, munition, artillery, boat, and other furniture, of and in the good ship vessel called the

whereof is master under God, for this present voyage,
or whosoever else shall go for master in the said ship, or by whatsoever other name or names the said ship, or the master thereof, is or shall be named or called; beginning the adventure upon the said goods and merchandises from the loading thereof aboard the said ship,

upon the said ship, &c.

and so shall continue and endure, during her abode there, upon the said ship &c. And further, until the said ship, with all her ordnance, tackle, apparel, &c., and goods and merchandises whatsoever shall be arrived at

upon the said ship, &c., until she hath moored at anchor twenty-four hours in good safety; and upon the goods and merchandises, until the same be there discharged and safely landed. And it shall be lawful for the said ship, &c., in this voyage, to proceed and sail to and touch and stay at any ports or places whatsoever

without prejudice to this insurance. The said ship, &c., goods and merchandises, &c., for so much as concerns the assured by agreement between the assured and assurers in this policy, are and shall be valued at

Touching the adventures and perils which we the assurers are contented to bear and do take upon us in this voyage: they are of the seas, men of war, fire, enemies, pirates, rovers, thieves, jettisons, letters of mart and countermart, surprisals, takings at sea, arrests, restraints, and detainments of all kings, princes, and people, of what nation, condition, or quality soever, barratry of the master and mariners, and of all other perils, losses, and misfortunes, that have or shall come to the hurt, detriment, or damage of the said goods and merchandises, and ship, &c., or any part thereof. And in case of any loss or misfortune it shall be lawful to the assured, their factors, servants and assigns, to sue, labour, and travel for, in and about the defence, safeguards, and recovery of the said goods and merchandises, and ship, &c., or any part thereof, without prejudice to this insurance: to the charges whereof we, the assurers, will contribute each one according to the rate and quantity of his sum herein assured. And it is especially declared and agreed that no acts of the insurer or insured in recovering, saving, or preserving the property insured shall be considered as a waiver, or acceptance of abandonment. And it is agreed by us, the insurers, that this writing or policy of assurance shall be of as much force and effect as the surest writing or policy of assurance heretofore made in Lombard Street, or in the Royal Exchange, or elsewhere in London. And so we, the assurers, are contented, and so hereby promise and bind ourselves, each one for his own part, our heirs, executors, and goods to the assured, their executors, administrators, and assigns, for the true performance of the premises, confessing ourselves paid the consideration due unto us for this assurance by the assured, at and after the rate of

IN WITNESS whereof we, the assurers, have subscribed our names and sums assured in London

N.B.—Corn, fish, salt, fruit, flour, and seed are warranted free from average, unless general, or the ship be stranded—sugar, tobacco, hemp, flax, hides and skins are warranted free from average, under five pounds per cent., and all other goods, also the ship and freight, are warranted free from average, under three pounds per cent unless general, or the ship be stranded.

RULES FOR CONSTRUCTION OF POLICY

The following are the rules referred to by this Act for the construction of a policy in the above or other like form, where the context does not otherwise require:

1. Where the subject-matter is insured "lost or not lost", and the loss has occurred before the contract is concluded, the risk attaches unless, at such time the assured was aware of the loss, and the insurer was not.
2. Where the subject-matter is insured "from" a particular place, the risk does not attach until the ship starts on the voyage insured.
3. (*a*) Where the ship is insured "at and from" a particular place, and she is at that place in good safety when the contract is concluded, the risk attaches immediately.
(*b*) If she be not at that place when the contract is concluded, the risk attaches as soon as she arrives there in good safety, and, unless the policy otherwise provides, it is immaterial that she is covered by another policy for a specified time after arrival.
(*c*) Where chartered freight is insured "at and from" a particular place, and the ship is at that place in good safety when the contract is concluded the risk attaches immediately. If she be not there when the contract is concluded, the risk attaches as soon as she arrives there in good safety.
(*d*) Where freight, other than chartered freight, is payable without special conditions and is insured "at and from" a particular place, the risk attaches pro rata as the goods or merchandise are shipped; provided that if there be cargo in readiness which belongs to the shipowner, or which some other person has contracted with him to ship, the risk attaches as soon as the ship is ready to receive such cargo.
4. Where goods or other movables are insured "from the loading thereof", the risk does not attach until such goods or movables are actually on board, and the insurer is not liable for them while in transit from the shore to the ship.
5. Where the risk on goods or other movables continues until they are "safely landed",

they must be landed in the customary manner and within a reasonable time after arrival at the port of discharge, and if they are not so landed the risk ceases.

6. In the absence of any further license or usage, the liberty to touch and stay "at any port or place whatsoever" does not authorise the ship to depart from the course of her voyage from the port of departure to the port of destination.

7. The term "perils of the seas" refers only to fortuitous accidents or casualties of the seas. It does not include the ordinary action of the winds and waves.

8. The term "pirates" includes passengers who mutiny and rioters who attack the ship from the shore.

9. The term "thieves" does not cover clandestine theft or a theft committed by any one of the ship's company, whether crew or passengers.

10. The term "arrests, &c., of kings, princes, and people" refers to political or executive acts, and does not include a loss caused by riot or by ordinary judicial process.

11. The term "barratry" includes every wrongful act wilfully committed by the master or crew to the prejudice of the owner, or, as the case may be, the charterer.

12. The term "all other perils" includes only perils similar in kind to the perils specifically mentioned in the policy.

13. The term "average unless general" means a partial loss of the subject-matter insured other than a general average loss, and does not include "particular charges".

14. Where the ship has stranded, the insurer is liable for the excepted losses, although the loss is not attributable to the stranding, provided that when the stranding takes place the risk has attached and, if the policy be on goods, that the damaged goods are on board.

15. The term "ship" includes the hull, materials and outfit, stores and provisions for the officers and crew, and, in the case of vessels engaged in a special trade, the ordinary fittings requisite for the trade, and also, in the case of a steamship, the machinery, boilers, and coals and engine stores, if owned by the assured.

16. The term "freight" includes the profit derivable by a shipowner from the employment of his ship to carry his own goods or movables, as well as freight payable by a third party, but does not include passage money.

17. The term "goods" means goods in the nature of merchandise, and does not include personal effects or provisions and stores for use on board.

In the absence of any usage to the contrary, deck cargo and living animals must be insured specifically, and not under the general denomination of goods.

SECOND SCHEDULE

(*This Schedule was repealed by the Statute Law Revision Act 1927; 24 Halsbury's Statutes (2nd edn) 426*)

THE MARINE INSURANCE (GAMBLING POLICIES) ACT 1909[1]
(9 Edw 7 c 12)

An Act to prohibit Gambling on Loss by Maritime Perils [20th October 1909]

1. Prohibition of gambling on loss by maritime perils.—(1) If—
    (*a*) any person effects a contract of marine insurance without having any bonâ fide interest, direct or indirect, either in the safe arrival of the ship in relation

---

[1] The Act is printed as amended.

(b) any person in the employment of the owners of a ship, not being a part owner of the ship, effects a contract of marine insurance in relation to the ship, and the contract is made "interest or no interest"; or "without further proof of interest than the policy itself", or "without benefit of salvage to the insurer", or subject to any other like term,

the contract shall be deemed to be a contract by way of gambling on loss by maritime perils, and the person effecting it shall be guilty of an offence, and shall be liable, on summary conviction, to imprisonment . . . for a term not exceeding six months or to a fine not exceeding level 3 on the standard scale, and in either case to forfeit to the Crown any money he may receive under the contract.

(2) Any broker or other person through whom, and any insurer with whom, any such contract is effected shall be guilty of an offence and liable on summary conviction to the like penalties if he acted knowing that the contract was by way of gambling on loss by maritime perils within the meaning of this Act.

(3) Proceedings under this Act shall not be instituted without the consent in England of the Attorney-General, in Scotland of the Lord Advocate, and in Ireland of the Attorney-General for Ireland.

(4) Proceedings shall not be instituted under this Act against a person (other than a person in the employment of the owner of the ship in relation to which the contract was made) alleged to have effected a contract by way of gambling on loss by maritime perils until an opportunity has been afforded him of showing that the contract was not such a contract as aforesaid, and any information given by that person for that purpose shall not be admissible in evidence against him in any prosecution under this Act.

(5) If proceedings under this Act are taken against any person (other than a person in the employment of the owner of the ship in relation to which the contract was made) for effecting such a contract, and the contract was made "interest or no interest", or "without further proof of interest than the policy itself", or "without benefit of salvage to the insurer", or subject to any other like term, the contract shall be deemed to be a contract by way of gambling on loss by maritime perils unless the contrary is proved.

(6) For the purpose of giving jurisdiction under this Act, every offence shall be deemed to have been committed either in the place in which the same actually was committed or in any place in which the offender may be.

(7) Any person aggrieved by an order or decision of a court of summary jurisdiction under this Act, may appeal to the Crown Court.

(8) For the purposes of this Act the expression "owner" includes charterer.

(9) Subsection (7) of this section shall not apply to Scotland.

2. Short title.—This Act may be cited as the Marine Insurance (Gambling Policies) Act 1909, and the Marine Insurance Act 1906, and this Act may be cited together as the Marine Insurance Acts 1906 and 1909.

THE MARINE AND AVIATION INSURANCE (WAR RISKS) ACT 1952[2]
(15 & 16 Geo 6 & 1 Eliz 2 c 57)

An Act to make provision for authorising the Minister of Transport to undertake the insurance of ships, aircraft and certain other goods against war risks and, in certain circumstances, other risks; for the payment by him of compensation in respect of certain goods lost or damaged in transit in consequence of war risks; and for purposes connected with the matters aforesaid. [30th October 1952]

---

[2] The Act is printed as amended.

1. Agreements for re-insurance by Minister of Transport of war risks in respect of ships, aircraft and cargoes.—(1) The Minister of Transport (hereinafter in this Act referred to as "the Minister") may, with the approval of the Treasury, enter into agreements with any authorities or persons—
  (a) whereby he undertakes the liability of re-insuring any war risks against which a ship or aircraft is for the time being insured; and
  (b) whereby he undertakes the liability of re-insuring any war risks against which the cargo carried in a ship or aircraft is for the time being insured:

Provided that the Minister shall not enter into an agreement whereby he undertakes the liability of re-insuring any war risks against which a ship or aircraft not being a British ship or British aircraft is for the time being insured, except in so far as they arise during the continuance of any war or other hostilities in which Her Majesty is engaged or arise after any such war or hostilities in consequence of things done or omitted during the continuance thereof.

(2) A copy of every agreement made in pursuance of this section shall, as soon as may be after the agreement is made, be laid before each House of Parliament; and if either House, within the period of fourteen days beginning with the day on which a copy of such an agreement is laid before it, resolves that the agreement be annulled, the agreement shall thereupon become void except in so far as it confers rights or imposes obligations in respect of things previously done or omitted to be done, without prejudice, however, to the making of a new agreement.

In reckoning for the purposes of this subsection any such period of fourteen days as aforesaid, no account shall be taken of any time during which Parliament is dissolved or prorogued or during which both Houses are adjourned for more than four days.

(3) The reference in paragraph (a) of subsection (1) of this section to a ship or aircraft shall be construed as including a reference to any machinery, tackle, furniture or equipment of a ship or aircraft, and to any goods on board of a ship or aircraft, not being cargo carried therein, and the first reference in the proviso to that subsection to a ship or aircraft shall accordingly be similarly construed.

2. Insurance by Minister of Transport of ships, aircraft and cargoes.—(1) The Minister may, with the approval of the Treasury, carry on business under and in accordance with all or any of the following provisions of this subsection, that is to say:
  (a) at any time when it appears to him that reasonable and adequate facilities for the insurance of British ships or British aircraft against war risks, or any description of such risks, are not available, for the insurance by him of such ships, or as the case may be, such aircraft, against such risks, or as the case may be, that description thereof;
  (b) during the continuance of any war or other hostilities in which Her Majesty is engaged, for the insurance by him of ships and aircraft (whether British or not);
  (c) at any time when it appears to him that reasonable and adequate facilities for the insurance of cargoes carried in ships or aircraft against war risks, or any description of such risks, are not available, for the insurance by him of such cargoes against such risks or, as the case may be, that description thereof;
  (d) during the continuance of any war or other hostilities in which Her Majesty is engaged, for the insurance by him of cargoes carried in ships or aircraft;
  (e) during the continuance of any such war or hostilities, for the insurance by him of goods consigned for carriage by sea or by air, while the goods are in transit between the premises from which they are consigned and the ship or aircraft or between the ship or aircraft and their destination:

Provided that the Minister shall not, by virtue of paragraph (b), (d) or (e) of this subsection, undertake the insurance of a ship, aircraft or cargo against risks other than war risks unless he is satisfied that, in the interests of the defence of the realm or the efficient prosecution of any such war or hostilities as aforesaid, it is necessary or expedient so to do.

(2) References in paragraphs (*a*) and (*b*) of the foregoing subsection to ships of any description and to aircraft of any description shall be construed as including references to any machinery, tackle, furniture or equipment of ships of that description and aircraft of that description respectively and to any goods on board of ships of that description and aircraft of that description respectively, not being cargo carried therein, and the reference in the proviso to that subsection to a ship or aircraft shall accordingly be similarly construed.

(3) In paragraph (*e*) of subsection (1) of this section the expression "the ship or aircraft", in relation to goods consigned for carriage by sea or by air, does not include a vessel from which the goods are discharged for the purpose of being carried by sea or by air or into which they are discharged for the purpose of being landed.

3. Transitional provisions for compensation in respect of goods lost or damaged in transit after discharge or before shipment.—(1) Where a person satisfies the Minister with respect to any goods—
- (*a*) that the goods, having been consigned for carriage by sea or by air from a place outside any one of the countries to which this paragraph applies to a place in that country,—
    - (i) were discharged in that country from the ship or aircraft before the expiration of the period of seven days beginning with such day as the Minister may declare to be the day as from which he will carry on business for the purpose mentioned in paragraph (*e*) of subsection (1) of the last foregoing section;
    - (ii) were, after the beginning of that day and before the expiration of the appropriate period, lost or damaged in consequence of a war risk, being one which the Minister was, on that day, prepared to insure under the said paragraph (*e*); and
    - (iii) were lost or damaged while in transit between the ship or aircraft and their destination;

  or, having been consigned for carriage by sea or by air from a place in any one of the countries to which this paragraph applies to a place outside that country before the expiration of the said period of seven days, were, after the beginning of the said, day, lost or damaged in consequence of such a war risk as aforesaid while in transit between the premises from which they were consigned and the ship or aircraft; and
- (*b*) that the goods were not insured against the risk in consequence of which they were lost or damaged; and
- (*c*) that he and his agents exercised all due diligence for securing that no delay occurred while the goods were in such transit as aforesaid; and
- (*d*) that at the time when the loss or damage occurred the property in the goods was vested in him;

the Minister shall pay to him, by way of compensation for that loss or damage, an amount ascertained in accordance with the next following subsection.

(2) The amount of compensation payable under the foregoing subsection shall be—
- (*a*) in the case of lost goods, an amount equal to the insurable value of the goods;
- (*b*) in the case of damaged goods—
    - (i) where the goods have been delivered at their destination, an amount equal to such proportion of the insurable value of the goods as the difference between the gross sound and damaged values at the place of arrival bears to the gross sound value;
    - (ii) where the goods have not been so delivered, an amount equal to such proportion of the insurable value of the goods as the difference between the

gross sound and damaged values at the premises from which they were consigned bears to the gross sound value.

(3) Where, at a time when the loss or damage for which compensation in respect of any goods has become payable under this section occurred, the goods were subject to a mortgage, charge or other similar obligation, the amount of the compensation shall be deemed to be comprised in that mortgage, charge or other obligation.

(4) The countries to which paragraph (*a*) of subsection (1) of this section applies are the United Kingdom, the Isle of Man and any of the Channel Islands.

(5) In this section—
- (*a*) the expression "the ship or aircraft", in relation to goods consigned for carriage by sea or by air to or from a country to which paragraph (*a*) of subsection (1) of this section applies, does not include a vessel into which the goods are discharged at a port or place in that country for the purpose of being landed at that port or place, or from which the goods are discharged for the purpose of being carried by sea or by air from that country, as the case may be;
- (*b*) the expression "the appropriate period" means—
    - (i) in a case where the destination of the goods is within the port or place at which they were discharged from the ship or aircraft, the period of fifteen days beginning with the day on which they were so discharged; or
    - (ii) in a case where the destination of the goods is outside the said port or place, the period of thirty days beginning with the day on which they were so discharged; and
- (*c*) the expression "insurable value" means, in relation to goods consigned for carriage by sea or by air, the prime cost of the goods plus the expenses of and incidental to the carriage thereof as aforesaid and the charges of insurance upon the whole;

and for the purposes of this section the gross value of goods shall be taken to be the wholesale price or, if there be no such price, the estimated value, with, in either case, the expenses of and incidental to the carriage of the goods.

4. Liabilities of re-insurer in the event of insurer's insolvency.—Where a sum becomes payable to a person (hereafter in this section referred to as "the insurer") in respect of any loss or damage arising from a risk against which the insurer has, either originally or by way of re-insurance, insured another person (hereafter in this section referred to as "the assured") and either—
- (*a*) the sum has become payable by the Minister by virtue of an agreement made under section one of this Act; or
- (*b*) the sum has become payable under a contract of insurance by some person other than the Minister (hereafter in this section referred to as "the intermediate insurer") and the risk has been re-insured under such an agreement as aforesaid,

then, if before payment of that sum is made by the Minister or the intermediate insurer, the insurer becomes bankrupt or, in a case where the insurer is a company, the company commences to be wound up, or a receiver is appointed on behalf of the holders of any debentures of the company secured by a floating charge or possession is taken by or on behalf of the holders of such debentures of any property comprised in or subject to the charge, that sum shall cease to be payable to the insurer and the amount thereof shall be paid to the assured by the Minister or the intermediate insurer, as the case may be, and the right of the assured to receive payment in respect of the loss or damage from the insurer shall, to the extent to which the risk has been re-insured by the Minister, be extinguished.

5. Establishment of fund for purposes of this Act.—(1) There shall be established under the control of the Minister a fund, to be called the "marine and aviation insurance (war risks) fund",—

(a) into which shall be paid—
  (i) all sums received by the Minister by virtue of this Act;
  (ii) . . .
  (iii) . . .
(b) out of which shall be paid—
  (i) all sums required for the fulfilment by the Minister of any of his obligations under this Act; and
  (ii) . . .

(2) If, at any time when a payment falls to be made out of the marine and aviation insurance (war risks) fund, the sum standing to the credit of that fund is less than the sum required for the making of that payment, an amount equal to the deficiency shall be paid into that fund out of moneys provided by Parliament, but if and so far as that amount is not paid out of such moneys, it shall be charged on and issued out of the Consolidated Fund of the United Kingdom . . . (hereinafter in this Act referred to as "the Consolidated Fund").

(3) If, at any time, the amount standing to the credit of the marine and aviation insurance (war risks) fund exceeds the sum which, in the opinion of the Minister and the Treasury, is likely to be required for the making of payments out of that fund, the excess shall be paid into the Exchequer; . . .

(4) The Minister shall prepare, in such form and manner as the Treasury may direct, an account of the sums received into and paid out of the marine and aviation insurance (war risks) fund in each financial year, and shall, on or before the thirtieth day of November in each year, transmit the account to the Comptroller and Auditor General, who shall examine and certify the account and lay copies thereof together with copies of his report thereon, before both Houses of Parliament:

Provided that if the Treasury certify that, in the interests of the defence of the realm or the efficient prosecution of any war or other hostilities in which Her Majesty is engaged, it is expedient that copies of the account for any year and of the report thereon should be laid before Parliament, a copy of the certificate shall be laid before both Houses of Parliament and, so long as the certificate remains in force, those copies of the account and of the report shall not be so laid.

6. [*repealed*].

7. Exemption of certain instruments from provisions of Stamp Act 1891, and Marine Insurance Act 1906.—(1) None of the following instruments shall . . . be inadmissible in evidence by reason only that it is not embodied in a marine policy in accordance with the Marine Insurance Act 1906, that is to say:
  (a) an agreement for re-insurance made in pursuance of section one of this Act between the Minister and any other authority or person, and a policy of re-insurance issued by the Minister in pursuance of such an agreement;
  (b) an agreement entered into by a body to which this paragraph applies, being an agreement for the re-insurance of a risk insured by another person which may be again re-insured by the Minister, and a policy issued in pursuance of such an agreement, being a policy for the re-insurance only of such a risk as aforesaid;
  (c) a contract of insurance entered into by the Minister in exercise of the powers conferred on him by section two of this Act, and a policy of insurance and a certificate of insurance issued by the Minister in connection with any such contract.

(2) [*repealed*]
(3) [*repealed*]
(4) Paragraph (b) of subsection (1) of this section applies to any body of persons for the time being approved for the purposes of this Act by the Minister, being a body the objects of which are or include the carrying on of business by way of the re-insurance of

risks which may be re-insured under any agreement for the purpose mentioned in paragraph (*b*) of subsection (1) of section one of this Act.

8. Consequential amendment of 2 & 3 Geo. 6 c. 120.—For paragraph (*b*) of subsection (2) of section one of the Restriction of Advertisement (War Risks Insurance) Act 1939 (which, as amended by Order in Council under the Ministers of the Crown (Transfer of Functions) Act 1946, excludes from the acts rendered unlawful by subsection (1) of that section anything done with a view to inducing persons to enter into any contract of insurance, if the Minister of Transport could, under section one or section two of the War Risks Insurance Act 1939, lawfully re-insure the person liable under that contract), there shall be substituted the following paragraph:

"(*b*) anything done with a view to inducing persons to enter into any contract of insurance, if the Minister of Transport could, under section one of the Marine and Aviation Insurance (War Risks) Act 1952, lawfully re-insure the person liable under that contract; or"

9. Expenses of the Minister of Transport.—The expenses incurred for the purposes of this Act by the Minister shall, except in so far as they are required to be defrayed out of the marine and aviation insurance (war risks) fund, be defrayed out of moneys provided by Parliament.

10. Interpretation and savings.—(1) In this Act, unless the context otherwise requires, the following expressions have the meanings hereby respectively assigned to them, that is to say:

"British aircraft" means aircraft registered in Her Majesty's dominions;

"goods" includes currency and any securities payable to bearer, not being either bills of exchange or promissory notes;

"war risks' means risks arising from any of the the following events, that is to say, hostilities, rebellion, revolution and civil war, from civil strife consequent on the happening of any of those events, or from action taken (whether before or after the outbreak of any hostilities, rebellion, revolution or civil war) for repelling an imagined attack or preventing or hindering the carrying out of any attack, and includes piracy.

(2) The provisions of this Act relating to British ships shall apply also to ships of India and ships of the Republic of Ireland, and references in this Act to British ships shall be construed accordingly.

(3) The provisions of this Act relating to British aircraft shall apply also to aircraft registered in India, the Republic of Ireland, the Federation of Malaya, a protectorate, a protected state, a trust territory or a mandated territory, and references in this Act to British aircraft shall be construed accordingly.

The references in this subsection to a protectorate, a protected state, a trust territory and a mandated territory shall be construed as if they were references contained in the British Nationality Act 1948.

(4) [*repealed*]

11. Short title, extent and repeal.—(1) This act may be cited as the Marine and Aviation Insurance (War Risks) Act 1952.

(2) It is hereby declared that this Act extends to Northern Ireland.

(3) [*repealed*]

SCHEDULE

[*repealed*].

APPENDIX II
Marine Policy Forms

(1) Lloyd's Form

LLOYD'S MARINE POLICY

We, The Underwriters, hereby agree, in consideration of the payment to us by or on behalf of the Assured of the premium specified in the Schedule, to insure against loss damage liability or expense in the proportions and manner hereinafter provided. Each Underwriting Member of a Syndicate whose definitive number and proportion is set out in the following Table shall be liable only for his own share of his respective Syndicate's proportion.

In Witness whereof the General Manager of Lloyd's Policy Signing Office has subscribed his Name on behalf of each of Us.

LLOYD'S POLICY SIGNING OFFICE
General Manager

For embossment
by
Lloyd's Policy
Signing Office

This insurance is subject to English jurisdiction.

510

SCHEDULE
POLICY NUMBER

NAME OF ASSURED

VESSEL

VOYAGE OR PERIOD OF INSURANCE

SUBJECT-MATTER INSURED

AGREED VALUE
(if any)

AMOUNT INSURED HEREUNDER

PREMIUM

CLAUSES, ENDORSEMENTS, SPECIAL CONDITIONS AND WARRANTIES

Appendix II

Definitive numbers of the Syndicates and proportions

The List of Underwriting Members of Lloyd's mentioned in the above Table shows their respective Syndicates and Shares therein and is deemed to be incorporated in and to form part of this Policy: It is available for inspection at Lloyd's Policy Signing Office by the Assured or his or their representatives and a true copy of the material parts of it certified by the General Manager of Lloyd's Policy Signing Office will be furnished to the Assured on application.

(2) **Insurance Companies' Form**

The Institute of London Underwriters Companies Marine Policy

We, The Companies, hereby agree, in consideration of the payment to us by or on behalf of the Assured of the premium specified in the Schedule, to insure against loss damage liability or expense in the proportions and manner hereinafter provided. Each Company shall be liable only for its own respective proportion.

In Witness whereof the General Manager and Secretary of The Institute of London Underwriters has subscribed his name on behalf of each Company.

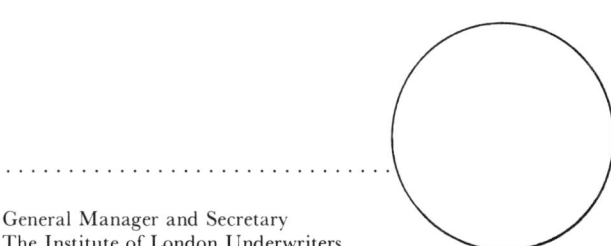

....
General Manager and Secretary
The Institute of London Underwriters

This Policy is not valid unless it bears the embossment of the Policy Department of The Institute of London Underwriters.

This insurance is subject to English jurisdiction.

SCHEDULE
POLICY NUMBER

NAME OF ASSURED

VESSEL

VOYAGE OR PERIOD OF INSURANCE

SUBJECT-MATTER INSURED

AGREED VALUE
(if any)

AMOUNT INSURED HEREUNDER

PREMIUM

CLAUSES, ENDORSEMENTS, SPECIAL CONDITIONS AND WARRANTIES

THE ATTACHED CLAUSES AND ENDORSEMENTS FORM PART OF THIS POLICY

COMPANIES' PROPORTIONS

For use by the Policy Department
of
The Institute of London Underwriters

APPENDIX III

The Institute Clauses

(1) CARGO CLAUSES

1/1/82 (FOR USE ONLY WITH THE NEW MARINE POLICY FORM)

INSTITUTE CARGO CLAUSES (A)

RISKS COVERED

1. Risks Clause. This insurance covers all risks of loss of or damage to the subject-matter insured except as provided in Clauses 4, 5, 6 and 7 below.

2. General Average Clause. This insurance covers general average and salvage charges, adjusted or determined according to the contract of affreightment and/or the governing law and practice, incurred to avoid or in connection with the avoidance of loss from any cause except those excluded in Clauses 4, 5, 6 and 7 or elsewhere in this insurance.

3. "Both to Blame Collision" Clause. This insurance is extended to indemnify the Assured against such proportion of liability under the contract of affreightment "Both to Blame Collision" Clause as is in respect of a loss recoverable hereunder. In the event of any claim by shipowners under the said Clause the Assured agree to notify the Underwriters who shall have the right, at their own cost and expense, to defend the Assured against such claim.

EXCLUSIONS

4. General Exclusions Clause. In no case shall this insurance cover
- 4.1. loss damage or expense attributable to wilful misconduct of the Assured
- 4.2 ordinary leakage, ordinary loss in weight or volume, or ordinary wear and tear of the subject-matter insured
- 4.3 loss damage or expense caused by insufficiency or unsuitability of packing or preparation of the subject-matter insured (for the purpose of this Clause 4.3 "packing" shall be deemed to include stowage in a container or liftvan but only when such stowage is carried out prior to attachment of this insurance or by the Assured or their servants)
- 4.4 loss damage or expense caused by inherent vice or nature of the subject-matter insured
- 4.5 loss damage or expense proximately caused by delay, even though the delay be caused by a risk insured against (except expenses payable under Clause 2 above)
- 4.6 loss damage or expense arising from insolvency or financial default of the owners managers charterers or operators of the vessel
- 4.7 loss damage or expense arising from the use of any weapon of war employing atomic or nuclear fission and/or fusion or other like reaction or radioactive force or matter.

5. Unseaworthiness and Unfitness Exclusion Clause.
- 5.1 In no case shall this insurance cover loss damage or expense arising from unseaworthiness of vessel or craft,

unfitness of vessel craft conveyance container or liftvan for the safe carriage of the subject-matter insured,

where the Assured or their servants are privy to such unseaworthiness or unfitness, at the time the subject-matter insured is loaded therein.

5.2   The Underwriters waive any breach of the implied warranties of seaworthiness of the ship and fitness of the ship to carry the subject-matter insured to destination, unless the Assured or their servants are privy to such unseaworthiness or unfitness.

6. War Exclusion Clause. In no case shall this insurance cover loss damage or expense caused by

6.1   war civil war revolution rebellion insurrection, or civil strife arising therefrom, or any hostile act by or against a belligerent power

6.2   capture seizure arrest restraint or detainment (piracy excepted), and the consequences thereof or any attempt thereat

6.3   derelict mines torpedoes bombs or other derelict weapons of war.

7. Strikes Exclusion Clause. In no case shall this insurance cover loss damage or expense

7.1   caused by strikers, locked-out workmen, or persons taking part in labour disturbances, riots or civil commotions

7.2   resulting from strikes, lock-outs, labour disturbances, riots or civil commotions

7.3   caused by any terrorist or any person acting from a political motive.

DURATION
8. Transit Clause.

8.1   This insurance attaches from the time the goods leave the warehouse or place of storage at the place named herein for the commencement of the transit, continues during the ordinary course of transit and terminates either

8.1.1   on delivery to the Consignees' or other final warehouse or place of storage at the destination named herein,

8.1.2   on delivery to any other warehouse or place of storage, whether prior to or at the destination named herein, which the Assured elect to use either

8.1.2.1   for storage other than in the ordinary course of transit or

8.1.2.2   for allocation or distribution,

or

8.1.3   on the expiry of 60 days after completion of discharge overside of the goods hereby insured from the oversea vessel at the final port of discharge,

whichever shall first occur.

8.2   If, after discharge overside from the oversea vessel at the final port of discharge, but prior to termination of this insurance, the goods are to be forwarded to a destination other than that to which they are insured hereunder, this insurance, whilst remaining subject to termination as provided for above, shall not extend beyond the commencement of transit to such other destination.

8.3   This insurance shall remain in force (subject to termination as provided for above and to the provisions of Clause 9 below) during delay beyond the control of the Assured, any deviation, forced discharge, reshipment or transhipment and during any variation of the adventure arising from the exercise of a liberty granted to shipowners or charterers under the contract of affreightment.

9. Termination of Contract of Carriage Clause. If owing to circumstances beyond the control of the Assured either the contract of carriage is terminated at a port or place other than the destination named therein or the transit is otherwise terminated before delivery of the goods as provided for in Clause 8 above, then this insurance shall also terminate *unless prompt notice is given to the Underwriters and continuation of cover is requested* *when the insurance shall remain in force, subject to an additional premium if required by the Underwriters,* either

9.1 until the goods are sold and delivered at such port or place, or, unless otherwise specially agreed, until the expiry of 60 days after arrival of the goods hereby insured at such port or place, whichever shall first occur, or

9.2 if the goods are forwarded within the said period of 60 days (or any agreed extension thereof) to the destination named herein or to any other destination, until terminated in accordance with the provisions of Clause 8 above.

10. Change of Voyage Clause. Where, after attachment of this insurance, the destination is changed by the Assured, *held covered at a premium and on conditions to be arranged subject to prompt notice being given to the Underwriters.*

CLAIMS
11. Insurable Interest Clause.

11.1 In order to recover under this insurance the Assured must have an insurable interest in the subject-matter insured at the time of the loss.

11.2 Subject to 11.1 above, the Assured shall be entitled to recover for insured loss occurring during the period covered by this insurance, notwithstanding that the loss occurred before the contract of insurance was concluded, unless the Assured were aware of the loss and the Underwriters were not.

12. Forwarding Charges Clause. Where, as a result of the operation of a risk covered by this insurance, the insured transit is terminated at a port or place other than that to which the subject-matter is covered under this insurance, the Underwriters will reimburse the Assured for any extra charges properly and reasonably incurred in unloading storing and forwarding the subject-matter to the destination to which it is insured hereunder.

This Clause 12, which does not apply to general average or salvage charges, shall be subject to the exclusions contained in Clauses 4, 5, 6 and 7 above, and shall not include charges arising from the fault negligence insolvency or financial default of the Assured or their servants.

13. Constructive Total Loss Clause. No claim for Constructive Total Loss shall be recoverable hereunder unless the subject-matter insured is reasonably abandoned either on account of its actual total loss appearing to be unavoidable or because the cost of recovering, reconditioning and forwarding the subject-matter to the destination to which it is insured would exceed its value on arrival.

14. Increased Value Clause.

14.1 If any Increased Value insurance is effected by the Assured on the cargo insured herein the agreed value of the cargo shall be deemed to be increased to the total amount insured under this insurance and all Increased Value insurances covering the loss, and liability under this insurance shall be in such proportion as the sum insured herein bears to such total amount insured.
In the event of claim the Assured shall provide the Underwriters with evidence of the amounts insured under all other insurances.

14.2 **Where this insurance is on Increased Value the following clause shall apply.**
The agreed value of the cargo shall be deemed to be equal to the total amount insured under the primary insurance and all Increased Value insurances covering the loss and effected on the cargo by the Assured, and liability under this insurance shall be in such proportion as the sum insured herein bears to such total amount insured.
In the event of claim the Assured shall provide the Underwriters with evidence of the amounts insured under all other insurances.

BENEFIT OF INSURANCE
15. Not to Inure Clause. This insurance shall not inure to the benefit of the carrier or other bailee.

MINIMISING LOSSES
16. Duty of Assured Clause. It is the duty of the Assured and their servants and agents in respect of loss recoverable hereunder
- 16.1 to take such measures as may be reasonable for the purpose of averting or minimising such loss, and
- 16.2 to ensure that all rights against carriers, bailees or other third parties are properly preserved and exercised

and the Underwriters will, in addition to any loss recoverable hereunder, reimburse the Assured for any charges properly and reasonably incurred in pursuance of these duties.

17. Waiver Clause. Measures taken by the Assured or the Underwriters with the object of saving, protecting or recovering the subject-matter insured shall not be considered as a waiver or acceptance of abandonment or otherwise prejudice the rights of either party.

AVOIDANCE OF DELAY
18. Reasonable Despatch Clause. It is a condition of this insurance that the Assured shall act with reasonable despatch in all circumstances within their control.

LAW AND PRACTICE
19. English Law and Practice Clause. This insurance is subject to English law and practice.

NOTE:—It is necessary for the Assured when they become aware of an event which is "held covered" under this insurance to give prompt notice to the Underwriters and the right to such cover is dependent upon compliance with this obligation.

1/1/82 (FOR USE ONLY WITH THE NEW MARINE POLICY FORM)

INSTITUTE CARGO CLAUSES (B)

RISKS COVERED
1. Risks Clause. This insurance covers, except as provided in Clauses 4, 5, 6 and 7 below,
- 1.1 loss of or damage to the subject-matter insured reasonably attributable to
- 1.1.1 fire or explosion
- 1.1.2 vessel or craft being stranded grounded sunk or capsized
- 1.1.3 overturning or derailment of land conveyance
- 1.1.4 collision or contact of vessel craft or conveyance with any external object other than water
- 1.1.5 discharge of cargo at a port of distress
- 1.1.6 earthquake volcanic eruption or lightning,
- 1.2 loss of or damage to the subject-matter insured caused by
- 1.2.1 general average sacrifice
- 1.2.2 jettison or washing overboard
- 1.2.3 entry of sea lake or river water into vessel craft hold conveyance container liftvan or place of storage,
- 1.3 total loss of any package lost overboard or dropped whilst loading on to, or unloading from, vessel or craft.

2. General Average Clause. This insurance covers general average and salvage charges, adjusted or determined according to the contract of affreightment and/or the governing law and practice, incurred to avoid or in connection with the avoidance of loss from any cause except those excluded in Clauses 4, 5, 6 and 7 or elsewhere in this insurance.

3. "Both to Blame Collision" Clause. This insurance is extended to indemnify the Assured against such proportion of liability under the contract of affreightment "Both to Blame Collision" Clause as is in respect of a loss recoverable hereunder.

In the event of any claim by shipowners under the said Clause the Assured agree to notify the Underwriters who shall have the right, at their own cost and expense, to defend the Assured against such claim.

EXCLUSIONS

4. General Exclusions Clause. In no case shall this insurance cover

- 4.1 loss damage or expense attributable to wilful misconduct of the Assured
- 4.2 ordinary leakage, ordinary loss in weight or volume, or ordinary wear and tear of the subject-matter insured
- 4.3 loss damage or expense caused by insufficiency or unsuitability of packing or preparation of the subject-matter insured (for the purpose of this Clause 4.3 "packing" shall be deemed to include stowage in a container or liftvan but only when such stowage is carried out prior to attachment of this insurance or by the Assured or their servants)
- 4.4 loss damage or expense caused by inherent vice or nature of the subject-matter insured
- 4.5 loss damage or expense proximately caused by delay, even though the delay may be caused by a risk insured against (except expenses payable under Clause 2 above)
- 4.6 loss damage or expense arising from insolvency or financial default of the owners managers charterers or operators of the vessel
- 4.7 deliberate damage to or deliberate destruction of the subject-matter insured or any part thereof by the wrongful act of any person or persons
- 4.8 loss damage or expense arising from the use of any weapon of war employing atomic or nuclear fission and/or fusion or other like reaction or radioactive force or matter.

5. Unseaworthiness and Unfitness Exclusion Clause.

- 5.1 In no case shall this insurance cover loss damage or expense arising from
    unseaworthiness of vessel or craft
    unfitness of vessel craft conveyance container or liftvan for the safe carriage of the subject-matter insured,
    where the Assured or their servants are privy to such unseaworthiness or unfitness, at the time the subject-matter insured is loaded therein.
- 5.2 The Underwriters waive any breach of the implied warranties of seaworthiness of the ship and fitness of the ship to carry the subject-matter insured to destination, unless the Assured or their servants are privy to such unseaworthiness or unfitness.

6. War Exclusion Clause. In no case shall this insurance cover loss damage or expense caused by

- 6.1 war civil war revolution rebellion insurrection, or civil strife arising therefrom, or any hostile act by or against a belligerent power
- 6.2 capture seizure arrest restraint or detainment, and the consequences thereof or any attempt thereat
- 6.3 derelict mines torpedoes bombs or other derelict weapons of war.

7. Strikes Exclusion Clause. In no case shall this insurance cover loss damage or expense

- 7.1 caused by strikers, locked-out workmen, or persons taking part in labour disturbances, riots or civil commotions
- 7.2 resulting from strikes, lock-outs, labour disturbances, riots or civil commotions
- 7.3 caused by any terrorist or any person acting from a political motive.

DURATION
8. Transit Clause.
    8.1   This insurance attaches from the time the goods leave the warehouse or place of storage at the place named herein for the commencement of the transit, continues during the ordinary course of transit and terminates either

    8.1.1   on delivery to the Consignees' or other final warehouse or place of storage at the destination named herein,

    8.1.2   on delivery to any other warehouse or place of storage, whether prior to or at the destination named herein, which the Assured elect to use either

    8.1.2.1   for storage other than in the ordinary course of transit or

    8.1.2.2   for allocation or distribution,

or

    8.1.3   on the expiry of 60 days after completion of discharge overside of the goods hereby insured from the oversea vessel at the final port of discharge,

whichever shall first occur.

    8.2   If, after discharge overside from the oversea vessel at the final port of discharge, but prior to termination of this insurance, the goods are to be forwarded to a destination other than that to which they are insured hereunder, this insurance, whilst remaining subject to termination as provided for above, shall not extend beyond the commencement of transit to such other destination.

    8.3   This insurance shall remain in force (subject to termination as provided for above and to the provisions of Clause 9 below) during delay beyond the control of the Assured, any deviation, forced discharge, reshipment or transhipment and during any variation of the adventure arising from the exercise of a liberty granted to shipowners or charterers under the contract of affreightment.

9. Termination of Contract of Carriage Clause.
If owing to circumstances beyond the control of the Assured either the contract of carriage is terminated at a port or place other than the destination named therein or the transit is otherwise terminated before delivery of the goods as provided for in Clause 8 above, then this insurance shall also terminate *unless prompt notice is given to the Underwriters and continuation of cover is requested when the insurance shall remain in force, subject to an additional premium if required by the Underwriters,* either

    9.1   until the goods are sold and delivered at such port or place, or, unless otherwise specially agreed, until the expiry of 60 days after arrival of the goods hereby insured at such port or place, whichever shall first occur,

or

    9.2   if the goods are forwarded within the said period of 60 days (or any agreed extension thereof) to the destination named herein or to any other destination, until terminated in accordance with the provisions of Clause 8 above.

10. Change of Voyage Clause.
Where, after attachment of this insurance, the destination is changed by the Assured, *held covered at a premium and on conditions to be arranged subject to prompt notice being given to the Underwriters.*

CLAIMS

11. Insurable Interest Clause.
    11.1   In order to recover under this insurance the Assured must have an insurable interest in the subject-matter insured at the time of the loss.

    11.2   Subject to 11.1 above, the Assured shall be entitled to recover for insured loss occurring during the period covered by this insurance, notwithstanding that the loss occurred before the contract of insurance was concluded, unless the Assured were aware of the loss and the Underwriters were not.

12. Forwarding Charges Clause.
Where, as a result of the operation of a risk covered by this insurance, the insured transit is terminated at a port or place other than that to which the subject-matter is covered under this insurance, the Underwriters will reimburse the Assured for any extra charges properly and reasonably incurred in unloading storing and forwarding the subject-matter to the destination to which it is insured hereunder.

This Clause 12, which does not apply to general average or salvage charges, shall be subject to the exclusions contained in Clauses 4, 5, 6 and 7 above, and shall not include charges arising from the fault negligence insolvency or financial default of the Assured or their servants.

13. Constructive Total Loss Clause. No claim for Constructive Total Loss shall be recoverable hereunder unless the subject-matter insured is reasonably abandoned either on account of its actual total loss appearing to be unavoidable or because the cost of recovering, reconditioning and forwarding the subject-matter to the destination to which it is insured would exceed its value on arrival.

14. Increased Value Clause.

14.1 If any Increased Value insurance is effected by the Assured on the cargo insured herein the agreed value of the cargo shall be deemed to be increased to the total amount insured under this insurance and all Increased Value insurances covering the loss, and liability under this insurance shall be in such proportion as the sum insured herein bears to such total amount insured.

In the event of claim the Assured shall provide the Underwriters with evidence of the amounts insured under all other insurances.

14.2 **Where this insurance is on Increased Value the following clause shall apply:**

The agreed value of the cargo shall be deemed to be equal to the total amount insured under the primary insurance and all Increased Value insurances covering the loss and effected on the cargo by the Assured, and liability under this insurance shall be in such proportion as the sum insured herein bears to such total amount insured.

In the event of claim the Assured shall provide the Underwriters with evidence of the amounts insured under all other insurances.

BENEFIT OF INSURANCE

15. Not to Inure Clause. This insurance shall not inure to the benefit of the carrier or other bailee.

MINIMISING LOSSES

16. Duty of Assured Clause. It is the duty of the Assured and their servants and agents in respect of loss recoverable hereunder

16.1 to take such measures as may be reasonable for the purpose of averting or minimising such loss, and

16.2 to ensure that all rights against carriers, bailees, or other third parties are properly preserved and exercised

and the Underwriters will, in addition to any loss recoverable hereunder, reimburse the Assured for any charges properly and reasonably incurred in pursuance of these duties.

17. Waiver Clause. Measures taken by the Assured or the Underwriters with the object of saving, protecting or recovering the subject-matter insured shall not be considered as a waiver or acceptance of abandonment or otherwise prejudice the rights of either party.

AVOIDANCE OF DELAY

18. Reasonable Despatch Clause. It is a condition of this insurance that the Assured shall act with reasonable despatch in all circumstances within their control.

LAW AND PRACTICE

19. English Law and Practice Clause. This insurance is subject to English law and practice.

NOTE:—It is necessary for the Assured when they become aware of an event which is "held covered" under this insurance to give prompt notice to the Underwriters and the right to such cover is dependent upon compliance with this obligation.

1/1/82   (FOR USE ONLY WITH THE NEW MARINE POLICY FORM)

INSTITUTE CARGO CLAUSES (C)

RISKS COVERED
1. Risks Clause. This insurance covers, except as provided in Clauses 4, 5 6 and 7 below,
 1.1 loss of or damage to the subject-matter insured reasonably attributable to
 1.1.1 fire or explosion
 1.1.2 vessel or craft being stranded grounded sunk or capsized
 1.1.3 overturning or derailment of land conveyance
 1.1.4 collision or contact of vessel craft or conveyance with any external object other than water
 1.1.5 discharge of cargo at a port of distress,
 1.2 loss of or damage to the subject-matter insured caused by
 1.2.1 general average sacrifice
 1.2.2 jettison.
2. General Average Clause. This insurance covers general average and salvage charges, adjusted or determined according to the contract of affreightment and/or the governing law and practice, incurred to avoid or in connection with the avoidance of loss from any cause except those excluded in Clauses 4, 5, 6 and 7 or elsewhere in this insurance.
3. "Both to Blame Collision" Clause. This insurance is extended to indemnify the Assured against such proportion of liability under the contract of affreightment "Both to Blame Collision" Clause as is in respect of a loss recoverable hereunder.
In the event of any claim by shipowners under the said Clause the Assured agree to notify the Underwriters who shall have the right, at their own cost and expense, to defend the Assured against such claim.

EXCLUSIONS
4. General Exclusions Clause. In no case shall this insurance cover
 4.1 loss damage or expense attributable to wilful misconduct of the Assured
 4.2 ordinary leakage, ordinary loss in weight or volume, or ordinary wear and tear of the subject-matter insured
 4.3 loss damage or expense caused by insufficiency or unsuitability of packing or preparation of the subject-matter insured (for the purpose of this Clause 4.3 "packing" shall be deemed to include stowage in a container or liftvan but only when such stowage is carried out prior to attachment of this insurance or by the Assured or their servants)
 4.4 loss damage or expense caused by inherent vice or nature of the subject-matter insured
 4.5 loss damage or expense proximately caused by delay, even though the delay be caused by a risk insured against (except expenses payable under Clause 2 above)
 4.6 loss damage or expense arising from insolvency or financial default of the owners managers charterers or operators of the vessel
 4.7 deliberate damage to or deliberate destruction of the subject-matter insured or any part thereof by the wrongful act of any person or persons
 4.8 loss damage or expense arising from the use of any weapon of war employing atomic or nuclear fission and/or fusion or other like reaction or radioactive force or matter.
5. Unseaworthiness and Unfitness Exclusion Clause.
 5.1 In no case shall this insurance cover loss damage or expense arising from unseaworthiness of vessel or craft,

unfitness of vessel craft conveyance container or liftvan for the safe carriage of the subject-matter insured,

where the Assured or their servants are privy to such unseaworthiness or unfitness, at the time the subject-matter insured is loaded therein.

5.2 The Underwriters waive any breach of the implied warranties of seaworthiness of the ship and fitness of the ship to carry the subject-matter insured to destination, unless the Assured or their servants are privy to such unseaworthiness or unfitness.

6. War Exclusion Clause. In no case shall this insurance cover loss damage or expense caused by

6.1 war civil war revolution rebellion insurrection, or civil strife arising therefrom, or any hostile act by or against a belligerent power

6.2 capture seizure arrest restraint or detainment, and the consequences thereof or any attempt thereat

6.3 derelict mines torpedoes bombs or other derelict weapons of war.

7. Strikes Exclusion Clause. In no case shall this insurance cover loss damage or expense

7.1 caused by strikers, locked-out workmen, or persons taking part in labour disturbances, riots or civil commotions

7.2 resulting from strikes, lock-outs, labour disturbances, riots or civil commotions

7.3 caused by any terrorist or any person acting from a political motive.

DURATION

8. Transit Clause.

8.1 This insurance attaches from the time the goods leave the warehouse or place of storage at the place named herein for the commencement of the transit, continues during the ordinary course of transit and terminates either

8.1.1 on delivery to the Consignees' or other final warehouse or place of storage at the destination named herein,

8.1.2 on delivery to any other warehouse or place of storage, whether prior to or at the destination named herein, which the Assured elect to use either

8.1.2.1 for storage other than in the ordinary course of transit or

8.1.2.2 for allocation or distribution,

or

8.1.3 on the expiry of 60 days after completion of discharge overside of the goods hereby insured from the oversea vessel at the final port of discharge,

whichever shall first occur.

8.2 If, after discharge overside from the oversea vessel at the final port of discharge, but prior to termination of this insurance, the goods are to be forwarded to a destination other than that to which they are insured hereunder, this insurance, whilst remaining subject to termination as provided for above, shall not extend beyond the commencement of transit to such other destination.

8.3 This insurance shall remain in force (subject to termination as provided for above and to the provisions of Clause 9 below) during delay beyond the control of the Assured, any deviation, forced discharge, reshipment or transhipment and during any variation of the adventure arising from the exercise of a liberty granted to shipowners or charterers under the contract of affreightment.

9. Termination of Contract of Carriage Clause. If owing to circumstances beyond the control of the Assured either the contract of carriage is terminated at a port or place other than the destination named therein or the transit is otherwise terminated before delivery of the goods as provided for in Clause 8 above, then this insurance shall also terminate *unless prompt notice is given to the Underwriters and continuation of cover is requested* when the insurance shall remain in force, subject to an additional premium if required by the Underwriters, either

    9.1   until the goods are sold and delivered at such port or place, or, unless otherwise specially agreed, until the expiry of 60 days after arrival of the goods hereby insured at such port or place, whichever shall first occur.

or

    9.2   if the goods are forwarded within the said period of 60 days (or any agreed extension thereof) to the destination named herein or to any other destination, until terminated in accordance with the provisions of Clause 8 above.

10. Change of Voyage Clause. Where, after attachment of this insurance, the destination is changed by the Assured, *held covered at a premium and on conditions to be arranged subject to prompt notice being given to the Underwriters.*

CLAIMS

11. Insurable Interest Clause.

    11.1   In order to recover under this insurance the Assured must have an insurable interest in the subject-matter insured at the time of the loss.

    11.2   Subject to 11.1 above, the Assured shall be entitled to recover for insured loss occurring during the period covered by this insurance, notwithstanding that the loss occurred before the contract of insurance was concluded, unless the Assured were aware of the loss and the Underwriters were not.

12. Forwarding Charges Clause. Where, as a result of the operation of a risk covered by this insurance, the insured transit is terminated at a port or place other than that to which the subject-matter is covered under this insurance, the Underwriters will reimburse the Assured for any extra charges properly and reasonably incurred in unloading storing and forwarding the subject-matter to the destination to which it is insured hereunder.

This Clause 12, which does not apply to general average or salvage charges, shall be subject to the exclusions contained in Clauses 4, 5, 6 and 7 above, and shall not include charges arising from the fault negligence insolvency or financial default of the Assured or their servants.

13. Constructive Total Loss Clause. No claim for Constructive Total Loss shall be recoverable hereunder unless the subject-matter insured is reasonably abandoned either on account of its actual total loss appearing to be unavoidable or because the cost of recovering, reconditioning and forwarding the subject-matter to the destination to which it is insured would exceed its value on arrival.

14. Increased Value Clause.

    14.1   If any Increased Value insurance is effected by the Assured on the cargo insured herein the agreed value of the cargo shall be deemed to be increased to the total amount insured under this insurance and all Increased Value insurances covering the loss, and liability under this insurance shall be in such proportion as the sum insured herein bears to such total amount insured.

In the event of claim the Assured shall provide the Underwriters with evidence of the amounts insured under all other insurances.

    14.2   **Where this insurance is on Increased Value the following clause shall apply:**

The agreed value of the cargo shall be deemed to be equal to the total amount insured under the primary insurance and all Increased Value insurances covering the loss and effected on the cargo by the Assured, and liability under this insurance shall be in such proportion as the sum insured herein bears to such total amount insured.

In the event of claim the Assured shall provide the Underwriters with evidence of the amounts insured under all other insurances.

BENEFIT OF INSURANCE
15. Not to Inure Clause. This insurance shall not inure to the benefit of the carrier or other bailee.

MINIMISING LOSSES
16. Duty of Assured Clause. It is the duty of the Assured and their servants and agents in respect of loss recoverable hereunder
- 16.1 to take such measures as may be reasonable for the purpose of averting or minimising such loss, and
- 16.2 to ensure that all rights against carriers, bailees or other third parties are properly preserved and exercised

and the Underwriters will, in addition to any loss recoverable hereunder, reimburse the Assured for any charges properly and reasonably incurred in pursuance of these duties.

17. Waiver Clause. Measures taken by the Assured or the Underwriters with the object of saving, protecting or recovering the subject-matter insured shall not be considered as a waiver or acceptance of abandonment or otherwise prejudice the rights of either party.

AVOIDANCE OF DELAY
18. Reasonable Despatch Clause. It is a condition of this insurance that the Assured shall act with reasonable despatch in all circumstances within their control.

LAW AND PRACTICE
19. English Law and Practice Clause. This insurance is subject to English law and practice.

NOTE:—*It is necessary for the Assured when they become aware of an event which is "held covered" under this insurance to give prompt notice to the Underwriters and the right to such cover is dependent upon compliance with this obligation.*

1/1/82   (FOR USE ONLY WITH THE NEW MARINE POLICY FORM)

INSTITUTE WAR CLAUSES (CARGO)

RISKS COVERED
1. Risks Clause. This insurance covers, except as provided in Clauses 3 and 4 below, loss of or damage to the subject-matter insured caused by
- 1.1 war civil war revolution rebellion insurrection, or civil strife arising therefrom, or any hostile act by or against a belligerent power
- 1.2 capture seizure arrest restraint or detainment, arising from risks covered under 1.1 above, and the consequences thereof or any attempt thereat
- 1.3 derelict mines torpedoes bombs or other derelict weapons of war.

2. General Average Clause. This insurance covers general average and salvage charges, adjusted or determined according to the contract of affreightment and/or the governing law and practice, incurred to avoid or in connection with the avoidance of loss from a risk covered under these clauses.

EXCLUSIONS
3. General Exclusions Clause. In no case shall this insurance cover
- 3.1 loss damage or expense attributable to wilful misconduct of the Assured

3.2 ordinary leakage, ordinary loss in weight or volume, or ordinary wear and tear of the subject-matter insured

3.3 loss damage or expense caused by insufficiency or unsuitability of packing or preparation of the subject-matter insured (for the purpose of this Clause 3.3 "packing" shall be deemed to include stowage in a container or liftvan but only when such stowage is carried out prior to attachment of this insurance or by the Assured or their servants)

3.4 loss damage or expense caused by inherent vice or nature of the subject-matter insured

3.5 loss damage or expense proximately caused by delay, even though the delay be caused by a risk insured against (except expenses payable under Clause 2 above)

3.6 loss damage or expense arising from insolvency or financial default of the owners managers charterers or operators of the vessel

3.7 any claim based upon loss of or frustration of the voyage or adventure

3.8 loss damage or expense arising from any hostile use of any weapon of war employing atomic or nuclear fission and/or fusion or other like reaction or radioactive force or matter.

4. Unseaworthiness and Unfitness Exclusion Clause.

4.1 In no case shall this insurance cover loss damage or expense arising from
unseaworthiness of vessel or craft,
unfitness of vessel craft conveyance container or liftvan for the safe carriage of the subject-matter insured,
where the Assured or their servants are privy to such unseaworthiness or unfitness, at the time the subject-matter insured is loaded therein.

4.2 The Underwriters waive any breach of the implied warranties of seaworthiness of the ship and fitness of the ship to carry the subject-matter insured to destination, unless the Assured or their servants are privy to such unseaworthiness or unfitness.

DURATION

5. Transit Clause.

5.1 This insurance

5.1.1 attaches only as the subject-matter insured and as to any part as that part is loaded on an oversea vessel
and

5.1.2 terminates, subject to 5.2 and 5.3 below, either as the subject-matter insured and as to any part as that part is discharged from an oversea vessel at the final port or place of discharge,
or
on expiry of 15 days counting from midnight of the day of arrival of the vessel at the final port or place of discharge,
whichever shall first occur;
nevertheless,
subject to prompt notice to the Underwriters and to an additional premium, such insurance

5.1.3 reattaches when, without having discharged the subject-matter insured at the final port or place of discharge, the vessel sails therefrom,
and

5.1.4 terminates, subject to 5.2 and 5.3 below, either as the subject-matter insured and as to any part as that part is thereafter discharged from the vessel at the final (or substituted) port or place of discharge,
or
on expiry of 15 days counting from midnight of the day of re-arrival of the

vessel at the final port or place of discharge or arrival of the vessel at a substituted port or place of discharge, whichever shall first occur.

5.2 If during the insured voyage the oversea vessel arrives at an intermediate port or place to discharge the subject-matter insured for on-carriage by oversea vessel or by aircraft, or the goods are discharged from the vessel at a port or place of refuge, then, subject to 5.3 below and to an additional premium if required, this insurance continues until the expiry of 15 days counting from midnight of the day of arrival of the vessel at such port or place, but thereafter reattaches as the subject-matter insured and as to any part as that part is loaded on an on-carrying oversea vessel or aircraft. During the period of 15 days the insurance remains in force after discharge only whilst the subject-matter insured and as to any part as that part is at such port or place. If the goods are on-carried within the said period of 15 days or if the insurance reattaches as provided in this Clause 5.2

5.2.1 where the on-carriage is by oversea vessel this insurance continues subject to the terms of these clauses,
or

5.2.2 where the on-carriage is by aircraft, the current Institute War Clauses (Air Cargo) (excluding sendings by Post) shall be deemed to form part of this insurance and shall apply to the on-carriage by air.

5.3 If the voyage in the contract of carriage is terminated at a port or place other than the destination agreed therein, such port or place shall be deemed the final port of discharge and such insurance terminates in accordance with 5.1.2. If the subject-matter insured is subsequently reshipped to the original or any other destination, then *provided notice is given to the Underwriters before the commencement of such further transit and subject to an additional premium,* such insurance reattaches

5.3.1 in the case of the subject-matter insured having been discharged, as the subject-matter insured and as to any part as that part is loaded on the on-carrying vessel for the voyage;

5.3.2 in the case of the subject-matter not having been discharged, when the vessel sails from such deemed final port of discharge;
therafter such insurance terminates in accordance with 5.1.4

5.4 The insurance against the risks of mines and derelict torpedoes, floating or submerged, is extended whilst the subject-matter insured or any part thereof is on craft whilst in transit to or from the oversea vessel, but in no case beyond the expiry of 60 days after discharge from the oversea vessel unless otherwise specially agreed by the Underwriters.

5.5 *Subject to prompt notice to Underwriters, and to an additional premium if required,* this insurance shall remain in force within the provisions of these Clauses during any deviation, or any variation of the adventure arising from the exercise of a liberty granted to shipowners or charterers under the contract of affreightment.

(for the purpose of Clause 5
"arrival" shall be deemed to mean that the vessel is anchored, moored or otherwise secured at a berth or place within the Harbour Authority area. If such a berth or place is not available, arrival is deemed to have occurred when the vessel first anchors, moors or otherwise secures either at or off the intended port or place of discharge
"oversea vessel" shall be deemed to mean a vessel carrying the subject-matter from one port or place to another where such voyage involves a sea passage by that vessel).

6. Change of Voyage Clause. Where, after attachment of this insurance, the destination is changed by the Assured, *held covered at a premium and on conditions to be arranged subject to prompt notice being given to the Underwriters.*

7. Anything contained in this contract which is inconsistent with Clauses 3.7, 3.8 or 5 shall, to the extent of such inconsistency, be null and void.

CLAIMS
8. Insurable Interest Clause.
- 8.1   In order to recover under this insurance the Assured must have an insurable interest in the subject-matter insured at the time of the loss.
- 8.2   Subject to 8.1 above, the Assured shall be entitled to recover for insured loss occurring during the period covered by this insurance, notwithstanding that the loss occurred before the contract of insurance was concluded, unless the Assured were aware of the loss and the Underwriters were not.

9. Increased Value Clause.
- 9.1   If any Increased Value insurance is effected by the Assured on the cargo insured herein the agreed value of the cargo shall be deemed to be increased to the total amount insured under this insurance and all Increased Value insurances covering the loss, and liability under this insurance shall be in such proportion as the sum insured herein bears to such total amount insured.

    In the event of claim the Assured shall provide the Underwriters with evidence of the amounts insured under all other insurances.
- 9.2   **Where this insurance is on Increased Value the following clause shall apply:**

    The agreed value of the cargo shall be deemed to be equal to the total amount insured under the primary insurance and all Increased Value insurances covering the loss and effected on the cargo by the Assured, and liability under this insurance shall be in such proportion as the sum insured herein bears to such total amount insured.

    In the event of claim the Assured shall provide the Underwriters with evidence of the amounts insured under all other insurances.

BENEFIT OF INSURANCE
10. Not to Inure Clause. This insurance shall not inure to the benefit of the carrier or other bailee.

MINIMISING LOSSES
11. Duty of Assured Clause. It is the duty of the Assured and their servants and agents in respect of loss recoverable hereunder
- 11.1   to take such measures as may be reasonable for the purpose of averting or minimising such loss, and
- 11.2   to ensure that all rights against carriers, bailees or other third parties are properly preserved and exercised

and the Underwriters will, in addition to any loss recoverable hereunder, reimburse the Assured for any charges properly and reasonably incurred in pursuance of these duties.

12. Waiver Clause. Measures taken by the Assured or the Underwriters with the object of saving, protecting or recovering the subject-matter insured shall not be considered as a waiver or acceptance of abandonment or otherwise prejudice the rights of either party.

AVOIDANCE OF DELAY
13. Reasonable Despatch Clause. It is a condition of this insurance that the Assured shall act with reasonable despatch in all circumstances within their control.

LAW AND PRACTICE.
14. English Law and Practice Clause. This insurance is subject to English law and practice.

NOTE:—It is necessary for the Assured when they become aware of an event which is "held covered" under this insurance to give prompt notice to the Underwriters and the right to such cover is dependent upon compliance with this obligation.

1/1/82   (FOR USE ONLY WITH THE NEW MARINE POLICY FORM)

INSTITUTE STRIKES CLAUSES (CARGO)

RISKS COVERED

1. Risks Clause. This insurance covers, except as provided in Clauses 3 and 4 below, loss of or damage to the subject-matter insured caused by
- 1.1 strikers, locked-out workmen, or persons taking part in labour disturbances, riots or civil commotions
- 1.2 any terrorist or any person acting from a political motive.

2. General Average Clause. This insurance covers general average and salvage charges, adjusted or determined according to the contract of affreightment and/or the governing law and practice, incurred to avoid or in connection with the avoidance of loss from a risk covered under these clauses.

EXCLUSIONS

3. General Exclusions Clause. In no case shall this insurance cover
- 3.1 loss damage or expense attributable to wilful misconduct of the Assured
- 3.2 ordinary leakage, ordinary loss in weight or volume, or ordinary wear and tear of the subject-matter insured
- 3.3 loss damage or expense caused by insufficiency or unsuitability of packing or preparation of the subject-matter insured (for the purpose of this Clause 3.3 "packing" shall be deemed to include stowage in a container or liftvan but only when such stowage is carried out prior to attachment of this insurance or by the Assured or their servants)
- 3.4 loss damage or expense caused by inherent vice or nature of the subject-matter insured
- 3.5 loss damage or expense proximately caused by delay, even though the delay be caused by a risk insured against (except expenses payable under Clause 2 above)
- 3.6 loss damage or expense arising from insolvency or financial default of the owners managers charterers or operators of the vessel
- 3.7 loss damage or expense arising from the absence shortage or withholding of labour of any description whatsoever resulting from any strike, lockout, labour disturbance, riot or civil commotion
- 3.8 any claim based upon loss of or frustration of the voyage or adventure
- 3.9 loss damage or expense arising from the use of any weapon of war employing atomic or nuclear fission and/or fusion or other like reaction or radioactive force or matter
- 3.10 loss damage or expense caused by war civil war revolution rebellion insurrection, or civil strife arising therefrom, or any hostile act by or against a belligerent power.

4. Unseaworthiness and Unfitness Exclusion Clause.
- 4.1 In no case shall this insurance cover loss damage or expense arising from
  unseaworthiness of vessel or craft,
  unfitness of vessel craft conveyance container or liftvan for the safe carriage of the subject-matter insured,
  where the Assured or their servants are privy to such unseaworthiness or unfitness, at the time the subject-matter insured is loaded therein.
- 4.2 The Underwriters waive any breach of the implied warranties of seaworthiness of the ship and fitness of the ship to carry the subject-matter insured to destination, unless the Assured or their servants are privy to such unseaworthiness or unfitness.

DURATION
5. Transit Clause.
- 5.1 This insurance attaches from the time the goods leave the warehouse or place of storage at the place named herein for the commencement of the transit, continues during the ordinary course of transit and terminates either
- 5.1.1 on delivery to the Consignees' or other final warehouse or place of storage at the destination named herein,
- 5.1.2 on delivery to any other warehouse or place of storage, whether prior to or at the destination named herein, which the Assured elect to use either
- 5.1.2.1 for storage other than in the ordinary course of transit or
- 5.1.2.2 for allocation or distribution,

    or
- 5.1.3 on the expiry of 60 days after completion of discharge overside of the goods hereby insured from the oversea vessel at the final port of discharge, whichever shall first occur
- 5.2 If, after discharge overside from the oversea vessel at the final port of discharge, but prior to termination of this insurance, the goods are to be forwarded to a destination other than that to which they are insured hereunder, this insurance, whilst remaining subject to termination as provided for above, shall not extend beyond the commencement of transit to such other destination.
- 5.3 This insurance shall remain in force (subject to termination as provided for above and to the provisions of Clause 6 below) during delay beyond the control of the Assured, any deviation, forced discharge, reshipment or transhipment and during any variation of the adventure arising from the exercise of a liberty granted to shipowners or charterers under the contract of affreightment.

6. Termination of Contract of Carriage Clause.
If owing to circumstances beyond the control of the Assured either the contract of carriage is terminated at a port or place other than the destination named therein or the transit is otherwise terminated before delivery of the goods as provided for in Clause 5 above, then this insurance shall also terminate *unless prompt notice is given to the Underwriters and continuation of cover is requested when the insurance shall remain in force, subject to an additional premium if required by the Underwriters,* either

- 6.1 until the goods are sold and delivered at such port or place, or, unless otherwise specially agreed, until the expiry of 60 days after arrival of the goods hereby insured at such port or place, whichever shall first occur,

    or
- 6.2 if the goods are forwarded within the said period of 60 days (or any agreed extension thereof) to the destination named herein or to any other destination, until terminated in accordance with the provisions of Clause 5 above.

7. Change of Voyage Clause.
Where, after attachment of this insurance, the destination is changed by the Assured, *held covered at a premium and on conditions to be arranged subject to prompt notice being given to the Underwriters.*

CLAIMS
8. Insurable Interest Clause.
- 8.1 In order to recover under this insurance the Assured must have an insurable interest in the subject-matter insured at the time of the loss.
- 8.2 Subject to 8.1 above, the Assured shall be entitled to recover for insured loss occurring during the period covered by this insurance, notwithstanding that the loss occurred before the contract of insurance was concluded, unless the Assured were aware of the loss and the Underwriters were not.

9. Increased Value Clause.

9.1 If any Increased Value insurance is effected by the Assured on the cargo insured herein the agreed value of the cargo shall be deemed to be increased to the total amount insured under this insurance and all Increased Value insurances covering the loss, and liability under this insurance shall be in such proportion as the sum insured herein bears to such total amount insured.
In the event of claim the Assured shall provide the Underwriters with evidence of the amounts insured under all other insurances.

9.2 **Where this insurance is on Increased Value the following clause shall apply:**
The agreed value of the cargo shall be deemed to be equal to the total amount insured under the primary insurance and all Increased Value insurances covering the loss and effected on the cargo by the Assured, and liability under this insurance shall be in such proportion as the sum insured herein bears to such total amount insured.
In the event of claim the Assured shall provide the Underwriters with evidence of the amounts insured under all other insurances.

BENEFIT OF INSURANCE

10. Not to Inure Clause. This insurance shall not inure to the benefit of the carrier or other bailee.

MINIMISING LOSSES

11. Duty of Assured Clause. It is the duty of the Assured and their servants and agents in respect of loss recoverable hereunder

11.1 to take such measures as may be reasonable for the purpose of averting or minimising such loss,
and

11.2 to ensure that all rights against carriers, bailees or other third parties are properly preserved and exercised.

and the Underwriters will, in addition to any loss recoverable hereunder, reimburse the Assured for any charges properly and reasonably incurred in pursuance of these duties.

12. Waiver Clause. Measures taken by the Assured or the Underwriters with the object of saving, protecting or recovering the subject-matter insured shall not be considered as a waiver or acceptance of abandonment or otherwise prejudice the rights of either party.

AVOIDANCE OF DELAY

13. Reasonable Despatch Clause. It is a condition of this insurance that the Assured shall act with reasonable despatch in all circumstances within their control.

LAW AND PRACTICE

14. English Law and Practice Clause. This insurance is subject to English law and practice.

NOTE:—It is necessary for the Assured when they become aware of an event which is "held covered" under this insurance to give prompt notice to the Underwriters and the right to such cover is dependent upon compliance with this obligation.

---

(2) HULL CLAUSES

1/10/83 (FOR USE ONLY WITH THE NEW MARINE POLICY FORM)

INSTITUTE TIME CLAUSES
HULLS

This insurance is subject to English law and practice

1. Navigation.
    1.1   The Vessel is covered subject to the provisions of this insurance at all times and has leave to sail or navigate with or without pilots, to go on trial trips and to assist and tow vessels or craft in distress, but it is warranted that the Vessel shall not be towed, except as is customary or to the first safe port or place when in need of assistance, or undertake towage or salvage services under a contract previously arranged by the Assured and/or Owners and/or Managers and/or Charterers. This Clause 1.1 shall not exclude customary towage in connection with loading and discharging.

    1.2   In the event of the Vessel being employed in trading operations which entail cargo loading or discharging at sea from or into another vessel (not being a harbour or inshore craft) no claim shall be recoverable under this insurance for loss of or damage to the Vessel or liability to any other vessel arising from such loading or discharging operations, including whilst approaching, lying alongside and leaving, unless previous notice that the Vessel is to be employed in such operations has been given to the Underwriters and any amended terms of cover and any additional premium required by them have been agreed.

    1.3   In the event of the Vessel sailing (with or without cargo) with an intention of being (a) broken up, or (b) sold for breaking up, any claim for loss of or damage to the Vessel occurring subsequent to such sailing shall be limited to the market value of the Vessel as scrap at the time when the loss or damage is sustained, unless previous notice has been given to the Underwriters and any amendments to the terms of cover, insured value and premium required by them have been agreed. Nothing in this Clause 1.3 shall affect claims under Clauses 8 and/or 11.

2. Continuation. Should the Vessel at the expiration of this insurance be at sea or in distress or at a port of refuge or of call, she shall, provided previous notice be given to the Underwriters, be held covered at a pro rata monthly premium to her port of destination.

3. Breach of Warranty. Held covered in case of any breach of warranty as to cargo, trade, locality, towage, salvage services or date of sailing, provided notice be given to the Underwriters immediately after receipt of advices and any amended terms of cover and any additional premium required by them be agreed.

4. Termination. *This Clause 4 shall prevail notwithstanding any provision whether written typed or printed in this insurance inconsistent therewith.*
Unless the Underwriters agree to the contrary in writing, this insurance shall terminate automatically at the time of
    4.1   change of the Classification Society of the Vessel, or change, suspension, discontinuance, withdrawal or expiry of her Class therein, provided that if the Vessel is at sea such automatic termination shall be deferred until arrival at her next port. However where such change, suspension, discontinuance or withdrawal of her Class has resulted from loss or damage covered by Clause 6 of this insurance or which would be covered by an insurance of the Vessel subject to current Institute War and Strikes Clauses Hulls–Time such automatic termination shall only operate should the Vessel sail from her next port without the prior approval of the Classification Society,

534 *Appendix III*

    4.2   any change, voluntary or otherwise, in the ownership or flag, transfer to new management, or charter on a bareboat basis, or requisition for title or use of the Vessel, provided that, if the Vessel has cargo on board and has already sailed from her loading port or is at sea in ballast, such automatic termination shall if required be deferred, whilst the Vessel continues her planned voyage, until arrival at final port of discharge if with cargo or at port of destination if in ballast. However, in the event of requisition for title or use without the prior execution of a written agreement by the Assured, such automatic termination shall occur fifteen days after such requisition whether the Vessel is at sea or in port.

A pro rata daily net return of premium shall be made.

5. Assignment. No assignment of or interest in this insurance or in any moneys which may be or become payable thereunder is to be binding on or recognised by the Underwriters unless a dated notice of such assignment or interest signed by the Assured, and by the assignor in the case of subsequent assignment, is endorsed on the Policy and the Policy with such endorsement is produced before payment of any claim or return of premium thereunder.

6. Perils.

    6.1   This insurance covers loss of or damage to the subject-matter insured caused by
        6.1.1   perils of the seas rivers lakes or other navigable waters
        6.1.2   fire, explosion
        6.1.3   violent theft by persons from outside the Vessel
        6.1.4   jettison
        6.1.5   piracy
        6.1.6   breakdown of or accident to nuclear installations or reactors
        6.1.7   contact with aircraft or similar objects, or objects falling therefrom, land conveyance, dock or harbour equipment or installation
        6.1.8   earthquake volcanic eruption or lightning.
    6.2   This insurance covers loss of or damage to the subject-matter insured caused by
        6.2.1   accidents in loading discharging or shifting cargo or fuel
        6.2.2   bursting of boilers breakage of shafts or any latent defect in the machinery or hull
        6.2.3   negligence of Master Officers Crew or Pilots
        6.2.4   negligence of repairers or charterers provided such repairers or charterers are not an Assured hereunder
        6.2.5   barratry of Master Officers or Crew,
provided such loss or damage has not resulted from want of due diligence by the Assured, Owners or Managers.
    6.3   Master Officers Crew or Pilots not to be considered Owners within the meaning of this Clause 6 should they hold shares in the Vessel.

7. Pollution Hazard. This insurance covers loss of or damage to the Vessel caused by any governmental authority acting under the powers vested in it to prevent or mitigate a pollution hazard, or threat thereof, resulting directly from damage to the Vessel for which the Underwriters are liable under this insurance, provided such act of governmental authority has not resulted from want of due diligence by the Assured, the Owners, or Managers of the Vessel or any of them to prevent or mitigate such hazard or threat. Master, Officers, Crew or Pilots not to be considered Owners within the meaning of this Clause 7 should they hold shares in the Vessel.

8. 3/4ths Collision Liability.

    8.1   The Underwriters agree to indemnify the Assured for three-fourths of any sum or sums paid by the Assured to any other person or persons by reason of the Assured becoming legally liable by way of damages for
        8.1.1   loss of or damage to any other vessel or property on any other vessel

8.1.2 delay to or loss of use of any such other vessel or property thereon

8.1.3 general average of, salvage of, or salvage under contract of, any such other vessel or property thereon,

where such payment by the Assured is in consequence of the Vessel hereby insured coming into collision with any other vessel.

8.2 The indemnity provided by this Clause 8 shall be in addition to the indemnity provided by the other terms and conditions of this insurance and shall be subject to the following provisions:

8.2.1 Where the insured Vessel is in collision with another vessel and both vessels are to blame then, unless the liability of one or both vessels becomes limited by law, the indemnity under this Clause 8 shall be calculated on the principle of cross-liabilities as if the respective Owners had been compelled to pay to each other such proportion of each other's damages as may have been properly allowed in ascertaining the balance or sum payable by or to the Assured in consequence of the collision.

8.2.2 In no case shall the Underwriters' total liability under Clauses 8.1 and 8.2 exceed their proportionate part of three-fourths of the insured value of the Vessel hereby insured in respect of any one collision.

8.3 The Underwriters will also pay three-fourths of the legal costs incurred by the Assured or which the Assured may be compelled to pay in contesting liability or taking proceedings to limit liability, with the prior written consent of the Underwriters.

EXCLUSIONS

8.4 Provided always that this Clause 8 shall in no case extend to any sum which the Assured shall pay for or in respect of

8.4.1 removal or disposal of obstructions, wrecks, cargoes or any other thing whatsoever

8.4.2 any real or personal property or thing whatsoever except other vessels or property on other vessels

8.4.3 the cargo or other property on, or the engagements of, the insured Vessel

8.4.4 loss of life, personal injury or illness

8.4.5 pollution or contamination of any real or personal property or thing whatsoever (except other vessels with which the insured Vessel is in collision or property on such other vessels).

9. Sistership. Should the Vessel hereby insured come into collision with or receive salvage services from another vessel belonging wholly or in part to the same Owners or under the same management, the Assured shall have the same rights under this insurance as they would have were the other vessel entirely the property of Owners not interested in the Vessel hereby insured; but in such cases the liability for the collision or the amount payable for the services rendered shall be referred to a sole arbitrator to be agreed upon between the Underwriters and the Assured.

10. Notice of Claim and Tenders.

10.1 In the event of accident whereby loss or damage may result in a claim under this insurance, notice shall be given to the Underwriters prior to survey and also, if the Vessel is abroad, to the nearest Lloyd's Agent so that a surveyor may be appointed to represent the Underwriters should they so desire.

10.2 The Underwriters shall be entitled to decide the port to which the Vessel shall proceed for docking or repair (the actual additional expense of the voyage arising from compliance with the Underwriters' requirements being refunded to the Assured) and shall have a right of veto concerning a place of repair or a repairing firm.

10.3 The Underwriters may also take tenders or may require further tenders to be taken for the repair of the Vessel. Where such a tender has been taken and a tender is accepted with the approval of the Underwriters, an allowance shall be made at the rate of 30% per annum on the insured value for time lost between the despatch of the invitations to tender required by Underwriters and the acceptance of a tender to the extent that such time is lost solely as the result of tenders having been taken and provided that the tender is accepted without delay after receipt of the Underwriters' approval.

Due credit shall be given against the allowance as above for any amounts recovered in respect of fuel and stores and wages and maintenance of the Master Officers and Crew or any member thereof, including amounts allowed in general average, and for any amounts recovered from third parties in respect of damages for detention and/or loss of profit and/or running expenses, for the period covered by the tender allowance or any part thereof. Where a part of the cost of the repair of damage other than a fixed deductible is not recoverable from the Underwriters the allowance shall be reduced by a similar proportion.

10.4 In the event of failure to comply with the conditions of this Clause 10 a deduction of 15% shall be made from the amount of the ascertained claim.

11. General Average and Salvage.

11.1 This insurance covers the Vessel's proportion of salvage, salvage charges and/or general average, reduced in respect of any under-insurance, but in case of general average sacrifice of the Vessel the Assured may recover in respect of the whole loss without enforcing their right of contribution from other parties.

11.2 Adjustment to be according to the law and practice obtaining at the place where the adventure ends, as if the contract of affreightment contained no special terms upon the subject; but where the contract of affreightment so provides the adjustment shall be according to the York–Antwerp Rules.

11.3 When the Vessel sails in ballast, not under charter, the provisions of the York–Antwerp Rules 1974 (excluding Rules XX and XXI) shall be applicable, and the voyage for this purpose shall be deemed to continue from the port or place of departure until the arrival of the Vessel at the first port or place thereafter other than a port or place of refuge or a port or place of call for bunkering only. If at any such intermediate port or place there is an abandonment of the adventure originally contemplated the voyage shall thereupon be deemed to be terminated.

11.4 No claim under this Clause 11 shall in any case be allowed where the loss was not incurred to avoid or in connection with the avoidance of a peril insured against.

12. Deductible.

12.1 No claim arising from a peril insured against shall be payable under this insurance unless the aggregate of all such claims arising out of each separate accident or occurrence (including claims under Clauses 8, 11 and 13) exceeds . . . . in which case this sum shall be deducted. Nevertheless the expense of sighting the bottom after stranding, if reasonably incurred specially for that purpose, shall be paid even if no damage be found. This Clause 12.1 shall not apply to a claim for total or constructive total loss of the Vessel or, in the event of such a claim, to any associated claim under Clause 13 arising from the same accident or occurrence.

12.2 Claims for damage by heavy weather occurring during a single sea passage between two successive ports shall be treated as being due to one accident. In the case of such heavy weather extending over a period not wholly covered by this insurance the deductible to be applied to the claim recoverable hereunder shall be the proportion of the above deductible that the number of days of such heavy weather falling within the period of this insurance bears to the number of days of heavy weather during the single sea passage.

The expression "heavy weather" in this Clause 12.2 shall be deemed to include contact with floating ice.

12.3   Excluding any interest comprised therein, recoveries against any claim which is subject to the above deductible shall be credited to the Underwriters in full to the extent of the sum by which the aggregate of the claim unreduced by any recoveries exceeds the above deductible.

12.4   Interest comprised in recoveries shall be apportioned between the Assured and the Underwriters, taking into account the sums paid by the Underwriters and the dates when such payments were made, notwithstanding that by the addition of interest the Underwriters may receive a larger sum than they have paid.

13. Duty of Assured (Sue and Labour).

13.1   In case of any loss or misfortune it is the duty of the Assured and their servants and agents to take such measures as may be reasonable for the purpose of averting or minimising a loss which would be recoverable under this insurance.

13.2   Subject to the provisions below and to Clause 12 the Underwriters will contribute to charges properly and reasonably incurred by the Assured their servants or agents for such measures. General average, salvage charges (except as provided for in Clause 13.5) and collision defence or attack costs are not recoverable under this Clause 13.

13.3   Measures taken by the Assured or the Underwriters with the object of saving, protecting or recovering the subject-matter insured shall not be considered as a waiver or acceptance of abandonment or otherwise prejudice the rights of either party.

13.4   When expenses are incurred pursuant to this Clause 13 the liability under this insurance shall not exceed the proportion of such expenses that the amount insured hereunder bears to the value of the Vessel as stated herein, or to the sound value of the Vessel at the time of the occurrence giving rise to the expenditure if the sound value exceeds that value. Where the Underwriters have admitted a claim for total loss and property insured by this insurance is saved, the foregoing provisions shall not apply unless the expenses of suing and labouring exceed the value of such property saved and then shall apply only to the amount of the expenses which is in excess of such value.

13.5   When a claim for total loss of the Vessel is admitted under this insurance and expenses have been reasonably incurred in saving or attempting to save the Vessel and other property and there are no proceeds, or the expenses exceed the proceeds, then this insurance shall bear its pro rata share of such proportion of the expenses, or of the expenses in excess of the proceeds, as the case may be, as may reasonably be regarded as having been incurred in respect of the Vessel; but if the Vessel be insured for less than its sound value at the time of the occurrence giving rise to the expenditure, the amount recoverable under this clause shall be reduced in proportion to the under-insurance.

13.6   The sum recoverable under this Clause 13 shall be in addition to the loss otherwise recoverable under this insurance but shall in no circumstances exceed the amount insured under this insurance in respect of the Vessel.

14. New for Old. Claims payable without deduction new for old.

15. Bottom Treatment. In no case shall a claim be allowed in respect of scraping gritblasting and/or other surface preparation or painting of the Vessel's bottom except that

15.1   gritblasting and/or other surface preparation of new bottom plates ashore and supplying and applying any "shop" primer thereto,

15.2   gritblasting and/or other surface preparation of:
the butts or area of plating immediately adjacent to any renewed or refitted plating damaged during the course of welding and/or repairs,

areas of plating damaged during the course of fairing, either in place or ashore,

15.3 supplying and applying the first coat of primer/anti-corrosive to those particular areas mentioned in 15.1 and 15.2 above,

shall be allowed as part of the reasonable cost of repairs in respect of bottom plating damaged by an insured peril.

16. Wages and Maintenance. No claim shall be allowed, other than in general average, for wages and maintenance of the Master, Officers and Crew, or any member thereof, except when incurred solely for the necessary removal of the Vessel from one port to another for the repair of damage covered by the Underwriters, or for trial trips for such repairs, and then only for such wages and maintenance as are incurred whilst the Vessel is under way.

17. Agency Commission. In no case shall any sum be allowed under this insurance either by way of remuneration of the Assured for time and trouble taken to obtain and supply information or documents or in respect of the commission or charges of any manager, agent, managing or agency company or the like, appointed by or on behalf of the Assured to perform such services.

18. Unrepaired Damage.

18.1 The measure of indemnity in respect of claims for unrepaired damage shall be the reasonable depreciation in the market value of the Vessel at the time this insurance terminates arising from such unrepaired damage, but not exceeding the reasonable cost of repairs.

18.2 In no case shall the Underwriters be liable for unrepaired damage in the event of a subsequent total loss (whether or not covered under this insurance) sustained during the period covered by this insurance or any extension thereof.

18.3 The Underwriters shall not be liable in respect of unrepaired damage for more than the insured value at the time this insurance terminates.

19. Constructive Total Loss.

19.1 In ascertaining whether the Vessel is a constructive total loss, the insured value shall be taken as the repaired value and nothing in respect of the damaged or break-up value of the Vessel or wreck shall be taken into account.

19.2 No claim for constructive total loss based upon the cost of recovery and/or repair of the Vessel shall be recoverable hereunder unless such cost would exceed the insured value. In making this determination, only the cost relating to a single accident or sequence of damages arising from the same accident shall be taken into account.

20. Freight Waiver. In the event of total or constructive total loss no claim to be made by the Underwriters for freight whether notice of abandonment has been given or not.

21. Disbursements Warranty.

21.1 Additional insurances as follows are permitted:

21.1.1 *Disbursements, Managers' Commissions, Profits or Excess or Increased Value of Hull and Machinery.* A sum not exceeding 25% of the value stated herein.

21.1.2 *Freight, Chartered Freight or Anticipated Freight, insured for time.* A sum not exceeding 25% of the value as stated herein less any sum insured, however described, under 21.1.1.

21.1.3 *Freight or Hire, under contracts for voyage.* A sum not exceeding the gross freight or hire for the current cargo passage and next succeeding cargo passage (such insurance to include, if required, a preliminary and an intermediate ballast passage) plus the charges of insurance. In the case of a voyage charter where payment is made on a time basis, the sum permitted for insurance shall be calculated on the estimated duration of the voyage, subject to the limitation of two cargo passages as laid down herein. Any sum insured under 21.1.2 to be taken into account and only the excess thereof may be insured, which excess shall be reduced as the freight or hire is advanced or earned by the gross amount so advanced or earned.

21.1.4 *Anticipated Freight if the Vessel sails in ballast and not under Charter.* A sum not exceeding the anticipated gross freight on next cargo passage, such sum to be reasonably estimated on the basis of the current rate of freight at time of insurance plus the charges of insurance. Any sum insured under 21.1.2 to be taken into account and only the excess thereof may be insured.

21.1.5 *Time Charter Hire or Charter Hire for Series of Voyages.* A sum not exceeding 50% of the gross hire which is to be earned under the charter in a period not exceeding 18 months. Any sum insured under 21.1.2 to be taken into account and only the excess thereof may be insured, which excess shall be reduced as the hire is advanced or earned under the charter by 50% of the gross amount so advanced or earned by the sum insured need not be reduced while the total of the sums insured under 21.1.2 and 21.1.5 does not exceed 50% of the gross hire still to be earned under the charter. An insurance under this Section may begin on the signing of the charter.

21.1.6 *Premiums.* A sum not exceeding the actual premiums of all interests insured for a period not exceeding 12 months (excluding premiums insured under the foregoing sections but including, if required, the premium or estimated calls on any Club or War etc. Risk insurance) reducing pro rata monthly.

21.1.7 *Returns of Premium.* A sum not exceeding the actual returns which are allowable under any insurance but which would not be recoverable thereunder in the event of a total loss of the Vessel whether by insured perils or otherwise.

21.1.8 *Insurance irrespective of amount against:*
Any risks excluded by Clauses 23, 24, 25 and 26 below.

21.2 Warranted that no insurance on any interests enumerated in the foregoing 21.1.1 to 21.1.7 in excess of the amounts permitted therein and no other insurance which includes total loss of the Vessel P.P.I., F.I.A., or subject to any other like term, is or shall be effected to operate during the currency of this insurance by or for account of the Assured, Owners, Managers or Mortgagees. Provided always that a breach of this warranty shall not afford the Underwriters any defence to a claim by a Mortgagee who has accepted this insurance without knowledge of such breach.

22. Returns for Lay-Up and Cancellation.

22.1 To return as follows:

22.1.1 Pro rata monthly net for each uncommenced month if this insurance be cancelled by agreement.

22.1.2 For each period of 30 consecutive days the Vessel may be laid up in a port or in a lay-up area provided such port or lay-up area is approved by the Underwriters (with special liberties as hereinafter allowed)
(a) .... per cent net not under repair
(b) .... per cent net under repair.
If the Vessel is under repair during part only of a period for which a return is claimable, the return shall be calculated pro rata to the number of days under (a) and (b) respectively.

22.2 PROVIDED ALWAYS THAT

22.2.1 a total loss of the Vessel, whether by insured perils or otherwise, has not occurred during the period covered by this insurance or any extension thereof

22.2.2 in no case shall a return be allowed when the Vessel is lying in exposed or unprotected waters, or in a port or lay-up area not approved by the Underwriters but, provided the Underwriters agree that such non-approved lay-up area is deemed to be within the vicinity of the approved port or lay-up area, days during which the Vessel is laid up in such non-approved lay-up area may be added to days in the approved port or lay-up area to calculate a period of 30 consecutive days and a return shall be allowed for the proportion of such period during which the Vessel is actually laid up in the approved port or lay-up area

22.2.3 loading or discharging operations or the presence of cargo on board shall not debar returns but no return shall be allowed for any period during which the Vessel is being used for the storage of cargo or for lightering purposes

22.2.4 in the event of any amendment of the annual rate, the above rates of return shall be adjusted accordingly

22.2.5 in the event of any return recoverable under this Clause 22 being based on 30 consecutive days which fall on successive insurances effected for the same Assured, this insurance shall only be liable for an amount calculated at pro rata of the period rates 22.1.2(a) and/or (b) above for the number of days which come within the period of this insurance and to which a return is actually applicable. Such overlapping period shall run, at the option of the Assured, either from the first day on which the Vessel is laid up or the first day of a period of 30 consecutive days as provided under 22.1.2(a) or (b), or 22.2.2 above.

The following clauses shall be paramount and shall override anything contained in this insurance inconsistent therewith.

23. War Exclusion. In no case shall this insurance cover loss damage liability or expense caused by

23.1 war civil war revolution rebellion insurrection, or civil strife arising therefrom, or any hostile act by or against a belligerent power

23.2 capture seizure arrest restraint or detainment (barratry and piracy excepted), and the consequences thereof or any attempt thereat

23.3 derelict mines torpedoes bombs or other derelict weapons of war.

24. Strikes Exclusion. In no case shall this insurance cover loss damage liability or expense caused by

24.1 strikers, locked-out workmen, or persons taking part in labour disturbances, riots or civil commotions

24.2 any terrorist or any person acting from a political motive.

25. Malicious Acts Exclusion. In no case shall this insurance cover loss damage liability or expense arising from

25.1 the detonation of an explosive

25.2 any weapon of war

and caused by any person acting maliciously or from a political motive.

26. Nuclear Exclusion. In no case shall this insurance cover loss damage liability or expense arising from any weapon of war employing atomic or nuclear fission and/or fusion or other like reaction or radioactive force or matter.

1/10/83 (FOR USE ONLY WITH THE NEW MARINE POLICY FORM)

INSTITUTE VOYAGE CLAUSES
HULLS

This insurance is subject to English law and practice

1. Navigation.

1.1 The Vessel is covered subject to the provisions of this insurance at all times and has leave to sail or navigate with or without pilots, to go on trial trips and to assist and tow vessels or craft in distress, but it is warranted that the Vessel shall not be towed, except as is customary or to the first safe port or place when in need of assistance, or undertake towage or salvage services under a contract previously arranged by the Assured and/or Owners and/or Managers and/or Charterers. This Clause 1.1 shall not exclude customary towage in connection with loading and discharging.

1.2 In the event of the Vessel being employed in trading operations which entail cargo loading or discharging at sea from or into another vessel (not being a harbour or inshore craft) no claim shall be recoverable under this insurance for loss of or damage to the Vessel or liability to any other vessel arising from such loading or discharging operations, including whilst approaching, lying alongside and leaving, unless previous notice that the Vessel is to be employed in such operations has been given to the Underwriters and any amended terms of cover and any additional premium required by them have been agreed.

2. Change of Voyage. Held covered in case of deviation or change of voyage or any breach of warranty as to towage or salvage services, provided notice be given to the Underwriters immediately after receipt of advices and any amended terms of cover and any additional premium required by them be agreed.

3. Assignment. No assignment of or interest in this insurance or in any moneys which may be or become payable thereunder is to be binding on or recognised by the Underwriters unless a dated notice of such assignment or interest signed by the Assured, and by the assignor in the case of subsequent assignment, is endorsed on the Policy and the Policy with such endorsement is produced before payment of any claim or return of premium thereunder.

4. Perils.

4.1 This insurance covers loss of or damage to the subject-matter insured caused by
4.1.1 perils of the seas rivers lakes or other navigable waters
4.1.2 fire, explosion
4.1.3 violent theft by persons from outside the Vessel
4.1.4 jettison
4.1.5 piracy
4.1.6 breakdown of or accident to nuclear installations or reactors
4.1.7 contact with aircraft or similar objects, or objects falling therefrom, land conveyance, dock or harbour equipment or installation
4.1.8 earthquake volcanic eruption or lightning.
4.2 This insurance covers loss of or damage to the subject-matter insured caused by
4.2.1 accidents in loading discharging or shifting cargo or fuel
4.2.2 bursting of boilers breakage of shafts or any latent defect in the machinery or hull
4.2.3 negligence of Master Officers Crew or Pilots
4.2.4 negligence of repairers or charterers provided such repairers or charterers are not an Assured hereunder
4.2.5 barratry of Master Officers or Crew,
provided such loss or damage has not resulted from want of due diligence by the Assured, Owners or Managers.
4.3 Master Officers Crew or Pilots not to be considered Owners within the meaning of this Clause 4 should they hold shares in the Vessel.

5. Pollution Hazard. This insurance covers loss of or damage to the Vessel caused by any governmental authority acting under the powers vested in it to prevent or mitigate a pollution hazard, or threat thereof, resulting directly from damage to the Vessel for which the Underwriters are liable under this insurance, provided such act of governmental authority has not resulted from want of due diligence by the Assured, the Owners, or Managers of the Vessel or any of them to prevent or mitigate such hazard or threat. Master, Officers, Crew or Pilots not to be considered Owners within the meaning of this Clause 5 should they hold shares in the Vessel.

6. 3/4ths Collision Liability.

6.1 The Underwriters agree to indemnify the Assured for three-fourths of any sum or sums paid by the Assured to any other person or persons by reason of the Assured becoming legally liable by way of damages for

6.1.1 loss of or damage to any other vessel or property on any other vessel

6.1.2 delay to or loss of use of any such other vessel or property thereon

6.1.3 general average of, salvage of, or salvage under contract of, any such other vessel or property thereon,

where such payment by the Assured is in consequence of the Vessel hereby insured coming into collision with any other vessel.

6.2 The indemnity provided by this Clause 6 shall be in addition to the indemnity provided by the other terms and conditions of this insurance and shall be subject to the following provisions:

6.2.1 Where the insured Vessel is in collision with another vessel and both vessels are to blame then, unless the liability of one or both vessels becomes limited by law, the indemnity under this Clause 6 shall be calculated on the principle of cross-liabilities as if the respective Owners had been compelled to pay to each other such proportion of each other's damages as may have been properly allowed in ascertaining the balance or sum payable by or to the Assured in consequence of the collision.

6.2.2 In no case shall the Underwriters' total liability under Clauses 6.1 and 6.2 exceed their proportionate part of three-fourths of the insured value of the Vessel hereby insured in respect of any one collision.

6.3 The Underwriters will also pay three-fourths of the legal costs incurred by the Assured or which the Assured may be compelled to pay in contesting liability or taking proceedings to limit liability, with the prior written consent of the Underwriters.

EXCLUSIONS

6.4 Provided always that this Clause 6 shall in no case extend to any sum which the Assured shall pay for or in respect of

6.4.1 removal or disposal of obstructions, wrecks, cargoes or any other thing whatsoever

6.4.2 any real or personal property or thing whatsoever except other vessels or property on other vessels

6.4.3 the cargo or other property on, or the engagements of, the insured Vessel

6.4.4 loss of life, personal injury or illness

6.4.5 pollution or contamination of any real or personal property or thing whatsoever (except other vessels with which the insured Vessel is in collision or property on such other vessels).

7. Sistership. Should the Vessel hereby insured come into collision with or receive salvage services from another vessel belonging wholly or in part to the same Owners or under the same management, the Assured shall have the same rights under this insurance as they would have were the other vessel entirely the property of Owners not interested in the Vessel hereby insured; but in such cases the liability for the collision or the amount payable for the services rendered shall be referred to a sole arbitrator to be agreed upon between the Underwriters and the Assured.

8. Notice of Claim and Tenders.

8.1 In the event of accident whereby loss or damage may result in a claim under this insurance, notice shall be given to the Underwriters prior to survey and also, if the Vessel is abroad, to the nearest Lloyd's Agent so that a surveyor may be appointed to represent the Underwriters should they so desire.

8.2 The Underwriters shall be entitled to decide the port to which the Vessel shall proceed for docking or repair (the actual additional expense of the voyage arising from compliance with the Underwriters' requirements being refunded to the Assured) and shall have a right of veto concerning a place of repair or a repairing firm.

8.3 The Underwriters may also take tenders or may require further tenders to be taken for the repair of the Vessel. Where such a tender has been taken and a tender is accepted with the approval of the Underwriters, an allowance shall be made at the rate of 30% per annum on the insured value for time lost between the despatch of the invitations to tender required by Underwriters and the acceptance of a tender to the extent that such time is lost solely as the result of tenders having been taken and provided that the tender is accepted without delay after receipt of the Underwriters' approval.

Due credit shall be given against the allowance as above for any amounts recovered in respect of fuel and stores and wages and maintenance of the Master Officers and Crew or any member thereof, including amounts allowed in general average, and for any amounts recovered from third parties in respect of damages for detention and/or loss of profit and/or running expenses, for the period covered by the tender allowance or any part thereof. Where a part of the cost of the repair of damage other than a fixed deductible is not recoverable from the Underwriters the allowance shall be reduced by a similar proportion.

8.4 In the event of failure to comply with the conditions of this Clause 8 a deduction of 15% shall be made from the amount of the ascertained claim.

9. General Average and Salvage.

9.1 This insurance covers the Vessel's proportion of salvage, salvage charges and/or general average, reduced in respect of any under-insurance, but in case of general average sacrifice of the Vessel the Assured may recover in respect of the whole loss without first enforcing their right of contribution from other parties.

9.2 Adjustment to be according to the law and practice obtaining at the place where the adventure ends, as if the contract of affreightment contained no special terms upon the subject; but where the contract of affreightment so provides the adjustment shall be according to the York–Antwerp Rules.

9.3 When the Vessel sails in ballast, not under charter, the provisions of the York–Antwerp Rules 1974 (excluding Rules XX and XXI) shall be applicable, and the voyage for this purpose shall be deemed to continue from the port or place of departure until the arrival of the Vessel at the first port or place thereafter other than a port or place of refuge or a port or place of call for bunkering only. If at any such intermediate port or place there is an abandonment of the adventure originally contemplated the voyage shall thereupon be deemed to be terminated.

9.4 No claim under this Clause 9 shall in any case be allowed where the loss was not incurred to avoid or in connection with the avoidance of a peril insured against.

10. Deductible.

10.1 No claim arising from a peril insured against shall be payable under this insurance unless the aggregate of all such claims arising out of each separate accident or occurrence (including claims under Clauses 6, 9 and 11) exceeds .... in which case this sum shall be deducted. Nevertheless the expense of sighting the bottom after stranding, if reasonably incurred specially for that purpose, shall be paid even if no damage be found. This Clause 10.1 shall not apply to a claim for total or constructive total loss of the Vessel, or in the event of such a claim, to any associated claim under Clause 11 arising from the same accident or occurrence.

10.2 Claims for damage by heavy weather occurring during a single sea passage between two successive ports shall be treated as being due to one accident. In the case of such heavy weather extending over a period not wholly covered by this insurance the deductible to be applied to the claim recoverable hereunder shall be the proportion of the above deductible that the number of days of such heavy weather falling within the period of this insurance bears to the number of days of heavy weather during the single sea passage. The expression "heavy weather" in this Clause 10.2 shall be deemed to include contact with floating ice.

10.3 Excluding any interest comprised therein, recoveries against any claim which is subject to the above deductible shall be credited to the Underwriters in full to the extent of the sum by which the aggregate of the claim unreduced by any recoveries exceeds the above deductible.

10.4 Interest comprised in recoveries shall be apportioned between the Assured and the Underwriters, taking into account the sums paid by the Underwriters and the dates when such payments were made, notwithstanding that by the addition of interest the Underwriters may receive a larger sum than they have paid.

11. Duty of Assured (Sue and Labour).

11.1 In case of any loss or misfortune it is the duty of the Assured and their servants and agents to take such measures as may be reasonable for the purpose of averting or minimising a loss which would be recoverable under this insurance.

11.2 Subject to the provisions below and to Clause 10 the Underwriters will contribute to charges properly and reasonably incurred by the Assured their servants or agents for such measures. General average, salvage charges (except as provided for in Clause 11.5) and collision defence or attack costs are not recoverable under this Clause 11.

11.3 Measures taken by the Assured or the Underwriters with the object of saving, protecting or recovering the subject-matter insured shall not be considered as a waiver or acceptance of abandonment or otherwise prejudice the rights of either party.

11.4 When expenses are incurred pursuant to this Clause 11 the liability under this insurance shall not exceed the proportion of such expenses that the amount insured hereunder bears to the value of the Vessel as stated herein, or to the sound value of the Vessel at the time of the occurrence giving rise to the expenditure if the sound value exceeds that value. Where the Underwriters have admitted a claim for total loss and property insured by this insurance is saved, the foregoing provisions shall not apply unless the expenses of suing and labouring exceed the value of such property saved and then shall apply only to the amount of the expenses which is in excess of such value.

11.5 When a claim for total loss of the Vessel is admitted under this insurance and expenses have been reasonably incurred in saving or attempting to save the Vessel and other property and there are no proceeds, or the expenses exceed the proceeds, then this insurance shall bear its pro rata share of such proportion of the expenses, or of the expenses in excess of the proceeds, as the case may be, as may reasonably be regarded as having been incurred in respect of the Vessel; but if the Vessel be insured for less than its sound value at the time of the occurrence giving rise to the expenditure, the amount recoverable under this clause shall be reduced in proportion to the under-insurance.

11.6 The sum recoverable under this Clause 11 shall be in addition to the loss otherwise recoverable under this insurance but shall in no circumstances exceed the amount insured under this insurance in respect of the Vessel.

12. New for Old. Claims payable without deduction new for old.

13. Bottom Treatment. In no case shall a claim be allowed in respect of scraping gritblasting and/or other surface preparation or painting of the Vessel's bottom except that

13.1 gritblasting and/or other surface preparation of new bottom plates ashore and supplying and applying any "shop" primer thereto,

13.2 gritblasting and/or other surface preparation of:
the butts or area of plating immediately adjacent to any renewed or refitted plating damaged during the course of welding and/or repairs,
areas of plating damaged during the course of fairing, either in place or ashore,

13.3 supplying and applying the first coat of primer/anti-corrosive to those particular areas mentioned in 13.1 and 13.2 above,

shall be allowed as part of the reasonable cost of repairs in respect of bottom plating damaged by an insured peril.

14. Wages and Maintenance. No claim shall be allowed, other than in general average, for wages and maintenance of the Master, Officers and Crew, or any member thereof, except when incurred solely for the necessary removal of the Vessel from one port to another for the repair of damage covered by the Underwriters, or for trial trips for such repairs, and then only for such wages and maintenance as are incurred whilst the Vessel is under way.

15. Agency Commission. In no case shall any sum be allowed under this insurance either by way of remuneration of the Assured for time and trouble taken to obtain and supply information or documents or in respect of the commission or charges of any manager, agent, managing or agency company or the like, appointed by or on behalf of the Assured to perform such services.

16. Unrepaired Damage.

16.1 The measure of indemnity in respect of claims for unrepaired damage shall be the reasonable depreciation in the market value of the Vessel at the time this insurance terminates arising from such unrepaired damage, but not exceeding the reasonable cost of repairs.

16.2 In no case shall the Underwriters be liable for unrepaired damage in the event of a subsequent total loss (whether or not covered under this insurance) sustained during the period covered by this insurance or any extension thereof.

16.3 The Underwriters shall not be liable in respect of unrepaired damage for more than the insured value at the time this insurance terminates.

17. Constructive Total Loss

17.1 In ascertaining whether the Vessel is a constructive total loss, the insured value shall be taken as the repaired value and nothing in respect of the damaged or break-up value of the Vessel or wreck shall be taken into account.

17.2 No claim for constructive total loss based upon the cost of recovery and/or repair of the Vessel shall be recoverable hereunder unless such cost would exceed the insured value. In making this determination, only the cost relating to a single accident or sequence of damages arising from the same accident shall be taken into account.

18. Freight Waiver. In the event of total or constructive total loss no claim to be made by the Underwriters for freight whether notice of abandonment has been given or not.

19. Disbursements Warranty.

19.1 Additional insurances as follows are permitted:

19.1.1 *Disbursements, Managers' Commissions, Profits or Excess or Increased Value of Hull and Machinery.* A sum not exceeding 25% of the value stated herein.

19.1.2 *Freight, Chartered Freight or Anticipated Freight, insured for time.* A sum not exceeding 25% of the value as stated herein less any sum insured, however described, under 19.1.1.

19.1.3 *Freight or Hire, under contracts for voyage.* A sum not exceeding the gross freight or hire for the current cargo passage and next succeeding cargo passage (such insurance to include, if required, a preliminary and an intermediate ballast passage) plus the charges of insurance. In the case of a voyage charter where payment is made on a time basis, the sum permitted for insurance shall be calculated on the estimated duration of the voyage, subject to the limitation of two cargo passages as laid down herein. Any sum insured under 19.1.2 to be taken into account and only the excess thereof may be insured, which excess shall be reduced as the freight or hire is advanced or earned by the gross amount so advanced or earned.

19.1.4 *Anticipated Freight if the Vessel sails in ballast and not under Charter.* A sum not exceeding the anticipated gross freight on next cargo passage, such sum to be reasonably estimated on the basis of the current rate of freight at time of insurance plus the charges of insurance. Any sum insured under 19.1.2 to be taken into account and only the excess thereof may be insured.

19.1.5 *Time Charter Hire or Charter Hire for Series of Voyages.* A sum not exceeding 50% of the gross hire which is to be earned under the charter in a period not exceeding 18 months. Any sum insured under 19.1.2 to be taken into account and only the excess thereof may be insured, which excess shall be reduced as the hire is advanced or earned under the charter by 50% of the gross amount so advanced or earned but the sum insured need not be reduced while the total of the sums insured under 19.1.2 and 19.1.5 does not exceed 50% of the gross hire still to be earned under the charter. An insurance under this Section may begin on the signing of the charter.

19.1.6 *Premiums.* A sum not exceeding the actual premiums of all interests insured for a period not exceeding 12 months (excluding premiums insured under the foregoing sections but including, if required, the premium or estimated calls on any Club or War etc. Risk insurance) reducing pro rata monthly.

19.1.7 *Returns of Premium.* A sum not exceeding the actual returns which are allowable under any insurance but which would not be recoverable thereunder in the event of a total loss of the Vessel whether by insured perils or otherwise.

19.1.8 *Insurance irrespective of amount against:*
Any risks excluded by Clauses 20, 21, 22 and 23 below.

19.2 Warranted that no insurance on any interests enumerated in the foregoing 19.1.1 to 19.1.7 in excess of the amounts permitted therein and no other insurance which includes total loss of the Vessel P.P.I., F.I.A., or subject to any other like term, is or shall be effected to operate during the currency of this insurance by or for account of the Assured, Owners, Managers or Mortgagees. Provided always that a breach of this warranty shall not afford the Underwriters any defence to a claim by a Mortgagee who has accepted this insurance without knowledge of such breach.

The following clauses shall be paramount and shall override anything contained in this insurance inconsistent therewith.

20. War Exclusion. In no case shall this insurance cover loss damage liability or expense caused by

20.1 war civil war revolution rebellion insurrection, or civil strife arising therefrom, or any hostile act by or against a belligerent power

20.2 capture seizure arrest restraint or detainment (barratry and piracy excepted), and the consequences thereof or any attempt thereat

20.3 derelict mines torpedoes bombs or other derelict weapons of war.

21. Strikes Exclusion. In no case shall this insurance cover loss damage liability or expense caused by

21.1 strikers, locked-out workmen, or persons taking part in labour disturbances, riots or civil commotions

21.2 any terrorist or any person acting from a political motive.

22. Malicious Acts Exclusion. In no case shall this insurance cover loss damage liability or expense arising from
  22.1   the detonation of an explosive
  22.2   any weapon of war
and caused by any person acting maliciously or from a political motive.

23. Nuclear Exclusion. In no case shall this insurance cover loss damage liability or expense arising from any weapon of war employing atomic or nuclear fission and/or fusion or other like reaction or radioactive force or matter.

1/10/83   (FOR USE ONLY WITH THE NEW MARINE POLICY FORM)

INSTITUTE WAR AND STRIKES CLAUSES

Hulls–Time

This insurance is subject to English law and practice

1. Perils. Subject always to the exclusions hereinafter referred to, this insurance covers loss of or damage to the Vessel caused by
  1.1   war civil war revolution rebellion insurrection, or civil strife arising therefrom, or any hostile act by or against a belligerent power
  1.2   capture seizure arrest restraint or detainment, and the consequences thereof or any attempt thereat
  1.3   derelict mines torpedoes bombs or other derelict weapons of war
  1.4   strikers, locked-out workmen, or persons taking part in labour disturbances, riots or civil commotions
  1.5   any terrorist or any person acting maliciously or from a political motive
  1.6   confiscation or expropriation.

2. Incorporation. The Institute Time Clauses—Hulls 1/10/83 (including 4/4ths Collision Clause) except Clauses 1.2, 2, 3, 4, 6, 12, 21.1.8, 22, 23, 24, 25 and 26 are deemed to be incorporated in this insurance in so far as they do not conflict with the provisions of these clauses.

Held covered in case of breach of warranty as to towage or salvage services provided notice be given to the Underwriters immediately after receipt of advices and any additional premium required by them be agreed.

3. Detainment. In the event that the Vessel shall have been the subject of capture seizure arrest restraint detainment confiscation or expropriation, and the Assured shall thereby have lost the free use and disposal of the Vessel for a continuous period of 12 months then for the purpose of ascertaining whether the Vessel is a constructive total loss the Assured shall be deemed to have been deprived of the possession of the Vessel without any likelihood of recovery.

4. Exclusions. This insurance excludes
  4.1   loss damage liability or expense arising from
    4.1.1   any detonation of any weapon of war employing atomic or nuclear fission and/or fusion or other like reaction or radioactive force or matter, hereinafter called a nuclear weapon of war
    4.1.2   the outbreak of war (whether there be a declaration of war or not) between any of the following countries:
        United Kingdom, United States of America, France,
        the Union of Soviet Socialist Republics,
        the People's Republic of China

4.1.3 requisition or pre-emption
4.1.4 capture seizure arrest restraint detainment confiscation or expropriation by or under the order of the government or any public or local authority of the country in which the Vessel is owned or registered
4.1.5 arrest restraint detainment confiscation or expropriation under quarantine regulations or by reason of infringement of any customs or trading regulations
4.1.6 the operation of ordinary judicial process, failure to provide security or to pay any fine or penalty or any financial cause
4.1.7 piracy (but this exclusion shall not affect cover under Clause 1.4),
4.2 loss damage liability or expense covered by the Institute Time Clauses—Hulls 1/10/83 (including 4/4ths Collision Clause) or which would be recoverable thereunder but for Clause 12 thereof,
4.3 any claim for any sum recoverable under any other insurance on the Vessel or which would be recoverable under such insurance but for the existence of this insurance,
4.4 any claim for expenses arising from delay except such expenses as would be recoverable in principle in English law and practice under the York–Antwerp Rules 1974.

5. Termination.
5.1 This insurance may be cancelled by either the Underwriters or the Assured giving 7 days notice (such cancellation becoming effective on the expiry of 7 days from midnight of the day on which notice of cancellation is issued by or to the Underwriters). The Underwriters agree however to reinstate this insurance subject to agreement between the Underwriters and the Assured prior to the expiry of such notice of cancellation as to new rate of premium and/or conditions and/or warranties.
5.2 Whether or not such notice of cancellation has been given this insurance shall TERMINATE AUTOMATICALLY
5.2.1 upon the occurrence of any hostile detonation of any nuclear weapon of war as defined in Clause 4.1.1 wheresoever or whensoever such detonation may occur and whether or not the Vessel may be involved
5.2.2 upon the outbreak of war (whether there be a declaration of war or not) between any of the following countries:
United Kingdom, United States of America, France,
the Union of Soviet Socialist Republics,
the People's Republic of China
5.2.3 in the event of the Vessel being requisitioned, either for title or use.
5.3 In the event either of cancellation by notice of automatic termination of this insurance by reason of the operation of this Clause 5, or of the sale of the Vessel, pro rata net return of premium shall be payable to the Assured.

This insurance shall not become effective if, subsequent to its acceptance by the Underwriters and prior to the intended time of its attachment, there has occurred any event which would have automatically terminated this insurance under the provisions of Clause 5 above.

1/10/83 (FOR USE ONLY WITH THE NEW MARINE POLICY FORM)

INSTITUTE WAR AND STRIKES CLAUSES

Hulls—Voyage

This insurance is subject to English law and practice

1. Perils. Subject always to the exclusions hereinafter referred to, this insurance covers loss of or damage to the Vessel caused by
- 1.1 war civil war revolution rebellion insurrection, or civil strife arising therefrom, or any hostile act by or against a belligerent power
- 1.2 capture seizure arrest restraint or detainment, and the consequences thereof or any attempt thereat
- 1.3 derelict mines torpedoes bombs or other derelict weapons of war
- 1.4 strikers, locked-out workmen, or persons taking part in labour disturbances, riots or civil commotions
- 1.5 any terrorist or any person acting maliciously or from a political motive
- 1.6 confiscation or expropriation.

2. Incorporation. The Institute Voyage Clauses—Hulls 1/10/83 (including 4/4ths Collision Clause) except Clauses 1.2, 10. 19.1.8, 20, 21, 22 and 23 are deemed to be incorporated in this insurance in so far as they do not conflict with the provisions of these clauses.

Held covered in case of breach of warranty as to towage or salvage services provided notice be given to the Underwriters immediately after receipt of advices and any additional premium required by them be agreed.

3. Detainment. In the event that the Vessel shall have been the subject of capture seizure arrest restraint detainment confiscation or expropriation, and the Assured shall thereby have lost the free use and disposal of the Vessel for a continuous period of 12 months then for the purpose of ascertaining whether the Vessel is a constructive total loss the Assured shall be deemed to have been deprived of the possession of the Vessel without any likelihood of recovery.

4. Exclusions. This insurance excludes
- 4.1 loss damage liability or expense arising from
- 4.1.1 any detonation of any weapon of war employing atomic or nuclear fission and/or fusion or other like reaction or radioactive force or matter, hereinafter called a nuclear weapon of war
- 4.1.2 the outbreak of war (whether there be a declaration of war or not) between any of the following countries:
    United Kingdom, United States of America, France,
    the Union of Soviet Socialist Republics,
    the People's Republic of China
- 4.1.3 requisition or pre-emption
- 4.1.4 capture seizure arrest restraint detainment confiscation or expropriation by or under the order of the government or any public or local authority of the country in which the Vessel is owned or registered
- 4.1.5 arrest restraint detainment confiscation or expropriation under quarantine regulations or by reason of infringement of any customs or trading regulations
- 4.1.6 the operation of ordinary judicial process, failure to provide security or to pay any fine or penalty or any financial cause
- 4.1.7 piracy (but this exclusion shall not affect cover under Clause 1.4),
- 4.2 loss damage liability or expense covered by the Institute Voyage Clauses—Hulls 1/10/83 (including 4/4ths Collision Clause) or which would be recoverable thereunder but for Clause 10 thereof,

4.3   any claim for any sum recoverable under any other insurance on the Vessel or which would be recoverable under such insurance but for the existence of this insurance,

4.4   any claim for expenses arising from delay except such expenses as would be recoverable in principle in English law and practice under the York–Antwerp Rules 1974.

5. Termination.

5.1   This insurance may be cancelled by either the Underwriters or the Assured giving 7 days notice (such cancellation becoming effective on the expiry of 7 days from midnight of the day on which notice of cancellation is issued by or to the Underwriters). The Underwriters agree however to reinstate this insurance subject to agreement between the Underwriters and the Assured prior to the expiry of such notice of cancellation as to new rate of premium and/or conditions and/or warranties.

5.2   Whether or not such notice of cancellation has been given this insurance shall TERMINATE AUTOMATICALLY

5.2.1   upon the occurrence of any hostile detonation of any nuclear weapon of war as defined in Clause 4.1.1 wheresoever or whensoever such detonation may occur and whether or not the Vessel may be involved

5.2.2   upon the outbreak of war (whether there be a declaration of war or not) between any of the following countries:
       United Kingdom, United States of America, France,
       the Union of Soviet Socialist Republics,
       the People's Republic of China

5.2.3   in the event of the Vessel being requisitioned, either for title or use.

5.3   In the event either of cancellation by notice or of automatic termination of this insurance by reason of the operation of this Clause 5, or of the sale of the Vessel, a return of premium shall be payable to the Assured.

This insurance shall not become effective if, subsequent to its acceptance by the Underwriters and prior to the intended time of its attachment, there has occurred any event which would have automatically terminated this insurance under the provisions of Clause 5 above.

---

(3)   FREIGHT CLAUSES

1/10/83   (FOR USE ONLY WITH THE NEW MARINE POLICY FORM)

INSTITUTE TIME CLAUSES
FREIGHT

This insurance is subject to English law and practice

1. Navigation. The Vessel has leave to dock and undock, to go into graving dock, to sail or navigate with or without pilots, to go on trial trips and to assist and tow vessels or craft in distress, but it is warranted that the Vessel shall not be towed, except as is customary or when in need of assistance, or undertake towage or salvage services under a contract previously arranged by the Assured and/or Owners and/or Managers and/or Charterers. This Clause 1 shall not exclude customary towage in connection with loading and discharging.

2. Craft Risk. Including risk of craft and/or lighter to and from the Vessel.

The Institute Clauses

3. Continuation. Should the Vessel at the expiration of this insurance be at sea or in distress or at a port of refuge or of call, the subject-matter insured shall, provided previous notice be given to the Underwriters, be held covered at a pro rata monthly premium to her port of destination.

4. Breach of Warranty. Held covered in case of any breach of warranty as to cargo, trade, locality, towage, salvage services or date of sailing, provided notice be given to the Underwriters immediately after receipt of advices and any amended terms of cover and any additional premium required by them be agreed.

5. Termination. This Clause 5 shall prevail notwithstanding any provision whether written typed or printed in this insurance inconsistent therewith. Unless the Underwriters agree to the contrary in writing, this insurance shall terminate automatically at the time of

- 5.1 change of the Classification Society of the Vessel, or change, suspension, discontinuance, withdrawal or expiry of her Class therein, provided that if the Vessel is at sea such automatic termination shall be deferred until arrival at her next port. However where such change, suspension, discontinuance or withdrawal of her Class has resulted from loss or damage covered by Clause 7 of this insurance or which would be covered by an insurance of the Vessel subject to current Institute War and Strikes Clauses Hulls–Time such automatic termination shall only operate should the Vessel sail from her next port without the prior approval of the Classification Society,
- 5.2 any change, voluntary or otherwise, in the ownership or flag, transfer to new management, or charter on a bareboat basis, or requisition for title or use of the Vessel, provided that, if the Vessel has cargo on board and has already sailed from her loading port or is at sea in ballast, such automatic termination shall if required be deferred, whilst the Vessel continues her planned voyage, until arrival at final port of discharge if with cargo or at port of destination if in ballast. However, in the event of requisition for title or use without the prior execution of a written agreement by the Assured, such automatic termination shall occur fifteen days after such requisition whether the Vessel is at sea or in port.

A pro rata daily net return of premium shall be made.

6. Assignment. No assignment of or interest in this insurance or in any moneys which may be or become payable thereunder is to be binding on or recognised by the Underwriters unless a dated notice of such assignment or interest signed by the Assured, and by the assignor in the case of subsequent assignment, is endorsed on the Policy and the Policy with such endorsement is produced before payment of any claim or return of premium thereunder.

7. Perils.
- 7.1 This insurance covers loss of the subject-matter insured caused by
- 7.1.1 perils of the seas rivers lakes or other navigable waters
- 7.1.2 fire, explosion
- 7.1.3 violent theft by persons from outside the Vessel
- 7.1.4 jettison
- 7.1.5 piracy
- 7.1.6 breakdown of or accident to nuclear installations or reactors
- 7.1.7 contact with aircraft or similar objects, or objects falling therefrom, land conveyance, dock or harbour equipment or installation
- 7.1.8 earthquake volcanic eruption or lightning.
- 7.2 This insurance covers loss of the subject-matter insured caused by
- 7.2.1 accidents in loading discharging or shifting cargo or fuel
- 7.2.2 bursting of boilers breakage of shafts or any latent defect in the machinery or hull
- 7.2.3 negligence of Master Officers Crew or Pilots

552 *Appendix III*

    7.2.4   negligence of repairers or charterers provided such repairers or charterers are not an Assured hereunder

    7.2.5   barratry of Master Officers or Crew,
provided such loss has not resulted from want of due diligence by the Assured, Owners or Managers.

    7.3   Master Officers Crew or Pilots not to be considered Owners within the meaning of this Clause 7 should they hold shares in the Vessel.

8. Pollution Hazard. This insurance covers loss of the subject-matter insured caused by any governmental authority acting under the powers vested in it to prevent or mitigate a pollution hazard, or threat thereof, resulting directly from a peril covered by this insurance, provided such act of governmental authority has not resulted from want of due diligence by the Assured, the Owners, or Managers of the Vessel or any of them to prevent or mitigate such hazard or threat. Master, Officers, Crew or Pilots not to be considered Owners within the meaning of this Clause 8 should they hold shares in the Vessel.

9. Freight Collision.

    9.1   It is further agreed that if the Vessel shall come into collision with any other vessel and the Assured shall in consequence thereof become liable to pay and shall pay by way of damages to any other person or persons any sum or sums in respect of the amount of freight taken into account in calculating the measure of the liability of the Assured for

    9.1.1   loss of or damage to any other vessel or property on any other vessel

    9.1.2   delay to or loss of use of any such other vessel or property thereon

    9.1.3   general average of, salvage of or salvage under contract of, any such other vessel or property thereon,

the Underwriters will pay the Assured such proportion of three-fourths of such sum or sums so paid applying to freight as their respective subscriptions hereto bear to the total amount insured on freight or, if greater, to the gross freight at risk at the time of the collision.

    9.2   Provided always that:

    9.2.1   liability of the Underwriters in respect of any one such collision shall not exceed their proportionate part of three-fourths of the total amount insured hereon on freight, and in cases in which, with the prior consent in writing of the Underwriters, the liability of the Vessel has been contested or proceedings have been taken to limit liability, they will also pay a like proportion of three-fourths of the costs, appertaining proportionately to the freight portion of damages, which the Assured shall thereby incur or be compelled to pay;

    9.2.2   no claim shall attach to this insurance:

    9.2.2.1   which attaches to any other insurances covering collision liabilities

    9.2.2.2   which is, or would be, recoverable in the terms of the Institute 3/4ths Collision Liability Clause if the Vessel were insured in the terms of such Institute 3/4ths Collision Liability Clause for a value per ton of her gross registered tonnage not less than the equivalent in pounds sterling, at the time of commencement of this insurance, of 66.67 Special Drawing Rights as defined by the International Monetary Fund;

    9.2.3   this Clause 9 shall in no case extend or be deemed to extend to any sum which the Assured may become liable to pay or shall pay for or in respect of:

    9.2.3.1   removal or disposal, under statutory powers or otherwise, of obstructions, wrecks, cargoes or any other thing whatsoever

    9.2.3.2   any real or personal property or thing whatsoever except other vessels or property on other vessels

    9.2.3.3   pollution or contamination of any real or personal property or thing whatsoever (except other vessels with which the insured Vessel is in collision or property on such other vessels)

9.2.3.4   the cargo or other property on or the engagements of the Vessel
9.2.3.5   loss of life, personal injury or illness.

10. Sistership. Should the Vessel named herein come into collision with or receive salvage services from another vessel belonging wholly or in part to the same Owners, or under the same management, the Assured shall have the same rights under this insurance as they would have were the other vessel entirely the property of Owners not interested in the Vessel named herein; but in such cases the liability for the collision or the amount payable for the services rendered shall be referred to a sole arbitrator to be agreed upon between the Underwriters and the Assured.

11. General Average and Salvage.

11.1   This insurance covers the proportion of general average salvage and/or salvage charges attaching to freight at risk of the Assured, reduced in respect of any under-insurance.

11.2   Adjustment to be according to the law and practice obtaining at the place where the adventure ends, as if the contract of affreightment contained no special terms upon the subject; but where the contract of affreightment so provides the adjustment shall be according to the York-Antwerp Rules.

11.3   No claim under this Clause 11 shall in any case be allowed where the loss was not incurred to avoid or in connection with the avoidance of a peril insured against.

12. Franchise. This insurance does not cover partial loss, other than general average loss, under 3% unless caused by fire, sinking, stranding or collision with another vessel. Each craft and/or lighter to be deemed a separate insurance if required by the Assured.

13. Measure of Indemnity.

13.1   The amount recoverable under this insurance for any claim for loss of freight shall not exceed the gross freight actually lost.

13.2   Where insurances on freight other than this insurance are current at the time of the loss, all such insurances shall be taken into consideration in calculating the liability under this insurance and the amount recoverable hereunder shall not exceed the rateable proportion of the gross freight lost, notwithstanding any valuation in this or any other insurance.

13.3   In calculating the liability under Clause 11 all insurances on freight shall likewise be taken into consideration.

13.4   Nothing in this Clause 13 shall apply to any claim arising under Clause 15.

14. Loss of Time. This insurance does not cover any claim consequent on loss of time whether arising from a peril of the sea or otherwise.

15. Total Loss.

15.1   In the event of the total loss (actual or constructive) of the Vessel named herein the amount insured shall be paid in full, whether the Vessel be fully or partly loaded or in ballast, chartered or unchartered.

15.2   In ascertaining whether the Vessel is a constructive total loss, the insured value in the insurances on hull and machinery shall be taken as the repaired value and nothing in respect of the damaged or break-up value of the Vessel or wreck shall be taken into account.

15.3   Should the Vessel be a constructive total loss but the claim on the insurances on hull and machinery be settled as a claim for partial loss, no payment shall be due under this Clause 15.

16. Returns for Lay-Up and Cancellation.

16.1   To return as follows:

16.1.1   Pro rata monthly net for each uncommenced month if this insurance be cancelled by agreement.

16.1.2   For each period of 30 consecutive days the Vessel may be laid up in a port or in a lay-up area provided such port or lay-up area is approved by the Underwriters (with special liberties as hereinafter allowed)

(a) .... per cent net not under repair
(b) .... per cent net under repair.
If the Vessel is under repair during part only of a period of which a return is claimable, the return shall be calculated pro rata to the number of days under (a) and (b) respectively.

16.2 PROVIDED ALWAYS THAT

16.2.1 a total loss of the Vessel, whether by insured perils or otherwise, has not occurred during the period covered by this insurance or any extension thereof

16.2.2 in no case shall a return be allowed when the Vessel is lying in exposed or unprotected waters, or in a port or lay-up area not approved by the Underwriters but, provided the Underwriters agree that such non-approved lay-up area is deemed to be within the vicinity of the approved port or lay-up area, days during which the Vessel is laid up in such non-approved lay-up area may be added to days in the approved port or lay-up area to calculate a period of 30 consecutive days and a return shall be allowed for the proportion of such period during which the Vessel is actually laid up in the approved port or lay-up area

16.2.3 loading or discharging operations or the presence of cargo on board shall not debar returns but no return shall be allowed for any period during which the Vessel is being used for the storage of cargo or for lightering purposes

16.2.4 in the event of any amendment of the annual rate, the above rates of return shall be adjusted accordingly

16.2.5 in the event of any return recoverable under this Clause 16 being based on 30 consecutive days which fall on successive insurances effected for the same Assured, this insurance shall only be liable for an amount calculated at pro rata of the period rates 16.1.2(a) and/or (b) above for the number of days which come within the period of this insurance and to which a return is actually applicable. Such overlapping period shall run, at the option of the Assured, either from the first day on which the Vessel is laid up or the first day of a period of 30 consecutive days as provided under 16.1.2(a) or (b), or 16.2.2 above.

The following clauses shall be paramount and shall override anything contained in this insurance inconsistent therewith.

17. War Exclusion. In no case shall this insurance cover loss damage liability or expense caused by

17.1 war civil war revolution rebellion insurrection, or civil strife arising therefrom, or any hostile act by or against a belligerent power

17.2 capture seizure arrest restraint or detainment (barratry and piracy excepted), and the consequences thereof or any attempt thereat

17.3 derelict mines torpedoes bombs or other derelict weapons of war.

18. Strikes Exclusion. In no case shall this insurance cover loss damage liability or expense caused by

18.1 strikers, locked-out workmen, or persons taking part in labour disturbances, riots or civil commotions

18.2 any terrorist or any person acting from a political motive.

19. Malicious Acts Exclusion. In no case shall this insurance cover loss damage liability or expense arising from

19.1 the detonation of an explosive

19.2 any weapon of war

and caused by any person acting maliciously or from a political motive.

20. Nuclear Exclusion. In no case shall this insurance cover loss damage liability or expense arising from any weapon of war employing atomic or nuclear fission and/or fusion or other like reaction or radioactive force or matter.

1/10/83 (FOR USE ONLY WITH THE NEW MARINE POLICY FORM)

INSTITUTE VOYAGE CLAUSES
FREIGHT

This insurance is subject to English law and practice

1. Navigation. The Vessel has leave to dock and undock, to go into graving dock, to sail or navigate with or without pilots, to go on trial trips and to assist and tow vessels or craft in distress, but it is warranted that the Vessel shall not be towed, except as is customary or when in need of assistance, or undertake towage or salvage services under a contract previously arranged by the Assured and/or Owners and/or Managers and/or Charterers. This Clause 1 shall not exclude customary towage in connection with loading and discharging.

2. Craft Risk. Including risk of craft and/or lighter to and from the Vessel.

3. Change of Voyage. Held covered in case of deviation or change of voyage or any breach of warranty as to towage or salvage services, provided notice be given to the Underwriters immediately after receipt of advices and any amended terms of cover and any additional premium required by them be agreed.

4. Assignment. No assignment of or interest in this insurance or in any moneys which may be or become payable thereunder is to be binding on or recognised by the Underwriters unless a dated notice of such assignment or interest signed by the Assured, and by the assignor in the case of subsequent assignment, is endorsed on the Policy and the Policy with such endorsement is produced before payment of any claim or return of premium thereunder.

5. Perils.

5.1	This insurance covers loss of the subject-matter insured caused by
5.1.1	perils of the seas rivers lakes or other navigable waters
5.1.2	fire, explosion
5.1.3	violent theft by persons from outside the Vessel
5.1.4	jettison
5.1.5	piracy
5.1.6	breakdown of or accident to nuclear installations or reactors
5.1.7	contact with aircraft or similar objects, or objects falling therefrom, land conveyance, dock or harbour equipment or installation
5.1.8	earthquake volcanic eruption or lightning.
5.2	This insurance covers loss of the subject-matter insured caused by
5.2.1	accidents in loading discharging or shifting cargo or fuel
5.2.2	bursting of boilers breakage of shafts or any latent defect in the machinery or hull
5.2.3	negligence of Master Officers Crew or Pilots
5.2.4	negligence of repairers or charterers provided such repairers or charterers are not an Assured hereunder
5.2.5	barratry of Master Officers or Crew,
	provided such loss has not resulted from want of due diligence by the Assured, Owners or Managers.
5.3	Master Officers Crew or Pilots not to be considered Owners within the meaning of this Clause 5 should they hold shares in the Vessel.

6. Pollution Hazard. This insurance covers loss of the subject-matter insured caused by any governmental authority acting under the powers vested in it to prevent or mitigate a pollution hazard, or threat thereof, resulting directly from a peril covered by this insurance, provided such act of governmental authority has not resulted from want of due diligence by the Assured, the Owners, or Managers of the Vessel or any of them to prevent or mitigate such hazard or threat. Master, Officers, Crew or Pilots not to be considered Owners within the meaning of this Clause 6 should they hold shares in the Vessel.

7. Freight Collision.

7.1 It is further agreed that if the Vessel shall come into collision with any other vessel and the Assured shall in consequence thereof become liable to pay and shall pay by way of damages to any other person or persons any sum or sums in respect of the amount of freight taken into account in calculating the measure of the liability of the Assured for

7.1.1 loss of or damage to any other vessel or property on any other vessel

7.1.2 delay to or loss of use of any such other vessel or property thereon

7.1.3 general average of, salvage of or salvage under contract of, any such other vessel or property thereon,

the Underwriters will pay the Assured such proportion of three-fourths of such sum or sums so paid applying to freight as their respective subscriptions hereto bear to the total amount insured on freight or, if greater, to the gross freight at risk at the time of the collision.

7.2 Provided always that:

7.2.1 liability of the Underwriters in respect of any one such collision shall not exceed their proportionate part of three-fourths of the total amount insured hereon on freight, and in cases in which, with the prior consent in writing of the Underwriters, the liability of the Vessel has been contested or proceedings have been taken to limit liability, they will also pay a like proportion of three-fourths of the costs, appertaining proportionately to the freight portion of damages, which the Assured shall thereby incur or be compelled to pay;

7.2.2 no claim shall attach to this insurance:

7.2.2.1 which attaches to any other insurances covering collision liabilities

7.2.2.2 which is, or would be, recoverable in the terms of the Institute 3/4ths Collision Liability Clause if the Vessel were insured in the terms of such Institute 3/4ths Collision Liability Clause for a value per ton of her gross registered tonnage not less than the equivalent in pounds sterling, at the time of commencement of this insurance, of 66.67 Special Drawing Rights as defined by the International Monetary Fund;

7.2.3 this Clause 7 shall in no case extend or be deemed to extend to any sum which the Assured may become liable to pay or shall pay for or in respect of:

7.2.3.1 removal or disposal, under statutory powers or otherwise, of obstructions, wrecks, cargoes or any other thing whatsoever

7.2.3.2 any real or personal property or thing whatsoever except other vessels or property on other vessels

7.2.3.3 pollution or contamination of any real or personal property or thing whatsoever (except other vessels with which the insured Vessel is in collision or property on such other vessels)

7.2.3.4 the cargo or other property on or the engagements of the Vessel

7.2.3.5 loss of life, personal injury or illness.

8. Sistership. Should the Vessel named herein come into collision with or receive salvage services from another vessel belonging wholly or in part to the same Owners, or under the same management, the Assured shall have the same rights under this insurance as they would have were the other vessel entirely the property of Owners not interested in the Vessel named herein; but in such cases the liability for the collision or the amount payable for the services rendered shall be referred to a sole arbitrator to be agreed upon between the Underwriters and the Assured.

9. General Average and Salvage.

9.1 This insurance covers the proportion of general average salvage and/or salvage charges attaching to freight at risk of the Assured, reduced in respect of any under-insurance.

9.2 Adjustment to be according to the law and practice obtaining at the place where the adventure ends, as if the contract of affreightment contained no special terms upon the subject; but where the contract of affreightment so provides the adjustment shall be according to the York–Antwerp Rules.

9.3 No claim under this Clause 9 shall in any case be allowed where the loss was not incurred to avoid or in connection with the avoidance of a peril insured against.

10. Franchise. This insurance does not cover partial loss, other than general average loss, under 3% unless caused by fire, sinking, stranding or collision with another vessel. Each craft and/or lighter to be deemed a separate insurance if required by the Assured.

11. Measure of Indemnity.

11.1 The amount recoverable under this insurance for any claim for loss of freight shall not exceed the gross freight actually lost.

11.2 Where insurances on freight other than this insurance are current at the time of the loss, all such insurances shall be taken into consideration in calculating the liability under this insurance and the amount recoverable hereunder shall not exceed the rateable proportion of the gross freight lost, notwithstanding any valuation in this or any other insurance.

11.3 In calculating the liability under Clause 9 all insurances on freight shall likewise be taken into consideration.

11.4 Nothing in this Clause 11 shall apply to any claim arising under Clause 13.

12. Loss of Time. This insurance does not cover any claim consequent on loss of time whether arising from a peril of the sea or otherwise.

13. Total Loss.

13.1 In the event of the total loss (actual or constructive) of the Vessel named herein the amount insured shall be paid in full, whether the Vessel be fully or partly loaded or in ballast, chartered or unchartered.

13.2 In ascertaining whether the Vessel is a constructive total loss, the insured value in the insurances on hull and machinery shall be taken as the repaired value and nothing in respect of the damaged or break-up value of the Vessel or wreck shall be taken into account.

13.3 Should the Vessel be a constructive total loss but the claim on the insurances on hull and machinery be settled as a claim for partial loss, no payment shall be due under this Clause 13.

The following clauses shall be paramount and shall override anything contained in this insurance inconsistent therewith.

14. War Exclusion. In no case shall this insurance cover loss damage liability or expense caused by

14.1 war civil war revolution rebellion insurrection, or civil strife arising therefrom, or any hostile act by or against a belligerent power

14.2 capture seizure arrest restraint or detainment (barratry and piracy excepted), and the consequences thereof or any attempt thereat

14.3 derelict mines torpedoes bombs or other derelict weapons of war.

15. Strikes Exclusion. In no case shall this insurance cover loss damage liability or expense caused by

15.1 strikers, locked-out workmen, or persons taking part in labour disturbances, riots or civil commotions

15.2 any terrorist or any person acting from a political motive.

16. Malicious Acts Exclusion. In no case shall this insurance cover loss damage liability or expense arising from

16.1 the detonation of an explosive

16.2 any weapon of war

and caused by any person acting maliciously or from a political motive.

17. Nuclear Exclusion. In no case shall this insurance cover loss damage liability or expense arising from any weapon of war employing atomic or nuclear fission and/or fusion or other like reaction or radioactive force or matter.

1/10/83 (FOR USE ONLY WITH THE NEW MARINE POLICY FORM)

INSTITUTE WAR AND STRIKES CLAUSES

Freight—Time

This insurance is subject to English law and practice

1. Perils. Subject always to the exclusions hereinafter referred to, this insurance covers
- 1.1 loss (total or partial) of the subject-matter insured caused by
- 1.1.1 war civil war revolution rebellion insurrection, or civil strife arising therefrom, or any hostile act by or against a belligerent power
- 1.1.2 capture seizure arrest restraint or detainment, and the consequences thereof or any attempt thereat
- 1.1.3 derelict mines torpedoes bombs or other derelict weapons of war,
- 1.2 loss (total or partial) of the subject-matter insured arising from loss of or damage to the Vessel caused by
- 1.2.1 strikers, locked-out workmen, or persons taking part in labour disturbances, riots or civil commotions
- 1.2.2 any terrorist or any person acting maliciously or from a political motive
- 1.2.3 confiscation or expropriation.

2. Incorporation. The Institute Time Clauses—Freight 1/10/83 except Clauses 2, 3, 4, 5, 12, 16, 17, 18, 19 and 20 are deemed to be incorporated in this insurance in so far as they do not conflict with the provisions of these clauses.

Held covered in case of breach of warranty as to towage or salvage services provided notice be given to the Underwriters immediately after receipt of advices and any additional premium required by them be agreed.

3. Detainment. In the event that a claim for a constructive total loss of the Vessel is paid on the war risks insurance of the Vessel under Clause 3 (Detainment) of the Institute War and Strikes Clauses—Hulls—Time 1/10/83 or the Institute War and Strikes Clauses—Hulls—Voyage 1/10/83 as a result of the loss of the free use and disposal of the Vessel for a continuous period of 12 months due to capture, seizure, arrest, restraint, detainment, confiscation or expropriation whilst this insurance is in force, the amount insured hereunder shall be paid in full less any claims otherwise arising during the said period of 12 months which have been paid or are recoverable hereunder or under insurances subject to the Institute Time Clauses—Freight 1/10/83 and/or the Institute Voyage Clauses—Freight 1/10/83 and any recoveries made in respect of the said period.

4. Exclusions. This insurance excludes
- 4.1 loss (total or partial) or expense arising from
- 4.1.1 any detonation of any weapon of war employing atomic or nuclear fission and/or fusion or other like reaction or radioactive force or matter, hereinafter called a nuclear weapon of war
- 4.1.2 the outbreak of war (whether there be a declaration of war or not) between any of the following countries:
   United Kingdom, United States of America, France,
   the Union of Soviet Socialist Republics,
   the People's Republic of China
- 4.1.3 requisition or pre-emption
- 4.1.4 capture seizure arrest restraint detainment confiscation or expropriation by

	or under the order of the government or any public or local authority of the country in which the Vessel is owned or registered
4.1.5	arrest restraint detainment confiscation or expropriation under quarantine regulations or by reason of infringement of any customs or trading regulations
4.1.6	the operation of ordinary judicial process, failure to provide security or to pay any fine or penalty or any financial cause
4.1.7	piracy (but this exclusion shall not affect cover under Clause 1.2.1),
4.2	loss (total or partial) or expense covered by the Institute Time Clauses—Freight 1/10/83 or which would be recoverable thereunder but for Clause 12 thereof,
4.3	any claim (not being a claim recoverable under the Institute War and Strikes Clauses Freight—Voyage 1/10/83) for any sum recoverable under any other insurance on the subject-matter insured or which would be recoverable under such insurance but for the existence of this insurance,
4.4	loss proximately caused by delay or any claim for expenses arising from delay except such expenses as would be recoverable in principle in English law and practice under the York–Antwerp Rules 1974,
4.5	any claim based upon loss of or frustration of any voyage or adventure.

5. Termination.

5.1 This insurance may be cancelled by either the Underwriters or the Assured giving 7 days notice (such cancellation becoming effective on the expiry of 7 days from midnight of the day on which notice of cancellation is issued by or to the Underwriters). The Underwriters agree however to reinstate this insurance subject to agreement between the Underwriters and the Assured prior to the expiry of such notice of cancellation as to new rate of premium and/or conditions and/or warranties.

5.2 Whether or not such notice of cancellation has been given this insurance shall TERMINATE AUTOMATICALLY

5.2.1 upon the occurrence of any hostile detonation of any nuclear weapon of war as defined in Clause 4.1.1 wheresoever or whensoever such detonation may occur and whether or not the Vessel may be involved

5.2.2 upon the outbreak of war (whether there be a declaration of war or not) between any of the following countries:
United Kingdom, United States of America, France,
the Union of Soviet Socialist Republics,
the People's Republic of China

5.2.3 in the event of the Vessel being requisitioned, either for title or use.

5.3 In the event either of cancellation by notice or of automatic termination of this insurance by reason of the operation of this Clause 5, or of the sale of the Vessel, pro rata net return of premium shall be payable to the Assured.

This Insurance shall not become effective if, subsequent to its acceptance by the Underwriters and prior to the intended time of its attachment, there has occurred any event which would have automatically terminated this insurance under the provisions of Clause 5 above.

1/10/83 (FOR USE ONLY WITH THE NEW MARINE POLICY FORM)

INSTITUTE WAR AND STRIKES CLAUSES

Freight—Voyage

This insurance is subject to English law and practice

1. Perils. Subject always to the exclusions hereinafter referred to, this insurance covers
- 1.1 loss (total or partial) of the subject-matter insured caused by
  - 1.1.1 war civil war revolution rebellion insurrection, or civil strife arising therefrom, or any hostile act by or against a belligerent power
  - 1.1.2 capture seizure arrest restraint or detainment, and the consequences thereof or any attempt thereat
  - 1.1.3 derelict mines torpedoes bombs or other derelict weapons of war,
- 1.2 loss (total or partial) of the subject-matter insured arising from loss of or damage to the Vessel caused by
  - 1.2.1 strikers, locked-out workmen, or persons taking part in labour disturbances, riots or civil commotions
  - 1.2.2 any terrorist or any person acting maliciously or from a political motive
  - 1.2.3 confiscation or expropriation.

2. Incorporation. The Institute Voyage Clauses—Freight 1/10/83 except Clauses 2, 10, 14, 15, 16 and 17 are deemed to be incorporated in this insurance in so far as they do not conflict with the provisions of these clauses.

Held covered in case of breach of warranty as to towage or salvage services provided notice be given to the Underwriters immediately after receipt of advices and any additional premium required by them be agreed.

3. Detainment. In the event that a claim for a constructive total loss of the Vessel is paid on the war risks insurance of the Vessel under Clause 3 (Detainment) of the Institute War and Strikes Clauses—Hulls—Time 1/10/83 or the Institute War and Strikes Clauses—Hulls—Voyage 1/10/83 as a result of the loss of the free use and disposal of the Vessel for a continuous period of 12 months due to capture, seizure, arrest, restraint, detainment, confiscation or expropriation whilst this insurance is in force, the amount insured hereunder shall be paid in full less any claims otherwise arising during the said period of 12 months which have been paid or are recoverable hereunder or under insurances subject to the Institute Time Clauses—Freight 1/10/83 and/or the Institute Voyage Clauses—Freight 1/10/83 and any recoveries made in respect of the said period.

4. Exclusions. This insurance excludes
- 4.1 loss (total or partial) or expense arising from
  - 4.1.1 any detonation of any weapon of war employing atomic or nuclear fission and/or fusion or other like reaction or radioactive force or matter, hereinafter called a nuclear weapon of war
  - 4.1.2 the outbreak of war (whether there be a declaration of war or not) between any of the following countries:
    United Kingdom, United States of America, France,
    the Union of Soviet Socialist Republics,
    the People's Republic of China
  - 4.1.3 requisition or pre-emption
  - 4.1.4 capture seizure arrest restraint detainment confiscation or expropriation by or under the order of the government or any public or local authority of the country in which the Vessel is owned or registered
  - 4.1.5 arrest restraint detainment confiscation or expropriation under quarantine regulations or by reason of infringement of any customs or trading regulations

4.1.6   the operation of ordinary judicial process, failure to provide security or to pay any fine or penalty or any financial cause
4.1.7   piracy (but this exclusion shall not affect cover under Clause 1.2.1),
4.2   loss (total or partial) or expense covered by the Institute Voyage Clauses—Freight 1/10/83 or which would be recoverable thereunder but for Clause 10 thereof,
4.3   any claim (not being a claim recoverable under the Institute War and Strikes Clauses Freight—Time 1/10/83) for any sum recoverable under any other insurance on the Vessel or which would be recoverable under such insurance but for the existence of this insurance,
4.4   loss proximately caused by delay or any claim for expenses arising from delay except such expenses as would be recoverable in principle in English law and practice under the York–Antwerp Rules 1974.
4.5   any claim based upon loss of or frustration of any voyage or adventure.

5. Termination.
5.1   This insurance may be cancelled by either the Underwriters or the Assured giving 7 days notice (such cancellation becoming effective on the expiry of 7 days from midnight of the day on which notice of cancellation is issued by or to the Underwriters). The Underwriters agree however to reinstate this insurance subject to agreement between the Underwriters and the Assured prior to the expiry of such notice of cancellation as to new rate of premium and/or conditions and/or warranties.
5.2   Whether or not such notice of cancellation has been given this insurance shall TERMINATE AUTOMATICALLY
5.2.1   upon the occurrence of any hostile detonation of any nuclear weapon of war as defined in Clause 4.1.1 wheresoever or whensoever such detonation may occur and whether or not the Vessel may be involved
5.2.2   upon the outbreak of war (whether there be a declaration of war or not) between any of the following countries:
    United Kingdom, United States of America, France,
    the Union of Soviet Socialist Republics,
    the People's Republic of China
5.2.3   in the event of the Vessel being requisitioned, either for title or use.
5.3   In the event either of cancellation by notice or of automatic termination of this insurance by reason of the operation of this Clause 5, or of the sale of the Vessel, a return of premium shall be payable to the Assured.

This Insurance shall not become effective if, subsequent to its acceptance by the Underwriters and prior to the intended time of its attachment, there has occurred any event which would have automatically terminated this insurance under the provisions of Clause 5 above.

---

(4) INSTITUTE WARRANTIES

1.7.76

1. Warranted no:
  (a)   Atlantic Coast of North America, its rivers or adjacent islands,
    (i)   north of 52° 10′ N. Lat. and west of 50° W. Long.;
    (ii)   south of 52° 10′ N. Lat. in the area bounded by lines drawn between Battle Harbour/Pistolet Bay; Cape Ray/Cape North; Port Hawkes-

bury/Port Mulgrave and Baie Comeau/Matane, between 21st December and 30th April both days inclusive.
(iii) west of Baie Comeau/Matane (but not west of Montreal) between 1st December and 30th April both days inclusive.
(b) Great Lakes or St Lawrence Seaway west of Montreal.
(c) Greenland Waters.
(d) Pacific Coast of North America its rivers or adjacent islands north of 54° 30' N. Lat., or west of 130° 50' W. Long.

2. Warranted no Baltic Sea or adjacent waters east of 15° E. Long.
(a) North of a line between Mo (63° 24' N. Lat.) and Vasa (63° 06' N. Lat.) between 10th December and 25th May b.d.i.
(b) East of a line between Viipuri (Vyborg) (28° 47' E. Long.) and Narva (28° 12' E. Long.) between 15th December and 15th may b.d.i.
(c) North of a line between Stockholm (59° 20' N. Lat.) and Tallinn (59° 24' N. Lat.) between 8th January and 5th May b.d.i.
(d) East of 22° E. Long., and south of 59° N. Lat. between 28th December and 5th May b.d.i.

3. Warranted not North of 70° N. Lat. other than voyages direct to or from any port or place in Norway or Kola Bay.

4. Warranted no Behring Sea, no East Asian waters north of 46° N. Lat. and not to enter or sail from any port or place in Siberia except Nakhodka and/or Vladivostock.

5. Warranted not to proceed to Kerguelen and/or Croset Islands or south of 50° S. Lat., except to ports and/or places in Patagonia and/or Chile and/or Falkland Islands, but liberty is given to enter waters south of 50° S. Lat., if *en route* to or from ports and/or places not excluded in this warranty.

6. Warranted not to sail with Indian Coal as cargo:
(a) between 1st March and 30th June, b.d.i.
(b) between 1st July and 30th September, b.d.i., except to ports in Asia, not West of Aden or East of or beyond Singapore.

APPENDIX IV

The York–Antwerp Rules 1974

Rule of Interpretation.—In the adjustment of general average the following lettered and numbered Rules shall apply to the exclusion of any Law and Practice inconsistent therewith.

Except as provided by the numbered Rules, general average shall be adjusted according to the lettered Rules.

Rule A.—There is a general average act, when, and only when, any extraordinary sacrifice or expenditure is intentionally and reasonably made or incurred for the common safety for the purpose of preserving from peril the property involved in a common maritime adventure.

Rule B.—General average sacrifices and expenses shall be borne by the different contributing interests on the basis hereinafter provided.

Rule C.—Only such losses, damages or expenses which are the direct consequence of the general average act shall be allowed as general average.

Loss or damage sustained by the ship or cargo through delay, whether on the voyage or subsequently, such as demurrage, and any indirect loss whatsoever, such as loss of market, shall not be admitted as general average.

Rule D.—Rights to contribution in general average shall not be affected, though the event which gave rise to the sacrifice or expenditure may have been due to the fault of one of the parties to the adventure, but this shall not prejudice any remedies or defences which may be open against or to that party in respect of such fault.

Rule E.—The onus of proof is upon the party claiming in general average to show that the loss or expense claimed is properly allowable as general average.

Rule F.—Any extra expense incurred in place of another expense which would have been allowable as general average shall be deemed to be general average and so allowed without regard to the saving, if any, to other interests, but only up to the amount of the general average expense avoided.

Rule G.—General average shall be adjusted as regards both loss and contribution upon the basis of values at the time and place when and where the adventure ends.

This rule shall not affect the determination of the place at which the average statement is to be made up.

Rule I. Jettison of Cargo.—No jettison of cargo shall be made good as general average unless such cargo is carried in accordance with the recognised custom of the trade.

Rule II. Damage by Jettison and Sacrifice for the Common Safety.—Damage done to a ship and cargo, or either of them, by or in consequence of a sacrifice made for the common safety, and by water which goes down a ship's hatches opened or other opening made for the purpose of making a jettison for the common safety, shall be made good as general average.

Rule III. Extinguishing Fire on Shipboard.—Damage done to a ship and cargo, or either of them, by water or otherwise, including damage by beaching or scuttling a burning ship, in extinguishing a fire on board the ship, shall be made good as general average; except that no compensation shall be made for damage by smoke or heat however caused.

Rule IV. Cutting away Wreck.—Loss or damage sustained by cutting away wreck or parts of the ship which have been previously carried away or are effectively lost by accident shall not be made good as general average.

Rule V. Voluntary Stranding.—When a ship is intentionally run on shore for the common safety, whether or not she might have been driven on shore, the consequent loss or damage shall be allowed in general average.

Rule VI. Salvage Remuneration.—Expenditure incurred by the parties to the adventure on account of salvage, whether under contract or otherwise, shall be allowed in general average to the extent that the salvage operations were undertaken for the purpose of preserving from peril the property involved in the common maritime adventure.

Rule VII. Damage to Machinery and Boilers.—Damage caused to any machinery and boilers of a ship which is ashore and in a position of peril, in endeavouring to refloat, shall be allowed in general average when shown to have arisen from an actual intention to float the ship for the common safety at the risk of such damage; but where a ship is afloat no loss or damage caused by working the propelling machinery and boilers shall in any circumstances be made good as general average.

Rule VIII. Expenses Lightening a Ship when Ashore, and Consequent Damage.—When a ship is ashore and cargo and ship's fuel and stores or any of them are discharged as a general average act, the extra cost of lightening, lighter hire and reshipping if incurred and the loss or damage sustained thereby, shall be admitted as general average.

Rule IX. Ship's Materials and Stores Burnt for Fuel.—Ship's materials and stores, or any of them, necessarily burnt for fuel for the common safety at a time of peril, shall be admitted as general average, when and only when an ample supply of fuel had been provided; but the estimated quantity of fuel that would have been consumed, calculated at the price current at the ship's last port of departure at the date of her leaving, shall be credited to the general average.

Rule X. Expenses at Port of Refuge etc.—(*a*) When a ship shall have entered a port or place of refuge or shall have returned to her port or place of loading in consequence of accident, sacrifice or other extraordinary circumstances, which render that necessary for the common safety, the expenses of entering such port or place shall be admitted as general average; and when she shall have sailed thence with her original cargo, or part of it, the corresponding expenses of leaving such port or place consequent upon such entry or return shall likewise be admitted as general average.

When a ship is at any port or place of refuge and is necessarily removed to another port or place because repairs cannot be carried out in the first port or place, the provisions of this Rule shall be applied to the second port or place as if it were a port or place of refuge and the cost of such removal including temporary repairs and towage shall be admitted as general average. The provisions of Rule XI shall be applied to the prolongation of the voyage occasioned by such removal.

(*b*) The cost of handling on board or discharging cargo, fuel or stores whether at a port or place of loading, call or refuge, shall be admitted as general average, when the handling or discharge was necessary for the common safety or to enable damage to the ship caused by sacrifice or accident to be repaired if the repairs were necessary for the safe prosecution of the voyage, except in cases where the damage to the ship is discovered at a port or place of loading or call without any accident or other extraordinary circumstance connected with such damage having taken place during the voyage.

The cost of handling on board or discharging cargo, fuel or stores shall not be admissible as general average when incurred solely for the purpose of restowage due to shifting during the voyage unless such restowage is necessary for the common safety.

(c) Whenever the cost of handling or discharging cargo, fuel or stores is admissible as general average, the costs of storage, including insurance if reasonably incurred, reloading and stowing of such cargo, fuel or stores shall likewise be admitted as general average.

But when the ship is condemned or does not proceed on her original voyage storage expenses shall be admitted as general average only up to the date of the ship's condemnation or of the abandonment of the voyage or up to the date of completion of discharge of cargo if the condemnation or abandonment takes place before that date.

Rule XI. Wages and Maintenance of Crew and other expenses Bearing up for and in a port of Refuge, etc.—(a) Wages and maintenance of master, officers and crew reasonably incurred and fuel and stores consumed during the prolongation of the voyage occasioned by a ship entering a port or place of refuge or returning to her port or place of loading shall be admitted as general average when the expenses of entering such port or place are allowable in general average in accordance with Rule X (a).

(b) When a ship shall have entered or been detained in any port or place in consequence of accident, sacrifice or other extraordinary circumstances which render that necessary for the common safety, or to enable damage to the ship caused by sacrifice or accident to be repaired, if the repairs were necessary for the safe prosecution of the voyage, the wages and maintenance of the master, officers, and crew reasonably incurred during the extra period of detention in such port or place until the ship shall or should have been made ready to proceed upon her voyage, shall be admitted in general average.

Provided that when damage to the ship is discovered at a port or place of loading or call without any accident or other extraordinary circumstance connected with such damage having taken place during the voyage, then the wages and maintenance of master, officers and crew and fuel and stores consumed during the extra detention for repairs to damage so discovered shall not be admissible as general average, even if the repairs are necessary for the safe prosecution of the voyage.

When the ship is condemned or does not proceed on her original voyage, wages and maintenance of the master, officers and crew and fuel and stores consumed shall be admitted as general average only up to the date of the ship's condemnation or of the abandonment of the voyage or up to the date of completion of discharge of cargo if the condemnation or abandonment takes place before that date.

Fuel and stores consumed during the extra period of detention shall be admitted as general average, except such fuel and stores as are consumed in effecting repairs not allowable in general average.

Port charges incurred during the extra period of detention shall likewise be admitted as general average except such charges as are incurred solely by reason of repairs not allowable in general average.

(c) For the purpose of this and the other Rules wages shall include all payments made to or for the benefit of the master, officers and crew, whether such payments be imposed by law upon the shipowners or be made under the terms or articles of employment.

(d) When overtime is paid to the master, officers or crew for maintenance of the ship or repairs, the cost of which is not allowable in general average, such overtime shall be allowed in general average only up to the saving in expense which would have been incurred and admitted as general average, had such overtime not been incurred.

Rule XII. Damage to Cargo in discharging, etc.—Damage to or loss of cargo, fuel or stores caused in the act of handling, discharging, storing, reloading and stowing shall be made good as general average, when and only when the cost of those measures respectively is admitted as general average.

Rule XIII. Deductions from Cost of Repairs.—Repairs to be allowed in general average shall not be subject to deductions in respect of "new for old" where old material or parts are replaced by new unless the ship is over fifteen years old in which case there shall be a deduction of one third. The deductions shall be regulated by the age of the ship from the 31st December of the year of completion of construction to the date of the general average act, except for insulation, life and similar boats, communications and navigational apparatus and equipment, machinery and boilers for which the deductions shall be regulated by the age of the particular parts to which they apply.

The deductions shall be made only from the cost of the new material or parts when finished and ready to be installed in the ship.

No deduction shall be made in respect of provisions, stores, anchors and chain cables.

Drydock and slipway dues and costs of shifting the ship shall be allowed in full.

The costs of cleaning, painting or coating of bottom shall not be allowed in general average unless the bottom has been painted or coated within the twelve months preceding the date of the general average act in which case one half of such costs shall be allowed.

Rule XIV. Temporary Repairs.—Where temporary repairs are effected to a ship at a port of loading, call or refuge, for the common safety, or of damage caused by general average sacrifice, the cost of such repairs shall be admitted as general average.

Where temporary repairs of accidental damage are effected in order to enable the adventure to be completed, the cost of such repairs shall be admitted as general average without regard to the saving, if any, to other interest, but only up to the saving in expense which would have been incurred and allowed in general average if such repairs had not been effected there.

No deductions "new for old" shall be made from the cost of temporary repairs allowable as general average.

Rule XV. Loss of Freight.—Loss of freight arising from damage to or loss of cargo shall be made good as general average, either when caused by a general average act, or when the damage to or loss of cargo is so made good.

Deduction shall be made from the amount of gross freight lost, of the charges which the owner thereof would have incurred to earn such freight, but has, in consequence of the sacrifice, not incurred.

Rule XVI. Amount to be made good for Cargo lost or Damaged by Sacrifice.— The amount to be made good as general average for damage to or loss of cargo sacrificed shall be the loss which has been sustained thereby based on the value at the time of discharge, ascertained from the commercial invoice rendered to the receiver or if there is no such invoice from the shipped value. The value at the time of discharge shall include the cost of insurance and freight except insofar as such freight is at the risk of interests other than the cargo.

When cargo so damaged is sold and the amount of the damage has not been otherwise agreed, the loss to be made good in general average shall be the difference between the net proceeds of sale and the net sound value as computed in the first paragraph of this Rule.

Rule XVII. Contributory Values.—The contribution to a general average shall be made upon the actual net value of the property at the termination of the adventure except that the value of cargo shall be the value at the time of discharge, ascertained from the commercial invoice rendered to the receiver or if there is no such invoice from the shipped value. The value of the cargo shall include the cost of insurance and freight unless and insofar as such freight is at the risk of interests other than the cargo, deducting therefrom any loss or damage suffered by the cargo prior to or at the time of discharge. The value of the ship shall be assessed without taking into account the beneficial or detrimental effect of any demise or time charterparty to which the ship may be committed.

To these values shall be added the amount made good as general average for property sacrificed, if not already included, deduction being made from the freight and passage money at risk of such charges and crew's wages as would not have been incurred in earning the freight had the ship and cargo been totally lost at the date of the general average act and have not been allowed as general average; deduction being also made from the value of the property of all extra charges incurred in respect thereof subsequently to the general average act, except such charges as are allowed in general average.

Where cargo is sold short of destination, however, it shall contribute upon the actual net proceeds of sale, with the addition of any amount made good as general average.

Passenger's luggage and personal effects not shipped under Bill of Lading shall not contribute in general average.

Rule XVIII. Damage to Ship.—The amount to be allowed as general average for damage or loss to the ship, her machinery and/or gear caused by a general average act shall be as follows:

(*a*) When repaired or replaced,

the actual reasonable cost of repairing or replacing such damage or loss subject to deduction in accordance with Rule XIII;

(*b*) When not repaired or replaced,

the reasonable depreciation arising from such damage or loss, but not exceeding the estimated cost of repairs. But where the ship is an actual total loss or when the cost of repairs of the damage would exceed the value of the ship when repaired, the amount to be allowed as general average shall be the difference between the estimated sound value of the ship after deducting therefrom the estimated cost of repairing damage which is not general average and the value of the ship in her damaged state which may be measured by the net proceeds of sale, if any.

Rule XIX. Undeclared or Wrongfully declared Cargo.—Damage or loss caused to goods loaded without the knowledge of the shipowner or his agent or to goods wilfully misdescribed at time of shipment shall not be allowed as general average but such goods shall remain liable to contribute, if saved.

Damage or loss caused to goods which have been wrongfully declared on shipment at a value which is lower than their real value shall be contributed for at the declared value, but such goods shall contribute upon their actual value.

Rule XX. Provision of Funds.—A commission of two per cent. of general average disbursements, other than the wages and maintenance of master, officers and crew and fuel and stores not replaced during the voyage, shall be allowed in general average, but when the funds are not provided by any of the contributing interests, the necessary cost of obtaining the funds required by means of a bottomry bond or otherwise, or the loss sustained by owners of goods sold for the purpose, shall be allowed in general average.

The cost of insuring money advanced to pay for general average disbursements shall also be allowed in general average.

Rule XXI. Interest on Losses made good in general average.—Interest shall be allowed on expenditure, sacrifices and allowances charged to general average at the rate of seven per cent. per annum, until the date of the general average statement, due allowance being made for any interim reimbursement from the contributory interests or from the general average deposit fund.

Rule XXII. Treatment of Cash Deposits.—Where cash deposits have been collected in respect of cargo's liability for general average, salvage or special charges, such deposits shall be paid without any delay into a special account in the joint names of a representative nominated on behalf of the shipowner and a representative nominated on behalf of the depositors in a bank to be approved by both. The sum so deposited together with accrued interest, if any, shall be held as security for payment to the parties entitled thereto of the general average, salvage or special charges payable by cargo in respect to which the deposits have been collected. Payments on account of refund of deposits may be made if certified to in writing by the average adjuster. Such deposits and payments or refunds shall be without prejudice to the ultimate liability of the parties.

APPENDIX V

Rules of Practice of the Association of Average Adjusters (1981)[1]

INTRODUCTION

In the middle of the 19th Century, when average adjusting as a separate profession was in its infancy, there was very little in the way of established law to guide the practising

---

[1] The membership of the Association, the function of the average adjuster, and the aims of the Association are described in the Preface to the Association's Rules as follows:

Membership of the Association of Average Adjusters
Members, Associate Members and Overseas Members of the Association are practising Average Adjusters who:
    being expert in the law and practice of general average and marine insurance,
    and
    having qualified by examination or other requirement of the Association of Average Adjusters,
apply their expertise for the benefit of the maritime and marine insurance communities.

The Function of the Average Adjuster
1. The functions of the Average Adjuster are principally the following:
   —the adjustment of General Average.
   —the adjustment of claims on policies of insurance on any interest directly or indirectly exposed to maritime perils,
   —the preparation of statements of claim against third parties,
   —the division of recoveries from third parties, or of proceeds of sale,
   —the arbitration of disputes arising in relation to the above or associated matters.
2. In the discharge of these functions the Average Adjuster may be appointed by any member of the maritime or marine insurance communities having an interest in the matter concerned, and, irrespective of the identity of the party appointing him, the Average Adjuster shall act in an impartial and independent manner.
3. The Average Adjuster may advise any party seeking his opinion on any matter within the area of his expertise.
4. The Average Adjuster may assist in the collection of General Average, Salvage or other security.
5. The Average Adjuster may assist in effecting settlements under an average adjustment, or otherwise as required.

The Aims of the Association of Average Adjusters.
The aims of the Association are:
1. To promote professional standards and correct principles in the adjustment of marine claims by ensuring, through examination or otherwise, that those entering into membership possess a high level of expertise.
2. To achieve uniformity of practice amongst Average Adjusters by providing a forum for discussion and by establishing rules of practice where necessary.
3. To ensure the independence and impartiality of its members by imposing a strict code of professional conduct.
4. To provide a service to the maritime community by establishing procedures by which advice on all aspects of marine claims may be obtained so as to facilitate their settlement.

adjuster, and consequently many points of practice had to be decided in accordance with custom. Some of these customs were subsequently ratified by legal decisions, but other were disapproved, and it became evident that unless steps were taken to establish a reasonable measure of uniformity among average adjusters, the profession would fall into disrepute. Those wishing to read further on this topic are recommended to the addresses delivered from the Chair of the Association by Mr Richard Lowndes (1873), Mr Charles McArthur (1883) and the Right Hon Lord Merrivale (1927), reprinted in 'From the Chair', published by the Association in 1976.

It was to remedy this situation that the Association of Average Adjusters was founded in 1869, with the object, among others, of 'the promotion of correct principles in the adjustment of Averages and uniformity of practice amongst average adjusters'.

After the formation of the Association, one of its first tasks was to consider the areas of divergency in practice, and decide how the various so-called 'customs' could be brought together into a uniform, if not universal, practice. This aim was largely achieved by the Association in the first fifteen years of its existence, by a two-fold approach:

(a) By the collection and refinement of the Customs of Lloyd's. This task was undertaken by a Special Committee which reported to the Association in 1876. In the preamble to the Customs it was stated: 'Nothing can be called a Custom of Lloyd's which is determined by a decision of the superior Courts; for whatever is thus sanctioned rests on a ground surer than custom. A Custom of Lloyd's then must relate to a point on which the law is doubtful, or not yet defined, but as to which, for practical convenience, it is necessary that there should be some uniform rule.'

(b) By the adoption of Rules of Practice, relating to the adjustment of averages and the duties of adjusters in connection therewith. In the early days of the Association it was hotly debated whether these Rules of Practice should bind Members or not, and in the event it was decided that they would not be binding, although, naturally, they would carry considerable authority. Even now, if an average adjuster draws up a statement which is at variance with a Rule of Practice, he must place a note in his adjustment referring to the Rule of Practice and stating why he differs from it.

Since 1890, when the Customs of Lloyd's were reviewed and assimilated into the Rules of Practice, various new Rules and amendments to existing Rules have been adopted from time to time in order to regulate the practice of average adjusters in areas where the law is silent. Since the Rules of Practice were last printed in 1971, new Rules or amendments have been introduced in Rules C2, C4, F3 and F19 in order to bring English practice on the subjects concerned into line with York–Antwerp Rules 1974.

The procedure for establishing a Rule of Practice is as follows:

By the Rules of the Association, Representatives Members (who are appointed by Underwriting bodies as well as by Shipowners, Merchants and similar institutions) are entitled, equally with Members, on giving appropriate notice, to move resolutions intended to become Rules of Practice at any General Meeting of the Association. After discussion such resolution will be voted upon by Members, and if carried by the votes of a simple majority of the Members voting, it becomes a probationary Rule until the next following General Meeting. During the intervening period the probationary Rule is considered by the Advisory Committee (or a Special Committee) of the Association, who may recommend its acceptance, rejection or amendment. At the next following General Meeting the probationary Rule, in the form approved by the Advisory Committee (or Special Committee), is again discussed, and if it is confirmed by a two-thirds majority, it becomes a Rule of Practice.

The Rules of Practice as printed herein are divided into six sections according to the subjects dealt with. The Rules relating to General Average now appear in two separate sections:

Section B
Rules which affect the adjustment of general average or the duties of adjusters in all cases, whatever may be the basis of adjustment.

570 Appendix V

Section F
Rules relating to the adjustment of general average under English law and practice. The Rules contained in section F may be considered by some readers to be of little more than historical interest, in view of the fact that the vast majority of general averages are now adjusted in accordance with York–Antwerp Rules, but these Rules of Practice have been retained not only to deal with the minority of cases where the adjustment is prepared in accordance with English law and practice, but also to demonstrate the early steps taken in the movement towards uniformity.

The Rules which have been rescinded in the past have not been printed in this edition of the Rules, but the Index to the Reports of the Association shows where the text of any rescinded Rule may be found. Readers who are not in possession of the Association's printed Reports may obtain photocopies of the appropriate pages, on payment of a small fee, by application to the Secretary.

December 1980

RULES OF PRACTICE

SECTION A—GENERAL RULES

A1. Adjustments for the consideration of underwriters

That any claim prepared for the consideration of underwriters shall include a statement of the reasons of the average adjuster for stating such a claim, and when submitted in conjunction with a claim for which underwriters are liable, shall be shown in such a manner as clearly to distinguish the claim for consideration from other claims embodied in the same adjustment.

An earlier Rule of Practice dealing with this subject was accepted in 1875, confirmed in 1876, and rescinded in 1894/95. The text of the earlier Rule is printed in the report for 1876, p 12.

A2. Interest and commission for advancing funds

That, in practice, interest and commission for advancing funds are only allowable in average when, proper and necessary steps having been taken to make a collection on account, an out-of-pocket expense for interest and/or commission for advancing funds is reasonably incurred.

See note under Rule A3.

A3. Agency commission and agency

That, in practice, neither commission (excepting bank commission) nor any charge by way of agency or remuneration for trouble is allowed to the shipowner in average, except in respect of services rendered on behalf of cargo when such services are not involved in the contract of affreightment.

An earlier Rule of Practice dealing with the subject of Agency fees chargeable by shipowners was accepted in 1879, confirmed in 1880, and rescinded in 1906/07, following the report of a Special Committee. The text of the earlier Rule is incorporated in the Committee's report, printed at 1906, p 21.

A4. Duty of adjusters in respect of cost of repairs

That in adjusting particular average on ship or general average which includes repairs, it is the duty of the adjuster to satisfy himself that such reasonable and usual precautions have been taken to keep down the cost of repairs as a prudent shipowner would have taken if uninsured.

A5. Claims on ship's machinery

That in all claims on ship's machinery for repairs, no claim for a new propeller or new shaft shall be admitted into an adjustment, unless the adjuster shall obtain and insert into his statement evidence showing what has become of the old propeller or shaft.

A6. Water casks

Water casks or tanks carried on a ship's deck are not paid for by underwriters as general or particular average; nor are warps or other articles when improperly carried on deck.

A7. Adjustment; policies of insurance and names of underwriters

That no adjustment shall be drawn up showing the amount of payments by or to the underwriters, unless the policies or copies of the policies of insurance or certificates of insurance, for which the statement is required, be produced to the average adjusters. Such statement shall set out sufficient details of the underwriters interested and the amounts due on the respective policies produced.

An earlier Rule of Practice dealing with this subject was accepted in 1889, confirmed in 1890, and rescinded in 1968/69. The text of the earlier Rule is printed in the report for 1890, p 33.

A8. Apportionment of costs in collision cases

That when a vessel sustains and does damage by collision, and litigation consequently results for the purpose of testing liability, the technicality of the vessel having been plaintiff or defendant in the litigation shall not necessarily govern the apportionment of the costs of such litigation, which shall be apportioned between claim and counter-claim in proportion to the amount, excluding interest, which has been or would have been allowed in respect of each in the event of the claim or counter-claim being established; provided that when a claim or counter-claim is made solely for the purpose of defence, and is not allowed, the costs apportioned thereto shall be treated as costs of defence.

A9. Franchise charges

The expenses of protest, survey, and other proofs of loss, including the commission or other expenses of a sale by auction, are not admitted to make up the percentage of a claim; and are only paid by the underwriters in case the loss amounts to a claim without them.

SECTION B—GENERAL AVERAGE

Rules of general application.

Note: In this edition, the Rules relating to the adjustment of general average under English law and practice have been transferred to Section F.

B1. Basis of adjustment

That in any adjustment of general average not made in accordance with British law it shall be prefaced on what principle or according to what law the adjustment has been made, and the reason for so adjusting the claim shall be set forth.

In all cases the adjuster shall give particulars in a prominent position in the average statement of the clause or clauses contained in the charter-party and/or bills of lading with reference to the adjustment of general average.

B2—B8 inclusive—*transferred to section F.*

B9. Claims arising out of deficiency of fuel

That in adjusting general average arising out of deficiency of fuel, the facts on which the general average is based shall be set forth in the adjustment, including the material dates and distances, and particulars of fuel supplies and consumption.

B10—B23 inclusive—*transferred to section F.*

B24. Contributory value of ship

That in any adjustment of general average there shall be set forth the certificate on which the contributory value of the ship is based or, if there be no such certificate, the information adopted in lieu thereof, and any amount made good shall be specified.

B25. Contributory value of freight

That in any adjustment of general average there shall be set forth the amount of the gross freight and the freight advanced, if any; also the charges and wages deducted and any amount made good.

The first paragraph of Rule B25, dealing with the basis of adjustment under English law and practice, has been transferred to Section F and re-numbered F22.

B26. Vessel in ballast and under charter: contributing interests

For the purpose of ascertaining the liability of Underwriters on British policies of insurance, the following provisions shall apply:

When a vessel is proceeding in ballast to load under a voyage charter entered into by the shipowner before the general average act, the interests contributing to the general average shall be the vessel, such items of stores and equipment as belong to parties other than the owners of the vessel (eg bunkers, wireless installation and navigational instruments) and the freight earned under the voyage charter computed in the usual way after deduction of contingent expenses subsequent to the general average act. Failing a prior termination of the adventure, the place where the adventure shall be deemed to end and at which the values for contribution to general average shall be calculated is the final port of discharge of the cargo carried under the charter but in the event of the prior loss of the vessel and freight, or either of them, the general average shall attach to any surviving interest or interests including freight advanced at the loading port deducting therefrom contingent expenses subsequent to the general average act.

When a vessel is proceeding in ballast under a time charter alone or a time charter and a voyage charter entered into by the time charterer, the general average shall attach to the vessel and such items of stores and equipment as are indicated above. Failing a prior termination of the adventure, the adventure shall be deemed to end and the values for contribution to general average calculated at the first loading port upon the commencement of loading cargo.

When the charter to which the shipowner is a party provides for York–Antwerp Rules, the general average shall be adjusted in accordance with those Rules and British law and practice and without regard to the law and practice of any foreign port at which the adventure may terminate; and in the interpretation of Rule XI it shall be immaterial whether the extra period of detention takes place at a port of loading, call or refuge, provided that the detention is in consequence of accident, sacrifice or other extraordinary circumstance occurring whilst the vessel is in ballast.

In practice neither time charter hire, as such, nor time charterer's voyage freight shall contribute to general average.

The earliest Rule of Practice dealing with this subject was accepted in 1896, confirmed in 1897 and rescinded in 1926, when after reference to a Special Committee it was replaced by a new Rule, which was in its turn referred to a Special Committee in 1944 and rescinded in 1945/46. The text of the original Rule is printed in the report for 1897, pp 34/35 and the subsequent Rule in the report for November 1926, p 9.

B27. Ulterior chartered freight: contribution to general average

That when at the time of a general average act the vessel has on board cargo shipped under charter-party or bills of lading, and is also under a separate charter to load another cargo after the cargo then in course of carriage has been discharged, the ulterior chartered freight shall not contribute to the general average.

B28. Deductions from freight at charterer's risk

That freight at the risk of the charterer shall be subject to no deduction for wages and charges, except in the case of charters in which the wages or charges are payable by the charterer, in which case such freight shall be governed by the same rule as freight at the risk of the shipowner.

B29. Forwarding charges on advanced freight

That in case of wreck, the cargo being forwarded to its destination, the charterer, who has paid a lump sum on account of freight, which is not to be returned in the event of the vessel being lost, shall not be liable for any portion of the forwarding freight and charges, when the same are less than the balance of freight payable to the shipowner at the port of destination under the original charter-party.

B30. Sacrifice for the common safety: direct liability of underwriters

That in case of general average sacrifice there is, under ordinary policies of insurance, a direct liability of an underwriter on ship for loss of or damage to ship's materials, and of an underwriter on goods or freight, for loss of or damage to goods or loss of freight so sacrificed as a general average loss; that such loss not being particular average is not taken into account in computing the memorandum percentages, and that the direct liability of an underwriter for such loss is consequently unaffected by the memorandum or any other warranty respecting particular average.

An earlier Rule of Practice dealing with this subject was accepted in 1874, confirmed in 1875 and rescinded in 1889. The text of this earlier Rule is printed in the report for 1875, p 18.

B31. Sacrifice of ship's stores: direct liability of underwriters

That underwriters insuring ship's stores, bunker coal or fuel, destroyed or used as part of a general average operation, shall only be liable for those articles as a direct claim on the policy when they formed part of the property at risk at the time of the peril giving rise to the general average act.

B32. Enforcement of general average lien by shipowners

That in all cases where general average damage to ship is claimed direct from the underwriters on that interest, the average adjusters shall ascertain whether the shipowners have taken the necessary steps to enforce their lien for general average on the cargo, and shall insert in the average statement a note giving the result of their enquiries.

B33. Underwriter's liability

If the ship or cargo be insured for more than its contributory value, the underwriter pays what is assessed on the contributory value. But where insured for less than the contributory value, the underwriter pays on the insured value; and when there has been a particular average for damage which forms a deduction from the contributory value of the ship that must be deducted from the insured value to find upon what the underwriter contributes.

This rule does not apply to foreign adjustments, when the basis of contribution is something other than the net value of the thing insured.

That in practice, in applying the above rule for the purpose of ascertaining the liability of underwriters for contribution to general average and salvage charges, deduction shall be made from the insured value of all losses and charges for which underwriters are liable and which have been deducted in arriving at the contributory value.

In adjusting the liability of underwriters on freight for general average contribution and salvage charges, effect shall be given to section 73 of the Marine Insurance Act 1906, by comparing the gross and not the net amount of freight at risk with the insured value in the case of a valued policy or the insurable value in the case of an unvalued policy.

B34. The duty of adjusters in cases involving refunds of general average deposits or apportionment of salvage, collision recoveries, or other funds

That in cases of general average where deposits have been collected and it is likely that repayments will have to be made, measures be taken by the adjuster to ascertain the names of underwriters who have reimbursed their assured in respect of such deposits; that the names of any such underwriters be set forth in the adjustment as claimants of refund, if any, to which they are apparently entitled; and that on completion of the adjustment, notice be sent to all underwriters whose names are so set forth as to any refund of which they appear as claimants and as to the steps to be taken in order to obtain payment of the same.

That in cases where the names of any underwriters are not to be ascertained on completion of the adjustment, notice be sent to the Secretary of Lloyd's, to the Institute of London Underwriters, to the Liverpool Underwriters' Association, and to the Association of Underwriters of Glasgow, notifying such interests as have not been appropriated to underwriters.

And that in cases of apportionment of salvage or other funds for distribution, similar measures be taken by the adjuster to safeguard the interests of any underwriters who may be entitled to benefit under the apportionment.

B35. Memorandum to statements showing refunds in respect of general average deposits

That the following memorandum shall appear at the end of statements which show refunds to be due in respect of General Average Deposits, viz:
Memorandum—Refunds of general average deposits shown in this statement should only be paid on production of the original deposit receipts.

B36. Interest on deposits

That, unless otherwise expressly provided, the interest accrued on deposits on account of salvage and/or general average and/or particular and/or other charges, or on the balance of such deposits after payments on account, if any, have been made, shall be credited to the depositor or those to whom his rights in respect of the deposits have been transferred.

B37. Apportionment of interest on amounts made good

That in practice (in the absence of express agreement between the parties concerned) interest allowed on amounts made good shall be apportioned between assured and underwriters, taking into account the sums paid by underwriters and the dates when such payments were made, notwithstanding that by the addition of interest the underwriter may receive a larger sum than he has paid.

SECTION C—YORK–ANTWERP RULES

C1. Salvage services rendered under an agreement

Expenses for salvage services rendered by or accepted under agreement shall in practice be treated as general average provided that such expenses were incurred for the common safety within the meaning of Rule 'A' of the York–Antwerp Rules, 1924 or York–Antwerp Rules 1950.

An earlier Rule of Practice dealing with this subject was accepted in 1927, confirmed in 1928, and rescinded in 1942/43. The text of the earlier Rule is printed in the report for 1928, p 32.

C2. Commission allowed under York–Antwerp Rules

That the commission of 2 per cent allowed on general average disbursements under Rule XXI of York–Antwerp Rules 1924 and Rule XX of York–Antwerp Rules 1950 or 1974, shall be credited in full to the party who has authorised the expenditure and is liable for payment, except that where the funds for payment are provided in the first instance in whole or in part from the deposit funds, or by other parties to the adventure, or by underwriters, the commission on such advances shall be credited to the deposit funds or to the parties or underwriters providing the funds for payment.

C3. York–Antwerp Rules 1924. Rules X(a) and XX

That, in practice, where a vessel is at any port or place in circumstances in which the wages and maintenance of crew during detention there for the purpose of repairs necessary for the safe prosecution of the voyage would be admissible in general average under Rule XI of the York–Antwerp Rules 1924, and the vessel is necessarily removed thence to another port or place because such repairs cannot be effected at the first port or place, the provisions of Rule X(a) shall be applied to the second port or place as if it were a port or place of refuge within that Rule and the provisions of Rule XX shall be applied to the prolongation of the voyage occasioned by such removal.

C4. York–Antwerp Rules 1950 and 1974. Rule X(a)

That in practice, in applying the second paragraph of Rule X(a), a vessel shall be deemed to be at a port or place of refuge when she is at any port or place in circumstances in which the wages and maintenance of the Master, Officers and crew incurred during any extra period of detention there would be admissible in General Average under the provisions of Rule XI.

SECTION D—DAMAGE AND REPAIRS TO SHIP

D1. Expenses of removing a vessel for repair

Where a vessel is in need of repair at any port, and is removed thence to some other port for the purpose of repairs, either because the repairs cannot be effected, or cannot be effected prudently:
  (a) The necessary expenses incurred in moving the vessel to the port of repair shall be allowed as part of the cost of repair, and where the vessel after repairing forthwith returns to the port from which she was removed, the necessary expenses incurred in so returning shall also be allowed.
  (b) Where by moving the vessel to the port of repair any new freight is earned, or any expenses are saved in relation to the current voyage of the vessel, such net earnings or savings shall be deducted from the expenses of moving her, and where the vessel loads a new cargo at the port of repair no expenses subsequent to the completion of repair shall be allowed.
  The expenses of removal include the cost of temporary repair, ballasting, wages and provisions of crew and/or runners, pilotage, towage, extra marine insurance, port charges, fuel and engine-room stores.
  (c) This rule shall not admit any ordinary expenses incurred in fulfilment of a contract of affreightment, though such expenses are increased by the removal to a port of repair.

D2. Fuel and stores used in repair of damage to the vessel

That the cost of replacing fuel and stores consumed either in the repair of damage to a vessel, in working the engines or winches to assist in the repairs of damage, or in moving her to a place of repair within the limits of the port where she is lying, shall be treated as part of the cost of repairs.

D3. Rigging chafed

Rigging injured by straining or chafing is not charged to underwriters, unless such injury is caused by blows of the sea, grounding, or contact; or by displacement, through sea peril, of the spars, channels, bulwarks, or rails.

D4. Sails split or blown away

Sails split by the wind, or blown away while set, unless occasioned by the ship's grounding or coming into collision, or in consequence of damage to the spars to which the sails are bent, are not charged to underwriters.

D5. Dry dock expenses

1. That, in practice, where repairs, for the cost of which underwriters are liable, are necessarily effected in dry dock as an immediate consequence of the casualty, or the vessel is taken out of service especially to effect such repairs in dry dock, the cost of entering and leaving the dry dock, in addition to so much of the dock dues as is necessary for the repair of the damage, shall be chargeable in full to the underwriters, notwithstanding that the shipowner may have taken advantage of the vessel being in dry dock to carry out survey for classification purposes or to effect repairs on his account which are not immediately necessary to make the vessel seaworthy.

2. (a) Where repairs on Owners' account which are immediately necessary to make the vessel seaworthy and which can only be effected in dry dock are executed concurrently with other repairs, for the cost of which underwriters are liable, and which also can only be effected in dry dock,
  (b) Where the repairs, for the cost of which underwriters are liable, are deferred until a routine dry-docking and are then executed concurrently with repairs on Owners' account which require the use of the dry dock, whether or not such Owners' repairs affect the seaworthiness of the vessel,

the cost of entering and leaving the dry dock, in addition to so much of the dock dues as is common to both repairs, shall be divided equally between the shipowner and the underwriters, irrespective of the fact that the repairs for which underwriters are liable may relate to more than one voyage or accident or may be payable by more than one set of underwriters.

3. Sub-division between underwriters of the proportion of dry-docking expenses chargeable to them shall be made on the basis of voyages, and/or such other franchise units as are specified in the policies.

4. In determining whether the franchise is reached the whole cost of dry-docking necessary for the repair of the damage, less the proportion (if any) chargeable to Owners when Section (a) of paragraph 2 applies, shall be taken into consideration, notwithstanding that there are other damages to which a portion of the cost of dry-docking has to be apportioned in ascertaining the amount actually recoverable.

An earlier Rule of Practice dealing with this subject was accepted in 1891, confirmed in 1892, and amended in 1903/4 after reference to a Special Committee. It was again referred to a Special Committee in November 1926, further amended in 1927/28, and rescinded in 1970/71. The texts are printed in the reports for 1892, p 28; 1904, p 42 and 1928, p 31.

D6. Tankers—treatment of the cost of tank cleaning and/or gas-freeing

1. That, in practice, where repairs, for the cost of which underwriters are liable, require the tanks to be rough cleaned and/or gas-freed as an immediate consequence of the casualty, or the vessel is taken out of service especially to effect such repairs, the cost of such rough cleaning and/or gas-freeing shall be chargeable in full to the underwriters, notwithstanding that the shipowner may have taken advantage of the vessel being rough cleaned and/or gas-freed to carry out survey for classification purposes or to effect repairs on his account which are not immediately necessary to make the vessel seaworthy.

2. (a) Where repairs on Owners' account which are immediately necessary to make the vessel seaworthy and which require the tanks being rough cleaned and/or gas-freed are executed concurrently with other repairs, for the cost of which underwriters are liable, and which also require the tanks being rough cleaned and/or gas-freed,
  (b) Where the repairs, for the cost of which underwriters are liable, are deferred until a routine dry-docking or repair period, at which time repairs on Owners' account which also require the tanks being rough cleaned and/or gas-freed are

effected, whether or not such Owners' repairs affect the seaworthiness of the vessel,

the cost of such rough cleaning and/or gas-freeing as is common to both repairs shall be divided equally between the shipowners and the underwriters, irrespective of the fact that the repairs for which underwriters are liable may relate to more than one voyage or accident or may be payable by more than one set of underwriters.

3. The cost of fine cleaning specifically for a particular repair or particular repairs shall be divided in accordance with the principles set forth above.

4. Sub-division between underwriters of the proportion of rough tank cleaning and/or gas-freeing and/or fine cleaning chargeable to them shall be made on the basis of voyages, and/or such other franchise units as are specified in the policies.

5. In determining whether the franchise is reached the whole cost of rough cleaning and/or gas-freeing and/or fine cleaning necessary for the repair of the damage, less the proportion (if any) chargeable to Owners when Section (a) of paragraph 2 applies, shall be taken into consideration, notwithstanding that there are other damages to which a portion of the cost of rough tank cleaning and/or gas-freeing and/or fine cleaning has to be apportioned in ascertaining the amount actually recoverable.

D7. Particular average on ship: deduction of one-third

The deduction for new work in place of old is fixed by custom at one-third, with the following exceptions:

Anchors are allowed in full. Chain cables are subject to one-sixth only.

Metal sheathing is dealt with, by allowing in full the cost of a weight equal to the gross weight of metal sheathing stripped off minus the proceeds of the old metal. Nails, felt, and labour metalling are subject to one-third.

The rule applies to iron as well as to wooden ships, and to labour as well as material. It does not apply to the expense of straightening bent ironwork, and to the labour of taking out and replacing it.

It does not apply to graving dock expenses and removals, cartages, use of shears, stages, and graving dock materials.

It does not apply to a ship's first voyage.

D8. Scraping and painting

Where the Policy includes a Clause to the effect that:
  'No claim shall in any case be allowed in respect of scraping or painting the vessel's bottom'.
  (a) Gritblasting and/or other surface preparation of new bottom plates ashore and supplying and applying any 'shop' primer thereto
  (b) Gritblasting and/or other surface preparation of:
      (i) the butts or area of plating immediately adjacent to any renewed or refitted plating damaged during the course of welding and/or repairs
      (ii) areas of plating damaged during the course of fairing, either in place or ashore
  (c) Supplying and applying the first coat of primer/anti-corrosive to those particular areas mentioned in (a) and (b) above

shall be allowed as part of the reasonable cost of repairs in respect of bottom plating damaged by an insured peril and shall be deemed not to be excluded by the wording of this Clause. The gritblasting and/or other surface preparation and the painting of all other areas of the bottom is excluded by the Clause.

SECTION E—PARTICULAR AVERAGE ON GOODS

E1. Adjustment on bonded prices

In the following cases it is customary to adjust particular average on a comparison of bonded, instead of duty-paid prices:

In claims for damage to tea, tobacco, coffee, wine, and spirits imported into this country.

E2. Adjustment of average on goods sold in bond

That in consequence of the facilities generally offered to bond goods at their destination, at which terms they are often sold, the term 'Gross Proceeds' shall, for the purpose of adjustment, be taken to mean the price at which the goods are sold to the consumer, after payment of freight and landing charges, but exclusive of Customs duty, in cases where it is the custom of the port to sell or deal with the goods in bond.

E3. Apportionment of insured value of goods

That where different qualities or descriptions of cargo are valued in the policy at a lump sum, such sum shall, for the purpose of adjusting claims, be apportioned on the invoice where the invoice value distinguishes the separate values of the said different qualities or descriptions; and over the net arrived sound values in all other cases.

E4. Allowance for water and/or impurities in picked cotton

When bales of cotton are picked, and the pickings are sold wet, the allowance for water in the pickings (where there are no means of ascertaining it) is by custom fixed at one-third.

There is a similar custom to deduct one-sixth from the gross weight of pickings of country damaged cotton to take account of dirt, moisture and other impurities.

E5. Allowance for water in cut tobacco

When damaged tobacco is cut off, the allowance for water in the cuttings is one-fourth if the actual increase cannot be ascertained.

E6. Allowance for water in wool

Damaged wool from Australia, New Zealand, and the Cape is subject to a deduction of 3 per cent for wet, if the actual increase cannot be ascertained.

E7. Extra charges

[*rescinded 1981*]

SECTION F—GENERAL AVERAGE ADJUSTMENT UNDER ENGLISH LAW AND PRACTICE

F1. Deckload jettison

The jettison of a deckload carried according to the usage of trade and not in violation of the contracts of affreightment is general average.

There is an exception to this rule in the case of cargoes of cotton, tallow, acids and some other goods.

F2. Damage by water used to extinguish fire

That damage done by water poured down a ship's hold to extinguish a fire be treated as general average.

F3. Extinguishing fire on shipboard

Damage done to a ship and cargo, or either of them, by water or otherwise, including damage by beaching or scuttling a burning ship, in extinguishing a fire on board the ship, shall be made good as general average; except that no compensation shall be made for damage by smoke or heat however caused.

The earliest Rule of Practice dealing with this subject entitled 'Damage caused by water thrown upon burning goods' was accepted in 1874, confirmed in 1875, and rescinded in 1968/69.
It was then replaced by a Rule under the present title which was in its turn rescinded in 1974/75. The text of the original Rule is printed in the report for 1875, p 22 and the subsequent Rule in the report for 1968, pp 18/19.

F4. Voluntary stranding

When a ship is intentionally run on shore and the circumstances are such that if that course were not adopted she would inevitably drive on shore or on rocks, no loss or damage caused to the ship, cargo and freight or any of them by such intentional running on shore shall be made good as general average, but loss or damage incurred in refloating such a ship shall be allowed as general average.

In all other cases where a ship is intentionally run on shore for the common safety, the consequent loss or damage shall be allowed as general average.

The original Custom of Lloyd's under this heading, amended in 1876, was rescinded in 1968/69. The text of the Custom is printed, as confirmed as a Rule of Practice, in the report for 1891, p 69.

F5. Expenses lightening a ship when ashore

When a ship is ashore in a position of peril and, in order to float her, cargo is put into lighters, and is then at once re-shipped, the whole cost of lightering, including lighter hire and re-shipping, is general average.

F6. Sails set to force a ship off the ground

Sails damaged by being set, or kept set, to force a ship off the ground or to drive her higher up the ground for the common safety, are general average.

F7. Stranded vessels: damage to engines in getting off

That damage caused to machinery and boilers of a stranded vessel, in endeavouring to refloat for the common safety, when the interests are in peril, be allowed in general average.

F8. Resort to port of refuge for general average repairs: treatment of the charges incurred

That when a ship puts into a port of refuge in consequence of damage which is itself the subject of general average, and sails thence with her original cargo, or a part of it, the outward as well as the inward port charges shall be treated as general average; and when cargo is discharged for the purpose of repairing such damage, the warehouse rent and reloading of the same shall, as well as the discharge, be treated as general average. (See *Attwood v Sellar*.)

F9. Resort to port of refuge on account of particular average repairs: treatment of the charges incurred

That when a ship puts into a port of refuge in consequence of damage which is itself the subject of particular average (or not of general average) and when the cargo has been discharged in consequence of such damage, the inward port charges and the cost of discharging the cargo shall be general average, the warehouse rent of cargo shall be a particular charge on cargo, and the cost of reloading and outward port charges shall be a particular charge on freight. (See *Svendsen v Wallace*.)

F10. Treatment of costs of storage and reloading at port of refuge

That when the cargo is discharged for the purpose of repairing, re-conditioning, or diminishing damage to ship or cargo which is itself the subject of general average, the cost of storage on it and of reloading it shall be treated as general average, equally with the cost of discharging it.

F11. Insurance on cargo discharged under average

That in practice, where the cost of insurance has been reasonably incurred by the shipowner, or his agents, on cargo discharged under average, such cost shall be treated as part of the cost of storage.

F12. Expenses at a port of refuge

When a ship puts into a port of refuge on account of accident and not in consequence of damage which is itself the subject of general average, then on the assumption that the ship was seaworthy at the commencement of the voyage, the Custom of Lloyd's is as follows:
  (a) All cost of towage, pilotage, harbour dues, and other extraordinary expenses incurred in order to bring the ship and cargo into a place of safety, are general average. Under the term 'extraordinary expenses' are not included wages or victuals of crew, coals, or engine stores, or demurrage.
  (b) The cost of discharging the cargo, whether for the common safety, or to repair the ship, together with the cost of conveying it to the warehouse, is general average. The cost of discharging the cargo on account of damage to it resulting from its own vice propre, is chargeable to the owners of the cargo.
  (c) The warehouse rent, or other expenses which take the place of warehouse rent, of the cargo when so discharged, is, except as under, a special charge on the cargo.
  (d) The cost of reloading the cargo, and the outward port charges incurred through leaving the port of refuge, are, when the discharge of cargo falls in general average, a special charge on freight.
  (e) The expenses referred to in clause (d) are charged to the party who runs the risk of freight—that is, wholly to the charterer—if the whole freight has been prepaid;

and, if part only, then in the proportion which the part prepaid bears to the whole freight.

(f) When the cargo, instead of being sent ashore, is placed on board hulk or lighters during the ship's stay in port, the hulk-hire is divided between general average, cargo, and freight, in such proportions as may place the several contributing interests in nearly the same relative positions as if the cargo has been landed and stored.

F13. Treatment of costs of extraordinary discharge

That no distinction be drawn in practice between discharging cargo for the common safety of ship and cargo, and discharging it for the purpose of effecting at an intermediate port or ports of refuge repairs necessary for the prosecution of the voyage.

F14. Towage from a port of refuge

That if a ship be in a port of refuge at which it is practicable to repair her, and if, in order to save expense, she be towed thence to some other port, then the extra cost of such towage shall be divided in proportion to the saving of expense thereby occasioned to the several parties to the adventure.

F15. Cargo forwarded from a port of refuge

That if a ship be in a port of refuge at which it is practicable to repair her so as to enable her to carry on the whole cargo, but, in order to save expense, the cargo, or a portion of it, be transhipped by another vessel, or otherwise forwarded, then the cost of such transhipment (up to the amount of expense saved) shall be divided in proportion to the saving of expense thereby occasioned to the several parties to the adventure.

F16. Cargo sold at a port of refuge

That if a ship be in a port of refuge at which it is practicable to repair her so as to enable her to carry on the whole cargo, or such portion of it as is fit to be carried on, but, in order to save expense, the cargo, or a portion of it, be, with the consent of the owners of such cargo, sold at the port of refuge, then the loss by sale including loss of freight on cargo so sold (up to the amount of expense saved) shall be divided in proportion to the saving of expense thereby occasioned to the several parties to the adventure; provided always that the amount so divided shall in no case exceed the cost of transhipment and/or forwarding referred to in the preceding rule of the Association.

F17. Interpretation of the rule respecting substituted expenses

That for the purpose of avoiding any misinterpretation of the resolution relating to the apportionment of substituted expenses, it is declared that the saving of expense therein mentioned is limited to a saving or reduction of the actual outlay, including the crew's wages and provisions, if any, which would have been incurred at the port of refuge, if the vessel has been repaired there, and does not include supposed losses or expenses, such as interest, loss of market, demurrage, or assumed damage by discharging.

F18. Treatment of damage to cargo caused by discharge, storing, and reloading

That damage necessarily done to cargo by discharging, storing, and reloading it, be treated as general average when, and only when the cost of those measures respectively is so treated.

A Custom of Lloyd's concerning cargo discharged at a port of refuge was rescinded in 1890/91, and an earlier Rule of Practice accepted in 1883 and confirmed in 1884 was rescinded in 1968/69. The text of the earlier Rule is printed in the report for 1884, p 37.

F19. Deductions from cost of repairs in adjusting general average

Repairs to be allowed in general average shall not be subject to deductions in respect of 'new for old' where old materials or parts are replaced by new unless the ship is over fifteen years old in which case there shall be a deduction of one-third. The deductions shall be regulated by the age of the ship from 31 December of the year of completion of construction to the date of the general average act, except for insulation, life and similar boats, communications and navigational apparatus and equipment, machinery and boilers for which the deductions shall be regulated by the age of the particular parts to which they apply.

The deductions shall be made only from the cost of the new material or parts when finished and ready to be installed in the ship.

No deduction shall be made in respect of provisions, stores, anchors and chain cables.

Drydock and slipway dues and costs of shifting the ship shall be allowed in full.

The costs of cleaning, painting or coating of bottom shall not be allowed in general average unless the bottom has been painted or coated within the twelve months preceding the date of the general average act in which case one half of such costs shall be allowed.

F20. Freight sacrificed: amount to be made good in general average

That the loss of freight to be made good in general average shall be ascertained by deducting from the amount of gross freight lost the charges which the owner thereof would have incurred to earn such freight, but has, in consequence of the sacrifice, not incurred.

F21. Basis of contribution to general average

When property saved by a general average act is injured or destroyed by subsequent accident, the contributing value of that property to a general average which is less than the total contributing value, shall, when it does not reach the port of destination, be its actual net proceeds; when it does it shall be its actual net value at the port of destination on its delivery there; and in all cases any values allowed in general average shall be added to and form part of the contributing value as above.

The above rule shall not apply to adjustments made before the adventure has terminated.

F22. Contributory value of freight

That freight at the risk of the shipowner shall contribute to general average upon its gross amount, deducting such charges and crew's wages as would not have been incurred in earning the freight had the ship and cargo been totally lost at the date of the general average act and have not been allowed as general average.

UNIFORMITY RESOLUTION

York–Antwerp Rules 1924: application of Rule XIV

That, in practice, in applying Rule XIV of the York–Antwerp Rules, 1924, the cost of the temporary repair of the accidental damage there referred to shall be allowed in general average up to the saving to the general average by effecting such temporary repair, without regard to the saving (if any) to other interests.

INDEX TO THE REPORTS OF THE ASSOCIATION CURRENT RULES OF PRACTICE

Number	Subject	Proposal		Amendments (if any)	
		Accepted	Confirmed	Accepted	Confirmed
	SECTION A— **GENERAL RULES**				
A1	Adjustments 'for the consideration of Underwriters'	1894, p 32	1895, p 25	1968, p 17	1969, p 22
A2	Interest and Commission for advancing funds	1906, p 21	1907, p 60		
A3	Agency commission and agency	1906, p 21	1907, p 60		
A4	Duty of adjusters in respect of cost of repairs	1879, p 24	1880, p 21		
A5	Claims on Ship's machinery	1890, p 32	1891, p 32		
A6	Water casks	Custom of Lloyd's		1876, p 20	
A7	Adjustment: policies of insurance and names of Underwriters	1968, p 25	1969, p 22		
A8	Apportionment of costs in collision cases	1889, p 42	1890, p 30	1930, p 32	1931, p27
A9	Franchise charges	Custom of Lloyd's			

INDEX TO THE REPORTS OF THE ASSOCIATION CURRENT RULES OF PRACTICE

Number	Subject	Proposal		Amendments (if any)	
		Accepted	Confirmed	Accepted	Confirmed
	SECTION B—GENERAL AVERAGE				
	Rules of general application				
B1	Basis of adjustment	1889, p 60	1890, p 33	1899, p 29	1900, p 20
B9	Claims arising out of a deficiency of fuel	1899, p 50	1900, p 25		
B24	Contributory value of ship	1899, p 41	1900, p 20		
B25	Contributory value of freight	1873			
B26	Vessel in ballast and under charter: contributing interests	1945, p 53	1946, p 45		
B27	Ulterior chartered freight: contribution to general average	1891, p 35	1892, p 27		
B28	Deductions from freight at charterers' risk	1873,		1968, p 23	1969, p 22
B29	Forwarding charges on advanced freight	1873,			
B30	Sacrifice for the common safety: direct liability of Underwriters	1890, p 42	1891, p 34		
B31	Sacrifice of ship's stores: direct liability of Underwriters	1921, p 50	1922, p 43		
B32	Enforcement of general average lien by shipowners	1890, p 56	1891, p 34		
B33	Underwriters' liability	Custom of Lloyd's		1922, p 56 1926, p 38	1923, p 19 1926 (Nov) p 7

INDEX TO THE REPORTS OF THE ASSOCIATION CURRENT RULES OF PRACTICE

Number	Subject	Proposal		Amendments (if any)	
		Accepted	Confirmed	Accepted	Confirmed
	SECTION B— GENERAL AVERAGE				
B34	The duties of adjusters in cases involving refunds of general average deposits or apportionment of salvage, collision recoveries, or other funds	1896, p 50	1897, p 34		
B35	Memorandum to statements showing refunds in respect of general average deposits	1904, p 50	1905, p 36		
B36	Interest on deposits	1923, p 32	1924, p 36		
B37	Apportionment of interest on amounts made good	1925, p 68	1926, p 38		

INDEX TO THE REPORTS OF THE ASSOCIATION CURRENT RULES OF PRACTICE

Number	Subject	Proposal		Amendments (if any)	
		Accepted	Confirmed	Accepted	Confirmed
	SECTION C— **YORK-ANTWERP** **RULES**				
C1	Salvage services rendered under an agreement	1942, p 50	1943, p 39	1950, p 28	1951, p 38
C2	Commission allowed under York-Antwerp Rules	1933, p 45	1934, p 40	1950, p 28 1974, p 13	1951, p 38 1975, p 15
C3	York-Antwerp Rules 1924. Rules X(a) and XX	1949, p 36	1950, p 27		
C4	York-Antwerp Rules 1950 and 1974 Rule X(a)	1957, p 24	1958, p 18	1974, p 13	1975, p 15

INDEX TO THE REPORTS OF THE ASSOCIATION CURRENT RULES OF PRACTICE

Number	Subject	Proposal		Amendments (if any)	
		Accepted	Confirmed	Accepted	Confirmed
	SECTION D—DAMAGE AND REPAIRS TO SHIP				
D1	Expenses of removing a vessel for repair	1896, p 23	1897, p 24	1928, p 13	1929, p 25
D2	Fuel and stores used in repair of damage to the vessel	1876, p 23	1877, p 53	1968, p 26	1969, p 22
D3	Rigging chafed	Custom of Lloyd's			
D4	Sails split or blown away	Custom of Lloyd's			
D5	Drydock expenses	1970, p 19	1971, p 21		
D6	Tankers – treatment of the cost of tank cleaning and/or gas-freeing	1970, p 19	1971, p 21		
D7	Particular Average on ship. Deduction of one-third	Custom of Lloyd's			
D8	Scraping and Painting	1980	1981		

INDEX TO THE REPORTS OF THE ASSOCIATION CURRENT RULES OF PRACTICE

Number	Subject	Proposal		Amendments (if any)	
		Accepted	Confirmed	Accepted	Confirmed
	SECTION E—PARTICULAR AVERAGE ON GOODS				
E1	Adjustment on bonded prices	Custom of Lloyd's			
E2	Adjustment of average on goods sold in bond	1885, p 64	1886, p 24		
E3	Apportionment of insured value of goods	1885, p 43	1886, p 23		
E4	Allowance for water and/or impurities in picked cotton	Custom of Lloyd's		1968, p 29	1969, p 22
E5	Allowance for water in cut tobacco	Custom of Lloyd's		1968, p 28	1969, p 22
E6	Allowance for water in wool	Custom of Lloyd's			
E7	Extra charges	Custom of Lloyd's			

INDEX TO THE REPORTS OF THE ASSOCIATION CURRENT RULES OF PRACTICE

Number	Subject	Proposal		Amendments (if any)	
		Accepted	Confirmed	Accepted	Confirmed
	SECTION F—GENERAL AVERAGE ADJUSTMENT UNDER ENGLISH LAW AND PRACTICE				
F1	Deckload jettison	Custom of Lloyd's		1890, p 34	1891, p 32
F2	Damage by water used to extinguish fire	1873, p 20	1874, p 18		
F3	Extinguishing fire on shipboard	1974, p 13	1975, p 15		
F4	Voluntary stranding	1968, p 20	1969, p 22		
F5	Expenses lightening a ship when ashore	Custom of Lloyd's		1890, p 34 1968, p 20	1891, p 33 1969, p 22
F6	Sails set to force a ship off the ground	Custom of Lloyd's			
F7	Stranded vessels: damage to engines in getting off	1890, p 64	1891, p 35	1906, p 15	1907, p 46
F8	Resort to port of refuge for general average repairs: treatment of the charges incurred	1888, p 45	1889, p 48		
F9	Resort to port of refuge for particular average repairs: treatment of the charges incurred	1888, p 47	1889, p 49		
F10	Treatment of costs of storage and reloading at port of refuge	1886, p 37	1887, p 36		
F11	Insurance on cargo discharged under average	1924, p 43	1925, p 43	1968, p 21	1969, p 22
F12	Expenses at a port of refuge	Custom of Lloyd's		1890, p 34	1891, p 32

INDEX TO THE REPORTS OF THE ASSOCIATION CURRENT RULES OF PRACTICE

Number	Subject	Proposal		Amendments (if any)	
		Accepted	Confirmed	Accepted	Confirmed
	SECTION F—GENERAL AVERAGE ADJUSTMENT UNDER ENGLISH LAW AND PRACTICE				
F13	Treatment of costs of extraordinary discharge	1886, p 37	1887, p 36		
F14	Towage from a port of refuge	1876, p 26	1877, p 54		
F15	Cargo forwarded from a port of refuge	1876, p 26	1877, p 54		
F16	Cargo sold at a port of refuge	1902, p 34	1903, p 18		
F17	Interpretation of the Rule respecting substituted expenses	1877, p 63	1878, p 18		
F18	Treatment of damage to cargo caused by discharge, storing and reloading	1886, p 37	1887, p 36		
F19	Deductions from cost of repairs in adjusting general average	1887, p 36	1888, p 28	1934, p 41 1950, p 30 1974, p 13	1935, p 22 1951, p 38 1975, p 15
F20	Freight sacrificed: amount to be made good in general average	1894, p 56	1895, p 29		
F21	Basis of contribution to general average	1873			
F22	Contributory value of freight	1873		1968, p 22	1969, p 22

INDEX TO THE REPORTS OF THE ASSOCIATION
RESCINDED RULES

Subject	Proposal		Rescission		Current Rule (if any)
	Accepted	Confirmed	Accepted	Confirmed	
Adjustments 'for the consideration of Underwriters'	1875, p 37	1876, p 12	1894, p 32	1895, p 25	A1
Agency fees chargeable by shipowners	1879, p 30	1880, p 28	1906, p 21	1907, p 46	A3
Adjustment: policies of insurance and names of Underwriters	1889, p 60	1890, p 33	1968, p 25	1969, p 22	A7
Adjustment of return of premium	Custom of Lloyd's		1968, p 28	1969, p 22	—
Vessel in ballast and under charter: contributing interests	1896, p 63	1897, p 34	1926, p 41	1926 (Nov) p 9	B26
Vessel in ballast and under charter: contributing interests (new Rule)	1926, p 41	1926 (Nov) p 9	1945, p 53	1946, p 45	B26
Underwriters' liability in respect of jettison	1874, p 20	1875, p 18	1889, p 50		B30
Under-insured interest made good in general average	1882, p 47	1883, p 48	1921, p 53	1922, p 43	—
Damage caused by water thrown upon burning goods	1874, p 23	1875, p 22	1968, p 18	1969, p 22	F3
Extinguishing fire on shipboard	1968, p 18	1969, p 22	1974, p 13	1975, p 15	F3
Voluntary Stranding	Custom of Lloyd's, amended 1876, p 13		1968, p 20	1969, p 22	F4
Damage to cargo in discharging	Custom of Lloyd's		1890, p 35	1891, p 33	F18

INDEX TO THE REPORTS OF THE ASSOCIATION RESCINDED RULES

Subject	Proposal		Rescission		Current Rule (if any)
	Accepted	Confirmed	Accepted	Confirmed	
Damage to cargo during forced discharge	1883, p 58	1884, p 37	1968, p 21	1969, p 22	F18
Salvage Expenses. Application of Rules XXI and XXII	1927, p 44	1928, p 32	1942, p 48	1943, p 39	C1
Allowance to be made in general under York-Antwerp Rules in respect of the cost of maintenance of officers and crew	1896, p 47	1897, p 33			
Allowance to be made in general average under York-Antwerp Rules in respect of the cost of maintenance of officers and crew (amended)	1913, p 27		1968, p 24	1969, p 22	—
Modification of York-Antwerp Rules in contracts of affreightment: Liability of Underwriters	1904, p 44	1905, p 32	1968, p 23	1969, p 22	—
Statement of particular average on ships	1874, p 23	1875, p 19	1968, p 25	1969, p 22	—
Claims for damage to ship's machinery	1880, p 31	1881, p 27	1968, p 18	1969, p 22	—
Drydock expenses	1891, p 26	1892, p 23			
Drydock expenses (amended)	1903, p 31	1904, p 41			
Drydock expenses (amended)	1927, p 18	1928, p 3	1970, p 19	1971, p 21	D5
Scraping and painting	1900, p 26	1901, p 41	1968, p 26	1969, p 22	D8

APPENDIX VI

Ship's Papers
Rules of the Supreme Court

(A) RSC Ord 72, r 10— Production of certain documents in marine insurance actions

10. (1) Where in an action in the commercial list relating to a marine insurance policy an application for an order under Order 24, rule 3, is made by the insurer, then, without prejudice to its powers under that rule, the Court, if satisfied that the circumstances of the case are such that it is necessary or expedient to do so, may make an order, either in Form No 94 in Appendix A or in such other form as it thinks fit, for the production of such documents as are therein specified or described.

(2) An order under this rule may be made on such terms, if any, as to staying proceedings in the action or otherwise, as the Court thinks fit.

(3) In this rule 'the Court' means the judge, the district registrar of Liverpool or the district registrar of Manchester, as the case may be.

(B) RSC Appendix A, Form No 94

Order for production of documents in marine insurance action

(Ord 72, r 10)

[*Heading as in action*]

Upon hearing   [and upon reading the affidavit of   filed the   day of   19]:

It is ordered that the plaintiff and all other persons interested in this action, and in the insurance the subject of this action, do produce and show to the defendant, his solicitors or agents on oath [*or* by oath of their proper officer] all insurance slips, policies, letters of instruction or other orders for effecting such slips or policies, or relating to the insurance or the subject-matter of the insurance on the ship   , or the cargo on board thereof, or the freight thereby, and also all documents relating to the sailing or alleged loss of the said ship, cargo or freight, and all correspondence with any person relating in any manner to the effecting of the insurance on the said ship, cargo or freight, or any other insurance whatsoever effected on the said ship, cargo or freight, on the voyage insured by the policy sued on in this action, or any other policy whatsoever effected on the said ship, or the cargo on board thereof, or the freight thereby on the same voyage. Also all correspondence between the captain or agent or the ship and any other person with the owner or any person before the commencement of or during the voyage on which the alleged loss happened. Also all books and documents, whatever their nature and whether originals, duplicates or copies, which in anyway relate or refer to any matter in question in this action and which are now in the custody, possession or power of the plaintiff or any other person on his behalf, his or their, or any of their brokers, solicitors or agents, with liberty for the defendant, his solicitors or agents to inspect and take copies of, or extracts from, any of those books or documents. And that in the like manner the plaintiff and every other person interested as aforesaid do account for all other books and documents relating or referring to any matter in question in this action which were once but are not now in his custody, possession and power.

And that [in the meantime all further proceedings be stayed and that] the costs of and occasioned by this application be costs in the action.

Dated the   day of   19

Index

Abandonment
  acceptance of, what constitutes 389, 390
  effect of 533
    right to freight 394–396
      take over matter insured 392–394
  generally 378
  insurer not obliged to accept 389
  irrevocability of 390–392
  notice of—
    broker's duty to give 331, 332
    cases in which to be given 382–385
    form of 385–387
    generally 378, 381
    statutory provisions 494, 495
    time within which to be given 387–389
    to whom to be given 387
    underwriters refusing to accept 377
    waiver of 392
  reasonable, amounting to constructive total loss 365, 366
  right to abandon, when arising 378–381
  statutory provisions, generally 493–495
  who may abandon 380, 381
Acceptance
  abandonment, of, generally 389, 390
Actual total loss. *See* TOTAL LOSS
Additional premium. *See* PREMIUM
Ademption
  where loss reduced from total to partial, 376
Advances
  insurance of, generally 9
Adventure
  marine, meaning 4
Agent. *See also* BROKER
  acts and intentions of 41
  ambiguous instructions received by 30 *n.*
  assured, of, sue and labour clause 450
  broker, as 30
  disclosure by, 41–44, 487
  fraud or neglect of, will not excuse principal 41
  insurable interest of 24
  nature of agency 42
  non-disclosure of loss of vessel by 55
All risks
  clause, form of 178
  effect of policy against 178, 179
  insurance of cargoes against, generally 178
  prima facie inference of loss under policy, 179

Alteration
  policy, of 278, 279
    how effected 279
Anchor
  part of vessel, as 172
Apprehension of loss
  loss not recoverable 230
Approval
  government authority, of, steps taken with 221
Arrival
  ship, of, rule as to 119
Assignee
  policy, of, defences available to insurer 316–319
Assignment
  policy, of—
    assignor and assignee, rights *inter se* 321
    form of 319, 320
    generally 315 *et seq.*
    notice to be given to insurers 551, 555
    person having no interest, assignment ineffective 320, 321
    right of assignee to sue in own name 315, 316
    statutory provisions as to 315, 492, 493
    time clauses provisions 315
Assigns
  suing and labouring by 442, 443
At and from
  meaning 115, 116
Average. *See* GENERAL AVERAGE, PARTICULAR AVERAGE
Average adjusters
  functions 569, 570
  generally, 568
  membership of Association of 569
  Rules of Practice 568 *et seq.*

Ballast
  vessel in 572, 573
Barge
  sunken, collision with 172
Barratry
  civil war, changing sides in 167, 168
  date of liability of underwriter 168, 169
  deviation excused where 134
  deviation, held to be 164, 165
  early example of 161

Barratry—*continued*
  evidence of loss by 169
  generally 161 *et seq.*
  intentional sinking of ship 236
  international or municipal regulations, breach of 164
  meaning 161, 162
  mistake not amounting to 166
  must be without owner's consent 162
  negligence, owner's, effect of 168
  part-owner may commit 164
  scuttling, arising from 164, 167
  shipowners, can only be committed against 163
  smuggling, by 164
  standard of proof 245, 246, 247
  theft, historical connection with 151
Beaching
  peril of seas, as 144, 145
Bill of lading
  missing ship 55
Boilers
  damage to, allowable in general average 190
Bond
  goods sold in, adjustment of average on 579
Both to blame. *See* COLLISION CLAUSE
Bottom treatment
  generally 421, 422, 537, 545
Bottomry
  lender of money on, insurable interest of 27
  not "goods" 108
Breakage
  not peril of seas 142
Brigands
  raid by 156
Broker. *See also* AGENT
  assured responsible for representations made by 71
  authority of—
    cancellation of policy 333
    generally 331
  brokerage, right to 333, 337
  duty of—
    cover note, no duty to state terms of 332, 333
    disclosure 40
    effecting policy, in 30 *et seq.*
    express instructions, where 331
    generally 331
    no express instructions 331
    notice of abandonment, to give 331, 332
    principal's instructions, to obey 30–32
    skill and care, to use 32–37
    sum insured, to collect 332
    to act *bona fide* 30
    transaction, to carry out 37, 38
    usual and ordinary clauses, to insert 32
  effect of illegality of policy on position of 34, 36
  misrepresentations by 73–77
  name of, to be specified in policy 108

Broker—*continued*
  negligence by 31, 32
  policy void, position where 36, 37
  premium on policy effected through 493
  responsibility for payment of 82
  presumption that all necessary information available 34
  rights of—
    lien, general 333–337
      particular 333, 334
Burning
  ship's fittings, of 226
    material and stores, of, as fuel 191
Burnt
  meaning 413, 414

Cancellation
  policy, of, generally 273
Cancellation clause
  cancel, meaning 267, 268, 539, 540, 553, 554
  freight policies, on 267
Captors
  insurable interest of 26
Capture
  doubtful, effect on insurance of ship 55
Cargo
  cattle, of 154
  damage to—
    cover by protection association 219
    discharging, in 191
  damaged, sale of 227
  deck—
    carriage on 65
    custom of trade as to 154
    not normally protected against jettison 153, 154
    qualification of insurer's undertaking as to 271, 272
  institute clauses. *See* INSTITUTE CLAUSES
  insurable interest of owner of 18, 19
  non-disclosure of character of 50, 51
  overvaluation, materiality 57, 58
  perishable, sale of 353
  sale of part to pay for repairs 226
  shortages, cover by protection association 219
  stoppage *in transitu* 18, 19
  undeclared or wrongfully declared, not allowable as general average 192
  wrongly described, effect 109
Carrier
  insurable interest of 24, 25
Casks
  leakage of 194, 195
Casting away
  vessel, of 233 *et seq.*
Cattle
  deck cargo of 154

Certainty
  need for, in designating subject matter in policy 106
Change of voyage. *See* VOYAGE
Chartered freight. *See* FREIGHT
Circumstance
  meaning of 54
Civil war
  changing sides in, as barratry 167, 168
  restraint of princes imposed in 265
Collision. *See also* COLLISION CLAUSE
  costs, apportionment 571
  crane, pontoon, held not ship or vessel 173
  fruit unloaded after, loss held not collision damage 228
  liability for, cover by protection association 217
  meaning 414
  peril of seas, as 144
    when not 144
  pilot boat, with 175
  proximate cause of loss, as 227, 228
  ship fouling nets of fishing vessel, held not 172
  sunken barge, with 172
  wreck, with, not collision with "ship or vessel" 172
Collision clause
  both to blame—
    cargo clauses 516, 520, 523
    generally 180
    freight collision 552, 556
    generally 170, 171, 534, 535, 542
  three-fourths liability, 261, 534, 535, 542
Commission
  insurance of, generally 9
Complaint
  customer's, as to state of goods, 62
Connivance. *See* MISCONDUCT
Consideration
  failure of, return of premium for 84
Construction
  policy, of. *See* POLICY
Constructive total loss
  contract, arising from 375
  damage to goods 374, 375
    ship 372–374
  definition, 342, 343, 362, 363, 494
    completeness of 363, 364
  deprivation of possession of ship or goods 367–371
  detainment clause 372
  doctrine of, generally 362, 363
  effect of 375, 376, 494
  freight, of 350 *n*
  generally 342, 343
  Institute clauses 407, 518, 538, 545
  notice of abandonment not essential ingredient 365
  reasonable abandonment of subject-matter 365, 366

Constructive total loss—*continued*
  value fixed by policy not conclusive for determining whether 97
Continuation clause
  reinsurer presumed to know of 46
  time policy, in 113
***Contra proferentem* rule**
  generally 328–330
Contraband
  carrying of, by neutral country 309
Contribution
  general average, to 192
  insurers, between—
    double insurance, on 499
    right of 461
Convoy
  ship sailing without 54
  warranty that vessel shall sail in 286
Cover note
  broker under no duty to state terms of 332, 333
Crane
  pontoon, held not ship or vessel 173
Crew
  inexperience of, clause qualifying liability of insurers 272
  insurable interest in respect of wages 23
  substitutes, expenses of, cover by protection association 216
  warranty as to number of 285, 286
Customs regulations
  exclusion of liability for loss by, infringement of, form of clause 261, 262

Decay
  ship's timbers, of, not peril of seas 141
Deck cargo. *See* CARGO
Deductible claims expenses
  form 536, 537, 543, 544
Delay
  duty to resume course after 138
  ice, by 136
  losses caused by, generally 247, 248
  unreasonable 136
  voyage, in, 492
    effect of 135–138
    excuses for 138, 492
Delivery
  meaning 19
  price of goods at port of, elements making up 19
Demurrage
  association to cover expenses arising from claims 224
Detainment clause
  generally 372, 408, 547, 549, 558, 560
Detention
  loss by, whether barratry 166
  vessel, of, as war risk 220–224
Devaluation
  effect of, on claim for total loss 442–443

Deviation
additional premium on 80, 81
barratry arising from 164–167
course of voyage specifically or not specifically designated 129, 130
duty to resume course after 134
excuses for 133, 134, 492
expenses of, cover by protection association 217
extent immaterial 129
geographical order, ports to be visited in 130
"held covered" clause 134, 135
ignorance or want of skill, from 166
intention immaterial 129
intermediate voyages 132
liberty to touch and stay 130–132
meaning 129
mere intention is not 130
omitting port of discharge is not 130
ports of discharge, order of calling at 130
revisiting is 130
statutory provisions as to 491, 492
trading at port of call is not 132, 133
war risk, as 223, 224

Directions
government department, of 220, 221

Disbursements
insurance of, generally 9

Disclosure
agent affecting insurance, by 41–44
assured, by 39–41
character of cargo, of 51
duty of—
   duration of 66–68
   generally 487, 488
enquiry, putting of businessman on 50
facts which need not be disclosed—
   information waived, facts as to which 50–53
   knowledge of insurer, facts within, 46–49
   risk, facts tending to diminish 46
   unnecessary by reason of warranty 53
good faith, duty of 39
material and immaterial facts 53–66
material facts, duty to disclose 39–44
materiality, test of 44, 45
misrepresentation and non-disclosure distinguished 71
non-disclosure—
   broker's liability to insurer for 69, 70
   effect of 68, 69
   may be fraudulent or innocent 40
part information, of 40
previous claims record 59
   convictions 60
prudent insurer as yardstick 45
re-insurance 40
source of facts to be disclosed 40

Discovery
ship's papers, of—
   discretion of court 397–400

Discovery—*continued*
ship's papers, of—*continued*
   generally 397
   persons against whom order can be made 400, 401

Distress
ship in, deviation excused where going to assistance of 134

Distressed seamen
expenses of, cover by protection association 217

Diversion
vessel, of, as war risk 223, 224

Dock
damage to, cover by protection association 217

Dock dues
inclusion in cost of repairs 416

Double insurance
contribution, right of 461, 499
definition 5 *n.*, 461
effect of over-insurance by 5
return of premiums on 85
statutory provisions 489, 490

Duty of assured clause
generally 451, 519, 522, 526, 529, 532, 537, 544. *See also* SUE AND LABOUR CLAUSE

Earnings
loss of, insurance against 229

Effects
loss of, cover by protection association 217

Embargo
vessel, on, prevents mooring in good safety 121
voyage not pursued for fear of 230

Enemy
presence of, materiality of information 54

Evidence
barratry, of loss by 169
connivance at scuttling, of 233–242
nationality, of 287
particulars of scuttling 242, 243
representations, as to 78, 79
seaworthiness, of 296, 297
slip as 500

Excess clause
reinsurance policy, in 467

Exclusions clauses
cargo clauses—
   general 256, 257, 516, 520, 523
   strikes 257, 517, 520, 524
   unseaworthiness 257, 516, 520, 523
   war 257, 517, 520, 524
general exclusions clause 516, 520, 523
hull clauses—
   generally 259–262
   malicious acts 260, 540
   navigation 260, 533, 540, 541
   nuclear 260, 540
   strikes 260, 540

Index   601

Exclusions clauses—*continued*
  hull clauses—*continued*
    three-fourths collision liability 261, 534, 535, 542
    war 260, 540
Executors
  insurable interest of 25
Express warranty. *See* WARRANTY

Factor
  suing and labouring by 442, 443
Fines
  cover by protection and indemnity association 219
Fire
  damage by water used to extinguish 580
  extinguishing, damage caused in 190
  extinguishing, generally 580
  generally 150, 151
  grounds under which assured may recover 150, 151
  inherent vice, caused by 150, 151
  negligence, caused by 150, 161
  spontaneous combustion 151
Floating objects
  damage by, cover by protection association 217
Floating policy
  advantages of 91
  all goods to be declared 91
  declarations—
    assured, by, necessity for 91
    endorsement or other customary manner 91
    erroneous, rectification of 92
    fraud in regard to 93
    must be made in order of despatch 92
    must comprise all consignments 92
    time for 92, 93
  definition 489
  fire risks, reinsurance of 92
  meaning 91
  several policies, effect of existence of 93
  undervaluation in 65
  vessels not necessarily stated 91
  when attaching to goods 92
Flying boat
  held not to be "ship or vessel" 174
Foreign adjustment clause
  general average, as to adjustment of 186, 187
Forwarding charges clause
  forms 518, 522, 525
Fraud
  effect of, on question of return of premium 84
Freight
  advance, insurable interest in 20
  associations to cover expenses arising from claims 224
  attachment of risk *pro rata* as goods shipped 118, 119
  cancellation clause in policies on 267

Freight—*continued*
  chartered—
    application of doctrine of proximate cause 228–230
    insurance of, generally 21
    insurable interest in 20–22
    meaning 10
    nature of payments of 20, 21
    "off-hire" clause 20
    payment in advance 20
      forms of 21
    waiver of information as to 52
  constructive total loss of 350 *n.*
  contributory value of 572, 583
  deductions from 573
  definition 9, 107, 500
  earning of, effect 361
  forwarding charges on 573
  insurable value of 98
  insurance of, generally 8–10
  interest in, insurable value of 10
  loss of, making good as general average 192
    measure of indemnity 553
  ordinary—
    as element in making up price of goods 19
    definition 19
    explained 9, 10
    insurable interest in owner 19
    loss of, how arising 19
    meaning 9
    payable though goods damaged 19
  owner's trading freight, meaning 10
  ownership of, giving rise to insurable interest 19–22
  partial loss of. *See* PARTIAL LOSS
  profit, insurance of 19
  right to wages not dependent on earning of 23
  time and voyage clauses 177, 550 *et seq.*
  total loss of—
    measure of indemnity for 407–409
    See also TOTAL LOSS
  trading, owner's, insurable interest in 22
  ulterior chartered 573
  voyage policies on 118, 119
From
  meaning 115
Frustration
  chartered voyage, of 353
  frustration clause, generally 264, 265
  loss of goods, inapplicability to claim for 265–267
  restraint of princes imposed in civil war 265
Fuel
  burning of ship's materials, etc., as 191

Gaming or wagering contracts
  contracts deemed to be 12
  detachable clauses 14, 15
  failure to disclose material fact 14

Gaming or wagering contracts—*continued*
  gambling policies 12, 13
    penalty for effecting 12, 13
  generally 11
  honour policies 13
  indemnity, departure from principle of 12
  "interest or no interest", policy made 12
  "policy proof of interest", contracts made 13
  position after 1745 . . . 11–15
    before 1745 . . . 11
  statutory provisions against 12
  void by statute 12
Gasoline
  vessel's carrying capacity 66
General average
  adjustment rules 571–575
  average adjusters', rules of practice 571–575
  ballast, vessel sailing in 186
  burning of materials and stores as fuel 191
  cargo—
    clauses 180, 516, 520, 523
    damage in discharging 191
    undeclared or wrongfully declared 192
  contribution to 192, 583
  cover by protection and indemnity association 219
  definition 495
  English law and practice 579 *et seq.*
  explained 182
  fire, damage caused in extinguishing 190
  foreign law, application of 186, 187
  general average act, definition 187
  general average contribution—
    different interests owned by same assured 184
    insurer's liability in respect of 183
    measure of indemnity 437, 497, 498
  general average expenditure—
    insurer's liability in respect of 182, 183
  general average loss—
    not to be added to particular average loss 417
  general average sacrifice—
    amount to be made good for cargo lost by 192
    common safety, for 573
    insurer's liability in respect of 183
    ship's stores, 574
  hulls clauses 176, 536, 543
  jettison 189
  lien, enforcement of 574
  lightening ship 190, 191
  limitation period 184, 185
  loss incurred not for avoidance of peril insured against 184
  machinery and boilers, damage to 190
  meaning 344
  port of refuge, expenses of 191
  repairs, deductions from cost of 583
  statutory provisions 495, 496
  stranding, voluntary 190

General average—*continued*
  strikes clauses (cargo) 530
  time clauses 553
  "unless general", meaning 411
  valuation in policy, insurer bound by, in ascertaining sacrifice 97
  voyage clauses 543, 556, 557
  war clauses (cargo) 526
  wreck, cutting away 190
  York–Antwerp Rules, 1974, application of 187–192
General exclusions clause. *See* EXCLUSIONS CLAUSES
Good faith
  duty of 39
Good safety
  clause, various forms of 121, 122
  embargo prevents vessel being in 121
  ice preventing mooring in 120
  meaning 115
  moored in, meaning 121, 122
  ship in sinking condition cannot be moored in 121
  warranty of 490
Goods
  condition of—
    customers' complaints as to 62
    shipment, on 62
  damage to, computation of amount 374
  definition 9, 107
  deprivation of, whether amounting to constructive total loss 367–371
  history of, whether material 56
  insurable value of 98, 99
  insurance of, generally 9
  meaning 107, 108
  misrepresentation as to condition 78
  partial loss of. *See* PARTIAL LOSS
  total loss of 349, 350
  transit, in. *See* TRANSIT CLAUSE
  unmerchantable condition, arrival in 352
  voyage policy on—
    general rule 117, 118
    "transit" clause 118
Greenwich mean time
  use of, in drawing up time policies 113
Grounding
  ship, of, materiality of information as to 55

Harbour
  damage to, cover by protection association 217
Heat
  damage by 195, 196
Hiring contract
  liability under, cover by protection association 274
Honour policy
  not enforceable at law 13
  "policy proof of interest" clause 13
    detachable 14, 15

Index 603

Hostilities
consequences of, examples 204–207
meaning 198
Hull
meaning 107

Ice
delay by 136
prevention of mooring in good safety by 120
ship damaged by, and abandoned 145, 146
vessel lost through leakage caused by 232, 233
Illegal adventure
examples of 308
Illegality
effect of, on question of return of premium 84, 85
Increased value clause
forms of 518, 522, 525
Indemnity
associations, protection and, risks covered by 215 *et seq.*
assured receiving sums in excess of 5
cardinal principal of insurance, as 11
gaming or wagering contracts depart from principle of 12
marine insurance as contract of 4–7
meaning 4
measure of—
 based on convention of parties 6, 7
 calculation 418 *et seq.*, 432
 freight, loss of 553
 general average contribution and salvage charges 437
 general provisions 497, 498
 generally 405, 406
 meaning 405
 partial loss of freight 427, 428
  ship 410 *et seq.*
 statutory provisions 496–498
 successive losses 440, 441
 sue and labour clause 442–451
 third parties, liabilities to 439
 total loss 407–409
 unrepaired damage, claim for 425, 538
partial loss 7
particular average loss 6
Indemnity association
risks covered by 215 *et seq.*
Inherent vice
contracting out of statutory protection 254, 255
fire caused by 150, 151
generally 250 *et seq.*
jettison rendered necessary by 153
not peril of seas 142
Injury
personal, cover by protection association 216
Institute clauses
cargo clauses—
 benefit of insurance 519, 522, 526

Institute clauses—*continued*
cargo clauses—*continued*
 change of voyage clause 128, 518, 521, 525
 claims 518, 521, 522, 525
 delay, avoidance of 519, 523, 526
 duration 517, 518, 521, 524, 525
 duty of assured 451, 519, 522, 526
 exclusions 256–258, 516, 520, 523
 generally 177 *et seq.*
 law and practice 519, 523, 526
 minimising losses 519, 522, 526
 risks covered 214, 519, 520, 523
 transit clause 118, 133, 517, 521, 524
generally 104, 105, 516 *et seq.*
strikes clauses (cargo)—
 benefit of insurance 532
 claims 531, 532
 delay, avoidance of 532
 duration 531
 exclusions 258, 259, 530
 law and practice 532
 minimising losses 532
 risks covered 214, 530
 transit clause 118, 531
time clauses—
 freight 114, 177, 262, 428, 550–554
 hulls 114, 140, 157, 170, 259, 418, 437, 451, 533–540
voyage clauses—
 freight 177, 262, 428, 555–558
 hulls 128, 140, 157, 170, 176, 259, 540–547
war and strikes clauses—
 freight-time 210, 211, 214, 558, 559
 freight-voyage 210, 211, 214, 560, 561
 hulls-time 114, 210, 214, 261, 547, 548
 hulls-voyage 114, 214, 269, 549, 550
war clauses (cargo)—
 benefit of insurance 529
 claims 529
 delay, avoidance of 529
 duration 527, 528
 exclusions 258, 526, 527
 generally 209–211
 law and practice 529
 minimising losses 529
 risks covered 526
 transit clause 118, 527, 528
warranties 561, 562
Institute of London underwriters
clauses for use with policies, issue and revision of 104, 104 *n. See also* INSTITUTE CLAUSES
Institute trading warranties
effect of 268
Insurable interest
assured lacking, cannot claim to be indemnified 5
definition 485
examples of persons having—
 agent 24
 captors 26

Insurable interest—*continued*
  examples of persons having—*continued*
    carrier 24, 25
    executors 25
    insurer 26
    lender of money on bottomry or respondentia 27
    lien holders 25
    master and crew 23
    mortgagor and mortgagee 22, 23
    owner of ship, cargo or freight 17–22
    pawnors 25
    persons expecting profit from marine adventure 26, 27
    reinsurer 26
    trustees 25
  generally 16
  Institute clauses, forms 518, 521, 522, 525, 529
  "lost or not lost", effect of insertion of words 28, 29
  marine adventure, in, what amounts to 16
  must exist at time of loss 27–29
  reinsurance 467, 468
  statutory provisions as to 485, 486
Insurable value
  freight, of 98
  goods, of 98, 99
  ship, of 98
    steamship 98
Insurance
  additional policies effected by insured 63–65
  "prudent insurer", meaning 44, 45
  speculation, as contract of 39
Insurance broker. *See* BROKER
Insurer
  facts within knowledge of, need not be disclosed 46, 49
  insurable interest of 26
  qualified undertakings of 268–272
Interest. *See also* INSURABLE INTEREST
  "interest insured", meaning 110
  meaning, in Act of 1906 . . . 111, 112
  subject-matter of policy, in. *See* POLICY
Interest or no interest
  policy deemed void as gaming or wagering contract 12

Jettison
  damage by 190
  deck cargo 153, 154, 579, 580
  general average and 189
  inherent vice, rendered necessary by 153
  justification of 153, 154
  meaning 153
  money, of 153
Jetty
  damage to, cover by protection association 217
Jewellery
  not "goods" 108

Knowledge
  presumption of 46–49

Land risk
  incidental to sea voyage 7, 8
Latent defect
  connecting rod breakage held not 159
  machinery or hull, in 250
  meaning 160
  pre-existing, affected by wear and tear 159
  shaft breaking through 158
  weakness of design held not to be 159
Lay-up
  returns for 539, 540, 553, 554
Leakage
  as peril of the seas 142
  casks and barrels, of 194, 195
  ice, caused by 233, 234
  liability of insurer for, generally 194, 195
  meaning 195
  must be specially insured against 194
Legal expenses
  recovery of, where insured by protection association 220
Legality
  adventure, of, implied warranty as to 308–310
  illegal adventure, examples of 308
Lien
  broker's 333–337
  insurable interest of holder of 25
  salvor's, on ship salved 25
  stoppage *in transitu* giving rise to 18
Life
  loss of, cover by protection association 216
Life salvage
  cover by protection association 216
  salvage award for 193, 194
Life saving
  deviation excused where for purpose of 134
Lightening of ship
  expenses of, allowable as general average 190, 191
Lightermen
  liability of, non-disclosure of 56
Lloyd's
  policy—
    form of 102–104, 510–512
    history 103
    signatures 105
Loading
  ports, at, insurer presumed to know trade usages 46
Loan
  insurance of, generally 9
Loss
  average loss. *See* GENERAL AVERAGE; PARTICULAR AVERAGE
  causa proxima non remota spectatur 226
  generally 341

Loss—*continued*
   must be attributed to actual and direct cause 225
   negligence as dominant cause 231, 232
   partial. *See* PARTIAL LOSS
   statutory provisions, generally 493–495
   successive losses, insurer's liability for 440, 441
   total. *See* CONSTRUCTIVE TOTAL LOSS; TOTAL LOSS
   types of 342–344

Lost or not lost
   entitlement to premium where risk attached 86
   policy where subject-matter insured whether 28, 29

Machinery
   damage to, allowable in general average 190
   ships, claim for repair of 571

Malicious acts
   exclusion clause 258, 260, 540

Marina operator
   liability of 27

Marine adventure
   definition 485
   losses incident to, generally 7
   meaning 4
   persons expecting profit from, insurable interest of 26, 27

Marine insurance
   contract of, when concluded 71
   defined 4, 484, 485
   indemnity, as contract of 4–7
   land risks incidental to sea voyage 7, 8
   mixed sea and land risks 485
   nature of 4 *et seq.*
   subject-matter, types of 8–10
   uberrima fides as ingredient of 487

Marine risks
   generally 140 *et seq. See also* PERILS OF THE SEAS

Maritime perils. *See also* PERILS OF THE SEAS
   definition 485
   meaning 4
   prohibition of gambling on loss, by 503, 504

Master of ship
   definition 161
   history of, whether material 56
   insurable interest in respect of wages 23
   negligence of, recovery 160, 161

Materiality
   question of fact, as, in considering representation 72, 73
   test of—
     in considering representation 72
     influencing judgment of insurer 44, 45

Measure of indemnity. *See* INDEMNITY

Medical aid
   deviation excused where need to obtain 134

Misconduct
   assured, of—
     connivance—
       at scuttling 232
       evidence of 233–242
       particulars of 242, 243
       burden of proof 243–247
     generally 232 *et seq.*
   insurer not liable for losses attributable to 232
   master and crew, of, does not absolve insurers from liability 231
   wilful, meaning 232

Misrepresentation
   assured, duty of 71
     duration 71–73
   construction of representation 72
   defence of, burden of proof 78
   effect of 78
   evidence 78, 79
   material and immaterial, examples of 73–77
   materiality—
     as question of fact 72, 73
     test of 72
   non-disclosure distinguished 71
   withdrawal or correction of representation 77

Missing ship
   presumption of loss 349, 494

Mistake
   contract annulled by 39
   mutual, must be, where rectification sought 274
   policy, in, rectification of, generally 274–277

Mixed policy
   meaning 91

Money
   jettison of 153

Moored
   good safety, in, meaning 121, 122. *See also* GOOD SAFETY

Mortgage
   insurable interests 22, 23

Moveables
   meaning 4 *n*

Mutual insurance
   certificates 479
   cesser of 478
   claims 478
   disputes 478, 479
   explained 475
   generally 475
   members, contribution by 476, 477
   membership, terms of entry and 475, 476
   period of insurance 477
   risks covered by 478
   rules of association 475
   statutory provisions 500

Nationality
  assured, of, materiality 59, 60
  evidence of 287
  warranty as to 286, 287
    none implied 286, 491
  what consituites 286, 287
Navigation clause
  terms of 533, 540, 541, 550, 555
Necessaries
  advances for, insurable interest in 25
Negligence
  broker, by 32
  dominant cause of loss, as 231, 232
  fire caused by 150, 160, 161
  master and crew, of—
    does not absolve insurers from liability 231, 232
  owner's, avoiding barratry 168
Nets
  fishing vessel, of, ship fouling 172
Neutrality
  condemnation for breach of 288
  proof of 287
  ship's papers 287, 288
  warranty of 490
    effect of breach of 288
    generally 287, 288
Non-disclosure. *See* DISCLOSURE
Notice of abandonment. *See* ABANDONMENT

Oil pollution
  indemnity for cleaning cost 217
Operation
  area of, clauses as to 268–270
Ordinary freight. *See* FREIGHT
Overvaluation
  vessel, of, avoidance on grounds of non-disclosure 61
Owner
  cargo, of—
    insurable interest 18, 19
    stoppage *in transitu* by 18, 19
  freight, of, insurable interest 19–22
  ship, of, insurable interest 17, 18
  vessel, of, ascertainment of who is 17, 18

Partial loss
  amount payable for, ascertainment of 426, 535, 542
  freight, of—
    franchise 427, 553
    generally 427
    losses amounting to specified percentage 427, 428
    measure of indemnity 496
    generally 342
  goods, of—
    deckload 430
    grounding 429, 430

Partial loss—*continued*
  goods of—*continued*
    measure of indemnity 496, 497
    particular average warranties 429–432
    salvage charges, etc., liability of insurer for 436
    total loss of part 430–432, 433
    valuation, apportionment of 432
  indemnity, measure of 6, 7
  ship, of—
    ascertainment of amount payable 426
    measure of indemnity 410 *et seq.*, 496
    no claim where insured against total loss only 410
    statutory provisions 495, 496
    stranding, arising from 411–413
Particular average
  average adjustment, rules of practice 579
  definition 495
  liability to indemnify limited to bargain under policy 6
  meaning 343, 344
  new work for old, deduction for 578
  subrogation 5
  warranty 410, 498
Particular charges
  definition 417
  exclusion of, in calculating partial loss 417
  liability of insurer for 417
Pawnor
  insurable interest of 25
Perils of the seas
  diligence, assured not guilty of want of 157 *et seq.*
  examples of 141 *et seq.*
  excepted perils 225 *et seq.*
  fortuitousness as ingredient of 141
  foundering 143, 144
  generally 141 *et seq.*
  Institute clauses 534, 541, 549, 551, 552, 555, 558, 560
  loss by apprehension of peril not recoverable 230
  losses not proximately caused by, exception of 225–232
  marine risks, generally 140 *et seq.*
  maritime perils, meaning 4, 485
  meaning 141
  ordinary action of winds and waves not included in 141
  rough weather 149
  sea or salt water must be destroying agent 142
  submarine, submerged, collision with 250
  waves 149
  wear and tear not included in 141
Pier
  damage to, cover by protection association 217
Pilot-boat
  collision with 175

Pirates
definition 154
   statutory 155
emigrants, seizure of ship by 156
force or violence as ingredients of piracy 157
mob boarding ship 156
mutineering crew 156
scuttling in time of war held not piracy 156, 157
territorial waters, piracy within 157
theft and piracy distinguished 157

Policy
alteration of 278, 279
assignment of 315 *et seq.*, 492, 493. *See also* ASSIGNMENT
attachment of risk 113 *et seq.*
cancellation of 273
   broker has no authority 333
classification 90 *et seq.*
clauses—
   attachment of slips, etc., containing 102
   See also INSTITUTE CLAUSES
construction of—
   context of words 327
   contra proferentem rule 328, 329
   doctrine of precedent and 322
   general rules of 322
   generally 322 *et seq.*
   intention of parties to be looked at 323
   ordinary meaning, words to be construed in 324–327
   reasonable, must be 327
   rules set out in Act of 1906 . . . 330
   terms in 489
   usage of trade 325–327
   whole, construction as 323
   written and printed words 323, 324
contract must be embodied in 488
definition 500
duration of risk 113 *et seq.*
duty, rights, etc., of broker in and after effecting. *See* BROKER
exceptions applicable to—
   generally. *See* EXCLUSIONS CLAUSES
   Institute clauses, under 256 *et seq.*
   Marine Insurance Act, under 225 *et seq.*
floating. *See* FLOATING POLICY
form of 501, 502
   criticised 102–104
   insurance companies' 515–517
   Lloyd's 102–105, 510–512
   new, as adopted in 1982 . . . 104, 105
   no restrictions of 101
   prior to 1982 . . . 102–104
   statutory 101, 102
gambling. *See* GAMING OR WAGERING CONTRACTS
generally 89
honour. *See* HONOUR POLICY
illegality of, effect on position of broker 34, 35

Policy—*continued*
marine risks 140 *et seq.*
matters to be specified in 488
   losses falling within 288
mixed 91, 306, 307
perils, additional 158 *et seq.*
premium payable. *See* PREMIUM
pre-requisites to recovery under 16
proof of interest, policy not enforceable at law 13
rectification of 274–277
reinsurance, of. *See* REINSURANCE
rules for construction of 502, 503
   recognised, incorporation of 102
   York–Antwerp 102
salvage, without benefit of 12
statutory provisions 488, 489
subject-matter—
   certainty, reasonable, need for 106–111
   description in brief 107, 108
   designation of, generally 106 *et seq.*
   error in description of 109
   interest in, nature and extent need not be specified 111
   interest intended to be covered 111, 112
   usage regulating designation of 106
termination of 273
time. *See* TIME POLICY
"tree to buyer" policy 123
unvalued. *See* UNVALUED POLICY
valued. *See* VALUED POLICY
variations in, by reference to other documents 102
void, position of broker where 36, 37
voyage. *See* VOYAGE POLICY
warranties in. *See* WARRANTY

Pollution
hazard from 170, 534, 541

Port
departure, of, alteration of 116, 491
discharge, of, several 492
expenses, cover by particular association 217
geographical order of visiting 130
"laid up in", meaning 83
   return of premium where 83
last port of discharge, extension of policy to 120, 121
nature of, non-disclosure of 56
order of calling at ports, whether deviation 130
refuge, of—
   expenses of, admission as general average 191
   wages and maintenance of crew in 191

Position
ship, of, warranty as to 285

Precedent
doctrine of, affects construction of policy 322

Premium
additional—
   change of voyage, in case of 80

Premium—*continued*
  additional—*continued*
    reasonable, payable where no arrangement made 80
    rule for ascertainment of 81
  amount of, generally 80–82
  "arranged", meaning 109
  definition 80
  index to nature of risk, as 44
  policy effected through 493
  rate of, as guidance to risk 78
  reasonable—
    must be, where none arranged 80, 489
  receipt of—
    acknowledged on policy 493
    effect of acknowledgement of 82
  responsibility for payment of 82
  return of—
    agreement, by 83
    attachment of risk, effect of 85
    double insurance, in cases of 85
    enforcement of 86
    failure of consideration, for 84–86
    fraud, effect of 84
    generally 82, 83
    illegality, effect of 84, 85
    insurance of goods on wrong ship, where 85
    responsibility of insurer to assured 86
    risk never attaching, effect of 85
    short interest 85
    statutory provisions 499, 500
    vessel laid up in port, where 83
      sold 83
  returnable where goods never imperilled 6
  when payable 82, 493

Prize
  insurable interest in 26

Profits
  as element in make-up of price of goods 19
  insurance of, generally 9
  not "goods" 108

Prolongation. *See* VOYAGE

Protection and indemnity associations
  risks covered by 215 *et seq.*

Proximate cause 225–230

Prudent insurer
  meaning 44, 45

Purchaser
  insurance cover until delivery to 123

Quarantine
  expenses of, cover by protection association 218
  protection of vessel whilst in 120

Ratification
  contract, of, by assured 500

Reasonableness
  standard of proof 446

Rectification
  policy, of 274–277

Reinsurance
  casualty slips at Lloyds, knowledge of 47
  continuation clause, reinsurer presumed to know of 46
  disclosure 40
  excess clause 467
  fire risks, of, under floating policy 92
  generally 467 *et seq.*
  goods already lost 59
  incorporates terms of original policy 466
  insurable interest 467, 468
    of insurer 26
  non-disclosure of material fact 48
  original policy—
    expiry of 466, 467
    payment under 466
  "pay as may be paid thereon", meaning of words 466
  policy, usual form of 465
  proximate cause of loss 469, 470
  relation between original assured and reinsurer 465
  relation between reassured and reinsurer 466 *et seq.*
  "total or constructive loss only" 470–472
  unseaworthiness, effect of 468, 469

Repairs
  duty of adjusters in respect of 570, 571
  ship, to. *See* SHIP

Repatriation
  expenses of, cover by protection association 216

Representation
  burden of proof of misrepresentation 78
  construction of 72
  correction of 77
  effect of misrepresentation 78
  evidence, as to 78, 79
  expectation or belief, as to 72
  first underwriter, to, effect of 78
  fraudulent 73
  material and immaterial misrepresentations 73–77
  materiality, test of 72
  must be true 71
  need not receive literal construction 72
  trade usages, regard must be had to 72
  untrue, avoids contract 71
  warranty distinguished 280
  withdrawal of 77

Respondentia
  lender of money on, insurable interest of 27
  not "goods" 108

Restraint of princes
  civil war, imposed in 265

Return of premium. *See* PREMIUM

Risk. *See also* ALL RISKS; PERILS OF THE SEAS; WAR RISKS

Risk—*continued*
    facts tending to diminish, need not be disclosed 46
    marine risks, generally 140 *et seq.*
    refusal of, by other insurers, not necessary to disclosure 58, 59
    risk clauses—
        cargo clauses 516, 519, 523
        generally 177–182
        strikes clauses 530
        war clauses 526

Sailing
    date of, materiality of 57
Sailing orders
    policy avoided by non-disclosure of 56
Sale of goods
    contract, effects of 483, 484
Salvage
    hulls clauses 176, 536, 543
    insurer's liability for salvage charges 417
    life. *See* LIFE SALVAGE
    policy without benefit of 12, 13
    remuneration 568
    salvage charges—
        assured entitled to indemnity in respect of 192
        definition 192, 193, 495, 496
        life salvage 193, 194
        measure of indemnity 497, 498
        recovery of 495
    salved ship, implied condition of seaworthiness 302
Scuttling
    barratry arising from 164, 167, 246
    in wartime, not piracy 156, 157
    circumstances to be considered in cases of 233, 234
    connivance at 233–242
        particulars of 242, 243
    intentional, not peril of seas 145
    proximate cause of loss, as, where insurers not liable 227
Seaworthiness
    burden of proof of 298, 299
    continuation of, not warranted 302
    dispensing with warranty of 302
    improper stowage, effect of 298
    meaning 296, 297
    requisites of 296
    salved ship 302
    types of policy, in relation to—
        time policy on ship 302–306
        voyage policy on goods 307
                ship 299–302
    voyage in stages 301
    waiver of breach of warranty of 311
    warranty of 490, 491
Servant
    suing and labouring by 442, 443

Shaft
    damage caused by breakage of 158, 159
Ship
    arrival of, rule as to 119
    contributory value of 572
    damage and repairs to, average adjuster rules 576–579
        assessment of value 372–374
    deprivation of, whether amounting to constructive total loss 367–371
    distress, in, aid as excuse for deviation 134
    flying boat held not 174
    grounding of 55
    insurable value of, how ascertained 97, 98
    insurance of, generally 9
    lightening 580
    loss of, before sailing 353
    meaning 107
        in collision clause 173
    missing 494
    materiality of bills of lading 55
    presumed lost 349, 350
    mixed policy on 306, 307
    navigability not test of 173
    not repaired or sold, measure of indemnity 423–425
    owner of, insurable interest 17, 18
    partial loss of. *See* PARTIAL LOSS
    partially repaired, measure of indemnity where 423
    pontoon crane held not 173
    position of, warranty as to 285
    readiness to sail 54
    repaired, measure of indemnity 419–422
    repairs to—
        dry dock expenses 577
        expenses of removal 576
        fuel and stores used in 576
        rigging 576
        sails 576
        scraping and painting 578
        tankers 577, 578
    sale of, by master 348
    sold but not repaired 425, 426
    total loss of. *See* CONSTRUCTIVE TOTAL LOSS; TOTAL LOSS
    unable to proceed, loss of freight where 354–361
    voyage policies on, attachment of risk 114–117
    yacht built from kit 53, 66
Shipment
    condition of goods on 62
Shipowner
    liability of, insurance generally 9
    meaning 9
Short interest
    return of premium on 85
Signatures
    policy, to 488

Sinking
  meaning 413
  ordinary wear and tear, through 249
Sister ship clause
  generally 171, 172, 535, 542
Slip
  evidence, as 79, 500
Smuggling
  barratry by 164
  seizure of ship by revenue authorities 226
Spontaneous combustion
  damage by 195, 196
  fire caused by 151
Steamship
  insurable value of, how ascertained 98
Stoppage in transitu
  lien given by 18, 19
  unpaid seller's right of 18, 19
Storm
  as peril of the seas 141
  ships parting in, materiality of information as to 55
Stowage
  deck, on, insurer presumed to know trade usages 46
  negligent, causing loss 231
Stowaway
  expenses of disposing of, cover by protection association 217
Stranding
  clause limiting effect of 413
  meaning 411
  voluntary, may be made good as general average 190, 580
  whole loss recoverable on 413
Strike
  clauses covering loss or damage by—
    cargo clauses 214, 530
    freight clauses 214, 558, 560
    generally 213, 214
    hull clauses 214, 547, 549
  exclusion clauses 257, 260, 517, 520, 524
Subrogation
  doctrine of—
    application on payment of total loss 5
    collision case 5
  effect of 458–460
  exercise of right of 458
  insurer's right of, generally 498, 499
  principle of, generally 455
  rights in respect of which arising 456, 457
Sue and labour clause
  breach of duty, effect 450
  'duty of assured' clause, now known as 451
  effect of 442
  expenses incurred by insurers not recoverable from assured 449
  expenses properly incurred 443–446
  factors, servants and assigns 442, 443
  form 442
  form and effect of, in Lloyd's policy 442 *et seq.*

Sue and labour clause—*continued*
  generally 442 *et seq.*
  independent contract, as 447
  modernisation 442
  necessity for existence of peril 447
  non-inclusion of, effect 450, 451
  peril must be covered by policy 447–449
  statutory provisions 498
Sweat
  damage from 195, 196
  meaning 195

Termination
  clause, generally 138, 139
  contract of carriage, of 517, 518, 521, 524
  policy, of 273
Theft. *See also* THIEVES
  by land thieves in port 152
    pirates and robbers 152
    violence 153
  committed on board ship 152
  meaning 151
Thieves
  furtum distinguished from *latrocinium* 152
  generally 151
  meaning 151, 152
Third party
  liability to, measure of indemnity 439
Time policy
  attachment and duration of risk 113
  continuation clause 113
  definition 90, 488
  Greenwich mean time to be used 113
  no restriction on length of time 113
  percentage of damage 414–416
  privity of the assured, meaning 303
  ship, on, warranty of seaworthiness 303–306
  specified event 113
Total loss
  actual—
    definition 342
    generally 342, 343
  constructive. *See* CONSTRUCTIVE TOTAL LOSS
  freight, of—
    effect of freight being earned 361
    frustration of chartered voyage 353
    generally 407, 408
    goods arriving in unmerchantable condition, where 352
    how arising 350–352
    loss of ship before sailing 353
    perishable cargo, sale of 353
    ship unable to proceed 354–361
  generally 342
  goods, of—
    damaged goods, test as to whether loss total or partial 350
    generally 349, 350
    measure of indemnity for 407–409, 494
  ship, of—
    examples 346–348

Total loss—*continued*
 ship, of—*continued*
  missing ships 349
  sale of vessel by master 348, 349
  scrap, vessel sold for 407
  statutory provisions 493, 494
  subrogation of rights where insurer pays 5
Touch and stay
 liberty to, generally 130–132
Towage
 general average act 187, 188
 liability under contracts for, cover by protection association 218
 peril of seas, as 144, 145
 qualification of insurer's undertaking, as to 270, 271
Trade usages
 insurer presumed to know 46
 regard to, in construing representation 72
Transhipment
 effect of 494
 generally 133
Transit
 associations to cover expenses arising from claims 224
Transit clause
 effect of 118
 in voyage policy 122–126
 forms of 22 *et seq.*, 517, 521, 524, 527, 528, 531
Trustees
 insurable interest of 25

Undervaluation
 floating policy, in 65
Underwriter. *See also* LLOYD'S
 first, effect of untrue representation to 78
 reliance upon assured for information 39, 40
Unloading
 ports of destination, at, insurer presumed to know trade usages 46
Unmerchantable condition
 arrival of goods in 352
Unseaworthiness
 Institute clauses—
  cargo clauses, 256, 257, 516, 520, 523
  generally 256–258, 259, 308
  war clauses 258
 vessel, of, non-disclosure 58
 See also SEAWORTHINESS
Unvalued policy
 ascertainment of value—
  of freight 98
   goods 98, 99
   ship 98
   other matters 99
 definition 97, 98, 489
 necessity for proof of value 99, 100
 rarity of 93
 treatment of floating policy as 93

Usage of trade
 effect of construction of policy, generally 325–327
 must be notorious 326
  not be contradictory to law 327
  contradict policy 326, 327
Usages
 insurer presumed to know 46
 meaning 108
 regulating designation of subject-matter of insurance 106

Valuation. *See* UNVALUED POLICY; VALUED POLICY
Valued policy
 definition 93, 94, 489
 valuation—
  conclusiveness of 94–96
  constructive total loss and 96, 97
  general average sacrifice and 97
  salvage charges and 97
Verification
 meaning 293
Vessel. *See also* SHIP
 already sailed, non-disclosure 60, 61
 anchor is part of 172
 casting away of 233, *et seq.*
 date of arrival of, materiality 57
 flying boat held not 174
 loss of, non-disclosure by agent 55
 meaning 172
 name of, non-disclosure 55, 56
 navigability not test of 173
 overvaluation of 61, 62
 pontoon crane held not 173
 previous history of, disclosure 56
 rock, damage by 55
 sunken, remains "vessel" if still salvageable 172, 173
Vice. *See* INHERENT VICE
Violence
 theft by 153
Voyage. *See also* VOYAGE POLICY
 alteration in nature of, policy avoided where 278
 change of 530
  effect of 127–129
  Institute clauses 518, 521, 525, 528, 531
  meaning 127
 chartered, frustration of 353
 commencement of risk, implied condition as to 491
 delay in 492
  effect of 135–138
 deviation 491, 492
  See also DEVIATION
 different destination, sailing for 491
 intermediate, whether amounting to deviation 132
 meaning 222

Voyage—*continued*
  must be prosecuted with reasonable despatch 136
  port of departure, alteration of 491
  prolongation of—
    as war risk 220–224
    meaning 221, 222
  stages, in, absence of equipment rendering ship unseaworthy 301

Voyage policy. *See also* VOYAGE
  "at and from", meaning 115–117
  attachment of risk—
    freight, policies on 118, 119
    generally 114
    goods, policies on 117, 118
    ship, policies on 115–117
  change of voyage 127–129
  definition 90, 488
  delay in voyage 135–138
  deviation 129–135
  duration of risk—
    generally 119
    goods, risk on 122–126
    ship, risk on 119–122
  "from", meaning 115
  "good safety", meaning 115
  goods, on, warranty of seaworthiness 307
  implied condition as to commencement of risk 126, 127
  percentage of damage, computation of 414
  port of departure, alteration of 116
  ship, on, warranty of seaworthiness 299–302
  ship sailing for different destination 116, 117
  transit clause, effect of 122–126

Wagering contract. *See* GAMING OR WAGERING CONTRACT

Wages
  insurance of, generally 9
  master and crew have insurable interest in 23
  seamen's right to, not dependent on earning of freight 23

Waiver
  breach of warranty, of, generally 311–314
  information of, generally 50–53
  non-disclosure, of, not proved 66
  not easily presumed 51
  notice of abandonment, of 392
  omission to make inquiry does not amount to 51
  civil—
    changing sides in, as barratry 167, 168
    restraint of princes imposed in 265
    imminence of, insurer presumed to know 46
    state of, insurer presumed to know 46

War clauses. *See* INSTITUTE CLAUSES

War risks
  detention of vessel and prolongation of voyage 220–223
  diversion of vessel 223, 224

War risks—*continued*
  generally 197, 198
  insurance of war risks by government 211–213
  meaning 203
  proof of loss or damage by 207–209
  statutory provisions 504–509

Warehouse
  "warehouse to warehouse" clause 122–126

Warlike operations
  examples of 199–201
  hostilities and, whether loss due to consequences of 204–207
  meaning 198, 199
  operations held not warlike 201–203

Warranty
  breach of—
    excuses for 310
    Institute form 533
    repudiation on grounds of 295
    result of 310, 311
    waiver 311–314
    when excused 490
  compliance with, must be exact 280
  convoy warranties 286
  crew, as to number of 285, 286
  disbursements, Institute form 538, 539, 545, 546
  disclosure unnecessary by reason of 53
  express warranty 490
    construction of 281, 282
    examples of 282 *et seq.*
    must be included in policy 282
    generally 280 *et seq.*
  good safety, of 490
  implied 296 *et seq.*
  Institute Trading Warranties, effect of 268
  legality, of 308, 491
  meaning 280
  nationality, as to 286, 287, 490
    compliance with 287
  nature of 280, 281, 490
  neutrality, as to 287, 288, 490
    effect of breach 288
  part uninsured, as to 288–291
  particular average warranty 410, 498
  position of ship, as to 285
  representation distinguished 280, 281
  sailing warranty—
    definition of "sailing" 282, 283
    generally 282, 283
    intention to proceed to sea 284
    readiness of vessel 283
    unmooring and proceeding on voyage 283, 284
    warranty to depart 284, 285
      sail from 285
      to 285
  seaworthiness, of 296 *et seq.*, 469
    See also SEAWORTHINESS
  types of 281

Wear and tear
  insurer not ordinarily liable for 248
  ordinary, generally 248, 249
Wilful misconduct. *See* MISCONDUCT
Words
  context of words, effect of 327
  ordinary meaning to be given to 324–326
  written and printed, in policy, construction of 323, 324
Wreck
  collision with 172
  cutting away 190
  removal of, expenses for, cover by protection association 218
  sunken vessel becomes, when not salvageable 173

Wreckers
  plundering cargo, as peril of seas 144

Yacht
  constructive total loss 277, 296
York–Antwerp Rules 1974
  average adjusters, Rules of Practice 575, 576
  commission allowed under 575
  general average, adjustment of 187
  incorporation in policy 102
  lettered rules 187–189
  numbered rules 189–192
  salvage services rendered under agreement 575
  text of 563–567